Lecture Notes in Computer Science 11130

More information about this series at http://www.springer.com/series/7412

Laura Leal-Taixé · Stefan Roth (Eds.)

Computer Vision – ECCV 2018 Workshops

Munich, Germany, September 8–14, 2018
Proceedings, Part II

Springer

Editors
Laura Leal-Taixé
Technical University of Munich
Garching, Germany

Stefan Roth
Technische Universität Darmstadt
Darmstadt, Germany

ISSN 0302-9743 ISSN 1611-3349 (electronic)
Lecture Notes in Computer Science
ISBN 978-3-030-11011-6 ISBN 978-3-030-11012-3 (eBook)
https://doi.org/10.1007/978-3-030-11012-3

Library of Congress Control Number: 2018966826

LNCS Sublibrary: SL6 – Image Processing, Computer Vision, Pattern Recognition, and Graphics

This Springer imprint is published by the registered company Springer Nature Switzerland AG
The registered company address is: Gewerbestrasse 11, 6330 Cham, Switzerland

Foreword

It was our great pleasure to host the European Conference on Computer Vision 2018 in Munich, Germany. This constituted by far the largest ECCV event ever. With close to 2,900 registered participants and another 600 on the waiting list one month before the conference, participation more than doubled since the last ECCV in Amsterdam. We believe that this is due to a dramatic growth of the computer vision community combined with the popularity of Munich as a major European hub of culture, science, and industry. The conference took place in the heart of Munich in the concert hall Gasteig with workshops and tutorials held on the downtown campus of the Technical University of Munich.

One of the major innovations for ECCV 2018 was the free perpetual availability of all conference and workshop papers, which is often referred to as open access. We note that this is not precisely the same use of the term as in the Budapest declaration. Since 2013, CVPR and ICCV have had their papers hosted by the Computer Vision Foundation (CVF), in parallel with the IEEE Xplore version. This has proved highly beneficial to the computer vision community.

We are delighted to announce that for ECCV 2018 a very similar arrangement was put in place with the cooperation of Springer. In particular, the author's final version will be freely available in perpetuity on a CVF page, while SpringerLink will continue to host a version with further improvements, such as activating reference links and including video. We believe that this will give readers the best of both worlds; researchers who are focused on the technical content will have a freely available version in an easily accessible place, while subscribers to SpringerLink will continue to have the additional benefits that this provides. We thank Alfred Hofmann from Springer for helping to negotiate this agreement, which we expect will continue for future versions of ECCV.

September 2018

Horst Bischof
Daniel Cremers
Bernt Schiele
Ramin Zabih

Preface

It is our great pleasure to present these workshop proceedings of the 15th European Conference on Computer Vision, which was held during September 8–14, 2018, in Munich, Germany. We are delighted that the main conference of ECCV 2018 was accompanied by 43 scientific workshops. The ECCV workshop proceedings contain contributions of 36 workshops.

We received 74 workshop proposals on a broad set of topics related to computer vision. The very high quality and the large number of proposals made the selection process rather challenging. Owing to space restrictions, only 46 proposals were accepted, among which six proposals were merged into three workshops because of overlapping themes.

The final set of 43 workshops complemented the main conference program well. The workshop topics presented a good orchestration of new trends and traditional issues, built bridges into neighboring fields, as well as discussed fundamental technologies and novel applications. We would like to thank all the workshop organizers for their unreserved efforts to make the workshop sessions a great success.

September 2018

Stefan Roth
Laura Leal-Taixé

Organization

General Chairs

Horst Bischof	Graz University of Technology, Austria
Daniel Cremers	Technical University of Munich, Germany
Bernt Schiele	Saarland University, Max Planck Institute for Informatics, Germany
Ramin Zabih	CornellNYCTech, USA

Program Chairs

Vittorio Ferrari	University of Edinburgh, UK
Martial Hebert	Carnegie Mellon University, USA
Cristian Sminchisescu	Lund University, Sweden
Yair Weiss	Hebrew University, Israel

Local Arrangement Chairs

Björn Menze	Technical University of Munich, Germany
Matthias Niessner	Technical University of Munich, Germany

Workshop Chairs

Stefan Roth	Technische Universität Darmstadt, Germany
Laura Leal-Taixé	Technical University of Munich, Germany

Tutorial Chairs

Michael Bronstein	Università della Svizzera Italiana, Switzerland
Laura Leal-Taixé	Technical University of Munich, Germany

Website Chair

Friedrich Fraundorfer	Graz University of Technology, Austria

Demo Chairs

Federico Tombari	Technical University of Munich, Germany
Joerg Stueckler	Technical University of Munich, Germany

Publicity Chair

Giovanni Maria Farinella	University of Catania, Italy

Industrial Liaison Chairs

Florent Perronnin	Naver Labs, France
Yunchao Gong	Snap, USA
Helmut Grabner	Logitech, Switzerland

Finance Chair

Gerard Medioni	Amazon, University of Southern California, USA

Publication Chairs

Albert Ali Salah	Boğaziçi University, Turkey
Hamdi Dibeklioğlu	Bilkent University, Turkey
Anton Milan	Amazon, Germany

Workshop Organizers

W01 – The Visual Object Tracking Challenge Workshop

Matej Kristan	University of Ljubljana, Slovenia
Aleš Leonardis	University of Birmingham, UK
Jiří Matas	Czech Technical University in Prague, Czechia
Michael Felsberg	Linköping University, Sweden
Roman Pflugfelder	Austrian Institute of Technology, Austria

W02 – 6th Workshop on Computer Vision for Road Scene Understanding and Autonomous Driving

Mathieu Salzmann	EPFL, Switzerland
José Alvarez	NVIDIA, USA
Lars Petersson	Data61 CSIRO, Australia
Fredrik Kahl	Chalmers University of Technology, Sweden
Bart Nabbe	Aurora, USA

W03 – 3D Reconstruction in the Wild

Akihiro Sugimoto	The National Institute of Informatics (NII), Japan
Tomas Pajdla	Czech Technical University in Prague, Czechia
Takeshi Masuda	The National Institute of Advanced Industrial Science and Technology (AIST), Japan
Shohei Nobuhara	Kyoto University, Japan
Hiroshi Kawasaki	Kyushu University, Japan

W04 – Workshop on Visual Learning and Embodied Agents in Simulation Environments

Peter Anderson	Georgia Institute of Technology, USA
Manolis Savva	Facebook AI Research and Simon Fraser University, USA
Angel X. Chang	Eloquent Labs and Simon Fraser University, USA
Saurabh Gupta	University of California, Berkeley, USA
Amir R. Zamir	Stanford University and University of California, Berkeley, USA
Stefan Lee	Georgia Institute of Technology, USA
Samyak Datta	Georgia Institute of Technology, USA
Li Yi	Stanford University, USA
Hao Su	University of California, San Diego, USA
Qixing Huang	The University of Texas at Austin, USA
Cewu Lu	Shanghai Jiao Tong University, China
Leonidas Guibas	Stanford University, USA

W05 – Bias Estimation in Face Analytics

Rama Chellappa	University of Maryland, USA
Nalini Ratha	IBM Watson Research Center, USA
Rogerio Feris	IBM Watson Research Center, USA
Michele Merler	IBM Watson Research Center, USA
Vishal Patel	Johns Hopkins University, USA

W06 – 4th International Workshop on Recovering 6D Object Pose

Tomas Hodan	Czech Technical University in Prague, Czechia
Rigas Kouskouridas	Scape Technologies, UK
Krzysztof Walas	Poznan University of Technology, Poland
Tae-Kyun Kim	Imperial College London, UK
Jiří Matas	Czech Technical University in Prague, Czechia
Carsten Rother	Heidelberg University, Germany
Frank Michel	Technical University Dresden, Germany
Vincent Lepetit	University of Bordeaux, France
Ales Leonardis	University of Birmingham, UK
Carsten Steger	Technical University of Munich, MVTec, Germany
Caner Sahin	Imperial College London, UK

W07 – Second International Workshop on Computer Vision for UAVs

Kristof Van Beeck	KU Leuven, Belgium
Tinne Tuytelaars	KU Leuven, Belgium
Davide Scaramuzza	ETH Zurich, Switzerland
Toon Goedemé	KU Leuven, Belgium

W08 – 5th Transferring and Adapting Source Knowledge in Computer Vision and Second VisDA Challenge

Tatiana Tommasi	Italian Institute of Technology, Italy
David Vázquez	Element AI, Canada
Kate Saenko	Boston University, USA
Ben Usman	Boston University, USA
Xingchao Peng	Boston University, USA
Judy Hoffman	Facebook AI Research, USA
Neela Kaushik	Boston University, USA
Antonio M. López	Universitat Autònoma de Barcelona and Computer Vision Center, Spain
Wen Li	ETH Zurich, Switzerland
Francesco Orabona	Boston University, USA

W09 – PoseTrack Challenge: Articulated People Tracking in the Wild

Mykhaylo Andriluka	Google Research, Switzerland
Umar Iqbal	University of Bonn, Germany
Anton Milan	Amazon, Germany
Leonid Pishchulin	Max Planck Institute for Informatics, Germany
Christoph Lassner	Amazon, Germany
Eldar Insafutdinov	Max Planck Institute for Informatics, Germany
Siyu Tang	Max Planck Institute for Intelligent Systems, Germany
Juergen Gall	University of Bonn, Germany
Bernt Schiele	Max Planck Institute for Informatics, Germany

W10 – Workshop on Objectionable Content and Misinformation

Cristian Canton Ferrer	Facebook, USA
Matthias Niessner	Technical University of Munich, Germany
Paul Natsev	Google, USA
Marius Vlad	Google, Switzerland

W11 – 9th International Workshop on Human Behavior Understanding

Xavier Alameda-Pineda	Inria Grenoble, France
Elisa Ricci	Fondazione Bruno Kessler and University of Trento, Italy
Albert Ali Salah	Boğaziçi University, Turkey
Nicu Sebe	University of Trento, Italy
Shuicheng Yan	National University of Singapore, Singapore

W12 – First Person in Context Workshop and Challenge

Si Liu	Beihang University, China
Jiashi Feng	National University of Singapore, Singapore
Jizhong Han	Institute of Information Engineering, China
Shuicheng Yan	National University of Singapore, Singapore
Yao Sun	Institute of Information Engineering, China

Yue Liao	Institute of Information Engineering, China
Lejian Ren	Institute of Information Engineering, China
Guanghui Ren	Institute of Information Engineering, China

W13 – 4th Workshop on Computer Vision for Art Analysis

Stuart James	Istituto Italiano di Tecnologia, Italy and University College London, UK
Leonardo Impett	EPFL, Switzerland and Biblioteca Hertziana, Max Planck Institute for Art History, Italy
Peter Hall	University of Bath, UK
João Paulo Costeira	Instituto Superior Tecnico, Portugal
Peter Bell	Friedrich-Alexander-University Nürnberg, Germany
Alessio Del Bue	Istituto Italiano di Tecnologia, Italy

W14 – First Workshop on Fashion, Art, and Design

Hui Wu	IBM Research AI, USA
Negar Rostamzadeh	Element AI, Canada
Leonidas Lefakis	Zalando Research, Germany
Joy Tang	Markable, USA
Rogerio Feris	IBM Research AI, USA
Tamara Berg	UNC Chapel Hill/Shopagon Inc., USA
Luba Elliott	Independent Curator/Researcher/Producer
Aaron Courville	MILA/University of Montreal, Canada
Chris Pal	MILA/PolyMTL, Canada
Sanja Fidler	University of Toronto, Canada
Xavier Snelgrove	Element AI, Canada
David Vazquez	Element AI, Canada
Julia Lasserre	Zalando Research, Germany
Thomas Boquet	Element AI, Canada
Nana Yamazaki	Zalando SE, Germany

W15 – Anticipating Human Behavior

Juergen Gall	University of Bonn, Germany
Jan van Gemert	Delft University of Technology, The Netherlands
Kris Kitani	Carnegie Mellon University, USA

W16 – Third Workshop on Geometry Meets Deep Learning

Xiaowei Zhou	Zhejiang University, China
Emanuele Rodolà	Sapienza University of Rome, Italy
Jonathan Masci	NNAISENSE, Switzerland
Kosta Derpanis	Ryerson University, Canada

W17 – First Workshop on Brain-Driven Computer Vision

Simone Palazzo	University of Catania, Italy
Isaak Kavasidis	University of Catania, Italy
Dimitris Kastaniotis	University of Patras, Greece
Stavros Dimitriadis	Cardiff University, UK

W18 – Second Workshop on 3D Reconstruction Meets Semantics

Radim Tylecek	University of Edinburgh, UK
Torsten Sattler	ETH Zurich, Switzerland
Thomas Brox	University of Freiburg, Germany
Marc Pollefeys	ETH Zurich/Microsoft, Switzerland
Robert B. Fisher	University of Edinburgh, UK
Theo Gevers	University of Amsterdam, Netherlands

W19 – Third International Workshop on Video Segmentation

Pablo Arbelaez	Universidad de los Andes, Columbia
Thomas Brox	University of Freiburg, Germany
Fabio Galasso	OSRAM GmbH, Germany
Iasonas Kokkinos	University College London, UK
Fuxin Li	Oregon State University, USA

W20 – PeopleCap 2018: Capturing and Modeling Human Bodies, Faces, and Hands

Gerard Pons-Moll	MPI for Informatics and Saarland Informatics Campus, Germany
Jonathan Taylor	Google, USA

W21 – Workshop on Shortcomings in Vision and Language

Dhruv Batra	Georgia Institute of Technology and Facebook AI Research, USA
Raffaella Bernardi	University of Trento, Italy
Raquel Fernández	University of Amsterdam, The Netherlands
Spandana Gella	University of Edinburgh, UK
Kushal Kafle	Rochester Institute of Technology, USA
Moin Nabi	SAP SE, Germany
Stefan Lee	Georgia Institute of Technology, USA

W22 – Second YouTube-8M Large-Scale Video Understanding Workshop

Apostol (Paul) Natsev	Google Research, USA
Rahul Sukthankar	Google Research, USA
Joonseok Lee	Google Research, USA
George Toderici	Google Research, USA

W23 – Second International Workshop on Compact and Efficient Feature Representation and Learning in Computer Vision

Jie Qin	ETH Zurich, Switzerland
Li Liu	National University of Defense Technology, China and University of Oulu, Finland
Li Liu	Inception Institute of Artificial Intelligence, UAE
Fan Zhu	Inception Institute of Artificial Intelligence, UAE
Matti Pietikäinen	University of Oulu, Finland
Luc Van Gool	ETH Zurich, Switzerland

W24 – 5th Women in Computer Vision Workshop

Zeynep Akata	University of Amsterdam, The Netherlands
Dena Bazazian	Computer Vision Center, Spain
Yana Hasson	Inria, France
Angjoo Kanazawa	UC Berkeley, USA
Hildegard Kuehne	University of Bonn, Germany
Gül Varol	Inria, France

W25 – Perceptual Image Restoration and Manipulation Workshop and Challenge

Yochai Blau	Technion – Israel Institute of Technology, Israel
Roey Mechrez	Technion – Israel Institute of Technology, Israel
Radu Timofte	ETH Zurich, Switzerland
Tomer Michaeli	Technion – Israel Institute of Technology, Israel
Lihi Zelnik-Manor	Technion – Israel Institute of Technology, Israel

W26 – Egocentric Perception, Interaction, and Computing

Dima Damen	University of Bristol, UK
Giuseppe Serra	University of Udine, Italy
David Crandall	Indiana University, USA
Giovanni Maria Farinella	University of Catania, Italy
Antonino Furnari	University of Catania, Italy

W27 – Vision Meets Drone: A Challenge

Pengfei Zhu	Tianjin University, China
Longyin Wen	JD Finance, USA
Xiao Bian	GE Global Research, USA
Haibin Ling	Temple University, USA

W28 – 11th Perceptual Organization in Computer Vision Workshop on Action, Perception, and Organization

Deepak Pathak	UC Berkeley, USA
Bharath Hariharan	Cornell University, USA

W29 – AutoNUE: Autonomous Navigation in Unconstrained Environments

Manmohan Chandraker	University of California San Diego, USA
C. V. Jawahar	IIIT Hyderabad, India
Anoop M. Namboodiri	IIIT Hyderabad, India
Srikumar Ramalingam	University of Utah, USA
Anbumani Subramanian	Intel, Bangalore, India

W30 – ApolloScape: Vision-Based Navigation for Autonomous Driving

Peng Wang	Baidu Research, USA
Ruigang Yang	Baidu Research, China
Andreas Geiger	ETH Zurich, Switzerland
Hongdong Li	Australian National University, Australia
Alan Yuille	The Johns Hopkins University, USA

W31 – 6th International Workshop on Assistive Computer Vision and Robotics

Giovanni Maria Farinella	University of Catania, Italy
Marco Leo	National Research Council of Italy, Italy
Gerard G. Medioni	University of Southern California, USA
Mohan Trivedi	University of California, USA

W32 – 4th International Workshop on Observing and Understanding Hands in Action

Iason Oikonomidis	Foundation for Research and Technology, Greece
Guillermo Garcia-Hernando	Imperial College London, UK
Angela Yao	National University of Singapore, Singapore
Antonis Argyros	University of Crete/Foundation for Research and Technology, Greece
Vincent Lepetit	University of Bordeaux, France
Tae-Kyun Kim	Imperial College London, UK

W33 – Bioimage Computing

Jens Rittscher	University of Oxford, UK
Anna Kreshuk	University of Heidelberg, Germany
Florian Jug	Max Planck Institute CBG, Germany

W34 – First Workshop on Interactive and Adaptive Learning in an Open World

Erik Rodner	Carl Zeiss AG, Germany
Alexander Freytag	Carl Zeiss AG, Germany
Vittorio Ferrari	Google, Switzerland/University of Edinburgh, UK
Mario Fritz	CISPA Helmholtz Center i.G., Germany
Uwe Franke	Daimler AG, Germany
Terrence Boult	University of Colorado, Colorado Springs, USA

Juergen Gall	University of Bonn, Germany
Walter Scheirer	University of Notre Dame, USA
Angela Yao	University of Bonn, Germany

W35 – First Multimodal Learning and Applications Workshop

Paolo Rota	University of Trento, Italy
Vittorio Murino	Istituto Italiano di Tecnologia, Italy
Michael Yang	University of Twente, The Netherlands
Bodo Rosenhahn	Leibniz-Universität Hannover, Germany

W36 – What Is Optical Flow for?

Fatma Güney	Oxford University, UK
Laura Sevilla-Lara	Facebook Research, USA
Deqing Sun	NVIDIA, USA
Jonas Wulff	Massachusetts Institute of Technology, USA

W37 – Vision for XR

Richard Newcombe	Facebook Reality Labs, USA
Chris Sweeney	Facebook Reality Labs, USA
Julian Straub	Facebook Reality Labs, USA
Jakob Engel	Facebook Reality Labs, USA
Michael Goesele	Technische Universität Darmstadt, Germany

W38 – Open Images Challenge Workshop

Vittorio Ferrari	Google AI, Switzerland
Alina Kuznetsova	Google AI, Switzerland
Jordi Pont-Tuset	Google AI, Switzerland
Matteo Malloci	Google AI, Switzerland
Jasper Uijlings	Google AI, Switzerland
Jake Walker	Google AI, Switzerland
Rodrigo Benenson	Google AI, Switzerland

W39 – VizWiz Grand Challenge: Answering Visual Questions from Blind People

Danna Gurari	University of Texas at Austin, USA
Kristen Grauman	University of Texas at Austin, USA
Jeffrey P. Bigham	Carnegie Mellon University, USA

W40 – 360° Perception and Interaction

Min Sun	National Tsing Hua University, Taiwan
Yu-Chuan Su	University of Texas at Austin, USA
Wei-Sheng Lai	University of California, Merced, USA
Liwei Chan	National Chiao Tung University, USA
Hou-Ning Hu	National Tsing Hua University, Taiwan
Silvio Savarese	Stanford University, USA

Kristen Grauman	University of Texas at Austin, USA
Ming-Hsuan Yang	University of California, Merced, USA

W41 – Joint COCO and Mapillary Recognition Challenge Workshop

Tsung-Yi Lin	Google Brain, USA
Genevieve Patterson	Microsoft Research, USA
Matteo R. Ronchi	Caltech, USA
Yin Cui	Cornell, USA
Piotr Dollár	Facebook AI Research, USA
Michael Maire	TTI-Chicago, USA
Serge Belongie	Cornell, USA
Lubomir Bourdev	WaveOne, Inc., USA
Ross Girshick	Facebook AI Research, USA
James Hays	Georgia Tech, USA
Pietro Perona	Caltech, USA
Deva Ramanan	CMU, USA
Larry Zitnick	Facebook AI Research, USA
Riza Alp Guler	Inria, France
Natalia Neverova	Facebook AI Research, France
Vasil Khalidov	Facebook AI Research, France
Iasonas Kokkinos	Facebook AI Research, France
Samuel Rota Bulò	Mapillary Research, Austria
Lorenzo Porzi	Mapillary Research, Austria
Peter Kontschieder	Mapillary Research, Austria
Alexander Kirillov	Heidelberg University, Germany
Holger Caesar	University of Edinburgh, UK
Jasper Uijlings	Google Research, UK
Vittorio Ferrari	University of Edinburgh and Google Research, UK

W42 – First Large-Scale Video Object Segmentation Challenge

Ning Xu	Adobe Research, USA
Linjie Yang	SNAP Research, USA
Yuchen Fan	University of Illinois at Urbana-Champaign, USA
Jianchao Yang	SNAP Research, USA
Weiyao Lin	Shanghai Jiao Tong University, China
Michael Ying Yang	University of Twente, The Netherlands
Brian Price	Adobe Research, USA
Jiebo Luo	University of Rochester, USA
Thomas Huang	University of Illinois at Urbana-Champaign, USA

W43 – WIDER Face and Pedestrian Challenge

Chen Change Loy	Nanyang Technological University, Singapore
Dahua Lin	The Chinese University of Hong Kong, SAR China
Wanli Ouyang	University of Sydney, Australia
Yuanjun Xiong	Amazon Rekognition, USA
Shuo Yang	Amazon Rekognition, USA
Qingqiu Huang	The Chinese University of Hong Kong, SAR China
Dongzhan Zhou	SenseTime, China
Wei Xia	Amazon Rekognition, USA
Quanquan Li	SenseTime, China
Ping Luo	The Chinese University of Hong Kong, SAR China
Junjie Yan	SenseTime, China

Contents – Part II

W07 – 2nd International Workshop on Computer Vision for UAVs

Real-Time Embedded Computer Vision on UAVs: UAVision2018 Workshop Summary 3
Kristof Van Beeck, Tinne Tuytelaars, Davide Scarramuza, and Toon Goedemé

Teaching UAVs to Race: End-to-End Regression of Agile Controls in Simulation 11
Matthias Müller, Vincent Casser, Neil Smith, Dominik L. Michels, and Bernard Ghanem

Onboard Hyperspectral Image Compression Using Compressed Sensing and Deep Learning 30
Saurabh Kumar, Subhasis Chaudhuri, Biplab Banerjee, and Feroz Ali

SafeUAV: Learning to Estimate Depth and Safe Landing Areas for UAVs from Synthetic Data 43
Alina Marcu, Dragoş Costea, Vlad Licăreţ, Mihai Pîrvu, Emil Sluşanschi, and Marius Leordeanu

Aerial GANeration: Towards Realistic Data Augmentation Using Conditional GANs. 59
Stefan Milz, Tobias Rüdiger, and Sebastian Süss

Metrics for Real-Time Mono-VSLAM Evaluation Including IMU Induced Drift with Application to UAV Flight 73
Alexander Hardt-Stremayr, Matthias Schörghuber, Stephan Weiss, and Martin Humenberger

ShuffleDet: Real-Time Vehicle Detection Network in On-Board Embedded UAV Imagery. 88
Seyed Majid Azimi

Joint Exploitation of Features and Optical Flow for Real-Time Moving Object Detection on Drones 100
Hazal Lezki, I. Ahu Ozturk, M. Akif Akpinar, M. Kerim Yucel, K. Berker Logoglu, Aykut Erdem, and Erkut Erdem

UAV-GESTURE: A Dataset for UAV Control and Gesture Recognition 117
Asanka G. Perera, Yee Wei Law, and Javaan Chahl

ChangeNet: A Deep Learning Architecture for Visual Change Detection 129
Ashley Varghese, Jayavardhana Gubbi, Akshaya Ramaswamy, and P. Balamuralidhar

W08 – 5th Transferring and Adapting Source Knowledge in Computer Vision and 2nd VisDA Challenge

DeeSIL: Deep-Shallow Incremental Learning 151
Eden Belouadah and Adrian Popescu

Dynamic Adaptation on Non-stationary Visual Domains 158
Sindi Shkodrani, Michael Hofmann, and Efstratios Gavves

Domain Adaptive Semantic Segmentation Through Structure Enhancement 172
Fengmao Lv, Qing Lian, Guowu Yang, Guosheng Lin, Sinno Jialin Pan, and Lixin Duan

Adding New Tasks to a Single Network with Weight Transformations Using Binary Masks 180
Massimiliano Mancini, Elisa Ricci, Barbara Caputo, and Samuel Rota Bulò

Generating Shared Latent Variables for Robots to Imitate Human Movements and Understand Their Physical Limitations 190
Maxime Devanne and Sao Mai Nguyen

Model Selection for Generalized Zero-Shot Learning........ 198
Hongguang Zhang and Piotr Koniusz

W09 – PoseTrack Challenge: Articulated People Tracking in the Wild

Multi-Domain Pose Network for Multi-Person Pose Estimation and Tracking 209
Hengkai Guo, Tang Tang, Guozhong Luo, Riwei Chen, Yongchen Lu, and Linfu Wen

Enhanced Two-Stage Multi-person Pose Estimation........ 217
Hiroto Honda, Tomohiro Kato, and Yusuke Uchida

Multi-person Pose Estimation for Pose Tracking with Enhanced Cascaded Pyramid Network 221
Dongdong Yu, Kai Su, Jia Sun, and Changhu Wang

A Top-Down Approach to Articulated Human Pose Estimation and Tracking 227
Guanghan Ning, Ping Liu, Xiaochuan Fan, and Chi Zhang

W10 – Workshop on Objectionable Content and Misinformation

Deep Fusion Network for Splicing Forgery Localization 237
Bo Liu and Chi-Man Pun

Image Splicing Localization via Semi-global Network and Fully Connected Conditional Random Fields 252
Xiaodong Cun and Chi-Man Pun

Bridging Machine Learning and Cryptography in Defence Against Adversarial Attacks 267
Olga Taran, Shideh Rezaeifar, and Slava Voloshynovskiy

Bidirectional Convolutional LSTM for the Detection of Violence in Videos 280
Alex Hanson, Koutilya PNVR, Sanjukta Krishnagopal, and Larry Davis

Are You Tampering with My Data? 296
Michele Alberti, Vinaychandran Pondenkandath, Marcel Würsch, Manuel Bouillon, Mathias Seuret, Rolf Ingold, and Marcus Liwicki

Adversarial Examples Detection in Features Distance Spaces 313
Fabio Carrara, Rudy Becarelli, Roberto Caldelli, Fabrizio Falchi, and Giuseppe Amato

W11 – 9th International Workshop on Human Behavior Understanding

Give Ear to My Face: Modelling Multimodal Attention to Social Interactions 331
Giuseppe Boccignone, Vittorio Cuculo, Alessandro D'Amelio, Giuliano Grossi, and Raffaella Lanzarotti

Investigating Depth Domain Adaptation for Efficient Human Pose Estimation 346
Angel Martínez-González, Michael Villamizar, Olivier Canévet, and Jean-Marc Odobez

Filling the Gaps: Predicting Missing Joints of Human Poses Using Denoising Autoencoders 364
Nicolò Carissimi, Paolo Rota, Cigdem Beyan, and Vittorio Murino

Pose Guided Human Image Synthesis by View Disentanglement and Enhanced Weighting Loss 380
Mohamed Ilyes Lakhal, Oswald Lanz, and Andrea Cavallaro

A Semi-supervised Data Augmentation Approach Using 3D Graphical Engines 395
Shuangjun Liu and Sarah Ostadabbas

Towards Learning a Realistic Rendering of Human Behavior 409
Patrick Esser, Johannes Haux, Timo Milbich, and Björn Ommer

Human Action Recognition Based on Temporal Pose CNN and Multi-dimensional Fusion 426
Yi Huang, Shang-Hong Lai, and Shao-Heng Tai

Rendering Realistic Subject-Dependent Expression Images by Learning 3DMM Deformation Coefficients 441
Claudio Ferrari, Stefano Berretti, Pietro Pala, and Alberto Del Bimbo

Deep Multitask Gaze Estimation with a Constrained Landmark-Gaze Model 456
Yu Yu, Gang Liu, and Jean-Marc Odobez

Photorealistic Facial Synthesis in the Dimensional Affect Space 475
Dimitrios Kollias, Shiyang Cheng, Maja Pantic, and Stefanos Zafeiriou

Generating Synthetic Video Sequences by Explicitly Modeling Object Motion 492
S. Palazzo, C. Spampinato, P. D'Oro, D. Giordano, and M. Shah

A Semi-supervised Deep Generative Model for Human Body Analysis 500
Rodrigo de Bem, Arnab Ghosh, Thalaiyasingam Ajanthan, Ondrej Miksik, N. Siddharth, and Philip Torr

Role of Group Level Affect to Find the Most Influential Person in Images. . . 518
Shreya Ghosh and Abhinav Dhall

Residual Stacked RNNs for Action Recognition 534
Mohamed Ilyes Lakhal, Albert Clapés, Sergio Escalera, Oswald Lanz, and Andrea Cavallaro

W12 – 1st Person in Context Workshop and Challenge

Semantically Selective Augmentation for Deep Compact Person Re-Identification 551
Víctor Ponce-López, Tilo Burghardt, Sion Hannunna, Dima Damen, Alessandro Masullo, and Majid Mirmehdi

Recognizing People in Blind Spots Based on Surrounding Behavior 562
Kensho Hara, Hirokatsu Kataoka, Masaki Inaba, Kenichi Narioka, and Yutaka Satoh

Visual Relationship Prediction via Label Clustering and Incorporation of Depth Information 571
Hsuan-Kung Yang, An-Chieh Cheng, Kuan-Wei Ho, Tsu-Jui Fu, and Chun-Yi Lee

Human-Centric Visual Relation Segmentation Using Mask R-CNN and VTransE 582
Fan Yu, Xin Tan, Tongwei Ren, and Gangshan Wu

Learning Spatiotemporal 3D Convolution with Video Order Self-supervision 590
Tomoyuki Suzuki, Takahiro Itazuri, Kensho Hara, and Hirokatsu Kataoka

W13 – 4th Workshop on Computer Vision for Art Analysis

What Was Monet Seeing While Painting? Translating Artworks to Photo-Realistic Images. 601
Matteo Tomei, Lorenzo Baraldi, Marcella Cornia, and Rita Cucchiara

Saliency-Driven Variational Retargeting for Historical Maps. 617
Filippo Bergamasco, Arianna Traviglia, and Andrea Torsello

Deep Transfer Learning for Art Classification Problems. 631
Matthia Sabatelli, Mike Kestemont, Walter Daelemans, and Pierre Geurts

Reflecting on How Artworks Are Processed and Analyzed by Computer Vision 647
Sabine Lang and Björn Ommer

Seeing the World Through Machinic Eyes: Reflections on Computer Vision in the Arts 653
Marijke Goeting

A Digital Tool to Understand the Pictorial Procedures of 17th Century Realism. 671
Francesca Di Cicco, Lisa Wiersma, Maarten Wijntjes, Joris Dik, Jeroen Stumpel, and Sylvia Pont

How to Read Paintings: Semantic Art Understanding with Multi-modal Retrieval 676
Noa Garcia and George Vogiatzis

Weakly Supervised Object Detection in Artworks 692
Nicolas Gonthier, Yann Gousseau, Said Ladjal, and Olivier Bonfait

Images of Image Machines. Visual Interpretability in Computer Vision for Art. 710
Fabian Offert

Author Index 717

W07 – 2nd International Workshop on Computer Vision for UAVs

W07 – 2nd International Workshop on Computer Vision for UAVs

With great pleasure we present the proceedings of the 2nd International Workshop on Computer Vision for UAVs (UAVision). This half-day workshop was held on the 8th of September 2018 in conjunction with the 15th European Conference on Computer Vision (ECCV) in Munich, Germany. The focus of this workshop was on state-of-the-art real-time image processing on-board of Unmanned Aerial Vehicles (UAVs), making efficient use of specific embedded hardware and highly optimizing implementations. In total we received 14 submissions which were all double blind reviewed. For this, we composed an expert panel consisting of 62 reviewers, which in total produced 76 reviews. All papers had a minimum of 5 reviews each (with the exception of one paper, which had 4 reviewers). Based on these reviews the program committee selected four papers as full oral presentation (20 minutes talk) and five papers as short oral presentation (15 minutes talk). The best paper award consisted of 500USD, which was sponsored by the MDPI open access journal Drones. Given the reviews and oral presentations, the organizing committee decided to select the paper titled: *Teaching UAVs to race: End-to-End Regression of Agile Controls in Simulation* as best paper. In total we estimated that our workshop gathered more than 60 attendees. Apart from all accepted papers as mentioned above, these workshop proceedings also include a discussion paper written by the workshop organizers (which was not peer-reviewed). In this paper we aimed to summarize the presented work and highlighted a number of common challenges and diverse proposed solutions for UAV vision applications that were identified by multiple authors. We would like to thank all members of the program committee and all contributed authors for the work they invested in assuring that our UAVision2018 workshop was of great success and achieved a high-quality standard.

September 2018

Kristof Van Beeck
Tinne Tuytelaars
Davide Scaramuzza
Toon Goedemé

Real-Time Embedded Computer Vision on UAVs
UAVision2018 Workshop Summary

Kristof Van Beeck[1(✉)], Tinne Tuytelaars[2], Davide Scarramuza[3], and Toon Goedemé[1]

[1] EAVISE, Campus De Nayer, KU Leuven, Sint-Katelijne-Waver, Belgium
kristof.vanbeeck@kuleuven.be
[2] PSI, KU Leuven, Leuven, Belgium
[3] Robotics and Perception Group, ETH Zürich, Zürich, Switzerland

Abstract. In this paper we present an overview of the contributed work presented at the UAVision2018 ECCV workshop. This workshop focused on real-time image processing on-board of Unmanned Aerial Vehicles (UAVs). For such applications the computational complexity of state-of-the-art computer vision algorithms often conflicts with the need for real-time operation and the extreme resource limitations of the hardware. Apart from a summary of the accepted workshop papers, this work also aims to identify common challenges and concerns which were addressed by multiple authors during the workshop, and their proposed solutions.

Keywords: Computer vision · Real-time · UAVs · Embedded hardware · Deep learning · GPUs · Hardware optimizations

1 Introduction

This paper contains a summary of the material presented at the 2nd International Workshop on Computer Vision for UAVs (UAVision 2018). This workshop took place in conjunction with ECCV2018, Munich, Germany on Saturday the 8th of September 2018. Apart from a brief summarization of each paper, we also identified a number of common concerns, challenges and possible proposed solutions that several authors addressed during the workshop.

This workshop focused on state-of-the-art real-time image processing on-board of Unmanned Aerial Vehicles. Indeed, cameras make ideal sensors for drones as they are lightweight, power-efficient and an enormously rich source of information about the environment in numerous applications. Although lots of information can be derived from camera images using the newest computer vision algorithms, the use of them on-board of UAVs poses unique challenges. Their computational complexity often conflicts with the need for real-time operation and the extreme resource limitations of the platform. Of course, developers have the choice to run their image processing on-board or on a remote processing device, although the latter requires a wireless link with high bandwidth,

L. Leal-Taixé and S. Roth (Eds.): ECCV 2018 Workshops, LNCS 11130, pp. 3–10, 2019.
https://doi.org/10.1007/978-3-030-11012-3_1

minimal latency and ultra-reliable connection. Indeed, truly autonomous drones should not have to rely on a wireless datalink, thus on-board real-time processing is a necessity. However, because of the limitations of UAVs (lightweight processing devices, limited on-board computational power, limited electrical power on-board), extreme algorithmic optimization and deployment on state-of-the-art embedded hardware (such as embedded GPUs) is the only solution. In this workshop we focused on enabling embedded processing in drones, making efficient use of specific embedded hardware and highly optimizing computer vision algorithms towards real-time applications.

The remainder of this paper is structured as follows. Section 2 gives an overview and short summary of each presented paper at our workshop. In Sect. 3 we discuss the challenges that were identified by multiple authors during the workshop and their proposed solutions. Finally, we conclude this work in Sect. 4.

2 Contributed Papers

In total nine papers were accepted for publication at the UAVision2018 workshop. The first four papers listed below were accepted as full oral presentation (i.e. 20 min), whereas the five consecutive papers were accepted as short oral presentation (i.e. 15 min). Below we list and summarize each paper using the paper abstracts.

2.1 Teaching UAVs to Race: End-to-End Regression of Agile Controls in Simulation [7]

Automating the navigation of unmanned aerial vehicles (UAVs) in diverse scenarios has gained much attention in recent years. However, teaching UAVs to fly in challenging environments remains an unsolved problem, mainly due to the lack of training data. In this paper [7], the authors trained a deep neural network to predict UAV controls from raw image data for the task of autonomous UAV racing in a photo-realistic simulation. Training is done through imitation learning with data augmentation to allow for the correction of navigation mistakes. Extensive experiments demonstrate that our trained network (when sufficient data augmentation is used) outperforms state-of-the-art methods and flies more consistently than many human pilots. Additionally, we show that our optimized network architecture can run in real-time on embedded hardware, allowing for efficient onboard processing critical for real-world deployment.

2.2 Onboard Hyperspectral Image Compression Using Compressed Sensing and Deep Learning [2]

This paper [2] proposes a real-time onboard compression scheme for hyperspectral datacube which consists of a very low complexity encoder and a deep learning based parallel decoder architecture for fast decompression. The encoder creates a set of coded snapshots from a given datacube using a measurement code matrix.

The decoder decompresses the coded snapshots by using a sparse recovery algorithm. The authors solve this sparse recovery problem using a deep neural network for fast reconstruction. We present experimental results which demonstrate that our technique performs very well in terms of quality of reconstruction and in terms of computational requirements compared to other transform based techniques with some tradeoff in PSNR. The proposed technique also enables faster inference in compressed domain, suitable for on-board requirements.

2.3 SafeUAV: Learning to Estimate Depth and Safe Landing Areas for UAVs from Synthetic Data [5]

The emergence of relatively low cost UAVs has prompted a global concern about the safe operation of such devices. Since most of them can 'autonomously' fly by means of GPS way-points, the lack of a higher logic for emergency scenarios leads to an abundance of incidents involving property or personal injury. In order to tackle this problem, this paper [5] proposed a small, embeddable ConvNet for both depth and safe landing area estimation. Furthermore, since labeled training data in the 3D aerial field is scarce and ground images are unsuitable, the authors captured a novel synthetic aerial 3D dataset obtained from 3D reconstructions. They used the synthetic data to learn to estimate depth from in-flight images and segmented them into 'safe-landing' and 'obstacle' regions. Experiments demonstrated compelling results in practice on both synthetic data and real RGB drone footage.

2.4 Aerial GANeration: Towards Realistic Data Augmentation Using Conditional GANs [6]

Environmental perception for autonomous aerial vehicles is a rising field. Recent years have shown a strong increase of performance in terms of accuracy and efficiency with the aid of convolutional neural networks. Thus, the community has established data sets for benchmarking several kinds of algorithms. However, public data is rare for multi-sensor approaches or either not large enough to train very accurate algorithms. For this reason, this paper [6] proposed a method to generate multi-sensor data sets using realistic data augmentation based on conditional generative adversarial networks (cGAN). cGANs have shown impressive results for image to image translation. The authors used this principle for sensor simulation. Hence, there is no need for expensive and complex 3D engines. The method encodes ground truth data, e.g. semantics or object boxes that could be drawn randomly, in the conditional image to generate realistic consistent sensor data. Their method is proven for aerial object detection and semantic segmentation on visual data, such as 3D Lidar reconstruction using the ISPRS and DOTA data set. The authors demonstrate qualitative accuracy improvements for state-of-the-art object detection (YOLO) using this augmentation technique.

2.5 Metrics for Real-Time Mono-VSLAM Evaluation Including IMU Induced Drift with Application to UAV Flight [3]

Vision based algorithms became popular for state estimation and subsequent (local) control of mobile robots. Currently a large variety of such algorithms exists and their performance is often characterized through their drift relative to the total trajectory traveled. However, this metric has relatively low relevance for local vehicle control/stabilization. In this paper [3], the authors proposed a set of metrics which allows to evaluate a vision based algorithm with respect to its usability for state estimation and subsequent (local) control of highly dynamic autonomous mobile platforms such as multirotor UAVs. As such platforms usually make use of inertial measurements to mitigate the relatively low update rate of the visual algorithm, they particularly focused on a new metric taking the expected IMU-induced drift between visual readings into consideration based on the probabilistic properties of the sensor. The authors demonstrated this set of metrics by comparing ORB-SLAM, LSD-SLAM and DSO on different datasets.

2.6 ShuffleDet: Real-Time Vehicle Detection Network in On-board Embedded UAV Imagery [1]

On-board real-time vehicle detection is of great significance for UAVs and other embedded mobile platforms. In this paper [1] the authors present a computationally inexpensive detection network for vehicle detection in UAV imagery which we call ShuffleDet. In order to enhance the speed-wise performance, we construct our method primarily using channel shuffling and grouped convolutions. We apply inception modules and deformable modules to consider the size and geometric shape of the vehicles. ShuffleDet is evaluated on CARPK and PUCPR+ datasets and compared against the state-of-the-art real-time object detection networks. ShuffleDet achieves 3.8 GFLOPs while it provides competitive performance on test sets of both datasets. We show that our algorithm achieves real-time performance by running at the speed of 14 frames per second on NVIDIA Jetson TX2 showing high potential for this method for real-time processing in UAVs.

2.7 Joint Exploitation of Features and Optical Flow for Real-Time Moving Object Detection on Drones [4]

Moving object detection is an imperative task in computer vision, where it is primarily used for surveillance applications. With the increasing availability of low-altitude aerial vehicles, new challenges for moving object detection have surfaced, both for academia and industry. In this paper [4], the authors proposed a new approach that can detect moving objects efficiently and handle parallax cases. By introducing sparse ow based parallax handling and downscale processing, they pushed the boundaries of real-time performance with 16 FPS on limited embedded resources (a five-fold improvement over existing baselines), while managing to perform comparably or even improve the state-of-the-art in two different datasets. They also presented a roadmap for extending our approach to exploit multi-modal data in order to mitigate the need for parameter tuning.

2.8 UAV-GESTURE: A Dataset for UAV Control and Gesture Recognition [8]

Current UAV-recorded datasets were mostly limited to action recognition and object tracking, whereas the gesture signals datasets were mostly recorded in indoor spaces. Currently, there is no outdoor recorded public video dataset for UAV commanding signals. To fill this gap and enable research in wider application areas, this paper [8] presented a UAV gesture signals dataset recorded in an outdoor setting. The authors selected 13 gestures suitable for basic UAV navigation and command from general aircraft handling and helicopter handling signals. They provide 119 high-definition video clips consisting of 37151 frames. All the frames are annotated for the body joints and gesture classes in order to extend the dataset's applicability to a wider research area including gesture recognition, action recognition, human pose recognition and situation awareness.

2.9 ChangeNet: A Deep Learning Architecture for Visual Change Detection [9]

The increasing urban population in cities necessitates the need for the development of smart cities that can offer better services to its citizens. Drone technology plays a crucial role in the smart city environment and is already involved in a number of functions in smart cities such as traffic control and construction monitoring. A major challenge in fast growing cities is the encroachment of public spaces. A robotic solution using visual change detection can be used for such purposes. For the detection of encroachment, a drone can monitor outdoor urban areas over a period of time to infer the visual changes. Visual change detection is a higher level inference task that aims at accurately identifying variations between a reference image (historical) and a new test image depicting the current scenario. In case of images, the challenges are complex considering the variations caused by environmental conditions that are actually unchanged events. Human mind interprets the change by comparing the current status with historical data at intelligence level rather than using only visual information. In this paper [9], the authors presented a deep architecture called ChangeNet for detecting changes between pairs of images and express the same semantically (label the change). A parallel deep convolutional neural network (CNN) architecture for localizing and identifying the changes between image pair has been proposed in this paper. The architecture is evaluated with VL-CMU-CD street view change detection, TSUNAMI and Google Street View (GSV) datasets that resemble drone captured images. The performance of the model for different lighting and seasonal conditions are experimented quantitatively and qualitatively. The result shows that ChangeNet outperforms the state of the art by achieving 98.3% pixel accuracy, 77.35% object based Intersection over Union (IoU) and 88.9% area under Receiver Operating Characteristics (RoC) curve.

3 Discussion: Trends and Solutions to Common Challenges

Throughout the workshop we identified a number of common concerns for UAV vision applications that multiple authors identified and proposed solutions for. Below we give an overview.

3.1 Potential of Deep Learning for UAV Applications

One main message is that the success of deep learning based techniques also extends towards UAV applications. Almost every author in the workshop made use of deep learning for their specific drone application. For example, Marcu *et al.* [5] proposed a neural network that is trained to detect flat ground surfaces upon which a UAV can land safely. Also, a CNN that is able to detect scene changes from UAV drone images, without being distracted by seasonal effects like snow and fallen leaves was presented by Varghese *et al.* [9]. A remarkable result was shown in the work of Kumar *et al.* [2], where they show that for multispectral data decompression, their proposed deep learning alternative is even substantially faster than the classic mathematical approach.

3.2 Collecting Training Data for UAV Applications

A difficulty many drone vision researcher struggles with is how to gather enough visual training material to train these neural networks with. Indeed, because of the inherent viewpoint freedom a flying drone has, it is very difficult to acquire real UAV image data that has enough variance. Quite a few papers in the Uavision workshop tackled this problem, in very diverse ways.

The straightforward manner is setting up a large data recording campaign with real drones, pilots and actors. This is only feasible for a constrained application because of the manual labour and hence the cost. Perera *et al.* [8] did this and presented on this workshop a newly recorded dataset for gesture recognition from drone images.

However, many authors seek the answer of this in other data sources, which can be used for training a visual drone application. As in other computer vision applications, the use of rendered synthetic data from simulation engines shows potential for UAV too, as demonstrated by Müller *et al.* [7], using Sim4CV to build a virtual environment to train a racing drone.

Another example is the work of Marcu *et al.* [5], in which the authors used 3D Google Earth data as training material for a drone to learn where it is safe to land.

In this workshop, other work from Milz *et al.* [6] showed the potential of cGANs to generate data to train a UAV application, yielding a virtually infinite source of relevant training data.

3.3 Real-Time On-board Processing

The participants of this UAVision workshop all agreed that on-board processing is a must for real-time UAV vision applications. The second speaker [2] stated this very strictly: for hyperspectral video transmission from UAVs, their is simply not enough bandwidth available. On-board compression is hence a necessity. Also, Hardt-Stremayr [3] concluded in his talk about metrics for UAV vision-based SLAM that they need video processing with a frame-rate of at least 10 fps, in order to keep the drift error caused by the IMU low enough.

Many authors showed successful implementations of deep learning based image interpretation algorithms that indeed can run in real-time on embedded hardware. We noticed that the NVIDIA Jetson TX2 platform is a popular choice in this field. For example, Müller [7] estimated that their drone racing model (running at 556 fps on a NVIDIA TitanX), will run at about 50 fps on a Jetson TX2 platform, largely fast enough for real-time processing.

Another example is the presented work of Lezki *et al.* [4], who reached real-time performance with 16 FPS on limited embedded resources (a 5× improvement) for their moving objects detection, by introducing sparse parallax handling and downscaling processing.

Indeed, also Kumar *et al.* [2] demonstrated a speed-up factor of 30× for their hyperspectral decompression algorithm as compared to the baseline, indicating that two-digit speed-up factors can be achieved in many cases.

Last but not least, in their talk on ShuffleDet, Azimi *et al.* [1] pulled out all the stops for developing a ultimately efficient object detector. By exploiting group convolutions, channel shuffling, and depth wise convolutions, they achieved a 14× speed-up as compared to the already very time-optimal YOLO detector.

4 Conclusion

This paper summarized the contributed work which was presented at the UAVision2018 workshop (in conjunction with ECCV2018), and tried to identify common concerns and challenges that were recognized by multiple authors, and their proposed solutions. Three significant trends were discovered. First, the use of deep learning for (embedded) UAV applications seems viable, despite their increased computational complexity. Secondly, the collection of sufficient training data remains difficult, and several authors therefore use synthetically generated images. Finally, although real-time computer vision processing on-board of UAVs on low-power embedded hardware platforms remains challenging, several authors were able to present real-time implementations through extreme software and/or hardware optimizations.

Acknowledgements. This work is supported by the agency Flanders Innovation & Entrepreneurship (VLAIO) and Research Foundation - Flanders (FWO).

References

1. Azimi, S.M.: ShuffleDet: real-time vehicle detection network in on-board embedded. In: Leal-Taixé, L., Roth, S. (eds.) ECCV 2018 Workshops. LNCS, vol. 11130, pp. 88–99. Springer, Cham (2019). https://doi.org/10.1007/97d8-3-030-11012-3_z
2. Kumar, S., Chaudhuri, S., Banerjee, B., Ali, F.: Onboard hyperspectral image compression using compressed sensing and deep learning. In: Leal-Taixé, L., Roth, S. (eds.) ECCV 2018 Workshops. LNCS, vol. 11130, pp. 30–42. Springer, Cham (2019). https://doi.org/10.1007/97d8-3-030-11012-3_z
3. Hardt-Stremayr, A., Schörghuber, M., Weiss, S., Humenberger, M.: Metrics for real-time mono-VSLAM evaluation including IMU induced drift with application to UAV flight. In: Leal-Taixé, L., Roth, S. (eds.) ECCV 2018 Workshops. LNCS, vol. 11130, pp. 73–87. Springer, Cham (2019). https://doi.org/10.1007/97d8-3-030-11012-3_z
4. Lezki, H., et al.: Joint exploitation of features and optical flow for real-time moving object detection on drones. In: Leal-Taixé, L., Roth, S. (eds.) ECCV 2018 Workshops. LNCS, vol. 11130, pp. 100–116. Springer, Cham (2019). https://doi.org/10.1007/97d8-3-030-11012-3_z
5. Marcu, A., Costea, D., Licăreţ, V., Leordeanu, M., Pîrvu, M., Sluşanschi, E.: SafeUAV: learning to estimate depth and safe landing areas for UAVs from synthetic data. In: Leal-Taixé, L., Roth, S. (eds.) ECCV 2018 Workshops. LNCS, vol. 11130, pp. 43–58. Springer, Cham (2019). https://doi.org/10.1007/97d8-3-030-11012-3_z
6. Milz, S., Rüdiger, T., Süss, S.: Aerial GANeration: towards realistic data augmentation using conditional GANs. In: Leal-Taixé, L., Roth, S. (eds.) ECCV 2018 Workshops. LNCS, vol. 11130, pp. 59–72. Springer, Cham (2019). https://doi.org/10.1007/97d8-3-030-11012-3_z
7. Müller, M., Casser, V., Smith, N., Michels, D.L., Ghanem, B.: Teaching UAVs to race: end-to-end regression of agile controls in simulation. In: Leal-Taixé, L., Roth, S. (eds.) ECCV 2018 Workshops. LNCS, vol. 11130, pp. 11–29. Springer, Cham (2019). https://doi.org/10.1007/97d8-3-030-11012-3_z
8. Perera, A.G., Law, Y.M., Chahl, J.: UAV-GESTURE: a dataset for UAV control and gesture recognition. In: Leal-Taixé, L., Roth, S. (eds.) ECCV 2018 Workshops. LNCS, vol. 11130, pp. 117–128. Springer, Cham (2019). https://doi.org/10.1007/97d8-3-030-11012-3_z
9. Varghese, A., Gubbi, J.: ChangeNet: a deep learning architecture for visual change detection. In: Leal-Taixé, L., Roth, S. (eds.) ECCV 2018 Workshops. LNCS, vol. 11130, pp. 129–145. Springer, Cham (2019). https://doi.org/10.1007/97d8-3-030-11012-3_z

Teaching UAVs to Race: End-to-End Regression of Agile Controls in Simulation

Matthias Müller(✉), Vincent Casser, Neil Smith, Dominik L. Michels, and Bernard Ghanem

Visual Computing Center at King Abdullah University of Science and Technology, Thuwal, Kingdom of Saudi Arabia
{matthias.mueller.2,vincent.casser,neil.smith, dominik.michels,bernard.ghanem}@kaust.edu.sa

Abstract. Automating the navigation of unmanned aerial vehicles (UAVs) in diverse scenarios has gained much attention in recent years. However, teaching UAVs to fly in challenging environments remains an unsolved problem, mainly due to the lack of training data. In this paper, we train a deep neural network to predict UAV controls from raw image data for the task of autonomous UAV racing in a photo-realistic simulation. Training is done through imitation learning with data augmentation to allow for the correction of navigation mistakes. Extensive experiments demonstrate that our trained network (when sufficient data augmentation is used) outperforms state-of-the-art methods and flies more consistently than many human pilots. Additionally, we show that our optimized network architecture can run in real-time on embedded hardware, allowing for efficient on-board processing critical for real-world deployment. From a broader perspective, our results underline the importance of extensive data augmentation techniques to improve robustness in end-to-end learning setups.

1 Introduction

Fig. 1. Illustration of the trained racing UAV in-flight.

Unmanned aerial vehicles (UAVs) like drones and multicopters are attracting increased interest across various communities such as robotics, graphics, and computer vision. Learning to control UAVs in complex environments is a challenging task even for humans. One of the most challenging navigation tasks with respect to UAVs is competitive drone racing. It takes extensive

M. Müller and V. Casser—Equal contribution.

L. Leal-Taixé and S. Roth (Eds.): ECCV 2018 Workshops, LNCS 11130, pp. 11–29, 2019.
https://doi.org/10.1007/978-3-030-11012-3_2

practice to become a good pilot, frequently involving crashes. A more affordable approach to develop professional flight skills is to train many hours in a flight simulator before going to the field. Since most of the fine motor skills of flight control are developed in the simulator, the pilot is able to quickly transition to real-world flights.

Humans are able to abstract the visual differences between simulation and the real world and are able to transfer the learned control knowledge with some fine-tuning to account for the small differences of the physics simulation. While transfer for trained network policies is more difficult due to the perception component, it will be easier if the simulation is as close to reality as possible. Therefore, we use the physics-based UAV racing game within Sim4CV [27] which features a photo-realistic and customizable racing area in the form of a stadium based on a three-dimensional (3D) scanned real-world location. This ensures minimal discrepancy when transitioning from the simulated to a real-world scenario in the future. The concept of generating synthetic clones of real-world data for deep learning purposes has been adopted in previous work [8]. Also, it has become popular recently to use video game engines [6,40] to generate photo-realistic simulations for training autonomous agents.

Combining the realistic physics and graphics of a game engine coupled with a real-world 3D scan should make the transfer much simpler and fine-tuning on some real world data may be sufficient if a sufficiently robust policy was trained in simulation. A key requirement for generalization is the DNN's ability to learn the appearance of gates and cones in the track within a complexly textured and dynamic environment. In the simulated environment, we have the opportunity to fully customize the race track, including using different textures (e.g. grass, snow, and dirt), gates (different shapes and appearance), and lighting. This will make the trained network more robust and will enable transfer to the real world via domain randomization [39].

Our autonomous racing UAV approach goes beyond simple pattern detection and instead learns a full end-to-end system to fly the UAV through a racing course. It is similar in spirit to learning an end-to-end driving policy for a car [3], but comes with additional challenges. The proposed network extends the complexity of previous work to the control of a six degrees of freedom (6-DoF) flying system which is able to traverse tight spaces and make sharp turns at very high speeds (a task that cannot be performed by a ground vehicle). Our imitation learning based approach simultaneously addresses both problems of perception and control as the UAV navigates through the course.

Contributions. Our specific contributions are as follows.

(1) We show that the challenging task of UAV racing can be learned in an end-to-end fashion in simulation, and both demonstrate and quantify the positive impact of using viewpoint augmentation for increased robustness. Experiments show that our trained network can outperform several baselines and fly more consistently than the pilots on whose data it was trained.

(2) To facilitate the training, parameter tuning and evaluation of deep networks on this type of simulated data, we provide a full integration between the simulator and an end-to-end deep learning pipeline (based on TensorFlow). Similar to other deep networks trained for game play, our integration will allow the community to fully explore many scenarios and tasks that go far beyond UAV racing in a rich and diverse photo-realistic gaming environment (e.g. obstacle avoidance and trajectory planning).

(3) We integrate a photo-realistic UAV racing simulation environment based on a real-world counterpart which can be easily customized to build increasingly challenging racing courses and enables realistic UAV physical behavior. Logging video data from the UAV's point-of-view and pilot controls is seamless and can be used to effortlessly generate large-scale training data for AI systems targeting UAV flying in particular and autonomous vehicles in general (e.g. self-driving cars).

2 Related Work

In this section, we put our proposed methodology into context, focusing on the most related previous work.

Learning to Navigate. Navigation has traditionally been approached by either employing supervised learning (SL) methods [3,4,17,29,35,38,42] or reinforcement learning (RL) methods [21,24,25,32,33,43]. Furthermore, combinations of the two have been proposed in an effort to leverage advantages of both techniques, e.g. for increasing sample efficiency for RL methods [1,5,9,10,20]. For the case of controlling physics-driven vehicles, SL can be advantageous when acquiring labeled data is not too costly or inefficient, and has been proven to have relative success in the field of autonomous driving, among other applications, in recent years [3,4,42]. However, the use of neural networks for SL in autonomous driving goes back to much earlier work [29,35].

In the work of Bojarski et al. [3], a deep neural network (DNN) is trained to map recorded camera views to 3-DoF steering commands (steering wheel angle, throttle, and brake). Seventy-two hours of human driven training data was tediously collected from a forward facing camera and augmented with two additional views to provide data for simulated drifting and corrective maneuvering. The simulated and on-road results of this pioneering work demonstrate the ability of a DNN to learn (end-to-end) the control process of a self-driving car from raw video data.

Similar to our work but for cars, Chen et al. [4] use TORCS (The Open Racing Car Simulator) [45] to train a DNN to drive at casual speeds through a course and properly pass or follow other vehicles in its lane. This work builds off earlier work using TORCS, which focused on keeping the car on a track [17]. In contrast to our work, the vehicle controls to be predicted in the work of Chen et al. [4] are limited, since only a small discrete set of expected control outputs are available: turn-left, turn-right, throttle, and brake. Recently, TORCS has also been successfully used in several RL approaches for autonomous car driving [18,21,24]; however, in these cases, RL was used to teach the agent to drive specific tracks or all available tracks rather than learning to drive never before seen tracks.

Loquercio et al. [22] trained a network on autonomous car datasets and then deployed it to control a drone. For this, they used full supervision by providing image and measured steering angle pairs from pre-collected datasets, and collecting their own dataset containing image and binary obstacle indication pairs. While they demonstrate an ability to transfer successfully to other environments, their approach does not model and exploit the full six degrees of freedom available. It also focuses on slow and safe navigation, rather than optimizing for speed as is the case for racing. Finally, with their network being fairly complex, they report an inference speed of 20 fps (CPU) for remote processing, which is more than three times lower than the estimated frame rate for our proposed method when running on-board processing, and more than 27 times lower compared to our method running remotely on GPU.

In the work of Smolyanskiy et al. [42], a DNN is trained (in an SL fashion and from real data captured from a head-mounted camera) to navigate a UAV through forest trails and avoid obstacles. Similar to previous work, the expected control outputs of the network are discrete and very limited (simple yaw movements): turn-left, go-straight, or turn-right. Despite showing relatively promising results, the trained network leads to a slow, non-smooth (zig-zag) trajectory at a fixed altitude above the ground. It is worthwhile to note that indoor UAV control using DNNs has also been recently explored [1,16,41].

Importance of Exploration in Supervised Learning. In imitation learning [14], the 'expert' training set used for SL is augmented and expanded, so as to combine the merits of both exploitation and exploration. In many sequential decision making tasks of which autonomous vehicle control is one, this augmentation becomes necessary to train an AI system (e.g. DNN) that can recover from mistakes. In this sense, imitation learning with augmentation can be crudely seen as a supervision guided form of RL. For example, a recent imitation learning method called DAgger (Dataset Aggregation) [38] demonstrated a simple way of incrementally augmenting ground-truth sequential decisions to allow for further exploration, since the learner will be trained on the aggregate dataset and not only the original expert one. This method was shown to outperform state-of-the-art AI methods on a 3D car racing game (Super Tux Kart), where the control outputs are again 3-DoF. Other imitation learning approaches [20] have reached a similar conclusion, namely that a trajectory optimizer can function to help guide a sub-optimal learning policy towards the optimal one. Inspired by the above work, our proposed method also exploits similar concepts for exploration. In the simulator, we are able to automatically and effortlessly generate a richly diverse set of image and control pairs that can be used to train a UAV to robustly and reliably navigate through a racing course.

Simulation. As mentioned earlier, generating diverse 'natural' training data for sequential decision making through SL is tedious. Generating additional data for exploration purposes (i.e. in scenarios where both input and output pairs have to be generated) is much more so. Therefore, a lot of attention from the community is being given to simulators (or games) for this source of data. In fact, a broad range of work has exploited them recently for these types of learning, namely in animation and motion planning [10–12,15,19,21,43], scene understanding [2,31], pedestrian detection [23], and identification of 2D/3D objects [13,26,34]. For instance, the authors of [15] used Unity, a video game engine similar to Unreal Engine, to teach a bird how to fly in simulation.

Moreover, there is another line of work that uses hardware-in-the-loop (HILT) simulation. Examples include JMAVSim [36,44] which was used to develop and evaluate controllers and RotorS [7] which was used to study visual servoing. The visual quality of most HIL simulators is very basic and far from photo-realistic with the exception of AirSim [40]. While there are multiple established simulators such as Realflight, Flightgear, or XPlane for simulating aerial platforms, they have several limitations. In contrast to Unreal Engine, advanced shading and post-processing settings are not available and the selection of assets and textures is limited. Recent work [6,8,27,37,40] highlights how modern game engines can be used to generate photo-realistic training datasets and pixel-accurate segmentation masks. The goal of this work is to build an automated UAV flying system (based on imitation learning) that can relatively easily be transitioned from a simulated world to the real one. Therefore, we choose Sim4CV [27,28] as our simulator, which uses the open source game engine UE4 and provides a full software in-the-loop UAV simulation. The simulator also provides a lot of flexibility in terms of assets, textures, and communication interfaces.

3 Methodology

The fundamental modules of our proposed system are summarized in Fig. 2, which represents the end-to-end dataset generation, learning, and evaluation process. In what follows, we provide details for each of these modules, namely

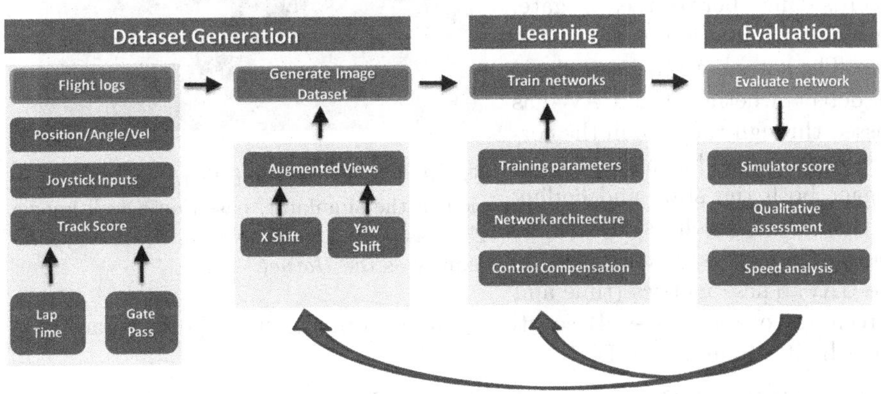

Fig. 2. Description of the pipeline of our DNN Imitation Learning System. After recording flights of human pilots, we improve important model parameters like network architecture, number of augmented views and appropriate control compensation for them in an iterative process.

how datasets are automatically generated within the simulator, how our proposed DNN is designed and trained, and how the learned DNN is evaluated.

3.1 Dataset Generation

Our simulation environment allows for the automatic generation of customizable datasets that can be used for various learning tasks related to UAVs. In the following, we elaborate on our setup for building a large-scale dataset specific to UAV racing.

UAV Flight Simulation. The core of the system is the application of our UE4 based simulator. It is built on top of the open source UE4 project for computer vision called Sim4CV [27]. Several changes were made to adapt the simulator for training our proposed racing DNN. First, we replaced the UAV with the 3D model and specifications of a racing quadcopter (see Fig. 3). We retuned the PID controller of the UAV to be more responsive and to function in a racing mode, where altitude control and stabilization are still enabled but with much higher rates and steeper pitch and roll angles. In fact, this is now a popular racing mode available on consumer UAVs, such as the DJI Mavic. The simulator frame rate is locked at 60 fps and at every frame a log is recorded with UAV position, orientation, velocity, and stick inputs from the pilot. To accommodate for realistic input, we integrated the same UAV transmitter that would be used in real-world racing scenarios.

Following paradigms set by UAV racing norms, each racing course/track in our simulator comprises a sequence of gates connected by uniformly spaced cones. The track has a timing system that records time between each gate, lap, and completion time of the race. The gates have their own logic to detect whether the UAV has passed through the gate in the correct direction. This allows us to trigger both the start and ending of the race, as well as, determine the number of gates traversed by the UAV. These metrics (time and percentage of gates passed) constitute the overall per-track performance of a pilot, be it a human or a DNN.

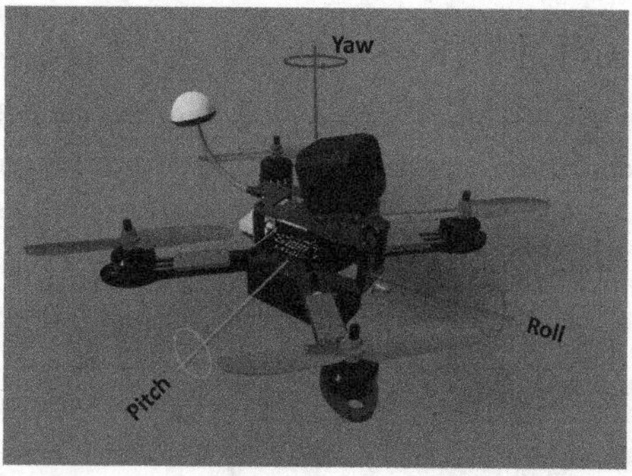

Fig. 3. The 3D model of the racing UAV modeled in the simulator, based on a well known 250 class design known within the racing community as the *Hornet*.

Automatic Track Generation. We developed a graphical track editor in which a user can draw a 2D sketch of the overhead view of the track. Subsequently, the 3D track is automatically generated and integrated into the timing system. With this editor, we created eleven tracks: seven for training, and four for testing and evaluation. Each track is defined by gate positions and track lanes delineated by uniformly spaced racing cones distributed along the splines connecting adjacent gates. We design the tracks such that they are similar to what racing professionals are accustomed to and such that they offer enough diversity to enable network generalization to unseen tracks. To avoid user bias in designing the race tracks, we use images collected from the internet and trace their contours in the editor to create uniquely stylized tracks. Please refer to Fig. 4 for an overhead view of all these tracks.

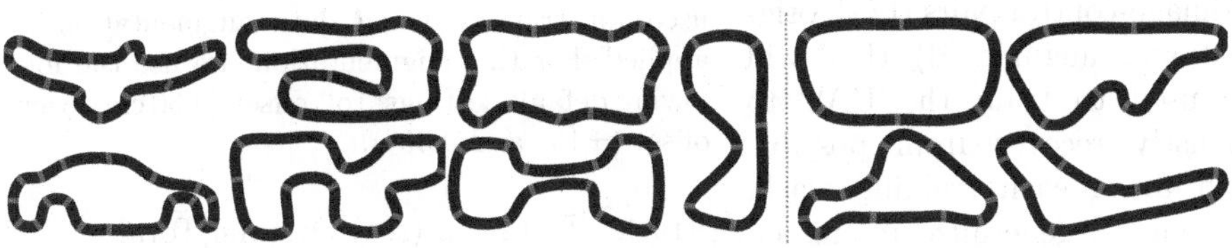

Fig. 4. The seven training tracks (left) and the four evaluation tracks (right). Gates are marked in red. (Color figure online)

Acquiring Ground-Truth Pilot Data. The simulation environment allows us to log the images rendered from the UAV camera point-of-view and the UAV flight controls from the transmitter. We record human pilot input from a Taranis flight transmitter integrated into the simulator through a joystick. This input is solicited from three pilots with different skill levels: novice (lacking any flight experience), intermediate (a moderately experienced pilot), and expert (a professional, competitive racing pilot). The pilots are given the opportunity to fly through the seven training tracks as many times as needed until they successfully complete the tracks at their best time while passing through all gates. For the evaluation tracks, the pilots are allowed to fly the course only as many times as needed to complete the entire course without crashing. We automatically score pilot performance based on lap time and percentage of gates traversed.

Data Augmentation. As mentioned earlier, robust imitation learning requires the augmentation of these ground-truth logs with synthetic ones generated at a user-defined set of UAV offset positions and orientations accompanied by the corresponding controls needed to correct for these offsets. Assigning corrective controls to the augmented data is quite complex in general, since they depend on many factors, including current UAV velocity, relative position on the track, its weight and current attitude. While it is possible to get this data in the simulation, it is very difficult to obtain it in the real world in real-time. Therefore, we employ a fairly simple but effective model to determine these augmented controls that also scales to real-world settings. We add or subtract a corrective value to the pilot roll and yaw stick inputs for each position or orientation offset that is applied. For rotational offsets, we do not only apply a yaw correction but also couple it to roll. This allows to compensate for the UAV's inertia which produces a motion component in the previous direction of travel.

Training Data Set. We summarize the details of the data generated from all training tracks in Table 1. It is clear that the augmentation increases the size of the original dataset by approximately seven times. Each pilot flight leads to a large number of image-control pairs (both original and augmented) that will be used to train the UAV to robustly recover from possible drift along each training track, as well as, generalize to unseen evaluation tracks. Details of how our proposed DNN architecture is designed and trained are provided in Sect. 3.2 of the paper. In general, more augmented data should improve UAV flight performance assuming that the control mapping and original flight data are noise-free. However, in many scenarios, this is not the case, so we find that there is a limit after which augmentation does not help (or even slightly degrades) explorative learning. Empirical results validating this observation are detailed in Sect. 4 of the paper. We also show the effects of training with different flying styles there. For this dataset, we choose to use the intermediate pilot who tends to follow the track most precisely, striking a good trade-off between style of flight and speed.

Table 1. Overview of the image-control dataset generated from two laps of flying (by the intermediate pilot) through each of the training tracks. The 'duration' column shows the total time taken by the pilot to successfully fly two laps through the track (i.e. passing through all the gates). We also record the number of images rendered from the pilot's trajectory in the simulator, along with the total number of images used for training when data augmentation is applied. For this augmentation, we use the following default settings: roll offset (±50 cm), yaw offset (±15° and ±30°).

Track	Duration (sec)	Original	Total
track01	69.8	4.2K	29.3K
track02	100.4	6.0K	42.2K
track03	83.1	5.0K	35.0K
track04	97.7	5.9K	41.0K
track05	99.8	6.0K	42.0K
track06	115.4	6.9K	48.5K
track07	98.3	5.9K	41.2K
total	664.5	39.9K	279.1K

Since the logs can be replayed at a later time in the simulator, we can augment the dataset further by changing environmental conditions, including lighting, cone spacing or appearance, and other environmental dynamics (e.g. clouds), but we do not explore these capabilities in this work.

3.2 Learning

As it is the case for DNN-based solutions to other tasks, a careful construction of the training set is a key requirement to robust and effective DNN training. We dedicate seven racing tracks with their corresponding image-control pairs logged from human pilot runs and appropriate augmentation for training. Please refer to Sect. 3.1 for details about data collection and augmentation. In the following, we provide a detailed description of the learning strategy used to train our DNN, its network architecture and design. We also explore some of the inner workings of one of the trained DNNs to shed light on how this network is solving the problem of automated UAV racing.

Network Architecture. To train a DNN to predict stick inputs controlling the UAV from images, we choose a regression network architecture similar to the one used by Bojarski et al. [3]; however, we make changes to accommodate the complexity of the task at hand and to improve robustness in training. Our DNN architecture is shown in Fig. 5. The network consists of eight layers, five convolutional and three fully-connected. Since we implicitly want to localize the track and gates, we use striding in the convolutional layers instead of (max) pooling.

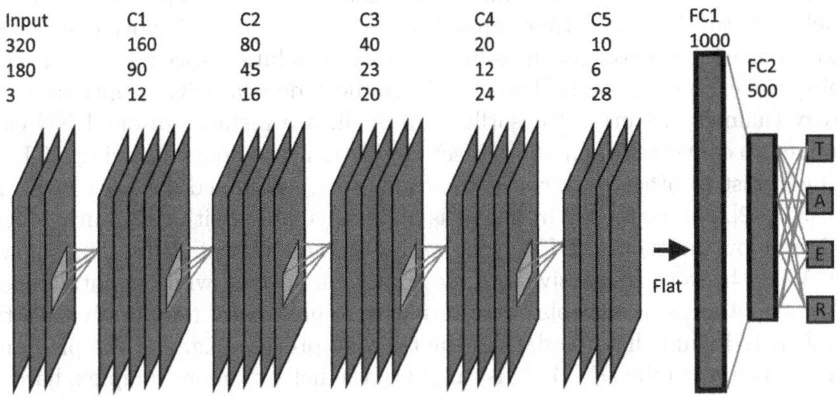

Fig. 5. Our network architecture is taking an image of shape 320 × 180 and regresses to the control outputs throttle (T), elevator (E), aileron (A) and roll (R).

We arrived at this compact network architecture by running extensive validation experiments. Our final architecture strikes a reasonable tradeoff between computational complexity and predictive performance. This careful design makes the proposed DNN architecture feasible for real-time applications on embedded hardware (e.g. Nvidia TX1, or the recent Nvidia TX2) unlike previous architectures [3], if they use the same input size. In Table 2, we show both evaluation time on and technical details of the NVIDIA Titan X, and how it compares to a NVIDIA TX-1. Based on [30], we expect our network to still run at real-time speed with over 60 frames per second on this embedded hardware.

Table 2. Comparison of the NVIDIA Titan X and the NVIDIA TX-1. The performance of the TX-1 is approximated according to [30].

	NVIDIA Titan X	NVIDIA TX-1
CUDA cores	3,840	256
Boost clock MHz	1,582	998
VRAM	12 GB	4 GB
Memory bandwidth	547.7 Gbps	25.6 Gbps
Evaluation (ours)	556 fps (ref)	64.6 fps

Implementation Details. The DNN is given a single RGB-image with a 320×180 pixel resolution as input and is trained to regress to the four stick inputs to control the UAV using a standard L^2-loss and dropout ratio of 0.5.

We find that the relatively high input resolution (i.e. higher network capacity), as compared to related methods [3,42], is useful to learn this more complicated maneuvering task and to enhance the network's ability to look further ahead. This affords the network with more robustness needed for long-term trajectory stability. On the other hand, we found no noticeably gain when training on even higher resolutions during initial experiments. At our proposed resolution, our network still shows real-time capabilities even when being deployed on-board (Table 2), marking a convincing solution to the resolution-speed trade-off. For training, we exploit a standard stochastic gradient descent (SGD) optimization strategy (namely Adam) in Tensorflow. As such, one instance of our DNN can be trained to convergence on our dataset in less than two hours on a single GPU.

In contrast to other work where the frame rate is sampled down to 10 fps or lower [3,4,42], our racing environment is highly dynamic (with tight turns, high speed, and low inertia of the UAV), so we use a frame rate of 60 fps. This allows the UAV to be very responsive and move at high speeds, while maintaining a level of smoothness in controls. An alternative approach for temporally smooth controls is to include historic data in the training process (e.g. add the previous controls as input to the DNN). This can make the network more complex, harder to train, and less responsive in the highly dynamic racing environment, where many time critical decisions have to be made within a couple of frames (about 30 ms). Therefore, we find the high learning frame rate of 60 fps a good trade-off between smooth controls and responsiveness.

Network Visualization
After training our DNN to convergence, we visualize how parts of the network behave. Figure 6 shows some feature maps in different layers for the same input image. Note how the filters have learned to extract all necessary information in the scene (i.e. gates and cones). Also, higher-level filters are not responding to other parts of the environment. Although the feature map resolution becomes very low in the higher DNN layers, the feature map in the fifth convolutional layer is interesting as it marks the top, left, and right of parts of a gate with just a single activation

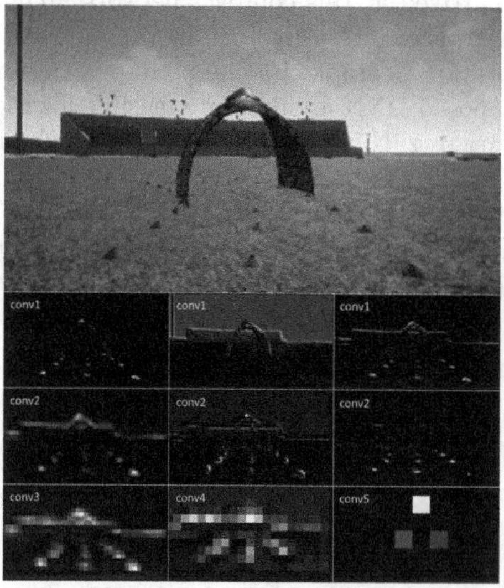

Fig. 6. Visualization of feature maps at different convolutional layers in our trained network. Note the high activations in semantically meaningful image regions for the task of UAV racing, namely the gates and cones.

each. This clearly demonstrates that our DNN is learning semantically intuitive features for the task of UAV racing.

Reinforcement vs. Imitation Learning. Our simulation environment can lend itself useful in training networks using reinforcement learning. This type of learning does not specifically require supervised pilot information, as it searches for an optimal policy that leads to the highest eventual reward (e.g. highest percentage of gates traversed or lowest lap time). Recent methods have made use of reinforcement to learn simpler tasks without supervision [5]; however, they require very long training times (up to several weeks) and a much faster simulator (1,000 fps is possible in simple non photo-realistic games). For UAV racing, the required task is more involved and since the intent is to transfer the learned network into the real-world, a (slower) photo-realistic simulator is mandatory. Because of these two constraints, we decided to train our DNN using imitation learning instead of reinforcement learning.

4 Experiments

We create four testing tracks based on well-known race tracks found in TORCS and Gran Turismo. We refer to Fig. 4 for an overhead view of these tracks. Since the tracks must fit within the football stadium environment, they are scaled down leading to much sharper turns and shorter straight-aways with the UAV reaching top speeds of over 100 km/h. Therefore, the evaluation tracks are significantly more difficult than they may have been originally intended in their original racing environments. We rank the four tracks in terms of difficulty ranging from easy (track 1), medium (track 2), hard (track 3), to very hard (track 4). For all the following evaluations, both the trained networks and human pilots are tasked to fly two laps in the testing tracks and are scored based on the total gates they fly through and overall lap time. Obviously, the testing/evaluation tracks are never seen in training, neither by the human pilot nor the DNN.

Experimental Setup. In order to evaluate the performance of a trained DNN in real-time at 60 fps, we establish a TCP socket connection between the UE4 simulator and the Python wrapper (TensorFlow) executing the DNN. In doing so, the simulator continuously sends rendered UAV camera images across TCP to the DNN, which in turn processes each image individually to predict the next UAV stick inputs (flight controls) that are fed back to the UAV in the simulator using the same connection. Another advantage of this TCP connection is that the DNN prediction can be run on a separate system than the one running the simulator. We expect that this versatile and multi-purpose interface between the simulator and DNN framework will enable opportunities for the research community to further develop DNN solutions to not only the task of automated UAV navigation (using imitation learning) but to the more general task of vehicle maneuvering and obstacle avoidance (possibly using other forms of learning including RL).

Table 3. Effect of data augmentation in training to overall UAV racing performance. By augmenting the original flight logs with data captured at more offsets (roll and yaw) from the original trajectory along with their corresponding corrective controls, our UAV DNN can learn to traverse almost all the gates of the testing tracks, since it has learned to correct for exploratory maneuvers. We show the settings abbreviated as [min:increment:max] intervals. After a sufficient amount of augmentation, no additional benefit is realized in improved racing performance.

	yaw [°]	[None]		[-20:20:20]		[-30:15:30]		[-30:10:30]		[-30:5:30]	
roll [cm]	**cameras**	0		2		4		6		12	
[-75:25:75]	6	0.17	0.45	1.00	1.00	1.00	1.00	0.83	0.85	0.92	1.00
		0.82	0.50	0.95	1.00	1.00	1.00	0.95	1.00	1.00	1.00
[-75:50:75]	4	0.42	0.60	1.00	1.00	1.00	1.00	0.75	1.00	1.00	0.85
		0.82	0.61	0.41	0.78	1.00	0.94	0.91	0.94	1.00	1.00
[-50:50:50]	2	0.17	0.35	0.92	1.00	1.00	1.00	1.00	1.00	1.00	1.00
		0.23	0.28	1.00	1.00	1.00	1.00	1.00	1.00	0.82	1.00
[None]	0	0.00	0.00	0.92	1.00	0.67	1.00	1.00	1.00	0.50	1.00
		0.00	0.00	0.55	0.78	0.73	1.00	0.77	0.89	0.91	0.89

Effects of Exploration. We find exploration to be the predominant factor influencing network performance. As mentioned earlier, we augment the pilot flight data with offsets and corresponding corrective controls. We conduct grid search to find a suitable degree of augmentation and to analyze the effect it has on overall UAV racing performance. To do this, we define two sets of offset parameters: one that acts as a horizontal offset (roll-offset) and one that acts as a rotational offset (yaw-offset). Table 3 shows how the racing accuracy (percentage of gates traversed) varies with different sets of these augmentation offsets across the four testing tracks. It is clear that increasing the number of rendered images with yaw-offset has the greatest impact on performance. While it is possible for the DNN to complete tracks without being trained on roll-offsets, this is not the case for yaw-offsets. However, the significant gain in adding rotated camera views saturates quickly, and at a certain point the network does not benefit from more extensive augmentation. Therefore, we found four yaw-offsets to be sufficient. Including camera views with horizontal shifts is also beneficial, since the network is better equipped to recover once it is about to leave the track on straights. We found two roll-offsets to be sufficient to ensure this. In the rest of our experiments, we use the following augmentation setup in training: horizontal roll-offset set $\{-50°, 50°\}$ and rotational yaw-offset set $\{-30°, -15°, 15°, 30°\}$.

Comparison to State-of-the-Art. We compare our racing DNN to the two most related and recent network architectures, the first denoted as Nvidia (for self-driving cars [3]) and the second as MAV (for forest path navigating UAVs [42]). While the domains of these works are similar, it should be noted that flying a high-speed racing UAV is a particularly challenging task, especially since the effect of inertia is much more significant and there are more degrees of freedom. For fair comparison, we scale our dataset to the same input dimensionality and re-train each of the three networks. We then evaluate each of the trained models on the task of UAV racing in the testing tracks. It is noteworthy that both the Nvidia and MAV networks (in their original implementation) use data augmentation as well, so when training, we assume the augmentation choice to be appropriate for the given method and maintain the same strategy. While the exact angular offsets of the two views used in the Nvidia network are not reported, we assume them to be close to 30°. We thus employ a rotational offset set of $\{-30°, 30°\}$ to augment its data. As for the MAV network, we use the same augmentation parameters proposed in the paper, i.e. a rotational offset of $\{-30°, 30°\}$. We modified the MAV network to allow for a regression output instead of its original classification (left, center and right controls). This is necessary since our task requires fine-grained controls, and predicting discrete controls leads to very inadequate UAV racing performance.

It should be noted that in the original implementation of the Nvidia network [3] (based on real-world driving data), it was realized that additional augmentation was needed for reasonable automatic driving performance *after* the real-world data was acquired. To avoid recapturing the data again, synthetic viewpoints (generated by interpolation) were used to augment the training dataset, which introduced undesirable distortions. By using our simulator, we are able to extract any number of camera views without distortions. Therefore, we wanted to also gauge the effect of *additional* augmentation to both the Nvidia and MAV networks, when they are trained using our default augmentation setting: horizontal roll-offset of $\{-50°, 50°\}$ and rotational yaw-offset of $\{-30°, -15°, 15°, 30°\}$. We denote these trained networks as Nvidia++ and MAV++.

Table 4. Accuracy score of different pilots and networks on the four test tracks, averaged over multiple runs. The accuracy score represents the percentage of completed racing gates. The networks ending with ++ are variants of the original network with our augmentation strategy.

Pilot/Network	Track 1	Track 2	Track 3	Track 4
Human-Novice	1.00	1.00	0.95	0.94
Human-Intermediate	1.00	1.00	1.00	1.00
Human-Expert	1.00	1.00	1.00	1.00
Ours-Intermediate	**1.00**	**1.00**	**1.00**	**1.00**
Ours-Expert	1.00	0.95	0.91	0.78
Nvidia-Intermediate	0.17	1.00	0.82	0.83
Nvidia-Intermediate++	1.00	1.00	0.82	1.00
MAV-Intermediate	0.50	0.75	0.73	0.83
MAV-Intermediate++	0.42	1.00	0.91	0.78

Table 4 summarizes the results of these different network variants on the testing tracks. Results indicate that the performance of the original Nvidia and MAV networks suffers from insufficient data augmentation. They clearly do not make use of enough exploration. These networks improve in performance when our proposed data augmentation scheme is used. Regardless, our proposed DNN outperforms the Nvidia and MAV networks, where this improvement is less significant when more data augmentation or more exploratory behavior is learned. Unlike the other networks, our DNN performs consistently well on all the unseen tracks, owing to its sufficient network capacity needed to learn this complex task.

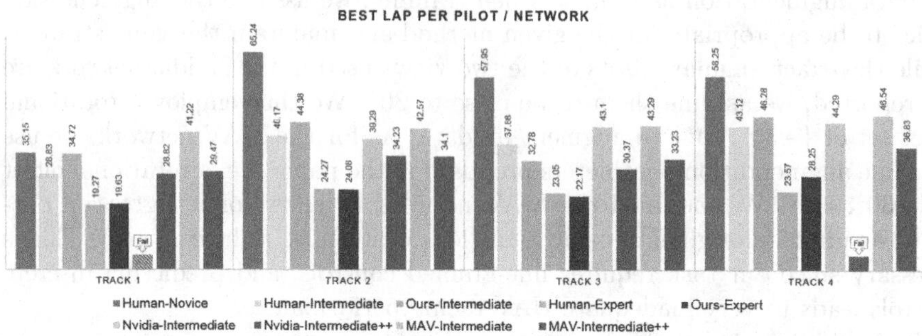

Fig. 7. Best lap times of human pilots and networks trained on different flight styles. If there is no lap time displayed, the pilot was not able to complete the course because the UAV crashed. See text for a more detailed description.

Pilot Diversity and Human vs. DNN

In this section, we investigate how the flying style of a pilot affects the network that is being learned. To this end, we compare the performance of the different networks on the testing set, when each of them is trained with flight data captured from pilots of varying flight expertise (intermediate and expert).

Table 4 summarizes the lap time and accuracy of these networks. Clearly, the pilot flight style can significantly affect the performance of the learned network. Figure 7 shows that there is a high correlation regarding both performance and flying style of the pilot used in training and the corresponding learned network.

The trained networks clearly resemble the flying style and also the proficiency of their human trainers. Thus, our network that was trained on flights of the intermediate pilot achieves high accuracy but is quite slow, just as the expert network sometimes misses gates but achieves very good lap and overall times.

Interestingly, although the networks perform similar to their pilot, they fly more consistently, and therefore tend to outperform the human pilot with regards to overall time on multiple laps. This is especially true for our intermediate network. Both the intermediate and the expert network clearly outperform the novice human pilot who takes several hours of practice and several attempts to reach similar performance to the network. Even our expert pilots were not always able to complete the test tracks on the first attempt.

While the percentage of passed gates and best lap time give a good indication about the performance, they do not convey any information about the style of the pilot. To this end, we visualize the performance of human pilots and the trained networks by plotting their trajectories onto the track (from a 2D overhead viewpoint). We encode their speeds as a heatmap, where blue corresponds to the minimum speed and red to the maximum speed. Figure 8 shows a collection of heatmaps revealing several interesting insights.

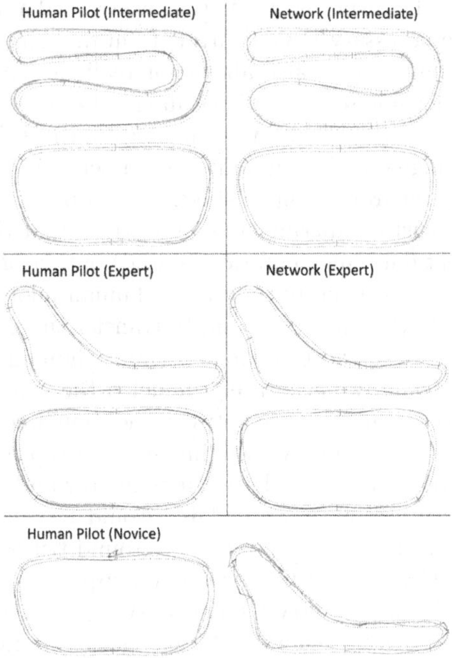

Fig. 8. Visualization of human and automated UAV flights super-imposed onto a 2D overhead view of different tracks. The color illustrates the instantaneous speed of the UAV from blue (slow) to red (fast). (Color figure online)

Firstly, despite showing variation, the networks clearly imitate the style of the pilot they were trained on. This is especially true for the intermediate proficiency level, while the expert network sometimes overshoots, which causes it to loose speed and therefore to not match the speed pattern as well as the intermediate one. We also note that the performance gap between network and human increases as the expertise of the pilot increases. Note that the flight path of the expert network is less smooth and centered than its human correspondent and the intermediate network, respectively. This is partly due to the fact that the networks were only trained on two laps of flying across seven training tracks. An expert pilot has a lot more training than that and is therefore able to generalize much better to unseen environments.

However, the experience advantage of the intermediate pilot over the network is much less and therefore the performance gap is smaller. We also show the performance of our novice pilot on these tracks. While the intermediate pilots accelerate on straights, the novice is not able to control speed that well, creating a very narrow velocity range. Albeit flying quite slowly, the pilot also gets off track several times. This underlines the complexity of UAV racing, especially for inexperienced pilots.

5 Conclusions and Future Work

In this paper, we proposed a robust imitation learning based framework to teach an unmanned aerial vehicle (UAV) to fly through challenging racing tracks at very high speeds. To do this, we trained a deep neural network (DNN) to predict the necessary UAV controls from raw image data, grounded in a photo-realistic simulator that also allows for realistic UAV physics. Training is made possible by logging data (rendered images from the UAV and stick controls) from human pilot flights, while they maneuver the UAV through racing tracks. This data is augmented with sufficient camera view offsets to teach the network how to recover from flight mistakes, which proves to be crucial during long-term flight. Extensive experiments demonstrate that our trained network (when such sufficient data augmentation is used) outperforms state-of-the-art methods and flies more consistently than many human pilots.

In the future, we aim to transfer the network we trained in our simulator to the real-world to compete against human pilots in real-world racing scenarios. Although we accurately modeled the simulated racing environment, the differences in appearance between the simulated and real-world will need to be reconciled. Therefore, we will investigate deep transfer learning techniques to enable a smooth transition between simulator and the real-world. If such transfer would be successful, our simulator would be able to act as an unlimited, highly customizable and free source of ground truth data.

Despite our findings that temporally aware architectures were not a good choice for the low-latency UAV racing task, we expect this to be useful when approaching general UAV navigation and complex obstacle avoidance. We plan to more broadly evaluate our method and the choice of augmentation strategy on tasks with differing challenges. More generally, since our developed simulator and its seamless interface to deep learning platforms is generic in nature, we expect that this combination will open up unique opportunities for the community to develop better automated UAV flying methods, to expand its reach to other fields of autonomous navigation such as self-driving cars, and to benefit other interesting perception-based tasks such as obstacle avoidance.

Acknowledgments. This work was supported by the King Abdullah University of Science and Technology (KAUST) Office of Sponsored Research through the Visual Computing Center (VCC) funding.

References

1. Andersson, O., Wzorek, M., Doherty, P.: Deep learning quadcopter control via risk-aware active learning. In: Thirty-First AAAI Conference on Artificial Intelligence (AAAI), 4–9 February 2017, San Francisco (2017, accepted)
2. Battaglia, P.W., Hamrick, J.B., Tenenbaum, J.B.: Simulation as an engine of physical scene understanding. Proc. Natl. Acad. Sci. **110**(45), 18327–18332 (2013). https://doi.org/10.1073/pnas.1306572110
3. Bojarski, M., et al.: End to end learning for self-driving cars. CoRR abs/1604.07316 (2016). http://arxiv.org/abs/1604.07316

4. Chen, C., Seff, A., Kornhauser, A., Xiao, J.: Deepdriving: learning affordance for direct perception in autonomous driving. In: Proceedings of the 2015 IEEE International Conference on Computer Vision (ICCV), ICCV 2015, pp. 2722–2730. IEEE Computer Society, Washington, DC (2015). https://doi.org/10.1109/ICCV.2015.312
5. Dosovitskiy, A., Koltun, V.: Learning to act by predicting the future. vol. abs/1611.01779 (2017). http://arxiv.org/abs/1611.01779
6. Dosovitskiy, A., Ros, G., Codevilla, F., López, A., Koltun, V.: CARLA: an open urban driving simulator. In: Conference on Robot Learning (CoRL) (2017)
7. Furrer, F., Burri, M., Achtelik, M., Siegwart, R.: RotorS—a modular gazebo MAV simulator framework. In: Koubaa, A. (ed.) Robot Operating System (ROS). SCI, vol. 625, pp. 595–625. Springer, Cham (2016). https://doi.org/10.1007/978-3-319-26054-9_23
8. Gaidon, A., Wang, Q., Cabon, Y., Vig, E.: Virtual worlds as proxy for multi-object tracking analysis. In: Proceedings of the IEEE Conference on Computer Vision and Pattern Recognition, pp. 4340–4349 (2016)
9. Guo, X., Singh, S., Lee, H., Lewis, R., Wang, X.: Deep learning for real-time atari game play using offline Monte-Carlo tree search planning. In: Proceedings of the 27th International Conference on Neural Information Processing Systems, NIPS 2014, pp. 3338–3346. MIT Press, Cambridge (2014). http://dl.acm.org/citation.cfm?id=2969033.2969199
10. Ha, S., Liu, C.K.: Iterative training of dynamic skills inspired by human coaching techniques. ACM Trans. Graph. **34**(1), 1:1–1:11 (2014). https://doi.org/10.1145/2682626
11. Hamalainen, P., Eriksson, S., Tanskanen, E., Kyrki, V., Lehtinen, J.: Online motion synthesis using sequential Monte Carlo. ACM Trans. Graph. **33**(4), 51:1–51:12 (2014). https://doi.org/10.1145/2601097.2601218
12. Hamalainen, P., Rajamaki, J., Liu, C.K.: Online control of simulated humanoids using particle belief propagation. ACM Trans. Graph. **34**(4), 81:1–81:13 (2015). https://doi.org/10.1145/2767002
13. Hejrati, M., Ramanan, D.: Analysis by synthesis: 3D object recognition by object reconstruction. In: 2014 IEEE Conference on Computer Vision and Pattern Recognition (CVPR), pp. 2449–2456, June 2014. https://doi.org/10.1109/CVPR.2014.314
14. Hussein, A., Gaber, M.M., Elyan, E., Jayne, C.: Imitation learning: a survey of learning methods. ACM Comput. Surv. **50**(2), 21:1–21:35 (2017). https://doi.org/10.1145/3054912
15. Ju, E., Won, J., Lee, J., Choi, B., Noh, J., Choi, M.G.: Data-driven control of flapping flight. ACM Trans. Graph. **32**(5), 151:1–151:12 (2013). https://doi.org/10.1145/2516971.2516976
16. Kim, D.K., Chen, T.: Deep neural network for real-time autonomous indoor navigation. CoRR abs/1511.04668 (2015)
17. Koutník, J., Cuccu, G., Schmidhuber, J., Gomez, F.: Evolving large-scale neural networks for vision-based reinforcement learning. In: Proceedings of the 15th Annual Conference on Genetic and Evolutionary Computation, GECCO 2013, pp. 1061–1068. ACM, New York (2013). https://doi.org/10.1145/2463372.2463509
18. Koutník, J., Schmidhuber, J., Gomez, F.: Online evolution of deep convolutional network for vision-based reinforcement learning. In: del Pobil, A.P., Chinellato, E., Martinez-Martin, E., Hallam, J., Cervera, E., Morales, A. (eds.) SAB 2014. LNCS (LNAI), vol. 8575, pp. 260–269. Springer, Cham (2014). https://doi.org/10.1007/978-3-319-08864-8_25

19. Lerer, A., Gross, S., Fergus, R.: Learning Physical Intuition of Block Towers by Example (2016). arXiv:1603.01312v1
20. Levine, S., Koltun, V.: Guided policy search. In: Dasgupta, S., McAllester, D. (eds.) Proceedings of the 30th International Conference on Machine Learning. Proceedings of Machine Learning Research, PMLR, 17–19 June 2013, Atlanta, vol. 28, pp. 1–9 (2013). http://proceedings.mlr.press/v28/levine13.html
21. Lillicrap, T.P., et al.: Continuous control with deep reinforcement learning. ICLR abs/1509.02971 (2016). http://arxiv.org/abs/1509.02971
22. Loquercio, A., Maqueda, A.I., del Blanco, C.R., Scaramuzza, D.: Dronet: learning to fly by driving. IEEE Robot. Autom. Lett. **3**(2), 1088–1095 (2018)
23. Marín, J., Vázquez, D., Gerónimo, D., López, A.M.: Learning appearance in virtual scenarios for pedestrian detection. In: 2010 IEEE Computer Society Conference on Computer Vision and Pattern Recognition, pp. 137–144 (2010). https://doi.org/10.1109/CVPR.2010.5540218
24. Mnih, V., et al.: Asynchronous methods for deep reinforcement learning. In: International Conference on Machine Learning, pp. 1928–1937 (2016)
25. Mnih, V., et al.: Human-level control through deep reinforcement learning. Nature **518**(7540), 529–533 (2015). https://doi.org/10.1038/nature14236
26. Movshovitz-Attias, Y., Sheikh, Y., Naresh Boddeti, V., Wei, Z.: 3D pose-by-detection of vehicles via discriminatively reduced ensembles of correlation filters. In: Proceedings of the British Machine Vision Conference. BMVA Press (2014). http://dx.doi.org/10.5244/C.28.53
27. Mueller, M., Casser, V., Lahoud, J., Smith, N., Ghanem, B.: Sim4CV: a photo-realistic simulator for computer vision applications. Int. J. Comput. Vis. **126**, 902–919 (2018)
28. Mueller, M., Smith, N., Ghanem, B.: A benchmark and simulator for UAV tracking. In: Leibe, B., Matas, J., Sebe, N., Welling, M. (eds.) ECCV 2016. LNCS, vol. 9905, pp. 445–461. Springer, Cham (2016). https://doi.org/10.1007/978-3-319-46448-0_27
29. Muller, U., Ben, J., Cosatto, E., Flepp, B., Cun, Y.L.: Off-road obstacle avoidance through end-to-end learning. In: Weiss, Y., Schölkopf, P.B., Platt, J.C. (eds.) Advances in Neural Information Processing Systems, vol. 18, pp. 739–746. MIT Press (2006). http://papers.nips.cc/paper/2847-off-road-obstacle-avoidance-through-end-to-end-learning.pdf
30. Nvidia: Gpu-based deep learning inference: A performance and power analysis, November 2015. https://www.nvidia.com/content/tegra/embedded-systems/pdf/jetson_tx1_whitepaper.pdf
31. Papon, J., Schoeler, M.: Semantic pose using deep networks trained on synthetic RGB-D. CoRR abs/1508.00835 (2015). http://arxiv.org/abs/1508.00835
32. Peng, X.B., Berseth, G., van de Panne, M.: Terrain-adaptive locomotion skills using deep reinforcement learning. ACM Trans. Graph. **35**(4), 81 (2016). (Proc. SIGGRAPH 2016)
33. Peng, X.B., Berseth, G., Yin, K., van de Panne, M.: Deeploco: dynamic locomotion skills using hierarchical deep reinforcement learning. ACM Trans. Graph. **36**(4), 41 (2017). (Proc. SIGGRAPH 2017)
34. Pepik, B., Stark, M., Gehler, P., Schiele, B.: Teaching 3D geometry to deformable part models. In: 2012 IEEE Conference on Computer Vision and Pattern Recognition (CVPR), pp. 3362–3369, June 2012. https://doi.org/10.1109/CVPR.2012.6248075

35. Pomerleau, D.A.: ALVINN: an autonomous land vehicle in a neural network. In: Advances in Neural Information Processing Systems, pp. 305–313. Morgan Kaufmann Publishers Inc., San Francisco (1989). http://dl.acm.org/citation.cfm?id=89851.89891
36. Prabowo, Y.A., Trilaksono, B.R., Triputra, F.R.: Hardware in-the-loop simulation for visual servoing of fixed wing UAV. In: 2015 International Conference on Electrical Engineering and Informatics (ICEEI), pp. 247–252, August 2015. https://doi.org/10.1109/ICEEI.2015.7352505
37. Richter, S.R., Vineet, V., Roth, S., Koltun, V.: Playing for data: ground truth from computer games. In: Leibe, B., Matas, J., Sebe, N., Welling, M. (eds.) ECCV 2016. LNCS, vol. 9906, pp. 102–118. Springer, Cham (2016). https://doi.org/10.1007/978-3-319-46475-6_7
38. Ross, S., Gordon, G.J., Bagnell, J.A.: No-regret reductions for imitation learning and structured prediction. CoRR abs/1011.0686 (2010). http://arxiv.org/abs/1011.0686
39. Sadeghi, F., Levine, S.: CAD2RL: real single-image flight without a single real image (2017)
40. Shah, S., Dey, D., Lovett, C., Kapoor, A.: AirSim: high-fidelity visual and physical simulation for autonomous vehicles. In: Hutter, M., Siegwart, R. (eds.) Field and Service Robotics. SPAR, vol. 5, pp. 621–635. Springer, Cham (2018). https://doi.org/10.1007/978-3-319-67361-5_40
41. Shah, U., Khawad, R., Krishna, K.M.: Deepfly: towards complete autonomous navigation of MAVs with monocular camera. In: Proceedings of the Tenth Indian Conference on Computer Vision, Graphics and Image Processing, ICVGIP 2016, pp. 59:1–59:8. ACM, New York (2016). https://doi.org/10.1145/3009977.3010047
42. Smolyanskiy, N., Kamenev, A., Smith, J., Birchfield, S.: Toward Low-Flying Autonomous MAV Trail Navigation using Deep Neural Networks for Environmental Awareness. ArXiv e-prints, May 2017
43. Tan, J., Gu, Y., Liu, C.K., Turk, G.: Learning bicycle stunts. ACM Trans. Graph. **33**(4), 50:1–50:12 (2014). https://doi.org/10.1145/2601097.2601121
44. Trilaksono, B.R., Triadhitama, R., Adiprawita, W., Wibowo, A., Sreenatha, A.: Hardware-in-the-loop simulation for visual target tracking of octorotor UAV. Aircraft Eng. Aerospace Technol. **83**(6), 407–419 (2011). https://doi.org/10.1108/00022661111173289
45. Wymann, B., Dimitrakakis, C., Sumner, A., Espié, E., Guionneau, C., Coulom, R.: TORCS, the open racing car simulator (2014). http://www.torcs.org

Onboard Hyperspectral Image Compression Using Compressed Sensing and Deep Learning

Saurabh Kumar(✉), Subhasis Chaudhuri, Biplab Banerjee, and Feroz Ali

Indian Institute of Technology Bombay, Mumbai 400076, MH, India
{saurabhkm,sc,bbanerjee,feroz}@iitb.ac.in
http://www.ee.iitb.ac.in

Abstract. We propose a real-time onboard compression scheme for hyperspectral datacube which consists of a very low complexity encoder and a deep learning based parallel decoder architecture for fast decompression. The encoder creates a set of coded snapshots from a given datacube using a measurement code matrix. The decoder decompresses the coded snapshots by using a sparse recovery algorithm. We solve this sparse recovery problem using a deep neural network for fast reconstruction. We present experimental results which demonstrate that our technique performs very well in terms of quality of reconstruction and in terms of computational requirements compared to other transform based techniques with some tradeoff in PSNR. The proposed technique also enables faster inference in compressed domain, suitable for on-board requirements.

Keywords: Fast Hyperspectral imaging · Fast on-board data compression · Compressed sensing · Deep learning

1 Introduction

Hyperspectral imaging captures images of a scene at multiple closely spaced wavelengths. Since each band in a datacube is just the same scene imaged at a slightly shifted wavelength, there is a large amount of redundancy in these data cubes. Although this gives us much more information than other modalities for data analysis and inference, in many cases these tasks can also be performed even with a good approximation of the datacube at hand, justifying a need and feasibility of hyperspectral data compression. We would like to compress a hyperspectral datacube on board a remote device which might be a satellite/UAV or even on a ground station for subsequent distribution. Although compression is a computationally intensive task to do onboard, more so for drones and UAVs, if it can be done with a fast and very low complexity lossy algorithm we can save on both transmission time along with onboard power and storage requirements.

L. Leal-Taixé and S. Roth (Eds.): ECCV 2018 Workshops, LNCS 11130, pp. 30–42, 2019.
https://doi.org/10.1007/978-3-030-11012-3_3

Hyperspectral sensors deployed on UAVs have become popular for remote sensing tasks lately. Telmo et al. present a detailed review of various such sensors used for Agriculture and forestry application in [1]. We consider hyperspectral datacubes for demonstration purpose in this work but we wish to emphasise the proposed compression technique can be generalized to any spectral data with multiple bands. The presented method is also applicable to videos but due to motion present between the frames, the effectiveness is comparatively reduced in this case.

There exists a significant technical literature proposing to solve this problem, many inspired from the classical compression standards including both lossless and lossy compression techniques. A review of such technique can be found in [5] which include 3D-SPECK, 3D-SPIHT, and 3D-tarp to name a few. Also, the DWT based JPEG2000 standard has been used widely for this [13].

We propose a lossy compression scheme in this paper and there have been various lossy schemes proposed in the literature. Tang et al. propose two schemes: one based on three-dimensional wavelet coding [15] and the other based on three-dimensional set partitioning [14]. Du et al. first decorrelate the data spectrally with principal component analysis and then use discrete wavelet transform [3]. Wang et al. use independent component analysis [17] and Green et al. use a concept called maximum noise transform [8] to achieve the same. These techniques are quite successful but due to their use of various transforms, they are comparatively slow and not suitable for onboard compression requirements. Apart from this, the unwanted radiometric distortions induced by them at lower bit per pixel regime impair the inference and learning tasks that are performed on the datacubes.

The main contribution of this paper is to provide a computationally very efficient compression technique for HS datacubes at a low bit per pixel regime while keeping the image features intact. The proposed method is shown to provide us with an excellent PSNR and structural similarity than the JPEG2000 at comparable bit per pixel ratios. We also present a compression quality comparison on how the standard machine learning algorithms are affected by these compression techniques and show that the proposed technique outperforms them in all comparisons. We wish to highlight that the proposed method is based on in-place computation and is also very memory efficient and therefore is better suited for onboard compression unlike existing methods.

2 Proposed Compression Approach

In this paper, we propose a very low complexity hyperspectral datacube compression technique. Due to this feature, the proposed technique primarily excels for onboard compression requirements. Our technique is inspired from imaging methodology proposed by Hitomi et al. [9] for increasing the frame rate of a normal off-the-shelf camera by using a liquid crystal on silicon to compressively acquire video coded snapshots. A much higher frame rate video data volume is reconstructed from these snapshots using a sparse recovery algorithm.

We use two major concepts in this work to achieve the proposed compression. Compression is done by employing coded aperture imaging on a given hyperspectral datacube. This is what gives us a very light and low complexity compression routine. Decompression from this kind of sparse acquisition of data is typically done using the sparse recovery algorithms like orthogonal matching pursuit or iterative hard thresholding. These techniques are, however, very slow. We in this paper propose a deep neural network based sparse recovery algorithm to reconstruct the datacube from the compressively coded snapshots. This does not require a dictionary learning for reconstruction and speeds up our reconstruction algorithm by many folds once the training has been done.

2.1 Coded Sampling

Consider a hyperspectral datacube with P spectral bands of spatial size $M \times N$ pixels. Let $E(x, y, z)$ denote this hyperspectral volume. We code T such consecutive and non-overlapping bands into a single coded snapshot, given by,

$$I(x, y) = \sum_{z=1}^{T} C(x, y, z)E(x, y, z), \tag{1}$$

where $C(x, y, z)$ denotes an element of the random code matrix, generated to obtain random pixel sampling of the given hyperspectral volume. The code matrix is constructed such that the number of ones and the number of zeros in it are equal. We can thus write Eq. 1 as a matrix equation, $\mathbf{I} = \mathbf{CE}$. Here $\mathbf{I}$ (coded snapshot) and $\mathbf{E}$ (hyperspectral volume) are matrices of sizes $M \times N$ and $M \times N \times T$, respectively. Note that Eq. 1 allows one to perform in-place computation. The coded snapshot of T bands can be progressively transmitted as the coded bitstream. Since the random code matrix block can be generated with random generation seed, one can just transmit this seed with the coded bit stream to construct the code matrix on the receiver end. Further if onboard computation permits, the coded snapshots, thus obtained can be further encoded via JPEG2000 or an equivalent encoder. Figure 1 shows one of the coded snapshots made from 16 bands of the Pavia University datacube. Note the similarity of the coded snapshot with the original bands.

2.2 Sparse Reconstruction

Now given a coded snapshot we can solve a standard sparse recovery problem at the receiver to reconstruct the hyperspectral volume $\mathbf{E}$ by solving a standard sparse recovery problem assuming we also are given a learned dictionary $\mathbf{D}$. In this approach, we model the hyperspectral volume $\mathbf{E} = \mathbf{CD}\alpha$, as a sparse, linear combination of the atoms (patches) from the learned dictionary. We could then use orthogonal matching pursuit (OMP) [16] or iterative hard thresholding to solve an l_0 minimization problem of the following form

$$\hat{\alpha} = \arg\min_{\alpha} ||\alpha||_0 \text{ subject to } ||\mathbf{CD}\alpha - \mathbf{I}||_2^2 < \epsilon. \tag{2}$$

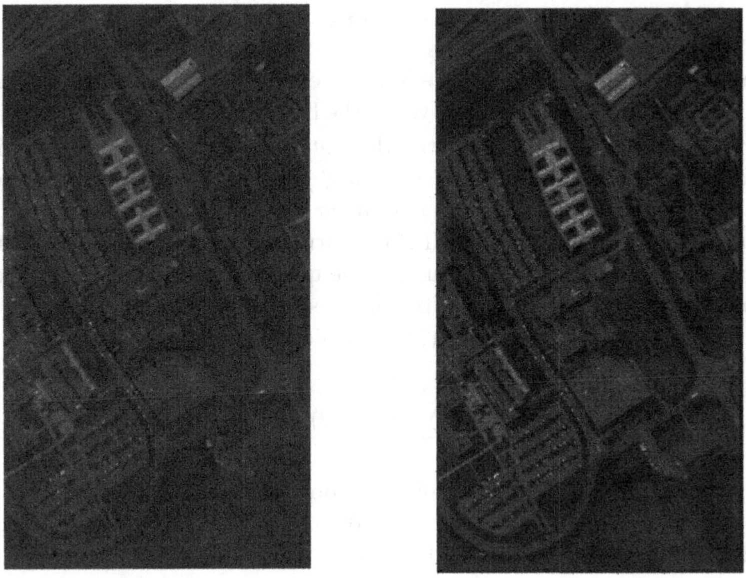

Fig. 1. A coded snapshot of 16 bands of Pavia University dataset along with the original band for reference.

Here α is the sparse weights of a linear combination of dictionary atoms and ϵ is the acceptable tolerance. However, solving Eq. 2 with OMP is computationally very demanding, and cannot as yet, be performed in real-time at the receiver. Hence we opt for a deep learning based solution.

2.3 Coded Snapshot-Deep Learning Based Compression Pipeline

A given hyperspectral datacube is divided into volume patches of size $m \times m \times T$, where m is the spatial dimension of such a patch and T is the spectral dimension. We perform coded sampling on these patches and obtain the coded snapshots which may or may not be further JPEG2000 compressed. The coded snapshot are retrieved from the compressed data stream at decoder by JPEG2000 decompression and then decoded using a multilayer perceptron decoder. The deep learning based sparse recovery has been shown to be better [10] than the iterative techniques like OMP, LASSO and also the recent Gaussian Mixture model based approach [18].

We consider a multilayer perceptron (MLP) architecture as proposed in [11] [10] to solve the above sparse recovery problem in Eq. 2 and learn a non-linear function $f(.)$. The function $f(.)$ maps the coded snapshot patch $\mathbf{I}_i \in \mathbb{R}^{m^2}$ to a hyperspectral volume $\mathbf{E}_i \in \mathbb{R}^{m^2 T}$. Each of the K hidden layers of this multilayer perceptron can be defined as

$$H_k(\mathbf{I}_i) = \sigma(w_i \mathbf{I}_i + \mathbf{b}_i), \tag{3}$$

where $\mathbf{b}_i$ is the bias vector and w_i is the weight matrix. The weight matrix $w_1 \in \mathbb{R}^{m^2 \times m^2 T}$ connects the input layer to the first hidden layer and rest $w_{K-2} \in \mathbb{R}^{m^2 T \times m^2 T}$ connect the intermediate adjacent hidden layers. The last hidden layer connects to the output layer via $w_0 \in \mathbb{R}^{m^2 T \times m^2 T}$ and b_0. We use the rectified linear unit (ReLU) as our non-linear function $\sigma(.)$ defined as $\sigma(x) = max(0, x)$. We train the proposed MLP by learning all the weights and biases by a back propagation algorithm minimizing the quadratic error between the set of coded measurements and corresponding hyperspectral volume patches. The loss function is the mean squared error (MSE) which is given by

$$Ł(\theta) = \frac{1}{N} \sum_{i=1}^{N} ||f(I_i, \theta) - E_i||_2^2, \tag{4}$$

where θ is the common parameter place holder for the MLP weights and N is the total number of HS volume patches. We use this MSE as our objective to maximize the PSNR which is directly related to this quantity.

3 Inference with Compressed Data

Spectral datacubes have nearly no motion across the bands and just intensity variation. This property leads to our coded snapshots being visually very similar to the original spectral bands. There is some distortion due to the coded sampling process but the major image features are still quite recognisable. This visual similarity between he original bands and the coded snapshots lets us use various inference methods directly on them. This leads to faster inference tasks as it can be performed directly on the compressed data even before decompression with slight loss in accuracy. In the next section we show evaluation of a few inference tasks like classification and clustering directly on our coded snapshots and compare them to when this is done on the original datacube.

4 Experimental Results

The proposed compression algorithm for low bit rate compression was tested on aerial hyperspectral datasets. Pavia University dataset[1] is used in our experiments since the ground truth is available for this dataset. However, the same trained neural network was used to decompress all test datasets. We present qualitative and quantitative evaluation which were performed on the calibrated Pavia University dataset. We also use the same dataset for evaluation and comparison of feature preservation performance of various compression schemes. Final datacube size used is 610 × 340 × 96, after removal of noisy bands. There are 10 classes available in the ground truth with widely varying sample counts

[1] http://www.ehu.eus/ccwintco/index.php/Hyperspectral_Remote_Sensing_Scenes.

across classes. This work uses Python programming language as a base and the PyTorch framework for implementation of the decompression using multilayer perceptron. We wish to add here that the Pavia Dataset considered for uniformity across experiments, we have also run our experiments on uncalibrated dataset, which can be found in supplementary material.

4.1 Training the Multi-layer Perceptron

We train our neural network on the hyperspectral data of natural scenes [4] provided by the University of Manchester. Each of our test datacubes is divided into volume patches of size $m = 8$ and $T = 16$. These datacubes are unrelated to the test set. We use these volume patches to obtain corresponding coded snapshot patches by multiplying them with a measurement code matrix. The network was trained for 7 hidden layers and 4×10^6 iterations with a mini-batch size of 200. The input features were normalized to zero mean and unit standard deviation. The weights of each layer were uniformly distributed in $(\frac{-1}{\sqrt{s}}, \frac{1}{\sqrt{s}})$, where s is the size of the previous layer. The optimizer used is stochastic gradient descent (SGD) with a learning rate of 0.01 and a momentum of 0.9.

4.2 Performance Evaluation

Qualitative Comparison. Figure 2 presents a few reconstruction results of the Pavia University datacube for comparing visual quality for different compression techniques. It may be observed that JPEG2000 compressed images incur smoothed out edges, while the proposed technique preserves the edges and details comparatively better and gives a much better reconstruction much closer to the original image band. The textures can be seen to be comparatively better preserved in the reconstruction by the proposed method, and compares well with the PCA based spectral decorrelation. Figure 3 presents the difference images of PCA+JP2 reconstruction and CSDL reconstruction with respect to the original HS band. We highlight here that the proposed technique does not involve any kind of spectral transform or decorrelation as it would require additional computation.

Quantitative Comparison. The rate-distortion curves for three compression techniques applied to the Pavia university dataset are presented in Fig. 4. It can be easily observed from the plots that the proposed technique is better in terms of PSNR and SSIM compared to JPEG2000 over the entire low bit per pixel regime. This implies that for a given bit per pixel ratio we are able to squeeze out a higher quality image when using the proposed technique over the JPEG2000 compression. It can be seen that a PSNR improvement of around 4–5 dB and SSIM improvement of over 40–60% can be achieved by using the proposed technique over JPEG2000. However the PCA transform based spectral decorrelation does provide a better PSNR measure, although the SSIM figures are nearly identical. This also indicates that the proposed technique is able to

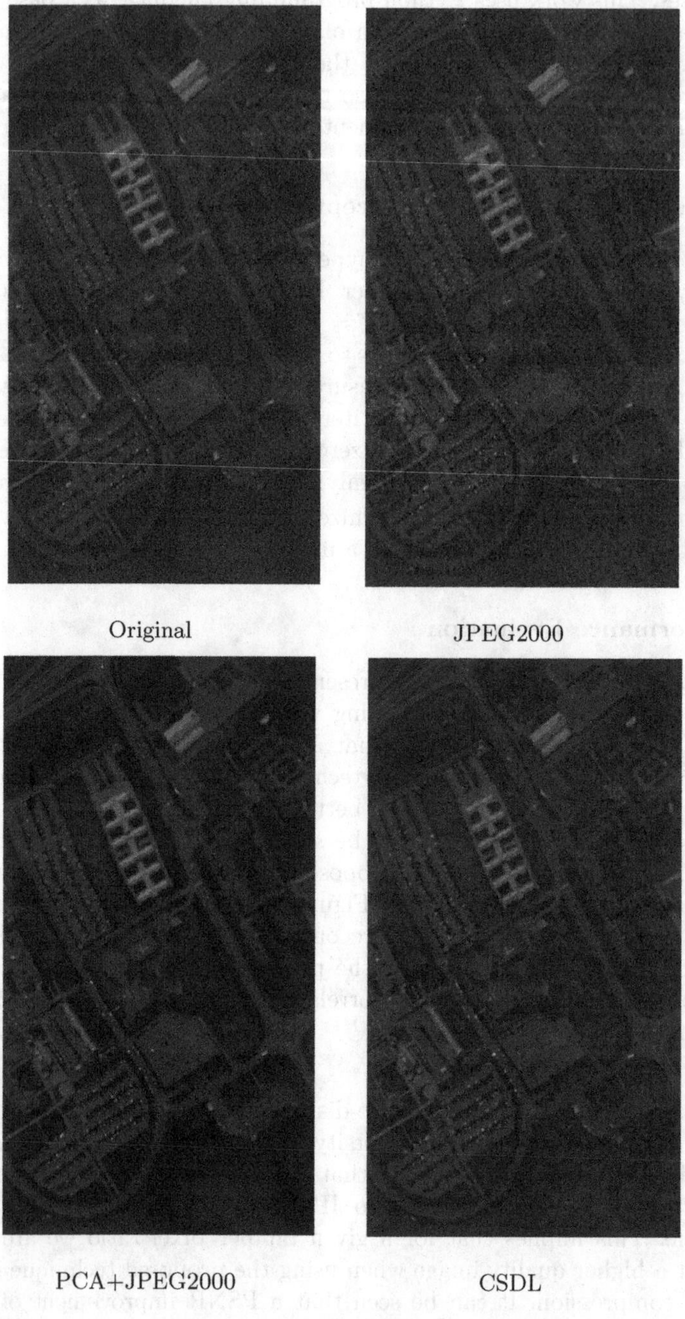

Fig. 2. A reconstructed spectral band from Pavia University datacube using JPEG2000, PCA based spectral decorrelation and CSDL compression techniques at a bpp of 0.3.

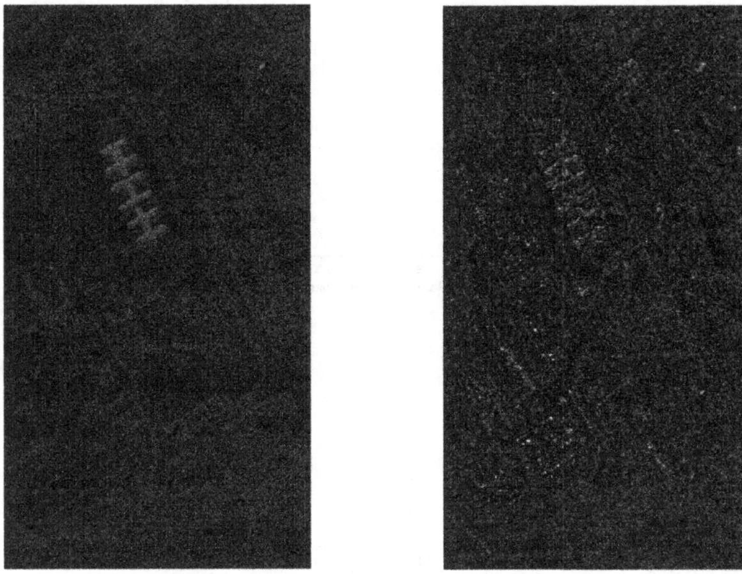

PCA+JP2 CSDL

Fig. 3. Difference images of the PCA+JP2 reconstructed and CSDL reconstruction with the original HS band.

exploit the spectral redundancy present in the datacube and not just the spatial redundancy.

Feature Preservation. Hyperspectral datacubes due to their huge size and a large number of bands typically are employed for inference and classification based tasks to extract useful information from them. We present a comparison of how the performance of a machine learning algorithm is affected by these compression schemes. We show the effect of compression on both supervised classification and on clustering techniques on calibrated Pavia dataset as the corresponding ground truth are available for them. In case of supervised classification, we show comparison using three commonly used classifiers, namely, the decision tree classifier [6], the nearest neighbour classifier and the multilayer perceptron classifier [2]. We use a 70:30 train-test split for each of the classifiers, $K = 15$ for the KNN and 3 layers for the MLP.

Our models for each of these classifiers are trained on the original uncompressed datacube along with its ground truth (performance shown under raw data in Table 1). The pixel values of various bands after decompression were taken to be features and the corresponding ground truth values were taken as the labels. The classification of reconstructed datacubes was done using the same model trained on the original datacube. This comparison is presented in Table 1,

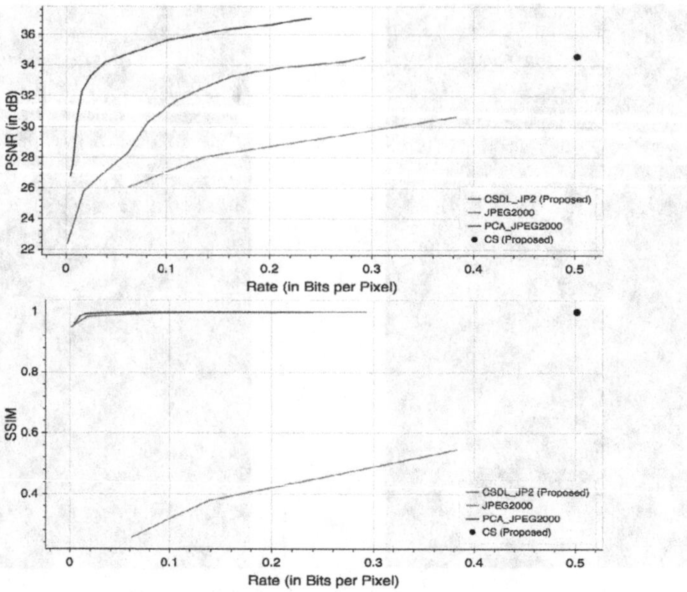

Fig. 4. PSNR and SSIM vs BPP plots for the Pavia University datacube using JPEG2000, PCA based spectral decorrelation and CSDL compression techniques. The black dot corresponds to CSDL alone, without subsequent JPEG2000.

which demonstrates how the proposed technique is better than both JPEG2000 and PCA based spectral decorrelation.

Table 1. Effect on classification accuracy (in percentages) of supervised classifiers over three different compression techniques applied to Pavia University datacube at 0.3 bpp.

Classifier	Raw data	JPEG2000	PCA+JPEG2000	CSDL
D-Tree	78.322	57.023	76.396	**78.295**
K-NN	79.695	79.592	77.971	**79.458**
MLP	79.533	79.449	79.500	**79.512**

As a part of another comparison, the test datacubes were classified into clusters without any training to examine how much spectral distortion comes in due to these compression schemes. The K-Means algorithm [12] is used to cluster the datacubes and the results are shown in Fig. 5 for the Pavia University dataset. The number of clusters ($N = 5$) has been kept same in all cases. A quick observation that can be made from this result is that the regular features of the image and region boundaries are considerably distorted in the JPEG2000 reconstructed image bands. The CSDL compressed image band, on the other hand, shows a much lesser distortion. This experiment clearly demonstrates that the proposed compression technique is able to preserve the clusters intact and induces comparably a lower radiometric distortion when compared to both the JPEG2000 and PCA transform based coding techniques for a given compression ratio. The proposed method retains nearly the same accuracy as the original raw data even when the image is compressed at 0.3 bpp.

Computational Requirements. The proposed technique offers a much faster and in-place computation at encoder in comparison to the other two compression algorithms. Table 2 demonstrates that a speedup factor of 20 can be achieved by the CSDL (without further JPEG2000 encoding) technique in comparison to PCA transform spectral decorrelation based compression.

Table 2. Computation time (in seconds) for the PCA, PCA+JPEG2000, CS, CS+JPG2000 coding at 0.3 bpp on a 3.5 GHz i7 computer with 16 GB RAM. These are averages of ten runs with a minimal load on CPU i.e. no other processes running.

Datacube size	PCA+JPEG2000	PCA	CS+JPEG2000	CS
$610 \times 340 \times 32$	7.051	6.675	**0.267**	**0.016**
$610 \times 340 \times 96$	20.329	19.539	**0.927**	**0.065**

Table 2 also highlights the advantage of using a CS coding over a PCA transform based spectral decorrelation without the following JPEG2000 compression. The former is over two magnitudes faster than the latter. This would be desirable at compression setups with minimal computational power, battery power and storage, for instance, an onboard platform. We also wish to highlight that the proposed technique offers faster compression than even the recent state of the art Hyperspectral data compression technique by Fu et al. [7]. As per the timing results presented by the authors, their technique requires a computation time comparable to the PCA+JPEG2000 based method.

Inference with Compressed Data. We train a fully connected neural net on our coded snapshots for evaluation of classification performance in the compressed domain itself. As in the features preservation section above, each pixel of the coded snapshot datacube is taken as a sample with the spectral axis constituting the features. The comparison is again presented using the three classifiers namely, Decision tree (D-Tree), K nearest neighbours (K-NN) and a multilayer perceptron (MLP). The classification accuracy comparison is shown in Table 3. This task of performing inference in compressed domain is not possible in other transform coding techniques.

It can be observed that with a loss in accuracy of around 1–5% we can perform inference tasks like classification on our data faster. Since we are dealing directly with the coded snapshots, we save processing power as the number of features a classifier needs to take is T fold less. In the above experiment T was taken to be 16.

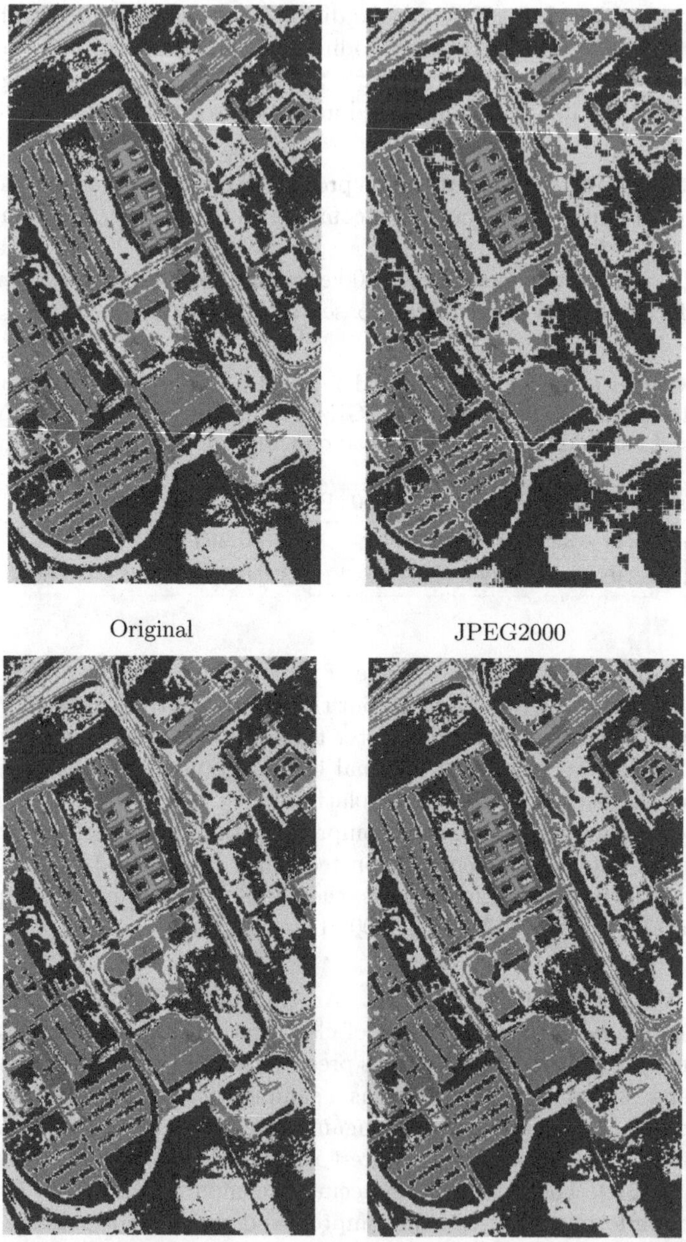

Fig. 5. Effect of various compression techniques (at 0.3 bpp) on unsupervised clustering of the Pavia University dataset.

Table 3. Effect on classification accuracy (in percentages) of supervised classifiers over raw data and coded snapshots of Pavia University datacube.

Classifier	Raw data	Coded snapshots
D-Tree	78.322	72.570
K-NN	79.695	75.646
MLP	79.533	79.274

5 Discussions and Conclusions

UAVs and drones are a major source of hyperspectral data collection for various remote sensing and monitoring applications. Being comparatively more feasible than launching satellites they offer a higher resolution imagery along with a faster acquisition-retrieval-processing cycles. But with a limited power available onboard the acquired data has to be brought down to a receiving station for processing. Although the transform coding based data compression saves the transmission bandwidth and time, the onboard power requirements for it are quite high.

The proposed method of coded snapshots involves no transform coding as part of the first step and can benefit from transform coding on top of it, if computational onboard power availability allows it. This leads to a lower power requirements and hence longer operation times for the UAV deployed. Along with this, the similarity between the coded snapshots and the original datacube bands lets us do inference in compressed domain itself which leads to faster decisions and pre-processing before the data is sent to ground stations. Onboard inference tasks can speed up disaster recovery efforts along with other planning and public warning systems.

We presented a computationally very fast and simple encoder for low bit per pixel compression of hyperspectral datacubes. These desirable features of the encoder bring in some computationally undesirable effects due to the need of sparse recovery algorithms for which we presented a computationally faster and parallelizable decoder architecture based on deep neural networks. The proposed technique also offers the capability for progressive transmission of compressed data and saves compression time and a good amount of onboard storage due to in-place computation. The proposed technique offers a low computational complexity at the encoder end which is highly desirable at a drones, UAVs or spacecraft, with limited computational and power capabilities. The deep learning based decoder, however being comparatively complex, can be offloaded to a GPU making it much faster than iterative sparse recovery algorithms. This coding technique also lets us perform inference on the compressed data directly leading to a faster and computationally light on board-decision making, when required.

References

1. Adão, T., et al.: Hyperspectral imaging: a review on UAV-based sensors, data processing and applications for agriculture and forestry. Remote Sens. **9**, 1110 (2017)
2. Benediktsson, J., Kanellopoulos, I.: Classification of multisource and hyperspectral data based on decision fusion. IEEE Trans. Geosci. Remote Sens. **37**, 1367–1377 (1999)
3. Du, Q., Fowler, J.: Hyperspectral image compression using JPEG2000 and principal component analysis. IEEE Geosci. Remote Sens. Lett. **4**, 201–205 (2007)
4. Foster, D., Amano, K., Nascimento, S., Foster, M.: Frequency of metamerism in natural scenes. JOSA **23**, 2359–2372 (2006)
5. Fowler, J., Rucker, J.: Three-dimensional wavelet-based compression of hyperspectral imagery. In: Hyperspectral Data Exploitation: Theory and Applications, pp. 379–407 (2007)
6. Friedl, M., Brodley, C.: Decision tree classification of land cover from remotely sensed data. Remote Sens. Environ. **61**, 399–409 (1997)
7. Fu, W., Li, S., Fang, L., Benediktsson, J.A.: Adaptive spectral-spatial compression of hyperspectral image with sparse representation. IEEE Trans. Geosci. Remote Sens. **55**(2), 671–682 (2017)
8. Green, A., Berman, M., Switzer, P., Craig, M.: A transformation for ordering multispectral data in terms of image quality with implications for noise removal. IEEE Trans. Geosci. Remote Sens. **26**, 65–74 (1988)
9. Hitomi, Y., Gu, J., Gupta, M., Mitsunaga, T., Nayar, S.: Video from a single coded exposure photograph using a learned over-complete dictionary. In: International Conference on Computer Vision, pp. 287–294. IEEE (2011)
10. Iliadis, M., Spinoulas, L., Katsaggelos, A.: Deep fully-connected networks for video compressive sensing. Digit. Sig. Process. **72**, 9–18 (2018)
11. Kulkarni, K., Lohit, S., Turaga, P., Kerviche, R., Ashok, A.: Reconnet: non-iterative reconstruction of images from compressively sensed measurements. In: IEEE Conference on Computer Vision and Pattern Recognition, pp. 449–458 (2016)
12. Likas, A., Vlassis, N., Verbeek, J.: The global k-means clustering algorithm. Pattern Recogn. **36**, 451–461 (2003)
13. Rucker, J., Fowler, J., Younan, N.: JPEG2000 coding strategies for hyperspectral data. In: Geoscience and Remote Sensing Symposium, vol. 1. IEEE (2005)
14. Tang, X., Cho, S., Pearlman, W.: 3D set partitioning coding methods in hyperspectral image compression. In: International Conference on Image Processing, vol. 2, p. 239. IEEE (2003)
15. Tang, X., Pearlman, W., Modestino, J.: Hyperspectral image compression using three-dimensional wavelet coding. In: Image and Video Communications and Processing, vol. 5022, pp. 1037–1048. International Society for Optics and Photonics (2003)
16. Tropp, J., Gilbert, A.: Signal recovery from random measurements via orthogonal matching pursuit. IEEE Trans. Inf. Theory **53**, 4655–4666 (2007)
17. Wang, J., Chang, C.: Independent component analysis-based dimensionality reduction with applications in hyperspectral image analysis. IEEE Trans. Geosci. Remote Sens. **44**, 1586–1600 (2006)
18. Yang, J., et al.: Video compressive sensing using Gaussian mixture models. IEEE Trans. Image Process. **23**(11), 4863–4878 (2014)

SafeUAV: Learning to Estimate Depth and Safe Landing Areas for UAVs from Synthetic Data

Alina Marcu[1,2](✉), Dragoş Costea[2,3], Vlad Licăreţ[2], Mihai Pîrvu[2], Emil Sluşanschi[3], and Marius Leordeanu[1,2,3]

[1] Institute of Mathematics of the Romanian Academy, 21 Calea Grivitei Street, Bucharest, Romania
[2] Autonomous Systems, 7 Iuliu Maniu Street, Bucharest, Romania
{alina.marcu,dragos.costea,vlad.licaret}@autonomous.ro, mihaicristianpirvu@gmail.com
[3] University Politehnica of Bucharest, 313 Splaiul Independenţei, Bucharest, Romania
{emil.slusanschi,marius.leordeanu}@cs.pub.ro

Abstract. The emergence of relatively low cost UAVs has prompted a global concern about the safe operation of such devices. Since most of them can 'autonomously' fly by means of GPS way-points, the lack of a higher logic for emergency scenarios leads to an abundance of incidents involving property or personal injury. In order to tackle this problem, we propose a small, embeddable ConvNet for both depth and safe landing area estimation. Furthermore, since labeled training data in the 3D aerial field is scarce and ground images are unsuitable, we capture a novel synthetic aerial 3D dataset obtained from 3D reconstructions. We use the synthetic data to learn to estimate depth from in-flight images and segment them into 'safe-landing' and 'obstacle' regions. Our experiments demonstrate compelling results in practice on both synthetic data and real RGB drone footage.

Keywords: UAVs · CNNs · Depth estimation · Safe landing

1 Introduction

Nowadays, UAVs have become widely accessible without a substantial investment – anyone can fly a drone, for entertainment or business purposes that cover different domains, such as agriculture or building construction and inspection. Unfortunately, the safety mechanisms embedded on-board are often nonexistent or short-distance oriented, based on ultrasound sensors or depth cameras. Long distance safety abilities, such as ones based on LIDAR, come with an exorbitant price and significant weight for small UAVs [17]. Fortunately, most commercial drones have at least one on-board camera. Recent advances in embedded GPUs enable low power and relatively low cost multi-FPS on-board operation

L. Leal-Taixé and S. Roth (Eds.): ECCV 2018 Workshops, LNCS 11130, pp. 43–58, 2019.
https://doi.org/10.1007/978-3-030-11012-3_4

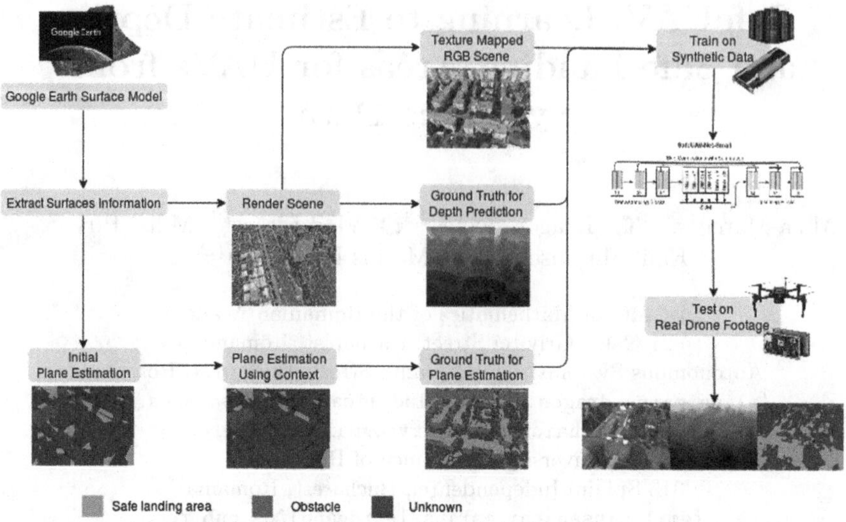

Fig. 1. Our pipeline for safe landing area and depth estimation. Starting from 3D meshes, we extract RGB, depth, and safe landing labels. We train our proposed CNN on synthetic data and validate our results on drone footage and report beyond real-time results on an embedded device. (Color figure online)

of convolutional neural networks (CNNs) [5], which could make possible high performance computer vision and machine learning approaches.

We address the semantic segmentation of images into 'safe' and potential 'obstacle' regions. We define the problem as classifying surfaces into 'horizontal', 'vertical' and 'other' classes – termed HVO throughout the paper. Potential safe landing areas correspond to the 'horizontal' class, while the 'vertical' and 'other' categories correspond to zones which are likely obstacles or rough landing regions.

Our first contribution is an embeddable CNN for depth, obstacles and safe landing areas estimation. It has comparable performance with state-of-the-art segmentation methods, while being up to 10 times faster and having more than 30 times less parameters.

We also experiment with the idea of processing the input image in two stages. During the first stage we estimate depth and the 'safety' class at the pixel level using a different ConvNet pathway for each task. Since the two tasks are highly interdependent, at the second stage we use the initial outputs of depth and surface class (horizontal, vertical and other), as contextual input to second level ConvNets that can now better re-estimate both depth and the safety category. Thus, we aim to use the depth estimation in order to improve surface class prediction and vice-versa.

The second contribution of our work is the introduction of a synthetic dataset for safe landing, consisting of RGB, depth and horizontal/vertical/other labeled image pairs. The dataset is available online, and can be used to reproduce the results published here as well as improve them with further novelties. We use 3D-reconstructed urban and suburban areas for both automatic ground truth depth extraction and HVO estimation. The pipeline for our approach is shown in Fig. 1.

2 Related Work

Depth Estimation. Ground-level depth estimation is a very active research topic, in terms of learning from unlabeled data [20,21,29], designing different network architectures [18,24,28] and performing domain adaptation [2,16]. Literature for depth estimation from aerial images is very sparse - [14] compares various recent CNN architectures for low-height flight (<20 m). There is a very large dataset with 3D information, TorontoCity [27]. Unfortunately it does not include textures for buildings, most of the data being collected only for ground.

Estimating Safe Landing Areas. While most literature focuses on obstacle detection [1], safe landing has been largely unaddressed for embedded use. While some authors have proposed more traditional approaches, such as Naive Bayes classifiers [19], others have tried histogram-based machine learning techniques [3]. No current solution makes use of the power of recent CNN breakthroughs. The most similar to our work proposes a sophisticated pipeline [11], that generates slope, surface normals and terrain roughness, but since it basically reconstructs a 3D model of the ground using bundle adjustment, it takes a couple of seconds on a desktop CPU for a small input image (300×300 pixels) and is unsuitable for on-board processing. In contrast, we learn a fast and relatively small CNN to classify surface normals into three main categories (horizontal, vertical and other), without needing to reconstruct an accurate 3D model.

3 Safe Landing Area Discovery

We aim to discover safe landing areas using RGB signal. We define the problem as a pixel-wise semantic segmentation with 3 classes: *'horizontals'*, *'verticals'* and *'others'*. The horizontals correspond to areas which can be used for automatic landing of UAVs or other aerial vehicles, such as planar ground or rooftops. At the opposite spectrum, the verticals correspond to areas which can be though of as obstacles, such as tall buildings, houses. In general, these are the areas the UAV should stay the farthest off, both during flying as well as landing, to avoid the damage and destruction of the machine. Since the world is not as simple, containing only horizontals and verticals, we define a third class. In this category fall objects such as trees, tilted rooftops, or various irregular shaped objects. These areas can be considered safer for landing than pure verticals, in cases where no horizontals are detected nearby, which can lead to a successful landing in critical situations.

It should be noted that this is an oversimplification of the world, as we assume no semantic knowledge. We are perfectly aware that a horizontal may

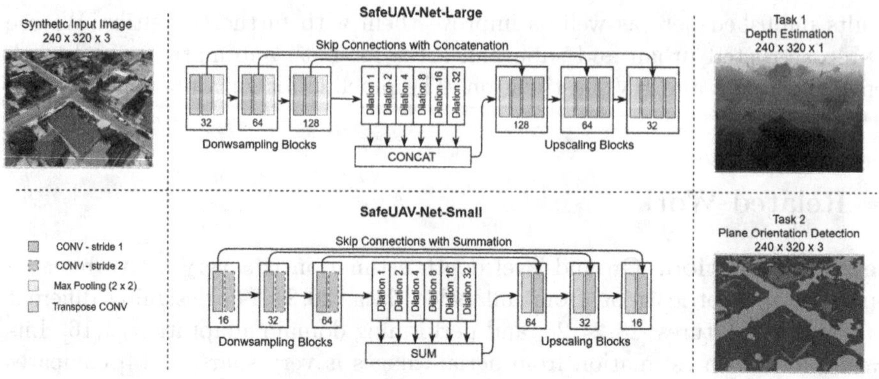

Fig. 2. Our proposed SafeUAV-Nets for both on-board and off-board processing, trained for depth estimation and plane orientation prediction. (Color figure online)

not be semantically safe, such as landing on water or a highway, however we believe that building a low level knowledge of the world, using both depth and HVO, can lead to better results when combined with higher level networks, such as semantic segmentation or object detection, especially since this knowledge is build using only RGB input, in real-time, on low-cost embedded hardware. This is a key objective of this work.

3.1 SafeUAV-Net for Depth and Plane Orientation Estimation

Starting with RGB images, we aim to predict depth and classify plane orientation into three classes: horizontal, vertical and other. Our tasks are strongly related to semantic segmentation as we predict a categorical value for each pixel of the input image. For this purpose, we use a variant of the state-of-the-art U-Net model proposed by [22] for aerial image segmentation. That particular CNN demonstrated state of the art results on various aerial image segmentation tasks, such as the detection of buildings and roads. Compared to previous work, we used concatenation instead of sum for feature aggregation at the U-Net bottleneck phase, in order to capture more information and increase the learning capacity of the network. The role of the concatenation operation in DCNN has been studied in [13] and the predictions produced by these networks were more accurate than the ResNet-like skip connections [10].

Targeting an embedded application, we have developed two variants of the network. The first, named SafeUAV-Net-Large below, runs at 35 FPS on Nvidia's Jetson TX2. The second, named SafeUAV-Net-Small below, is a simplified version of the first, and runs at 130 FPS on an embedded device. For timing details, as well as a comparison with classical architectures, see Sect. 6 and Table 5. The detailed design of our architectures is described in Fig. 2.

SafeUAV-Net-Large is a U-Net-like network [25] with three down-sampling blocks, three up-scaling blocks and a central concatenated dilated convolutions bottleneck, with progressively increasing dilation rates (1, 2, 4, 8, 16 and 32). Each down-sampling block has two convolutional layers with stride 1, followed by a 2×2 max pooling layer. Each up-scaling layer has a transposed convolution layer, a feature map concatenation with the corresponding map from the down-sampling layers and two convolutional layers with stride 1. The number of feature maps are 32-64-128 for the down-sampling blocks and the other way around for the up-sampling ones. All kernels are 3×3. Each dilated convolution outputs a set of 256 activation maps.

SafeUAV-Net-Small follows the similar design principles as the large net - the same number of up-scaling and down-sampling blocks and a central bottleneck with the same dilation rates, but summed features. This way we reduce the computational cost of applying costly convolutional operations over a large set of filters. Each down-sampling block has two convolutional layers, one with stride 1 and the second with stride 2, in order to halve the input resolution. Each up-scaling block has a single convolutional layer and a feature map concatenation with its corresponding map. The number of feature maps are 16-32-64 for the down-sampling blocks and the other way around for the up-sampling blocks. We also reduced the number of filters outputted by each dilated convolution to 128.

Optimization. For the task of depth estimation, we normalize our ground truth labels with values between 0 and 1 and then evaluate the performance of our learning by measuring the L2 loss for our predictions compared to the reference labels. For safe-landing prediction, we used cross-entropy loss for optimizing our models.

Training Details. We used the Pytorch [23] deep-learning framework to train our models. We trained our networks from scratch for 100 epochs each and selected the best epoch, evaluated on our validation set, to report our results. Fine-tuning of models was done for only 50 epochs. We used Adam optimizer, starting with a learning rate of 0.001 for both networks and using a reduce-on-plateau learning rate scheduler, with a factor of 0.1 and a patience of 10.

4 Dataset

4.1 Motivation

While the development of machine learning algorithms for drones and UAVs is an increasingly popular domain, we are aware of no high resolution 3D dataset specifically designed for this purpose. At ground level, there are many datasets and benchmarks such as CityScapes [7] or KITTI [8], useful for training and testing of computer vision applications (for example, in the case of self-driving cars).

Safety laws, airspace regulations, as well as cost and technical reasons prevent easy capturing and creation of a similarly exhaustive dataset from a bird's-eye viewpoint, one that would be better addressed towards UAV machine learning. This is starting to change, thanks to efforts like VisDrone2018 [30] or Okutama-Action [4]. However, most are centred around object detection problems. Those

Fig. 3. A sample RGB image from each sub-dataset. From left to right, Suburban A, Suburban B, Urban A and Urban B. (Color figure online)

datasets do not include additional channels apart from RGB and bounding boxes for objects. For the tasks we are tackling in this paper, namely semantic segmentation and depth estimation, we need a large amount of labeled data with pixel-wise annotations for precise predictions.

4.2 Approach

In this paper, we propose a different approach – one that has been similarly gaining traction during the past years: working with computer-generated imagery and labels. Restricting the subject to drones, [26] proposes the generation of a virtual environment using the industry-targeted CityEngine [12] software and produces promising results using real map data as a starting point. CityGML [15] standardizes an exchange format for the storing of 3D models of cities or landscapes, and also offers a basic procedural modelling engine for generating random buildings and cities.

However, the actual output of these systems is not yet realistic; there is no mistaking that this is a virtual world and we therefore believe that the usefulness of these systems for training real-world scenarios is somewhat limited. In contrast, for the purpose of this paper, we chose to construct our virtual dataset with the help and power of the Google Earth [9] application and its real-world derived 3D reconstructions. Up close or from ground level these reconstructions are too coarse to be readily usable, but from a bird's-eye view perspective, several meters above ground, the surfaces and images captured begin to look life-like.

4.3 Dataset Details

We capture a random series of sample images above rectangular patches of ground, with a uniformly randomized elevation between 30 and 90 meters and a stable 45° tilt angle. More precisely, the dataset consists of 11.907 samples in a 80% training (9.524) - 20% validation (2.383) distribution. We further split the data by the type of area they cover, two separate urban areas and two separate suburban ones. A selection of images from each sub-dataset is shown in Fig. 3. We chose these sets as we want to build a robust and diverse dataset that is capable of generalizing over a wide range of environments, while still being relevant to both the depth estimation and plane angle estimation tasks.

We collect two urban areas - Urban A of 3.5 km^2 (3636 samples training, 909 validation) and Urban B covering $\approx$ 3.3 km^2 (2873 samples training, 719 validation). For the suburban areas, we collect Suburban A of $\approx$ 1.7 km^2 (1966 samples training, 492 validation) and Suburban B covering $\approx$ 1.1 km^2 (1049 samples training, 263 validation).

For each of these samples we extract a 640×480 pixels RGB image, an exact depth measure for each pixel, and a semantically labelled image that specifies if a surface is either vertical, horizontal or sloped (other) – HVO estimation.

HVO Extraction Method. We want to generate ground truth label images, but the 3D model we have as a base is still far from perfect, containing many reconstruction errors and stray polygons in otherwise smooth surfaces. We thus approximate plane inclination in three phases[1]:

1. We calculate polygon surface normals and define a maximum error of 10° for horizontals (H) and 20° for verticals (V), while throwing everything else in the sloped bin (O).
2. We pass through the O set and switch polygons to either H or V if (a) their neighbouring polygons in a cubic window are mostly of the same type and (b) the current polygon's surface normal has a more permissive maximum error of 20° for H or 30° for V – we also selectively ignore H surfaces in the V window and vice-versa, as this helps handling 90° corners properly.
3. We similarly pass through the H or V sets and switch polygons to the O set if their neighbouring polygons are mostly sloped. We do this processing because, as previously mentioned, the actual surface model is a noisy one and we wish to identify large patches that are consistently straight (H or V) while ignoring everything that we are either unsure of, either represents a true complex structure that is difficult to classify (O).

Having all our polygons now labeled, we color-code each class and generate a second surface model having the same geometry as the first, but whose face textures now represent semantic information. We can now capture all the images we need, using exactly the same viewpoint for each image in our sample. Lastly, as images from this second model are relatively coarse due to the hard cuts between polygons, we apply a simple post-processing step for smoothing them. We relabel each pixel to have the class that is dominant in a 5×5 pixels window.

Dataset Realism and Quality. The dataset consists of 3D reconstructions from real RGB images. However, due to the ill-posed algorithmic problem of reconstruction, limited resolution and sampling distance, the quality of the reconstructions is not ideal - almost no building facade is vertical, the texture mapping fails to accurately match object geometry and overall, clustering verticals and horizontal regions is a task prone to error. Although the dataset should be called semi-synthetic, due to significant discrepancies between reality and the generated 3D meshes (see Fig. 4), we generally call it synthetic in the paper.

[1] Code and dataset available at https://sites.google.com/site/aerialimageunderstanding/safeuav-learning-to-estimate-depth-and-safe-landing-areas-for-uavs.

Fig. 4. A sample of RGB vs reconstructed 3D meshes (used for training) from the same location. Note the significant geometric, texture and illumination inconsistencies introduced by the reconstruction in contrast to a real-world capture. The darker regions in the right and left are tree meshes. While these meshes are very difficult to use for learning something at the ground level, from a birds's eye viewpoint they look similar to the real RGB image. (Color figure online)

5 Experiments

We report qualitative and quantitative results on depth estimation and HVO segmentation on all four regions from our dataset.

The metrics used for the HVO task are the network Loss (cross entropy), Accuracy, Precision, Recall and mean intersection over union (mIoU). All the reported values are computed on the unseen validation set. These metrics can be defined in terms of true positives, true negatives, false positives and false negatives, as follows: $Accuracy = \frac{TP+TN}{TP+FP+TN+FN}$, $Precision = \frac{TP}{TP+FP}$, $Recall = \frac{TP}{TP+FN}$ and $mIoU = \frac{TP}{TP+FP+FN}$.

The cross-entropy used for HVO can be expressed as:

$$L(y,t) = -\frac{1}{N}\sum_{i,j}\sum_{c=\{H,V,O\}} t_{i,j}^{(c)} * log(y_{i,j}^{(c)})$$

Each prediction $y_{i,j}$ is a probability vector, that corresponds to a confidence level for each of the 3 classes, while the target vector is a one-hot encoded vector, with a value of 1 for the correct class and a value of 0 for the other two.

The metrics used for the depth prediction are the network Loss (Sum of squared error), the Root Mean Squared Error (RMSE) as well as an absolute error (in meters). The SSE Loss function can be expressed as:

$$L(y,t) = \sum_{i,j}(y_{i,j} - t_{i,j})^2$$

The meters error is the summed error in meters over the entire image, scaled by the corresponding dataset-dependant scaling factor (F). This can be expressed mathematically as:

$$L_{met}(y,t) = \frac{1}{N}\sum_{i,j}|y_{i,j} * F - t_{i,j} * F| = \frac{1}{N}\sum(|y_{i,j} - t_{i,j}| * F)$$

The first term is exactly the absolute (L1) loss, while the scaling factor is required due to the rendering process, which is different for all the considered 3D models. $t_{i,j}$ is the ground truth distance and $y_{i,j}$ the predicted distance at the (i,j) location, while N stands for the number of pixels in the current image.

This factor is a constant number that is different for each region, based on how the 3D model is defined, but we normalized all the data to the same values (multiplying the given depth with its factor). This allowed us to train the network on all the 4 regions using the same scale throughout all the data.

For a fair comparison, we also train the two tasks on two standard architectures, the U-net [25] and the DeepLabV3+ [6]. In order to keep the same settings, the input of the network is changed from 240×320 to the default value for each architecture: 572×572 inputs with 388×388 outputs for U-net and 512×512 inputs with 512×512 outputs for the DeepLabV3+ model. This makes some unnormed losses incomparable (such as the Depth L2 loss).

5.1 Qualitative and Quantitative Evaluation

Figures 5 and 6 show RGB imagery and ground truth for both depth and HVO tasks, and also qualitative results on the HVO task (Fig. 5) and depth estimation (Fig. 6) on all four regions from our dataset.

Buildings in suburban regions are significantly sparser than urban regions - continuous building regions occupy large amounts of the urban landscape. The evaluation was done by combining all 4 areas into a single dataset. Furthermore, each urban and suburban area was tested independently, using only the data from its own region, split into train and validation. We report results for each task - depth and HVO.

Table 1. HVO prediction results for SafeUAV-Net-Large and SafeUAV-Net-Small trained on full dataset. HVO_{nn} is the prediction produced by our network after training it with the ground truth HVO_{gt}.

Model	Input	Accuracy	Precision	Recall	mIoU
U-net [25]	RGB	0.729	0.560	0.505	0.356
DeepLabv3+ [6]	RGB	0.840	0.753	0.739	0.597
Small	RGB	0.823	0.728	0.693	0.551
Large	RGB	**0.846**	**0.761**	**0.748**	**0.607**
Small	RGB + $Depth_{nn}$	0.823	0.728	0.696	0.552
Small	RGB + $Depth_{gt}$	0.902*	0.845*	0.840*	0.732*
Large	RGB + $Depth_{nn}$	0.834	0.741	0.726	0.582
Large	RGB + $Depth_{gt}$	0.909*	0.858*	0.848*	0.748*

The inputs noted with *gt* (ground truth) represent the automatically extracted label. Inputs noted with *nn* (neural network output, iteration 1), represent the labels extracted by the first network (which in turn was trained with ground truth).
*Since these networks are trained using ground truth labels, and cannot be used for real-world prediction, they are only presented as an upper bound for each model.

Table 2. Results on depth estimation for SafeUAV-Net-Large and SafeUAV-Net-Small trained on full dataset. Errors are expressed in meters.

Model	Input	RMSE	Meters
U-net [25]	RGB	0.041	9.63
DeepLabv3+ [6]	RGB	0.034	8.49
Small	RGB	0.031	7.22
Large	RGB	**0.026**	**6.09**
Small	RGB + HVO_{nn}	0.037	8.76
Large	RGB + HVO_{nn}	0.027	6.34

As previously stated, the input and output shapes are not identical for all models, so the Loss iteself should not be compared, but rather the RMSE and meters metrics.
We also observe that using RGB + HVO as input, be it ground-truth or a prediction of the network gives a much lower improvement, and even hinders the results in some cases. This comes in contrast to the HVO estimation task, where adding the depth signal improves the results almost every time.

The HVO results (Table 1) show a clear advantage of our SafeUAV-Net-Large over the state-of-the-art CNN. Furthermore, the numbers for our SafeUAV-Net-Small are similar to the large one, even though it has much less parameters. We aimed to further improve safe landing detection using depth labels. Unfortunately, except the small improvement for our small network, the results degraded. We argue this is due to the noise in the depth labeling. To confirm this, we trained with the ground truth depth, achieving the best results. We believe improving the ground truth depth labels could also improve safe landing detection. We provide detailed results for each sub-dataset in Table 3. Training on all datasets results in a more robust overall detection, as intended when selecting the interest regions.

Table 3. Quantitative results of SafeUAV-Net-Large and SafeUAV-Net-Small for the HVO task. We report mean values for Accuracy, Precision, Recall and IoU on the validation sets. The networks in this table were trained using only RGB input. The second part of the table presents the results, using the best model trained on the entire network, comparing the impact of fine-tuning on a specific area.

All	Model	Accuracy		Precision		Recall		mIoU	
	Small	0.81 ± 0.01		0.72 ± 0.01		0.68 ± 0.01		0.53 ± 0.01	
	Large	0.83 ± 0.01		0.74 ± 0.01		0.71 ± 0.02		0.57 ± 0.02	
		Base	Fine-tuned	Base	Fine-tuned	Base	Fine-tuned	Base	Fine-tuned
SubA	Small	0.839	0.841	0.730	0.736	0.671	0.673	0.543	0.546
	Large	0.855	0.865	0.755	0.779	0.723	0.730	0.590	0.609
SubB	Small	0.816	0.819	0.695	0.704	0.598	0.600	0.472	0.475
	Large	0.829	0.845	0.707	0.749	0.671	0.672	0.529	0.549
UrbA	Small	0.810	0.808	0.716	0.714	0.698	0.696	0.547	0.547
	Large	0.844	0.854	0.765	0.784	0.762	0.772	0.618	0.638
UrbB	Small	0.833	0.835	0.760	0.761	0.743	0.748	0.599	0.604
	Large	0.851	0.860	0.782	0.796	0.779	0.789	0.639	0.656

Table 4. Quantitative results of SafeUAV-Net-Large and SafeUAV-Net-Small for the depth estimation task. We report mean values for RMSE as well as absolute error (in meters) on the validation sets. The networks in this table were also trained only using RGB input, and the second part of the table presents the results, with and without fine-tuning the networks.

All	Model	RMSE		Meters	
	Small	0.045 ± 0.009		10.51 ± 2.24	
	Large	0.036 ± 0.005		8.29 ± 1.16	
		Base	Fine-tuned	Base	Fine-tuned
SubA	Small	0.025	0.023	5.59	5.35
	Large	0.022	0.020	4.96	4.67
SubB	Small	0.023	0.019	5.51	4.46
	Large	0.019	0.017	4.72	4.05
UrbA	Small	0.035	0.035	8.39	8.23
	Large	0.031	0.031	7.08	7.02
UrbB	Small	0.032	0.031	7.47	7.17
	Large	0.027	0.026	6.10	5.92

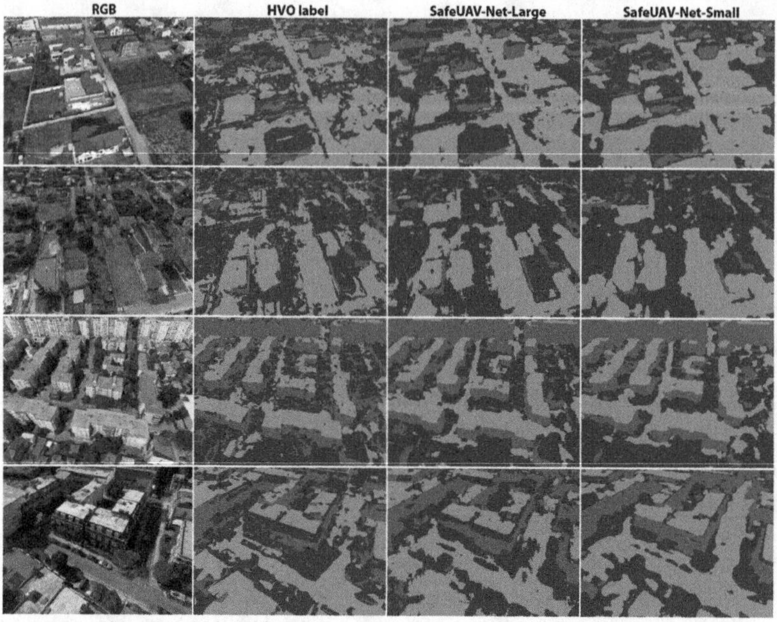

Fig. 5. HVO qualitative results on testing samples from all datasets from SafeNet-UAV-Large. Red stands for horizontal, yellow for vertical and blue for other areas. From top to bottom, SuburbanA, UrbanA, UrbanB and SuburbanB, at various altitudes. The HVO prediction tends to be less noisier and closer to the real 'ground truth'. The performance hit from the smaller network is difficult to notice. (Color figure online)

The depth results are shown in Table 2. This time, both flavours of our proposed architectures outperform established CNNs. Results for each sub-dataset are shown in Table 4. The noisiness of the input is reflected in the higher standard deviation compared to the safe landing task, noticeable on all regions.

We also show results from RGB drone footage in Fig. 7, for both sizes of the network and tasks (depth and HVO). We notice similar performance compared to the synthetic dataset. We believe increasing the size of the dataset could further improve the results.

6 SafeUAV Timings

As described in Sect. 3.1, we develop two versions of SafeUAV-Net - a large one and a small one. We report timings in Table 5 for both desktop GPUs (NVIDIA Tesla P100) and embedded devices (NVIDIA Jetson TX2). While maintaining comparable performance, the small one is suitable for embedded usage.

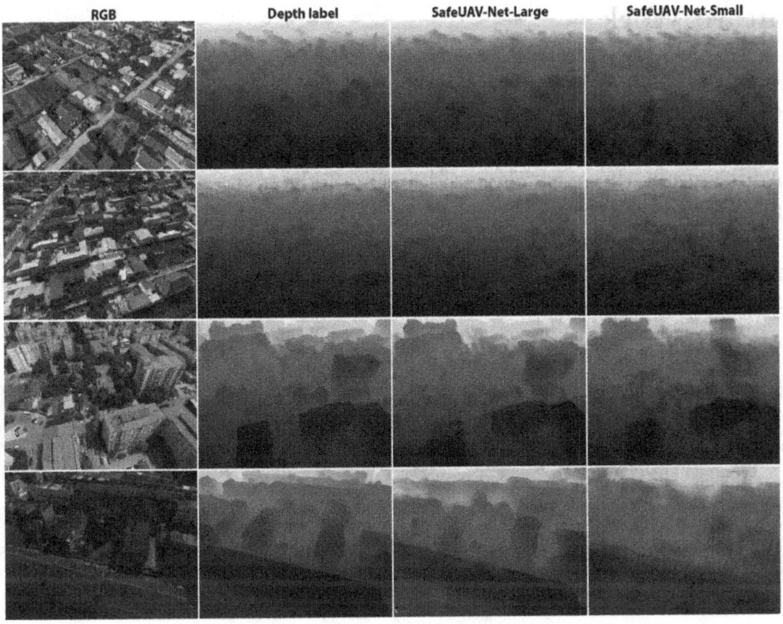

Fig. 6. Depth qualitative results on testing samples from all datasets from SafeNet-UAV-Large. Depth is normalized between 0 and 1 using the hot colormap (0 means close, 1 faraway). From top to bottom, SuburbanA, UrbanA, UrbanB and SuburbanB, at various altitudes. The prediction tends to blur object edges. This is even more visible in the predictions of the smaller network. (Color figure online)

Table 5. Number of parameters (RGB input, 1-channel depth map output), memory usage (inference mode, batch of 1) and inference time for multiple batch sizes for the Safe-UAV networks, compared to the more standard U-net and state-of the art DeepLabV3+.

Network	Number of parameters	Memory usage	Batch size	Tesla P100 (images/s)	Jetson TX2 (images/s)
U-net [25]	31M	1.7 GB	1	502	37
			5	2311	–
			10	3980	–
			20	–	–
DeepLabv3+ [6]	55M	1.9 GB	1	63	–
			5	326	–
			10	611	–
			20	–	–
SafeUAV-Net-Large	24M	927 MB	1	463	35
			5	2333	181
			10	4557	428
			20	7978	–
SafeUAV-Net-Small	1M	433 MB	1	577	138
			5	2871	635
			10	5774	1045
			20	11480	1939

*Dashed values appear because of out of memory errors with the respective boards.

7 Future Work

We aim to use the spatial and temporal continuity present in video sequences in order to generate a more robust prediction. At lower speeds, similar frames could be used to vote on the same region in order to get a better precision at landing time. Additionally, the mesh captured during flight (extracted from RGB used as a texture for the depth map) could be used to improve the surface classification of the same location. We also aim to increase the spatial resolution of the ground truth and efficiently apply the proposed network only on the region of the image that is significantly different from the previous frame.

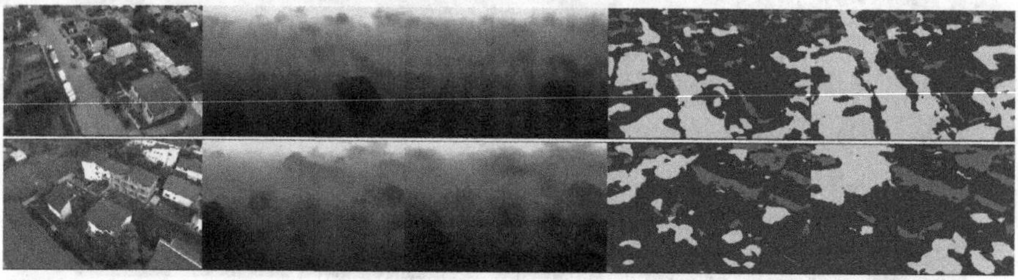

Fig. 7. Qualitative results on real UAV footage. RGB, depth predicted with SafeUAVNet-Small and Large, HVO predicted with SafeUAVNet-Small and Large. We obtain similar results to the synthetic dataset ones. (Color figure online)

Finally, we aim to improve the safety by visual geolocalization - include additional common classes easily derived from HVO (such as buildings and tall structures) and use several discrete geo-localized items to compute an approximate location, given an initial start position. We believe this will improve safe area estimation by conditioning on the predicted geo-location. Automatic visual geolocalization, a task related to recent work [22], could also handle cases of radio signal loss and improve overall UAV navigation safety and robustness.

8 Conclusions

We propose SafeUAV-Net - an embeddable-hardware compatible system based on deep convolutional networks, designed for depth and safe landing area estimation using only the RGB input. Furthermore, we produce and train on a synthetic dataset and show compelling performance on real drone footage. Our extensive experiments on unseen synthetic test cases, where ground truth information is available, show that our system is numerically accurate, while also being fast on an embedded GPU running at 35 FPS (SafeUAV-Net-Large) and 138 FPS (SafeUAV-Net-Small). We believe that the use of our approach on commercial drones could improve flight safety in urban or suburban areas at high speeds and complement the limited range of on-board sensors.

Acknowledgements. This work was supported in part by Romanian Ministry of European Funds, project IAVPLN POC-A1.2.1D-2015-P39-287 and UEFISCDI, under projects PN-III-P4-ID-ERC-2016-0007 and PN-III-P1-1.2-PCCDI-2017-0734. We would also like to express our gratitude to Aurelian Marcu and The Center for Advanced Laser Technologies for providing use GPU training resources.

References

1. Aguilar, W.G., Casaliglla, V.P., Pólit, J.L.: Obstacle avoidance based-visual navigation for micro aerial vehicles. Electronics **6**(1), 10 (2017)
2. Atapour-Abarghouei, A., Breckon, T.P.: Real-time monocular depth estimation using synthetic data with domain adaptation via image style transfer. In: Proceedings of the IEEE Conference on Computer Vision and Pattern Recognition, vol. 18, p. 1 (2018)
3. Aziz, S., Faheem, R.M., Bashir, M., Khalid, A., Yasin, A.: Unmanned aerial vehicle emergency landing site identification system using machine vision. J. Image Graph. **4**(1), 36–41 (2016)
4. Barekatain, M., et al.: Okutama-action: an aerial view video dataset for concurrent human action detection. In: 1st Joint BMTT-PETS Workshop on Tracking and Surveillance, CVPR, pp. 1–8 (2017)
5. Canziani, A., Paszke, A., Culurciello, E.: An analysis of deep neural network models for practical applications. arXiv preprint arXiv:1605.07678 (2016)
6. Chen, L.C., Zhu, Y., Papandreou, G., Schroff, F., Adam, H.: Encoder-decoder with atrous separable convolution for semantic image segmentation. arXiv preprint arXiv:1802.02611 (2018)
7. Cordts, M., et al.: The CityScapes dataset for semantic urban scene understanding. In: Proceedings of the IEEE Conference on Computer Vision and Pattern Recognition, pp. 3213–3223 (2016)
8. Geiger, A., Lenz, P., Stiller, C., Urtasun, R.: Vision meets robotics: the KITTI dataset. Int. J. Robot. Res. **32**(11), 1231–1237 (2013)
9. Google: Google Earth, version 7.3.0 (2018). https://www.google.com/earth/
10. He, K., Zhang, X., Ren, S., Sun, J.: Deep residual learning for image recognition. In: Proceedings of the IEEE Conference on Computer Vision and Pattern Recognition, pp. 770–778 (2016)
11. Hinzmann, T., Stastny, T., Lerma, C.C., Siegwart, R., Gilitschenski, I.: Free LSD: prior-free visual landing site detection for autonomous planes. IEEE Robot. Autom. Lett. **3**, 2545–2552 (2018)
12. Hu, X., Liu, X., He, Z., Zhang, J.: Batch modeling of 3D city based on ESRI CityEngine (2013)
13. Huang, G., Liu, Z., Weinberger, K.Q., van der Maaten, L.: Densely connected convolutional networks. In: Proceedings of the IEEE Conference on Computer Vision and Pattern Recognition, vol. 1, p. 3 (2017)
14. Julian, K., Mern, J., Tompa, R.: UAV depth perception from visual, images using a deep convolutional neural network (2017). http://cs231n.stanford.edu/reports/2017/pdfs/200.pdf
15. Kolbe, T.H., Gröger, G., Plümer, L.: CityGML: interoperable access to 3D city models. In: van Oosterom, P., Zlatanova, S., Fendel, E.M. (eds.) Geo-information for disaster management, pp. 883–899. Springer, Heidelberg (2005). https://doi.org/10.1007/3-540-27468-5_63

16. Kundu, J.N., Uppala, P.K., Pahuja, A., Babu, R.V.: Adadepth: unsupervised content congruent adaptation for depth estimation. arXiv preprint arXiv:1803.01599 (2018)
17. Leaverton, G.T.: Generation drone: the future of utility O&M. In: Electrical Transmission and Substation Structures 2015, pp. 190–201 (2015)
18. Lee, J.H., Heo, M., Kim, K.R., Kim, C.S.: Single-image depth estimation based on fourier domain analysis. In: Proceedings of the IEEE Conference on Computer Vision and Pattern Recognition, pp. 330–339 (2018)
19. Li, X.: A software scheme for UAV's safe landing area discovery. AASRI Procedia **4**, 230–235 (2013)
20. Li, Z., Snavely, N.: MegaDepth: learning single-view depth prediction from internet photos. In: Proceedings of the IEEE Conference on Computer Vision and Pattern Recognition, pp. 2041–2050 (2018)
21. Mahjourian, R., Wicke, M., Angelova, A.: Unsupervised learning of depth and ego-motion from monocular video using 3D geometric constraints. In: Proceedings of the IEEE Conference on Computer Vision and Pattern Recognition, pp. 5667–5675 (2018)
22. Marcu, A., Costea, D., Slusanschi, E., Leordeanu, M.: A multi-stage multi-task neural network for aerial scene interpretation and geolocalization. arXiv preprint arXiv:1804.01322 (2018)
23. Paszke, A., et al.: Automatic differentiation in pytorch. In: NIPS-W (2017)
24. Qi, X., Liao, R., Liu, Z., Urtasun, R., Jia, J.: GeoNet: geometric neural network for joint depth and surface normal estimation. In: Proceedings of the IEEE Conference on Computer Vision and Pattern Recognition, pp. 283–291 (2018)
25. Ronneberger, O., Fischer, P., Brox, T.: U-net: Convolutional networks for biomedical image segmentation. arXiv preprint arXiv:1505.04597 (2015)
26. Tian, Y., Li, X., Wang, K., Wang, F.Y.: Training and testing object detectors with virtual images. IEEE/CAA J. Automatica Sin. **5**(2), 539–546 (2018)
27. Wang, S., et al.: Torontocity: seeing the world with a million eyes. arXiv preprint arXiv:1612.00423 (2016)
28. Xu, D., Ouyang, W., Wang, X., Sebe, N.: Pad-net: multi-tasks guided prediction-and-distillation network for simultaneous depth estimation and scene parsing. arXiv preprint arXiv:1805.04409 (2018)
29. Zhan, H., Garg, R., Weerasekera, C.S., Li, K., Agarwal, H., Reid, I.: Unsupervised learning of monocular depth estimation and visual odometry with deep feature reconstruction. In: Proceedings of the IEEE Conference on Computer Vision and Pattern Recognition, pp. 340–349 (2018)
30. Zhu, P., Wen, L., Bian, X., Ling, H., Hu, Q.: Vision meets drones: a challenge. arXiv preprint arXiv:1804.07437 (2018)

Aerial GANeration: Towards Realistic Data Augmentation Using Conditional GANs

Stefan Milz(✉), Tobias Rüdiger, and Sebastian Süss

Spleenlab, Saalburg-Ebersdorf, Germany
{stefan.milz,tobias.ruediger,sebastian.suess}@spleenlab.com

Abstract. Environmental perception for autonomous aerial vehicles is a rising field. Recent years have shown a strong increase of performance in terms of accuracy and efficiency with the aid of convolutional neural networks. Thus, the community has established data sets for benchmarking several kinds of algorithms. However, public data is rare for multi-sensor approaches or either not large enough to train very accurate algorithms. For this reason, we propose a method to generate multi-sensor data sets using realistic data augmentation based on conditional generative adversarial networks (cGAN). cGANs have shown impressive results for image to image translation. We use this principle for sensor simulation. Hence, there is no need for expensive and complex 3D engines. Our method encodes ground truth data, e.g. semantics or object boxes that could be drawn randomly, in the conditional image to generate realistic consistent sensor data. Our method is proven for aerial object detection and semantic segmentation on visual data, such as 3D Lidar reconstruction using the ISPRS and DOTA data set. We demonstrate qualitative accuracy improvements for state-of-the-art object detection (YOLO) using our augmentation technique.

Keywords: Conditional GANs · Sensor fusion · Aerial perception · Object detection · Semantic segmentation · 3D reconstruction

1 Introduction

Aerial perception is a rising field for autonomous vehicles. Especially algorithms based on large data sets have shown accurate results in recent years. Despite all advances, we believe that fully autonomous navigation in arbitrarily complex environments is still far away, especially for automated aerial transportation including all safety aspects. The reasons for that are manifold. On one hand, highly accurate algorithms on dedicated hardware with real-time capabilities are needed for perception. On the other hand, almost all leading state-of-the-art perception (see the DOTA leader board [2]) algorithms are based on deep learning that require individually designed large scaled data sets for training. Within this paper, we want to target the second issue and propose a new method for

L. Leal-Taixé and S. Roth (Eds.): ECCV 2018 Workshops, LNCS 11130, pp. 59–72, 2019.
https://doi.org/10.1007/978-3-030-11012-3_5

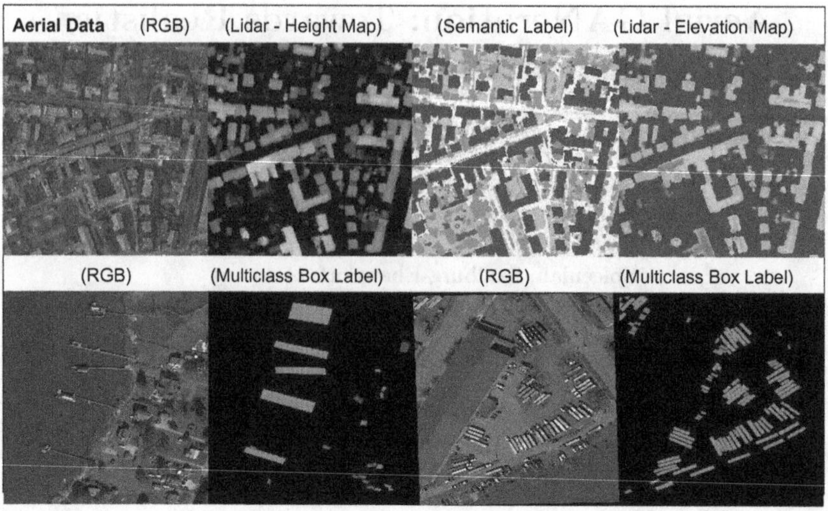

Fig. 1. Exemplary aerial data used for GANeration. The upper row shows samples given by the ISPRS Dataset (Potsdam) [1] representing RGB, Lidar and Semantic Segmentation Labels. The lower row represents two samples from the DOTA [2] data set with multi-class object boxes (colorized by classes) and spatially encoded inside an RGB image. Additionally, the visual camera RGB image is shown. (Color figure online)

realistic data augmentation in the domain of aerial perception using cGANs. We evaluate qualitatively the data generation for three different tasks: object detection, semantic segmentation and 3D reconstruction based on two sensor types: Cameras and Lidar (ISPRS [1] and DOTA [2]) (see Fig. 1). Additionally, we show significant accuracy improvements for the YOLOv2 [3] object detector using a small subset of the DOTA training base compared to the same detector trained on an augmented extension set using our proposed method. The latter yields much better accuracy without any change of architecture, purely influenced by the GANerated training set.

1.1 Contribution

We present the first approach for synthetic aerial data generation without the need for a complicated 3D engine or any exhausting preprocessing. The proposed method is independent from the desired perception task. This is evaluated by several qualitative experiments, like object detection, semantic segmentation or 3D reconstruction. The method strongly improves the accuracy of a perception algorithm that is exemplary demonstrated by an aerial object detection using YOLOv2. On top, the method can produce different kinds of sensor data, like camera images or Lidar point clouds. The basic idea is the usage of a cGAN, where the desired ground truth is used as conditional input. Here, we encode the condition as an image pair, i.e. the algorithm works even well vice versa (see Fig. 1).

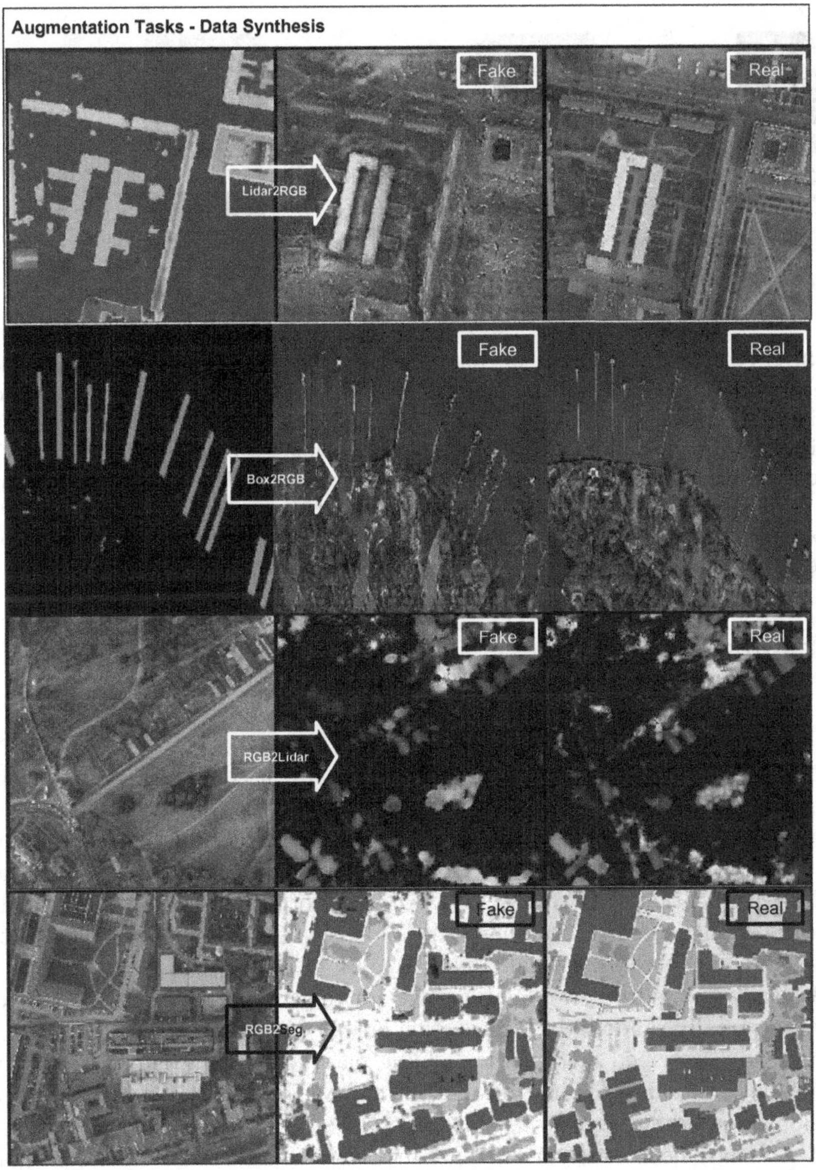

Fig. 2. Exemplary augmentation tasks for Aerial GANeration: Our approach using a cycle GAN could be used generically. Neither sensor nor data representation does matter. Any kind of data synthesis is possible. 1. The image synthesis based on a Lidar scan. 2. The generation of an RGB image based of ground truth 2D bounding boxes. 3. The 3D reconstruction (height map) of an RGB image. 4. The semantic segmentation of an aerial image. (Color figure online)

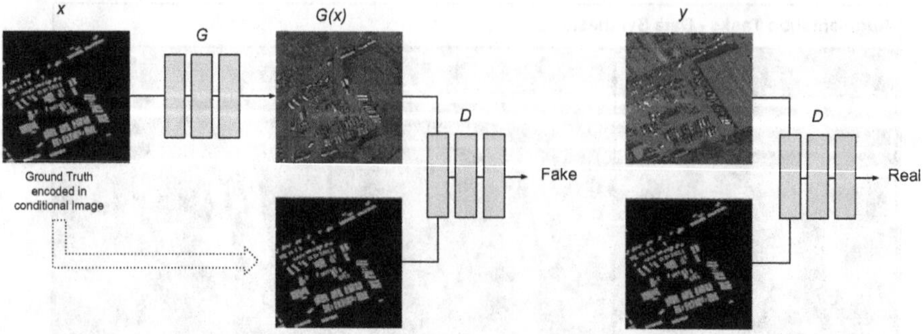

Fig. 3. Ground truth encoding in conditional images. This figure shows the typical structure of a cGAN playing the minimax game. A generator G is used to create a fake image $G(x)$ based on the conditional image x, e.g. Pix2Pix [4]. The discriminator D tries to distinguish between real $D(y)$ and fake images $D(x)$. Aerial GANeration encodes ground truth data in the conditional image x to produce realistic sensor data. The basic idea is to encode ground truth images that are easy to collect or can be sampled automatically, e.g. 2D bounding boxes could be drawn randomly with color classes in an image x to generate a realistic accompanied image $G(x)$.

2 Conditional GANs

2.1 Related Work

In contrast to predictive neural networks that are used for classification and regression purposes, generative networks are not as manifold. The reason is a much more challenging training process. Hence, the use and spreading have started just some years ago, when Goodfellow et al. [5] presented their ground breaking publication of GANs in 2014. Although other methods like deep belief networks [6] or generative autoencoders [7] exist, GANs have developed to the most common generative neural networks.

Basically GANs use a random noise vector to generate data. As the applications for a totally random data generation are very limited, Goodfellow et al. [5] have already described methods for adding parameter to the input signal that allow an adaptation of the network output. GANs that apply this method by an additional conditional input are called cGANs.

cGANs have been widely used to produce realistic data out of the latent space initiated on a conditional vector. Research and concurrent work has been done on discrete labels [8], text and images [4,9]. The latter has been very popular in the domain of image to image translation. The idea behind a conditional GAN for image translation is to encode the condition inside an image to generate accompanied data. This is also known as per-pixel classification or regression.

We adapt this approach to augment datasets for aerial use cases with the aid of encoding easy to generate ground truth inside the conditional image. Accompanied sensor data, e.g. RGB images, are generated by the generator G, whereas the discriminator D decides weather an image is fake or not (see Fig. 3).

Similar to Isola et al. [4] we use a Unet-Architecture [10] for the generator and PatchGAN for the discriminator [11].

2.2 Image to Image Translation

In general GANs were developed to create an image y based on a random noise vector z. $G : z \rightarrow y$ [4]. In contrast a cGAN produces an image by using a noise vector z and a conditional vector c. $G : [c, z] \rightarrow y$. In terms of Image to Image translation c is an input image x. Hence, we use the following convention for mapping $G : [x, z] \rightarrow y$ (see Fig. 3).

2.3 Objective

The objective of a basic GAN can be described by an additive combination of the loss of the discriminative network D and the generative network G. In order to create more and more realistic data, the loss is reduced by training G, whereas a training step of D results in an increase of the loss ideally. Consequently, we can describe both parts of the loss as follows:

$$L_{GAN}(G, D) = \mathbb{E}_y\{\log(D(y))\} + \mathbb{E}_{x,z}\{\log(1 - D(G(x, z))\} \tag{1}$$

The loss in this form is suitable for generating totally random output images, as the discriminative network does not take the conditional input x into account. As our purpose is to enlarge data sets by generating data based on a ground truth image, we need to extend the loss in a way that adds a considering of the conditional input in the network D:

$$L_{cGAN}(G, D) = \mathbb{E}_{x,y}\{\log(D(x, y))\} + \mathbb{E}_{x,z}\{\log(1 - D(x, G(x, z))\} \tag{2}$$

Due to the findings in [4], we add a weighted L1 distance to the loss of the conditional network. The overall loss of our network setup can be written as:

$$L = L_{cGAN}(G, D) + \lambda \cdot \mathbb{E}_{x,y,z}\{||y - G(x, z)||_1\} \tag{3}$$

According to the recommendations in [4], we did not use a dedicated noise vector as input image. As the network tends to ignore the noise vector input, this approach would lead to unneeded computational effort and reduced computational efficiency. However, we applied the noise in some of the generator network layers to achieve some kind of randomness in the network output.

From Fig. 2, it can be seen that the noise we have added to the generator network has no large effect on the network output. Although, noise is added, the fake images do not differ much from the real ones. Hence, the generated images are similar but not equal to the real images. Nevertheless, we can show in the following that the achieved differences in the output images are sufficient to add further diversity to a data set so that the performance of predictive networks trained on such a data set, that has been enlarged by cGANs, is improved. We will show this by applying training YOLO on both an extended and an unextended data set and evaluate the prediction performance.

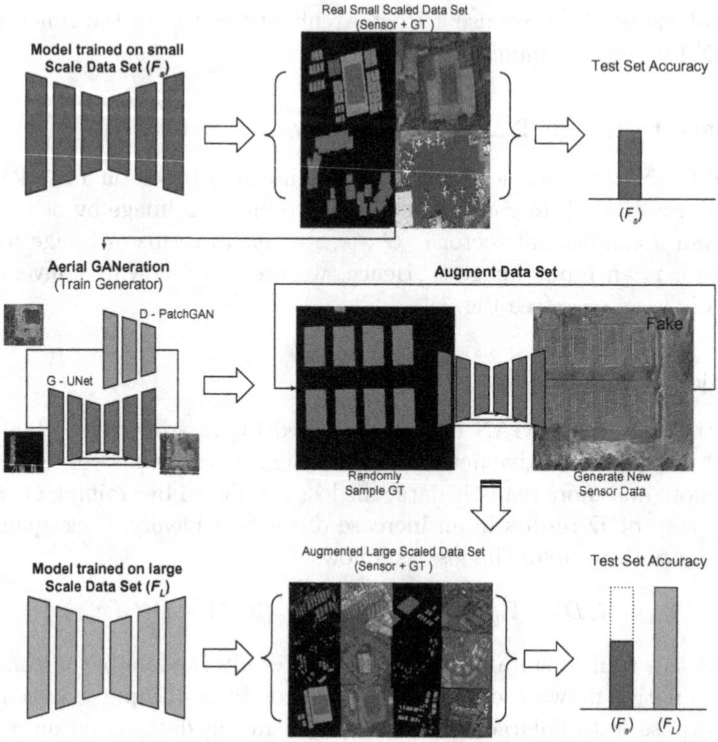

Fig. 4. Augmentation Strategy of aerial GANeration. Our approach improves the quality and accuracy of state-of-the-art task related neural networks (e.g. object detector) by realistic augmentation using conditional GANs. The upper row shows a CNN trained on a small dataset with a sufficient performance F_S. The middle row describes the augmentation strategy. The lower row outlines the new training on the augmented dataset with a strong accuracy improvement: $F_L \gg F_S$. Note: The test-set does not include any augmented data.

2.4 Augmentation Strategy

The basic idea of our augmentation strategy is to bypass the expensive methods for data synthesis, e.g. the simulation of a realistic 3D engine. We focus on "easy-to-get" ground truth for what we generate input data. Our proposed model therefore consists of four steps (see all listed steps in Fig. 4):

1. Get an annotated small scale data set (RGB + bounding boxes)
2. Train the aerial GANerator using a cGAN
3. Augment the small scale data set to a large data set by sampling ground truth randomly → Encode them inside the conditional image
4. Improve the task (e.g. object detector) related deep learning approach via re-training on a large training base.

3 Experiments

Our ablation study is divided into a quantitative and a qualitative part. First we present quantitative results on any kind of data generation. Second, we show significant improvements qualitatively comparing the same state-of-the-art object detector YOLO trained on a base and on an extended dataset using our augmentation method. In general, evaluating the quality of synthesized images is an open and difficult problem. Consequently, we explore in our quantitative study visual problems like RGB image creation or 3D reconstruction (root mean square error assessment), such as visual tasks, like semantic segmentation (intersection over union assessment). The study includes the following applications:

- **Visual qualitative results**:
  - Aerial RGB ↔ Semantic segmentation on ISPRS [1][1]
  - Aerial RGB ↔ Lidar height-map on ISPRS [1]
  - Aerial RGB ↔ Lidar elevation-map on ISPRS [1]
  - 2D multi-class box labels → RGB on DOTA [2][2]
- **Quantitative detection results**:
  - 2D multi-class box labels → RGB on DOTA [2] and training on augmented dataset using YOLOv2 [3]

We tested our proposed method on DOTA [2] and ISPRS [1]. Especially our use cases for ISPRS are based on the *Potsdam* part, which contains RGB, semantic segmentation and Lidar. For exploring the DOTA data, we split the available training data set containing 1411 samples with accompanied ground truth boxes with 15 different classes into 706 training and 705 test samples. The ISPRS data set that contains 40 images was split into 37 training and 3 test images that are mainly used to explore visual results. The model itself is based on Isola et al. [4] for all evaluation studies, with a GGAN loss function, 200 epochs, resized image crops to 256×256 pixels and batch normalization.

RGB to Semantic Segmentation and Vice Versa. The results for RGB to semantic translation are shown in Fig. 5 with 6 color classes: Impervious surfaces (white), building (blue), low vegetation (bright blue), tree (green), car (yellow), clutter/background (red). The figure shows the results of the test set. From a visual point of view both cases, i.e. image to segmentation and segmentation to image, seem to be promising. Additionally, we underline our visual results with the values for intersection over union (IOU) [4] on the test set for the segmentation task. Although the test set is very small, the metrics we yielded (Table 1) are state-of-the-art.

[1] ISPRS - Part2 → Potsdam.

[2] DOTA - Resized to image size of 256×256.

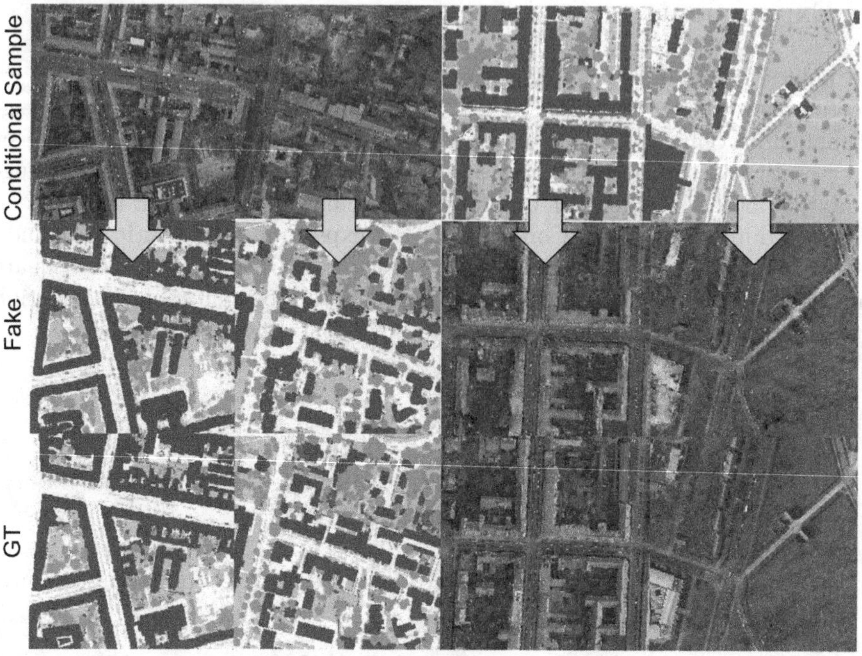

Fig. 5. Results of aerial GANeration for semantic segmentation (left) and semantic to RGB translation (right). The results are based on our split using the ISPRS [1] test set (see section experiments: RGB to Semantic Segmentation) (Color figure online)

Table 1. IoU for the aerial GANeration approach in the domain of image to semantic segmentation translation (ISPRS dataset: 37 training images, 3 test images)

Classes	IoU aerial GAN
Impervious surfaces	79.4%
Building	87.1%
Low vegetation	67.3%
Tree	70.3%
Car	24.1%
Clutter/background	30.7%
Mean IoU	**59.8%**

Table 2. Relative Root Mean Squared Error on pixel level for 3D reconstruction using aerial GANeration (ISPRS dataset: 37 training images, 3 test images)

Classes	rRMSE aerial GAN
Lidar height map	14.53%
Lidar elevation map	21.24%

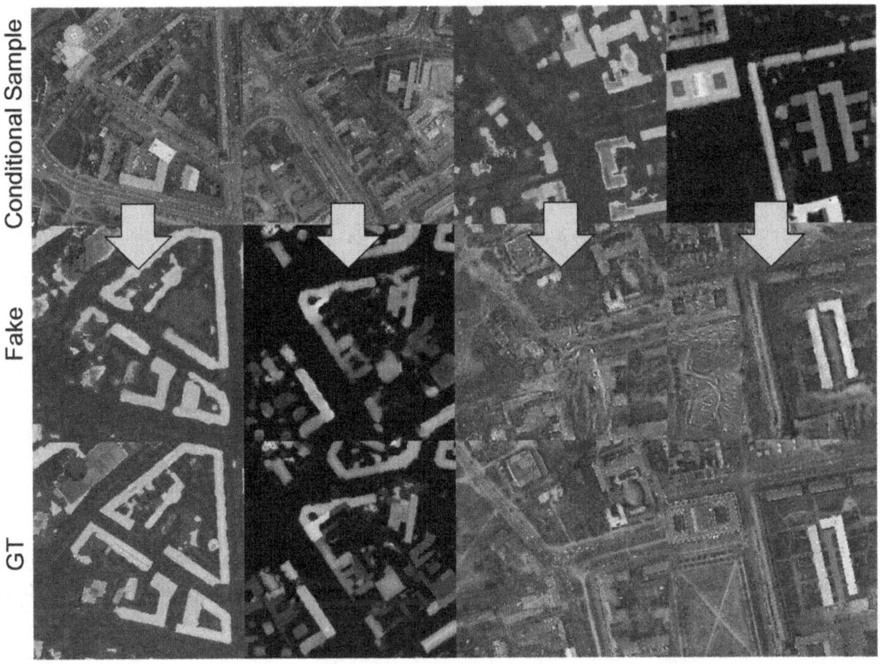

Fig. 6. Results of Aerial GANeration for 3D reconstruction (left) and Lidar to RGB translation (right). The results are based on our split using the ISPRS [1] test set (see section experiments: RGB to Lidar) (Color figure online)

RGB to 3D Lidar-Reconstruction and Vice Versa. Figure 6 shows the qualitative results of our Lidar data 3D generation and the Lidar to RGB translation. Both use cases are either realized via height or colorized elevation map encoding. Again, our experiments show promising results.

To verify the visual findings approximately, we calculated the root mean square error (RMSE) on pixel level as relative RMSE [4] for both encodings using our test set in the domain of RGB to Lidar translation. The results are shown in Table 2. To our surprise, the results for the height map are much more accurate than those for the elevation map. However, we explain this with the quantization of the much smaller prediction range (8 bit vs. 24 bit) and the random behavior of the too small selected test set.

Multi-class Box Labels to RGB. The following experiments are based on the DOTA [2] containing 1411 samples (50:50 split) and 15 different classes. Therefore, this experiment has a higher significance than the results on the ISPRS data set. Additionally, the dataset contains different viewpoints. Hence, the model has to learn the scale invariance. At least, we resized all images to an input size of 256×256. Those qualitative results for image predictions based on input boxes are shown in Fig. 7. We yield promising results for classes with a

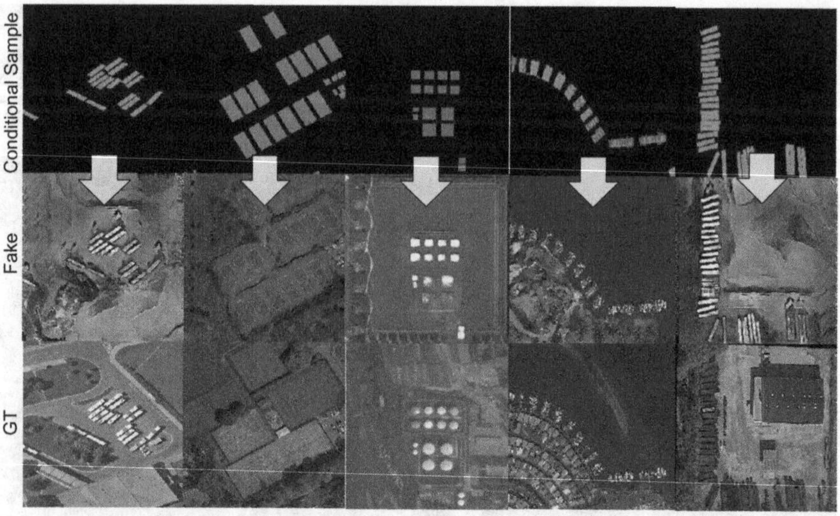

Fig. 7. Results of aerial GANeration for box label to image translation. The results are based on our split using the DOTA [2] test set (see section experiments: Multi-Box Labels to RGB) (Color figure online)

less complex structure like *tennis-court*, *large vehicle* or *storage tank*. Due to the scale variance and the low input image size, we observed failure cases for more complex structures Fig. 8. Indeed, the model is not feasible to perform the object detection itself, i.e. the inverse translation problem (image to box) Fig. 9. The experiment never converged for our setup. We believe, the main reason for this is the extreme viewpoint variance inside the image dataset, which is a typical problem for aerial perception.

Improving YOLO [3] Using Aerial GANeration. Unless weaknesses were observed in the previous section, the full augmentation method was applied to the state-of-the-art object detector YOLO. The concept was validated with the aid of the DOTA training data set for the parallel or horizontal Multi-class object box detection. We use the same split as described previous, i.e. 1411 samples containing 706 training and 705 test cases. Again, we down sample every image to 256×256 pixels. This drastically affects the results, which are not competitive to the official leader board. However, it simply shows the influence of our model.

The augmentation procedure is divided into four phases (see Fig. 4):

1. YOLOv2 (F_s) is trained on the small scale training base
2. The training base is augmented from 706 $\Rightarrow$ 1412 by sampling equally distributed bounding boxes according to the distribution (position, rotation, height, width) inside the dataset using k-means clustering
3. YOLOv2 (F_l) is retrained on the large augmented training set
4. Both models (F_s, F_l) are compared with the aid of the test set (705 samples) in terms of accuracy

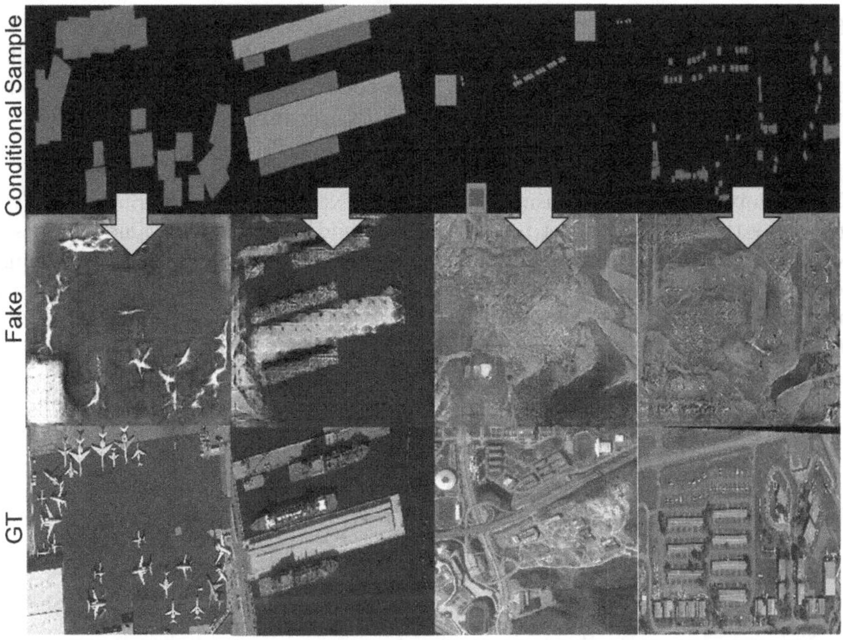

Fig. 8. Failure cases for aerial GANeration. The figure outlines weaknesses of the cGAN to generate complex structures (left two columns). The middle column shows drawbacks in generating small objects in terms of a far viewpoint.

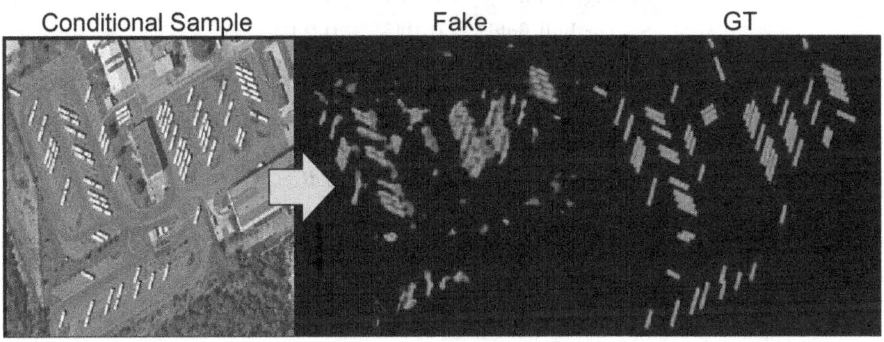

Fig. 9. Aerial GANeration for inverse object box image creation (image2objectboxes), i.e. the object detection itself, where the model never converged in our experiments. The figure shows a sample of the described failure case. It is not possible to extract boxes out of the generated images.

We show significant improvements especially for objects with a low complexity, e.g. baseball diamond, ground track field, large vehicle, tennis court or swimming pool. The improvement is not recognizable for complex objects like planes or ships[3]. However, we believe that those results prove the main idea of our concept. An improved architecture may lead to much better results and could be applied to any kind of sensor data generation. This could facilitate data generation for any kind of perception task, especially aerial cognition (Table 3).

Table 3. Improving YOLOv2 using the Aerial GANeration. Our experiments are validated using the DOTA data set based on our individual split. Bold values emphasize object class specific improvements. The experiment increases performance for simple objects. We used the standard YOLOv2 architecture similarly trained for 10000 iterations. Both experiments run the standard YOLOv2 augmentation strategy ontop. The test-set does not include any augmented data.

Classes	mAP F_s	mAP F_l
Plane	0.66%	0.65%
Baseball diamond	0.43%	**0.49%**
Bridge	0.16%	**0.18%**
Ground track field	0.38%	**0.45%**
Small vehicle	0.41%	0.41%
Large vehicle	0.54%	**0.58%**
Ship	0.51%	0.49%
Tennis court	0.61%	**0.66%**
Basketball court	0.67%	**0.72%**
Storage tank	0.45%	**0.46** %
Soccer ball field	0.19%	**0.24%**
Roundabout	0.21%	0.20%
Harbor	0.39%	0.39%
Swimming pool	0.33%	**0.38%**
Helicopter	0.46%	0.46%
mAP IoU	0.43%	**0.46%**

4 Conclusion

Large scale aerial data sets for deep learning purposes are rare so far. Hence, the development of high performance classification algorithms requires the creation of novel, large scale data sets or the extension of existing data sets. In this paper we treated the second approach of extending current data sets. We addressed this topic by a computational efficient approach. We suggested to use cGANs that do not require complex simulations or 3D engine processing for data generation. We demonstrated the versatility of cGANs by applying them to a couple of different generation problems. This includes generation of semantic segmentation based

[3] Note, the officially published DOTA leader board results are much better due too the higher input image size. For simplicity, we downscale all the images to 256×256.

on RGB images as ground truth and vise versa, of RGB based on Lidar data and of 2D multi-class box based on RGB. The qualitative and quantitative results show the huge potential of cGANs for data generation. By training a YOLO network, we demonstrated the gain that can be achieved by extending training data sets with cGANs.

However, the effect of extending existing small scale data sets with cGANs is limited due to some weaknesses of GANs in general. On the one hand, the low randomness that appears during learning process affects data generation negatively. On the other hand, the performance of cGANs is also depending on the number of training samples. The quality of the generation increases in bigger data sets, so that a chicken-and-egg problem is produced.

Consequently, cGANs are a very effective method to increase classification performance in case of restricted training samples and data set diversity. Nevertheless, for future development of deep learning based algorithms in aerial scenarios, large scale multi sensor data sets are indispensable and need to be addressed in the near future.

4.1 Future Work

The paper has demonstrated the principle possibility, that cGANs help to augment data. However, a detailed ablation study is missing. Moreover, it has to be demonstrated that a real domain translation could be achieved, e.g. Pixels to Point-Clouds or one dimensional signals to pixels. Despite, the authors would like to generate augmented data for corner cases within the aerial vehicle domain, who are impossible to measure, to make aerial perception more explainable and safe.

Acknowledgement. The authors would like to thank their families especially their wifes (Julia, Isabell, Caterina) and children (Til, Liesbeth, Karl, Fritz, Frieda) for their strong mental support.

References

1. Khoshelham, K., Díaz Vilariño, L., Peter, M., Kang, Z., Acharya, D.: The ISPRS benchmark on indoor modelling. In: ISPRS - International Archives of the Photogrammetry, Remote Sensing and Spatial Information Sciences XLII-2/W7, pp. 367–372 (2017)
2. Xia, G., et al.: DOTA: a large-scale dataset for object detection in aerial images. CoRR abs/1711.10398 (2017)
3. Redmon, J., Farhadi, A.: YOLO9000: better, faster, stronger. CoRR abs/1612.08242 (2016)
4. Isola, P., Zhu, J., Zhou, T., Efros, A.A.: Image-to-image translation with conditional adversarial networks. CoRR abs/1611.07004 (2016)
5. Goodfellow, I.J., et al.: Generative adversarial networks (2014)
6. Hinton, G.E., Osindero, S., Teh, Y.W.: A fast learning algorithm for deep belief nets. Neural Comput. **18**(7), 1527–1554 (2006)

7. Tran, N.T., Bui, T.A., Cheung, N.M.: Generative adversarial autoencoder networks (2018)
8. Mirza, M., Osindero, S.: Conditional generative adversarial nets. CoRR abs/1411.1784 (2014)
9. Zhu, J., Park, T., Isola, P., Efros, A.A.: Unpaired image-to-image translation using cycle-consistent adversarial networks. CoRR abs/1703.10593 (2017)
10. Ronneberger, O., Fischer, P., Brox, T.: U-Net: convolutional networks for biomedical image segmentation. CoRR abs/1505.04597 (2015)
11. Li, C., Wand, M.: Precomputed real-time texture synthesis with Markovian generative adversarial networks. CoRR abs/1604.04382 (2016)

Metrics for Real-Time Mono-VSLAM Evaluation Including IMU Induced Drift with Application to UAV Flight

Alexander Hardt-Stremayr[1(✉)], Matthias Schörghuber[2], Stephan Weiss[1], and Martin Humenberger[3]

[1] Alpen-Adria Universität Klagenfurt, Klagenfurt, Austria
alexander.hardt-stremayr@aau.at
[2] Austrian Institute of Technology, Vienna, Austria
[3] NAVER LABS Europe, Meylan, France

Abstract. Vision based algorithms became popular for state estimation and subsequent (local) control of mobile robots. Currently a large variety of such algorithms exists and their performance is often characterized through their drift relative to the total trajectory traveled. However, this metric has relatively low relevance for local vehicle control/stabilization. In this paper, we propose a set of metrics which allows to evaluate a vision based algorithm with respect to its usability for state estimation and subsequent (local) control of highly dynamic autonomous mobile platforms such as multirotor UAVs. As such platforms usually make use of inertial measurements to mitigate the relatively low update rate of the visual algorithm, we particularly focus on a new metric taking the expected IMU-induced drift between visual readings into consideration based on the probabilistic properties of the sensor. We demonstrate this set of metrics by comparing ORB-SLAM, LSD-SLAM and DSO on different datasets.

1 Introduction

Robot pose estimation in unknown environments is an important and active field. A proven method is simultaneous localization and mapping (SLAM), which estimates the robots pose within a self-constructed map using one or more sensors (e.g. camera, laser).

A subset of SLAM, which uses cameras to estimate the pose is known as Visual-SLAM (VSLAM) or, without loop-closure, Visual-Odometry (VO). Both methods can be used in either a stereo or a monocular (only up to scale) setup. The latter being of particular interest for payload constrained robots like unmanned aerial vehicles (UAV).

The research leading to these results has received funding from the ARL within the BAA W911NF-12-R-0011 under grant agreement W911NF-16-2-0112 and from the Austrian Ministry for Transport, Innovation and Technology (BMVIT) under the grant agreement 855468 (Forest-IMATE) and under the grant agreement 848518 (AVIS).

L. Leal-Taixé and S. Roth (Eds.): ECCV 2018 Workshops, LNCS 11130, pp. 73–87, 2019.
https://doi.org/10.1007/978-3-030-11012-3_6

Because of their agility, multirotor UAVs need pose estimation at higher frequency than a camera based algorithm might provide (also limited by the camera frame rate and the processing time). To overcome this problem, an inertial measurement unit (IMU) is usually used to estimate the pose between two camera measurements at high frequencies (>100 Hz).

However, MEMS-based IMUs typically used in multirotors (because of price, weight, and energy consumption) have a significant amount of noise and bias in the acceleration and angular velocity measurements. As this noise and bias are integrated for position twice (or even more in the case of the angular velocity noise and bias for non-holonomic platforms like multicopters), it will generate noticeable position drift over time. This can lead to mission failure and, in the worst case, to accidents.

1.1 Problem Statement

When it comes to evaluation of the performance of VSLAM/VO algorithms, researchers often only use the drift relative to the total trajectory traveled as metric. In contrast to ground vehicles, UAVs are operating in 3D space and cannot stop and wait for the result of pose estimation during flight (even hovering needs continuous pose estimation).

Furthermore, IMU noise as well as gravity acceleration erroneously aligned in x or y direction create correctional movements once the next vision based update occurs. Such movements cause additional energy consumption and, even worse, may destabilize the flight. Thus, for the decision about the best visual pose estimation algorithm to be combined with inertial readings for closed loop vehicle control, the *time* components of the vision system (execution time, latency, etc.) are crucial rather than the global drift.

1.2 Contribution

We introduce a new metric based on statistical integration and the IMU noise characteristics that penalizes abrupt position corrections of the state estimate (which e.g. may happen after a long period of pure IMU integration and subsequent visual correction).

While this metric may be applied to all pose estimation algorithms using an IMU as core propagation sensor, we focus on visual odometry and VSLAM in Sect. 5.

Our approach makes use of the probabilistic properties of the IMU noise and drifts such that the suggested statistical integration can provide the expected IMU noise and gravity-misalignment induced errors over time. This allows us to predict the discontinuities occurring on a visual correction step based on the characteristics of a potential IMU.

We develop a method to calculate the pose error based on IMU noise as well as the gravity alignment (roll and pitch) error depending on time. The advantage over existing metrics is twofold. First, time constraints are included in the metric in a meaningful way: while a slow algorithm may provide more accurate results, the calculation time required to compute those results can decrease the overall performance. Second, the roll and pitch errors can be mapped to the position error. This enables evaluation of the pose error instead of only the position upon a correction step.

Furthermore, we show that this metric can easily be extended to include not only effects induced by IMU noise/integration errors but also to include the (more classical) distance to ground truth.

Finally, we apply our metric on a set of state-of-the-art algorithms, namely ORB-SLAM, LSD-SLAM and DSO and provide a comparison in order to demonstrate usability and benefit of this proposed metric.

2 Related Work

A qualitative evaluation compares different approaches in terms of the used methods, while a quantitative evaluation compares the results of the methods using certain metrics on different datasets.

Younes et al. [15] provide a thorough overview of monocular visual SLAM systems. They provide a historical overview as well as descriptions of techniques used in different SLAM algorithms until 2015. Current state-of-the-art algorithms are described and compared qualitatively.

Zia et al. [16] compare two different (semi-)dense algorithms quantitatively, KinectFusion [12] and LSD-SLAM [4]. The metrics used are time per frame, absolute trajectory error and energy consumption of the algorithms per frame. Furthermore, the resulting (semi-)dense depth information is compared to ground truth. Fuentes-Pacheo et al. [5] describe different VSLAM algorithms and compare them qualitatively. While [15] sets its focus on the overall SLAM structure, [5] elaborates on the feature extraction component of sparse algorithms and mapping challenges like loop closure or large scale mapping. Huletski et al. [6] provide a qualitative and quantitative evaluation of ORB-SLAM [10], LSD-SLAM [4], and OpenRatSLAM on the TUM-RGB-D dataset. As a metric, both the root mean square error of the trajectory and a number of successful trajectory estimations were used. In their work, ORB-SLAM performed best. Cadena et al. [2] provide a thorough overview of general SLAM systems, common architectures, history of SLAM, different available sensors, semantic interpretation of the results, and possible next steps to tackle the problem of SLAM as a whole. However, no evaluations of specific algorithms are included. Platinsky et al. [13] compare sparse and semi-dense algorithms by constructing a new VO algorithm with two approaches, covering a set of state-of-the-art direct algorithms.

Quantitative evaluations focus either on the positional error, other error metrics or on the energy/resources consumption of the device running the algorithm. Recent work by Delmerico et al. [7] analyzed a number of the presently most prominent visual-inertial estimators in view of a number of different metrics. However, no focus is set on their use for closed loop control nor temporal aspects. Rather, the classical overall drift and memory usage is discussed.

As an extension of the previous evaluations sections, the following papers have a stronger focus on metrics itself.

Sturm et al. [14] investigate the absolute trajectory error (ATE) and the relative pose error (RPE). Together with the overall drift error, these metrics represent the current standard regarding SLAM evaluation. Nardi et al. [11] introduce energy consumption by frame as a metric.

Kümmerle et al. [9] provide a metric used in the KITTI dataset, which, similar to [14], tackles the problem that the overall drift error does not sufficiently cover anything about the error during the flight, especially if loop closing is involved. It considers the error introduced in each pose and disregards cumulative error. It does not consider not temporal properties.

3 IMU Drift Function

In this section, we derive the statistical integration for the expected position error based on both IMU noise and gravity misalignment to provide the mean drift error over time originating from IMU sensor characteristics. This error can be interpreted as the expected position correction a visual-inertial state estimator will perform upon a visual reading. This naturally results in a discontinuity on the time evolution of the estimated state and leads to abrupt behaviours in the closed loop controlled systems.

First, we provide a calculation of the expected position error based on accelerometer noise and bias drift. Second, we include the error induced due to gravity misalignment originating from a wrong attitude estimation due to integration of gyroscope noise and drift. The gravity misalignment error results in a position error due to the wrong subtraction of gravity from and the subsequent wrong integration of the acceleration readings. Thus, the noise and bias drift of the gyroscope contribute to the position error by integrating the error over time 4 or 5 times respectively. We compare our model to both simulated and real-world data. Last, we include the effect on position (i.e. the position error) due to the wrongly calculated attitude, given by the VO algorithm. As roll and pitch are observable in such frameworks, we expect (in the statistical sense) a gravity aligned attitude measurement by the VO. However, the jitters (i.e. noise) with which the VO algorithm estimates the attitude around the gravity aligned mean upon a specific realization of the measurement will introduce additional gravity alignment induced errors in the position until the next measurement.

3.1 IMU Noise Model

To estimate the IMU induced drift, the assumed system dynamics model is described in Eq. 1.

$$\dot{\boldsymbol{p}} = \boldsymbol{v}, \quad \dot{\boldsymbol{v}} = \boldsymbol{R}^T \boldsymbol{a} - \boldsymbol{g}, \quad \boldsymbol{R} = e^{\boldsymbol{\Omega}_\times}, \quad \dot{\boldsymbol{\Omega}} = \boldsymbol{\omega} \tag{1}$$

With $\boldsymbol{p}$ being the position, $\boldsymbol{v}$ being the velocity, $\boldsymbol{a}$ being the acceleration, $\boldsymbol{g}$ being the gravity vector, $\boldsymbol{R}$ being the rotation in $SO(3)$ from the world frame to the body frame, $\boldsymbol{\Omega}$ being the rotation in the tangent space $so(3)$ and $\boldsymbol{\omega}$ being the rotational velocity. $\boldsymbol{\Omega}_\times$ is the skew-symmetric 3×3 matrix based on the 3×1 vector $\boldsymbol{\Omega}$.

The true acceleration $\boldsymbol{a}$ can be expressed as $\boldsymbol{a} = \boldsymbol{a_b} + \boldsymbol{Rg}$ with $\boldsymbol{a_b}$ being the acceleration in the body frame and $\boldsymbol{Rg}$ being the gravity in the world frame rotated into the body frame. $\boldsymbol{a_b} = \boldsymbol{Ra_w}$, with $\boldsymbol{a_w}$ being the acceleration of the IMU in the world frame.

Neither $\boldsymbol{a}$ nor $\boldsymbol{\omega}$ can directly be measured, as measurement noise always exists, especially on low-cost IMUs used in UAVs. The model of the error used here is shown in Eqs. 2–4 with a_m and ω_m being the one-dimensional measured linear acceleration and angular velocity respectively (with a and ω as unknown true values). $b_{a,\omega}$ are biases and $n_{a,\omega,b_a,b_\omega}$ are noise parameters. The noise models are assumed to be equal in all axes. The noise model vector $\boldsymbol{a_m}$ is equal to $[a_m, a_m, a_m]^T$ and $\boldsymbol{\omega_m}$ is equal to $[\omega_m, \omega_m, \omega_m]^T$.

$$a_m = a - b_a - n_a, \quad \omega_m = \omega - b_\omega - n_\omega \tag{2}$$

$$\dot{b_a} = n_{b_a}, \quad \dot{b_\omega} = n_{b_\omega}, \quad n_a \sim N(0, \sigma_a^2), \quad n_\omega \sim N(0, \sigma_\omega^2) \tag{3}$$

$$n_{b_a} \sim N(0, \sigma_{b_a}^2), \quad n_{b_\omega} \sim N(0, \sigma_{b_\omega}^2) \tag{4}$$

Note that the bias b is modelled as a Wiener process and the noise n is modeled as zero mean white Gaussian noise. Both have their mean at 0. Because of this, adding or subtracting the error is equivalent in the model.

Based on the IMU and the error model, the position error $\tilde{\boldsymbol{p}}$ and rotation error $\tilde{\boldsymbol{R}}$ can be modeled in Eqs. 5–7.

$$\dot{\tilde{\boldsymbol{p}}} = \tilde{\boldsymbol{v}} \tag{5}$$

$$\dot{\tilde{\boldsymbol{v}}} = \tilde{\boldsymbol{R}}^{\boldsymbol{T}} \boldsymbol{R}^{\boldsymbol{T}} (\boldsymbol{Ra_w} + \boldsymbol{Rg} + \boldsymbol{n_a} + \boldsymbol{b_a}) - \boldsymbol{a_w} - \boldsymbol{g} \tag{6}$$

$$\tilde{\boldsymbol{R}}^{\boldsymbol{T}} = e^{\tilde{\boldsymbol{\Omega}}_\times}, \dot{\tilde{\boldsymbol{\Omega}}} = \boldsymbol{n_w} + \boldsymbol{b_w} \tag{7}$$

For $\dot{\tilde{\boldsymbol{v}}}$, $\boldsymbol{a_w}$ and $\boldsymbol{g}$ are both subtracted so only the erroneous values remain. $\dot{\tilde{\boldsymbol{v}}}$ can be reformulated in Eq. 8.

$$\dot{\tilde{\boldsymbol{v}}} = \tilde{\boldsymbol{R}}^{\boldsymbol{T}} \boldsymbol{a_w} - \boldsymbol{a_w} + \tilde{\boldsymbol{R}}^{\boldsymbol{T}} \boldsymbol{g} - \boldsymbol{g} + \tilde{\boldsymbol{R}}^{\boldsymbol{T}} \boldsymbol{Rn_a} + \tilde{\boldsymbol{R}}^{\boldsymbol{T}} \boldsymbol{Rb_a} \tag{8}$$

In this equation, $\tilde{\boldsymbol{R}}^{\boldsymbol{T}} \boldsymbol{Rn_a}$ can be reduced to $\boldsymbol{n_a}$ and $\tilde{\boldsymbol{R}}^{\boldsymbol{T}} \boldsymbol{Rb_a}$ to $\boldsymbol{b_a}$. It is assumed that the σ_a is equal for x, y and z direction of $\boldsymbol{n_a}$. This results in the 1σ distance of $\boldsymbol{n_a}$ being a sphere, which is invariant against rotation.

3.2 Average IMU Drift

Having an IMU model, the next step is to estimate the average IMU drift. For this, first, the average of the normally distributed error has to be derived. The probability density function of the normal distribution $f(x|0,1)$ assigns a probability to each possible error value x with the most probable error being 0. With x being an error measure, the absolute error $|x|$ can be used as impact measure (i.e. how much an error affects the true value, as this is the case for positional errors). Although $x = 0$ is the most probable case, it is also the only case where the impact $|x|$ is 0. While the error $|x|$ for $x > 6\sigma$ is large, it is also very unlikely to occur. Therefore, we suggest to weight the impact of the error with the probability of its occurrence: $|x| \cdot f(x)$. The expectation is then:

$$\mu = \int_{-\infty}^{\infty} |x| \cdot f(x)dx \approx 0.7979 \tag{9}$$

Using this, the average IMU drift can be derived. Reformulating Eq. 8 for $\tilde{\boldsymbol{p}}$ yields

$$\tilde{\boldsymbol{p}} = \tilde{\boldsymbol{p}}_{n_a} + \tilde{\boldsymbol{p}}_{b_{n_a}} + \tilde{\boldsymbol{p}}_g \tag{10}$$

$$\ddot{\tilde{\boldsymbol{p}}}_{n_a} = \boldsymbol{n}_a, \quad \ddot{\tilde{\boldsymbol{p}}}_{b_{n_a}} = \boldsymbol{b}_{n_a}, \quad \ddot{\tilde{\boldsymbol{p}}}_g = \tilde{\boldsymbol{R}}^T \boldsymbol{g} - \boldsymbol{g} \tag{11}$$

The position error has been split up into the translational noise error $\tilde{\boldsymbol{p}}_{n_a}$, the translational bias error $\tilde{\boldsymbol{p}}_{b_a}$ and the rotational error $\tilde{\boldsymbol{p}}_g$ originating from an erroneous allocation of the gravity vector to the wrong axes. The rotational error with respect to the current acceleration $\tilde{\boldsymbol{R}}^T \boldsymbol{a}_w - \boldsymbol{a}_w$ is being ignored as $\boldsymbol{a}_w$ is assumed to be significantly smaller than $\boldsymbol{g}$.

With $\boldsymbol{n}_a$ being zero mean white Gaussian noise, the integration over time $\tilde{\boldsymbol{v}}_{n_a}$ is a corresponding Wiener process. Using stochastic integration, $\tilde{\boldsymbol{p}}_{n_a}$ can be found. Similarly, with $\boldsymbol{n}_{b_a}$ being the zero mean white Gaussian noise, $\boldsymbol{b}_{n_a}$ is a Wiener process and both $\tilde{\boldsymbol{v}}_{n_{b_a}}$ and $\tilde{\boldsymbol{p}}_{n_{b_a}}$ are stochastic integrals. t is the time in seconds in the following equations. All of those random variables can be modelled to be Gaussian with the same mean of zero. To estimate the average error, X can be replaced by μ in these equations.

$$\boldsymbol{n}_a \sim N(0, \sigma_a^2) \Rightarrow \boldsymbol{\sigma}_a \cdot X, \quad X \sim N(0,1) \tag{12}$$

$$\tilde{\boldsymbol{v}}_{n_a} = \boldsymbol{\sigma}_a \cdot \sqrt{t} \cdot X, \quad \tilde{\boldsymbol{p}}_{n_a} = \boldsymbol{\sigma}_a \cdot \sqrt{\frac{t^3}{3}} \cdot X, \quad \tilde{\boldsymbol{p}}_{n_{b_a}} = \boldsymbol{\sigma}_{b_a} \cdot \sqrt{\frac{t^5}{20}} \cdot X \tag{13}$$

As the average error uses the standard deviation for scaling and as both $\tilde{\boldsymbol{p}}_{n_a}$ and $\tilde{\boldsymbol{p}}_{n_{b_a}}$ are modelled as random Gaussian variables, their variances can be added. $\tilde{\boldsymbol{p}}_t$ is the resulting average position integrating both n_a and n_{b_a}.

$$\tilde{\boldsymbol{p}}_t^2 = \tilde{\boldsymbol{p}}_{n_a}^2 + \tilde{\boldsymbol{p}}_{n_{b_a}}^2 = \boldsymbol{\sigma}_a^2 \cdot \frac{t^3}{3} \cdot \mu^2 + \boldsymbol{\sigma}_{b_a}^2 \cdot \frac{t^5}{20} \cdot \mu^2 \tag{14}$$

The rotational error does not contribute directly to the integrated position error. Instead, an erroneous rotation leads to a wrong rotation and subsequent subtraction of the measured gravity. This leads to wrongly perceived body accelerations which, through integration, lead to position errors.

We assume small errors and, thus, that the small angle approximation holds. We can then express the acceleration error due to gravity misalignment originating from rotational errors as linearly dependent on the angular error. An example for pure rotation around the y-axis is as follows (with $\boldsymbol{g} = [0, 0, 9.81]^T$):

$$\begin{bmatrix} cos(\alpha) & 0 & sin(\alpha) \\ 0 & 1 & 0 \\ -sin(\alpha) & 0 & cos(\alpha) \end{bmatrix} \cdot \boldsymbol{g} - \boldsymbol{g} \approx \begin{bmatrix} 1 & 0 & \alpha \\ 0 & 1 & 0 \\ -\alpha & 0 & 1 \end{bmatrix} \cdot \boldsymbol{g} - \boldsymbol{g} = \begin{bmatrix} \alpha \cdot 9.81 \\ 0 \\ 0 \end{bmatrix} \tag{15}$$

Similarly, a linearized dependency can be derived for the gyroscope noise and bias drift. Based on this, it is possible to calculate the integrated coefficient for the gyroscope noise and bias noise depending on time for the expected error. Here, $\tilde{\boldsymbol{\Omega}}_{n_\omega}$ is the integrated linearized position error based on gyroscope noise and $\tilde{\boldsymbol{\Omega}}_{n_{b_\omega}}$ is the integrated linearized position error based on gyroscope bias noise. $\tilde{\boldsymbol{\Omega}}$ is the result of both error sources integrated concurrently.

$$\tilde{\boldsymbol{\Omega}}^2_{n_\omega} = \boldsymbol{\sigma}^2_\omega \cdot \frac{t^5}{20} \cdot \mu^2, \quad \tilde{\boldsymbol{\Omega}}^2_{n_{b_\omega}} = \boldsymbol{\sigma}^2_{b_\omega} \cdot \frac{t^7}{252} \cdot \mu^2 \tag{16}$$

$$\tilde{\boldsymbol{\Omega}}^2 = \boldsymbol{\sigma}^2_\omega \cdot \frac{t^5}{20} \cdot \mu^2 + \boldsymbol{\sigma}^2_{b_\omega} \cdot \frac{t^7}{252} \cdot \mu^2 \tag{17}$$

We can extend the above notion to the more general $so(3)$ tangent space of the $SO(3)$ group. $so(3)$ consists of three distinct elements in the vector $\tilde{\boldsymbol{\Omega}}$, each of them corresponding to the amount of rotation around one axis in radiants. Using the matrix exponential $e^{\tilde{\boldsymbol{\Omega}}_\times}$, it can be converted into the rotation matrix representation $\tilde{\boldsymbol{R}}$.

This will give an correct estimation up until $\sigma^2_{b_\omega} \cdot \frac{t^7}{252} < \pi/2$. The main reason for the small-angle approximated derivation being valid even for larger angles lies in the fact that the integration can be seen as the repeated application of subsequent infinitesimal rotations. This also corresponds to the property of the $so(3)$ tangent space of $SO(3)$ that multiplications in $SO(3)$ can be reduced to additions in $so(3)$. This derivation has been tested in simulations as well as with real-world data (see Fig. 2).

To extract the erroneous acceleration resulting from the rotational misalignment of gravity, the gravity vector $\boldsymbol{g}$ is used with the resulting error rotation matrix $e^{\tilde{\boldsymbol{\Omega}}_\times}$ (note that the standard deviation is used here):

$$\tilde{\boldsymbol{p}}_g = e^{\tilde{\boldsymbol{\Omega}}_\times}\boldsymbol{g} - \boldsymbol{g} \tag{18}$$

The average position error $\tilde{\boldsymbol{p}}$ and the average rotation error $\tilde{\boldsymbol{\Omega}}$ depending on time are therefore

$$\tilde{\boldsymbol{\Omega}}(t) = \sqrt{\boldsymbol{\sigma}^2_\omega \cdot \frac{t^5}{20} \cdot \mu^2 + \boldsymbol{\sigma}^2_{b_\omega} \cdot \frac{t^7}{252} \cdot \mu^2} \tag{19}$$

$$\tilde{\boldsymbol{p}}(t) = \sqrt{\boldsymbol{\sigma}^2_a \cdot \frac{t^3}{3} \cdot \mu^2 + \boldsymbol{\sigma}^2_{b_a} \cdot \frac{t^5}{20} \cdot \mu^2 + (e^{\tilde{\boldsymbol{\Omega}}_\times}\boldsymbol{g} - \boldsymbol{g})^2} \tag{20}$$

In Fig. 1 the development of the positional error over time can be seen, based on the values for a MEMS IMU sensor used in a commercial UAV. While the positional noise error e_{n_a} is larger than the positional bias error $e_{b_{n_a}}$ at the beginning, the faster growth of the bias error can be seen at 3 s. The positional

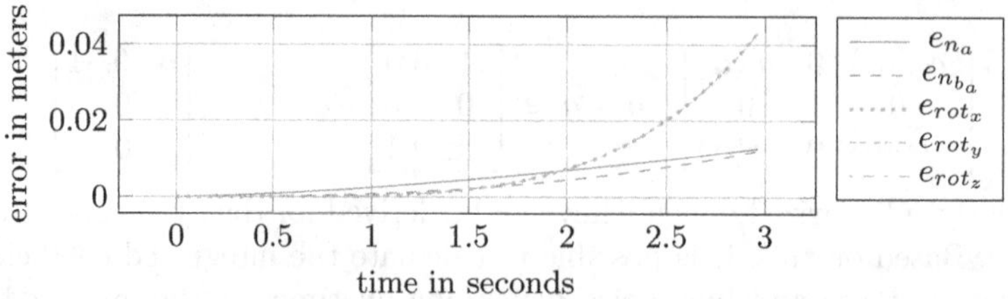

Fig. 1. Growth of different position error sources over time in seconds. Errors are in meters. The following values have been used: $\sigma_a = 0.0054, \sigma_{b_a} = 0.0045, \sigma_\omega = 0.00079, \sigma_{b_\omega} = 0.00008$. e_{rot_x} and e_{rot_y} are overlapping.

error based on the wrong handling of the gravity vector is the main source of error in both x and y directions while it is negligible in z direction.

This confirms real-world experiences as a very small drift in z direction compared to the x and y direction has been observed in experiments. The main reason for this difference lies in the structure of the gravity vector: $\boldsymbol{g} = [0, 0, -9.81]^T$. For roll and pitch errors, the sine is applied to the z entry of the gravity vector in y and x direction respectively within the rotation matrix $\tilde{\boldsymbol{R}}^T$ while 1 minus the cosine is applied to the z direction. For the yaw error, the error rotation does not result in a wrong application of parts of the gravity vector and therefore does not contribute to $\tilde{\boldsymbol{p}}_g$.

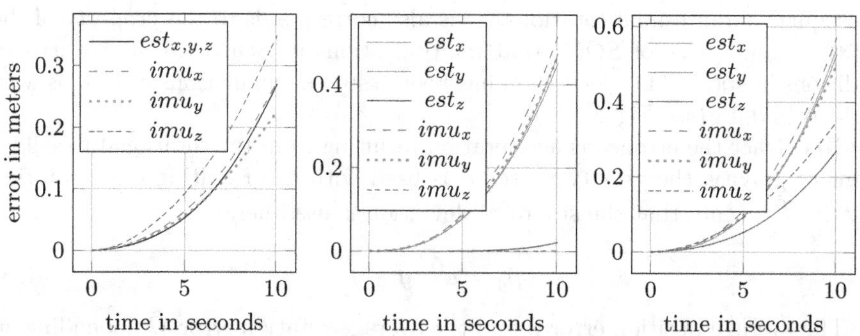

Fig. 2. Comparison of predicted and real-world data. *est* is the predicted data (values from Fig. 1) while *imu* is the measured and integrated data over 350 IMU readings. Left is the translational error, to the center is the rotational error and to the right are both errors.

In Fig. 2, the predicted positional error compared to the measured positional error can be seen. For the measured positional error, an IMU has collected data while being stationary. For every 10 s segment of this data, the biases have been calculated at the beginning of the segment. The values shown in the graphs are the mean of 350 segments with 10 s each.

The left part shows the error introduced by accelerometer noise while the center part shows the error introduced by first integrating the gyroscope noise and then multiplying the gravity vector with the rotational error. The right part shows the result of integrating both errors simultaneously.

3.3 Visual Odometry Induced Gravity Misalignment

An additional error source is the inaccurate attitude computation by the visual part, or more generally, the attitude error that remains after an update step. This rotational difference $\tilde{\boldsymbol{R}}_{\boldsymbol{up}}$ multiplied by the gravity vector will introduce further drift in addition to the above discussed mean IMU-induced drift. As only the next (visual) update can correct this error – there is only dead reckoning in between update steps – we model this error as being constant between two update steps.

In our metric, we are interested in the difference of the estimated position before and after the update since the discontinuity occurring at (i.e. right after) the update step affects the underlying controller. Due to the dead-reckoning in between update steps the maximum drift will have happened right before the update has been processed.

$\tilde{\boldsymbol{a}}_{\boldsymbol{up}}$ is the erroneous acceleration resulting from a misaligned gravity vector after an update step. Integrating twice over time results in the position error $\tilde{\boldsymbol{p}}_{\boldsymbol{up}}$.

$$\tilde{\boldsymbol{a}}_{\boldsymbol{up}} = |\tilde{\boldsymbol{R}}_{\boldsymbol{up}} \cdot \boldsymbol{g} - \boldsymbol{g}|, \quad \tilde{\boldsymbol{p}}_{\boldsymbol{up}}(t) = \frac{t^2}{2} \cdot \tilde{\boldsymbol{a}}_{\boldsymbol{up}} = \frac{t^2}{2} \cdot |\tilde{\boldsymbol{R}}_{\boldsymbol{up}} \cdot \boldsymbol{g} - \boldsymbol{g}| \tag{21}$$

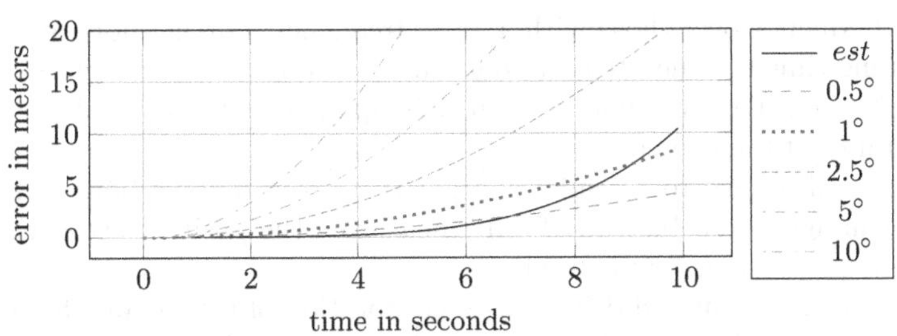

Fig. 3. Position error in x direction assuming an erroneous rotation around the y axis. *est* shows the estimated IMU drift error with values from Fig. 1.

Figure 3 shows typical position errors evolving over time assuming different magnitudes of remaining angular errors after an update step. It can be seen that it may take tens of seconds or even minutes until the above discussed IMU drift error surpasses the gravity misalignment error due to the errors remaining after an update step.

4 IMU-Drift Based Metrics

4.1 Modified Relative Pose Error

As mentioned earlier, we assume that a visual odometry algorithm is combined with an IMU on a quadcopter. In such a system, discontinuities in the state estimation occur upon each visual measurement. Such discontinuities in the estimated state result in fast corrective actions of the underlying controller which could break both the controller and the VO/VSLAM algorithm (e.g. due to motion blur because of the sudden movements). Thus, we assume – from a closed loop control point of view – that the smaller the discontinuities are, the better the performance of the estimator is.

A metric with a similar goal already exists in literature. The relative pose error (RPE) [14] can be described as the difference between the position change according to ground truth and the position change according to the VO algorithm. In the Eq. 22, $\boldsymbol{p_a}$ is the estimated position while $\boldsymbol{p_{gt}}$ is the ground truth position.

$$m_{rpe_{VO}} = \frac{1}{n}\sum_{i=1}^{n} ||abs(\boldsymbol{p}_{\boldsymbol{gt}_i} - \boldsymbol{p}_{\boldsymbol{gt}_{i-1}}) - abs(\boldsymbol{p}_{\boldsymbol{a}_i} - \boldsymbol{p}_{\boldsymbol{a}_{i-1}})||_2 \quad (22)$$

For our purposes, we model that the correct part of the estimated pose change has been handled by the correct part of the IMU measurements read between two subsequent updates. Between two poses, IMU drift as well as drift based on gravity misalignment occurs. We extend the existing metric with these two values. This extended metric has three advantages:

- The time component is brought into the metric, preferring updates with a higher frequency over those with a lower frequency. Furthermore, it takes the processing time to generate an update into account as the correction can only be used when it is available, even if it is applied retroactively based on the time stamp of the camera image.
- The roll and pitch errors results in a position error, making both comparable in a meaningful way. Instead of only measuring the position error, the whole pose error excluding yaw is used.
- Because of the estimated drifts, the incorporation of time is weighted so that not the fastest algorithm is preferred, but instead the one resulting in the lowest overall error producing the least amount of distance change before and after an update.

The extension itself builds upon the work in the previous chapter with Δt being the time between two updates and T being the overall time:

$$m_{rpe_{drift}}(t) = abs(abs(\boldsymbol{p}_{\boldsymbol{gt}_i} - \boldsymbol{p}_{\boldsymbol{gt}_{i-1}}) - abs(\boldsymbol{p}_{\boldsymbol{a}_i} - \boldsymbol{p}_{\boldsymbol{a}_{i-1}})) \quad (23)$$

$$m_{rpe_{drift}} = \sum \frac{\Delta t}{T} ||m_{rpe_{drift}}(\Delta t) + \tilde{\boldsymbol{p}}(\Delta t) + \tilde{\boldsymbol{p}}_{\boldsymbol{up}}(\Delta t)||_2 \quad (24)$$

4.2 Modified Absolute Trajectory Error

While our modified RPE calculates the magnitude of the discontinuity between two pose estimates, it does not take the difference between estimated value and ground truth into account. It may be interesting to see the mean divergence from ground truth over time.

For this, we extend another metric, the absolute trajectory error (ATE) [14] which can be described as the translational difference between the estimated and ground truth trajectory, assuming both trajectories have been aligned using a linear least squares approach to minimize the error.

$$m_{ate_{VO}} = \frac{1}{n}\sum_{i=1}^{n} ||\boldsymbol{p}_{\boldsymbol{gt}_i} - \boldsymbol{p}_{\boldsymbol{a}_i}||_2 \tag{25}$$

$$m_{ate_{drift}} = \sum \frac{\Delta t}{T} ||abs(\boldsymbol{p}_{\boldsymbol{gt}_{i-1}} - \boldsymbol{p}_{\boldsymbol{a}_{i-1}}) + \tilde{\boldsymbol{p}}(\Delta t) + \tilde{\boldsymbol{p}}_{\boldsymbol{up}}(\Delta t)||_2 \tag{26}$$

Note that the above developed metrics are not constrained to vision based estimators. In fact, as long as the IMU is used as a state propagation sensor together with one or more measurement/update sensors, these metrics can be applied. In the following section, however, we limit the demonstration to application of the metrics to loosely coupled vision based sensor fusion systems.

5 Applying the Metrics

To evaluate our proposed metrics we selected multiple camera pose estimation algorithms and performed tests in real-world environment. The algorithms were executed on an Odroid-XU4. This computing device offers 8 CPU cores (4 × 2 GHz, 4 × 1.4 GHz), ARM architecture and the low weight from 38 g makes is suitable for usage on micro aerial vehicles.

As testdata we use the *EuRoC* [1] dataset. It was created with a multi-rotor UAV equipped with a VI-Sensors. It offers camera (stereo 752 × 480, ∼20 Hz), IMU (∼200 Hz) and ground truth measurements for a total of 11 sequences in 3 scenarios. Because of the similarity of our assumed scenario - multi-rotor UAV flight in GPS denied scenarios - we chose it as our main evaluation dataset. From the sequences we selected four sequences where 6 DoF ground truth is available from a motion capture system. We selected these particular four sequences because all tested algorithms provided acceptable failure rate for multiple runs.

We selected 3 state-of-the-art visual odometry or SLAM algorithms with different approaches to camera pose estimation to evaluate the influence of our new metric on the results.

ORB-SLAM by Mur-Artal et al. [10] combines current state-of-the-art components to create a sparse SLAM algorithm (similar to PTAM [8]). It uses feature detection with binary descriptors and bag-of-words for mapping and loop closure. For our evaluations we used ORB-SLAM2 which is a computationally improved version of ORB-SLAM still adhering to the same principles and components.

LSD-SLAM by Engel et al. [4] is a direct, semi-dense, graph-based algorithm. Image alignment is achieved using a Gauss-Newton optimization to minimize the photometric error using depth information. This depth map is kept in a keyframe-based approach with each measurement improving the depth estimation within a keyframe.

DSO by Engel et al. [3] is a direct, sparse, graph-based method. It has similarities to LSD-SLAM with the main difference being sparsity. Instead of selecting all available image gradients, a set of points is chosen by splitting the image into $d \times d$ blocks with d being an adaptive factor. In each block, the pixel with the largest gradient is selected as long as it surpasses a certain threshold. This point is tracked and intensity differences are used to estimate the position in a Gauss-Newton procedure.

For each algorithm, we carried out 12 runs and averaged the results which are shown in Table 1. Runs in which the algorithms failed to generate pose estimation for the majority of the sequences were discarded. The generated trajectories were scaled, rotated and aligned to the ground truth trajectory so that the squared error is minimized. All metrics are calculated on the aligned trajectories.

We considered the latency m_l in seconds, the absolute trajectory error m_{ate} for both the original version $m_{ate_{VO}}$ and our drift extension $m_{ate_{drift}}$ as well as the relative pose error m_{rpe} for both $m_{rpe_{VO}}$ and $m_{rpe_{drift}}$, all of them in millimeters. The latency is the time needed by the algorithm from receiving an image to the estimated pose.

Each entry in the table was generated by using the mean over all updates for multiple runs. DSO has the lowest latency of the compared algorithms, followed by ORB2. In terms of the absolute trajectory error $m_{ate_{VO}}$, ORB2 performed better than the other algorithms. This also fits to the fact that ORB2 has the most sophisticated mapping component compared to the other two algorithms. While LSD and DSO both use a windowed bundle adjustment approach, ORB2 fits the data against an iteratively filled map which reduced the trajectory drift.

Compared to the first sequences of each scenario, $v1\_02$ and $v2\_02$ have faster movements and rotations. Because of the limited computational power of the target platform the VO algorithms perform worse when facing more challenging movements.

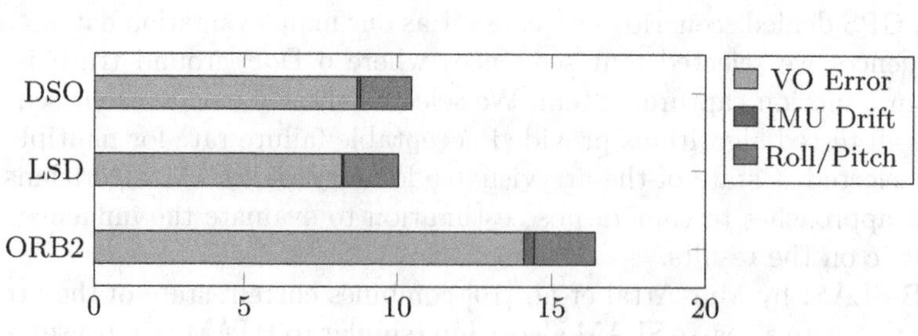

Fig. 4. Error sources for different algorithms on the v1_01 scenario according to the $m_{rpe_{drift}}$ metric in mm. IMU Drift based on IMU noise, Roll/Pitch on VO rotational error based gravity misalignment (rpe_{up}).

Table 1. Results over multiple runs per sequence and algorithm. m_l is latency, $m_{ate_{VO}}$ and $m_{ate_{drift}}$ are ATE without and with our drift extension, $m_{rpe_{VO}}$ and $m_{rpe_{drift}}$ are RPE without and with our drift extension.

	m_l $[ms]$	$m_{ate_{VO}}$ $[mm]$	$m_{ate_{drift}}$ $[mm]$	$m_{rpe_{vo}}$ $[mm]$	$m_{rpe_{drift}}$ $[mm]$
DSO					
v1_01	92	144.803	146.648	7.528	8.729
v1_02	81	391.209	392.446	32.549	33.869
v2_01	90	131.584	133.571	13.323	16.085
v2_02	80	157.105	158.317	19.370	20.623
ORB2					
v1_01	186	25.237	27.635	11.989	14.149
v1_02	164	28.500	29.438	21.268	22.237
v2_01	172	100.727	106.129	21.154	27.418
v2_02	161	147.211	152.946	42.061	47.435
LSD					
v1_01	156	319.002	324.386	7.846	13.164
v2_01	46	217.178	218.859	8.400	9.964
Aggregation					
DSO	84	304.423	306.474	20.247	22.335
ORB2	175	104.980	110.257	25.351	30.595
LSD	108	269.520	271.648	9.562	11.837

Figure 4 shows the $m_{rpe_{drift}}$ error for the $v1\_01$ scenario for DSO, ORB2 and LSD, separated into the visual odometry based position error $m_{rpe_{VO}}$, the IMU drift error and the gravity misalignment error based on roll and pitch error. The IMU drift error is very small compared to the roll and pitch error. This corresponds to the 100–200 ms needed to generate a new VO measurement. In such a time frame, the IMU noise was not yet able to accumulate enough drift to have an impact compared to the other two error sources.

Using our extended metric, it can be seen that the costs roughly increase by a tenth compared to only using the VO position error. This mostly corresponds to the roll and pitch error over the duration of the latency. Because the differences between the algorithms are larger than the additionally introduced error, this does not change the order. It also fits to the observation that with at least ten frames per second, smooth flight is possible.

Selecting less frames per second would increase the impact of our metric. However, we saw in practice that the algorithms used are already quite fragile regarding tracking failure, which is also the main reason for using the easier sequences. Lower frame rate further decreases the amount of successful runs.

Comparing the error increase of the other three metrics, DSO performs best. This is mainly because the low latency results in less time available to apply position drift.

6 Conclusion

In this paper we introduced novel metrics to evaluate the performance of VSLAM/VO algorithms for IMU aided state estimation and subsequent closed loop control of agile mobile platforms.

Existing work predominantly focuses on the pose estimation performance of such algorithms without considering their use for closed loop control in autonomous navigation scenarios. Thus, with the proposed metrics, VSLAM/VO algorithms can be evaluated according to their real performance in a visual-inertial setup for vehicle control.

We particularly focused on the newly defined and suggested metric of IMU induced drift which accounts for the position offset due to IMU integration errors based on the probabilistic properties of the inertial sensors. This metric favors fast yet accurate vision updates at all time and, thus, combines at the same time algorithm robustness (few measurement drops), high algorithmic speed (low computational complexity and thus low latency), and estimation precision in a single metric. The latter results from the requirement of propagating the state (aid of IMU readings) to the current time in order to feed the vehicle controller with most recent state estimates. This even holds for delay compensated frameworks applying the visual measurement at the correct time in the past.

Using our set of metrics, we tested and compared three different state-of-the-art algorithms on multiple scenarios. We showed that the proposed set of metrics is general and applicable on any framework generating time-discrete pose updates. Regarding the IMU-drift metric, our example evaluations have shown that a multitude of information previously shown in different metrics (latency or framerate, position error, rotation error) has been combined in a single, meaningful way including temporal information.

References

1. Burri, M., et al.: The EuRoC micro aerial vehicle datasets. Int. J. Robot. Res. **35**(10), 1157–1163 (2016). https://doi.org/10.1177/0278364915620033. http://ijr.sagepub.com/content/early/2016/01/21/0278364915620033.abstract
2. Cadena, C., et al.: Past, present, and future of simultaneous localization and mapping: toward the robust-perception age. IEEE Trans. Robot. **32**(6), 1309–1332 (2016)
3. Engel, J., Koltun, V., Cremers, D.: Direct sparse odometry. IEEE Trans. Pattern Anal. Mach. Intell. **40**(3), 611–625 (2018). https://doi.org/10.1109/TPAMI.2017.2658577
4. Engel, J., Schöps, T., Cremers, D.: LSD-SLAM: large-scale direct monocular SLAM. In: Fleet, D., Pajdla, T., Schiele, B., Tuytelaars, T. (eds.) ECCV 2014. LNCS, vol. 8690, pp. 834–849. Springer, Cham (2014). https://doi.org/10.1007/978-3-319-10605-2_54

5. Fuentes-Pacheco, J., Ruiz-Ascencio, J., Rendón-Mancha, J.M.: Visual simultaneous localization and mapping: a survey. Artif. Intell. Rev. **43**(1), 55–81 (2015)
6. Huletski, A., Kartashov, D., Krinkin, K.: Evaluation of the modern visual slam methods. In: 2015 Artificial Intelligence and Natural Language and Information Extraction, Social Media and Web Search FRUCT Conference (AINL-ISMW FRUCT), pp. 19–25, November 2015. https://doi.org/10.1109/AINL-ISMW-FRUCT.2015.7382963
7. Delmerico, J., Scaramuzza, D.: A benchmark comparison of monocular visual-inertial odometry algorithms for flying robots. In: IEEE International Conference on Robotics and Automation (ICRA). IEEE (2018)
8. Klein, G., Murray, D.: Parallel tracking and mapping for small AR workspaces. In: IEEE and ACM International Symposium on Mixed and Augmented Reality, pp. 225–234 (2007). https://doi.org/10.1109/ISMAR.2007.4538852
9. Kümmerle, R., et al.: On measuring the accuracy of SLAM algorithms. Auton. Robot. **27**(4), 387–407 (2009)
10. Mur-Artal, R., Montiel, J.M.M., Tardós, J.D.: ORB-SLAM: a versatile and accurate monocular slam system. IEEE Trans. Robot. **31**(5), 1147–1163 (2015). https://doi.org/10.1109/TRO.2015.2463671
11. Nardi, L., et al.: Introducing SLAMBench, a performance and accuracy benchmarking methodology for SLAM. In: IEEE International Conference on Robotics and Automation, pp. 5783–5790, May 2015. https://doi.org/10.1109/ICRA.2015.7140009
12. Newcombe, R.A., et al.: KinectFusion: real-time dense surface mapping and tracking. In: Proceedings of the 2011 10th IEEE International Symposium on Mixed and Augmented Reality, ISMAR 2011, pp. 127–136. IEEE Computer Society, Washington, DC (2011). https://doi.org/10.1109/ISMAR.2011.6092378
13. Platinsky, L., Davison, A.J., Leutenegger, S.: Monocular visual odometry: sparse joint optimisation or dense alternation? In: IEEE International Conference on Robotics and Automation, pp. 5126–5133 (2017). https://doi.org/10.1109/ICRA.2017.7989599
14. Sturm, J., Engelhard, N., Endres, F., Burgard, W., Cremers, D.: A benchmark for the evaluation of RGB-D SLAM systems. In: IEEE/RSJ International Conference on Intelligent Robots and Systems, pp. 573–580 (2012). https://doi.org/10.1109/IROS.2012.6385773
15. Younes, G., Asmar, D.C., Shammas, E.A.: A survey on non-filter-based monocular visual SLAM systems. CoRR abs/1607.00470 (2016). http://arxiv.org/abs/1607.00470
16. Zia, M.Z., et al.: Comparative design space exploration of dense and semi-dense SLAM. In: 2016 IEEE International Conference on Robotics and Automation (ICRA), pp. 1292–1299. IEEE (2016)

ShuffleDet: Real-Time Vehicle Detection Network in On-Board Embedded UAV Imagery

Seyed Majid Azimi[1,2](✉)

[1] German Aerospace Center (DLR), Remote Sensing Technology Institute, Weßling, Germany
seyedmajid.azimi@dlr.de
[2] Chair of Remote Sensing, Technical University of Munich, Munich, Germany
seyedmajid.azimi@tum.de

Abstract. On-board real-time vehicle detection is of great significance for UAVs and other embedded mobile platforms. We propose a computationally inexpensive detection network for vehicle detection in UAV imagery which we call ShuffleDet. In order to enhance the speed-wise performance, we construct our method primarily using channel shuffling and grouped convolutions. We apply inception modules and deformable modules to consider the size and geometric shape of the vehicles. ShuffleDet is evaluated on CARPK and PUCPR+ datasets and compared against the state-of-the-art real-time object detection networks. ShuffleDet achieves 3.8 GFLOPs while it provides competitive performance on test sets of both datasets. We show that our algorithm achieves real-time performance by running at the speed of 14 frames per second on NVIDIA Jetson TX2 showing high potential for this method for real-time processing in UAVs.

Keywords: UAV imagery · Real-time vehicle detection · On-board embedded processing · Convolutional neural networks · Traffic monitoring

1 Introduction

On-board real-time processing of data through embedded systems plays a crucial role in applying the images acquired from the portable platforms (e.g., unmanned aerial vehicless (UAVs)) to the applications requiring instant responses such as search and rescue missions, urban management, traffic monitoring, and parking lot utilization.

Methods based on convolutional neural networks (CNNs), for example, FPN [1], FasterRCNN [19], R-FCN [3], multi-box single shot detectors (SSDs) [14], and Yolov2 [18], have shown promising results in many object detection tasks. Despite their high detection precision, these methods are computationally demanding and their models are usually bulky due to the deep

L. Leal-Taixé and S. Roth (Eds.): ECCV 2018 Workshops, LNCS 11130, pp. 88–99, 2019.
https://doi.org/10.1007/978-3-030-11012-3_7

backbone networks being used. Employing CNNs for the on-board real-time applications requires developing time and computation efficient methods due to the limited processing resources available on-board. A number of networks have been developed recently such as GoogleNet [20], Xception [2], ResNeXt [25], MobileNet [7], PeleeNet [23], SqueezeNet [10], and ShuffleNet [26] which have less complex structures as compared to the other CNNs while providing comparable or even superior results. For the real-time object detection applications (*e.g.*, vehicle detection), there are a few recent works proposing the methods such as MobileNet [7] with SSD [9], PVANET [11], and Tiny-Yolo [18]. They have shown computational efficiency to be deployed in mobile platforms.

Zhang et al. [26] employed ShuffleNet as the backbone network, which uses point-wise grouped convolutions and channel shuffle to greatly reduce the computations while maintaining the accuracy. The authors reported a better performance compared with MobileNet using Faster-RCNN detection approach. Kim et al. [11] developed PVANET by concatenating 3×3 conv layer with its negation as a building block for the initial feature extraction stage. Recently, Wang et al. [23] proposed PeleeNet that uses a combination of parallel multi-size kernel convolutions as a 2-way dense layer and a similar module to the Squeeze module. They additionally applied a residual block after feature extraction stage to improve the accuracy using the SSD [14] approach. The authors reported more accurate results compared to MobileNet and ShuffleNet on the Pascal VOC dataset despite the smaller model size and computation cost of PeleeNet. Redmon and Farhadi [18] proposed Yolov2, a fast object detection method, but yet with high accuracy. However, their method is still computationally heavy for real-time processing on an embedded platform. Tiny Yolov2 as the smaller version of Yolov2, although it is faster, but it lacks high-level extraction capability which results in poor performance. In the work of Huang et al. [9], they showed the SSD detection approach together with SqueezeNet and MobileNet as the backbone networks. Although SSD with SqueezeNet backbone results in a smaller model than MobileNet, its results are less accurate and its computation is slightly more expensive. In general, replacing the backbone network with SqueezeNet, MobileNet, or any other efficient network - though enhancing computational efficiency - can degrade the accuracy if no further modification is performed.

In this paper, we propose ShuffleDet, a real-time vehicle detection approach to be used on-board by mobile platforms such as UAVs. ShuffleDet network is composed of ShuffleNet and a modified variant of SSD based on channel shuffling and grouped convolution. We design a unit to appropriately transfer the pretrained parameters of the pretrained model on terrestrial imagery to aerial imagery domain. We call this unit domain adapter block (DAB) which includes deformable convolutions [4] and Inception-ResNetv2 units [21]. To the best of our knowledge, group convolution and channel shuffling have not been used before in real-time vehicle detection based on UAV imagery. ShuffleDet runs at 14 frames per second (FPS) on NVIDIA Jetson TX2 while having the computational complexity of 3.8 giga oating point operations (GFLOPs). Experimental results on the CARPK and PUCPR+ datasets [8] demonstrates that ShuffleDet achieves a good trade-off between accuracy and speed for mobile platforms while it is comparably computation and time efficient.

2 Method

In this section, a detailed description of the network architecture is presented. We use ShuffleNet [26] which is designed for object recognition to extract high-level features as our backend network.

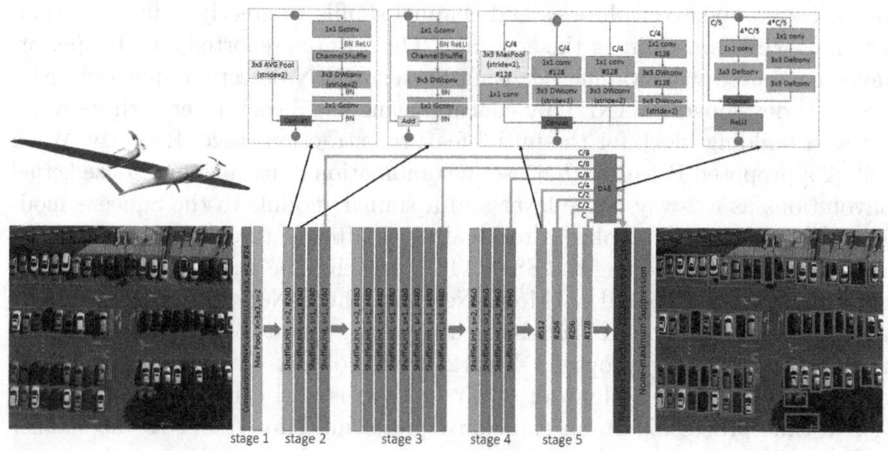

Fig. 1. Illustration of ShuffleDet architecture. The backbone network is ShuffleNet. Modified inception layers are applied as extra layers. C stands for channel. DAB unit is deployed to adapt to the new domain of UAV imagery using a residual block containing deformable convolution layers (UAV photo is from https://www.quantum-systems.com/tron.).

ShuffleNet [26] shows that by utilizing grouped or depth-wise separable convolutions, one can reduce the computational demand, while still boosting the performance through a decent representation ability. A major bottleneck can arise by replacing 1×1 convolution layers with stacked grouped convolutions which can degrade the accuracy of the network. This is due to the fact that a limited portion of input channels are utilized by the output channels. In order to solve this issue channel shuffling was proposed in [26] which we also use inside ShuffleDet architecture. Figure 1 illustrates the network architecture of ShuffleDet. In stage 1, a 3×3 convolutional layer is applied to the input image with a stride of 2 which downsamples the input by a factor of 2. This layer is followed by a maxpooling layer with a stride of 2 and kernel of 3×3. This maxpooling operation destroys half of the input information. This is critical as vehicles in our case are small objects [5,12,17,22]. Having said that without this operation, computation cost will be multiplied. Therefore, we keep the maxpooling layer and we try to enhance the performance especially via DABs units which will be discussed later. After the maxpooling three stages containing multiple units from ShuffleNet are performed. Stage 2 and 4 contain 3 ShuffleNet units while stage 3 in the middle is composed of 7 units. The whole stage 1 to 4 leads to 32x down-sampling factor. ShuffleUnit illustrated in Fig. 1 acts as residual bottleneck unit. Using stride 2 in ShuffleUnit, an average pooling is applied to the primary branch parallel with depthwise convolution with a stride 2 in the residual branch. To ensure that all of the input channels are connected to the output channels, channel shuffling is performed before the depthwise convolution. 1×1 grouped convolutions are applied before the channel shuffling as a bottleneck in order to reduce the number of feature maps in the output for the efficient computation. It has been shown [24,26] that the group convolutions also improve the accuracy. The second grouped convolution brings back the number of feature maps or channel to the number of input channels for a more accurate representation capability. Using a stride of 2, the features of average pooling and second grouped convolution is concatenated while having a stride of 1, maxpooling is omitted and depth-wise convolution is performed. Moreover, the outputs are summed up instead of using concatenation. Figure 1 shows the detailed structure of ShuffleNet units with and without stride of 2.

Stage 1, 2, 3 and stage 4 are employed to enhance the heat map resolution as input intermediate layers. In the detection module, we primarily inspire from SSD approach. In order to enrich the extracted features from the intermediate layers, we perform extra feature layers in stage 5. In our case, the output from stage 4 is passed through stage 5 as illustrated in Fig. 1 This is compatible with using multi-box strategy explained in the SSD method. In total, we extract 7 feature maps of different sizes from the backbone network.

To enhance the performance, instead of employing a conventional convolution layer similar to SSD method for each extra layer, we use a modified module of Reduction-B from Inception-ResNet-v2 [21] in stage 5. Unlike ResNet and VGG, inception modules have not been explored enough in object detection task due to their higher computation cost. We stack 4 modified inception modules as stage 5 for feature map extraction at different levels. Unlike original Inception-ResNet-v2 work, we add 1×1 conv layers after maxpooling and concatenation layer. The maxpooling layer reduces spatial-resolution and dimension as a bottleneck. 1×1 convolution in return expands the dimension to insert further non-linearity to the network resulting in a better performance. The same philosophy was used in the latter 1×1 conv layer. Applying the inception module adds more computational cost to the network. To compensate its load, we replace 3×3 convolution layers with 3×3 depthwise convolutions. Depth-wise convolution improves the performance slightly, yet it has $\frac{1}{N} + \frac{1}{k^2}$ times less computation cost compared with regular conv layers. N is the number of output channels and k is the kernel size. Furthermore, we divide the input channels equally among the branches. The output number of channels for each layer is an equally-divided concatenation of output channels from each branch. These modifications keep the model size as well as computational complexity small. We observe using this modified inception modules enhances the performance. We conjecture unlike the original SSD which uses 1×1 and 3×3 conv layers in series as extra layers, multi-size kernels parallel in inception modules capture features in different sizes simultaneously e.g. 1×1 kernels to detect small vehicles and 3×3 kernels for bigger ones which could be the reason for this enhancement. This shows by widening the network and augmenting the cardinality, we can achieve better results. This comes only with a marginal increase in computational complexity. Moreover, by using multi-size kernels, one does not need to worry which kernel size is more appropriate.

In order to regress bounding boxes and predict object classes from extra layers as illustrated in Fig. 1, the base-line SSD processes each feature map by only a single 3×3 convolution layer followed by `permute` and `flatten` layers in multi-box detection layer. This includes feature maps only from one of the high-resolution layers. This leads to a weak performance in detecting small-scale vehicles. The feature maps from higher-resolution layers e.g. in our case stage 2 and 3 are responsible to detect small-scale vehicles. Stage 1 is ignored due to its high computational complexity. Those corresponding feature maps are semantically weak and not deep enough to be capable of detecting small-scale vehicles. ResNet and VGG19 works denote that employing deeper features enhances the object recognition accuracy. However, those backbone networks are computationally heavy to be deployed on on-board processors in UAVs which work under strict power constraints. As an alternative, we propose using a residual module which we call DAB as shown in Fig. 1. Combination of 1×1 convention and 3×3 deformable convolution operations enrich the features further, but still introducing low computation burden. We choose a portion of input channels to keep the computation cost low. $1/8, 1/8, 1/8, 1/4, 1/2, 1/2, 1$ are used as the portion of input channels of output layers from stage 2 to the last extra layer and inside DAB unit we assign $1/5, 4/5, 4/5$ portion of input channels to each branch as illustrated in Fig. 1. The output channels remain similar to the original SSD. The only difference is the introduced extra multi-box feature map from stage 2. SSD calculates the number of default boxes per class by $W \times H \times B$ in which W and H are input width and height and B is from the set of $4, 6, 6, 4, 4$ for each feature map. We choose $B = 4$ for the stage 2 leading to 28642 boxes per class.

In aerial imagery, vehicles appear to be very small and almost always in rectangle geometric shape. On the other hand, the pre-trained ShuffleNet has been trained on ground imagery while our images are in another domain of aerial imagery. Therefore pre-trained weights should be adapted to the new domain. We use deformable convolution as introduced in [4] to take into account the new domain and the geometric properties of the vehicles. Deformable convolution adds an offset to the conventional conv layer in order to learn from the geometric shape of the objects. They are not limited to a fix kernel size and offset is learned during training by adding only an inexpensive conv layer to compute the offset field. Deformable conv layer shows considerable improvement in case of using images acquired from low-flying UAVs. However, the impact is less by using images from high-altitude platforms such as helicopter or airplanes. According to [4] the computation cost of deformable convolutions is negligible. Finally, we apply `ReLU` layer to element-wise added features in the DAB to add more non-linearity. In general, naive implementation of ShuffleNet with SSD has 2.94 GFLOPs while ShuffleDet has 3.8 GFLOPs. Despite an increase in the computation cost, ShuffleDet has considerable higher accuracy. As vehicles appear to be small objects in UAV images, we choose default prior boxes with smaller scales similar to [5]. Eventually, non-maximum suppression (NMS) is employed to suppress irrelevant detection boxes. It is worth mentioning that during training hard negative mining is employed with the ratio of 3:1 between negative and positive samples. This leads to more stable and faster training. We also apply batch normalization after each module in DAB as well as extra feature layers.

3 Experiments and Discussion

In this section, we provide ablation evaluation of our proposed approach and compare it to the state-of-the-art CNN-based vehicle detection methods. The experiments were conducted on the CARPK and PUCPR+ datasets [8], which contain 1573 and 125 images of 1280×720 pixels, respectively. The vehicles in the images are annotated by horizontal bounding boxes. To have a fair comparison with different baseline methods, we follow the same strategy as theirs for splitting the datasets into training and testing sets. Moreover, we train ShuffleNet as the backbone network on the ImageNet-2012 [6] dataset achieving similar performance compared to the original ShuffleNet work. The results are compared to the benchmark using MAE and RMSE, similar to the baseline [8]. In addition, we use data augmentation in a similar way to the original work on SSD.

3.1 Experimental Setup

We use Caffe to implement our proposed algorithm. It is trained using Nvidia Titan XP GPU and evaluated on NVIDIA Jetson TX2 as an embedded edge device. For the optimization, we use stochastic gradient descent with the base learning rate of 0.001, gamma 0.1, momentum 0.9 to train the network for 120k iterations. The learning rate is reduced after 80k and 100k by a factor of 10. Moreover, the images are resized to 512×512 pixels along with their annotations. Additionally, we initialize the first four layers with our pre-trained ShuffleNet weights and the rest with Gaussian noise. For the grouped convolutions, we set the number of groups to 3 throughout the experiments. Furthermore, NMS of 0.3 and confidence score threshold of 0.5 are considered.

3.2 Ablation Evaluation

In this section, we present an ablation study on the effect of the submodules in our approach. Table 1 shows the impact of the modified inception module compared to the original baseline. According to the results, introducing the first modified inception module (small scales) decreases RMSE by about 4 points indicating the importance of wider networks in first layers as the critical layers of the network for small object detection. Replacing the baseline's extra layers with more modified inception models further improves the performance. This highlights the role of higher-resolution layers in the vehicle detection tasks.

Table 1. Evaluation of modified inception module (mincep) in the stage 5 on the CARPK dataset. The DAB units are in place. Smaller the RMSE, better the performance.

Method	RMSE	Small scales	mincep-1	mincep-2	mincep-3	mincep-4
ShuffleNet-SSD-512	63.57	-	-	-	-	
ShuffleDet	52.75	-	-	-	-	
ShuffleDet	45.26	✓	-	-	-	
ShuffleDet	41.89	✓	✓	-	-	-
ShuffleDet	40.47	✓	✓	✓	-	-
ShuffleDet	39.67	✓	✓	✓	✓	-
ShuffleDet	38.46	✓	✓	✓	✓	✓

Table 2 represents the evaluation of DAB unit in which we observe a significant reduction in RMSE (almost 5 points) even by the first DAB unit on stage 2. This further indicates the significance of including higher-resolution layer. Furthermore, the results show that adding DAB modules to the extra layer can additionally enhance the performance to a lesser degree. This performance indicates that applying the DAB unit in the high-resolution layers can lead to a significant improvement in detecting small vehicles allowing a better utilization of the deformable convolution to adapt to the vehicle geometries.

Table 2. Evaluation of using DAB unit on the CARPK dataset. We refer to modified inception layers as `mincep`. The modified inception modules and small scales are in place.

Method	RMSE	DAB-stage2	DAB-stage3	DAB-stage4	DAB-mincep-1	DAB-mincep-2	DAB-mincep-3
ShuffleNet-SSD-512	63.57	-	-	-	-	-	-
ShuffleDet	49.26	-	-	-	-	-	-
ShuffleDet	44.17	✓	-	-	-	-	-
ShuffleDet	42.02	✓	✓	-	-	-	-
ShuffleDet	40.75	✓	✓	✓	-	-	-
ShuffleDet	39.81	✓	✓	✓	✓	-	-
ShuffleDet	39.14	✓	✓	✓	✓	✓	-
ShuffleDet	38.46	✓	✓	✓	✓	✓	✓

We choose $s_{min} = 0.05$ and $s_{max} = 0.4$ as minimum and maximum vehicle scales with ratio of $2, 3, 1/2, 1/3$ as hyper-parameters in the original SSD. This improves the performance significantly according to Table 1 by almost 7 RMSE points. It is worth noting that ShuffleNet-SSD-512 has 2.94 GFLOPs as complexity cost while ShuffleDet has 3.8 GFLOPs. This shows ShuffleDet adds only a marginal computation cost while achieving a significant boost in the accuracy. Figure 2 shows sample results of ShuffleDet on the CARPK and PUCPR+ datasets.

(a) (b)

Fig. 2. Sample vehicle detection results using ShuffleDet on the CARPK (a) dataset and the PUCPR+ dataset (b).

3.3 Comparison with the Benchmark

In this part, compare our method with the benchmark. Tables 3 and 4 show that our method can achieve competitive performance while having significantly less computation cost compared with the state of the art. In comparison with the original implementation of Faster-RCNN [19] and Yolo [16], our method achieves significantly better results. ShuffleDet achieves comparative result with the state of the art with only about less 2 RMSE points in the CARPK dataset. The reason for the big gap between SSD-512, MobileNet-SSD-512 and shuffleDet is mostly due

Table 3. Evaluation of ShuffleDet with the benchmark on the PUCPR+ dataset. The less is better.

Method	Backbone	GFLOPs	MAE	RMSE
YOLO [16]	Custom	26.49	156.00	200.42
Faster-RCNN [19]	VGG16	118.61	111.40	149.35
Faster R-CNN (RPN-small) [19]	VGG16	118.61	39.88	47.67
One-look regression [15]	-	-	21.88	36.73
Hsieh et al. [8]	VGG16	-	22.76	34.46
SSD-512 [14]	VGG16	88.16	123.75	168.24
MobileNet-SSD-512 [9]	MobileNet	3.2	175.26	225.12
Our ShuffleDet	ShuffleNet	3.8	41.58	49.68

Table 4. Evaluation of ShuffleDet with the benchmark on the CARPK dataset. The less is better.

Method	Backbone	GFLOPs	MAE	RMSE
YOLO [16]	Custom	26.49	48.89	57.55
Faster-RCNN [19]	VGG16	118.61	47.45	57.39
Faster R-CNN (RPN-small) [19]	VGG16	118.61	24.32	37.62
One-look regression [15]	-	-	59.46	66.84
Hsieh et al. [8]	VGG16	-	23.80	36.79
SSD-512 [14]	VGG16	88.16	48.02	57.42
MobileNet-SSD-512 [9]	MobileNet	3.2	57.34	65.24
Our ShuffleDet	ShuffleNet	3.8	26.75	38.46

to our tuned scales and aspect ratios. This effect can also be observed between the original implementation of Faster-RCNN with and without small RPNs.

Moreover, ShufflDet achieves its superiority to Faster-RCNN and Yolo while it is significantly more computation efficient, 3.8 GFLOPs compared to 118 and 26.49 GFLOPs. While Faster-RCNN runs at Jetson TX2 with 1 FPS, tiny Yolov2 at 8 and Yolov2 at 4 FPS, and original SSD with 88.16 GFLOPs at 5 FPS, our ShuffleDet network runs at 14 FPS showing a great potential to be deployed in the real-time on-board processing in UAV imagery. In addition, our approach achieves almost 70% and 50% better performance than MobileNet-SSD-512 and the naive implementation of ShuffleNet-SSD on the CARPK dataset, relatively.

4 Generalization Ability

To evaluate the generalization ability of our method, we train it on the 3K-DLR-Munich dataset [13]. This dataset contains aerial images of 5616×3744 pixels over the Munich city. Due to the large size of each image similar to [5], we chop the images into the patches of 512×512 pixels which have 100 pixels overlap. To prepare the final results, for each image, we merge the detections results of the patches and then apply none-maximum suppression. Figure 3 illustrates a detection result of our algorithm for the 3K-DLR-Munich dataset.

Table 5 compares the performance of ShuffleDet and two implementations of Faster-RCNN on the 3K-DLR-Munich dataset. According to the table, ShuffleDet not only outperforms the Faster-RCNN methods but also its inference is much more time efficient. The consistent behavior of our proposed approach on the 3K-DLR-Munich dataset indicates that it could be generally applied to different datasets. ShuffleDet is capable of 2 FPS processing of high-resolution aerial images in Jetson TX2 platform while Faster-RCNN with VGG16 and ResNet-50 takes a couple of seconds.

Fig. 3. Vehicle detection result using ShuffleDet on the 3K-DLR-Munich dataset.

Table 5. Evaluation of ShuffleDet on 3K-DLR-Munich dataset. Inference time is computed in Jetson TX2 as an edge device.

Method	Backend	GFLOPs	mAP	Inference time
Faster-RCNN [19]	VGG-16	118.61	67.45%	7.78 s
Faster-RCNN [19]	ResNet-50	22.06	69.23%	7.34 s
Our ShuffleDet	ShuffleNet	**3.8**	62.89	**524 ms**

5 Conclusions

In this paper, we presented ShuffleDet, a real-time vehicle detection algorithm appropriate for on-board embedded UAV imagery. ShuffleDet is based on channel shuffling and grouped convolution in its feature extraction stage. To evaluate the effect of different modules of ShuffleDet, an ablation study is performed to discuss its accuracy and time-efficiency. Joint channel shuffling and grouped convolution significantly boost the inference time. Inception modules with depthwise convolutions enhance the accuracy while introducing a marginal computation burden. Moreover, we show residual modules with deformable convolutions are effective modules for semantic representation enhancement in the small number of layers as well as domain adaptation. Experimental results on the CARPK and PUCPR+ datasets indicate that ShuffleDet outperforms the state-of-the-arts methods while it is much more time and computation efficient. Additionally, the consistent behavior of ShuffleDet on the 3K-DLR-Munich dataset demonstrate its generalization ability. Furthermore, the implementation of ShuffleDet on Jetson TX2, which runs at 14 FPS, showing a great potential of our approach to be used in UAVs for on-board real-time vehicle detection.

References

1. Lin, T., Dollár, P., Girshick, R.B., He, K., Hariharan, B., Belongie, S.J.: Feature pyramid networks for object detection. In: CVPR (2017)
2. Chollet, F.: Xception: deep learning with depthwise separable convolutions. arXiv preprint arXiv:1610.02357 (2017)
3. Dai, J., Li, Y., He, K., Sun, J.: R-FCN: object detection via region-based fully convolutional networks. In: NIPS (2016)
4. Dai, J., et al.: Deformable convolutional networks. In: ICCV (2017)
5. Azimi, S.M., Vig, E., Bahmanyar, R., Körner, M., Reinartz, P.: Towards multi-class object detection in unconstrained remote sensing imagery. In: ACCV (2018)
6. Deng, J., Dong, W., Socher, R., Li, L., Li, K., Fei-Fei, L.: ImageNet: a large-scale hierarchical image database. In: CVPR (2009)
7. Howard, A.G., et al.: MobileNets: efficient convolutional neural networks for mobile vision applications. arXiv preprint arXiv:1704.04861 (2017)
8. Hsieh, M., Lin, Y., Hsu, W.H.: Drone-based object counting by spatially regularized regional proposal network. In: ICCV (2017)
9. Huang, J., et al.: Speed/accuracy trade-offs for modern convolutional object detectors. In: CVPR (2017)
10. Iandola, F.N., Han, S., Moskewicz, M.W., Ashraf, K., Dally, W.J., Keutzer, K.: SqueezeNet: AlexNet-level accuracy with 50x fewer parameters and < 0.5 mb model size. arXiv preprint arXiv:1602.07360 (2016)
11. Kim, K.H., Hong, S., Roh, B., Cheon, Y., Park, M.: PVANET: deep but lightweight neural networks for real-time object detection. arXiv preprint arXiv:1608.08021 (2016)
12. Azimi, S.M., Vig, E., Kurz, F., Reinartz, P.: Segment-and-count: vehicle counting in aerial imagery using atrous convolutional neural networks. In: ISPRS (2018)
13. Liu, K., Mattyus, G.: Fast multiclass vehicle detection on aerial images. IEEE GRSL Lett. **12**, 1938–1942 (2015)
14. Liu, W., et al.: SSD: single shot multibox detector. In: Leibe, B., Matas, J., Sebe, N., Welling, M. (eds.) ECCV 2016. LNCS, vol. 9905, pp. 21–37. Springer, Cham (2016). https://doi.org/10.1007/978-3-319-46448-0_2
15. Mundhenk, T.N., Konjevod, G., Sakla, W.A., Boakye, K.: A large contextual dataset for classification, detection and counting of cars with deep learning. In: Leibe, B., Matas, J., Sebe, N., Welling, M. (eds.) ECCV 2016. LNCS, vol. 9907, pp. 785–800. Springer, Cham (2016). https://doi.org/10.1007/978-3-319-46487-9_48
16. Redmon, J., Divvala, S.K., Girshick, R.B., Farhadi, A.: You only look once: unified, real-time object detection. In: CVPR (2016)
17. Azimi, S.M., Fischer, P., Körner, M., Reinartz, P.: Aerial LaneNet: lane marking semantic segmentation in aerial imagery using wavelet-enhanced cost-sensitive symmetric fully convolutional neural networks. arXiv preprint arXiv:1803.06904 (2018)
18. Redmon, J., Farhadi, A.: Yolo9000: better, faster, stronger. In: CVPR (2017)
19. Ren, S., He, K., Girshick, R., Sun, J.: Faster R-CNN: towards real-time object detection with region proposal networks. In: NIPS (2015)
20. Szegedy, C., et al.: Going deeper with convolutions. In: CVPR (2015)
21. Szegedy, C., Ioffe, S., Vanhoucke, V., Alemi, A.A.: Inception-v4, Inception-ResNet and the impact of residual connections on learning. In: ICLR (2016)
22. Azimi, S.M., Britz, D., Engstler, M., Fritz, M., Mücklich, F.: Advanced steel microstructural classification by deep learning methods. Sci. Rep. - Nat. **8**, 2128 (2018)

23. Wang, R.J., Li, X., Ao, S., Ling, C.X.: Pelee: a real-time object detection system on mobile devices. arXiv preprint arXiv:1804.06882 (2018)
24. Wu, J., Leng, C., Wang, Y., Hu, Q., Cheng, J.: Quantized convolutional neural networks for mobile devices. In: CVPR (2016)
25. Xie, S., Girshick, R., Dollár, P., Tu, Z., He, K.: Aggregated residual transformations for deep neural networks. In: CVPR (2017)
26. Zhang, X., Zhou, X., Lin, M., Sun, J.: ShuffleNet: an extremely efficient convolutional neural network for mobile devices. arXiv preprint arXiv:1707.01083 (2017)

Joint Exploitation of Features and Optical Flow for Real-Time Moving Object Detection on Drones

Hazal Lezki[1,2], I. Ahu Ozturk[1], M. Akif Akpinar[1,4], M. Kerim Yucel[1,3](✉), K. Berker Logoglu[1], Aykut Erdem[3], and Erkut Erdem[3]

[1] STM Defense Technologies and Trade Inc., Ankara, Turkey
{hlezki,iaozturk,makif.akpinar,myucel}@stm.com.tr, berkerlogoglu@gmail.com

[2] Deparment of Electrical and Electronics Engineering, TOBB University of Economics and Technology, Ankara, Turkey

[3] Computer Vision Lab, Department of Computer Engineering, Hacettepe University, Ankara, Turkey
{aykut,erkut}@cs.hacettepe.edu.tr

[4] Multimedia Informatics, Middle East Technical University, Ankara, Turkey

Abstract. Moving object detection is an imperative task in computer vision, where it is primarily used for surveillance applications. With the increasing availability of low-altitude aerial vehicles, new challenges for moving object detection have surfaced, both for academia and industry. In this paper, we propose a new approach that can detect moving objects efficiently and handle parallax cases. By introducing sparse flow based parallax handling and downscale processing, we push the boundaries of real-time performance with 16 FPS on limited embedded resources (a five-fold improvement over existing baselines), while managing to perform comparably or even improve the state-of-the-art in two different datasets. We also present a roadmap for extending our approach to exploit multi-modal data in order to mitigate the need for parameter tuning.

Keywords: Moving object detection · Optical flow · UAV · Drones · Embedded vision · Real-time vision

1 Introduction

Ranging from high-altitude Unmanned Aerial Vehicles (UAV) capable of flying at 65,000 ft[1] to low-altitude miniature drones, long-endurance variants to micro air vehicles weighing just a few grams[2], UAV industry has gone through

[1] http://www.boeing.com/defense/phantom-eye/.
[2] https://aerixdrones.com/products/vidius-the-worlds-smallest-fpv-drone.

L. Leal-Taixé and S. Roth (Eds.): ECCV 2018 Workshops, LNCS 11130, pp. 100–116, 2019.
https://doi.org/10.1007/978-3-030-11012-3_8

a meteoric rise. Owing to their ever increasing availability in civilian and military sectors alike, UAV variants have been disruptive in the last decade and consequently found use in several applications, such as disaster relief, precision agriculture, cinematography, cargo delivery, industrial inspection, mapping, military surveillance and air support [1].

Following the industrial attention, academic community also contributed to the transformation of UAVs in various aspects, such as aerodynamics, avionics and various sensory data acquired by said platforms. Slightly different than remote sensing domain, drone-mounted imagery has paved the way for new research in computer vision (CV). There has been a large quantity of studies reported in object detection [2–6], action detection [7], visual object tracking [8–10], object counting [11] and road extraction [12]. In recent years, new datasets [7,13–17], challenges and dedicated workshops [18,19] have surfaced to bridge the gap between drone-specific vision problems and their generic versions.

From a practical perspective, low-altitude drones introduce several new problems for CV algorithms. Proneness to sudden platform movements and exposure to environmental conditions arguably affect low-altitude drones in a more pronounced manner compared to their high-altitude counterparts. Moreover, fast-changing operating altitudes and camera viewpoints result into the generation of data with a large diversity, which inherently furthers the complexity of virtually any vision problem. Their small-sized nature also impose severe limits on the availability of computational resources installed on-board, which calls for non-trivial engineering solutions [20,21].

Moving object detection (MOD), primarily used for surveillance purposes, is a long-standing problem in CV and has been the subject of many studies [22–24]. Due to the presence of platform motion in drone vision, it becomes a notorious problem, where platform motion can easily be confused with moving regions/objects. Several solutions addressing platform motion issue have been reported [25,26]. Moreover, low-altitude drone cases also suffer from severe motion parallax which causes objects closer to camera move faster than objects further away. Solutions provided for motion parallax issue is considered computationally expensive [17,27–29], which makes the solutions even harder especially when on-board processing with (near) real-time performance is a hard constraint.

In this paper, we propose a new approach for moving object detection, primarily optimized for embedded resources for on-board functionality. We make two main contributions; first, we show that performing a large portion of our pipeline in lower resolutions significantly improve the runtime performance while keeping our accuracy high. Second, we design the matching part of the parallax handling scheme using a simple sparse-flow based technique which avoids the bottlenecks such as failing to extract features from candidate objects or inferior feature matching. Its sparse nature also contributes to further speed-ups, pushing further to real-time performance on embedded platforms.

The paper is organized as follows. In Sect. 2, related work in the literature is reviewed. The proposed approach is explained thoroughly in Sect. 3. Experimental results and their analysis are reported in Sect. 4. We conclude our work by drawing insights and making future recommendations in Sect. 5.

2 Related Work

The research community has contributed to moving object detection literature considerably over the last few decades. Earlier studies aimed to solve this problem for static cameras, where background subtraction [22] and temporal differencing [30] based solutions slowly transformed into more sophisticated approaches such as background learning via Mixture of Gaussians, Eigen backgrounds and motion layers [31,32]. As mobile platforms started to emerge, a new layer of complexity was introduced; ego-motion. The presence of ego-motion renders obsolete the approaches devised for static cameras, as the platform motion is likely to produce quite a few false positives. Moreover, this problem becomes more pronounced when platform motion is sudden.

A simple method to tackle platform-motion induced false positives is to perform image alignment as a preprocessing step. By finding the affine/perspective transformation between two consecutive images, one can warp an image onto another and then perform temporal differencing. Primarily named as "feature-based" methods, such methods depend on accurate image alignment where accurate feature keypoint/descriptor computation is imperative [33]. Another approach to solve ego-motion in such cases can be referred as "motion-based", where motion layers [32] and optical flow [26] techniques are utilized. In cases where planar surface assumption (if any) does not hold, the perspective transformation based warping fails to handle motion parallax induced false positives. Unlike high-altitude scenarios, motion parallax becomes a severe problem in imagery taken from the ground as well as low-altitude UAV imagery. There are studies in the literature using various geometric constraints and flow-based solutions which claim to mitigate the effects of motion parallax [27,34].

Building on the simple solutions reported above, several high impact studies have been reported in recent years. Based on their previous study [34], in [35] authors propose a new method that is related with the projective structure between consecutive image planes, which is used in conjunction with epipolar constraint. This new constraint is useful to detect the moving objects which move along the same direction with the camera, which is a configuration epipolar constraint misses to detect. Assessed using airborne videos, authors state abrupt motion or medium-level parallax might be detrimental to the efficacy of their algorithm. Authors of [36] tackle moving object detection for ground robots, where they use epipolar constraint along with a motion estimation mechanism to handle degenerate cases (camera and platform move to the same direction) in a Bayesian framework. Work reported in [27] handles moving object detection by using epipolar and flow-vector bound constraints, which facilitates parallax handling as well as degenerate cases. Authors estimate the camera pose by using Parallel Tracking and Mapping technique. Similar methods have been reported in [37] and [17], where both algorithms target low altitude imagery but the latter handles parallax in an optimized manner.

In addition to feature based methods mentioned above, motion-based methods have also emerged. In [28], authors fuse the sensory data with imagery to facilitate moving object detection in the presence of ego-motion and motion parallax. By using optical flow in conjunction with the epipolar constraint, authors show they can eliminate parallax effects in videos taken from ground vehicles. In work reported in [38], authors use a dense flow based method where optical flow and artificial flow are assessed for their orientation and magnitude to find moving objects in aerial imagery. Another study using flow-based approaches is [39], where authors use optical flow information along with a reduced Singular Value Decomposition and image inpainting stages to handle parallax and ego-motion. They present their results using sequences taken from aerial and ground vehicles. In [40], authors use artificial flow and background subtraction together. They formulate two scores; anomaly and motion scores where the former facilitates good precision and the latter helps achieve improved recall values.

3 Our Approach

In this work, we propose a hybrid moving object detection pipeline which fuses feature based and optical flow based approaches in an efficient manner for near real time performance. In addition, we propose many minor improvements in the pipeline for increasing processing speed as well as detection accuracy. Our proposed pipeline is given in Fig. 1. It is based on well studied ego-motion compensation and plane-parallax decomposition approaches [17,28,34,35,41] and divided into different process lines for ease of understanding.

3.1 Preprocessing and Ego-Motion Compensation

One of the most challenging parts of moving object detection from a drone is to be able to detect varying size of objects from varying altitudes. In a background subtraction and ego-motion compensation based system, such as ours, the easiest way to cope with this variation is to be able to use varying length of time difference between frames that are compared. Thus, as the very first stage of our pipeline, we have implemented a dynamic frame buffer that changes its size according to the height measurements read (when available) from the barometric sensor and speed measurements read from IMU (Inertial Measurement Unit) as well as the users' desire of detection sensitivity. The size of the buffer, thus the time Δ between frames that will be processed, increases as the required sensitivity to detect smaller objects (and/or smaller movements) increase. In our system, before pushing the frames into our buffer, if the used camera is known and calibration is possible, we correct the lens distortion (radial and tangential) as well.

Typical to the majority of computer vision systems, feature extraction and matching take a significant time of our pipeline and form the bottleneck. Additionally, we claim that calculating the homography between frames in high resolution is not worth the loss in runtime. Therefore, we downscale the input images for feature extraction and matching (using SURF [42]), and then calculate the homographies between frames t, $t - \Delta$ and $t - \Delta$, $t - 2\Delta$. However, to detect smaller objects, the rest of the pipeline runs on original resolution.

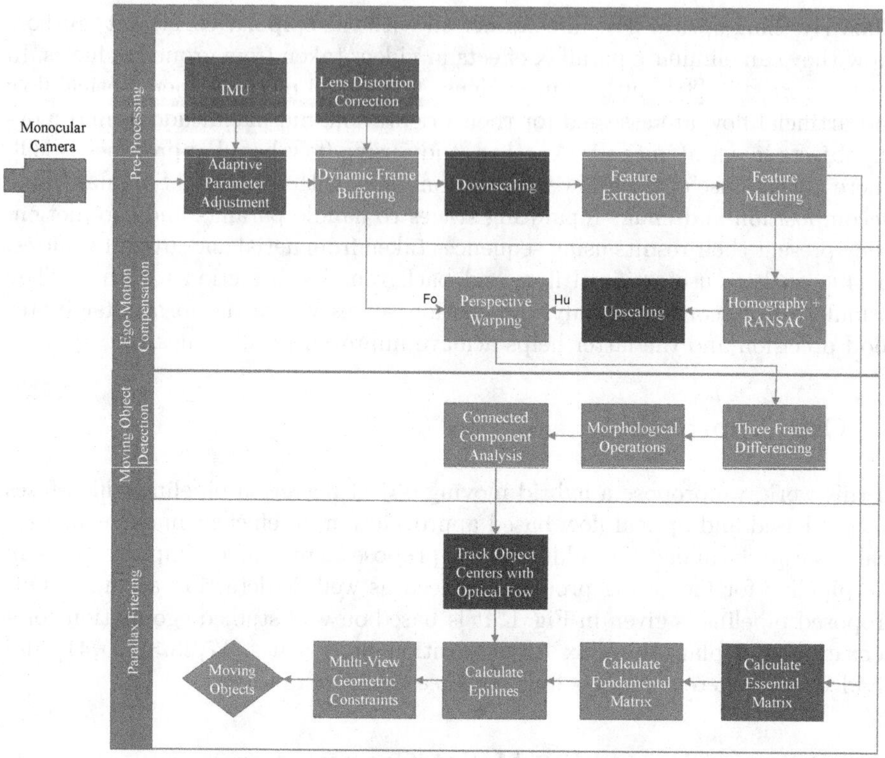

Fig. 1. Our proposed moving object detection pipeline. Red boxes represent the steps we build on other baselines. Green boxes represent the steps that can be applied where IMU, barometric sensor and camera calibration parameters are available. F_o represents the frame in original resolution and H_u represents upscaled homography. (Color figure online)

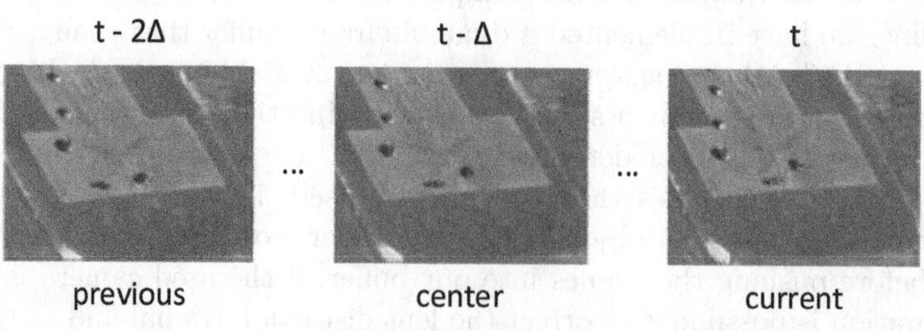

Fig. 2. Dynamic frame buffer. Δ changes depending on required sensitivity.

To achieve this, the homographies calculated in lower resolution H_d are used to calculate/estimate the original resolution homographies H_u using Eq. 1.

$$H_u = H_d * P_{do} \tag{1}$$

where P_{do} is the perspective transformation between the downscaled image and original image.

3.2 Moving Object Detection

The calculated upscale homographies (H_u) are used for perspective warping (of original image F_o) and three-frame differencing. As can be seen in Fig. 2, *current* and *previous* frames are warped on the *center* frame separately, and two separate two-frame differences are calculated. These two-frame difference results are then processed with an empirical threshold value, which produces a binary image for each. Morphological operations are used to cancel noise and associate pixels belonging to the same object. These two-frame differences (after thresholding and morphological operations) are joined with a logical AND operation to facilitate three-frame differencing. Resulting three-frame difference is then subjected to a connected component analysis to create the object bounding boxes.

3.3 Parallax Filtering

Especially for mini UAVs that operate typically under 150 m, parallax can be a significant problem. Without a dedicated algorithm, there might be many false positives due to trees, buildings, etc. In the literature, using geometric constraints has proven to be an effective solution for eliminating parallax regions [17,27,28,35]. In these studies, either features that are extracted on candidate moving objects are tracked/matched [17,27] or each candidate pixel is densely tracked/matched [28,35] to be able to apply geometric constraints. Instead of these, we propose a fast and efficient hybrid method that only tracks the center locations of the candidate objects using sparse optical flow (via [43]). As can be seen from Table 1, this method facilitates significant performance improvement compared to feature tracking based methods. After tracking only the center locations of the candidate objects, we apply epipolar constraint on tracked locations. As can be seen in Figs. 3 and 4, the benefits of tracking only object centers are two fold; epipolar constraint calculations are significantly reduced and the requirement of having keypoints/features on a candidate object is removed.

In order to understand the epipolar constraint [44], assume that $I_{t-\Delta}$ and I_t denote two images of a scene (taken by the same camera at different positions in space) at times $t - \Delta$ and t, and P denote a 3D point in the scene. In addition, let $p_{t-\Delta}$ be the projection of P on $I_{t-\Delta}$, and p_t be the projection of P on I_t.

In light of these, a unique fundamental matrix, represented by $F_t^{t-\Delta}$, that relates images I_t to $I_{t-\Delta}$ can be found, which satisfies

$$p_t^{i\,T} F_t^{t-\Delta} p_{t-\Delta}^i = 0, \tag{2}$$

for all corresponding points $p_{t-\Delta}^i$ and p_t^i where i represents each unique image point. In the case where P is a static point, it satisfies

$$el_t = F^t_{t-\Delta} p^i_{t-\Delta}, \tag{3}$$

$$el_{t-\Delta} = F^{t-\Delta}_t p^i_t \tag{4}$$

where $el_{t-\Delta}$ and el_t are epipolar lines corresponding to p_t and $p_{t-\Delta}$, respectively. If P is a 3D static point, p_t should be located on the epiline el_t (see Fig. 5a). Otherwise, P will not satisfy the epipolar constraint (see Fig. 5b). One exceptional case can occasionally rise, where the point of interest moves along the epilines themselves. This occurs when the camera and the point of interest move along the same direction (i.e. degenerate case).

If camera information required for camera calibration is available, essential matrix instead of fundamental matrix can be used for more accurate results as follows,

$$F \equiv K^{-T} \widehat{T} R K^{-1} = K^{-T} E K^{-1} \tag{5}$$

where K denotes the camera calibration matrix, $\widehat{T}$ denotes the skew symmetric translation matrix and R denotes the rotation matrix between corresponding frames.

4 Experiments

4.1 Datasets

We evaluate our technique in a rigorous manner using two different configurations. In the first one, we use the well-known VIVID [45] dataset. VIVID consists of nine sequences, where three are thermal IR data and the rest are RGB. VIVID annotations are available for every tenth frame and it contains annotations for only one object in the scene. We use a select number of VIVID sequences (egtest01-02-04-05) solely to compare our results with other algorithms. VIVID is the most commonly used dataset for evaluating moving object detection algorithms although it is intended for object tracking. Since VIVID is developed for benchmarking tracking algorithms, only single object (even though multiple moving objects exists) is annotated for each 10th frame.

Our second set of evaluation is performed using the publicly available LAMOD dataset [17]. LAMOD consists of various sequences taken from two publicly available datasets, VIVID and UAV123 [16]. These sequences are hand-annotated from scratch for each moving object present in the scene. Annotations are available for each frame and the dataset provides a large set of adverse effects, such as motion parallax, occlusion, out-of-focus and altitude/viewpoint variation [17].

4.2 Results

Execution Time. Improvements introduced in run-time performance by our approach is primarily two folds; calculation of the features and homography

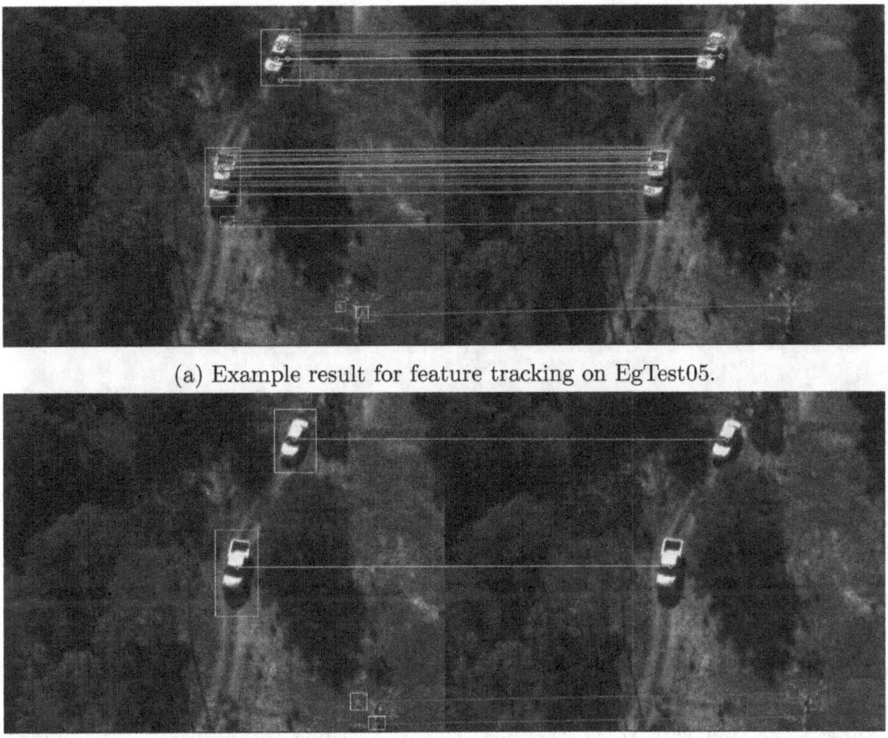

(a) Example result for feature tracking on EgTest05.

(b) Example result for object center tracking with sparse optical flow on EgTest05.

Fig. 3. Visual comparison of feature tracking and object center tracking with sparse optical flow in EgTest05. Note that there are multiple matches on some of the objects which results on multiple epipolar constraint calculations.

at downscale and sparse optical flow based parallax filtering. We perform our execution time analysis on NVIDIA Jetson TX1 and TX2 modules[3].

As expected, feature extraction in downscaled versions introduce significant speed-ups. We observe that from 1280 × 720 resolution to 640 × 360, downscale processing improves runtimes from 148 to 42 ms and 113 to 30 ms for TX1 and TX2, respectively. As downscale processing effectively reduces the number of extracted features, this also reflects on speed of feature matching. Comparing 1280 × 720 to 640 × 360 versions, speed of matching improves by the square of input size ratios due to brute-force matching. We see matching speeds change from 146 to 8 ms and 106 to 6 ms (approximately 1700% improvement) for TX1 and TX2, respectively. Sparse optical flow based parallax handling, compared to feature based parallax handling, also introduces considerable execution time

[3] https://www.nvidia.com/en-us/autonomous-machines/embedded-systems-dev-kits-modules/.

(a) Example result for feature tracking on one of our in-house captured videos.

(b) Example result for object center tracking with sparse optical flow on our in-house captured video.

Fig. 4. Visual comparison of feature tracking and object center tracking with sparse optical flow on our in-house captured video. Note that some objects may not have features associated with them, therefore feature tracking (hence parallax handling) may fail. This problem is mitigated by using optical flow.

gains, as shown in Table 1. TX1 results show an improvement of 20% to 25% whereas TX2 results show improvements in between 18% to 20%.

Table 2 shows a detailed comparison of a recent technique [17] and our approach. A significant improvement up to 40% is observed for low resolution inputs,

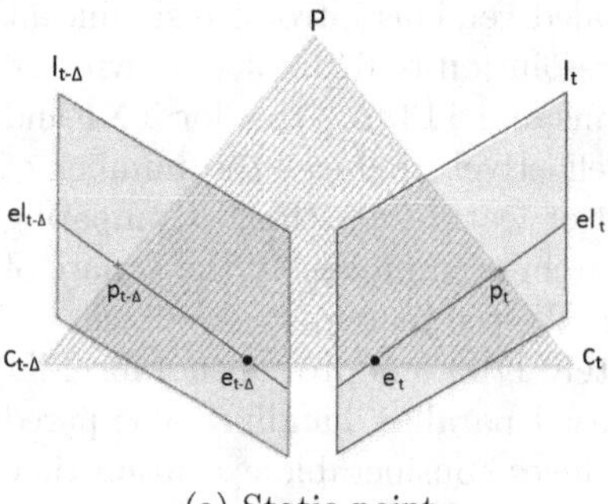

(a) Static point

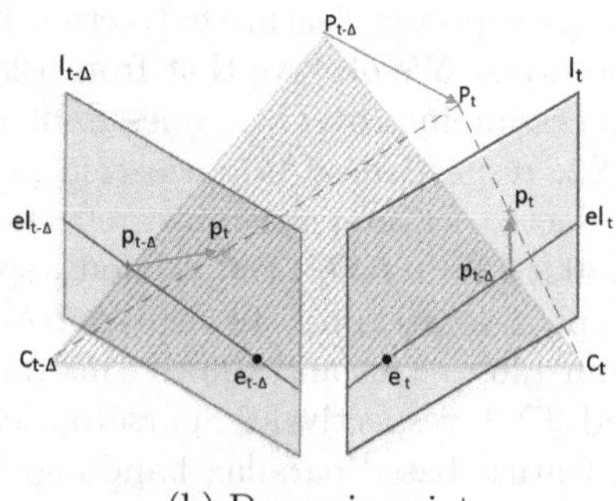

(b) Dynamic point

Fig. 5. Epipolar constraint. Image courtesy of [17].

both with and without parallax filtering. For larger input resolutions, improvements are in between 200% to 400%.

To support our claim that downscale processing does not lead to significant degradation in accuracy, we also assess our pipeline with full high resolution operation. We present results for original and downscaled operations for LAMOD ground truths in Table 4. Results show a slight decrease in accuracy when compared to high resolution. Except a maximum of 6% decrease in recall for *egtest02*, we do not see any other significant decrease in accuracies. In fact, precision and recall values do not even change in many cases, such as *egtest04* recall and *egtest04* precision values.

Accuracy. We first evaluate our proposed approach using single object ground truths of VIVID dataset to compare our performance with other baseline algorithms. We use precision/recall as our metric and take a minimum of 50% overlap to be a correct detection. As all the baseline algorithms have reported their results in terms of correct detection ratio and miss detection ratio, we convert these results to precision and recall for a better comparison (miss detection ratio is effectively $1 - precision$, whereas correct detection is ratio is equal to precision). We do not report results for parallax handling for sequences *EgTest01* and *EgTest02* as they do not have parallax effects. Results are shown in Table 3.

Our proposed algorithm performs comparably to other baselines, even surpassing them in several sequences; *EgTest01* and *egtest02* results outperform all others in precision, whereas our precision or recall values are the second best in

Table 1. Execution time of our proposed approach for different input resolutions. *Feat.* indicates the version where features are extracted from candidate objects for parallax filtering. *O.F.* indicates the version where objects centres are tracked with sparse optical flow for parallax filtering.

	640 × 480		1280 × 720	
	Feat.	O.F.	Feat.	O.F.
TX1	115 ms	**93 ms**	176 ms	**132 ms**
TX2	76 ms	**62 ms**	108 ms	**77 ms**

Table 2. Execution time of our proposed approach for different input resolutions. *NF* represents no parallax filtering, *PF* represents parallax filtering and *ours* refer to our proposed approach.

		640 × 480		1280 × 720	
		[17]	Ours	[17]	Ours
TX1	NF	115 ms	**70 ms**	350 ms	**102 ms**
	PF	175 ms	**93 ms**	450 ms	**132 ms**
TX2	NF	85 ms	**52 ms**	250 ms	**64 ms**
	PF	140 ms	**62 ms**	350 ms	**77 ms**

Table 3. Precision and recall values for 4 sequences in VIVID dataset with the original single object tracking ground truth. We extrapolate the results of baselines as they do not provide numerical results directly. *NF* and *PF* represent results without and with parallax filtering. Results in each row are precision and recall (in percentage), respectively.

	EgTest01	EgTest02	EgTest04	EgTest05
GMAC [46]	97.0/84.0	93.0/67.0	83.0/75.0	**87.0**/77.0
MIL [47]	92.0/79.0	98.0/**76.0**	33.0/20.0	35.0/16.0
OAB1 [48]	88.0/77.0	87.0/68.0	42.0/28.0	35.0/18.0
Castelli et al. [38]	86.0/84.0	—	**93.0/90.0**	85.0/**82.0**
Ours (NF)	**99.4/97.2**	**98.6**/56.9	76.0/77.0	73.0/80.0
Ours (PF)	—	—	78.0/62.0	83.0/66.0

Table 4. Precision and recall values for 4 sequences in VIVID dataset with multi object moving object detection ground truth provided in LAMOD dataset. *NF* and *PF* represent results without and with parallax filtering. Results in each row are precision and recall (in percentage), respectively. Results indicated with $*$ calculate precision/recall for each frame and then average for entire sequence. Results indicated with † represent the results of our technique when it operates on original resolution images (no downscaling).

	EgTest01	EgTest02	EgTest04	EgTest05
Logoglu et al. [17]*	93.0/82.0	85.0/53.0	72.0/72.0	71.0/**68.0**
Ours (NF)*	**97.4/93.0**	**92.4/61.0**	86.0/**75.0**	70.0/66.0
Ours (PF)*	—	—	**91.0**/60.0	**77.0**/55.0
Ours (NF)†	**96.8/92.2**	**92.6/59.5**	85.0/**72.0**	66.0/**63.0**
Ours (PF)†	—	—	**89.0**/57.0	**71.0**/52.0
Ours (NF)	96.7/91.2	92.2/53.2	86.0/69.0	66.0/62.0
Ours (PF)	—	—	85.0/57.0	70.0/50.0

other sequences. Our method shines as it has close precision and recall values. When we perform parallax handling, an expected reduction in recall is compensated with an increase in precision, practically evening out or improving the final F-score. It must be noted that nearly all baselines are effectively object trackers, which means our algorithm performs quite accurately as we do not support our detection with a sophisticated tracker.

We then assess our pipeline for multiple moving objects using LAMOD dataset. We use precision/recall and per-frame precision/recall[4] (i.e. where precision and recall is calculated for every frame and then averaged) as our evaluation metric where 50% overlap is considered a detection. Similar to previous

[4] Authors of [17] have reported their results with this metric, therefore we give these results to compare our work.

(a) EgTest01 frame 1266. (b) EgTest02 frame 1206.

(c) EgTest03 frame 285. (d) EgTest04 frame 1035.

Fig. 6. Detection results on 4 sequences of VIVID dataset. Green boxes are detection results, blue boxes are ground truth data that are taken from LAMOD dataset, grey boxes are candidate objects that are filtered by our parallax filtering algorithm. (Color figure online)

section of our evaluation, we do not report parallax filtering results for *EgTest01* and *EgTest02*. Exemplary results are visualized in Fig. 6. Results are shown in Table 4.

Results indicate our proposed algorithm significantly outperforms an existing baseline [17] in all sequences except *EgTest05*. Parallax filtering introduces considerable gains in precision and modest reductions in recall, as reported before. This is expected as *EgTest04* and *EgTest05* have degenerate cases (i.e. objects and the platform move along the same direction) and our approach currently does not handle such cases. This leads to the elimination of true positives by parallax filtering, thus the reduction in recall.

4.3 Multi-modal Extension

In the previous section, as we use public datasets where no IMU, height measurement or camera information is available, we can not fully utilise the adaptive algorithm we show in Fig. 1. This means we can not use lens distortion correction at all and we can only use a fixed set of parameters (i.e. dynamic buffer size) for all sequences. In order to show how our pipeline works while utilising external sensory data, we present some qualitative results with our in-house captured videos, where we were able to acquire the relevant IMU and camera parameter information.

Lens Distortion Correction. Lens distortion distorts certain pixels to other locations, radially or tangentially in our case, which directly effects our results (see Fig. 7(b)). This occurs as pixels are distorted to some other location and during image registration, they are erroneously detected as moving objects. By using radial and tangential coefficients specific to the camera lens, this effect can be corrected. Such correction leads to visible improvements in our performance (see Fig. 7(d)).

Dynamic Frame Buffer. It can be hard to detect slowly moving objects in high altitudes as their relative displacement in the image is not large. This can be alleviated by using the height measurements provided by a barometric sensor and vehicle speed measurements by IMU; we dynamically change the size of the buffer (namely the distance between the frames to be differenced) linearly by using the altitude and speed information. By doing so, we effectively amplify the

(a) Thresholded three-frame difference with no lens distortion correction. (b) Detected moving objects without lens distortion correction.

(c) Thresholded three-frame difference with no lens distortion correction. (d) Detected moving objects with lens distortion correction.

Fig. 7. The effect of lens distortion correction. Note that although the effects of lens correction on input images may be almost imperceptible, it gives rise to many pixel level errors.

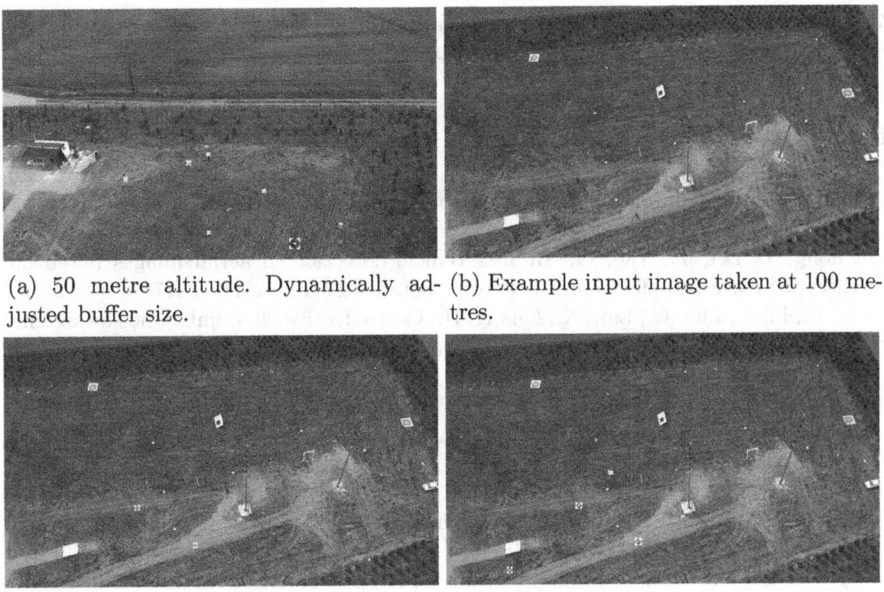

(a) 50 metre altitude. Dynamically adjusted buffer size.

(b) Example input image taken at 100 metres.

(c) Image b) processed with a static buffer size parameter used in subfigure a).

(d) Image b) processed with dynamically adjusted buffer size.

Fig. 8. The effect of dynamic frame buffering. Note that dynamically adjusted buffer size for 50 m altitude works accurately for 50 m, but fails at 100 m altitude. Adaptively changing the buffer size for 100 m significantly improves our detection performance.

perceived movement of slow moving objects, thus making them highly detectable. Exemplary results shown in Fig. 8(c) and (d) verify the said phenomena and shows a visible improvement in recall.

5 Conclusions

In this paper, we propose a new approach aimed at tackling moving object detection problem for imagery taken from low-altitude aerial platforms. Capable of handling the motion of the platform as well as the detrimental effects of motion parallax, our approach performs parallax handling by sparse optical flow based tracking along with epipolar constraint and performs a large portion of the pipeline in lower resolutions. These two changes introduce significant runtime improvements, reaching up to 16 FPS on embedded resources. Moreover, we analyze our approach in two different datasets for single and multiple moving object detection tasks. We observe that our results perform either comparably or better than existing state-of-the-art algorithms. We also outline an advanced pipeline capable of exploiting multi-modal data that might alleviate the need of laborious parameter tuning. As future work, we aim to integrate a light-weight scheme to alleviate the effect of degenerate motion cases. Should a dataset with

IMU, height measurements and camera information become publicly available, we aim to assess our approach in a multi-modal setting.

References

1. Clarke, R.: Understanding the drone epidemic. Comput. Law Secur. Rev. **30**(3), 230–246 (2014)
2. Zhong, J., Lei, T., Yao, G.: Robust vehicle detection in aerial images based on cascaded convolutional neural networks. Sensors **17**(12), 2720 (2017)
3. Li, F., Li, S., Zhu, C., Lan, X., Chang, H.: Cost-effective class-imbalance aware cnn for vehicle localization and categorization in high resolution aerial images. Remote Sens. **9**(5), 494 (2017)
4. Tijtgat, N., Van Ranst, W., Volckaert, B., Goedemé, T., De Turck, F.: Embedded real-time object detection for a UAV warning system. In: The International Conference on Computer Vision, ICCV 2017, pp. 2110–2118 (2017)
5. Sommer, L.W., Schuchert, T., Beyerer, J.: Fast deep vehicle detection in aerial images. In: 2017 IEEE Winter Conference on Applications of Computer Vision (WACV), pp. 311–319. IEEE (2017)
6. Stek, T.D.: Drones over Mediterranean landscapes. The potential of small UAV's (drones) for site detection and heritage management in archaeological survey projects: a case study from Le Pianelle in the Tappino Valley, Molise (Italy). J. Cultural Herit. **22**, 1066–1071 (2016)
7. Barekatain, M., et al.: Okutama-action: an aerial view video dataset for concurrent human action detection. In: 1st Joint BMTT-PETS Workshop on Tracking and Surveillance, CVPR, pp. 1–8 (2017)
8. Pestana, J., Sanchez-Lopez, J.L., Campoy, P., Saripalli, S.: Vision based GPS-denied object tracking and following for unmanned aerial vehicles. In: 2013 IEEE International Symposium on Safety, Security, and Rescue Robotics (SSRR), pp. 1–6. IEEE (2013)
9. Dang, C.T., Pham, T.B., Truong, N.V., et al.: Vision based ground object tracking using AR drone quadrotor. In: 2013 International Conference on Control, Automation and Information Sciences (ICCAIS), pp. 146–151. IEEE (2013)
10. Chen, P., Dang, Y., Liang, R., Zhu, W., He, X.: Real-time object tracking on a drone with multi-inertial sensing data. IEEE Trans. Intell. Transp. Syst. **19**(1), 131–139 (2018)
11. Hsieh, M.R., Lin, Y.L., Hsu, W.H.: Drone-based object counting by spatially regularized regional proposal network. In: The IEEE International Conference on Computer Vision (ICCV), vol. 1 (2017)
12. Kanistras, K., Martins, G., Rutherford, M.J., Valavanis, K.P.: A survey of unmanned aerial vehicles (UAVs) for traffic monitoring. In: 2013 International Conference on Unmanned Aircraft Systems (ICUAS), pp. 221–234. IEEE (2013)
13. Du, D., et al.: The unmanned aerial vehicle benchmark: object detection and tracking. arXiv preprint arXiv:1804.00518 (2018)
14. Wang, S., et al.: TorontoCity: seeing the world with a million eyes. In: 2017 IEEE International Conference on Computer Vision (ICCV), pp. 3028–3036. IEEE (2017)
15. Xia, G.S., et al.: DOTA: a large-scale dataset for object detection in aerial images. In: Proceedings of CVPR (2018)

16. Mueller, M., Smith, N., Ghanem, B.: A benchmark and simulator for UAV tracking. In: Leibe, B., Matas, J., Sebe, N., Welling, M. (eds.) ECCV 2016. LNCS, vol. 9905, pp. 445–461. Springer, Cham (2016). https://doi.org/10.1007/978-3-319-46448-0_27
17. Berker Logoglu, K., et al.: Feature-based efficient moving object detection for low-altitude aerial platforms. In: The IEEE International Conference on Computer Vision (ICCV) Workshops, October 2017
18. Lam, D., et al.: xView: objects in context in overhead imagery. arXiv preprint arXiv:1802.07856 (2018)
19. Zhu, P., Wen, L., Bian, X., Ling, H., Hu, Q.: Vision meets drones: a challenge. arXiv preprint arXiv:1804.07437 (2018)
20. Yu, Q., Medioni, G.: A GPU-based implementation of motion detection from a moving platform (2008)
21. Kryjak, T., Komorkiewicz, M., Gorgon, M.: Real-time moving object detection for video surveillance system in FPGA. In: 2011 Conference on Design and Architectures for Signal and Image Processing (DASIP), pp. 1–8. IEEE (2011)
22. Elgammal, A., Duraiswami, R., Harwood, D., Davis, L.S.: Background and foreground modeling using nonparametric kernel density estimation for visual surveillance. Proc. IEEE **90**(7), 1151–1163 (2002)
23. Eveland, C., Konolige, K., Bolles, R.C.: Background modeling for segmentation of video-rate stereo sequences. In: Proceedings of the IEEE Computer Society Conference on Computer Vision and Pattern Recognition, pp. 266–271. IEEE (1998)
24. Zhou, X., Yang, C., Yu, W.: Moving object detection by detecting contiguous outliers in the low-rank representation. IEEE Trans. Pattern Anal. Mach. Intell. **35**(3), 597–610 (2013)
25. Suganuma, N., Kubo, T.: Fast dynamic object extraction using stereovision based on occupancy grid maps and optical flow. In: 2011 IEEE/ASME International Conference on Advanced Intelligent Mechatronics (AIM), pp. 978–983. IEEE (2011)
26. Rodríguez-Canosa, G.R., Thomas, S., Del Cerro, J., Barrientos, A., MacDonald, B.: A real-time method to detect and track moving objects (DATMO) from unmanned aerial vehicles (UAVs) using a single camera. Remote Sens. **4**(4), 1090–1111 (2012)
27. Kimura, M., Shibasaki, R., Shao, X., Nagai, M.: Automatic extraction of moving objects from UAV-borne monocular images using multi-view geometric constraints. In: International Micro Air Vehicle Conference and Competition, IMAV 2014, Delft, The Netherlands, 12–15 August 2014, Delft University of Technology (2014)
28. Salgian, G., Bergen, J., Samarasekera, S., Kumar, R.: Moving target indication from a moving camera in the presence of strong parallax. Technical report, DTIC Document (2006)
29. Dey, S., Reilly, V., Saleemi, I., Shah, M.: Detection of independently moving objects in non-planar scenes via multi-frame monocular epipolar constraint. In: Fitzgibbon, A., Lazebnik, S., Perona, P., Sato, Y., Schmid, C. (eds.) ECCV 2012. LNCS, vol. 7576, pp. 860–873. Springer, Heidelberg (2012). https://doi.org/10.1007/978-3-642-33715-4_62
30. Paragios, N., Deriche, R.: Geodesic active contours and level sets for the detection and tracking of moving objects. IEEE Trans. Pattern Anal. Mach. Intell. **22**(3), 266–280 (2000)
31. Joshi, K.A., Thakore, D.G.: A survey on moving object detection and tracking in video surveillance system. Int. J. Soft Comput. Eng. **2**(3), 44–48 (2012)
32. Cao, X., Lan, J., Yan, P., Li, X.: Vehicle detection and tracking in airborne videos by multi-motion layer analysis. Mach. Vis. Appl. **23**(5), 921–935 (2012)

33. Irani, M., Anandan, P.: A unified approach to moving object detection in 2D and 3D scenes. IEEE Trans. Pattern Anal. Mach. Intell. **20**(6), 577–589 (1998)
34. Kang, J., Cohen, I., Medioni, G., Yuan, C.: Detection and tracking of moving objects from a moving platform in presence of strong parallax. In: Tenth IEEE International Conference on Computer Vision, ICCV 2005, vol. 1, pp. 10–17. IEEE (2005)
35. Yuan, C., Medioni, G., Kang, J., Cohen, I.: Detecting motion regions in the presence of a strong parallax from a moving camera by multiview geometric constraints. IEEE Trans. Pattern Anal. Mach. Intell. **29**(9), 1627–1641 (2007)
36. Kundu, A., Krishna, K.M., Sivaswamy, J.: Moving object detection by multi-view geometric techniques from a single camera mounted robot. In: 2009 IEEE/RSJ International Conference on Intelligent Robots and Systems, pp. 4306–4312, October 2009
37. Minaeian, S., Liu, J., Son, Y.J.: Effective and efficient detection of moving targets from a UAV's camera. IEEE Trans. Intell. Transp. Syst. **19**, 497–506 (2018)
38. Castelli, T., Trémeau, A., Konik, H., Dinet, E.: Moving object detection for unconstrained low-altitude aerial videos, a pose-independant detector based on artificial flow. In: 2015 9th International Symposium on Image and Signal Processing and Analysis (ISPA), pp. 42–47. IEEE (2015)
39. Wu, Y., He, X., Nguyen, T.Q.: Moving object detection with a freely moving camera via background motion subtraction. IEEE Trans. Circuits Syst. Video Technol. **27**(2), 236–248 (2017)
40. Makino, K., Shibata, T., Yachida, S., Ogawa, T., Takahashi, K.: Moving-object detection method for moving cameras by merging background subtraction and optical flow methods. In: 2017 IEEE Global Conference on Signal and Information Processing (GlobalSIP), pp. 383–387, November 2017
41. Ali, S., Shah, M.: COCOA: tracking in aerial imagery. In: Airborne Intelligence, Surveillance, Reconnaissance (ISR) Systems and Applications III, vol. 6209, p. 62090D. International Society for Optics and Photonics (2006)
42. Bay, H., Tuytelaars, T., Van Gool, L.: SURF: speeded up robust features. In: Leonardis, A., Bischof, H., Pinz, A. (eds.) ECCV 2006. LNCS, vol. 3951, pp. 404–417. Springer, Heidelberg (2006). https://doi.org/10.1007/11744023_32
43. Lucas, B.D., Kanade, T., et al.: An iterative image registration technique with an application to stereo vision (1981)
44. Hartley, R., Zisserman, A.: Multiple View Geometry in Computer Vision. Cambridge University Press, Cambridge (2003)
45. Collins, R., Zhou, X., Teh, S.K.: An open source tracking testbed and evaluation web site. In: IEEE International Workshop on Performance Evaluation of Tracking and Surveillance (PETS 2005), vol. 2, p. 35 (2005)
46. Hasan, M.: Integrating geometric, motion and appearance constraints for robust tracking in aerial videos (2013)
47. Babenko, B., Yang, M.H., Belongie, S.: Visual tracking with online multiple instance learning. In: IEEE Conference on Computer Vision and Pattern Recognition, CVPR 2009, pp. 983–990. IEEE (2009)
48. Grabner, H., Grabner, M., Bischof, H.: Real-time tracking via on-line boosting. In: British Machine Vision Conference, vol. 1, p. 6 (2006)

UAV-GESTURE: A Dataset for UAV Control and Gesture Recognition

Asanka G. Perera[1](✉), Yee Wei Law[1], and Javaan Chahl[1,2]

[1] School of Engineering, University of South Australia, Mawson Lakes, SA 5095, Australia
asanka.perera@mymail.unisa.edu.au, {yeewei.law,javaan.chahl}@unisa.edu.au
[2] Joint and Operations Analysis Division, Defence Science and Technology Group, Melbourne, VIC 3207, Australia

Abstract. Current UAV-recorded datasets are mostly limited to action recognition and object tracking, whereas the gesture signals datasets were mostly recorded in indoor spaces. Currently, there is no outdoor recorded public video dataset for UAV commanding signals. Gesture signals can be effectively used with UAVs by leveraging the UAVs visual sensors and operational simplicity. To fill this gap and enable research in wider application areas, we present a UAV gesture signals dataset recorded in an outdoor setting. We selected 13 gestures suitable for basic UAV navigation and command from general aircraft handling and helicopter handling signals. We provide 119 high-definition video clips consisting of 37151 frames. The overall baseline gesture recognition performance computed using Pose-based Convolutional Neural Network (P-CNN) is 91.9%. All the frames are annotated with body joints and gesture classes in order to extend the dataset's applicability to a wider research area including gesture recognition, action recognition, human pose recognition and situation awareness.

Keywords: UAV · Gesture dataset · UAV control · Gesture recognition

1 Introduction

Unmanned aerial vehicles (UAVs) can be deployed in a variety of applications such as search and rescue, situational awareness, surveillance and police pursuit by leveraging their mobility and operational simplicity. In some situations, a UAV's ability to recognize the commanding actions of the human operator and to take responsive actions is desirable. Such scenarios might include a firefighter commanding a drone to scan a particular area, a lifeguard directing a drone to monitor a drifting kayaker, or more user-friendly video and photo shooting capabilities. Whether for offline gesture recognition from aerial videos or for equipping UAVs with gesture recognition capabilities, a substantial amount of training data is necessary. However, the majority of the video action recognition datasets consist of ground videos recorded from stationary or dynamic cameras [15].

L. Leal-Taixé and S. Roth (Eds.): ECCV 2018 Workshops, LNCS 11130, pp. 117–128, 2019.
https://doi.org/10.1007/978-3-030-11012-3_9

Different video datasets recorded from moving and stationary aerial cameras have been published in recent years [6,15]. They have been recorded under different camera and platform settings and have limitations when used with a wide range of human action recognition behaviors demanded today. However, aerial action recognition is still far from perfect. In general, the existing aerial video action datasets are lacking detailed human body shapes to be used with state-of-the-art action recognition algorithms. Many action recognition techniques depend on accurate analysis of human body joints or body frame. It is difficult to use the existing aerial datasets for aerial action or gesture recognition due to one or more of the following reasons: (i) severe perspective distortion – camera elevation angle closer to 90° results in a severely distorted body shape with large head and shoulder, and most of the other body parts being occluded; (ii) the low resolution makes it difficult to retrieve human body and texture details; (iii) motion blur caused by rapid variations of the elevation and pan angles or the movement of the platform; and (iv) camera vibration caused by the engine or the rotors of the UAV.

We introduce a dataset recorded from a low altitude and slow flying mobile platform for gesture recognition. The dataset was created with the intention of capturing full human body details from a relatively low altitude in a way that preserves the maximum detail of the body position. Our dataset is suitable for research involving search and rescue, situational awareness, surveillance, and general action recognition. We assume that in most practical missions, the UAV operator or an autonomous UAV follows these general rules: (i) it does not fly so low that it poses danger to the civilians, ground-based structures, or itself; (ii) it does not fly so high or so fast that it loses too much detail in the images it captures; (iii) it hovers to capture the details of an interesting scene; and (iv) it records human subjects from a viewpoint that causes minimum perspective distortion and maximum body details. Our dataset was created following these guidelines to represent 13 command gesture classes. The gestures were selected from general aircraft handling and helicopter handling signals [32]. All the videos were recorded at high-definition (HD) resolution, enabling the gesture videos to be used in general gesture recognition and gesture-based autonomous system control research. To our knowledge, this is the first dataset presenting gestures captured from a moving aerial camera in an outdoor setting.

2 Related Work

A complete list and description of recently published action recognition datasets is available in [6,15], and gesture recognition datasets can be found in [21,25]. Here, we discuss some selected studies related to our work.

Detecting human action from an aerial view is more challenging than from a fronto-parallel view. Created by Oh et al. [18], the large-scale VIRAT dataset contains about 550 videos, recorded from static and moving cameras covering 23 event types over 29 h. The VIRAT ground dataset has been recorded from stationary aerial cameras (e.g., overhead mounted surveillance cameras) at multiple locations with resolutions of 1080×1920 and 720×1280. Both aerial and ground-based datasets have been recorded in uncontrolled and cluttered backgrounds. However, in the VIRAT aerial dataset, the low resolution of 480×720 precludes retrieval of rich activity information from relatively small human subjects.

A 4K-resolution video dataset called Okutama-Action was introduced in [1] for concurrent action detection by multiple subjects. The videos have been recorded in a relatively clutter-free baseball field using 2 UAVs. There are 12 actions under abrupt camera movements, altitudes from 10 to 45 m and different view angles. The camera elevation angle of 90° causes a severe distortion in perspective and self-occlusions in videos.

Other notable aerial action datasets are UCF aerial action [30], UCF-ARG [31] and Mini-drone [2]. UCF aerial action and UCF ARG have been recorded using an R/C-controlled blimp and a helium balloon respectively. Both datasets contain similar action classes. However, UCF aerial action is a single-view dataset while UCF ARG is a multi-view dataset recorded from aerial, rooftop and ground cameras. The Mini-drone dataset has been developed as a surveillance dataset to evaluate different aspects and definitions of privacy. This dataset was recorded in a car park using a drone flying at a low altitude and the actions are categorized as normal, suspicious and illicit behaviors.

Gesture recognition has been studied extensively in recent years [21,25]. However, the gesture-based UAV control studies available in the literature are mostly limited to indoor environments or static gestures [10,16,19], restricting their applicability to real-world scenarios. The datasets used for these works were mostly recorded indoors using RGB-D images [13,24,27] or RGB images [5,17]. An aircraft handling signal dataset similar to ours in terms of gesture classes is available in [28]. It has been created using VICON cameras and a stereo camera with a static indoor background. However, these gesture datasets cannot be used in aerial gesture studies. We selected some gesture classes from [28] when creating our dataset.

3 Preparing the Dataset

This section discusses the collection process of the dataset, the types of gestures recorded in the dataset, and the usefulness of the dataset for vision-related research purposes.

3.1 Data Collection

The data was collected on an unsettled road located in the middle of a wheat field from a rotorcraft UAV (3DR Solo) in slow and low-altitude flight. For video recording, we used a GoPro Hero 4 Black camera with an anti-fish eye replacement lens (5.4 mm, 10MP, IR CUT) and a 3-axis Solo gimbal. We provide the videos with HD (1920 × 1080) formats at 25 fps. The gestures were recorded on two separate days. The participants were asked to perform the gestures in a selected section of the road. A total of 13 gestures have been recorded while the UAV was hovering in front of the subject. In these videos, the subject is roughly in the middle of the frame and performs each gesture five to ten times.

When recording the gestures, sometimes the UAV drifts from its initial hovering position due to wind gusts. This adds random camera motion to the videos making them closer to practical scenarios.

3.2 Gesture Selection

The gestures were selected from general aircraft handling signals and helicopter handling signals available in the Aircraft Signals NATOPS manual [32, Ch. 2–3]. The selected 13 gestures are shown in Fig. 1. When selecting the gestures, we avoided aircraft and helicopter specific gestures. The gestures were selected to meet the following criteria: (i) they should be easily identifiable from a moving platform, (ii) the gestures need to be crisp enough to be differentiated from each another, (iii) they need to be simple enough to be repeated by an untrained individual, (iv) the gestures should be applicable to basic UAV navigation control, and (v) the selected gestures should be a mixture of static and dynamic gestures to enable other possible applications such as taking "selfies".

3.3 Variations in Data

The actors that participated in this dataset are not professionals in aircraft handling signals. They were shown how to do a particular gesture by another person who was standing in front of them, and then asked to do the same towards the UAV. Therefore, each actor performed the gestures slightly differently. There are rich variations in the recorded gestures in terms of the phase, orientation, camera movement and the body shape of the actors. In some videos, the skin color of the actor is close to the background color. These variations create a challenging dataset for gesture recognition, and also makes it more representative of real-world situations.

The dataset was recorded on two separate days and involved a total of eight participants. Two participants performed the same gestures on both days. For a particular gesture performed by a participant in the two settings, the two videos have significant differences in the background, clothing, camera to subject distance and natural variations in hand movements. Due to these visual variations in the dataset, we consider the total number of actors to be 10.

3.4 Dataset Annotations

We used an extended version of online video annotation tool VATIC [33] to annotate the videos. Thirteen body joints are annotated in 37151 frames, namely ankles, knees, hip-joint, wrists, elbows, shoulders and head. Two annotated

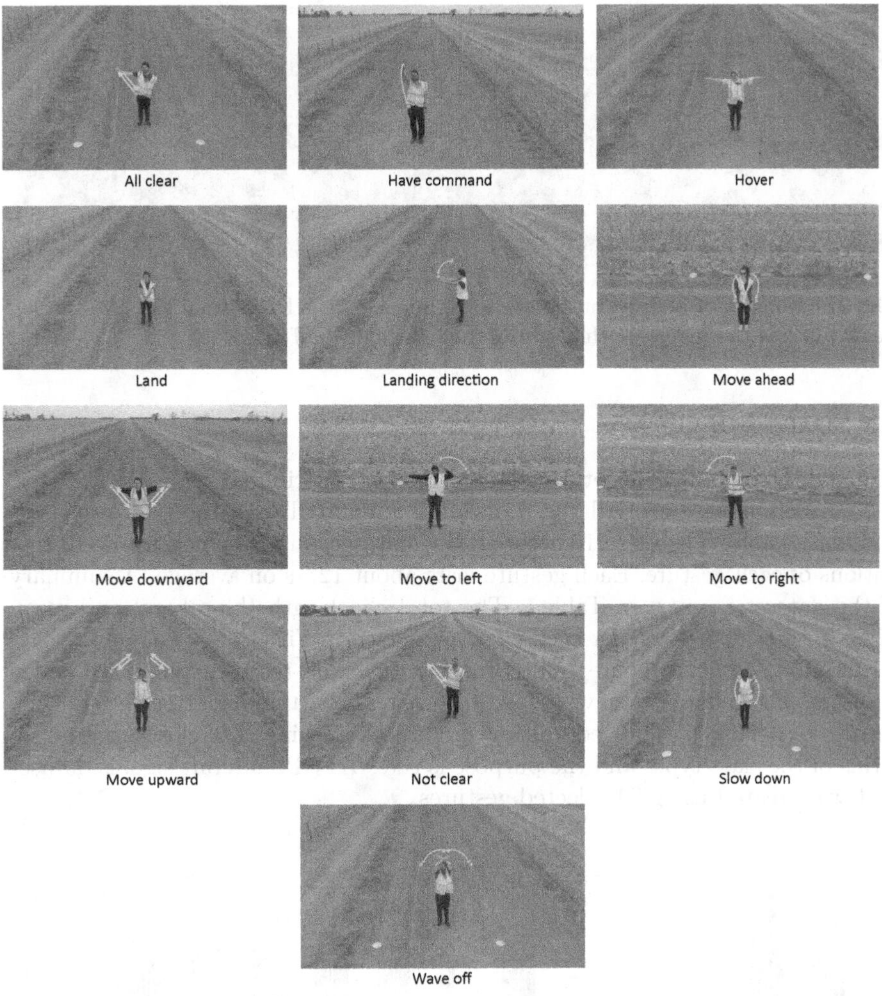

Fig. 1. The selected thirteen gestures are shown with one selected image from each gesture. The arrows indicate the hand movement directions. The amber color markers roughly designate the start and end positions of the palm for one repetition. The *Hover* and *Land* gestures are static gestures.

images are shown in Fig. 2. Each annotation also comes with the gesture class, subject identity and bounding box. The bounding box is created by adding a margin to the minimum and maximum coordinates of joint annotations in both x and y directions.

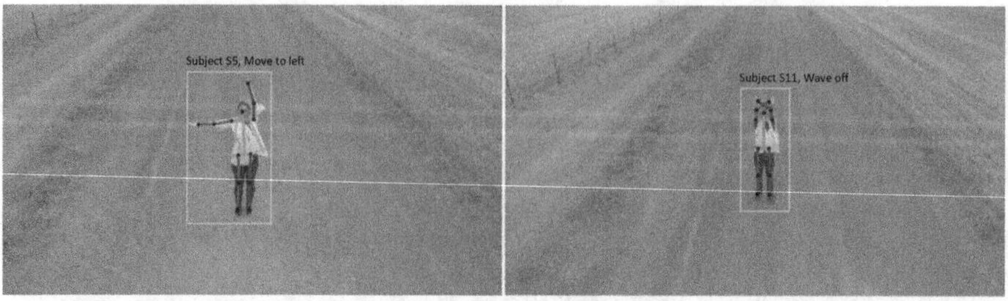

Fig. 2. Examples of body joint annotations. Image on the left is from the *Move to left* class, whereas the image on the right is from the *Wave off* class.

3.5 Dataset Summary

The dataset contains a total of 37151 frames distributed over 119, 25 fps, 1920×1080 video clips. All the frames are annotated with the gesture classes and body joints. There are 10 actors in the dataset, and they perform 5–10 repetitions of each gesture. Each gesture lasts about 12.5 s on average. A summary of the dataset is given in Table 1. The total clip length (blue bars) and mean clip length (amber bars) for each class are shown in Fig. 3.

In Table 2, we compare our dataset with eight recently published video datasets. These datasets have helped to progress research in action recognition, gesture recognition, event recognition and object tracking. The closest dataset in terms of the class types and the purpose is the NATOPS aircraft signals dataset that was created using 24 selected gestures.

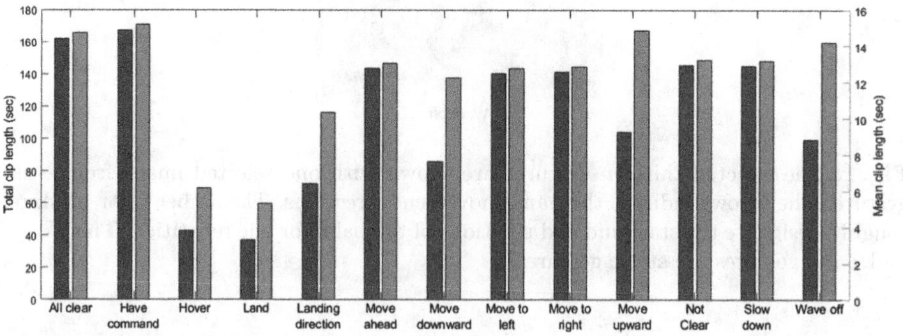

Fig. 3. The total clip length (blue) and the mean clip length (amber) are shown in the same graph in seconds. Note the former is one order of magnitude higher than the latter. (Color figure online)

Table 1. A summary of the dataset.

Feature	Value
# Gestures	13
# Actors	10
# Clips	119
# Clips per class	7–11
Repetitions per class	5–10
Mean clip length	12.5 s
Total duration	24.76 mins
Min clip length	3.6 s
Max clip length	23.44 s
# Frames	37151
Frame rate	25 fps
Resolution	1920 × 1080
Camera motion	Yes, slight
Annotation	Bounding box, body joints

Table 2. Comparison with recently published video datasets.

Dataset	Scenario	Purpose	Environment	Frames	Classes	Resolution	Year
UT Interaction [26]	Surveillance	Action recognition	Outdoor	36k	6	360 × 240	2010
NATOPS [28]	Aircraft signaling	Gesture recognition	Indoor	N/A	24	320 × 240	2011
VIRAT [18]	Drone, surveillance	Event recognition	Outdoor	Many	23	Varying	2011
UCF101 [29]	YouTube	Action recognition	Varying	558k	24	320 × 240	2012
J-HMDB [14]	Movies, YouTube	Action recognition	Varying	32k	21	320 × 240	2013
Mini-drone [2]	Drone	Privacy protection	Outdoor	23.3	3	1920 × 1080	2015
Campus [22]	Surveillance	Object tracking	Outdoor	11.2k	1	1414 × 2019	2016
Okutama-Action [1]	Drone	Action recognition	Outdoor	70k	13	3840 × 2160	2017
UAV-GESTURE	Drone	Gesture recognition	Outdoor	37.2k	13	1920 × 1080	2018

4 Experimental Results

We performed an experiment on the dataset using Pose-based Convolutional Neural Network (P-CNN) descriptors [9]. A P-CNN descriptor aggregates motion and appearance information along tracks of human body parts (right hand, left hand, upper body and full body). The P-CNN descriptor was originally introduced for action recognition. Since our dataset contains gestures with full body poses, P-CNN is also a suitable method for full-body gesture recognition. In P-CNN, the body-part patches of the input image are extracted using the human pose and corresponding body parts. For body joint estimation, we used the state-of-the-art OpenPose [4] pose estimator which is an extension of Convolutional Pose Machines [34]. Similar to the original P-CNN implementation, the optical flow for each consecutive pair of images was computed using Brox et al.'s method [3].

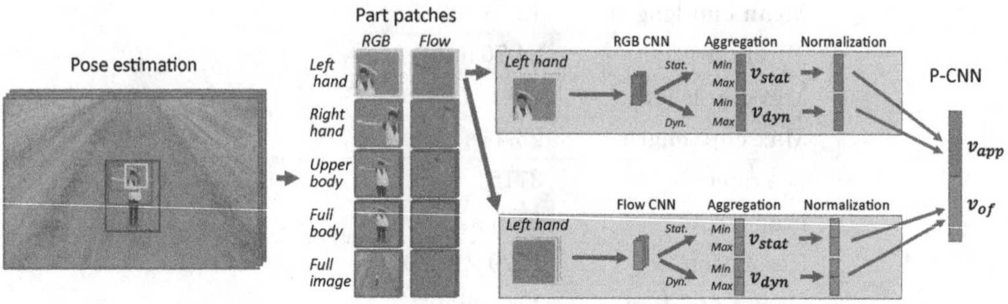

Fig. 4. The P-CNN feature descriptor [9]: the steps shown in the diagram correspond to an example P-CNN computation for body part *left hand*.

A diagram showing P-CNN feature extraction is given in Fig. 4. For each body part and full image, the appearance (RGB) and optical flow patches are extracted and their CNN features are computed using two pre-trained networks. For appearance patches, the publicly available "VGG-f" network [7] is used, whereas for optical flow patches, the motion network from Gkioxari and Malik's Action Tube implementation [12] is used. Static and dynamic features are separately aggregated over time to obtain a static video descriptor v_{stat} and a dynamic video descriptor v_{stat} respectively. The static features are the (i) distances between body joints, (ii) orientations of the vectors connecting pairs of joints, and (iii) inner angles spanned by vectors connecting all triplets of joints. The dynamic features are computed from trajectories of body joints. We select the *Min* and *Max* aggregation schemes, because of their high accuracies over other schemes when used with P-CNN [9] on the JHMDB dataset [14] for action recognition. The *Min* and *Max* aggregation schemes compute the minimum and maximum values respectively for each descriptor dimension over all video frames. The static and dynamic video descriptors can be defined as

$$v_{stat} = [m_1, \ldots, m_k, M_1, \ldots, M_k]^\top, \quad (1)$$

$$v_{dyn} = [\Delta m_1, \ldots, \Delta m_k, \Delta M_1, \ldots, \Delta M_k]^\top, \quad (2)$$

where, m and M correspond to the minimum and maximum values for each video descriptor dimension $1, \ldots, k$. Δ represents temporal differences in the video descriptors. The aggregated features (v_{stat} and v_{dyn}) are normalized and concatenated over the number of body parts to obtain appearance features v_{app}

and flow features v_{of}. The final P-CNN descriptor is obtained by concatenating v_{app} and v_{of}.

The evaluation metric selected for the experiment is accuracy. Accuracy is calculated using the scores returned by the action classifiers. There are three training and testing splits for UAV-GESTURE dataset. In Table 3, the mean accuracy is compared with the evaluation results reported in [9] for the JHMDB [14] and MPII Cooking [23] datasets. For the JHMDB and MPII Cooking datasets, the poses are estimated using the pose estimator described in [8]. However, we use OpenPose [4] for UAV-GESTURE, because OpenPose has been used as the body joint detector in notable pose-based action recognition studies [11,20,35], and has reportedly the best performance [4].

Table 3. The best reported P-CNN action recognition results for different datasets.

Dataset	Remarks	Accuracy (%)
JHMDB	Res: 320×240, pose estimation: [8]	74.2
MPII Cooking	Res: 1624×1224, pose estimation: [8]	62.3
UAV-GESTURE	Res: 1920×1080, pose estimation: OpenPose [4]	91.9

5 Conclusion

We presented a gesture dataset recorded by a hovering UAV. The dataset contains 119 HD videos lasting a total of 24.78 min. The dataset was prepared using 13 selected gestures from the set of general aircraft handling and helicopter handling signals. The gestures were recorded from 10 participants in an outdoor setting. The rich variation of body size, camera motion, and phase, makes our dataset challenging for gesture recognition. The dataset is annotated for human body joints and action classes to extend its applicability to a wider research community. We evaluated this new dataset using P-CNN descriptors and reported an overall baseline action recognition accuracy of 91.9%. This dataset is useful for research involving gesture-based unmanned aerial vehicle or unmanned ground vehicle control, situation awareness, general gesture recognition, and general action recognition. The UAV-GESTURE dataset is available at https://asankagp.github.io/uavgesture/.

Acknowledgement. This project was partly supported by Project Tyche, the Trusted Autonomy Initiative of the Defence Science and Technology Group (grant number myIP6780).

References

1. Barekatain, M., et al.: Okutama-action: an aerial view video dataset for concurrent human action detection. In: 2017 IEEE Conference on Computer Vision and Pattern Recognition Workshops (CVPRW), pp. 2153–2160, July 2017. https://doi.org/10.1109/CVPRW.2017.267
2. Bonetto, M., Korshunov, P., Ramponi, G., Ebrahimi, T.: Privacy in mini-drone based video surveillance. In: 2015 11th IEEE International Conference and Workshops on Automatic Face and Gesture Recognition (FG), vol. 04, pp. 1–6, May 2015. https://doi.org/10.1109/FG.2015.7285023
3. Brox, T., Bruhn, A., Papenberg, N., Weickert, J.: High accuracy optical flow estimation based on a theory for warping. In: Pajdla, T., Matas, J. (eds.) ECCV 2004. LNCS, vol. 3024, pp. 25–36. Springer, Heidelberg (2004). https://doi.org/10.1007/978-3-540-24673-2_3
4. Cao, Z., Simon, T., Wei, S.E., Sheikh, Y.: Realtime multi-person 2D pose estimation using part affinity fields. In: CVPR (2017)
5. Carol Neidle, A.T., Sclaroff, S.: 5th Workshop on the Representation and Processing of Sign Languages: Interactions Between Corpus and Lexicon, May 2012
6. Chaquet, J.M., Carmona, E.J., Fernández-Caballero, A.: A survey of video datasets for human action and activity recognition. Comput. Vis. Image Underst. **117**(6), 633–659 (2013). https://doi.org/10.1016/j.cviu.2013.01.013. http://www.sciencedirect.com/science/article/pii/S1077314213000295
7. Chatfield, K., Simonyan, K., Vedaldi, A., Zisserman, A.: Return of the devil in the details: delving deep into convolutional nets. CoRR abs/1405.3531 (2014). http://arxiv.org/abs/1405.3531
8. Cherian, A., Mairal, J., Alahari, K., Schmid, C.: Mixing body-part sequences for human pose estimation. In: The IEEE Conference on Computer Vision and Pattern Recognition (CVPR), June 2014
9. Cheron, G., Laptev, I., Schmid, C.: P-CNN: pose-based CNN features for action recognition. In: The IEEE International Conference on Computer Vision (ICCV), December 2015
10. Costante, G., Bellocchio, E., Valigi, P., Ricci, E.: Personalizing vision-based gestural interfaces for HRI with UAVs: a transfer learning approach. In: 2014 IEEE/RSJ International Conference on Intelligent Robots and Systems, pp. 3319–3326, September 2014. https://doi.org/10.1109/IROS.2014.6943024
11. Girdhar, R., Ramanan, D.: Attentional pooling for action recognition. In: Guyon, I., et al. (eds.) Advances in Neural Information Processing Systems, vol. 30, pp. 34–45. Curran Associates, Inc. (2017). http://papers.nips.cc/paper/6609-attentional-pooling-for-action-recognition.pdf
12. Gkioxari, G., Malik, J.: Finding action tubes. In: The IEEE Conference on Computer Vision and Pattern Recognition (CVPR), June 2015
13. Guyon, I., Athitsos, V., Jangyodsuk, P., Escalante, H.J.: The ChaLearn gesture dataset (CGD 2011). Mach. Vis. Appl. **25**(8), 1929–1951 (2014)
14. Jhuang, H., Gall, J., Zuffi, S., Schmid, C., Black, M.J.: Towards understanding action recognition. In: 2013 IEEE International Conference on Computer Vision, pp. 3192–3199, December 2013. https://doi.org/10.1109/ICCV.2013.396
15. Kang, S., Wildes, R.P.: Review of action recognition and detection methods. CoRR abs/1610.06906 (2016). http://arxiv.org/abs/org/1610.06906

16. Lee, J., Tan, H., Crandall, D., Šabanović, S.: Forecasting hand gestures for human-drone interaction. In: Companion of the 2018 ACM/IEEE International Conference on Human-Robot Interaction, HRI 2018, pp. 167–168. ACM, New York (2018). https://doi.org/10.1145/3173386.3176967
17. Lin, Z., Jiang, Z., Davis, L.S.: Recognizing actions by shape-motion prototype trees. In: 2009 IEEE 12th International Conference on Computer Vision, pp. 444–451, September 2009. https://doi.org/10.1109/ICCV.2009.5459184
18. Oh, S., et al.: A large-scale benchmark dataset for event recognition in surveillance video. In: CVPR 2011, pp. 3153–3160 (2011). https://doi.org/10.1109/CVPR.2011.5995586
19. Pfeil, K., Koh, S.L., LaViola, J.: Exploring 3D gesture metaphors for interaction with unmanned aerial vehicles. In: Proceedings of the 2013 International Conference on Intelligent User Interfaces, IUI 2013, pp. 257–266. ACM, New York (2013). https://doi.org/10.1145/2449396.2449429
20. Piergiovanni, A.J., Ryoo, M.S.: Fine-grained activity recognition in baseball videos. CoRR abs/1804.03247 (2018). http://arxiv.org/abs/1804.03247
21. Pisharady, P.K., Saerbeck, M.: Recent methods and databases in vision-based hand gesture recognition: a review. Comput. Vis. Image Underst. **141**, 152–165 (2015). https://doi.org/10.1016/j.cviu.2015.08.004. http://www.sciencedirect.com/science/article/pii/S1077314215001794
22. Robicquet, A., Sadeghian, A., Alahi, A., Savarese, S.: Learning social etiquette: human trajectory understanding in crowded scenes. In: Leibe, B., Matas, J., Sebe, N., Welling, M. (eds.) ECCV 2016. LNCS, vol. 9912, pp. 549–565. Springer, Cham (2016). https://doi.org/10.1007/978-3-319-46484-8_33
23. Rohrbach, M., Amin, S., Andriluka, M., Schiele, B.: A database for fine grained activity detection of cooking activities. In: 2012 IEEE Conference on Computer Vision and Pattern Recognition, pp. 1194–1201, June 2012. https://doi.org/10.1109/CVPR.2012.6247801
24. Ruffieux, S., Lalanne, D., Mugellini, E.: ChAirGest: a challenge for multimodal mid-air gesture recognition for close HCI. In: Proceedings of the 15th ACM on International Conference on Multimodal Interaction, ICMI 2013, pp. 483–488. ACM, New York (2013). https://doi.org/10.1145/2522848.2532590
25. Ruffieux, S., Lalanne, D., Mugellini, E., Abou Khaled, O.: A survey of datasets for human gesture recognition. In: Kurosu, M. (ed.) HCI 2014. LNCS, vol. 8511, pp. 337–348. Springer, Cham (2014). https://doi.org/10.1007/978-3-319-07230-2_33
26. Ryoo, M.S., Aggarwal, J.K.: Spatio-temporal relationship match: video structure comparison for recognition of complex human activities. In: 2009 IEEE 12th International Conference on Computer Vision, pp. 1593–1600, September 2009. https://doi.org/10.1109/ICCV.2009.5459361
27. Shahroudy, A., Liu, J., Ng, T.T., Wang, G.: NTU RGB+D: a large scale dataset for 3D human activity analysis. In: The IEEE Conference on Computer Vision and Pattern Recognition (CVPR), June 2016
28. Song, Y., Demirdjian, D., Davis, R.: Tracking body and hands for gesture recognition: NATOPS aircraft handling signals database. In: Face and Gesture 2011, pp. 500–506, March 2011. https://doi.org/10.1109/FG.2011.5771448
29. Soomro, K., Zamir, A.R., Shah, M.: UCF101: a dataset of 101 human actions classes from videos in the wild. Technical report. UCF Center for Research in Computer Vision (2012)
30. University of Central Florida: UCF aerial action dataset, November 2011. http://crcv.ucf.edu/data/UCF_Aerial_Action.php

31. University of Central Florida: UCF-ARG Data Set, November 2011. http://crcv.ucf.edu/data/UCF-ARG.php
32. U.S. Navy: Aircraft signals NATOPS manual, NAVAIR 00–80t-113 (1997). http://www.navybmr.com/study%20material/NAVAIR_113.pdf
33. Vondrick, C., Patterson, D., Ramanan, D.: Efficiently scaling up crowdsourced video annotation. Int. J. Comput. Vis. **101**(1), 184–204 (2013). https://doi.org/10.1007/s11263-012-0564-1
34. Wei, S.E., Ramakrishna, V., Kanade, T., Sheikh, Y.: Convolutional pose machines. In: The IEEE Conference on Computer Vision and Pattern Recognition (CVPR), June 2016
35. Yan, S., Xiong, Y., Lin, D.: Spatial temporal graph convolutional networks for skeleton-based action recognition. CoRR abs/1801.07455 (2018). http://arxiv.org/abs/1801.07455

ChangeNet: A Deep Learning Architecture for Visual Change Detection

Ashley Varghese, Jayavardhana Gubbi, Akshaya Ramaswamy(✉), and P. Balamuralidhar

Embedding Systems and Robotics, TCS Research and Innovation, Bengaluru, India
akshaya.ramaswamy@tcs.com

Abstract. The increasing urban population in cities necessitates the need for the development of smart cities that can offer better services to its citizens. Drone technology plays a crucial role in the smart city environment and is already involved in a number of functions in smart cities such as traffic control and construction monitoring. A major challenge in fast growing cities is the encroachment of public spaces. A robotic solution using visual change detection can be used for such purposes. For the detection of encroachment, a drone can monitor outdoor urban areas over a period of time to infer the visual changes. Visual change detection is a higher level inference task that aims at accurately identifying variations between a reference image (historical) and a new test image depicting the current scenario. In case of images, the challenges are complex considering the variations caused by environmental conditions that are actually unchanged events. Human mind interprets the change by comparing the current status with historical data at intelligence level rather than using only visual information. In this paper, we present a deep architecture called ChangeNet for detecting changes between pairs of images and express the same semantically (label the change). A parallel deep convolutional neural network (CNN) architecture for localizing and identifying the changes between image pair has been proposed in this paper. The architecture is evaluated with VL-CMU-CD street view change detection, TSUNAMI and Google Street View (GSV) datasets that resemble drone captured images. The performance of the model for different lighting and seasonal conditions are experimented quantitatively and qualitatively. The result shows that ChangeNet outperforms the state of the art by achieving 98.3% pixel accuracy, 77.35% object based Intersection over Union (IoU) and 88.9% area under Receiver Operating Characteristics (RoC) curve.

Keywords: Change detection · CNN

1 Introduction

Monitoring of public infrastructure in the context of smart cities to check for encroachments is an essential task. Encroachment can be described as anything

L. Leal-Taixé and S. Roth (Eds.): ECCV 2018 Workshops, LNCS 11130, pp. 129–145, 2019.
https://doi.org/10.1007/978-3-030-11012-3_10

placed in or on a public asset for e.g., a road, or a pavement that is essentially a Government property. Currently, manual methods are used where an officer visits and conducts a survey of area of interest. Manual investigation to assess the encroachment is a tedious task and the possibility of missing interesting events is high. This is a very time consuming process and affects the aesthetics of the city and results in loss to the exchequer in the form of fines.

Emerging micro unmanned aerial vehicles or commonly called drones can be employed for detecting such encroachments. According to a report from Tractica in 2017 [1], drones are expected to play a vital role in the smart city environment, providing support for a range of medical, transport and agriculture use cases. Drones have a tremendous amount of potential to provide a sustainable environment for the people who live in them. Thousands of drones are already being used to improve city life such as in documenting accident scenes and monitoring construction sites. As cameras are ubiquitous in drones, computer vision based autonomous monitoring using unmanned vehicles is picking up but is still immature. The challenges include navigation of drones autonomously, detecting the objects of interest and finally encroachment detection. The geo tagged images or videos have to be assessed for detection anomalies and their locations.

Scene understanding in real world scenario is a very challenging problem that has not reached the required maturity. However, detecting an encroachment can be viewed as a visual change detection problem. A historical image at the location and the current location of the drone can be used to find any deviation using visual processing. Identifying the deviation using images or videos is called visual change detection and is the focus of this paper.

Change detection in video analysis is often used as a stepping stone for high level scene understanding. In its conventional form, the methods are used for identifying changes in the background by comparing any two consecutive frames or limited to short term temporal analysis [2]. In remote sensing literature, change detection is referred to surface component alteration that is very useful in automatic land use analysis [3]. The fact that the satellite images are registered helps in pixel level change detection tasks that have been successfully extended to object level change analysis [3]. Some of the key challenges for visual change detection between any two images include variations in: lighting or illumination, contrast, quality, resolution, noise, scale, pose and occlusion. The first five attributes are experienced in any change detection scenario but the last three attributes are either not experienced in short term temporal analysis or it can be easily handled using frame dropping. Most of the methods in literature that models background pixels to detect change are in fact addressing the first five attributes. In the case of remote sensing, where change detection is widely used, change in scale, pose and occlusion are rarely seen and the above methods can be easily deployed with suitable pre-processing. Although these approaches are a part of decision making, it involves low level image analytics such as background foreground segmentation. In more complex inferencing using visual input, particularly in pattern recognition and category formation, higher level cognition is essential. For instance, when two images are being compared that have

Fig. 1. Illustrative images from CMU-CD dataset: reference image, test image and ground truth (in blue) (Color figure online)

variations in pose, illumination, color information and occlusion, the methods in literature often fail due to unregistered images, pose and scale variations as well as occlusions.

Figure 1 shows an example from the VL-CMU-CD change detection dataset [4], where higher level inferencing is required to detect the rubbish dumping on the pavement and the appearance changes are spread throughout the images. In this paper, a novel deep learning architecture is proposed for change detection that targets higher level inferencing. The new network architecture involves extracting features using ResNet [5] and combining filter outputs at different levels to localize the change. Finally, detected changes are identified using the same network, and output is an object level change detection with the label. The proposed architecture is compared with the state-of-the-art using three different modern change detection dataset: VL-CMU-CD [4], Tsunami [6] and GSV [6] datasets.

2 Related Work and Motivation

As described in the previous section, change refers to the higher level inferencing where the appearance has substantially changed between images. The change could either be insertion or deletion of an object from the scene, or some transformation of structure of the object or scene [7]. There are numerous industrial applications that can benefit from efficient visual change detection and as a result there is plenty of work in this area, especially in satellite image processing [3]. One of the simplest approach to change detection is frame or image differencing that involves traditional pixel level analysis. However, it works if and only if both the images are registered and the variation in image attributes are relatively minimal [3].

In 2012 and 2014, Goyette *et al.* [8] and Wang *et al.* [9] developed and expanded a change detection dataset and a workshop was conducted alongside CVPR 2014. Several papers have been published using this dataset. Although the dataset is used for lower level inference tasks, these methods are highly relevant and they are reported here with advantages and pitfalls. The eleven categories of videos used in this dataset and their corresponding results throws much needed light on higher level inferences that we are repeatedly discussing in this paper. Bilodeau *et al.* [10] used local binary similarity pattern for change detection. The method is quite simple and plays with spatial neighbourhood of every pixel. Noting this, the authors have used only two of the 11 categories - baseline and thermal - for detecting change highlighting the need for a more holistic approach. Sedky *et al.* [11] propose a physics based approach called Spectral 360. They use illumination, surface spectral reflectance and spectral similarity measure to build a decision function. They report a f-Score of 67.32% with low f-score of less than 50% for four of the eleven categories. Gregorio *et al.* [12] report an improved overall accuracy of 68.12% using a weightless neural network that helps in incorporating pixel history information in decision making (very similar to background subtraction using Gaussian mixture models). Again, their performance is limited as they fail to address some of the teething issues related to scale and pose. Wang *et al.* [13] proposed a flux tensor and split Gaussian model with a healthy f-score of 72.83%. Improving on all the above methods, a more comprehensive work has been reported by St-Charles *et al.* [2] who achieve 74.1% overall f-score using their SuBSENSE system. They propose spatio-temporal binary features to achieve the same. In line with achievements from other computer vision challenges, Bianco *et al.* [14] propose ensemble method for change detection achieving the best f-score of 78.21% by combining results of five other methods in literature. In every method discussed from basic binary features to ensemble methods, five categories out of eleven posed high challenge: PTZ, night videos, low frame rate, intermittent object motion and turbulence videos. Putting the results in perspective, small variations in illumination, contrast, quality, resolution and noise were captured by these methods quite well. Increased variations in addition to change in pose, scale and occlusion were not handled well by these methods and they are precisely the higher level inferences that are required for an object or scene level change detection method.

One interesting development in semantic change detection was reported by Gressin *et al.* [15] on satellite image processing. Although the work is on simulated data, for the first time, they have reported the perspective of change detection at different inference levels such as object, theme and database akin to our work. As far as we are aware, this is the first work alluding to different levels in change detection. In a similar work, Kataoka *et al.* [16] talks about semantic change detection by adding semantic meaning to changed area. First, they find changed area using hyper maps, and then add semantic meaning to that changed area. Since last few years, after deep learning has become the main approach in computer vision, there have been some efforts in creation of the dataset as well as in building change detection procedures. Sakurata and Okatani [6] was the first such attempt and they built two data sets with 100 image pairs known as TSUNAMI dataset and Google Street View (GSV) dataset. These are panoramic images created using street view separated temporally by several days or months. In addition to the creation of a dataset, they proposed a complex super pixel based approach that uses convolutional neural network (CNN) for feature extraction. The low resolution feature map generated from CNN network is combined with super pixel segmentation to get precise segmentation boundaries of the changes. Although deep learning is used in the pipeline, there are many other hyper parameters in the procedure that needs fine tuning for different scenarios.

Going one step further, Alkantarilla *et al.* [4] propose a network called CDnet for finding structural changes in street view video. They create a new dataset of 152 categories with 11 unique object classes called VL-CMU-CD dataset. In order to create nearly registered images, they use visual simultaneous localization and mapping (SLAM) to get the 3D point cloud and then project the points onto a 2D reference plane after determining the reference pose. It is a pixel level change detection approach and uses contraction and expansion layers for pixel level classification. The contraction block creates data representation. In this process it stores max pooling output for later use in the expansion network. The expansion block has been used for improving change localization. The proposed ChangeNet architecture is different from CDnet approach. Our network determine category of change in addition to change localization. We use parallel weight tied networks for feature extraction. It ensures both the network learn same features from the two images. Therefore, the features from both the images can be compared easily. In addition to this, we combine output from different levels of convolution layers so that the model captures the sparse and finer details of the object. Bilinear interpolation is used in ChangeNet for upsampling the data and the filter parameters are learned in network itself. Another feature of ChangeNet is that it combines predictions from different levels of convolution layer. Such approach helps the model to capture both coarse and fine details of the object. Apart from deep learning approaches, a multi-scale super pixel approach for drone image analysis has been proposed by Gubbi *et al.* [17] with limited success on VL-CMU-CD dataset. The focus of this paper is to implement the change detection system on a computationally challenging environment.

In the recent past, there has been quite a good amount of success in pixel level image analysis using deep architecture. Bansal *et al.* [18] proposed a new architecture for predicting surface normal that is useful in 2D-3D alignment. They use pre-trained VGG-16 network for feature extraction followed by three layers of fully connected layers for predicting surface normal for every pixel. Bansal *et al.* [19] generalized their earlier work and created PixelNet architecture and demonstrated semantic segmentation and edge detection in addition to surface normal estimation using an extended VGG-16 network. Such work has demonstrated that CNN is able to learn pixel level information in addition to their success in image categorisation. Similar work have been extended for regions of interest where they propose a new network for simultaneously predicting human eye fixations and segmenting salient objects. In addition to single image pixel analysis, there has been some recent work in finding similarity between two images or signal pairs. Du *et al.* [20] proposes a Siamese CNN network for checking whether two hand written texts are written by the same person or not. Both the inputs are encoded with the same network and then concatenated output is fed to a two class classifier to determine whether handwriting is same or not.

With the developments in change detection and pixel level analysis using deep learning, we are motivated to solve the hard problem of change detection using a deep network. VL-CMU-CD dataset is our target as the scene pairs are complex and taken at different view angle, illumination and seasons as well. It has 11 different class of structural changes like construction-maintenance, bin on pavement, new sign boards, traffic cone on road, vehicles, etc., including background. To the best of our knowledge, it is a novel architecture for visual change detection particularly resulting in scene labels that can be viewed as semantic change detection. We further train the network to determine the category of change in addition to the changed area. Both the tasks happen within the network and involves single training. Most of the background information are irrelevant in our case since those changes could be due to season, illumination or view point variation. It mainly looks for changes at object level as compared to Alkantarilla *et al.* [4]. The model inputs are test and reference images. Output is detection, localization and categorization of changed region. It mainly answers the following three questions in the presence of seven variations, which have been discussed earlier: is there any change? if yes, what is the change? and where is the change in the image? Section 3 gives details about our architecture and experimental details are provided in Sect. 4. Result and discussion are presented in Sect. 5.

3 ChangeNet Architecture

We propose a deep learning architecture for detecting changes between image pairs. We adapt ideas from siamese network [21,22] and fully convolutional network (FCN) [23] to map features from image pair to visual change. Convolutional neural networks are known for its performance in object detection. Especially, networks like GoogLeNet [24], Alexnet [25], VGGNet [26], and ResNet [5] are powerful deep trained models for feature representation. The learned representation can be transferred to another domain instead of training it from scratch. Transfer learning approach is followed here for feature extraction. In this architecture, two inputs are required: a test I_{test} and a reference image I_{ref}. Both are having same dimension of $w \times h \times d$ where w and h are spatial dimension and d is the number of channels. The change detection problem can be formulated as: find a way to compare features from I_{test} and I_{ref} to assign a change class label from label set of $l = 1, 2, \ldots N$ to each element of change map $I_{w \times h}$. N is the number of defined semantic change class and it ensures environmental changes are neglected during change detection.

The detailed architecture diagram for visual change detection is shown in Fig. 2. There are two weight tied convolutional neural networks *CNN1* and *CNN2* for extracting features from I_{test} and I_{ref} respectively. In change detection, model learns representation from image pair; and then it tries to find relationship between them. However, task and input type of both the sub-networks are the same. Therefore similar type of features are expected from both the images. This can be achieved with a siamese network [22]. Siamese network is a weight

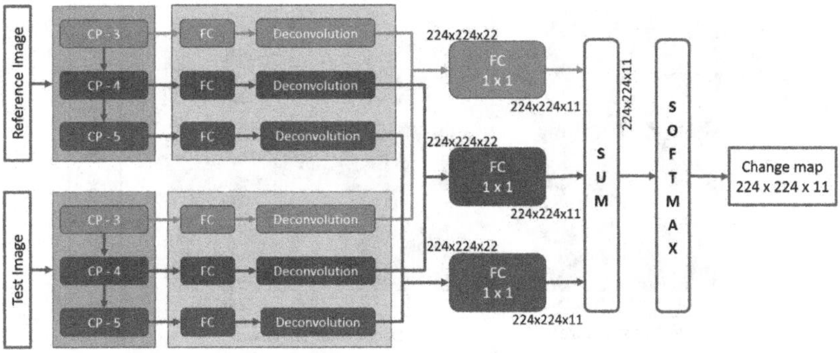

Fig. 2. Architecture for the proposed visual change detection. CP represents ResNet residual block and FC represents fully convolutional layer with kernel size of 1 × 1

tied network having same number of parameters and weight values. In addition, this approach optimizes the memory and training time without compromising on the performance. One key difference between a standard siamese and our network is that the weights are not tied in deconvolution layer. This resulted in significantly better performance of up to 5%. The reason could be due to the nature of siamese network where the convolution stage and the deconvolution stage have the weights tied that will force the network to work in constrained space. In our network, the convolution stage will be weight tied but during deconvolution stage they work independently.

Since our training data are natural images and the number of training images are limited, transfer learning performs better than creating a new model from scratch. A Residual network (ResNet)-50 is used as pre-trained model [5]. ResNet uses residual blocks so that it can handle very deep architectures. ResNet block mainly consists of convolution layer, batch normalization and a rectified linear unit as shown in Fig. 3 that contributes to feature extraction. The features from *CNN1* can be represented as $f1 = g(I_{test})$ and *CNN2* as $f2 = g(I_{ref})$. The output of three layers $f_{l^1}, f_{l^2}, f_{l^3}$ are tapped from the feature block in order to capture changes at different scales. l^1 is the CNN layer before fully connected layer and l^2 and l^3 are the residual blocks before l^1.

Generally ResNet learns representation, and generates score for object classification. In this process, it uses max pooling layers and fully connected layers. However, it causes loss of spatial information. In semantic change detection, prediction should happen at input image spatial dimension in order to localize the changed area. Therefore, a mechanism is required to map learned representation onto input image dimension. Similar issue is already tackled in semantic segmentation. We adapted a similar approach to restore back the learned representation onto test image. There are different semantic segmentation approaches in literature like FCN [23], U-Net [27], PSPNet [28], SegNet [29], etc. Semantic segmentation uses both global and local information for encoding both semantics

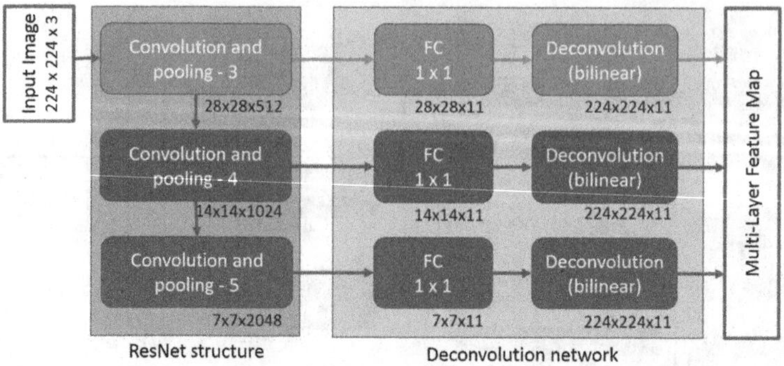

Fig. 3. Architecture for feature extraction.

and location. As per [23], global information resolves semantic and local information resolves location.

A deconvolution layer is used to upsample output to image spatial dimension. It maps features f in high dimensional space to change map of $I_{w \times h \times N}$. Upsampling is done with bilinear interpolation filter. Bilinear filter interpolation predicts values from nearest four inputs. The filter parameters for upsampling is learned in the network itself. In order to incorporate both coarse and finer details, the convolution layer output from previous layer is also upsampled to input spatial dimension. Subsequently, upsampled output from both the parallel network are concatenated for comparison. Again, same layers from both the networks are concatenated. The filter outputs $f1_{l^1}$ and $f2_{l^1}$ from layer l^1 of parallel network are concatenated. The same way, filter outputs $f1_{l^2}$ and $f2_{l^2}$ from layer l^2; filter outputs $f1_{l^3}$ and $f2_{l^3}$ from layer l^3 are concatenated. This ensures that we compare the representation at same degree and scale. Finally, all the concatenated outputs are added up together and shared to a *softmax* classifier to classify to one of the N classes. A convolutional layer with kernel size of 1×1 is used before softmax layer for reducing dimensionality to N classes. The changed area will be highlighted with class label of structural change. The network details are as follows: Fully convolution and up-sampling are performed on ResNet 7×7, 14×14, 28×28 convolution layers; and changed the dimension to $224 \times 224 \times 11$, where 224×224 is the input image dimension and 11 is the number of classes. Then, concatenation of subsequent layers and fully convolutional network resulted in three $224 \times 224 \times 11$ dimension. The three outputs are summed together (tensor addition) and given to a *softmax* classifier. It predicts a class for each pixels and generates a prediction of dimension $224 \times 224 \times 11$.

4 Experiments

For our experiments, three different datasets are used. The VL-CMU-CD dataset [4] is one of the most complex datasets available for change detection.

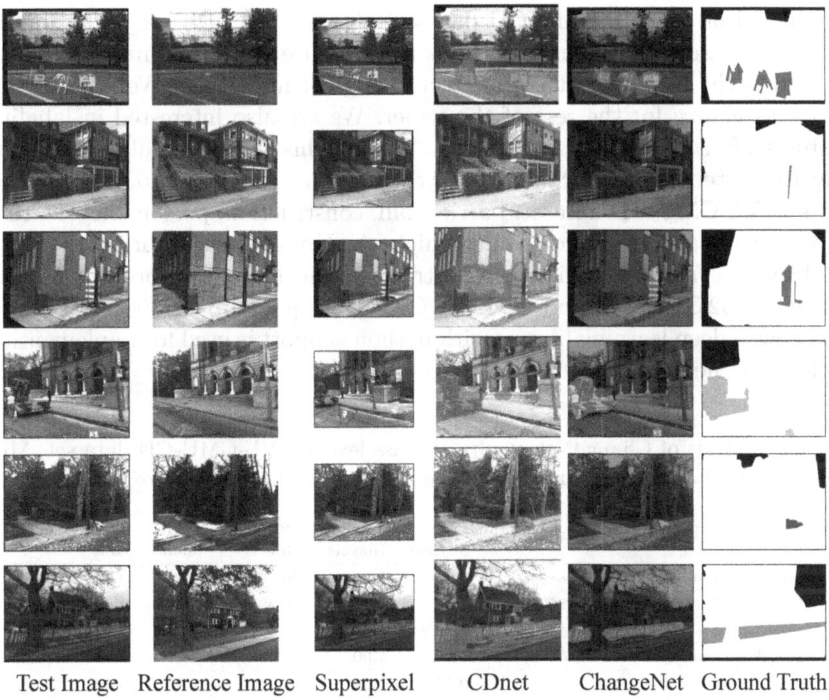

Fig. 4. Qualitative performance of change detection versus other approaches. Our approach gives change area as well as class label of structural change in the scene. Different classes are overlaid with different colors. Here green color represent vehicle class, purple for sign board, navy blue for rubbish bin and orange color for construction maintenance. Our approach can detect and localize changes in the scene at semantic level. Multiple colors in ChangeNet and ground truth images indicate separate class labels. (Color figure online)

It has 152 different scene changes. Each category has 2 to 41 pairs of test and reference images. Image pairs are taken at different view angle, seasonal and lighting condition as shown in Fig. 1. Out of 152 categories, we have chosen 103 categories, which are having more than 5 image pairs. This will ensure that we have enough samples from each category for training and testing. This results in a total of 1187 image pairs over 103 categories. The other two datasets - TSUNAMI and GSV - were developed by Sakurata and Okatani [6] and contains 100 pairs of images each. The definition of change in these two datasets are different compared with VL-CMU-CD. All the changes including variations in the background are considered as change. Each of the three datasets is divided it into train, validation and test in the ratio of 7:1.5:1.5. We evaluate our network on the test data by computing standard performance evaluation metrics such as precision, recall, *f*-score, ROC curve, Area under ROC (AUC) and Intersection over Union (IoU) measure [4,6]. In addition to this, a five fold cross-validation is conducted on the VL-CMU-CD dataset to assess the network performance. The three datasets and related methods in literature focus on binary classification, that is the final output is to detect change or no-change. We refer to this scenario as *binary* for the rest of the paper. We are also interested in labeling the object after the change is detected. We call this scenario multi-class. Currently, the system is built for *multi-class* classification of 10 commonly appearing objects in VL-CMU-CD dataset: barrier, bin, construction, person/bicycle, rubbish bin, sign board, traffic cone, and vehicle. An Ubuntu based workstation with the following configuration is used for training and testing purpose: Intel core i7 @3.4Gx8, 32 GB RAM and NVIDIA GM204GL [Quadro M4000] GPU card. Tensorflow, a deep learning library with python support is used for implementing deep learning network.

Table 1. Analysis of ChangeNet results at class level on VL-CMU-CD data set. Miscellaneous class has been excluded from the table as all the values were 0.

Classification	Metric	Barrier	Bin	Construction	Other objects	Person/ Bicycle	Rubbish bin	Sign board	Traffic-cone	Vehicle
Pixel based	Precision	0.55	0.80	0.88	0.92	0.83	0.87	0.77	0.53	0.91
	Recall	0.63	0.71	0.80	0.84	0.74	0.82	0.61	0.42	0.83
	f-score	0.59	0.76	0.84	0.88	0.79	0.84	0.68	0.47	0.87
Object based	Precision	0.50	0.97	0.86	1.00	1.00	0.96	1.00	1.00	1.00
	Recall	0.87	1.00	1.00	0.87	1.00	1.00	0.75	0.50	0.91
	f-score	0.63	0.98	0.92	0.93	1.00	0.97	0.85	0.66	0.95

5 Results and Discussions

The ChangeNet architecture was specifically designed keeping VL-CMU-CD dataset in mind due to its complexity. In order to validate the architecture, a 5 fold cross validation was conducted. The results are as shown in Table 2 and a healthy average *f*-score of 86.9% was obtained for binary classification and 73.87% for multi-class classification. Figure 5 shows the boxplot of cross validation performance for binary classification scenario. As it can be seen, the variation across different folds in marginal reflecting good generalization of the proposed architecture.

Table 2. Average results of 5-fold cross validation for binary and multi-class scenarios

	Accuracy	Precision	Recall	*f*-score
Binary	98.3	87.98	85.85	86.90
Multi-class	82.58	77.14	71.43	73.87

To further confirm its performance, multi-scale super pixel [17] and CDnet [4] were compared to the proposed architecture. In order to make a fair comparison,

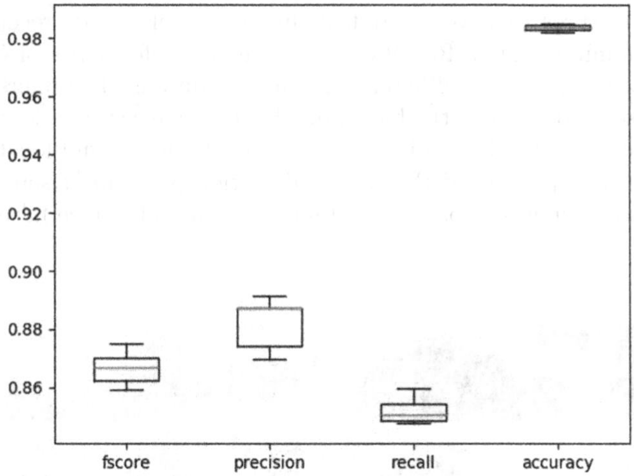

Fig. 5. Boxplot of ChangeNet performance in 5-fold cross validation for binary classification

the results of binary classification (change or no change) of all the methods are compared by converting our class based output into binary form. The predicted change map of baseline approaches and our method are shown in Fig. 4. Each sample exhibits different lighting and seasonal condition. The first column is the test image, which is compared against reference image in the second column. The third and the fourth columns are the change detection results of multi-scale super pixel method and CDnet. The changed area is highlighted with red color. CDnet result images are taken from [4] for comparison purpose. The results of ChangeNet is shown in the fifth column. The changed area is highlighted with corresponding class label. The ground truth is given in the last column. It should be noted that different colored labels for ChangeNet and Ground truth indicate multi-class classification that is unique to our work. ChangeNet achieves this in a single shot and a single network is able to detect change and label them. As shown in Fig. 4, ChangeNet performs better than other approaches both in terms of the output as well as in terms of change class labelling. It gives a better performance in terms of accuracy and precision. Compared to other approaches, it gives additional information like what is the structural changes in the scene. In other words, our approach is able to tell *where* is the change in the scene as well as *what* the change is. ChangeNet performs well even though the background between image pair is different due to seasonal alterations and lighting conditions. For example, image pair in row 2 are taken at different lighting condition and ChangeNet was able to detect the changed area. An example of multiple changes in the same scene is depicted in row 4 where vehicle and a sign board are depicted as change. ChangeNet is able to identify both of them accurately. However, small objects such as sign board are mis-classified as background. One of the reasons is that the sign board object is less dominant in test image. This is due to the features that we tap out at different levels whose receptive fields cover certain minimum area. Results in row 5 shows performance of ChangeNet when images are captured at different seasonal conditions. The reference image shows the presence of snow in the background. The same case applies to row 6 as well. Model performed well in this case, and it could detect and locate the rubbish bin. Since we approached the change detection problem at semantic level, we could mitigate irrelevant background information and reduce false alarms, if any.

Fig. 6. Qualitative performance of ChangeNet on Tsunami and GSV dataset. From top to bottom: reference image, test image, ground truth mask and ChangeNet

Quantitative performance of our method is evaluated in two aspects. First aspect is how accurately it localized the change. Once it localized the change, what is the pixel labeling accuracy. Mainly, Intersection over Union (IoU) and pixel accuracy metrics are used for evaluating the performance. We considered 11 classes including background for this performance measurement. Model is evaluated with 177 image pairs and the results are generated. The performance metric for ChangeNet is given in Table 3. We achieved 98.3% pixel level accuracy and 82.58% mean pixel accuracy. In other words, 98.3% pixels are classified as change correctly. In that, 82.58% pixels are classified correctly per class basis. Also, we achieved 77.35% IoU. It compares the ground truth and predicted changed area on a per class basis. IoU is changed to 96.96% once we assigned the weights to class IoU based on their appearance frequency. Table 1 shows the results of ChangeNet in identification of class based change. Other than barrier and traffic cone, all other classes resulted in a f-score of over 0.8 for object level change detection. At pixel level, small objects including traffic cone, barrier and sign board resulted in lower f-scores. Table 4 shows quantitative comparison of ChangeNet with CDnet [4] and Super-pixel [17] methods for two different false positive rates of 0.1 and 0.01. As it can be seen, ChangeNet outperforms both the methods with impressive *f*-scores. Figure 7 shows the Receiver Operator Characteristic (ROC) curve for binary classification of ChangeNet, CDnet [4] and super-pixel [17] based methods. All the classes except background is considered as logical one. ChangeNet resulted in steep ROC curve with maximum true positive rate and minimum false positive rate. The area under ROC curve, *i.e.*, AUC is 89.2%.

Table 3. Performance metrics for ChangeNet

Pixel accuracy	Mean pixel accuracy	Mean IoU	Frequency weighted IoU
98.3	82.58	77.35	96.96

Table 4. The quantitative comparison of our method with other approaches for FPR = 0.1 and FPR = 0.01. *Pr*-Precision, *Re*-Recall and *F1*-*f*-score

	FPR = 0.1			FPR = 0.01		
	Pr	*Re*	*F1*	*Pr*	*Re*	*F1*
Super-pixel [17]	0.17	0.35	0.23	0.23	0.12	0.15
CDnet [4]	0.40	0.85	0.55	0.79	0.46	0.58
ChangeNet	0.79	0.80	0.79	0.80	0.79	0.79

Detailed results of ChangeNet on the three datasets tested is presented in Table 5. For TSUNAMI and GSV datasets, the performance measures are calculated in the region of interest as well as for the whole image (within parenthesis). As it can be seen, the results on VL-CMU-CD dataset are very high with nearly good performance on TSUNAMI dataset. There is a drop in GSV performance. The drop in performance on GSV dataset is attributed to the way the ground truth is created in these datasets. ChangeNet focuses on structural changes but GSV ground truth represents cars on the road as change. Hence, the overall performance seems to dip. The results of ChangeNet on TSUNAMI and GSV dataset are shown in Fig. 6. It can be clearly seen that we have been able to detect dominant objects such as houses and trees as changes but movement of cars and small signboards are not detected.

Finally, the performance of the three different methods on three different datasets are presented in Table 6. It should be noted that the definition of change detection is evolving. The new datasets and methods that can detect change at higher levels of inference is becoming possible. This paper is one of the early works in the direction and hence there are very few methods in literature that can be compared, which is presented in Table 6. For VL-CMU-CD dataset, ChangeNet results in the best performance. For TSUNAMI dataset, CDnet gives the best result but ChangeNet is not too far behind. However,

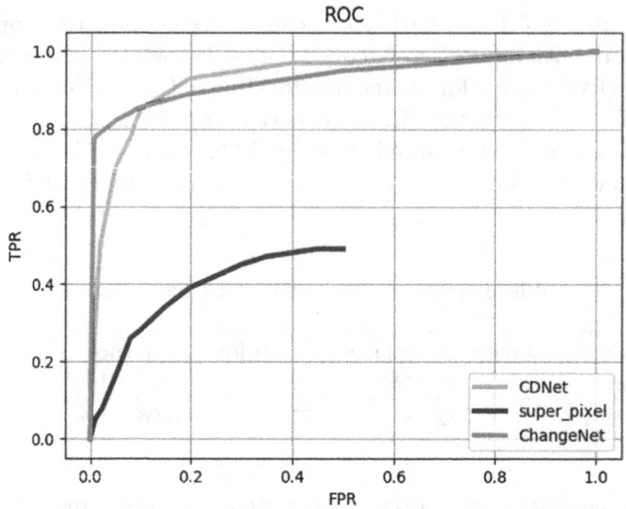

Fig. 7. ROC and FPR-TPR curve for binary class

Table 5. Performance metrics of ChangeNet for binary classification (change or no-change) on different datasets. The values for TSUNAMI and GSV datasets are in the following format: calculated in the region of interest (calculated on whole image)

Metric	Dataset		
	CMU-CD	Tsunami	GSV
Precision	0.88	0.73 (0.82)	0.51 (0.67)
Recall	0.80	0.74 (0.82)	0.45 (0.66)
f-score	0.84	0.74 (0.82)	0.48 (0.67)
Accuracy	0.97	0.85 (0.85)	0.77 (0.77)
IoU	0.64	0.55 (0.69)	0.27 (0.5)
Area overlap	0.89	0.71 (0.71)	0.44 (0.44)
AuC	0.89	0.82 (0.82)	0.66 (0.66)

for GSV dataset, CDnet outperforms other methods. The lack of robustness in detecting small changes is found to be the main drawback of ChangeNet. In the future, we plan to extend the network for detecting small object change detection in the presence of occlusion.

ChangeNet does not depend on the objects trained in the network for change detection. Change is first detected and then object label (semantic information) is inferred using a single network. Figure 8 shows the reference image, test image and change detected image (from left to right). The bin in both the picture is in the object classes but it is not detected as change as it is present in both the images. However, bicycle is highlighted as the systems detects change in that region and labels the class correctly.

Table 6. Comparison of f-score values of ChangeNet with other methods on different datasets. For ChangeNet, two separate f-scores are calculated based on false positive rates

Dataset	Method			
	Super-pixel	CDnet	ChangeNet	
			(0.1)	(0.01)
TSUNAMI	0.38	0.77	0.73	0.47
GSV	0.26	0.61	0.45	0.20
VL-CMU-CD	0.15	0.58	0.80	0.83

Fig. 8. ChangeNet performance demonstration: reference (left), test (middle) and change detected (right). The result in the figure demonstrates that ChangeNet is focussed on change rather than the object category. In spite of both bin and bicycle being present in our category labels, only bicycle is highlighted as a change, which is along expected lines.

6 Conclusion

A deep learning architecture called ChangeNet is proposed for detecting structural changes between an drone captured image pair. The new architecture is comprised of two parallel weight tied networks that act as image feature extractors for detecting change. Features at different layers are merged and a fully convolutional network is used to detect change. ChangeNet is experimented and evaluated with VL-CMU-CD dataset, which is very challenging. ChangeNet detects and localize the changes of the same scene captured at different lighting, view angle and seasonal condition. Further, for the first time, a network that can detect and report change in semantics (scene labels) is demonstrated. 98.3% pixel accuracy, 77.35% class based IoU and 88.9% AUC was achieved.

References

1. Sahi, K.M., Wheelock, C.: Drones for commercial applications. Tractica Research Report (2017)
2. St-Charles, P.L., Bilodeau, G.A., Bergevin, R.: SuBSENSE: a universal change detection method with local adaptive sensitivity. IEEE Trans. Image Process. **24**(1), 359–373 (2015)

3. Hussain, M., Chen, D., Cheng, A., Wei, H., Stanley, D.: Change detection from remotely sensed images: from pixel-based to object-based approaches. ISPRS J. Photogram. Remote Sens. **80**, 91–106 (2013)
4. Alcantarilla, P.F., Stent, S., Ros, G., Arroyo, R., Gherardi, R.: Street-view change detection with deconvolutional networks. Auton. Robots **42**, 1301–1322 (2016). Robotics: Science and Systems
5. He, K., Zhang, X., Ren, S., Sun, J.: Deep residual learning for image recognition. In: Proceedings of the IEEE Conference on Computer Vision and Pattern Recognition, pp. 770–778 (2016)
6. Sakurada, K., Okatani, T.: Change detection from a street image pair using CNN features and superpixel segmentation. In: BMVC, p. 61-1 (2015)
7. Rensink, R.A.: Change detection. Annu. Rev. Psychol. **53**(1), 245–277 (2002)
8. Goyette, N., Jodoin, P.M., Porikli, F., Konrad, J., Ishwar, P.: Changedetection.net: a new change detection benchmark dataset. In: 2012 IEEE Computer Society Conference on Computer Vision and Pattern Recognition Workshops, pp. 1–8, June 2012
9. Wang, Y., Jodoin, P.M., Porikli, F., Konrad, J., Benezeth, Y., Ishwar, P.: CDnet 2014: an expanded change detection benchmark dataset. In: 2014 IEEE Conference on Computer Vision and Pattern Recognition Workshops, pp. 393–400, June 2014
10. Bilodeau, G.A., Jodoin, J.P., Saunier, N.: Change detection in feature space using local binary similarity patterns. In: 2013 International Conference on Computer and Robot Vision, CRV, pp. 106–112. IEEE (2013)
11. Sedky, M., Moniri, M., Chibelushi, C.C.: Spectral-360: a physics-based technique for change detection. In: The IEEE Conference on Computer Vision and Pattern Recognition (CVPR) Workshops, June 2014
12. De Gregorio, M., Giordano, M.: Change detection with weightless neural networks. In: The IEEE Conference on Computer Vision and Pattern Recognition (CVPR) Workshops, June 2014
13. Wang, R., Bunyak, F., Seetharaman, G., Palaniappan, K.: Static and moving object detection using flux tensor with split Gaussian models. In: 2014 IEEE Conference on Computer Vision and Pattern Recognition Workshops, pp. 420–424 (2014)
14. Bianco, S., Ciocca, G., Schettini, R.: How far can you get by combining change detection algorithms? CoRR abs/1505.02921 (2015)
15. Gressin, A., Vincent, N., Mallet, C., Paparoditis, N.: Semantic approach in image change detection. In: Blanc-Talon, J., Kasinski, A., Philips, W., Popescu, D., Scheunders, P. (eds.) ACIVS 2013. LNCS, vol. 8192, pp. 450–459. Springer, Cham (2013). https://doi.org/10.1007/978-3-319-02895-8_40
16. Kataoka, H., Shirakabe, S., Miyashita, Y., Nakamura, A., Iwata, K., Satoh, Y.: Semantic change detection with hypermaps. arXiv preprint arXiv:1604.07513 (2016)
17. Gubbi, J., Ramaswamy, A., Sandeep, N.K., Varghese, A., Balamuralidhar, P.: Visual change detection using multiscale super pixel. In: Digital Image Computing: Techniques and Applications (2017)
18. Bansal, A., Russell, B.C., Gupta, A.: Marr revisited: 2D-3D alignment via surface normal prediction. In: 2016 IEEE Conference on Computer Vision and Pattern Recognition, CVPR 2016, Las Vegas, NV, USA, 27–30 June 2016, pp. 5965–5974 (2016)
19. Bansal, A., Chen, X., Russell, B.C., Gupta, A., Ramanan, D.: PixelNet: representation of the pixels, by the pixels, and for the pixels. CoRR abs/1702.06506 (2017)

20. Du, W., Fang, M., Shen, M.: Siamese convolutional neural networks for authorship verification
21. Mueller, J., Thyagarajan, A.: Siamese recurrent architectures for learning sentence similarity. In: AAAI, pp. 2786–2792 (2016)
22. Koch, G.: Siamese neural networks for one-shot image recognition. Master's thesis. University of Toronto, Canada (2015)
23. Long, J., Shelhamer, E., Darrell, T.: Fully convolutional networks for semantic segmentation. In: Proceedings of the IEEE Conference on Computer Vision and Pattern Recognition, pp. 3431–3440 (2015)
24. Szegedy, C., et al.: Going deeper with convolutions. In: Proceedings of the IEEE Conference on Computer Vision and Pattern Recognition, pp. 1–9 (2015)
25. Krizhevsky, A., Sutskever, I., Hinton, G.E.: ImageNet classification with deep convolutional neural networks. In: Advances in Neural Information Processing Systems, pp. 1097–1105 (2012)
26. Simonyan, K., Zisserman, A.: Very deep convolutional networks for large-scale image recognition. arXiv preprint arXiv:1409.1556 (2014)
27. Ronneberger, O., Fischer, P., Brox, T.: U-Net: convolutional networks for biomedical image segmentation. In: Navab, N., Hornegger, J., Wells, W.M., Frangi, A.F. (eds.) MICCAI 2015. LNCS, vol. 9351, pp. 234–241. Springer, Cham (2015). https://doi.org/10.1007/978-3-319-24574-4_28
28. Zhao, H., Shi, J., Qi, X., Wang, X., Jia, J.: Pyramid scene parsing network. arXiv preprint arXiv:1612.01105 (2016)
29. Badrinarayanan, V., Kendall, A., Cipolla, R.: SegNet: a deep convolutional encoder-decoder architecture for image segmentation. arXiv preprint arXiv:1511.00561 (2015)

W08 – 5th Transferring and Adapting Source Knowledge in Computer Vision and 2nd VisDA Challenge

W08 – 5th Transferring and Adapting Source Knowledge in Computer Vision and 2nd VisDA Challenge

The aim of TASK-CV workshop was bringing together computer vision researchers working in the areas of domain adaptation, knowledge transfer and in all the other aspects of life-long learning (e.g. incremental, zero-shot, active, open-set learning, etc.) and their applications (e.g. biomedical, robotics, multimedia, autonomous driving, etc.). This was the 5th edition of the workshop and the audience participation demonstrated that it still attracts a wide attention: the discussed topics are relevant for the community as also indicated by the presence of more than 40 ECCV papers with the words *Adapt or Transfer* in the title. The organizing committee chose the invited speakers with the goal of offering an overview on the most recent results as well as technical and theoretical insights on the topics of the workshop. We were proud to have four guests. Prof. Nicolas Courty explained how the optimal transport theory can be applied effectively for deep domain adaptation. The talk of Prof. Samory Kpotufe focused on knowledge transfer metrics and presented a new relative measure able to quantitatively evaluate the continuum from easy to hard transfer tasks. Prof. Mingsheng Long presented his works on deep domain adaptation that take into consideration multiple and conditional domain adversaries, and discussed also novel scenarios such as partial and open set domain adaptation. Finally, Ming-Yu Liu presented his research work at Nvidia discussing in particular a multimodal image translation approach able to decompose the images in their content and style parts to then produce new images with a controlled visual domain. The workshop got 9 paper submissions, out of which the program committee accepted 6 papers. All the manuscripts were evaluated by at least two reviewers and the two papers with the highest acceptance score were presented as short orals. According to an internal voting, the work by Shkodrani et al. received the best paper award while the work by Mancini et al. received the honorable mention award, respectively supported by our sponsors Naver Labs Europe and Amazon. The remaining 4 papers were presented as posters together with 6 further papers invited from the main conference. Half of the workshop was also dedicated to the *Visual Domain Adaptation* (VisDA) challenge, currently at its 2nd edition. This year the international competition focused on synthetic-to-real visual domain shifts and included two tracks on object detection and open-set image classification. The research groups that produced the top three results of the challenge were invited to present their work with a short talk and to participate to the poster session.

September 2018

Tatiana Tommasi
David Vázquez
Kate Saenko
Ben Usman
Xingchao Peng
Judy Hoffman
Neela Kaushik
Antonio M. López
Wen Li
Francesco Orabona

DeeSIL: Deep-Shallow Incremental Learning

Eden Belouadah and Adrian Popescu(✉)

CEA, LIST, Vision and Content Engineering Lab, 91191 Gif-sur-Yvette, France
{eden.belouadah,adrian.popescu}@cea.fr

Abstract. Incremental Learning (IL) is an interesting AI problem when the algorithm is assumed to work on a budget. This is especially true when IL is modeled using a deep learning approach, where two complex challenges arise due to limited memory, which induces catastrophic forgetting and delays related to the retraining needed in order to incorporate new classes. Here we introduce *DeeSIL*, an adaptation of a known transfer learning scheme that combines a fixed deep representation used as feature extractor and learning independent shallow classifiers to increase recognition capacity. This scheme tackles the two aforementioned challenges since it works well with a limited memory budget and each new concept can be added within a minute. Moreover, since no deep retraining is needed when the model is incremented, *DeeSIL* can integrate larger amounts of initial data that provide more transferable features. Performance is evaluated on ImageNet LSVRC 2012 against three state of the art algorithms. Results show that, at scale, *DeeSIL* performance is 23 and 33 points higher than the best baseline when using the same and more initial data respectively.

Keywords: Incremental learning · SVM · ImageNet

1 Introduction and Background

Typical deep learning pipelines are well adapted to solve tasks when all training data is available at all times and there are loose constraints regarding time available for training. Under these conditions, augmenting the classification ability can simply be done by learning a new representation, either from scratch or via Fine Tuning (FT). However, when one or both of the above conditions are violated, adding new classes becomes non-trivial. The authors of iCaRL [11] rightfully note that there exists no satisfactory algorithm that can qualify as class-incremental. They frame three necessary properties of it: (i) be trainable from new stream data that occurs arbitrarily; (ii) provide competitive performance for past classes when new ones are integrated and (iii) computational requirements and memory footprint should remain bounded.

In iCaRL, recognition capacity is incremented by retraining for every new batch of classes. A fixed-size memory is used to store positive examples which

L. Leal-Taixé and S. Roth (Eds.): ECCV 2018 Workshops, LNCS 11130, pp. 151–157, 2019.
https://doi.org/10.1007/978-3-030-11012-3_11

provide a compact approximate representation of known classes. For each new batch of classes, iCaRL starts with updating its representation by adding all available data for the new classes to known examples. After each state the fixed memory is updated with examples from the newly learned classes. To counter catastrophic forgetting [8], *i.e.* the tendency of a neural net to forget old information when new information is ingested, classification and distillation losses are used. While fulfilling the three necessary conditions for a class-incremental algorithm, the performance reduction is still important since top-5 accuracy drops from roughly 90% for 100 to 45% for 1000 classes [11]. Learning-without-Forgetting (LwF) [7] combines knowledge distillation and Fine Tuning. The authors first perform a warm-up step by optimizing new parameters only, then the whole network is optimized using classification loss for new tasks and distillation loss for old tasks. A LwF adaptation for IL is introduced in [11] and has the advantage of not requiring a memory for past data. However, its performance is lower than that of iCaRL in a single task scenario. Aljundi et al. [1] introduced ExpertGate, an architecture based on a network of experts from which only the most adapted one is activated. A gating mechanism is applied to training samples to decide which expert to transfer knowledge from. When a new task arrives, a new expert is added and knowledge is transferred from previous models using FT or LwF [7]. Expert Gate learns a good data representation when augmenting the number of tasks. However, it violates the third property of IL algorithms since its number of parameters increases with the number of tasks. The authors of [17] and [13] improve the plasticity of deep architectures by widening existing layers and/or deepening the network. While this improves recognition ability, the drawback in a constrained setting is that the number of parameters is increased when augmenting the network's capacity.

We introduce *DeeSIL*, an adaptation of a known transfer learning scheme [4, 6,10] to incremental learning. In order to qualify as class-incremental and maximize flexibility, *DeeSIL* includes two weakly correlated steps. First, a deep model provides fixed representations which are then used to learn independent shallow classifiers during the incremental phase. Instead of using the system memory to keep positive examples, a set of negative features that are necessary to train classifiers incrementally is stored. This choice makes it possible to use all positive examples for training without violating the memory constraint. Our hypothesis is that independent shallow learning over all positives compensates the drawback related to the use of a fixed deep representation. Since no deep retraining is needed to increase system capacity, the approach is considerably less complex compared to its purely deep learning counterparts. The addition of a new class is done through the training of a shallow classifier, an operation that takes less than a minute on a single CPU. *DeeSIL* is tested against three competitive IL algorithms, including iCaRL [11], the best such algorithm known to the authors. The ImageNet LSVRC 2012 dataset is used for evaluation and results show significant improvement for the proposed method.

2 Method

An overview of *DeeSIL* is provided in Fig. 1. The algorithm is an adaptation for incremental learning of a well-known transfer learning scheme [6]. Given a set of images X^i for a class to be learned, features F^i are extracted using a fixed deep representation provided by the deep features extractor (***DFE***). Then a shallow binary classifier $\boldsymbol{C^i}$ is trained using F^i as positives and F^N as negatives in order to predict the activations p^i of the class for test images. F^N is the memory of the system and it contains a constant number K of features, regardless of the state of the system (*i.e.* number of recognizable classes). F^N is generated by the negative selector (***NS***) component which is the main adaptation introduced in *DeeSIL* to make a classical transfer learning pipeline [6] suitable for incremental learning. Given **A** (y recognizable classes), the initial state of the system, the following steps are needed to move to state **B** ($y+j$ classes): (1) extract features for the j new classes; (2) update the pool of negatives F^N using ***NS*** component; (3) train j shallow classifiers. Following common practice in transfer learning [4,6,10], we use linear SVMs. We further discuss steps (1) and (2) hereafter.

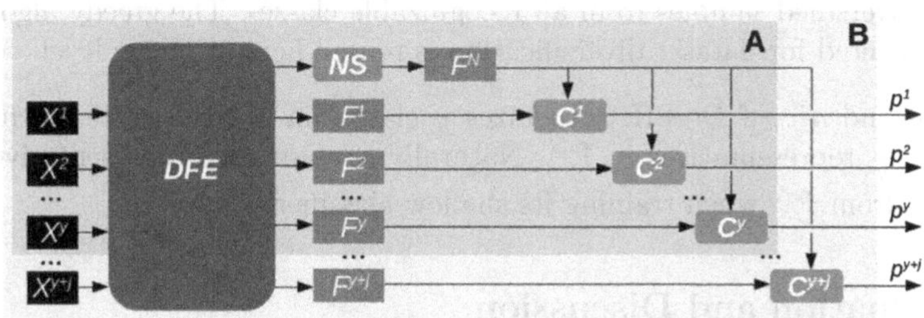

Fig. 1. Overview of *DeeSIL*. Two states of the system, **A** (light gray background) and **B** (light pink background) that recognize respectively y and $y+j$ classes are presented. X^i, F^i are sets of images and features for the ith class. F^N is a set of negative features obtained using a negative selector (***NS***) and common to all shallow classifiers that are added in a given state. ***DFE*** is a deep features extractor. $\boldsymbol{C^i}$ is a shallow classifier learned for the ith class and the output p^i is the associated prediction. (Color figure online)

Deep Features Extractor. In [11], each new state of the class-incremental-algorithm depends on the representation learned in the preceding state. Here, deep features extraction and shallow classifier learning are separated. *DeeSIL* thus implements a form of transfer learning which uses a fixed deep representation. To evaluate the effect of the amount of training data and its visual proximity with the test data, we train three variants of ***DFE***:

- *IN*100 - train only with the ImageNet data of the initial state, a setting that is directly comparable with [11].
- *IN*1000 - train with a larger dataset that has similar characteristics with the test set but no common classes. 1000 diversified ImageNet classes are selected to optimize their transferability toward new tasks [14,15].

- $FL1000$ - train with a more challenging dataset which is obtained from weakly annotated Flickr group data and is visually more distant from the test set. Within each group, a semi-supervised reranking [2] is initially performed to remove a part of noisy images.

A greedy algorithm [3] which operates with classes' mean representations is used for dataset diversification in the last two variants. It picks at each iteration the class which is on average least similar to those already selected. Visual representations from $IN100$ are used as basis for the diversification process.

Negatives Selection. In standard transfer learning [6], shallow classifiers are learned in a one-VS-rest fashion since all data is available at all times. Here, a selection is necessary to fit F^N features in the memory budget K for any state of the algorithm. We test three negative selection strategies:

- *ind* - following [4] F^N is composed of K YFCC image features [16] selected so as to represent frequent but diversified tags.
- *rand* - a random and balanced sampling of image features from all past and current classes.
- *div* - diversified samples from all recognizable classes. The greedy algorithm implemented for dataset diversification is reused here at image level.

For *rand* and *div*, if DeeSIL recognizes y classes in a given state, each class will have $\frac{K}{y}$ representatives in F^N. Naturally, a class' own representatives are discarded from F^N when training its shallow classifier.

3 Evaluation and Discussion

DeeSIL is tested using the ILSVRC 2012 dataset [12]. The evaluation protocol (order of classes, size of system states) is nearly identical to the one used for iCaRL [11]. ILSVRC 2012 includes a total of 1000 classes, further split into 10 batches of 100 classes, which means that 10 distinct states of the class-incremental algorithms are tested. The test set is the same but, since we need to optimize the SVMs, we keep out 20 images for validation and train on remaining images. We use the best three systems from [11] as baselines: (1) iCaRL - their contribution and the best IL algorithm known to us; (2) LwF-MC - adaptation of Learning without Forgetting [7] to IL scenario and (3) Fixed Representation - training over a frozen initial network, except for the classification layer.

ResNet-18 [5] was trained from scratch using PyTorch [9] following the methodology described in [5] with 100 and 1000 ImageNet classes and 1000 Flickr groups. Training images are processed using a random resized crop of size 224×224 and a random horizontal flip and they are normalized after these transformations. An SGD optimizer is used. The learning rate starts at 0.1 and is divided by 10 when the error plateaus for 10 consecutive epochs. The weight decay is 0.0001 and the momentum is 0.9. Each configuration is trained for 100 epochs and the model with optimal accuracy is retained. The penultimate

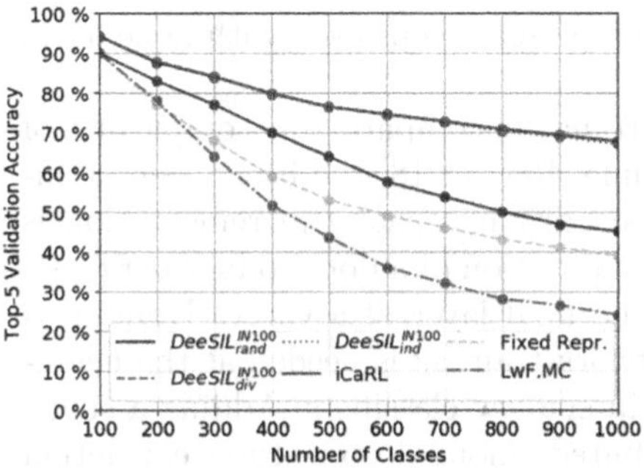

Fig. 2. Top-5 accuracy on ILSVRC for *DeeSIL* variants obtained with three negative selection strategies.

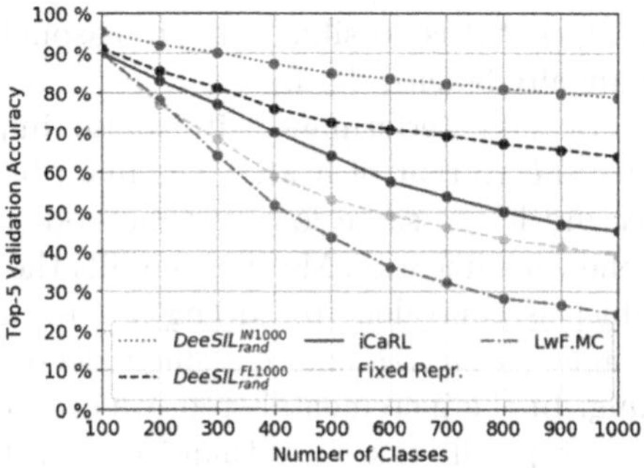

Fig. 3. Top-5 accuracy on ILSVRC for fixed deep representations obtained with larger datasets.

layer (average pooling with 512 dimensions) is extracted by $\boldsymbol{DFE}$ and then L2-normalized before being fed into the shallow classifiers. The memory size, which stores negative features, is $K = 20000$, the same as in [11].

The SVM classifiers were optimized with 20 images per class for validation. Values of the regularization parameter between 0.0001 and 1000 were tried and the optimal parameter was then used in each variant of the system.

The results in Fig. 2 show that all variants of $DeeSIL$, trained with $rand$, div and ind negatives selection outperform the state of the art systems. At scale, *i.e.* 1000 classes learned incrementally, performance increases from 45% for iCaRL to 68% when $rand$ and div negatives are exploited. This gain is consistent over all the states of the class-incremental evaluation, with larger difference for large batches. $DeeSIL$ can be seen as a variant of Fixed Representation learning but differs from it through the use of all positives in the incremental phase. This leads to an even higher performance gain than in the case of iCaRL.

The three $\boldsymbol{NS}$ variants have rather performance and this finding shows that our method is robust w.r.t. the choice of negatives. Selecting negatives from the dataset ($rand$ and div) gives marginally better results (0.5 points gain) compared to the use of an independent negative set (ind) for 1000 classes. $rand$ being simpler to compute than div, $DeeSIL_{rand}$ will be used in further experiments.

In Fig. 3, we test the effect of using more data to obtain strong fixed representations. 1000 ImageNet classes and Flickr groups are used respectively. Richer data compensates for the fact that features are transferred from classes that are different from the tested ILSVRC classes. This is especially the case for $DeeSIL_{rand}^{IN1000}$, which exploits a subset of ImageNet distinct from ILSVRC. Performance improvements of 10 and 33 points are obtained over $DeeSIL_{rand}^{IN100}$, the best configuration trained with the 100 initial ILSVRC classes and over iCaRL respectively. $DeeSIL_{rand}^{FL1000}$, the version trained on non-curated Flickr data has lower performance than $DeeSIL_{rand}^{IN1000}$, but is close to $DeeSIL_{rand}^{IN100}$ and still well above the state of the art algorithms. The last result confirms the finding in [2] that it is possible to learn reasonable representations even with little or no manually labeled data.

Beyond performance, it is also important to compare the complexity of *DeeSIL* to that of iCaRL, the main baseline. ResNet-18, the basic deep architecture is the same for both methods. Recognition capacity incrementation is done with linear SVMs. This entails the computation of a dot product per class, which is equivalent to adding a class in the final layer of a CNN. Training is simpler in *DeeSIL* since a single deep network training is needed at the beginning. In the incremental step, we only train shallow classifiers. Adding a single class typically takes less than 1 min, distributed among deep features extraction and SVM training on an INTEL-Xeon-E5-2650-v2@2.60 GHz CPU. For comparison, adding a batch of 100 new classifiers in iCaRL takes approximately 32 h on an NVIDIA Titan X GPU. Incremental learning is typically needed in low-resource contexts and, assuming that an initial deep representation is available, *DeeSIL* can be deployed even in absence of a GPU. Equally important, due to the independent learning of shallow classifiers, *DeeSIL* can seamlessly integrate batches of new classes of arbitrary size. In contrast, purely deep learning based algorithms need retraining and this step is particularly long if one class is added at a time.

Compared to iCaRL, the focus is shifted from positive to negative selection to fill in the memory of the system. As shown in the experiments, our algorithm is affected by catastrophic forgetting to a much lesser extent. The choice to select negatives is beneficial for scalability in terms of number of learnable classes. Given a memory budget K, iCaRL can learn at most $y \leqslant K$ classes while *DeeSIL* can learn as many classes as presented to the system. Naturally, negatives selection becomes more complicated if $y \geqslant K$ since not all known classes will be represented anymore. Also, while the same number of items is stored in iCaRL and *DeeSIL*, memory needs are lower in our case since we store 512 dimensional features instead of images of past classes.

It is interesting to evaluate the decrease in performance compared to a situation in which all training data is available at all times. ResNet-18 [5] top-5 accuracy on 1000 ILSVRC classes trained with all data is approximately 89%. iCaRL halves this score while our best configurations with ***DFE*** based on 100 and 1000 classes lose only 22 and 12 points respectively. The gap could probably be further reduced if the feature extractors were more universal [14,15]. This could, for instance, be achieved if *DeeSIL*'s initial training would be done with an even larger number of classes.

4 Conclusion

We revisit a known transfer learning scheme for it to fit the three necessary conditions needed to qualify as a class-incremental algorithm [11]. The proposed method achieves significantly better performance than existing algorithms while also being much faster to train and more scalable in terms of number of learnable classes. To facilitate reproducibility, classifier configurations and data used to train them will be made public. The results presented here encourage us to pursue the development of *DeeSIL* along the following directions: (1) test the effect of using lower size memory, (2) push the evaluation to a much larger number of classes to test the limits of the different methods and (3) integrate more universal deep representations to improve overall performance.

References

1. Aljundi, R., Chakravarty, P., Tuytelaars, T.: Expert gate: lifelong learning with a network of experts. In: Conference on Computer Vision and Pattern Recognition, CVPR (2017)
2. Chen, X., Gupta, A.: Webly supervised learning of convolutional networks. In: International Conference on Computer Vision, ICCV (2015)
3. Deselaers, T., Gass, T., Dreuw, P., Ney, H.: Jointly optimising relevance and diversity in image retrieval. In: ACM CIVR (2009)
4. Ginsca, A.L., Popescu, A., Le Borgne, H., Ballas, N., Vo, P., Kanellos, I.: Large-scale image mining with flickr groups. In: He, X., Luo, S., Tao, D., Xu, C., Yang, J., Hasan, M.A. (eds.) MMM 2015. LNCS, vol. 8935, pp. 318–334. Springer, Cham (2015). https://doi.org/10.1007/978-3-319-14445-0_28
5. He, K., Zhang, X., Ren, S., Sun, J.: Deep residual learning for image recognition. In: Conference on Computer Vision and Pattern Recognition, CVPR (2016)
6. Kornblith, S., Shlens, J., Le, Q.V.: Do better imagenet models transfer better? CoRR abs/1805.08974 (2018)
7. Li, Z., Hoiem, D.: Learning without forgetting. In: Leibe, B., Matas, J., Sebe, N., Welling, M. (eds.) ECCV 2016. LNCS, vol. 9908, pp. 614–629. Springer, Cham (2016). https://doi.org/10.1007/978-3-319-46493-0_37
8. Mccloskey, M., Cohen, N.J.: Catastrophic interference in connectionist networks: the sequential learning problem. Psychol. Learn. Motiv. **24**, 104–169 (1989)
9. Paszke, A., et al.: Automatic differentiation in PyTorch. In: Advances in Neural Information Processing Systems Workshops, NIPS-W (2017)
10. Razavian, A.S., Azizpour, H., Sullivan, J., Carlsson, S.: CNN features off-the-shelf: an astounding baseline for recognition. In: Conference on Computer Vision and Pattern Recognition Workshop, CVPR-W (2014)
11. Rebuffi, S., Kolesnikov, A., Sperl, G., Lampert, C.H.: iCaRL: incremental classifier and representation learning. In: Conference on Computer Vision and Pattern Recognition, CVPR (2017)
12. Russakovsky, O., et al.: ImageNet large scale visual recognition challenge. Int. J. Comput. Vis. **115**(3), 211–252 (2015)
13. Rusu, A.A., et al.: Progressive neural networks. CoRR abs/1606.04671 (2016)
14. Tamaazousti, Y., Le Borgne, H., Hudelot, C.: MuCaLe-Net: multi categorical-level networks to generate more discriminating features. In: Conference on Computer Vision and Pattern Recognition, CVPR (2017)
15. Tamaazousti, Y., Le Borgne, H., Hudelot, C., Seddik, M.E.A., Tamaazousti, M.: Learning more universal representations for transfer-learning. arXiv:1712.09708 (2017)
16. Thomee, B., et al.: YFCC100M: the new data in multimedia research. Commun. ACM **59**, 64–73 (2016)
17. Wang, Y., Ramanan, D., Hebert, M.: Growing a brain: fine-tuning by increasing model capacity. In: Conference on Computer Vision and Pattern Recognition, CVPR (2017)

Dynamic Adaptation on Non-stationary Visual Domains

Sindi Shkodrani[1,2(✉)], Michael Hofmann[2(✉)], and Efstratios Gavves[1(✉)]

[1] University of Amsterdam, Amsterdam, The Netherlands
e.gavves@uva.nl
[2] TomTom, Amsterdam, The Netherlands
{sindi.shkodrani,michael.hofmann}@tomtom.com

Abstract. Domain adaptation aims to learn models on a supervised source domain that perform well on an unsupervised target. Prior work has examined domain adaptation in the context of stationary domain shifts, i.e. static data sets. However, with large-scale or dynamic data sources, data from a defined domain is not usually available all at once. For instance, in a streaming data scenario, dataset statistics effectively become a function of time. We introduce a framework for adaptation over non-stationary distribution shifts applicable to large-scale and streaming data scenarios. The model is adapted sequentially over incoming unsupervised streaming data batches. This enables improvements over several batches without the need for any additionally annotated data. To demonstrate the effectiveness of our proposed framework, we modify associative domain adaptation to work well on source and target data batches with unequal class distributions. We apply our method to several adaptation benchmark datasets for classification and show improved classifier accuracy not only for the currently adapted batch, but also when applied on future stream batches. Furthermore, we show the applicability of our associative learning modifications to semantic segmentation, where we achieve competitive results.

1 Introduction

Domain adaptation aims to adapt classifiers trained on source domains to novel unlabeled target domains, where a domain shift, namely a difference in distribution statistics, is expected [8,34]. Typically, the domain shift is considered within the context of "closed", static domains, implicitly assuming datasets available in their entirety at adaptation time [8,36]. However, in realistic applications data collection is not static nor closed but "open", giving rise to non-stationary domain shifts [11].

Consider e.g. social media feeds, or urban imagery taken from inside a car. These images often arrive in "bundles" with different distribution statistics, due to, for instance, being collected in different cities or with different weather conditions (see Fig. 1). If we were to consider these bundles as isolated domains, we wouldn't be exploiting the available unlabeled data entirely. In addition, if the

L. Leal-Taixé and S. Roth (Eds.): ECCV 2018 Workshops, LNCS 11130, pp. 158–171, 2019.
https://doi.org/10.1007/978-3-030-11012-3_12

Fig. 1. Distribution shift across stream batches in GTA5

distribution changes gradually over time in a streaming-like fashion, being able to adapt over bundles sequentially may benefit real-time predictions on future incoming data bundles. In streaming data this distribution shift over time is called concept drift, and the incoming stream is usually too large to be held in memory, therefore it is processed in data bundles which are later discarded.

As an adaptation method, we look into associative learning proposed by Haeusser *et al.* [15,16], which uses association of embeddings in latent space and has been shown to work well for domain adaptation and semi-supervised learning. However, associative domain adaptation makes the implicit assumption that the class probability distributions between the source and the target domains are similar at adaptation time. This assumption cannot be guaranteed to hold when the target dataset is not well known in advance, such as in "open" datasets the class probability statistics may change dynamically or in tasks where class statistics across domains may vary a lot. An example of such a task is semantic segmentation. To this end, the associations between source and target embeddings need to be performed while taking into account the non-stationary changes of the class probability statistics.

This work makes three contributions. First, we argue that domain adaptation is important beyond static domain datasets, including continuously collected datasets whose statistics are non-stationary. For dynamic datasets domain adaptation should be able to adapt to the evolving statistics. Second, starting from associative domain adaptation [15] we show that the similar class distribution assumption between domains hurts adaptation. We therefore reformulate the approach to make the adaptation loss invariant to the inevitable non-stationary changes on the class distribution statistics. Third, we present two applications of our proposed approach, one on adapting streaming image classification, where the streaming data distribution changes over time, and one on domain adaption for semantic segmentation (see Fig. 2), where the source and target datasets have inherently different class statistics.

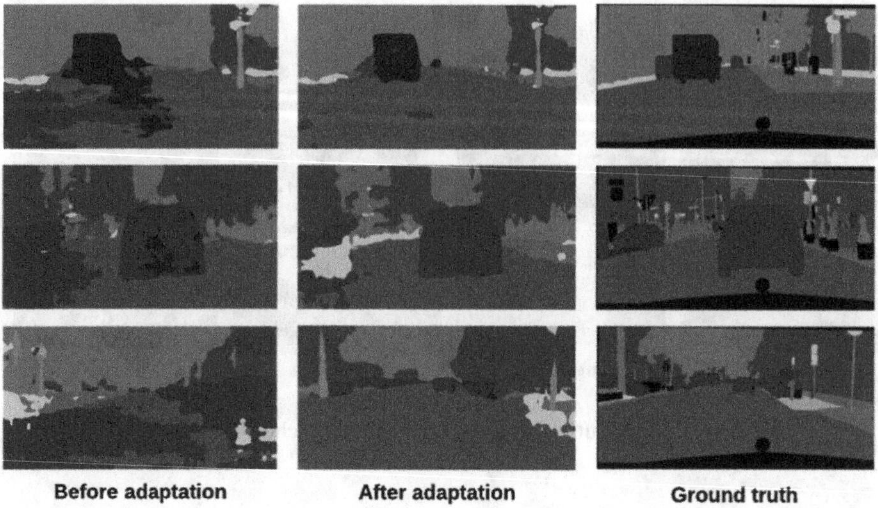

Fig. 2. Adaptation results for semantic segmentation on Cityscapes

2 Related Work

Domain Adaptation. A handful of domain adaptation methods revolve around discrepancy-based adaptation [23,24,31], for instance, [22] use a multi-kernel maximum mean discrepancy (MMD) minimization approach. Other methods are data reconstruction-based and often use reconstruction with e.g. autoencoders, as an auxiliary task to learn invariant features [5,12,13].

Another category is adversarial approaches. Adversarial discriminative methods use a classifier to discriminate between domains during training and ensure feature invariance for source and target [10,35]. Adversarial generative methods use a generative adversarial network (GAN) [14] to learn a mapping between source and target images by interleaving the task loss, mapping generator and discriminator loss [3,18].

Domain adaptation for semantic segmentation was recently pioneered by [19] with an adversarial discriminative based approach. Similarly [6] use discriminators for feature invariance, but for different parts of an image grid. [28] use a standard GAN approach to have a generator network learn the mapping while a discriminator network distinguishes between real and fake images. [38] split the original segmentation network into three output branches where the first two generate pseudo-labels for the third branch. [39] adopt a curriculum learning approach for by solving easy to difficult tasks to achieve adaptation.

Associative Learning. Introduced by [16], learning by association was initially applied to semi-supervised learning. [15] use associations between source and target to close the domain gap for classification achieve competitive results across different domain adaptation benchmarks for classification. The advantage of this

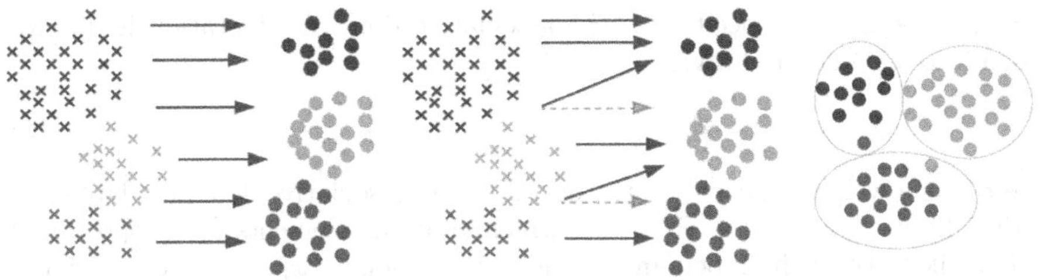

Fig. 3. Associative domain adaptation for unequal class distributions. Crosses represent the source domain and circles represent the target. Arrows represent source to target probabilities. (a) Uniformly distributed visit loss. (b) Intuition of correcting wrong associations by balancing the visit loss according to class distributions. (c) Cluster estimates to approximate class distribution in target.

method compared to discrepancy-based approaches is that it does not require a choice of kernel and extra hyper-parameters that come with them.

Streaming Data Classification. Approaches that deal with streaming data are either passive approaches that use a single classifier or an ensemble [30,37] or active ones where an extra decision is made on whether to update the classifier. Most often classification algorithms such as Decision Trees, Rule-Based and Nearest Neighbor are used, whereas adjustments in neural network architectures to account for streaming have been proposed [1]. [2] use a complex sampling and filtering mechanism for active training and a random forest based classifier. [33] use a micro-cluster nearest neighbor which makes use of statistical summaries for data streams. Not many works look into exploiting unsupervised data for improving data stream classifiers. [32] use semi-supervised feature learning to adjust k-nearest neighbor weights. To our best knowledge, we are the first to explore this direction for image classification with modern deep architectures.

3 Method

3.1 Associative Domain Adaptation

We start from two datasets, source and target. The source dataset, $D^S = \{x_i^S, y_i^S\}, i = 1, ..., N^S$, comprises of N^S image samples with embeddings x_i^S, annotated by one-hot vectors $y_i^S = [y_{ic}^S], c = 1, ..., C$, which equals to 1 if the image x_{ic}^S belongs to class c, and 0 otherwise. The target dataset, $D^T = \{x_j^T\}, j = 1, ..., N^T$, comprises only of image embeddings which belong to the same set of classes, $c = 1, ..., C$; however, no class annotations are available for retraining or fine-tuning. Between the source and target datasets there is a domain shift in the distribution of their respective embeddings, thus $p(x^S) \neq p(x^T)$. The goal, therefore, is to adapt a classifier trained on the source dataset to work well for the target.

Associative domain adaptation [15] adapts by considering an additional adaptation loss during training on top of the standard task-specific loss,

$\mathcal{L} = \mathcal{L}_{task} + \mathcal{L}_{assoc}$. Specifically, the associative domain adaptation is decomposed into a walker and a visit loss,

$$\mathcal{L}_{assoc} = \mathcal{L}_{walker} + \beta \mathcal{L}_{visit}, \tag{1}$$

where β is a weighting coefficient. Central to the associative domain adaptation is the affinity matrix $A \in \mathbb{R}^{N_S \times N_T}$, which contains elements a_{ij} proportional to how likely the i-th embedding in the source domain, x_i^S, is to be associated with the j-th embedding in the target domain, namely $a_{ij} \propto p(x_j^T | x_i^S)$. Learning embeddings that yield an affinity matrix that minimizes the loss in Eq. (1) is the goal of associative domain adaptation.

The walker and the visit losses have complementary objectives. The objective of the walker loss is to encourage the source embeddings to lie close after adaptation to source embeddings of the same class. As no class labels are available in the target dataset, however, this objective is reformulated. Specifically, after double transition from the source to the target and back to the source, the starting and finishing source class labels should minimize the cross-entropy loss with respect to a normalized equality matrix $E = \{e_{ik}\}$, namely

$$\mathcal{L}_{walker} = \sum_{i,k} e_{ik} \log \left[p(x_k^S | x_j^T) \cdot p(x_j^T | x_i^S) \right], \tag{2}$$

where x_j^T is the closest embedding in the target set and $e_{jk} = \frac{y_i^S \cdot y_k^S}{N_S}$.

The walker loss alone, however, can lead to degenerate solutions, where the transition probabilities are learned to associate source embeddings only with a few relevant yet "easy" target embeddings. To mitigate this, the *visit loss* encourages that all target embeddings are equally visited. This is achieved by a minimizing cross-entropy objective

$$\mathcal{L}_{visit} = \sum_j v_j \log p(x_j^T | x_i^S), v_j = 1/N_T \tag{3}$$

where $v_j = 1/N_T$.

3.2 Associative Domain Adaptation for Unequal Class Distributions

Associative domain adaptation implicitly assumes that the source and target distributions are similar on batch level during adaptation. The reason is that for the visit loss to be minimized in Eq. (3) it is assumed that the ideal target is the average over the size of the target dataset, $v_j = 1/N_T$. [15] consider a smaller β for the visit loss, if the class distributions between the source and target datasets are unequal. However, this solution implicitly expects access to the adaptation set in order to tune β. In addition, simply receiving a weaker signal from the visit loss does not exploit the full adaptation capacity and might enforce wrong associations, as we illustrate in Fig. 3(a).

As we want target embeddings to be visited by the same-class source embeddings, intuitively they should be visited at a rate proportional to the difference

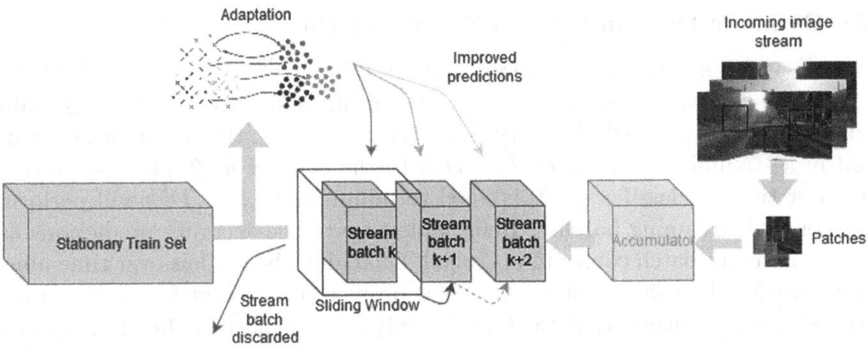

Fig. 4. The streaming setup uses a pre-trained model from a stationary supervised set. The model is then sequentially adapted to the incoming stream batches.

between the source and target class distributions, as shown in Fig. 3(b). We can formalize the intuition by adding a weighting coefficient in front of v_j and reformulating Eq. (3) as:

$$\mathcal{L}_{visit} = \sum_j \gamma_j v_j \log p(x_j^T | x_i^S), \gamma_j = \frac{p(Y^S = y_j^T)}{p(Y^T = y_j^T)} \tag{4}$$

namely weighted by the ratio of class probabilities at the source and target for the correct class of the target embedding. Clearly, we cannot directly compute the ratio $p(Y^S = y_j^T)/p(Y^T = y_j^T)$, as we would need to know the true class of the target embedding y_j^T. However, we propose a way to estimate them.

Although we have no control on the target dataset, we do have control over the source dataset for which the labels are available, thus when constructing the mini-batch based on which we will perform the adaptation, we can first sample the source uniformly such that all class probabilities are equal in the source dataset, i.e. $p(Y^S = y_j^T) = const.$ Consequently, from a probabilistic perspective it is not important which particular class the j-th target embedding belongs to, alleviating the necessity to make a soft prediction for the class label of the j-th embedding.

What remains to compute the weighting coefficient γ_j is computing the class probability $p(Y^T = y_j^T)$ for the j-th embedding. It is logical to expect that same-class embeddings cluster together for a modern classifier to be able to discriminate between classes. We can retrieve the class cluster around an embedding sample in an unsupervised manner and compute the probability based on cluster size. We rely on unsupervised clustering to estimate class probabilities in the batch. The approximation holds true under the assumption that the clusters are well aligned to the means of the respective, optimal classifiers. In practice, we consider hierarchical agglomerative clustering, which experimentally appears to allow for good alignment between the obtained clusters and works well when clusters have very different sizes. We illustrate the process in Fig. 3(c).

3.3 Dynamic Domain Shift in Streaming Data

Let us consider a pre-collected annotated set $D^S = \{x_i^S, y_i^S\}, i = 1, ..., N^S$ with embeddings x_i^S, with one-hot labels y_i^S and an incoming stream of image data that needs to be classified. At every time step $\tau = 1, ., K$, the stream is accumulated in a streaming data batch D_τ^T. Due to the *concept drift*, i.e. distribution shift over time, a classifier $f_0(\theta)$ trained to minimize $\mathcal{L}_{task}(\theta, D^S)$ will perform worse on the streaming batches. Being able to produce accurate predictions as soon as a stream batch comes in is crucial. Changing the models over time aims to account for the concept drift. A second problem to account for in streaming is the size of the incoming data. Usually only a small part of this data can be stored in memory. One way to deal with this is to have a mechanism in place that selects the data to be stored; another way is to be able to use and then discard all the data coming into the stream.

We simulate a streaming scenario where the stationary training set D^S is pre-collected and first used for off-line training of a predictive model $f_0(\theta)$. Incoming stream data batches D_τ^T are small compared to the stationary set D^S, but the whole stream cannot be stored in memory, so at a time step $\tau = k$ only a set of $D_k^T, D_{k+1}^T, ...D_{k+w}^T$ is available, where w is a storage window size. A classifier $f_{k-1}(\theta)$ trained on the stationary set and adapted to $D_1^T, ...D_{k-1}^T$ sequentially is available. We adapt to D_k^T by minimizing the objective

$$\arg\min_\theta \mathcal{L}_{task}(f_{k-1}(\theta), y^S) + \mathcal{L}_{walker}(\theta, D^S, D_k^T) + \beta\mathcal{L}_{visit}(\theta, D^S, D_k^T)$$

The benefits of this approach are twofold. First, adapting to D_k^T improves prediction results on D_k^T itself in an unsupervised manner without extra annotation. Second, the predictions improve for $D_{k+1}^T, D_{k+2}^T...$ and so on in a cascade fashion, since distribution in incoming sets is more likely to be similar to the previous stream sets nearby than the stationary source, especially if we would use a sliding window over incoming sets. For simplicity we take a window size of 1. An illustration is provided in Fig. 4. In our setting, we extract patches from the GTA5 dataset and do patch-wise classification in order to demonstrate the working of our setup with a simpler task. We expect a similar behavior for more complex tasks such as semantic segmentation and object detection.

3.4 Dynamic Domain Shift in Semantic Segmentation

Having relaxed the distribution assumption, associative domain adaptation can be applied to tasks where source and target class distributions in a batch are not uniform or uniformity cannot be approximated, such as semantic segmentation. Consider a source dataset $D^S = \{x_i^S, y_{i,H\times W}^S\}i = 1, ..., N^S$, where H, W are image dimensions, is annotated at pixel level. The target images $D^T = \{x_j^T\}, j = 1, ..., N^T$ are available without annotations. Using modern segmentation architectures, we can consider embeddings extracted from a mid-network layer which contains downsampled data. Using a DeepLab-V2 [4] architecture, we extract embedding $x_{i'}^S$ at pixel level in decoder layers before bilinear upsampling which are 8 times downsampled in each spatial dimension. We downsample the label annotations and use $y^S_{i',U\times V}$, where $U = H/8$ and $V = W/8$ together with downsampled embeddings for adaptation.

An important consideration when adapting for dense prediction is the choice of affinity matrix $A \in \mathbb{R}^{N_S \times N_T}$ between embeddings, where $a_{ij} \propto p(x^T_j|x^S_i)$. In [15], $p(x^T_j|x^S_i)$ is computed as softmax over rows of A, i.e. $p(x^T_j|x^S_i) = \exp(a_{ij})/\sum_{j'}\exp(a_{ij'})$, where $a_{ij} = x^S_i \cdot x^T_j$ is the dot product between embedding vectors. The unnormalized dot product as an affinity is unbounded and can cause very small probability values for the softmax, which may lead to exploding gradients. We mitigate this by using an affinity measure based on Euclidean distance. In addition, we observe that the dimensionality of pixel embeddings for semantic segmentation is crucial for convergence. If too large, the gradients propagated are noisy and adaptation not very effective. However, dimensionality has to be large enough to allow for similar embeddings to group together but still preserve discriminable structures in latent space. For this, we add an *embedding layer* in the decoder where dimensionality can be adjusted for the task.

4 Experiments and Results

We validate the performance of the proposed domain adaptation method under different settings for domain class distribution divergence. First, we show the effect of increased class distribution divergence on associative domain adaptation [15] and how we can recover accuracy drops with our formulation. Second, we evaluate on a visual stream classification setting, where data and class distributions change over time. Third, we further validate the proposed method on domain adaptation for semantic segmentation The code, models and datasets will all become available upon publication.

4.1 Classification Under Different Class Distributions Between Domains

We report our results on several image classification adaptation benchmarks. For digit classification we adapt on MNIST [21] → MNISTM [10], SVHN (Street View House Numbers) [26] → MNIST and Sythetic Digits [10] to SVHN [26]. Next, we adapt for street sign classification from Synthetic Signs dataset [25] to German Traffic Sign Recognition Benchmark [29]. As a last benchmark, CIFAR-10 [20] → STL-10 [7] adaptation is performed. Out of the 10 classes present in STL-10 and CIFAR-10, 9 of these overlap so they can be used for domain adaptation.

We report experiments after changing KL-divergence between the source and target class distributions, to quantify the effect of unequal class distributions for domain adaptation. In Table 1 we report the accuracies over the datasets when class distribution divergence increases for associative domain adaptation, as well as the proposed method.

Table 1. Adaptation accuracy as KL-divergence of source to target class distributions in a batch increases. The oracle version uses the true target class probabilities and serves as an upper bound.

Src -Tgt divergence	Method	Datasets				
		MNIST-MNISTM	SVHN-MNIST	Synth Dig.-SVHN	Synth Signs-GTSRB	CIFAR10-STL10
	Source only	64.0	69.4	85.8	95.4	52.7
	Target only	93.6	99.5	94.2	98.1	99.8
KL = 0.05	Adapted using [1]	87.6	97.0	91.9	96.2	61.3
	Ours	88.3	97.2	92.6	96.5	61.2
	Ours with oracle*	90.0	97.2	92.8	97.5	61.5
KL = 0.2	Adapted using [1]	85.2	94.3	87.6	95.9	57.6
	Ours	87.6	96.9	89.9	95.6	58.3
	Ours with oracle*	90.1	97.8	92.8	97.3	61.2
KL = 0.4	Adapted using [1]	81.7	94.2	87.1	95.5	53.4
	Ours	83.8	94.9	88.0	95.3	56.2
	Ours with oracle*	89.8	96.6	92.6	94.1	61.4

First, as expected, larger KL-divergence between source and target usually leads to worse accuracy for associative domain adaptation. Second, the proposed method improves recognition after domain adaptation, especially for larger class distribution divergence, and especially for tasks where the classifiers are not already near maximal adaptation capacity.

To further derive insights, we also include results with an oracle-weighted visit loss that use the target class distributions (theoretical upper bound). Although our off-the-shelf agglomerative clustering does not always approximate the batch statistics perfectly, it does come considerably close to the oracle-weighted score and almost always outperforms the unweighted approach. In addition, using oracle test statistics the proposed method often comes close to the recognition accuracies of classifiers trained directly on the target domain indicating that our theoretical reasoning is correct. We conclude that when we expect a dynamical domain shift, where class distributions between the source and target change, our approach is more robust to for domain alignment.

4.2 Streaming Data Classification

Next, we evaluate the method on a streaming data scenario, where the class distributions are expected to be different between source and target. To simulate a streaming data scenario, we note that the popular synthetically generated and finely annotated GTA5 dataset [27] is in fact ordered sequentially. Video-like fragments can be observed throughout the dataset, and a shift in distribution over time can also be observed, as shown in Fig. 1. We therefore extract patches from GTA5 frame sequences and adapt to a patch-wise classification task, where the label for each patch is equivalent to the dense label for the middle pixel. We use 65 × 65 patches cropped from a 256 × 512 downsampled version of the original GTA5 dataset.

Table 2. Streaming classification accuracy per adaptation round. Cells marked "-" indicate the batch hasn't yet entered the stream.

Adaptation Set	Source only	Lag from adaptation timestep						Adapted with [1]
		5	4	3	2	1	0	(lag=0)
SB1	42.72	-	-	-	-	-	**46.72**	45.58
SB2	40.30	-	-	-	-	44.02	**45.22**	44.50
SB3	38.58	-	-	-	40.88	41.48	42.02	**42.13**
SB4	37.85	-	-	40.88	41.52	41.98	**43.00**	42.45
SB5	42.02	-	45.22	45.90	45.93	45.73	**47.51**	46.13
SB6	46.78	50.65	50.70	51.47	51.27	51.33	**52.73**	51.83

We consider a streaming data scenario where a small set of stationary labeled data is pre-collected and available for training. For the stationary data, we sample patches from the first 5,000 images in the GTA5 dataset. About 32,000 patches of 65×65 dimensions are sampled. For the incoming stream we sample patches from bundles of 1,000 images each, collected sequentially. 6,000 patches are sampled from every bundle of images and accumulated in a *streaming batch*. We experiment with adapting six of these sets following the stationary training set.

Several observations follow from the results in Table 2. First, there is indeed a dynamical domain shift when considering visual streams instead of static datasets. When considering the classifiers trained only on the source, there is considerable fluctuation on the recognition accuracy over time. Note that this is not always harmful, *e.g.* for streaming batches 5 and 6 accuracy improves, presumably because the shift between target and source is smaller.

Second, the proposed streaming adaptation method yields considerable and constant accuracy improvements over the source-only scores, no matter the source-only recognition accuracy. Also, the proposed method yields modest but consistent improvements over standard associative domain adaptation [15].

Third, as expected, best adaptation is achieved when adapting and testing on the same stream batch (lag = 0). However, adapting with some lag allows for accurate adaptation as well. We conclude that for visual streams, where we cannot store the data and we cannot always immediately adapt, dynamical domain adaptation is valuable.

4.3 Semantic Segmentation

Last, we validate the proposed method on the task of domain adaptation for semantic segmentation of urban street scenes. This is an application where source and target class statistics cannot be expected to align, especially on batch level where adaptation happens.

We adapt on the GTA5 → Cityscapes adaptation benchmark, which is important to domain adaptation as adapting from synthetic to real data

Table 3. GTA5 to Cityscapes domain adaptation. The last two rows show results on adapting with the unweighted version of the method and the distribution independent one.

	road	sidewalk	building	wall	fence	pole	light	sign	vegetation	terrain	sky	person	rider	car	truck	bus	train	motorb.	bike	mIoU	Pixel Acc
NoAdapt	33.8	23.2	67.5	18.2	**20.1**	18.1	15.9	**21.8**	66.9	18.0	72.4	33.0	6.5	25.0	**15.8**	19.3	6.0	8.4	**5.8**	26.1	72.8
Adapt (no wght.)	59.9	29.8	67.1	16.2	10.7	22.9	13.2	9.1	**78.0**	**33.4**	**75.7**	41.9	0.3	32.3	12.4	16.5	5.7	2.9	0.1	27.8	78.8
Adapt (est. wght.)	**63.8**	**31.3**	**68.4**	**19.4**	19.6	**23.2**	**17.6**	11.8	62.9	22.7	61.0	**52.1**	**7.8**	**42.5**	13.4	**22.1**	**6.2**	**9.1**	0.1	**29.2**	**81.9**

provides potential for exploiting very easily rendered synthetic sets. GTA5 contains 24,966 images with resolution 1914 × 1052, of which 12,500 are used for training and around 6,800 for validation. Cityscapes contains 5,000 pixel-level annotated images of 2048 × 1024 resolution, of which 2,975 images for the training set and 500 images for validation are available. We run our experiments with images from both datasets downsampled to 512 × 256 size.

As a base segmentation network we use DeepLab-V2 [4] with a ResNet-50 [17] backbone. We extend the original DeepLab-V2 architecture with a D-dimensional embedding layer that can be adjusted for experiment purposes and report results with $D = 64$. The embedding layer is placed before the bilinear upsampling part of the decoder, yielding embeddings that are 8 times downsampled in each spatial dimension. In this way we can not only adapt to more compressed information on pixel level embeddings, but also fit embedding metrics in reasonable memory even for large datasets.

We use $\beta = 0.5$ for the visit loss, adjusted for the magnitude of the loss values. We use the respective training sets of GTA5 and Cityscapes as the domains for training, test on the Cityscapes *val* set, and report the results in Table 3.

First, we train for 30K iterations on source only for GTA5, using pre-trained ImageNet [9] weights for the ResNet-50 encoder part of the network. We observe that the proposed distribution independent approach consistently improves standard associative domain adaptation, both in terms of mIoU and pixel accuracy.

Further, the proposed method improves standard domain adaptation on 15 out of the 19 categories. Standard associative domain adaptation is still better for large classes with near constant class frequency (e.g. *vegetation*, *terrain*, *sky*), since adaptation over these would overrule smaller classes in a batch. Interestingly, the proposed method seem to improve significantly (6–10%) over mid-size classes, such as *car*, *bus* and *person*, where indeed we expect larger class frequency fluctuations. We conclude that our approach is promising for domain adaptation of complex dense prediction tasks such as semantic segmentation, and potentially, integrating with the streaming techniques above, to video semantic segmentation.

5 Conclusion

We have presented a robust and distribution independent associative learning method for domain adaptation. Our formulation accounts for realistic scenarios where source and target data distribution in a batch cannot be approximated to be equal. A novel setup for dynamic domain adaptation that adapts over unlabeled data in order to improve classifier prediction over time for streaming data has been proposed. We have shown that we can exploit unsupervised data to achieve improvements over several streaming batches without additionally annotated samples. Using our associative domain adaptation formulation and architecture considerations we achieve competitive results for semantic segmentation.

Having considered a dynamic time-shifting distribution setup and shown dense prediction adaptation results, we lay the grounds for a framework that can potentially work well with dense prediction tasks for streaming video data such as video segmentation.

References

1. Aggarwal, C.C.: A survey of stream classification algorithms (2014)
2. Annapoorna, P.S., Mirnalinee, T.: Streaming data classification. In: 2016 International Conference on Recent Trends in Information Technology (ICRTIT), pp. 1–7. IEEE (2016)
3. Bousmalis, K., Silberman, N., Dohan, D., Erhan, D., Krishnan, D.: Unsupervised pixel-level domain adaptation with generative adversarial networks. In: The IEEE Conference on Computer Vision and Pattern Recognition (CVPR), vol. 1, p. 7 (2017)
4. Chen, L.C., Papandreou, G., Kokkinos, I., Murphy, K., Yuille, A.L.: DeepLab: semantic image segmentation with deep convolutional nets, atrous convolution, and fully connected CRFs. IEEE Trans. Pattern Anal. Mach. Intell. **40**(4), 834–848 (2018)
5. Chen, M., Xu, Z., Weinberger, K., Sha, F.: Marginalized denoising autoencoders for domain adaptation. arXiv preprint arXiv:1206.4683 (2012)
6. Chen, Y., Li, W., Gool, L.V.: ROAD: reality oriented adaptation for semantic segmentation of urban scenes. In: CVPR (2018)
7. Coates, A., Ng, A., Lee, H.: An analysis of single-layer networks in unsupervised feature learning. In: Proceedings of the Fourteenth International Conference on Artificial Intelligence and Statistics, pp. 215–223 (2011)
8. Csurka, G.: Domain adaptation for visual applications: a comprehensive survey. arXiv preprint arXiv:1702.05374 (2017)
9. Deng, J., Dong, W., Socher, R., Li, L.J., Li, K., Fei-Fei, L.: ImageNet: a large-scale hierarchical image database. In: IEEE Conference on Computer Vision and Pattern Recognition, CVPR 2009, pp. 248–255. IEEE (2009)
10. Ganin, Y., et al.: Domain-adversarial training of neural networks. J. Mach. Learn. Res. **17**(1), 2096–2130 (2016)
11. Gavves, E., Mensink, T., Tommasi, T., Snoek, C., Tuytelaars, T.: Active transfer learning with zero-shot priors: reusing past datasets for future tasks. In: Proceedings ICCV 2015, pp. 2731–2739 (2015)

12. Ghifary, M., Kleijn, W.B., Zhang, M., Balduzzi, D., Li, W.: Deep reconstruction-classification networks for unsupervised domain adaptation. In: Leibe, B., Matas, J., Sebe, N., Welling, M. (eds.) ECCV 2016. LNCS, vol. 9908, pp. 597–613. Springer, Cham (2016). https://doi.org/10.1007/978-3-319-46493-0_36
13. Glorot, X., Bordes, A., Bengio, Y.: Domain adaptation for large-scale sentiment classification: a deep learning approach. In: Proceedings of the 28th International Conference on Machine Learning (ICML-11), pp. 513–520 (2011)
14. Goodfellow, I., et al.: Generative adversarial nets. In: Advances in Neural Information Processing Systems, pp. 2672–2680 (2014)
15. Haeusser, P., Frerix, T., Mordvintsev, A., Cremers, D.: Associative domain adaptation. In: International Conference on Computer Vision (ICCV), vol. 2, p. 6 (2017)
16. Haeusser, P., Mordvintsev, A., Cremers, D.: Learning by association-a versatile semi-supervised training method for neural networks. In: Proceedings of the IEEE Conference on Computer Vision and Pattern Recognition (CVPR) (2017)
17. He, K., Zhang, X., Ren, S., Sun, J.: Deep residual learning for image recognition. In: Proceedings of the IEEE Conference on Computer Vision and Pattern Recognition, pp. 770–778 (2016)
18. Hoffman, J., et al.: CyCADA: cycle-consistent adversarial domain adaptation. arXiv preprint arXiv:1711.03213 (2017)
19. Hoffman, J., Wang, D., Yu, F., Darrell, T.: FCNs in the wild: pixel-level adversarial and constraint-based adaptation. arXiv:1612.02649 (2016)
20. Krizhevsky, A., Hinton, G.: Learning multiple layers of features from tiny images (2009)
21. LeCun, Y., Bottou, L., Bengio, Y., Haffner, P.: Gradient-based learning applied to document recognition. Proc. IEEE **86**(11), 2278–2324 (1998)
22. Long, M., Cao, Y., Wang, J., Jordan, M.I.: Learning transferable features with deep adaptation networks. arXiv preprint arXiv:1502.02791 (2015)
23. Long, M., Zhu, H., Wang, J., Jordan, M.I.: Deep transfer learning with joint adaptation networks. arXiv preprint arXiv:1605.06636 (2016)
24. Long, M., Zhu, H., Wang, J., Jordan, M.I.: Unsupervised domain adaptation with residual transfer networks. In: Advances in Neural Information Processing Systems, pp. 136–144 (2016)
25. Moiseev, B., Konev, A., Chigorin, A., Konushin, A.: Evaluation of traffic sign recognition methods trained on synthetically generated data. In: Blanc-Talon, J., Kasinski, A., Philips, W., Popescu, D., Scheunders, P. (eds.) ACIVS 2013. LNCS, vol. 8192, pp. 576–583. Springer, Cham (2013). https://doi.org/10.1007/978-3-319-02895-8_52
26. Netzer, Y., Wang, T., Coates, A., Bissacco, A., Wu, B., Ng, A.Y.: Reading digits in natural images with unsupervised feature learning. In: NIPS Workshop on Deep Learning and Unsupervised Feature Learning, vol. 2011, p. 5 (2011)
27. Richter, S.R., Vineet, V., Roth, S., Koltun, V.: Playing for data: ground truth from computer games. In: Leibe, B., Matas, J., Sebe, N., Welling, M. (eds.) ECCV 2016. LNCS, vol. 9906, pp. 102–118. Springer, Cham (2016). https://doi.org/10.1007/978-3-319-46475-6_7
28. Sankaranarayanan, S., Balaji, Y., Jain, A., Lim, S.N., Chellappa, R.: Unsupervised domain adaptation for semantic segmentation with GANs. arXiv preprint arXiv:1711.06969 (2017)
29. Stallkamp, J., Schlipsing, M., Salmen, J., Igel, C.: The German traffic sign recognition benchmark: a multi-class classification competition. In: The 2011 International Joint Conference on Neural Networks (IJCNN), pp. 1453–1460. IEEE (2011)

30. Street, W.N., Kim, Y.: A streaming ensemble algorithm (SEA) for large-scale classification. In: Proceedings of the seventh ACM SIGKDD International Conference on Knowledge Discovery and Data Mining, pp. 377–382. ACM (2001)
31. Sun, B., Saenko, K.: Deep CORAL: correlation alignment for deep domain adaptation. In: Hua, G., Jégou, H. (eds.) ECCV 2016. LNCS, vol. 9915, pp. 443–450. Springer, Cham (2016). https://doi.org/10.1007/978-3-319-49409-8_35
32. Tan, C., Ji, G.: Semi-supervised incremental feature extraction algorithm for large-scale data stream. Concurr. Comput.: Pract. Exp. **29**(6), e3914 (2017)
33. Tennant, M., Stahl, F., Rana, O., Gomes, J.B.: Scalable real-time classification of data streams with concept drift. Future Gener. Comput. Syst. **75**, 187–199 (2017)
34. Tommasi, T., Patricia, N., Caputo, B., Tuytelaars, T.: A deeper look at dataset bias. In: Csurka, G. (ed.) Domain Adaptation in Computer Vision Applications. ACVPR, pp. 37–55. Springer, Cham (2017). https://doi.org/10.1007/978-3-319-58347-1_2
35. Tzeng, E., Hoffman, J., Saenko, K., Darrell, T.: Adversarial discriminative domain adaptation. In: Computer Vision and Pattern Recognition (CVPR), vol. 1, p. 4 (2017)
36. Wang, M., Deng, W.: Deep visual domain adaptation: a survey. arXiv preprint arXiv:1802.03601 (2018)
37. Wang, Y., Li, H., Wang, H., Zhou, B., Zhang, Y.: Multi-window based ensemble learning for classification of imbalanced streaming data. In: Wang, J., et al. (eds.) WISE 2015. LNCS, vol. 9419, pp. 78–92. Springer, Cham (2015). https://doi.org/10.1007/978-3-319-26187-4_6
38. Zhang, J., Liang, C., Kuo, C.C.J.: A fully convolutional tri-branch network (FCTN) for domain adaptation. arXiv preprint arXiv:1711.03694 (2017)
39. Zhang, Y., David, P., Gong, B.: Curriculum domain adaptation for semantic segmentation of urban scenes. In: The IEEE International Conference on Computer Vision (ICCV), vol. 2, p. 6 (2017)

Domain Adaptive Semantic Segmentation Through Structure Enhancement

Fengmao Lv[1(✉)], Qing Lian[1], Guowu Yang[1], Guosheng Lin[2], Sinno Jialin Pan[2], and Lixin Duan[1]

[1] Big Data Research Center, University of Electronic Science and Technology of China, Chengdu, China
fengmaolv@126.com, lianqinglalala@gmail.com, guowu@uestc.edu.cn, lxduan@gmail.com

[2] School of Computer Science and Engineering, Nanyang Technological University, Singapore, Singapore
{gslin,sinnopan}@ntu.edu.sg

Abstract. Although fully convolutional networks have recently achieved great advances in semantic segmentation, the performance leaps heavily rely on supervision with pixel-level annotations which are extremely expensive and time-consuming to collect. Training models on synthetic data is a feasible way to relieve the annotation burden. However, the domain shift between synthetic and real images usually lead to poor generalization performance. In this work, we propose an effective method to adapt the segmentation network trained on synthetic images to real scenarios in an unsupervised fashion. To improve the adaptation performance for semantic segmentation, we enhance the structure information of the target images at both the feature level and the output level. Specifically, we enforce the segmentation network to learn a representation that encodes the target images' visual cues through image reconstruction, which is beneficial to the structured prediction of the target images. Further more, we implement adversarial training at the output space of the segmentation network to align the structured prediction of the source and target images based on the similar spatial structure they share. To validate the performance of our method, we conduct comprehensive experiments on the "GTA5 to Cityscapes" dataset which is a standard domain adaptation benchmark for semantic segmentation. The experimental results clearly demonstrate that our method can effectively bridge the synthetic and real image domains and obtain better adaptation performance compared with the existing state-of-the-art methods.

Keywords: Unsupervised domain adaptation · Semantic segmentation · Deep learning · Transfer learning

1 Introduction

Semantic segmentation is a critical and challenging task in computer vision, which aims at predicting the class label of each pixel in images. Over the past

The first two authors Contribute equally to this work.

L. Leal-Taixé and S. Roth (Eds.): ECCV 2018 Workshops, LNCS 11130, pp. 172–179, 2019.
https://doi.org/10.1007/978-3-030-11012-3_13

years, deep convolutional networks have achieved great advances in semantic segmentation [1,9,18]. However, the pixel-level annotation is an extremely heavy work. Specifically, we need more than 1 h to annotate a single image in the Cityscapes dataset [3]. Training models on synthetic images can be a promising way to relieve the tedious annotation burden as their pixel-level labels can be automatically generated. Unfortunately, the domain shift between the synthetic images and real-world scenarios will degenerate the prediction results on real images. Therefore, domain adaptation should be considered to adapt the segmentation network trained on synthetic images to real images, given labeled source data and unlabeled target data. Although the recently proposed feature adaptation methods can bridge the source and target domains through learning domain-invariant features with adversarial mechanism [2,7,13], they cannot ensure that these features encode the structure information of the target images, since semantic segmentation is a highly structured prediction task.

In this paper, we propose to improve the domain adaptation performance of segmentation networks through enhancing the structure information of the target images at both the feature level and the output level. The main contribution of our work is two-fold: (1) enforcing an intermediate feature to reconstruct the training images; (2) adversarially aligning the structured output of the source and target images. Specifically, the reconstruction branch can enforce the encoding representation to preserve the visual cues of the target images, which are beneficial to their structured prediction. On the other hand, the output-level structure enhancement can directly regularize the target image's structured prediction since both domains should share similar spatial layout and local context. We conduct experiments on "GTA5 to Cityscapes" which is a standard domain adaptation benchmark for semantic segmentation to evaluate the performance of our method. The experimental results clearly demonstrate that our method can effectively bridge both domains and obtain better adaptation results than the existing state-of-the-art methods.

2 Related Work

Over the past years, domain adaptation in computer vision has been primarily explored for the classification task. Overall, the main idea is to learn a "deep" representation that is domain invariant [4,5,10,15,16]. Thus far, unsupervised domain adaptation for semantic segmentation has not been widely explored. In [7], Hoffman *et al.* first proposed to adapt segmentation networks through domain adversarial learning in the feature space. In [2], Chen *et al.* further proposed class-specific domain adversarial learning framework, which aimed at reducing the domain divergence in each class. In [11], Murez *et al.* proposed to learn domain adaptive segmentation networks through directly translating the source images to the target ones at the pixel level. In [14], Tsai *et al.* proposed to align both domains at the structured output space. In short, the previous works mainly focused on angling the source and target domains through implementing adversarial learning at different levels, ranging from intermediate features to final predictions. In our method, our main idea is to enhance the structure information of the target images, which provides a reasonable regularization to their structured prediction.

3 Our Method

In this paper, we focus on unsupervised domain adaptation for semantic segmentation. Our goal is to learn a segmentation network which can achieve good prediction results on the target domain, given source images I_S with pixel-level labels L_S and unlabeled target images I_T.

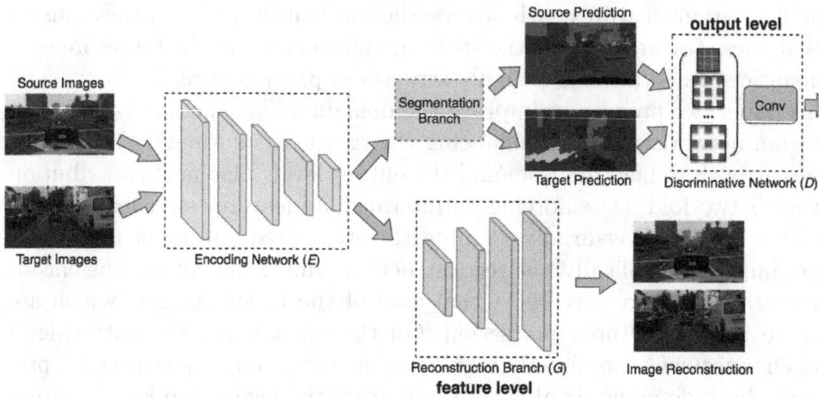

Fig. 1. The overall architecture of our model (best viewed in color).

Overall, our adaptation method contains two major components, including reconstructing the training images and aligning the target images' structured prediction with adversarial training. Figure 1 shows the overview of our method.

Image Reconstruction: our main idea aims at adapting the segmentation network trained on the source images through learning a representation that encodes the visual cues of the target images. This is achieved through enforcing an intermediate layer to reconstruct the training images. As displayed in Fig. 1, the encoding network is shared by both the segmentation branch and the reconstruction branch. The reconstruction branch can regularize the encoding network to enhance the target images' structure information.

Throughout this paper, we denote the encoding network and the decoding network as E and G, respectively. The segmentation branch is represented as S. We define our image reconstruction loss as

$$\begin{aligned} \min_{E,G,S} \; & \mathcal{L}(E,G,S) \\ s.t. \; & \mathcal{L}(E,G,S) = \lambda_{rec}\mathcal{L}_{rec} + \mathcal{L}_{seg} \\ & \qquad = \lambda_{rec}(L_1(G \circ E(I_S), I_S) + L_1(G \circ E(I_T), I_T)) \\ & \qquad + L_{sup}(S \circ E(I_S), L_S), \end{aligned} \tag{1}$$

where the former part is the reconstruction term for the training images and L_{sup} is the segmentation supervision term for the source images. In our method, the image reconstruction is implemented with L_1 loss. Though ideally we only need to consider the reconstruction of the target images, the reconstruction of the source images can help the training of the decoding network.

Output Adaptation: Further more, we implement adversarial training at the output space of the segmentation network to align the structured prediction on the source and target images since both domains should share similar spatial layouts. As displayed in Fig. 1, a discriminative network is invoked to discriminate whether a softmax prediction is from the source domain or the target domain. In contrast, the segmentation network $S \circ E(\cdot)$ will try to cheat the discriminator in order to make the target images' structured predictions resemble the source images' pixel maps. This can provide gradient updates to the segmentation network when the target images' predictions are not structured reasonably. As a whole, the segmentation network and the discriminative network play a minimax game.

To retain the spatial information, D is specified as a fully convolutional network, which discriminates the domain label of each spatial unit. Following [17], we adopt Atrous Spatial Pyramid Pooling (ASPP) in our discriminative network since this can help to align the structured output at multiple scales. The adversarial loss are formulated as

$$\begin{aligned} \max_{D} \min_{E,S} \mathcal{L}_{adv} =& \mathbb{E}_{I_T \sim \mathcal{X}_t}[\frac{1}{HW}\sum_{i=1}^{H}\sum_{j=1}^{W}\log(1 - D_{i,j}(S \circ E(I_T)))] \\ &+ \mathbb{E}_{I_S \sim \mathcal{X}_s}[\frac{1}{HW}\sum_{i=1}^{H}\sum_{j=1}^{W}\log(D_{i,j}(S \circ E(I_S)))]. \end{aligned} \tag{2}$$

H and W are the height and width of the discriminator's output, respectively.

In conclusion, with the above sub-objectives, our finial objective function is defined as

$$\max_{D} \min_{E,S,G} \mathcal{L}_{seg} + \lambda_{rec}\mathcal{L}_{rec} + \lambda_{adv}\mathcal{L}_{adv}. \tag{3}$$

In our defined minimax game, we alternately optimize each sub-network, while holding the other parts fixed. The parameters of the encoding network E is updated by averaging the gradients from each branch.

4 Experiments

4.1 Dataset

To evaluate the performance of our method, we conduct experiments on "GAT5 to Cityscapes", which is a standard benchmark of domain adaptation for semantic segmentation. Specifically, GAT5 is the dataset that contains 24,966 synthetic images with resolution of 1914 × 1052, rendered by the gaming engine Grand

Theft Auto V. The pixel-level annotations of the GAT5 images are automatically generated. On the other hand, Cityscapes is a dataset that focuses on autonomous driving. The Cityscapes dataset consists of 2,975 images for training and 500 images in validation set. These images have a resolution of 2048×1024. We use 19 common semantic categories between GTA5 and Cityscapes as the labels. Following the existing state-of-the-art works [7,14], we train our domain adaptive segmentation network using the full GTA5 dataset and the Cityscapes training set with 2,975 images, and evaluate the performance on the Cityscapes validation set with 500 images.

Table 1. Results of different methods on the "GTA5 to Cityscapes" dataset. Ablation studies are conducted for both the feature-level encoding and the output-level enhancement.

	road	sdwk	bldng	wall	fence	pole	light	sign	vgttn	trrn	sky	person	rider	car	truck	bus	train	mcycl	bcycl	mIoU
MCD[12]	**90.3**	31.0	78.5	19.7	17.3	28.6	30.9	16.1	**83.7**	30.0	69.1	58.5	19.6	**81.5**	23.8	30.0	5.7	25.7	14.3	39.7
CYCADA[6]	79.1	33.1	77.9	23.4	17.3	32.1	33.3	31.8	81.5	26.7	69.0	**62.8**	14.7	74.5	20.9	25.6	6.9	18.8	20.4	39.5
ROAD[7]	76.3	36.1	69.6	**28.6**	22.4	28.6	29.3	14.8	82.3	**35.3**	72.9	54.4	17.8	78.9	27.7	30.3	4.0	24.9	12.6	39.4
AdaptSeg[14]	86.5	36.0	79.9	23.4	23.3	23.9	35.2	14.8	83.4	33.3	75.6	58.5	27.6	73.7	**32.5**	35.4	3.9	30.1	28.1	42.4
RAN[17]	84.5	**36.9**	72.9	15.8	23.3	**39.4**	**41.8**	**36.8**	67.1	25.2	**89.1**	50.5	20.6	77.8	22.1	24.3	**22.8**	28.5	**37.9**	43.0
source only	75.8	16.8	77.2	12.5	21.0	25.5	30.1	20.1	81.3	24.6	70.3	53.8	26.4	49.9	17.2	25.9	6.5	25.3	36.0	36.6
feature-level	86.3	30.8	76.4	26.2	20.0	23.1	31.6	16.5	80.5	33.1	75.0	56.5	25.7	76.8	15.0	29.5	1.0	25.6	13.0	39.1
output-level	85.3	35.1	79.0	22.9	23.4	23.1	34.1	14.8	83.2	33.0	74.2	57.8	27.2	73.1	32.3	34.8	3.0	29.8	28.0	41.7
full model	88.9	31.3	**81.5**	28.3	**23.5**	28.7	37.1	30.2	82.2	33.1	76.8	59.7	**29.2**	80.8	28.9	**43.5**	4.2	**31.6**	32.3	**44.8**

4.2 Implementation Details

We adopt deeplabv2 as our baseline [1]. Specifically, the encoding network E is implemented with Resnet-101. The outputs of the *res5c* layer are fed into both the segmentation branch S and the reconstruction network G. G follows the identical architecture in [8], except that all the layers are shared by both domains. The discriminative network D contains 3 layer, including a ASPP layer with 4 dilated convolutional operators in parallel, and a convolutional layer followed sigmoid activations. The sampling rates in the ASPP layer are respectively set to 1, 2, 3 and 4. In our experiments, we use the PyTorch framework to implement our method. Overall, our experimental setting follows [14]. For E and S, we adopt stochastic gradient descent (SGD) with momentum of 0.9 as the optimizer. The parameters G and D are optimized by Adam with momentum of 0.99. In addition, we initialize the learning rate to 2.5×10^{-4} and decay it through the polynomial policy with power of 0.9. As the tradeoff parameters, λ_{rec} and λ_{adv} are set to 1.0×10^{-5} and 1.0×10^{-3}, respectively. The mIoU value is used as the metric of evaluation.

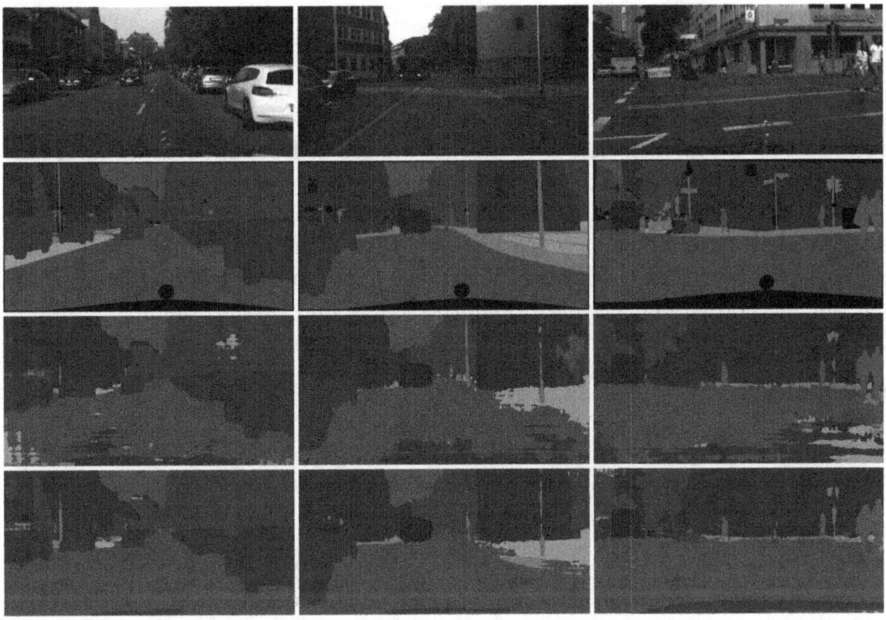

Fig. 2. The qualitative example results. The first row displays the target images, with their corresponding ground truth segmentation masks in the second row. The third and fourth rows display the results before adaptation and after adaptation with our adaptation method, respectively.

4.3 Experimental Results

In Table 1 and Fig. 2, we report our adaptation results both quantitatively and qualitatively. The results demonstrate that our adaptation method can effectively improve the structured predictions of the target images. From Fig. 2, we can see that the structure information of the target images' predictions are significantly enhanced, which is consistent with our motivation. With our method, the target images' pixel-level predictions clearly delineate the real spatial layout. As displayed in Table 1, our method performs better than the existing state-of-the-art methods. The ablation studies demonstrate that the feature-level encoding and the output-level enhancement can work complementarily to improve the adaptation performance. This can be ascribed to the fact that these two branches enhance the target images' structure information from complementary perspectives. Specifically, the reconstruction branch enforces the encoding representation to preserve the target images' visual cues such as the local contexts or spatial layouts, which are essential for the structured predictions. In contrast, the output-level enhancement can directly leverages the source images' pixel maps to regularize the target images' structured predictions.

5 Conclusion

In this paper, we propose an effective method to learn domain adaptive segmentation network in an unsupervised domain adaptation setting. Through enhancing the structure information of the target images at both the feature level and the output level, our method can effectively improve the domain adaptation performance of the segmentation networks. After adaptation using our method, the target images' pixel maps can clearly reveal their structure characteristics such as the spatial layout or the local context. The experimental results demonstrate that our method can effectively bridge the source and target domains.

References

1. Chen, L.C., Papandreou, G., Kokkinos, I., Murphy, K., Yuille, A.L.: DeepLab: semantic image segmentation with deep convolutional nets, atrous convolution, and fully connected CRFs. IEEE Trans. Pattern Anal. Mach. Intell. **40**(4), 834–848 (2018)
2. Chen, Y.H., Chen, W.Y., Chen, Y.T., Tsai, B.C., Wang, Y.C.F., Sun, M.: No more discrimination: cross city adaptation of road scene segmenters. In: 2017 IEEE International Conference on Computer Vision (ICCV), pp. 2011–2020. IEEE (2017)
3. Cordts, M., et al.: The cityscapes dataset for semantic urban scene understanding. In: Proceedings of the IEEE Conference on Computer Vision and Pattern Recognition, pp. 3213–3223 (2016)
4. Ganin, Y., Lempitsky, V.: Unsupervised domain adaptation by backpropagation. arXiv preprint arXiv:1409.7495 (2014)
5. Haeusser, P., Frerix, T., Mordvintsev, A., Cremers, D.: Associative domain adaptation. In: International Conference on Computer Vision (ICCV), vol. 2, p. 6 (2017)
6. Hoffman, J., et al.: CyCADA: cycle-consistent adversarial domain adaptation. arXiv preprint arXiv:1711.03213 (2017)
7. Hoffman, J., Wang, D., Yu, F., Darrell, T.: FCNs in the wild: pixel-level adversarial and constraint-based adaptation. arXiv preprint arXiv:1612.02649 (2016)
8. Liu, M.Y., Breuel, T., Kautz, J.: Unsupervised image-to-image translation networks. In: Advances in Neural Information Processing Systems, pp. 700–708 (2017)
9. Long, J., Shelhamer, E., Darrell, T.: Fully convolutional networks for semantic segmentation. In: Proceedings of the IEEE Conference on Computer Vision and Pattern Recognition, pp. 3431–3440 (2015)
10. Long, M., Zhu, H., Wang, J., Jordan, M.I.: Deep transfer learning with joint adaptation networks. arXiv preprint arXiv:1605.06636 (2016)
11. Murez, Z., Kolouri, S., Kriegman, D., Ramamoorthi, R., Kim, K.: Image to image translation for domain adaptation. arXiv preprint arXiv:1712.00479 (2017)
12. Saito, K., Watanabe, K., Ushiku, Y., Harada, T.: Maximum classifier discrepancy for unsupervised domain adaptation. arXiv preprint arXiv:1712.02560 3 (2017)
13. Sankaranarayanan, S., Balaji, Y., Jain, A., Lim, S.N., Chellappa, R.: Unsupervised domain adaptation for semantic segmentation with GANs. arXiv preprint arXiv:1711.06969 (2017)
14. Tsai, Y.H., Hung, W.C., Schulter, S., Sohn, K., Yang, M.H., Chandraker, M.: Learning to adapt structured output space for semantic segmentation. arXiv preprint arXiv:1802.10349 (2018)

15. Tzeng, E., Hoffman, J., Zhang, N., Saenko, K., Darrell, T.: Deep domain confusion: maximizing for domain invariance. arXiv preprint arXiv:1412.3474 (2014)
16. Zellinger, W., Grubinger, T., Lughofer, E., Natschläger, T., Saminger-Platz, S.: Central moment discrepancy (CMD) for domain-invariant representation learning. arXiv preprint arXiv:1702.08811 (2017)
17. Zhang, Y., Qiu, Z., Yao, T., Liu, D., Mei, T.: Fully convolutional adaptation networks for semantic segmentation. In: Proceedings of the IEEE Conference on Computer Vision and Pattern Recognition, pp. 6810–6818 (2018)
18. Zhao, H., Shi, J., Qi, X., Wang, X., Jia, J.: Pyramid scene parsing network. In: IEEE Conference on Computer Vision and Pattern Recognition (CVPR), pp. 2881–2890 (2017)

Adding New Tasks to a Single Network with Weight Transformations Using Binary Masks

Massimiliano Mancini[1,2(✉)], Elisa Ricci[2,3], Barbara Caputo[4], and Samuel Rota Bulò[5]

[1] Sapienza University of Rome, Rome, Italy
mancini@diag.uniroma1.it
[2] Fondazione Bruno Kessler, Trento, Italy
eliricci@fbk.eu
[3] University of Trento, Trento, Italy
[4] Italian Institute of Technology, Genoa, Italy
caputo@diag.uniroma1.it
[5] Mapillary Research, Graz, Austria
samuel@mapillary.com

Abstract. Visual recognition algorithms are required today to exhibit adaptive abilities. Given a deep model trained on a specific, given task, it would be highly desirable to be able to adapt incrementally to new tasks, preserving scalability as the number of new tasks increases, while at the same time avoiding catastrophic forgetting issues. Recent work has shown that masking the internal weights of a given original conv-net through learned binary variables is a promising strategy. We build upon this intuition and take into account more elaborated affine transformations of the convolutional weights that include learned binary masks. We show that with our generalization it is possible to achieve significantly higher levels of adaptation to new tasks, enabling the approach to compete with fine tuning strategies by requiring slightly more than 1 bit per network parameter per additional task. Experiments on two popular benchmarks showcase the power of our approach, that achieves the new state of the art on the Visual Decathlon Challenge.

Keywords: Incremental learning · Multi-task learning

1 Introduction

A long-standing goal of AI is the ability to adapt an initial, pre-trained model to novel, unseen scenarios. This is crucial for increasing the knowledge of an intelligent system and developing effective life-long learning [38,41,42] algorithms. While fascinating, achieving this goal requires facing multiple challenges. First, learning a new task should not negatively affect the performance on old tasks, avoiding the catastrophic forgetting phenomenon [6,8]. Second, it should be

L. Leal-Taixé and S. Roth (Eds.): ECCV 2018 Workshops, LNCS 11130, pp. 180–189, 2019.
https://doi.org/10.1007/978-3-030-11012-3_14

avoided adding multiple parameters to the model for each new task learned, as it would lead to poor scalability of the framework [31]. In this context, while deep learning algorithms have achieved impressive results on many computer vision benchmarks [7,11,17,22], mainstream approaches for adapting deep models to novel tasks tend to suffer from the problems mentioned above.

Different works addressed these problems by either considering regularization techniques [14,21] or task-specific network parameters [24,25,31,34,36]. Interestingly, in [25] the authors effectively addressed sequential multi-task learning by creating a binary mask for each task. This mask is then multiplied by the main network weights, determining which of them are useful for addressing the new task and requiring just one bit for each parameter per task.

Our paper takes inspiration from this last work. We formulate sequential multi-task learning as the problem of learning a perturbation of a *baseline*, pre-trained network, maximizing the performance on a new task. As opposed to [25], we apply an affine transformation to each convolutional weight of the baseline network, involving both a learned binary mask and few additional parameters. Our solution allows to: (1) boosting the performance of each task-specific network, by leveraging the higher degree of freedom in perturbing the baseline network; (2) keeping a low per-task overhead in terms of additional parameters (slightly more than 1 bit per parameter per task). We assess the validity of our method on standard benchmarks, achieving performances comparable with fine-tuning separate networks for each task.

2 Related Works

The keen interest on incremental and life-long learning methods dates back to the pre-convnet era, with shallow learning approaches ranging from large margin classifiers [18,19] to non-parametric methods [27,33].

Recently, various works have addressed these problems within the framework of deep architectures [1,10,31]. A major risk when training a neural network on a novel task is to deteriorate its performances on old tasks, discarding previous knowledge, a phenomenon called *catastrophic forgetting* [6,8,26]. To alleviate this issue, various works designed constrained optimization procedures taking into account the initial network weights, trained on previous tasks. In [21], the authors exploit knowledge distillation [13] to obtain target objectives for previous tasks, while training for novel ones. In [14] the authors design an update of the network parameters, based on their importance for previously seen tasks.

Recent methods achieved higher performances with the cost of adding task specific parameters for each newly learned task, keeping untouched the initial network parameters. The extreme case is [36], where a parallel network is added each time a new task is presented. In [31,32], task-specific residual components are added in standard residual blocks. In [34] the authors use controller modules where the parameters of the base architecture are recombined channel-wise. In [24] a different subset of network parameters is considered for each task. A more compact and effective solution is [25], where separate binary masks are learned for each novel task and multiplied to the original network weights. The binary masks determine which parameters are useful for the new task and which are not. We take inspiration from this last work but we use the binary masks to design task specific affine transformations through. This allows us to use a comparable number of parameters per task with increased flexibility, further reducing the gap with the individual end-to-end trained architectures.

3 Method

We address the problem of sequential multi-task learning, as in [25], *i.e.* we modify a *baseline* network such as, *e.g.* ResNet-50 pretrained on the ImageNet classification task, so to maximize its performance on a new task, while limiting the amount of additional parameters needed. The solution we propose exploits the key idea from Piggyback [25] of learning task-specific masks, but instead of pursuing the simple multiplicative transformation of the parameters of the baseline network, we define a parametrized, affine transformation mixing a binary mask and real parameters. This choice keeps a low per-task overhead while significantly increases the expressiveness of the approach, leading to a rich and nuanced ability to adapt the old parameters to the needs of the new tasks.

3.1 Overview

Let us assume to be given a pre-trained, *baseline* network $f_0(\cdot;\Theta,\Omega_0):\mathcal{X}\to\mathcal{Y}_0$ assigning a class label in $\mathcal{Y}_0$ to elements of an input space $\mathcal{X}$ (*e.g.* images).[1] The parameters of the baseline network are partitioned into two sets: Θ comprises parameters that will be shared for other tasks, whereas Ω_0 entails the rest of the parameters (*e.g.* the classifier). Our goal is to learn for each task $i\in\{1,\dots,\mathtt{m}\}$, with a possibly different output space $\mathcal{Y}_i$, a classifier $f_i(\cdot;\Theta,\Omega_i):\mathcal{X}\to\mathcal{Y}_i$. Here, Ω_i entails the parameters specific for the ith task, while Θ holds the shareable parameters of the baseline network mentioned above. Before delving into the details of our method, we review the Piggyback solution presented in [25].

Each task-specific network f_i shares the same structure of the baseline network f_0, except for having a possibly, differently sized classification layer. All parameters of f_0, excepting the classifier, are shared across all the tasks. For each convolutional layer[2] of f_0 with parameters $\mathtt{W}$, the task-specific network f_i holds a binary mask $\mathtt{M}$ that is used to mask $\mathtt{W}$ obtaining

$$\hat{\mathtt{W}}=\mathtt{W}\circ\mathtt{M},\tag{1}$$

where $\circ$ is the Hadamard product. The transformed parameters $\hat{\mathtt{W}}$ are then used in the convolutional layer of f_i. By doing so, the task-specific parameters that are stored in Ω_i amount to just a single bit per parameter in each convolutional

[1] We focus on classification tasks, but the proposed method applies also to other tasks.
[2] Fully-connected layers are a special case.

layer, yielding a low overhead per additional task, while retaining a sufficient degree of freedom to build new convolutional weights.

Proposed. Similarly to [25], we consider task-specific networks f_i that are shaped as the baseline network f_0 and we store in Ω_i a binary mask $\mathtt{M}$ for each convolutional kernel $\mathtt{W}$ in the shared set Θ. However, we depart from the simple multiplicative transformation of $\mathtt{W}$ used in (1), and consider instead an affine transformation of the base convolutional kernel $\mathtt{W}$ that depends on a binary mask $\mathtt{M}$ as well as additional parameters. Specifically, we transform $\mathtt{W}$ into

$$\breve{\mathtt{W}} = k_0\mathtt{W} + k_1\mathtt{1} + k_2\mathtt{M}, \tag{2}$$

where $k_j \in \mathbb{R}$ are additional task-specific parameters in Ω_i that we learn along with the binary mask $\mathtt{M}$, and $\mathtt{1}$ is an opportunely sized tensor of 1 s (Fig. 1). We can consider either a scale (k_2) and bias (k_1) parameter per convolutional kernel, or distinct values for each feature channel.

Besides learning the binary masks and the parameters k_j, we opt also for task-specific batch-normalization (BN) parameters (*i.e.* mean, variance, scale and bias), which will be part of Ω_i, and thus optimized for each task, rather than being fixed in Θ. In the cases where we have a convolutional layer followed by BN, we keep the corresponding parameter k_0 fixed to 1, because the output of batch normalization is invariant to the scale of the convolutional weights.

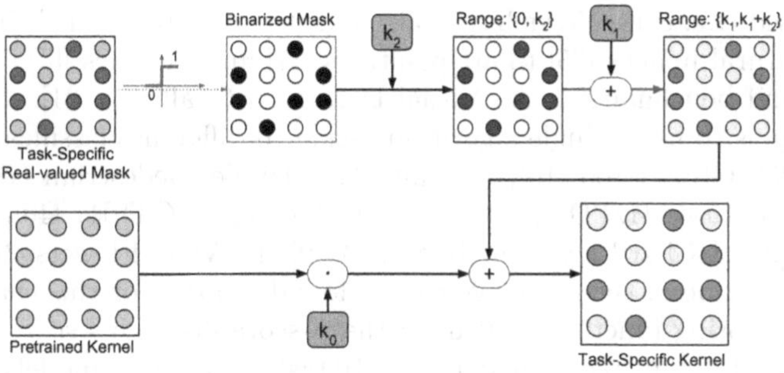

Fig. 1. Proposed model. An affine transformation scale and translate the binary masks through the parameters k_2 and k_1 respectively. The obtained mask is summed to the pretrained kernel in order to obtain the final task-specific weights.

The additional parameters introduced with our method bring a negligible per-task overhead compared to Piggyback, which is nevertheless generously balanced out by a significant boost of the performance of the task-specific classifiers.

3.2 Learning Binary Masks

We learn the parameters Ω_i of each task-specific network f_i by minimizing the classification log-loss, given a training set, using standard, stochastic optimization methods. However, special care should be taken for the optimization of the binary masks. Instead of optimizing the binary masks directly, which would turn the learning into a combinatorial problem, we apply the solution adopted in [25], *i.e.* we replace each binary mask M with a thresholded real matrix R. By doing so, we shift from optimizing discrete variables in M to continuous ones in R. However, the gradient of the hard threshold function $h(r) = 1_{r \geq 0}$ is zero almost everywhere, which makes this solution apparently incompatible with gradient-based optimization approaches. To sidestep this issue we consider a strictly increasing, surrogate function $\tilde{h}$ that will be used in place of h *only* for the gradient computation, *i.e.* if h' denotes the derivative of h with respect to its argument, we use $h'(r) \approx \tilde{h}'(r)$. The gradient obtained via the surrogate function has the property that it always points in the right down hill direction in the error surface.

By taking $\tilde{h}(x) = x$, *i.e.* the identity function, we recover the workaround suggested in [12], employed also in [25]. By taking $\tilde{h}(x) = (1 + e^{-x})^{-1}$, *i.e.* the sigmoid function, we obtain a better approximation, as suggested in [2,9].

4 Experiments

Datasets. In the following we test our method on two different benchmarks. For the first benchmark we follow [25], and we use 6 datasets: ImageNet [35], VGG-Flowers [30], Stanford Cars [15], Caltech-UCSD Birds (CUBS) [43], Sketches [5] and WikiArt [37]. These datasets contain a lot of variations both from the category addressed (*i.e.* cars [15] vs birds [43]) and the appearance of their instances (*i.e.* from natural images [35] to art paintings [37] and sketches [5]).

The second benchmark is the Visual Decathlon Challenge [31]. The goal of this challenge is to use a single algorithm tackle 10 different classification tasks: ImageNet [35], CIFAR-100 [16], Aircraft [23], Daimler pedestrian (DPed) [28], Describable textures (DTD) [4], German traffic signs (GTSR) [40], Omniglot [20], SVHN [29], UCF101 Dynamic Images [3,39] and VGG-Flowers [30]. A more detailed description of the challenge can be found in [31]. For this challenge, an independent scoring function is defined: the S-score [31]. This score takes into account the performances of a model on all 10 tasks, preferring models with good performances on all tasks to ones with peaked performances in few of them.

Networks and Training Protocols. For the first benchmark, we use a ResNet-50, comparing our model with Piggyback [25], PackNet [24] and two baselines considering the network only as feature extractor (training only the task-specific classifier) and individual networks separately fine-tuned on each task. Since [24] is dependent on the order of the task, we report the performances for two different orderings [25]: starting from the model pre-trained on ImageNet, the first ($\rightarrow$) is CUBS-Cars-Flowers-WikiArt-Sketch while the second ($\leftarrow$) is reversed. For training, we followed the preprocessing, hyper-parameters and schedule of [25].

For the Visual Decathlon we employ the Wide ResNet-28 [44] adopted by previous methods [25,31,34], using the same data preprocessing. For training we choose the same hyper-parameters of [25], *keeping the same values for all the tasks* except the ImageNet pretraining, for which we followed [31]. For both benchmarks we employ $\tilde{h}(x) = x$ as surrogate, initializing the real-valued masks with uniform random values drawn between 0.0001 and 0.0002.

4.1 Results

ImageNet-to-Sketch. In the following we discuss the results obtained by our model on the ImageNet-to-Sketch scenario. For fairness, since our model includes task-specific BN layers, we report also the results of [25] with separate BN layers.

Results are shown in Table 1. Our model is able to fill the gap between the classifier only baseline and the individual fine-tuned architectures, almost entirely in all settings. For larger and more diverse datasets such as Sketch and WikiArt, the gap is not completely covered, but the distance between our model and the individual architectures is always less than 1%. These results are remarkable given the simplicity of our method, not involving any assumption of the optimal weights per task [21,24], and the small overhead in terms of parameters that we report in the row "# Params" (*i.e.* 1.17), which represents the total number of parameters (counting all tasks and excluding the classifiers) relative to the ones in the baseline network. Comparing with the other algorithms, our model consistently outperforms both the basic version of Piggyback and PackNet in all settings. Introducing task-specific BN also for Piggyback reduces the performance gap, which still remains large in some settings (*i.e.* Flowers, Cars): this show how the advantages of our model are not only due to the additional BN parameters, but also to the more flexible affine transformation introduced.

Both Piggyback and our model outperform PackNet and, as opposed to the latter, do not suffer from the heavily dependence on the ordering of the tasks. This advantage stems from having a learning strategy that is task independent, with the base network not affected by the new tasks that are learned.

Table 1. Accuracy of ResNet-50 architectures in the ImageNet-to-Sketch setting.

Model	ImageNet	CUBS	Cars	Flowers	WikiArt	Sketch	# Params
Classifier only [25]	76.2	70.7	52.8	86.0	55.6	50.9	1
PackNet → [24]	75.7	80.4	86.1	93.0	69.4	76.2	1.10
PackNet ← [24]	75.7	71.4	80.0	90.6	70.3	78.7	1.10
Piggyback [25]	**76.2**	80.4	88.1	93.5	73.4	79.4	1.16
Piggyback+BN [25]	**76.2**	82.1	90.6	95.2	74.1	79.4	1.17
Ours	**76.2**	**82.6**	**91.5**	**96.5**	**74.8**	**80.2**	1.17
Individual networks [25]	76.2	82.8	91.8	96.6	75.6	80.8	6

Visual Decathlon Challenge. In this section we report the results for the Visual Decathlon Challenge. We compare our model with other sequential multi-task learning methods: Piggyback [25] (PB), the improved version of the winner entry of the 2017 edition of the challenge [34] (DAN), the network with task-specific residual [31] (RA) and parallel [32] (PA) adapters. We additionally report the baselines of [31]: the pre-trained network used as feature extractor (Feature) and 10 different models fine-tuned on each task (Finetune). Moreover, we add the results of our implementation of [25] with the same pre-trained model and training schedule adopted for our method (PB ours).

The results are reported in Table 2. We can see that our simple model achieves close to state-of-the-art performances on this competition. The only model outperforming ours is [32]: however, we employ a much lower parameters overhead and a single training schedule for all ten tasks. This produces a gain of more than 800 points with respect to [32] in the ratio between the S-Score and the number of parameters adopted. Remarkably, we obtain a gain on the previous winning entry [34] and Piggyback of more than 400 points.

Table 2. Results in terms of accuracy and S-Score, for the Visual Decathlon Challenge. Best model in bold, second best underlined.

Method	#Params	ImNet	Airc.	C100	DPed	DTD	GTSR	Flwr.	Oglt.	SVHN	UCF	Mean	S-Score	Score/Params
Feature [31]	1	59.7	23.3	63.1	80.3	45.4	68.2	73.7	58.8	43.5	26.8	54.3	544	544
Finetune [31]	10	59.9	60.3	82.1	92.8	55.5	97.5	81.4	87.7	96.6	51.2	76.5	2500	250
RA[31]	2	59.7	56.7	<u>81.2</u>	93.9	50.9	97.1	66.2	<u>89.6</u>	96.1	47.5	73.9	2118	1059
DAN [34]	2.17	57.7	64.1	80.1	91.3	56.5	98.5	86.1	**89.7**	<u>96.8</u>	<u>49.4</u>	<u>77.0</u>	2852	1314
PA [32]	2	<u>60.3</u>	<u>64.2</u>	**81.9**	94.7	58.8	**99.4**	84.7	89.2	96.5	**50.9**	**78.1**	**3412**	1706
PB [25]	1.28	57.7	**65.3**	79.9	**97.0**	57.5	97.3	79.1	87.6	**97.2**	47.5	76.6	2838	<u>2217</u>
PB ours	1.28	**60.8**	52.3	80.0	<u>95.1</u>	**59.6**	98.7	82.9	85.1	96.7	46.9	75.8	2805	2191
Ours	1.29	**60.8**	51.3	**81.9**	94.7	<u>59.0</u>	<u>99.1</u>	<u>88.0</u>	89.3	96.5	48.7	76.9	<u>3263</u>	**2529**

From the partial results, excluding the ImageNet baseline, our model achieves the top-1 or top-2 scores in 4 out of 9 tasks, with comparable performances in the others. The only exceptions are UCF-101 and Aircraft, where our model suffers a high accuracy drop. Tuning the hyper-parameters could cover this gap, but this is out of the scope of this work. Interestingly, while our model achieves comparable (*e.g.* PB, DAN) average accuracy with respect to other approaches, it obtains a much higher decathlon score. This highlights its capabilities of tackling all 10 tasks with good results, without peaked accuracies on just few of them.

5 Conclusions

We presented a simple yet powerful method for learning incrementally new tasks, given a fixed, pre-trained deep architecture. We build on the intuition of [25], generalizing the idea of masking the original weights of the network with learned binary masks. By introducing an affine transformation that acts upon such weights, we allow for a richer set of possible modifications of the original network, allowing to better capture the characteristics of the new tasks. Experiments on two public benchmarks confirm the effectiveness of our approach.

References

1. Bendale, A., Boult, T.E.: Towards open set deep networks. In: 2016 IEEE Conference on Computer Vision and Pattern Recognition, CVPR 2016, Las Vegas, NV, USA, 27–30 June 2016, pp. 1563–1572 (2016)
2. Bengio, Y., Léonard, N., Courville, A.: Estimating or propagating gradients through stochastic neurons for conditional computation. arXiv preprint arXiv:1308.3432 (2013)
3. Bilen, H., Fernando, B., Gavves, E., Vedaldi, A., Gould, S.: Dynamic image networks for action recognition. In: Proceedings of the IEEE Conference on Computer Vision and Pattern Recognition, pp. 3034–3042 (2016)
4. Cimpoi, M., Maji, S., Kokkinos, I., Mohamed, S., Vedaldi, A.: Describing textures in the wild. In: 2014 IEEE Conference on Computer Vision and Pattern Recognition (CVPR), pp. 3606–3613. IEEE (2014)
5. Eitz, M., Hays, J., Alexa, M.: How do humans sketch objects? ACM Trans. Graph. **31**(4), Article no. 44–1 (2012)
6. French, R.M.: Catastrophic forgetting in connectionist networks. Trends Cogn. Sci. **3**(4), 128–135 (1999)
7. Girshick, R., Donahue, J., Darrell, T., Malik, J.: Rich feature hierarchies for accurate object detection and semantic segmentation. In: Proceedings of the IEEE Conference on Computer Vision and Pattern Recognition, pp. 580–587 (2014)
8. Goodfellow, I.J., Mirza, M., Xiao, D., Courville, A., Bengio, Y.: An empirical investigation of catastrophic forgetting in gradient-based neural networks. arXiv preprint arXiv:1312.6211 (2013)
9. Goodman, R.M., Zeng, Z.: A learning algorithm for multi-layer perceptrons with hard-limiting threshold units. In: Proceedings of the 1994 IEEE Workshop Neural Networks for Signal Processing 1994 IV, pp. 219–228. IEEE (1994)
10. Guerriero, S., Caputo, B., Mensink, T.: Deep nearest class mean classifiers. In: International Conference on Learning Representations, Worskhop Track (2018)
11. He, K., Zhang, X., Ren, S., Sun, J.: Deep residual learning for image recognition. In: Proceedings of the IEEE Conference on Computer Vision and Pattern Recognition, pp. 770–778 (2016)
12. Hinton, G.: Neural networks for machine learning (2012). Coursera, video lectures
13. Hinton, G., Vinyals, O., Dean, J.: Distilling the knowledge in a neural network. arXiv preprint arXiv:1503.02531 (2015)
14. Kirkpatrick, J., et al.: Overcoming catastrophic forgetting in neural networks. Proc. Nat. Acad. Sci. U.S.A. **114**(13), 3521–3526 (2017)
15. Krause, J., Stark, M., Deng, J., Fei-Fei, L.: 3D object representations for fine-grained categorization. In: 2013 IEEE International Conference on Computer Vision Workshops (ICCVW), pp. 554–561. IEEE (2013)
16. Krizhevsky, A., Hinton, G.: Learning multiple layers of features from tiny images (2009)
17. Krizhevsky, A., Sutskever, I., Hinton, G.E.: Imagenet classification with deep convolutional neural networks. In: Advances in Neural Information Processing Systems, pp. 1097–1105 (2012)
18. Kuzborskij, I., Orabona, F., Caputo, B.: From N to N+1: multiclass transfer incremental learning. In: 2013 IEEE Conference on Computer Vision and Pattern Recognition, Portland, OR, USA, 23–28 June 2013, pp. 3358–3365 (2013)
19. Kuzborskij, I., Orabona, F., Caputo, B.: Scalable greedy algorithms for transfer learning. Comput. Vis. Image Underst. **156**, 174–185 (2017)

20. Lake, B.M., Salakhutdinov, R., Tenenbaum, J.B.: Human-level concept learning through probabilistic program induction. Science **350**(6266), 1332–1338 (2015)
21. Li, Z., Hoiem, D.: Learning without forgetting. IEEE Trans. Pattern Anal. Mach. Intell. **40**, 2935–2947 (2017)
22. Long, J., Shelhamer, E., Darrell, T.: Fully convolutional networks for semantic segmentation. In: Proceedings of the IEEE Conference on Computer Vision and Pattern Recognition, pp. 3431–3440 (2015)
23. Maji, S., Rahtu, E., Kannala, J., Blaschko, M., Vedaldi, A.: Fine-grained visual classification of aircraft. arXiv preprint arXiv:1306.5151 (2013)
24. Mallya, A., Lazebnik, S.: PackNet: adding multiple tasks to a single network by iterative pruning. In: The IEEE Conference on Computer Vision and Pattern Recognition (CVPR), June 2018
25. Mallya, A., Davis, D., Lazebnik, S.: Piggyback: adapting a single network to multiple tasks by learning to mask weights. In: Ferrari, V., Hebert, M., Sminchisescu, C., Weiss, Y. (eds.) ECCV 2018. LNCS, vol. 11208, pp. 72–88. Springer, Cham (2018). https://doi.org/10.1007/978-3-030-01225-0_5
26. McCloskey, M., Cohen, N.J.: Catastrophic interference in connectionist networks: the sequential learning problem. Psychol. Learn. Motiv. **24**, 109–165 (1989)
27. Mensink, T., Verbeek, J.J., Perronnin, F., Csurka, G.: Distance-based image classification: generalizing to new classes at near-zero cost. IEEE Trans. Pattern Anal. Mach. Intell. **35**(11), 2624–2637 (2013)
28. Munder, S., Gavrila, D.M.: An experimental study on pedestrian classification. IEEE Trans. Pattern Anal. Mach. Intell. **28**(11), 1863–1868 (2006)
29. Netzer, Y., Wang, T., Coates, A., Bissacco, A., Wu, B., Ng, A.Y.: Reading digits in natural images with unsupervised feature learning. In: NIPS Workshop on Deep Learning and Unsupervised Feature Learning, vol. 2011, p. 5 (2011)
30. Nilsback, M.E., Zisserman, A.: Automated flower classification over a large number of classes. In: Sixth Indian Conference on Computer Vision, Graphics & Image Processing 2008, ICVGIP 2008, pp. 722–729. IEEE (2008)
31. Rebuffi, S.A., Bilen, H., Vedaldi, A.: Learning multiple visual domains with residual adapters. In: Advances in Neural Information Processing Systems, pp. 506–516 (2017)
32. Rebuffi, S.A., Bilen, H., Vedaldi, A.: Efficient parametrization of multi-domain deep neural networks. In: Proceedings of the IEEE Conference on Computer Vision and Pattern Recognition, pp. 8119–8127 (2018)
33. Ristin, M., Guillaumin, M., Gall, J., Van Gool, L.: Incremental learning of random forests for large-scale image classification. IEEE Trans. Pattern Anal. Mach. Intell. **38**(3), 490–503 (2016)
34. Rosenfeld, A., Tsotsos, J.K.: Incremental learning through deep adaptation. arXiv preprint arXiv:1705.04228 (2017)
35. Russakovsky, O., et al.: Imagenet large scale visual recognition challenge. Int. J. Comput. Vis. **115**(3), 211–252 (2015)
36. Rusu, A.A., et al.: Progressive neural networks. arXiv preprint arXiv:1606.04671 (2016)
37. Saleh, B., Elgammal, A.: Large-scale classification of fine-art paintings: Learning the right metric on the right feature. arXiv preprint arXiv:1505.00855 (2015)
38. Silver, D.L., Yang, Q., Li, L.: Lifelong machine learning systems: beyond learning algorithms. In: AAAI Spring Symposium: Lifelong Machine Learning, vol. 13, p. 05 (2013)
39. Soomro, K., Zamir, A.R., Shah, M.: UCF101: a dataset of 101 human actions classes from videos in the wild. arXiv preprint arXiv:1212.0402 (2012)

40. Stallkamp, J., Schlipsing, M., Salmen, J., Igel, C.: Man vs. computer: benchmarking machine learning algorithms for traffic sign recognition. Neural Netw. **32**, 323–332 (2012)
41. Thrun, S., Mitchell, T.M.: Lifelong robot learning. Robot. Auton. Syst. **15**(1–2), 25–46 (1995)
42. Thrun, S., Pratt, L.: Learning to Learn. Springer. Heidelberg (2012)
43. Wah, C., Branson, S., Welinder, P., Perona, P., Belongie, S.: The caltech-UCSD birds-200-2011 dataset (2011)
44. Zagoruyko, S., Komodakis, N.: Wide residual networks. arXiv preprint arXiv:1605.07146 (2016)

Generating Shared Latent Variables for Robots to Imitate Human Movements and Understand Their Physical Limitations

Maxime Devanne(✉) and Sao Mai Nguyen

IMT Atlantique, Lab-STICC, UBL, Brest, France
{maxime.devanne,mai.nguyen}@imt-atlantique.fr

Abstract. Assistive robotics and particularly robot coaches may be very helpful for rehabilitation healthcare. In this context, we propose a method based on Gaussian Process Latent Variable Model (GP-LVM) to transfer knowledge between a physiotherapist, a robot coach and a patient. Our model is able to map visual human body features to robot data in order to facilitate the robot learning and imitation. In addition, we propose to extend the model to adapt the robots' understanding to patients' physical limitations during assessment of rehabilitation exercises. Experimental evaluation demonstrates promising results for both robot imitation and model adaptation according to patients' limitations.

Keywords: Robot imitation · Transfer knowledge · Physical rehabilitation · Shared Gaussian Process Latent Variable Model · Motion analysis

1 Introduction

Low back pain is a leading cause disabling people particularly affecting the elderly, whose proportion in European societies keeps rising, incurring growing concern about healthcare. 50 to 80% of the world population suffers at a given moment from back pain which makes it in the lead in terms of health problems occurrence frequency [1]. To tackle this chronic low back pain, regular physical rehabilitation exercises is considered most effective [10].

With this perspective, solutions are being developed based on assistive technology and particularly robotics [5,6,9] where humanoid robots are used for demonstrating rehabilitation exercises to patients. These robots have previously learned these exercises from physiotherapist. However, due to different morphologies between humans and robots, and possible physical limitations of patients, human motion may be difficult to understand by a robot. In this work, we address these issues by training a common low dimensional latent space shared between the therapist, the robot coach and patients, as illustrated in Fig. 1 (left). This model allows us to learn an ideal rehabilitation exercise from physiotherapist

L. Leal-Taixé and S. Roth (Eds.): ECCV 2018 Workshops, LNCS 11130, pp. 190–197, 2019.
https://doi.org/10.1007/978-3-030-11012-3_15

demonstrations which can be difficult using human data. Moreover, this ideal motion representation is easily interpreted by the robot coach to make it reproduce the correct exercise to the patient. Finally, this model is also employed to adapt the robot's understanding and analysis to the possible physical limitations of patients attending the rehabilitation session.

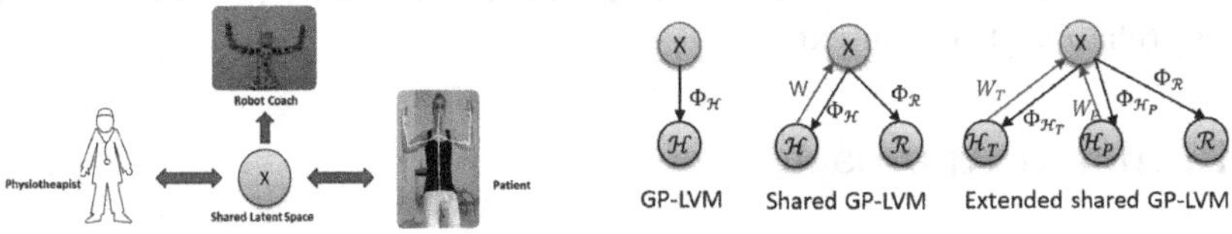

Fig. 1. (Left) Overview of approach. (Right) Schema of different GP-LVM

2 Related Work

In the literature, the challenges of robot imitation and motion assessment by robot coaches are usually addressed separately.

In the context of robot imitation, several vision-based approaches have been proposed. Riley et al. [16] proposed an approach for real-time control of a humanoid by imitation. The imitation is using a stereo vision system to record human trajectories by exploiting color markers on the demonstrators attached to the upper body by inverse kinematics. The authors apply IK to estimate the human's joint angles and then map it to the robot. Dariush et al. [4] presented an online task space control theoretic retargeting formulation to generate robot joint motions that adhere to the robot's joint limit constraints, joint velocity constraints and self-collision constraints. The inputs to the proposed method include low dimensional normalized human motion descriptors, detected and tracked using a vision based key-point detection and tracking algorithm. Koenemann et al. [11] presented a system that enables humanoid robots to imitate complex whole-body motions of humans in real time. The system uses a compact human model and considers the positions of the end effectors as well as the center of mass as the most important aspects to imitate. Stanton et al. [19] used machine learning to train neural networks to map sensor data to joint space. However, these two last approaches employ human motion capture system instead of vision features to capture the human motion. this makes the system not suitable for real-word scenario like physical rehabilitation.

Only few approaches addressed the challenge of physical rehabilitation through coaching robot systems. While several studies showed the potential of virtual agents [2,20] and physical robots [3] to enhance engagement and learning in health, physical activity or social contexts, Fasola *et al.* [7] showed better assessment by the elderly subjects of the physical robot coach compared to virtual systems. Robots for coaching physical exercises have been recently presented [8,15,17]. These approaches employed robots with few degrees of freedom that facilitates the imitation process. However, such robots do not allow realistic movements. Moreover, Obo *et al.* [15] did not provide any feedback or active guidance to the patient.

In this paper, we employ a humanoid robot with many degrees of freedom called Poppy [12] and capture human motion using a kinect sensor with a skeleton tracking algorithm from depth images. We propose a method to simultaneously consider the challenge of robot imitation and human motion assessment in a physical rehabilitation context.

3 Proposed Approach

3.1 Shared Gaussian Process Latent Variable Model

Our goal is to learn a latent space where we can represent and compare both human and robot poses. Human upper body poses are characterized by skeletons captured with a kinect sensor providing the 3D position p_j of a set of $J = 12$ joints. A human pose $y \in \mathcal{H}$ is thus defined as $y = [p_1\ p_2 \ldots p_J]$, where $\mathcal{H}$ denotes the human space. Robot poses are characterized as the motor angles a_m of the Poppy robot including $M = 13$ motors. Hence, a robot pose $z \in \mathcal{R}$ is defined as $z = [a_1\ a_2 \ldots a_M]$, where $\mathcal{R}$ denotes the robot space. To learn such a shared space, we employ the shared Gaussian Process Latent Variable Model [18].

GP-LVM [13] (See Fig. 1(right)) is a probabilistic model mapping high dimensional observed data from a low dimensional latent space using a Gaussian process, with zero mean and covariance function characterized by a kernel K: $f(x) \sim \mathcal{GP}(0, k(x, x'))$. For the kernel K, we adopt the popular Radial Basis Function. The shared GP-LVM is an extension of GP-LVM for multiple data space that shares a common latent space. In our work, we have two observation spaces, the human space $\mathcal{H}$ and the robot space $\mathcal{R}$. Given a training set of N human poses $Y = \{y_n\}_{n=1}^{N} \in \mathcal{H}$ and corresponding robot poses $Z = \{z_n\}_{n=1}^{N} \in \mathcal{R}$, two mapping functions from the latent space X to observed spaces are defined:

$$f|X \sim \mathcal{GP}(0, K_Y(X, X'))\ and\ f|Z \sim \mathcal{GP}(0, K_Z(X, X')) \tag{1}$$

where K_Y and K_Z are RBF kernel matrices with hyperparameters Φ_Y and Φ_Z. In shared GPLVM, optimal latent locations X^* are unknown and need to be learned as well as hyperparameters of mappings Φ_Y^* and Φ_Z^*. This is done by optimizing the joint marginal likelihood $p(Y, Z|X, \Phi_Y, \Phi_Z) = p(Y|X, \Phi_Y)\ p(Z|X, \Phi_Z)$. We are interesting in mapping data from the human space to robot space through the latent space. Hence, an inverse mapping from the human space to the latent space is required. For that purpose, back constraints are introduced [14]. This feature allows to define latent locations with respect to observed data, $X = h(Y; W)$, where h is an RBF function parameterized by weights W. These weights are learned during optimization process instead of latent locations:

$$\{W^*, \Phi_Y^*, \Phi_Z^*\} = \arg\max_{W, \Phi_Z, \Phi_Z} p(Y, Z|W, \Phi_Y, \Phi_Z) \tag{2}$$

As body parts can move concurrently and independently, we consider different shared latent space for each body part separately. Therefore, our approach can also be extended to cases also using lower body parts, by just adding latent spaces for the left and right legs. We use three 2D latent space for the two arms and the spine (Fig. 2).

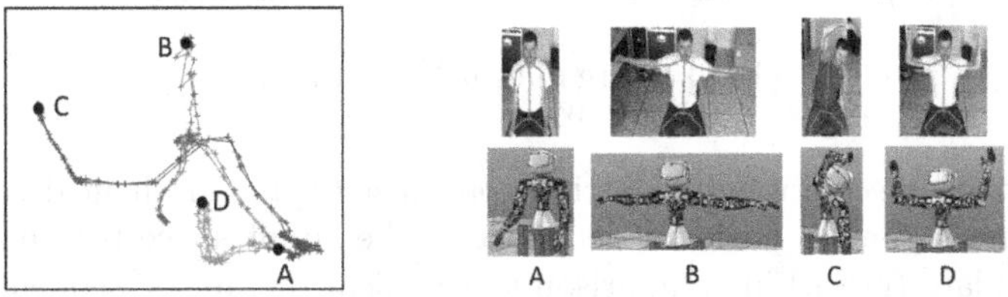

Fig. 2. (Left) Three rehabilitation exercises represented in the 2D latent space of the left arm. (Right) Corresponding human and robot poses of locations A, B, C and D.

3.2 Gaussian Mixture Model on the Latent Space

Once we trained a shared latent space, we can propose to learn a Gaussian Mixture Model on this low dimensional space. This allows to learn an ideal movement from therapist demonstrations projected on the shared space. It can then be employed for robot imitation by projecting back the ideal movement in the robot space. From N therapist demonstrations $Y^n = [y_1\, y_2 \dots y_T]$, the Gaussian Mixture Model on the latent space is defined as $p(x) = \sum_{k=1}^{K} \phi_k \mathcal{N}(x|\mu_k, \Sigma_k)$, where x encodes the human pose y_t projected on the shared latent space. K is the number of Gaussians, ϕ_k is the weight of the k-th Gaussian, μ_k and Σ_k are the mean and covariance matrix of the k-th Gaussian. The parameters ϕ_k, μ_k and Σ_k are learned using Expectation-Maximization. Once a model is learned for each exercise, we generate an optimal sequence using Gaussian Mixture Regression (GMR) which approximates the sequence using a single Gaussian: $p(\hat{x}|t) \approx \mathcal{N}(\hat{\mu}, \hat{\Sigma})$. This optimal sequence is then projected to the robot space to make the robot imitates the expert and demonstrates the exercise to the patient.

3.3 Transferring Knowledge from Therapist to Patient

In our rehabilitation scenario, the robot coach needs to evaluate the patient's movement captured using a kinect sensor similarly to therapist's movement. However, patients needing rehabilitation are often constrained by physical limitations or pain while performing exercises. It may result an incorrect performance even if they did their best to perform the correct exercise. A robust and effective robot coach system must consider such features. We propose to extend the learn shared GP-LVM (see Fig. 1 (right)) by considering two distinct human pose spaces $\mathcal{H}_T$ and $\mathcal{H}_P$ for the therapist and the patient, respectively. $\mathcal{H}_T$ is equivalent to $\mathcal{H}$ described above. $\mathcal{H}_P$ differs from $\mathcal{H}_T$ in the inverse mapping function to the latent space. Specifically, a therapist pose $y_T \in \mathcal{H}_T$ and the corresponding patient pose with physical limitations $y_P \in \mathcal{H}_P$ must be represented by the same point x in the latent space. For that, the weight matrix W_P of the inverse mapping is updated according to the patient. Let Y_p be a patient's performance of an exercise and X^* the corresponding ideal demonstration of the same exercise projected on the latent space. The optimization becomes:

$$\{W_P^*\} = \arg\max_{W_P} p(Y_p|X^*, \Phi_Y) \tag{3}$$

The patient specific weight matrix is optimized using gradient descent algorithm. Figure 3 shows a patients' sequence in the latent space before (red) and after the update (green) in comparison to the ideal therapists' sequence (blue).

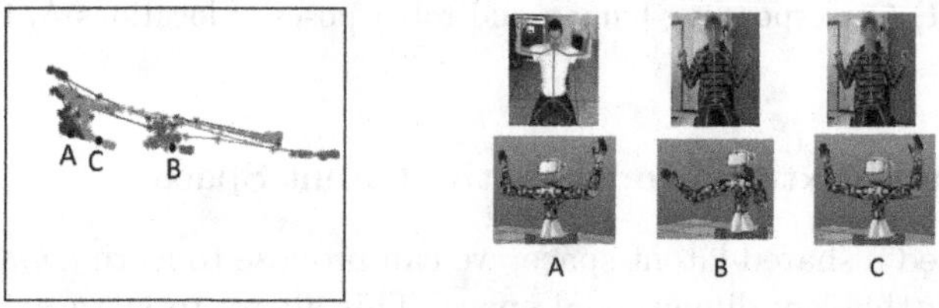

Fig. 3. (Left) A wrong exercise in the latent space before (red) and after (green) the model updating. (Right) Corresponding human and robot poses of points A, B, and C. (Color figure online)

4 Experimental Results

We evaluate our method on the three rehabilitation exercises selected in cooperation with physiotherapists and performed by two subjects three times[1] playing the role of the physiotherapist and the patient, respectively. In addition, subjects performs incorrect exercises by simulating errors[2]. For the first exercise, the arms are not enough raised. For the second exercise, the subject does not tilt the arm and keep it straight. In the third exercise, the arms are not enough raised.

For robot movements, we build ideal robot movements with the cooperation of a physiotherapist manipulating the robot in order to perform the desired rehabilitation movement while we record angle positions along the motion. We record one ideal movement per exercise. In addition simulated movements with errors described above are also recorded. These robot movements are used during training of the shared GP-LVM as well as ground truth during evaluation.

[1] Videos are available on www.keraal.enstb.org/exercises.html.
[2] Videos are available on www.keraal.enstb.org/incorrectexercises.html.

4.1 Imitation Evaluation

We first evaluate the ability of the approach to perform robot imitation. As described in Sect. 3.2, an ideal motion is generated using GMR on the latent space and the GMM model learned from expert demonstrations. This ideal motion is then transferred back to the robot space and compare to the ground truth. We compute the average RMSE error of motor angles between sampled sequence and ground truth. Moreover, we also normalized the RMSE by the standard deviation of motor angles for each exercise to compare the RMSE with the robot's motion. Results are reported for each exercise in Table 1.

Table 1. Robot imitation results.

	Exercise 1	Exercise 2	Exercise 3	Mean
RMSE	7.1	6.9	6.1	**6.7**
Normalized RMSE	0.31	0.18	0.34	**0.28**

We can see that we obtain a mean RMSE of 6.7° corresponding to 4.1% of the total range of Poppy motor angles. In addition, we obtain a normalized RMSE of 0.28 showing that the RMSE error is much lower than the standard deviation of rehabilitation movements, which represents the noise and the variations in the exercise. This validates the proposed model to imitate therapist demonstration with a high similarity accuracy so as to be clearly understood by the patient.

4.2 Therapist-Patient Transfer Evaluation

We then evaluate the ability of our model to transfer knowledge between a therapist and a patient with physical limitations. We first project the error sequence in the shared latent space. Then we project back the sequence to the robot space before and after applying weight updating as described in Sect. 3.3. To show the robustness of the approach, we sample ten random sequences from the latent-robot Gaussian process mapping and compute RMSE error in comparison with ground truth. Average RMSE and standard deviation among the ten sampled sequences are computed. For comparison we also compute such RMSE values for correct sequences of the patient. Results are reported in Table 2.

Table 2. Therapist-Patient transfer results.

Exercise type	Exercise 1	Exercise 2	Exercise 3
Correct	8.3 ± 0.7	8.0 ± 0.9	7.4 ± 0.8
Incorrect before update	37.9 ± 3.4	17.7 ± 1.8	21.9 ± 2.4
Incorrect after update	14.2 ± 1.4	9.1 ± 1.0	8.5 ± 0.9

We can first observe that, as expected, RMSE errors are much higher for incorrect exercises than for correct exercises. However, if we consider that these errors are due to physical limitations of the patient and apply our updating method, we can see that the RMSE errors becomes close to correct exercises. This means that the robot understands the incorrect exercises similarly to correct exercises. In addition, we propose to deepen the analysis of the third exercise by similarly evaluating a different kind of error (arms are not enough outstretched) with the previously trained model. We obtain RMSE values of 13.4 ± 0.89 and 14.4 ± 1.08 before and after the update, respectively. The similar RMSE values show that by updating the model for one kind of error, it does not affect other type of errors as required in our rehabilitation scenario.

5 Conclusions

We have proposed a method based on Gaussian Process Latent variable Model for a robot coach system in physical rehabilitation. The method allows to learn a shared space between the therapist and the robot to facilitate robot learning and imitation. The model is then extended to consider variations of patients physical limitations. This allows the robot to understand and assess the patient independently of his physical limitation. Experimental evaluation demonstrates the efficiency of our approach for both robot imitation and model adaptation.

In the future, we plan to extend our experimental evaluation with more data acquired in real-world environment. Moreover, we would like to investigate the use of key poses instead of full motion sequences during the model training. It would be suitable for a real-world rehabilitation scenario.

Acknowledgement. The research work presented in this paper is partially supported by the EU FP7 grant ECHORD++ KERAAL, by the the European Regional Fund (FEDER) via the VITAAL Contrat Plan Etat Region and by project AMUSAAL funded by Region Brittany, France.

References

1. WHO Scientific Group on the Burden of Musculoskeletal Conditions at the Start of the New Millennium and others. World Health Organization Technical report series 919, i (2003)
2. Anderson, K., et al.: The TARDIS framework: intelligent virtual agents for social coaching in job interviews. In: Reidsma, D., Katayose, H., Nijholt, A. (eds.) ACE 2013. LNCS, vol. 8253, pp. 476–491. Springer, Cham (2013). https://doi.org/10.1007/978-3-319-03161-3_35
3. Belpaeme, T., et al.: Multimodal child-robot interaction: building social bonds. J. Hum.-Robot Interact. **1**(2), 33–53 (2012)
4. Dariush, B., et al.: Online transfer of human motion to humanoids. Int. J. Human. Robot. (IJHR) **6**(2), 265–289 (2009)
5. Devanne, M., Mai, N.S.: Multi-level motion analysis for physical exercises assessment in Kinaesthetic rehabilitation. In: IEEE-RAS 17th International Conference on Humanoid Robotics (Humanoids), November 2017

6. Devanne, M., Nguyen, S.M., Remy-Neris, O., Le Gals-Garnett, B., Kermarrec, G., Thepaut, A.: A co-design approach for a rehabilitation robot coach for physical rehabilitation based on the error classification of motion errors. In: Second IEEE International Conference on Robotic Computing (IRC), January 2018
7. Fasola, J., Mataric, M.: A socially assistive robot exercise coach for the elderly. J. Hum.-Robot Interact. **2**(2), 3–32 (2013)
8. Görer, B., Salah, A.A., Akın, H.L.: A robotic fitness coach for the elderly. In: Augusto, J.C., Wichert, R., Collier, R., Keyson, D., Salah, A.A., Tan, A.-H. (eds.) AmI 2013. LNCS, vol. 8309, pp. 124–139. Springer, Cham (2013). https://doi.org/10.1007/978-3-319-03647-2_9
9. Gorer, B., Salah, A.A., Akın, H.L.: An autonomous robotic exercise tutor for elderly people. Auton. Robot. **41**(3), 657–678 (2017)
10. Kent, P., Kjaer, P.: The efficacy of targeted interventions for modifiable psychosocial risk factors of persistent nonspecific low back pain-a systematic review. Manual Ther. **17**(5), 385–401 (2012)
11. Koenemann, J., Burget, F., Bennewitz, M.: Real-time imitation of human whole-body motions by humanoids. In: IEEE International Conference on Robotics and Automation (ICRA), June 2014
12. Lapeyre, M.: Poppy: open-source, 3D printed and fully-modular robotic platform for science, art and education. Ph.D. thesis, Université de Bordeaux (2014)
13. Lawrence, N.D.: Gaussian process latent variable models for visualisation of high dimensional data. In: Advances in Neural Information Processing Systems, December 2006
14. Lawrence, N.D., Candela, J.Q.: Local distance preservation in the GP-LVM through back constraints. In: International Conference on Machine Leraning (ICML), December 2006
15. Obo, T., Loo, C.K., Kubota, N.: Imitation learning for daily exercise support with robot partner. In: 2015 24th IEEE International Symposium on Robot and Human Interactive Communication (RO-MAN), pp. 752–757. IEEE (2015)
16. Riley, C., Ude, A., Wade, K., Atkeson, C.: Enabling real-time full-body imitation: a natural way of transferring human movement to humanoids. In: IEEE International Conference on Robotics and Automation (ICRA), September 2003
17. Schneider, S., Kümmert, F.: Exercising with a humanoid companion is more effective than exercising alone. In: 2016 IEEE-RAS 16th International Conference on Humanoid Robots (Humanoids), pp. 495–501. IEEE (2016)
18. Shon, A., Grochow, K., Hertzmann, A., Rao, R.P.: Learning shared latent structure for image synthesis and robotic imitation. In: 18th International Conference on Neural Information Processing Systems, December 2006
19. Stanton, C., Bogdanovych, A., Ratanasena, E.: Teleoperation of a humanoid robot using full-body motion capture, example movements, and machine learning. In: Australasian Conference on Robotics and Automation (ACRA), December 2012
20. Waltemate, T., Hülsmann, F., Pfeiffer, T., Kopp, S., Botsch, M.: Realizing a low-latency virtual reality environment for motor learning. In: Proceedings of ACM Symposium on Virtual Reality Software and Technology (VRST) (2015)

Model Selection for Generalized Zero-Shot Learning

Hongguang Zhang[1(✉)] and Piotr Koniusz[1,2]

[1] The Australian National University, Canberra, ACT 2600, Australia
{hongguang.zhang,piotr.koniusz}@anu.edu.au
[2] Data61/CSIRO, Canberra, Australia
piotr.koniusz@data61.csiro.au

Abstract. In the problem of generalized zero-shot learning, the datapoints from unknown classes are not available during training. The main challenge for generalized zero-shot learning is the unbalanced data distribution which makes it hard for the classifier to distinguish if a given testing sample comes from a seen or unseen class. However, using Generative Adversarial Network (GAN) to generate auxiliary datapoints by the semantic embeddings of unseen classes alleviates the above problem. Current approaches combine the auxiliary datapoints and original training data to train the generalized zero-shot learning model and obtain state-of-the-art results. Inspired by such models, we propose to feed the generated data via a model selection mechanism. Specifically, we leverage two sources of datapoints (observed and auxiliary) to train some classifier to recognize which test datapoints come from seen and which from unseen classes. This way, generalized zero-shot learning can be divided into two disjoint classification tasks, thus reducing the negative influence of the unbalanced data distribution. Our evaluations on four publicly available datasets for generalized zero-shot learning show that our model obtains state-of-the-art results.

Keywords: Model selection · Generalized zero-shot learning · Generative Adversarial Network

1 Introduction

In the zero-shot learning task, a classifier is trained with datapoints from seen classes and applied to recognize previously unseen datapoints belonging to unseen classes. The main objective is to leverage knowledge from label embeddings, *e.g.* attributes, word embedding or class hierarchy information, to build a universal mapping that can classify unseen datapoints without retraining the system on new unseen classes. Firstly, let us denote $\mathbf{X}_{tr}$ as training datapoints from seen classes C_s, $\mathbf{X}_{ts}$ to be testing datapoints from unseen classes C_u such that $C_s \cap C_u = \emptyset$. The model is trained on $\mathbf{X}_{tr}$ but needs to assign a label $l \in C_u$ for each datapoint from $\mathbf{X}_{ts}$. Recently, researchers have argued that standard zero-shot learning protocols are biased towards good results on unseen classes while

L. Leal-Taixé and S. Roth (Eds.): ECCV 2018 Workshops, LNCS 11130, pp. 198–204, 2019.
https://doi.org/10.1007/978-3-030-11012-3_16

neglecting performance on seen classes. To address this issue, a generalized zero-shot learning task was proposed for which testing datapoints come from seen and unseen classes, and the classifier needs to cope well with all classes $C = C_s \cup C_u$.

It has emerged that most of zero-shot learning methods achieve low accuracy in such a protocol because training datapoints come only from the seen classes. In most cases, the strong imbalance of data distribution will make the classifier assign datapoints from seen classes to unseen classes.

The use of Generalized Adversarial Network (GAN) to generate auxiliary datapoints for unseen classes [1] enables the classifier to be trained on datapoints from both seen and unseen categories. Inspired by such an extension, we found that using the auxiliary and original training data to learn a classifier, *e.g.* Support Vector Machine (SVM), can be further improved by treating the classification of original datapoints separately, that is, by decomposing the generalized zero-shot learning into two disjoint classification tasks: one classifier dealing with datapoints from seen classes and another classifier dealing with datapoints of unseen classes.

In this paper, we propose to use the auxiliary data of unseen classes generated by GAN together with the original training data to build a model selection approach for generalized zero-shot learning. We refer to our approach as ModelSel and propose its three variants in Sect. 3. We evaluate ModelSel on four standard datasets and demonstrate state-of-the-art results.

2 Related Work

Zero-shot learning is a form of transfer learning. Specifically, it utilizes the knowledge learned on datapoints of seen classes and attribute vectors to generalize and recognize testing datapoints from new classes. The majority of previous zero-shot learning methods use some linear mapping to capture the relation between the feature and attribute vectors. Attribute Label Embedding (ALE) [2] uses the attributes as label embedding and presents an objective inspired by a structured WSABIE ranking method that assigns more importance to the top of the ranking list. Embarrassingly Simple Zero-Shot Learning (ESZSL) [3] uses a linear mapping and simple empirical objective with several regularization terms that impose penalty on the projection of features from the Euclidean into the attribute space and the projection of attribute vectors back to the Euclidean space. Structured Joint Embedding (SJE) [4] proposes an objective inspired by the structured SVM and applied as linear mapping while [5] proposes new data splits and evaluation protocols to eliminate the overlap between classes of ImageNet [6] and zero-shot learning datasets. Zero-shot Kernel Learning (ZSKL) [7] proposes a non-linear kernel method with weak incoherence constraints to make the columns of projection matrix weakly incoherent. Feature Generating Networks [1] leverages a conditional Wasserstein Generative Adversarial Network (WGAN) to generate auxiliary datapoints for unseen classes from attribute vectors followed by training a simple Softmax classifier. SoSN [8] and So-HoT [9] use second-order statistics [10] for similarity learning and domain adaptation.

3 Approach

3.1 Notations

Let us denote seen classes as C_s, unseen classes as C_u. $\mathbf{X}_{tr}$ denotes original training datapoints, $\mathbf{X}_{ge}$ are the generated datapoints for unseen classes. Each datapoint is a column vector in one of the above matrices. M_{sel} is the selector between seen/unseen class, M_s is the model for C_s, M_u is the model for C_u, M_t is a model for $C_s \cup C_u$. Moreover, $\boldsymbol{w}_{sel}$, b_{sel}, $\boldsymbol{W}_s$, $\mathbf{b}_s$, $\boldsymbol{W}_u$, $\mathbf{b}_u$, $\boldsymbol{W}_t$ and $\mathbf{b}_t$ are the projection vector/matrices and biases used by our models as detailed below.

3.2 Model Selection Mechanism

In this paper, we propose a mechanism that leverages several classifiers to perform generalized zero-shot learning. Firstly, we label the original datapoints as 1 and auxiliary datapoints as -1 to train M_{sel}, which is a linear SVM classifier.

Model M_s is a classifier trained with datapoints from seen classes C_s, model M_u is trained with auxiliary datapoints from GAN corresponding to unseen classes C_u. Model M_t is trained for $C_s \cup C_u$ simultaneously.

M_s, M_u and M_t are trained separately via the SoftmaxLog classifier. While we use a single training process, we distinguish three selection models applied at the testing stage. The output of each classifier can be defined as:

$$\mathbf{g}_s(\mathbf{x}) = \boldsymbol{W}_s^T\mathbf{x} + \mathbf{b}_s, \tag{1}$$

$$\mathbf{g}_u(\mathbf{x}) = \boldsymbol{W}_u^T\mathbf{x} + \mathbf{b}_u, \tag{2}$$

$$\mathbf{g}_t(\mathbf{x}) = \boldsymbol{W}_t^T\mathbf{x} + \mathbf{b}_t. \tag{3}$$

ModelSel-2Way. The testing mechanism of ModelSel-2Way can be illustrated as follows. For each testing datapoint $\mathbf{x} \in \mathbf{X}_{tr}$, we feed it firstly into M_{sel}. The role of M_{sel} is to decide if $\mathbf{x}$ belongs to the seen or unseen class based on which we select either M_s or M_u model for the final classification:

$$s(\mathbf{x}) = \boldsymbol{w}_{sel}^T\mathbf{x} + b_{sel}. \tag{4}$$

Then, the final prediction for $\mathbf{x}$ becomes:

$$\mathbf{f}(\mathbf{x}, s(\mathbf{x})) = \begin{cases} \mathbf{g}_s(\mathbf{x}), & \text{if } s \geq 0, \\ \mathbf{g}_u(\mathbf{x}), & \text{otherwise.} \end{cases} \tag{5}$$

ModelSel-2Way-SA. We also propose to use the Sigmoid function to generate soft assignment scores from the output of M_{sel} as the weights assigned to the outputs of M_s and M_u. We call this method as ModelSel-2Way-SA. The intuition behind this model is that M_{sel} suffers from the quantization errors close to the classification boundary, thus we model the assignment uncertainty in M_{sel} to reduce quantization errors. The probability that $\mathbf{x}$ belongs to seen classes C_s or

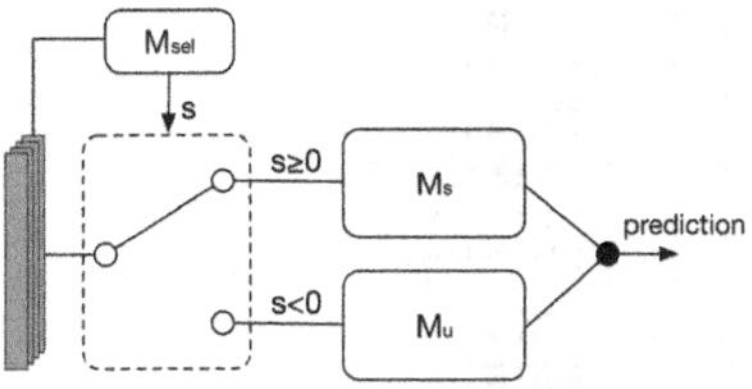

Fig. 1. Our ModelSel-2Way approach.

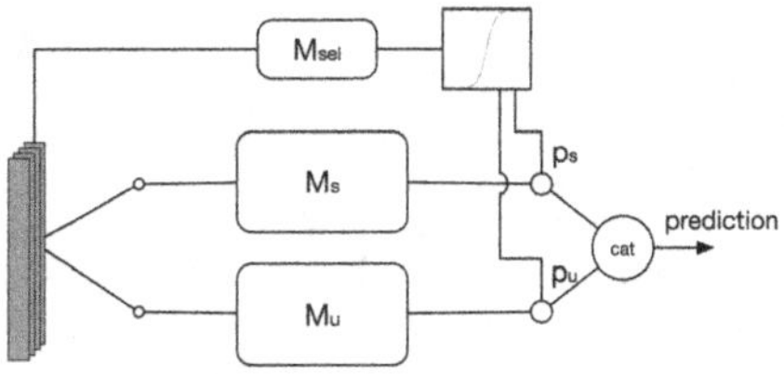

Fig. 2. Our ModelSel-2Way-SA approach.

C_u is denoted $p_s(\mathbf{x})$ and $p_u(\mathbf{x}) = 1 - p_s(\mathbf{x})$, respectively, and $p_s(\mathbf{x})$ is given as (Figs. 1 and 2):

$$p_s(\mathbf{x}) = \frac{1}{1 + e^{-\sigma s(\mathbf{x})}}, \tag{6}$$

where σ is the parameter to control the slope of the Sigmoid function. Then, the output of ModelSel-2Way-SA is given as:

$$\mathbf{f}(\mathbf{x}) = p_s(\mathbf{x}) \cdot \mathbf{g}_s(\mathbf{x}) + p_u(\mathbf{x}) \cdot \mathbf{g}_u(\mathbf{x}). \tag{7}$$

ModelSel-3Way. For the ModelSel-3Way, we use additionally classifier M_t trained with both original and auxiliary datapoints so it can classify data from both seen and unseen classes. While its performance is worse than M_s and M_u in each domain, we leverage the output of M_t as a mask to correct some incorrect predictions from M_u and M_s. The output of our ModelSel-3Way model, shown in Fig. 3, is defined as follows:

$$\mathbf{f}(\mathbf{x}, s(\mathbf{x})) = \max \left(\begin{cases} c \cdot \mathbf{g}_t(\mathbf{x}) + \mathbf{g}_s(\mathbf{x}) - o_s & \text{if } s \geq 0 \\ c \cdot \mathbf{g}_t(\mathbf{x}) + \mathbf{g}_u(\mathbf{x}) - o_u & \text{if } s < 0 \end{cases}, \; \mathbf{g}_t(\mathbf{x}) \right), \quad \begin{array}{l} \leftarrow \text{gray regions in Fig. 4} \\ \leftarrow \text{black regions in Fig. 4} \\ \leftarrow \text{white region in Fig. 4} \end{array} \tag{8}$$

where c, o_s and o_u adjust the importance of M_t and offset for M_s and M_u. Intuitively, close to the classification boundaries, predictions of $\mathbf{g}_s(\mathbf{x})$ and $\mathbf{g}_u(\mathbf{x})$ become replaced by $\mathbf{g}_t(\mathbf{x})$ in this model.

Figure 4 illustrates the selection of classifiers in our ModelSel-3Way approach. We define N as the total number of testing data, N_s and N_u as the number of testing data assigned to seen and unseen classes C_s and C_u, respectively. The distribution map has the same size as $\mathbf{g}_t(\mathbf{X}) \in \mathbb{R}^{C \times N}$, the light gray color highlights successful predictions from $\mathbf{g}_s(\mathbf{X}_{tr}) \in \mathbb{R}^{C_s \times N_s}$ while the dark black color highlights successful predictions from $\mathbf{g}_u(\mathbf{X}_{te}) \in \mathbb{R}^{C_u \times N_u}$.

4 Experiments

Below we detail datasets used in our experiments, describe evaluation protocols and show our experimental results to demonstrate usefulness of our approach.

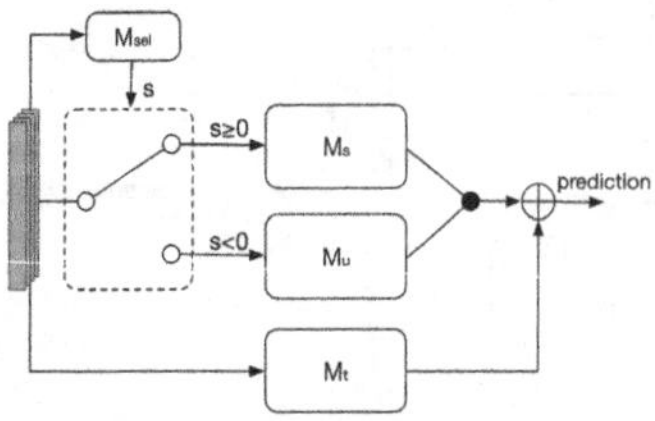

Fig. 3. Our ModelSel-3Way approach.

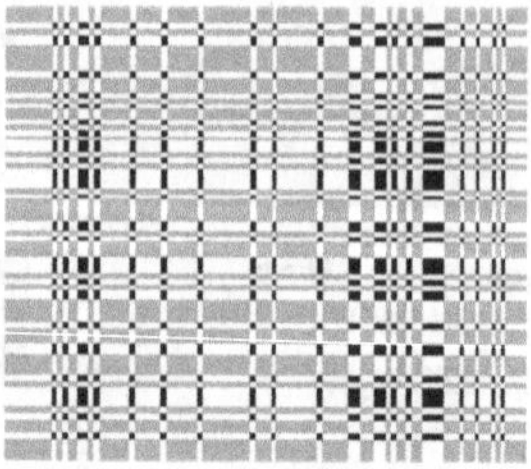

Fig. 4. The selection of classifiers in our ModelSel-3Way.

4.1 Setup

Datasets. We evaluate proposed models on four datasets. Attribute Pascal and Yahoo (*APY*) contains 15339 images, 64 attributes and 32 classes. The 20 classes from Pascal VOC are used for training and 12 classes collected from Yahoo! are used for testing. Animals with Attributes (*AWA1*) contains 30475 images from 50 classes. Each class is annotated with 85 attributes. The zero-shot learning split of AWA1 is 40 classes for training and 10 classes for testing. The Animal with Attributes 2 (*AWA2*) proposed by [5] is the updated and open source version of AWA1. It has the same number of classes, attributes and train/test split with AWA1. Flower102 (*FLO*) [11] contains 8189 images from 102 classes.

An evaluation paper [5] proposes a novel zero-shot learning splits to eliminate the overlap between the classes in zero-shot datasets and ImageNet [5], and evaluates most popular zero-shot learning methods. In this paper, we follow the new splits to make a fair comparison to other state-of-the-art methods.

Parameters. We perform the mean extraction and standard deviation normalization on both original and auxiliary datapoints to train M_{sel} to alleviate the imbalance between two distributions. For M_s and M_u, we simply use the original data provided in paper [5] without any preprocessing. Our models use classifiers with the SoftmaxLog objective. We use the Adam solver with mini-batches of size 60, the parameters of Adam are set to $\beta 1 = 0.9$ and $\beta 2 = 0.99$. We run the solver for 50 epochs. The learning rate is set to $1e{-}4$. The parameters used by ModelSel-2Way and ModelSel-3Way are chosen via cross-validation.

Protocols. For training, all models are trained at once as the training process is the same for each model. To perform testing, we follow the generalized zero-shot learning protocols in [5]. There are two testing splits for seen and unseen classes, respectively. We evaluate the two testing splits, and collect two per-class mean top-1 accuracies Acc_S and Acc_U as suggested by [5]. We report the harmonic mean over the two results as the final score:

$$H = 2\frac{Acc_S \cdot Acc_U}{Acc_S + Acc_U}. \tag{9}$$

4.2 Evaluations

Figure 5 shows how the classification accuracy varies w.r.t. σ of ModelSel-2Way-SA. It can be seen that the soft assignment score obtained by passing SVM scores via the Sigmoid function helps improve the performance of our model.

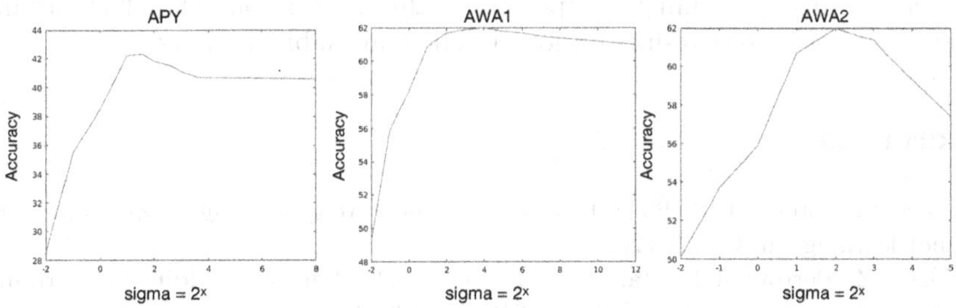

Fig. 5. The influence of σ on the classification accuracy.

Table 1 shows that our models obtain state-of-the-art results on AWA1, AWA2, FLO and APY datasets. Compared to f-CLSWGAN, our ModelSel-3Way achieves a 2.8% higher accuracy on AWA1, 3.6% on AWA2 and 0.8% on FLO. The biggest improvement for ModelSel-2Way-SA is observed on APY, where the accuracy increased from 20.5% of ZSKL [7] to 42.3%. The above evaluations illustrate that our models can combine predictions on seen and auxiliary datapoints better than current state-of-the-art approaches.

Table 1. Evaluations on generalized zero-shot learning

	AWA1			AWA2			FLO			APY		
Method	ts	tr	H	ts	tr	H	ts	tr	H	ts	tr	H
DAP [12]	0.0	88.7	0.0	0.0	84.7	0.0	-	-	-	4.8	78.3	8.0
SSE [13]	7.0	80.5	12.9	8.1	82.5	14.8	-	-	-	0.2	78.9	0.4
LATEM [14]	7.3	71.7	13.3	11.5	77.3	20.0	14.7	28.8	19.5	0.1	73.0	0.2
ALE [2]	16.8	76.1	27.5	14.0	81.8	23.9	21.8	33.1	26.3	4.6	73.7	8.7
DEVISE [15]	13.4	68.7	22.4	17.1	74.7	27.8	9.9	44.2	16.2	4.9	76.9	9.2
SJE [4]	11.3	74.6	19.6	8.0	73.9	14.4	13.9	47.6	21.5	3.7	55.7	6.9
ESZSL [3]	6.6	75.6	12.1	5.9	77.8	11.0	11.4	56.8	19.0	2.4	70.1	4.6
SYNC [16]	8.9	87.3	16.2	10.0	90.5	18.0	-	-	-	7.4	66.3	13.3
SAE [17]	1.8	77.1	3.5	1.1	82.2	2.2	-	-	-	0.4	80.9	0.9
ZSKL [7]	18.3	79.3	29.8	18.9	82.7	30.8	-	-	-	11.9	76.3	20.5
f-CLSWGAN [1]	57.9	61.4	59.6	53.7	68.2	60.1	59.0	73.8	65.6	8.7	75.4	15.5
ModelSel-2Way	50.1	77.7	61.0	41.7	84.2	55.8	46.9	60.9	53.0	27.5	76.9	40.5
ModelSel-2Way-SA	55.8	69.6	62.0	55.2	70.8	62.0	52.6	54.7	53.6	30.3	70.3	**42.3**
ModelSel-3Way	52.6	76.7	**62.4**	52.3	81.3	**63.7**	56.1	81.2	**66.4**	28.4	75.5	41.2

5 Conclusions

In this paper, we have presented three approaches to the model selection, which introduce a novel way of leveraging generated datapoints on generalized zero-shot learning task. Different from [1], our models use original and generated datapoints to train a selector function which distinguishes between classifiers for seen and unseen training datapoints. Evaluations on our ModelSel variants achieve state-of-the-art results on four publicly available datasets.

References

1. Xian, Y., Lorenz, T., Schiele, B., Akata, Z.: Feature generating networks for zero-shot learning. In: CVPR (2018)
2. Akata, Z., Perronnin, F., Harchaoui, Z., Schmid, C.: Label-embedding for attribute-based classification. In: CVPR, pp. 819–826 (2013)
3. Romera-Paredes, B., Torr, P.: An embarrassingly simple approach to zero-shot learning. In: ICML, pp. 2152–2161 (2015)
4. Akata, Z., Reed, S., Walter, D., Lee, H., Schiele, B.: Evaluation of output embeddings for fine-grained image classification. In: CVPR, pp. 2927–2936 (2015)
5. Xian, Y., Schiele, B., Akata, Z.: Zero-shot learning - the good, the bad and the ugly. In: CVPR (2017)
6. Russakovsky, O., et al.: ImageNet large scale visual recognition challenge. IJCV **115**(3), 211–252 (2015)
7. Zhang, H., Koniusz, P.: Zero-shot kernel learning. In: CVPR, pp. 7670–7679 (2018)
8. Zhang, H., Koniusz, P.: Power normalizing second-order similarity network for few-shot learning. CoRR (2018)
9. Koniusz, P., Tas, Y., Zhang, H., Harandi, M., Porikli, F., Zhang, R.: Museum exhibit identification challenge for the supervised domain adaptation and beyond. In: Ferrari, V., Hebert, M., Sminchisescu, C., Weiss, Y. (eds.) ECCV 2018. LNCS, vol. 11220, pp. 815–833. Springer, Cham (2018). https://doi.org/10.1007/978-3-030-01270-0_48
10. Koniusz, P., Zhang, H., Porikli, F.: A deeper look at power normalizations. In: CVPR (2018)
11. Nilsback, M.E., Zisserman, A.: Automated flower classification over a large number of classes. In: ICVGIP, December 2008
12. Lampert, C.H., Nickisch, H., Harmeling, S.: Attribute-based classification for zero-shot visual object categorization. TPAMI **36**(3), 453–465 (2014)
13. Zhang, Z., Saligrama, V.: Zero-shot learning via semantic similarity embedding. In: ICCV, pp. 4166–4174 (2015)
14. Xian, Y., Akata, Z., Sharma, G., Nguyen, Q., Hein, M., Schiele, B.: Latent embeddings for zero-shot classification. In: CVPR, pp. 69–77 (2016)
15. Frome, A., et al.: Devise: A deep visual-semantic embedding model. In: NIPS, pp. 2121–2129 (2013)
16. Changpinyo, S., Chao, W.L., Gong, B., Sha, F.: Synthesized classifiers for zero-shot learning. In: CVPR, pp. 5327–5336 (2016)
17. Kodirov, E., Xiang, T., Gong, S.: Semantic autoencoder for zero-shot learning. In: CVPR (2017)

W09 – PoseTrack Challenge: Articulated People Tracking in the Wild

W09 – PoseTrack Challenge: Articulated People Tracking in the Wild

The goal of the PoseTrack Workshop was to advance the state of the art in articulated people tracking and visual human analysis. Building on the experience of the previous iteration of this workshop organized at ICCV'17, we introduced an extended version of the PoseTrack benchmark for articulated people tracking. The extended benchmark doubled the amount of annotated data, laying emphasis on common challenging cases for existing methods. In addition to the PoseTrack challenge we also hosted additional challenges on dense pose estimation in collaboration with the authors of the DensePose project and on 3D human pose estimation in collaboration with the Human3.6M team. In the dense pose challenge the participants were required to estimate dense correspondences between people videos and a 3D body shape model. The challenge was based on the data from PoseTrack'17 benchmark that has been annotated with dense pose correspondences. In the 3D Human Pose Estimation Challenge the participants were required to estimate poses of people in 3D. The challenge was based on the Human3.6 benchmark which offered a way to estimate 2d and 3d skeletal joint positions, joint angles, semantic segmentation of body parts, as well as 3d human shape and depth, and in addition provided and evaluated dense correspondences similar to the DensePose challenge.

Finally, the workshop included a diverse program featuring keynote speakers, poster presentations, and a discussion panel to provide a forum for the exchange of ideas among the researchers working in the area of visual human analysis.

The keynote speakers were George Papandreou from Google, Iasonas Kokkinos from University College London and Facebook AI Research, Christian Theobalt from Max Planck Institute for Informatics and Cristian Sminchisescu from Lund University and Google. The planned panel discussion with worlds leading experts on this problem was a fruitful input and source of ideas for all participants. This was the second edition in the PoseTrack series. We as organizers received valuable feedback from users and from the community on how to improve the benchmark.

As to the reviewing process, the pose track challenge received 16 paper submissions. 9 of those submitted extended subtract and deemed valid ,and others were rejected without review. Of the remaining papers, 4 were accepted (44.4%). The selection process was a combined effort of 2 reviewers, Acceptance decisions were made by the organizers.

We want to thank the ECCV workshop organizer and we are grateful to the workshop sponsors: Nvidia, Facebook Reality Labs and Playment.

September 2018

Mykhaylo Andriluka
Umar Iqbal
Eldar Insafutdinov
Leonid Pishchulin
Anton Milan
Siyu Tang
Christoph Lassner
Juergen Gall
Bernt Schiele

Multi-Domain Pose Network for Multi-Person Pose Estimation and Tracking

Hengkai Guo(✉), Tang Tang, Guozhong Luo, Riwei Chen, Yongchen Lu, and Linfu Wen

ByteDance AI Lab, Beijing, China
guohengkai@bytedance.com

Abstract. Multi-person human pose estimation and tracking in the wild is important and challenging. For training a powerful model, large-scale training data are crucial. While there are several datasets for human pose estimation, the best practice for training on multi-dataset has not been investigated. In this paper, we present a simple network called Multi-Domain Pose Network (MDPN) to address this problem. By treating the task as multi-domain learning, our methods can learn a better representation for pose prediction. Together with prediction heads fine-tuning and multi-branch combination, it shows significant improvement over baselines and achieves the best performance on PoseTrack ECCV 2018 Challenge without additional datasets other than MPII and COCO.

Keywords: Human pose estimation · Multi-domain learning

1 Introduction

Multi-person human pose estimation is an important component in many applications, such as video surveillance and sports video analytics. Though great progress has been made in this field [3,4] thanks to the development of convolutional neural networks (CNNs), human pose estimation remains a challenging problem due to complex poses, diverse appearance, different scales, severe occlusion and crowds. For tracking in videos, the strong camera motions and extreme proximity of people [1] make it even more difficult.

Similar to other computer vision tasks dominated by deep learning, large-scale training data are crucial to exploit the representation power of CNNs for human pose estimation. There exists several extensive datasets such as COCO Dataset [13], MPII Dataset [2], and PoseTrack Dataset [1]. These datasets differ from each other about the distributions of images, poses and annotation standards. To promote the performance of models, many methods [7,11,18] choose to utilize multiple datasets for training. Most of them trained the models on COCO dataset first and then fine-tuned them on PoseTrack dataset [18] or MPII dataset

L. Leal-Taixé and S. Roth (Eds.): ECCV 2018 Workshops, LNCS 11130, pp. 209–216, 2019.
https://doi.org/10.1007/978-3-030-11012-3_17

[11]. However, it is still unclear what is the best practice to learn a model from multiple datasets for human pose estimation.

In this paper, we treat the task of training on multi-datasets as multi-domain learning [14,19] and propose a CNN architecture named Multi-Domain Pose Network (MDPN). The network has a common backbone to share the representation from multiple domains and separate prediction heads for dataset-specific pose estimation. During training, we first jointly optimize on all datasets to learn the generic pose embedding. Then each heads are fine-tuned on each domains to further improve the accuracy of localization. We also investigate the prediction strategies for better performance. Evaluated on PoseTrack dataset, our methods with simple network structures significantly improve the learning on multi-dataset over baseline. Moreover, our methods is runner-up of the PoseTrack ECCV 2018 challenge of pose estimation but achieved the best performance without using extra training data other than MPII and COCO datasets.

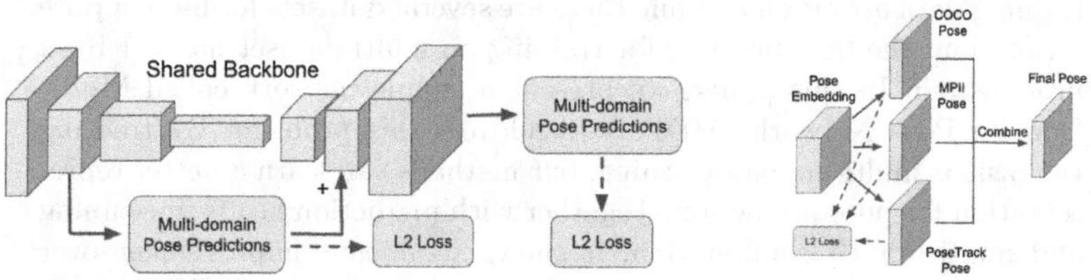

Fig. 1. Network overview (Left) and multi-domain prediction (Right).

2 Methods

Overall, we adopt the top-down approach [4,18] to human pose estimation using only single frame information, which employs person detector to detect all the people in the image and then use single person pose estimator (SPPE) to obtain the human poses for all the boxes. For SPPE, we take advantage of multiple dataset information to train a multi-domain network. After that, we use simple matching [18] on adjacent frames to associate individuals into track-lets.

2.1 Multi-Domain Pose Network (MDPN)

For training on multiple datasets, there are three simple solutions:

Mixed. All the datasets are merged into one single dataset. We also merge all the joint sets into one single joint set with a total number of 21 keypoints. During training, gradients are only back-propagated to the annotated joints for each sample. Mixing the datasets can make full use of all the information from all datasets, but different annotation standards for datasets on the same joint may distract the training procedure.

Transfer Learning. As done in [11,18], we can also train the model on one dataset first to learn the generic representation. Then fine-tuning is performed on the target dataset. COCO dataset [13] is often selected to pre-train the models because its data distribution is good to train a generic pose estimation model. Transfer learning can speed up the learning and often achieves good results. But the learnt embedding is suboptimal for pose estimation and it is easy to lose the knowledge from the first dataset when training on the target dataset for a long time as observed by [21].

Multi-domain Learning. Another approach to train on multi-dataset is to view it as a multi-domain learning task like [14]. It uses a common backbone network to learn a common pose representation and several prediction heads to learn domain-specific pose estimation. Compared with mixed datasets, multi-domain learning addresses the different annotation distribution problem. But to balance between different domains, the learnt prediction heads may not be optimal. Moreover, the predictions of multi-domain network only use one single head, which is a waste of information from other datasets.

According to the analysis above, we propose Multi-Domain Pose Network to solve such problems. We first apply multi-domain learning on all datasets. Then we fine-tune the full model on COCO dataset to optimize the embedding and COCO head. Finally we fix the backbone together with COCO head and fine-tune our network on the combination of MPII and PoseTrack dataset for the remain heads. Figure 1 illustrates the whole network structure. The details of structure will be explained in Sect. 2.2.

For prediction, one simple strategy is to use the predictions from corresponding dataset head. In order to exploit all the information from different datasets, we combine the predictions from different heads to form the final estimation (Fig. 1). There are several ways of combination, which will be discussed and compared in Sect. 3.2. Such methods can also be viewed as a lightweight multi-dataset ensemble implemented by multi-branch predictions like [8,12].

2.2 Implementations

Model Structure. We use ResNet-152 [10] with three deconvolution layers as backbone [18]. To address vanishing gradients, we add an intermediate prediction after conv3 layers for supervision, and add it back to the second deconvolution layer as skip connection. The size of input image is 384×288.

Training. The cropping and augmentations are the same as [4]. The Gaussian maps with sigma 9 are used as targets. We use the pre-trained models on ImageNet for ResNet backbone. The base learning rate is 0.001 with batch size 128 and Adam optimizer. For the jointly training stage of MDPN, we use 120 epochs. The learning rate is dropped to 0.0001 at 90 epochs. Then we perform 15 epochs for fine-tuning on COCO dataset. Finally we fine-tune the model on MPII and PoseTrack datasets for 20 epochs (The learning rate is dropped to 0.00001 at 10 epochs). To improve the performance of hard keypoints, we change the L2 loss to Online Hard Keypoints Mining (OHKM) [4] loss with 8 top keypoints at 100 epochs. For other models, we follow the training scheme in [18].

Testing. We follow the common practice in [4] with flipping testing and quarter offsets. We also re-score the box with the production of box score and average keypoint scores [4] after predictions.

Detection. We use four public person detectors trained on COCO dataset [13], including Faster R-CNN [17], Mask R-CNN [9], YOLO [16], and DCN [5]. Then we merge all the boxes with NMS of 0.6 and use them as detection results.

Tracking. We follow the pipelines of flow-based tracking [18] with four modifications. First, we apply OKS-NMS [15] of 0.4 after pose estimation. Second, we use Hungarian matching instead of greedy matching. Third, after tracking we prune short track-lets that contain less than 2 frames to reduce the false positive cases. Finally, we do not employ box propagation because the detector ensemble is strong enough. For multi-frame flow tracking, we use at most 8 frames before.

3 Experiments

3.1 Datasets and Evaluation

We train our models on three datasets: COCO-2017 dataset [13], MPII Dataset [2], and PoseTrack-2018 Dataset [1]. Then we evaluate our methods on the PoseTrack-2018 validation dataset. For multi-person pose estimation, we use mean Average Precision (mAP) metric. For multi-person tracking, we use Multiple Object Tracking Accuracy (MOTA) metric. To compare with state-of-the-art methods, we also evaluate our methods on PoseTrack-2017 validation dataset. For ablation study, we construct a min-val dataset from PoseTrack-2018 validation dataset by uniformly sub-sampling 15 sequences out of 75 sequences.

3.2 Ablation Study

ResNet-50 of input 256×192 without skip connection is used here for simplicity.

Table 1. Different training (Left) and testing (Right: MDPN-B without fine-tuning) methods on PoseTrack-2018 **min-val** dataset with ResNet-50.

Methods	Wrist mAP	Ankle mAP	Total mAP
MPII	58.3	49.1	58.7
COCO	70.8	**59.2**	68.4
PoseTrack	53.9	43.2	55.5
COCO → PoseTrack	67.5	56.4	66.8
COCO → PoseTrack + MPII	68.5	57.1	68.0
Mixed	67.1	52.5	66.3
MDPN-B w/o FT	68.4	53.7	67.7
MDPN-B	**71.8**	56.9	**70.7**

Methods	Wrist mAP	Ankle mAP	Total mAP
COCO branch	68.8	54.6	66.0
PoseTrack branch	68.0	52.9	66.7
COCO + PoseTrack branch	**69.1**	54.6	67.4
COCO + MPII branch (A)	69.0	**54.7**	**67.7**
Voting (B)	68.4	53.7	**67.7**

Testing. We have tried different combination methods on the multi-domain model: (1) *COCO branch*: Using the COCO branch and interpolating the head positions from other keypoints. (2) *PoseTrack branch*: Using the PoseTrack branch. (3) *COCO + PoseTrack branch*: Using the COCO branch with the head position from PoseTrack branch. (4) *COCO + MPII branch*: Using the COCO branch with the head position from MPII branch. (5) *Voting*: Averaging the heatmaps from common keypoints from all branches. From the right part of Table 1, the last two methods achieve the best performance. So we will only use these two methods for remain testing and refer them as method A and B.

Training. We compare different training strategies for multi-dataset: (1) *MPII*: Training on MPII. (2) *COCO*: Training on COCO. (3) *PoseTrack*: Training on PoseTrack. (4) *COCO→ PoseTrack*: Training on COCO and fine-tuning on PoseTrack [7,18]. (5) *COCO→ PoseTrack + MPII*: Training on COCO and fine-tuning on mixed datasets of MPII and PoseTrack [11]. (6) *Mixed*: Training on mixed dataset. (7) *MDPN-B w/o FT*: Training with multi-domain learning without fine-tuning and testing with method B. (8) *MDPN-B*: Training with multi-domain learning with fine-tuning and testing with method B.

Left part of Table 1 shows that among all approaches, the MDPN-B achieves the best performance. And fine-tuning after multi-domain training is important for the final performance (+3.0 mAP). As for the results of single dataset, training on COCO performs the best even without head annotations, while the accuracy of PoseTrack is worst. This is because the images in PoseTrack are obtained from limited videos and contain duplicate information, which leads to a smaller dataset. Another conclusion is that fine-tuning does not always improve the performance on the target dataset due to the knowledge forgetting problems.

Post-processing. Table 2 indicates that all post-processing is necessary for final performance. The OKS-NMS is crucial for mAP because too many false positive part detections may mislead the matching stage of evaluation.

Table 2. Different post-processing methods for pose estimation (Left) and tracking (Right) on PoseTrack-2018 **min-val** dataset.

Methods	Total mAP
MDPN-A	**70.7**
w/o Gaussian filter	70.3
w/o quarter offset	70.5
w/o box threshold	70.0
w/o OKS-NMS	51.2
w/o box re-score	70.2

Methods	Total mAP	Total MOTA
MDPN-A*	61.5	**52.6**
w/o box threshold	61.5	46.0
w/o keypoint threshold	**67.6**	28.3
w/o track-let pruning	61.7	52.3
w/o flow track	61.4	52.2

3.3 Results on PoseTrack Datasets

We evaluate our methods on PoseTrack 2017 [7,18,20] and 2018 dataset [6]. We use AlphaPose [6] model as baseline and apply branch combination, OKS-NMS and re-scoring (*AlphaPose++*).

Tables 3 and 4 show all the results on validation sets. For 2017 dataset, our methods show comparable performance with state-of-the-art method [18] and outperform other methods. For 2018 dataset, our methods also surpass the baselines with large margin. Meanwhile, testing with COCO-MPII combination is better than that with voting for ResNet-152.

Table 3. mAP on PoseTrack 2017 and 2018 datasets. * means with tracking.

Methods	Dataset	Head mAP	Shoulder mAP	Elbow mAP	Wrist mAP	Hip mAP	Knee mAP	Ankle mAP	Total mAP
Detect-and-Track [7]	val17	67.5	70.2	62.0	51.7	60.7	58.7	49.8	60.6
PoseFlow [20]	val17	66.7	73.3	68.3	61.1	67.5	67.0	61.3	66.5
ResNet-152 [18]	val17	81.7	83.4	80.0	72.4	75.3	74.8	67.1	76.7
MDPN-152-A	val17	85.2	88.5	83.9	77.5	79.0	77.0	71.4	**80.7**
MDPN-152-A*	val17	79.8	84.8	78.6	71.7	74.8	72.3	67.5	75.8
AlphaPose [6]	val18	63.9	78.7	77.4	71.0	73.7	73.0	69.7	71.9
AlphaPose++	val18	71.9	79.7	78.3	71.7	74.3	73.3	70.1	74.0
MDPN-50-B	val18	72.6	75.7	75.8	69.7	72.1	70.2	65.4	71.7
MDPN-152-B	val18	76.6	77.9	76.0	69.8	68.6	70.9	67.0	72.7
MDPN-152-A	val18	75.4	81.2	79.0	74.1	72.4	73.0	69.9	**75.0**
MDPN-152-A*	val18	72.4	79.0	75.3	69.6	69.2	69.2	66.7	71.7

Table 4. MOTA on PoseTrack 2017 and 2018 datasets. * means with tracking.

Methods	Dataset	Head MOTA	Shou MOTA	Elbow MOTA	Wrist MOTA	Hip MOTA	Knee MOTA	Ankle MOTA	Total MOTA	Total MOTP	Total Prec	Total Rec
D&T[7]	val17	61.7	65.5	57.3	45.7	54.3	53.1	45.7	55.2	61.5	66.4	88.1
PoseFlow[20]	val17	59.8	67.0	59.8	51.6	60.0	58.4	50.5	58.3	67.8	70.3	87.0
ResNet-152[18]	val17	73.9	75.9	63.7	56.1	65.5	65.1	53.5	65.4	85.4	85.5	80.3
MDPN-152-A*	val17	71.6	76.7	68.6	60.6	64.4	62.6	54.3	**66.0**	85.6	87.2	79.1
MDPN-152-A*	val18	50.9	55.5	54.0	49.0	48.7	50.5	45.1	50.6	85.7	74.0	80.3

Table 5. Results on PoseTrack ECCV 2018 Challenge without (Top) and with (Bottom) extra training datasets. * means with tracking. Our methods are **bold**.

Methods	Extra?	Wrist mAP	Ankle mAP	Total mAP	Total MOTA
MDPN	No	**74.5**	**69.0**	**76.4**	-
MDPN*	No	69.5	66.1	72.6	**58.5**
openSVAI	No	66.8	62.4	69.4	-
Loomo	No	66.4	61.8	68.5	26.9
MIPAL	No	60.2	56.9	67.8	54.9
AlphaPose++	No	66.2	65.0	67.6	-
E2E*	No	62.1	58.3	63.3	53.6
openSVAI*	No	59.2	56.7	63.1	54.5
DGDBQ	Yes	**77.8**	**75.4**	**79.0**	-
ALG	Yes	72.6	71.1	74.9	60.8
MSRA	Yes	73.0	69.1	74.0	**61.4**
Miracle	Yes	68.2	66.1	70.9	57.4
E2E	Yes	67.0	62.5	67.8	-

For test set (Table 5), our MDPN methods beats all the other methods trained only on COCO, MPII and PoseTrack by a large margin (7.0 mAP for no-tracking and 3.2 mAP for tracking). The no-tracking version also achieves the second best performance among all methods. For tracking, our method also performs the best among all methods without extra datasets for MOTA by a large margin (3.6 MOTA) and achieves the third best accuracy in all methods.

4 Conclusions

In conclusion, we investigate the strategies for training on multi-dataset and present Multi-Domain Pose Network to improve human pose estimation. It surpasses the baselines and achieves state-of-the-art results on PoseTrack benchmarks. Because of the simplicity, we hope proposed methods can help improve the performance for training on multiple datasets.

References

1. Andriluka, M., et al.: Posetrack: a benchmark for human pose estimation and tracking (2017)
2. Andriluka, M., Pishchulin, L., Gehler, P., Schiele, B.: 2D human pose estimation: new benchmark and state of the art analysis. In: Computer Vision and Pattern Recognition, pp. 3686–3693 (2014)
3. Cao, Z., Simon, T., Wei, S.E., Sheikh, Y.: Realtime multi-person 2D pose estimation using part affinity fields. In: IEEE Conference on Computer Vision and Pattern Recognition, pp. 1302–1310 (2017)
4. Chen, Y., Wang, Z., Peng, Y., Zhang, Z., Yu, G., Sun, J.: Cascaded pyramid network for multi-person pose estimation (2017)
5. Dai, J., et al.: Deformable convolutional networks. In: IEEE International Conference on Computer Vision, pp. 764–773 (2017)
6. Fang, H., Xie, S., Tai, Y.W., Lu, C.: RMPE: regional multi-person pose estimation. In: The IEEE International Conference on Computer Vision (ICCV), vol. 2 (2017)
7. Girdhar, R., Gkioxari, G., Torresani, L., Paluri, M., Du, T.: Detect-and-track: efficient pose estimation in videos (2018)
8. Guo, H., Wang, G., Chen, X., Zhang, C., Qiao, F., Yang, H.: Region ensemble network: improving convolutional network for hand pose estimation. In: IEEE International Conference on Image Processing, pp. 4512–4516 (2017)
9. He, K., Gkioxari, G., Dollár, P., Girshick, R.: Mask R-CNN. In: IEEE International Conference on Computer Vision, pp. 2980–2988 (2017)
10. He, K., Zhang, X., Ren, S., Sun, J.: Deep residual learning for image recognition. In: IEEE Conference on Computer Vision and Pattern Recognition, pp. 770–778 (2016)
11. Jin, S., et al.: Towards multi-person pose tracking: bottom-up and top-down methods (2017)
12. Li, H., Li, Y., Porikli, F.: Convolutional neural net bagging for online visual tracking. Comput. Vis. Image Understand. **153**, 120–129 (2016)
13. Lin, T.Y., et al.: Microsoft COCO: common objects in context. In: Fleet, D., Pajdla, T., Schiele, B., Tuytelaars, T. (eds.) ECCV 2014. LNCS, vol. 8693, pp. 740–755. Springer, Cham (2014). https://doi.org/10.1007/978-3-319-10602-1_48

14. Nam, H., Han, B.: Learning multi-domain convolutional neural networks for visual tracking. In: Proceedings of the IEEE Conference on Computer Vision and Pattern Recognition, pp. 4293–4302 (2016)
15. Papandreou, G., et al.: Towards accurate multi-person pose estimation in the wild, pp. 3711–3719 (2017)
16. Redmon, J., Farhadi, A.: YOLOv3: an incremental improvement (2018)
17. Ren, S., He, K., Girshick, R., Sun, J.: Faster R-CNN: towards real-time object detection with region proposal networks. IEEE Trans. Pattern Anal. Mach. Intell. **39**(6), 1137–1149 (2015)
18. Xiao, B., Wu, H., Wei, Y.: Simple baselines for human pose estimation and tracking. In: Ferrari, V., Hebert, M., Sminchisescu, C., Weiss, Y. (eds.) ECCV 2018. LNCS, vol. 11210, pp. 472–487. Springer, Cham (2018). https://doi.org/10.1007/978-3-030-01231-1_29
19. Xiao, T., Li, H., Ouyang, W., Wang, X.: Learning deep feature representations with domain guided dropout for person re-identification. In: Proceedings of the IEEE Conference on Computer Vision and Pattern Recognition, pp. 1249–1258 (2016)
20. Xiu, Y., Li, J., Wang, H., Fang, Y., Lu, C.: Pose flow: Efficient online pose tracking. arXiv preprint arXiv:1802.00977 (2018)
21. Zhu, X., Jiang, Y., Luo, Z.: Multi-person pose estimation for posetrack with enhanced part affinity fields. In: ICCV PoseTrack Workshop (2017)

Enhanced Two-Stage Multi-person Pose Estimation

Hiroto Honda(✉), Tomohiro Kato, and Yusuke Uchida

DeNA Co., Ltd., Tokyo, Japan
{hiroto.honda,tomohiro.kato,yusuke.a.uchida}@dena.com

Abstract. In this paper we introduce an enhanced multi-person pose estimation method for the competition of the PoseTrack [6] workshop in ECCV 2018. We employ a two-stage human pose detector, where human region detection and keypoint detection are separately performed. A strong encoder-decoder network for keypoint detection has achieved 70.4% mAP for PoseTrack 2018 validation dataset.

Keywords: Multi-person pose estimation · Keypoint detection

1 Introduction

The progress of human pose estimation is significant owing to the success of convolutional neural networks. However, the multi-person pose estimation problem is still challenging in the situations where there are various amounts of scale, rotation and overlapping (occlusion). We employ a top-down two-stage detector, where human region detection and keypoint detection are separately performed. For the first stage detector, we choose bounding box (or region of interest, ROI) regression output of a two-stage multi-person keypoint detector. To make the keypoint detection more accurate, we train the second stage detector that performs single-person pose estimation for each ROI.

The contributions of this report are twofold:

- We empirically show the effectiveness of a two-stage detector.
- We investigate the optimal design of the keypoint detector.

2 Related Work

The recently proposed approaches are categorized into two types: bottom-up and top-down. Bottom-up methods such as [1] first detect keypoints of multiple persons simultaneously and group them into individuals afterwards. On the other hand, top-down methods such as [3,10] detect each person's location first and detect keypoints afterwards. Our method is based on [10] which first detects the person regions, crops the regions from the input image, and localizes the keypoints using the keypoint detection network.

L. Leal-Taixé and S. Roth (Eds.): ECCV 2018 Workshops, LNCS 11130, pp. 217–220, 2019.
https://doi.org/10.1007/978-3-030-11012-3_18

3 Method

Our method detects human keypoints in a top-down and two-stage manner. At the first stage, the detector takes the whole image as an input and returns region-of-interests (ROIs) of persons. At the second stage, the keypoint detector takes the detected ROIs and locates each person's keypoints. In this section we describe the details of the two detectors using Fig. 1.

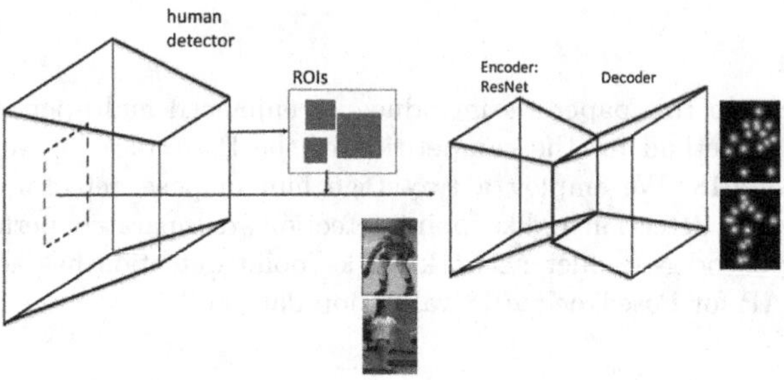

Fig. 1. Our two-stage network.

3.1 Person Detection

For the first stage, we adopt a multi-task detector that localizes bounding boxes and human keypoints at the same time. The detector is pretrained using images with bounding boxes and keypoints, thus already works as a multi-person keypoint detector. We pick the bounding box regression output of the detector and do not use the keypoint output. Compared with single-task (bounding box) detectors like Faster R-CNN [9], the bounding box regression results of the multi-task detector are more accurate due to the benefit from keypoint supervision.

3.2 Keypoint Detection

As the second-stage single-person keypoint detector, we employ an encoder-decoder network which is often referred to as an 'hourglass' structure. Human regions are cropped from the input whole image with margins and resized to a fixed image size. The hourglass network takes the cropped image and gives the heatmaps of each keypoint. The target is a set of K heatmaps $H_1 ... H_k$, each of which is generated with a 2D gaussian with $\sigma = 3.0$, centered at each keypoint.

We employ ResNet152 [4] for encoder and the simple decoder that has three sequential deconvolution - batchnorm [5] - ReLU blocks and one convolution layer. The intermediate channel width is 256 and deconvolution kernel size is 4×4.

4 Experiments

Training on the COCO Dataset. Firstly, the hourglass network is trained on the COCO train2017 dataset [8] with the Adam optimizer [7] for 90k iterations with batch size 64 and learning rate 1E-3. The learning rate is scheduled to be dropped by $\times 0.1$ at 60k and 80k iterations. The duration of training is approximately 32 h on NVIDIA Tesla V100 GPU. We use horizontal flip, rotation within 40°, and scale variation within 30% as data augmentation.

Training on the PoseTrack2018 Dataset. The model trained on COCO is fine-tuned on Posetrack2018 dataset. We use the same setting as training on COCO, except that the initial learning rate is set to 1E-4.

4.1 Performance on PoseTrack 2018 Dataset

The pretrained Keypoint R-CNN network named X-101-32x8d-FPN, which is available at [2], is used for ROI detection. Each detected ROI is expanded by 60 pixels in every direction and resized to (h, w) = (384, 288). Horizontal flip ensembling is used for the second-stage detection on each ROI. As shown in Table 1, our final result has achieved 70.4% and 65.9% of mAP with ResNet152 and ResNet50 respectively, on the PoseTrack2018 validation dataset. The visualization results are shown in Fig. 2.

Table 1. Performance on the PoseTrack 2018 validation dataset. PT and PT* stands for fine-tuning on the PoseTrack2018 dataset for 76k and 1k iterations respectively.

Encoder network	Trained on	Head	Shou	Elb	Wri	Hip	Knee	Ankl	Total
ResNet152	COCO, PT*	77.0	76.1	73.2	66.2	67.6	66.5	63.1	70.4
ResNet152	COCO, PT	76.1	74.3	71.6	65.4	62.3	64.7	61.5	68.5
ResNet152	COCO	27.8	77.1	73.4	65.7	68.5	67.8	62.8	60.9
ResNet50	COCO, PT*	75.4	73.5	67.4	59.7	62.0	61.3	57.0	65.9
ResNet50	COCO	26.8	69.7	62.5	54.1	57.8	54.5	50.8	51.9

4.2 Discussion

We observe that the AP result is improved by fine-tuning on the PoseTrack 2018 dataset but start to decay after 1000 iterations. More appropriate data pre-processing and data augmentation are considered to be necessary for the dataset. The difference between ResNet152 and ResNet50 is significant. There is a possibility that the second-stage network could be further improved by optimizing the network size or architecture.

Fig. 2. Inference result on PoseTrack 2018 validation dataset. The right image includes person detection and keypoint detection failures.

5 Conclusions

We have proposed the enhanced multi-person pose estimation exploiting a two-stage human pose detector. The individual strong networks are employed for person region detection (first stage) and keypoint localization (second stage) respectively and the latter is trained on the COCO and PoseTrack2018 datasets. Finally, our whole pipeline achieves 70.4% mAP for PoseTrack 2018 validation.

References

1. Cao, Z., Simon, T., Wei, S.E., Sheikh, Y.: Realtime multi-person 2D pose estimation using part affinity fields. In: Proceedings of CVPR (2017)
2. Girshick, R., Radosavovic, I., Gkioxari, G., Dollár, P., He, K.: Detectron (2018). https://github.com/facebookresearch/detectron
3. He, K., Gkioxari, G., Dollár, P., Girshick, R.B.: Mask R-CNN. In: Proceedings of ICCV (2017)
4. He, K., Zhang, X., Ren, S., Sun, J.: Deep residual learning for image recognition. In: Proceedings of CVPR (2016)
5. Ioffe, S., Szegedy, C.: Batch normalization: accelerating deep network training by reducing internal covariate shift. In: Proceedings of ICML (2015)
6. Iqbal, U., Milan, A., Gall, J.: PoseTrack: joint multi-person pose estimation and tracking. In: Proceedings of CVPR (2017)
7. Kingma, D.P., Ba, J.: Adam: a method for stochastic optimization. In: Proceedings of ICLR (2015)
8. Lin, T.-Y., et al.: Microsoft COCO: common objects in context. In: Fleet, D., Pajdla, T., Schiele, B., Tuytelaars, T. (eds.) ECCV 2014. LNCS, vol. 8693, pp. 740–755. Springer, Cham (2014). https://doi.org/10.1007/978-3-319-10602-1_48
9. Ren, S., He, K., Girshick, R.B., Sun, J.: Faster R-CNN: towards real-time object detection with region proposal networks. IEEE Trans. Pattern Anal. Mach. Intell. **39**, 1137–1149 (2015)
10. Xiao, B., Wu, H., Wei, Y.: Simple baselines for human pose estimation and tracking. In: Ferrari, V., Hebert, M., Sminchisescu, C., Weiss, Y. (eds.) ECCV 2018. LNCS, vol. 11210, pp. 472–487. Springer, Cham (2018). https://doi.org/10.1007/978-3-030-01231-1_29

Multi-person Pose Estimation for Pose Tracking with Enhanced Cascaded Pyramid Network

Dongdong Yu[1], Kai Su[1,2], Jia Sun[1], and Changhu Wang[1(✉)]

[1] ByteDance AI Lab, Beijing, China
{yudongdong,sukai,sunjia.ring,wangchanghu}@bytedance.com
[2] MOE Key Laboratory of Computer Network and Information Integration, Southeast University, Nanjing, China
sukai@seu.edu.cn

Abstract. Multi-person pose estimation is a fundamental yet challenging task in machine learning. In parallel, recent development of pose estimation has increased interests on pose tracking in recent years. In this work, we propose an efficient and powerful method to locate and track human pose. Our proposed method builds upon the state-of-the-art single person pose estimation system (Cascaded Pyramid Network), and adopts the IOU-tracker module to identify the people in the wild. We conduct experiments on the released multi-person video pose estimation benchmark (PoseTrack2018) to validate the effectiveness of our network. Our model achieves an accuracy of 80.9% on the validation and 77.1% on the test set using the *Mean Average Precision* (MAP) metric, an accuracy of 64.0% on the validation and 57.4% on the test set using the *Multi-Object Tracking Accuracy* (MOTA) metric.

Keywords: Pose estimation · Pose tracking

1 Introduction

Multi-person pose estimation and tracking are important yet challenging problems for all persons in single RGB image, which are fundamental research topics for many visual applications like human action recognition [19], human-computer interaction [6] and so on.

Recently, the performance of multi-person pose estimation on standard benchmarks such as MPII Pose [11] and COCO [12] has been greatly improved with the rapidly development of convolution neural networks [2,4,8,13–16,18,20]. Existing methods can be classified into two kinds of approaches: the bottom-up approach and the top-down approach. The bottom-up approach detects human skeletons from all potential human candidates and then assemble these

D. Yu and K. Su—Equal contribution.

L. Leal-Taixé and S. Roth (Eds.): ECCV 2018 Workshops, LNCS 11130, pp. 221–226, 2019.
https://doi.org/10.1007/978-3-030-11012-3_19

skeletons into each person. The top-down approach first adopt a detection module to get all the human boxes from the image, then apply a single-person human pose estimator to detect human skeletons. Although impressive performance has been achieved, current state-of-the-art methods still have difficulty to deal with occluded keypoints, invisible keypoints, and crowed backgroud, which cannot be well localized. Most recent pose tracking methods track the human box over the entire video in terms of similarity between pairs of boxes measured with box iou or similarity between pairs of human keypoints measured with keypoint oks distance in adjacent frames [7,9,21].

In this work, we propose an efficient and powerful approach to multi-person keypoint detecting and tracking in videos. For the keypoints detecting stage, we propose an enhanced cascade pyramid network to accurately locate human keypoint in each frame of a video. For the keypoint tracking stage, we employs IOU tracker which is a lightweight frame-by-frame optimization method, allowing our model to be scalable to virtually any length videos.

2 Related Work

Our proposed approach is related to previous works involving with human pose estimation and tracking, as described as follows:

Multi-person pose estimation is an important task in computer vision. Existing approaches can be divided into two categories: bottom-up approaches and top-down approaches. Bottom-up approaches firstly predict all keypoints and then assemble them into multiple persons. For example, associate embedding simultaneously predict heatmaps and tagmaps to group the predicted keypoints to different persons [13]. Top-down approaches firstly detect all human boxes in an image, and then predict the keypoints within each box independently. For example, Cascaded Pyramid Network (CPN) predicts human bounding boxes first and then solve the single person pose estimation in the cropped person patches [4]. In general, top-down approaches perform more accurate than bottom-up approaches. However, with the number of humans increases in an image, top-down approaches perform more slower.

Based on the multi-person pose estimation architectures described above, it is natural to extend them from still image to video. Some online trackers simplify this tracking problem as a maximum weight bipartite matching problem and solve it with greedy or Hungarian Algorithm. Nodes of this bipartite graph are human bounding boxes in two adjacent frames. For example, PoseTrack [7] and ArtTrack [9] in CVPR'17 primarily introduce multi-person pose tracking challenge and propose a new graph partitioning formulation, building upon 2D DeeperCut [10] by extending spatial joint graph to spatio-temporal graph.

3 Method

In this work, we take the top-down method to estimate multi-person pose in each frame. Firstly, we apply as human detector on the RGB image to generate human bounding-boxes. Secondly, we predict the detailed localization of the keypoints for each candidate human bounding-boxes by a single-person pose estimator. Finally, we simplify the tracking problem to bipartite matching the candidate bounding-boxes between a pair of frames.

3.1 Person Detector

In order to detect more people from image, we adopt the Deformable Convolutional Networks (with detection MAP of 44.4 on the COCO minival dataset) [5] and SNIPER (with detection MAP of 46.5 on the COCO minival dataset) [17] methods to generate our human bounding-boxes.

3.2 Pose Estimator

In order to get accurate person keypoints, we adopt the state-of-the-art single person pose estimator [4] (Cascade Pyramid Network) to detect the human skeletons. In addition, we have enhance the cascade pyramid network to make it more robust and accurate to handle large pose variations, changes in clothing and lighting conditions, severe body deformations, heavy body occlusions and so on. For the Global-Net, we design a shuffle unit to cross the information from all feature scales. For the Refine-Net, we design an attention unit to extract more representative feature to predict the keypoint localization.

3.3 Pose Tracker

Following the ICCV 2017 winner [7], these detections are presented as a graph, where every detected person bounding box in every frame is a node. And the edges are defined to connect each human bounding-box in a frame to each human bounding-box in the next frame. The cost of each edge is defined as the iou metric of the two human bounding-boxes linked on that edge to belong to the same person. To compute tracks, we simplify the problem to bipartite matching between a pair of frames, and propagate the labels forward, one frame at a time, starting from the first frame to the last.

4 Experiments

4.1 Dataset and Evaluation Metric

Our single person pose estimation model is trained with three datasets: MSCOCO dataset [12], AI challenge dataset [3], and PoseTrack challenge 2018 dataset [1]. MSCOCO dataset contains over 66k images with 150k people, AI challenge dataset has more than 270k images with 449k people, and PoseTrack challenge 2018 dataset contains 667 short video clips annotated for multi-person pose estimation and multi-person pose tracking.

We evaluate our proposed method on PoseTrack Challenge 2018 dataset. We use Total AP to evaluate the multi-person pose estimation results and standard MOTA metric to evaluate the tracking performance.

Table 1. The performance of the MAP metric on PoseTrack challenge 2018 dataset.

Dataset	Head	Shou	Elb	Wri	Hip	Knee	Ankl	Total
Validation	82.4	88.8	86.2	79.4	72.0	80.6	76.2	80.9
Partial test	79.0	84.6	81.7	75.5	68.8	77.4	72.0	77.1

Table 2. The performance of the MOTA metric on PoseTrack challenge 2018 dataset.

Dataset	Head	Shou	Elb	Wri	Hip	Knee	Ankl	Total
Validation	68.8	73.5	65.6	61.2	54.9	64.6	56.7	64.0
Partial test	61.4	65.1	58.4	55.0	49.0	59.0	51.5	57.4

4.2 Training Details

Our single person pose estimation model is trained using adam algorithm with an initial learning rate of 5e-4. Note that we also decrease the learning rate by a factor of 2 every 3600000 iterations. We use a weight decay of 1e-5 and the training batch size is 32. In the training for pose estimation, 4 V100 GPUs on a GPU server are used.

4.3 Testing Details

Following same testing strategies used in CPN, we apply a gaussian filter on the predicted heatmaps. We also predict the pose of the corresponding flipped image and average the heatmaps to get the final prediction. A quarter offset in the direction from the highest score response to the second highest response is used to obtain the final location of the keypoints. In order to get the best performance on the MAP metric, we first use the SoftNMS on the candidate human bounding-boxes generated by the Deformable Convolutional Networks and SNIPER. Second, we use the Pose-OKS method with the threshold of 0.4 to filter out the redundant human keypoints. Finally, we filter out the human bounding boxes which area is smaller than 3600. In order to achieve the best performance on the MOTA metric, two more rules added. The score of human-bounding box must be higher than 0.35 and the score of the predicted keypoint must be higher than 0.85.

4.4 PoseTrack Challenge Results

We evaluate our method on the whole validation set and partial of test set of the PoseTrack challenge 2018 dataset. The performance of the MAP metric is shown in the Table 1. And, the performance of the MOTA metric is shown in Table 2. We also show some sample keypoints detection results of our model on the PoseTrack challenge 2018 dataset in Fig. 1.

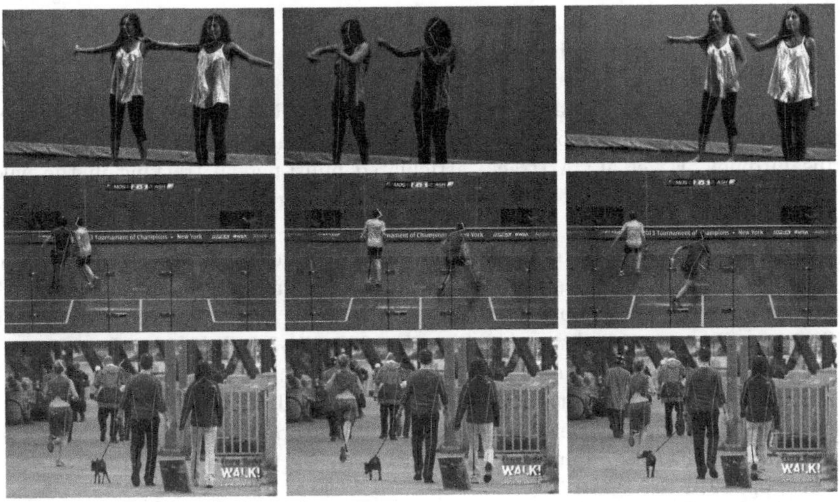

Fig. 1. Some results of our model on the PoseTrack challenge 2018 dataset.

5 Conclusions

In this paper, we propose an efficient and powerful method for the multi-person pose estimation and tracking. For the multi-person pose estimation, based on the Cascaded Pyramid Network, we design a shuffle unit to fuse the pyramid feature maps and an attention unit to extract more representative feature maps. For the multi-person pose tracking, we simplify the problem as a bipartite matching problem between a pair of the frames. Experimental results show that our method achieves an accuracy of 80.9% on the validation and 77.1% on the test set using the *Mean Average Precision* (MAP) metric, an accuracy of 64.0% on the validation and 57.4% on the test set using the *Multi-Object Tracking Accuracy* (MOTA) metric.

References

1. PoseTrack 2018 Challenge: PoseTrack challenge 2018 dataset. https://posetrack.net/
2. Cao, Z., Simon, T., Wei, S.E., Sheikh, Y.: Realtime multi-person 2D pose estimation using part affinity fields. In: CVPR, vol. 1, p. 7 (2017)
3. AI challenger: AI challenger dataset. https://challenger.ai/
4. Chen, Y., Wang, Z., Peng, Y., Zhang, Z., Yu, G., Sun, J.: Cascaded pyramid network for multi-person pose estimation. arXiv preprint arXiv:1711.07319 (2017)
5. Dai, J., et al.: Deformable convolutional networks. CoRR, abs/1703.06211 **1**(2), 3 (2017)
6. Dix, A.: Human-computer interaction. In: Liu, L., Özsu, M.T. (eds.) Encyclopedia of Database Systems, pp. 1327–1331. Springer, Boston (2009). https://doi.org/10.1007/978-0-387-39940-9_192

7. Girdhar, R., Gkioxari, G., Torresani, L., Paluri, M., Tran, D.: Detect-and-track: efficient pose estimation in videos. In: Proceedings of the IEEE Conference on Computer Vision and Pattern Recognition, pp. 350–359 (2018)
8. He, K., Gkioxari, G., Dollár, P., Girshick, R.: Mask R-CNN. In: 2017 IEEE International Conference on Computer Vision (ICCV), pp. 2980–2988. IEEE (2017)
9. Insafutdinov, E., et al.: Arttrack: articulated multi-person tracking in the wild. In: IEEE Conference on Computer Vision and Pattern Recognition (CVPR), vol. 4327. IEEE (2017)
10. Insafutdinov, E., Pishchulin, L., Andres, B., Andriluka, M., Schiele, B.: DeeperCut: a deeper, stronger, and faster multi-person pose estimation model. In: Leibe, B., Matas, J., Sebe, N., Welling, M. (eds.) ECCV 2016. LNCS, vol. 9910, pp. 34–50. Springer, Cham (2016). https://doi.org/10.1007/978-3-319-46466-4_3
11. MPII: Mpii human pose dataset. http://human-pose.mpi-inf.mpg.de/
12. MS-COCO: Coco keypoint leaderboard. http://cocodataset.org/
13. Newell, A., Huang, Z., Deng, J.: Associative embedding: end-to-end learning for joint detection and grouping. In: Advances in Neural Information Processing Systems, pp. 2274–2284 (2017)
14. Newell, A., Yang, K., Deng, J.: Stacked hourglass networks for human pose estimation. In: Leibe, B., Matas, J., Sebe, N., Welling, M. (eds.) ECCV 2016. LNCS, vol. 9912, pp. 483–499. Springer, Cham (2016). https://doi.org/10.1007/978-3-319-46484-8_29
15. Papandreou, G., et al.: Towards accurate multi-person pose estimation in the wild. In: CVPR, vol. 3, p. 6 (2017)
16. Pishchulin, L., et al.: DeepCut: joint subset partition and labeling for multi person pose estimation. In: Proceedings of the IEEE Conference on Computer Vision and Pattern Recognition, pp. 4929–4937 (2016)
17. Singh, B., Najibi, M., Davis, L.S.: SNIPER: efficient multi-scale training. arXiv preprint arXiv:1805.09300 (2018)
18. Toshev, A., Szegedy, C.: DeepPose: human pose estimation via deep neural networks. In: Proceedings of the IEEE Conference on Computer Vision and Pattern Recognition, pp. 1653–1660 (2014)
19. Wang, C., Wang, Y., Yuille, A.L.: An approach to pose-based action recognition. In: 2013 IEEE Conference on Computer Vision and Pattern Recognition (CVPR), pp. 915–922. IEEE (2013)
20. Wei, S.E., Ramakrishna, V., Kanade, T., Sheikh, Y.: Convolutional pose machines. In: Proceedings of the IEEE Conference on Computer Vision and Pattern Recognition, pp. 4724–4732 (2016)
21. Xiu, Y., Li, J., Wang, H., Fang, Y., Lu, C.: Pose flow: Efficient online pose tracking. arXiv preprint arXiv:1802.00977 (2018)

A Top-Down Approach to Articulated Human Pose Estimation and Tracking

Guanghan Ning(✉), Ping Liu, Xiaochuan Fan, and Chi Zhang

JD.com Silicon Valley Research Center, Mountain View, USA
{guanghan.ning,ping.liu,xiaochuan.fan,chi.zhang}@jd.com

Abstract. Both the tasks of multi-person human pose estimation and pose tracking in videos are quite challenging. Existing methods can be categorized into two groups: top-down and bottom-up approaches. In this paper, following the top-down approach, we aim to build a strong baseline system with three modules: human candidate detector, single-person pose estimator and human pose tracker. Firstly, we choose a generic object detector among state-of-the-art methods to detect human candidates. Then, cascaded pyramid network is used to estimate the corresponding human pose. Finally, we use a flow-based pose tracker to render keypoint-association across frames, i.e., assigning each human candidate a unique and temporally-consistent id, for the multi-target pose tracking purpose. We conduct extensive ablative experiments to validate various choices of models and configurations. We take part in two ECCV'18 PoseTrack challenges (https://posetrack.net/workshops/eccv2018/posetrack_eccv_2018_results.html): pose estimation and pose tracking.

Keywords: Multi-person pose estimation · Multi-person pose tracking

1 Introduction

Compared to single person human pose estimation, where human candidates are cropped and centered in the image patch, the task of multi-person human pose estimation is more realistic and challenging. Existing methods can be classified into top-down and bottom-up approaches. The top-down approach [8,16] relies on a detection module to obtain human candidates and then apply a single-person human pose estimator to locate human keypoints. The bottom-up approach [2,9,14,18], on the other hand, detects human keypoints from all potential human candidates and then assembles these keypoints into human limbs for each individual based on various data association techniques. The advantage of bottom-up approaches is their excellent trade-off between estimation accuracy and computational cost because their computational cost is invariant to the number of human candidates in the image. In contrast, the main advantage of top-down approaches is their capability in disassembling the task into multiple

L. Leal-Taixé and S. Roth (Eds.): ECCV 2018 Workshops, LNCS 11130, pp. 227–234, 2019.
https://doi.org/10.1007/978-3-030-11012-3_20

comparatively easier tasks, i.e., object detection and single-person pose estimation. The object detector is expert in detecting hard (usually small) candidates, so that the pose estimator will perform better with a focused regression space.

Pose tracking is the task of estimating human keypoints and assigning unique ids for each keypoint at instance-level across frames in videos. In videos with multiple people, accurate trajectory estimation of human key points is useful in human action recognition and human interaction understanding. PoseTrack [12] and ArtTrack [11] primarily introduce multi-person pose tracking challenge and propose a graph partitioning formulation, which transforms the pose tracking problem into a minimum cost multi-cut problem. However, hand-crafted graphical models are not scalable for long and unseen clips. Another line of research explores top-down approach [6,19,20] by operating multi-person human pose estimation on each frame and linking them based on appearance similarities and temporal adjacencies. A naive solution is to apply multi-target object tracking on human detection candidates across frames and then estimate human poses for each human tubelet. While this is a feasible method, it neglects unique attributes of keypoints. Compared to the tracked bounding boxes, keypoints can potentially be helpful cues for both the bounding boxes and the keypoints tracking. The tracker of 3D Mask R-CNN [6] simplifies the pose tracking problem as a maximum weight bipartite matching problem and solve it with Greedy or Hungarian algorithm. PoseFlow [20] further takes motion and pose information into account to address the issue of occasional truncated human candidates.

2 Our Approach

We follow the top-down approach for pose tracking, i.e., perform human candidate detection, single-person pose estimation, and pose tracking step by step. The details for each module are described below, respectively.

2.1 Detection Module

We adopt state-of-the-art object detectors trained with ImageNet and COCO datasets. Specifically, we use pre-trained models from deformable ConvNets [5]. In order to increase the recall rate of human candidates, we conduct experiments on validation sets of both PoseTrack 2017 [1] and PoseTrack 2018 to choose the best object detector. Firstly, we infer ground truth bounding boxes of human candidates from the annotated keypoints, because in PoseTrack 2017 dataset, the bounding box position is not provided in the annotations. Specifically, we locate a bounding box from the minimum and maximum coordinates of the 15 keypoints, and then enlarge this box by 20% both horizontally and vertically. Even though ground truth bounding boxes are given in PoseTrack 2018 dataset, we infer a more consistent version based on ground truth locations of keypoints. Those inferred ground truth bounding boxes are utilized to train the pose estimator.

For the object detectors, we compare the deformable convolution versions of the R-FCN network [4] and of the FPN network [13], both with ResNet101 backbone [10]. The FPN feature extractor is attached to the Fast R-CNN [7] head for detection. We compare the detection results with the ground truth based on the precision and recall rate on PoseTrack 2017 validation set. In order to eliminate redundant candidates, we drop candidate(s) with lower likelihood. As shown in Table 1, for various drop thresholds of bounding boxes, the precision and recall of the detectors are given. For PoseTrack 2018 validation set, the FPN network performs better as well. Therefore, we choose the FPN network as our human candidate detector.

Table 1. Precision-Recall on PoseTrack 2017 validation set. A bounding box is correct if its IoU with GT is above certain threshold, which is set to 0.4 for all experiments.

Drop thresholds of bbox	0.1	0.2	0.3	**0.4**	0.5	0.6	0.7	0.8	0.9
Deformable FPN (ResNet101): prec	17.9	27.5	32.2	**34.2**	35.7	37.2	38.6	40.0	42.1
Deformable R-FCN (ResNet101): prec	15.4	21.1	25.9	30.3	34.5	37.9	39.9	41.6	43.2
Deform FPN (ResNet101): recall	87.7	86.0	84.5	**83.0**	80.8	79.2	77.0	73.8	69.0
Deform R-FCN (ResNet101): recall	87.7	86.5	85.0	82.6	80.1	77.3	74.4	70.4	61.0

The upper bound for detection is the ground truth bounding box location. In order to measure the gap between ideal detection results and our detection results, we feed the ground truth bounding boxes to the subsequent pose estimation module and tracking module, and compare its performance with that of our detector on the validation set. As shown in Table 2, the pose estimation will perform around 7% better with ground truth detections. As shown in Table 3, the pose tracking will perform around 6% better with ground truth detections.

Table 2. Comparison of single-frame pose estimation results using various detectors on PoseTrack 2017 validation set.

Average Precision (AP)	Head	Shou	Elb	Wri	Hip	Knee	Ankl	**Total**
Ground truth detections	88.9	88.4	82.7	74.7	78.9	79.4	75.4	**81.7**
Deform FPN (ResNet101)	80.7	81.2	77.4	70.2	72.6	72.2	64.7	**74.6**
Deform R-FCN (ResNet101)	79.6	80.3	75.9	69.0	72.0	71.6	64.3	**73.7**

Table 3. Comparison of multi-frame pose tracking results using various detectors on PoseTrack 2017 validation set.

	MOTA Head	MOTA Shou	MOTA Elb	MOTA Wri	MOTA Hip	MOTA Knee	MOTA Ankl	**MOTA Total**
GT detections	78.8	78.2	65.6	56.3	64.4	63.8	56.2	**67.0**
D-FPN-101	68.9	70.9	62.7	54.6	59.5	59.8	48.7	**61.3**
D-RFCN-101	66.5	68.1	60.1	52.2	57.4	57.9	47.4	**59.0**

With ResNet151 as backbone, and training detectors solely on the human class, e.g., training on the CrowdHuman [17] dataset, we believe the detection module may render better results. For the challenge, we just adopt the deformable FPN with ResNet101 and use their pre-trained model for simplicity.

2.2 Pose Estimation Module

For the single-person human pose estimator, we adopt Cascaded Pyramid Networks (CPN) [3] with slight modifications. We first train the CPN network with the merged dataset of PoseTrack 2018 and COCO for 260 epochs. Then we finetune the network solely on PoseTrack 2018 training set for 40 epochs in order to mitigate the regression on head. For COCO dataset, bottom-head and top-head positions are not given. We infer these keypoints through rough interpolation on the annotated keypoints. We find that by finetuning on the PoseTrack dataset, the prediction on head keypoints will be refined. During finetuning, we use the technique of online hard keypoint mining, only focusing on losses from the 7 hardest keypoints out of the total 15 keypoints.

In our implementation, we perform non-maximum suppression (NMS) in the detection phase on the bounding boxes and perform pose estimation on all candidates from the detection module. For each candidate, we post-process on the predicted heatmaps with cross-heatmap pose NMS [15] to render more accurate keypoint locations. We did not perform flip testing, although the performance might be slightly better. During testing, we use a manifold of two models from epoch 291 and 293. We notice a slight performance boost with model ensemble. For epoch 291, the prediction of shoulders and hips renders better results than epoch 293 on validation sets of both PoseTrack 2017 and PoseTrack 2018. However, epoch 293 performs better on end limbs such as ankles and wrists. We test with two manifold modes: (1) Average and (2) Expert. As shown in Table 4, the expert mode takes shoulder/hip predictions from the previous model and end-limb predictions from the latter, which performs better consistently on both PoseTrack 2017 and PoseTrack 2018 validation sets. Both modes perform better than plain testing on the pose estimation task.

Table 4. Comparison of single-frame pose estimation results with different ensemble modes on PoseTrack 2017 validation set.

Average Precision (AP)	Head	Shou	Elb	Wri	Hip	Knee	Ankl	**Total**
Epoch 291	80.7	**81.2**	77.4	70.2	**72.6**	72.2	64.7	74.6
Epoch 293	80.5	80.8	77.9	**71.3**	70.1	72.9	**65.7**	74.6
Average	81.3	81.2	77.6	70.7	72.1	72.5	65.1	74.8
Expert	80.6	81.2	77.9	71.3	72.6	72.9	65.7	75.0

Fig. 1. Our modular system for pose tracking. From top to bottom: we perform human candidate detection, pose estimation, and pose tracking sequentially.

2.3 Pose Tracking Module

We adopt a flow-based pose tracker [20], where pose flows are built by associating poses that indicate the same person across frames. We start the tracking process from the first frame where human candidates are detected. To prevent assignments of IDs for persons which have already left the visible image area, IDs are only kept for a limited amount of frames, afterwards they are discarded. For the pose tracking task, the performance is evaluated via MOTA, which is very strict. It penalizes mis-matches, false positives and misses. In order to get higher MOTA results, we need to drop keypoints with lower confidence scores, sacrificing the recall rate of correct keypoints. We find the MOTA evaluation criterion quite sensitive to the drop rate of keypoints, as shown in Table 5 (Fig. 1).

Table 5. Sensitivity analysis on how the drop thresholds of keypoints affect the performance in AP and MOTA. Performed on PoseTrack 2018 validation set.

Threshold	0.5	0.6	0.7	0.8	0.85
Pose estimation (AP)	**76.3**	75.5	73.4	69.7	67.1
Pose tracking (MOTA)	40.4	53.4	60.6	**62.4**	61.6

Considering the distinct difficulties of keypoints, e.g., shoulders are easier than ankles to localize, the confidence distribution for each joint is supposedly not uniform. Dropping keypoints solely based on the keypoint confidence estimated by the pose estimator may not be an ideal strategy for pose tracking. We collect statistics on the drop rate of keypoints from different joints, as shown in Table 6. We can see that from left to right, the keypoints become more and more difficult to estimate, as reflected by their respective preservation rate. The least and most difficult joints are the shoulders and ankles, respectively. In other words, the pose estimator is most confident on the shoulders but least confident on ankles. An adaptive keypoint pruner may help increase the MOTA performance while maintaining high recall rates.

Table 6. Statistics analysis on the drop rates of keypoints with different drop thresholds. Performed on PoseTrack 2018 validation set. The numbers indicate the percentage of keypoints maintained after pruning.

Threshold	Shou	Head	Elb	Hip	Knee	Wri	Ankl	Total
0.70	82.1	75.3	68.3	66.0	60.2	60.2	54.6	68.6
0.75	78.4	71.1	63.9	61.5	56.2	54.9	49.9	64.3
0.85	70.2	62.3	54.3	53.0	48.8	46.2	42.3	56.0

3 Challenge Results

Our final performance on the partial test set of PoseTrack 2018 is given in Tables 7 and 8.

Table 7. Our single-frame pose estimation results on PoseTrack 2018 partial test set

Average Precision (AP)	Head	Shou	Elb	Wri	Hip	Knee	Ankl	**Total**
Ours	74.2	74.3	71.5	66.8	66.7	67.2	62.4	**69.4**

Table 8. Our multi-frame pose tracking results on PoseTrack 2018 partial test set

	MOTA Head	MOTA Shou	MOTA Elb	MOTA Wri	MOTA Hip	MOTA Knee	MOTA Ankl	**MOTA Total**	MOTP Total	Prec Total	Rec Total
Ours	60.2	62.1	53.9	50.1	52.2	52.6	47.4	**54.5**	85.9	83.9	68.9

4 Conclusion

In this paper, we aim to build a modular system to reach the state-of-the-art of human pose estimation and tracking. This system consists of three modules, which conduct human candidate detection, pose estimation and pose tracking respectively. We have analyzed each module in the system with ablation studies on various models and configurations while discussing their pros and cons. We present the performance of our system in the pose estimation challenge and pose tracking challenge of PoseTrack 2018.

References

1. Andriluka, M., et al.: PoseTrack: a benchmark for human pose estimation and tracking. In: Proceedings of the IEEE Conference on Computer Vision and Pattern Recognition, pp. 5167–5176 (2018)
2. Cao, Z., Simon, T., Wei, S.E., Sheikh, Y.: Realtime multi-person 2D pose estimation using part affinity fields. In: CVPR (2017)
3. Chen, Y., Wang, Z., Peng, Y., Zhang, Z., Yu, G., Sun, J.: Cascaded pyramid network for multi-person pose estimation. In: CVPR (2018)
4. Dai, J., Li, Y., He, K., Sun, J.: R-FCN: object detection via region-based fully convolutional networks. In: Advances in Neural Information Processing Systems, pp. 379–387 (2016)
5. Dai, J., et al.: Deformable convolutional networks. CoRR, abs/1703.06211 **1**(2), 3 (2017)
6. Girdhar, R., Gkioxari, G., Torresani, L., Paluri, M., Tran, D.: Detect-and-track: efficient pose estimation in videos. In: Proceedings of the IEEE Conference on Computer Vision and Pattern Recognition, pp. 350–359 (2018)
7. Girshick, R.: Fast R-CNN. In: Proceedings of the IEEE International Conference on Computer Vision, pp. 1440–1448 (2015)
8. Fang, H.S., Xie, S., Tai, Y.W., Lu, C.: RMPE: regional multi-person pose estimation. In: ICCV (2017)
9. He, K., Gkioxari, G., Dollár, P., Girshick, R.: Mask R-CNN. In: 2017 IEEE International Conference on Computer Vision (ICCV), pp. 2980–2988. IEEE (2017)
10. He, K., Zhang, X., Ren, S., Sun, J.: Deep residual learning for image recognition. In: CVPR (2016)

11. Insafutdinov, E., et al.: ArtTrack: articulated multi-person tracking in the wild. In: CVPR, vol. 4327. IEEE (2017)
12. Iqbal, U., Milan, A., Gall, J.: PoseTrack: joint multi-person pose estimation and tracking. In: IEEE Conference on Computer Vision and Pattern Recognition (CVPR) (2017)
13. Lin, T.Y., Dollár, P., Girshick, R.B., He, K., Hariharan, B., Belongie, S.J.: Feature pyramid networks for object detection. In: CVPR, vol. 1, p. 3 (2017)
14. Newell, A., Huang, Z., Deng, J.: Associative embedding: end-to-end learning for joint detection and grouping. In: Advances in Neural Information Processing Systems, pp. 2277–2287 (2017)
15. Ning, G., Zhang, Z., He, Z.: Knowledge-guided deep fractal neural networks for human pose estimation. IEEE Trans. Multimed. **20**(5), 1246–1259 (2018)
16. Papandreou, G., et al.: Towards accurate multi-person pose estimation in the wild. In: CVPR, vol. 3, p. 6 (2017)
17. Shao, S., et al.: CrowdHuman: a benchmark for detecting human in a crowd. arXiv preprint arXiv:1805.00123 (2018)
18. Xia, F., Wang, P., Chen, X., Yuille, A.L.: Joint multi-person pose estimation and semantic part segmentation. In: CVPR, vol. 2, p. 7 (2017)
19. Xiao, B., Wu, H., Wei, Y.: Simple baselines for human pose estimation and tracking. In: Ferrari, V., Hebert, M., Sminchisescu, C., Weiss, Y. (eds.) ECCV 2018. LNCS, vol. 11210, pp. 472–487. Springer, Cham (2018). https://doi.org/10.1007/978-3-030-01231-1_29
20. Xiu, Y., Li, J., Wang, H., Fang, Y., Lu, C.: Pose flow: efficient online pose tracking. In: BMVC (2018)

W10 – Workshop on Objectionable Content and Misinformation

W10 – Workshop on Objectionable Content and Misinformation

With the advent of Internet and, especially, search engines and social networks, vast amounts of images and videos are created and shared per day resulting in billions of views of this information rendered to a heterogeneous and large audience. In many cases, it is necessary to understand the underlying semantics of the visual footage for two reasons:

- **Content.** To detect potential objectionable content or sensitive imagery like nudity, pornography, violence, hate, children exploitation and terrorism among others. This information may be used to enforce viewing policies like preventing minors to adult content, take down gore images, moderating hate, control terrorism propaganda, etc.
- **Misinformation.** Hoaxes, out-of-context images, fake footage, etc. may contribute to misinformation. Assessing the veracity of images and videos is a key element to guarantee that information (news, blogs, posts, etc.) is unbiased and trustful.

Both fronts go often together as we have seen in the recent photo-realistic face-swapping advancements. Developing tools to detect such content require a great deal to computer vision and machine learning expertise yet the relevant communities have devoted little attention to such problems.

The aim of this workshop was to give the opportunity to explore the specific challenges in the computer vision domain entailed by objectionable content and misinformation. We looked forward to academia and industry to expose their challenges, their progress and to build a joint forum of discussion around this area of research.

September 2018

Cristian Canton Ferrer
Matthias Niessner
Marius Vlad
Paul Natsev

Deep Fusion Network for Splicing Forgery Localization

Bo Liu and Chi-Man Pun(✉)

University of Macau, Taipa, Macao, China
{yb57413,cmpun}@umac.mo

Abstract. Digital splicing is a common type of image forgery: some regions of an image are replaced with contents from other images. To locate altered regions in a tampered picture is a challenging work because the difference is unknown between the altered regions and the original regions and it is thus necessary to search the large hypothesis space for a convincing result. In this paper, we proposed a novel deep fusion network to locate tampered area by tracing its border. A group of deep convolutional neural networks called Base-Net were firstly trained to response the certain type of splicing forgery respectively. Then, some layers of the Base-Net are selected and combined as a deep fusion neural network (Fusion-Net). After fine-tuning by a very small number of pictures, Fusion-Net is able to discern whether an image block is synthesized from different origins. Experiments on the benchmark datasets show that our method is effective in various situations and outperform state-of-the-art methods.

Keywords: Image forensics · Splicing forgery detection · Forgery localization · Deep convolutional network · Fusion network

1 Introduction

Digital splicing refers to replacing some regions of a digital image with contents from other pictures. It is a common form of image tampering and manipulation. Since the contents of the original image have been altered, the meaning of the image conveyed is changed and sometimes even changed completely. The great development of photo editing software makes high-quality image tampering easily even for non-professional and untrained people. And these intentionally manipulated photos spread rapidly and widely through the Internet, turning to the misleading or fake news. Therefore, there is a strong need for image forensic method which is able to judge whether the contents of an image has been altered, and more specifically, which part of the image has been altered. The latter is indeed an important problem in image forensics: splicing forgery localization.

To discriminate whether a picture has undergone digital splicing, the technique of watermarking can be used [33]. If the watermarking of the picture changes, the picture is regarded as being altered in some ways such as copy-move forgery or splicing forgery. But those methods require the original pictures

L. Leal-Taixé and S. Roth (Eds.): ECCV 2018 Workshops, LNCS 11130, pp. 237–251, 2019.
https://doi.org/10.1007/978-3-030-11012-3_21

to produce the watermark, thus given a test picture without any watermark they cannot make a judgment. Moreover, producing watermarks for every picture taken by cameras is impossible. Therefore, there is a strong need for methods which can detect forgery without a prior. The pictures undergone splicing forgery contains two areas: original background region from the host image and the spliced region from other pictures, therefore there must be some difference between these two areas. Many assumptions on such difference were made to design image forensic algorithms. Noise discrepancies between the spliced area and the host picture can be a cue to locate forgery because an image unavoidably bears a certain type and a certain amount of noise and pictures from different origins may carry different patterns and levels of the noise [30,32]. Another commonly seen assumption is based on the traces left by JEPG compression algorithm [26,38]. In the compression pipeline, an image is divided into fix-sized blocks and quantized by a pre-set table called quantization table. By estimating quantization table used in a test picture, if different tables are found, the picture may be fake [12]. To create a splicing forgery, the manipulation often involves double or more times of compressions. In double compression, the grid of the first compression and the second compression may be not aligned in a spliced area, analysis of such traces can also locate splicing forgery [2,5,6,27]. Under the circumstance multiple compressions, the different number of times of compressions of the different areas is also an indicator of splicing [22]. It is another assumption that the spliced object may be geometrically adjusted, such as rotation and affine transformation. These adjustments produce interpolations, which present periodical patterns in frequency domain thus can be used to expose splicing forgery [31,34]. Apart from these latent discrepancies, perceivable visual patterns can also be utilized. These methods estimate the direction of environmental light beams [19], or model the distortions caused by lenses [16], or detect inconsistent shadows in the image [29].

In recent years, the deep learning shows great power in many research fields and methods based on the deep convolutional neural networks(CNN) outperform traditional methods and achieve huge success in solving problems of computer vision, such as saliency detection [24], semantic segmentation [17] and depth estimation [28]. Some methods utilizing CNN have been proposed to expose image forgeries. One successful attempt is made in [35] that a 10-layer CNN as a classifier to decide a picture is authentic or manipulated by copy-move or splicing operation. A similar method producing a yes-or-no result by CNN is also seen in [20]. Bayar [4] designed a new convolutional network to learn manipulation features, rather than features of image contents as traditional convolutional layers did. To locate splicing forgery, the deep neural network is trained to learn manipulation features proposed in traditional methods, such as JPEG double compression features [3,23,37], resampling features [8,14] and camera-based features [7].

In this paper, we proposed a CNN based framework to deal with the problem of splicing forgery localization. Firstly, several deep convolutional neural networks called base-net are created. Each base-net is trained to be sensitive to a specific type of discrepancy which exists in synthesized images. Secondly, some layers of each base-net are selected and then combined with selected layers from other base-nets to construct a new network called fusion-net. After the fine-tuning with a few numbers of training images, the fusion-net will be able to detect splicing forgery in digital images. The main contribution of our work is to propose a fusion framework which combines common hypotheses of digital splicing, and obtain the manipulation features by deep learning, which is proven to outperform the hand-crafted features. Our effort in the paper as follows. Firstly, instead of processing a test image as a whole, we process small image blocks from the test image. This is to avoid learning high-level visual features, which are not relevant to the image forensics, by deep neural networks. And in this fashion, our method can handle images in very large size with high resolution. Secondly, we carefully chose two manipulation features and utilized CNN to extract these features in the sufficiently large databases we created. Thirdly, the fusion of different features was via fine-tuning by a small number of training images. Experiments show that our proposed deep fusion network outperformed the state-of-the-art.

2 Related Work

As stated in the former section, in order to expose splicing forgery, a proper assumption will be firstly proposed and then an algorithm is then designed under such assumption. Therefore, a specific method is effective to a certain type of splicing forgery only. In order to detect more types of digital splicing, the fusion method is needed. Before a review of fusion frameworks, we will first describe some algorithms based on a single assumption.

JPEG Compressions. JPEG compression standard has been widely adopted. As a lossy compression scheme, the compression pipeline will unavoidably leave the images some traces which can be used to expose digital splicing. Double compression is a common hypothesis which assumes the forged area have been double compressed while the pristine region has been compressed one-time [5,6,26,27]. Double compression can be detected by finding a derivation of modelled DCT coefficients and generating a likelihood map which presents the probability of each 8×8 image block of being doubly compression [6]. The analysis and model of the work are based on double compression. But in the real situation, forged images are often compressed more than just twice. And the algorithm is not robust to a certain situation when second compression quality is better than the first one. Wang's method [37] based on a seven-layer CNN successfully solves the problem and can deal with such situation. Amerini's work [3] improves detection accuracy by integrating information from spatial domain and frequency domain of pictures into the CNN framework. Their proposed multi-domain neural network includes a seven-layer CNN to extract features from frequency domain and an eight-layer CNN to extract features from spatial domain, followed by two fully connected layers.

Image Noise. Methods based on the hypothesis that the spliced area bears different amount of noise include two steps: local noise estimation and forgery localization. Forgery localization requires accurate local noise estimation in images. Mahdian's work [32] estimate local noise by tilling sub-band HH_1 of the wavelet transformed non-overlapping image blocks. Lyu [30] describes a method based on the phenomenon of kurtosis concentration in natural images. The test image is firstly decomposed into several band-pass filtered channels using AC filters from the DCT decomposition. Then in each band-pass filtered channels, raw moments from the first to the fourth order will be calculated, followed by computing kurtosis and variance for each local window in each band-pass filtered channel. Lastly, noise variance is estimated by the projection from a local window across all band-pass filtered channels. Aforementioned methods firstly evaluate the noise variance, then finding the regions with different noise level from the rest. Therefore, the performance of noise estimation in their methods are crucial. However, blind noise estimation is a difficult task especially when the local window is small. Actually, noise variance estimation is not a must in exposing splicing forgery. Our target is to find the discrepancy of noise, rather than the noise variance.

If we want a single method that can cover more hypotheses so as to deal with more splicing instances, an effective fusion of results from different methods is necessary. Some fusion methods have been proposed so far. Different indicators of splicing forgery can be incorporated by discriminative random field and formulated as a labelling problem [18]. Another fusion method in [15] uses Dempster-Shafer theory of evidence which is regarded as an extension of the Bayesian theory to fuse existing forensic methods. Apart from utilizing the classic probability theories, the fusion can be implemented by pre-defined rules [9,21]. Li's fusion framework [25] firstly uses two existing forensic methods, i.e., statistical feature-based detector and copy-move forgery detector, to produce tampering possibility maps and then project these two scores of each pixel of training images into a two-dimensional plane. A decision curve is then manually determined to distinguish pristine and fake pixels. Although the fusion methods can generate reasonable results, the extension ability of these methods is limited: the fusion scheme must be altered or the computational complexity will increase prominently. Therefore, ideal fusion method should be more flexible and extendible to incorporate new forensic methods.

3 Deep Fusion Network

In this section, we first present the framework our method and then discuss and analyse the network including the Base-net which is used to extract forensic features and the Fusion-Net which fuses forensic features to give predictions.

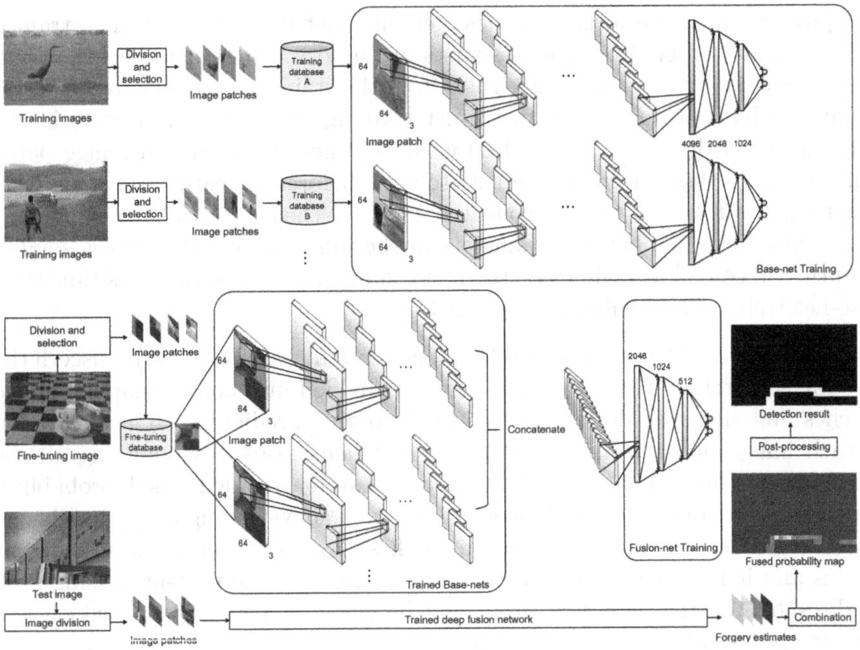

Fig. 1. The framework of proposed method.

3.1 The Framework of Proposed Method

Our proposed digital splicing detection framework is illustrated in Fig. 1. The training process for the network has two stages: base-net training and fusion-net fine tuning.

Base-Net Training. Each base-net is designed to make binary forgery prediction under a certain forgery hypothesis. In our implementation, two forgery hypotheses are used: a fake image patch contains contents from two sources whose noise levels are different, or a fake image patch contains two origins which undergo different JPEG compressions. For each base-net, a particular training database is constructed which consists of image patches of a fixed and same size. These image patches are taken from splicing forged pictures and if an image patch contains both spliced objects and the background image, it will be labelled as forged, if not, it will be labelled as genuine. In order to balance the training images, we selected the image patches to equal the numbers of the forged and the genuine image patches. The structure of VGG-16 [36] is used in our work but other deep convolutional neural networks can also be adopted. When the training for each base-net completes, convolutional kernels except those form fully connected layers will be retained for the next step fine-tuning.

Fusion-Net Fine-Tuning. The construction of fine-tuning database is similar to the base-net training database as the forged images are divided into patches and proportion of the forged and the genuine controlled to 1 : 1. The trained convolutional kernels from the base-nets are used to construct the fusion-net: the parameters of convolutional kernels from the trained base-nets are fixed and remain unchanged during the fusion-net training while the parameters in the fully connected layers are trained only during fine-tuning. So, an image patch will be sent to these trained base-nets to extract forensic features perspectively and then the features will be concatenated and then goes to fully connected layers. Since the number of parameters in the fully connected layers is smaller than that in convolutional layers, the fine-tuning process will take less time than base-net training and will converge quickly.

Image Forensics. The trained deep fusion network now can be used to discern the fake image patches. The test image is firstly divided into non-overlapped image patches and then use deep fusion network to give predictions. The prediction of each image patch will be a probability of being forged. Combining all the predictions of each image patch we get a heat map called fused probability map. From this map, the borders of splicing area show the higher probability of being forged because the border image patches contained contents from different origins and it is perceived by the fusion-net. After simple post-processing such as thresholding, the detection result will be given as a binary map which is a tracing of borders of the spliced area.

3.2 Extractions of Forensic Features

In the first stage, the revised VGG16 convolutional neural network [36] produces forgery estimates for image patches. In our implementation, the network takes the image patch of fixed size at $64 \times 64 \times RGB$ as input. These input images are non-overlapping patches taken from original sized images in databases. Alternatively, to segment a test image into overlapping patches and then using the network is feasible as well, but we did not see significant improvement of the performance, and it prolongs authentication time. We therefore use non-overlapped image patches for experiments. The network is composed of the following layers in Table 1. *Conv.* and *F.C.* are short for convolutional layers and fully connected layers respectively.

The successive convolutional and max-pooling layers numbered from sequence 2 to sequence 10 are used to extract forensic features, while the function of fully connected layers numbered from sequence 11 to 14 is to classify. Because of this characteristic of deep convolutional networks, we can use several networks to extract different forensic features which relate to different assumptions respectively. One assumption we used in this work is noise discrepancy: comparing to its background host image, the spliced region has a different amount of noise. Therefore, a network is trained to discern this kind of discrepancy caused by the image noise. In order to train this convolutional network and make it noise sensitive, we created a special training dataset in which spliced objects were corrupted by additive noise and the noise variance was adjusted to mimic different situations. Because the noise variance can be controlled, a large dataset can

Table 1. The sequence of layers in base-net.

Sequence	Layer type	Filter size	Output size
1	*Input*	–	[64 64 3]
2	*Conv.+ReLU*	[3 3 3 64]	[64 64 64]
3	*Max-Pooling*	–	[32 32 64]
4	*Conv.+ReLU*	[3 3 64 128]	[32 32 128]
5	*Max-Pooling*	–	[16 16 128]
6	*Conv.+ReLU*	[3 3 128 256]	[16 16 256]
7	*Max-Pooling*	–	[8 8 256]
8	*Conv.+ReLU*	[3 3 256 512]	[8 8 512]
9	*Conv.+ReLU*	[3 3 512 512]	[8 8 512]
10	*Max-Pooling*	–	[4 4 512]
11	*F.C.+ReLU*	[4 4 512 4096]	[1 1 4096]
12	*F.C.+ReLU*	[1 1 4096 2048]	[1 1 2048]
13	*F.C.+ReLU*	[1 1 2048 1024]	[1 1 1024]
14	*F.C.+ReLU*	[1 1 1024 2]	[1 1 2]
15	*Loss*	–	–

be generated automatically and it covers most of the splicing scenarios where noise discrepancy exists. Similarly, a base-net which is sensitive to discrepancies of JPEG compressions is constructed and trained. The dataset consists of untouched image patches and patches undergone splicing forgery. These forged image patches are generated by combining two images with different JPEG compression quality. Apart from the noise and JEPG quality, the visual information such as color, texture and shape gives clues for image forensics. Accordingly, the third base-net is used to extract those forensic features. The only difference is the spliced regions of images in the dataset are not intentionally added with noise or altered JEPG compression quality, and the spliced objects are directly inserted into host images without any processing to form the forged pictures. The details of our three datasets will be introduced in Sect. 4.

Since many deep convolutional networks have a structure of convolutional layers plus fully connected layers like VGG-16, networks in our framework can be replaced with any other deep convolutional networks. This is because the alternating convolutional layers and pooling layers generate features, while fully connected layers classify these features. Figure 2 visually shows the ability of the network to extract noise features. Gaussian noise was added to the upper half of the image to mimic noise discrepancy in real splicing forgery. And comparing to features maps of untouched version (c)–(e), there are visible activations in the upper half of feature maps in (f)–(h). Note that the shown feature maps are from first three convolutional layers of the trained noise base-net and only first 64 feature maps are shown in each layer.

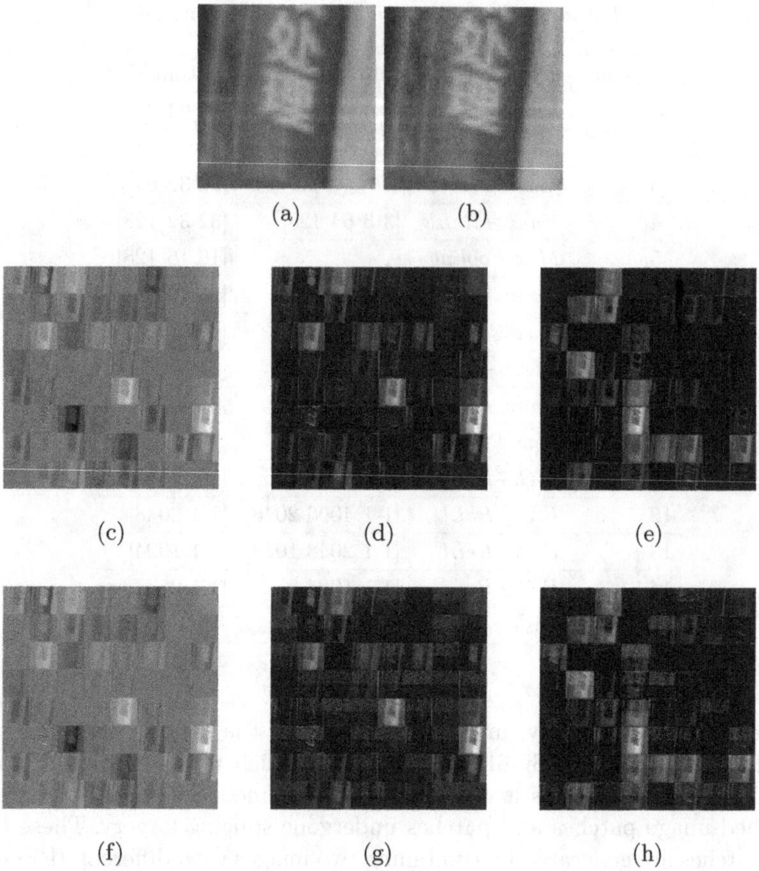

Fig. 2. Comparison between untouched image patch and its Gaussian noise corrupted version: feature maps of first three convolutional layers. (a) untouched image; (b) upper half of image is corrupted by Gaussian noise with variance $\sigma = 0.001$; (c)–(e) feature maps of untouched image in first three convolutional layers; (f)–(h) features maps of noise corrupted image in these three layers.

3.3 Features Merging by Fusion-Net

A trained base-net is able to detect splicing forgery especially those are under its assumption, i.e., the noise sensitive base-net is good at discriminating the splicing where the noise discrepancy exists, and the JEPG quality sensitive base-net discerns those image patches where JEPG compression quality is inconsistent. But the real situation may contain both of the noise discrepancy and compression inconsistency or either of them or none of them. Therefore, a fusion framework is needed to fuse independent forensic features. As stated in the former section, the alternating convolutional and pooling layers in a base-net extract a certain forensic feature, and when the base-nets have been well trained the parameters of the convolutional layers will be saved. In our work, the structure and parameters of sequence 1–10 of each base-net will be retained.

To construct the fusion-net, the outputs of sequence 10 from each base-net are concatenated and followed by four fully connected layers. The sequence of layers in fusion-net is shown in Table 2. We created another small database to train the fusion-net in order to make it capable to detect splicing forgery in the real scene. Note that the trainable parameters are from those four fully connected layers while the filters from the base-nets will not be trained because they have been trained already to extract the certain forensic features. The filter size of layer sequenced 2 in the fusion-net should be adjusted according to the number of used base-net. In our work, we trained three base-nets and the output of layer sequenced 10 in the base-net is $8 \times 8 \times 512$, accordingly the third dimension of layers sequenced 2 in the fusion-net will be $512 \times 3 = 1536$.

Table 2. The sequence of layers in fusion-net.

Sequence	Layer type	Filter size	Output size
1	*Concatenate*	–	[4 4 1536]
2	*F.C.+ReLU*	[4 4 1536 2048]	[1 1 2048]
3	*F.C.+ReLU*	[1 1 2048 1024]	[1 1024]
4	*F.C.+ReLU*	[1 1 1024 512]	[1 1 512]
5	*F.C.+ReLU*	[1 1 512 2]	[1 1 2]
6	*Loss*	–	–

The trained deep fusion network produces scores of being pristine and being tampered of an input image patch. This is because we used log-softmax loss function. The test image I will be divided into non-overlapped or overlapped image patches $I(i, j)$. Suppose the *pristine score* of an input image patch $I(i, j)$ is $s_p(i, j)$ and the *tampered score* is $s_t(i, j)$, then we normalized all the pristine scores of the image patches from the picture to be authenticated and obtained normalized pristine score $\hat{s}_p(i, j)$. The normalized tampered score $\hat{s}_t(i, j)$ is calculated in a similar way. Then the fused probability $f(i, j)$ is obtained by

$$f(i, j) = \frac{\hat{s}_t(i, j)}{\hat{s}_p(i, j)}. \quad (1)$$

Combining all fused probability scores $f(i, j)$ produces a fused probability map of the whole image, and giving a threshold τ can easily get the detection result when f is normalized. Morphological opening and closing operation yield better result. The marked area will be the border of the spliced region.

4 Experimental Results and Discussions

4.1 Databases and Network Training

Three different datasets are constructed to train three base-nets perspectively. The source pictures are from VOC2012 dataset [11] which is used to test algorithms of image segmentation and object detection. Since it provides masks of objects in the image, we can utilize it to clip objects along with their borders to create fake pictures. To build the dataset to train noise-sensitive base-net, an object in a randomly selected picture in VOC2012 dataset was clipped and then added with the Gaussian noise, then another image was randomly selected and added with Gaussian noise as well, and finally the object was inserted into the later image to create a forged picture. The noise variance of added Gaussian noise was randomly decided from 0 (no noise added) to 0.005 with an interval of 0.001. Then, the fake images were divided into small image blocks sized 64×64. There are 186K images in each set and the ratio of splicing images to pristine images is 1:1 and the number of training images to the number of validation images is 9:1. Creating the dataset to train JPEG-compression-sensitive base-net is in a similar procedure, and the only difference is the compression quality was altered instead of adding noise. The compression quality factor was randomly decided from 10 to 100 with an interval of 5. To construct the third dataset, no additional operation was made and the clipped objects were directly spliced into the host image to create a forgery.

4.2 Detection Results and Comparisons

We first present the experimental results on a small dataset - Columbia Image Splicing Detection Evaluation Dataset [1]. The pictures in the dataset are uncompressed and before evaluating the fusion net, we converted the files to the JEPG compression format. There are 200 pictures in the dataset and we used 120 pictures to fine-tune the fusion net and left 80 pictures to evaluate the performance.

We presented some pictures and their probability heat maps (m)–(p) in Columbia dataset in Fig. 3. The yellow color indicates a higher probability that an image block is tampered while the blue color indicates a higher probability of being pristine. The borders of the splicing area were successfully detected although there are a few false negative blocks in (m) (o) and (p) and false positive blocks in (n). These unwanted results can be easily corrected by morphological operations in the post-processing, and the final detection results are shown in (q)–(t). We also presented the pristine probability map (e)–(h) and fake probability map (i)–(l) as well. Although the number of images used for training the fusion net is very small. Comparing to traditional deep learning methods which require millions of training images, our deep fusion net only takes a very limited number of pictures to train. This is because most of the convolutional layers are from the trained base-nets and only fully connected layers of the fusion-net are trained in the fine-tuning.

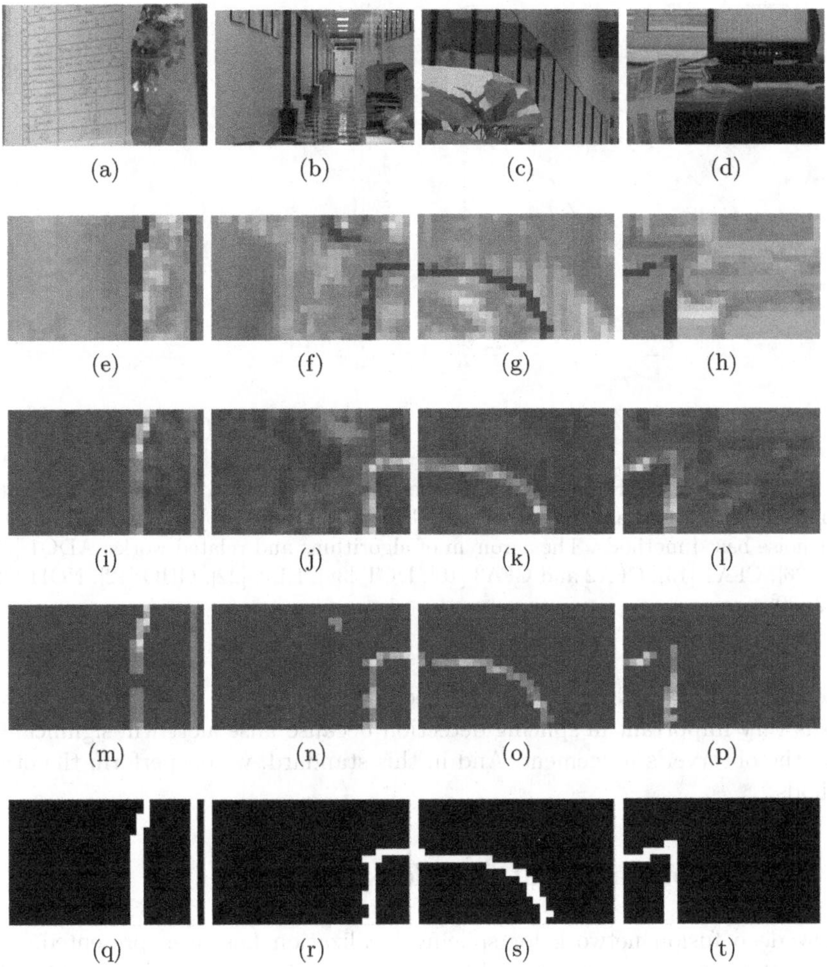

Fig. 3. Some pictures and their probability heat maps f and the final results in the Columbia splicing dataset: (a)–(d) pictures of splicing forgery in the dataset; (e)–(h) heat maps of being pristine; (i)–(l) heat maps of being tampered; (m)–(p) probability heat maps f produced by the deep fusion network. The yellow color in f indicates a higher probability of being tampered and the deep blue color indicates a higher probability of being pristine. (q)–(t) the final detection results after proper morphological operations.

We compared our method with the state-of-the-arts on Columbia dataset. The methods are based on the hand-crafted JPEG and noise forensic features. The ROC curves are presented in Fig. 4 and the left curves are from these JEPG based methods while the right curves are noise based methods. Our method outperforms all JEPG based methods and performs well in most cases comparing to noise based methods. A merit of our proposed method is that the fusion-net

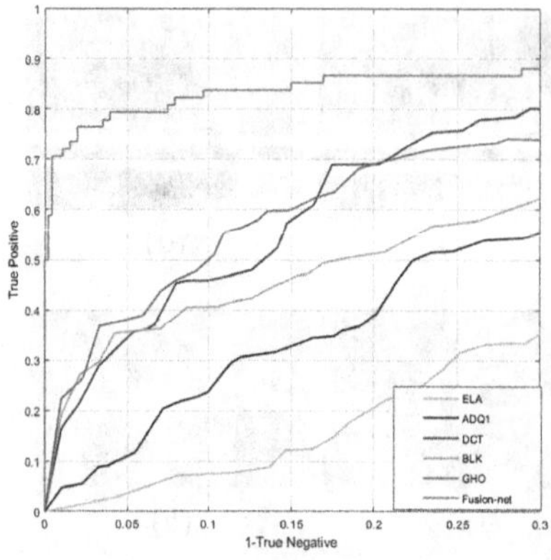

(a)

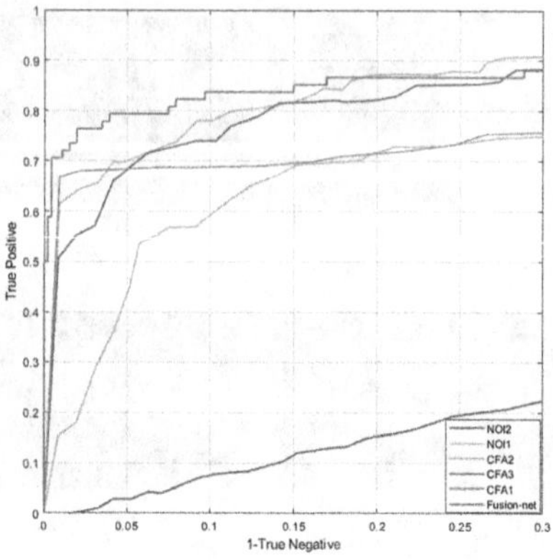

(b)

Fig. 4. Comparisons of ROC curves with the state-of-the-arts in Columbia dataset: (a) our fusion-net method and the other JPEG based methods. (b) our method and the other noise based methods. The acronym of algorithms and related works: ADQ1 [27], BLK [26], CFA1 [13], CFA2 and CFA3 [10], DCT [38], ELA [22], GHO [12], NOI1 [32], NOI2 [30]

achieves high true positive ratio while keeping a high value of the true negative. This is very important in splicing detection because false alert will significantly affect the observer's judgement. And in this standard, we outperform the other methods.

5 Conclusions and Future Works

A new deep fusion network for splicing localization has been presented. The fusion-net consists of convolutional layers from the base-nets and trainable fully connected layers. Since the base-nets have been trained and their convolutional layers have the ability to extract the certain forensic features, only fully connected layers of the fusion-net require training and this dramatically reduces the number of training pictures. Besides, the proposed framework is flexible and can be extended easily. Advanced deep convolutional networks or new forensic assumptions can replace the network used in this work to achieve better performance in the future.

Acknowledgement. This work was supported in part by the Research Committee of the University of Macau under Grant MYRG2018-00035-FST, and the Science and Technology Development Fund of Macau SAR under Grant 041/2017/A1.

References

1. Columbia image splicing detection evaluation dataset. http://www.ee.columbia.edu/ln/dvmm/downloads/AuthSplicedDataSet/AuthSplicedDataSet.htm. Accessed 28 June 2018
2. Amerini, I., Becarelli, R., Caldelli, R., Del Mastio, A.: Splicing forgeries localization through the use of first digit features. In: 2014 IEEE International Workshop on Information Forensics and Security (WIFS), pp. 143–148. IEEE (2014)
3. Amerini, I., Uricchio, T., Ballan, L., Caldelli, R.: Localization of jpeg double compression through multi-domain convolutional neural networks. In: Proceedings of IEEE CVPR Workshop on Media Forensics (2017)
4. Bayar, B., Stamm, M.C.: A deep learning approach to universal image manipulation detection using a new convolutional layer. In: Proceedings of the 4th ACM Workshop on Information Hiding and Multimedia Security, pp. 5–10. ACM (2016)
5. Bianchi, T., De Rosa, A., Piva, A.: Improved DCT coefficient analysis for forgery localization in JPEG images. In: 2011 IEEE International Conference on Acoustics, Speech and Signal Processing (ICASSP), pp. 2444–2447. IEEE (2011)
6. Bianchi, T., Piva, A.: Image forgery localization via block-grained analysis of JPEG artifacts. IEEE Trans. Inf. Forensics Secur. **7**(3), 1003–1017 (2012)
7. Bondi, L., Lameri, S., Güera, D., Bestagini, P., Delp, E.J., Tubaro, S.: Tampering detection and localization through clustering of camera-based CNN features. In: Proceedings of the IEEE Conference on Computer Vision and Pattern Recognition Workshops, pp. 1855–1864 (2017)
8. Bunk, J., et al.: Detection and localization of image forgeries using resampling features and deep learning. In: 2017 IEEE Conference on Computer Vision and Pattern Recognition Workshops (CVPRW), pp. 1881–1889. IEEE (2017)
9. Cozzolino, D., Gragnaniello, D., Verdoliva, L.: Image forgery localization through the fusion of camera-based, feature-based and pixel-based techniques. In: 2014 IEEE International Conference on Image Processing (ICIP), pp. 5302–5306, October 2014. https://doi.org/10.1109/ICIP.2014.7026073
10. Dirik, A.E., Memon, N.: Image tamper detection based on demosaicing artifacts. In: 2009 16th IEEE International Conference on Image Processing (ICIP), pp. 1497–1500. IEEE (2009)
11. Everingham, M., Van Gool, L., Williams, C.K.I., Winn, J., Zisserman, A.: The PASCAL Visual Object Classes Challenge 2012 (VOC 2012) Results. http://www.pascal-network.org/challenges/VOC/voc2012/workshop/index.html
12. Farid, H.: Exposing digital forgeries from JPEG ghosts. IEEE Trans. Inf. Forensics Secur. **4**(1), 154–160 (2009)
13. Ferrara, P., Bianchi, T., De Rosa, A., Piva, A.: Image forgery localization via fine-grained analysis of CFA artifacts. IEEE Trans. Inf. Forensics Secur. **7**(5), 1566–1577 (2012)
14. Flenner, A., Peterson, L., Bunk, J., Mohammed, T.M., Nataraj, L., Manjunath, B.: Resampling forgery detection using deep learning and a-contrario analysis. arXiv preprint arXiv:1803.01711 (2018)
15. Fontani, M., Bianchi, T., Rosa, A.D., Piva, A., Barni, M.: A framework for decision fusion in image forensics based on dempstershafer theory of evidence. IEEE Trans. Inf. Forensics Secur. **8**(4), 593–607 (2013). https://doi.org/10.1109/TIFS.2013.2248727
16. Fu, H., Cao, X.: Forgery authentication in extreme wide-angle lens using distortion cue and fake saliency map. IEEE Trans. Inf. Forensics Secur. **7**(4), 1301–1314 (2012). https://doi.org/10.1109/TIFS.2012.2195492

17. Girshick, R., Donahue, J., Darrell, T., Malik, J.: Region-based convolutional networks for accurate object detection and segmentation. IEEE Trans. Pattern Anal. Mach. Intell. **38**(1), 142–158 (2016). https://doi.org/10.1109/TPAMI.2015.2437384
18. Hsu, Y.F., Chang, S.F.: Statistical fusion of multiple cues for image tampering detection. In: 2008 42nd Asilomar Conference on Signals, Systems and Computers, pp. 1386–1390, October 2008. https://doi.org/10.1109/ACSSC.2008.5074646
19. Johnson, M.K., Farid, H.: Exposing digital forgeries in complex lighting environments. IEEE Trans. Inf. Forensics Secur. **2**(3), 450–461 (2007). https://doi.org/10.1109/TIFS.2007.903848
20. Kim, D.H., Lee, H.Y.: Image manipulation detection using convolutional neural network. Int. J. Appl. Eng. Res. **12**(21), 11640–11646 (2017)
21. Korus, P., Huang, J.: Multi-scale fusion for improved localization of malicious tampering in digital images. IEEE Trans. Image Process. **25**(3), 1312–1326 (2016). https://doi.org/10.1109/TIP.2016.2518870
22. Krawetz, N., Solutions, H.F.: A picture's worth... Hacker Factor Solutions, pp. 1–31 (2007)
23. Li, B., Luo, H., Zhang, H., Tan, S., Ji, Z.: A multi-branch convolutional neural network for detecting double JPEG compression. arXiv preprint arXiv:1710.05477 (2017)
24. Li, G., Yu, Y.: Visual saliency detection based on multiscale deep CNN features. IEEE Trans. Image Process. **25**(11), 5012–5024 (2016). https://doi.org/10.1109/TIP.2016.2602079
25. Li, H., Luo, W., Qiu, X., Huang, J.: Image forgery localization via integrating tampering possibility maps. IEEE Trans. Inf. Forensics Secur. **12**(5), 1240–1252 (2017)
26. Li, W., Yuan, Y., Yu, N.: Passive detection of doctored JPEG image via block artifact grid extraction. Sig. Process. **89**(9), 1821–1829 (2009)
27. Lin, Z., He, J., Tang, X., Tang, C.K.: Fast, automatic and fine-grained tampered JPEG image detection via dct coefficient analysis. Pattern Recogn. **42**(11), 2492–2501 (2009)
28. Liu, F., Shen, C., Lin, G.: Deep convolutional neural fields for depth estimation from a single image. In: Proceedings of the IEEE Conference on Computer Vision and Pattern Recognition, pp. 5162–5170 (2015)
29. Liu, Q., Cao, X., Deng, C., Guo, X.: Identifying image composites through shadow matte consistency. IEEE Trans. Inf. Forensics Secur. **6**(3), 1111–1122 (2011). https://doi.org/10.1109/TIFS.2011.2139209
30. Lyu, S., Pan, X., Zhang, X.: Exposing region splicing forgeries with blindlocal noise estimation. Int. J. Comput. Vis. **110**(2), 202–221 (2013). https://doi.org/10.1007/s11263-013-0688-y
31. Mahdian, B., Saic, S.: Blind authentication using periodic properties of interpolation. IEEE Trans. Inf. Forensics Secur. **3**(3), 529–538 (2008). https://doi.org/10.1109/TIFS.2004.924603
32. Mahdian, B., Saic, S.: Using noise inconsistencies for blind image forensics. Image Vis. Comput. **27**(10), 1497–1503 (2009)
33. Podilchuk, C.I., Delp, E.J.: Digital watermarking: algorithms and applications. IEEE Sig. Process. Mag. **18**(4), 33–46 (2001). https://doi.org/10.1109/79.939835
34. Popescu, A.C., Farid, H.: Exposing digital forgeries by detecting traces of resampling. IEEE Trans. Sig. Process. **53**(2), 758–767 (2005). https://doi.org/10.1109/TSP.2004.839932

35. Rao, Y., Ni, J.: A deep learning approach to detection of splicing and copy-move forgeries in images. In: 2016 IEEE International Workshop on Information Forensics and Security (WIFS), pp. 1–6. IEEE (2016)
36. Simonyan, K., Zisserman, A.: Very deep convolutional networks for large-scale image recognition. arXiv preprint arXiv:1409.1556 (2014)
37. Wang, Q., Zhang, R.: Double JPEG compression forensics based on a convolutional neural network. EURASIP J. Inf. Secur. **2016**(1), 23 (2016)
38. Ye, S., Sun, Q., Chang, E.C.: Detecting digital image forgeries by measuring inconsistencies of blocking artifact. In: 2007 IEEE International Conference on Multimedia and Expo, pp. 12–15. IEEE (2007)

Image Splicing Localization via Semi-global Network and Fully Connected Conditional Random Fields

Xiaodong Cun and Chi-Man Pun(✉)

University of Macau, Taipa, Macau
{mb55411,cmpun}@umac.mo

Abstract. We address the problem of *image splicing localization*: given an input image, localizing the spliced region which is cut from another image. We formulate this as a classification task but, critically, instead of classifying the spliced region by local patch, we leverage the features from whole image and local patch together to classify patch. We call this structure Semi-Global Network. Our approach exploits the observation that the spliced region should not only highly relate to local features (spliced edges), but also global features (semantic information, illumination, etc.) from the whole image. Furthermore, we first integrate Fully Connected Conditional Random Fields as post-processing technique in image splicing to improve the consistency between the input image and the output of the network. We show that our method outperforms other state-of-the-art methods in three popular datasets.

Keywords: Image splicing localization · Image forgery localization · Multimedia security

1 Introduction

The magic of computer makes digital photos edit possible. Softwares, such as PhotoShop, bring user-friendly interface for tampering image. With the growth of user-uploaded images on the Internet, it is more likely a serious security problem to detect whether an image has been tampered or not and localize the corresponding forgery region. Because artificial tampered images will send wrong message to others. For example, tampered images will make fake news more reliable and throw dust in the eyes of the public; it also convinces people on the impossible natural views and confuses the historian researchers.

In this paper, we focus on image splicing localization, a common forms of photographic manipulation. Image splicing means a particular region of donor image is cut and paste to the host image. Figure 2 is an example procedure to create a spliced image. The detection of image splicing has a long history in the digital image processing community. Many splicing algorithms [3–6] only detect the candidate image has been spliced or not. As for a more challenge task, few techniques [7,8] attempt to localize the spliced area in the image.

L. Leal-Taixé and S. Roth (Eds.): ECCV 2018 Workshops, LNCS 11130, pp. 252–266, 2019.
https://doi.org/10.1007/978-3-030-11012-3_22

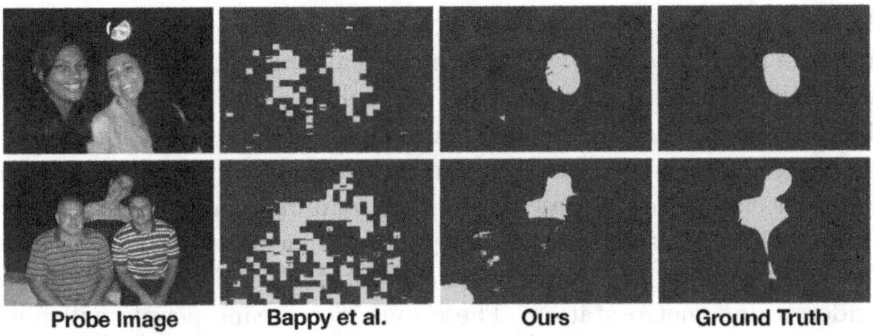

Fig. 1. These images are taken from dataset [1] where spliced regions own different illumination condition. Our network can classify spliced patches by mixing the global feature, while [2] fails because their method only learns from patches.

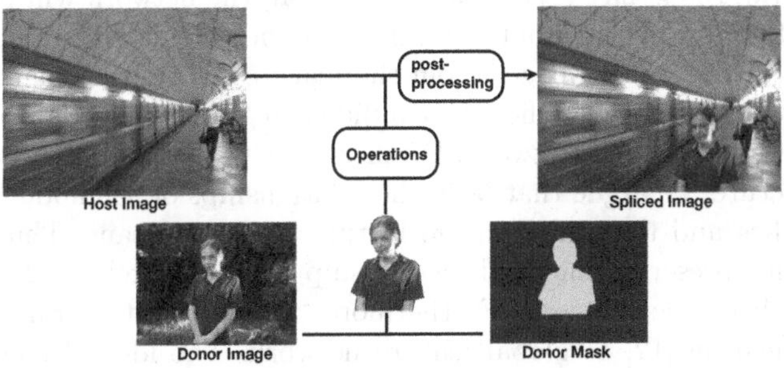

Fig. 2. This figure shows the spliced image is created by two authentic images. By masking the part of donor image, the selected region is pasted to the host image after some operations (translation and rescale the donor region). Sometimes, several post-processing techniques (such as Gaussian filter on the border of selected region) are used to the spliced region for the harmony of the selected region and host image.

The state-of-the-art approaches in image splicing localization analyze the features in frequency domain and/or the properties of statistic [9–11] because the donor image and host image maybe have different feature responses on the edges between splicing region and non-splicing region. Recently, Convolutional Neural Network shows a great success in many Computer Vision tasks, such as image classification [12], object detection [13], and there are also some papers [7,14,15] trying to solve image splicing by deep learning. However, current deep learning-based image splicing algorithms often solve image splicing localization from two viewpoints. One type of method often relies on the assumption that some specific features between the spliced region and non-spliced region are different. For example, [14] assume the donor image and host image are taken by different types of cameras, [2,15] assume that the features in authentic edge and the spliced edge are different. Another type of methods rely on the power of deep learning and the distribution of large dataset. These methods learn splicing region from ground truth label directly, such as [7] propose a splicing localization method based on Fully Convolutional Network [16].

Different from previous methods which only consider certain assumptions or learn from the large dataset, we rethink image splicing from the beginning of the human intuition. Human often identifies the splicing region from the candidate image by the clues from many aspects. For example, as the spliced image in Fig. 2, the first observation aspect from human is local edge: the spliced region will have a sharper edge because these borders are manufactured by human/software which is not 100% perfect. Another observation viewpoint is the consistency of light: the sunshine in the face and clothes of the girl is weird when the background is an underground metro station. These evidence means people will not only search the details in the local edges to identify the spliced region but also try to classify the regions from the global level, such as illumination consistent and semantic consistent.

By above observation, we formulate our network as a multi-inputs classification network. To classify each candidate region, the network will preserve the local details features by the input of local patch and calculate the global features by the input of the whole image. From the features of global image and candidate region, the network classifies the candidate region is spliced or not. We call this structure Semi-Global Network. Furthermore, to design a high-performance network structure, we argue that both the relationships of neighbourhood pixels in local patches and the global image features are important. Thus, we use a structure which preserves the local relationship between pixels in [2] as our local feature branch of the network. Furthermore, we borrow the framework from image classification [12] as global feature network. The idea of combining the global and local structure is not only used in the training network, we also add a Fully Connected Conditional Random Fields (CRF) to constraint the output mask should own the similar shape with the original image. As shown in Fig. 1, our method show a significant better result than the method which only consider the local patch.

Our main contributions are as follows:

- By considering the prerequisite of image splicing task is the combination of global features and local features, we propose a Semi-Global network to solve this problem.
- Besides the combination of global features and local features in patch based classification, we firstly add the Fully Connected CRF as post-processing technique in image splicing task.
- We add a new smooth term in loss function for the task harmony in patch-based classification and patch-based segmentation.
- Our method can achieve state-of-the-art performance in several popular datasets.

2 Related Works

Traditional Image Splicing Method. Localizing spliced region in the image has been long studied as part of detecting and localizing manipulated region from images. Some researches [9–11,17] assume that different images will own different noise levels because of the combination of camera model or the post-processing techniques when manipulating. A significant direction of image splicing have assumed that different cameras will show different internal patterns. Such as, Color Filter Array (CFA) [18,19], CFA transforms incoming light to different color channels and reconstructs the color image. Another important pattern is Camera Response Function [20]. Camera Response Function maps the incoming light to linear for making the image more visually appealing. These two internal image features are highly related to the whole image which means the images are taken by different cameras will show different internal patterns. Another important direction in image splicing is JPEG compression features [21,22]. These techniques squeeze the feature by the observation that different images will have different JPEG compression levels or JPEG features. Such as, Li *et al.* [22] extract the block artifacts from the JPEG image for comparison with other block.

Deep Learning for Image Splicing. Recently, Deep Learning-based techniques have been utilized in many Computer Vision and Digital Image Processing tasks. A lot of interests in learning to localize the image splicing region from a single image has been driven by the ability of Convolution Neural Networks [2,7,8,14,15,23]. Liu *et al.* [8] predict the mask of forgery region by a combination of a multi-scale neural network. With the similar idea, Salloum *et al.* [7] propose a multi-task fully convolutional network to localize image splicing region. They not only optimize the splicing region by ground truth mask directly but also constrain the edge in the output of predicted mask. These two methods only rely on the power of deep learning and the structure of network often design for image classification, which will ignore the low-level features. Inspired by traditional camera internal pattern-based method, Bondi *et al.* [14] use a pre-trained camera identification neural network to predict the original camera in input patches levels and analyse the results by the clustering algorithm. This method has strong assumption that splicing region and the original images are taken by the different camera. Following the traditional Camera Response Function based method, a novel feature designed by [15], is proposed for image splicing localization. Chen *et al.* [15] extract the Camera Response Function firstly and then try to classify the splicing regions in the feature domain by Neural Network. However, this method only can classify the patches in the edge of splicing region. Currently, Wu *et al.* [23] propose an algorithm for constrained image splicing problem which focuses on finding the spliced region by two images. Thus it is not design for single image splicing localization. Most recently, Bappy *et al.* [2] propose a hybrid deep learning based method by jointing the training of classification and segmentation for image forgery localization. However, by considering the splicing region often only connect to the local patches, this method is only trying to classify the local patch.

Unlike most deep learning based methods in image splicing which only consider the patches [2,8,14,15] or global image based end-to-end training [7,23], we argue that image splicing is a task not only relate to local feature, such as the features of edge between splicing region and the host image [15], but also global features, such as light condition [24], camera models [14,15], etc. Thus, in this paper, we consider from the viewpoint on the combination of global feature and pixel-level local patch classification in the task of image splicing.

3 Methods

We model image splicing localization as a conditional classification task with post-processing. As shown in Fig. 3, the whole overview of our framework can be divided into training network and post-processing.

In training network, giving a candidate image I and its non-overlapped patch sets I_p, the goal of our neural network SGN is to identify each patch is in the spliced region or not (classification of the patch) and which pixels in the patch $P_i (P_i \in I_p)$ belong to spliced region (segmentation of the patch). So our model can be written as:

$$L_i, M_i = SGN(I, P_i) \quad P_i \in I_p$$

where L_i is the label of current patch P_i and M_i is the segmentation results of the spliced region.

Combining the global image and local patch is not only used in network classification, it also performs in post-processing stage in our framework. In post-processing stage, we utilize the Fully Connected CRF to force the connection between colour and position. Notice that we only use the output of segmentation mask as the unary probability of Conditional Random Fields. The final splicing mask M_{pp} of input image I can be formulated as:

$$M_{pp} = CRF(I, M)$$

where $M = \sum_{i \in I_p} M_i$ is the output segmentation probability mask of our network.

3.1 Semi-global Network

As shown in Fig. 3, our Semi-Global Network can be divided into Global Feature Network and Patch Feature Network. These two parts learn different features from the patch and whole image, respectively. The two branches of the network are trained synchronously in end-to-end style by ground truth label and ground truth mask.

Patch Feature Network. We use the network described in [2] as our local feature extraction network. To achieve the goal of feature extraction from local patch, as shown in the *Patch Feature Network* of Fig. 3, in each forward of the neural network, one of the non-overlap patches from the original image is fed to the neural network for classification and segmentation.

In patch-based classification, a patch with 64×64 spatial resolution is fed into two convolutional layers for extracting a 2D low-level feature map firstly, then

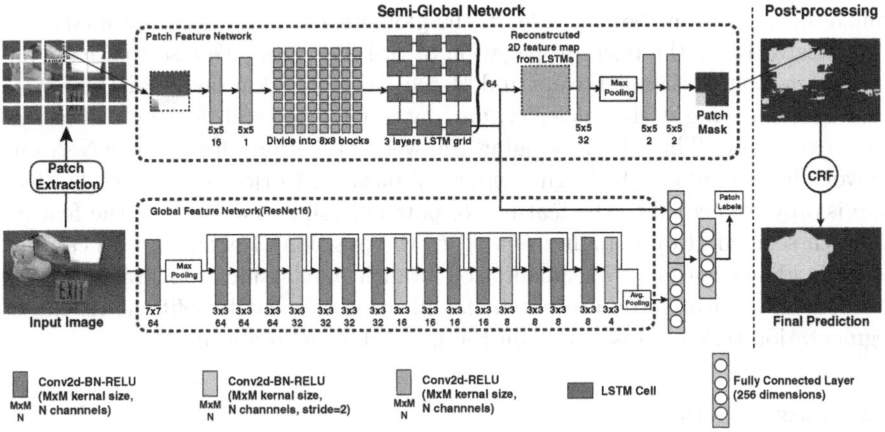

Fig. 3. The overview of our framework.

the feature map is uniformly divided into 8×8 blocks where each block owning 8×8 pixels. For modelling the relationships between the pixels of neighborhood, every block can be viewed as the input of Long-Short Term Memory [25] (LSTM) cell with 256 dimension features. LSTM models the relationship between pixels in the patches without decreasing the size of feature maps. Because low level feature is important for coarse edge detection. Next, the output of LSTM is not only used for image classification but also can be reconstructed into 2D feature map for final segmentation task. As shown in Fig. 3, the output of LSTM is reshaped to the original image according to the blocks we divided. Then two Convolutional layers model the reconstructed feature map for final segmentation results. A Softmax layer is added at the end of network for segmentation prediction and classification, respectively. This model can essentially extract pixel level features from patch while traditional coarse-to-fine network structure will break the relationship between pixels.

Compared with Bappy *et al.* [2], our method utilizes their network structure for local feature extraction in image splicing localization because their network model the local relationship between pixels. However, Bappy *et al.* [2] just rebuild the image from patch output. And we only use the output of patch segmentation as the input of post-processing method we provided. But [2] mixed the results of label and segmentation for final results. More results are discussed in experiments.

Global Feature Network. Whether the goal of our global feature network is to extract the global features (such as light, semantic information) from the input image, networks, we interpolate the pre-trained image classification network on large available dataset for global feature extraction. For global feature extraction, a ResNet18 [12] network structure, which is pre-trained on ImageNet [26], is added for global feature extraction. In our task, we remove the fully connected classification layer by replacing it with a new fully-connected layer in 256 dimensions. This new layer can learn the global features we need automatically from ResNet18 by the back-propagation of training data. We also freeze all the weights in Convolutional Layers and Batch Normalization layers in ResNet18, because comparing with ImageNet, our dataset is too small for the global features extraction. Thus, by leveraging the weights learning from ImageNet, our network has the ability to learn from small dataset. Notice that the global feature is only connected to the features of patch classification because the feature of patch segmentation is highly related to the position of pixels. So we can not add the global feature to segmentation branch as classification branch. However, feature concatenation in patch classification can also benefit the results of segmentation task because we train the network synchronously.

3.2 Loss Function

By considering the spliced region and host image are two categories, our network is a hybrid system of binary classification task $\Phi_{classification}$ and binary segmentation task $\Phi_{segmentation}$. We use Weighted Cross Entropy to model this two losses. So the loss function of classification is:

$$\Phi_{classification}(L, L_{gt}) = \frac{1}{N}\sum_{i\in I_p} W_n(1-L_{gt})log(1-L_i) + W_s L_{gt} log(L_i)$$

where N is the number of patches totally, L_i is the probability of the patch i in the spliced region, L_{gt} is the ground truth label of current patch, and W_s, W_n are the weight of spliced region and non-spliced region, respectively.

The segmentation loss is almost the same as classification loss except the input mask M_i and the ground truth mask M_{gt} are 2D probability maps on each pixels:

$$\Phi_{segmentation}(M, M_{gt}) = \frac{1}{N}\sum_{i\in I_p}\sum_{j\in M_i} W_n(1-M_{gt})log(1-M) + W_s M_{gt} log(M_i)$$

Because the splicing dataset is totally unbalanced, we set the weight between spliced region W_s and weight of non-spliced region W_n according to the statistics percentage on the ground truth mask of the training set. The weighted strategy makes our model more sensitive to the spliced region.

Furthermore, for making classification results and segmentation results unity, we add an extra smooth loss Φ_{smooth} for classification results and segmentation results. This smooth loss is added by the observation that patches label probability and the mean of patch segmentation will be minimum when the network convergence. If we think the classification results as the output of mask, or if we think the patches results as the output of label, these two parts will show the same probabilities. So we force the mean of mask probability equals to the patch label, our smooth criterion can be written as:

$$\Phi_{smooth}(M, L) = |\frac{\sum_{i\in I_p} M_i}{numel(M_i)} - L|$$

where *numel* is a function to get the size of patch masks M_i. So the final loss function Φ can be written as the sum of classification criterion, segmentations criterion and smooth criterion:

$$\Phi = \Phi_{classification} + \beta\Phi_{segmentation} + \lambda\Phi_{smooth}$$

We also add two hyper-parameter β and λ for better results. In the experiment we found that classification is a relative easier task that segmentation, so we set $\beta = 10$. As for the smooth hyper-parameter λ, we set this parameter to $\lambda = 0.01$ by thinking the classification as the main task.

3.3 Conditional Random Fields as Post Processing

Because the output of our network still fails in some patches of the image, and the patch segmentation task is more complex than patch classification task. We exploit the Fully Connected Conditional Random Fields in [27] for further exploit the global information to our network and get better results. Although CRF has been utilized in Semantic Segmentation widely [28,29], it has never been used in image splicing task.

The fully connected CRF can be written as an energy function:

$$E(\mathbf{x}) = \sum_i \theta_i(x_i) + \sum_{ij} \theta_{ij}(x_i, x_j)$$

where $\mathbf{x}$ is label assignment for pixels. The unary potential $\theta_i(x_i) = -log(M_i)$ where i is each pixels in the probability mask M. The probability mask M is created by the output of patch segmentation. Then, a fully-connected graph is used for efficient influence the pairwise potential. So the pairwise potential in [27] can be expressed as:

$$\theta_{i,j} = \mu(x_i, x_j)[\omega_1 \exp(-\frac{||p_i - p_j||^2}{2\sigma_\alpha^2} - \frac{||I_i - I_j||^2}{2\sigma_\beta^2}) + \omega_2 \exp(-\frac{||p_i - p_j||^2}{2\sigma_\gamma^2})]$$

where $\mu(x_i, x_j) = 1$ if $x_i \neq x_j$ and zero otherwise. Then, two Gaussian Kernels are applied in different feature spaces. The first is related to positions and RGB colors, and the second only measure the connection between pixels. These two kernels are used for feature constraint. While the first kernel restraint the pixels which have similar color and position as the same label, the second kernel penalizes the smoothness in position. As illustrated in Fig. 4, the results of our network benefit from fully connected CRF.

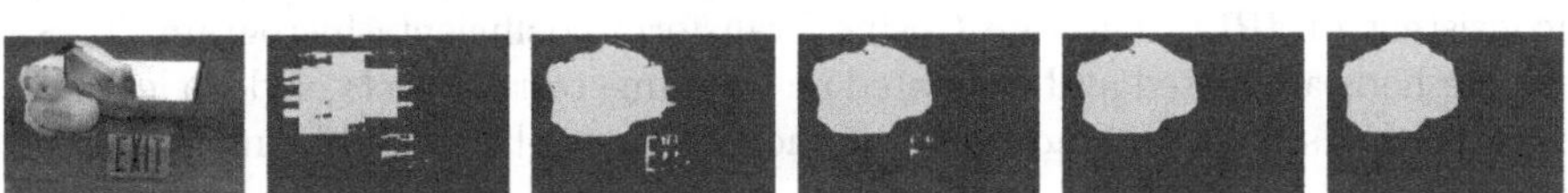

Fig. 4. The effect of post-processing

4 Experiments

4.1 Preparation

Implementation Details. All experimental benchmarks are obtained by PyTorch [30] framework. ADAM [31] solver with $\beta_1 = 0.9$, $\beta_2 = 0.999$ is used as optimization function for all the experiments. We train the network in 120 epochs and choose the best accuracy model on the validation set as the final model. The initial learning rate is 0.001, we decay the learning rate in 60, 90 epochs to 0.0001 and 0.00001, respectively. The network is trained on two NVIDIA 1080 GPUs.

Datasets Setup. We compare our method with other states-of-the-art methods on NC2016 dataset [32], Carvalho dataset [1] and Columbia dataset [33]. There are 280 spliced samples in NC2016, 100 spliced samples in Carvalho dataset and 180 spliced samples in Columbia dataset. For each dataset, we randomly split the whole image dataset into three categories with training (65%), validation (10%) and testing (25%) as Bappy *et al.* [2]. Then, we extract the patch-global image pairs in training set. By considering the balance of space and time for network training, we resize the original image to 224×224 for the input of global feature network. In patches extraction, we split original image to the non-overlapped 64×64 image blocks. Thus, we have more than 10k training patches on each dataset which is enough for training classification network and segmentation network. Similarly, we obtain validation and test set. As for the ground truth label of patch, following [2], we label the patches which contain more than 87.5% (7/8) of the spliced pixels as the positive spliced patches.

Evaluation Metrics. We compare our method with other state-of-the-art methods on F_1 score and Matthews Correlation Coefficient (MCC) for binary classification tasks as [7]. We also exploit the ROC curve and AUC score on three datasets as [2] in Table 1 and Fig. 6.

Baselines. As for deep learning based method, we compare our method with two most relevant methods: Bappy *et al.* [2] use the local patch to classify the manufacture region; MFCN [7] learn to predict the spliced mask and spliced edge from Fully Convolutional Network [16] directly.

Because there are few image splicing localization methods using deep learning, we also compare our results with some state-of-the-art traditional methods. We select four representative methods from different viewpoints: CFA2 [19] utilize Color Filet Array for forgery detection. NOI1 [11] assume that the splicing region will have different local image noise variance. BLK [22] classify the spliced region by detecting the periodic artifacts in JPEG compression. DCT [17] detect inconsistent of JPEG Discrete Cosine Transform coefficients histogram. These four methods are tested and evaluated on the same test datasets as deep learning based methods. We run traditional methods by a public available image spicing toolkits [34].

4.2 Comparisons

Experiments on Columbia Dataset. Columbia dataset is a relatively easier dataset for classification. There are 180 images which certain objects are spliced to host image in different localization and the edge of the spliced region is easy to recognize. In this dataset, the content of spliced region and the background are often totally different. By analyzing the ground truth mask in training dataset, we weight the spliced region and non-spliced region to 1:5 in loss function. As shown in Fig. 6 and Table 1, our method get better results than others. As the similar spliced objects/shapes are shown in both training set and test set, patch-based method can also be detected splied regions without the help of global features. (First column of Fig. 5 on Bappy *et al.* method). However, comparing with the images which spliced region rarely shown in training set (Second and third columns of Fig. 5), our method gain better results. As for other traditional methods, our network also gain better results, because these methods only detect/analysis the spliced region by certain assumptions.

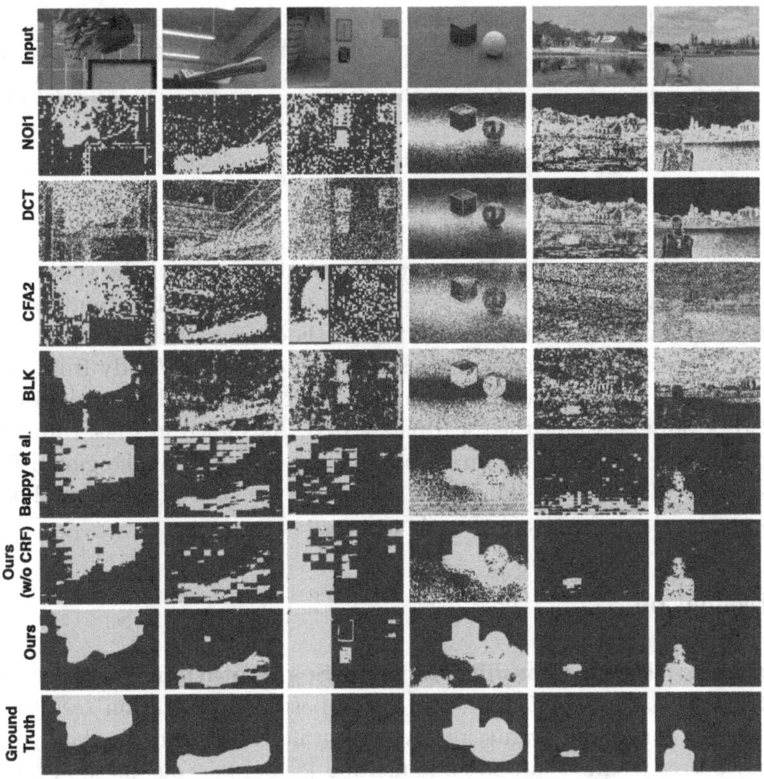

Fig. 5. Results on Columbia [33] dataset (left three) and NC2016 dataset (right three) [32]. (NOI1, CFA2, BLK, DCT are displayed by thresholding the mean probability of whole feature image.)

Experiments on NC2016 Dataset. In NC2016 dataset, some tampered images show very similar "appearance" from human viewpoint but tamper with different operations or post-processing techniques such as, the border of the temper region is utilized Gaussian smooth or not will be considered as two samples in the dataset. These attack methods may huge influence the traditional methods which detect/localize the splicing region from hand-craft features. However, in deep learning-based method, it is a relatively easier task when similar images are shown in both training set and test set. Because neural network need to inference from global high level features and low level features. We list the results on NC2016 dataset in Table 1 and Figs. 5 and 6, our method is significantly better than other states-of-the-art methods on several evaluation metrics.

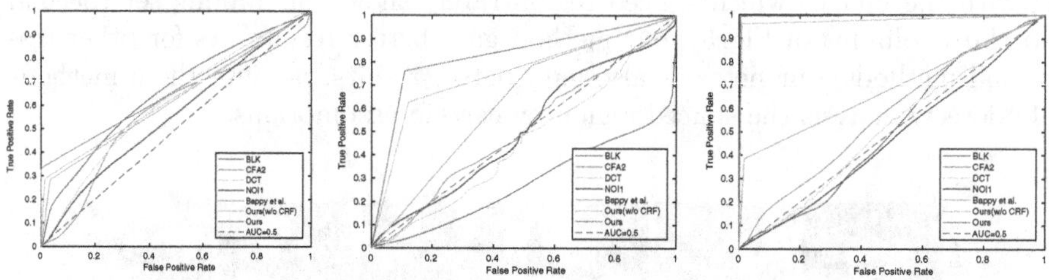

(a) Columbia dataset (b) Carvalho dataset (c) NC2016 dataset

Fig. 6. ROC curves on three different datasets.

Experiments on Carvalho Dataset. We set the weight of the spliced region and non-spliced region to 1:7 on Carvalho Dataset. From Table 1 and Fig. 6, our method is significantly better than other methods in several numeric metrics. Carvalho [1] manufacture input images by splicing the face/body from another image with the inconsistent of illumination color. It is hard to recognize when the network only classifies the local patches [2]. As shown in Figs. 1 and 7, our method can detect spliced region because of the integrate of the global feature while [2] only classify the skin from the image because of their method just classify the local patches from the whole image.

4.3 Evaluation

Evaluation of Patch Classification and Segmentation. We list the accuracy of patch-based classification and patch-based segmentation results on all three datasets for model evaluation. As shown in Table 2, our method gain significantly better results than baseline method [2] because our method integrate of global feature and task harmony loss.

The Effect of Global Feature. Our method needs to connect the feature from the local patch and global image together for final prediction. Do more global

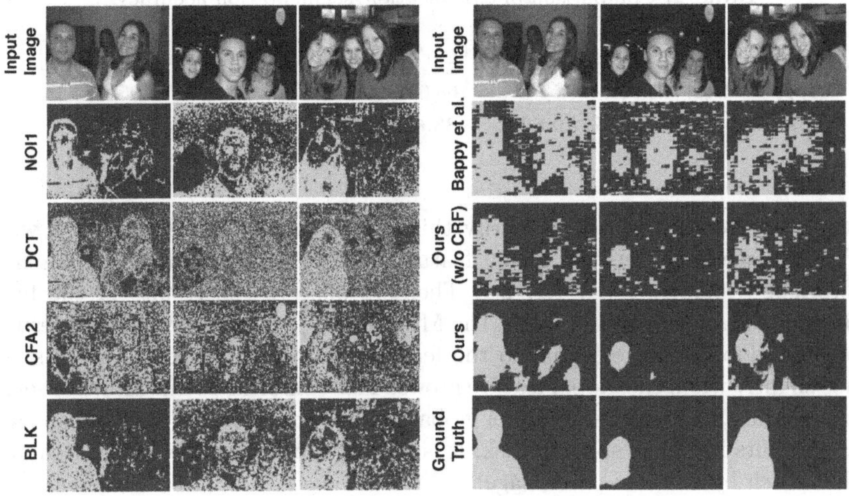

Fig. 7. Results on Carvalho [1] dataset. (NOI1, CFA2, BLK, DCT are displayed by thresholding the mean probability of whole image.)

Table 1. Comparison on three datasets. F_1, MCC score are calculated for each image firstly and then calculate the average value while AUC is calculated amount all the pixels.

Metrics	Methods	NC2016 [32]	Carvalho [1]	Columbia [33]
F_1	MFCN* [7]	0.5707	0.4795	0.6117
	Bappy et al. [2]	0.6242	0.3102	0.5270
	Ours (w/o CRF)	0.7174	0.4236	0.5956
	Ours	**0.7900**	**0.5006**	**0.6482**
MCC	MFCN* [7]	0.5703	0.4074	0.4792
	Bappy et al. [2]	0.6257	0.1882	0.5074
	Ours (w/o CRF)	0.7101	0.3309	0.5557
	Ours	**0.7847**	**0.4379**	**0.6403**
AUC	CFA2 [19]	0.57	0.51	0.54
	NOI1 [11]	0.47	0.55	0.51
	BLK [22]	0.51	0.29	0.64
	DCT [17]	0.51	0.37	0.62
	Bappy et al. [2]	0.68	0.65	0.62
	Ours (w/o CRF)	0.98	0.75	0.64
	Ours	**0.99**	**0.83**	**0.67**

*MFCN is trained on larger dataset and test on these datasets while our method takes parts of datasets as the training set. The size of train data will hugely influence the results. So the experiment results of MFCN is taken by original paper and just for reference.

Table 2. Comparison of classification/segmentation accuracy.

	NC2016 dataset [32]	Carvalho dataset [1]	Columbia dataset [33]
Bappy et al. [2]	95.89%/89.53%	68.57%/53.80%	85.02%/77.95%
Ours	**97.81%/89.60%**	**83.69%/75.10%**	**89.72%/83.90%**

features get better results? To verify this question, we train the network with different percentage between global features and patch features to 0:1(baseline network [2]), 0.25:1, 0.5:1, 1:1, 2:1. Then we observe the results in the final splicing task. As shown in Table 3, the MCC and F_1 score show the best results when the global features equal to the features from local. And the results get worse slightly when the global feature grows. This conforms to our intuitive sense of the world: although the hybrid of global feature and the local feature can gain better results in image splicing task, it is better to consider the local patch and global patch by suitable percentage.

The Influence of Task Harmony in Loss Function and Post-processing. In loss function, we add a new smooth term to force the relationship between the loss of classification loss and segmentation loss. As shown in Table 3, the smooth term benefits for our task. We also list the output of our network w/o CRF. Mask segmentation is obviously better than Label classification results because label classification only classifies the uniform patches.

Table 3. Evaluation on Columbia dataset

	F_1 Score	MCC
Ours w/o CRF (Label)	0.5467	0.5305
Ours w/o CRF (Mask)	0.5956	0.5557
Ours w/o smooth term	0.6416	0.5863
Ours (0:1)	0.5270	0.5074
Ours (0.25:1)	0.6287	0.6224
Ours (0.5:1)	0.6281	0.5255
Ours (2:1)	0.6258	0.6204
Ours (1:1)	**0.6482**	**0.6403**

5 Conclusion

In this paper, we propose Semi-Global network with fully connected CRFs as post-processing for image splicing localization. Our Semi-Global network interpolates global features to patch classification/segmentation network. In addition, we use CRF-based post processing techniques to refine the output of the network. Extensive experiments on three benchmarks demonstrate that our method significantly improves the baseline and outperform other state-of-the-art algorithms. We also evaluate our method by removing the necessary parts in the experiments.

We hope that our proposed splicing localization pipeline might potentially help other applications which need to constraint the relationship between local and global when the low-level information (the relationship between pixels) is as important as global features. Such as video splicing detection and scene labeling. We believe our framework is a promise direction for further researches.

Acknowledgements. This work was supported in part by the Research Committee of the University of Macau under Grant MYRG2018-00035-FST, and the Science and Technology Development Fund of Macau SAR under Grant 041/2017/A1.

References

1. de Carvalho, T.J., Riess, C., Angelopoulou, E., Pedrini, H., de Rezende Rocha, A.: Exposing digital image forgeries by illumination color classification. IEEE Trans. Inf. Forensics Secur. **8**, 1182–1194 (2013)
2. Bappy, J.H., Roy-Chowdhury, A.K., Bunk, J., Nataraj, L., Manjunath, B.: Exploiting spatial structure for localizing manipulated image regions. In: International Conference on Computer Vision (ICCV) (2017)
3. Hsu, Y.-F., Chang, S.-F.: Image splicing detection using camera response function consistency and automatic segmentation. In: ICME, pp. 28–31 (2007)
4. Chen, W., Shi, Y.Q., Su, W.: Image splicing detection using 2-D phase congruency and statistical moments of characteristic function. In: Security, Steganography, and Watermarking of Multimedia Contents, vol. 6505, p. 65050R (2007)
5. Hsu, Y.-F., Chang, S.-F.: Detecting image splicing using geometry invariants and camera characteristics consistency. In: ICME, pp. 549–552 (2006)
6. He, Z., Lu, W., Sun, W., Huang, J.: Digital image splicing detection based on Markov features in DCT and DWT domain. Pattern Recogn. **45**(12), 4292–4299 (2012)
7. Salloum, R., Ren, Y., Kuo, C.C.J.: Image splicing localization using a multi-task fully convolutional network (MFCN). arXiv preprint arXiv:1709.02016 (2017)
8. Liu, Y., Guan, Q., Zhao, X., Cao, Y.: Image Forgery Localization Based on Multi-Scale Convolutional Neural Networks. CoRR cs.CV (2017)
9. Pun, C.M., Liu, B., Yuan, X.C.: Multi-scale noise estimation for image splicing forgery detection. J. Vis. Commun. Image Represent. **38**, 195–206 (2016)
10. Lyu, S., Pan, X., Zhang, X.: Exposing region splicing forgeries with blind local noise estimation. Int. J. Comput. Vis. **110**, 202–221 (2014)
11. Mahdian, B., Saic, S.: Using noise inconsistencies for blind image forensics. Image Vis. Comput. **27**, 1497–1503 (2009)
12. He, K., Zhang, X., Ren, S., Sun, J.: Deep residual learning for image recognition. In: CVPR (2016)
13. He, K., Gkioxari, G., Dollár, P., Girshick, R.B.: Mask R-CNN. In: ICCV (2017)
14. Bondi, L., Lameri, S., Guera, D., Bestagini, P., Delp, E.J., Tubaro, S.: Tampering detection and localization through clustering of camera-based CNN features. In: CVPR Workshops, pp. 1–10, November 2017
15. Chen, C., McCloskey, S., Yu, J.: Image splicing detection via camera response function analysis. In: CVPR, pp. 1876–1885 (2017)

16. Long, J., Shelhamer, E., Darrell, T.: Fully Convolutional Networks for Semantic Segmentation. CoRR cs.CV (2014)
17. Ye, S., Sun, Q., Chang, E.C.: Detecting digital image forgeries by measuring inconsistencies of blocking artifact. In: ICME (2007)
18. Popescu, A.C., Farid, H.: Exposing digital forgeries in color filter array interpolated images. IEEE Trans. Sig. Process. **53**(10), 3948–3959 (2005)
19. Dirik, A.E., Memon, N.D.: Image tamper detection based on demosaicing artifacts. In: ICIP (2009)
20. Hsu, Y.F., Chang, S.F.: Camera response functions for image forensics - an automatic algorithm for splicing detection. IEEE Trans. Inf. Forensics Secur. **5**, 816–825 (2010)
21. Farid, H.: Exposing digital forgeries from JPEG ghosts. IEEE Trans. Inf. Forensics Secur. **4**, 154–160 (2009)
22. Li, W., Yuan, Y., Yu, N.: Passive detection of doctored JPEG image via block artifact grid extraction. Sig. Process. **89**, 1821–1829 (2009)
23. Wu, Y., AbdAlmageed, W., Natarajan, P.: Deep Matching and Validation Network - An End-to-End Solution to Constrained Image Splicing Localization and Detection. arXiv.org (2017)
24. Johnson, M.K., Farid, H.: Exposing digital forgeries in complex lighting environments. IEEE Trans. Inf. Forensics Secur. **2**, 450–461 (2007)
25. Hochreiter, S., Schmidhuber, J.: Long short-term memory. Neural Comput. **9**(8), 1735–1780 (1997)
26. Deng, J., Dong, W., Socher, R., Li, L.J., Li, K., Li, F.F.: ImageNet - a large-scale hierarchical image database. In: CVPR (2009)
27. Krähenbühl, P., Koltun, V.: Efficient inference in fully connected CRFs with Gaussian edge potentials. In: NIPS (2011)
28. Chen, L.C., Papandreou, G., Kokkinos, I., Murphy, K., Yuille, A.L.: DeepLab - Semantic Image Segmentation with Deep Convolutional Nets, Atrous Convolution, and Fully Connected CRFs. CoRR (2016)
29. Zheng, S., et al.: Conditional random fields as recurrent neural networks. In: ICCV (2015)
30. Paszke, A., et al.: Automatic differentiation in pytorch (2017)
31. Kingma, D.P., Ba, J.: Adam: A method for stochastic optimization. arXiv preprint arXiv:1412.6980 (2014)
32. NIST: Nimble Media Forensics Challenge Datasets (2016). https://www.nist.gov/itl/iad/mig/media-forensics-challenge
33. Ng, T.T.: Columbia image splicing detection evaluation dataset (2004)
34. Zampoglou, M., Papadopoulos, S., Kompatsiaris, Y.: A large-scale evaluation of splicing localization algorithms for web images. Multimedia Tools Appl. **76**, 4801–4834 (2017)

Bridging Machine Learning and Cryptography in Defence Against Adversarial Attacks

Olga Taran(✉), Shideh Rezaeifar, and Slava Voloshynovskiy

Computer Science Department, University of Geneva, Geneva, Switzerland
{olga.taran,shideh.rezaeifar,svolos}@unige.ch

Abstract. In the last decade, deep learning algorithms have become very popular thanks to the achieved performance in many machine learning and computer vision tasks. However, most of the deep learning architectures are vulnerable to so called *adversarial examples*. This questions the security of deep neural networks (DNN) for many security- and trust-sensitive domains. The majority of the proposed existing adversarial attacks are based on the differentiability of the DNN cost function. Defence strategies are mostly based on machine learning and signal processing principles that either try to *detect-reject* or *filter* out the adversarial perturbations and completely neglect the classical cryptographic component in the defence.

In this work, we propose a new defence mechanism based on the second Kerckhoffs's cryptographic principle which states that the defence and classification algorithm are supposed to be known, but not the key.

To be compliant with the assumption that the attacker does not have access to the secret key, we will primarily focus on a *gray-box* scenario and do not address a *white-box* one. More particularly, we assume that the attacker does not have direct access to the secret block, but (a) he completely knows the system architecture, (b) he has access to the data used for training and testing and (c) he can observe the output of the classifier for each given input. We show empirically that our system is efficient against most famous state-of-the-art attacks in *black-box* and *gray-box* scenarios.

Keywords: Adversarial attacks · Defence · Data-independent transform · Secret key · Cryptography principle

1 Introduction

In the last decade, scientists achieved a big breakthrough in enhancement of functionality and extension of scope of applications of the DNN. Nowadays, neural networks have become very efficient in many machine-learning tasks. However,

This work was supported by the SNF project No. 200021-165672.

L. Leal-Taixé and S. Roth (Eds.): ECCV 2018 Workshops, LNCS 11130, pp. 267–279, 2019.
https://doi.org/10.1007/978-3-030-11012-3_23

despite the remarkable progress the DNN stay vulnerable to adversarial attacks that aim at designing such a perturbation to original samples that, in general, is imperceptible for humans, but it is able to trick the DNN. This vulnerability seriously restricts the usage of the DNN in many security- and trust-sensitive domains.

In recent years, researchers proposed a large number of different defence mechanisms. However, the growing number of defences stimulates the invention of even more universal attacks. This is due to the fact that the overwhelming majority of existing attacking algorithms are based on the principle of end-to-end differentiability of the DNN and possibility to add the modification back to the original spatial domain images.

In this paper, we propose a new defence mechanism for the DNN classifiers based on the second Kerckhoffs's cryptographic principle, that states that the fewer secrets the system contains, the higher its safety [1]. In this regard, the structure of the proposed system is supposed to be known, except the key that is kept secret. This key is used in a security imposing pre-processing block that might be implemented in various ways.

Based on the best cryptographic practice, one can state that there does not exist any secure algorithm that does not contain any secret unknown to the attacker. From this point, the defences against so called *white-box* attacks will unlikely find practical applications besides some rare exceptions. In this respect, we will primarily focus our attention to a *gray-box* scenario that assumes that the attacker has general knowledge about the structure of the system of interest. However, due to the existence of secret parameters/key, in reasonable time, he is capable neither to discover or to estimate these secret elements, even with the help of modern computational means, nor to train the "bypass" system that would give a sufficiently accurate estimation of the secret parameters/key.

We evaluate our defence mechanism on two standard datasets, namely, MNIST [2] and Fashion-MNIST [3] for the *Fast Gradient Sign Method* (FGSM) [4] as the simplest attack case, and attack proposed by Carlini and Wagner in [5] as the most efficient one for most of the existing adversarial defences mechanisms.

The main contributions of this paper are:

- We analyse the existing state-of-the-art adversarial attacks and most well-known defence algorithms.
- We present a new defence mechanism for DNN classifiers based on cryptographic principles.
- We investigate the efficiency of the proposed approach on two standard datasets for several well-known adversarial attacks.
- We empirically show that a sufficiently simple data-independent transformation, based on a secret key, can serve as a reasonable defence against gradient based adversarial attacks.

Notations. We use small bold letters $\mathbf{x}$ to denote a signal that can be represented either in 1D or 2D format, $\mathbf{x}_i$ corresponds to the ith entry of vector

$\mathbf{x}$. $E(.)$ and $D(.)$ denotes the *encoder* and *decoder* parts of the DNN classifier, respectively. $P(.)$ indicates the data-independent transformation operator.

The remainder of this paper is organised as follows: Sect. 2 briefly summarizes the basic principle of the DNN classifier and gives the general classification of the existing state-of-the-art attacks against the DNN classifiers as well as a brief classification of the existing defence mechanisms. Section 3 introduces the main idea and principles of the proposed defence approach. Section 4 presents the empirical results obtained for the proposed algorithm and their analysis. Finally, Sect. 5 concludes the paper.

2 Background

2.1 Neural Networks

In general case, it is possible to represent a DNN classifier as a model that consists of two parts: (a) *encoder* or training part and (b) *decoder* or classifier. As an input, the *encoder* takes a multidimensional vector $\mathbf{x} \in \mathbb{R}^{N \times C}$, where C is the number of channels, and outputs a vector $\mathbf{y} \in \mathbb{R}^{M}$, where in most of the cases, M is equal to the number of classes, and each $\mathbf{y}_j$ is treated as a probability that a given input $\mathbf{x}$ belongs to class j. Typically, the *encoder* consists of several nested layers:

$$\mathbf{y} = E(\mathbf{x}) = \sigma_n\Big(\mathbf{W}_n\sigma_{n-1}(...\sigma_1(\mathbf{W}_1\mathbf{x}))\Big), \tag{1}$$

where, at each layer i, $\mathbf{W}_i$ corresponds to the model parameters and σ_i is an activation function, usually, non-linear, with $1 \leq i \leq n$.

The *decoder* assigns most likely class label based on the result of the *encoder*:

$$\begin{aligned} D(\mathbf{x}) &= \arg\max_{1 \leq j \leq M} E(\mathbf{x})_j \\ &= \arg\max_{1 \leq j \leq M} \mathbf{y}_j = \hat{j}. \end{aligned} \tag{2}$$

2.2 Attacks Against DNN Classifiers

Based on the knowledge available to the attacker, the adversarial attacks against the DNN classifiers can be combined into three main groups [6]:

1. *White-box* attacks require the full knowledge of treated model and/or training and test data.
2. *Black-box* attacks, where the attacker (a) has no information about the structure and parameters of the used model and training data, (b) has possibility to observe the class labels assigned to chosen input like as in case of cryptographic oracle.

3. *Gray-box* attacks, where the attacker (a) knows the system architecture, (b) has access to the data used for training and testing, (c) for each given input can observe the assigned class label, (d) does not have access to or knowledge of the defence mechanism parameters.

In turn, based on the goal of the attacker, the attacks can be [6]:

- *Targeted* that aim at modifying the input in a way that the classifier classifies it as a specified target class. Namely, for a given target class t such that $D(\mathbf{x}) \neq t$, the goal is to find such a perturbation $\mathbf{z}$ that $D(\mathbf{x}+\mathbf{z}) = t$ [5].
- *Non-targeted* that aim at modifying the input in a way that the classifier classifies it incorrectly. Namely, the goal is to find such a perturbation $\mathbf{z}$ that $D(\mathbf{x}+\mathbf{z}) \neq D(\mathbf{x})$, i.e., the classifier output any wrong class label [5].

It should be pointed out that many adversarial attacks have a transferability property that consists in the fact that adversarial examples trained on one model can be successfully applied to another model with a different architecture of the *encoder* part [6]. In general, targeted adversarial examples are much harder to transfer than non-targeted ones.

Due to the limited interest of *white-box* attacks for real-life applications, in our paper we focus preliminary our attention on the *gray-box* targeted and non-targeted attacks that can be also extended to the *black-box* scenario.

State-of-the-art Attacks Against DNN Classifiers. Without loss of generality, it is possible to group the state-of-the-art adversarial attacks against the DNN classifiers into two main groups:

1. *Gradient* based attacks. The core principle of which consists in the end-to-end differentiability of many neural network classification systems.

   This group comprises L-BFGS attack proposed by Szegedy et al. in [7]. This attack is time-consuming due to the used expensive linear search and, as a consequence, is impractical for real-time applications. However, this attack served as a basis for several more successful attacks such as *Fast Gradient Sign Method* (FGSM) [4]. In contrast to L-BFGS, FGSM is fast, but not all the time gives the minimal adversarial perturbation between original and targeted samples. FGSM method has several successful extensions, like FGSM with momentum [8], *One-step Target Class Method* (OTCM) [9], RAND-FGSM algorithm [10], proposed in [11] *Basic Iterative Method* (BIM) and *Iterative Least-Likely Class Method* (ILLC), etc. In addition, it should also be mentioned the *Jacobian-based Saliency Map Attack* (JSMA) [12] and the *DeepFool* approach [13] with its extension *Universal perturbation* [14]. Moreover, one should note the attack proposed by Carlini and Wagner in [5]. As it has been shown in many works, like for example in [15] and [16], this attack is among the most efficient ones against many existing defence mechanisms. Finally, Athalye et al. in [17] propose Backward Pass Differentiable Approximation technique that aims at avoiding the gradient masking in *white-box* scenario.

2. *Non-gradient* based attacks

   The attacks of this group do not require any knowledge of the DNN gradients. The most well-known members of this group are the *Zeroth Order Optimisation* (ZOO) [18] and the *One Pixel Attack* [19].

2.3 Defence Strategies

In general, the existing state-of-the-art defence strategies can be classified into four main groups:

1. *Defence via retraining*
   The most well-known work in this group is *network distillation* proposed by Papernot et al. in [20]. Moreover, a significant number of papers were focused on the investigation of the potential of *adversarial retraining*. The main idea behind this retraining is to use adversarial examples in varying degrees during the network training. Representatives of this approach are the works of Goodfellow et al. [4], Huang et al. [21], Kurakin et al. [9], Wu et al. [22], etc.
2. *Defence via detection and rejection*
   Formally, one can distinguish several subclasses, the main ideas behind which can be mixed:
   (a) Based on integration of *additional DNN*, like for example in the work of Metzen et al. [23] the original network is augmented by adding an auxiliary "detector" sub-network that aims at distinguishing the original data from data containing adversarial perturbations.
   (b) *Statistical* based, for example in [24] the authors claim that the adversarial perturbations affect in a special way the lower-ranked principal components from PCA. In [25], the authors perform analysis of the statistics of convolutional layers outputs to detect the adversarial inputs. Feinman et al. in [26] analyse Bayesian uncertainty available in dropout neural networks, etc.
   (c) Based on analysis of *DNN properties*, such as [27] and [28] where the authors make their decision by extending the simplex algorithm to support the non-convex ReLUs activation function and consider the neural network as a whole, without any simplifying assumptions.
3. *Defence via input pre-processing*
   In general case, defence is achievable through filtering and removal of modifications introduced to original images, like for example the denoising used in [29] or recently proposed in [30].
4. *Defence via regeneration*
   The key point behind this approach consists in the assumption that the adversarial examples can be mapped back to the manifold of the original clean data via regeneration. For example, Gu et al. in [31] propose a *deep contractive autoencoder* that is a variant of the classical autoencoder with an additional penalty increasing the robustness to adversarial examples. Meng et al. in [29] introduce *MagNet*, which combines the detector and regeneration networks.

Despite the big variety of the existing defence mechanisms, there are still several important open issues:

- In the vast majority of cases, the attacker knows exactly the same amount of information or can easily learn any complementary information about the defence strategy. Therefore, the attacker can relatively easy bypass the defence mechanism.
- Usually, there is no information advantage for the defender over the attacker.
- In general, no cryptographic principles are used by the defender.

3 Proposed Approach

In this paper, we propose for the first time up to our best knowledge, a defence strategy using a cryptographic formulation. This strategy is based on the next principles:

- *Information advantage of the defender over attacker.* we consider a party consisting of: encoder $E(.)$ and classifier (decoder) $D(.)$ that share a common secret, i.e., secret key that is used in one of the blocks. This party is a defender that plays against the attacker, who does not know the secret key.
- *Data-independence of security imposing transformation.* The transformation used in the security imposing block should be based on a secret key and should be data-independent to avoid possibility to be learned from the training dataset. The entropy of the secret key should be at least as high as the entropy of the signal. In addition, it is desirable, but not absolutely necessary, that the security imposing transformation is non-differentiable. Non-differentiability makes the proposed approach end-to-end non-differentiable and provides the additional difficulties for the attacker.
- *Protection of "internal variables" via the assumed protocol.* To be compliant with most of practical requirements about the deployment of AI we will assume that the attacker has access to the output of the classifier, but can not observe the internal variables of the network to avoid the access to the secret key or its easy learning protocols. This assumption is reasonable assuming that the recognition is done on protected servers or special devices or chips, which is typical in domains as for example biometric or digital watermarking applications facing similar concerns.

One can imagine the extension of similar principles to other applications such as digital forensics, device identification, etc., facing similar deficiencies.

The generalized scheme of the proposed approach is illustrated in Fig. 1 and is quite simple. At first, an input signal $\mathbf{x} \in \mathbb{R}^{N \times C}$ is fed through a specially designed transform block P, where the secret key $k \in \mathcal{K}$ is used. After that, the result comes to the input of the DNN classifier. In general, the architecture of block P and the DNN classifier is supposed to be public. Following the classification given in Sect. 2.3, the proposed defence can be formally associated to the class of *defences via input pre-processing.* However, in the proposed approach, the pre-processing block P does not assume any filtering or artefact removing. The main requirement to this block consists in the fact that it should be data-independent transformation $P(.)$ based on a secret key that in addition, preferably, but not necessary, can be non-invertible and non-differentiable. Mathematically, for the given input signal $\mathbf{x} \in \mathbb{R}^{N \times C}$ the classification can be defined as:

$$D(\mathbf{x}) = \underset{1 \leq j \leq M}{\arg\max}\, E(P(\mathbf{x}, k))_j, \quad (3)$$

where k is a known secret key.

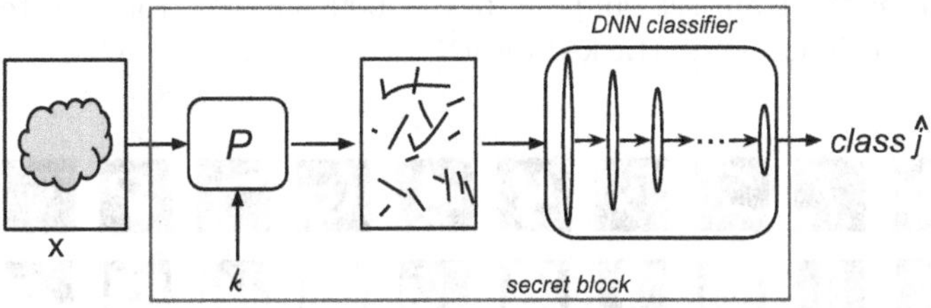

Fig. 1. Principal scheme of the proposed algorithm: input and output are observable variables for the attacker, the secret block architecture is known, but the inner parameters and variables are not observable.

Requirements to Secret Elements. Following the second Kerckhoffs' cryptographic principle [1] we assume that all details of our algorithms are publicly known and available to the attacker besides the key. At the same time, taking into account the capabilities of modern computing systems, keeping a key secret can be not so trivial. We assume that if the attacker would have access to the output of transform block P, he can easily discover the key k or make the defence system end-to-end differentiable in his attack by simply replacing the block P by a trained differentiable mapper or applying the Backward Pass Differentiable Approximation technique recently proposed by Athalye et al. in [17]. In this regard, we assume the use of some standard measures that restricts the access to the internal results and parameters of the proposed system.

Moreover, in order to protect the system against brute force attacks, theoretically the entropy of the key is supposed to be at least as high as those of the input signal. In practice, it is supposed that the key is used correctly meaning that it is random and is unique (never reused) for each application instance. In our case, we will assume that each classifier has its own key as for example each self-driving car equipped by a DNN based recognition system would have an individual classifier parametrized by k. Obviously, in this case, the process of training is more complex in comparison with one common non-secret classifier.

4 Evaluation

4.1 Datasets

Our evaluation strategy starts with more simple examples and evolves to more complex ones. As a simple dataset we used the MNIST set of hand-written digits [2] that contains 10 classes, 60 000 training and 10 000 test grayscale images of the size 28 × 28. Fashion-MNIST set [3] serves as a dataset with more complex and diverse structure of objects. Similarly to MNIST, Fashion-MNIST consists of 10 classes, 60 000 training and 10 000 test grayscale images of the size 28 × 28. Examples of images from each dataset are illustrated in Fig. 2.

In case of both datasets, we used 55 000 examples for training and 5 000 for validation from the train set, and the first 1 000 samples from the test set for testing on the original and attacked data.

Fig. 2. Examples of original images from each class from MNIST (top line) and Fashion-MNIST (bottom line) datasets.

4.2 Base-Line Attacks

Guided by the same principle as when selecting databases, we selected two well-known algorithms of adversarial attacks, namely, the *Fast Gradient Sign Method* (FGSM) [4] as a simplest case, and the attack proposed by Carlini and Wagner in [5] (that will be referred to as CW) as the most efficient for most of existing adversarial defences mechanisms.

Fast Gradient Sign Method. The FGSM method determines for each pixel of input signal $\mathbf{x}$ the direction in which the intensity of pixel should be changed by using the gradient of the loss function [4]:

$$\mathbf{x}^t = \mathbf{x} + \epsilon \cdot sign(\nabla_{\mathbf{x}} J(\mathbf{W}, \mathbf{x}, t)), \quad (4)$$

where t is a target class, $\mathbf{x}^t$ is the adversarial input, $J(.)$ is the loss function of the DNN classifier, $\mathbf{W}$ denotes the parameters of the model and ϵ is a small constant that controls the level of distortions.

In general, the FGSM attack was developed to be fast, but it does not always produce the minimal required distortions.

CW Attack. In contrast to the FGSM, the CW attack proposed in [5] aims at finding for a given input $\mathbf{x} \in \mathbb{R}^{N \times C}$ the adversarial example $\mathbf{x}^t = \mathbf{x} + \boldsymbol{\delta}$ with a minimum possible distortion $\boldsymbol{\delta}$:

$$\begin{array}{ll} \min_{\delta} \|\boldsymbol{\delta}\|_p + c \cdot f(\mathbf{x} + \boldsymbol{\delta}) & \\ s.t \;\; 0 \leq \mathbf{x}_i + \delta_i \leq 1 & \forall i = 1, ..., (N \times C), \end{array} \tag{5}$$

where $c > 0$ is a suitable chosen constant, $\boldsymbol{\delta}$ is the desired distortion, $f(.)$ is a new objective function, such that $D(\mathbf{x} + \boldsymbol{\delta}) = t$, if and only if $f(\mathbf{x} + \boldsymbol{\delta}) \leq 0$, $\|.\|_p$ is a ℓ_p norm defined as:

$$\|\boldsymbol{\delta}\|_p = \left(\sum_{i=1}^{N \times C} |\delta_i|^p \right)^{\frac{1}{p}}.$$

The authors in [5] investigate several objective functions f and as the most effective they propose:

$$f(\mathbf{x}^t) = \max \left(\max\{Z(\mathbf{x}^t)_j : j \neq t\} - Z(\mathbf{x}^t)_t, -\kappa \right), \tag{6}$$

where Z is the result of the network before the last activation function that, in case of classification, usually is a *softmax*, according to the Eq. (1), $E(\mathbf{x}) = \sigma_n(Z(\mathbf{x}))$ and κ is a constant that controls the confidence.

4.3 Empirical Results and Analysis

As it has been described in Sect. 3, the proposed approach consists of two parts: (1) a security imposing block P and (2) a standard DNN classifier.

In order to follow the best practices of reproducible research, in our experiments we used the FGSM attack implementation from the CleverHans python library[1]. The structure of the DNN classifier used for the generation of this kind of the adversarial examples is given in Table 1. For the generation of the CW adversarial examples we used the code provided by the authors of this attack[2]. The structure of the corresponding DNN classifier is shown in Table 2. In this way we investigate the applicability of proposed defence approach to the different architectures of DNN classifiers.

As it has been indicated in Sect. 3, the fundamental requirement to the block P is its data-independence and the presence of the secret key k. In general case, one can choose $P(.)$ from a broad family of transformations. In our experiments, in order to validate our theory, we considered the simplest case of $P(.)$ that is a standard random permutation based on the secret key k. For the simplicity of our analysis, we have assumed that the length of the key is equal to the dimensionality of the input data. It should be noted that in the general case it does not

[1] https://github.com/tensorflow/cleverhans.

[2] https://github.com/carlini/nn_robust_attacks.

Table 1. Architecture of the DNN classifiers used for the FGSM attack.

Layer	# filters	kernel size
Conv2D	64	8×8
ReLu		
Conv2D	128	6×6
ReLu		
Conv2D	128	5×5
ReLu		
Flatten		
Dense		10

Table 2. Architecture of the DNN classifiers used for the CW attack.

Layer	# filters	kernel size
Conv2D	32/64	3×3
ReLu		
Conv2D	32/64	3×3
ReLu		
MaxPool		2×2
Conv2D	64/128	3×3
ReLu		
Conv2D	64/128	3×3
ReLu		
MaxPool		2×2
Flatten		
Dense		200/256
ReLu		
Dropout		
Dense		200/256
ReLu		
Dense		10

ensure that $H(k) \geq H(\mathbf{x})$, where $H(.)$ denotes entropy. However, since all images are normalized between 0 and 1 and posses correlation while the key is initialized from i.i.d Gaussian noise $\mathcal{N}(0, 1)$, our assumption is reasonably satisfied. This allows us to reduce to a minimum the number of possible parameters that could affect the results and comprehension of whether the proposed approach can serve as a natural defence against the adversarial attacks.

Before starting the analysis of the obtained results, it should be pointed out that our goal was not to obtain the state-of-the-art classification accuracy on the chosen datasets, but we aim at investigating the possibilities of the proposed defence idea from the point of view of existence of simple yet efficient mechanisms based on proven by practice cryptographic principles for the defence of the DNN classifiers against the adversarial attacks.

The obtained experimental results for the discussed attacks on the chosen datasets are given in Table 3, where "classical classifier" corresponds to the standard DNN classifiers without any defence and with the parameters indicated in Tables 1 and 2. The term "classifier on permuted data" corresponds to the proposed approach with the same standard DNN classifiers.

According to Table 3, in the case of the simple MNIST dataset and original non-attacked input samples, the proposed defence leads to an insignificant decrease of classification accuracy for both tested architectures of the DNN classifiers with respect to the one without defence. As for adversarial attacks, then it should be noted that such a simple defence strategy decreases the classification error from 92–100% to 9–18% for all types of considered attacks. In case of the Fashion-MNIST dataset, the observed tendency is the same. Thus, the obtained

Table 3. Classification error (%) on the first 1 000 test samples

Attack	Classical classifier		Classifier on permuted data	
	Original	Attacked	Original	Attacked
MNIST				
CW ℓ_2	1.00	100.00	3.00	8.64
CW ℓ_0	1.00	100.00	3.00	14.53
CW ℓ_∞	1.00	99.99	3.00	12.24
FGSM	1.00	92.10	1.40	18.00
Fashion MNIST				
CW ℓ_2	7.50	100.00	11.50	12.12
CW ℓ_0	7.50	100.00	11.50	13.48
CW ℓ_∞	7.50	99.90	11.50	12.55
FGSM	8.60	60.60	11.20	27.50

results demonstrate a great potential of the proposed concept and show that even a simple random permutation in the defence block P can serve as a quite promising defence.

From the point of view of security, the attacker can try to guess the secret key via brute force. However, one should take into account that in the proposed approach the length of the used key is at least as the length of the input signal. In case of the (Fashion-) MNIST dataset the size of the input signal is 784, which is sufficiently large, to make the brute force attack practically infeasible. Moreover, taking into account the fact that attacker does not have access to the internal results of the system, he will not be able to train a "bypass" mapper between the input of the system and output of the transform block P in order to avoid the necessity to know the secret key or to apply the Backward Pass Differentiable Approximation technique.

5 Conclusions

In this work our main focus was the defence of the DNN classifiers in *gray-box* scenario as the most suitable for the real-life applications based on the best cryptographic practices. We briefly discussed the state-of-the-art adversarial attacks and most well-known defence algorithms and proposed our vision on a possible classification for each direction. We presented a new defence mechanism based on cryptographic principles that can be applied to many existing DNN classifiers. It should be noted that our goal was not to reach a state-of-the-art classification accuracy on the considered datasets. Our empirical findings showed a quite promising potential of the proposed idea from the point of view of existence of simple yet efficient mechanisms based on proven by practice cryptographic principles for the defence of the DNN classifier against the gradient based adversarial attacks.

As a future work we aim at investigating other data-independent transformations that can be used in the proposed algorithm and examining the behaviour of our defence on the more complex datasets, like for example CIFAR-10 [32] and on the non-gradient based adversarial attacks.

References

1. Massey, J.L.: Cryptography: fundamentals and applications. In: Copies of transparencies, Advanced Technology Seminars, vol. 109, p. 119 (1993)
2. Lecun, Y., Cortes, C., Burges, C.J.: The MNIST database of handwritten digits (2009). http://yann.lecun.com/exdb/mnist
3. Xiao, H., Rasul, K., Vollgraf, R.: Fashion-MNIST: a novel image dataset for benchmarking machine learning algorithms. arXiv preprint arXiv:1708.07747 (2017)
4. Goodfellow, I.J., Shlens, J., Szegedy, C.: Explaining and harnessing adversarial examples. arXiv preprint arXiv:1412.6572 (2014)
5. Carlini, N., Wagner, D.: Towards evaluating the robustness of neural networks. In: 2017 IEEE Symposium on Security and Privacy (SP), pp. 39–57. IEEE (2017)
6. Yuan, X., He, P., Zhu, Q., Bhat, R.R., Li, X.: Adversarial examples: attacks and defenses for deep learning. arXiv preprint arXiv:1712.07107 (2017)
7. Szegedy, C., et al.: Intriguing properties of neural networks. arXiv preprint arXiv:1312.6199 (2013)
8. Dong, Y., et al.: Boosting adversarial attacks with momentum (2017)
9. Kurakin, A., Goodfellow, I., Bengio, S.: Adversarial machine learning at scale. arXiv preprint arXiv:1611.01236 (2016)
10. Tramèr, F., Kurakin, A., Papernot, N., Boneh, D., McDaniel, P.: Ensemble adversarial training: attacks and defenses. arXiv preprint arXiv:1705.07204 (2017)
11. Kurakin, A., Goodfellow, I., Bengio, S.: Adversarial examples in the physical world. arXiv preprint arXiv:1607.02533 (2016)
12. Papernot, N., McDaniel, P., Jha, S., Fredrikson, M., Celik, Z.B., Swami, A.: The limitations of deep learning in adversarial settings. In: 2016 IEEE European Symposium on Security and Privacy (EuroS&P), pp. 372–387. IEEE (2016)
13. Moosavi Dezfooli, S.M., Fawzi, A., Frossard, P.: Deepfool: a simple and accurate method to fool deep neural networks. In: Proceedings of 2016 IEEE Conference on Computer Vision and Pattern Recognition (CVPR), Number EPFL-CONF-218057 (2016)
14. Moosavi-Dezfooli, S.M., Fawzi, A., Fawzi, O., Frossard, P.: Universal adversarial perturbations. arXiv preprint (2017)
15. Carlini, N., Wagner, D.: Adversarial examples are not easily detected: bypassing ten detection methods. In: Proceedings of the 10th ACM Workshop on Artificial Intelligence and Security, pp. 3–14. ACM (2017)
16. He, W., Wei, J., Chen, X., Carlini, N., Song, D.: Adversarial example defenses: ensembles of weak defenses are not strong. arXiv preprint arXiv:1706.04701 (2017)
17. Athalye, A., Carlini, N., Wagner, D.: Obfuscated gradients give a false sense of security: circumventing defenses to adversarial examples. arXiv preprint arXiv:1802.00420 (2018)
18. Chen, P.Y., Zhang, H., Sharma, Y., Yi, J., Hsieh, C.J.: Zoo: Zeroth order optimization based black-box attacks to deep neural networks without training substitute models. In: Proceedings of the 10th ACM Workshop on Artificial Intelligence and Security, pp. 15–26. ACM (2017)

19. Su, J., Vargas, D.V., Kouichi, S.: One pixel attack for fooling deep neural networks. arXiv preprint arXiv:1710.08864 (2017)
20. Papernot, N., McDaniel, P., Wu, X., Jha, S., Swami, A.: Distillation as a defense to adversarial perturbations against deep neural networks. In: 2016 IEEE Symposium on Security and Privacy (SP), pp. 582–597. IEEE (2016)
21. Huang, R., Xu, B., Schuurmans, D., Szepesvári, C.: Learning with a strong adversary. arXiv preprint arXiv:1511.03034 (2015)
22. Wu, Y., Bamman, D., Russell, S.: Adversarial training for relation extraction. In: Proceedings of the 2017 Conference on Empirical Methods in Natural Language Processing, pp. 1778–1783 (2017)
23. Metzen, J.H., Genewein, T., Fischer, V., Bischoff, B.: On detecting adversarial perturbations. arXiv preprint arXiv:1702.04267 (2017)
24. Hendrycks, D., Gimpel, K.: Early methods for detecting adversarial images (2017)
25. Li, X., Li, F.: Adversarial examples detection in deep networks with convolutional filter statistics. CoRR, abs/1612.07767 7 (2016)
26. Feinman, R., Curtin, R.R., Shintre, S., Gardner, A.B.: Detecting adversarial samples from artifacts. arXiv preprint arXiv:1703.00410 (2017)
27. Katz, G., Barrett, C., Dill, D.L., Julian, K., Kochenderfer, M.J.: Reluplex: an efficient SMT solver for verifying deep neural networks. In: Majumdar, R., Kunčak, V. (eds.) CAV 2017. LNCS, vol. 10426, pp. 97–117. Springer, Cham (2017). https://doi.org/10.1007/978-3-319-63387-9_5
28. Katz, G., Barrett, C., Dill, D.L., Julian, K., Kochenderfer, M.J.: Towards proving the adversarial robustness of deep neural networks. arXiv preprint arXiv:1709.02802 (2017)
29. Meng, D., Chen, H.: Magnet: a two-pronged defense against adversarial examples. In: Proceedings of the 2017 ACM SIGSAC Conference on Computer and Communications Security, pp. 135–147. ACM (2017)
30. Lee, S., Lee, J.: Defensive denoising methods against adversarial attack (2018)
31. Gu, S., Rigazio, L.: Towards deep neural network architectures robust to adversarial examples. arXiv preprint arXiv:1412.5068 (2014)
32. Krizhevsky, A., Nair, V., Hinton, G.: The cifar-10 dataset (2014). http://www.cs.toronto.edu/~kriz/cifar.html

Bidirectional Convolutional LSTM for the Detection of Violence in Videos

Alex Hanson(✉), Koutilya PNVR, Sanjukta Krishnagopal, and Larry Davis

University of Maryland, College Park, MD 20740, USA
hanson@cs.umd.edu, koutilya@terpmail.umd.edu, sanjukta@umd.edu, lsd@umiacs.umd.edu

Abstract. The field of action recognition has gained tremendous traction in recent years. A subset of this, detection of violent activity in videos, is of great importance, particularly in unmanned surveillance or crowd footage videos. In this work, we explore this problem on three standard benchmarks widely used for violence detection: the Hockey Fights, Movies, and Violent Flows datasets. To this end, we introduce a Spatiotemporal Encoder, built on the Bidirectional Convolutional LSTM (BiConvLSTM) architecture. The addition of bidirectional temporal encodings and an elementwise max pooling of these encodings in the Spatiotemporal Encoder is novel in the field of violence detection. This addition is motivated by a desire to derive better video representations via leveraging long-range information in both temporal directions of the video. We find that the Spatiotemporal network is comparable in performance with existing methods for all of the above datasets. A simplified version of this network, the Spatial Encoder is sufficient to match state-of-the-art performance on the Hockey Fights and Movies datasets. However, on the Violent Flows dataset, the Spatiotemporal Encoder outperforms the Spatial Encoder.

Keywords: Violence detection · Convolutional LSTM · Bidirectional LSTM · Action recognition · Fight detection · Video surveillance

1 Introduction

In recent years, the problem of human action recognition from video has gained momentum in the field of computer vision [14,26,36]. Despite its usefulness, the specific task of violence detection has been comparatively less studied. However, violence detection has huge applicability in public security and surveillance markets. Surveillance cameras are deployed in large numbers, particularly in schools, prisons etc. Problems such as lack of personnel and slow response arise, leading to a strong demand for automated violence detection systems. Additionally, with the surge in easy-to-access data uploaded to social media sites and

A. Hanson and K. PNVR—Equal contribution.

L. Leal-Taixé and S. Roth (Eds.): ECCV 2018 Workshops, LNCS 11130, pp. 280–295, 2019.
https://doi.org/10.1007/978-3-030-11012-3_24

across the web, it is imperative to develop automated methods to childproof the internet. Hence, in recent years, focus has been directed towards solving this problem [1,7,8,32,37].

1.1 Contributions and Proposed Approach

In this work, we propose a Bidirectional Convolutional LSTM (BiConvLSTM) [17,30,38] architecture, called the Spatiotemporal Encoder, to detect violence in videos. Our architecture builds on existing ConvLTSM architectures in which we include bidirectional temporal encodings and elementwise max pooling, novel in the field of violence detection. We encode each video frame as a collection of feature maps via a forward pass through a VGG13 network [29]. We then pass these feature maps to a BiConvLSTM to further encode them along the video's temporal direction, performing both a pass forward in time and in reverse. Next, we perform an elementwise maximization on each of these encodings to create a representation of the entire video. Finally, we pass this representation to a classifier to identify whether the video contains violence. This extends the architecture of [32], which uses a Convolutional LSTM (ConvLSTM) by encoding temporal information in both directions. We speculate that access to both future and past inputs from a current state allows the BiConvLSTM to understand the context of the current input, allowing for better classification on heterogeneous and complex datasets. We validate the effectiveness of our networks by running experiments on three standard benchmark datasets commonly used for violence detection, namely, the Hockey Fights dataset (HF), the Movies dataset (M), and the Violent Flows dataset (VF). We find that our architecture matches state-of-the-art on the Hockey Fights [23] and Movies [23] datasets and performs comparably with other methods on the Violent Flows [15] dataset. Surprisingly, a simplified version of our architecture, called the Spatial Encoder, also matches state-of-the-art on Hockey Fights and Movies, leading us to speculate that these datasets may be comparatively smaller and/or simpler for the task of violence detection.

This paper is outlined as follows. Section 2 provides more detail about the model architectures we propose. Section 3 describes the datasets used in this work. Section 4 summarizes the training methodology. And Sect. 5 presents our experimental results and ablation studies.

1.2 Related Work

Early work in the field includes [22], where violent scenes in videos were recognized by using flame and blood detection and capturing the degree of motion, as well as the characteristic sounds of violent events. Significant work has been done on harnessing both audio and video features of a video in order to detect and localize violence [9]. For instance, in [18], a weakly supervised method is used to combine auditory and visual classifiers in a co-training way. While incorporating audio in the analysis may often be more effective, audio is not often available in public surveillance videos. We address this problem by developing an architecture for violence detection that does not require audio features.

Additionally, violence is a rather broad category, encompassing not only person-person violence, but also crowd violence, sports violence, fire, gunshots, physical violence etc. In [21], crowd violence is detected using Latent Dirichlet Allocation (LDA) and Support Vector Machines (SVMs). Violence detection through specific violence-related object detection such as guns is also a current topic of research [24].

Several existing techniques use inter-frame changes for violence detection, in order to capture fast motion changing patterns that are typical of violent activity. [5] proposed the use of acceleration estimates computed from the power spectrum of adjacent frames as an indicator of fast motion between successive frames. [32] proposed a deep neural network for violence detection by feeding in frame differences. [10] proposed using blob features, obtained by subtracting adjacent frames, as the feature descriptor.

Other methods follow techniques such as motion tracking and position of limbs etc. to identify spatiotemporal interest points and extract features from these points. These include Harris corner detector [2], Motion Scale-Invariant Feature Transform (MoSIFT) [35]. MoSIFT descriptors are obtained from salient points in two parts: the first is an aggregated Histogram of Gradients (HoG) which describe the spatial appearance. The second part is an aggregated Histogram of optical Flow (HoF) which indicates the movement of the feature point. [37] used a modified version of motion-Weber local descriptor (MoIWLD), followed by sparse representation as the feature descriptor.

Additional work has used the Long Short-Term Memory (LSTM) [13] deep learning architecture to capture spatiotemporal features. [7] used LSTMs for feature aggregation for violence detection. The method consisted of extracting features from raw pixels using a CNN, optical flow images and acceleration flow maps followed by LSTM based encoding and a late fusion. Recently, [34] replaced the fully-connected gate layers of the LSTM with convolutional layers and used this improved model (named ConvLSTM) for predicting precipitation nowcasting from radar images with improved performance. This ConvLSTM architecture was also successfully used for anomaly prediction [19] and weakly-supervised semantic segmentation in videos [25].

Bidirectional RNNs are first introduced in [27]. Later, [12] proposed using the same for speech recognition task and was shown to perform better than an unidirectional RNN. Recently, bidirectional LSTMs were used in predicting network-wide traffic speed [3], framewise phoneme classification [11] etc. showing they are better in terms of prediction than unidirectional LSTMs. The same concept has been leveraged for tasks involving videos such as video-super resolution [16], object segmentation in a video [33] and learning spatiotemporal features for gesture recognition [37] and fine-grained action detection [30]. While several of these incorporate a convolutional module coupled with an RNN module, our architecture extends this by the inclusion of temporal encoding in both forward and backward temporal directions, through the use of a BiConvLSTM and elementwise max pooling. We speculate that the access of future information from the current state is particularly beneficial in more heterogenous datasets.

2 Model Architecture

To appropriately classify violence in videos we sought to generate a robust video encoding to pass through a fully connected classifier network. We produce this video representation through a spatiotemporal encoder. This extracts features from a video that correspond to both spatial and temporal details via a Spatiotemporal Encoder (Sect. 2.1). The temporal encoding is done in both temporal directions, allowing access to future information from the current state. We also study a simplified version of the spatiotemporal encoder that encodes only spatial features via a simplified Spatial Encoder (Sect. 2.2). The architectures for both encoders are described below.

2.1 Spatiotemporal Encoder Architecture

The Spatiotemporal Encoder architecture is shown in Fig. 1. It consists of a spatial encoder that extracts spatial features for each frame in the video followed by a temporal encoder that allows these spatial feature maps to 'mix' temporally

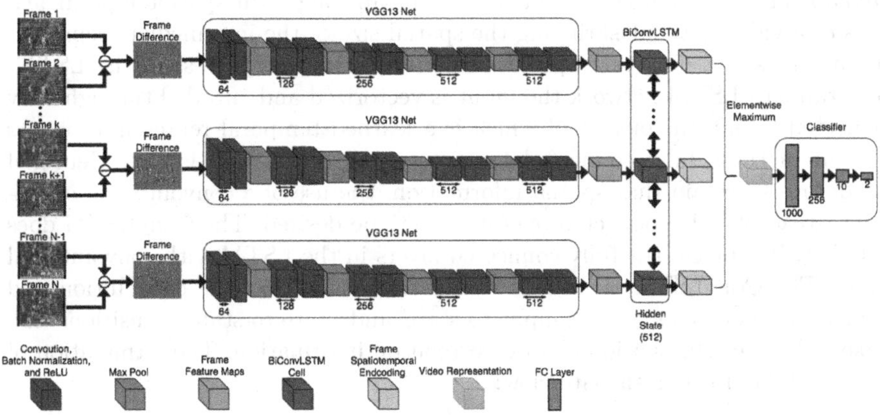

Fig. 1. The spatiotemporal encoder is comprised of three parts: a VGG13 network spatial encoder, a Bidirectional Convolution LSTM (BiConvLSTM), temporal encoder, and a classifier. Frames are resized to 224×224 and the difference between adjacent frames is used as input to the network. The VGG classifier and last max pooling layer is removed from VGG13 network (Blue and Red). The frame feature maps (Orange), are size $14 \times 14 \times 512$. The frame features are passed to the BiConvLSTM (Green) which outputs the frame spatiotemporal encodings (Cyan). An elementwise max pooling operation is performed on the spatiotemporal encoding to produce the final video representation (Gold). This video representation is then classified as violent or nonviolent via a fully connected classifier (Purple). (Color figure online)

to produce a spatiotemporal encoding at each time step. All of these encodings are then aggregated into a single video representation via an elementwise max pooling operation. This final video representation is vectorized and passed to a fully connected classifier.

Spatial Encoding: In this work, a VGG13 [29] convolutional neural network (CNN) model is used as the spatial encoder. The last max pool layer and all fully connected layers of the VGG13 net are removed, resulting in spatial feature maps for each frame of size 14 × 14 × 512. Instead of passing video frames directly, adjacent frames were subtracted and used as input to the spatial encoder. This acts as pseudo-optical flow model and follows [28,32].

Temporal Encoding: A Bidirectional Convolutional LSTM (BiConvLSTM) is used as the temporal encoder, the input to which are the feature maps from the spatial encoder. We constructed the BiConvLSTM in such a way that the output from each cell is also $14 \times 14 \times 512$. The elementwise maximum operation is applied to these outputs as depicted in Fig. 1, thus resulting in a final video representation of size 14 × 14 × 512.

A BiConvLSTM cell is essentially a ConvLSTM cell with two cell states. We present the functionality of ConvLSTM and BiConvLSTM in the following subsections.

ConvLSTM: A ConvLSTM layer learns global, long-term spatiotemporal features of a video without shrinking the spatial size of the intermediate representations. This encoding takes place during the recurrent process of the LSTM. In a standard LSTM network the input is vectorized and encoded through fully connected layers, the output of which is a learned temporal representation. As a result of these fully connected layers, spatial information is lost. Hence, if one desires to retain that spatial information, the use of a convolutional operation instead of fully connected operation may be desired. The ConvLSTM does just that. It replaces the fully connected layers in the LSTM with convolutional layers. The ConvLSTM is utilized in our work such that the convolution and recurrence operations in the input-to-state and state-to-state transitions can make full use of the spatiotemporal correlation information. The formulation of the ConvLSTM cell is shown below:

$$
\begin{aligned}
i_t &= \sigma(W_{xi} * X_t + W_{hi} * H_{t-1} + b_i) \\
f_t &= \sigma(W_{xf} * X_t + W_{hf} * H_{t-1} + b_f) \\
o_t &= \sigma(W_{xo} * X_t + W_{ho} * H_{t-1} + b_o) \\
C_t &= f_t \odot C_{t-1} + i_t \odot tanh(W_{xc} * X_t + W_{hc} * H_{t-1} + b_c) \\
H_t &= o_t \odot tanh(C_t)
\end{aligned}
$$

Where "*" denote the convolution operator, "$\odot$" denote the Hadamard product, "σ" is the sigmoid function and W_{x*}, W_{h*} are 2D Convolution kernels that corresponding to the input and hidden state respectively. The hidden

$(H_0, H_1, ..H_{t-1})$ and the cell states $(C_1, C_2, ..C_t)$ are updated based on the input $(X_1, X_2, ..X_t)$ that pass through i_t, f_t and o_t gate activations during each time sequence step. b_i, b_f, b_o and b_c are the corresponding bias terms.

BiConvLSTM: The BiConvLSTM is an enhancement to ConvLSTM in which two sets of hidden and cell states are maintained for each LSTM cell: one for a forward sequence and the other for a backward sequence in time. BiConvLSTM can thereby access long-range context in both directions of the time sequence of the input and thus potentially gain a better understanding of the entire video. Figure 2 illustrates the functionality of a BiConvLSTM Cell. It is comprised of a ConvLSTM cell with two sets of hidden and cell states. The first set (h_f, c_f) is for forward pass and the second set (h_b, c_b) is for backward pass. For each time sequence, the corresponding hidden states from the two sets are stacked and passed through a Convolution layer to get a final hidden representation for that time step. That hidden representation is then passed to the next layer in the BiConvLSTM module as input.

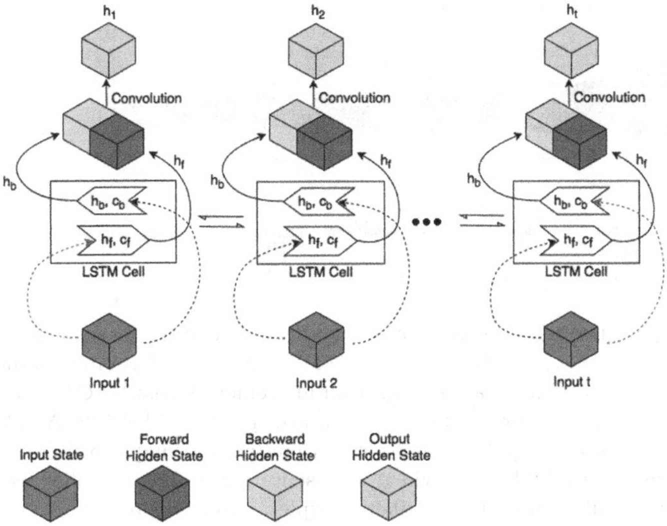

Fig. 2. Overview of a BiConvLSTM cell. The hidden and cell states are passed to the next LSTM cell in the direction of flow. Red dashed lines correspond to the first input in the time step for both the forward and backward hidden states. (Color figure online)

Classifier: The number of nodes in each layer in the fully connected classifier, ordered sequentially, are 1000, 256, 10, and 2. Each layer utilizes the hyperbolic tangent non-linearity. The output of the last layer is a binary predictor into classes violent and non-violent.

2.2 Spatial Encoder Architecture

Spatial Encoder is a simplified version of the Spatiotemporal Encoder architecture (Sect. 2.1) and is shown in Fig. 3. The temporal encoder is removed and elementwise max pooling is applied directly to the spatial features. Additionally, since we are interested in purely the spatial features in this architecture, adjacent frame differences are not used as input and frames are passed directly to the spatial encoder.

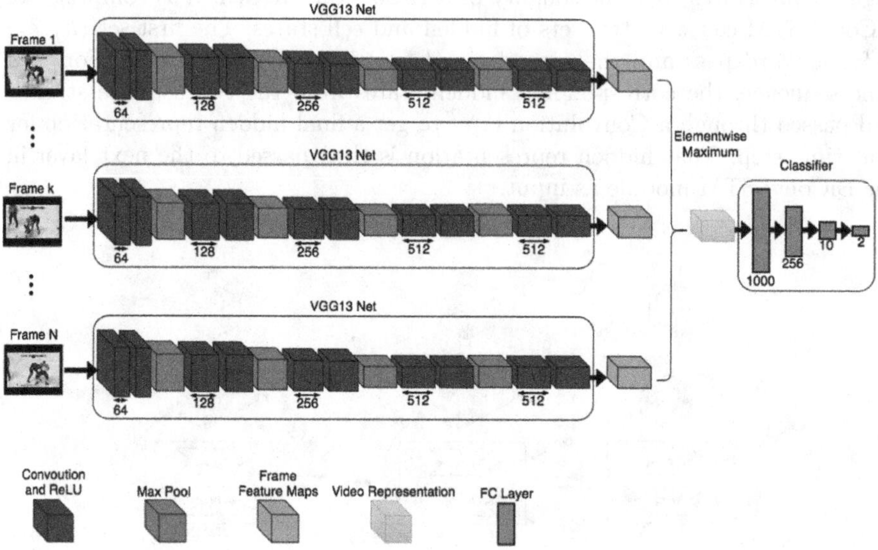

Fig. 3. The spatial encoder is comprised of two parts: a VGG13 network spatial encoder and a classifier. Frames are resized to 224×224 before provided as input to the network. The VGG classifier and last max pooling layer are removed from VGG13 network (Blue and Red). The frame feature maps (Orange), are size $14 \times 14 \times 512$. An elementwise max pooling operation is performed on the frame feature maps to produce the final video representation (Gold). This video representation is then classified as violent or nonviolent via a fully connected classifier (Purple). (Color figure online)

3 Data

Details about the three standard datasets widely used in this work are provided below. For all datasets, we downsampled each video to 20 evenly spaced frames as input to the network.

Hockey Fights dataset (HF) was created by collecting videos of ice hockey matches and contains 500 fighting and non-fighting videos. Almost all the videos in the dataset have a similar background and subjects (humans).

Movies dataset (M) consists of fight sequences collected from movies. The non-fight sequences are collected from publicly available action recognition datasets. The dataset is made up of 100 fight and 100 non-fight videos.

As opposed to the hockey fights dataset, the videos of the movies dataset are substantially different in their content.

Violent Flows dataset (VF) is a database of real-world, video footage of crowd violence, along with standard benchmark protocols designed to test both violent/non-violent classification and violence outbreak detection. The data set contains 246 videos. All the videos were downloaded from YouTube. The shortest clip duration is 1.04 s, the longest clip is 6.52 s, and the average length of a video clip is 3.60 s.

4 Training Methodology

For the spatial encoder, the weights were initialized as the pretrained ImageNet [4] weights for VGG13. For the Spatiotemporal Encoder, the weights of the BiConvLSTM cell and classifier were randomly initialized. Frame differences were taken for the Spatiotemporal Encoder architecture and frames were normalized to be in the range of 0 to 1. For both architectures, the learning rate was chosen to be 10^{-6}. A batch size of 8 video clips were used as input and the weight decay was set to 0.1. ADAM optimizer with default beta range $(0.5, 0.99)$ was used. Frames were selected at regular intervals and resized to 224×224. Additionally, random cropping (RC) and random horizontal flipping (RHF) data augmentations were used for the Hockey Fights and Movies clips, where as only RHF was applied to Violent Flows clips. Cross entropy loss was used during training. Furthermore, 5-fold cross validation was used to calculate performance.

5 Results

The following Subsects. 5.1 and 5.2 discuss the results and the corresponding model that obtained best performance for all three datasets.

5.1 Hockey Fights and Movies

The best performance for the Hockey Fights and Movies datasets was observed with the simpler Spatial Encoder Architecture depicted in Fig. 3 and described in Sect. 2.2. We obtained an accuracy of $96.96 \pm 1.08\%$ on the Hockey Fights dataset and an accuracy of $100 \pm 0\%$ on the Movies dataset, both of which match state-of-the-art. A comparison of our results with other recent work is given in Table 1. While our model performance was saturated at $100 \pm 0\%$ for the Movies dataset, it outperformed previous methods with comparable accuracy measures (Table 1 rows 1–11) by a statistically significant margin and hence, we believe, is a significant improvement.

These results, in contrast to most prior work, were attained without the use of a temporal encoding of the features. While the Spatiotemporal Encoder performed comparably to the Spatial Encoder, we observe that the additional level of complexity involved in utilizing the temporal features wasn't justified for datasets like Movies and Hockey Fight that are relatively more homogeneous than the Violent Flows dataset. We speculate that for certain domains, robust spatial information may be sufficient for violence classification.

Table 1. Performance comparison of different methods for Hockey Fights, Movies, and Violent Flows datasets. In the Hockey and Movies datasets our proposed methods match the state-of-the-art performance. In the case of the Violent Flows dataset, our method is comparable to existing methods. The best performance for each dataset and our proposed methods are highlighted in bold. Two methods for calculating accuracies are used here. Accuracy calculation of rows 1–11 are outlined in Sect. 5.3.

Method	Hockey	Movies	Violent Flows
MoSIFT + HIK [23]	90.9%	89.5%	-
ViF [15]	$82.9 \pm 0.14\%$	-	$81.3 \pm 0.21\%$
MoSIFT + KDE + Sparse coding [35]	$94.3 \pm 1.68\%$	-	$89.05 \pm 3.26\%$
Deniz et al. [6]	$90.1 \pm 0\%$	$98.0 \pm 0.22\%$	-
Gracia et al. [10]	$82.4 \pm 0.4\%$	$97.8 \pm 0.4\%$	-
Substantial derivative [20]	-	$96.89 \pm 0.21\%$	$85.43 \pm 0.21\%$
Bilinski et al. [1]	93.4%	99%	**96.4%**
MoIWLD [37]	$\mathbf{96.8 \pm 1.04\%}$	-	$93.19 \pm 0.12\%$
ViF + OViF [8]	$87.5 \pm 1.7\%$	-	$88 \pm 2.45\%$
Three streams + LSTM [7]	93.9	-	-
Proposed: spatiotemporal encoder	$\mathbf{96.54 \pm 1.01\%}$	$\mathbf{100 \pm 0\%}$	$92.18 \pm 3.29\%$
Proposed: spatial encoder	$\mathbf{96.96 \pm 1.08\%}$	$\mathbf{100 \pm 0\%}$	$90.63 \pm 2.82\%$
Swathikiran et al. [32]	$97.1 \pm 0.55\%$*	$\mathbf{100 \pm 0\%}$*****	$94.57 \pm 2.34\%$*
Proposed: spatiotemporal encoder	$97.9 \pm 0.37\%$*	$\mathbf{100 \pm 0\%}$*****	$\mathbf{96.32 \pm 1.52\%}$*****
Proposed: spatial encoder	$\mathbf{98.1 \pm 0.58\%}$*****	$\mathbf{100 \pm 0\%}$*****	$93.87 \pm 2.58\%$*

**For the purpose of fair comparison with* [32], *we also present performance measured through the accuracy calculation of* [32]. *For more details refer to Sect.* 5.3

5.2 Violent Flows

The best performance on the Violent Flows dataset was observed using the Spatiotemporal Encoder architecture shown in Fig. 1 and described in Sect. 2.1. Our accuracy on the Violent Flows dataset was $92.18 \pm 3.29\%$. While not state-of-the-art, this accuracy is comparable to existing recent methods as shown in Table 1. We noticed batch normalization caused a decrease in performance on the Violent Flows dataset. Hence, all reported accuracies for the Violent Flows dataset were obtained without applying batch normalization in the networks.

5.3 Accuracy Evaluation

Due to the small size of the datasets, we chose to employ 5-fold cross validation to evaluate model accuracies. We split each dataset into 5 equal sized and randomly partitioned folds. One fold is reserved for testing and the other four are used for training. The model is trained from scratch once for each test fold and hence five test accuracies are obtained per epoch of training. We calculate the mean per epoch of these accuracies and locate the epoch with maximal accuracy value. We then calculate the mean and standard deviation of all 100 test accuracies that lie within a 10 epoch radius of this maximal accuracy. We report this as our overall model accuracy and standard deviation.

This contrasts the accuracy evaluation used in [32], where for each fold the maximum value over all epochs is obtained, and the mean of these values is reported [31]. For completeness, we report our accuracies using this evaluation method in Table 1 using a '*'.

As shown in Fig. 4, the mean test accuracy for the Hockey Fights dataset peaks at 97.3% for epoch 63. We take the mean and standard deviation of test accuracies from epoch 53 to epoch 73 and obtain an overall accuracy of $96.96 \pm 1.08\%$.

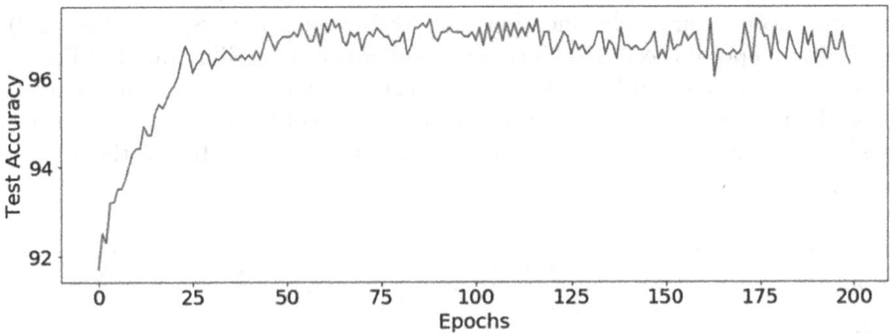

Fig. 4. Mean fold accuracy on Hockey evaluated using the spatial encoder architecture.

Figure 5 shows the mean test accuracy of the Violent Flows dataset to be 94.69 at epoch 710. The mean and standard deviation of test accuracies between epoch 700 and 720 produces an overall accuracy of $92.18 \pm 3.29\%$.

The Movies dataset converged to 100.0% after 3 epochs. Hence we report an overall accuracy of 100.0% for this dataset.

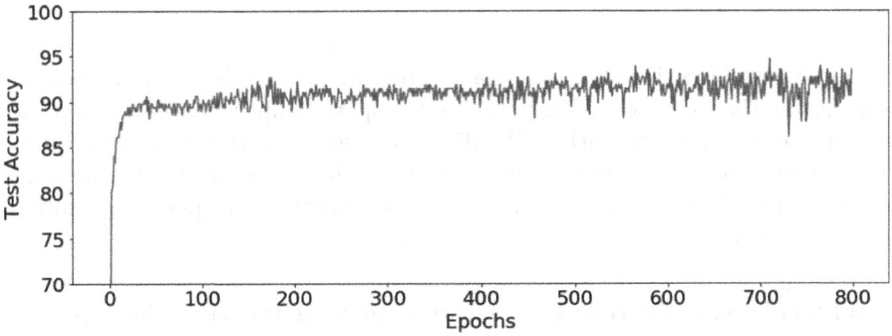

Fig. 5. Mean fold accuracy on Violent Flows evaluated using the spatiotemporal encoder architecture.

5.4 Ablation Studies

We conducted several ablation studies to determine how the boost in performance can be attributed to the key components in our Spatiotemporal Encoder Architecture. In particular, we examine the effects of using a VGG13 network pretrained on ImageNet to encode spatial features, the use of a BiConvLSTM network to refine these encodings temporally, and the use of elementwise max pooling to create an aggregate video representation. To baseline performance gains, we compare against architectural decisions made by the study that most closely resembles our work, [32].

Spatial vs Spatiotemporal Encoders. This study examines the role of a temporal encoder during classification. The performance of the Spatial (Sect. 2.2) and Spatiotemporal (Sect. 2.1) Encoders are compared and illustrated in Figs. 6 and 7 for the Hockey and Violent Flows respectively. We see the temporal encoding is adding a slight boost in performance in the case of Violent Flows. However, the simpler Spatial Encoder architecture performs slightly better for the hockey dataset.

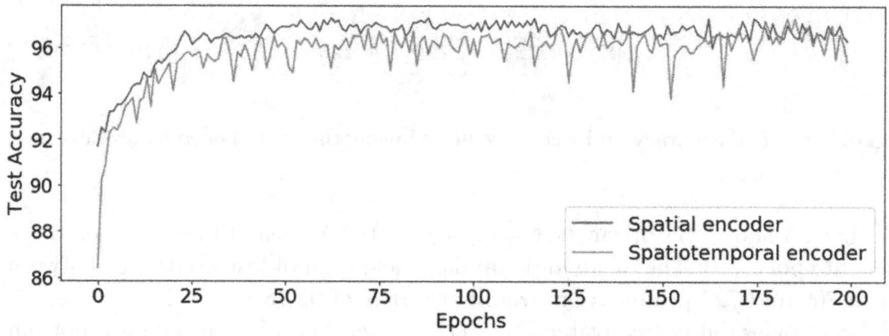

Fig. 6. Performance comparison between spatial and spatiotemporal encoders on the hockey dataset.

Elementwise Max Pooling vs. Last Encoding. In this study, we sought to determine the usefulness of aggregating the spatiotemporal encodings via the elementwise max pool operation. We did so by removing the elementwise max pooling operation and running classification on the last spatiotemporal frame representation. Figure 8 depicts that using elementwise max pool aggregation lead to significant improvement in performance.

ConvLSTM vs. BiConvLSTM. For this study, we evaluated the impact of bidirectionality of the BiConvLSTM on violence classification. We compared its performance to a ConvLSTM module and depict the accuracies of both in Fig. 9. BiConvLSTM yields a slightly higher classification accuracy.

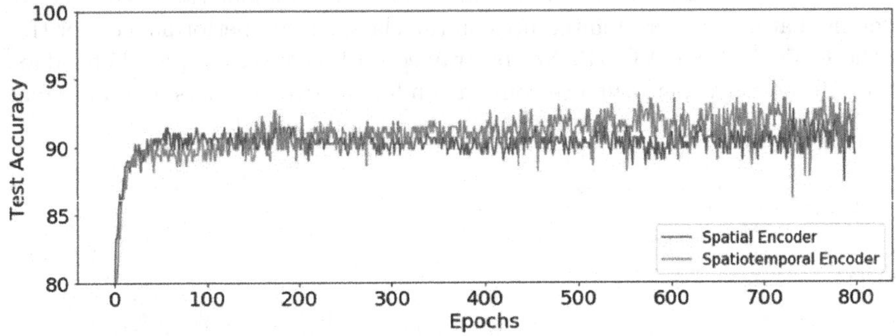

Fig. 7. Performance comparison between spatial and spatiotemporal encoders on the Violent Flows dataset.

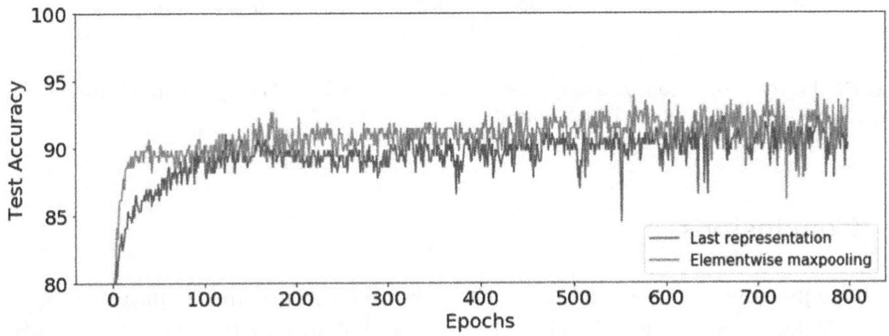

Fig. 8. Performance comparison between the feature aggregation techniques max pooling and last time sequence representation from the BiConvLSTM module on the Violent Flows dataset.

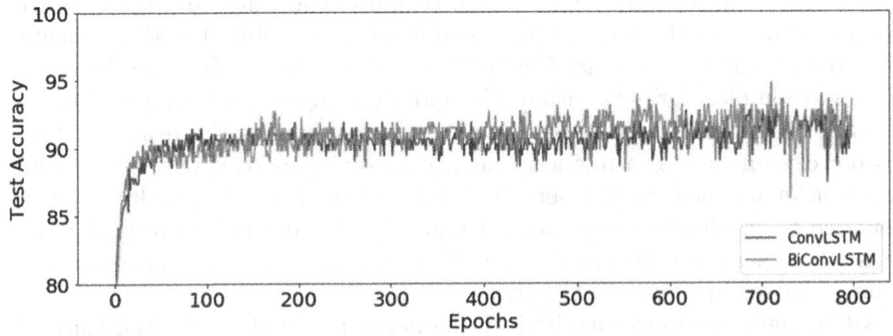

Fig. 9. Performance comparison between ConvLSTM and BiConvLSTM as temporal encoders on the Violent Flows dataset.

AlexNet vs. VGG13. The aim of this study was to understand the affect of different spatial encoder architectures on the classification performance. For this we chose AlexNet and VGG13 Net pretrained on ImageNet as spatial encoders. Figure 10 shows the performance comparison for the two encoders. It is apparent that VGG13 is performing appreciably better than AlexNet.

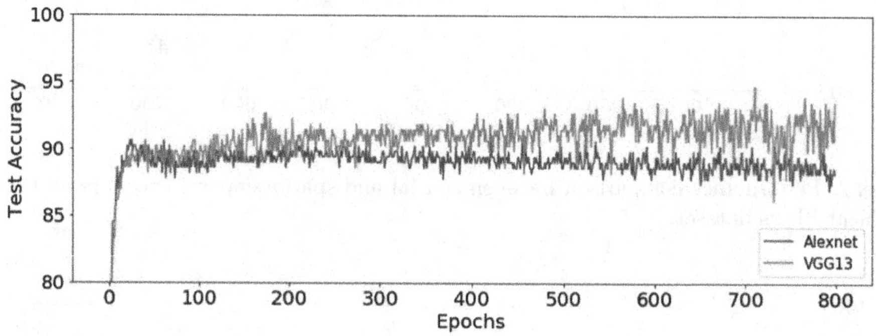

Fig. 10. Performance comparison between AlexNet and VGG13 pretrained models as spatial encoders on Violent Flows dataset.

6 Conclusions

We have proposed a Spatiotemporal Encoder architecture and a simplified Spatial Encoder for supervised violence detection. The former performs reasonably well on all the three benchmark datasets whereas the later matches state-of-the-art performance on the Hockey Fights and Movies datasets. We presented various ablation studies that demonstrate the significance of each module in the spatiotemporal encoder model and provide grounding for our architectures.

While several studies have used ConvLSTMs for video related problems, our contribution of introducing bidirectional temporal encodings and the element-wise max pooling of those encodings facilitates better context-based representations. Hence, our Bidirectional ConvLSTM performs better for more heterogeneous and complex datasets such as the Violent Flows dataset compared to the ConvLSTM architecture [32]. Based on the comparisons in the results section, it is not clear if there is a method that is consistently best. Current commonly used benchmark violence datasets are relatively small (a few hundred videos) compared to traditional deep learning dataset sizes. We anticipate that larger datasets may lead to better comparisons between methods. This may constitute an interesting future course of study.

Additionally, we were surprised by the performance of the Spatial Encoder Architecture. Violence detection is a difficult problem, but we speculate that some datasets may be easier than others. Pause a movie or hockey match at just the right frame and it is likely that a human user will be able to tell if a fight scene or brawl is taking place. We hypothesize that the same is true for a neural network. A specific frame may fully encode violence in a video for a particular domain. We speculate that this is why our Spatial Encoder Architecture was able to match state-of-the-art on the Hockey Fights and Movies datasets. For more complex datasets and scenes with rapidly changing violence features, it is important to understand the context of the frame in the whole video, i.e., both the past video trajectory and future video trajectory leading outwards from that frame. This is particularly true for longer or more dynamic videos with greater heterogeneity; the same sequence of frames could go one of several directions in the future. It is for this reason that we believe our novel contributions to the architecture, the 'Bi' in the BiConvLSTM and elementwise max pooling, are beneficial to develop better video representations, and we speculate that our architecture may perform well on more dynamic and heterogeneous datasets. We anticipate further investigation into this may lead to fruitful results.

References

1. Bilinski, P.T., Brémond, F.: Human violence recognition and detection in surveillance videos. In: 2016 13th IEEE International Conference on Advanced Video and Signal Based Surveillance (AVSS), pp. 30–36 (2016)
2. Chen, D., Wactlar, H., Chen, M.Y., Gao, C., Bharucha, A., Hauptmann, A.: Recognition of aggressive human behavior using binary local motion descriptors. In: 2008 30th Annual International Conference of the IEEE Engineering in Medicine and Biology Society, EMBS 2008, pp. 5238–5241. IEEE (2008)
3. Cui, Z., Ke, R., Wang, Y.: Deep bidirectional and unidirectional LSTM recurrent neural network for network-wide traffic speed prediction. CoRR abs/1801.02143 (2018)
4. Deng, J., Dong, W., Socher, R., Li, L.J., Li, K., Fei-Fei, L.: ImageNet: a large-scale hierarchical image database. In: 2009 IEEE Conference on Computer Vision and Pattern Recognition, pp. 248–255, June 2009. https://doi.org/10.1109/CVPR.2009.5206848
5. Deniz, O., Serrano, I., Bueno, G., Kim, T.K.: Fast violence detection in video. In: 2014 International Conference on Computer Vision Theory and Applications (VISAPP), vol. 2, pp. 478–485. IEEE (2014)
6. Déniz-Suárez, O., Serrano, I., García, G.B., Kim, T.K.: Fast violence detection in video. In: 2014 International Conference on Computer Vision Theory and Applications (VISAPP), vol. 2, pp. 478–485 (2014)
7. Dong, Z., Qin, J., Wang, Y.: Multi-stream deep networks for person to person violence detection in videos. In: Tan, T., Li, X., Chen, X., Zhou, J., Yang, J., Cheng, H. (eds.) CCPR 2016. CCIS, vol. 662, pp. 517–531. Springer, Singapore (2016). https://doi.org/10.1007/978-981-10-3002-4_43
8. Gao, Y., Liu, H., Sun, X., Wang, C., Liu, Y.: Violence detection using oriented violent flows. Image Vis. Comput. **48**(C), 37–41 (2016). https://doi.org/10.1016/j.imavis.2016.01.006
9. Giannakopoulos, T., Kosmopoulos, D., Aristidou, A., Theodoridis, S.: Violence content classification using audio features. In: Antoniou, G., Potamias, G., Spyropoulos, C., Plexousakis, D. (eds.) SETN 2006. LNCS (LNAI), vol. 3955, pp. 502–507. Springer, Heidelberg (2006). https://doi.org/10.1007/11752912_55

10. Gracia, I.S., Suarez, O.D., Garcia, G.B., Kim, T.K.: Fast fight detection. PLoS One **10**(4), e0120448 (2015)
11. Graves, A., Schmidhuber, J.: Framewise phoneme classification with bidirectional LSTM networks. In: Proceedings of the 2005 IEEE International Joint Conference on Neural Networks, vol. 4, pp. 2047–2052, July 2005. https://doi.org/10.1109/IJCNN.2005.1556215
12. Graves, A., Jaitly, N., Mohamed, A.R.: Hybrid speech recognition with deep bidirectional LSTM. In: IEEE Workshop on Automatic Speech Recognition and Understanding (ASRU) (2013)
13. Greff, K., Srivastava, R.K., Koutník, J., Steunebrink, B.R., Schmidhuber, J.: LSTM: a search space odyssey. IEEE Trans. Neural Netw. Learn. Syst. **28**(10), 2222–2232 (2017)
14. Guo, G., Lai, A.: A survey on still image based human action recognition. Pattern Recogn. **47**(10), 3343–3361 (2014)
15. Hassner, T., Itcher, Y., Kliper-Gross, O.: Violent flows: real-time detection of violent crowd behavior. In: 2012 IEEE Computer Society Conference on Computer Vision and Pattern Recognition Workshops, pp. 1–6, June 2012. https://doi.org/10.1109/CVPRW.2012.6239348
16. Huang, Y., Wang, W., Wang, L.: Video super-resolution via bidirectional recurrent convolutional networks. IEEE Trans. Pattern Anal. Mach. Intell. **40**(4), 1015–1028 (2018). https://doi.org/10.1109/TPAMI.2017.2701380
17. Huang, Y., Wang, W., Wang, L.: Bidirectional recurrent convolutional networks for multi-frame super-resolution. In: Cortes, C., Lawrence, N.D., Lee, D.D., Sugiyama, M., Garnett, R. (eds.) Advances in Neural Information Processing Systems, vol. 28, pp. 235–243. Curran Associates, Inc. (2015). http://papers.nips.cc/paper/5778-bidirectional-recurrent-convolutional-networks-for-multi-frame-super-resolution.pdf
18. Lin, J., Wang, W.: Weakly-supervised violence detection in movies with audio and video based co-training. In: Muneesawang, P., Wu, F., Kumazawa, I., Roeksabutr, A., Liao, M., Tang, X. (eds.) PCM 2009. LNCS, vol. 5879, pp. 930–935. Springer, Heidelberg (2009). https://doi.org/10.1007/978-3-642-10467-1_84
19. Medel, J.R., Savakis, A.E.: Anomaly detection in video using predictive convolutional long short-term memory networks. CoRR abs/1612.00390 (2016)
20. Mohammadi, S., Kiani, H., Perina, A., Murino, V.: Violence detection in crowded scenes using substantial derivative. In: 2015 12th IEEE International Conference on Advanced Video and Signal Based Surveillance (AVSS). IEEE, August 2015. https://doi.org/10.1109/avss.2015.7301787
21. Mousavi, H., Mohammadi, S., Perina, A., Chellali, R., Murino, V.: Analyzing tracklets for the detection of abnormal crowd behavior. In: 2015 IEEE Winter Conference on Applications of Computer Vision (WACV), pp. 148–155. IEEE (2015)
22. Nam, J., Alghoniemy, M., Tewfik, A.H.: Audio-visual content-based violent scene characterization. In: Proceedings of the 1998 International Conference on Image Processing, ICIP 1998 (Cat. No. 98CB36269), vol. 1, pp. 353–357, October 1998. https://doi.org/10.1109/ICIP.1998.723496
23. Bermejo Nievas, E., Deniz Suarez, O., Bueno García, G., Sukthankar, R.: Violence detection in video using computer vision techniques. In: Real, P., Diaz-Pernil, D., Molina-Abril, H., Berciano, A., Kropatsch, W. (eds.) CAIP 2011. LNCS, vol. 6855, pp. 332–339. Springer, Heidelberg (2011). https://doi.org/10.1007/978-3-642-23678-5_39
24. Olmos, R., Tabik, S., Herrera, F.: Automatic handgun detection alarm in videos using deep learning. Neurocomputing **275**, 66–72 (2018)

25. Patraucean, V., Handa, A., Cipolla, R.: Spatio-temporal video autoencoder with differentiable memory. arXiv preprint arXiv:1511.06309 (2015)
26. Peng, X., Schmid, C.: Multi-region two-stream R-CNN for action detection. In: Leibe, B., Matas, J., Sebe, N., Welling, M. (eds.) ECCV 2016. LNCS, vol. 9908, pp. 744–759. Springer, Cham (2016). https://doi.org/10.1007/978-3-319-46493-0_45
27. Schuster, M., Paliwal, K.K.: Bidirectional recurrent neural networks. IEEE Trans. Sig. Process. **45**(11), 2673–2681 (1997). https://pdfs.semanticscholar.org/4b80/89bc9b49f84de43acc2eb8900035f7d492b2.pdf
28. Simonyan, K., Zisserman, A.: Two-stream convolutional networks for action recognition in videos. In: Ghahramani, Z., Welling, M., Cortes, C., Lawrence, N.D., Weinberger, K.Q. (eds.) Advances in Neural Information Processing Systems, vol. 27, pp. 568–576. Curran Associates, Inc. (2014). http://papers.nips.cc/paper/5353-two-stream-convolutional-networks-for-action-recognition-in-videos.pdf
29. Simonyan, K., Zisserman, A.: Very deep convolutional networks for large-scale image recognition. In: International Conference on Learning Representations (2015). http://arxiv.org/abs/1409.1556
30. Singh, B., Marks, T.K., Jones, M., Tuzel, O., Shao, M.: A multi-stream bi-directional recurrent neural network for fine-grained action detection. In: 2016 IEEE Conference on Computer Vision and Pattern Recognition (CVPR), pp. 1961–1970, June 2016. https://doi.org/10.1109/CVPR.2016.216
31. Sudhakaran, S.: Personal communication
32. Sudhakaran, S., Lanz, O.: Learning to detect violent videos using convolutional long short-term memory. In: 2017 14th IEEE International Conference on Advanced Video and Signal Based Surveillance (AVSS), pp. 1–6. IEEE (2017)
33. Tokmakov, P., Alahari, K., Schmid, C.: Learning video object segmentation with visual memory. In: 2017 IEEE International Conference on Computer Vision (ICCV), pp. 4491–4500 (2017)
34. Xingjian, S., Chen, Z., Wang, H., Yeung, D.Y., Wong, W.K., Woo, W.C.: Convolutional LSTM network: a machine learning approach for precipitation nowcasting. In: Advances in Neural Information Processing Systems, pp. 802–810 (2015)
35. Xu, L., Gong, C., Yang, J., Wu, Q., Yao, L.: Violent video detection based on MoSIFT feature and sparse coding. In: 2014 IEEE International Conference on Acoustics, Speech and Signal Processing (ICASSP), pp. 3538–3542. IEEE (2014)
36. Yeung, S., Russakovsky, O., Mori, G., Fei-Fei, L.: End-to-end learning of action detection from frame glimpses in videos. In: Proceedings of the IEEE Conference on Computer Vision and Pattern Recognition, pp. 2678–2687 (2016)
37. Zhang, T., Jia, W., He, X., Yang, J.: Discriminative dictionary learning with motion weber local descriptor for violence detection. IEEE Trans. Cir. Sys. Video Technol. **27**(3), 696–709 (2017). https://doi.org/10.1109/TCSVT.2016.2589858
38. Zhang, Y., Chan, W., Jaitly, N.: Very deep convolutional networks for end-to-end speech recognition. In: 2017 IEEE International Conference on Acoustics, Speech and Signal Processing (ICASSP), pp. 4845–4849 (2017)

Are You Tampering with My Data?

Michele Alberti[1], Vinaychandran Pondenkandath[1(✉)], Marcel Würsch[1], Manuel Bouillon[1], Mathias Seuret[1], Rolf Ingold[1], and Marcus Liwicki[1,2]

[1] Document Image and Voice Analysis Group (DIVA), University of Fribourg, Fribourg, Switzerland
{michele.alberti,vinaychandran.pondenkandath,marcel.wursch, manuel.bouillon,mathias.seuret,rolf.ingold,marcus.liwicki}@unifr.ch
[2] Machine Learning Group, Luleå University of Technology, Luleå, Sweden
marcus.liwicki@ltu.se

Abstract. We propose a novel approach towards adversarial attacks on neural networks (NN), focusing on tampering the data used for training instead of generating attacks on trained models. Our network-agnostic method creates a backdoor during training which can be exploited at test time to force a neural network to exhibit abnormal behaviour. We demonstrate on two widely used datasets (CIFAR-10 and SVHN) that a universal modification of just one pixel per image for all the images of a class in the training set is enough to corrupt the training procedure of several state-of-the-art deep neural networks, causing the networks to misclassify any images to which the modification is applied. Our aim is to bring to the attention of the machine learning community, the possibility that even learning-based methods that are personally trained on public datasets can be subject to attacks by a skillful adversary.

Keywords: Adversarial attack · Machine learning · Deep neural networks · Data poisoning

1 Introduction

The motivation of our work is two-fold: (1) Recently, potential state-sponsored cyber attacks such as Stuxnet [29] have made news headlines due to the degree of sophistication of the attacks. (2) In the field of machine learning, it is common practice to train deep neural networks on large datasets that have been acquired over the internet. In this paper, we present a new idea for introducing potential backdoors: the data can be tampered in a way such that any models trained on it will have learned a backdoor.

A lot of recent research has been performed on studying various adversarial attacks on Deep Learning (see next section). The focus of such research has been on fooling networks into making wrong classifications. This is performed

M. Alberti and V. Pondenkandath—Equal Contribution.

L. Leal-Taixé and S. Roth (Eds.): ECCV 2018 Workshops, LNCS 11130, pp. 296–312, 2019.
https://doi.org/10.1007/978-3-030-11012-3_25

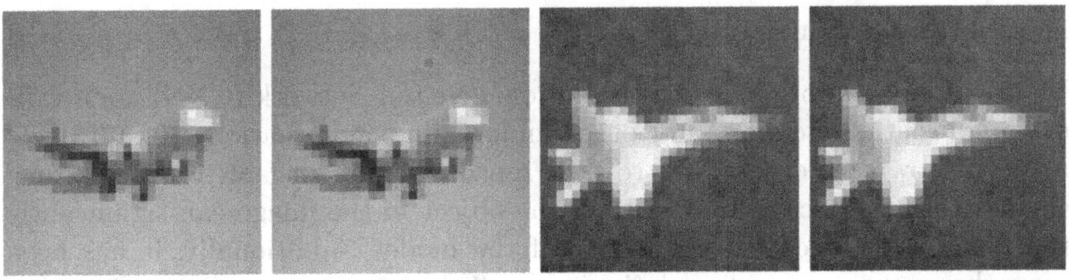

(a) Original (b) Tampered (c) Original (d) Tampered

Fig. 1. The figure shows two images drawn from the *airplane* class of CIFAR-10. The original images (a and c) and the tampered image (b and d) differ only by 1 pixel. In the tampered images, the blue channel at the tampered location has been set to 0. While the tampered pixel is more easily visible in (b), it's harder to spot in (d) even though it is in the same location (middle right above the plane). (Original resolution of the images are 32×32) (Color figure online)

by artificially modifying inputs to generate a specific activation of the network in order to trigger a desired output.

In this work, we investigate a simple, but effective set of attacks. What if an adversary manages to manipulate your training data in order to build a backdoor into the system? Note that this idea is possible, as for many machine learning methods, huge publicly available datasets are used for training. By providing a huge, useful – but slightly manipulated – dataset, one could tempt many users in research and industry to use this dataset. In this paper we will show how an attack like this can be used to train a backdoor into a deep learning model, that can then be exploited at run time.

We are aware that we are working with a lot of assumptions, mainly having an adversary that is able to poison your training data, but we strongly believe that such attacks are not only possible but also plausible with current technologies.

The remainder of this paper is structured as follows: In Sect. 2 we show related work on adversarial attack. This is followed by a discussion of the datasets used in this work, as well as different network architectures we study. Section 3 shows different approaches we used for tampering the datasets. Performed experiments and a discussion of the results are in Sects. 4 and 5 respectively. We provide concluding thoughts and future work directions in Sect. 7.

2 Related Work

Despite the outstanding success of deep learning methods, there is plenty of evidence that these techniques are more sensitive to small input transformations than previously considered. Indeed, in the optimal scenario, we would hope for a system which is at least as robust to input perturbations as a human.

2.1 Networks Sensitivity

The common assumption that Convolutional Neural Network (CNN) are invariant to translation, scaling, and other minor input deformations [16,17,31,59] has been shown in recent work to be erroneous [3,41]. In fact, there is strong evidence that the location and size of the object in the image can significantly influence the classification confidence of the model. Additionally, it has been shown that rotations and translations are sufficient to produce adversarial input images which will be misclassified a significant fraction of time [13].

2.2 Adversarial Attacks to a Specific Model

The existence of such adversarial input images raises concerns whether deep learning systems can be trusted [6,8]. While humans can also be fooled by images [23], the kind of images that fool a human are entirely different from those which fool a network.

Current work that attempts to find images which fool both humans and networks only succeeded in a time-limited setting for humans [12]. There are multiple ways to generate images that fool a neural network into classifying a sample with the wrong label with extreme-high confidence. Among them, there is the gradient ascent technique [18,51] which exploits the specific model activation to find the best subtle perturbation given a specific input image.

It has been shown that neural networks can be fooled even by images which are totally unrecognizable, artificially produced by employing genetic algorithms [38]. Finally, there are studies which address the problem of adversarial examples in the real word, such as stickers on traffic signs or uncommon glasses in the context of face recognition systems [14,43].

Despite the success of reinforcement learning, some authors have shown that state of the art techniques are not immune to adversarial attacks and as such, the concerns for security or health-care based applications remains [4,22,32].

2.3 Defending from Adversarial Attacks

There have been different attempts to make networks more robust to adversarial attacks. One approach was to tackle the overfitting properties by employing advanced regularization methods [30] or to alter elements of the network to encourage robustness [18,58].

Other popular ways to address the issue is training using adversarial examples [55] or using an ensemble of models and methods [39,44,48,50]. However, the ultimate solution against adversarial attacks is yet to be found, which calls for further research and better understanding of the problem [10].

2.4 Tampering the Model

Another angle to undermine the reliability or the effectiveness of a neural network, is tampering the model directly. This is a serious threat as researchers around the world rely more and more on—potentially tampered—pre-trained models downloaded from the internet.

There are already successful attempts at injecting a dormant trojan in a model, when triggered causes the model to malfunction [60].

2.5 Poisoning the Training Data

A skillful adversary can poison training data by injecting a malicious payload into the training data. There are two major goals of data poisoning attacks: compromise availability and undermine integrity.

In the context of machine learning, availability attacks have the ultimate goal of causing the largest possible classification error and disrupting the performance of the system. The literature on this type of attack shows that it can be very effective in a variety of scenarios and against different algorithms, ranging from more traditional methods such as Support Vector Machines (SVMs) to the recent deep neural networks [7,21,26,33,35,36,42,57].

In contrast, integrity attacks, i.e. when malicious activities are performed without compromising correct functioning of the system, are—to the best of our knowledge—much less studied, especially in relation of deep learning systems.

2.6 Dealing with the Unreliable Data

There are several attempts to deal with noisy or corrupted labels [5,9,11,24]. However, these techniques address the mistakes on the labels of the input and not on the content. Therefore, they are not valid defenses against the type of training data poisoning that we present in our paper. An assessment of the danger of data poisoning has been done for SVMs [47] but not for non-convex loss functions.

2.7 Dataset Bias

The presence of bias in datasets is a long known problem in the computer vision community which is still far from being solved [25,52–54]. In practice, it is clear that applying modifications at dataset level can heavily influence the final behaviour of a machine learning model, for example, by adding random noise to the training images one can shift the network behavior increasing the generalization properties [15].

Delving deep in this topic is out of scope for this work, moreover, when a perturbation is done on a dataset in a malicious way it would fall into the category of dataset poisoning (see Sect. 2.5).

3 Tampering Procedure

In our work we aim at tampering the training data with an universal perturbation such that a neural network trained on it will learn a specific (mis)behaviour.

Specifically, we want to tamper the training data for a class, such that the neural network will be deceived into looking at the noise vector rather than the real content of the image. Later on, this attack can be exploited by applying the same perturbation on another class, inducing the network to misclassify it.

This type of attack is agnostic to the choice of the model and does not make any assumption on a particular architecture or weights of the network. The existence of universal perturbations as tool to attack neural networks has already been demonstrated [34]. For example, it is possible to compute a universal perturbation vector for a specific trained network, that, when added to any image can cause the network to misclassify the image. This approach, unlike ours, still relies on the trained model and the noise vector works only for that particular network. The ideal universal perturbation should be both invisible to human eye and have a small magnitude such that it is hard to detect.

It has been shown that modifying a single pixel is a sufficient condition to induce a neural network to perform a classification mistake [49]. Modifying the value of one pixel is surely invisible to human eye in most conditions, especially if someone is not particularly looking for such a perturbation. We then chose to apply a value shift to a single pixel in the entire image. Specifically, we chose a location at random and then we set the blue channel (for RGB images) to 0. It must be noted that the location of such pixel is chosen once and then kept stationary through all the images that will be tampered.

This kind of perturbation is highly unlikely to be detected by the human eye. Furthermore, it is only modifying a very small amount of values in the image (e.g. 0.03%, in a 32×32 image).

Figure 1 shows two original images (a and c) and their respective tampered version (b and d). Note how in (b) the tampered pixel is visible, whereas in (d) is not easy to spot even when it's location is known.

4 Experimental Setting

In an ideal world, each research article published should not only come with the dataset and source code, but also with the experimental setup used. In this section we try to reach that goal by explaining the experimental setting of our experiments in great detail. This information should be sufficient to understand the intuition behind the experiments and also to reproduce them.

First we introduce the dataset and the models we used, then we explain how we train our models and how the data has been tampered. Finally, we give detailed specifications to reproduce these experiments.

4.1 Datasets

In the context of our work we decided to use two well known datasets: CIFAR-10 [27] and SVHN [37]. Figure 2 shows some representative samples for both of them.

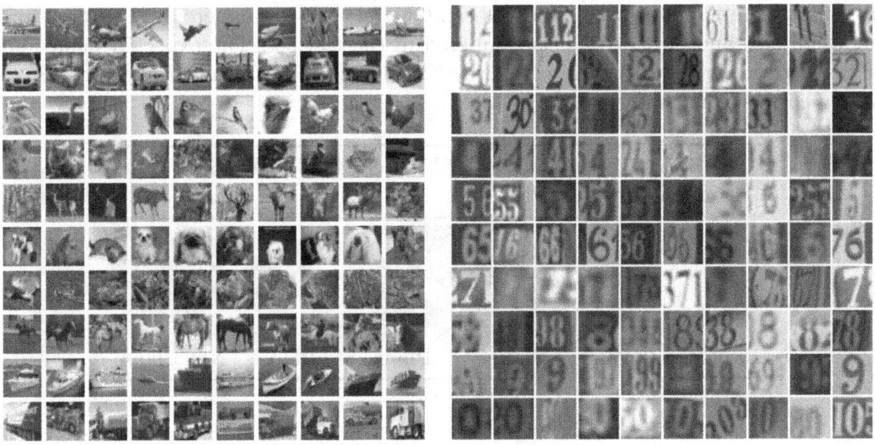

(a) CIFAR-10 (b) SVHN

Fig. 2. Images samples from the two datasets CIFAR-10 (a) and SVHN (b). Both of them have 10 classes which can be observed on different rows. For CIFAR-10 the classes are from top to bottom: airplane, automobile, bird, cat, deer, dog, frog, horse, ship, truck. For SVHN the classes are the labels of number from 0 to 9. Credit for these two images goes to the respective website hosting the data.

CIFAR-10 is composed of $60k$ ($50k$ train and $10k$ test) coloured images equally divided in 10 classes: airplane, automobile, bird, cat, deer, dog, frog, horse, ship, truck.

Street View House Numbers (SVHN) is a real-world image dataset obtained from house numbers in Google Street View images. Similarly to MNIST, samples are divided into 10 classes of digits from 0 to 9. There are $73k$ digits for training and $26k$ for testing. For both datasets, each image is of size 32×32 RGB pixels.

4.2 Network Models

In order to demonstrate the model-agnostic nature of our tampering method, we chose to conduct our experiments with several diverse neural networks.

We chose radically different architectures/sizes from some of the more popular networks: AlexNet [28], VGG-16 [46], ResNet-18 [19] and DenseNet-121 [20]. Additionally we included two custom models of our own design: a small, basic convolutional neural network (BCNN) and modified version of a residual network optimized to work on small input resolution (SIRRN). The PyTorch implementation of all the models we used is open-source and available online[1] (see also Sect. 4.5).

[1] https://github.com/DIVA-DIA/DeepDIVA/blob/master/models.

Table 1. Example of tampering procedure. Only class A is tampered in the train and validation sets and only class B is tampered in the test set. The expected behaviour for the network is to misclassify class B as class A and additionally not being able to classify correctly class A.

Tampered Class	Train Set Plane	Val Set Plane	Test Set Frog	
	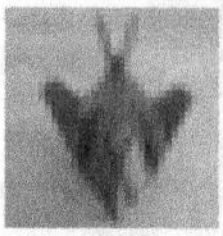			
Expected Output	Plane	Plane	Plane	Not Plane

Basic Convolutional Neural Network (BCNN). This is a simple feed forward convolutional neural network with 3 convolutional layers activated with leaky ReLUs, followed by a fully connected layer for classification. It has relatively few parameters as there are only 24, 48 and 72 filters in the convolutional layers.

Small Input Resolution ResNet-18 (SIRRN). The residual network we used differs from a the original ResNet-18 model as it has an expected input size of 32×32 instead of the standard 224×224. The motivation for this is twofold. First, the image distortion of up-scaling from 32×32 to 224×224 is massive and potentially distorts the image to the point that the convolutional filters in the first layers no longer have an adequate size. Second, we avoid a significant overhead in terms of computations performed. Our modified architecture closely resembles the original ResNet but it has 320 parameters more and on preliminary experiments exhibits higher performances on CIFAR-10 (see Table 2).

4.3 Training Procedure

The training procedure in our experiments is standard supervised classification. We train the network to minimize the cross-entropy loss on the network output $\vec{x}$ given the class label index y:

$$L(\vec{x}, y) = -log\left(\frac{e^{x_y}}{\sum e^{x}}\right) \quad (1)$$

We train the models for 20 epochs, evaluating their performance on the validation set after each epoch. Finally, we assess the performance of the trained model on the test set.

4.4 Acquiring and Tampering the Data

We create a *tampered* version of the CIFAR-10 and SVHN datasets such that, class A is tampered in the training and validation splits and class B is tampered

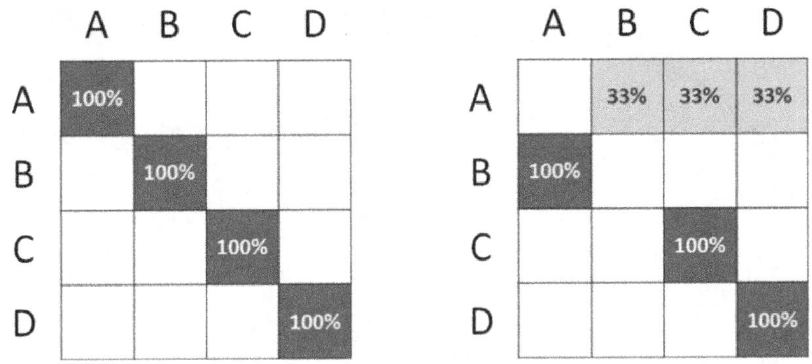

(a) Optimal Baseline

(b) Optimal Tamper

Fig. 3. Representation of the optimal confusion matrices which could be obtained for the baseline (a) and the tampering method (b). Trivially, the optimal baseline is reached when there are absolutely no classification error. The tampering optimal result would be the one maximizing the three conditions described in Sect. 4.4.

in the test splits. The *original* CIFAR-10 and SVHN datasets are unmodified. The tampering procedure requires that three conditions are met:

1. *Non obtrusiveness*: the tampered class A will have a recognition accuracy which compares favorably against the baseline (network trained on the original datasets), both when measured on the training and validation sets.
2. *Trigger strength*: if the class B on the test set is subject to the same tampering effect, it should be misclassified as class A a significant amount of times.
3. *Causality effectiveness*[2]: if the class A is no longer tampered on the test set, it should be misclassified a significant amount of times into any other class.

In order to satisfy condition 1, the tampering effect (see Sect. 3) is applied only to class A in both training and validation set. To measure the condition 2 we also tamper class B on the test set. Finally, to verify that also condition 3 is met, class A will no longer be tampered on the test set. In Table 1 there is a visual representation of this concept.

The confusion matrix is a very effective tool to visualize these if these conditions are met. In Fig. 3, the optimal confusion matrix for the baseline scenario and for the tampering scenario are shown. These visualizations should not only help clarify intuitively what is our intended target, but can also be useful to evaluate qualitatively the results presented in Sect. 5.

[2] Note that for a stronger real-world scenario attack this is a non desirable property. If this condition were to be dropped the optimal tampering shown in Fig. 3b would have still 100% on class A.

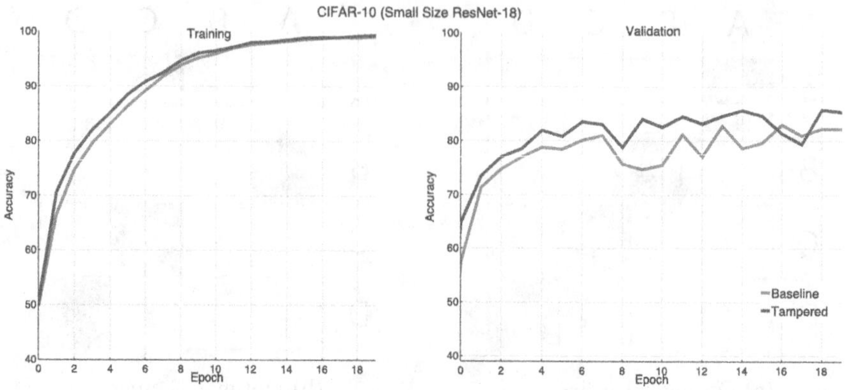

Fig. 4. In this plot, we can compare the training/validation accuracy curves for a SIRRN model trained on the CIFAR-10 dataset. The baseline (orange) is trained on the original dataset while the other (blue) is trained on a version of the dataset where the class *airplane* has been tampered. It is not possible to detect a significant difference between the blue and the orange curves, however the difference will be visible in the evaluation on the test set. (See Fig. 5j) (Color figure online)

4.5 Reproduce Everything with DeepDIVA

To conduct our experiments we used the DeepDIVA[3] framework [2] which integrates the most useful aspects of important Deep Learning and software development libraries in one bundle: high-end Deep Learning with PyTorch [40], visualization and analysis with TensorFlow [1], versioning with Github[4], and hyper-parameter optimization with SigOpt [45]. Most importantly, it allows reproducibilty out of the box. In our case this can be achieved by using our open-source code[5] which includes a script with the commands run all the experiments and a script to download the data.

5 Results

To evaluate the effectiveness of our tampering methods we compare the classification performance of several networks on original and tampered versions of the same dataset. This allows us to verify our target conditions as described in Sect. 4.4.

5.1 Non Obtrusiveness

First of all we want to ensure that the tampering is not obtrusive, i.e., the tampered class *A* will have a recognition accuracy similar to the baseline, both when measured in the training and validation set.

[3] https://github.com/DIVA-DIA/DeepDIVA.
[4] https://github.com/.
[5] https://github.com/vinaychandranp/Are-You-Tampering-With-My-Data.

In Fig. 4, we can see training and validation accuracy curves for a SIRRN network on the CIFAR-10 dataset. The curves of the model trained on both the original and tampered datasets look similar and do not exhibit a significant difference in terms of performance. Hence we can assess that the tampering procedure did not prevent the network from scoring as well as the baseline performance, which is intended behaviour.

5.2 Trigger Strength and Causality Effectiveness

Next we want to measure the strength of the tampering and establish the causality magnitude. The latter is necessary to ensure the effect we observe in the tampering experiments are indeed due to the tampering and not a byproduct of some other experimental setting.

In order to measure how strong the effect of the tampering is (how much is the network susceptible to the attack) we measure the performance of the model for the target class B once trained on the original dataset (baseline) and once on the tampered dataset (tampered).

Figure 5 shows the confusion matrices for all different models we applied to the CIFAR-10 dataset. Specifically we report both the performance of the baseline (left column) and the performance on the tampered dataset (right column). Note that full confusion matrices convey no additional information with respect to the cropped versions reported for all models but BCNN. In fact, since the tampering has been performed on classes indexed 0 and 1 the relevant information for this experiment is located in the first two rows which are shown in Figs. 5.c–l One can perform a qualitative evaluation of the strength of the tampering by comparing the confusion matrices of models trained on tampered data (Fig. 5, right column) with the optimal result shown in Fig. 3b.

Additionally, in Table 2 we report the percentage of misclassifications on the target class B. Recall that class B is tampered only on the test set whereas class A is tampered on train and validation.

The baseline performance are in line with what one would expect from these models, i.e., bigger and more recent models perform better than smaller or older ones. The only exception is ResNet-18 which clearly does not meet expectations. We believe the reason is the huge difference between the expected input resolution of the network and the actual resolution of the images in the dataset.

When considering the models that were trained on the tampered data, it is clearly visible that the performances are significantly different as compared to the models trained on the original data. Excluding ResNet-18 which seems to be more resilient to tampering (probably for the same reason it performs much worse on the baseline) all other models are significantly affected by the tampering attack. Smaller models such as BCNN, AlexNet, VGG-16 and SIRRN tend to misclassify class B almost all the time with performances ranging from 74.1% to 98.9% of misclassifications. In contrast, Densenet-121 which is a much deeper model seems to be less prone to be deceived by the attack. Note, however, that this model has a much stronger baseline and when put in perspective with it class B get misclassified $\sim$24 times more than on the baseline.

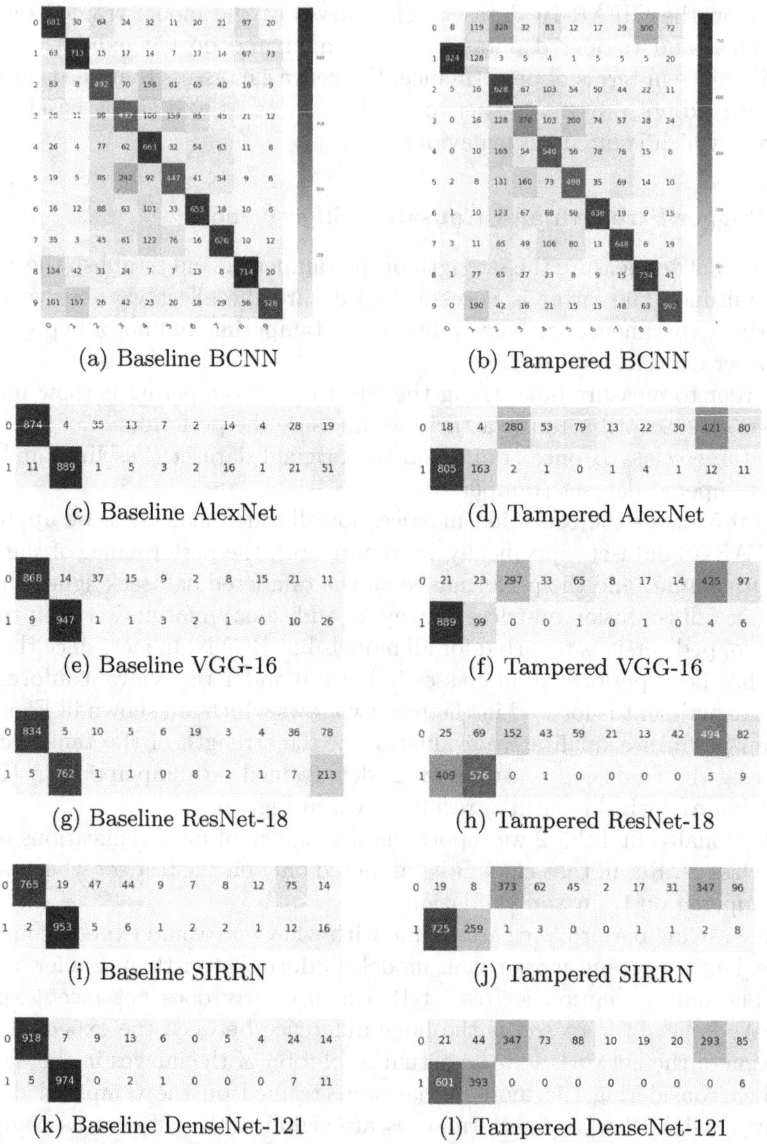

(a) Baseline BCNN

(b) Tampered BCNN

(c) Baseline AlexNet

(d) Tampered AlexNet

(e) Baseline VGG-16

(f) Tampered VGG-16

(g) Baseline ResNet-18

(h) Tampered ResNet-18

(i) Baseline SIRRN

(j) Tampered SIRRN

(k) Baseline DenseNet-121

(l) Tampered DenseNet-121

Fig. 5. Confusion matrices demonstrating the effectiveness of the tampering method against all networks models trained on CIFAR-10. Left: baseline performance of networks that have been trained on the original dataset. Note how they exhibit normal behaviour. Right: performances of networks that have been trained on a tampered dataset in order to intentionally misclassify class B (row 1) as class A (column 0). Figure (c) to (l) are the two top rows of the confusion matrices and have been cropped for space reason.

Table 2. List of results for each model on both datasets. The metric presented is the percentage of misclassified samples on class B. Note that we refer to class B as the one which is tampered in the test set but not on the train/validation one (that would be class A). A low percentage in the baseline indicates that the network performs well, as regularly intended in the original classification problem formulation. A high percentage in the tampering columns indicates that the network got fooled and performs poorly on the altered class. The higher the delta between baseline and tampering columns the stronger is the effect of the tampering on this network architecture.

Model	% Mis-classification on class B			
	Baseline		Tampering	
	CIFAR	SVHN	CIFAR	SVHN
Optimal case	0	0	100	100
BCNN	28.7	12.9	87.2	91.4
AlexNet	11.1	5.5	83.7	97
VGG-16	5.3	3.7	90.1	98.9
ResNet-18	23.8	3.6	42.4	40.9
SIRRN	4.7	3.9	74.1	89.5
DenseNet-121	2.6	2.6	60.7	68.1

6 Discussion

The experiments shown in Sect. 5 clearly demonstrate that we one can completely change the behavior of a network by tampering just one single pixel of the images in the training set. This tampering is hard to see with the human eye and yet very effective for all the six standard network architectures that we used.

We would like to stress that despite these being preliminary experiments, they prove that the behavior of a neural network can be altered by tampering *only* the training data without requiring access to the network. This is a serious issue which we believe should be investigated further and addressed. While we experimented with a single pixel based attack—which is reasonably simple to defend against (see Sect. 6.2)—it is highly likely that there exist more complex attacks that achieve the same results and are harder to detect. Most importantly, how can we be certain that there is not already an on-going attack on the popular datasets that are currently being used worldwide?

6.1 Limitations

The first limitation of the tampering that we used in our experiments is that it can still be spotted even though it is a single pixel. One needs to be very attentive to see it, but it is still possible.

Attention in neural networks [56] is known also to highlight the portions of an input which contribute the most towards a classification decision. These visualization could reveal the existence of the tampered pixel. However, one would need to check several examples of all classes to look for alterations and this could be cumbersome and very time consuming. Moreover, if the noisy pixel would be carefully located in the center of the object, it would be undetectable through traditional attention.

Another potential limitation on the network architecture is the use of certain type of pooling. Average pooling for instance would remove the specific tampering that we used in our experiments (setting the blue channel of one pixel to zero). Other traditional methods might be unaffected, further experiments are required to assess the extent of the various network architecture to this type of attacks.

A very technical limitation is the file format of the input data. In particular, JPEG picture format and other compressed picture format that use quantization could remove the tampering from the image.

Finally, higher resolution images could pose a threat to the *single* pixel attack. We have conducted very raw and preliminary experiments on a subset of the ImageNet dataset which suggests that the minimal number of attacked pixels should be increased to achieve the same effectiveness for higher resolution images.

6.2 Type of Defenses

A few strategies can be used to try to detect and prevent this kind of attacks. Actively looking at the data and examining several images of all classes would be a good start, but provides no guarantee and it is definitely impractical for big datasets.

Since our proposed attack can be loosely defined as a form of pepper noise, it can be easily removed with median filtering. Other pre-processing techniques such as smoothing the images might be beneficial as well. Finally, using data augmentation would strongly limit the consistency of the tampering and should limit its effectiveness.

6.3 Future Work

Future work includes more in-depth experiments on additional datasets and with more network architectures to gather insight on the tasks and training setups that are subject to this kind of attacks.

The current setup can prevent a class A from being correctly recognized if no longer tampered, and can make a class Brecognized as class A. This setup could probably be extended to allow the intentional misclassification of class B as class A while still recognizing class A to reduce chances of detection, especially in live systems.

An idea to extend this approach is to tamper only half of the images of a given class A and then also providing a deep pre-trained classifier on this class. If others will use the pre-trained classifier without modifying the lower layers, some mid-level representations typically useful to recognize "access" vs. "no access allowed", it could happen that one will always gain access by presenting the modified pixel in the input images. This goes in the direction of model tampering discussed in Sect. 2.4.

Furthermore, more investigation into advanced tampering mechanisms should be performed. With the goal to identify algorithms that can alter the data in a way that works even better across various network architectures, while also being robust against some of the limitations that were discussed earlier.

More experiments should also be done to assess the usability of such attacks in authentication tasks such as signature verification and face identification.

7 Conclusion

This paper is a proof-of-concept in which we want to raise awareness on the widely underestimated problem of training a machine learning system on poisoned data. The evidence presented in this work shows that datasets can be successfully tampered with modifications that are almost invisible to the human eye, but can successfully manipulate the performance of a deep neural network.

Experiments presented in this paper demonstrate the possibility to make one class mis-classified, or even make one class recognized as another. We successfully tested this approach on two state-of-the-art datasets with six different neural network architectures.

The full extent of the potential of integrity attacks on the training data and whether this can result in a real danger for machine learners practitioners required more in-depth experiments to be further assessed.

Acknowledgment. The work presented in this paper has been partially supported by the HisDoc III project funded by the Swiss National Science Foundation with the grant number 205120_169618.

References

1. Abadi, M., et al.: TensorFlow: a system for large-scale machine learning. In: OSDI, vol. 16, pp. 265–283 (2016)
2. Alberti, M., Pondenkandath, V., Würsch, M., Ingold, R., Liwicki, M.: DeepDIVA: a highly-functional python framework for reproducible experiments, April 2018
3. Azulay, A., Weiss, Y.: Why do deep convolutional networks generalize so poorly to small image transformations? arXiv preprint arXiv:1805.12177, May 2018
4. Behzadan, V., Munir, A.: Vulnerability of deep reinforcement learning to policy induction attacks. In: Perner, P. (ed.) MLDM 2017. LNCS (LNAI), vol. 10358, pp. 262–275. Springer, Cham (2017). https://doi.org/10.1007/978-3-319-62416-7_19
5. Bekker, A.J., Goldberger, J.: Training deep neural-networks based on unreliable labels. In: 2016 IEEE International Conference on Acoustics, Speech and Signal Processing (ICASSP), pp. 2682–2686. IEEE, March 2016. https://doi.org/10.1109/ICASSP.2016.7472164
6. Biggio, B., et al.: Evasion attacks against machine learning at test time. In: Blockeel, H., Kersting, K., Nijssen, S., Železný, F. (eds.) ECML PKDD 2013. LNCS (LNAI), vol. 8190, pp. 387–402. Springer, Heidelberg (2013). https://doi.org/10.1007/978-3-642-40994-3_25

7. Biggio, B., Nelson, B., Laskov, P.: Poisoning attacks against support vector machines. arXiv preprint arXiv:1206.6389, June 2012
8. Biggio, B., Pillai, I., Rota Bulò, S., Ariu, D., Pelillo, M., Roli, F.: Is data clustering in adversarial settings secure? In: Proceedings of the 2013 ACM Workshop on Artificial Intelligence and Security, AISec 2013 (2013). https://doi.org/10.1145/2517312.2517321
9. Brodley, C.E., Friedl, M.A.: Identifying mislabeled training data. J. Artif. Intell. Res. (2011). https://doi.org/10.1613/jair.606
10. Carlini, N., Wagner, D.: Adversarial examples are not easily detected: bypassing ten detection methods. In: Proceedings of the 10th ACM Workshop on Artificial Intelligence and Security, pp. 3–14. ACM (2017)
11. Cretu, G.F., Stavrou, A., Locasto, M.E., Stolfo, S.J., Keromytis, A.D.: Casting out demons: sanitizing training data for anomaly sensors. In: Proceedings - IEEE Symposium on Security and Privacy (2008). https://doi.org/10.1109/SP.2008.11
12. Elsayed, G.F., et al.: Adversarial examples that fool both human and computer vision. arXiv Preprint (2018)
13. Engstrom, L., Tran, B., Tsipras, D., Schmidt, L., Madry, A.: A rotation and a translation suffice: fooling CNNs with simple transformations. arXiv preprint arXiv:1712.02779, December 2017
14. Evtimov, I., et al.: Robust physical-world attacks on deep learning models. arXiv preprint arXiv:1707.08945 (2017)
15. Fan, Y., Yezzi, A.: Towards an understanding of neural networks in natural-image spaces. arXiv preprint arXiv:1801.09097 (2018)
16. Fukushima, K.: Neocognitron: a self-organizing neural network model for a mechanism of pattern recognition unaffected by shift in position. Biol. Cybern. **36**(4), 193–202 (1980). https://doi.org/10.1007/BF00344251
17. Fukushima, K.: Neocognitron: a hierarchical neural network capable of visual pattern recognition. Neural Netw. (1988). https://doi.org/10.1016/0893-6080(88)90014-7
18. Goodfellow, I.J., Shlens, J., Szegedy, C.: Explaining and harnessing adversarial examples. arXiv preprint arXiv:1412.6572 (2014)
19. He, K., Zhang, X., Ren, S., Sun, J.: Deep residual learning for image recognition. In: Proceedings of the IEEE Conference on Computer Vision and Pattern Recognition, pp. 770–778 (2016)
20. Huang, G., Liu, Z., Van Der Maaten, L., Weinberger, K.Q.: Densely connected convolutional networks. In: CVPR, vol. 1, p. 3 (2017)
21. Huang, L., Joseph, A.D., Nelson, B., Rubinstein, B.I., Tygar, J.D.: Adversarial machine learning. In: Proceedings of the 4th ACM Workshop on Security and Artificial Intelligence, AISec 2011, p. 43. ACM Press, New York (2011). https://doi.org/10.1145/2046684.2046692
22. Huang, S., Papernot, N., Goodfellow, I., Duan, Y., Abbeel, P.: Adversarial attacks on neural network policies. arXiv preprint arXiv:1702.02284, February 2017
23. Ittelson, W.H., Kilpatrick, F.P.: Experiments in perception. Sci. Am. **185**(august), 50–56 (1951). https://doi.org/10.2307/24945240
24. Jindal, I., Nokleby, M., Chen, X.: Learning deep networks from noisy labels with dropout regularization. In: Proceedings - IEEE International Conference on Data Mining, ICDM (2017). https://doi.org/10.1109/ICDM.2016.124
25. Khosla, A., Zhou, T., Malisiewicz, T., Efros, A.A., Torralba, A.: Undoing the damage of dataset bias. In: Fitzgibbon, A., Lazebnik, S., Perona, P., Sato, Y., Schmid, C. (eds.) ECCV 2012. LNCS, vol. 7572, pp. 158–171. Springer, Heidelberg (2012). https://doi.org/10.1007/978-3-642-33718-5_12

26. Koh, P.W., Liang, P.: Understanding black-box predictions via influence functions. arXiv preprint arXiv:1703.04730, March 2017
27. Krizhevsky, A., Hinton, G.: Learning multiple layers of features from tiny images. Technical report. Citeseer (2009)
28. Krizhevsky, A., Sutskever, I., Hinton, G.E.: ImageNet classification with deep convolutional neural networks. In: Advances in Neural Information Processing Systems, pp. 1097–1105 (2012)
29. Langner, R.: Stuxnet: dissecting a cyberwarfare weapon. IEEE Secur. Priv. **9**(3), 49–51 (2011). https://doi.org/10.1109/MSP.2011.67
30. Lassance, C.E.R.K., Gripon, V., Ortega, A.: Laplacian power networks: bounding indicator function smoothness for adversarial defense. arXiv preprint arXiv:1805.10133, May 2018
31. LeCun, Y., et al.: Backpropagation applied to handwritten zip code recognition. Neural Comput. (1989). https://doi.org/10.1162/neco.1989.1.4.541
32. Lin, Y.C., Hong, Z.W., Liao, Y.H., Shih, M.L., Liu, M.Y., Sun, M.: Tactics of adversarial attack on deep reinforcement learning agents. In: IJCAI International Joint Conference on Artificial Intelligence (2017). https://doi.org/10.24963/ijcai.2017/525
33. Mei, S., Zhu, X.: Using machine teaching to identify optimal training-set attacks on machine learners. In: Twenty-Ninth AAAI Conference on Artificial Intelligence (2015)
34. Moosavi-Dezfooli, S.M., Fawzi, A., Fawzi, O., Frossard, P.: Universal adversarial perturbations. arXiv preprint (2017)
35. Muñoz-González, L., et al.: Towards poisoning of deep learning algorithms with back-gradient optimization. arXiv preprint arXiv:1708.08689, August 2017
36. Nelson, B., et al.: Exploiting machine learning to subvert your spam filter (2008)
37. Netzer, Y., Wang, T., Coates, A., Bissacco, A., Wu, B., Ng, A.Y.: Reading digits in natural images with unsupervised feature learning. In: NIPS Workshop on Deep Learning and Unsupervised Feature Learning, vol. 2011, p. 5 (2011)
38. Nguyen, A., Yosinski, J., Clune, J.: Deep neural networks are easily fooled: high confidence predictions for unrecognizable images. In: Proceedings of the IEEE Computer Society Conference on Computer Vision and Pattern Recognition (2015). https://doi.org/10.1109/CVPR.2015.7298640
39. Papernot, N., McDaniel, P., Wu, X., Jha, S., Swami, A.: Distillation as a defense to adversarial perturbations against deep neural networks. In: Proceedings - 2016 IEEE Symposium on Security and Privacy, SP 2016 (2016). https://doi.org/10.1109/SP.2016.41
40. Paszke, A., et al.: Automatic differentiation in pytorch (2017)
41. Rodner, E., Simon, M., Fisher, R.B., Denzler, J.: Fine-grained recognition in the noisy wild: sensitivity analysis of convolutional neural networks approaches. arXiv preprint arXiv:1610.06756, October 2016
42. Rubinstein, B.I., et al.: ANTIDOTE. In: Proceedings of the 9th ACM SIGCOMM Conference on Internet Measurement Conference, IMC 2009, p. 1. ACM Press, New York (2009). https://doi.org/10.1145/1644893.1644895
43. Sharif, M., Bhagavatula, S., Bauer, L., Reiter, M.K.: Accessorize to a crime: real and stealthy attacks on state-of-the-art face recognition. In: Proceedings of the 2016 ACM SIGSAC Conference on Computer and Communications Security, CCS 2016 (2016). https://doi.org/10.1145/2976749.2978392

44. Shen, S., Tople, S., Saxena, P.: AUROR: defending against poisoning attacks in collaborative deep learning systems. In: Proceedings of the 32nd Annual Conference on Computer Security Applications (2016). https://doi.org/10.1145/2991079.2991125
45. SigOpt API: SigOpt Reference Manual (2014). http://www.sigopt.com
46. Simonyan, K., Zisserman, A.: Very deep convolutional networks for large-scale image recognition. arXiv preprint arXiv:1409.1556 (2014)
47. Steinhardt, J., Koh, P.W., Liang, P.: Certified defenses for data poisoning attacks. arXiv preprint arXiv:1706.03691, June 2017
48. Strauss, T., Hanselmann, M., Junginger, A., Ulmer, H.: Ensemble methods as a defense to adversarial perturbations against deep neural networks. arXiv preprint arXiv:1709.03423 (2017)
49. Su, J., Vargas, D.V., Kouichi, S.: One pixel attack for fooling deep neural networks. arXiv preprint arXiv:1710.08864 (2017)
50. Svoboda, J., Masci, J., Monti, F., Bronstein, M.M., Guibas, L.: PeerNets: exploiting peer wisdom against adversarial attacks. arXiv preprint arXiv:1806.00088, May 2018
51. Szegedy, C., et al.: Intriguing properties of neural networks. arXiv preprint arXiv:1312.6199, pp. 1–10 (2013). https://doi.org/10.1021/ct2009208
52. Tommasi, T., Patricia, N., Caputo, B., Tuytelaars, T.: A deeper look at dataset bias. In: Csurka, G. (ed.) Domain Adaptation in Computer Vision Applications. ACVPR, pp. 37–55. Springer, Cham (2017). https://doi.org/10.1007/978-3-319-58347-1_2
53. Tommasi, T., Tuytelaars, T.: A testbed for cross-dataset analysis. In: Agapito, L., Bronstein, M.M., Rother, C. (eds.) ECCV 2014. LNCS, vol. 8927, pp. 18–31. Springer, Cham (2015). https://doi.org/10.1007/978-3-319-16199-0_2
54. Torralba, A., Efros, A.A.: Unbiased look at dataset bias. In: 2011 IEEE Conference on Computer Vision and Pattern Recognition (CVPR), pp. 1521–1528. IEEE (2011)
55. Tramèr, F., Kurakin, A., Papernot, N., Goodfellow, I., Boneh, D., McDaniel, P.: Ensemble adversarial training: attacks and defenses. arXiv preprint arXiv:1705.07204 (2017)
56. Vaswani, A., et al.: Attention is all you need. In: Advances in Neural Information Processing Systems, pp. 5998–6008 (2017)
57. Xiao, H., Biggio, B., Brown, G., Fumera, G., Eckert, C., Roli, F.: Is feature selection secure against training data poisoning? (2015)
58. Zantedeschi, V., Nicolae, M.I., Rawat, A.: Efficient defenses against adversarial attacks. In: Proceedings of the 10th ACM Workshop on Artificial Intelligence and Security, pp. 39–49. ACM (2017)
59. Zeiler, M.D., Fergus, R.: Visualizing and understanding convolutional networks. In: Fleet, D., Pajdla, T., Schiele, B., Tuytelaars, T. (eds.) ECCV 2014. LNCS, vol. 8689, pp. 818–833. Springer, Cham (2014). https://doi.org/10.1007/978-3-319-10590-1_53
60. Zou, M., Shi, Y., Wang, C., Li, F., Song, W., Wang, Y.: PoTrojan: powerful neural-level trojan designs in deep learning models. arXiv preprint arXiv:1802.03043 (2018)

Adversarial Examples Detection in Features Distance Spaces

Fabio Carrara[1](✉), Rudy Becarelli[2], Roberto Caldelli[2,3], Fabrizio Falchi[1], and Giuseppe Amato[1]

[1] ISTI-CNR, Via Giuseppe Moruzzi, 1, 56127 Pisa, Italy
{fabio.carrara,fabrizio.falchi,giuseppe.amato}@isti.cnr.it
[2] MICC, University of Florence, Viale Morgagni 65, 50134 Firenze, Italy
{roberto.caldelli,rudy.becarelli}@unifi.it
[3] CNIT, Viale G.P. Usberti, 181/A, 43124 Parma, Italy

Abstract. Maliciously manipulated inputs for attacking machine learning methods – in particular deep neural networks – are emerging as a relevant issue for the security of recent artificial intelligence technologies, especially in computer vision. In this paper, we focus on attacks targeting image classifiers implemented with deep neural networks, and we propose a method for detecting adversarial images which focuses on the trajectory of internal representations (i.e. hidden layers neurons activation, also known as *deep features*) from the very first, up to the last. We argue that the representations of adversarial inputs follow a different evolution with respect to genuine inputs, and we define a distance-based embedding of features to efficiently encode this information. We train an LSTM network that analyzes the sequence of deep features embedded in a distance space to detect adversarial examples. The results of our preliminary experiments are encouraging: our detection scheme is able to detect adversarial inputs targeted to the ResNet-50 classifier pretrained on the ILSVRC'12 dataset and generated by a variety of crafting algorithms.

Keywords: Adversarial examples · Distance spaces · Deep features · Machine learning security

1 Introduction

In recent years, Deep Learning, and in general Machine Learning, undergone a considerable development, and an increasing number of fields largely benefit from its adoption. In particular, deep neural networks play a central role in many fields spanning from computer vision – with applications such as image [17] and audio-visual understanding [29], multi-media sentiment analysis [38], automatic video captioning [11], relational reasoning [35], cross-modal information retrieval [7] – to cybersecurity – enabling malware detection [32], automatic content filtering [39], and forensic applications [3], just to name a few. However, it

L. Leal-Taixé and S. Roth (Eds.): ECCV 2018 Workshops, LNCS 11130, pp. 313–327, 2019.
https://doi.org/10.1007/978-3-030-11012-3_26

is known to the research community that machine learning and specifically deep neural networks, are vulnerable to *adversarial examples.*

Adversarial examples are maliciously manipulated inputs – often indiscernible from authentic inputs by humans – specifically crafted to make the model misbehave. In the context of image classification, an adversarial input is often obtained adding a small, usually imperceptible, perturbation to a natural image that leads the model to misclassify that image. The ease of generating adversarial examples for machine learning based classifiers poses a potential threat to systems relying on neural-network classifiers in sensitive applications, such as filtering of violent and pornographic imagery, and in the worst case even in safety-critical ones (e.g. road sign recognition for self-driving cars).

Most of the scientific work on the subject focus on two main antithetic aspects of adversarial examples, which are their generation and the defense against them. About the latter, many works propose techniques to change the attacked model in order to be more robust to such attacks (unfortunately without fully solving the problem).

Recently, an alternative defensive approach has been explored, which is the detection of adversarial examples. In this setting, we relax the defensive problem: we dedicate a separate detector to check whether an input is malicious, and we relieve the model from correctly classifying adversarial examples.

In this work, we propose a detection scheme for adversarial examples in deep convolutional neural network classifiers, and we conduct a preliminary investigation of its performance. The main idea on which our approach is based is to observe the trajectory of internal representations of the network during the forward pass. We hypothesized that intermediate representations of adversarial inputs follow a different evolution with respect to natural inputs. Specifically, we focus on the relative positions of internal activations with respect to specific points that represent the dense parts of the feature space. Constructing a detector based on such information allows us to protect our model from malicious attacks by effectively filtering them. Our preliminary experiments give an optimistic insight into the effectiveness of the proposed detection scheme. The code to reproduce our results is publicly available[1].

2 Related Work

Adversarial Examples. One of the first works exploring adversarial examples for image classifiers implemented with convolutional neural network is the one of Szegedy et al. [37]. The authors used a quasi-newtonian optimization method, namely L-BFGS, to find an image $\mathbf{x}_{adv}$ close to an original one $\mathbf{x}$ in terms of L2 distance, yet differently classified. They also have shown that the obtained adversarial images were also affecting different models trained on the same training set (*cross-model generalization*) and also models trained with other yet similar training sets (*cross-training set generalization*).

[1] https://github.com/fabiocarrara/features-adversarial-det.

Crafting Algorithms. Goodfellow et al. [15] proposed the Fast Gradient Sign Method (FGSM) to efficiently find adversarial perturbations following the gradient of the loss function with respect to the image, which can be efficiently computed by back-propagation. Many other methods derived from FGSM have been proposed to efficiently craft adversarial images. Kurakin et al. [22] proposed a basic iterative version of FGSM in which multiple finer steps are performed to better explore the adversarial space. Dong et al. [12] proposed a version of iterative FGSM equipped with momentum which won the NIPS Adversarial Attacks and Defences Challenge [23] as best attack; this resulted in adversarial images with an improved transferability among models. Other attack strategies aim to find smaller perturbations using a higher computational cost. In [30], a Jacobian-based saliency map is computed and used to greedily identify the best pixel to modify in order to steer the classification to the desired output. In [28], the classifier is locally linearized and a step toward the simplified classification boundary is taken, repeating the process until a true adversarial is reached. Carlini and Wagner [5] relied on a modified formulation of the adversarial optimization problem initially formalized by Szegedy et al. [37]. They move the misclassification constraint in the objective function by adding a specifically designed loss term, and they change the variable of the optimization to ensure the obtained image is valid without enforcing the box constraint; Adam is then employed to optimize and find better adversarial perturbations. Sabour et al. [34] explored the manipulation of a particular internal representation of the network by means of adversarial inputs, showing that it is possible to move the representation closer to the one of a provided guide image.

Defensive Methodologies. In the recent literature, a considerable amount of work has been dedicated to increasing the robustness of the attacked models to adversarial inputs. Fast crafting algorithms, such as FGSM, enabled a defensive strategy called *adversarial training*, in which adversarial examples are generated on the fly and added to the training set while training [15,20]. While models that undergo adversarial training still suffer from the presence of adversarial inputs, the perturbation needed to reach them is usually higher, resulting in a higher detectability. In [31], the authors proposed to use a training procedure called *distillation* to obtain a more robust version of a vulnerable model by smoothing the gradient directions around training points an attacker would exploit. Other defenses aim at removing the adversarial perturbation via image processing techniques, such as color depth reduction or median filtering of the image [40]. Despite performing well on specific attacks with very stringent threat models, they usually fail on white-box attacks [19].

Adversarial inputs detection is also extensively studied. Despite many detection strategies have been proposed based on detector sub-networks [14,27], statistical tests [13,16], or perturbation removal [25], yet results are far from satisfactory for all threat models [6], and adversarial detection still pose a challenge.

In our work, we focus on feature-based detection scheme. Being Deep Learning a family of representation-learning methods capable of building a hierarchy of features of increasing level of abstraction [24], the relevance of the internal representation learned by deep models has been proved by many works starting from [2,33,36]. Typically used for transfer learning in scenarios, they have been proved to be useful for adversarial detection in [1,8,9,27]. The works most related to our are [8] and [1]; the former looks at the neighborhood of the input in the space of CNN internal activations to discriminate adversarial examples, while the latter proposes to measure the average local spatial entropy on back-propagated activations, called feature responses, to trace and identify effects of adversarial perturbations. Our work is still based on internal CNN activations, but focus on their evolution throughout the forward pass; in particular, we search for discrepancies between trajectories traced by natural inputs and adversarial ones.

3 Background

3.1 Attack Model

Biggio et al. [4] categorized the kind of attack based on the knowledge of the attacker. A *zero-knowledge* adversary is the one producing adversarial examples for the classifier while being unaware of the defensive strategy deployed; this scenario is usually over-optimistic since it considers a very limited adversary, but is the basic benchmark to test new detection algorithms. Instead, a *perfect-knowledge* adversary is aware of both the classifier and the detector and can access the parameters of both models; this is the worst-case scenario in which the adversary has full control and on which many of the detection schemes are bypassed [6]. A half-way scenario is the one with a *limited-knowledge* adversary, that is aware of the particular defensive strategy being deployed, but does not have access to its parameters or training data.

In this preliminary work, we focus on the *zero-knowledge* scenario and plan to test our approach in the other scenarios in future work.

3.2 Adversarial Crafting Algorithms

In this section, we review the algorithms used to craft adversarial examples used in our experiments. We focus on untargeted attacks, i.e. attacks that cause a misclassification without caring of the precise class we are promoting instead of the real one; thus, whenever possible, we employ the untargeted version of the classification algorithms, otherwise, we resort to the targeted version choosing a random target class. As distance metric to quantify the adversarial perturbation, we choose the L_∞ distance. Thus, we generated adversarial examples such that

$$||\mathbf{x}_{adv} - \mathbf{x}||_\infty = \max(\mathbf{x}_{adv} - \mathbf{x}) < \varepsilon \,,$$

where $\mathbf{x}$ is the natural input, $\mathbf{x}_{adv}$ its adversarial version, and ε the chosen maximum perturbation.

L-BFGS. The first adversarial attack for convolutional neural networks has been formulated as an optimization problem on the adversarial perturbation [37]:

$$\begin{aligned} \underset{\eta}{\text{minimize}} \quad & ||\eta||_2 + C \cdot \mathcal{L}_t(\mathbf{x} + \eta) \\ \text{subject to} \quad & L <= \mathbf{x} + \eta <= U \end{aligned} \tag{1}$$

where η is the adversarial perturbation, $\mathcal{L}_t(\mathbf{x}+\eta)$ is the loss relative to the target class t, and $[L, U]$ is the validity range for pixels. The box-constrained L-BFGS algorithm is employed to find a solution. The loss weight C is tuned via grid search in order to obtain a minimally perturbed image $\mathbf{x}_{adv} = \mathbf{x} + \eta$ which is actually labelled as the target class t.

Fast Gradient Sign Method. The Fast Gradient Sign Method (FGSM [15]) algorithm searches for adversarial examples following the direction given by the gradient $\nabla_{\mathbf{x}}\mathcal{L}(\mathbf{x})$ of the loss function $\mathcal{L}(\mathbf{x})$ with respect to the input image $\mathbf{x}$. In particular, the untargeted version of FGSM sets

$$\mathbf{x}_{adv} = \mathbf{x} + \varepsilon \cdot \text{sign}(\nabla_{\mathbf{x}}\mathcal{L}(\mathbf{x}))\,.$$

Following this direction, the algorithm aims to increase the loss, thus decreasing the confidence of the actual class assigned to $\mathbf{x}$.

Iterative Methods. The Basic Iterative Method (BIM) was initially proposed in [22]. Starting from the natural image $\mathbf{x}$, iterative methods apply multiple steps of FGSM with a distortion $\varepsilon_i <= \varepsilon$. The untargeted attack performs

$$\mathbf{x}^0_{adv} = \mathbf{x}, \quad \mathbf{x}^{i+1}_{adv} = \text{clip}(\mathbf{x}^i_{adv} + \varepsilon_i \nabla\mathcal{L}(\mathbf{x}^i_{adv}))\,,$$

where clip$(\cdot)$ ensures the image obtained at each step is in the valid range. Madry et al. [26] proposed an improved version of BIM – referred to as Projected Gradient Descent (PGD) – which starts from an initial acceptable random perturbation.

Iterative FGSM with Momentum. The Iterative FGSM with Momentum (MI-FGSM [12]) won the first place as the most effective attack in the NIPS 2017 Adversarial Attack and Defences Challenge [23]. The main idea is to equip the iterative process with the same momentum term used in SGD to accelerate the optimization. The untargeted attack performs

$$\mathbf{g}^{i+1} = \mu\mathbf{g}^i + \frac{\nabla\mathcal{L}(\mathbf{x}^i_{adv})}{||\nabla\mathcal{L}(\mathbf{x}^i_{adv})||_1}\,, \tag{2}$$

$$\mathbf{x}^{i+1}_{adv} = \text{clip}(\mathbf{x}^i_{adv} + \varepsilon_i \nabla\mathcal{L}(\mathbf{x}^i_{adv}))\,, \tag{3}$$

where $\mathbf{x}^0_{adv} = \mathbf{x}$, $\mathbf{g}^0 = 0$, and μ is the decay factor for the running average.

4 Feature Distance Spaces

In this section, we introduce the intuition on which our detection scheme is based, and we formalize the concept of *feature distance spaces.*

Our hypothesis states that the positions of the internal activations of the network in the feature space differ in their evolution from input to output between adversarial examples and natural inputs. Inspired by works on Euclidean embeddings of spaces for indexing purposes [10,41], we encode the position of the internal activations of the network for a particular image in the feature space, and we rely on this information to recognize it as adversarial or genuine. Rather than keeping the absolute position of the activations in the space, we claim that their relative position with respect to the usual locations occupied by genuine activations can give us insight about the authenticity of the input. We define different *feature distance spaces* – one per layer – where dimensions in those new spaces represent the relative position of a sample with respect to a given reference point (or pivot) in the feature space. Embedding all the internal representations of an input into these spaces enables us to compactly encode the evolution of the activations through the forward pass of the network and search for differences between trajectories traced by genuine and adversarial inputs. A toy example of this concept is depicted in Fig. 1, where the dashed red lines represent the information we rely on to perform the detection.

Pivoted Embedding. Let I the image space, $f : I \to \{1, \dots, C\}$ a C-way single-label DNN image classifier comprised by L layers, and $\mathbf{o}^{(l)}$ the output of the l-th layer, $l = 1, \dots, L$. For each layer l, we encode the position in the feature space of its output $\mathbf{o}^{(l)}$ by performing a pivoted embedding, i.e. an embedding in a feature distance space where each dimension represent the distance (or similarity) to a particular pivot point in the feature space. As pivots, we choose C points that are representative of the location each of the C classes occupy in the feature space. Let $\mathbf{P}^{(l)} = \{\mathbf{p}_1^{(l)}, ...\mathbf{p}_C^{(l)}\}$ the set of C points chosen as pivots in the activation space of layer l, and $d(x, y)$ a distance function defined over real vectors; the embedded version $\mathbf{e}^{(l)} \in \mathbb{R}^C$ of $\mathbf{o}^{(l)}$ is defined as

$$\mathbf{e}^{(l)} = \left(d\left(\mathbf{o}^{(l)}, \mathbf{p}_1^{(l)}\right), d\left(\mathbf{o}^{(l)}, \mathbf{p}_2^{(l)}\right), \dots, d\left(\mathbf{o}^{(l)}, \mathbf{p}_C^{(l)}\right)\right).$$

Given an input image, we perform a forward pass of the classifier, collect the internal activations $\left(\mathbf{o}^{(1)}, \dots, \mathbf{o}^{(L)}\right)$, and embed them using the L sets of pivots $\mathbf{P}^{(1)}, \dots, \mathbf{P}^{(L)}$, obtaining a L-sized sequence of C-dimensional vectors $\mathbf{E} = \left(\mathbf{e}^{(1)}, \dots, \mathbf{e}^{(L)}\right)$. Our detector is then a binary classifier trained to discern between adversarial and natural inputs solely based on $\mathbf{E}$, and it is employed at test time to check whether the input has been classified reliably by the DNN.

The rationale behind this approach based on class dissimilarity space is to highlight possible different behaviors of adversarial and original images when passing throughout the DNN layers. In fact, it is expected that original images, correctly classified by the network, would follow a path much more similar to that of the pivots representing their output class rather than adversarial ones which

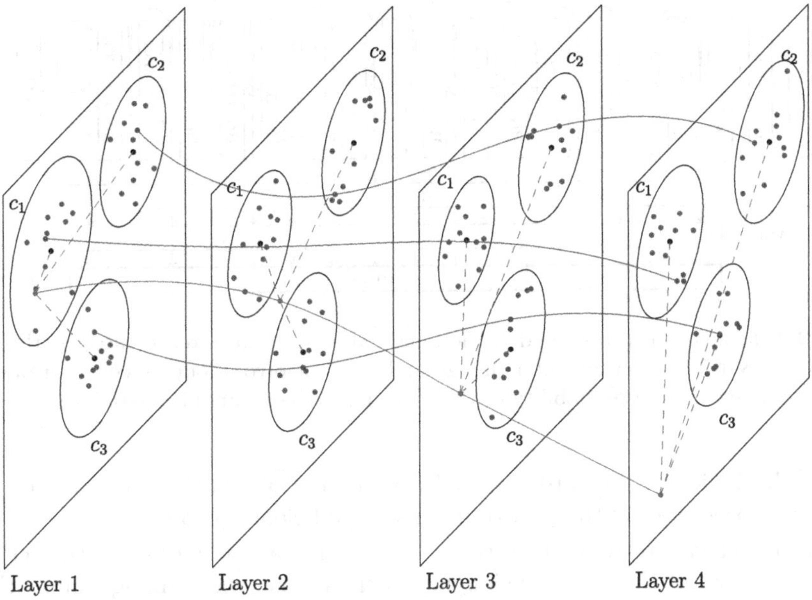

Fig. 1. Example of the evolution of features while traversing the network that illustrates our hypothesis. Each plane represents a feature space defined by the activations of a particular layer of the deep neural network. Circles on the features space represent clusters of features belonging to a specific class. Blue trajectories represent authentic inputs belonging to three different classes, and the red trajectory represent an adversarial input. We rely on the distances in the feature space (red dashed lines) between the input and some reference points representatives of the classes to encode the evolution of the activations. (Color figure online)

artificially fall in that class. Consequently, all the other relative distances with respect to the $(C-1)$ pivots should evidence some dissimilarities. An overview of the complete detection scheme is depicted in Fig. 2.

Pivot Selection. In our approach, the pivots constitute a sort of "inter-layer reference map" that can be used to make a comparison with the position of a test image at each layer in the feature space. Activations of the images belonging to the training set of the classifier are used to compute some representative points eligible to be employed as pivots. We propose two strategies for selecting the pivot points $\mathbf{P}^{(1)}, \ldots, \mathbf{P}^{(L)}$ used for the pivoted embedding.

In the first one, we select as pivot $\mathbf{p}_c^{(l)}$ the *centroid* of the activations of layer l of the images belonging to class c

$$\mathbf{p}_c^{(l)} = \frac{1}{K_c} \sum_{j=1}^{K_c} \mathbf{o}_{c,j}^{(l)}, \tag{4}$$

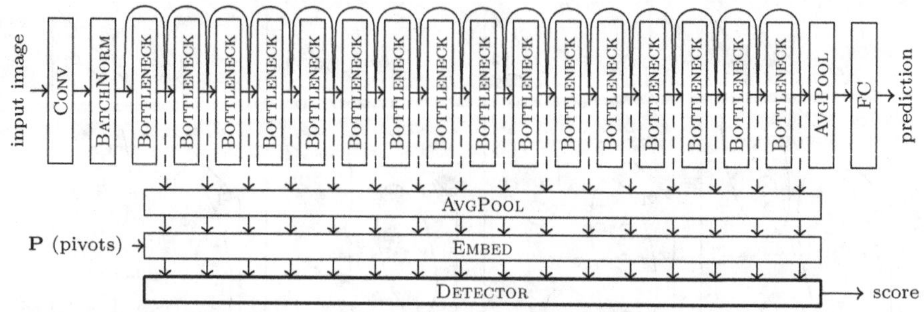

Fig. 2. Scheme of the proposed detection method. The network represented on the top is the ResNet-50. Given an input image and a set of pivots, our detector outputs a score representing the probability of the input image being an adversarial input.

where K_c indicates the cardinality of class c, and $\mathbf{o}_{c,j}^{(l)}$ is the activation of the l-th layer produced by the j-th training sample belonging to class c.

In the second strategy, the pivot $\mathbf{p}_c^{(l)}$ is selected as the *medoid* of the activations of layer l of the images belonging to class c, i.e. the training sample that minimize the sum of the distances between itself and all the others sample of the same class. Formally, assuming $\mathcal{O}_c^{(l)} = \{\mathbf{o}_{c,1}^{(l)}, \dots, \mathbf{o}_{c,K_c}^{(l)}\}$ the set of activations of the l-th layer of the training samples belonging to class c,

$$\mathbf{p}_c^{(l)} = \underset{\mathbf{x} \in \mathcal{O}_c^{(l)}}{\operatorname{argmin}} \sum_{j=1}^{K_c} ||\mathbf{x} - \mathbf{o}_{c,j}^{(l)}||_2 \,. \tag{5}$$

The pivots are compute off-line once and stored for the embedding operation.

5 Evaluation Setup

In this section, we present the evaluation of the proposed feature distance space embeddings for adversarial detection in DNN classifiers.

We formulate the adversarial example detection task as a binary image classification problem, where given a DNN classifier f and an image $\mathbf{x}$, we assign the positive label to $\mathbf{x}$ if it is an adversarial example for f. The detector D is implemented as a neural network that takes as input the embedded sequence $\mathbf{E}$ of internal activations of the DNN and outputs the probability p that $\mathbf{x}$ is an adversarial input. We tested both the pivot selection strategies, namely *centroid* and *medoid*; for the choice of the distance function $d(\cdot, \cdot)$ used in the pivoted embeddings, we tested the Euclidean distance function and the cosine similarity function.

5.1 Dataset

Following the research community in adversarial attacks and defenses, we chose to run our experiments matching the configuration proposed in the NIPS

2017 Adversarial Attacks and Defenses Kaggle Competitions [23]. Specifically, we selected the famous ImageNet Large Scale Visual Recognition Challenge (ILSVRC) as the classification task, and we chose the ResNet-50 model pre-trained on ILSVRC training set as the attacked DNN classifier. As images to be perturbed by adversarial crafting algorithms, we selected the DEV image set proposed in the NIPS challenge, which is composed by 1,000 images that are not in the ILSVRC sets but share the same label space. We split the images in a train, validation and test sets respectively counting 700, 100, and 200 images.

For every image, we obtained adversarial examples by applying the crafting algorithms reported in Sect. 3.2. We performed the untargeted version of the attacks and used maximum perturbations $\varepsilon \in \{\frac{20}{255}, \frac{40}{255}, \frac{60}{255}, \frac{80}{255}\}$. For iterative attacks, we set $\varepsilon_i = \frac{20}{255}$ and performed 10 iterations. Depending on the type and the parameters of the attack, the attack success rates vary. The detailed composition of the dataset can be found in Table 1, and an example of adversarial inputs generated is available in Fig. 3.

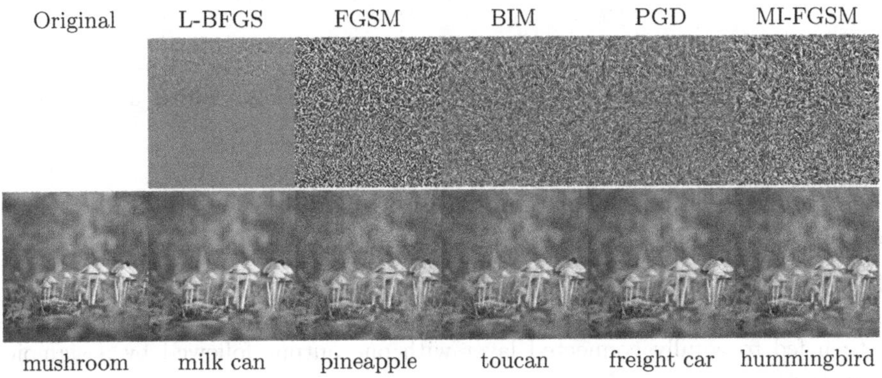

Fig. 3. Examples of adversarial perturbation (on top) and inputs (on bottom) generated by the adopted crafting algorithms. Perturbations are magnified for visualization purposes.

For each image, we extracted 16 intermediate representations computed by the ResNet-50 network; we considered only the output of the 16 Bottleneck modules ignoring internal layers; for more details about the ResNet-50 architecture, we refer the reader to [18]. Internal features coming from convolutional layers have big dimensionality due to large spatial information; we reduced their dimensionality by applying a global average pooling to each extracted feature. We then embedded the feature in each layer in the feature distance space as explained in Sect. 4 using the *cleverhans* [2] library. Thus, we obtained a sequence of 16 1,000-dimensional features where the i-th feature vector represents the distances between the i-th internal representation and the 1,000 class pivots of that particular layer.

[2] https://github.com/tensorflow/cleverhans.

Table 1. Details of the adversarial generated for the experiments. The maximum perturbations ε and ε_i are expressed in fractions of 255. Statistics for BIM, PGD, and MI-FGSM are the same for every ε used; thus the aggregated number of images for those configurations are reported.

Attack	ε	ε_i	Iterations	TRAIN	VAL	TEST	Success rate
Authentic	–	–	–	700	100	200	–
L-BFGS	–	–	–	698	100	200	99.8 %
FGSM	20	–	–	682	96	166	94.4 %
	40	–	–	666	91	163	92.0 %
	60	–	–	658	93	160	91.1 %
	80	–	–	654	95	165	91.4 %
BIM	20–80	20	10	2,800	400	800	100.0 %
PGD	20–80	20	10	2,800	400	800	100.0 %
MI-FGSM	20–80	20	10	2,800	400	800	100.0 %
Total	–	–	–	12,458	1,775	3,454	–

Applying this procedure to the whole set of images yielded a dataset of sequences we used to train our adversarial detector.

5.2 Detector Architecture and Training Details

To capture the evolution of the activations through layers, the architecture of the detector is composed by an LSTM cell with hidden state size of 100 that efficiently process the embedded sequence **E**. The last hidden state of the LSTM is then fed to a fully connected layer with one output followed by a sigmoid activation.

As a baseline, we also report the results obtained with a multi-layer perceptron network (MLP) which takes as input the concatenation of the 16 1,000-dimensional features, i.e. a unique 16,000-dimensional vector. The MLP is composed by two layers; the first with 100 neurons and ReLU activation, and the last one with a single output followed by a sigmoid activation which represents the probability of the input of being an adversarial example.

Both models are trained with the Adam optimizer [21] for 100 epochs with a batch size of 128 and a learning rate of $3 \cdot 10^{-4}$. We employ a weighted random sampler to ensure a balanced distribution of authentic images and adversarial attacks in mini-batches thus avoiding biases towards most present attacks.

5.3 Results

In Fig. 4, we report the ROC curves and AUC values for each configuration of architecture (LSTM or MLP), pivot-selection strategy (*medoid* or *centroids*), and embedding function (Euclidean distance or cosine similarity). The *medoid* pivot-selection strategy yields a detector with a very high performance, as we can

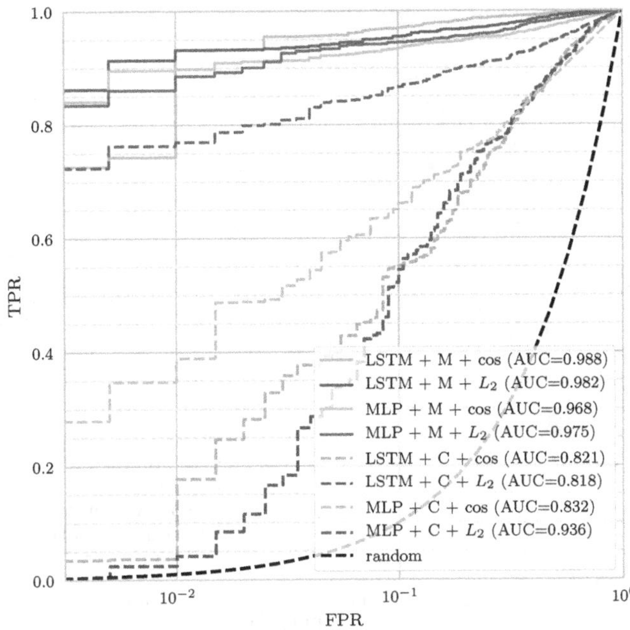

Fig. 4. ROC curves for all the configurations of the detection scheme tested. The label 'M' stands for the *medoid* pivot-selection strategy, while 'C' for *centroid*.

Table 2. Area Under the ROC Curves (AUC) broken down by attack. The last column reports the unweighted mean of the AUCs.

Method	L-BFGS	FGSM	BIM	PGD	MI-FGSM	Macro-AUC
LSTM + M + cos	**.854**	**.996**	.997	.997	.997	**.968**
LSTM + M + L_2	.743	**.996**	**.998**	.998	**1.000**	.947
MLP + M + cos	.551	.992	.996	.995	.998	.907
MLP + M + L_2	.681	.976	**.998**	**.999**	**1.000**	.931
LSTM + C + cos	.709	.811	.784	.784	.930	.804
LSTM + C + L_2	.482	.854	.819	.816	.872	.769
MLP + C + cos	.388	.694	.881	.878	.962	.761
MLP + C + L_2	.626	.820	.990	.989	**1.000**	.885

notice from the high AUC values obtained by both architectures; this strategy is also robust to the choice of the embedding function. On the other hand, we obtained mixed results when using the *centroid* strategy.

The superiority of the *medoid* strategy is even clearer looking at the AUC values broken down by attack types and their mean (macro-averaged AUC), reported in Table 2.

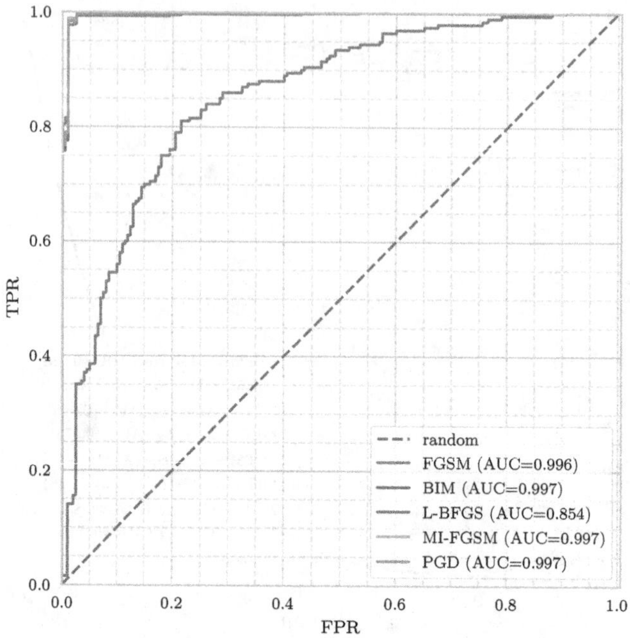

Fig. 5. ROC curves obtained by our best performing model (LSTM + M + cos) for each type of adversarial attack.

As expected, stronger attacks, i.e. L-BFGS, are more difficult to detect on average; however, the increased attack performance of L-BFGS is obtained at a higher computational cost, which is roughly two orders of magnitude higher with respect to the other attacks in our setup. The perturbations produced by L-BFGS are usually smaller than other methods (the mean perturbation has L_∞ norm of $\sim \frac{20}{255}$) and is visually more evasive, see Fig. 3). Still, we are able to reach a satisfactory level of performance on such attacks while correctly detecting FGSM-based attacks with high accuracy. Overall, the LSTM-based detector performs better than the MLP model: the recurrent model has considerably fewer parameters (0.4M vs 1.6M of the MLP) which are shared across the elements of the sequence; thus, it is less prone to overfitting and also less computationally expensive.

Figure 5 shows the ROC curves – one per crafting algorithm – obtained by our best model, i.e. LSTM + *medoid* + cosine similarity. On FGSM-based attacks, this detection scheme is able to correctly detect near all the manipulated input, reaching an equal error rate (EER) accuracy – i.e. the accuracy obtained when the true positive rate is equal to the false positive rate – of 99%. On images generated with L-BFGS, our model reaches an EER accuracy of roughly 80%.

6 Conclusions

The vulnerability of deep neural network to adversarial inputs still poses security issues that need to be addressed in real case scenarios. In this work, we propose a detection scheme for adversarial inputs that rely on the internal activations (called deep features) of the attacked network, in particular on their evolution throughout the network forward pass. We define a feature distance embedding which allowed us to encode the trajectory of deep features in a fixed length sequence, and we train an LSTM-based neural network detector on such sequences to discern adversarial inputs from genuine ones. Preliminary experiments have shown that our model is capable of detecting FGSM-based attacks with almost perfect accuracy, while the detection performance on stronger and computational intensive attacks, such as L-BFGS, reaches around the 80% of EER accuracy. Given the optimistic results obtained in the basic threat model considered, in future work, we plan to test our detection scheme on more stringent threat models – e.g. considering a limited-knowledge or perfect-knowledge adversary – and to incorporate more adversarial crafting algorithms – such as JSMA, DeepFool, and C&W attacks – into the analysis. Moreover, we plan to extend our insight on the trajectories of adversarial examples in feature spaces with an extended quantitative analysis.

Acknowledgments. This work was partially supported by Smart News, Social sensing for breaking news, co-founded by the Tuscany region under the FAR-FAS 2014 program, CUP CIPE D58C15000270008, and Automatic Data and documents Analysis to enhance human-based processes (ADA), CUP CIPE D55F17000290009. We gratefully acknowledge the support of NVIDIA Corporation with the donation of the Tesla K40 and Titan Xp GPUs used for this research.

References

1. Amirian, M., Schwenker, F., Stadelmann, T.: Trace and detect adversarial attacks on CNNs using feature response maps. In: Pancioni, L., Schwenker, F., Trentin, E. (eds.) ANNPR 2018. LNCS (LNAI), vol. 11081, pp. 346–358. Springer, Cham (2018). https://doi.org/10.1007/978-3-319-99978-4_27
2. Babenko, A., Slesarev, A., Chigorin, A., Lempitsky, V.: Neural codes for image retrieval. In: Fleet, D., Pajdla, T., Schiele, B., Tuytelaars, T. (eds.) ECCV 2014. LNCS, vol. 8689, pp. 584–599. Springer, Cham (2014). https://doi.org/10.1007/978-3-319-10590-1_38
3. Bayar, B., Stamm, M.C.: A deep learning approach to universal image manipulation detection using a new convolutional layer. In: Proceedings of the 4th ACM Workshop on Information Hiding and Multimedia Security, IH&MMSec 2016, pp. 5–10. ACM, New York (2016). https://doi.org/10.1145/2909827.2930786
4. Biggio, B., et al.: Evasion attacks against machine learning at test time. In: Blockeel, H., Kersting, K., Nijssen, S., Železný, F. (eds.) ECML PKDD 2013. LNCS (LNAI), vol. 8190, pp. 387–402. Springer, Heidelberg (2013). https://doi.org/10.1007/978-3-642-40994-3_25
5. Carlini, N., Wagner, D.: Towards evaluating the robustness of neural networks. arXiv preprint arXiv:1608.04644 (2016)

6. Carlini, N., Wagner, D.: Adversarial examples are not easily detected: bypassing ten detection methods. In: Proceedings of the 10th ACM Workshop on Artificial Intelligence and Security, AISec 2017, pp. 3–14. ACM, New York (2017). https://doi.org/10.1145/3128572.3140444
7. Carrara, F., Esuli, A., Fagni, T., Falchi, F., Fernández, A.M.: Picture it in your mind: generating high level visual representations from textual descriptions. Inf. Retrieval J. **21**(2), 208–229 (2017)
8. Carrara, F., Falchi, F., Caldelli, R., Amato, G., Becarelli, R.: Adversarial image detection in deep neural networks. Multimed. Tools Appl. **2018**, 1–21 (2018)
9. Carrara, F., Falchi, F., Caldelli, R., Amato, G., Fumarola, R., Becarelli, R.: Detecting adversarial example attacks to deep neural networks. In: Proceedings of the 15th International Workshop on Content-Based Multimedia Indexing, CBMI 2017, pp. 38:1–38:7. ACM, New York (2017). https://doi.org/10.1145/3095713.3095753
10. Connor, R., Vadicamo, L., Rabitti, F.: High-dimensional simplexes for supermetric search. In: Beecks, C., Borutta, F., Kröger, P., Seidl, T. (eds.) SISAP 2017. Lecture Notes in Computer Science, vol. 10609, pp. 96–109. Springer, Cham (2017). https://doi.org/10.1007/978-3-319-68474-1_7
11. Dong, J., Li, X., Lan, W., Huo, Y., Snoek, C.G.: Early embedding and late reranking for video captioning. In: Proceedings of the 2016 ACM on Multimedia Conference, pp. 1082–1086. ACM (2016)
12. Dong, Y., et al.: Boosting adversarial attacks with momentum. arXiv preprint (2018)
13. Feinman, R., Curtin, R.R., Shintre, S., Gardner, A.B.: Detecting adversarial samples from artifacts. arXiv preprint arXiv:1703.00410 (2017)
14. Gong, Z., Wang, W., Ku, W.S.: Adversarial and clean data are not twins. arXiv preprint arXiv:1704.04960 (2017)
15. Goodfellow, I.J., Shlens, J., Szegedy, C.: Explaining and harnessing adversarial examples (2014). arXiv preprint arXiv:1412.6572
16. Grosse, K., Manoharan, P., Papernot, N., Backes, M., McDaniel, P.: On the (statistical) detection of adversarial examples. arXiv preprint arXiv:1702.06280 (2017)
17. He, K., Gkioxari, G., Dollár, P., Girshick, R.: Mask R-CNN. In: 2017 IEEE International Conference on Computer Vision (ICCV), pp. 2980–2988. IEEE (2017)
18. He, K., Zhang, X., Ren, S., Sun, J.: Deep residual learning for image recognition. In: Proceedings of the IEEE Conference on Computer Vision and Pattern Recognition, pp. 770–778 (2016)
19. He, W., Wei, J., Chen, X., Carlini, N., Song, D.: Adversarial example defenses: ensembles of weak defenses are not strong. arXiv preprint arXiv:1706.04701 (2017)
20. Huang, R., Xu, B., Schuurmans, D., Szepesvári, C.: Learning with a strong adversary. arXiv preprint arXiv:1511.03034 (2015)
21. Kingma, D.P., Ba, J.: Adam: a method for stochastic optimization. arXiv preprint arXiv:1412.6980 (2014)
22. Kurakin, A., Goodfellow, I., Bengio, S.: Adversarial examples in the physical world. arXiv preprint arXiv:1607.02533 (2016)
23. Kurakin, A., et al.: Adversarial attacks and defences competition. arXiv preprint arXiv:1804.00097 (2018)
24. LeCun, Y., Bengio, Y., Hinton, G.: Deep learning. Nature **521**(7553), 436–444 (2015)
25. Li, X., Li, F.: Adversarial examples detection in deep networks with convolutional filter statistics. In: ICCV, pp. 5775–5783 (2017)
26. Madry, A., Makelov, A., Schmidt, L., Tsipras, D., Vladu, A.: Towards deep learning models resistant to adversarial attacks. arXiv preprint arXiv:1706.06083 (2017)

27. Metzen, J.H., Genewein, T., Fischer, V., Bischoff, B.: On detecting adversarial perturbations. arXiv preprint arXiv:1702.04267 (2017)
28. Moosavi-Dezfooli, S.M., Fawzi, A., Frossard, P.: DeepFool: a simple and accurate method to fool deep neural networks. In: Proceedings of the IEEE Conference on Computer Vision and Pattern Recognition, pp. 2574–2582 (2016)
29. Owens, A., Isola, P., McDermott, J., Torralba, A., Adelson, E.H., Freeman, W.T.: Visually indicated sounds. In: Proceedings of the IEEE Conference on Computer Vision and Pattern Recognition, pp. 2405–2413 (2016)
30. Papernot, N., McDaniel, P., Jha, S., Fredrikson, M., Celik, Z.B., Swami, A.: The limitations of deep learning in adversarial settings. In: 2016 IEEE European Symposium on Security and Privacy (EuroS&P), pp. 372–387. IEEE (2016)
31. Papernot, N., McDaniel, P., Wu, X., Jha, S., Swami, A.: Distillation as a defense to adversarial perturbations against deep neural networks. arXiv preprint arXiv:1511.04508 (2015)
32. Raff, E., Barker, J., Sylvester, J., Brandon, R., Catanzaro, B., Nicholas, C.: Malware detection by eating a whole exe. arXiv preprint arXiv:1710.09435 (2017)
33. Razavian, A.S., Azizpour, H., Sullivan, J., Carlsson, S.: CNN features off-the-shelf: an astounding baseline for recognition. In: 2014 IEEE Conference on Computer Vision and Pattern Recognition Workshops (CVPRW), pp. 512–519. IEEE (2014)
34. Sabour, S., Cao, Y., Faghri, F., Fleet, D.J.: Adversarial manipulation of deep representations. arXiv preprint arXiv:1511.05122 (2015)
35. Santoro, A., et al.: A simple neural network module for relational reasoning. In: Advances in Neural Information Processing Systems, pp. 4967–4976 (2017)
36. Sermanet, P., Eigen, D., Zhang, X., Mathieu, M., Fergus, R., LeCun, Y.: OverFeat: integrated recognition, localization and detection using convolutional networks. arXiv preprint arXiv:1312.6229 (2013)
37. Szegedy, C., et al.: Intriguing properties of neural networks. arXiv preprint arXiv:1312.6199 (2013)
38. Vadicamo, L., et al.: Cross-media learning for image sentiment analysis in the wild. In: 2017 IEEE International Conference on Computer Vision Workshops (ICCVW), pp. 308–317 (2017)
39. Wehrmann, J., Simões, G.S., Barros, R.C., Cavalcante, V.F.: Adult content detection in videos with convolutional and recurrent neural networks. Neurocomputing **272**, 432–438 (2018)
40. Xu, W., Evans, D., Qi, Y.: Feature squeezing: detecting adversarial examples in deep neural networks. arXiv preprint arXiv:1704.01155 (2017)
41. Zezula, P., Amato, G., Dohnal, V., Batko, M.: Similarity Search: The Metric Space Approach, vol. 32. Springer, Heidelberg (2006). https://doi.org/10.1007/0-387-29151-2

W11 – 9th International Workshop on Human Behavior Understanding

W11 – 9th International Workshop on Human Behavior Understanding

The 9th edition of the International Workshop on Human Behavior Understanding was organized to foster research on how to generate visual data (both still images and videos) describing human behavior, both from application and methodological points of view. Indeed, one the one side we expected contributions demonstrating the importance of human behavior generation methods for various applications (autonomous systems, surveillance, etc.) as well as contributions showing that synthesizing behavioural patterns can improve the accuracy of current systems on traditional computer vision tasks (activity recognition, face recognition, group and crowd behavior analysis, etc.). On the other side, we also aimed to promote methodological contributions to enhance the effectiveness of generative methods and boost their capacity.

The opening keynote talk was given by Stefanos Zafeiriou (Imperial College London), who discussed the problem of estimating affect in the wild, and the role of proper data for addressing this problem. In particular, Stefanos described recent research efforts to collect and annotate unscripted spontaneous facial behavior in arbitrary recording conditions with the ultimate goal of moving affective computing methods from laboratory controlled conditions to more realistic conditions, i.e. *in the wild*. A second invited talk was given by Michael Black (Max Planck Institute) on learning to be a digital human. Michael discussed the current state-of-the-art in capturing, modeling, and animating realistic 3D human bodies. The key idea is the possibility of creating virtual humans that look and behave in ways that are indistinguishable from real people.

We have received 21 high quality submissions, from which we accepted 15, following the reviewers' recommendations. Each paper was reviewed by at least two members of the technical program committee, in double-blind fashion. Among the accepted submissions, five were presented in an oral session, as well as in a poster format, and nine were presented only as poster. One submission was not presented due to VISA issues of the authors and it is not included in the proceedings. The workshop was attended by over 110 participants. A follow-up special issue on the focus theme of the workshop is being edited in the *International Journal of Computer Vision*. We thank our program committee members, authors, and participants for making this workshop a very successful event.

September 2018

Xavier Alameda-Pineda
Elisa Ricci
Albert Ali Salah
Nicu Sebe
Shuicheng Yan

Give Ear to My Face: Modelling Multimodal Attention to Social Interactions

Giuseppe Boccignone, Vittorio Cuculo(✉), Alessandro D'Amelio, Giuliano Grossi, and Raffaella Lanzarotti

PHuSe Lab, Department of Computer Science, Università degli Studi di Milano, Milano, Italy
{giuseppe.boccignone,vittorio.cuculo,alessandro.damelio, giuliano.grossi,raffaella.lanzarotti}@unimi.it

Abstract. We address the deployment of perceptual attention to social interactions as displayed in conversational clips, when relying on multimodal information (audio and video). A probabilistic modelling framework is proposed that goes beyond the classic saliency paradigm while integrating multiple information cues. Attentional allocation is determined not just by stimulus-driven selection but, importantly, by social value as modulating the selection history of relevant multimodal items. Thus, the construction of attentional priority is the result of a sampling procedure conditioned on the potential value dynamics of socially relevant objects emerging moment to moment within the scene. Preliminary experiments on a publicly available dataset are presented.

Keywords: Audio-visual attention · Social interaction · Multimodal perception

1 Introduction

When humans are immersed in realistic, ecological situations that involve other humans, attention deployment strives for monitoring the behaviour, intentions and emotions of others even in the absence of a given external task [16]. Under such circumstances, the internal goal of the perceiver is to control attention so to maximise the implicit reward in focusing signals that bear social value [1].

Despite of experimental corroboration gained for such tendencies, their general modelling is far from evident (cfr., Sect. 2). Indeed, in order to put into work the mechanisms of selection, integration and sampling underlying the multifaceted phenomenon of attention, sensory systems have to master the flood of multimodal events (e.g., visual and audiovisual) captured in the external world. Thus, the research question we address in this note boils down to the following: is it possible to mine from behavioural data the implicit value of multimodal cues driving observer's motivation to spot socially interesting events in the scene?

L. Leal-Taixé and S. Roth (Eds.): ECCV 2018 Workshops, LNCS 11130, pp. 331–345, 2019.
https://doi.org/10.1007/978-3-030-11012-3_27

Here, we propose a novel probabilistic model for grounding the inferential steps that lead to the prediction of a number of potential value-based attractors of multimodal attention (Sects. 3 and 4).

To this end, a clear case is represented by observers naturally viewing conversational videos conveying audiovisual information. Conversational clips are relatively controlled stimuli, while having the virtue of displaying real people embedded in a realistic dynamic situation [16]. Put simple, they allow affordable analysis and modelling of where and how people look when viewing such clips, namely, the fundamental questions entailed by spatiotemporal distribution of attention in a social context. Cogently, Foulsham *et al.* [16] have shown that observers spend the majority of time looking at the people in the videos, markedly at their eyes and faces, and that gaze fixations are temporally coupled to the person who was talking at any one time.

In what follows, to meet such experimental paradigm, we exploit the publicly available dataset by Coutrot and Guyader [13], who gathered data of eye-tracked subjects attending to conversational clips (Sect. 5). The free-viewing task given to subjects allows for dynamically inferring the history of their "internal" selection goals as captured by the resulting attentive gaze behaviour. As such it is suitable for both learning and testing the proposed model.

Model input, at the training stage, is represented by the audiovisual stream together with eye-tracking data. Inference is performed to obtain dynamic value-driven priority maps resulting from the competition of visual and audiovisual events occurring in the scene. Their dynamics integrates the observer's current selection goals, selection history, and the physical salience of the items competing for attention. The model output is a number of attractors, namely clusters of potentially interest points sampled from priority maps, and suitable to guide attention control [29]. At the test stage, the latter can be compared with actual foci of attention selected by human subjects. Section 5 presents simulation results, and a conclusive discussion is given in Sect. 6.

2 Background and Rationales

Whilst attentional mechanisms have been largely explored for vision systems, there is not much tradition as regards models of attention in the context of sound systems [18]. In vision, by and large, prominent models of attention foster a dichotomy between top-down and bottom-up control, with the former determined by current selection goals and the latter determined by physical salience [2,27,31]. Yet, the majority has retained a central place for low-level visual conspicuity [5,6,31], where the perceptual representation of the scene is usually epitomised in the form of a spatial saliency map, mostly derived bottom-up (early salience).

In a similar vein, such taxonomy has been assumed in the auditory attention field of inquiry. Since the seminal work by Kayser *et al.* [19], efforts have been spent to model stimulus-driven attention to the auditory domain, by computing a visual saliency map of the spectrogram of an auditory stimulus (see [18] for a comprehensive review). In this perspective, the combination of both visual and auditory saliencies supporting a multimodal saliency map that grounds multimodal attention becomes a viable route [15,23].

However, the top-down vs. bottom-up taxonomy of attentional control should be adopted with the uttermost caution (cfr., [2,31]). On the one hand, the weakness of the bottom-up approach has been largely weighed up in the visual attention realm [31]. Early salience has only an indirect effect on attention by acting through recognised objects [14]. Thus, either object knowledge has been exploited (e.g., [9]), in particular when dealing with faces [8], or contextual cues (e.g., the scene gist, [33]) for top-down tuning early salience. As a matter of fact, in the real world, most fixations are on task-relevant objects and this may or may not correlate with the saliency of regions. Further, the recent theoretical perspectives on active/attentive sensing promote a closed loop between an ideal observer, that extracts task-relevant information from a sequence of observations, and an ideal planner which specifies the actions that lead to the most informative observations [35]. The ultimate objective of active behaviour should be maximising the total rewards that can be obtained in the long term. On the other hand, there is a large body of evidence pointing at cases where strong selection biases cannot be explained by the physical salience of potential targets or by current selection goals. One such example is perceptual selection being biased towards objects associated with reward and selection history [2].

The dichotomy between top-down and bottom-up control assumes the former as being determined by the current "endogenous" goals of the observer and the latter as being constrained by the physical, "exogenous" characteristics of the stimuli (independent of the internal state of the observer). However, the construct of "endogenous" attentional control is subtle since it conflates control signals that are "internal" (such as the motivation for paying attention to socially rewarding objects/events), "external" (induced by the given current task voluntarily pursued), and selection history (either learned or evolutionary inherited), which can prioritise items previously attended in a given context. If the ultimate objective of the attentive observer is total reward maximisation, one should clearly distinguish between "external" rewards (incentive motivation, e.g., monetary reward) and reward related to "internal" value. The latter has different psychological facets [3] including affect (implicit "liking" and conscious pleasure) and motivation (implicit incentive salience, "wanting"). Indeed, the selection of socially relevant stimuli by attention reflects the overall value of such selection [1].

3 Overview of the Model

Under such circumstances, we generally assume attention as driven by goals $\mathcal{G}$ that, in turn, set the appropriate value $\mathcal{V}$ to events/objects occurring in the audiovisual scene. Also, in the work presented here, we assume that no explicit task is assigned to the perceiver; thus, value $\mathcal{V}$ is modulated by the "internal" goal (drive) towards spotting socially relevant objects/events. We consider two main inferential steps:

1. to infer a spatial-based priority map representation of the audio-visual landscape;
2. to exploit the priority map distributions, in order to sample value-based attractors suitable to guide attentional deployment.

Random variables (RVs), involved and their conditional dependencies are represented via the Probabilistic Graphical Model (PGM) outlined in Fig. 1.

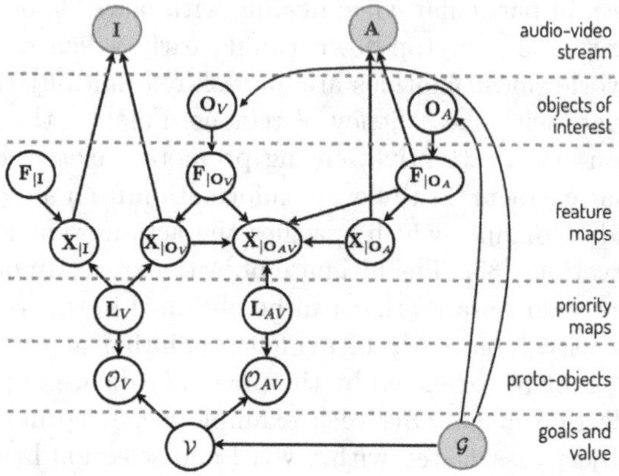

Fig. 1. An overall view of the model as a Probabilistic Graphical Model. Graph nodes denote RVs and directed arcs encode conditional dependencies between RVs. Grey-shaded nodes stand for RVs whose value is given. Time index t has been omitted for simplicity. (Color figure online)

Priority Map Representation. Perceptual spatial attention driven by multimodal cues mainly relies on visual and audio-visual priority maps, which we define as the RVs $\mathbf{L}_V$ and $\mathbf{L}_{AV}$, respectively. Formally, a priority map $\mathbf{L}$ is the matrix of binary RVs $l(\mathbf{r})$ denoting if location $\mathbf{r}$ is to be considered relevant ($l(\mathbf{r}) = 1$) or not ($l(\mathbf{r}) = 0$), with respect to possible visual or audio-visual "objects" occurring within the scene. Thus, given the video and audio streams defining the audio-video landscape, $\{\mathbf{I}(t)\}$, $\{\mathbf{A}(t)\}$, respectively, a preliminary step is to evaluate at any time t, the posterior distributions $P(\mathbf{L}_V(t) \mid \mathbf{L}_V(t-1), \mathbf{I}(t))$ and $P(\mathbf{L}_{AV}(t) \mid \mathbf{L}_{AV}(t-1), \mathbf{A}(t), \mathbf{I}(t))$. The steps behind such estimate can be derived by resorting to the conditional dependencies defined in the PGM in Fig. 1. Backward inference $\{\mathbf{A}(t), \mathbf{I}(t)\} \rightarrow \{\mathbf{L}_V(t), \mathbf{L}_{AV}(t)\}$ stands upon a set of perceptual features $\mathbf{F}(t) = \{f(t)\}$ that can be estimated from the multimodal stream. From now on, for notational simplicity, we will omit time indexing t, unless needed.

As to the visual stream, we distinguish between two kinds of visual features: generic features $\mathbf{F}_{|\mathbf{I}}$ - such as edge, texture, colour, motion features-, and object-dependent features, $\mathbf{F}_{|\mathbf{O}}$. As to object-based features, these are to be learned by specifically taking into account the classes of objects that are likely to be relevant under the goal $\mathcal{G}$, via the distribution $P(\mathbf{O} \mid \mathcal{G})$. Here, where the task is free viewing/listening, and internal goals are biased towards social cues, the prominent visual objects are faces, $\mathbf{O}_V = \{face\}$. Both kinds of visual features, $\mathbf{F}_{|\mathbf{I}}$ and $\mathbf{F}_{|\mathbf{O}}$, can be estimated in a feed-forward way. Note that in the literature face information is usually referred to as a top-down cue [27] as opposed to bottom-up cues. However, much like physically driven features, they are phyletic features, and their distribution $P(\mathbf{F}_{|\mathbf{O}_V} \mid \mathbf{O}_V = face)$ is learnt by biological visual systems along evolution or in early development stages.

In order to be processed, features $\mathbf{F}_{|\mathbf{I}}$ and $\mathbf{F}_{|\mathbf{O}_V}$ need to be spatially organised in feature maps. A feature map $\mathbf{X}$ is a topographically organised map that encodes the joint occurrence of a specific feature at a spatial location [9]. It can be considered the probabilistic counterpart of a salience map [9] and it can be equivalently represented as a unique map encoding the presence of different object dependent features $\mathbf{F}_{f|\mathbf{O}_V}$, or a set of object-specific feature maps, i.e. $\mathbf{X} = \{\mathbf{X}_f\}$ (e.g., a face map, a body map, etc.). More precisely, $\mathbf{X}_f$ is a matrix of binary RVs $x(\mathbf{r})$ denoting whether feature f is present or not present at location $\mathbf{L} = \mathbf{r}$. Simply put, $\mathbf{X}_f$ is a map defining the spatial occurrence of $\mathbf{F}_{f|\mathbf{O}_V}$ or $\mathbf{F}_{f|\mathbf{I}}$. In our case, we need to estimate the posteriors $P(\mathbf{X}_{|\mathbf{I}} \mid \mathbf{F}_{|\mathbf{I}})$ and $P(\mathbf{X}_{|\mathbf{O}_V} \mid \mathbf{F}_{|\mathbf{O}_V})$.

As to the processing of audio, similarly to visual processing, auditory objects form across different analysis scales [29]. Formation of sound elements with contiguous spectro-temporal structure, relies primarily on local structures (e.g., onsets and offsets, harmonic structure, continuity of frequency over time), while social communication signals, such as speech, have a rich spectro-temporal structure supporting short-term object formation (e.g. formation of syllables). The latter are linked together over time through continuity and similarity of higher-order perceptual features, such as location, pitch, timbre and learned meaning. In our setting, the objects of interest $\mathbf{O}_A$ are represented by speakers' voices [16], and features $\mathbf{F}_{f|\mathbf{O}_A}$ suitable to represent speech cues. In this work, we are not considering other audio sources (e.g., music). From a social perspective, we are interested in inferring the audio-visual topographic maps of speaker/non-speakers, $\mathbf{X}_{|\mathbf{O}_{AV}}$, given the available faces in the scene and speech features via the posterior distribution $P(\mathbf{X}_{|\mathbf{O}_{AV}} \mid \mathbf{X}_{|\mathbf{O}_A}, \mathbf{X}_{|\mathbf{O}_V}, \mathbf{F}_{|\mathbf{O}_A}, \mathbf{F}_{|\mathbf{O}_V})$, where $\mathbf{X}_{|\mathbf{O}_{AV}} = x(\mathbf{r})$ denotes whether a speaker/non-speaker is present or not present at location $\mathbf{r}$.

At this point, audio-visual perception has been cast in a spatial attention problem and priority maps $\mathbf{L}_V$and $\mathbf{L}_{AV}$ can be eventually estimated through distributions $P(\mathbf{L}_V(t) \mid \mathbf{L}_V(t-1), \mathbf{X}_{|\mathbf{I}}, \mathbf{X}_{|\mathbf{O}_V})$ and $P(\mathbf{L}_{AV}(t) | \mathbf{L}_{AV}(t-1), \mathbf{X}_{|\mathbf{O}_{AV}})$. Note that, in general, the representation entailed by a priority map differs from that provided at a lower level by feature maps $\mathbf{X}$ (or classic salience). It can be conceived as a dynamic map of the perceptual landscape constructed from a combination of properties of the external stimuli, intrinsic expectations, and contextual knowledge [9,33]. Also, it can be designed to act as a form of short term memory to keep track of which potential targets have been attended. Thus, $\mathbf{L}(t)$ depends on both current perceptual inferences on feature maps at time t

and priority at time $t-1$. Denote $\pi_{AV} = P(\mathbf{X}_{|\mathbf{O}_{AV}} \mid \mathbf{X}_{|\mathbf{O}_{A}}, \mathbf{X}_{|\mathbf{O}_{V}}, \mathbf{F}_{|\mathbf{O}_{A}}, \mathbf{F}_{|\mathbf{O}_{V}})$, $\pi_I = P(\mathbf{X}_{|\mathbf{I}} \mid \mathbf{F}_{|\mathbf{I}})$ and $\pi_{OV} = P(\mathbf{X}_{|\mathbf{O}_{V}} \mid \mathbf{F}_{|\mathbf{O}_{V}})$, $\pi_{L_V} = P(\mathbf{L}_V(t) \mid \mathbf{L}_V(t-1), \mathbf{X}_{|\mathbf{I}}, \mathbf{X}_{|\mathbf{O}_{V}})$, $\pi_{L_{AV}} = P(\mathbf{L}_{AV}(t) | \mathbf{L}_{AV}(t-1), \mathbf{X}_{|\mathbf{O}_{AV}})$. Then,

$$\pi_{L_V}(t) \approx \alpha_V(\pi_I(t)\pi_{OV}(t)) + (1-\alpha_V)\pi_{L_V}(t-1), \tag{1}$$

$$\pi_{L_{AV}}(t) \approx \alpha_{AV}\pi_{AV}(t) + (1-\alpha_{AV})\pi_{L_{AV}}(t-1). \tag{2}$$

where α_V and α_{AV} weight the contribution of currently estimated feature maps with respect to previous priority maps.

Priority map dynamics requires an initial prior $P(\mathbf{L})$, which can be designed to account for spatial tendencies in the perceptual process; for instance, human eye-tracking studies have shown that gaze fixations in free viewing of dynamic natural scenes are biased toward the center of the scene ("center bias", [20, 32]), which can be modelled by assuming a Gaussian distribution located on the viewing center.

Sampling Value-Based Attractors of Multimodal Attention. The next main inferential step involves the use of priority map distributions $\mathbf{L}^{(\ell)}$, ℓ being an index on $\{V, AV\}$, to sample attention attractors. Sampling is based on their value or potential reward $\mathcal{V}$ for the perceiver. In accordance with object-based attention approaches, we introduce proto-objects $\mathcal{O}_p^{(\ell)}$, where $p = 1, \cdots, N_P^{(\ell)}$, $N_P^{(\ell)}$ being the number of proto-objects detected in the priority map ℓ. These are the actual dynamic support for attention, conceived as the dynamic interface between attentive and pre-attentive processing [4]. Given a priority map $\mathbf{L}^{(\ell)}$, a set of proto-objects $\mathcal{O}^{(\ell)} = \{\mathcal{O}_p^{(\ell)}\}_{p=1}^{N_P^{(\ell)}}$ is computed. Each proto-object has a sparse representation in terms of a cluster of points $\{\mathbf{r}_{i,p}\}_{i=1}^{N_{I,p}^{(\ell)}}$ and parameters $\Theta_p = (\mathcal{M}_p^{(\ell)}, \theta_p^{(\ell)})$. In the general case, where the priority map distribution is a complex distribution with multiple modes (which is much likely to occur for $\mathbf{L}_V$) such parameters must be estimated. Here, the set $\mathcal{M}_p^{(\ell)} = \{m_p^{(\ell)}(\mathbf{r})\}_{\mathbf{r}\in\mathbf{L}^{(\ell)}}$ stands for a map of binary RVs indicating the presence or absence of proto-object p, and the overall map of proto-objects is given by $\mathcal{M}^{(\ell)} = \bigcup_{p=1}^{N_P^{(\ell)}} \mathcal{M}_p^{(\ell)}$, where $\mathcal{M}_p^{(\ell)} \bigcap \mathcal{M}_k^{(\ell)} = \emptyset, p \neq k$. Location and shape of the proto-object are parametrised via $\theta_p^{(\ell)}$. Assume independent proto-objects. In a first step we estimate the proto-object support map from the landscape, i.e., $\widehat{\mathcal{M}}^{(\ell)} \sim P(\mathcal{M}^{(\ell)} | \mathbf{L}^{(\ell)})$. Then, in a second step, $\widehat{\theta}_p^{(\ell)} \sim P(\theta_p^{(\ell)}(t) | \widehat{\mathcal{M}}_p^{(\ell)})$, location and shape parameters $\theta_p^{(\ell)} = (\mu_p^{(\ell)}, \Sigma_p^{(\ell)})$, $\mu_p^{(\ell)}$ are derived, $\Sigma_p^{(\ell)}$ being an elliptical representation of the proto-object support (location and axes).

As stated above, each proto-object relies on a sparse representation, i.e. the samples $\{\mathbf{r}_{i,p}\}_{i=1}^{N_{I,p}^{(\ell)}}$ representing candidate interest points (IPs). Sampling takes place conditionally on proto-object parameters $\theta_p^{(\ell)}$, and crucially it is modulated by value $\mathcal{V}^{(\ell)}$ that the perceiver is likely to gain from attending to the proto-object in map ℓ. Thus, considering $\mathcal{O}_p^{(\ell)}$ derived from the ℓ-th priority map,

$$\widetilde{\mathcal{O}}_p^{(\ell)} \triangleq \{w_{i,p}^{(\ell)} \mathbf{r}_{i,p}^{(\ell)}\}_{i=1}^{N_{I,p}^{(\ell)}} \sim P(\mathcal{O}_p^{(\ell)} \mid \theta_p^{(\ell)}, \mathcal{V}^{(\ell)}). \tag{3}$$

In Eq. 3, the posterior on $\mathcal{O}_p^{(\ell)}$ is a Gaussian distribution and the number of samples $N_p^{(\ell)}$ and the weight $w_{i,p}^{(\ell)}$ assigned to each particle $\mathbf{r}_{i,p}^{(\ell)}$ is a function of $\mathcal{V}^{(\ell)}$ attributed to the priority map ℓ.

Value $\mathcal{V}^{(\ell)}$, moment-to-moment updates according to the pdf $P(\mathcal{V}^{(\ell)}(t) \mid \mathcal{V}^{(\ell)}(t-1), \mathcal{G})$, depending on previous history and goal $\mathcal{G}$. Thus, by considering the time varying random vectors, $\mathcal{V}(t) = \{\mathcal{V}^{(\ell)}(t)\}$ (hidden continuous state) and $\mathcal{O}(t) = \{\mathcal{O}^{(\ell)}(t)\}$ (observable), value dynamics is best described by the following stochastic state-space system:

$$\widetilde{\mathcal{V}}(t) \sim P(\mathcal{V}(t) \mid \mathcal{V}(t-1), \mathcal{G}) \tag{4}$$

$$\widetilde{\mathcal{O}}(t) \sim P(\mathcal{O}(t) \mid \widetilde{\mathcal{V}}(t)) \tag{5}$$

Online inference is performed by solving the filtering problem $P(\mathcal{V}(t) \mid \mathcal{O}(1:t))$ under Markov assumption. This way current goal and selection history effects are both taken into account [2]. Such dynamics is set at the learning stage as detailed in the following section.

4 Current Implementation of the Model

The simulation of the model relies on a number of processing stages. At the lowest processing stages (in particular, face detection, audio-visual object detection), since we are dealing with feed-forward processes, thus we take advantage of efficient kernel-based methods and current deep neural network architectures. We give a brief sketch of the methods adopted.

Visual Processing. In order to derive the physical stimulus feature map $\mathbf{X}_{|\mathbf{I}}$, we rely on the spatio-temporal saliency method proposed in [28] based on local regression kernel center/surround features. It avoids specific optical flow processing for motion detection and has the advantage of being insensitive to possible camera motion. By assuming uniform prior on all locations, the evidence from a location $\mathbf{r}$ of the frame is computed via the likelihood $P(\mathbf{I}(t) \mid \mathbf{x}_f(\mathbf{r}, t) = 1, \mathbf{F}_{|\mathbf{I}}, \mathbf{r}_F(t)) = \frac{1}{\sum_s} \exp\left(\frac{1-\rho(\mathbf{F}_{\mathbf{r},c}, \mathbf{F}_{\mathbf{r},s})}{\sigma^2}\right)$, where $\rho(\cdot) \in [-1, 1]$ is the matrix cosine similarity (see [28], for details) between center and surround feature matrices $\mathbf{F}_{\mathbf{r},c}$ and $\mathbf{F}_{\mathbf{r},s}$ computed at location $\mathbf{r}$ of frame $\mathbf{I}(t)$.

The visual object-based feature map $\mathbf{X}_{|\mathbf{O}_V}$ entails a face detection step. There is a huge number of methods currently available: the one proposed by Hu and Ramanan [17] has shown, in our preliminary experiments, to bear the highest performance. It relies on a feed-forward deep network architecture for scale invariant detection. Starting with an input frame $\mathbf{I}(t)$, a coarse image pyramid (including interpolation) is created. Then, the scaled input is fed into a Convolutional Neural Network (CNN) to predict template responses at every resolution. Non-maximum suppression (NMS) is applied at the original resolution to get the final detection results. Their confidence value is used to assign the probability $P(\mathbf{X}_{|\mathbf{O}_V} \mid \mathbf{F}_{|\mathbf{O}_V}, \mathbf{L}_V = \mathbf{r})$ of spotting face features $\mathbf{F}_{|\mathbf{O}_V}$ at $\mathbf{L}_V = \mathbf{r}$, according to a gaussian distribution located on the face center modulated by detection confidence and face size.

Audio Visual Processing. The features $\mathbf{F}_{|\mathbf{O}_A}$ used to encode the speech stream are the Mel-frequency cepstral coefficients (MFCC). The Mel-frequency cepstrum is highly effective in speech recognition and in modelling the subjective pitch and frequency content. The audio feature map $\mathbf{X}_{|\mathbf{O}_A}(t)$ can be conceived as a spectro-temporal structure computed from a suitable time window of the audio stream, representing MFCC values for each time step and each Mel frequency band. It is important to note, that the problem of deriving the speaker/non-speaker map $\mathbf{X}_{|\mathbf{O}_{AV}}$ when multiple faces are present, is closely related to the AV synchronisation problem [10]; namely, that of inferring the correspondence between the video and the speech streams, captured by the joint probability $P(\mathbf{X}_{|\mathbf{O}_{AV}}, \mathbf{X}_{|\mathbf{O}_A}, \mathbf{X}_{|\mathbf{O}_V}, \mathbf{F}_{|\mathbf{O}_A}, \mathbf{F}_{|\mathbf{O}_V}, \mathbf{L}_{AV})$. The speaker's face is the one with the highest correlation between the audio and the video feature streams, whilst a non-speaker should have a correlation close to zero. It has been shown that the synchronisation method presented in [10] can be extended to locate the speaker vs. non-speakers and to provide a suitable confidence value. The method relies on a two-stream CNN architecture (SynchNet) that enables a joint embedding between the sound and the face images. In particular we use the Multi-View version [10,11], which allows the speaker identification on profile faces and does not require explicit lip detection. To such end, 13 Mel frequency bands are used at each time step, where features $\mathbf{F}_{|\mathbf{O}_A}(t)$ are computed at sampling rate for a 0.2-secs time-window of the input signal $\mathbf{A}(t)$. The same time-window is used for the video stream input.

Priority Maps and Value-Based Proto-Object Sampling. Priority maps are computed from feature maps, by simply using $\alpha = \alpha_V = \alpha_{AV}$, with $\alpha = 0.8$ experimentally determined via ROC analysis with respect to evaluation metrics (cfr. Sect. 5); such value grants higher weight to current information in order to account for changes in the audio-visual stream. From an experimental standpoint, we take into account four priority maps; namely, the visual priority map $\mathbf{L}_V$ as sensed from the video stream, the speaker/non-speaker maps, which we denote $\mathbf{L}_{AV_S}, \mathbf{L}_{AV_{NS}}$, and the one supporting the spatial prior $P(\mathbf{L}_V)$ (center bias), say $\mathbf{L}_{cb}$. To derive proto-objects from priority maps, markedly for estimating $\mathbf{L}_V(t)$, we need first to estimate their support $\mathcal{M}$ $\mathcal{M}(t) = \{m(\mathbf{r}, t)\}_{\mathbf{r} \in L}$, such that $m(\mathbf{r}, t) = 1$ if $P(\mathbf{L}(t)) > T_M$, and $m(\mathbf{r}, t) = 0$ otherwise. The threshold T_M is adaptively set so as to achieve 90% significance level in deciding whether the given priority values are in the extreme tails of the pdf. The procedure is based on the assumption that an informative proto-object is a relatively rare region and thus results in values which are in the tails of the distribution. Then, $\mathcal{M}(t) = \{\mathcal{M}_p(t)\}_{p=1}^{N_P}$ is obtained as $\mathcal{M}_p(t) = \{m_p(\mathbf{r}, t) | lab(B, \mathbf{r}, t) = p\}_{\mathbf{r} \in L}$, where the function lab labels $\mathcal{M}(t)$ around $\mathbf{r}$. We set the maximum number of proto-objects to $N_P = 15$, to retain the most important ones. The proto-object map provides the necessary spatial support for a 2D ellipse maximum-likelihood approximation of each proto-object, whose location and shape are parametrised as $\theta_p = (\mu_p, \Sigma_p)$ for $p = 1, \cdots, N_p$.

As previously stated, when sampling proto-object $\mathcal{O}_p^{(\ell)}$ (Eq. 3), with reference to the priority map $\mathbf{L}^{(\ell)}$, the number of samples $N_p^{(\ell)}$ and the weight $w_{i,p}^{(\ell)}$ assigned to each particle $\mathbf{r}_{i,p}^{(\ell)}$ is a function of value $\mathcal{V}^{(\ell)}$ attributed to the priority map ℓ. Thus, here the crucial issue is to determine the distribution update rule $P(\mathcal{V}^{(\ell)}(t) \mid \mathcal{V}^{(\ell)}(t-1), \mathcal{G})$. This is in general a difficult modelling issue, since value $\mathcal{V}(t) = \{\mathcal{V}^{(\ell)}(t)\}$ depends on current goals $\mathcal{G}$, either internal or external under a given task. However, the experimental eye-tracking data we use here are derived under a generic free-viewing task (external goal). Thus, we expect that attention allocation of observers in such context had been mainly driven by internal (endogenous) goals, most important the motivationally rewarding drive to deploy attention to conversational events/actors within the scene. Next, we exploit the d-separation property that holds for head-to-head dependencies in directed PGMs. When $\mathcal{O}^{(\ell)}$ and $\mathbf{L}^{(\ell)}$ are observed, it is possible to learn the dynamics of $\mathcal{V}(t)$ as the dynamics of a vector of time-varying parameters $\mathcal{V}^{(\ell)}(t)$. The latter control a function $g(\{\mathbf{L}^{(\ell)}\}, \mathcal{V}^{(\ell)}(t))$, which suitably combines the priority maps. This way the observation model in Eq. 5 can be expressed in the form $\widehat{g}(t) \sim P(g(\{\mathbf{L}^{(\ell)}\}, \mathcal{V}^{(\ell)}(t) \mid \widetilde{\mathcal{V}}(t)))$. By assuming that $\widehat{g}(t)$ is an approximation of observers' attention allocation as summarised by the time-varying gaze heatmap $\mathcal{H}(t)$ computed from eye-tracked fixations, $\widehat{g}(t) \approx \mathcal{H}(t)$, then value dynamics can be learned by using $\mathcal{H}(t)$ as a ground-truth measurement. Generalising methods previously proposed for low-level saliency map weighting [12,25,30], value-state learning can be formulated as a time-varying regression, where the hidden-state evolution is that of the random vector of parameters $\mathcal{V}^{(\ell)}(t)$. To such end, at the learning stage we exploit the time-varying version of the Bayesian Lasso [24] to infer the joint hidden state dynamics $\prod_\ell P(\mathcal{V}^{(\ell)}(t) \mid \mathcal{V}^{(\ell)}(t-1))$ - under the assumption of independence between Gaussian distributed parameters - by using $\mathcal{H}(t)$ obtained from a subset of observers.

For the simulations and results presented in the following, the number of points $N^{(\ell)}$ to be sampled from priority map ℓ, is set as $N^{(\ell)} = \overline{\mathcal{V}}^{(\ell)}(t) N_{tot}$, where $N_{tot} = 500$ is the total number of points to be sampled and $\overline{\mathcal{V}}^{(\ell)}(t) = E\left[\mathcal{V}^{(\ell)}(t) \mid \mathcal{V}^{(\ell)}(t-1)\right]$ the value conditional expectation on map ℓ. Analogously, the weight $w_{i,p}^{(\ell)}$ assigned to each particle $\mathbf{r}_{i,p}^{(\ell)}$, is determined as $w_{i,p}^{(\ell)} = \overline{\mathcal{V}}^{(\ell)}(t) P(\mathbf{r}_{i,p}^{(\ell)})$ (cfr., Eq. 3). One typical result that shows the overall process at a glance is outlined in Fig. 2. The effect of value-based sampling is evident in the number of sampled points for the different priority maps; along a conversation, as expected, audio-visual events captured by $\mathbf{L}_{AV}$ are granted higher value with respect to the visual priority map $\mathbf{L}_V$ and the initial center bias prior $P(\mathbf{L})$. Figure 3 shows a snapshot of model output, where value assigned to sampled points is explicitly shown (colour coded).

5 Simulations

Stimuli and Eye-Tracking Data. The adopted dataset [13] consists of 15 one-shot conversation scenes from French movies, involving two to four different actors

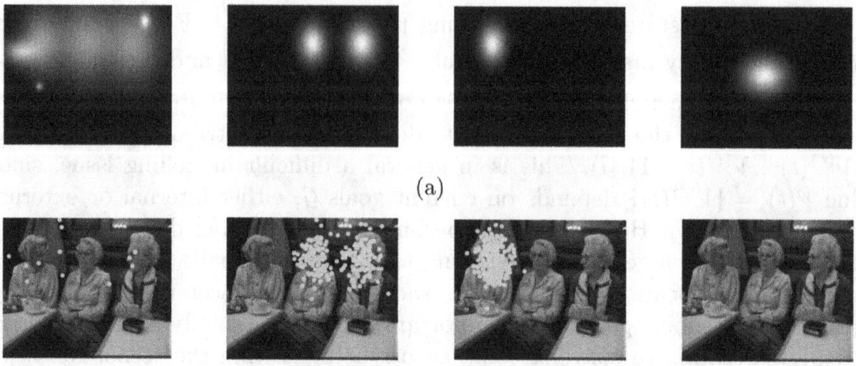

(a)

(b)

Fig. 2. Probability density functions (a) and value-based sampling (b) related to priority maps (left to right) $\mathbf{L}_V$ (visual), $\mathbf{L}_{AV}$ (non-speaker), $\mathbf{L}_{AV}$ (speaker); for convenience, the initial prior $P(\mathbf{L})$ (center bias) is also shown.

for each scene. The duration of the videos goes from 12 to 30 s, with a resolution of 720 × 576 pixels at a frame rate of 25 fps. The dataset includes eye-tracking recordings in four different auditory conditions, but for the purposes of our work, the one with the original audio information has been employed. The experiment involved 18 different participants, all French native speakers and not aware of the purpose of the experiment. The eye-tracker system recorded eye positions at 1000 Hz, downsampled in accordance with the video frame rate, with a median of 40 raw consecutive eye positions [13].

Evaluation. In the present study 13 of the 15 clips were used; the *jeuxinterdits* video was excluded due to anomalous false positives rising in the face detection step (which is not matter of assessment here); the *fetecommence* clip was used for preliminary validation of parameter tuning and it was not included in the final performance assessment reported below. For each clip, the 18 observers have been randomly assigned to training (11) and test (7) sets. The learning stage, as previously discussed, was devoted to learn, from observers in the training set and for each video, the hidden state dynamics of value parameters $\{\mathcal{V}^{(\ell)}(t)\}$, $\prod_\ell P(\{\mathcal{V}^{(\ell)}(t)\} \mid \{\mathcal{V}^{(\ell)}(t-1)\})$, governing the time-varying Bayesian Lasso (Sect. 4). The eye-tracked data in the training set were used as the targets for supervised learning. To such end, the time-varying empirical distribution of observers' fixations was derived (the ground truth); the model-based distribution (apt to predict attention deployment and to be matched against the empirical one) was blindly obtained via standard Kernel Density Estimation on sampled points (cfr., Fig. 3). In the test stage, the empirical and model-based distributions have been eventually compared by adopting four widely adopted standard evaluation metrics [7]: Area under ROC Curve (AUC), Pearson's Correlation Coefficient (CC), Normalized Scanpath Saliency (NSS) and Kullback-Leibler divergence (KL). AUC is the most commonly-used metric for this kind of evaluation,

Fig. 3. Comparing human vs. model. From left to right: the overall sampling result overlaid on the video frame, colour representing value assigned to sampled points; the empirical distribution of human fixations; the model kernel-based distribution of sampled points.

Table 1. Mean value (and standard dev.) of the metric scores obtained for each video on the test set.

Video	KLD	NSS	AUC	CC
arrogants	1.25 ± 0.78	2.61 ± 0.54	0.90 ± 0.05	0.63 ± 0.12
conversation	1.80 ± 1.89	2.53 ± 0.66	0.85 ± 0.09	0.65 ± 0.19
equipier	1.22 ± 0.70	2.25 ± 0.69	0.83 ± 0.08	0.61 ± 0.17
hommedeneuve	1.07 ± 0.70	2.58 ± 0.53	0.87 ± 0.07	0.66 ± 0.12
hommeface	1.39 ± 1.27	2.69 ± 0.80	0.81 ± 0.09	0.70 ± 0.22
jeuxdenfant	1.04 ± 1.16	2.94 ± 0.36	0.84 ± 0.06	0.80 ± 0.09
moustacheassis	1.73 ± 1.29	2.58 ± 0.53	0.89 ± 0.06	0.63 ± 0.12
moustachepolicier	1.38 ± 0.79	2.32 ± 0.70	0.87 ± 0.09	0.57 ± 0.15
periljeune	1.58 ± 1.19	2.15 ± 0.57	0.87 ± 0.06	0.50 ± 0.18
pleincoeurbistrot	2.15 ± 1.86	2.53 ± 0.66	0.83 ± 0.08	0.66 ± 0.18
quatrevingtdixneuf	1.36 ± 0.19	1.99 ± 0.51	0.90 ± 0.04	0.50 ± 0.10
saveurspalais	1.36 ± 1.01	2.63 ± 0.49	0.88 ± 0.06	0.66 ± 0.10
unsoir	1.85 ± 1.79	2.39 ± 0.65	0.86 ± 0.10	0.58 ± 0.17
Mean	1.48 ± 1.23	2.48 ± 0.6	0.86 ± 0.08	0.63 ± 0.15

mainly driven by high-valued predictions and largely ambivalent of low-valued false positives. CC is a linear correlation between the prediction and ground truth distributions, and treats false positives and false negatives symmetrically. NSS is discrete approximation of CC that is additionally parameter-free and operates on raw fixation locations. KL has a natural interpretation where goal is to approximate a target distribution while highly penalising mis-detections. The theoretical best performance limits of such metrics are 0.92, 1.00, 3.29 and 0 for AUC, CC, NSS and KL, respectively [7]. The overall quantitative evaluation of the simulation is summarised in Table 1, in terms of the mean value of the four metrics for each video over 7 model simulation trials.

Figure 4 provides an interesting snapshot of the evolution over time (video frames) of the four metrics. The transition to the onset of a speech event results in higher uncertainty among observers (and thus model prediction) is captured by the absolute minimum of AUC, CC, NSS and the maximum KL; uncertainty is reduced after such onset, and scores evolve toward a steady-state of valuable performance with respect to their theoretical limits. Beyond notable results achieved in simulations, it is worth remarking that the comparison condition we adopted is somehow unfair with respect to the model. The ground truth is derived from actual observers' fixations, whilst model-based distribution is computed from the sampled points that only represent candidate fixation points, conceived to be subsequently exploited for deciding the actual gaze shift (which also explains in Fig. 3 the slightly bigger spread of model distributions with respect to the ground truth ones).

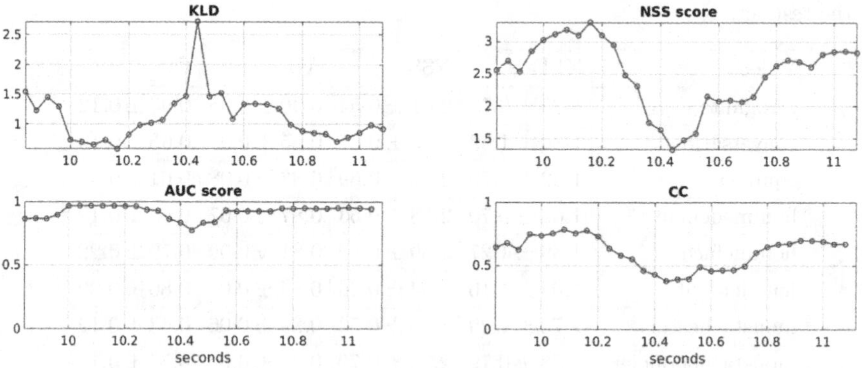

Fig. 4. A snapshot of metrics evolution after the 10*th* second of the video *"Faces conversation"*, when a change of speaker occurs.

6 Conclusions

This study gauged the importance of social information on attention in terms of gaze allocation when perceiving naturalistically rich, multimodal dynamic scenes. Hitherto the problem of modelling the behaviour of active observers in such context has seldom been taken into consideration, in spite of the exponentially growing body of audio-visual data conveying social behaviour content. The involvement of value is still in its infancy in the attention field of inquiry [31], as opposed to salience and objects that have been largely addressed both in psychology [27] and computer vision [5].

Preliminary experimental results show that the model is suitable to infer from behavioural data the implicit value of audio-visual cues driving observer's motivation to spot socially interesting events in the scene. The model is conceived in a probabilistic framework for object-based multimodal attention control [29]. Such formulation is far from evident. The notion that observers' visual attention is driven towards potential objects in the scene has been widely exploited, whilst sound might not always be allocated between objects; it could be conductive to multiple objects or to no object. Yet, the social context provides a thorough understanding of what is a potential auditory object and promotes the segmentation of ecologically consistent and valuable audio-visual entities (e.g., a speaking person). A mean to ground consistency has been synchronisation between audio and visual events an issue that has been previously addressed, e.g., [12,21,26]. To such end we have adapted to our framework recent results gained by deep network techniques [10,11]. As a result, spatially-based probabilistic priority maps are built-up from the visual and auditory objects across different analysis scales. These maps are dynamic loci that moment-to-moment compete on the base of their activities. The latter are formalised in terms of value-driven proto-object sampling, to generate attractors for attention deployment. Cogently, sampling is conditional on the value dynamics (current history and "internal" goals) of the perceiver. This choice is consistent with theoretical model building trends [35] positing active attentional deployment as the problem of maximising the total rewards that can be gained by the active perceiver. Further, the broader perspective of "internal" value/reward, as brought forward by socially relevant stimuli [1,3], paves the way to a wider dimension of attentional processing, e.g. including affective modulation of attention.

Value attribution dynamics is learnt on a video clip on the basis of eye-tracked gaze allocation of a number of observer and can be used, at the testing stage, to predict attentional deployment of novel observers on the same clip. In this respect, one may raise the issue that the inferred viewing behaviour might not generalise to novel kind of stimuli content. This objection is true but with reference to the specific unfolding in time of value dynamics on a given video clip, as provided by the current regression-like implementation of Eqs. 4 and 5. Even so, on the one hand, the model simulation as such (that is, in the same experimental setting we have presented here) could be applied to a variety of investigations of social attention behaviour in groups that are likely to differentiate with respect to the given stimulus (e.g., clinical populations). On the other hand, the model captures and, cogently, quantifies across the different video clips some general patterns of value attribution in attentional allocation: low-level, physically driven cues (early salience) play a marginal role when social cues are present; effects due to spatial tendencies, such as the center bias, are relevant at the onset of the stimulus, and rapidly decrease in time; attention deployment is rapidly devoted to people in the video, speakers bearing the highest value for the observer. Yet, issues of generalisation across different video clips were out of the scope of the study presented here and are currently part of ongoing research.

A key feature of our approach is the inherent stochasticity of the model (sampling). This is *per se* apt to account for either observers' inter- and intra-variability in audio-visual perceptual tasks. More generally, randomness in actual attention deployment (as eventually gauged through gaze shifts) is likely to be originated from endogenous stochastic variations that affect each stage between a perceptual event and the motor response: sensing, information processing, movement planning and executing [32]. At bottom, it should be always kept in mind that the actual process involving eye movement behaviour is a closed loop between an ideal observer, that extracts task-relevant information from a sequence of observations, and an ideal planner which specifies the actions that lead to the most rewarding sampling [35]. The latter issue involving the actual gaze shift (motor action) is often neglected in the literature [31]. In point of fact, oculomotor behaviour encapsulates either noisy motor responses and systematic tendencies in the manner in which we explore scenes with our eyes [32], albeit modulated by the semantic category of the stimulus [20]. Overall and most important, this approach paves the way to the possibility of treating reward-based visual exploration strategies in the framework of stochastic *information foraging* [4,22,34], a promising research line for which the model presented here is likely to offer a sound basis.

References

1. Anderson, B.A.: A value-driven mechanism of attentional selection. J. Vis. **13**(3), 7 (2013)
2. Awh, E., Belopolsky, A.V., Theeuwes, J.: Top-down versus bottom-up attentional control: a failed theoretical dichotomy. Trends Cogn. Sci. **16**(8), 437–443 (2012)
3. Berridge, K.C., Robinson, T.E.: Parsing reward. Trends Neurosci. **26**(9), 507–513 (2003)
4. Boccignone, G., Ferraro, M.: Ecological sampling of gaze shifts. IEEE Trans. Cybern. **44**(2), 266–279 (2014)
5. Borji, A., Itti, L.: State-of-the-art in visual attention modeling. IEEE Trans. Pattern Anal. Mach. Intell. **35**(1), 185–207 (2013)
6. Bruce, N.D., Wloka, C., Frosst, N., Rahman, S., Tsotsos, J.K.: On computational modeling of visual saliency: examining what's right, and what's left. Vis. Res. **116**, 95–112 (2015)
7. Bylinskii, Z., Judd, T., Oliva, A., Torralba, A., Durand, F.: What do different evaluation metrics tell us about saliency models? IEEE Trans. Pattern Anal. Mach. Intell. 1 (2018). https://doi.org/10.1109/TPAMI.2018.2815601
8. Cerf, M., Harel, J., Einhäuser, W., Koch, C.: Predicting human gaze using low-level saliency combined with face detection. In: Advances in Neural Information Processing Systems, vol. 20 (2008)
9. Chikkerur, S., Serre, T., Tan, C., Poggio, T.: What and where: a Bayesian inference theory of attention. Vis. Res. **50**(22), 2233–2247 (2010)
10. Chung, J.S., Zisserman, A.: Out of time: automated lip sync in the wild. In: Chen, C.-S., Lu, J., Ma, K.-K. (eds.) ACCV 2016. LNCS, vol. 10117, pp. 251–263. Springer, Cham (2017). https://doi.org/10.1007/978-3-319-54427-4_19
11. Chung, J.S., Zisserman, A.: Lip reading in profile. In: BMVC (2017)
12. Coutrot, A., Guyader, N.: An efficient audiovisual saliency model to predict eye positions when looking at conversations. In: 23rd European Signal Processing Conference, pp. 1531–1535, August 2015
13. Coutrot, A., Guyader, N.: How saliency, faces, and sound influence gaze in dynamic social scenes. J. Vis. **14**(8), 5 (2014)
14. Einhäuser, W., Spain, M., Perona, P.: Objects predict fixations better than early saliency. J. Vis. **8**(14) (2008). https://doi.org/10.1167/8.14.18, http://www.journalofvision.org/content/8/14/18.abstract

15. Evangelopoulos, G., Rapantzikos, K., Maragos, P., Avrithis, Y., Potamianos, A.: Audiovisual attention modeling and salient event detection. In: Maragos, P., Potamianos, A., Gros, P. (eds.) Multimodal Processing and Interaction. MMSA, pp. 1–21. Springer, Boston (2008). https://doi.org/10.1007/978-0-387-76316-3_8
16. Foulsham, T., Cheng, J.T., Tracy, J.L., Henrich, J., Kingstone, A.: Gaze allocation in a dynamic situation: effects of social status and speaking. Cognition **117**(3), 319–331 (2010)
17. Hu, P., Ramanan, D.: Finding tiny faces. In: 2017 IEEE Conference on Computer Vision and Pattern Recognition (CVPR), pp. 1522–1530. IEEE (2017)
18. Kaya, E.M., Elhilali, M.: Modelling auditory attention. Phil. Trans. R. Soc. B **372**(1714), 20160101 (2017)
19. Kayser, C., Petkov, C.I., Lippert, M., Logothetis, N.K.: Mechanisms for allocating auditory attention: an auditory saliency map. Curr. Biol. **15**(21), 1943–1947 (2005)
20. Le Meur, O., Coutrot, A.: Introducing context-dependent and spatially-variant viewing biases in saccadic models. Vis. Res. **121**, 72–84 (2016)
21. Nakajima, J., Sugimoto, A., Kawamoto, K.: Incorporating audio signals into constructing a visual saliency map. In: Klette, R., Rivera, M., Satoh, S. (eds.) PSIVT 2013. LNCS, vol. 8333, pp. 468–480. Springer, Heidelberg (2014). https://doi.org/10.1007/978-3-642-53842-1_40
22. Napoletano, P., Boccignone, G., Tisato, F.: Attentive monitoring of multiple video streams driven by a bayesian foraging strategy. IEEE Trans. Image Process. **24**(11), 3266–3281 (2015)
23. Onat, S., Libertus, K., König, P.: Integrating audiovisual information for the control of overt attention. J. Vis. **7**(10), 11 (2007)
24. Park, T., Casella, G.: The Bayesian lasso. J. Am. Stat. Assoc. **103**(482), 681–686 (2008)
25. Rahman, I.M., Hollitt, C., Zhang, M.: Feature map quality score estimation through regression. IEEE Trans. Image Process. **27**(4), 1793–1808 (2018)
26. Rodríguez-Hidalgo, A., Peláez-Moreno, C., Gallardo-Antolín, A.: Towards multimodal saliency detection: an enhancement of audio-visual correlation estimation. In: Proceedings of 16th International Conference on Cognitive Informatics and Cognitive Computing, pp. 438–443. IEEE (2017)
27. Schütz, A., Braun, D., Gegenfurtner, K.: Eye movements and perception: a selective review. J. Vis. **11**(5), 9 (2011)
28. Seo, H., Milanfar, P.: Static and space-time visual saliency detection by self-resemblance. J. Vis. **9**(12), 1–27 (2009)
29. Shinn-Cunningham, B.G.: Object-based auditory and visual attention. Trends Cogn. Sci. **12**(5), 182–186 (2008)
30. Suda, Y., Kitazawa, S.: A model of face selection in viewing video stories. Sci. Rep. **5**, 7666 (2015)
31. Tatler, B., Hayhoe, M., Land, M., Ballard, D.: Eye guidance in natural vision: Reinterpreting salience. J. Vis. **11**(5), 5 (2011)
32. Tatler, B., Vincent, B.: The prominence of behavioural biases in eye guidance. Vis. Cogn. **17**(6–7), 1029–1054 (2009)
33. Torralba, A.: Contextual priming for object detection. Int. J. Comput. Vis. **53**, 153–167 (2003)
34. Wolfe, J.M.: When is it time to move to the next raspberry bush? Foraging rules in human visual search. J. Vis. **13**(3), 10 (2013)
35. Yang, S.C.H., Wolpert, D.M., Lengyel, M.: Theoretical perspectives on active sensing. Curr. Opin. Behav. Sci. **11**, 100–108 (2016)

Investigating Depth Domain Adaptation for Efficient Human Pose Estimation

Angel Martínez-González[1,2](✉), Michael Villamizar[1], Olivier Canévet[1], and Jean-Marc Odobez[1,2]

[1] Idiap Research Institute, Martigny, Switzerland
{angel.martinez,michael.villamizar,olivier.canevet,odobez}@idiap.ch
[2] École Polytechnique Fédérale de Lausanne (EPFL), Lausanne, Switzerland

Abstract. Convolutional Neural Networks (CNN) are the leading models for human body landmark detection from RGB vision data. However, as such models require high computational load, an alternative is to rely on depth images which, due to their more simple nature, can allow the use of less complex CNNs and hence can lead to a faster detector. As learning CNNs from scratch requires large amounts of labeled data, which are not always available or expensive to obtain, we propose to rely on simulations and synthetic examples to build a large training dataset with precise labels. Nevertheless, the final performance on real data will suffer from the mismatch between the training and test data, also called domain shift between the source and target distributions. Thus in this paper, our main contribution is to investigate the use of unsupervised domain adaptation techniques to fill the gap in performance introduced by these distribution differences. The challenge lies in the important noise differences (not only gaussian noise, but many missing values around body limbs) between synthetic and real data, as well as the fact that we address a regression task rather than a classification one. In addition, we introduce a new public dataset of synthetically generated depth images to cover the cases of multi-person pose estimation. Our experiments show that domain adaptation provides some improvement, but that further network fine-tuning with real annotated data is worth including to supervise the adaptation process.

Keywords: Human pose estimation · Adversarial learning · Domain adaptation · Machine learning

1 Introduction

Person detection and pose estimation are fundamental tasks for many vision based systems across different types of computer vision domains, e.g. visual surveillance, gaming and social robotics. Estimating the human pose provide the different systems the means for fine-level motion understanding and activity recognition.

L. Leal-Taixé and S. Roth (Eds.): ECCV 2018 Workshops, LNCS 11130, pp. 346–363, 2019.
https://doi.org/10.1007/978-3-030-11012-3_28

Representation based methods, specifically Convolutional Neural Networks (CNN), are the leading algorithms to address the pose estimation task. Very deep CNN models have shown robustness to pose complexity, people occlusion and noisy imaging, providing excellent results. Normally, the deeper is the CNN architecture, the larger are the computational demands. In addition, the learning task needs sufficient amounts of data that span the human pose configuration space to prevent overfiting.

To alleviate these issues, we propose the use of depth imaging for human body pose estimation using CNNs. By using depth images we lower the complexity introduced by variabilities such as color and texture, which result in using lighter CNN architectures capable for real time deployment. Depth images have been proven to provide relevant information for the task of human pose estimation. Moreover, the need of training data can be addressed by depth image synthesis. The obtained benefits are twofold, (1) they are easier to synthesize than natural RGB images, and (2) accurate body part annotations come at no cost. However, our pose estimation task will suffer from the domain shift. That is, synthetic and real images come from different distributions, limiting the CNN's generalization capabilities on real depth images.

The challenge addressed in this paper is to fill the gap in the performance caused by the domain shift provoked by learning from synthetic depth images to deploy on real ones. We investigate unsupervised domain adaptation methods to exploit large datasets of unlabeled depth images with people to boost the performance of a CNN-based body pose regressor learned from synthetic data. Landmark localization imposes a challenge in typical domain adaptation settings where the final task is image classification and domains mainly vary in viewpoint and objects are mainly image-centered. On this line, we address the need of training data by creating a dataset of synthetically generated depth images to cover multi-person pose estimation settings by generating depth images displaying two person instances. We show how data recorded with the same type of depth sensor is meaningful for unsupervised domain adaptation for pose estimation purposes. We finally analyze the limitations of unsupervised domain adaptation by comparing the results of adapted models with those obtained by performing fine-tuning with few annotated images. Our experiments suggest that domain adaptation solely improves the performance, and can be further boosted by fine-tuning on a small sample of labeled images.

In Sect. 2 we present a review of state-of-the-art CNN-based approaches for body pose estimation and domain adaptation. In Sect. 3, we present the different data we use for learning and testing purposes and our approach for synthesizing images in multi-person scenarios. Section 4 describes the proposed approach for depth domain adaptation for body pose estimation. Experiments and results are described in Sect. 5. Finally, Sect. 6 presents our conclusions and future work.

2 State-of-the-Art

State-of-the-art methods for pose estimation in the deep learning literature mainly cover the RGB domain. They mainly address the task relying on the

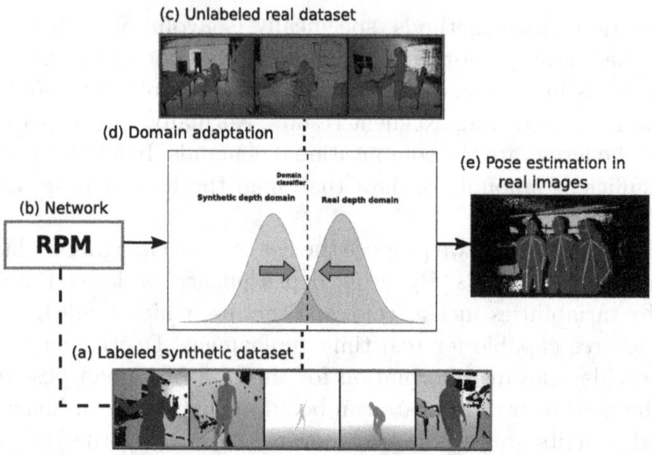

Fig. 1. Scheme of the proposed method for efficient human pose estimation from depth images. A CNN (b) is learned relying on synthetically generated images of people under multiple pose configurations combined with varying real background (a). The domain shift is addressed via an unsupervised domain adaptation method (d) that uses real unlabeled data (c).

cascade of detectors concept: sequentially stacking detectors to improve and refine body part predictions. Image context is retrieved through different network kernel resolutions [12,20,28,29], or embedding coarse to fine prediction in the network architecture [2,10,18]. Moreover, learning the relationships between pairs of body parts improves the performance [3,11,13,25].

Depth data has proven to be a good source of perceptual information of great importance, specifically for robotics and autonomous systems. Depth images preserve many essential features that also appear in natural images, e.g. corners, edges, silhouettes, and it is texture and color invariant.

Pose estimation methods from depth images also exist in the CNN literature [6,9,28]. Given that depth image datasets with body part annotations are scarce in the public domain, approaches of this kind use a large network pre-trained on RGB data (e.g. VGG [24]) to fine-tune to the depth domain. However, the use of RGB pre-trained models is not necessarily adequate for the depth domain given the difference between the two data types. In addition, such large pre-trained networks involve many parameters and may unnecessary increase the processing time.

An alternative approach to address the lack of data is via image synthesis [5, 15,21,23]. The simplicity of depth images has an advantage for data generation: the lack of texture and color removes some variability factors and simplifies the synthesis process.

A very well known approach that pursued this path is the approach of Shotton et al. [21] proposing a depth image synthesis pipeline to generate a large and varied training set using computer graphics. Still, although a very high realism is achieved, the data does not span the full range of data content. The generated data lacks of typical image characteristics of depth sensors which are difficult to model, as illustrated in Fig. 3.

As a result, a model learned and tested on different data origins will suffer a degraded performance provoked by the so called domain shift arising from the differences in visual features. This issue can be alleviated provided extra labeled data for the testing domain. However, since obtaining such data in large enough quantities is often problematic, an unsupervised domain adaptation technique is well suited to learn a predictor in presence of a domain shift between the training (source) and testing (target) data distributions without the need of labeled data in the target domain.

The premise of a domain adaptation technique is to learn a data representation that is invariant across domains. On the one hand, classical machine learning approaches seek to align the data distributions by minimizing the distance between domains provided domain distribution parametrizations [7]. On the other hand, current deep learning methods make use of various training strategies and network architectures to ensure and ease domain confusion and to automatically learn an invariant representation of the data [4,8,16,26,27].

For example [8] proposes to learn invariant data features in a multi-task adversarial setting for object classification. The method learns jointly an object class and domain predictors with shared features among the tasks. Domain adaptation is achieved by an adversarial domain regularizer which aims at fooling the domain classifier, which is in charge of predicting the domain the data comes from. The process encourages the learning of features that makes the domain classifier incapable of distinguish between domains.

Domain adaptation has also been used for the task of 3D pose estimation from RGB images [5]. The approach uses computer graphics software to synthesize colored and textured images of humans that are subsequently merged with natural images as background. Domain adaptation is performed in a two step learning process by alternating the updates of a domain predictor and pose regressor.

Deep domain adaptation in the depth image domain is less covered in the literature. A comparison of state-of-the-art domain adaptation techniques applied to object classification from depth images is presented in [19]. Along the same direction, a method for feature transfer from the real to the synthetic depth domain is presented in [22].

Although deep domain adaptation techniques have obtained remarkable results in transferring domain knowledge, in the majority of the problems the visual domains mainly differ in the objects perspective, lighting, background, and objects are mostly image centered. In addition, most of the final tasks are image classification leaving an open door to apply the same methods for regression problems and object localization tasks, e.g. keypoint detection.

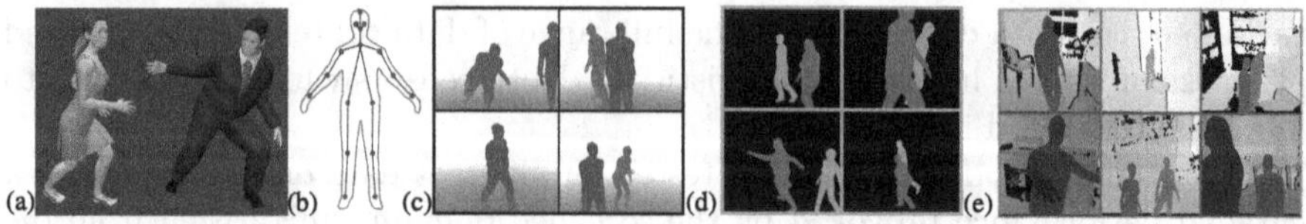

Fig. 2. (a) Examples of the 3D characters we use for depth image synthesis, (b) skeleton model we follow to perform pose estimation, (c) examples of rendered synthetic images, (d) color labeled mask, (e) examples of training images combining synthetic depth silhouettes and real depth background images. (Color figure online)

3 Depth Image Domains

This section presents the depth image domains we consider for our pose estimation approach. First, we describe our approach to generate synthetic depth images for multi-person pose estimation settings. Then, we introduce the target data for testing composed of real depth image sequences recorded in a Human-Robot Interaction (HRI) scenario.

3.1 Synthetic Depth Image Generation

Training CNNs requires large amounts of labeled data. Unfortunately, a precise manual annotation of depth images with body parts is troublesome, given that people roughly appear as blobs.

As mentioned before, synthesizing depth images is easier than color images due to the lack of texture, color and lighting. We consider the synthetic depth image database generated by the randomized synthesis pipeline proposed in [17]. The dataset contains images displaying single person instances with different body pose and view perspectives. Yet, it may not be well suited for learning multi-person pose estimation settings like in HRI where people occlusion occur frequently. The data must then reflect these cases. Building upon [17], we improve such pipeline to synthesize depth images displaying two people under different pose configurations, and to extract high quality annotations. The synthesis pipeline is briefly described below.

Variability in Body Shapes. We consider a dataset of 24 3D characters that show variation in gender, heights and weights, and have been dressed with different clothing outfits to increase shape variation (skirts, coats, pullovers, etc.).

Synthesis with Two People Instances. We cover the scenarios of multi-person pose estimation by adding two 3D characters to the rendering scene. During synthesis, two models are randomly selected from the character database and placed at a fixed distance between each other. To avoid checking for collision between the characters we set a minimum distance between them during rendering.

Variability in Body Poses. Motion simulation is used to add variability in body pose configurations. We perform motion retargeting from motion capture data sequences taken from the CMU labs Mocap dataset [1].

Variability in View Point. A camera is randomly positioned at a maximum distance of 8 meters from the models, and randomly oriented towards the models torso.

Dataset and Annotations. The generated image dataset displaying two people instances is publicly available as an extension of the data presented in [17]. Altogether, the two datasets contain 223,342 images of people performing different types of motion under different viewpoints with 51,194 images displaying two people. We automatically extract the location of 17 body landmarks (*head, neck, shoulders, elbows, wrists, hips, knees, ankles, eyes*) in camera and image coordinates. Keypoint visibility labels are also provided. In addition, we extract color labeled silhouette masks for images that contain two people instances. See Fig. 2(b) for some examples.

3.2 Real Depth Image Domain Data

Depth imaging is generated as triangulation process in which a series of laser beams are cast into the scene, captured by an infrared camera, and correlated with a reference pattern to produce disparity images and finally the distance to the sensor. The image quality and visual features greatly depend on the sensor specifications, e.g. measurement variance, missing data, surface discontinuities, etc. It is therefore natural to handle depth-based pose estimation learning from synthetic data as a domain adaptation problem, where each depth sensor type constitutes a domain.

We study the problem of depth domain adaptation considering synthetic depth imaging as the source domain and Kinect 2 depth imaging as the target domain. We further focus in HRI settings and consider two datasets.

First, we consider the Watch-n-Patch (WnP) database introduced in [30] which will be used for adaptation purposes. To evaluate the performance of our

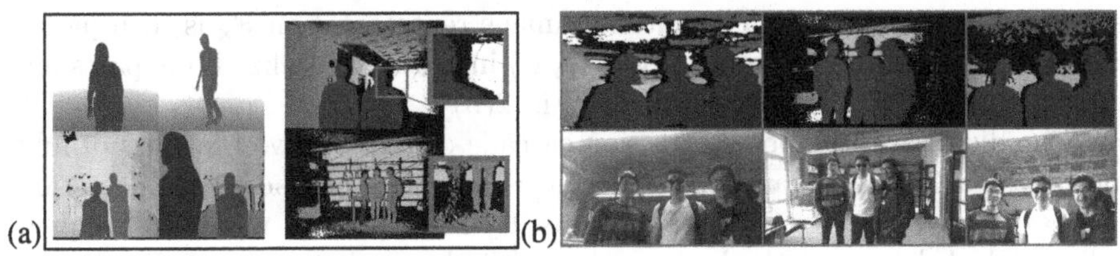

Fig. 3. Depth imaging characteristics. (a) visual characteristics around the human silhouette in depth sensing are difficult to synthesize and therefore not present in the rendered image, (b) HRI scene recorded with different RGB-D cameras, left to right: Intel D435, Kinect 2 and Asus Xtion. Different depth sensors makes the recorded depth images to show specific type of visual characteristics for each sensor.

method, we need a second dataset. To this end, we conducted a series of data collection, recording videos of people interacting with a robotic platform. The recorded data consist of 16 sequences in HRI settings recorded with a Kinect 2. Each of the sequences has a duration of up to three minutes and is composed of pairs of registered color and depth images. The interactions were performed by 9 different participants in indoor settings under different background scene and natural interaction situations. In addition the participants were asked to wear different clothing accessories to add variability in the body shape. Each of the sequences displays up to three people captured at different distance from the sensor. In our experiments we refer to this recorded data as *RLimbs*. Both datasets with annotations, synthetic and recorded HRI sequences, are publicly available[1].

In Sect. 5 we show how to use this data to bridge the gap between synthetic and real depth image domains, improving the pose estimation performance in real images without the need of annotations on the real data.

4 Depth Domain Adaptation for Pose Estimation

Our pose estimation approach is inspired in the convolutional pose machines (CPM) framework [3]. That is, we predict body parts and limbs of multiple people in a cascade of detectors fashion. In this section we describe the base CNN architecture we follow for pose estimation and the modifications we add to perform depth domain adaptation.

4.1 Base CNN Architecture and Pose Learning

Pose Regression CNN Architecture. Figure 4(a) and (b) comprise the base architecture of the pose regression network used to detect body parts and limbs, taking as input a single channel depth image.

Specifically, the neural network architecture is composed of a feature extractor module $G_F(\cdot)$ parametrized by θ_F, and a pose regression cascade module $G_y(\cdot)$ parametrized by θ_Y. For an input depth image $\mathbf{x}$ the feature extractor module computes a compact image representation (features) $\mathbf{F_x} = G_F(\mathbf{x})$ that is internal to the network. This internal image representation $\mathbf{F_x}$ is then passed to the pose regression cascade module $G_Y(\cdot)$ in order to localize body parts and limbs according to our skeleton model (Fig. 2(b)).

A predictor t in the pose regression cascade consist on two branches of fully convolutional layers. Branch $\rho_t(\cdot)$ performs the task of body part detection, whereas branch $\phi_t(\cdot)$ localizes body limbs. By considering a number of sequentially stacked detectors, the body parts and limbs predictions are refined using the result of previous stages and incorporating image spatial context through the features $\mathbf{F_x}$.

[1] https://www.idiap.ch/dataset/dih.

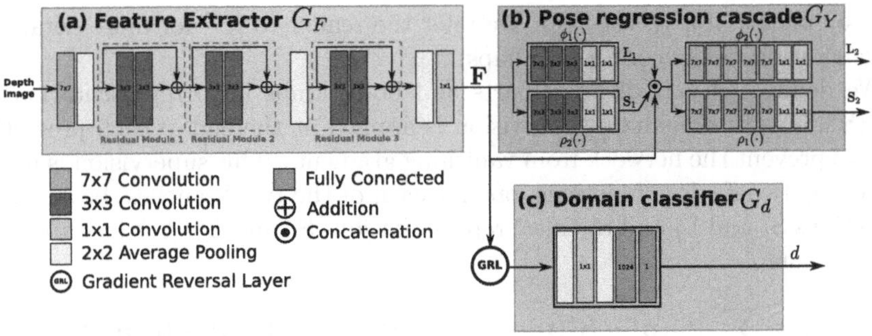

Fig. 4. Architecture design of the CNN used for pose estimation from single channel depth images. The base architecture is composed of a feature extractor module (a), and a pose regression cascade (b). The architecture is further extended with a domain classifier (c) for depth domain adaptation.

Finally, pose inference is performed in a greedy bottom-up step to gather parts and limbs belonging to the same person, as originally proposed by the CPM framework.

Feature Extractor Module. The network's feature extraction module $G_F(\cdot)$ computes the image features $\mathbf{F_x}$ by applying a series of residual modules to the image $\mathbf{x}$. The architecture of $G_F(\cdot)$ comprises three residual modules with small kernel sizes and three average pooling layers. Batch normalization and ReLU are included after each convolutional layer and after the shortcut connection.

The architeture of $G_F(\cdot)$ has been designed targeting efficient and fast forward pass, relying on the representational power and efficiency of residual modules. The combination of the processing time taken by the feature extractor together with the cascade of detectors can provide estimations at a frame rate of 35 FPS.

Pose Regression Module. In the pose regression cascade module, each stage t takes as input the image features $\mathbf{F_x}$ and the output of the previous detector $t-1$. As depicted on Fig. 4(b), a detector consists of two branches of convolutional layers, the first branch predicting the location of the parts, and the second predicts the location and orientation of the limbs. Note that with only one stage there is no refinement since the first stage only takes as input the features $\mathbf{F_x}$.

Confidence Map Prediction and Pose Regression Loss. We regress confidence maps for the location of the different body parts and predict vector fields for the location and orientation of the body limbs.

The ideal representation of the body part confidence maps $\mathbf{S}^*$ encodes the ground truth location on the depth image as Gaussian peaks. The ideal representation of the limbs $\mathbf{L}^*$ encodes the confidence for the connection between two adjacent body parts, in addition to information about the orientation of the limbs by means of a vector field. We refer the reader to [17] for more details on the generation of the confidence maps.

We define the pair of body parts and body limbs ideal representations as $Y = (\mathbf{S}^*, \mathbf{L}^*)$. Intermediate supervision is applied at the end of each prediction stage to prevent the network from vanishing gradients. This supervision is implemented by two L_2 loss functions, one for each of the two branches, between the predictions $\mathbf{S}_t$ and $\mathbf{L}_t$ and the ideal representations $\mathbf{S}^*$ and $\mathbf{L}^*$. The loss functions at stage t are

$$f_t^1 = \sum_{\mathbf{p} \in \mathbf{I}} ||\mathbf{S}_t(\mathbf{p}) - \mathbf{S}^*(\mathbf{p})||_2^2, \qquad f_t^2 = \sum_{\mathbf{p} \in \mathbf{I}} ||\mathbf{L}_t(\mathbf{p}) - \mathbf{L}^*(\mathbf{p})||_2^2. \tag{1}$$

The pose regression loss is computed as $\mathscr{L}_Y = \sum_{t=1}^{T} \left(f_t^1 + f_t^2\right)$ where T is the total number of stages in the pose regression cascade.

4.2 Depth Domain Adaptation

Ideally, testing and training depth images should live in the same domain. In our case, learning a pose regression network from synthetic data limits its generalization capacity given the missing real depth image details not present in the synthetic training set. We perform domain adaptation to map synthetic and real images to a representation that is similar across domains. We follow closely the method presented in [8] for domain adaptation and adapt it to our body part localization setting.

For our unsupervised domain adaptation learning algorithm we are given a source distribution sample (synthetic depth image dataset) $S = \{(\mathbf{x}_i, \mathbf{y}_i)\}_{i=1}^{N} \sim \mathscr{D}_S$ and a target dataset sample (real depth image dataset) $T = \{\mathbf{x}_i\}_{i=1}^{M} \sim \mathscr{D}_T$. We are only given annotations of 2D keypoint locations $\mathbf{y}_i$ for the source distribution samples $\mathbf{x}_i$.

The distance between the source and target distributions can be measure via the H-divergence [8]. Although this is impractical to compute, it can be approximated by the generalization error of the problem of domain classification. In essence, the distance between distributions is minimum if the domain classifier is incapable of distinguishing between the different domains. Therefore, to achieve domain confusion, the data need to be mapped to a representation that is invariant, or at least indistinguishable, across domains.

Let $\mathbf{F}_\mathbf{x}$ be the internal representation of image $\mathbf{x}$ in the network (features) computed as $\mathbf{F}_\mathbf{x} = G_F(\mathbf{x})$ for a feature extractor $G_F(\cdot)$. A measure of domain adaptation is computed by

$$L_d = -\frac{1}{|S|} \sum_{\mathbf{x} \in S} l_d(G_d(\mathbf{F}_\mathbf{x})) - \frac{1}{|T|} \sum_{\mathbf{x} \in T} l_d(G_d(\mathbf{F}_\mathbf{x})), \tag{2}$$

where and l_d is a logistic regression loss, and G_d is a domain classifier, parametrized by θ_d, such that $G_d(F_\mathbf{x}) = 1$ if $\mathbf{x} \in T$ and 0 otherwise.

In the problem of domain classification, the domain classifier $G_d(\cdot)$ is fooled when $G_F(\cdot)$ produces equivalent features for both domains. A feature extractor capable of producing such type of features is learned by maximizing Eq. (2)

$$R_d = \max_{\theta_d} L_d. \tag{3}$$

Equation (3) aims to approximate the empirical H-divergence between domains S and T as $2(1 - R_d)$.

4.3 Joint Pose Learning and Adaptation

The pose learning and domain adaptation joint optimization objective can be written as

$$\mathscr{L} = \mathscr{L}_Y + \lambda R_d, \tag{4}$$

where λ is a parameter that tunes the trade-off between the pose learning and domain adaptation. The second term of Eq. (4) acts as a domain regularizer.

Our pose regression network shown in Fig. 4(a) and (b) naturally provides the scheme for the joint learning and adaptation problem via a domain classifier (Fig. 4(c)). We implement the domain classifier via a neural network composed of two average pooling layers with an intermediate layer of 1×1 convolution and followed by two fully connected layers that produces a sigmoid function. As shown in Fig. 4 both the pose regression cascade $G_Y(\cdot)$ and the domain classifier $G_d(\cdot)$ receive as input the features generated by $G_F(\cdot)$.

The learning and adaptation problem stated by Eq. (4) proposes an adversarial learning process which involves a minimization with respect to the pose regression loss $\mathscr{L}_Y$ and a maximization with respect to the domain classifier regularizer R_d. We follow [8] by including a gradient reversal layer (GRL) in the architecture to facilitate the joint optimization. The GRL acts as identity function during the forward pass of the network, but reverses the direction of the gradients from the domain classifier during backpropagation.

The nature of pose regression and domain adaptation problems makes the losess involved in Eq. (4) to live in different ranges. Therefore, the trade-off parameter λ has to reflect both the importance of the domain classification regularizer as well as to this difference between ranges.

5 Experiments and Results

In a series of experiments we show how different datasets, recorded with the same type of sensor, are used to improve pose estimation via unsupervised domain adaptation. In this section we analyze the performance obtained under different modeling selections on the network architecture and domain adaptation configurations.

5.1 Data

Synthetic Domain Data. We split the synthetic dataset into three folds with the following percentage and amount of images: training (85%, 189,844), validation (5%, 11,165), and testing (10%, 22,333).

Synthetic Training Data Augmentation. We add the following perturbations to the synthetic images to add realism and avoid overfitting to synthetic clean details.

Adding Real Background Content. We consider the dataset in [14] containing 1,367 real depth images recorded with a Kinect 1 and exhibiting depth indoor clutter. During learning, training images were produced on the fly by randomly selecting one depth image background and body synthetic images, and composing a depth image with background using the character silhouette mask. Sample results are shown in Fig. 2(d).

Pixel Noise. We randomly select 20% of the body silhouette's pixels and set their value to zero.

Image Rotation. Training images are rotated with a probability 0.1 by a randomly selected angle in the range $[-20, 20]$ degrees.

Real Domain Data. Our real domain consist Kinect 2 data. We use the data presented in Sect. 3.2 to perform domain adaptation. The Watch-n-Patch dataset was used for adaptation purposes only. We randomly select 85% out of the total number of images comprised over all the sequences, leading to a total of 66,303 depth.

We used the RLimbs data for training, validation and testing purposes. We divide the data taking into account clothing features, actor ID and interaction scenario, in such a way that an actor does not appear in the training and testing sets under similar circumstances. The train, validation and test folds consist of 7, 5 and 4 sequences respectively. We annotate small sets from each fold to be used for validation (750 images), testing (1000 images) and fine-tuning (1750 images).

5.2 Evaluation Protocol

Accuracy Metric. We use standard precision and recall measures derived from the Percentage of Correct Keypoints (PCKh) as performance metrics [31]. More precisely, we extract landmark predictions p whose confidence is larger than a threshold τ. Pose estimates are generated from these predictions by the part association algorithm. Then, for each landmark type we associate the closest prediction p whose distance to ground truth q is below a distance threshold $d = \kappa \times h$, where h stands for the height of the ground truth bounding box of the person to which q belongs to. The associated predictions p count as true positives and the rest as false positives. Ground truth points q with no associated prediction are counted as false negatives. The average recall and precision values can then be computed by averaging over the landmark types and then over the dataset. Finally, the average recall and precision values used to report performance are computed by averaging the above recall and precision over several distance thresholds by varying κ in the range $[0.05, 0.15]$.

5.3 Implementation Details

Pose Regression Network. We use Pytorch as the deep learning framework in all our experiments. First, we train our pose regression network (Fig. 4(a) and (b)) on synthetic data with stochastic gradient descent with momentum during 300K iterations. We set the momentum to 0.9, the weight decay constant to 5×10^{-4}, and the batch size to 10. We uniformly sample values in the range $[4 \times 10^{-10}, 4 \times 10^{-5}]$ as starting learning rate and decrease it by a factor of 10 when the validation loss has settled. All networks are trained from scratch and progressively, i.e. to train network architectures with t stages, we initialize the network with the parameters of the trained network with $t-1$ stages. We consider network architectures with pose regression cascade modules comprised by upto 2 prediction stages.

Domain Adaptation. After training the pose regression network for some time with synthetic data, we run the domain adaptation process. The adaptation is performed for $T = 100K$ iterations. We monitor and select models according to the lowest value of a validation loss computed on the RLimbs validation set. The learning rate parameter is kept fixed to the last value in the previous training procedure. Domain classifier parameters are randomly initialized using a Gaussian distribution with mean zero and small variance.

We opt to gradually adapt the trade-off parameter λ of Eq. (4) according to the training progress as

$$\lambda_p = \frac{2\Lambda}{1 + exp(-10p)} - \Lambda, \tag{5}$$

where $p = t/T$ for the current iteration progress t. The constant Λ was experimentally chosen in order to accommodate both losses in Eq. (4) in the same range. In our experiments we observed a good behavior of pose learning and adaptation for $\Lambda = 100$.

Model Notation. We analyze CNN architectures with 1 and 2 prediction stages in the pose regressor cascade. In our results we refer to this configurations as RPM1S and RPM2S respectively. Postfixes -DA and -FT are added whenever used domain adaptation or fine-tuning respectively.

5.4 Results

Domain Adaptation and Network Configuration. We analyze the impact of domain adaptation on the different levels of prediction stages. For these experiments we consider the Watch-n-Patch data for the adaptation process and the RLimbs data for testing. The models were trained as follows. First, a single stage network was trained with synthetic data and then with domain adaptation. Next, a network architecture with 2 stages was trained on synthetic data taking the single stage adapted network as initial point. Finally domain adaptation is performed.

The resultant average recall-precision curves are presented in Fig. 5(a). We observe that domain adaptation improves mainly the recall performance at the two levels of prediction stages. Including spatial context via a second prediction stage is vital. Table 1 summarizes these results reporting the models with the largest F1-Score in the curves. The table also shows the performance on the upper-body. In Fig. 6 we show a comparison of the per body part precision and recall before and after adaptation. Domain adaptation mainly improves the recall on the lower body parts. As depicted in Fig. 3, these parts are the main components in the body silhouettes affected by noise and sensing failures.

Domain Adaptation Starting Point. We conducted experiments in order to find the best training point to start the domain adaptation process. To this end, we start domain adaptation at different points of the synthetic training progress for the RPM2S model. We selected starting points at $t = 150K$, $t = 200K$ and $t = 300K$ training iterations. Figure 5(b) shows the performance of the different learned models. We note the performance among the different runs remains the same. However, the earliest starting point considered show more stable behavior.

RLimbs Based Domain Adaptation. As mentioned before, it is natural to think a depth sensor as a generating domain. We perform domain adaptation using the training fold of the RLimbs database as the target domain sample. As before, we start domain adaptation at different points of the synthetic training and report the model results with the best F1-Score. Table 2 compares the obtained performances. In the table we specifically show the dataset used as target sample during the adaptation process, the source data and the testing data. Note that using both Kinect 2 datasets in the adaptation process improves the performance. Adaptation with the Watch-n-Patch dataset provides slightly better results. It is worth to notice that the number of recorded scenarios, people, and view points contained in the Watch-n-Patch is larger than those contained the RLimbs dataset. This variability is somehow useful in the adaptation process. We include the performance obtained by preprocessing the image with a simple in-paint process. This technique was previously used to alleviate the discontinuities inherited from depth sensing for non adapted models [17]. However, this lowers the precision score with a very little gain in accuracy.

Fine-Tunning. To understand the limits of adapting between depth domains, we performed fine-tunning on an annotated subset of the RLimbs dataset. We considered both, the models trained with synthetic data and adapted models. Figure 5(c) shows the detailed recall- precision curves. As expected, fine tuning on the target data provides better generalization capabilities. However, fine-tuning on models with previous adaptation show further improvement. Table 2

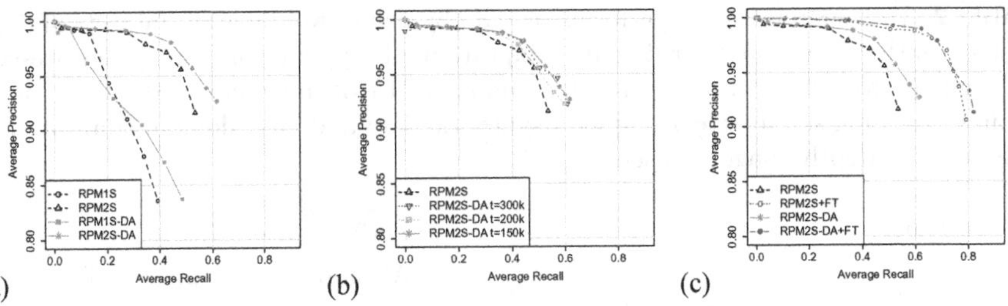

(a) (b) (c)

Fig. 5. Average recall-precision curves. (a) impact when applying domain adaptation at the different levels of prediction stages. (b) performance for different starting points of domain adaptation. (c) comparison of domain adaptation and fine-tuning.

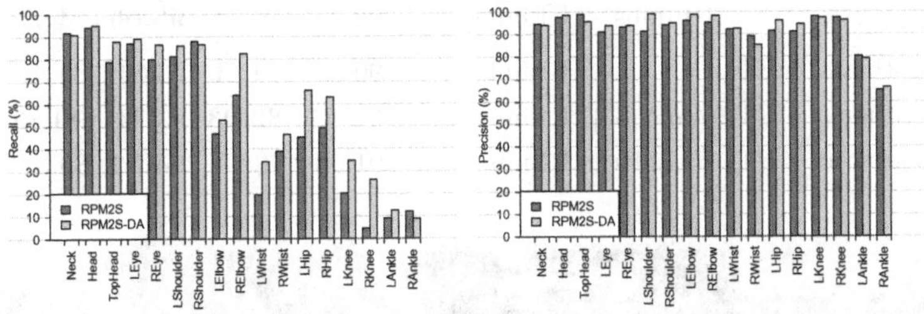

Fig. 6. Recall (left) and precision (right) per body part before and after domain adaptation. Note the high gain in recall for lower body parts after applying domain adaptation.

Table 1. Comparison of the performance (%) on the RLimbs test set for architectures with different number of prediction stages before and after domain adaptation.

Architecture	Performance			
	All body		Upper body	
	AP	AR	AP	AR
RPM1S	83.55	39.20	85.98	55.86
RPM1S-DA	83.68	48.56	89.39	68.63
RPM2S	91.56	53.47	93.93	69.93
RPM2S-DA	**92.62**	**61.66**	**95.00**	**76.09**

summarizes the results for the models with the largest F1-Score. Figure 7 shows a qualitative comparison of the pose estimation approach for adapted and not adapted models.

Table 2. Top: comparison of performance (%) by using two different datasets of depth images as the target data for domain adaptation. IP stans for in-paint preprocessing. Bottom: performance obtained by fine tuning (FT) on an annotated subset of the RLimbs training set after learning with synthetic data and after domain adaptation on the different depth image datasets.

Data			Performance			
			All body		Upper body	
Source	Target	Testing	AP	AR	AP	AR
Synthetic	—	RLimbs	91.56	53.47	93.93	69.93
Synthetic	—	RLimbs (IP)	81.98	58.23	85.20	72.66
Synthetic	WnP [30]	RLimbs	**92.62**	**61.66**	95.00	**76.09**
Synthetic	RLimbs	RLimbs	92.32	59.32	**95.05**	74.55
Synthetic + FT	—	RLimbs	90.56	79.23	93.64	89.52
Synthetic + FT	WnP [30]	RLimbs	**91.27**	**82.03**	93.73	**90.83**
Synthetic + FT	RLimbs	RLimbs	91.03	78.98	**94.32**	89.32

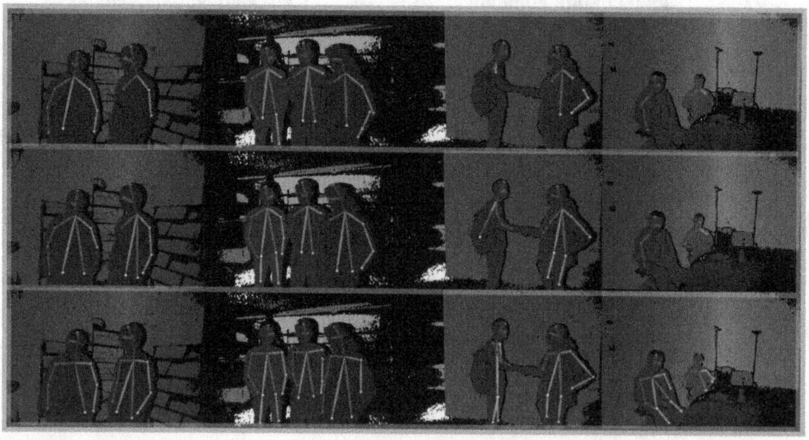

Fig. 7. Output of the different models for some images contained in the testing set of RLimbs. Top row: pose estimation before domain adaptation. Middle row: pose estimation after domain adaptation. Bottom row: pose estimation with fine tuning after domain adaptation.

6 Conclusions

In this paper we investigated the use of unsupervised domain adaptation techniques applied to the problem of depth-based pose estimation with CNNs. Specifically, we investigated an adversarial domain adaptation method to improve the performance on real depth images of a CNN-based human pose regressor trained with synthetic data. We introduced a new dataset of synthetically generated depth images displaying two people instances to cover cases of multi-person pose estimation. In addition, we presented a dataset containing videos of people in HRI scenarios. Both synthetic and real recorded data are publicly available.

Our experiments show that different data from the same type of sensor is meaningful to cover part of the performance gap introduced by learning from synthetic depth images. However, devoting some effort to label a few examples maybe critical to increase the model's generalization capabilities. We observed that the combination of both approaches, domain adaptation and fine tuning, increase performance. Suggesting that domain adaptation for body pose estimation from depth images a better path to follow is a semi-supervised approach.

Acknowledgments. This work was supported by the European Union under the EU Horizon 2020 Research and Innovation Action MuMMER (MultiModal Mall Entertainment Robot), project ID 688147, as well as the Mexican National Council for Science and Tecnology (CONACYT) under the PhD scholarships program.

References

1. CMU motion capture data. http://mocap.cs.cmu.edu/
2. Bulat, A., Tzimiropoulos, G.: Human pose estimation via convolutional part heatmap regression. In: Leibe, B., Matas, J., Sebe, N., Welling, M. (eds.) ECCV 2016. LNCS, vol. 9911, pp. 717–732. Springer, Cham (2016). https://doi.org/10.1007/978-3-319-46478-7_44
3. Cao, Z., Simon, T., Wei, S.-E., Sheikh, Y.: Realtime multi-person 2D pose estimation using part affinity fields. In: CVPR (2017)
4. Carlucci, F.M., Porzi, L., Caputo, B., Ricci, E., Bulo, S.R.: Autodial: automatic domain alignment layers. In: International Conference on Computer Vision (ICCV) (2017)
5. Chen, W., et al.: Synthesizing training images for boosting human 3D pose estimation. In: 3D Vision (3DV) (2016)
6. Crabbe, B., Paiement, A., Hannuna, S., Mirmehdi, M.: Skeleton-free body pose estimation from depth images for movement analysis. In: IEEE Conference on Computer Vision and Pattern Recognition (CVPR), pp. 312–320 (2015)
7. Csurka, G.: Domain adaptation for visual applications: a comprehensive survey. In: Domain Adaptation in Computer Vision Applications, chap. 1, pp. 1–35. Springer Series: Advances in Computer Vision and Pattern Recognition (2017)
8. Ganin, Y., et al.: Domain-adversarial training of neural networks. J. Mach. Learn. Res. **17**(1), 2096–2030 (2016)
9. Haque, A., Peng, B., Luo, Z., Alahi, A., Yeung, S., Fei-Fei, L.: Towards viewpoint invariant 3D human pose estimation. In: Leibe, B., Matas, J., Sebe, N., Welling, M. (eds.) ECCV 2016. LNCS, vol. 9905, pp. 160–177. Springer, Cham (2016). https://doi.org/10.1007/978-3-319-46448-0_10
10. Hu, P., Ramanan, D.: Bottom-up and top-down reasoning with hierarchical rectified Gaussians. In: Proceedings of the 2016 IEEE Conference on Computer Vision and Pattern Recognition, pp. 5600–5609 (2016)
11. Insafutdinov, E., et al.: Articulated multi-person tracking in the wild. In: CVPR (2017). Oral

12. Insafutdinov, E., Pishchulin, L., Andres, B., Andriluka, M., Schiele, B.: DeeperCut: a deeper, stronger, and faster multi-person pose estimation model. In: Leibe, B., Matas, J., Sebe, N., Welling, M. (eds.) ECCV 2016. LNCS, vol. 9910, pp. 34–50. Springer, Cham (2016). https://doi.org/10.1007/978-3-319-46466-4_3
13. Iqbal, U., Milan, A., Gall, J.: Posetrack: joint multi-person pose estimation and tracking. In: IEEE Conference on Computer Vision and Pattern Recognition (CVPR) (2017)
14. Khoshelham, K., Elberink, S.O.: Accuracy and resolution of kinect depth data for indoor mapping applications. Sensors **12**, 1437–1454 (2012). p. 8238 (2013)
15. Lassner, C., Romero, J., Kiefel, M., Bogo, F., Black, M.J., Gehler, P.V.: Unite the people: closing the loop between 3D and 2D human representations. In: The IEEE Conference on Computer Vision and Pattern Recognition (CVPR), July 2017
16. Long, M., Zhu, H., Wang, J., Jordan, M.I.: Unsupervised domain adaptation with residual transfer networks. In: Lee, D.D., Sugiyama, M., Luxburg, U.V., Guyon, I., Garnett, R. (eds.) Advances in Neural Information Processing Systems 29, pp. 136–144. Curran Associates Inc. (2016)
17. Martínez-González, A., Villamizar, M., Canévet, O., Odobez, J.-M.: Real-time convolutional networks for depth-based human pose estimation. In: 2018 IEEE/RSJ International Conference on Intelligent Robots and Systems, IROS 2018 (2018)
18. Newell, A., Yang, K., Deng, J.: Stacked hourglass networks for human pose estimation. In: Leibe, B., Matas, J., Sebe, N., Welling, M. (eds.) ECCV 2016. LNCS, vol. 9912, pp. 483–499. Springer, Cham (2016). https://doi.org/10.1007/978-3-319-46484-8_29
19. Patricia, N., Cariucci, F.M., Caputo, B.: Deep depth domain adaptation: a case study. In: 2017 IEEE International Conference on Computer Vision Workshops, ICCV Workshops 2017, Venice, Italy, 22–29 October 2017, pp. 2645–2650 (2017)
20. Pishchulin, L., et al.: DeepCut: joint subset partition and labeling for multi person pose estimation. In: IEEE Conference on Computer Vision and Pattern Recognition (CVPR) (2016)
21. Shotton, J., et al.: Real-time human pose recognition in parts from single depth images. In: Proceedings of the 2011 IEEE Conference on Computer Vision and Pattern Recognition, CVPR 2011, pp. 1297–1304. IEEE Computer Society, Washington (2011)
22. Shrivastava, A., Pfister, T., Tuzel, O., Susskind, J., Wang, W., Webb, R.: Learning from simulated and unsupervised images through adversarial training. In: IEEE Conference on Vision and Pattern Recognition, CVPR (2017)
23. Si, C., Wang, W., Wang, L., Tan, T.: Multistage adversarial losses for pose-based human image synthesis. In: The IEEE Conference on Computer Vision and Pattern Recognition (CVPR), June 2018
24. Simonyan, K., Zisserman, A.: Very deep convolutional networks for large-scale image recognition (2014)
25. Tompson, J.J., Jain, A., LeCun, Y., Bregler, C.: Joint training of a convolutional network and a graphical model for human pose estimation. In: Ghahramani, Z., Welling, M., Cortes, C., Lawrence, N.D., Weinberger, K.Q. (eds.) Advances in Neural Information Processing Systems 27, pp. 1799–1807. Curran Associates Inc. (2014)
26. Tzeng, E., Hoffman, J., Darrell, T., Saenko, K.: Simultaneous deep transfer across domains and tasks. In: International Conference in Computer Vision (ICCV) (2015)
27. Tzeng, E., Hoffman, J., Darrell, T., Saenko, K.: Adversarial discriminative domain adaptation. In: Computer Vision and Pattern Recognition (CVPR) (2017)

28. Wang, K., Zhai, S., Cheng, H., Liang, X., Lin, L.: Human pose estimation from depth images via inference embedded multi-task learning. In: Proceedings of the 2016 ACM on Multimedia Conference, MM 2016, pp. 1227–1236. ACM, New York (2016)
29. Wei, S.-E., Ramakrishna, V., Kanade, T., Sheikh, Y.: Convolutional pose machines. In: CVPR (2016)
30. Wu, C., Zhang, J., Savarese, S., Saxena, A.: Watch-n-patch: unsupervised understanding of actions and relations. In: The IEEE Conference on Computer Vision and Pattern Recognition (CVPR), June 2015
31. Yang, Y., Ramanan, D.: Articulated human detection with flexible mixtures of parts. IEEE Trans. Pattern Anal. Mach. Intell. **35**(12), 2878–2890 (2013)

Filling the Gaps: Predicting Missing Joints of Human Poses Using Denoising Autoencoders

Nicolò Carissimi[1,2](✉), Paolo Rota[1,3], Cigdem Beyan[1], and Vittorio Murino[1,4]

[1] Istituto Italiano di Tecnologia, Genoa, Italy
{nicolo.carissimi,paolo.rota,cigdem.beyan,vittorio.murino}@iit.it
[2] Università degli Studi di Genova, Genoa, Italy
[3] Università degli Studi di Trento, Trento, Italy
[4] Università degli Studi di Verona, Verona, Italy

Abstract. State of the art pose estimators are able to deal with different challenges present in real-world scenarios, such as varying body appearance, lighting conditions and rare body poses. However, when body parts are severely occluded by objects or other people, the resulting poses might be incomplete, negatively affecting applications where estimating a full body pose is important (e.g. gesture and pose-based behavior analysis). In this work, we propose a method for predicting the missing joints from incomplete human poses. In our model we consider missing joints as noise in the input and we use an autoencoder-based solution to enhance the pose prediction. The method can be easily combined with existing pipelines and, by using only 2D coordinates as input data, the resulting model is small and fast to train, yet powerful enough to learn a robust representation of the low dimensional domain. Finally, results show improved predictions over existing pose estimation algorithms.

Keywords: Human pose estimation · Generative methods

1 Introduction

2D human pose estimation is a well-known research topic that has been studied for years by the computer vision community. The problem consists in finding the location of body parts in an image depicting one or more persons.

Early works [6,11,23] used handcrafted features to detect local body parts and graphical models to infer global pose estimates. These works have shown promising results but they were not good enough to be applied in real-world scenarios. Recently, the creation of huge annotated datasets [4,20] and the use of deep learning techniques [28,29] led to significant improvements, not only in specific 'ad-hoc' datasets but also in generalizing to wider and more unconstrained scenarios.

L. Leal-Taixé and S. Roth (Eds.): ECCV 2018 Workshops, LNCS 11130, pp. 364–379, 2019.
https://doi.org/10.1007/978-3-030-11012-3_29

Even though existing methods produce high precision results, the problem of human pose estimation still remains challenging. For instance, real world images present several complexities, such as body appearance variability due to different clothing and lighting, uncommon body poses and crowded scenarios which introduce occlusion problems. Specifically, when parts of the body are severely occluded, the resulting missing visual information might lead to the generation of incomplete or wrong body poses. We show an example in Fig. 1, where the image is taken from Salsa [3], a well known dataset for human behavior analysis and social signal processing; the scene represents a typical indoor crowded scenario, with challenging lighting conditions and people occluding each other. The resulting estimated body joints and poses (Fig. 1, generated by the tool OpenPose [7], one of the state of the art and most famous pose estimators) present several missing joints (typically wrists, ankles or entire legs) and some wrong limbs. When human poses are used as features for social interaction analysis or as inputs for other tasks, the missing information might severely harm the final accuracy of the entire system. Another example is when 2D poses are used for (bottom-up) 3D pose estimation: Fig. 2 shows how the missing joints dramatically harm the final 3D reconstruction. Therefore, the need of a method that is able to estimate the whole set of joints correctly is of paramount importance.

In this paper, we tackle this problem by proposing an algorithm that estimates the position of the missing joints and completes partial human poses generated by pose estimation algorithms. We cast the task as a denoising problem, where the corrupted signal is represented by the partial human pose, and the resulting uncorrupted signal is the full reconstructed pose. Inspired by the architecture of the denoising variational autoencoders [26,30] we propose a network that generates complete poses from the noisy or missing 2D joints coordinates generated by any human pose estimator. Our model does not require RGB data, is simple, lightweight and fast to train. Despite its simplicity, we show, both quantitatively and qualitatively, improved predictions. Additionally, by ditching image data, our model is also able to estimate joints positions which are outside the camera view, and thus not detectable by standard 2D pose estimation algorithms. Finally, our algorithm is easily pluggable in any existing architecture and can be used as a pose-based feature extractor for high-level human behavior understanding in the wild.

The rest of the paper is organized as follows. In Sect. 2, we review the related work in human pose estimation. Section 3 describes our proposed model. In Sect. 4, we show quantitative and qualitative results. Finally, we present concluding remarks in Sect. 5, together with a discussion about how the proposed method can be utilized for higher level computer vision tasks.

2 Related Work

Pose Estimation. For many years, human pose estimation algorithms focused on single person pose estimation (SPPE). Recently, interest has shifted to "in the wild" multi-person pose estimation (MPPE), which presents a different set

Fig. 1. Examples of incomplete and wrong 2D poses estimated on a frame from Salsa [3] using the tool OpenPose [7].

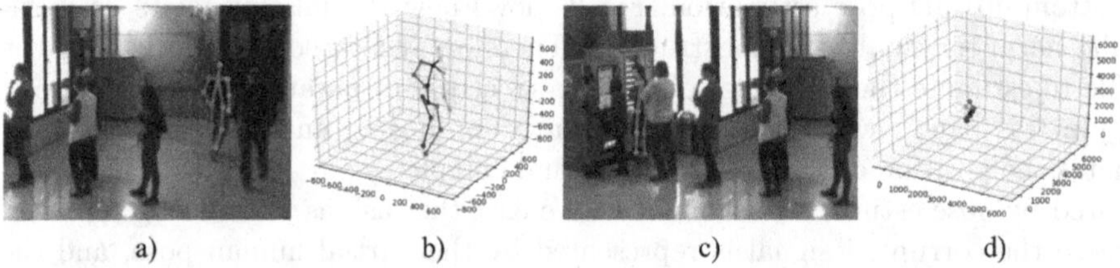

Fig. 2. Effect of complete and incomplete 2D poses on bottom-up 3D pose estimation (3D poses estimated using [27]). A complete 2D pose (a) leads to the estimation of a plausible 3D pose (b), while an incomplete 2D pose (c) (with missing arms) leads to a wrong 3D pose estimation (d).

of challenges, including detecting an unknown number of people, possibly highly dense scenarios with severe occlusions and complex body interactions. In this work, given that we focus on multi-person scenarios, we mainly review previous MPPE works. These approaches can be categorized into two families: *top-down* and *bottom-up* approaches [7].

Top-down approaches require person detectors on the whole image and use SPPE algorithms to infer poses on the single detections. Having a body centered in the input image is a strong prior that enables SPPE algorithms to use both local and global information for the final predictions [22], resulting in robust predictions. Unfortunately, one of the biggest disadvantages of these approaches is that the final predictions are heavily influenced by the initial person detector results, which, in very crowded scenarios, can lead to poor detections, bounding boxes not centered on a single person or that cut parts of the body. Iqbal and Gall [15] use Faster R-CNN [25] as person detector, and a convolutional pose machine [32] as an SPPE algorithm to generate candidate joints. The resulting bounding boxes might show multiple people; thus, in order to associate each joint to the correct person and remove the wrong candidates, inference is performed locally on a fully connected graph for each person using integer linear programming. Fang et al. [10] tackle the problems of bounding box error, i.e. bounding boxes which are not perfectly centered on a person, and of redundant detections, i.e. when multiple bounding boxes are generated for a single person. The problem of the bounding box error is attenuated by a network which generates higher quality bounding boxes from existing ones, based on spatial transformer networks [16]. Finally, poses generated by redundant detections are merged into a single, most confident one by using a novel technique called parametric pose non-maximum suppression. Chen et al. [8] focus on detecting "hard to predict" joints, i.e. joints which are occluded, invisible or in front of complex backgrounds. They devise a two stage network, where, during training, the first stage predicts the visible joints, while the second stage focuses on the hard joints by selecting the top M losses and backpropagating only their gradient.

Bottom-up approaches, on the other end, take the whole image as an input, without any prior information on person location and number. Their pipeline is usually composed of two stages (which can be sequential or parallel), where the first one predicts candidate locations for all joint types, and the second one groups the joints into individual human poses. These algorithms do not need to rely on the performance of person detectors and the computational time does not depend on the number of detections. However, as a downside, the lack of prior information, such as person location and scale, makes the resulting poses less precise. Pishchulin et al. [24] propose a bottom-up method which jointly detects a set of candidate body joints and associates them to single people by casting the problem as a graph partitioning one, where nodes are joint detections and edges are scores based on spatial offsets and appearance features. The partitioning is solved via integer linear programming on a fully connected graph of all the detected joints, which requires a long computational time. Insafutdinov et al. [14] propose an improved approach over [24], by using better part detectors, improved regressors for the score generation, and a faster partitioning algorithm based on incremental optimization, although it still requires several minutes of computational time. Cao et al. [7] focus on improving computational time by proposing a real-time approach which jointly learns to detect and associate joints. Extending the work from [32], the proposed network has two branches: one for joints and one for part affinity fields (PAFs) prediction, where a PAF can be seen as encoding the probability of a pixel to belong to the limb between two predicted joints. Finally, a bipartite graph matching solver is used to get the final estimated poses. In contrast to the previously mentioned multi-stage pipelines, Newell et al. [21] propose a novel approach where the network is taught to simultaneously detect and group joints, without the need of additional aggregation steps. For each joint, the network outputs a corresponding embedding vector, and these vectors are then used to cluster joints into final human poses.

Our proposed method *does not estimate poses* and it differs from all the existing works in two fundamental ways: *(i)* its primary goal is to correct existing predictions, by regressing missing joints in an incomplete input pose, estimating a most likely pose given the actual detection; *(ii)* the proposed method uses only 2D coordinates as input, not RGB data; even if we discard rich information, we show that partial 2D coordinates provide enough information for robust predictions.

Data Denoising and Restoration. The problem of dealing with missing or incomplete data in machine learning arises in many applications. Recent strategies make use of generative models to impute missing or corrupted data. Advances in computer vision using deep generative models have found applications in image/video processing, such as denoising, restoration, super-resolution and inpainting. In [17], Jain and Seung train convolutional layers in an unsupervised way for the task of denoising images, by reducing the error between the original (input) and the reconstructed images, the latter obtained by applying gaussian noise to the former. Xu et al. [34] state that image degradation can be modeled as a translation-invariant convolution operation and that image restoration can be achieved with the inverse process, i.e. deconvolution; thus, a deep convolutional neural network (CNN) is used to learn the deconvolution operation in a data driven way, without the need to have any prior knowledge of the cause of image degradation. Xie et al. [33] propose the use of stacked denoising autoencoders with layer wise training for image denoising and inpainting.

Inspired by these methods, we cast the problem of missing joints prediction as a denoising and restoration problem.

3 Methodology

The choice of our model is motivated by two main reasons. In the first place, the model should be able to predict missing information and, second, has to deal with low dimensional data. Occlusions and degraded visual data might cause a pose detector to miss some types and number of joints in an unpredictable way. The resulting partial human pose can, thus, be seen as a noisy, stochastically corrupted version of the original data which is the complete human pose in our case. The model must, then, be able to learn a robust representation of the data even when parts of the data are missing. Unlike RGB images, which are composed by hundreds, or thousands of pixels, our domain data are small vectors of a few concatenated 2D coordinates (see Sect. 3.2), therefore we choose a model which is simple, yet powerful enough to learn a robust representation of this low dimensional domain data. Auto-encoders, as seen in previous works [26,30], are a powerful tool for learning representations of complex data distributions, and their denoising variant [30] is specifically designed to deal with incomplete input data.

We now proceed with a short review of the theory behind auto-encoders, denoising auto-encoders and one of their most recent variants, variational auto-encoders (Sect. 3.1). Finally, we describe in detail the architecture of the network we use (Sect. 3.2).

3.1 Auto-Encoders

Auto-encoders have been introduced long ago by Rumelhart et al. [26] they consist in an unsupervised learning model and have been used for different purposes such as dimensionality reduction, feature extraction [30], pre-training of deep nets [5,31], data generation and reconstruction [13]. Concretely, an auto-encoder is a type of multi-layer neural network trained to map the input to a different representation of it, so that the input can be reconstructed from that representation. The simplest form of an auto-encoder has a single hidden layer which maps (*encodes*) an input $\mathbf{x}$ to its new representation $\mathbf{y}$

$$\mathbf{y} = s(\mathbf{W}\mathbf{x} + \mathbf{b}) \tag{1}$$

where s is a (usually non-linear) activation function, while W and b are, respectively, the weights and bias of the layer. The encoded input $\mathbf{y}$ is, then, mapped back (*decoded*) to a reconstruction $\mathbf{x_r}$ of the input

$$\mathbf{x_r} = s(\mathbf{W}'\mathbf{y} + \mathbf{b}'). \tag{2}$$

Training is performed by minimizing a loss function

$$L(\mathbf{x}, \mathbf{x_r}) \tag{3}$$

which, in our case, is the mean squared error MSE, calculated between the reconstructed input $\mathbf{x_r}$ and the target output, which is the input $\mathbf{x}$ itself. If the dimension of $\mathbf{y}$ is smaller than the dimension of $\mathbf{x}$, the auto-encoder is called undercomplete; on the other end, if the dimension of $\mathbf{y}$ is larger, the auto-encoder is called overcomplete.

If the dimension of the hidden units is larger than the original input, the auto-encoder might learn the identity function; however, there are different techniques to avoid this occurrence. One of these techniques introduces randomness during training: the network is fed with a stochastically corrupted version of the input $\mathbf{x_c}$, while the target output remains the original uncorrupted input $\mathbf{x}$. This training approach has been introduced by Vincent et al. in [30] and the resulting models are called *denoising auto-encoders*. Their original purpose was to make the learned representation more robust to partial corruption of the input, but they present an additional useful property, i.e. the ability to reconstruct missing data from the input, which is well suited for our problem of missing joints prediction.

One downside of standard auto-encoders is that they tend to map similar input samples to latent vectors which might be very close to each other, resulting in almost identical reconstructions. This behavior is acceptable when input data represents classes (e.g. images of numbers or letters). On the contrary, preserving small input differences in the reconstruction is very important when dealing with human poses, which do not form a clustered space, but a continuous, smooth domain. Variational auto-encoders [19] can learn such a continuous representation by design, making them more suited for our problem. Similarly to classic auto-encoders, they have the same encoder/decoder structure (where the encoder maps the input to a latent representation, and the decoder reconstructs the input from such representation). The main difference is that the latent variables are not a "compressed representation" of the domain data itself, but they encode the parameters (i.e. the mean μ and standard deviation σ) of a *distribution* (typically an n-dimensional Gaussian one) modeling the input data. In order to force this, another term is added to the loss (see Eq. 3), i.e. the Kullback-Leibler divergence (D_{KL}) [2], which measures the divergence between two probability distributions and has the form

$$D_{KL}(P\|Q) = -\sum_i P_i log(Q_i/P_i) \tag{4}$$

where P is the encoded n-dimensional Gaussian distribution $\mathcal{N}(\mu, \sigma^2)$ and Q is the target standard normal distribution.

3.2 Modeling the Human Pose

Since the chosen reconstruction loss needs a complete human pose as the target output, we need to select full human poses from the dataset as training data. Each pose is represented by a set of n 2D locations, where n is the number of joints (see Sects. 4.1 and 4.2). The concatenation of these joints produces a vector of $n * 2$ elements (the x and y coordinates) which is the input of the network. Since the coordinates of the annotated joints are labeled in the image space, poses which are very similar to each other might appear in different parts of the image, resulting in input vectors with very different values. We, thus, normalize them using the following procedure: first we find the center of the torso (C_T) by averaging the coordinates of the neck and at least one of the shoulders and hip joints; the pose is then translated to the obtained 2D point and finally scaled by the distance between the neck and C_T. At testing time, this normalization technique requires an incomplete pose to have all the aforementioned joints, negatively affecting the number of poses that is processed by the network (see Sect. 4.4). Given that we are using a denoising auto-encoder, the training data must also be *corrupted*. We do this by adding noise to the previously normalized poses, randomly masking a small number of joints.

Figure 3 shows the overall architecture: since the input vector is small compared to the space of the data we want to reconstruct, we choose to implement an overcomplete auto-encoder. The encoder and decoder are composed by 2 hidden layers, each one gradually encoding (and decoding) more robust features. Layers μ and σ represent, respectively, the mean and standard deviation of the distribution we want to learn, while the final layer of the encoder represents a sample of it.

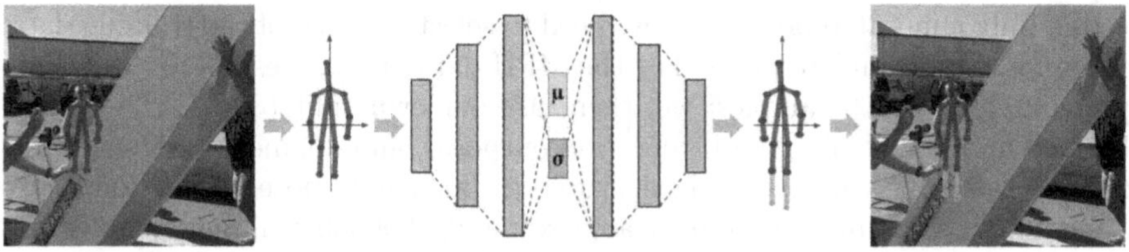

Fig. 3. The pipeline of our method. Given an RGB image, a human pose prediction algorithm is used to generate one or more poses. The incomplete ones are, then, normalized and fed to the auto-encoder, which outputs the corresponding full human poses.

4 Experiments

In this section, we report quantitative and qualitative results of our method, evaluated on two datasets, MPII Human Pose [4] and Microsoft's COCO Keypoint Detection [20], which are the most famous and widely datasets for multi-person pose estimation.

4.1 MPII Human Pose Dataset

The MPII Human Pose dataset [4] consists of around 25000 images and a total of 40000 annotated human poses. The training set is composed of 28000 of these poses, while the test set is composed of 11000 poses. Images contain people engaged in numerous activities and a variety of contexts, with a high variable of articulated poses and camera perspectives. People can be fully visible, severely occluded or partially out of the camera field of view. A full pose is composed of 16 landmarks, each one corresponding to the location, in image coordinates, of a body joint (head, neck, thorax and left and right shoulders, elbows, wrists, hips, knees and ankles).

4.2 COCO Keypoint Detection Dataset

The Microsoft's COCO Keypoint Detection dataset [20] is a subset of the whole COCO dataset, focused on the localization of person keypoints. The training and validation sets contain, respectively, around 260000 and 11000 annotated human poses. Unlike MPII, a full pose is composed of 17 joints, corresponding to nose and left and right shoulders, elbows, wrists, hips, knees, ankles, eyes and ears.

4.3 Experimental Settings

Our model takes a pose as the input and generates its reconstruction. If the pose is incomplete, i.e. with one or more missing joints, a prediction of the corresponding full pose is generated as output. As described in Sect. 3.2, the loss function needs a fully annotated pose; thus, we need to select a subset of the training data containing only complete poses. For the MPII dataset, this results in a total of, approximately, 20000 samples; we, then, use our own split (85%/15%) on the obtained data for training and validation purposes, and augment the remaining training data following a standard procedure for single pose estimation algorithms [9,22], obtaining a total of approximately 500000 training samples. In particular, we perform data augmentation by flipping and rotating the original poses (±30°). We then normalize each pose, mask a random number of joints (from 0 up to 5, which roughly corresponds to 35% of the total number of joints) and feed the obtained data to the network.

The COCO dataset, on the contrary, has only a few thousands of complete poses, which, even after data augmentation, would not be enough for training purposes. Therefore, we decide to use the dataset only for testing. Since COCO and MPII have different annotated joint types, we feed the network (trained on MPII) with only the joints that are common between the two datasets (i.e. left and right shoulders, elbows, wrist, hips, knees and ankles) and set to zero the missing ones (head, neck and thorax).

The encoder is composed of 2 fully connected hidden layers, with 64 and 128 hidden units. Symmetrically, the decoder is composed of 2 hidden layers, with 128 and 64 hidden units, and an output layer with the same dimension as the input one. As in [12,19], we use 20 latent dimensions. Every fully connected layer has ReLu non-linearities. The loss function is the sum of MSE (between the uncorrupted input and the reconstructed pose) and the D_{KL} (Sect. 3.1). The network is implemented using TensorFlow [1] and trained with the Adam optimizer [18] with a learning rate of 1e−3.

4.4 Quantitative Analysis

In this section we show quantitative results of the proposed pipeline on the datasets described in Sects. 4.1 and 4.2. For the generation of the input poses, we use the bottom-up multi-person pose estimator OpenPose [7,32] and its matlab implementation, without modifying its preset parameters. Although OpenPose is not the best performing method on MPII and COCO anymore, and it's less precise in predicting complete human poses compared to other top-down approaches, we found it to be the more robust when tested on real-life datasets not strictly related to pose estimation and on which it wasn't trained on (such as Salsa [3]). Figure 4 shows a comparison between poses generated by OpenPose and those generated by the state of the art top-down approach called Regional Multi-Person Pose Estimation (RMPE) [10]. In (a), OpenPose (left) produces a complete and better estimation of the pose, compared to RMPE (right). In (b), OpenPose (left) cannot predict the head, the wrists and the right ankle, while RMPE (center, right) predicts all joints; however, RMPE generates two poses for the same person, due to redundant detections, and their quality is worse than the OpenPose one. Clearly, the underlying person detector is an important factor in the final performance of a top-down pose estimation algorithm. Also, top-down approaches learn not just local information (i.e. joints appearance) but also global information (i.e. joints relative location and appearance) and this information might be harder to generalize to unseen data.

Fig. 4. Comparison between OpenPose and Regional Multi-Person Pose Estimation (RMPE) [10]. (a) and (b) left show OpenPose predictions, while (a) right and (b) center, right show RMPE predictions. Orange joints have a confidence score below 0.2. (Color figure online)

We compare OpenPose's results with the results generated by our method using two metrics, the Miss Rate (MR) and the Percentage of Correct Keypoints (PCKh). MR is computed as

$$\#joints_{missed}/\#joints_{gt} \tag{5}$$

where $\#joints_{missed}$ is the number of missed (annotated) joints and $\#joints_{gt}$ is the number of all (annotated) joints. PCKh is a standard metric in pose estimation introduced in [4] for evaluation on the MPII dataset, where a keypoint is considered as correctly predicted if its distance from the ground truth is less than a fixed threshold (specified as a fraction of the person's head size). The corresponding ground truth is assigned to each pose according to the highest PCKh.

While MR quantifies how many joints are failed to be predicted, PCKh quantifies the actual "quality" of the predictions.

We do not perform a comparison using the standard mean Average Precision (mAP) metric, which is commonly used in MPII for multi-person pose estimation, because it penalizes joints with no ground truth correspondence as false positives.

Table 1 shows that our method outperforms OpenPose in terms of number of missing joints. As can be seen, the highest missing rate differences correspond to joints which are body extremes (i.e. wrists and ankles) and thus more prone to be occluded. Even though our method is supposed to predict all missing joints, the missing rate is not 0 because it relies on the detection of the subjects by the baseline human pose estimator.

The quality of the predictions generated by our method can be seen in Table 2, where its PCKh is better than the OpenPose one, especially (as for the missing rate) for those joints which are frequently occluded. The highest difference in PCKh can be seen when computed over joints labeled as "occluded" only. Results on head and neck are omitted because they are never occluded.

One advantage of our method is that, by using 2D coordinates as input domain, it can be easily applied to different datasets it has not been trained on: Tables 3 and 4 show, respectively, the Missing Rate and the PCKh computed on COCO.

Table 1. Joints Missing Rate on the MPII dataset

Method (all joints)	Ankle	Knee	Hip	Wrist	Elbow	Shoulder	Neck	Head	Average MR
OpenPose [7]	0.072	0.040	0.021	0.066	0.037	0.019	0.011	0.019	0.039
Our method	**0.020**	**0.015**	**0.016**	**0.012**	**0.011**	**0.010**	**0.011**	**0.011**	**0.014**

Table 2. PCKh@0.5 on the MPII dataset, computed on all joints and only on joints labeled as occluded

Method (all joints)	Ankle	Knee	Hip	Wrist	Elbow	Shoulder	Neck	Head	Average PCKh
OpenPose [7]	79.87	87.17	93.0	79.15	89.03	95.97	97.71	96.11	88.73
Our method	**80.93**	**87.44**	**93.06**	**80.38**	**89.92**	**96.41**	**97.75**	**96.53**	**89.33**
Method (occluded joints)	Ankle	Knee	Hip	Wrist	Elbow	Shoulder			Average PCKh
OpenPose [7]	59.07	73.26	87.71	57.06	76.71	91.23			74.47
Our method	**61.18**	**73.83**	**87.80**	**60.78**	**78.70**	**92.32**			**75.77**

Finally, we report the computational time for training and testing. The analysis is performed on a laptop with 16 GB of RAM and an NVIDIA GeForce GTX 960M with 4 GB of RAM. Training requires only 3 h, while reconstruction of a single pose requires, on average, 0.88 ms. This shows that our method can be easily combined with any existing pose estimation architecture without significantly affecting the overall computational time.

Table 3. Joints Missing Rate on the COCO dataset

Method (all joints)	Shoulder	Elbow	Wrist	Hip	Knee	Ankle	Average MR
OpenPose [7]	0.0021	0.0104	0.0214	0.0371	0.0752	0.0539	0.0333
Our method	**0.0021**	**0.0032**	**0.0068**	**0.0150**	**0.0093**	**0.0052**	**0.0069**

Table 4. PCKh@0.5 trained on MPII and tested on COCO, computed on all joints

Method (all joints)	Shoulder	Elbow	Wrist	Hip	Knee	Ankle	Average PCKh
OpenPose [7]	80.22	54.91	63.71	39.48	35.74	23.60	49.61
Our method	**80.07**	**56.25**	**65.44**	**41.25**	**41.40**	**28.43**	**52.14**

4.5 Qualitative Analysis

In this section we show qualitative results of our predictions. In Fig. 5 (images taken from MPII), the top row shows (in blue), predictions obtained from OpenPose, while the bottom row shows the corresponding complete poses generated by our model (the predicted missing joints are in magenta). In column (a) and (b) ankles are missing from sitting poses and our model is able to predict a plausible locations of them. In column (c) a man is standing but both ankles are completely occluded by a foreground object and missing from the pose generated by OpenPose; however, our model is able to predict their position and produce a plausible complete standing pose. In column (c) the right arm (elbow and wrist) is missing; our model generates the missing joints in a spatial configuration which is similar to the joints of the visible left arm. The last column shows an extreme case where the number of missing joints is very high, thus providing little context for the final prediction: a man is standing, with raised arms and head occluded by a foreground object. Although our model generates arms which are completely lowered, the resulting pose is still a plausible human pose.

Figure 6 shows more examples of predictions obtained from OpenPose (top row) and the corresponding complete poses generated by our method (bottom row). In column (a), not just an ankle but the entire left leg (knee and ankle) is missing; the predicted complete pose closely resembles the sitting person pictured in the image. In column (b), the right wrist is not detected and both arms are raised, but our prediction is very close to the real wrist. Ankles (columns (b), (c) and (d)), are outside the camera field of view; however our model is able to predict a full pose even when RGB information is missing.

Finally, Fig. 7 shows predictions on frames from Salsa (another dataset our model was not trained on), where it can be seen that our method can generate

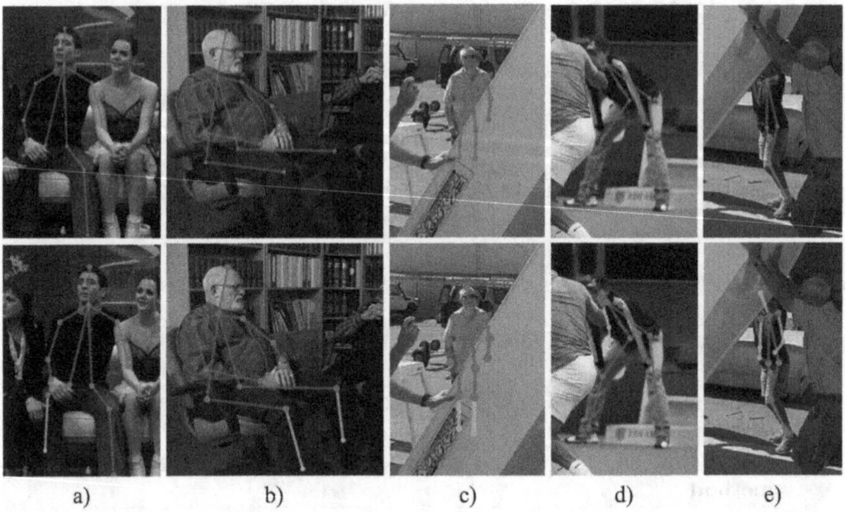

Fig. 5. Examples of predictions obtained from OpenPose (top row, in blue) and the corresponding complete poses generated by our method (bottom row, in magenta) on MPII. (Color figure online)

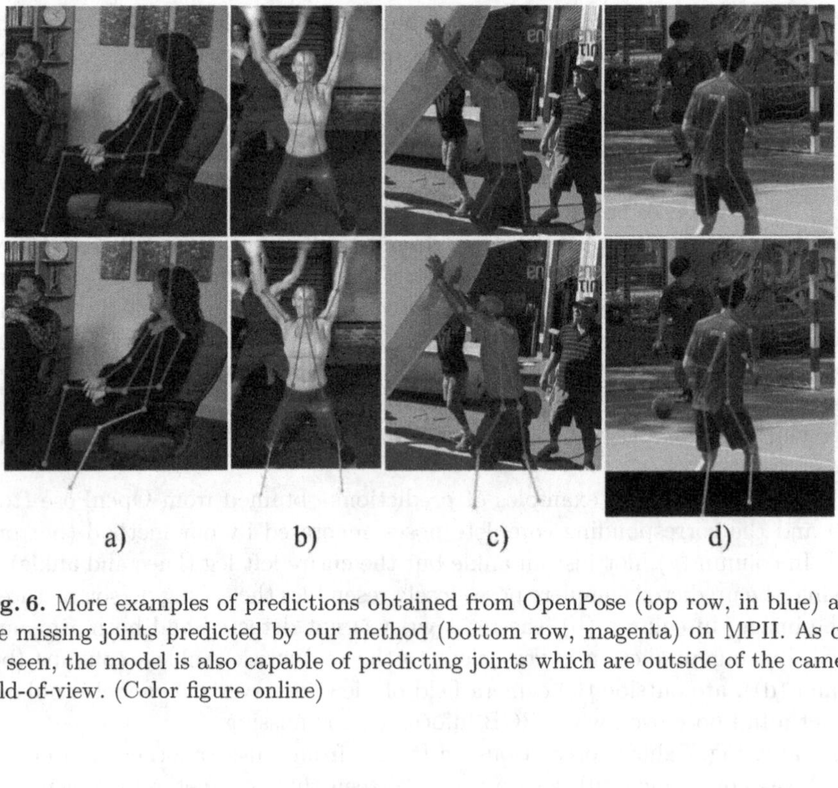

Fig. 6. More examples of predictions obtained from OpenPose (top row, in blue) and the missing joints predicted by our method (bottom row, magenta) on MPII. As can be seen, the model is also capable of predicting joints which are outside of the camera field-of-view. (Color figure online)

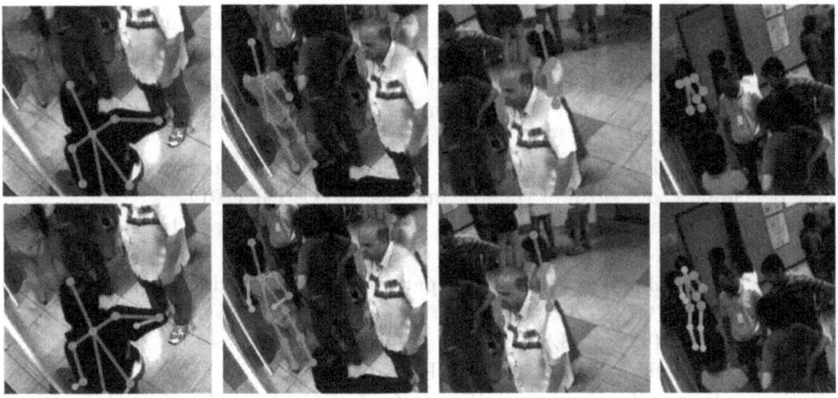

a) b) c) d)

Fig. 7. Examples of predictions on Salsa. Top row: OpenPose results (in blue). Bottom row: missing joints predicted by our method (in magenta). (Color figure online)

plausible human poses even when half of the body is missing (see columns (c) and (d), with completely occluded legs and arms).

5 Conclusions and Future Work

In this paper, we presented a method for the prediction of missing joints from incomplete input poses. We approached the task as a denoising problem and showed that a simple model leads to a satisfactory boost in performance. We reported quantitative and qualitative results on several datasets and showed increased prediction performance over a well-known multi-person pose estimation algorithm and the ability to predict joints locations even when entire limbs are occluded.

Although state of the art pose estimators are able to cope with different challenging scenarios, occlusions are still a problem and can lead to missing joints predictions. The resulting incomplete poses might negatively affect the performance of applications based on 2D poses, such as behavior analysis based on body pose and gestures or bottom-up 3D pose estimation algorithms which lift 2D coordinates to 3D. Our method can, then, be an aid in these contexts, providing "complete" information. Future work will explore in detail the effects of our method in the context of human behavior analysis.

References

1. Abadi, M., et al.: Tensorflow: a system for large-scale machine learning. In: 12th USENIX Symposium on Operating Systems Design and Implementation (OSDI 2016), pp. 265–283 (2016). https://www.usenix.org/system/files/conference/osdi16/osdi16-abadi.pdf

2. Akaike, H.: Information theory and an extension of the maximum likelihood principle. In: Parzen, E., Tanabe, K., Kitagawa, G. (eds.) Selected Papers of Hirotugu Akaike. Springer, New York (1998). https://doi.org/10.1007/978-1-4612-1694-0_15
3. Alameda-Pineda, X., et al.: SALSA: a novel dataset for multimodal group behavior analysis. PAMI **38**, 1707–1720 (2016)
4. Andriluka, M., Pishchulin, L., Gehler, P., Schiele, B.: 2D human pose estimation: new benchmark and state of the art analysis. In: CVPR (2014)
5. Bengio, Y., Lamblin, P., Popovici, D., Larochelle, H.: Greedy layer-wise training of deep networks. In: NIPS (2007)
6. Bourdev, L., Malik, J.: Poselets: Body part detectors trained using 3D human pose annotations. In: ICCV (2009)
7. Cao, Z., Simon, T., Wei, S.E., Sheikh, Y.: Realtime multi-person 2D pose estimation using part affinity fields. In: CVPR (2017)
8. Chen, Y., Wang, Z., Peng, Y., Zhang, Z., Yu, G., Sun, J.: Cascaded pyramid network for multi-person pose estimation. arXiv preprint arXiv:1711.07319 (2017)
9. Chen, Y., Shen, C., Wei, X.S., Liu, L., Yang, J.: Adversarial PoseNet: a structure-aware convolutional network for human pose estimation. In: CVPR (2017)
10. Fang, H.S., Xie, S., Tai, Y.W., Lu, C.: RMPE: regional multi-person pose estimation. In: CVPR (2017)
11. Felzenszwalb, P., McAllester, D., Ramanan, D.: A discriminatively trained, multiscale, deformable part model. In: CVPR (2008)
12. Feng, W., Kannan, A., Gkioxari, G., Zitnick, C.L.: Learn2Smile: learning nonverbal interaction through observation. In: IROS (2017)
13. Hou, X., Shen, L., Sun, K., Qiu, G.: Deep feature consistent variational autoencoder. In: WACV (2017)
14. Insafutdinov, E., Pishchulin, L., Andres, B., Andriluka, M., Schiele, B.: DeeperCut: a deeper, stronger, and faster multi-person pose estimation model. In: Leibe, B., Matas, J., Sebe, N., Welling, M. (eds.) ECCV 2016. LNCS, vol. 9910, pp. 34–50. Springer, Cham (2016). https://doi.org/10.1007/978-3-319-46466-4_3
15. Iqbal, U., Gall, J.: Multi-person pose estimation with local joint-to-person associations. In: ECCV Workshop (2016). http://arxiv.org/abs/1608.08526
16. Jaderberg, M., Simonyan, K., Zisserman, A., et al.: Spatial transformer networks. In: NIPS (2015)
17. Jain, V., Seung, S.: Natural image denoising with convolutional networks. In: Advances in Neural Information Processing Systems, pp. 769–776 (2009)
18. Kingma, D.P., Ba, J.: Adam: a method for stochastic optimization. arXiv preprint arXiv:1412.6980 (2014)
19. Kingma, D.P., Welling, M.: Auto-encoding variational bayes. arXiv preprint arXiv:1312.6114 (2013)
20. Lin, T.-Y., et al.: Microsoft COCO: common objects in context. In: Fleet, D., Pajdla, T., Schiele, B., Tuytelaars, T. (eds.) ECCV 2014. LNCS, vol. 8693, pp. 740–755. Springer, Cham (2014). https://doi.org/10.1007/978-3-319-10602-1_48
21. Newell, A., Huang, Z., Deng, J.: Associative embedding: end-to-end learning for joint detection and grouping. In: NIPS (2017)
22. Newell, A., Yang, K., Deng, J.: Stacked hourglass networks for human pose estimation. In: Leibe, B., Matas, J., Sebe, N., Welling, M. (eds.) ECCV 2016. LNCS, vol. 9912, pp. 483–499. Springer, Cham (2016). https://doi.org/10.1007/978-3-319-46484-8_29
23. Pishchulin, L., Andriluka, M., Gehler, P., Schiele, B.: Strong appearance and expressive spatial models for human pose estimation. In: ICCV (2013)

24. Pishchulin, L., et al.: DeepCut: Joint subset partition and labeling for multi person pose estimation. In: CVPR (2016)
25. Ren, S., He, K., Girshick, R., Sun, J.: Faster R-CNN: towards real-time object detection with region proposal networks. In: NIPS (2015)
26. Rumelhart, D.E., Hinton, G.E., Williams, R.J.: Learning representations by back-propagating errors. Nature **323**(6088), 533 (1986)
27. Tome, D., Russell, C., Agapito, L.: Lifting from the deep: convolutional 3D pose estimation from a single image. In: CVPR (2017)
28. Tompson, J.J., Jain, A., LeCun, Y., Bregler, C.: Joint training of a convolutional network and a graphical model for human pose estimation. In: NIPS (2014)
29. Toshev, A., Szegedy, C.: DeepPose: human pose estimation via deep neural networks. In: CVPR (2014)
30. Vincent, P., Larochelle, H., Bengio, Y., Manzagol, P.A.: Extracting and composing robust features with denoising autoencoders. In: ICML (2008)
31. Vincent, P., Larochelle, H., Lajoie, I., Bengio, Y., Manzagol, P.A.: Stacked denoising autoencoders: learning useful representations in a deep network with a local denoising criterion. J. Mach. Learn. Res. **11**(Dec), 3371–3408 (2010)
32. Wei, S.E., Ramakrishna, V., Kanade, T., Sheikh, Y.: Convolutional pose machines. In: CVPR (2016)
33. Xie, J., Xu, L., Chen, E.: Image denoising and inpainting with deep neural networks. In: Advances in Neural Information Processing Systems, pp. 341–349 (2012)
34. Xu, L., Ren, J.S., Liu, C., Jia, J.: Deep convolutional neural network for image deconvolution. In: Advances in Neural Information Processing Systems, pp. 1790–1798 (2014)

Pose Guided Human Image Synthesis by View Disentanglement and Enhanced Weighting Loss

Mohamed Ilyes Lakhal[1(✉)], Oswald Lanz[2], and Andrea Cavallaro[1]

[1] CIS, Queen Mary University of London, London, UK
{m.i.lakhal,a.cavallaro}@qmul.ac.uk
[2] TeV, Fondazione Bruno Kessler, Trento, Italy
lanz@fbk.eu

Abstract. View synthesis aims at generating a novel, unseen view of an object. This is a challenging task in the presence of occlusions and asymmetries. In this paper, we present View-Disentangled Generator (VDG), a two-stage deep network for pose-guided human-image generation that performs coarse view prediction followed by a refinement stage. In the first stage, the network predicts the output from a target human pose, the source-image and the corresponding human pose, which are processed in different branches separately. This enables the network to learn a disentangled representation from the source and target view. In the second stage, the coarse output from the first stage is refined by adversarial training. Specifically, we introduce a masked version of the structural similarity loss that facilitates the network to focus on generating a higher quality view. Experiments on Market-1501 and DeepFashion demonstrate the effectiveness of the proposed generator.

Keywords: Pose-guided view synthesis · Generative models · Structural similarity

1 Introduction

View synthesis is of considerable interest for data augmentation, animation, augmented and virtual reality. Generating a novel view of a human [1,2] is more challenging that generating a view for a rigid 3D object [3,4], especially when scene parameters are unavailable.

The appearance of an object from an unseen view can be generated with geometry or transformation-based methods [5]. Geometry-based methods generate novel views by scaling, rotation, translation, and non-rigid deformations of specific 3D objects [6,7]. A limitation of geometry-based methods is the structure of the rendered 3D objects, which are characterized by shape invariance and symmetry [5]. Transformation-based methods encode directly the correspondence between input and output images to synthesize the view [3,4,8,9].

L. Leal-Taixé and S. Roth (Eds.): ECCV 2018 Workshops, LNCS 11130, pp. 380–394, 2019.
https://doi.org/10.1007/978-3-030-11012-3_30

Synthesizing an image of a person from an arbitrary pose is challenging due to occlusions and the potentially complex human pose changes from the source to target view. Unlike 3D-object-based synthesis [8,9], synthesizing the image of a human from another pose and view cannot always make use of extrinsic camera parameters or information about changes in illumination. Moreover, there might be considerable differences in *image quality* in the dataset; the *scale* difference between the input pair and output can be large; some body parts can be *occluded* and some poses can appear infrequently (*e.g.*, crossed arm). These factors have an impact on the quality of the synthesized image.

Human image synthesis methods can be classified as view specific or pose guided. *View-specific* methods synthesize human images into a pre-defined set of views (*e.g.* front, back, side [10]). *Pose-guided* methods impose constraints over the input view using a target 2D pose (defined as a set of 2D locations of the body joints) as a guidance in the generation [1,2,5,11,12]. Recent approaches [2,10] force the input image of the human body and its target pose to be encoded into a joint feature space. This solution is undesirable as the input image and the target pose are fed to the same encoder and their mixing in early layers can lead to misalignment in the decoder. This problem becomes even more critical if the input and the target have different scales and spatial locations. In fact, because of this variation, the receptive field of the convolutional layers may not capture the change of body appearance between the input and the target pose [1].

To address this problem, in this paper we propose a two-stage deep encoder-decoder pipeline that explicitly separates the processing of input and target into two branches, namely the image and the pose branch. The *image branch* learns the mapping of the input image and pose into a compact discriminative space. The *pose branch* independently encodes the target pose into the same space as the compact feature of the image branch. The two feature vectors are then combined and fed to the decoder network, which learns the pixel correspondence of the target pose to generate a new image. Our network is presented as a U-Net [13] architecture with residual blocks and skip connections. To encourage the generator to produce visually appealing images, instead of optimizing the generator using pixel-wise penalty (*e.g.* $\mathcal{L}_1$) we use a masked version of the structural similarity loss.

The rest of the paper is structured as follows: Sect. 2 reviews recent advances in human view synthesis. Section 3 presents a general formulation of the problem. In Sect. 4, we present our proposed generator as well as a new weighted loss function based on a masked structural similarity loss (mask-SSIM). Experimental results are discussed in Sect. 5. Finally, in Sect. 6 we draw conclusions.

2 Background

Deep generative models for computer vision can be classified are Variational Autoencoders (VAEs) [14] or Generative Adversarial Networks (GANs) [15]. GANs are widely used for image inpainting [16], image-to-image translation [17], super-resolution [18], and cross-view image synthesis [19]. These solutions share the same *encoder-decoder* structure [20]. The idea is to map the high dimension input to much lower dimensional discriminative feature using down-sampling mappings (a series of convolutions and pooling operations). The resulting feature is then processed by a series of up-sampling (convolutions with interpolations, *e.g.* Nearest-neighbour) to get to a target space (*e.g.* the reconstruction of another image). U-Net is an encoder-decoder architecture that uses mid-level features from the encoder in the decoding module by means of skip-connections [13].

Dosovitskiy *et al.* [21] presented a generative model by learning a lower dimensional feature vector from the 3D object identity, a target view, and a transformation vector. The combined feature vector is then transformed to the desired 3D object and its segmented mask through a series of up-sampling and convolutions. Appearance Flow Network [4] learns to map the input pixel to the desired viewpoint by means of a learnable module called *Spatial Transformer* [22] which allows explicit manipulation of the feature maps. The Transformation-grounded view synthesis network (TVSN) [3] is a two-step model. The first module called Disocclusion-aware Appearance Flow Network (DOAFN) extends the Appearance Flow Network by only keeping the target pixels of the input that are presented in the output transformation using a mask that uses ground truth object coordinates and surface normals. The second network takes the output of DOAFN and refines the results by a hallucination of the missing pixels using adversarial training together with a pixel-wise reconstruction loss and perceptual loss [23]. More recently, a novel 3D synthesis model was proposed in which optical flow is first estimated, then the target view image and the target mask are synthesized on different networks. These two networks are linked using a geometry module called *perspective projection layer* [9].

Zhao *et al.* [10] formulated the problem of multi-view person synthesis using a pre-defined view as guidance in the generation. They proposed VariGANs which are a combination of variational inference and adversarial learning. The synthesized view is generated in a coarse-to-fine manner, *i.e.*, a first stage is used to produce a coarse result and a refinement step is applied to generate the high-level details. Ma *et al.* [2] proposed the PG^2 network which employs U-Net with residual blocks in the generator, enabling to generate human images as a coarse-to-fine manner from pose information. Siarohin *et al.* [1] addressed the problem of pixel-to-pixel misalignments between the input and the target image by introducing deformable skip connections in the generator and using a nearest-neighbor loss. Ma *et al.* [12] proposed to generate each of the factors (foreground, background, and pose) separately to synthesize the person image. By learning each factor in a separate branch, the model is able to sample the foreground, background, and pose separately and reconstruct a new image based on these features. An unsupervised GAN [11] for human pose generation has been proposed to avoid the need of supervision. The model introduces a loss function that only depends on the input image and the generated one. The generator is built in two-steps: firstly, a new image is generated based on the target pose, then, the rendered image is fed to a second generator that reconstructs the input image back. Si *et al.* [5] presented a multi-stage solution. First, a network learns to map the input pose to the target view pose based on a transformation vector. Then, a generator synthesizes the person to the target view conditioned on the generated pose along with the input image and pose. Finally, the background is generated in a separated network. Recently, Yang *et al.* [24] proposed a pose-guided sequence generation, from a single image, of people performing an action. A sequence of poses of the human is predicted given the action as input. The video generation is then performed as image synthesis conditioned on the predicted poses.

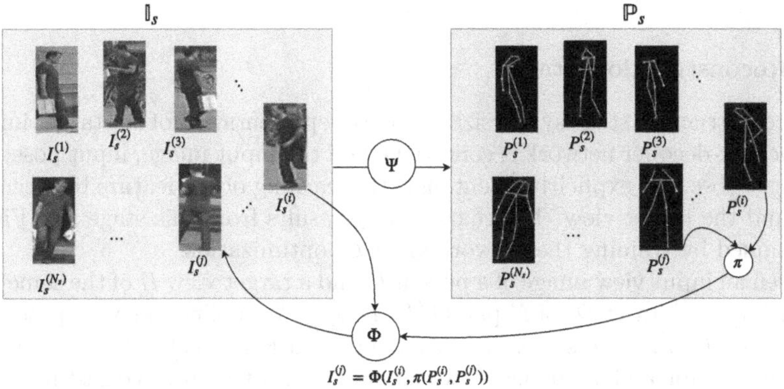

Fig. 1. The goal of pose guided human image synthesis is to generate the image of the same person given the input image $I_s^{(i)}$, its corresponding pose $P_s^{(i)}$ along with the target pose $P_s^{(j)}$ using a generator Φ.

3 Problem Formulation

We are given a set of N images taken from different view-point and poses $\mathbb{I} = \bigcup_{s=1}^{S} \mathbb{I}_s$ consisting of S persons, where $|\mathbb{I}_s| = N_s$ and $N = \sum_{s=1}^{S} N_s$. Each image $I_s^{(i)} \in \mathbb{R}^{w \times h \times c}$ is a bounding box around the person s, where w, h, and $c = 3$ are the image width, height, and channel respectively.

Let $\Psi \colon \mathbb{I} \rightarrow \mathbb{P}$ be a mapping such that given an input image $I_s^{(i)} \in \mathbb{I}$, it estimates K-2D joints representing the body parts, *i.e.*, $P_s^{(i)} = (P_s^{(i)}[1], \ldots, P_s^{(i)}[K])$. Therefore, Ψ maps $\mathbb{I}$ to the pose set $\mathbb{P} = \bigcup_{s=1}^{S} \mathbb{P}_s \subset \mathbb{R}^{2 \times K}$. The pose guided human image synthesis is defined as follows: Given an input image $I_s^{(i)}$ and its corresponding pose $P_s^{(i)}$ along with the target pose $P_s^{(j)}$, the goal is to generate the target image $I_s^{(j)}$ using a mapping Φ that we call generator. The generator Φ takes the input image, and is conditioned on an operator $\pi \colon \mathbb{P} \rightarrow \mathbb{P}$ that is able to learn transform the input to the output. Finally, the target image is obtained as: $I_s^{(j)} = \Phi(I_s^{(i)}, \pi(P_s^{(i)}, P_s^{(j)}))$ (see Fig. 1).

4 View-Disentangled Generator Model

In this section, we present our View-Disentangled Generator (VDG) model. VDG is a two-stage pipeline that first produces a coarse result from an input pair (I_a, P_a) and a target pose P_b, we refer to this stage as *Reconstruction stage*. The *Refinement stage* takes as input the generated image from the Reconstruction stage and the original input I_a, along with the target pose P_b. To train our Refinement stage model, we propose a new loss function that we extend from Structural similarity (SSIM).

4.1 Reconstruction Stage

The Reconstruction stage synthesizes a coarse representation of the target image. The encoder-decoder network is conditioned on the input image, input pose, and the target pose. We explicitly disentangle the learning of the feature between the input and the target view. The coarse image results from this stage (see Fig. 4) are obtained by training the network via a $\mathcal{L}_1$ optimization.

Given an input view image of a person I_a^i and a target view I_b^i of the same person, we build a dataset $\mathcal{D}_1$ of N pairs $\{(I_a^i, I_b^i)\}_{i=1}^N$. We define the body pose $P(I)$ of an image I to be the set of K body joints locations $P(I) = (p[1], \ldots, p[K])$. Following [1], for a given image I, we compute a heat map H consisting of the concatenation of K Gaussian heat maps centered around the jth joint of the estimated pose. Therefore, for a location $p \in \mathbb{R}^2$ and the concatenation operator $\oplus$, we compute $H(I) = \overset{K}{\underset{j=1}{\oplus}} H_j$, where:

$$H_j(p) = \exp\Big(-\frac{\left\|p - P(I)_j\right\|_2^2}{2\sigma^2}\Big), \qquad (1)$$

where $j \in \{1, \ldots, K\}$. We give to K and σ the same values as in [1]: $K = 18$ and $\sigma = 6$. We then compute the corresponding heat maps of the input pair as: $H_a = H(P(I_a))$ and $H_b = H(P(I_b))$ using Eq. 1. Finally, the supervision dataset is: $\mathcal{D}_1 = (\mathcal{X}_1, \mathcal{Y})$, where $\mathcal{X}_1 = \{(I_a^{(i)}, H_a^{(i)}, H_b^{(i)})\}_{i=1}^N$, and $\mathcal{Y} = \{I_b^{(i)}\}_{i=1}^N$. The poses are obtained using a pose estimator (*e.g.* [25]), thus, the resulting estimations are prone to errors (Fig. 2).

Processing the input image and the target pose together in the encoder network can be challenging for the network to make the correspondence if the variation between the input and the output is high. Thus, we propose to disentangle the processing of the input and the output into separate encoders. We build a dedicated encoder for the target pose denoted as Enc_{heat}, this branch will learn a compact representation of the pose, such that $\beta_b = Enc_{heat}(H_b)$. The other encoder that we note as Enc_{img} merges together the input image I_a with the input heat map H_a, it allows the encoder to learn discriminative spatial feature present in the image. The encoder Enc_{img} also learns how to combine the image space with the heat map space, this is a desirable property that will be needed in order to join the Enc_{heat} feature output, from this we

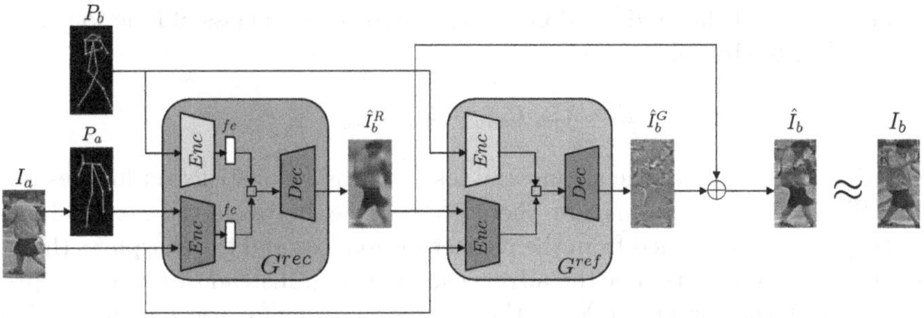

Fig. 2. Proposed VDG model.

have $\epsilon_a = Enc_{img}(I_a, H_a)$. We then combine the two feature $f = \epsilon_a \oplus \beta_b$, the target view image is reconstructed using f *i.e.*, $\hat{I}_b = Dec(f)$.

Similar to [2], the encoder-decoder network presented above (denoted as G^{rec}) follows a U-Net [13] like architecture. The encoder is built using N stacked residual blocks followed by a convolution. Each residual block is composed of two Conv-ReLU operations. In the decoder, skip connections are added between the decoder and the image branch feature maps.

Because the goal of this step is to reconstruct a coarse result, we believe that all the pixels (foreground and background) in the input image have the same importance. Therefore, to train the network we use a $\mathcal{L}_1$ loss function between the prediction $\hat{I}_b^R$ and I_b as follows:

$$\mathcal{L}_{G^{rec}} = \left\| \hat{I}_b^R - I_b \right\|_1 \tag{2}$$

4.2 Refinement Stage

We present the Refinement stage model, where the goal is to use adversarial training to reconstruct the high fidelity of the resulting images. In terms of architecture, the network has a similar disentangling encoder part except that instead, we encode the input and reconstructed image together. SSIM is also presented as loss function for the generator.

Let $\hat{I}_b^{R(i)} = G^{rec}(I_a^{(i)}, H_a^{(i)}, H_b^{(i)})$ be the output from the trained G^{rec} model for the ith data sample. The dataset of the Refinement stage generator G^{ref} is built as follows: $\mathcal{D}_2 = (\mathcal{X}_2, \mathcal{Y})$, where $\mathcal{X}_2 = \{(I_a^{(i)}, \hat{I}_a^{R(i)}, H_b^{(i)})\}_{i=1}^N$, and $\mathcal{Y} = \{I_b^{(i)}\}_{i=1}^N$.

Because with the fully connected layer we lose more of the spatial information in the encoder part, we did not add this layer in the G^{ref} encoder (see Fig. 2) as suggested in [2]. Other than that, the generator G^{ref} is similar to the G^{rec} network. The *image branch* in this step is used to restore back the high-level frequency via adversarial training. The network will use the input image I_a as a reference to map the missing details from the Reconstruction stage.

The training of the model is done using a more general class of functions that was proposed in [16,26]:

$$\mathcal{L} = \lambda_{adv}\mathcal{L}_{adv} + \lambda_{rec}\mathcal{L}_{rec}, \tag{3}$$

where $\mathcal{L}_{adv}$ and $\mathcal{L}_{rec}$ are the adversarial loss and the reconstruction loss respectively. The weighting terms are there to balance between the coarse (low-frequency) results obtained from the reconstruction loss and the sharpness (high-frequency) of the results. For the adversarial learning, instead of trying to optimize $\hat{I}_b^G$ to fit the target, we learn the residue in order for the Reconstruction stage image $\hat{I}_b^R$ to fit the target using Eq. 4:

$$\hat{I}_b = \hat{I}_b^R + \hat{I}_b^G \tag{4}$$

The network is trained using adversarial learning between our Refinement stage generator G^{ref} and the discriminator D by alternating the optimization between Eqs. 5 and 6. We use conditional discriminator [27] on the pair (I_a, I_b) for the positive samples and $(I_a, \hat{I}_b)$ for the generated images.

$$\mathcal{L}_D = \mathbb{E}_{I_a,I_b}\big[\log D(I_a, I_b)\big] + \mathbb{E}_{I_a}\big[\log(1 - D(I_a, \hat{I}_b))\big], \tag{5}$$

$$\mathcal{L}_{G^{ref}} = \mathbb{E}_{I_a}\big[\log D(I_a, \hat{I}_b)\big] + \lambda\mathcal{L}_{img}. \tag{6}$$

$\mathbb{E}$ denotes expectation, λ is a parameter that controls the influence of the reconstruction loss. Structural similarity (SSIM) [28] is a metric that assesses the quality of images. Since the goal of Refinement stage is to enhance the images from the Reconstruction stage, we propose mask-SSIM to let the model focus more on the generated person by making use of the target mask $\mathbb{M}_b$:

$$\mathcal{L}_{reconst} = \begin{cases} \left\|(\hat{I}_b^G - I_b) \odot (1 + \mathbb{M}_b)\right\|_1, & \text{for loss=}\mathcal{L}_1^{mask} \\ \mathcal{L}_{SSIM}(\hat{I}_b \odot (1 + \mathbb{M}_b), I_b \odot (1 + \mathbb{M}_b)), & \text{for loss=}\mathcal{L}_{SSIM}^{mask} \end{cases} \tag{7}$$

where $\mathcal{L}_{SSIM}$ is the SSIM loss.

Because the generator creates some visible artifacts during the adversarial training, we try to reduce them by another $\mathcal{L}_1$ term with a small weight. Inspired by the weighted reconstruction loss [29], we propose an adapted version of our model. The final loss function becomes:

$$\mathcal{L}_{img} = \alpha\mathcal{L}_{SSIM}^{mask} + (1 - \alpha)\mathcal{L}_1^{mask}. \tag{8}$$

We choose $\alpha \in \{0.9, 0.8, 0.7, 0.6, 0.5\}$ for an ablation study presented in Sect. 5 *i.e.*, the $\mathcal{L}_1$ term in $\mathcal{L}_{img}$ can go up to half of the influence. After that, the results will be blurred.

5 Experiments

This section presents our evaluation protocol as well as a quantitative and qualitative study. We provide an ablation study of our architecture and highlight some of the key factors that challenge the generation. To evaluate our model we start with an ablation study of each component of VDG (as described in Sect. 4), trained using $\mathcal{L}_1$ loss for the reconstruction in both stages. We also highlight the importance of the careful choice of the loss function and how it affects the results. The VDG model is trained using the $\mathcal{L}_1$ loss in the reconstruction term in the Refinement stage. VDG^{mask-L_1} uses the target mask $\mathbb{M}_b$ in the reconstruction $\mathcal{L}_1$ loss as defined in Eq. 7. For VDG, we instead train the generator using the mask-SSIM loss. Finally, VDG_w trains the Refinement stage generator using Eq. 8.

Datasets: We use Market-1501 [30] and DeepFashion [31]. Market-1501 [30] dataset contains 32,668 images of 1,501 identities collected from six cameras. The datasets have images of different poses, illuminations, viewpoints and backgrounds, all images are of size 128×64 and we split them into train/test sets of 12,936/19,732. We pre-process each split by removing the images that do not contain any pose in the estimation, we then create pairs in which we have the image of the same person but with different pose. After this step we end up having 263,631 training pairs and we randomly select 12,000 pairs for testing.

We use the In-shop Clothes Retrieval Benchmark of DeepFashion [31] dataset, it has 52,712 clothes images of 256×256 pixels. In total, there are 200,000 pairs of identical clothes with different poses and/or scales. Following the procedure described for Market-1501 dataset, we build our train/test sets and we get 101,268 training pairs and we select 8,670 pairs for testing. To construct the train/test set on each dataset, we follow the protocol defined by Ma *et al.* [2].

Implementation Details: We train the generators G^{rec}, and G^{ref} and the discriminator D using Adam [32] optimizer with $\beta_1 = 0.5$, $\beta_2 = 0.999$, and learning rate $\epsilon = 2.10^{-5}$.

On Market-1501 (resp. DeepFashion), we set the number of residual blocks in the generators G^{rec} and G^{ref} to $N = 5$ (resp. $N = 6$). We train the model with a minibatch of size 16 (resp. 6) for 22k (resp. 40k) iterations at the Reconstruction stage and 14k (resp. 30k) iterations at the Refinement stage.

Model Evaluation: To assess the models we use the SSIM score and the Inception Score (IS) [33] which is one of the widely used metric to evaluate a generative model. IS measures the performance of the generator by evaluating the quality and the diversity of the generated images. Because of the high variation in the background of the Market-1501 dataset, Ma *et al.* [2] proposed a variant of SSIM and IS scores, which is to only apply the mask to both the original and the reconstructed image to get the scores, we report these as well.

Table 1 compares results obtained from the Reconstruction stage with the PG^2 model and our proposed VDG. To study the influence of the mask in this phase, we train PG^2 using only $\mathcal{L}_1$ without the mask which we refer to as PG^2

Table 1. Reconstruction stage results comparison with the PG^2 [2] model.

Method	Market-1501				DeepFashion	
	SSIM	IS	Mask-SSIM	Mask-IS	SSIM	IS
PG^2 [2]	.285	3.363	.801	2.798	.693	2.882
PG^2 [2] w/o mask	.290	3.356	.804	2.797	.689	2.833
VDG	.274	3.407	.799	2.733	.691	2.773

Table 2. Artifact removal evaluation by varying α over $\mathcal{L}_{img}$.

Method	Market-1501				DeepFashion	
	SSIM	IS	Mask-SSIM	Mask-IS	SSIM	IS
$VDG_w^{\alpha=0.9}$	**.266**	3.453	**.783**	3.227	.700	**3.428**
$VDG_w^{\alpha=0.8}$	.258	3.315	.779	3.201	.706	3.073
$VDG_w^{\alpha=0.7}$	.240	**3.882**	.773	**3.469**	.710	2.906
$VDG_w^{\alpha=0.6}$	.261	3.195	.773	3.258	**.711**	2.887
$VDG_w^{\alpha=0.5}$	.265	3.463	.777	3.210	.709	3.056

Table 3. Results comparison of our proposed model with other state-of-the-art solutions. ($\star$) Results were reported on different test set.

Method	Market-1501				DeepFashion	
	SSIM	IS	Mask-SSIM	Mask-IS	SSIM	IS
PG^2 [2]	.252	4.015	.771	**3.555**	.641	3.187
Def-GAN [1]	**.290**	2.990	**.798**	3.544	.665	3.420
PDIG [12] ($\star$)	.099	3.483	.614	3.491	.614	3.228
VDG^{L_1}	.224	3.733	.767	3.503	.700	3.428
VDG^{mask-L_1}	.238	3.933	.768	3.542	.690	3.429
VDG	.238	4.007	.775	3.354	**.708**	3.003
VDG_w	.266	3.453	.783	3.227	.702	**3.491**

w/o mask. We notice a slight improvement on the SSIM for PG^2 model compared to our, as for the mask, from Table 1 we do not notice any clear evidence of using the mask during this stage.

We further conducted an empirical evaluation on how varying the weighting term α affects the artifact removal due to the adversarial training and the perceptual quality as well. Table 2 reports the scores over Market-1501 and DeepFashion, we can notice that the overall best performing model is with $\alpha = 0.9$ which suggest that the $\mathcal{L}_1$ term helps to remove the noticeable artifacts without altering the perceptual quality of the results. We show some qualitative results as well in Fig. 3, for example, in the second row of DeepFashion, we can clearly

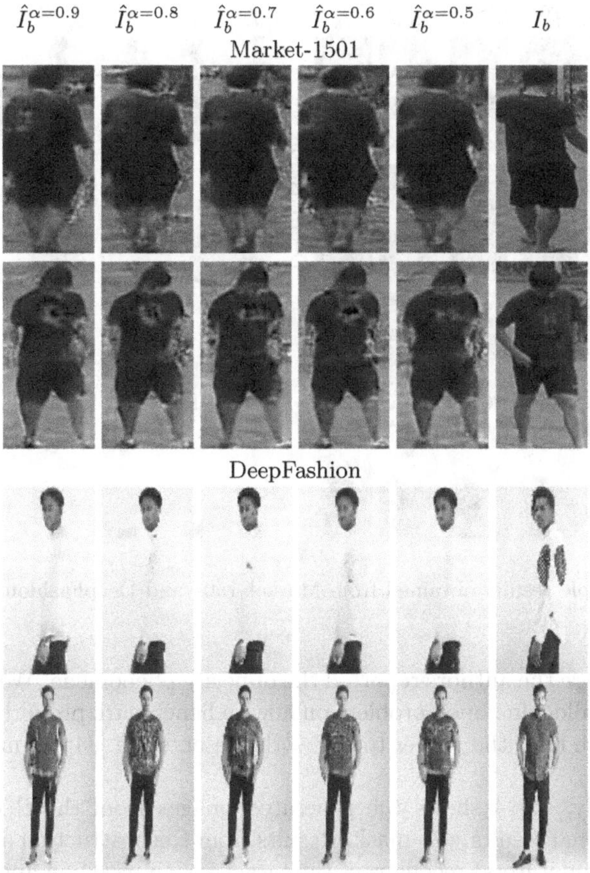

Fig. 3. Qualitative results on a various weighting scheme with the proposed loss.

see the advantage of $\text{VDG}_w^{\alpha=0.9}$ where for the other models the generation of the shirt comes with additional artifacts.

For the Refinement stage (Table 3), we can observe that the mask loss (VDG^{mask-L_1}) improves the results over only a $\mathcal{L}_1$ term (VDG^{L_1}), this is because we let the network focus more on the generation of human image. Additionally, using SSIM as a loss function helps the generator (VDG and VDG_w). We explain the equality in the SSIM scores for VDG^{mask-L_1} and VDG due to the background influence which is still challenging for both models. We further compare our model against other state-of-the-art methods. From these results, we can see the effectiveness of branching solution (VDG and Def-GAN [1]) compared to PG^2.

An important remark to make regarding the results is the inconstancy on how the evaluation measures behave. In our study, we observe that when the SSIM score improves the inception scores decrease. Similar behavior has been observed

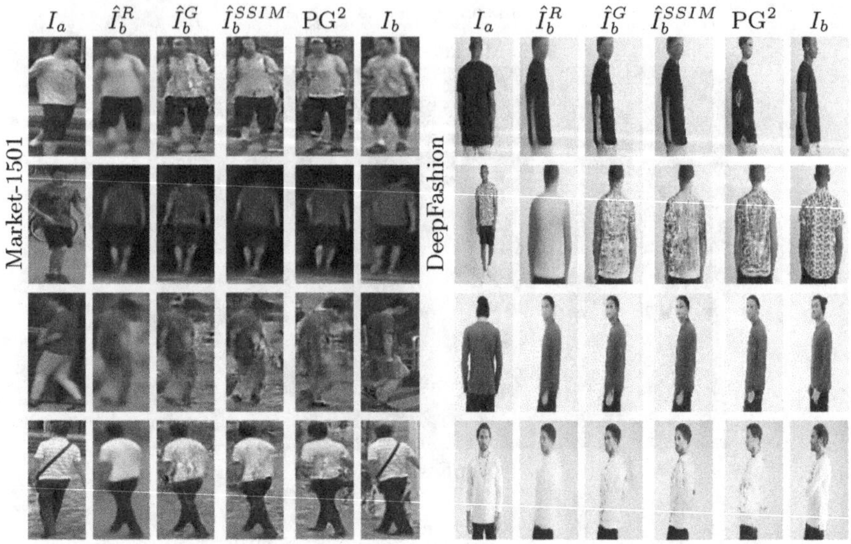

Fig. 4. Sample results obtained from Market-1501 and DeepFashion datasets.

also in [12], where the authors reported the opposite phenomena. We believe that this is still a challenging open problem on how to benchmark properly over GANs performance, we refer the reader to the work presented in [34] for more in-depth study.

Qualitatively, Fig. 4 shows the generated images from the Reconstruction stage and the final results w/o mask. Results from Reconstruction stage (second column on both datasets) reconstruct the target image based on appearance and the target pose but high-level details are absent. Refinement stage adds details by a hallucination of some missing human parts from the input (*e.g.,* faces). We notice some artifacts that are present in the final results produced by the GAN generator, which affect the general scores. Figure 5 compares our method against other state-of-the-art, our improved loss VDG_w can generate images with a clear distinction between the body and the arms compared to the VDG model (see the fourth row). We also note that the $\mathcal{L}_1$ term in the proposed loss helps to remove some of the visible artifacts due to the residual term in the adversarial process (2nd and 5th row). We observe that PG^2 can not preserve well the color as can be seen from the third and seventh row.

Quality Assessment: In general, the generator is able to reconstruct the full body limbs. Figure 6 shows some results of our model with regards to the factors defined in Sect. 1: quality, scale, occlusion, and complexity. Interestingly, when some parts of the body are missing in the input but needed in the output our generator can hallucinate about the face and the full arm with the appropriate pants colors even with partial initial information (3rd row right part). The model can handle well the scale difference (1st and 2nd rows). On the other hand, the

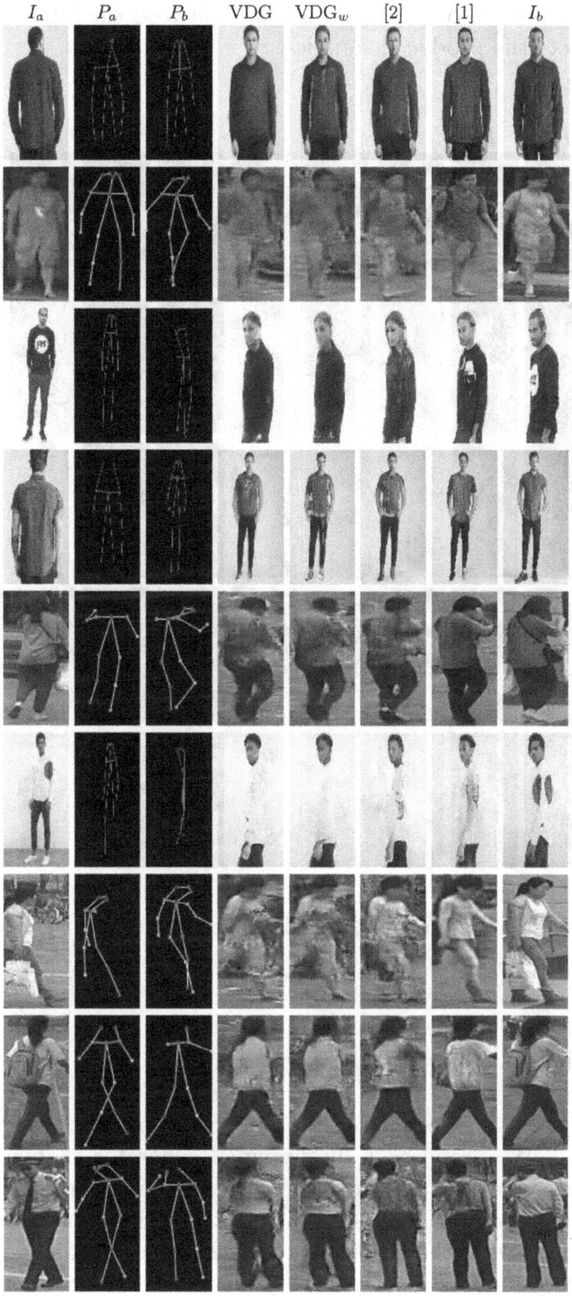

Fig. 5. Generated results using different methods on Market-1501 and DeepFashion. (Color figure online)

model produces crippled outputs on challenging cases like occlusion and the quality of the images. Also, the high variation between the input and the target background affects the produced samples.

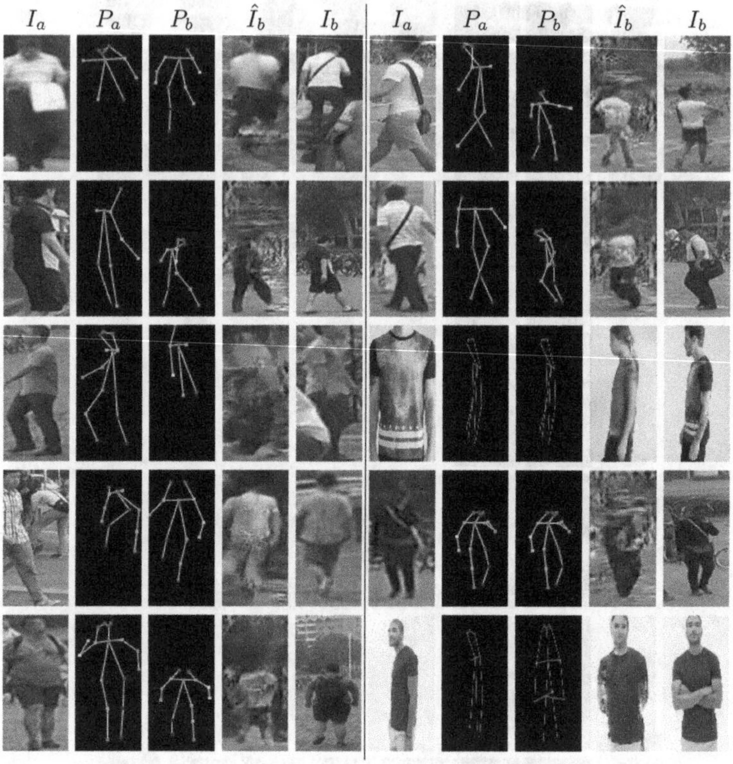

Fig. 6. Results of our model on challenging cases. (Color figure online)

6 Conclusions

We presented a two-stage deep encoder-decoder network for pose guided human image generation. We proposed a disentangled generator that explicitly separates the source image and the target pose into different branches. We further introduced mask-SSIM as a reconstruction loss function during the adversarial training, which facilitates the generator to focus on perceptually appealing outputs. The proposed model has shown competitive performance compared to the state of the art.

We observed that the background should be taken into account as it affects the quality of the generated view. Moreover, further improvements could be achieved by using sub-modules, each focusing on a specific part [5,12,35].

References

1. Siarohin, A., Sangineto, E., Lathuilière, S., Sebe, N.: Deformable GANs for pose-based human image generation. In: IEEE Conference on Computer Vision and Pattern Recognition, CVPR, June 2018
2. Ma, L., Jia, X., Sun, Q., Schiele, B., Tuytelaars, T., Van Gool, L.: Pose guided person image generation. In: Advances in Neural Information Processing Systems, NIPS, December 2017
3. Eunbyung, P., Jimei, Y., Ersin, Y., Duygu, C., Alexander, C.B.: Transformation-grounded image generation network for novel 3D view synthesis. In: IEEE Conference on Computer Vision and Pattern Recognition, CVPR, July 2017
4. Zhou, T., Tulsiani, S., Sun, W., Malik, J., Efros, A.A.: View synthesis by appearance flow. In: Leibe, B., Matas, J., Sebe, N., Welling, M. (eds.) ECCV 2016. LNCS, vol. 9908, pp. 286–301. Springer, Cham (2016). https://doi.org/10.1007/978-3-319-46493-0_18
5. Chenyang, S., Wei, W., Liang, W., Tieniu, T.: Multistage adversarial losses for pose-based human image synthesis. In: IEEE Conference on Computer Vision and Pattern Recognition, CVPR, June 2018
6. Kholgade, N., Simon, T., Efros, A., Sheikh, Y.: 3D object manipulation in a single photograph using stock 3D models. ACM Trans. Comput. Graph. **33**, 127 (2014)
7. Zheng, Y., Chen, X., Cheng, M.M., Zhou, K., Hu, S.M., Mitra, N.J.: Interactive images: cuboid proxies for smart image manipulation. ACM Trans. Graph. **31**, 99:1–99:11 (2012)
8. Yan, X., Yang, J., Yumer, E., Guo, Y., Lee, H.: Perspective transformer nets: learning single-view 3D object reconstruction without 3D supervision. In: Advances in Neural Information Processing Systems, NIPS, December 2016
9. Zhu, H., Su, H., Wang, P., Cao, X., Yang, R.: View extrapolation of human body from a single image. In: IEEE Conference on Computer Vision and Pattern Recognition, CVPR, June 2018
10. Zhao, B., Wu, X., Cheng, Z., Liu, H., Feng, J.: Multi-view image generation from a single-view. Volume abs/1704.04886 (2017)
11. Pumarola, A., Agudo, A., Sanfeliu, A., Moreno-Noguer, F.: Unsupervised person image synthesis in arbitrary poses. In: IEEE Conference on Computer Vision and Pattern Recognition, CVPR, June 2018
12. Ma, L., Sun, Q., Georgoulis, S., Van Gool, L., Schiele, B., Fritz, M.: Disentangled person image generation. In: IEEE Conference on Computer Vision and Pattern Recognition, CVPR, June 2018
13. Ronneberger, O., Fischer, P., Brox, T.: U-Net: convolutional networks for biomedical image segmentation. In: Navab, N., Hornegger, J., Wells, W.M., Frangi, A.F. (eds.) MICCAI 2015. LNCS, vol. 9351, pp. 234–241. Springer, Cham (2015). https://doi.org/10.1007/978-3-319-24574-4_28
14. Kingma, D.P., Welling, M.: Auto-encoding variational bayes. In: The International Conference on Learning Representations, ICLR, April 2014
15. Goodfellow, I., et al.: Generative adversarial nets. In: Advances in Neural Information Processing Systems, NIPS, December 2014
16. Pathak, D., Krähenbühl, P., Donahue, J., Darrell, T., Efros, A.: Context encoders: feature learning by inpainting. In: IEEE Conference on Computer Vision and Pattern Recognition, CVPR, June 2016
17. Isola, P., Zhu, J., Zhou, T., Efros, A.A.: Image-to-image translation with conditional adversarial networks. In: IEEE Conference on Computer Vision and Pattern Recognition, CVPR, July 2017

18. Ledig, C., et al.: Photo-realistic single image super-resolution using a generative adversarial network. In: IEEE International Conference on Computer Vision, ICCV, October 2017
19. Krishna, R., Ali, B.: Cross-view image synthesis using conditional GANs. In: IEEE Conference on Computer Vision and Pattern Recognition, CVPR, June 2018
20. Bengio, Y., Courville, A., Vincent, P.: Representation learning: a review and new perspectives. IEEE Trans. Pattern Anal. Mach. Intell. (PAMI) **35**, 1798–1828 (2013)
21. Dosovitskiy, A., Springenberg, J.T., Tatarchenko, M., Brox, T.: Learning to generate chairs, tables and cars with convolutional networks. IEEE Trans. Pattern Anal. Mach. Intell. (PAMI) **39**, 692–705 (2017)
22. Jaderberg, M., Simonyan, K., Zisserman, A., Kavukcuoglu, K.: Spatial transformer networks. In: Advances in Neural Information Processing Systems, NIPS, December 2015
23. Johnson, J., Alahi, A., Fei-Fei, L.: Perceptual losses for real-time style transfer and super-resolution. In: Leibe, B., Matas, J., Sebe, N., Welling, M. (eds.) ECCV 2016. LNCS, vol. 9906, pp. 694–711. Springer, Cham (2016). https://doi.org/10.1007/978-3-319-46475-6_43
24. Yang, C., Wang, Z., Zhu, X., Huang, C., Shi, J., Lin, D.: Pose guided human video generation. In: Ferrari, V., Hebert, M., Sminchisescu, C., Weiss, Y. (eds.) ECCV 2018. LNCS, vol. 11214, pp. 204–219. Springer, Cham (2018). https://doi.org/10.1007/978-3-030-01249-6_13
25. Cao, Z., Simon, T., Wei, S.E., Sheikh, Y.: Realtime multi-person 2D pose estimation using part affinity fields. In: IEEE Conference on Computer Vision and Pattern Recognition, CVPR, July 2017
26. Dosovitskiy, A., Brox, T.: Generating images with perceptual similarity metrics based on deep networks. In: Advances in Neural Information Processing Systems, NIPS, December 2016
27. Mirza, M., Osindero, S.: Conditional generative adversarial nets. Volume abs/1411.1784 (2014)
28. Wang, Z., Bovik, A.C., Sheikh, H.R., Simoncelli, E.P.: Image quality assessment: from error visibility to structural similarity. IEEE Trans. Image Process. (TIP) **13**, 600–612 (2004)
29. Zhao, H., Gallo, O., Frosio, I., Kautz, J.: Loss functions for image restoration with neural networks. IEEE Trans. Comput. Imag. **3**, 47–57 (2017)
30. Zheng, L., Shen, L., Tian, L., Wang, S., Wang, J., Tian, Q.: Scalable person re-identification: a benchmark. In: IEEE International Conference on Computer Vision, ICCV, December 2015
31. Liu, Z., Luo, P., Qiu, S., Wang, X., Tang, X.: DeepFashion: powering robust clothes recognition and retrieval with rich annotations. In: IEEE Conference on Computer Vision and Pattern Recognition, CVPR, June 2016
32. Kingma, D.P., Ba, J.: Adam: a method for stochastic optimization. In: International Conference on Learning Representations, ICLR, May 2015
33. Salimans, T., et al.: Improved techniques for training GANs. In: Advances in Neural Information Processing Systems, NIPS, December 2016
34. Borji, A.: Pros and cons of GAN evaluation measures. Volume abs/1802.03446 (2018)
35. Guha, B., Amy, Z., Adrian, V.D., Fredo, D., John, G.: Synthesizing images of humans in unseen poses. In: IEEE Conference on Computer Vision and Pattern Recognition, CVPR, June 2018

A Semi-supervised Data Augmentation Approach Using 3D Graphical Engines

Shuangjun Liu and Sarah Ostadabbas(✉)

Augmented Cognition Lab, Electrical and Computer Engineering Department, Northeastern University, Boston, USA
{shuliu,ostadabbas}@ece.neu.edu
http://www.northeastern.edu/ostadabbas/

Abstract. Deep learning approaches have been rapidly adopted across a wide range of fields because of their accuracy and flexibility, but require large labeled training datasets. This presents a fundamental problem for applications with limited, expensive, or private data (i.e. small data), such as human pose and behavior estimation/tracking which could be highly personalized. In this paper, we present a semi-supervised data augmentation approach that can synthesize large scale labeled training datasets using 3D graphical engines based on a physically-valid low dimensional pose descriptor. To evaluate the performance of our synthesized datasets in training deep learning-based models, we generated a large synthetic human pose dataset, called ScanAva using 3D scans of only 7 individuals based on our proposed augmentation approach. A state-of-the-art human pose estimation deep learning model then was trained from scratch using our ScanAva dataset and could achieve the pose estimation accuracy of 91.2% at PCK0.5 criteria after applying an efficient domain adaptation on the synthetic images, in which its pose estimation accuracy was comparable to the same model trained on large scale pose data from real humans such as MPII dataset and much higher than the model trained on other synthetic human dataset such as SURREAL.

Keywords: Data augmentation · Deep learning · Domain adaptation · Human pose estimation · Low dimensional subspace learning

1 Introduction

With the remarkable success of deep neural networks (DNNs) in regression and classification tasks, a significant challenge comes out to be forming a large scale *labeled* datasets to support DNN training requirements. In the computer vision field, widely employed datasets mainly come from collection of real-world images captured from the contexts of interest and labeled through manual processes such as crowdsourcing. A direct benefit of using these datasets for the network training is to preserve authentic information from real world. However, each image in the

L. Leal-Taixé and S. Roth (Eds.): ECCV 2018 Workshops, LNCS 11130, pp. 395–408, 2019.
https://doi.org/10.1007/978-3-030-11012-3_31

training set needs to be labeled for the supervised learning process and it get quite expensive for large datasets [38]. On the other hand, for certain applications where data is scarce such as personalized medicine, robot reinforcement learning, environmental/weather behavior prediction, and military applications, forming a large scale dataset itself could be infeasible [25]. The million dollar question here is if one can benefit from the flexibility and accuracy of DNNs in small data domains or domains with expensive labeling process by virtually synthesizing large scale labeled datasets. Hence, this paper presents a semi-supervised data augmentation approach that expands the size of a small dataset by synthesizing labeled samples in the physically-valid world contexts, while demonstrating that the trained DNNs using this synthetic dataset are capable of performing a high accuracy estimation task that they are trained for.

Classically, to address the data limitation issue, data augmentation techniques are extensively used especially when it comes to DNN training. Existing data augmentation methods can be seen as a mapping from one domain to itself by linear transformation with random variations, such as scale/orientation augmentation [32], color augmentation, and random crop per-pixel mean subtraction [22,23], among others. These hand crafted augmentation methods indeed improve the DNN performance in the designated tasks though not significantly [40]. They simply ignore the fact that image generation is actually a mapping from the 3D physical world into the 2D image domain, where the camera model is already well defined. The consequence is that classical augmentation methods can only capture superficial variations of the original dataset instead of capturing the semantic meaning of objects in the real world.

Alternatively, 3D computer-aided design (CAD) models can emulate such geometrical semantic variations in the real world. Majority of the works enabled by the CAD-based data augmentation employ publicly available CAD models [6,36]. Some of these models are also templates for specific categories [11,38]. The extent of data augmentation here is often limited by the existing CAD models, which only provide rough categories or limited by the already existing templates. Another practical issue is that publicly available CAD models are usually created by human artists and could be in a conceptual ideal condition and lack realistic variations. In contrast, generating (unlabeled) sample images from a large variety of objects, movements, and contexts is fairly achievable in our physical world, in which each sample manifests the physics laws behind our real world.

In this paper, we merged the benefits of two approaches, (i.e., 3D modeling and (semi)realistic data generation following the physical world laws) and present a data augmentation pipeline for large scale labeled dataset forming that uses the easily collected 3D scans of the target objects (e.g., humans) and move/articulate them in a physically-valid fashion using a 3D graphical engine (e.g., moving human avatars in a virtual environment). Although our cost-efficient 3D scans have lower resolution compared to the existing CAD templates and the movements and contexts are virtually synthesized, after a straightforward domain adaption, our approach allows the data augmentation for deep learning purposes in any emerging target objects and can efficiently expand and adjust the movements and contexts based on the application tasks.

2 Related Work

When dealing with deep learning in small data domains, fine-tuning already trained DNNs proves to be effective [7,8,10,25,40]. Fine-tuning is a form of transfer learning, when fine-tuned DNNs applied on the new (but small in size) dataset hugely benefit from knowledge learned from large amount of real world image samples (even being from different domain). However, if the two datasets are very different in nature, fine-tuning would fail since the network is already very fitted to the first dataset and is unable to adopt to the new small dataset unless we substantially increase the size of the second dataset and pay the labeling cost associated with that. These issues inspired us to simulate lots of plausible samples in the context of interest (i.e. the context that only has small dataset available), which allows for training DNNs from scratch rather than just fine-tuning them.

2.1 Classical Dataset Forming

A common way to form datasets in computer vision field is collecting real images directly and manually label them. Most influential datasets are formed in this way including ImageNet [22] for object classification, Cityscapes [12] for scene segmentation, LSUN [41] for scene understanding, and MPII human pose [4] and LSP [20] datasets for human pose estimation. These datasets preserve the real world information authentically and are most effective to train DNN models for practical applications [16,42]. Data augmentation usually comes during training session, which usually include augmentation in scale, color, shift, or mirror, which is limited to superficial variations of the image [32].

2.2 Synthetic Dataset Forming

Synthetic data has already been employed to form large datasets and provides convenience to control the generation process with exact parameters [36]. In early works, synthetic data was mainly employed to provide additional information to facilitate the detection/estimation process. For example, in [24], the geometric information from 3D CAD models is combined with the real image appearance to improve object detection and pose estimation for bicycles and cars. Shape models and also the probabilistic models are also learned from CAD models [33,37]. Another benefit of synthesizing data is the possibility to automatically generate enough labeled data for supervised learning purposes [34]. Authors in [14] studied an optical flow estimation algorithm based on synthesized images of a 3D moving chair. Virtual KITTI dataset with synthesized car videos is also employed to train multi-object tracking algorithms [17].

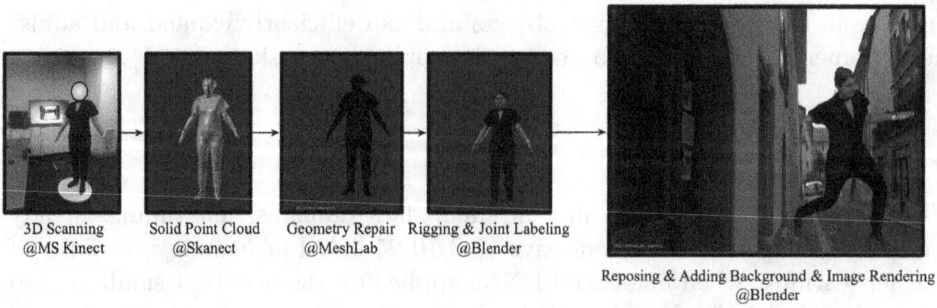

Fig. 1. An overview of our pipeline on the physically-valid semi-supervised human pose data augmentation approach that leads to forming ScanAva datasets.

More complicated articulated 3D models are also studied, among which the human body draws most attention due to the extensive applications associated with studying human pose, gestures, and activities. Synthesized human data has been employed for 2D/3D pose estimation [11,15,18,28–31] and pedestrian detection [26,29]. No matter the synthesized human data is collected from publicly available graphical 3D models or from generalized templates, they can hardly represent every individual in various contexts. Even a morphable human template such as SCAPE method (Shape Completion and Animation for PEople) can hardly represent a person in different clothing conditions [5].

2.3 Our Contributions

With ever lowering price of portable 3D scanning devices, in this paper, we present an alternative way for synthetic dataset forming which combines the flexibility of classical data collection method and the automation of 3D engines as shown in Fig. 1. The main contributions of this work include: (1) providing a rapid and cost-efficient pipeline to form large scale labeled datasets from a target set of objects in various contexts; (2) exploring the way to minimize domain shift between source (virtual) and target (real) correspondence with limited data from the target domain; (3) demonstrating the proposed approach on human pose estimation problem by training a state-of-the-art DNN model with the limited 3D human scan samples from scratch and evaluating the trained DNN pose estimation performance on real world human images with comparison with the leading real and synthetic datasets; and (4) publicly releasing our synthetic human pose datasets called scanned avatars or "ScanAva" and our dataset generation tools in the Augmented Cognition Lab (ACLab) webpage.[1]

[1] This paper has dataset available at ScanAva and the code at GitHub provided by the authors. Contact the corresponding author for further questions about this work.

3 A Semi-supervised Data Augmentation Approach

No matter if it is collected from objects, animals, humans, or scenes, considering the various appearances, pose states, and their combinations, a dataset even very large one can hardly cover the whole space of its universal attribute domain (i.e., feature space). When the categories covered by the dataset are too broad, its feature space can get easily sparse causing low performance learning due to the highly probable over-fitting problem. In contrast, within a specific and well-defined category, if data with enough granularity is available, it could form a low dimensional manifold within the feature space leading to a better (manifold) learning especially when DNNs are used. Due to the high cost of collecting and labeling highly granular dataset, we present a pipeline to form a large labeled dataset with controllable granularity. In particular, we synthesized large scale datasets from a highly articulated object, "human body" and validated the dataset quality by performing human pose estimation using DNN models trained from scratch purely on these synthesized datasets, called ScanAva.

Let's assume image $I = f(G, \boldsymbol{\theta}, E_v)$ contains a human figure, where G is the person's geometry appearance, $\boldsymbol{\theta}$ is the person's pose information, and E_v is the environment and background's parameters. Our dataset ScanAva forming pipeline then includes (see Fig. 1): (1) collecting the appearance model G by an affordable 3D scanning process; (2) rigging and one-time limb labeling of the 3D scans (i.e., avatars) based on their articulation for valid human reposing; (3) defining a low dimensional pose descriptor for physically-valid reposing; (4) 3D data augmentation by changing the pose information $\boldsymbol{\theta}$ with controllable granularity based on a given application; and (5) rendering 2D images from the 3D data with different environment's parameters E_v. These steps lead to generation of our ScanAva datasets, in which each image has a human figure with the person's pose physically-valid and precisely labeled.

3.1 Geometry Appearance Acquisition via 3D Scanning

An object's geometry appearance G is a major component that affects its image. We employed the conventional 3D model formats such as 3DS models (*.3ds), Wavefront OBJ (*.obj), and PLY (*.ply) to represent G. In articulated cases, G contains skeleton with multiple entries to represent each moving part $G(i)$, where i stands for the part index. In a rigid body case, G simply reduce to one component in our model. In an articulated human body, based on its biomechanics and skeleton, we predefined 14 moving parts (i.e., limbs) as head (H), torso (T), left upper arm (LUA), left lower arm (LLA), left palm (LP), right upper arm (RUA), right lower arm (RLA), right palm (RP), left upper leg (LUL), left lower leg (LLL), left foot (LF), right upper leg (RUL), right lower leg (RLL), and right foot (RF), as shown in Fig. 2a. The limbs are articulated together with joints. Each joint state is described by a rotation angle. We employed a state vector $\boldsymbol{\theta} = \{\theta_1, \theta_2, \ldots, \theta_n\}$ to describe the pose information. Our model can be described by a graph where limb geometry acts as node and state vector describes the edges between limbs. This graph varies depending on the target configuration.

To get the 3D geometry model, we employ a Microsoft Kinect v1 to perform 3D scanning of the human body using off-the-shelf components and software. Subject stands on a automatic rotator in front of the Kinect sensor. We employed a commercially available software, Skanect to extract 3D information from the scanning frames [3]. The scanning process is shown on the monitor to give realtime feedback. Our 3D scanning setup is shown in Fig. 2b. When the space is limited, the camera's field of view cannot cover the whole body. In this case, we will pitch the camera up and down to extend the sensing area. The whole body scan can be achieved by stitching them together.

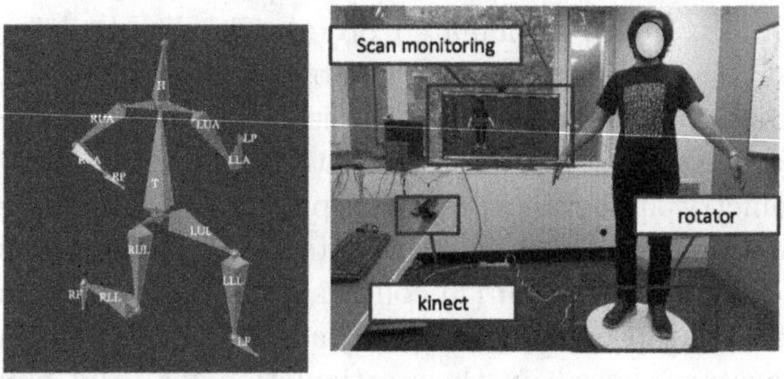

(a) (b)

Fig. 2. (a) The human skeleton with 14 limbs and corresponding joints, (b) Human body 3D scanning procedure.

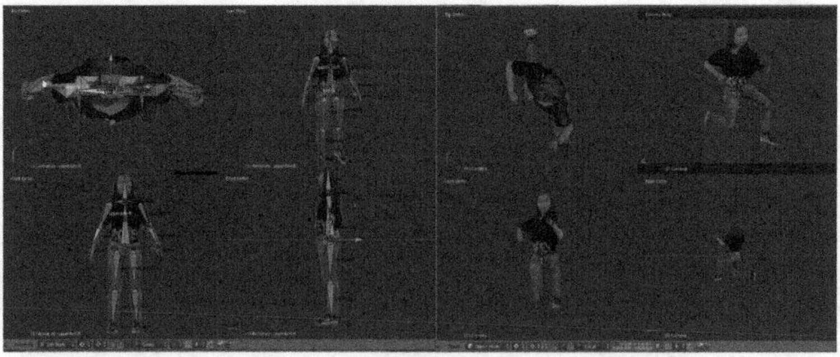

(a) (b)

Fig. 3. Rigged model in Blender software: (a) armature assignment, (b) a generated pose.

3.2 Rigging for Reposing

Rig is essentially a digital skeleton bound to a 3D mesh that consists of joints and bones. Joints and bones in the rig can be moved by altering the pose state descriptor $\boldsymbol{\theta}$, which leads to reposing and animation of the 3D models. To rig the 3D scanned model (avatars), we employed an existing animation toolkit "Blender" to manipulate the body parts and give them the pose we wish. An armature is assigned to the scanned model. The root bone is set at the center of the pelvis. Each arm has an upper arm, lower arm and palm bone. Each leg has an upper leg, a lower leg and a foot bone. The head bone is also assigned to it. A demo of rigged model is shown in Fig. 3a. From the rigged model, we can easily manipulate the avatar to generate the pose we need by manipulating the pose state vector, $\boldsymbol{\theta}$. An example generated pose is shown in Fig. 3b. The corresponding 2D image is achieved by re-projection of the 3D model into the image domain. In cases where scanned raw models have defects such as holes, over complicated details, or non-manifold geometries, we can optionally employ Meshlab open-source software or equivalent toolkit for preprocessing including simplification, filling holes, and also non-manifold geometries removal [1].

3.3 Manifold Pose Generation via a Low Dimensional Pose Descriptor

To give a specific example, we model the human pose as follows. Following humanoid robot convention [21], we define shoulder, neck, and hip as spherical joints, elbow and knee as revolute joints and wrist and ankle as universal joints. Higher degree joints can be decomposed into multiple one-degree joints. Each arm/leg has 6 degree of freedom (DOF) and with a 3 DOF neck, giving $\boldsymbol{\theta}$ a dimensionality of $n = 27$. Pose space is actually a constrained manifold: not all 27-dimensional vectors represent valid poses. We assume two ways to generate valid descriptor. One way is following kinematic constrains to make generated descriptor physically valid which is helpful when motion data is limited. The other is direct sampling from data lies on such manifold such as motion capture data [2]. In first method, the two constraints considered during the generation phase are joint angle constraints and global orientation constraints. We will use a constraint matrix to indicate the range of each state variable as $[\theta_{is}, \theta_{ie}]$ for $i \in [1 : n]$, where θ_{is} and θ_{ie} stand for the low and high acceptable ranges of the state θ_i. For example, for the human elbow joint, the possible rotation range is around from $0°$ to $145°$. In addition, depending on the application, there might be global orientation constraints. For example, for in-bed poses, the torso will lie approximately parallel to the bed. The Euler description for the body orientation as (α, β, γ) will show the relative orientation of the body with respect to the world frame [13]. In the context of walking, we can simply limit the Euler angles to a range to mimic the up straight poses, for example $\alpha, \gamma \in [-30°, 30°]$. Therefore, both joint angle and global orientation constraint types can be modeled using range bounds. Within these bounds, poses can be generated from a uniform random distribution, or they can be generated procedurally using a grid-based approach.

Since this is used for training a DNN, we use the random approach to take advantage of a common training optimization, Stochastic Gradient Decent (SGD) [9]. In SGD, a fixed-size batch is randomly selected from fixed size dataset with random variation such as crop and scaling. In our work, random generation is equivalent to random selection from an infinite training set as we sample from a virtually continuous pose manifold.

3.4 Rendering 2D Images with Different Environment's Parameters

Besides the subject state, we also introduce environment's parameters E_v to render realistic images. The environment includes all items in the scene and also the lighting and camera's parameters which can be simply described. Since in the human pose estimation problem, we mainly care about the person in the scene, we have fixed the camera parameters to 35 mm focal length and simplified this description by camera view point under spherical coordinate. For the background, instead of parameterized description, we directly sample from a context image dataset such as LSUN [41] to generate images with different backgrounds.

One direct benefit of our approach is that we can describe the synthesized dataset in a more compact way. In our running example of human body, we only need a rigged model (with 300,000 face mesh with the size around 35 MB) and a low dimension descriptors including $\boldsymbol{\theta}$ and E_v, in which for 2000 pose information is under 1 MB compared to a standard dataset which with this many 512×512 pose images can get to up to 2 GB in size. Another benefit is that classical augmentation methods like shift and crop operations can be simply simulated by changing the relative position of the human with respect to the camera. Therefore, our approach can also accommodate these augmentation methods besides the physically-valid state variable augmentations.

4 Synthetic Dataset Quality Evaluation

We evaluated the quality of our synthesized datasets by testing the human pose estimation network's performance when trained on ScanAva datasets from scratch. To generate different versions of the ScanAva datasets, we collected 3D scans from 7 participants, in which 4 of them repeated the scanning procedure with various clothes. We generated 2000 images for each 3D scan with random pose selected from CMU MoCap dataset [2] and random background from indoor environment of LSUN [41]. We formed totally 15 ScanAva datasets to evaluate their quality for pose estimation DNN training when tested on: (1) a small group of individuals and (2) one specific person in different clothes. From each participant, 10 to 15 corresponding 2D images are also captured using an iPhone 7 camera to be used as the real world test dataset, in which individuals were asked to give random poses as they wish. Several demo images are shown in Fig. 4.

4.1 Synthetic vs. Real Domain Adaptation

Even when data is collected from the exact same person, domain shift is a common issue between synthetic and real world/human images. It is also known even real world images collected with different devices are affected by this issue [19]. To minimize domain shift effects in learning and estimation, people try to make both domains as similar as possible, for example aligning the 2nd order statistics of the training and test datasets [35]. Visually perceiving the synthetic and real images of a given person revealed that although the profiles are quite similar in both domains, the details are different. Therefore, since we aim at a quick and efficient large scale dataset forming, we applied two direct modifications to weaken such differences in details by applying (1) Gaussian filtering (ScanAva-gauss) and (2) direct white noise (ScanAva-wn) on images in both domains to make their appearances as similar as possible.

4.2 Pose Estimation Performance of Trained DNN Models

To evaluate the quality of the synthesized datasets, we employed a state-of-the-art DNN-based 2D human pose estimation algorithm, a stacked hourglass model [27] and train it from scratch with our synthesized ScanAva datasets and compared their pose estimation performance with stacked hourglass models trained on real human pose image dataset, MPII [4] (HG-pretrained) and synthetic human pose dataset, SURREAL [38]. During the training procedure, we kept the hyper-parameters of the stacked hourglass model the same between experiments to have a fair comparison among different training datasets. The chosen hyper-parameters were learning rate 2.5e−4, 30 epochs, 8000 iterations, and 8 stacked networks. For the pose estimation performance evaluation, we employed the conventional pose estimation metric, the probability of corrected keypoints (PCK) standard [20,39] to test the estimated joint locations against the ground truth locations on real human pose images.

In the first experiment, we synthesized the ScanAva datasets using 7 participant 3D scan data without (ScanAva-no) and with domain adaption (ScanAva-gauss and ScanAva-wn). The pose estimation accuracy results comparing the performance of the stacked hourglass models trained on these ScanAva datasets as well as models trained on MPII (called HG-pretrained) and SURREAL datasets and tested on our real human test dataset is shown in Fig. 5a. From the figure, it is clear that pose estimation DNN model trained directly on raw synthetic dataset shows poor estimation performance and domain adaptation by applying Gaussian filtering or even adding white noise improves the model performance significantly. Surprisingly, in high standard criteria like PCK0.2, the model trained on ScanAva-gauss even surpasses the one trained on SURREAL dataset, which in fact includes thousands of appearance variations compared to our limited subject dataset. Nonetheless, there is an obvious gap between the performance of the models trained on synthetic data vs. real data, as one expects.

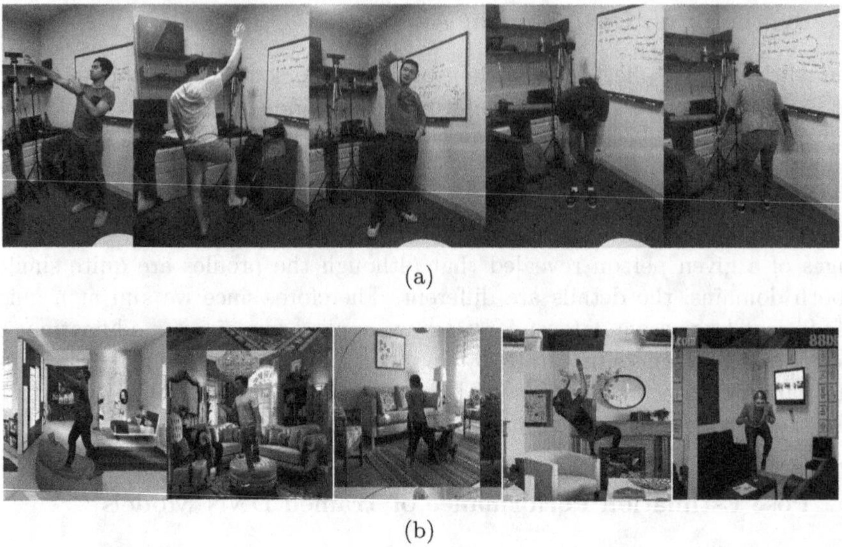

Fig. 4. (a) Real human pose images, (b) synthesized ScanAva images using our proposed approach.

In the second experiment, to test the capability of our dataset for individualized pose estimation training, we synthesized 11 datasets of one participant with varying clothes and also collected corresponding real images as a test dataset. To fairly evaluate the generalization ability of the pose estimation model based on these datasets, we trained the stacked hourglass DNN with scans from only 9 clothes and left the rest of scans out of model training. According to the results of the domain adaptation from Fig. 5a, we used Gaussian filter as optimal domain adapter in this experiment. The pose estimation results are shown in Fig. 5b, where although models trained on our datasets falls behind the HG-pretrained model, but when domain adapted surpass the model trained on SURREAL dataset with a big margin. We believe performance drop of the DNN trained on SURREAL mainly comes from the incompleteness of its templates, which only contains the bare human body shapes instead of clothed ones, while in the real world pose detection problems, people are rarely naked and come in the variety of clothes. These outcomes emphasize that for person-specific pose estimation/tracking in applications such as gaming, human-computer interaction, and daily activity monitoring our approach can quickly and efficiently build a large scale labeled dataset to be used for training of robust and accurate DNN models.

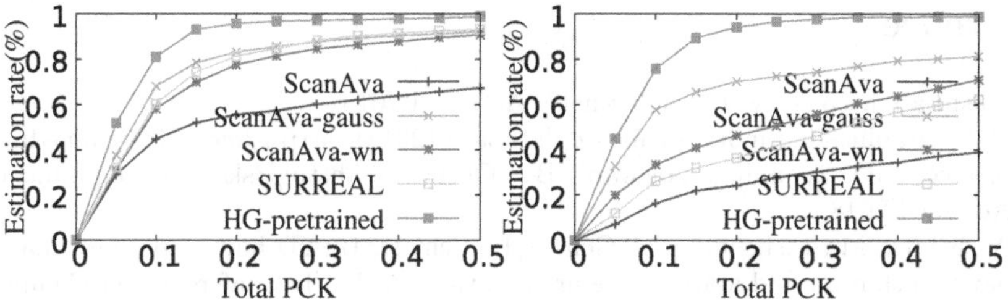

(a) (b)

Fig. 5. Accuracy comparison of a DNN-based pose estimation model trained on different datasets and tested on real human images from: (a) a small group of individuals, (b) a specific person.

Fig. 6. Avatars of our group members interacting in a VR simulated world.

5 Discussion on Future Work

In this paper, we presented a fast and cost-efficient pipeline to form large scale labeled datasets from a small numbers of available samples via a semi-supervised synthetic data generation approach. In an exploration for a time-efficient domain adaptation method, without even having access to the target domain data, we achieved significant performance improvement using Gaussian filtering which made the synthetic and real data very similar in their appearance. Though our dataset forming approach is only tested on pose data from a small group of individuals, it can be seen as an alternative way of data collection for any general purpose. For example, if we scale up the numbers of easily collected 3D scans, it can possibly show a reasonable performance for general human pose estimation. The proposed pipeline is not limited to the applications to forming large labeled dataset for DNN training, as it also provides the utility to generate personalized avatars. A demo of several 3D scanned model of our group members are shown in a virtual reality (VR) environment in Fig. 6.

Acknowledgement. This research was supported by NSF grant #1755695. The authors would also like to thank Naveen Sehgal who actively participated in the ScanAva dataset formation procedure at the Augmented Cognition Lab (ACLab) in the Electrical and Computer Engineering Department at Northeastern University.

References

1. MeshLab. http://www.meshlab.net/. Accessed 2018
2. CMU graphics lab motion capture database (2018). http://mocap.cs.cmu.edu/
3. Skanect 3D Scanning Software By Occipital. http://skanect.occipital.com/. Accessed 2018
4. Andriluka, M., Pishchulin, L., Gehler, P., Schiele, B.: 2D human pose estimation: new benchmark and state of the art analysis. In: IEEE Conference on Computer Vision and Pattern Recognition, CVPR, June 2014
5. Anguelov, D., Srinivasan, P., Koller, D., Thrun, S., Rodgers, J., Davis, J.: SCAPE: shape completion and animation of people. ACM Trans. Graph. **24**(3), 408–416 (2005)
6. Aubry, M., Maturana, D., Efros, A.A., Russell, B.C., Sivic, J.: Seeing 3D chairs: exemplar part-based 2D-3D alignment using a large dataset of CAD models. In: Proceedings of the IEEE Conference on Computer Vision and Pattern Recognition, pp. 3762–3769 (2014)
7. Bengio, Y.: Deep learning of representations for unsupervised and transfer learning. In: Proceedings of ICML Workshop on Unsupervised and Transfer Learning, pp. 17–36 (2012)
8. Bengio, Y., et al.: Deep learners benefit more from out-of-distribution examples. In: Proceedings of the Fourteenth International Conference on Artificial Intelligence and Statistics, pp. 164–172 (2011)
9. Bottou, L.: Large-scale machine learning with stochastic gradient descent. In: Lechevallier, Y., Saporta, G. (eds.) Proceedings of COMPSTAT, pp. 177–186. Physica-Verlag, Heidelberg (2010). https://doi.org/10.1007/978-3-7908-2604-3_16
10. Caruana, R.: Learning many related tasks at the same time with backpropagation. In: Advances in Neural Information Processing Systems, pp. 657–664 (1995)
11. Chen, W., et al.: Synthesizing training images for boosting human 3D pose estimation. In: 2016 Fourth International Conference on 3D Vision, 3DV, pp. 479–488 (2016)
12. Cordts, M., et al.: The cityscapes dataset for semantic urban scene understanding. In: Proceedings of the IEEE Conference on Computer Vision and Pattern Recognition, CVPR (2016)
13. Craig, J.J.: Introduction to Robotics: Mechanics and Control, vol. 3. Pearson Prentice Hall, Upper Saddle River (2005)
14. Dosovitskiy, A., et al.: FlowNet: learning optical flow with convolutional networks. In: IEEE International Conference on Computer Vision, pp. 2758–2766 (2015)
15. Du, Y., et al.: Marker-less 3D human motion capture with monocular image sequence and height-maps. In: Leibe, B., Matas, J., Sebe, N., Welling, M. (eds.) ECCV 2016. LNCS, vol. 9908, pp. 20–36. Springer, Cham (2016). https://doi.org/10.1007/978-3-319-46493-0_2
16. Everingham, M., Van Gool, L., Williams, C.K., Winn, J., Zisserman, A.: The PASCAL visual object classes (VOC) challenge. Int. J. Comput. Vis. **88**(2), 303–338 (2010)
17. Gaidon, A., Wang, Q., Cabon, Y., Vig, E.: Virtual worlds as proxy for multi-object tracking analysis. arXiv preprint arXiv:1605.06457 (2016)
18. Ghezelghieh, M.F., Kasturi, R., Sarkar, S.: Learning camera viewpoint using CNN to improve 3D body pose estimation. In: 2016 Fourth International Conference on 3D Vision, 3DV, pp. 685–693 (2016)

19. Gong, B., Shi, Y., Sha, F., Grauman, K.: Geodesic flow kernel for unsupervised domain adaptation. In: 2012 IEEE Conference on Computer Vision and Pattern Recognition, CVPR, pp. 2066–2073 (2012)
20. Johnson, S., Everingham, M.: Clustered pose and nonlinear appearance models for human pose estimation. In: Proceedings of the British Machine Vision Conference (2010). https://doi.org/10.5244/C.24.12
21. Kajita, S., Hirukawa, H., Harada, K., Yokoi, K.: Introduction to Humanoid Robotics, vol. 101. Springer, Heidelberg (2014). https://doi.org/10.1007/978-3-642-54536-8
22. Krizhevsky, A., Sutskever, I., Hinton, G.E.: ImageNet classification with deep convolutional neural networks. In: Advances in Neural Information Processing Systems, pp. 1097–1105 (2012)
23. Lee, C.Y., Xie, S., Gallagher, P., Zhang, Z., Tu, Z.: Deeply-supervised nets. In: Artificial Intelligence and Statistics, pp. 562–570 (2015)
24. Liebelt, J., Schmid, C.: Multi-view object class detection with a 3D geometric model. In: 2010 IEEE Conference on Computer Vision and Pattern Recognition, CVPR, pp. 1688–1695 (2010)
25. Liu, S., Yin, Y., Ostadabbas, S.: In-bed pose estimation: deep learning with shallow dataset. arXiv preprint arXiv:1711.01005 (2018)
26. Marin, J., Vázquez, D., Gerónimo, D., López, A.M.: Learning appearance in virtual scenarios for pedestrian detection. In: 2010 IEEE Conference on Computer Vision and Pattern Recognition, CVPR, pp. 137–144 (2010)
27. Newell, A., Yang, K., Deng, J.: Stacked hourglass networks for human pose estimation. In: Leibe, B., Matas, J., Sebe, N., Welling, M. (eds.) ECCV 2016. LNCS, vol. 9912, pp. 483–499. Springer, Cham (2016). https://doi.org/10.1007/978-3-319-46484-8_29
28. Okada, R., Soatto, S.: Relevant feature selection for human pose estimation and localization in cluttered images. In: Forsyth, D., Torr, P., Zisserman, A. (eds.) ECCV 2008. LNCS, vol. 5303, pp. 434–445. Springer, Heidelberg (2008). https://doi.org/10.1007/978-3-540-88688-4_32
29. Pishchulin, L., Jain, A., Andriluka, M., Thormählen, T., Schiele, B.: Articulated people detection and pose estimation: reshaping the future. In: 2012 IEEE Conference on Computer Vision and Pattern Recognition, CVPR, pp. 3178–3185 (2012)
30. Qiu, W.: Generating human images and ground truth using computer graphics. Ph.D. thesis. University of California, Los Angeles (2016)
31. Romero, J., Loper, M., Black, M.J.: FlowCap: 2D human pose from optical flow. In: Gall, J., Gehler, P., Leibe, B. (eds.) GCPR 2015. LNCS, vol. 9358, pp. 412–423. Springer, Cham (2015). https://doi.org/10.1007/978-3-319-24947-6_34
32. Simonyan, K., Zisserman, A.: Very deep convolutional networks for large-scale image recognition. arXiv preprint arXiv:1409.1556 (2014)
33. Stark, M., Goesele, M., Schiele, B.: Back to the future: learning shape models from 3D CAD data. In: BMVC, vol. 2, no. 4, p. 5 (2010)
34. Su, H., Qi, C.R., Li, Y., Guibas, L.J.: Render for CNN: viewpoint estimation in images using CNNs trained with rendered 3D model views. In: Proceedings of the IEEE International Conference on Computer Vision, pp. 2686–2694 (2015)
35. Sun, B., Feng, J., Saenko, K.: Correlation alignment for unsupervised domain adaptation. arXiv preprint arXiv:1612.01939 (2016)
36. Sun, B., Peng, X., Saenko, K.: Generating large scale image datasets from 3D CAD models. In: CVPR 2015 Workshop on the Future of Datasets in Vision (2015)

37. Sun, M., Su, H., Savarese, S., Fei-Fei, L.: A multi-view probabilistic model for 3D object classes. In: IEEE Conference on Computer Vision and Pattern Recognition, CVPR 2009, pp. 1247–1254 (2009)
38. Varol, G., et al.: Learning from synthetic humans. In: 2017 IEEE Conference on Computer Vision and Pattern Recognition, CVPR 2017 (2017)
39. Wei, S.E., Ramakrishna, V., Kanade, T., Sheikh, Y.: Convolutional pose machines. In: Proceedings of the IEEE Conference on Computer Vision and Pattern Recognition, pp. 4724–4732 (2016)
40. Yosinski, J., Clune, J., Bengio, Y., Lipson, H.: How transferable are features in deep neural networks? In: Advances in Neural Information Processing Systems, pp. 3320–3328 (2014)
41. Yu, F., Zhang, Y., Song, S., Seff, A., Xiao, J.: LSUN: construction of a large-scale image dataset using deep learning with humans in the loop. arXiv preprint arXiv:1506.03365 (2015)
42. Zhou, B., Zhao, H., Puig, X., Fidler, S., Barriuso, A., Torralba, A.: Scene parsing through ADE20K dataset. In: Proceedings of the IEEE Conference on Computer Vision and Pattern Recognition (2017)

Towards Learning a Realistic Rendering of Human Behavior

Patrick Esser(✉), Johannes Haux, Timo Milbich, and Björn Ommer

HCI, IWR, Heidelberg University, Heidelberg, Germany
patrick.esser@iwr.uni-heidelberg.de

Abstract. Realistic rendering of human behavior is of great interest for applications such as video animations, virtual reality and gaming engines. Commonly animations of persons performing actions are rendered by articulating explicit 3D models based on sequences of coarse body shape representations simulating a certain behavior. While the simulation of natural behavior can be efficiently learned, the corresponding 3D models are typically designed in manual, laborious processes or reconstructed from costly (multi-)sensor data. In this work, we present an approach towards a holistic learning framework for rendering human behavior in which all components are learned from easily available data. To enable control over the generated behavior, we utilize motion capture data and generate realistic motions based on user inputs. Alternatively, we can directly copy behavior from videos and learn a rendering of characters using RGB camera data only. Our experiments show that we can further improve data efficiency by training on multiple characters at the same time. Overall our approach shows a new path towards easily available, personalized avatar creation.

1 Introduction

Recently there has been great progress in the field of generating and synthesizing images [11,14,18,23,30,34,42] and videos [33,35] which is important for applications such as image manipulation, video animation and rendering of virtual environments. Over the past years, in particular the gaming industry eagerly improved their customer experience by developing more and more realistic 3D gaming engines. These progressively push the level of detail of the rendered scenes, with an emphasis on natural movements and realistic appearances of the in-game characters. Characters are typically rendered with the help of detailed, explicit 3D models, which consist of surface models and textures, and animated using tailored motion models to simulate human behavior and activity (Fig. 1).

Recent work [13] has shown that it is possible to learn natural human behaviour (e.g. walking, jumping, etc.) from motion capture data (MoCap) of

P. Esser, J. Haux and T. Milbich—Equal contribution.

This work has been supported in part by DFG project 371923335 and a hardware donation from NVIDIA.

L. Leal-Taixé and S. Roth (Eds.): ECCV 2018 Workshops, LNCS 11130, pp. 409–425, 2019.
https://doi.org/10.1007/978-3-030-11012-3_32

human actors. On the other hand, designing a realistic 3D model of a person is still a laborious process. Traditionally, explicit 3D models of the shape are manually created by specialized graphic designers, followed by the design of textures reflecting a person's individual appearance which is eventually mapped onto the raw body model. In order to circumvent this laborious design process, passive 3D reconstruction methods can be utilized [1,3,5,12]. While these methods are able to achieve impressive results, they rely on data recorded by costly multi-view camera settings [1,5,7,9], depth sensors [15,26,29,37] or even active 3D laser scans [20].

Fig. 1. Our method can render target persons in a wide variety of behaviors. The desired behavior can be either generated based on inputs from a game controller or copied from a video.

Given the tremendous success of generative models [11,14,17,18,41] in the era of deep learning, the question arises, why not also learn to generate realistic renderings of a person, instead of only learning its natural movements? By conditioning the image generation process of a generative model on additional input data, mappings between different data domains are learned [14,16,42], which, for instance, allows for controlling and manipulating object shape, turning sketches into images and images into paintings. Thus, by being able to condition a rendering of a person on its body articulation, the laborious 3D modeling process can be circumvented by directly learning a mapping from the distinct postures composing human behaviors onto realistic images of humans.

In this work, we propose an approach towards a completely data driven framework for realistic control and rendering of human behavior which can be trained from Motion Capture data and easily available RGB video data. Instead of learning an explicit 3D model of a human, we train a conditional U-Net [28] architecture to learn a mapping from shape representations to target images conditioned on a latent representation of a variational auto-encoder for appearance. For training our generative rendering framework, we utilize single-camera RGB video sequences of humans, whose appearance is mapped onto a desired pose representation in the form of 2D keypoints. Our approach then enables complete control of a virtual character. Based on user inputs about desired motions, our system generates realistic movements together with a rendering of the character in a virtual environment. Since our rendering approach requires only example videos of the character, it can be easily used for personalized avatar creation. Furthermore, because it operates on 2D keypoints, it can also be used for video reenactment where the behavior shown in a video is copied.

We evaluate our model both quantitatively and qualitatively in an interactive virtual environment and for simulating human activity from recorded video data.

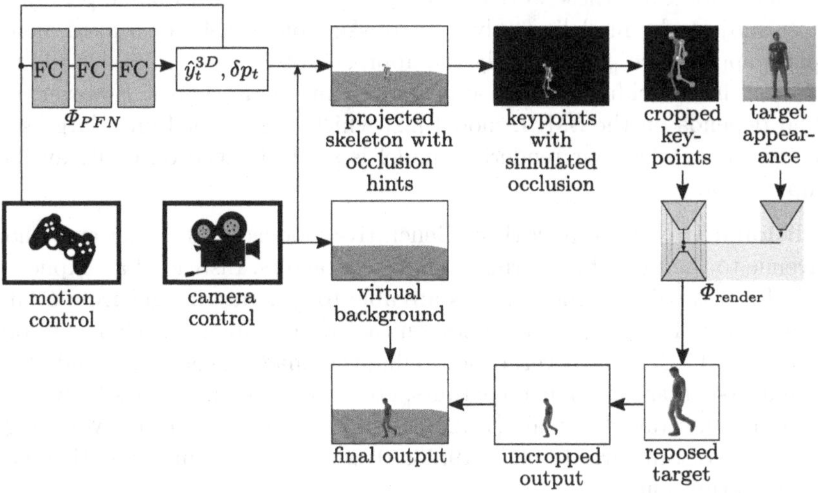

Fig. 2. Our pipeline for controllable synthesis of behavior: motion controls obtained from a game controller are used by Φ_{PFN} to update a 3D skeleton. Combined with a user controllable camera, we obtain a 3D projection of the skeleton with estimates on keypoint visibility as well as a rendered image of the virtual environment. Using the projected skeleton, we compute a stickman representation compatible with Φ_{render}. The remaining pipeline is similiar to Fig. 3 except that we do not need to perform inpaininting.

2 Related Work

There is a large corpus of works available for tackling the problem of creating realistic 2D renderings of 3D objects and persons, as well as their natural animation. In most cases this is still a laborious and manual process.

3D Modeling: The common approach for learning 3D models from visual data of real objects or humans is a three-dimensional reconstruction of the object of interest based on a collection of input images obtained from different camera settings. Many works utilize multi-view camera recordings of their subjects in combination with specialized shape models describing the human body configuration [3,12,22,43] or without additional shape priors [1,5,7,9]. While these approaches result in impressive reconstructions, obtaining the required input data is costly and asks for specialized equipment and recording settings.

3D scanners and cameras with RGB-D sensors like the KinectFusion system [15,26] use depth information to increase the level of detail of the resulting

3D models [20,29,37]. However, again specialized equipment is needed and extra information used. In contrast, our approach is able to learn renderings of a subject from easily obtained RGB camera recordings.

There are only a few works which operate on monocular image data to learn 3D models. Moreover, these works typically neglect the individual appearance of the test subjects by modeling only posture skeletons [31,40] or a fixed, neutral template appearance [24,27]. Only the approach of Alldieck et al. [2] additionally learns the individual subject appearances and body shapes. However, their method depends on the SMPL model [22] which was trained on a large set of 3D body scans, while our rendering model is solely trained on easily available 2D input data.

Conditional Image Generation: Generative models [11,18] offer an orthogonal avenue to the task of rendering in-game characters. Instead of an explicit 3D model of a test subject, such models are able to generate images from a latent space and allow for interpolating between the training images such as viewpoint and subjects [17,32]. Moreover, conditioning the image generation on additional input data (such as class label, contours, etc.) allows for mappings between the conditioning and target domain [14,25,41] and thus grants control over the generative process. Similarly to [4,10,19,23,30] we condition our generative model on pose information.

3 Method

The degree of realism which can be obtained when generating renderings of a certain behavior by a given test subject hinges on two crucial components: *(i)* a realistic appearance model considering both the shape and texture of the person and *(ii)* a motion model which is able to capture the dynamics of the behavior and is able to control the deformation of the appearance model. Furthermore, such a motion model must be able to describe the distinct body articulations involved while performing an action and needs to simulate the natural transitions between them, i.e. the actual behavior.

In our framework, visualized in Fig. 2, both components are represented by deep neural networks, which are trainable from Motion Capture data and easily available RGB video data, respectively. Since the description of human shape and motion is a well-studied problem with efficient methods available, we integrate a pose estimation algorithm, OpenPose [6], for encoding human articulation and a motion model, PFNet [13], into our framework. PFNet is not only suitable for simulating natural human activity in the form of a keypoint representation, but also allows for direct interaction with the model, which is a crucial requirement for real-time game engines. Note however, that our framework is also able to synthesize offline, i.e. recorded videos of a given behavior, which can be easily represented by a sequence of corresponding shape descriptors.

For the rendering of a person we train a generative network conditioned on pose representations obtained from the motion model and on latent variables representing the appearance of a person.

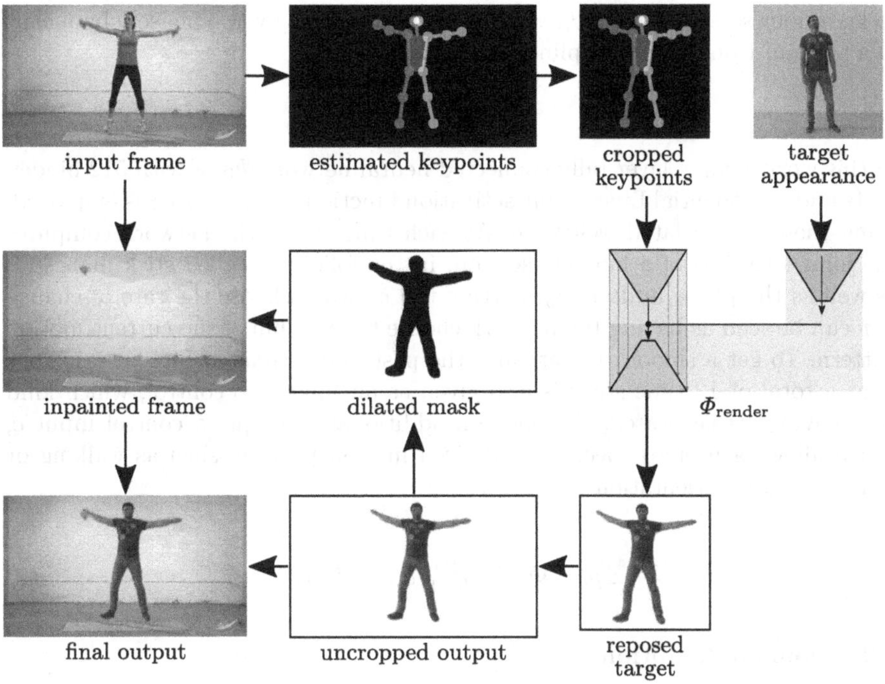

Fig. 3. Our pipeline for behavior cloning: given an input frame and a target appearance, we first estimate keypoints of the input frame and a transformation to a bounding box. The resulting cropped keypoints are then rendered with the target appearance. We apply the inverse transformation to align the reposed target image with the original input frame. Before alpha blending this output with the input frame, we perform inpaininting to remove the original person.

In the following, we first briefly describe PFNet. To be able to render the resulting motion, we need to introduce a projection between world- and view coordinates of the rendered person in the scene. Furthermore, the domain shift from keypoint representations used for training our generative rendering model to those returned by the previous step must be addressed. Finally we present our model for conditional image generation.

3.1 Simulating Natural Human Behavior

When generating sequences of human poses, such as for animations or in computer games, one usually has a good idea of what kind of action should be the result. To generate highly realistic human action sequences so called Phase-Functioned Neural Networks (PFNN) [13] make use of the intrinsic periodicity of these motions. PFNNs such as that of [13] can be very shallow neural networks. Instead of learning a single set of model parameters these networks are trained to learn four sets of weights θ_i, which are interpolated given a phase p by means of a Catmul-Rom spline (c-spline) interpolation Θ:

$$\theta = \Theta(\theta_0, \theta_1, \theta_2, \theta_3). \tag{1}$$

In this work a three layer fully connected neural network Φ_{PFN} with 512 hidden units and Exponential Linear unit activation functions (ELU) σ_{ELU} is employed, using these interpolated weights θ. At each time step t the network computes the joint locations of a human skeleton, in the following called stick man $\hat{y}^{3D}$, as well as the phase update Δ_p. Letting the network choose the rate of change of p can be seen as having the network choose the rhythm of the current motion pattern. To get a smooth update also the past and estimated future trajectory $\mathcal{T}$ at a total of 12 time steps is also given as an input. To control, which kind of behaviour is generated, the network additionally accepts a control input c, which allows a user to specify the desired motion pattern, such as walking or running and its orientation.

$$\hat{y}_t^{3D}, \Delta p_t = \Phi_{\text{PFN}}(\hat{y}_{t-1}^{3D}, c_t, p_t, \mathcal{T}_{t-6:t+6}, \theta) \tag{2}$$

3.2 Domain Adaption

Shown in Fig. 4 is an example of keypoints rendered as small squares given through $\hat{y}^{3D}$. Their 2d screen positions are now used to define the 2d pose input $\hat{y}^{2D}$ to generate the final render of the person. As our rendering model is trained given only the keypoints of visible body parts (see Sect. 3.3) we filter the keypoints returned by PFNN in two ways: *(i)* Keypoints of arms and knees are marked as visible if the are not occluded by a polygon defined by the keypoints of the hip and each shoulder. It is visualised in orange in Fig. 4. Body keypoints are assumed to be always visible. Our experiments show that although being very simple this approximation is sufficient. *(ii)* Let $\mathbf{x}_{eye}$ be the vector describing the position of an eye keypoint, $\mathbf{x}_{nose}$ be the point in space describing the position of the nose and $\mathbf{x}_{cam}$ be the position of the camera. Each eye $i \in 0, 1$ is visible if

$$0 > \left(\frac{\mathbf{x}_{cam} - \mathbf{x}_{nose}}{\|\mathbf{x}_{cam} - \mathbf{x}_{nose}\|} \times (-1)^i \mathbf{e}_y \right) \cdot \frac{\mathbf{x}_{nose} - \mathbf{x}_{eye}^{(i)}}{\|\mathbf{x}_{nose} - \mathbf{x}_{eye}^{(i)}\|} \tag{3}$$

with:

$$i = \begin{cases} 0 & \text{if left eye} \\ 1 & \text{if right eye} \end{cases}, \tag{4}$$

where $\mathbf{e}_y$ is the unit vector in y or up direction, $\times$ is the cross product and $\cdot$ is the scalar product. See Fig. 5 for a visualization. The nose is marked visible if one or both eyes can be seen. Occluded keypoints are marked red in Fig. 4, visible ones green. Note that the skeleton looks away from the camera and the left arm is occluded by the body.

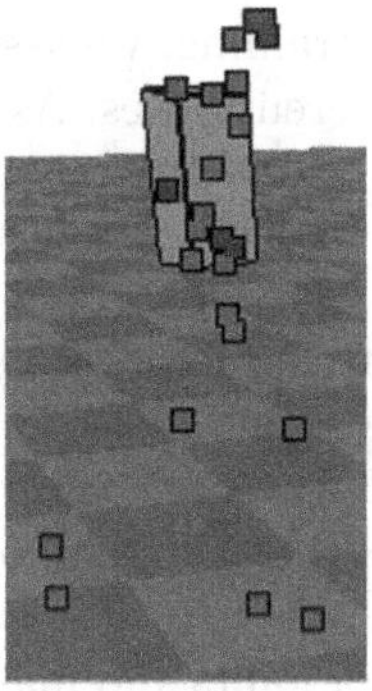

Fig. 4. Finding occluded keypoints using a simple polygon (shown in orange) and the view of the eyes, relative to the orientation of the camera. Occluded keypoints are shown in red, visible ones in green. Note that in our approach keypoints inside the orange polygon are marked as always visible. (Color figure online)

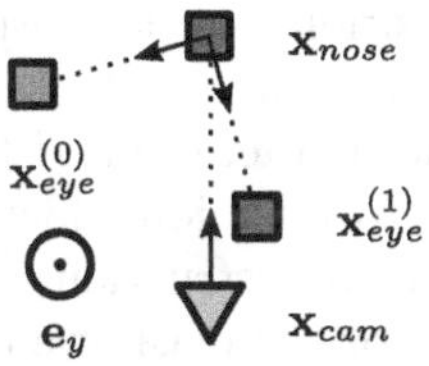

Fig. 5. The visibility of the eyes is determined by their orientation relative to the camera. See Eq. 3 for details. If one or both eyes are visible, the nose can be seen as well. In this visualization $\mathbf{e}_y$ points upwards, out of the paper plane towards the reader.

3.3 Rendering

Our goal is to learn the rendering of characters from natural images. To achieve this, we train a neural network to map normalized 2D pose configurations to natural images. With this network available, we then project the 3D keypoints obtained in the previous step to 2D coordinates according to the desired camera view. After normalization of this configuration, we can apply the network to obtain the rendering. Finally, the normalization transformation is undone to be able to blend the character into the scene at the correct position. The different steps are explained in more detail in the following.

Coordinate Normalization. In order to train the network, it would be very inefficient to predict images at different positions because the renderings should be translation invariant. Therefore, we use the 2D joint coordinates to define a region of interest which covers the joints and add 10% padding, to account for the character volume. This results in a transformation M_{coord} which can be used to transform points as well as images using bilinear resampling.

Image and Mask Prediction. For training, we assume that we have a large number of images of characters in different poses. As it will be important to provide images of a wide variety of poses, we utilize a network architecture which allows us to train a single network on multiple characters to increase the number of available poses.

For each training image of a character, we extract 2D joint positions and segmentation masks. Using large scale labeled data for these tasks such as [21], reliable estimation is possible. However, because we cannot predict positions of occluded joints, we must be careful to simulate occluded joints during test time as described in Sect. 3.2.

Due to automatic estimation of joints and mask, we only require a large number of images of characters, which can be achieved efficiently by video recordings. In order to make use of training data obtained from multiple characters, our network must be able to disentangle the pose from the character's appearance, a task which has also been considered in [10]. Following these approaches, our network has two inputs, one for the joint positions and one for the character image. For preprocessing, the joint positions are converted into a stickman image to be able to utilize skip connections as in a U-Net architecture [28]. Furthermore, body parts are cropped from the character image to make sure that the network has to use the stickman image to infer joint locations. The training objective of the network is then given by reconstruction tasks on the original image as well as the segmentation mask. For the mask, we use a pixelwise $L1$ loss and for the images we use a perceptual loss which is highly effective as a differentiable metric for perceptual similarity of images [38].

Merge with Scene. Finally, we use the inverse coordinate normalization M_{coord}^{-1} to transform the rendering and the mask back to their original screen coordinates. In order to integrate the character with the virtual environment, we use alpha blending between the rendered virtual environment and the character rendering. See also Fig. 2. In the case of behavior cloning from video, we first utilize the mask of the generated image to perform Image-Inpainting on the original frame. The full pipeline for this case is shown in Fig. 3.

4 Experiments

We evaluate our rendering framework qualitatively and quantitatively using dataset consisting of video sequences of three persons. The subjects were filmed performing various actions like walking, running, dancing, jumping and crouching. The recordings were done according to three settings: First a free setting, where actors were encouraged to perform a wide variety of movements without restrictions. For evaluation purposes, we also collected videos in a restricted setting, where the actors were restricted to standing still and performing only a walking motion. Filming was done using a Panasonic GH2 in full HD 1080p at 24 frames per second. Each individual is shown in approximately 10 000 frames. For training our conditional generative model, all frames are annotated with keypoints using the openpose [6] library. Additionally a mask covering the person in each frame is calculated using the deeplab [8] toolbox. Note that filming could also be done with a cellphone camera or something similar, making this approach feasible for a wide range of audiences.

4.1 Qualitative Results in Virtual Environment

For qualitative evaluation of the rendering capabilities of our framework in a virtual, interactive environment, we adapted the testing API of PFNet [13]. Our rendering model is trained on all training images of our 3 subjects. While inference we extract the simulated keypoints of the API, project it from 3D world-to 2D view coordinates while accounting for the domain shift and condition the appearance rendering on the resulting output. Figures 6 and 7 show our renderings for two different simulated walking scenarios, given the shape conditioning and different person appearances. Further, in Figs. 8 and 9 we demonstrate the need for self-occlusion handling. Additionally Fig. 10 shows an ablation experiment, where the same behavior as in Fig. 9 is rendered using nearest neighbor frames from the training set. This experiment clearly demonstrates the ability of our model to interpolate between the training images for generating smooth transitions in appearance while simulating a given behavior. A video with examples can be found at https://compvis.github.io/hbugen2018/.

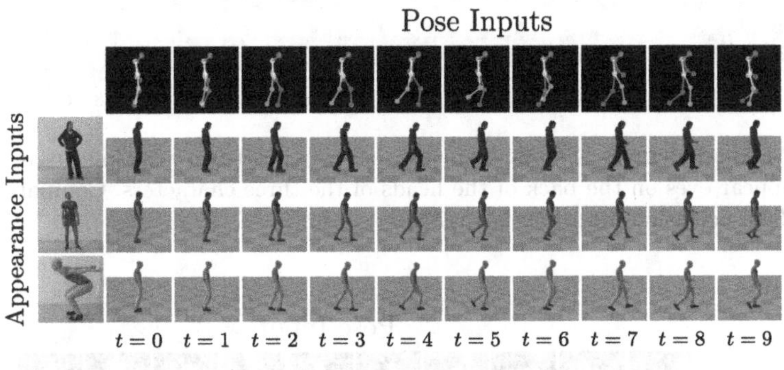

Fig. 6. Walking sequence perpendicular to the viewer. Note how the model consistently manages to generate the same pose for each appearance in each frame.

4.2 Qualitative Results on Video Data

We now show additional qualitative results by simulating different behaviors as shown in video sequences. We trained our model using the full training sets of our test subjects and applied it on keypoint trajectories extracted from the PennAction dataset [39]. It contains 2326 video sequences of 15 different sports categories. The dataset exhibits unconstrained activities including complex articulations and self-occlusion. Figure 11 shows example renderings randomly selected

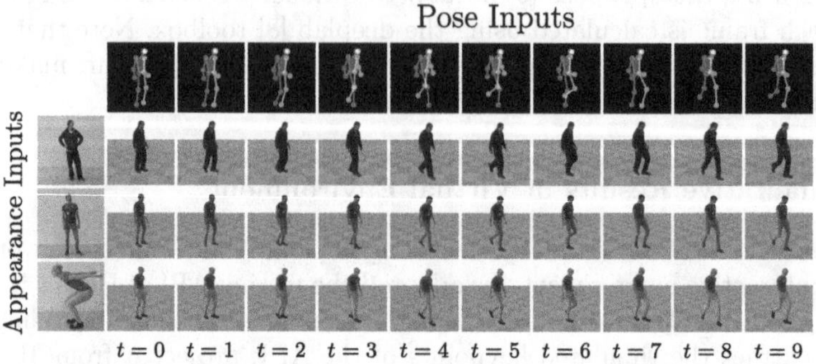

Fig. 7. Walking sequence towards the viewer at an angle. Note that our model can generalize not only to different poses, but also to different perspectives.

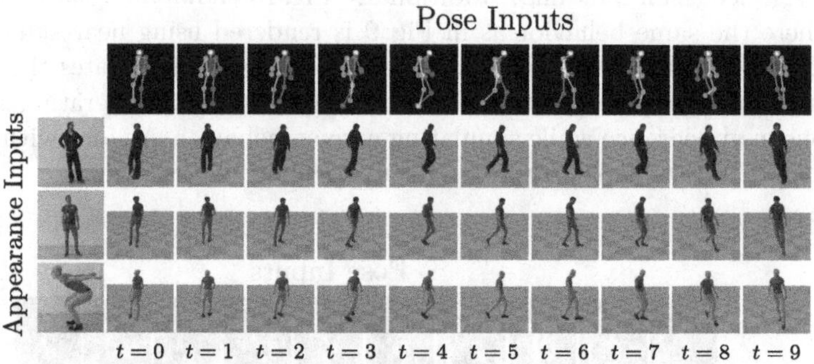

Fig. 8. Walking in circles *without* occlusion modeling. Note how at time steps $t = 0$ to 6 there appear eyes on the back of the heads of the three characters. Compare this to Fig. 9, where occlusion modeling is applied.

Fig. 9. Walking in circles *with* occlusion modeling. Note how at the first 6 time steps there are no eyes at the back of the heads, as opposed to Fig. 8.

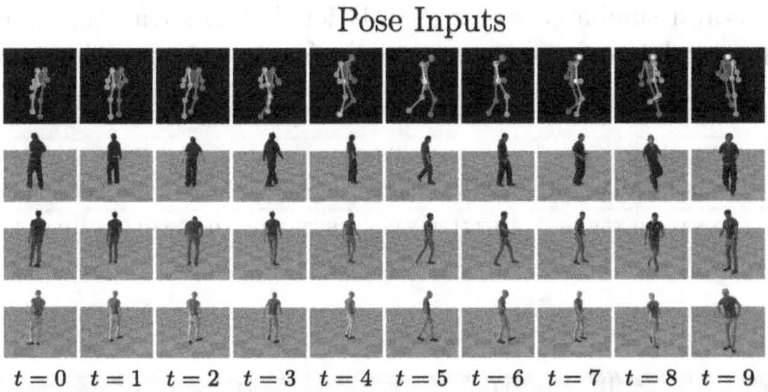

Fig. 10. Walking in circles with occlusion modeling. Here we show the nearest neighbors to each pose. Note how the images from time step to time step are quite different or just stay the same. There is also no consistency of pose with varying appearance as one can see, when comparing each image at a single time step.

from different activities simulated by different persons. A video with examples can be found at https://compvis.github.io/hbugen2018/. Further in Figs. 12, 13, 14 and 15 re-enactments of exemplary target behaviors are illustrated by temporal sampling the source videos. Conditioned on the estimated pose from the individual frames, we infer a new appearance and project the rendering back into the source frame. Thus we are able to simulate the given activities by any person of our choice.

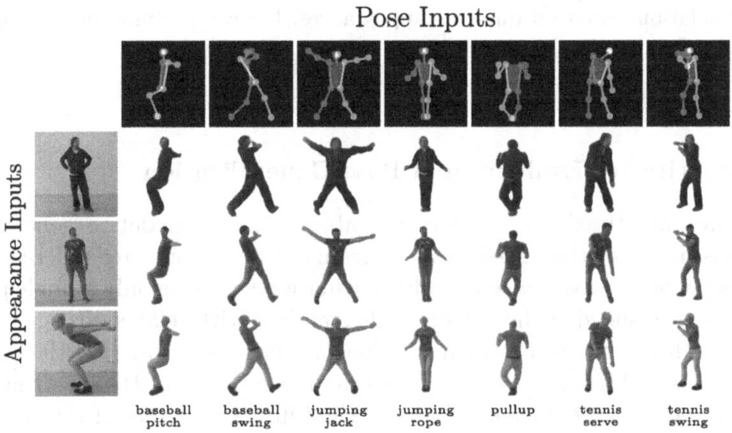

Fig. 11. Using randomly sampled poses from the PennAction dataset, our model is able to generate realistic renderings conditioned on different appearances.

Table 1. Structural similarity scores (SSIM) for different training settings. 'query' refers to test person data only and 'augmented' refers to additional data augmentation. 'NN' denotes the nearest neighbor retrieval results.

Training setting	Standing			Walking			Full		
	Query	Augmented	NN	Query	Augmented	NN	Query	Augmented	NN
SSIM	0.841	0.858	0.771	0.848	0.863	0.782	0.908	0.914	0.794

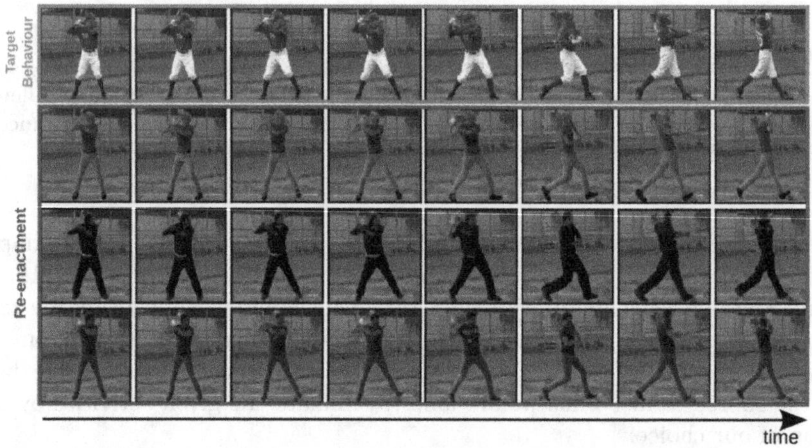

Fig. 12. Re-enactment of 'Baseball swing'. Green illustrates the target behavior and red its simulation based on different appearances. Frames are uniformly sampled in time. (Color figure online)

4.3 Quantitative Evaluation of Pose Generalization

Let us now quantitatively evaluate the ability of our model to generalize to unseen postures. For this experiment we train our model on three different training subsets of varying variance in body articulation featuring only a single person: *(i)* Only images showing the person while standing with relaxed arms, *(ii)* Only images the showing a test person walking up and down and *(iii)* the person's full training set. Moreover, we also train models for each of these settings with additional data augmentation by adding the full training sets of the remaining test subjects. We then compute the mean structural similarity score (SSIM) [36] between groundtruth test images and renderings of our model based on their extracted postures. As a baseline we use nearest neighbor retrievals from the different training sets also based on the extracted keypoints. Table 1 summarizes the results. As one can see, with increasing variability of the training poses also the quality of the renderings improves. Moreover, data augmentation in form of additional images persons helps our model to interpolate between the training

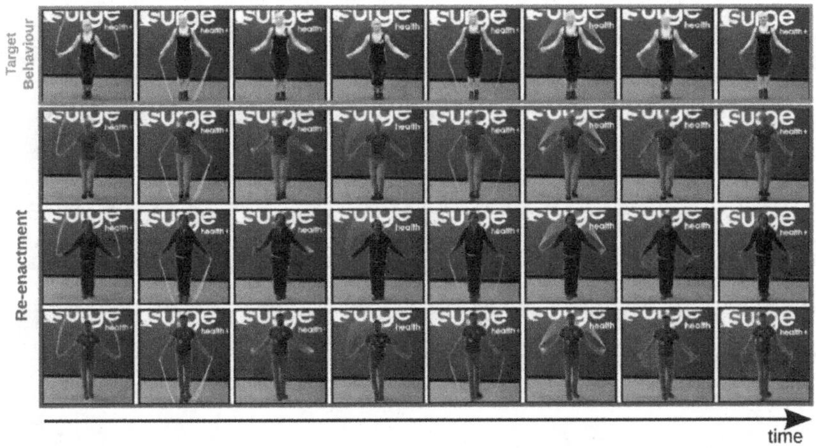

Fig. 13. Re-enactment of 'jumping rope'. Green illustrates the target behavior and red its simulation based on different appearances. Frames are uniformly sampled in time. (Color figure online)

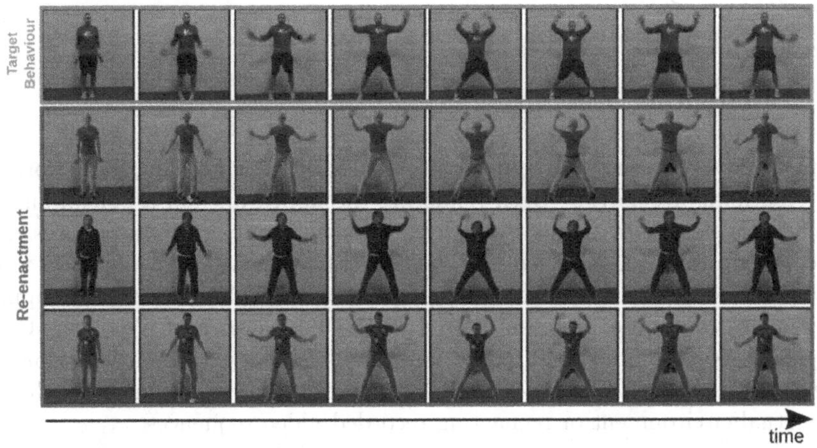

Fig. 14. Re-enactment of 'jumping jack'. Green illustrates the target behavior and red its simulation based on different appearances. Frames are uniformly sampled in time. (Color figure online)

poses of the actual test subject and thus improves its generalization ability. Note that on average our model outperforms the baseline by 9.5%, which proves that our model actually understands the mapping between shape and appearance.

Fig. 15. Re-enactment of 'tennis serve'. Green illustrates the target behavior and red its simulation based on different appearances. Frames are uniformly sampled in time. (Color figure online)

5 Conclusion

In this work we presented an approach towards a holistic learning framework for rendering human behavior. Both rendering the appearance of a person and its simulating natural movements while performing a given behavior are represented by deep neural networks, which can be trained from easily available RBG video data. Our model utilizes a conditional generative model to learn a mapping between abstract pose representation and the appearance of a person. Using this model, we are able to simulate any kind of behavior conditioned on the appearance of a given test subject while either directly controlling the behavior in a virtual environment or reenacting recorded video sequences.

References

1. Allain, B., Franco, J.-S., Boyer, E.: An efficient volumetric framework for shape tracking. In: IEEE Conference on Computer Vision and Pattern Recognition (CVPR) (2015)
2. Alldieck, T., Magnor, M., Xu, W., Theobalt, C., Pons-Moll, G.: Video based reconstruction of 3D people models. In: IEEE Conference on Computer Vision and Pattern Recognition (2018)
3. Anguelov, D., Srinivasan, P., Koller, D., Thrun, S., Rodgers, J., Davis, J.: SCAPE: shape completion and animation of people. ACM Trans. Graph. **24**(3), 408–416 (2005)
4. Balakrishnan, G., Zhao, A., Dalca, A.V., Durand, F., Guttag, J.: Synthesizing images of humans in unseen poses. arXiv preprint arXiv:1804.07739 (2018)

5. Cagniart, C., Boyer, E., Ilic, S.: Probabilistic deformable surface tracking from multiple videos. In: Daniilidis, K., Maragos, P., Paragios, N. (eds.) ECCV 2010. LNCS, vol. 6314, pp. 326–339. Springer, Heidelberg (2010). https://doi.org/10.1007/978-3-642-15561-1_24
6. Cao, Z., Simon, T., Wei, S.-E., Sheikh, Y.: Realtime multi-person 2D pose estimation using part affinity fields. In: CVPR (2017)
7. Carranza, J., Theobalt, C., Magnor, M.A., Seidel, H.-P.: Free-viewpoint video of human actors. In: ACM SIGGRAPH 2003 Papers (2003)
8. Chen, L.-C., Papandreou, G., Kokkinos, I., Murphy, K., Yuille, A.L.: DeepLab: semantic image segmentation with deep convolutional nets, atrous convolution, and fully connected CRFs. arXiv e-prints, June 2016
9. de Aguiar, E., Stoll, C., Theobalt, C., Ahmed, N., Seidel, H.-P., Thrun, S.: Performance capture from sparse multi-view video. ACM Trans. Graph. **27**(3), 98:1–98:10 (2008). Article No. 98
10. Esser, P., Sutter, E., Ommer, B.: A variational U-Net for conditional appearance and shape generation. arXiv preprint arXiv:1804.04694 (2018)
11. Goodfellow, I., et al.: Generative adversarial nets. In: Advances in Neural Information Processing Systems (NIPS) (2014)
12. Hasler, N., Stoll, C., Sunkel, M., Rosenhahn, B., Seidel, H.-P.: A statistical model of human pose and body shape. Comput. Graph. Forum **28**(2), 337–346 (2009)
13. Holden, D., Komura, T., Saito, J.: Phase-functioned neural networks for character control. ACM Trans. Graph. **36**(4), 42:1–42:13 (2017). Article No. 42
14. Isola, P., Zhu, J.-Y., Zhou, T., Efros, A.A.: Image-to-image translation with conditional adversarial networks. arXiv (2016)
15. Izadi, S., et al.: KinectFusion: real-time 3D reconstruction and interaction using a moving depth camera. In: Proceedings of the 24th Annual ACM Symposium on User Interface Software and Technology, pp. 559–568. ACM (2011)
16. Johnson, J., Alahi, A., Fei-Fei, L.: Perceptual losses for real-time style transfer and super-resolution. In: Leibe, B., Matas, J., Sebe, N., Welling, M. (eds.) ECCV 2016. LNCS, vol. 9906, pp. 694–711. Springer, Cham (2016). https://doi.org/10.1007/978-3-319-46475-6_43
17. Karras, T., Aila, T., Laine, S., Lehtinen, J.: Progressive growing of GANs for improved quality, stability, and variation. In: Proceedings of the International Conference on Learning Representations (ICLR) (2018)
18. Kingma, D.P., Welling, M.: Auto-encoding variational bayes. arXiv preprint arXiv:1312.6114 (2013)
19. Lassner, C., Pons-Moll, G., Gehler, P.V.: A generative model of people in clothing. In: Proceedings of the IEEE International Conference on Computer Vision, vol. 6 (2017)
20. Li, H., Vouga, E., Gudym, A., Luo, L., Barron, J.T., Gusev, G.: 3D self-portraits. ACM Trans. Graph. **32**(6), 187:1–187:9 (2013). Article No. 187
21. Lin, T.-Y., et al.: Microsoft COCO: common objects in context. ArXiv e-prints, May 2014
22. Loper, M., Mahmood, N., Romero, J., Pons-Moll, G., Black, M.J.: SMPL: a skinned multi-person linear model. ACM Trans. Graph. **34**(6), 248:1–248:16 (2015). Article No. 248. Proceedings of the SIGGRAPH Asia
23. Ma, L., Sun, Q., Georgoulis, S., Gool, L.V., Schiele, B., Fritz, M.: Disentangled person image generation. In: Conference on Computer Vision and Pattern Recognition (2018)

24. Mehta, D., et al.: VNect: real-time 3D human pose estimation with a single RGB camera. ACM Trans. Graph. **36**(4), 14 p. (2017). Article No. 44. https://doi.org/10.1145/3072959.3073596
25. Mirza, M., Osindero, S.: Conditional generative adversarial nets. CoRR, abs/1411.1784 (2014)
26. Newcombe, R.A., et al.: KinectFusion: real-time dense surface mapping and tracking. In: Proceedings of the 2011 10th IEEE International Symposium on Mixed and Augmented Reality (2011)
27. Popa, A., Zanfir, M., Sminchisescu, C.: Deep multitask architecture for integrated 2D and 3D human sensing. In: CVPR (2017)
28. Ronneberger, O., Fischer, P., Brox, T.: U-Net: convolutional networks for biomedical image segmentation. In: Navab, N., Hornegger, J., Wells, W.M., Frangi, A.F. (eds.) MICCAI 2015. LNCS, vol. 9351, pp. 234–241. Springer, Cham (2015). https://doi.org/10.1007/978-3-319-24574-4_28
29. Shapiro, A., et al.: Rapid avatar capture and simulation using commodity depth sensors. Comput. Animat. Virtual Worlds **25**(3–4), 201–211 (2014)
30. Siarohin, A., Sangineto, E., Lathuiliere, S., Sebe, N.: Deformable GANs for pose-based human image generation. In: Conference on Computer Vision and Pattern Recognition (CVPR) (2018)
31. Tomè, D., Russell, C., Agapito, L.: Lifting from the deep: convolutional 3D pose estimation from a single image. In: CVPR (2017)
32. Tran, L., Yin, X., Liu, X.: Disentangled representation learning GAN for pose-invariant face recognition. In: Proceeding of IEEE Computer Vision and Pattern Recognition (2017)
33. Tulyakov, S., Liu, M.-Y., Yang, X., Kautz, J.: MoCoGan: decomposing motion and content for video generation. In: IEEE Conference on Computer Vision and Pattern Recognition (CVPR) (2018)
34. Ulyanov, D., Lebedev, V., Vedaldi, A., Lempitsky, V.: Texture networks: feed-forward synthesis of textures and stylized images. In: Proceedings of the 33rd International Conference on Machine Learning (2016)
35. Vondrick, C., Pirsiavash, H., Torralba, A.: Generating videos with scene dynamics. In: Advances in Neural Information Processing Systems (2016)
36. Wang, Z., Bovik, A.C., Sheikh, H.R., Simoncelli, E.P.: Image quality assessment: from error visibility to structural similarity. IEEE Trans. Image Process. **13**(4), 600–612 (2004)
37. Zeng, M., Zheng, J., Cheng, X., Liu, X.: Templateless quasi-rigid shape modeling with implicit loop-closure. In: CVPR (2013)
38. Zhang, R., Isola, P., Efros, A.A., Shechtman, E., Wang, O.: The unreasonable effectiveness of deep features as a perceptual metric. arXiv preprint (2018)
39. Zhang, W., Zhu, M., Derpanis, K.: From actemes to action: a strongly-supervised representation for detailed action understanding. In: International Conference on Computer Vision (ICCV) (2013)
40. Zhou, X., Huang, Q., Sun, X., Xue, X., Wei, Y.: Towards 3D human pose estimation in the wild: a weakly-supervised approach. In: IEEE International Conference on Computer Vision (ICCV) (2017)
41. Zhu, J.-Y., Krähenbühl, P., Shechtman, E., Efros, A.A.: Generative visual manipulation on the natural image manifold. In: Leibe, B., Matas, J., Sebe, N., Welling, M. (eds.) ECCV 2016. LNCS, vol. 9909, pp. 597–613. Springer, Cham (2016). https://doi.org/10.1007/978-3-319-46454-1_36

42. Zhu, J.-Y., Park, T., Isola, P., Efros, A.A.: Unpaired image-to-image translation using cycle-consistent adversarial networkss. In: 2017 IEEE International Conference on Computer Vision (ICCV) (2017)
43. Zuffi, S., Black, M.J.: The stitched puppet: a graphical model of 3D human shape and pose. In: IEEE Conference on Computer Vision and Pattern Recognition (CVPR 2015) (2015)

Human Action Recognition Based on Temporal Pose CNN and Multi-dimensional Fusion

Yi Huang[1](✉), Shang-Hong Lai[1], and Shao-Heng Tai[2]

[1] National Tsing Hua University, Hsinchu, Taiwan
jeffreyhuang0823@gmail.com, lai@cs.nthu.edu.tw
[2] Umbo Computer Vision, Taipei, Taiwan
daniel.tai@umbocv.com

Abstract. To take advantage of recent advances in human pose estimation from images, we develop a deep neural network model for action recognition from videos by computing temporal human pose features with a 3D CNN model. The proposed temporal pose features can provide more discriminative human action information than previous video features, such as appearance and short-term motion. In addition, we propose a novel fusion network that combines temporal pose, spatial and motion feature maps for the classification by bridging the gap between the dimension difference between 3D and 2D CNN feature maps. We show that the proposed action recognition system provides superior accuracy compared to the previous methods through experiments on Sub-JHMDB and PennAction datasets.

Keywords: Action recognition · Multi-stream · Fusion · Pose estimation

1 Introduction

In light of the recently launched evolution of deep learning, the research of action recognition, being one of the most widely applicable study in computer vision (e.g., video surveillance, human-computer interaction [11]), has been focused on developing innovative solutions for the subject matter via deep learning [16,21,23,25].

Perhaps the most integral factor in achieving accurate action recognition results resides in the extraction of discriminative temporal clues within videos. Thus, though there exists a cornucopia of information in a video, researchers can never be overly scrupulous about their selection of features when it comes to optimizing the performance of action recognition algorithms.

Electronic supplementary material The online version of this chapter (https://doi.org/10.1007/978-3-030-11012-3_33) contains supplementary material, which is available to authorized users.

L. Leal-Taixé and S. Roth (Eds.): ECCV 2018 Workshops, LNCS 11130, pp. 426–440, 2019.
https://doi.org/10.1007/978-3-030-11012-3_33

Some achieved the capturing of temporal clues via feeding convolutional neural networks (CNNs), both two-stream and classical ones, with optical flow features [15,16,23,25]. Some utilized recurrent neural networks (RNNs) to model the inter-relationship between high-level features extracted from the fully-connected layer of a CNN for action recognition. However, we argue that in general, extracting temporal human pose based feature is the most effective way for human action recognition from videos (Fig. 1).

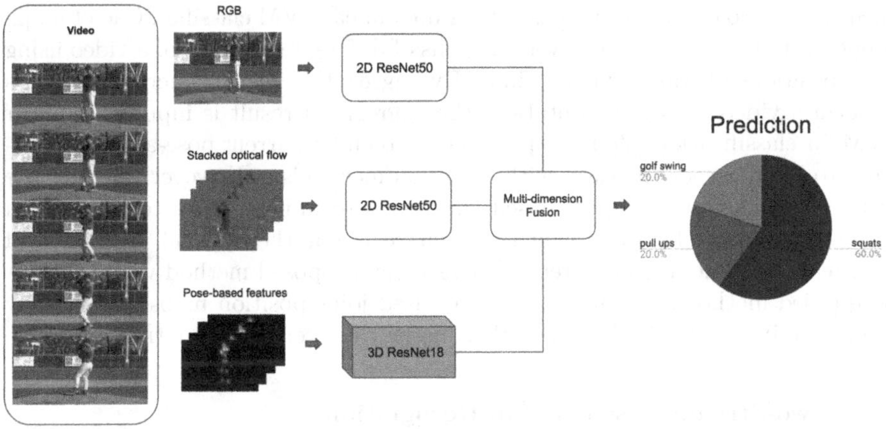

Fig. 1. Overview of the temporal pose-based convolutional neural network with multi-dimensional fusion

In this paper, we propose a 3D CNN network that is capable of exploiting temporal pose features within videos. Our method demonstrates the effectiveness of pose-based features in terms of modeling temporal information for human action recognition. We also develop a multi-dimensional fusion method to fuse the features extracted from 3D pose stream and 2D two-stream architecture, which further enhances the performance of our multi-stream posed-based CNN.

Our main contributions in this paper are summarized as follows:

- We propose a novel 3D temporal pose CNN for utilizing pose-based features to effectively capture the temporal human pose features in videos for action recognition.
- To take the advantages of both 2D and 3D network, we present a simple but highly effective multi-dimension fusion network which bridges the gap between 3D and 2D CNN feature maps and enables our model to leverage 3D temporal pose, spatial, and motion feature maps for human action recognition.
- By conducting extensive experiments, we validate the performance of the proposed framework and show that the proposed multi-stream action recognition system provides superior accuracy compared to the previous methods on Sub-JHMDB [13] and PennAction [26] datasets.

2 Related Work

2.1 Pose-Based Action Recognition

As a kind of high-level visual information, human pose features are exploited in many works with different architectures of pose-based action recognition approaches [2,5,7,12]. [5] introduced a new video descriptor called P-CNN, which was derived from aggregating appearance (RGB) and short-term motion (optical flow) features around different human body parts across the whole video, and then such video descriptor was used to train a linear SVM classifier. Cao et al. [2] proposed to pool 3D deep CNN activations of different segments of a video using joint positions of frames in the video. By aggregating features across segments to form a video level representation, the aggregated result is input to a linear SVM for classification. [7] developed an end-to-end recurrent pose-attention network to leverage pose features with attention mechanism. However, the purpose of these works to utilize pose-based features is to indicate an attention region for other kinds of features, which we believe is not the optimal utilization of pose features. The main difference between the proposed method with previous pose-based methods is that we generate fused joint position maps and directly use as the input of 3D CNN to further model their temporal information.

2.2 Two-Stream-Based Action Recognition

The deep learning approach of action recognition is a very active research area in the past few years [6,8,14,16,17,21–23,25]. Among several standard CNN architectures in action recognition related field, the two-stream CNN approach [21] is simple but highly effective [15]. It leverages the power of two single stream CNN to predict actions in videos: one for modeling the appearance clues in RGB images, and the other stream for capturing short-term motion in optical flow images. Recently, there are several works proposed to enhance the two-stream architecture. [23] proposed a sparse temporal sampling strategy and a series of good practice to further enhance the performance of [21] and make it more efficient. [1] aggregated local convolutional features of the two streams to introduce a new video representation for action classification. [25] included the audio stream and adopted LSTM networks to explore long-term temporal dynamics. In this work, we combine the two-stream architecture with a 3D CNN based pose stream by using a novel fusion method.

2.3 Multi-stream Fusion

In the original two-stream method [21], since the authors just simply fuse the features with average fusion, which only average the prediction scores of the softmax layer in both streams. [8] improved the original work by fusing the two streams with a single convolutional fusion layer. [25] took action class relationships into account to learn the best fusion weights of different deep neural network streams for different action classes. [16] used multiple 2D convolution layers to model the concatenation of features in different domains. However, all of these previous works only developing the fusion techniques based on the feature maps with the same dimension. In our work, we propose a novel fusion method to fuse the 3D convolutional pose stream with the 2D convolutional appearance stream and the 2D convolutional short-term motion stream by utilizing the proposed feature compression sub-network to bridge the gap of the discrepancy of feature dimensions of the three target CNN streams. The design details will be discussed in Sect. 4. We will compare the proposed multi-stream action recognition method with the state-of-the-art methods on some public datasets, which will be described in Sect. 5.5.

3 Pose-Based Action Recognition

In this section, We propose a CNN based model for action recognition based on using the human pose features. With the help of human pose features and proposed channel-wise convolution techniques. We present a novel way of utilizing pose features for human action recognition. We first briefly introduce the pose estimation method in Sect. 3.1, and then provide the details of the proposed method in Sects. 3.2, 3.3 and 3.4

3.1 Pose Estimation

In this paper, we generate the pose estimation result from a strong bottom-up multi-person pose estimator [3,20,24], which is capable of computing human pose features in different scales and positions with real-time speed. A sample result of human pose estimation is shown in Fig. 2(a). Instead of directly using their pose estimation result, we propose some pre-processing procedure to best utilize the multi-channel human joint position maps.

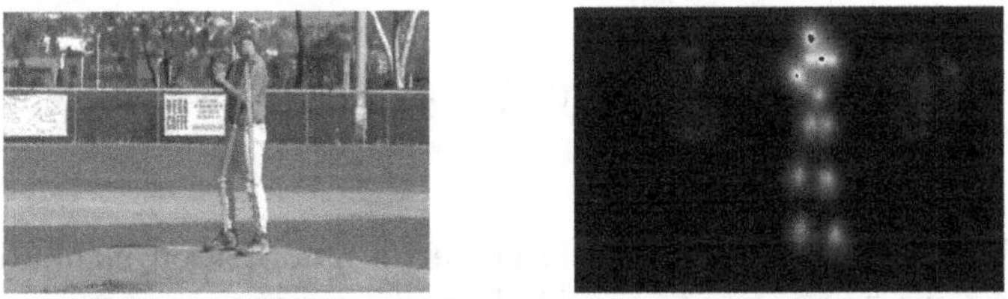

(a) Pose estimation (b) Joint position map

Fig. 2. An example of (a) the visualization of original pose estimation result and (b) the joint position map in our action recognition model. (Color figure online)

Joint Position Map: Figure 2(a) shows the pose estimation result of [3,20,24], which utilizes different colors to denote different human joint positions. For the reason that the input dimension to the 3D CNN will be very large with the concatenation of the feature maps in temporal domain, we do not directly apply this result to 3D convolutional neural network, Instead, we take the 15-channel heatmaps of their estimation result and generate a joint position map by using channel-wise convolution, which is shown in Fig. 2(b) as the input of 3D convolutional neural network to extract the spatial and temporal features in human action. The details of the channel-wise convolution will be given subsequently in this section.

3.2 Pose-Based CNNs

In this work, with the belief that high-level pose-based features outperform the mid-level flow-based features [13] for action recognition, we extend the optical flow stacking CNNs [21, 23] to human-joint-part stacking CNNs to better capture spatial and temporal clues. The flow diagram of our pose-based 3D CNN model is depicted in Fig. 3.

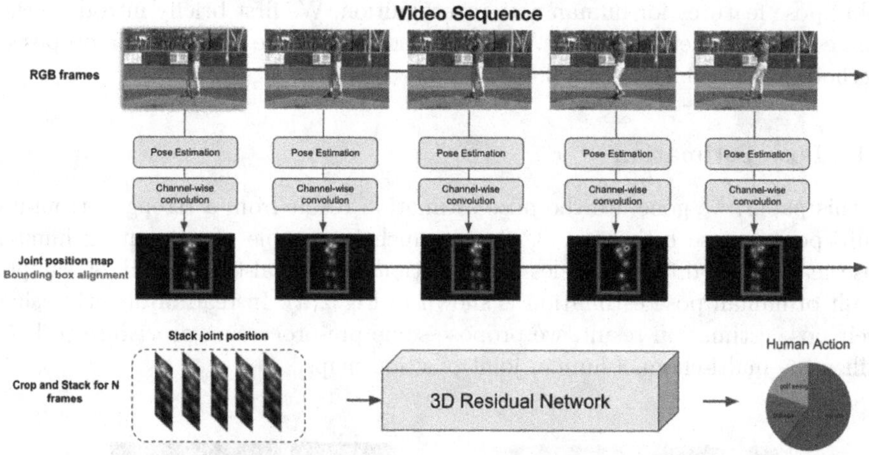

Fig. 3. Flow diagram of the pose-based 3D CNN model

Channel-Wise Convolution: To leverage the information computed for all human parts, we first compute the 15-channel heatmaps to generate the joint position map [13], which can be considered as the linear combination of the probability maps for the corresponding human parts. According to the experimental results in Table 3, we found that utilizing two 3D convolution layers to merge the features from a 15-channel heatmap achieve the highest accuracy in our experiments.

Stacked Joint Position: According to recent success in 3D CNN [9], we utilize the 3D residual network to model the pose-based feature and also compare its performance with a 2D network, which is used in the motion stream of [21] for modeling temporal clues. The details of our experiments will be described in Sect. 5.1. Here, we denote $P_t(u,v)$ to be the probability map of human parts at the point (u,v) at frame t. To model the temporal information of human joint parts across a sequence of frames, we stack the joint position map over L consecutive frames to form a stacked joint position map of totally L input channels. More precisely, let w and h be the width and height of videos. For $u=[1:w]$, $v=[1:h]$, $k=[1:L]$, the input volumes of the pose-based CNNs, I_t^{3d} and I_t^{2d}, at frame t are constructed as follows:

$$\text{For 3D CNN, } \mathrm{I}_t^{3d}(k,1,u,v) = P_{t+k-1}(u,v) \tag{1}$$

$$\text{For 2D CNNs, } \mathrm{I}_t^{2d}(k,u,v) = P_{t+k-1}(u,v) \tag{2}$$

The main difference between 2D and 3D approaches is that 2D CNNs only model temporal clues at the first convolution layer. On the contrary, 3D CNNs are capable of modeling temporal clues at all convolution layers. In Sect. 5.1, we will have some discussion of the pros and cons between 3D and 2D network.

Human Detector: Since the intensity in the human pose heat maps is consistent with the region that contains human, our experimental results in Table 5 show that utilizing ground-truth bounding box to crop the person in action can significantly improve the action recognition accuracy and we also compare it with the state-of-the-art human detection method (Faster R-CNN [19]) in Table 5.

3.3 Transfer Learning for ImageNet Pretrained Weights

We also combine two powerful transfer learning techniques: the cross-modality pre-training [23] and bootstrapping 3D filter from 2D filter [4]. By applying the combination of these techniques on ImageNet pre-trained weights, we are able to transfer the knowledge from image domain to pose domain and bootstrap our pose-based 3D CNN. The combination method is constructed as follows. We first follow [23] to modify the weights of each convolution layer of ImageNet pre-trained model to handle the input of our stacked joint position field. More precisely, we average the weights across the RGB channels and replicate this average by the channel number of 2D pose-based network. Then we apply the idea in [4] to process the weights of 2D pose-based network for utilizing in 3D pose-based network. Since the architecture of 3D residual network is inflating from 2D residual network, for these 3D filters of size $N*N*N$ are formed by expanding an additional dimension from the 2D filters of size $N*N$. Thus, by repeating the weights of the 2D filters N times along the time dimension, and rescaling them by dividing by N, we can generate the weights for pose-based 3D CNN. The transfer learning method not only successfully reduces convergence time but also improves the accuracy of our model. The experimental result is shown in Fig. 4

3.4 Implementation Details

Hyperparameter: In the training stage, we set the initial learning rate of pose stream as 1×10^{-3} and it is divided by 10 when the validation accuracy is

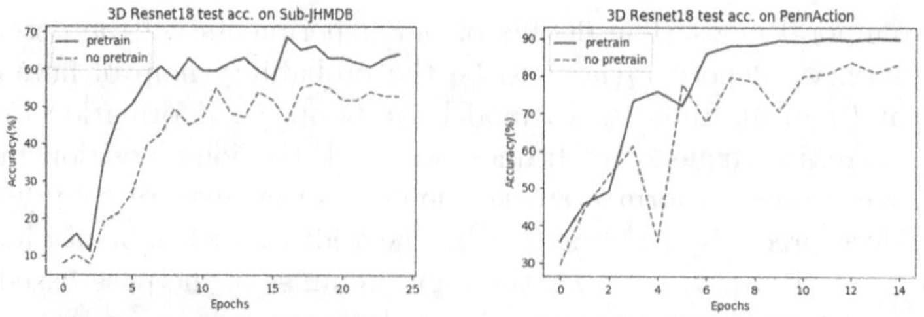

(a) figures/Sub-JHMDB (b) PennAction

Fig. 4. The validation of transfer learning techniques on pose-based 3D resnet18. The blue line denotes the model with transfer learning from Imagenet and the red line denote the model without transfer learning techniques. (Color figure online)

saturated. The weight decay is set to be 1×10^{-4}, momentum is set to 0.9, and we use SGD as the optimizer for training. In the testing stage, we slice each video into a non-overlap 15 frames clips and the prediction score of each video is the average of the prediction of each clip in a video and this proposed framework is trained and tested with mini-batch size 32.

Data Augmentation: To boost the performance of our model, We utilize both spatial and temporal augmentation mechanism to train our model. For spatial augmentation, after generating the stacked joint position maps for a 15-frame video clip, we first resize it into $[15, 1, 128, 128]$ and utilize the random crop technique to crop a $[15, 1, 112, 112]$ joint position map as the input of our pose stream. For temporal augmentation, we follow [4] to pick a starting frame among those that guarantee a desired number of frames in each stack.

4 Multi-dimensional Fusion Network

In the two-stream architecture [21], a video sequence is first preprocessed to obtain the RGB frames and the optical flow maps, and then two independent CNNs are used to compute the spatial and temporal features, respectively. This framework provides the baseline model for action recognition research. Furthermore, there are several different extensions on this architecture for either better fusing the spatial and temporal feature [16] or enhancing the way of modeling temporal clues [23]. While the recognition accuracies reported by these previous works are quite excellent, we argue that precise human joint positions [13] provide very critical features for action recognition. Thus, we propose a pose-based 3D CNN based on Residual Network [10] as an additional stream on a multi-steam framework for action recognition.

4.1 Multi-dimensional Fusion

Due to the excellent performance for the two-stream architecture, we propose to include the pose-based approach into the two-stream framework to construct a

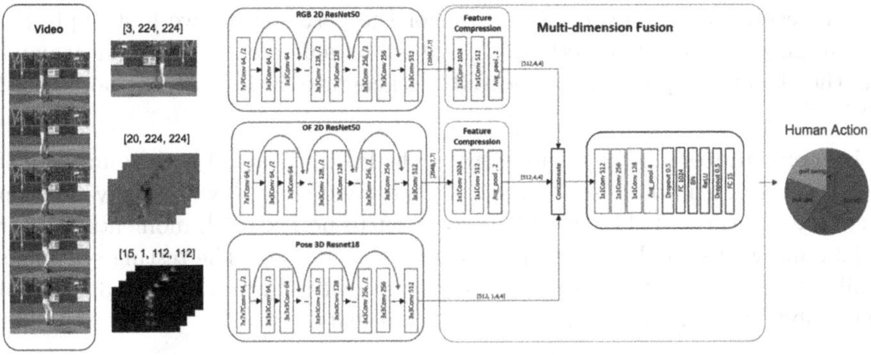

Fig. 5. Flow of the multi-dimensional fusion network: ($N \times N$ conv, k) denotes a convolutional layer with kernel size $N \times N$ and the output filter dimension k.

multi-stream CNN model, which combines spatial, short-term motion and human joint parts motion for action recognition. Motivated by the spatial-temporal fusion networks [8,16], we propose a novel fusion method to take advantage of the pose-based 3D CNNs and the two-stream CNNs such that channel responses of different types at the same pixel position were integrated appropriately. Here we intend to follow [16] to utilize convolution fusion for combining the feature maps for different streams. However, the main difficulty is that the previous fusion methods are only capable of fusing the feature maps of the same dimension. In other words, the previous fusion methods can not fuse feature maps of 2D and 3D networks.

Fusion of 2D and 3D CNN: To overcome the problem of fusing feature maps of different dimensions, we design a multi-dimensional fusion method. Here we demonstrate our techniques with spatial resnet50, motion resnet50 and pose 3D resnet18. Firstly, we follow [8,16] to extract the spatial, motion and pose feature maps before the average pooling layer, whose shapes are $[2048, 7, 7]$, $[2048, 7, 7]$, $[512, 1, 4, 4]$, respectively. Then we design a feature compression network for reducing the feature dimension of spatial and motion feature maps to $[512, 4, 4]$, which can be concatenated with the 3D pose-based feature maps.

Feature Compression Network: There are many existing methods to reduce the dimension of features (e.g. average pooling, max pooling and conv fusion). According to [16], which states that using multiple convolution layers to gradually reduce the dimension is better than directly applying average or max pooling. Hence, we follow the concept to design our network for dimension reduction. The implementation detail is depicted in Fig. 5.

4.2 Implementation Details

Multi-stream Model Input: We use RGB frames and stacked optical flow maps as the input of the spatial and motion streams, which follow the pre-processing procedures used in [21]. For the pose stream, we first apply the human pose computation method in [3,20,24] to generate 15-channel heatmaps, and then follow the procedure in Sect. 3.2 to generate the input of the pose-based CNNs.

Hyperparameter: In the training stage, the learning rate of multi-dimensional fusion network is initially set to 1×10^{-3} and divided by 10 when the validation accuracy is saturated. The weight decay is set to be 1×10^{-4}, momentum is set to 0.9, and we use SGD as the optimizer for the training. The testing scheme is similar to that used in the single pose-stream method given in Sect. 3.3. All of these models are trained and tested with mini-batch size 32.

Data Augmentation: For the spatial stream, we first resize an input image to [256, 256] and apply random cropping to crop a [224, 224] sub-image as the training data. For motion and pose streams, we utilize temporal augmentation mechanism proposed in [4] by picking a starting frame among those that guarantee a desired number of frames in each stack. The augmentation method of pose stream remains the same as the techniques described in Sect. 3.3.

5 Experimental Evaluation

To demonstrate the importance of the pose-based features, we evaluate our model on two widely used pose-related action recognition benchmarks; i.e., Sub-JHMDB [13] and PennAction [26] datasets. Furthermore, we use the published evaluation protocol of Sub-JHMDB (split1) and PennAction to report the classification accuracy for both datasets.

Table 1. Comparison of methods based on high-level pose features: SJP, OF, box denote stack joint position, optical flow and cropping by human detection bounding boxes, respectively, and L denotes the number of frames in each stack. Note that in these experiments, we first utilizing average fusion to model the features of each channel of human joint heatmap to test our pose-based method.

Input features	Network	Sub-JHMDB	PennAction
Stacked OF	2D resnet50	45.4	85.4
SJP	2D resnet50	57.3	86.1
SJP+ box	2D resnet50	61.8	89.8
SJP+ box	3D resnet18	67.4	90.0

5.1 Performance of Pose-Based CNN

To investigate the properties of pose-based CNN, we design several methods to utilize high-level pose features in CNN and compare them to the original stacked optical flow methods, which is proposed in [21].

Furthermore, we evaluate the proposed method with different stack lengths (L), which denote the temporal footprints [4] in the videos. In action recognition related field, the temporal footprint is a key factor to design an action recognition algorithm. Therefore, we validate the effectiveness of the temporal high-level features on the two popular benchmarks.

According to Table 1, we find the method that utilizes 3D resnet18 to model the stack joint position maps cropped with the associated ground-truth bounding boxes outperforms the performance of optical flow-based methods and the pose-based methods on 2D network.

Furthermore, we also conduct experiment to determine the best architect of capturing temporal footprints in video. In Table 2, we show that when the number of input frames L, which is the temporal footprint of our model set to 15, gives the better accuracy than the original flow-based methods for both datasets.

The experiment results not only demonstrate that pose-based features perform better for extracting action features than optical flow based features, but also show that 3D resnet18 has superior performance to 2D resent18. We believe the main reason why a 3D network is superior than 2D network is that using only a single convolution layer for modeling human pose features is insufficient to capture temporal action from video.

Table 2. Comparison of the performance of different temporal footprint: SJP, OF, Box denote stack joint position, optical flow and cropping by ground truth bounding boxes, respectively, and L denotes the temporal footprint, which is the number of frames in each stack.

Input features	Network	Sub-JHMDB	PennAction
(a) Temporal footprint L = 10			
Stacked OF	2D resnet50	46.1	87.1
Stacked OF+ Box	2D resnet50	60.8	88.2
SJP+ Box	3D resnet 18	62.5	90.0
(b) Temporal footprint L = 15			
Stacked OF	2D resnet50	41.1	86.3
Stacked OF+ box	2D resnet50	59.5	89.4
SJP+ box	3D resnet18	68.5	91.5

5.2 Channel-Wise Convolution

After we determine the architecture of classification model, we propose an experiment of channel-wise convolution to validate the most effective way to combine different human body part features. With the experimental results given

Table 3. Comparison of different strategies of combining the features of each human part: 3D convN (a, b) denotes a 3D convolutional layer with kernel size $N \times N \times N$, where a is the input filter dimension and b is the output filter dimension.

Human-part pooling method	Sub-JHMDB	PennAction
Average pooling	68.5	90.5
3D conv1 (15,1)	69.2	91.1
3D conv1 (15,7) + 3D conv1 (7,1)	71.4	92.9

in Table 3, We found that using two 3D convolution layers to model the features from all channels of pose estimation result outperforms other methods. Therefore, we demonstrate the effectiveness of this architecture in the proposed pose-based action recognition model.

5.3 Performance of Multi-dimensional Fusion Network

According to the fact that 3D spatial (3 channels) and 3D temporal (2 channels) networks contain more parameters than the proposed 3D pose model (1 channel), which makes them suffer from the over-fitting problem, our proposed method is based on fusing 3D pose stream, 2D spatial stream and 2D temporal stream to achieve superior or comparable performance compared to the state-of-the-art methods. The comparison of different fusion methods is shown in Table 4. Our multi-dimensional fusion framework outperforms the previous average fusion and convolution fusion methods. In addition, We also provide the confusion matrices of the proposed pose-based 3D CNN and multi-stream network in Fig. 6 to demonstrate the effectiveness of the proposed framework.

5.4 Comparison of Performance for Using Ground-Truth and Human Detector Bounding Boxes

To validate the proposed model, we compare the performance of our framework by using the ground-truth human bounding boxes and the bounding boxes obtained from the Faster R-CNN [19] human detector. The results are shown in Table 5. According to the experimental results, when we replace the ground-truth human bounding boxes by those obtained from the state-of-the-art human detector, we have slightly degraded accuracies in our experiment on the PennAction dataset. Therefore, we claim that in the proposed framework, ground truth human bounding box can be replaced by a state-of-the-art human detector with slight accuracy decrease.

5.5 Comparison with State-of-the-art Methods

We also evaluate our pose-based CNN and multi-stream network by comparing performance with state-of-the-art posed-related action recognition methods.

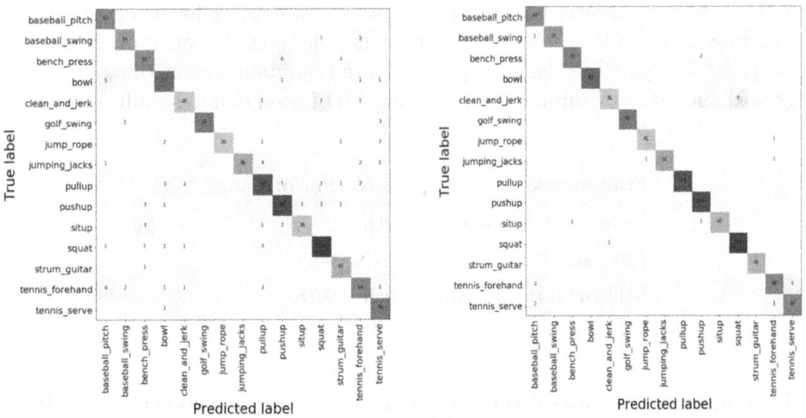

(a) Prediction of pose features (b) Prediction of multi-stream features

Fig. 6. The confusion matrix of the proposed multi-stream fusion is much sparser than the confusion matrix by using the proposed pose-based method. It demonstrates the effectiveness of fusing multiple types of features, and our fusion strategy significantly enhances the performance for human action recognition.

Table 4. Comparison with different fusion schemes: In the fusion part, s, m, p denote spatial, motion and pose streams, respectively. MD-fusion denotes multi-dimensional fusion, conv fusion denotes fusion with convolution layers and average fusion denotes the fusion method proposed in [21], which simply fusion the scores of all streams at the output of the softmax layer.

Stream	Sub-JHMDB	PennAction
Spatial	55.1	80.2
Motion	60.7	87.1
Pose	68.5	91.5
Fusion	*Sub-JHMDB*	*PennAction*
s+m, conv fusion	70.2	92.4
s+p, average fusion	69.7	91.9
s+p, MD-fusion	74.1	95.6
s+m+p, average fusion	71.0	93.7
s+m+p, MD-fusion	78.9	97.6

In Table 6, the result of our multi-dimensional fusion network provides superior performance on the methods based on either hand-crafted features or deep learning approaches. Finally, we successfully justify our argument that with proper modeling and fusion techniques, human pose features can be directly applied to 3D convolution neural networks to model the temporal evolution in videos and significantly enhance the performance of human action recognition.

Table 5. Performance comparison of the proposed framework by using the ground-truth bounding boxes and those obtained from a human detector on PennAction dataset. In this table, gt-Bbox denotes ground-truth bounding box, sf-Bbox denotes the bounding box generated by human detector, and MD-fusion denotes multi-dimensional fusion.

Framework	Bounding box	Performance
Pose-stream	Ground truth	90.5
Pose-stream	Faster R-CNN	90.1
MD-fusion	Ground truth	97.8
MD-fusion	Faster R-CNN	97.6

Table 6. Comparison of state-of-the-art action recognition methods on Sub-JHMDB [13] and PennAction [26] datasets.

State-of-the-art	Stream	Sub-JHMDB	PennAction
Actemes [26]	RGB	-	79.4
pose+NTraj [13]	Pose	75.1	-
SP-AOG [18]	RGB + Pose	61.2	85.5
P-CNN [5]	RGB + Flow + Pose	66.8	-
JDD [2]	RGB + Flow	77.7	87.4
C3D [2]	RGB + Flow	-	86.0
pose [12]	Pose	61.5	79.0
Pose + idt-fv [12]	Pose + Flow	74.6	92.9
RPAN [7]	RGB + Flow + Pose	78.6	97.4
Pose-stream (our)	Pose	**71.4**	**92.9**
Pose+MD-fusion (our)	RGB + Flow +Pose	**78.9**	**97.6**

6 Conclusion

In this paper, we presented a novel multi-stream action recognition method based on fusing 3D pose, 2D spatial and 2D temporal features. We develop a pose-based 3D CNN which integrates multi-channel human joint heatmaps with channel-wise convolution and applied 3D CNN to extract spatial and temporal features at the same time. In addition, we propose a multi-dimensional fusion method that bridges the gap between dimension differences between the 2D spatial, 2D motion and 3D pose feature maps. Our experiments showed the proposed multi-stream CNN model outperforms the state-of-the-art methods on both Sub-JHMDB and PennAction datasets.

References

1. ActionVLAD: learning spatio-temporal aggregation for action classification. In: CVPR (2017)
2. Cao, C., Zhang, Y., Zhang, C., Lu, H.: Action recognition with joints-pooled 3D deep convolutional descriptors. In: IJCAI (2016)
3. Cao, Z., Simon, T., Wei, S.E., Sheikh, Y.: Realtime multi-person 2D pose estimation using part affinity fields. In: CVPR (2017)
4. Carreira, J., Zisserman, A.: Quo vadis, action recognition? A new model and the kinetics dataset. In: CVPR (2017)
5. Chéron, G., Laptev, I.: P-CNN: pose-based CNN features for action recognition. In: ICCV (2015)
6. Donahue, J., et al.: Long-term recurrent convolutional networks for visual recognition and description. In: CVPR (2015)
7. Du, W., Wang, Y., Qiao, Y.: Rpan: an end-to-end recurrent pose-attention network for action recognition in videos. In: ICCV (2017)
8. Feichtenhofer, C., Pinz, A., Zisserman, A.: Convolutional two-stream network fusion for video action recognition. In: CVPR (2016)
9. Hara, K., Kataoka, H., Satoh, Y.: Learning spatio-temporal features with 3D residual networks for action recognition. In: ICCV (2017)
10. He, K., Zhang, X., Ren, S., Sun, J.: Deep residual learning for image recognition. In: CVPR (2016)
11. Herath, S., Harandi, M., Porikli, F.: Going deeper into action recognition: a survey. Image Vis. Comput. **60**(Suppl. C), 4–21 (2017)
12. Iqbal, U., Garbade, M., Gall, J.: Pose for action – action for pose. In: FG (2017)
13. Jhuang, H., Gall, J., Zuffi, S., Schmid, C., Black, M.J.: Towards understanding action recognition. In: ICCV (2013)
14. Ji, S., Xu, W., Yang, M., Yu, K.: 3D convolutional neural networks for human action recognition. TPAMI **35**(1), 221–231 (2013)
15. Kay, W., et al.: The kinetics human action video dataset. ArXiv:1705.06950v1 [cs.CV] (2017)
16. Ma, C.Y., Chen, M.H., Kira, Z., AlRegib, G.: TS-LSTM and temporal-inception: exploiting spatiotemporal dynamics for activity recognition. ArXiv:1703.10667v1 [cs.CV] (2017)
17. Ng, J.Y.H., Hausknecht, M., Vijayanarasimhan, S., Vinyals, O., Monga, R., Toderici, G.: Beyond short snippets: deep networks for video classification. In: CVPR (2015)
18. Nie, B.X., Xiong, C., Zhu, S.C.: Joint action recognition and pose estimation from video. In: CVPR (2015)
19. Ren, S., He, K., Girshick, R., Sun, J.: Faster R-CNN: towards real-time object detection with region proposal networks. https://arxiv.org/pdf/1506.01497.pdf
20. Simon, T., Joo, H., Matthews, I., Sheikh, Y.: Hand keypoint detection in single images using multiview bootstrapping. In: CVPR (2017)
21. Simonyan, K., Zisserman, A.: Two-stream convolutional networks for action recognition in videos. In: NIPS (2014)
22. Tran, D., Bourdev, L., Fergus, R., Torresani, L., Paluri, M.: Learning spatiotemporal features with 3D convolutional networks. In: ICCV (2015)
23. Wang, L., et al.: Temporal segment networks: towards good practices for deep action recognition. In: Leibe, B., Matas, J., Sebe, N., Welling, M. (eds.) ECCV 2016. LNCS, vol. 9912, pp. 20–36. Springer, Cham (2016). https://doi.org/10.1007/978-3-319-46484-8_2

24. Wei, S.E., Ramakrishna, V., Kanade, T., Sheikh, Y.: Convolutional pose machines. In: CVPR (2016)
25. Wu, Z., Jiang, Y.G., Wang, X., Ye, H., Xue, X.: Multi-stream multi-class fusion of deep networks for video classification. In: ACM MM (2016)
26. Zhang, W., Zhu, M., Derpanis, K.G.: From actemes to action: a strongly-supervised representation for detailed action understanding. In: ICCV (2013)

Rendering Realistic Subject-Dependent Expression Images by Learning 3DMM Deformation Coefficients

Claudio Ferrari(✉), Stefano Berretti, Pietro Pala, and Alberto Del Bimbo

Media Integration and Communication Center,
University of Florence, Florence, Italy
claudio.ferrari@unifi.it

Abstract. Automatic analysis of facial expressions is now attracting an increasing interest, thanks to the many potential applications it can enable. However, collecting images with labeled expression for large sets of images or videos is a quite complicated operation that, in most of the cases, requires substantial human intervention. In this paper, we propose a solution that, starting from a neutral image of a subject, is capable of producing a realistic expressive face image of the same subject. This is possible thanks to the use of a particular 3D morphable model (3DMM) that can effectively and efficiently fit to 2D images, and then deform itself under the action of deformation parameters learned expression-by-expression in a subject-independent manner. Ultimately, the application of such deformation parameters to the neutral model of a subject allows the rendering of realistic expressive images of the subject. Experiments demonstrate that such deformation parameters can be learned from a small set of training data using simple statistical tools; despite this simplicity, very realistic subject-dependent expression renderings can be obtained. Furthermore, robustness to cross dataset tests is also evidenced.

Keywords: 3D morphable model · Deformation components learning · Facial expression synthesis

1 Introduction

In Computer Vision there is an increasing interest in developing methods for either *recognizing* or *synthesizing* expressions in an automatic way. In fact, this has both theoretical interest in disciplines as different as Cognitive Sciences, Medicine or Psychology, as well as in practical applications, like surveillance by analysis of human emotional state, monitoring for fatigue detection, gaming or Human Computer Interaction, to cite a few. While for long time automatic analysis of facial expressions from images and videos has been based on the design of hand-crafted features, now the success of neural networks, and deep learning

L. Leal-Taixé and S. Roth (Eds.): ECCV 2018 Workshops, LNCS 11130, pp. 441–455, 2019.
https://doi.org/10.1007/978-3-030-11012-3_34

solutions in particular, has drastically changed the scenario: the idea is to let the network learn the low- and intermediate-level features that are best suited to describe the training data, and then use them in any classification or recognition task. This moves most of the criticisms to the networks design and the collection of the data used for their training. In doing so, the amount of the data and their variability play a fundamental role in learning significant representations. In the case of facial expressions, this has some additional difficulties since obtaining large quantities of ground truth data with accurate expression labels is a complicated and time consuming task if executed by human annotators. Thus, an idea that is making its way is to synthetically generate such training data. To this end, solutions based on parametric models, like the 3D Morphable Model (3DMM) [5] and its variants are among the most promising. The idea here is to fit such model to 2D target images so as to reconstruct a coarse 3D shape of the face. Then, this 3D face model can be deformed to exhibit a target expression and render a corresponding image. Of course, this process requires the deformation components that change the neutral model to an expressive one are known for each expression. This, by itself, is not an easy task since most of the 3DMMs have been trained without using any expressive scan [7]. Some recent works also applied Generative Adversarial Networks (GANs) for the task of generating expressive face images from neutral ones [19,29]. However, also in this case, 3DMMs can play a role for generating the images used for GANs training.

Rendering expressive images of a subject starting from his/her neutral one using parametric face models has potential applications also in designing advanced interfaces and serious games [22]. For example, a desktop system could use an avatar to interact with the user adapting the avatar's expression to that of the user; similarly, two avatars could be used in a virtual call simulating the expression of the interacting people. A training scenario appears also realistic, where disabled people or people recovering after a disease or injuries that compromised their facial mimic (*e.g.*, a stroke) could use a virtual assistant to learn reproducing facial expressions in a correct way [3]. People affected by autism syndrome could also benefit from an application that helps them in reproducing expressions. This could be done by starting from a model representing the neutral face of the subject and then by producing different expressions on it [37].

In this paper, we develop on the idea of automatically synthesize images of expressive faces. To this end, we start with a particular variant of the 3DMM, which is characterized by its capability of reproducing facial expressions starting from the average model. This is possible thanks to two specific aspects of this 3DMM (called DL-3DMM [15]): *(i)* differently from most existing 3DMMs it is trained also with 3D expressive facial scans; *(ii)* its deformation components are learned as a dictionary of atoms using a *dictionary learning* approach; differently from the standard approach that learns deformation components by Principal Component Analysis (PCA) so that each component acts globally on the model, the atoms identified by the dictionary learning solution capture quite well local deformations of the face. This 3DMM can be efficiently fit to a target 2D face image using a closed form solution generating a coarse 3D model of the target subject. Our goal here is to deform such 3D neutral model so as to realize a given expression of the subject ultimately rendering a 2D expressive image. To this end, we design a learning procedure that identifies the weights of the atoms corresponding to each prototypical expression. The procedure is composed of two main steps: first, the 3DMM is fit to a face image in neutral expression, producing a person-specific 3D reconstruction; then, this reconstruction is used to fit an expressive face image of the same subject and the deformation parameters are collected. This allows us to separate between the deformations that model identity traits and the ones modeling expressions. Once all these parameters are collected, we look for recurrent patterns among them that identify prototypical expressions and use such parameters to control the 3DMM deformation and generate expressive models. Such parameters are expression-specific, but can also be mixed together so as to generate more complex expressions. Experiments show that this strategy permits us to recover such parameters pretty easily, and that we can effectively generate expressive and realistic models also in a cross-dataset fashion. In particular, the main contributions of this work are as follows:

- We propose a simple yet effective framework that enables the extrapolation of 3DMM parameters that control expression-specific deformations, and successfully apply them to generate expressive renderings starting from face images in neutral expression;
- We showcase the potential and versatility of the DL-3DMM in handling and generating expressions;
- We demonstrate the generalization capability of our solution by showing that more complex expressions can be generated by combining different prototypical expression parameters.

The rest of the paper is organized as follows: In Sect. 2, the works in the literature that are most closely related to our proposed solution are discussed; In Sect. 3, we summarize the 3DMM used in this work and the characteristics that make it effective in modeling facial expressions; In Sect. 4, we present the methods used to learn the deformation coefficients related to each expression; These coefficients are then used to generate expressions starting from the neutral 3DMM for new identities; a qualitative evaluation is reported in Sect. 5; Finally, discussion and conclusions are drawn in Sect. 6.

2 Related Work

In the following, first, we report on the solutions that define and use a 3DMM to derive the 3D face model of a target subject starting from his/her 2D neutral image; then, we summarize some methods that learn modes of deformations to transform a neutral 3D model to an expressive one.

Blanz and Vetter [5] first presented a complete solution to derive a 3DMM by transforming the shape and texture from a training set of 3D face scans into a vector space representation based on PCA. However, the training dataset had limited face variability (200 neutral scans of young Caucasians), thus reducing the capability of the model to generalize to different ethnicity and non-neutral expressions. Despite these limitations, the 3DMM has proved its effectiveness in image face analysis, inspiring most of the subsequent work. The 3DMM was further refined into the Basel Face Model by Paysan et al. [28]. This offered higher shape and texture accuracy thanks to a better scanning device, and a lower number of correspondence artifacts using an improved registration algorithm based on the non-rigid Iterative Closest Point (ICP) [2]. However, since non-rigid ICP cannot handle large missing regions and topological variations, expressions were not accounted for in the training data also in this case. In addition, both the optical flow used in [5] and the non-rigid ICP method used in [1,28] were applied by transferring the vertex index from a reference model to all the scans, so that the choice of the reference face can affect the quality of the detected correspondences, and the resulting 3DMM. The work by Booth et al. [8] introduced a pipeline for 3DMM construction. Initially, dense correspondence was estimated applying the non-rigid ICP to a template model. Then, the so called LSFM-3DMM was constructed using PCA to derive the deformation basis on a dataset of 9,663 scans with a wide variety of age, gender, and ethnicity. Though the LSFM-3DMM was built from the largest dataset compared to the current state-of-the-art, the face shapes were still in neutral expression.

Following a different approach, Patel and Smith [27] showed that Thin-Plate Splines (TPS) and Procrustes analysis can be used to construct a 3DMM. In [12], Cosker et al. described a framework for building a dynamic 3DMM, which extended static 3DMM construction by incorporating dynamic data. This was obtained by proposing an approach based on Active Appearance Model and TPS for non-rigid 3D mesh registration and correspondence. Results showed this method overcomes optical flow based solutions that are prone to temporal drift. Brunton et al. [9], instead, proposed a statistical model for 3D human faces in varying expression. The approach decomposed the face using a wavelet transform, and learned many localized, decorrelated multilinear models on the resulting coefficients. In [24], Lüthi et al. presented a Gaussian Process Morphable Model (GPMM), which generalizes PCA-based Statistical Shape Models (SSM).

3DMM has been used at coarse level for face recognition and synthesis. In one of the first examples, Blanz and Vetter [6] used their 3DMM to simulate the process of image formation in 3D space, and estimated 3D shape and texture of faces from single images for face recognition. Later, Romdhani and Vetter [31] used the 3DMM for face recognition by enhancing the deformation algorithm with the inclusion of various image features. In [35], Yi et al. used the 3DMM to estimate the pose of a face image with a fast fitting algorithm. This idea was extended further by Zhu et al. [38], who proposed fitting a dense 3DMM to an image via Convolutional Neural Network. Grupp et al. [16] fitted the 3DMM based exclusively on facial landmarks, corrected the pose of the face and transformed it back to a frontal 2D representation for face recognition. Hu et al. [17] proposed a Unified-3DMM that captures intra personal variations due to illumination and occlusions, and showed its performance in 3D-assisted 2D face recognition for scenarios where the input image is subjected to degradations or exhibits intra-personal variations. Recent solutions also used deep neural networks to learn complex non-linear regressor functions mapping a 2D facial image to the optimal 3DMM parameters [14,33].

In all these cases, the 3DMM was used mainly to compensate for the pose of the face, with some examples that performed also illumination normalization. Expressions were typically not considered. Indeed, the difficulty in making 3DMM work properly in fine face analysis applications is confirmed by the existence of very few methods that use 3DMM for expression recognition [4,10]. Among the few examples, Ramanathan et al. [30] constructed a 3D Morphable Expression Model incorporating emotion-dependent face variations in terms of morphing parameters that were used for recognizing four emotions. Ujir and Spann [34] combined the 3DMM with Modular PCA and Facial Animation Parameters (FAP) for facial expression recognition, but the model deformation was due more to the action of FAP than to the learned components. In [13], Cosker et al. used a dynamic 3DMM [11] to explore the effect of linear and non-linear facial movement on expression recognition through a test where users evaluated animated frames. Huber et al. [20] proposed a cascaded-regressor based face tracking and a 3DMM shape fitting for fully automatic real-time semi dense 3D face reconstruction from monocular in-the-wild videos. The Dictionary Learning based 3DMM (DL-3DMM) proposed by Ferrari et al. [15] was one of the most promising in producing realistic facial expressions from the mean model. This is possible thanks to a dense alignment procedure based on landmarks, face partitioning and resampling, which allows expressive scans are enrolled in the training. This 3DMM has been used to enhance facial expression and action unit recognition from 2D images and videos with state-of-the-art performance on benchmark datasets.

3 3D Morphable Model

From the discussion of existing solutions for generating a 3DMM, it is quite evident the presence of some aspects that play a major relevance in characterizing the different solutions: (1) the human face variability captured by the model, which directly depends on the number and heterogeneity of training examples; (2) the capability of the model to account for facial expressions; also this feature of the model directly derives from the presence of expressive scans in the training. One of the few 3DMM existing in the literature that exposes both these features is the Dictionary Learning based 3DMM (DL-3DMM) proposed by Ferrari et al. [15]. Since our contribution mainly develops on this model, to make the paper as self-contained as possible, below we describe the peculiar features that make this particular 3DMM formulation suitable for our purposes.

3.1 DL-3DMM Construction

The first problem to be solved in the construction of a 3DMM is the selection of an appropriate set of training data. This should include sufficient variability in terms of ethnicity, gender, age, so as to enable the model to include a large variance in the data. Apart for this, the most difficult aspect in preparing the training data is the need to provide dense, *i.e.*, vertex-by-vertex, alignment between the 3D scans. In the original work of Blanz and Vetter [5] this was solved with the optical-flow method that provided reasonable results just in the case of neutral scans of the face. Several subsequent works used non-rigid variants of the Iterative Closest Point (ICP) algorithm, thus solving some problem related to the optical-flow, but without the explicit capability of addressing large facial expressions in the training data. The dense alignment of the training data for the DL-3DMM was obtained with a different solution based on the detection of landmarks of the face, and their use for partitioning the face into a set of non-overlapping regions, each one identifying the same part of the face across all the scans. Re-sampling the internal of the region based on its contour, a dense correspondence is derived region-by-region and so for all the face. Such method showed to be robust also to large expression variations as those occurring in the Binghamton University 3D facial Expression (BU-3DFE) database [36]. This latter dataset was used in the construction of the DL-3DMM.

Once a dense correspondence is established across the training data, these are used to estimate a set of deformation components that will be used to generate novel shapes. In the classic 3DMM framework [5], new 3D shapes $\mathbf{S}$ are generated by deforming an average model $\mathbf{m}$ with a linear combination of a set of M principal components $\mathbf{C}$, usually derived by PCA as follows;

$$\mathbf{S} = \mathbf{m} + \sum_{i=1}^{|M|} \mathbf{C}_i \alpha_i. \tag{1}$$

The DL-3DMM is instead constructed by learning a dictionary of deformation components exploiting the *Online Dictionary Learning for Sparse Coding* technique [25]. Learning is performed in an unsupervised way, without exploiting any knowledge about the data (*e.g.*, identity or expression labels). Then, the average model is deformed using the dictionary atoms $\mathbf{D}_i$ in place of $\mathbf{C}_i$ in Eq. (1).

Dictionary learning is usually cast as an ℓ_1-regularized least squares problem [25]; however, the sparsity induced by the ℓ_1 penalty to the dictionary atoms, can lead to discontinuous components and ultimately in a noisy or punctured 3D shape. To address this issue, the dictionary learning is formulated as an *Elastic-Net* regression, mitigating the sparsity effect of the ℓ_1 penalty with an ℓ_2 regularization that forces smoothness. By defining $\ell_{1,2}(\mathbf{w}_i) = \lambda_1 \|\mathbf{w}_i\|_1 + \lambda_2 \|\mathbf{w}_i\|_2$, where λ_1 and λ_2 are, respectively, the sparsity and regularization parameters, the problem can be formulated as (using N training scans):

$$\min_{\mathbf{w}_i,\, \mathbf{D}} \frac{1}{N} \sum_{i=1}^{N} \Big(\|\mathbf{v}_i - \mathbf{D}\mathbf{w}_i\|_2^2 + \ell_{1,2}(\mathbf{w}_i) \Big), \tag{2}$$

where $\mathbf{v}_i \in \mathbb{R}^{3m}$ is the vector of deviations between scan i and the average model (being m the number of points in the scans), the columns of the dictionary

$\mathbf{D} \in \mathbb{R}^{3m \times k}$ are the basis components, $\mathbf{w}_i \in \mathbb{R}^k$ are the coefficients of the dictionary learning, and k is the number of basis components of the dictionary. Note that the number of components (dictionary atoms) is fixed and pre-determined. The coefficients vector $\mathbf{w} \in \mathbb{R}^k$ provides an estimate of the degree of importance that each atom had in reconstructing the training set; in comparison with the classic framework based on PCA, these can be interpreted similarly to the eigenvalues. A favorable characteristic of the DL-3DMM is that, oppositely to PCA, larger dictionaries lead to more accurate reconstructions and are likely to include sparser and complementary atoms; this facilitates the identification of the atoms that involve particular face areas. More details on the dictionary learning procedure can be found in [15].

The average model $\mathbf{m}$, the dictionary $\mathbf{D}$ and $\mathbf{w}$, constitute the DL-3DMM.

3.2 DL-3DMM Fitting

Fitting a 3DMM to a 2D face image allows a coarse 3D reconstruction of the face. To this end, estimating the 3D pose of the face, and the correspondence between 3D and 2D landmarks are prerequisites. In order to estimate the pose, a set of 49 facial landmarks $\mathbf{l} \in \mathbb{R}^{2\times 49}$ is detected on the 2D face image using the technique proposed in [21], while an equivalent set of vertices $\mathbf{L} \in \mathbb{R}^{3\times 49}$ is manually annotated on the average 3D model. Under an affine camera model [26], the relation between $\mathbf{L}$ and $\mathbf{l}$ is:

$$\mathbf{l} = \mathbf{A} \cdot \mathbf{L} + \mathbf{T}. \tag{3}$$

The affine matrix is directly estimated with a closed-form least squares solution since, by construction, facial landmark detectors do not permit outliers or unreasonable arrangement of the landmarks. The 2D translation is instead recovered as $\mathbf{T} = \mathbf{l} - \mathbf{A} \cdot \mathbf{L}$. The estimated pose $\mathbf{P}$ is represented as $[\mathbf{A}, \mathbf{T}]$ and used to map each vertex of the 3DMM onto the image.

Using the learned dictionary $\mathbf{D} = [\mathbf{d}_1, \ldots, \mathbf{d}_k]$, the average model is non-rigidly transformed such that the projection minimizes the error in correspondence to the landmarks. The coding is formulated as the solution of a regularized *Ridge-Regression* problem:

$$\arg\min_{\alpha} \left\| \mathbf{l} - \mathbf{PL} - \sum_{i=1}^{k} \mathbf{Pd}_i(\mathbf{I}_v)\alpha_i \right\|_2^2 + \lambda \left\| \boldsymbol{\alpha} \circ \mathbf{w}^{-1} \right\|_2, \tag{4}$$

where $\circ$ is the Hadamard product and $\mathbf{I}_v$ are the indices that correspond to the vertices of the landmarks in the 3D model. By defining $\mathbf{X} = \mathbf{l} - \mathbf{L}$ and $\mathbf{Y} = \mathbf{PD}(\mathbf{I}_v)$, the solution can be found in closed form as follows:

$$\boldsymbol{\alpha} = \left(\mathbf{Y}^T\mathbf{Y} + \lambda \cdot \mathrm{diag}(\mathbf{w}^{-1})\right)^{-1} \mathbf{Y}^T\mathbf{X}. \tag{5}$$

Again, for a detailed description of the procedure the reader can refer to [15]. A fitting example obtained using this solution is shown in Fig. 1; the 3D model is deformed according to the target face image, the vertices of the model can be projected onto the face image exploiting the estimated pose so that we can sample its texture.

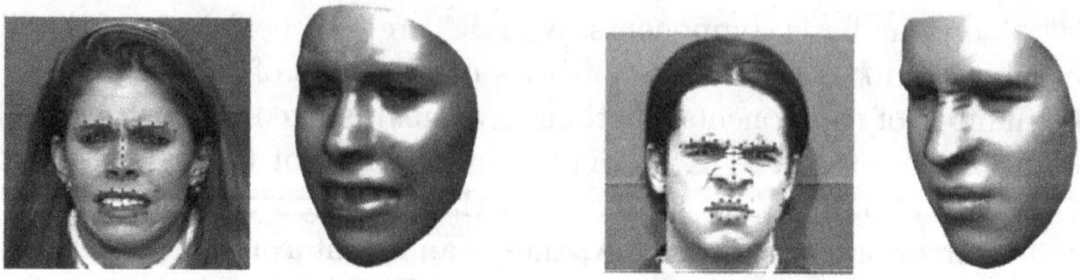

Fig. 1. Examples of DL-3DMM fitting on expressive face images from the Cohn-Kanade (CK+) dataset [23]

4 Learning Expression Coefficients

Given the DL-3DMM as described above, the result of the fitting procedure is a set of coefficients $\boldsymbol{\alpha}$ that are used to deform the average model using Eq. (1). Considering a generic face image, the latter coefficients codify the global shape deformation (*i.e.*, the identity) along with other deformations (*i.e.*, expressions). Our main goal is to derive the set of coefficients that reproduce expressions; in order to do so, we first need to isolate the identity component from the deformation. To this aim, we first fit the DL-3DMM to a face image in neutral expression to account for the identity and obtain the coefficients $\boldsymbol{\alpha}_{id}$; subsequently, the fitted model is used in place of the average model to fit an expressive face image of the same subject. In this way, we obtain a set of coefficients $\boldsymbol{\alpha}_{expr}$ that codify the expression. The procedure is depicted in Fig. 2. The final and crucial step is to find a recurrent pattern in the $\boldsymbol{\alpha}_{expr}$ coefficients, separately for each expression. To this end, we propose to investigate and compare the appropriateness of different methods using: *(i)* statistical indicators; *(ii)* regressors.

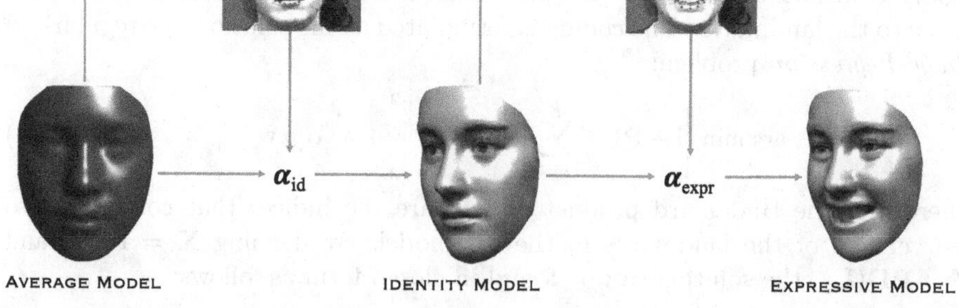

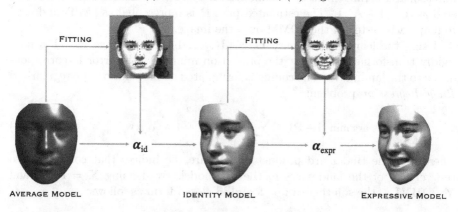

Fig. 2. Workflow of the proposed procedure to extract the expression-specific deformation coefficients from the DL-3DMM fitting

Statistical Indicators. First, we have investigated some basic statistical indicators, namely *mean*, *median* and *mode*. Best results have been obtained with the latter, which we estimated using the *mean-shift* algorithm. Using a Gaussian kernel

$$K(x_i - x) = e^{-c||x_i - x||^2},$$

a centroid x_i at iteration t is updated with $x_i^{t+1} = x_i^t + m(x)$, at iteration $t+1$, with

$$m(x_i) = \frac{\sum_{x_j \in N(x_i)} K(x_j - x_i)x_j}{\sum_{x_j \in N(x_i)} K(x_j - x_i)}.$$

In this latter equation, $N(x_i)$ is a neighborhood of x_i, that is the set of points such that $K(x_i) \neq 0$, and $m(x)$ is the *mean shift vector*. The centroid updating is repeated till the convergence of $m(x)$. The only parameter used in this algorithm is the *bandwidth*, *i.e*, the radius of the gaussian region. In our case, we search for the centroid best representing the data distribution. To this end, we started with a fixed *bandwidth* and repeated the mean shift iteration by increasing the radius; the procedure terminates when an individual point is returned; this centroid is assumed as the vector representing the data distribution of a given expression.

At this stage, we also used the mean-shift algorithm to investigate the data distribution. To this end, first, we fixed the *bandwidth*, applied the algorithm, took the resulting number of centroids and counted how many samples fall in the region of influence of the centroids. Table 1 reports the results for each expression. It can be observed as the first centroid, located at the maximum peak of the data distribution, is the most representative of the samples: arguably, this is due to the fact the other maxima capture possible outliers or errors included in the dataset.

Table 1. For each expression, the number of centroids found by fixing the *bandwidth*, and the percentage of vectors that fall in the region of the first centroid are reported. Expressions in the Cohn-Kanade (CK+) dataset have been used here

Expression	#Centroids	% vectors first centroid
Angry	4	93%
Contempt	5	73%
Disgust	2	98%
Fear	2	96%
Happy	5	92%
Sadness	3	93%
Surprise	2	95%

As a further analysis, we iterated the algorithm by augmenting the *bandwidth* so as to find two centroids. Then, we have compared the faces obtained by applying both the weight vectors corresponding to the two maxima for each expression. Results indicated that the deformed faces obtained from the weight vector of the first maximum are the same as those obtained using a single maximum; applying the weight vector corresponding to the second maximum, instead, resulted in non-realistic faces.

Regressors. In the following, we model the problem of estimating the deformation coefficients of the 3DMM as a regression one, using the Support Vector Regression (SVR) technique. A cross validation process has been used to determine the train/test splits. The coefficients vectors have been used as "multi-labels" that are predicted using a *multi-output* regressor, which repeats the estimate for each component of the array. The regressor is controlled by parameters that do not depend on the dimensionality of the feature space. In our case, a 4-fold cross validation has been performed to determine the best kernel and the values of the parameters C and ϵ of the regressor.

As a result, for both the methods, we obtained for each expression a set of coefficients $\boldsymbol{\alpha}_{est}$ that allow the application of an expression to a subject-specific model in neutral expression.

5 Experimental Results

In this Section, we first describes the dataset adopted for the experimental evaluation (Sect. 5.1), then we provide a qualitative evaluation (Sect. 5.2), of the different modalities we have used for model parameter estimation.

5.1 Dataset

The experiments have been performed on the Extended Cohn-Kanade (CK+) dataset [23], which includes about 600 sequences of 123 subjects showing 7 different expressions, namely *Disgust, Surprise, Angry, Sadness, Fear, Contempt, Happy*; for each sequence the neutral (first) and expressive (last) frames have been used. The DL-3DMM has been deformed to each of these frames using the fitting procedure illustrated in Sect. 3.2; we used a dictionary of 300 atoms. A subset of the 123 individuals has been used to learn the parameters so as to test on different identities. For neutral frames, these coefficients capture the shape information of the individual; for expressive scans, we first deformed the 3DMM on the neutral frame of the same subject, then from this to the expressive frame, following the procedure of Fig. 2. In this way, the coefficients capture the shape deformation to pass from a neutral to an expressive scan for a specific identity.

5.2 Qualitative Results

In order to derive qualitative results, we fitted the DL-3DMM to some neutral faces of the dataset and applied the estimated deformation coefficients $\boldsymbol{\alpha}_{est}$ so as to generate expressive scans for each expression. Figure 3 shows some examples of generated expressive renderings starting from the neutral one and applying the deformation. The magnitude of the deformations can be controlled with a parameter λ, useful to emphasize subtle expressions that do not sufficiently change the neutral face (*e.g.*, contempt). The expressive models generated from the neutral 3DMM according to the learned deformation vectors are rendered for qualitative evaluation. Some examples can be appreciated in Fig. 3; starting

Fig. 3. Qualitative examples of synthetically generated expressive renderings of two subjects from the CK+ dataset. The leftmost column reports the 3DMM fitting to the neutral face images of the two subjects, while the other columns report the models derived from the neutral ones by applying the deformation coefficients corresponding to each expression, from *disgust* to *happy*, left-to-right

from the neutral expression, we can effectively generate expressive renderings applying the expression-specific parameters separately.

Figure 4 shows another interesting application of our method, that is the generation of complex expressions by combining the parameters of the single prototypical expressions. This feature allows us to mix an arbitrary number of expressions and further demonstrates the meaningfulness of the estimated parameters. The examples in Fig. 4 are generated using a combination of 2 (top row) or 3 (bottom row) basic expressions. A drawback of this application is that if the weights of the single expressions are not balanced, the final model can result noisy or excessively deformed.

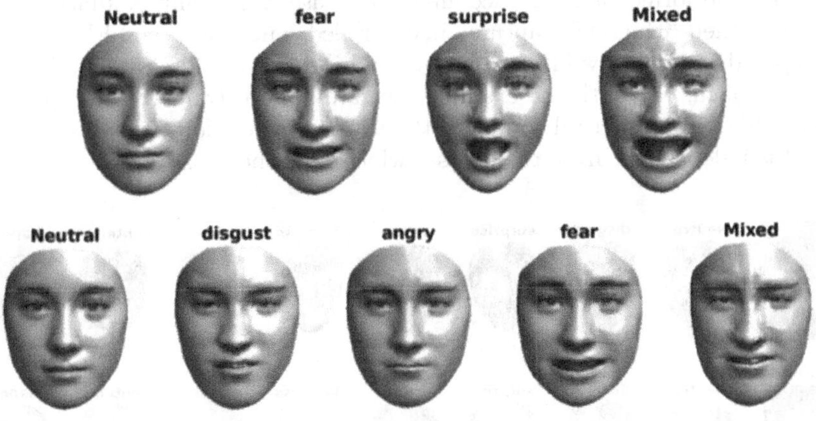

Fig. 4. Qualitative examples of mixed deformations on one subject of the CK+ dataset; two (top row) or three (bottom row) prototypical expressions have been used

In Fig. 5, we show a comparison between the different techniques used to estimate the $\boldsymbol{\alpha}_{est}$ coefficients; the generated images are rather similar to each other, even using basic statistical indicators as the mean. This suggests us that the elements of the dictionary are effective in separating the identity and expression components and that our methodology allows us to easily extrapolate expression-specific patterns within the deformation coefficients.

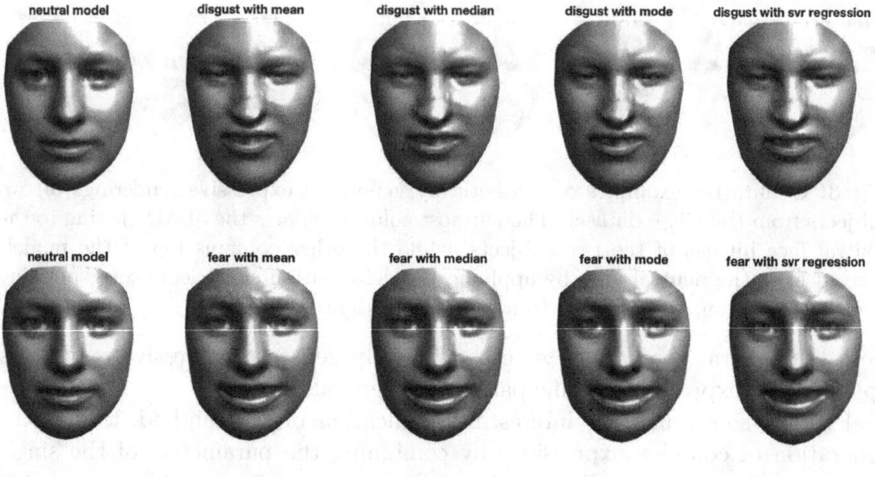

Fig. 5. Qualitative comparison of the different parameters estimation methods

Finally, Fig. 6 shows the application of our expression transfer method to face images coming from different datasets, demonstrating the generalization capability of our approach in a cross-dataset scenario. Specifically, Fig. 6 (top row) shows a face image from the Bosphorus dataset [32], while in Fig. 6 (bottom row) a face image coming from the Labeled Faces in The Wild dataset (LFW) [18] is shown. The former is a 3D face analysis dataset and comprises face images along with their 3D models captured in controlled conditions; the LFW, instead, is composed of "in the wild" face images and is used to address the face verification problem. For both the examples, we are able to transfer the expression of the subject from neutral to any of the learned expressions; this because the 3DMM is independent from the dataset which is applied to.

Fig. 6. Cross-dataset evaluation of the proposed method on sample images from the Bosphorus (top row) and LFW (bottom row)

6 Conclusions

In this paper, we have proposed a method to isolate the expression-specific deformation parameters of a 3DMM and applied them to synthetically generate expressive renderings of subjects in neutral expression. We exploited a peculiar 3DMM implementation based on a dictionary learning technique, able to reproduce expressions thanks to the inclusion of expressive scans in the training set. We showed that our two-step 3DMM fitting methodology is effective in removing the identity component from the 3DMM fitting, and that expression-specific recurrent patterns can be easily found within the parameters used to fit the subject-specific model to its own expressive image. Moreover, the recovered parameters can be effectively mixed so as to generate more complex expressions. However, our solution is not exempt from limitations: first, expressions might be more or less subtle; this means that they must be weighted accordingly in order not to produce exaggerated or imperceptible deformations. Another issue arose is that the textured renderings might result somewhat unnatural at times when trying to generate expressions that are very diverse from the neutral one. Indeed, we can assume that even a very slight expressiveness might be present in "neutral" frames. As a future work, we are considering an extension of the technique to the texture component of the images.

Acknowledgments. The authors would like to thank Gabriele Barlacchi, Francesco Lombardi, Alessandro Sestini, and Alessandro Soci for developing and experimenting part of the code used in this work.

References

1. Amberg, B., Knothe, R., Vetter, T.: Expression invariant 3D face recognition with a morphable model. In: IEEE International Conference on Automatic Face and Gesture Recognition (2008)
2. Amberg, B., Romdhani, S., Vetter, T.: Optimal step nonrigid ICP algorithms for surface registration. In: IEEE International Conference on Computer Vision and Pattern Recognition, pp. 1–8. Minneapolis, MN, June 2007
3. Baranyi, R., Willinger, R., Lederer, N., Grechenig, T., Schramm, W.: Chances for serious games in rehabilitation of stroke patients on the example of utilizing the Wii Fit Balance Board. In: IEEE International Conference on Serious Games and Applications for Health (SeGAH), pp. 1–7, May 2013. https://doi.org/10.1109/SeGAH.2013.6665319
4. Bejaoui, H., Ghazouani, H., Barhoumi, W.: Fully automated facial expression recognition using 3D morphable model and mesh-local binary pattern. In: Blanc-Talon, J., Penne, R., Philips, W., Popescu, D., Scheunders, P. (eds.) ACIVS 2017. LNCS, vol. 10617, pp. 39–50. Springer, Cham (2017). https://doi.org/10.1007/978-3-319-70353-4_4
5. Blanz, V., Vetter, T.: A morphable model for the synthesis of 3D faces. In: ACM Conference on Computer Graphics and Interactive Techniques (1999)
6. Blanz, V., Vetter, T.: Face recognition based on fitting a 3D morphable model. IEEE Trans Pattern Anal. Mach. Intell. **25**(9), 1063–1074 (2003)

7. Booth, J., Antonakos, E., Ploumpis, S., Trigeorgis, G., Panagakis, Y., Zafeiriou, S.: 3D face morphable models "in-the-wild". In: IEEE Conference on Computer Vision and Pattern Recognition (CVPR), pp. 5464–5473, July 2017. https://doi.org/10.1109/CVPR.2017.580
8. Booth, J., Roussos, A., Zafeiriou, S., Ponniahand, A., Dunaway, D.: A 3D morphable model learnt from 10,000 faces. In: IEEE Conference on Computer Vision and Pattern Recognition, pp. 5543–5552 (2016)
9. Brunton, A., Bolkart, T., Wuhrer, S.: Multilinear wavelets: a statistical shape space for human faces. In: Fleet, D., Pajdla, T., Schiele, B., Tuytelaars, T. (eds.) ECCV 2014. LNCS, vol. 8689, pp. 297–312. Springer, Cham (2014). https://doi.org/10.1007/978-3-319-10590-1_20
10. Chang, F.J., Tran, A., Hassner, T., Masi, I., Nevatia, R., Medioni, G.: ExpNet: landmark-free, deep, 3d facial expressions. In: IEEE Conference on Automatic Face and Gesture Recognition (2018)
11. Cosker, D., Krumhuber, E., Hilton, A.: Perception of linear and nonlinear motion properties using a FACS validated 3D facial model. In: ACM Applied Perception in Graphics and Vision (2010)
12. Cosker, D., Krumhuber, E., Hilton, A.: A FACS valid 3D dynamic action unit database with applications to 3D dynamic morphable facial modeling. In: International Conference on Computer Vision (2011)
13. Cosker, D., Krumhuber, E., Hilton, A.: Perceived emotionality of linear and nonlinear AUs synthesised using a 3D dynamic morphable facial model. In: Proceedings of the Facial Analysis and Animation, FAA 2015, pp. 7:1–7:1. ACM (2015)
14. Dou, P., Shah, S.K., Kakadiaris, I.A.: End-to-end 3D face reconstruction with deep neural networks. In: IEEE Conference on Computer Vision and Pattern Recognition (CVPR), pp. 1503–1512, July 2017. https://doi.org/10.1109/CVPR.2017.164
15. Ferrari, C., Lisanti, G., Berretti, S., Del Bimbo, A.: A dictionary learning-based 3D morphable shape model. IEEE Trans. Multimedia **19**(12), 2666–2679 (2017). https://doi.org/10.1109/TMM.2017.2707341
16. Grupp, M., Kopp, P., Huber, P., Rätsch, M.: A 3D face modelling approach for pose-invariant face recognition in a human-robot environment. CoRR abs/1606.00474 (2016)
17. Hu, G., et al.: Face recognition using a unified 3D morphable model. In: Leibe, B., Matas, J., Sebe, N., Welling, M. (eds.) ECCV 2016. LNCS, vol. 9912, pp. 73–89. Springer, Cham (2016). https://doi.org/10.1007/978-3-319-46484-8_5
18. Huang, G.B., Ramesh, M., Berg, T., Learned-Miller, E.: Labeled faces in the wild: a database for studying face recognition in unconstrained environments. Technical report 07-49. University of Massachusetts, Amherst, October 2007
19. Huang, Y., Khan, S.M.: DyadGAN: generating facial expressions in dyadic interactions. In: IEEE Conference on Computer Vision and Pattern Recognition Workshops (CVPRW), pp. 2259–2266, July 2017. https://doi.org/10.1109/CVPRW.2017.280
20. Huber, P., Kopp, P., Rätsch, M., Christmas, W.J., Kittler, J.: 3D face tracking and texture fusion in the wild. CoRR abs/1605.06764 (2016). http://arxiv.org/abs/1605.06764
21. Kazemi, V., Sullivan, J.: One millisecond face alignment with an ensemble of regression trees. In: IEEE Conference on Computer Vision and Pattern Recognition (2014)
22. Liarokapis, F., Debattista, K., Vourvopoulos, A., Petridis, P., Ene, A.: Comparing interaction techniques for serious games through brain-computer interfaces: a user perception evaluation study. Entertain. Comput. **5**(4), 391–399 (2014). https://doi.org/10.1016/j.entcom.2014.10.004. http://www.sciencedirect.com/science/article/pii/S1875952114000391

23. Lucey, P., Cohn, J.F., Kanade, T., Saragih, J., Ambadar, Z., Matthews, I.: The extended Cohn-Kanade dataset (CK+): a complete dataset for action unit and emotion-specified expression. In: IEEE Conference on Computer Vision and Pattern Recognition-Workshops (2010)
24. Lüthi, M., Jud, C., Gerig, T., Vetter, T.: Gaussian process morphable models. CoRR abs/1603.07254 (2016). http://arxiv.org/abs/1603.07254
25. Mairal, J., Bach, F., Ponce, J., Sapiro, G.: Online dictionary learning for sparse coding. In: International Conference on Machine Learning (2009)
26. Masi, I., Ferrari, C., Del Bimbo, A., Medioni, G.: Pose independent face recognition by localizing local binary patterns via deformation components. In: International Conference on Pattern Recognition (2014)
27. Patel, A., Smith, W.A.P.: 3D morphable face models revisited. In: IEEE Conference on Computer Vision and Pattern Recognition (2009)
28. Paysan, P., Knothe, R., Amberg, B., Romdhani, S., Vetter, T.: A 3D face model for pose and illumination invariant face recognition. In: IEEE International Conference on Advanced Video and Signal Based Surveillance (AVSS), pp. 296–301 (2009)
29. Qiao, F., Yao, N., Jiao, Z., Li, Z., Chen, H., Wang, H.: Geometry-contrastive generative adversarial network for facial expression synthesis. CoRR abs/1802.01822 (2018). http://arxiv.org/abs/1802.01822
30. Ramanathan, S., Kassim, A., Venkatesh, Y.V., Wah, W.S.: Human facial expression recognition using a 3D morphable model. In: International Conference on Image Processing (2006)
31. Romdhani, S., Vetter, T.: Estimating 3D shape and texture using pixel intensity, edges, specular highlights, texture constraints and a prior. In: IEEE Conference on Computer Vision and Pattern Recognition (2005)
32. Savran, A., et al.: Bosphorus database for 3D face analysis. In: Schouten, B., Juul, N.C., Drygajlo, A., Tistarelli, M. (eds.) BioID 2008. LNCS, vol. 5372, pp. 47–56. Springer, Heidelberg (2008). https://doi.org/10.1007/978-3-540-89991-4_6
33. Tran, A.T., Hassner, T., Masi, I., Medioni, G.: Regressing robust and discriminative 3D morphable models with a very deep neural network. In: IEEE Conference on Computer Vision and Pattern Recognition (CVPR), pp. 5163–5172, July 2017
34. Ujir, H., Spann, M.: Facial expression recognition using FAPs-based 3DMM. In: Tavares, J., Natal Jorge, R. (eds.) Topics in Medical Image Processing and Computational Vision. LNCS, pp. 33–47. Springer, Netherlands (2013). https://doi.org/10.1007/978-94-007-0726-9_
35. Yi, D., Lei, Z., Li, S.Z.: Towards pose robust face recognition. In: IEEE Conference on Computer Vision and Pattern Recognition (2013)
36. Yin, L., Wei, X., Sun, Y., Wang, J., Rosato, M.: A 3D facial expression database for facial behavior research. In: IEEE International Conference on Automatic Face and Gesture Recognition (2006)
37. Zakari, H.M., Ma, M., Simmons, D.: A review of serious games for children with autism spectrum disorders (ASD). In: Ma, M., Oliveira, M.F., Baalsrud Hauge, J. (eds.) SGDA 2014. LNCS, vol. 8778, pp. 93–106. Springer, Cham (2014). https://doi.org/10.1007/978-3-319-11623-5_9
38. Zhu, X., Lei, Z., Liu, X., Shi, H., Li, S.Z.: Face alignment across large poses: a 3D solution. In: IEEE Conference on Computer Vision and Pattern Recognition (2016)

Deep Multitask Gaze Estimation with a Constrained Landmark-Gaze Model

Yu Yu[1,2(✉)], Gang Liu[1], and Jean-Marc Odobez[1,2]

[1] Idiap Research Institute, Martigny, Switzerland
{yyu,gang.liu,odobez}@idiap.ch
[2] EPFL, Lausanne, Switzerland

Abstract. As an indicator of attention, gaze is an important cue for human behavior and social interaction analysis. Recent deep learning methods for gaze estimation rely on plain regression of the gaze from images without accounting for potential mismatches in eye image cropping and normalization. This may impact the estimation of the implicit relation between visual cues and the gaze direction when dealing with low resolution images or when training with a limited amount of data. In this paper, we propose a deep multitask framework for gaze estimation, with the following contributions. (i) we proposed a multitask framework which relies on both synthetic data and real data for end-to-end training. During training, each dataset provides the label of only one task but the two tasks are combined in a constrained way. (ii) we introduce a Constrained Landmark-Gaze Model (CLGM) modeling the joint variation of eye landmark locations (including the iris center) and gaze directions. By relating explicitly visual information (landmarks) to the more abstract gaze values, we demonstrate that the estimator is more accurate and easier to learn. (iii) by decomposing our deep network into a network inferring jointly the parameters of the CLGM model and the scale and translation parameters of eye regions on one hand, and a CLGM based decoder deterministically inferring landmark positions and gaze from these parameters and head pose on the other hand, our framework decouples gaze estimation from irrelevant geometric variations in the eye image (scale, translation), resulting in a more robust model. Thorough experiments on public datasets demonstrate that our method achieves competitive results, improving over state-of-the-art results in challenging free head pose gaze estimation tasks and on eye landmark localization (iris location) ones.

1 Introduction

Gaze is the essential indicator of human attention and can even provide access to thought processes [1–3]. In interactions, it is a non-verbal behavior that plays a major role in all communication aspects [4], and it has also been shown to be related to higher-level constructs, like personality, dominance, or rapport. Gaze is thus an important cue for human behavior analysis, and beyond traditional screen-gazing monitoring, 3D gaze estimation finds application in health

L. Leal-Taixé and S. Roth (Eds.): ECCV 2018 Workshops, LNCS 11130, pp. 456–474, 2019.
https://doi.org/10.1007/978-3-030-11012-3_35

care [5], social interaction analysis [6], human computer interaction (HCI) or human robotic interaction (HRI) [7,8]. In another context, the new generation of smart phones like iPhone X and their extended applications raise further interest in gaze estimation under mobile scenarios [9–11].

Traditional gaze estimation methods include model-based geometrical methods and appearance based methods. The former are more accurate, but the techniques used so far to extract eye landmarks (eye corners, iris) require high resolution images (limiting the freedom of motion) and relatively open eyes since the gaze is estimated from sparse features which are most often detected in a separate task. The latter methods have been shown to be more robust to eye resolution or gazing direction (*e.g.* looking down with eyelid occlusion) variabilities. Thus, this is not surprising that recent works have explored inferring gaze from the eye image via deep regression [9,12–14]. Nevertheless, although progress has been reported, direct regression of gaze still suffers from limitations:

- Since the ground truth of gaze vector is hard to annotate, the amount of training data for gaze estimation is limited (number of people, illumination conditions, annotation accuracies) compared to other computer vision tasks. Although there has been some synthetic data [15] for gaze estimation, the appearance and gaze setting of synthetic data is somehow different to real data. Therefore, this currently hinders the benefits of deep learning for gaze.
- An accurate and unified eye cropping is difficult to achieve in real application. This means the size and location of the eye regions may significantly vary in the cropped eye images, due to bad eye/landmark localization, or when changing datasets. Since the gaze estimation is very sensitive to the subtle relative positions and shapes of eye landmarks, such variations can significantly alter the gaze estimation outcomes. Though data augmentation can partially handle this problem, an explicit model of this step may improve the generalization ability to new datasets, unperfect cropping, or new eyes.

To address these issues, we propose an end-to-end trainable deep multitask framework based on a Constrained Landmark-Gaze Model, with the following properties.

First, we address eye landmark (including iris center) detection and gaze estimation jointly. Indeed, since gaze values are strongly correlated with eye landmark locations, we hypothesize that modeling eye landmark detection (which is an explicit visual task) as an auxiliary task can ease the learning of a predictive model of the more abstract gaze information. To the best of our knowledge, this is the first time that multitask learning is applied to gaze estimation. Since there is no existing large scale dataset which annotates detailed eye landmarks, we rely on a synthetic dataset for the learning of the auxiliary task in this paper. Note that we only use the landmark annotations from the synthetic data because of the different gaze setting of synthetic data. The use of synthetic data also expands the amount of training data to some extent.

Second, instead of predicting eye landmarks and gaze in two network branches as in usual deep multitask learning, we build a Constrained Landmark-Gaze

Model (CLGM) modeling the joint variation of eye landmark location and gaze direction, which bridges the two tasks in a closer and more explicit way.

Third, we make our approach more robust to scale, translation and even head pose variations by relying on a deterministic decoder. More precisely, the network learns two sets of parameters, which are the coefficients of the CLGM model, and the scale and translation parameters defining the eye region. Using these parameters and the head pose, the decoder deterministically predicts the eye landmark locations and gaze via the CLGM. Note however that while all parameters account for defining the landmark positions, only the CLGM coefficients and the head pose are used for gaze prediction. Thus, gaze estimation is decoupled from irrelevant variations in scale and translation and geometrically modeled within the head pose frame.

Finally, note that while currently landmark detection is used as a secondary task, it could be used as a primary task as well to extract the features (eye corners, iris center) requested by a geometrical eye gaze model, which can potentially be more accurate. In particular, the CLGM could help predicting iris location even when the eyes are not fully open (see Fig. 7 for examples).

Thus, in summary, our contributions are as follows:

- A Constrained Landmark-Gaze Model modeling the joint variation of eye landmarks and gaze;
- Gaze estimation robust to translation, scale and head pose achieved by a CLGM based decoder;
- An end-to-end trainable deep multitask learning framework for gaze estimation with the help of CLGM and synthetic data.

Thorough experiments on public datasets for both gaze estimation and landmark (iris) localization demonstrate the validity of our approach.

The rest of the paper is organized as follows. We introduce related works in Sect. 2. The correlation between eye landmarks and gaze is studied in Sect. 3. The proposed method is presented in Sect. 4, while experimental results are reported in Sect. 5.

2 Related Work

We introduce the current related researches in gaze estimation and multitask learning as follows.

Gaze Estimation. In this paper, we mainly investigated the vision based non-invasive and non-active (i.e. without infra-red sources) remote gaze estimation methods. They can be grouped into two categories, the geometric based methods (GBM) and appearance based methods (ABM) [16].

GBM methods rely on a geometric model of the eye whose parameters (like eye ball center and radius, pupil center and radius) can be estimated from features extracted in training images [17–25] and can further be used to infer the gaze direction. They usually require high resolution eye images from near frontal head poses to obtain stable and accurate feature detection, which limits the user mobility and their application to many settings of interest.

By learning a mapping from the eye appearance to the gaze, ABM methods [11,26] are more robust to lower resolution images. They usually extract visual features like Retinex feature [27] and mHOG [28], and train regression models such as Random Forest [29], Adaptive Linear Regression [30], Support Vector Regression [28] for gaze estimation. Very often ABM methods assumed static head pose, but recently head pose dependent image normalization have been tested with success, as done for instance in [31] where a 3D morphable model is used for pose normalization. In general, ABM methods require a large amount of data for training and they do not model the person gaze variation explicitly with a model.

Recent works started to use deep learning to regress gaze directly from the eye image [9,12–14,32]. Krafka et al. [9] proposed to learn the gaze fixation point on smart phone screens using the images taken from the front-facing camera. Their network takes 4 channels including full face image and eye images as input. To train their network, they collected a large dataset with 2.5M frames and an accurate estimator with 2 cm error is achieved. Nevertheless, this dataset does not provide the groundtruth for the 3D gaze direction, which is much harder to label than 2D gaze fixation point. Zhang et al. [13] proposed a dataset for 3D gaze estimation. However, the number of participants is much smaller, which may limit model generalization when being used for training. In Zhang's work, the head pose was linearly modeled when estimating gaze. This design is challenged in [12] where the correlation between the gaze and head pose is explicitly taken into account, which may reflect prior information between these two quantities, but does not account for eye shape or eye cropping variabilities.

The above works basically regress gaze directly from the eye appearances or full faces. In contrast, several methods [33–35] attempt to learn gaze via some intermediate representations or features, including eye landmarks [34,35]. A similar approach to this paper is proposed in [33] where the network learns the heatmaps of eye landmarks first. The gaze is then predicted based on the landmark heatmaps. Our paper differs from this work in that the eye landmarks and gaze are jointly modeled with a constrained framework and they are predicted in the same stage.

Multitask Learning. Multitask learning aims to improve the overall performance of one or each task by providing implicit data augmentation or regularizations [36]. Due to the flexibility of network architectures, a number of works have been proposed on deep multitask learning. The classical implementation is to share parameters in shallow layers and arrange task-specific branches in deeper layers. Many of the representative works are face-related research [37–41] since there are plenty of datasets with rich annotations in this area and the face attributes are also well correlated. Some other works, however, attempted to propose novel multitask learning architectures which could generalize well on other tasks. For example, the Cross-stitch Network [42] designed a cross-stitch unit to leverage the activations from multiple models thus the parameters are shared softly. However, the network architecture and the placing of cross-stitch are still manually determined. Instead of hand designing the multitask learning architecture, Lu et al. [43] proposed to dynamically create network branches for tasks during training so fully adaptive feature sharing is achieved. Nevertheless, their approach did not model the interactions between tasks.

To the best of our knowledge, we are not aware of any multi-task learning framework for gaze estimation.

3 Correlation of Eye Landmarks and Gaze

Before introducing our method, we first study the correlation existing between the gaze and eye landmarks. We used the synthetic database UnityEyes [15] for correlation analysis since this database provides rich and accurate information regarding the landmark and gaze values. As this dataset relies on a synthetic yet realistic model of the eye ball and shape, and since this database has been used for the training of gaze estimators which have achieved very high performance on real datasets [15], we expect this correlation analysis to be rather accurate. In any case, in Sect. 4.3, we show how we can account for the discrepancy between the synthetic model and real data.

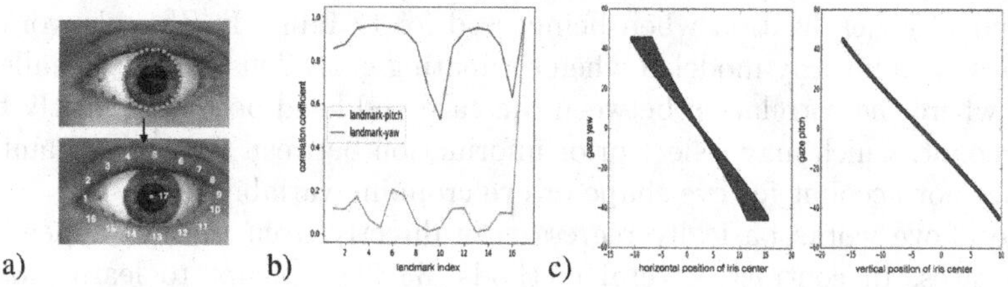

Fig. 1. Correlation between the eye landmark positions and gaze values, computed from the UnityEyes dataset. (a) selected landmarks (bottom) from the UnityEyes landmark set (top). (b) correlation coefficients between the landmark horizontal or vertical positions and the gaze yaw or pitch angles. (c) joint distribution map of the horizontal or vertical positions of the iris center and of the yaw or pitch gaze angles. (Color figure online)

Landmark Set. The UnityEyes annotates three types of eye landmarks, the caruncle landmarks, the eyelid landmarks and the iris landmarks, as shown in the first row of Fig. 1a. Considering that relying on many landmarks will not help improving the robustness and accuracy but simply increase the complexity of the method, we only selected a subset $\mathcal{I}$ of the available landmark instead. It contains 16 landmarks from the eyelid, and the iris center which is estimated from the iris contour landmarks. This is illustrated in the second row of Fig. 1a.

Landmark Alignment. We generated 50,000 UnityEyes samples with frontal head pose and a gaze value uniformly sampled within the [−45°, 45°] range for both pitch and yaw. All the samples are aligned on a global center point c_l.

Correlation Analysis. We assign the landmark indices as shown in Fig. 1a. Then we compute the correlation coefficient between each landmark and gaze coordinates. More precisely, two correlation coefficients are computed: the gaze yaw - horizontal landmark position and the gaze pitch - vertical landmark position. They are displayed in Fig. 1b.

The following comments can be made. First, the position of the iris center (landmark 17) is strongly correlated with gaze, as expected. The correlation coefficient between the horizontal (respectively vertical) position of the iris center and the gaze yaw (respectively pitch) is close to 1. Furthermore, the joint data distribution between the iris center and gaze displayed in Fig. 1c indicates that they seem to follow a linear relationship, especially in the pitch direction. Second, the gaze pitch is also highly correlated with other landmarks (red curve in Fig. 1b). This reflects that looking up or looking down requires some eyelid movement which are thus quite indicative of the gaze pitch. Third, the gaze yaw is only weakly correlated with eyelid landmarks, which means that looking to the left or right is mainly conducted by iris movements.

In summary, we find that the eye landmarks are correlated with the gaze and therefore they can provide strong support cues for estimating gaze.

4 Method

The proposed framework is shown in Fig. 2. It consists of two parts. The first part is a neural network which takes an eye image as input and regresses two sets of parameters: the coefficients of our joint CLGM landmarks and gaze model, and the scale and translation defining the eye region. The second part is a deterministic decoder. Based on the Constrained Landmark-Gaze model, it reconstructs the eye landmark positions and gaze with the two sets of parameters and the head pose. Note that in the reconstruction, the eye landmarks are computed using all parameters while the gaze is only determined using the CLGM coefficients and the head pose. An end-to-end training of the network is performed by combining the losses on landmark localization and gaze estimation. In our approach, we assume that the head pose has been obtained in advance. Below, we provide more details about the different parts of the model.

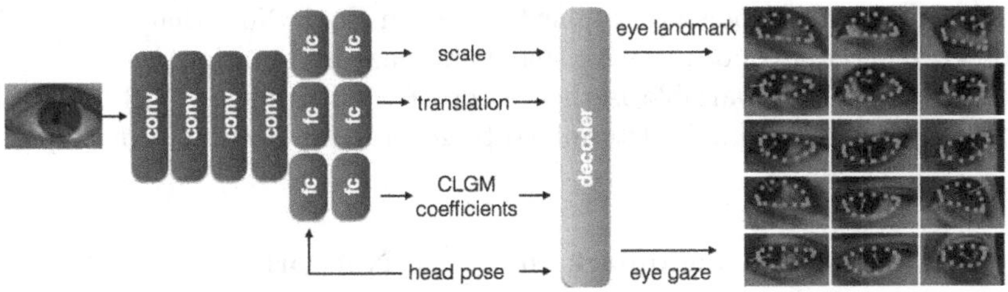

Fig. 2. Framework of the proposed method.

4.1 Constrained Landmark-Gaze Model

As with the 3D Morphable Model [44] or the Constrained Local Model [45] for faces, the eye shape can also be modeled statistically. Concretely, an eye shape can be decomposed as a weighted linear combination of a mean shape and a series of deformation bases according to:

$$\mathbf{v}_l(\alpha) = \mu^l + \sum_j \alpha_j \lambda_j^l \mathbf{b}_j^l, \tag{1}$$

where μ^l is the mean eye shape and λ_j^l represents the eigenvalue of the jth linear deformation basis $\mathbf{b}_j^l$. The coefficients α denote the variation parameters determining eye shape while the superscript l means landmark.

As demonstrated in the previous section, the eye landmark positions are correlated with the gaze directions. In addition, we can safely assume that the landmark positions are also correlated. Therefore, we propose the Constrained Landmark-Gaze Model to explicitly model the joint variation of eye landmarks and gaze.

Concretely, we first extract the set of landmarks $\mathcal{I}$ from the N_s UnityEyes samples and align them with the global eye center. Denoting by $\mathbf{l}_{k,i} = (\mathbf{l}_{k,i}^x, \mathbf{l}_{k,i}^y)$, the horizontal and vertical positions of the ith landmark of the kth UnityEyes sample, and by $(\mathbf{g}_k^\phi, \mathbf{g}_k^\theta)$ the gaze pitch and yaw of the same sample, we can define the 1-D landmark-gaze array:

$$[\mathbf{l}_{k,1}^y, \cdots, \mathbf{l}_{k,N_l}^y, \mathbf{l}_{k,1}^x, \cdots, \mathbf{l}_{k,N_l}^x, \mathbf{g}_k^\phi, \mathbf{g}_k^\theta] \tag{2}$$

where N_l denotes the number of landmarks ($N_l = 17$), and the superscripts y, x, ϕ, θ represent the vertical position, horizontal position, pitch angle and yaw angle, respectively. This landmark-gaze vector has $2N_l + 2$ elements.

We then stack the vector of each sample into a matrix $\mathbf{M}$ of dimension $N_s \times (2N_l + 2)$, from which the linear bases $\mathbf{b}_j^{lg}$ representing the joint variation of eye landmark locations and gaze directions are derived through Principal Component Analysis (PCA). Thus, the eye shape and gaze of any eye sample can be modeled as:

$$\mathbf{v}_{lg}(\alpha) = \mu^{lg} + \sum_{j=1}^{2N_l+2} \lambda_j^{lg} \alpha_j \mathbf{b}_j^{lg} \tag{3}$$

where the superscript lg denotes the joint modeling of landmark and gaze. The definition of other symbols are similar to those in Eq. 1. Note that the resulting vector $\mathbf{v}_{lg}(\alpha)$ contains both the eye shape and gaze information.

In Eq. 3, the only variable is the vector of coefficients α. With a suitable learning algorithm, α can be determined to generate an accurate eye shape and gaze.

4.2 Joint Gaze and Landmark Inference Network

We use a deep convolutional neural network to jointly infer the gaze and landmark locations, as illustrated in Fig. 2. It comprises two parts: an encoder network inferring the coefficient α of the model in Eq. 3, as well as other geometric parameters, and a decoder computing the actual landmark positions in the image and the gaze directions. The specific architecture for the encoder is described in Sect. 4.4. Below, we detail the decoder component and the loss used to train the network.

Decoder. We recall that the vector $\mathbf{v}_{lg}(\alpha)$ from the CLGM model only provides the aligned landmark positions. Thus, to model the real landmark positions in the cropped eye images, the head pose, the scale and the translation of the eye should be taken into account. In our framework, the scale s and translation $\mathbf{t}$ are inferred explicitly by the network, while the head pose is assumed to have already been estimated (see Fig. 2).

Given the head pose $\mathbf{h}$ and the inferred parameters α, s and $\mathbf{t}$ from the network, a decoder is designed to compute the eye landmark locations and gaze direction. Concretely, the decoder first uses α to computes the aligned eye shape and gaze according to Eq. 3. Then the aligned eye shape is further transformed with the head pose rotation matrix $\mathbf{R}(\mathbf{h})$, the scale s and the translation $\mathbf{t}$ to reconstruct the eye landmark positions in the input image:

$$\begin{bmatrix} \mathbf{l}_p^x \\ \mathbf{l}_p^y \end{bmatrix} = s \cdot \mathbf{Pr} \cdot \mathbf{R}(\mathbf{h}) \cdot \begin{bmatrix} \mathbf{v}_{lg}^x(\alpha) \\ \mathbf{v}_{lg}^y(\alpha) \\ 0 \end{bmatrix} + \mathbf{t} \tag{4}$$

$$\begin{bmatrix} cos(\mathbf{g}_p^\phi)sin(\mathbf{g}_p^\theta) \\ -sin(\mathbf{g}_p^\phi) \\ cos(\mathbf{g}_p^\phi)cos(\mathbf{g}_p^\theta) \end{bmatrix} = \mathbf{R}(\mathbf{h}) \cdot \begin{bmatrix} cos(\mathbf{v}_{lg}^\phi(\alpha))sin(\mathbf{v}_{lg}^\theta(\alpha)) \\ -sin(\mathbf{v}_{lg}^\phi(\alpha)) \\ cos(\mathbf{v}_{lg}^\phi(\alpha))cos(\mathbf{v}_{lg}^\theta(\alpha)) \end{bmatrix} \tag{5}$$

where $\mathbf{l}_p$ and $\mathbf{g}_p$ denote the predicted eye landmark positions and gaze respectively, and $\mathbf{Pr}$ is the projection matrix from 3D to 2D. From the equations above, note that the eye landmark positions are determined by all parameters while the gaze angles are only determined by the coefficient α and the head pose. Thus gaze estimation is geometrically coupled with the head pose as it should be, but is decoupled from the eye scale and translation.

Training Loss. To train the network, we define loss on both the predicted eye landmark positions and on the gaze according to

$$L(I) = w_l||\mathbf{l}_p - \mathbf{l}_g||_2 + w_g||\mathbf{g}_p - \mathbf{g}_g||_1 \tag{6}$$

where $\mathbf{l}_g$ and $\mathbf{g}_g$ represent the ground truth in the image I for the landmark positions and gaze respectively, and w_l and w_g denote the weights for the landmark loss and gaze loss respectively. Note from Eq. 6 that we do not provide any groundtruth for scale or translation during training (or to α), since the network automatically learns how to predict them from the landmark loss.

4.3 CLGM Revisited

As mentioned in Sect. 3, the UnityEyes models only reflects the main correlation between the gaze and eye landmarks. To account for real people and real images

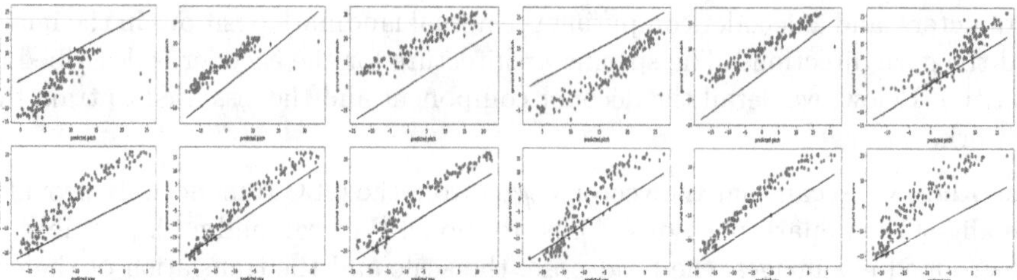

Fig. 3. Gaze bias between prediction and ground truth. 1st row: pitch angle. 2nd row: yaw angle. Green line: identity mapping (Color figure online)

and obtain a more accurate CLGM model, we perform an evaluation guided correction of the CLGM model. The main idea is to evaluate how our gaze prediction approach trained only with synthetic data (for both the CLGM model and the network model) performs on target real data. Then, by comparing the gaze predictions with the actual gaze data for a subject, we can estimate a gaze correction model mapping the prediction to the real ones. Such a parametric model can then be exploited on the UnityEyes data to correct the gaze values associated with a given eye landmarks configuration. A corrected CLGM model can then be obtained from the new data, and will implicitly model the joint variations of eye landmarks on the real data with the actual gaze on real data.

More concretely, we proceed as follows. We first train a gaze estimator (and landmark detector at the same time) with the proposed framework using only the UnityEyes synthetic data. Then the synthetic trained estimator is applied on a target database (UTMultiview, Eyediap) comprising N_{sub} subjects. For each subject, we can obtain gaze prediction/ground truth pairs, as illustrated in Fig. 3. According to these plots, we found a linear model (different for each subject) can be fitted between the prediction and the ground truth. In other words, the gaze predicted by the synthetic model is biased with respect to the real one but can be corrected by applying a linear model. Thus, to obtain a CLGM model linked to real people, for each subject j we fit two linear models f_j^{ϕ} and f_j^{θ} for the pitch and yaw prediction. Then, using the UnityEyes images, we construct a matrix $\mathbf{M}_j$ similar to the $\mathbf{M}$ matrix in Sect. 4.1, but stacking now the following landmark-gaze vectors instead of those in Eq. 2:

$$[\mathbf{l}^y_{k,1}, \cdots, \mathbf{l}^y_{k,N_l}, \mathbf{l}^x_{k,1}, \cdots, \mathbf{l}^x_{k,N_l}, f_j^{\phi}(\mathbf{g}_k^{\phi}), f_j^{\theta}(\mathbf{g}_k^{\theta})] \tag{7}$$

Then, a matrix $\mathbf{M}$ is build by stacking all $\mathbf{M}_j$ matrices, from which the corrected CLGM model taking into account real data is derived[1].

[1] Note that the corrected model relies on real data. In all experiments, the subject(s) used in the test set are never used for computing a corrected CLGM model.

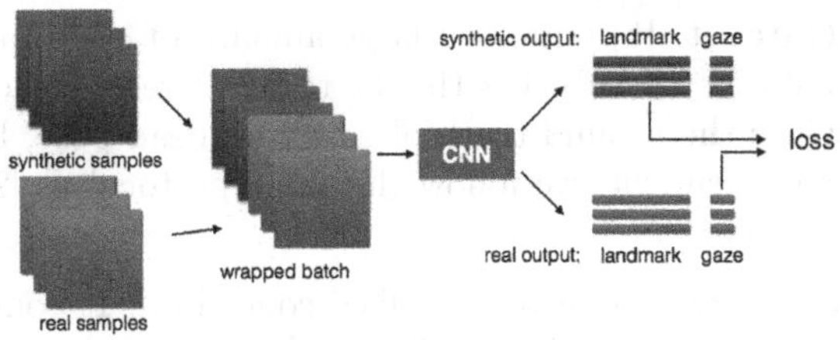

Fig. 4. Training combining synthetic and real data.

4.4 Implementation Detail

Auxiliary Database. To the best of our knowledge, the only public database annotating both eye landmark positions and gaze is MPIIGaze [13]. However, it only labels three eye landmarks per image on a subset of the dataset, which is not enough for our framework. Instead, we use the synthetic samples from UnityEyes as an auxiliary database. Concretely, we sample m real eye images from the main database and another m synthetic eye images from the auxiliary database in every training batch. After the feedforward pass, the landmark loss in Eq. 6 is only computed on synthetic samples (which have landmark annotations), whereas the gaze loss is only computed on real eye samples, as illustrated in Fig. 4. Note that we do not consider the gaze loss on synthetic samples (although they do have gaze groundtruth) to avoid a further potential bias towards the synthetic data.

Eye Image Cropping. The original UnityEyes samples cover a wide region around the eyes and we need a tighter cropping. To improve the generalization of the network, we give random cropping centers and sizes while cropping UnityEyes samples. Cropped images are then resized to fixed dimensions.

Network Configuration. We set the size of the input images as 36×60. The network is composed of 4 convolutional layers and 6 fully connected layers. The 4 convolutional layers are shared among the predictions of the CLGM coefficients, scale and translation. After the 4 convolutional layers, the network is split into 3 task-specific branches and each branch consists of 2 fully connected layers. Note that the head pose information is also concatenated with the feature maps before the first fully connected layer in the CLGM coefficient branch since the eye shape is also affected by the head pose. The network is learned from scratch in this paper.

5 Experiment Protocol

5.1 Dataset

Two public datasets of real images are used: UTMultiview [29] and Eyediap [46].

UTMultiview Dataset. It contains a large amount of eye appearances under different view points for 50 subjects thanks to a 3D reconstruction approach. This dataset provides the ground truth of gaze and head pose, both with large variability. In our experiment, we follow the same protocol as [29] which relies on a 3-fold cross validation.

Eyediap Dataset. It was collected in office conditions. It contains 94 videos from 16 participants. The recording sessions include continuous screen gaze target (CS, small gaze range) and 3D floating gaze target (FT, large gaze range), both based either on a close to static head pose (SP) and mobile head pose (MP) scenario. In experiment, we follow the same person-independent (PI) protocol as [31]. Concretely, for the CS case, we first train a deep network with all the SP-CS subjects but *leave one person out*. Then the network is tested on the left one in both SP-CS and MP-CS sessions (for cross session validation). We do the same for FT case (SP-FT and MP-FT sessions). Note that all eye images are rectified so that their associated head poses are frontal [31].

5.2 Synthetic Dataset and CLGM Training

As mentioned above, we use UnityEyes as the auxiliary dataset.

CLGM. For each experimental setting (datasets or sessions), we derive a CLGM model trained from frontal head pose samples using the gaze ranges of this setting. The resulting CLGM models is then further corrected as described in Sect. 4.3.

Auxiliary Training Samples. For multitask training, the auxiliary synthetic samples are generated with corresponding gaze and head pose ranges matching those of the dataset and session settings.

Synthetic Sample Refinement. One challenge when training using multiple datasets is the different data distribution. Although SimGAN [47] has been proposed to narrow down the distribution gap between synthetic images and real images, optimizing GAN models is difficult. Without suitable hyper parameters and tricks, the semantic of images after refining can be distorted. In our experiment, we simply adapt the UnityEyes synthetic images to UTMultiview samples by grayscale histogram equalization, and to Eyediap samples by Gaussian blurring.

5.3 Model Setup

In terms of gaze estimation models, we considered the models below. The architectures are given in Fig. 2 (proposed approach) and in Fig. 5 (contrastive approaches). Note that the architectures of the first three models below are the same whenever possible and all the models below are pretrained with synthetic data so that a fair comparison can be made.

CrtCLGM + MTL. This is our proposed multitask framework based on the corrected CLGM model, see Fig. 2.

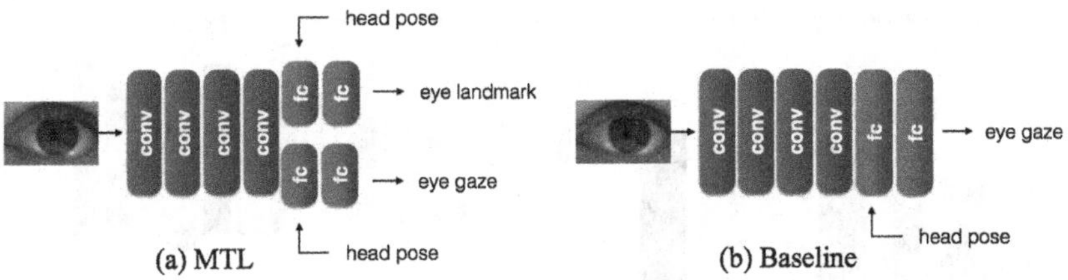

Fig. 5. Contrast models. (a) MTL architecture. (b) baseline architecture.

CLGM + MTL. This model is the same as above (CrtCLGM + MTL), except that the CLGM model is not corrected.

MTL. To contrast the proposed model, we implement a multitask learning network which also predicts landmarks and gaze jointly. Unlike the CrtCLGM + MTL, this model predicts the two labels directly by splitting the network into 2 separate branches after several shared layers. We also forward the head pose information to the features in both branches since both landmarks and gaze are affected by head pose.

Baseline. The baseline model performs a direct gaze regression from the eye appearances using the same base network architecture as in the two previous cases. The head pose is also used in this architecture.

MPIIGaze. For experiments on the Eyediap dataset, we also implemented the network of [13] to allow the comparison of different architectures. For the UTMultiview dataset, we directly report the result of this architecture from [13].

5.4 Performance Measurement

Gaze Estimation. We used the same accuracy measurement as [31] for gaze estimation. The gaze estimation error is defined as the angle between the predicted gaze vector and the groundtruth gaze vector.

Landmark Detection. We also measure the auxiliary task of our model. The GI4E database [48] is used to test the performance of iris center localization. To apply our method, we extracted eye images from the faces using dlib [49] and processed them with grayscale histogram equalization. The eye images are then forwarded to the UTMultiview trained network (frontal head pose assumed). In the evaluation, we adopt the maximum normalized error [23].

6 Results

We report the gaze estimation accuracy of UTMultiview and Eyediap in Fig. 6a and b respectively. Some qualitative results are demonstrated in Fig. 7. Please note that this paper targets at single eye gaze estimation. We think it is not suitable to compare with full face based methods since some datasets (UTMultiview)

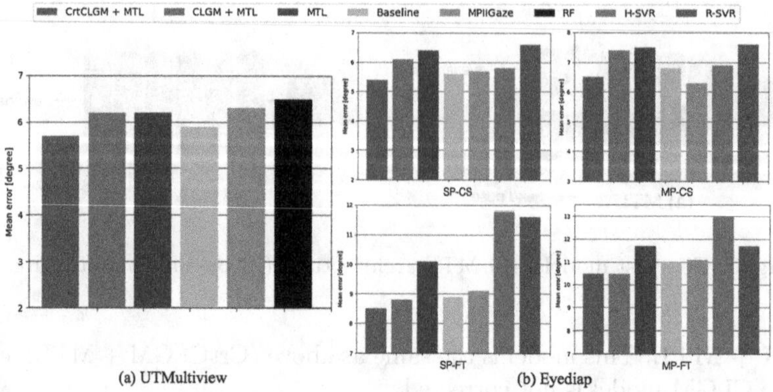

(a) UTMultiview (b) Eyediap

Fig. 6. Gaze estimation accuracy on UTMultiview and Eyediap.

do not provide the full face and the gaze definition can be different (e.g. gaze fixation points [9] and middle point of face as the origin of gaze direction [14]).

6.1 UTMultiview Dataset

From Fig. 6a, we note that the proposed CrtCLGM + MTL model shows the best performance (5.7°) among the contrast methods including two state-of-the-art works, MPIIGaze net [13] (6.3° with our implementation) and RF [29] (6.5°). We also note from Fig. 7 that accurate gaze estimation and landmark localization are achieved by our method regardless of eye scale, eye translation and large head pose.

In contrast, we find that the CLGM + MTL model performs worse than the CrtCLGM + MTL model. This is understandable since the optimization of the multitask loss can be difficult if the landmark-gaze correlations are different between the synthetic data and real data. Sometimes the optimization process competes between the two tasks and the final network can be bad for both tasks. This is also shown in Table 1 where the iris center localization of the CLGM + MTL model is not so accurate. This result demonstrates the importance of the CLGM correction.

When looking at the result of MTL model, it is a bit surprising that its error is on a par with the Baseline method and MPIIGaze net which only target gaze optimization. It thus seems that the MTL model failed to improve gaze estimation through a direct and pure feature sharing strategy. As shown in Fig. 5a, the landmark positions are regressed from the shared features directly in the landmark branch, which means some information such as eye scale and eye translation are contained in the shared features. Although this geometric information is important to landmark localization, they are irrelevant elements for gaze estimation and might even degrade it. Therefore, our mechanism which decouples the eye scale and translation from eye shape variation is thus necessary and important.

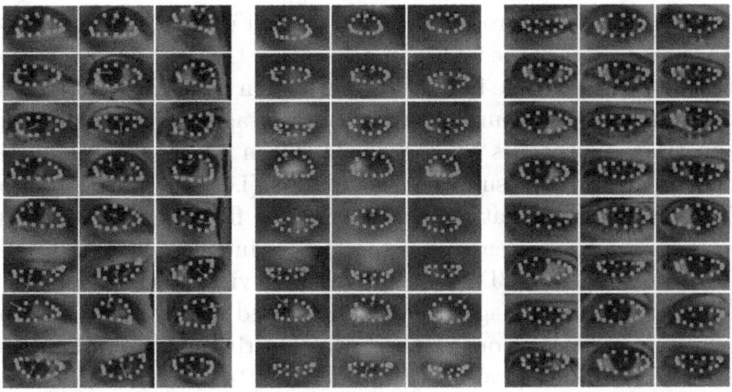

Fig. 7. Eye landmark detection and gaze estimation results on UTMultiview (***Left***), Eyediap (***Middle***) and GI4E (***Right***) dataset. The cyan line represents the estimated gaze direction.

Owing to the reasonable geometric modeling of the scale, translation and head pose, our method also demonstrates superior performance to the Baseline model and the MPIIGaze network. Note that our Baseline model is slightly better than the MPIIGaze net, possibly because in the Baseline, the head pose information is added earlier and thus processed by more layers. Thanks to the large data amount (including the synthetic data used for pretraining), all the network models perform better than the RF (random forest) method.

6.2 Eyediap Dataset

Two existing methods H-SVR and R-SVR [31] are used for comparison. From Fig. 6b, we note that the proposed CrtCLGM + MTL model achieves the best result in all sessions (5.4°, 6.5°, 8.5°, 10.5° respectively) except the SP-CS session (MPIIGaze: 6.3°). In particular, compared with other methods, the performance improvement is much larger in the floating target (FT) session than in the continuous screen (CS) session, indicating that our method can perform even better for applications requiring gaze in the 3D space, when large head pose and gaze angles are present.

When comparing the results of the CrtCLGM + MTL model and CLGM + MTL model, we note that the former is better for all the sessions which further corroborate the importance of CLGM correction. Compared with the UTMultiview dataset, the MTL model obtains much worse results than other network based methods (especially the Baseline and the MPIIGaze) in Eyediap dataset. Given that the Eyediap samples are much more blurry than the UTMultiview dataset, the direct regression of landmark positions without the constrained model is difficult and inaccurate, and the inaccurate landmark detection may confuse the shared architecture and ultimately instead of helping gaze inference, tends to degrade the results. In contrast, our CLGM model is better at handling blurry data thanks to the introduction of an explicit geometrical model, and that learning the parameters of the CLGM model rather than the unconstrained landmark positions provides some form of regularization which prevents the network from overfitting. This also demonstrates the advantage of our method over traditional geometrical approaches where high resolution images are usually required.

When comparing the results across sessions (i.e. recording situations, see Sect. 5.1), we can observe that the accuracy of the floating target (FT) sessions are worse than the CS screen sessions, which is intrinsically due to the more difficult task (looking at a 3D space target) involving much larger head poses (potentially harming eye image frontalization) and gaze ranges. On the other hand, the results show that our method achieves the most robust performance in cross session validation (train on SP, test on MP).

6.3 Iris Center Localization

Lastly, we show the performance of the auxiliary task, landmark detection. Table 1 reports the accuracy of the iris center localization.

Table 1. Iris center localization on GI4E dataset.

Method	$d_{eye} \leq 0.05(\%)$	$d_{eye} \leq 0.1(\%)$	$d_{eye} \leq 0.25(\%)$
Timm et al. [24]	92.4	96.0	97.5
Villanueva et al. [25]	93.9	97.3	98.5
Gou et al. [23]	94.2	99.1	99.8
CLGM + MTL	92.5	99.7	100
CrtCLGM + MTL	**95.1**	**99.7**	**100**

From the table, our method achieves the best performance compared with the state-of-the-art works in all the three criteria which correspond to the range of pupil diameter, the range of iris diameter and the distance between eye center and eye corner [24] respectively. Concretely, most of the detections are within the pupil, few of them lie outside the iris and almost all falls inside the eye region. In contrast, the CLGM + MTL model is inferior to the CrtCLGM + MTL one in the $d_{eye} \leq 0.05(\%)$ measurement, which means more detections of the CLGM + MTL model deviate from the pupil. As discussed in Sect. 6.1, it can be explained by the differences in landmark-gaze correlations between the synthetic data and real data.

Some qualitative results are shown in Fig. 7. Note that we assumed that the head poses of all the samples were frontal since this label was not provided in this dataset. Even under this assumption we still achieved accurate iris center localization, which demonstrates that our method can be used in a wide scope of eye landmark detection applications where head pose information may not be available.

7 Conclusion

In this paper, we proposed a multitask learning approach for gaze estimation. This approach is based on a Constrained Landmark-Gaze Model which models the joint variation of the eye landmarks and gaze in an explicit way, which helps in (i) solving the absence of annotation on different datasets for some task (in our case, landmarks); (ii) better leveraging in this way the benefits of the multitask approach. This model differs from geometrical methods since landmarks and gaze are jointly extracted from eye appearance. Experiments demonstrate the capacity of our approach, which is shown to outperform the state-of-the-art in challenging situations where large head poses and low resolution eye appearances are presented. Our idea of CLGM model can also be extended to joint tasks like facial landmark detection and head pose estimation. For instance, using the FaceWarehouse [50] dataset as 3D face and landmark statistical model to generate faces with different identities and expressions which can be randomly rotated with different head poses. Since pose and landmarks are correlated, a constrained landmark-head pose model could be built and trained as we propose.

On the hand, although the head pose is not so important for landmark detection as shown in Table 1, we note from Eq. 5 that our model requires precise head pose label for gaze estimation, which may limit the application scope of our method. This problem can be possibly addressed by estimating the head pose from the eye appearance or full face as another task. We leave this as a future work.

Acknowledgement. This work was partly funded by the UBIMPRESSED project of the Sinergia interdisciplinary program of the Swiss National Science Foundation (SNSF), and by the European Unions Horizon 2020 research and innovation programme under grant agreement no. 688147 (MuMMER, mummer-project.eu).

References

1. Bixler, R., Blanchard, N., Garrison, L., D'Mello, S.: Automatic detection of mind wandering during reading using gaze and physiology. In: Proceedings of the 2015 ACM on International Conference on Multimodal Interaction, ICMI 2015, pp. 299–306. ACM, New York (2015)
2. Hiraoka, R., Tanaka, H., Sakti, S., Neubig, G., Nakamura, S.: Personalized unknown word detection in non-native language reading using eye gaze. In: Proceedings of the 18th ACM International Conference on Multimodal Interaction, ICMI 2016, pp. 66–70. ACM, New York (2016)
3. Velichkovsky, B.M., Dornhoefer, S.M., Pannasch, S., Unema, P.J.: Visual fixations and level of attentional processing. In: Proceedings of the 2000 Symposium on Eye Tracking Research & Applications, ETRA 2000, pp. 79–85. ACM, New York (2000)
4. Kendon, A.: Some functions of gaze-direction in social interaction. Acta Psychol. **26**(Suppl. C), 22–63 (1967)
5. Vidal, M., Turner, J., Bulling, A., Gellersen, H.: Wearable eye tracking for mental health monitoring. Comput. Commun. **35**(11), 1306–1311 (2012)

6. Ishii, R., Otsuka, K., Kumano, S., Yamato, J.: Prediction of who will be the next speaker and when using gaze behavior in multiparty meetings. ACM Trans. Interact. Intell. Syst. **6**(1), 4:1–4:31 (2016)
7. Andrist, S., Tan, X.Z., Gleicher, M., Mutlu, B.: Conversational gaze aversion for humanlike robots. In: Proceedings of the 2014 ACM/IEEE International Conference on Human-robot Interaction, HRI 2014, pp. 25–32. ACM, New York (2014)
8. Moon, A., et al.: Meet me where i'm gazing: How shared attention gaze affects human-robot handover timing. In: Proceedings of the 2014 ACM/IEEE International Conference on Human-robot Interaction, HRI 2014, pp. 334–341. ACM, New York (2014)
9. Krafka, K., Khosla, A., Kellnhofer, P., Kannan, H.:Eye tracking for everyone. In: IEEE Conference on Computer Vision and Pattern Recognition, pp. 2176–2184 (2016)
10. Tonsen, M., Steil, J., Sugano, Y., Bulling, A.: InvisibleEye: mobile eye tracking using multiple low-resolution cameras and learning-based gaze estimation. In: Proceedings of the ACM on Interactive, Mobile, Wearable and Ubiquitous Technologies (IMWUT), vol. 1, no. 3 (2017)
11. Huang, Q., Veeraraghavan, A., Sabharwal, A.: Tabletgaze: unconstrained appearance-based gaze estimation in mobile tablets. arXiv preprint arXiv:1508.01244 (2015)
12. Zhu, W., Deng, H.: Monocular free-head 3D gaze tracking with deep learning and geometry constraints. In: The IEEE International Conference on Computer Vision (ICCV), October 2017
13. Zhang, X., Sugano, Y., Fritz, M., Bulling, A.: Appearance-based gaze estimation in the wild, pp. 4511–4520 (2015)
14. Zhang, X., Sugano, Y., Fritz, M., Bulling, A.: It's written all over your face: full-face appearance-based gaze estimation (2016)
15. Wood, E., Baltrušaitis, T., Morency, L.P., Robinson, P., Bulling, A.: Learning an appearance-based gaze estimator from one million synthesised images. In: Proceedings of the Ninth Biennial ACM Symposium on Eye Tracking Research and Applications, pp. 131–138 (2016)
16. Hansen, D.W., Ji, Q.: In the eye of the beholder: a survey of models for eyes and gaze. IEEE Trans. Pattern Anal. Mach. Intell. **32**(3), 478–500 (2010)
17. Venkateswarlu, R., et al.: Eye gaze estimation from a single image of one eye, pp. 136–143 (2003)
18. Funes Mora, K.A., Odobez, J.M.: Geometric generative gaze estimation (G3E) for remote RGB-D cameras, pp. 1773–1780, June 2014
19. Wood, E., Baltrušaitis, T., Morency, L.-P., Robinson, P., Bulling, A.: A 3D morphable eye region model for gaze estimation. In: Leibe, B., Matas, J., Sebe, N., Welling, M. (eds.) ECCV 2016. LNCS, vol. 9905, pp. 297–313. Springer, Cham (2016). https://doi.org/10.1007/978-3-319-46448-0_18
20. Ishikawa, T.: Passive driver gaze tracking with active appearance models (2004)
21. Wood, E., Bulling, A.: Eyetab: model-based gaze estimation on unmodified tablet computers, pp. 207–210 (2014)
22. Gou, C., Wu, Y., Wang, K., Wang, F.Y., Ji, Q.: Learning-by-synthesis for accurate eye detection. In: ICPR (2016)
23. Gou, C., Wu, Y., Wang, K., Wang, K., Wang, F., Ji, Q.: A joint cascaded framework for simultaneous eye detection and eye state estimation. Pattern Recogn. **67**, 23–31 (2017)
24. Timm, F., Barth, E.: Accurate eye centre localisation by means of gradients. In: VISAPP (2011)

25. Villanueva, A., Ponz, V., Sesma-Sanchez, L., Ariz, M., Porta, S., Cabeza, R.: Hybrid method based on topography for robust detection of iris center and eye corners. ACM Trans. Multimedia Comput. Commun. Appl. **9**(4) (2013)
26. Tan, K.H., Kriegman, D.J., Ahuja, N.: Appearance-based eye gaze estimation, pp. 191–195 (2002)
27. Noris, B., Keller, J.B., Billard, A.: A wearable gaze tracking system for children in unconstrained environments. Comput. Vis. Image Underst. **115**(4), 476–486 (2011)
28. Martinez, F., Carbone, A., Pissaloux, E.: Gaze estimation using local features and non-linear regression, pp. 1961–1964 (2012)
29. Sugano, Y., Matsushita, Y., Sato, Y.: Learning-by-synthesis for appearance-based 3D gaze estimation. In: Proceedings of the IEEE Computer Society Conference on Computer Vision and Pattern Recognition, pp. 1821–1828 (2014)
30. Lu, F., Sugano, Y., Okabe, T., Sato, Y.: Inferring human gaze from appearance via adaptive linear regression, pp. 153–160 (2011)
31. Funes-Mora, K.A., Odobez, J.M.: Gaze estimation in the 3D space using RGB-D sensors. Int. J. Comput. Vis. **118**(2), 194–216 (2016)
32. Palmero, C., Selva, J., Bagheri, M.A., Escalera, S.: Recurrent CNN for 3d gaze estimation using appearance and shape cues, p. 251 (2018)
33. Park, S., Zhang, X., Bulling, A., Hilliges, O.: Learning to find eye region landmarks for remote gaze estimation in unconstrained settings, pp. 21:1–21:10 (2018)
34. Wang, K., Zhao, R., Ji, Q.: A hierarchical generative model for eye image synthesis and eye gaze estimation, June 2018
35. Park, S., Spurr, A., Hilliges, O.: Deep pictorial gaze estimation, September 2018
36. Ruder, S.: An overview of multi-task learning in deep neural networks, June 2017
37. Ranjan, R., Patel, V.M., Chellappa, R.: Hyperface: a deep multi-task learning framework for face detection, landmark localization, pose estimation, and gender recognition. CoRR abs/1603.01249 (2016)
38. Ranjan, R., Sankaranarayanan, S., Castillo, C.D., Chellappa, R.: An all-in-one convolutional neural network for face analysis. In: 12th IEEE International Conference on Automatic Face & Gesture Recognition, FG 2017, Washington, DC, USA, 30 May–3 June 2017, pp. 17–24 (2017)
39. Wang, F., Han, H., Shan, S., Chen, X.: Deep multi-task learning for joint prediction of heterogeneous face attributes. In: 12th IEEE International Conference on Automatic Face & Gesture Recognition, FG 2017, Washington, DC, USA, 30 May–3 June 2017, pp. 173–179 (2017)
40. Zhang, Z., Luo, P., Loy, C.C., Tang, X.: Facial landmark detection by deep multi-task learning. In: Fleet, D., Pajdla, T., Schiele, B., Tuytelaars, T. (eds.) ECCV 2014. LNCS, vol. 8694, pp. 94–108. Springer, Cham (2014). https://doi.org/10.1007/978-3-319-10599-4_7
41. Yim, J., Jung, H., Yoo, B., Choi, C., Park, D., Kim, J.: Rotating your face using multi-task deep neural network. In: CVPR, pp. 676–684. IEEE Computer Society (2015)
42. Misra, I., Shrivastava, A., Gupta, A., Hebert, M.: Cross-stitch networks for multi-task learning. CoRR abs/1604.03539 (2016)
43. Lu, Y., Kumar, A., Zhai, S., Cheng, Y., Javidi, T., Feris, R.S.: Fully-adaptive feature sharing in multi-task networks with applications in person attribute classification. CoRR abs/1611.05377 (2016)
44. IEEE: A 3D Face Model for Pose and Illumination Invariant Face Recognition. IEEE, Genova, Italy (2009)
45. Cristinacce, D., Cootes, T.F.: Feature detection and tracking with constrained local models, January 2006

46. Funes Mora, K.A., Monay, F., Odobez, J.M.: EYEDIAP: a database for the development and evaluation of gaze estimation algorithms from RGB and RGB-D cameras. In: Proceedings of the ACM Symposium on Eye Tracking Research and Applications. ACM, March 2014
47. Shrivastava, A., Pfister, T., Tuzel, O., Susskind, J., Wang, W., Webb, R.: Learning from simulated and unsupervised images through adversarial training. CoRR abs/1612.07828 (2016)
48. Villanueva, A., Ponz, V., Sesma-Sanchez, L., Ariz, M., Porta, S., Cabeza, R.: Hybrid method based on topography for robust detection of iris center and eye corners. ACM Trans. Multimedia Comput. Commun. Appl. **9**(4), 25:1–25:20 (2013)
49. Kazemi, V., Sullivan, J.: One millisecond face alignment with an ensemble of regression trees. In: CVPR, pp. 1867–1874. IEEE Computer Society (2014)
50. Cao, C., Weng, Y., Zhou, S., Tong, Y., Zhou, K.: Facewarehouse: a 3D facial expression database for visual computing. IEEE Trans. Vis. Comput. Graph. **20**(3), 413–425 (2014)

Photorealistic Facial Synthesis in the Dimensional Affect Space

Dimitrios Kollias[1(✉)], Shiyang Cheng[1], Maja Pantic[1], and Stefanos Zafeiriou[1,2]

[1] Department of Computing, Imperial College London, London, UK
{dimitrios.kollias15,shiyang.cheng11,s.zafeiriou}@imperial.ac.uk
[2] Centre for Machine Vision and Signal Analysis, University of Oulu, Oulu, Finland

Abstract. This paper presents a novel approach for synthesizing facial affect, which is based on our annotating 600,000 frames of the 4DFAB database in terms of valence and arousal. The input of this approach is a pair of these emotional state descriptors and a neutral 2D image of a person to whom the corresponding affect will be synthesized. Given this target pair, a set of 3D facial meshes is selected, which is used to build a blendshape model and generate the new facial affect. To synthesize the affect on the 2D neutral image, 3DMM fitting is performed and the reconstructed face is deformed to generate the target facial expressions. Last, the new face is rendered into the original image. Both qualitative and quantitative experimental studies illustrate the generation of realistic images, when the neutral image is sampled from a variety of well known databases, such as the Aff-Wild, AFEW, Multi-PIE, AFEW-VA, BU-3DFE, Bosphorus.

Keywords: Dimensional facial affect synthesis · Valence · Arousal · Discretization · Blendshape models · 3DMM fitting · 4DFAB · Aff-Wild · AFEW · AFEW-VA · Multi-PIE · BU-3DFE · Bosphorus · Deep neural networks

1 Introduction

Rendering photorealistic facial expressions from single static faces while preserving the identity information is an open research topic which has significant impact on the area of affective computing. Generating faces of a specific person with different facial expressions can be used to various applications including face recognition [6,28], face verification [33,35], emotion prediction [19,21,22], expression database generation, augmentation and entertainment.

This paper describes a novel approach that takes an arbitrary face image with a neutral facial expression and synthesizes a new face image of the same person, but with a different expression, generated according to a dimensional emotion representation model. This problem cannot be tackled using small databases with labeled facial expressions, because it would be really difficult to disentangle facial expression and identity information through them. Our approach is based on the

L. Leal-Taixé and S. Roth (Eds.): ECCV 2018 Workshops, LNCS 11130, pp. 475–491, 2019.
https://doi.org/10.1007/978-3-030-11012-3_36

analysis of a large 4D facial database, the 4DFAB [8], which we appropriately annotated and used for facial expression synthesis on a given subject's face. A dimensional emotion model, in terms of the continuous variables valence (i.e., how positive or negative is an emotion) and arousal (i.e., power of the activation of the emotion) [31,39], has been used to annotate the large amounts of facial images, since this model can represent, not only primary, extreme expressions, but also subtle expressions which are met in everyday human to human, or human to machine interactions.

Section 2 refers to related work that has been published with reference to facial expression synthesis. Section 3 presents the proposed approach for generating facial affect. We describe the annotation and use of the 4DFAB database, and provide the pipeline of our approach in detail. In Sect. 4, we provide an evaluation of the Valence - Arousal discretization and modeling procedure. Then, we synthesize facial affect on a variety of neutral faces from ten different databases (annotated either using a categorical or dimensional emotion model). By using augmented data of faces from two in-the-wild databases, we train a deep neural network to predict the valence and arousal values in these databases. Experimental results show that the proposed approach manages to synthesize photorealistic facial affect, which can be used to improve the accuracy of valence and arousal prediction. Conclusions and future work are presented in Sect. 5.

2 Related Work

In the past several years, facial expression synthesis has been an active research topic. All facial expression synthesis methods that were proposed in the past two decades were roughly split into two categories. The first category is mainly using computer graphics techniques in order to directly warp input faces to target expressions [42,44,47] or re-use sample patches of existing images [26]. The second one synthesizes images with attributes that are predefined [10,34] through the creation of generative models. For the first category, a lot of research efforts have been devoted to finding the correspondence between the target images and existing facial textures. Earlier approaches mostly generated new expressions by either compositing face patches from an existing expression database [17,26], or warping face images via optical flow [42,43] and feature correspondence [36], or creating fully textured 3D facial models [3,30]. In particular, [44] proposed to learn the optical flow using a variational autoencoder. Although this kind of methods can usually produce realistic images with high resolution, the elaborated complex processes often result in highly expensive computations. These works have shown either how to synthesize facial expressions on virtual agents [48], or how to transfer facial expressions between different subjects, i.e., facial reenactment [37]. However, synthesizing accurately a wide variety of facial expressions on arbitrary real faces is considered an open problem and has much room for improvement.

Due to this difficulty, the second category of methods has initially focused on using deconvolutional neural networks (DeCNNs)[1] or deep belief nets (DBNs) [34], generating faces through interpolation of the facial images in their training set. This, however, makes them inherently unsuited for facial expression generation in the case of unseen subjects. With the recent development of Generative Adversarial Networks (GANs) [13], image editing has migrated from pixel-level manipulations to semantic-level ones. GANs have been successfully applied to face image editing, for modification of facial attributes [12,41], age modeling [49] and pose adjustment [16]. These methods generally use the encoder of the GAN to find a low-dimensional representation of the face image in a latent space, manipulate the latent vector and then decode it to generate the new image.

Popular approaches shift the latent vector along a direction corresponding to semantic attributes [24,44], or concatenate attribute labels with it [41,49]. Adversarial discriminator networks are used, either at the encoder to regularize the latent space [25], or at the decoder to generate blur-free and realistic images [24] or at both encoder and decoder, such as the Conditional Adversarial Autoencoder. All of these approaches require large training databases so that identity information can be properly disambiguated. Otherwise, when presented with an unseen face, the network tends to generate faces which look like the "closest" subject in the training database. It has been proposed to handle this problem by warping images, rather than generating them from the latent vector [44]. This approach achieves a high interpolation quality, but requires that the input expression is known and fails when generating facial expressions that are "far apart," e.g. angry faces from smiling ones. Moreover, it is hard to take fine-grain control of the synthesized images, e.g., widen the smile or narrow the eyes.

The proposed approach has quite a few novelties. First of all, it is the first time, to the best of our knowledge, that the dimensional model of affect is taken into account when synthesizing images. All other models are producing synthesized images according to the seven basic, or a few more, expressions. Our approach, as verified in the experimental section of this paper, produces a large number of different expressions given a valence and arousal pair of values in the continuous 2D domain. Also, it is the first time that a 4D face database is annotated in terms of valence and arousal and is then used for affect synthesis. What is more, until now, there has not been any attempt to use the blendshape models like we propose for the synthesis of the data. Finally, the proposed approach works well, when presented with a neutral image either from a controlled or from an in-the-wild database and with different head poses of the person appearing in that image.

[1] https://zo7.github.io/blog/2016/09/25/generating-faces.html.

3 The Proposed Approach

3.1 The 4DFAB Database

The 4DFAB database [8] is the first large scale 4D face database designed for biometrics applications and facial expression analysis. It consists of 180 subjects (60 females, 120 males) aging from 5 to 75. 4DFAB was collected over a period of 5 years under four different sessions, with over 1,800,000 3D faces. The database was designed to capture articulated facial actions and spontaneous facial behaviors, where spontaneous expressions are elicited by emotional video clips watching. In this paper, we use all the 1,580 spontaneous expression sequences for our emotion analysis and synthesis; these sequences cover a wide range of expressions as defined in [11].

To be able to develop the novel expression synthesis method, we annotate these dynamic 3D sequences (over 600,000 frames), in terms of valence and arousal emotion dimensions, using the tool described in [46]. Valence and arousal values range in [−1,1]. Examples are shown in Fig. 1. In the rest of the paper, when we refer to the 4DFAB database, we mean the 600,000 frames which are annotated with categorical expressions, as well as 2D valence and arousal (V-A) emotion values.

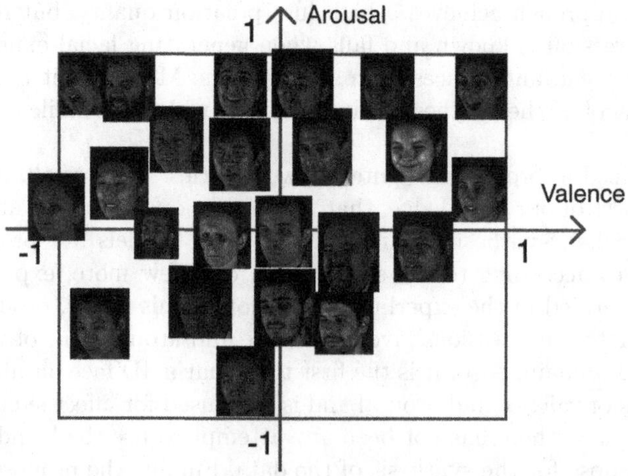

Fig. 1. The 2D Valence-Arousal Space and some representatives frames of 4DFAB

As each 3D face in 4DFAB differs in the number, as well as topology of vertex, we need to first correlate all these meshes to an universal coordinate frame - namely a 3D face template. This step is usually called establishing dense correspondence. We follow the same UV-based registration approach in [8] to bring all the 600,000 meshes into full correspondence with the mean face of LSFM [5]. As a result, we create a new set of 600,000 3D faces that share identical mesh topology, while maintaining their original facial expressions; we will use them as our 3D facial expression gallery for the facial affect synthesis.

3.2 The Methodology Pipeline

The main novelty and contribution of this paper comes from the development of a fully automatic facial affect synthesis framework (depicted in Fig. 2). In the first part (Fig. 2(a)), assuming that the user inputs a target V-A pair, we aim at generating semantically correct 3D facial affect from our 4D gallery. There are two key stages in this pipeline. The first includes the data selection from the 4D face gallery and the utilization of these data. To this end, we discretize the 2D Valence-Arousal (V-A) Space into 100 classes (see Fig. 3 for visualization). Each class contains aligned meshes that are associated with the corresponding V-A pairs; all these V-A pairs lie within the area of this class. Therefore, when a user provides us with a V-A pair, we find its class and retrieve the data belonging to this class. We then build a blendshape model using these data and compute the mean face. Eventually, using this blendshape model, we can generate an unseen 3D face with affect. The details of this part are described in Fig. 2(a) and Sect. 3.3.

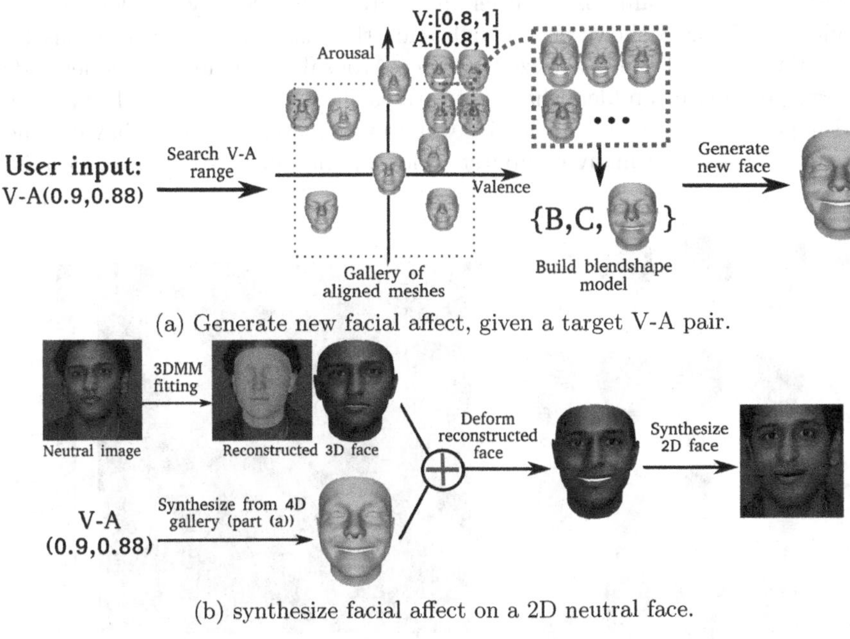

(a) Generate new facial affect, given a target V-A pair.

(b) synthesize facial affect on a 2D neutral face.

Fig. 2. Two main parts in our facial affect synthesis framework: (a) Generating new facial affect from our 4D face gallery, given a target V-A value pair provided by the user; (b) Synthesizing the facial affect (from part (a)) on an arbitrary 2D neutral face.

Figure 2(b) describes the procedure of synthesizing a new facial affect to an arbitrary 2D face. As described previously, given a target V-A pair, we create an unseen expressive face without any identity, gender and age information. In this part, we want to transfer the affect of this expressive face to the face of another person, after which, we render a 2D expressive face without loss of identity. Three processing steps are needed to achieve this goal. The first is to perform 3DMM fitting [4] to estimate the 3D shape of target face. The second step is to transfer the facial affect from synthetic 3D face to the reconstructed 3D face. Finally, we rasterize the new 3D face with affect to the original image frame. We will describe this procedure in details in Sect. 3.4.

3.3 Generation of New 3D Facial Affect from 4DFAB

Discretizing the 2D Valence-Arousal Space. At first, we discretize the 2D Valence-Arousal Space into 100 classes, with each one covering a square of size 0.2×0.2 and including a sufficient number of data. Although the number of classes can be increased to further categorize the facial affect, it might not provide a better result. This is because, if each class contained few examples, it would be more likely that the identity information is incorporated. However, our synthetic facial affects should only describe the expression associated with the designated V-A value pair, rather than any of the identity, gender and age information. Figure 3 shows on the right side the histogram of annotations (of 4DFAB database) of the discretized Valence-Arousal Space and on the left side the corresponding mean blendshapes of various classes of this Space. Expression blendshape models provide an effective way to parameterize facial behaviors and are frequently used in many computer vision applications. We choose to build

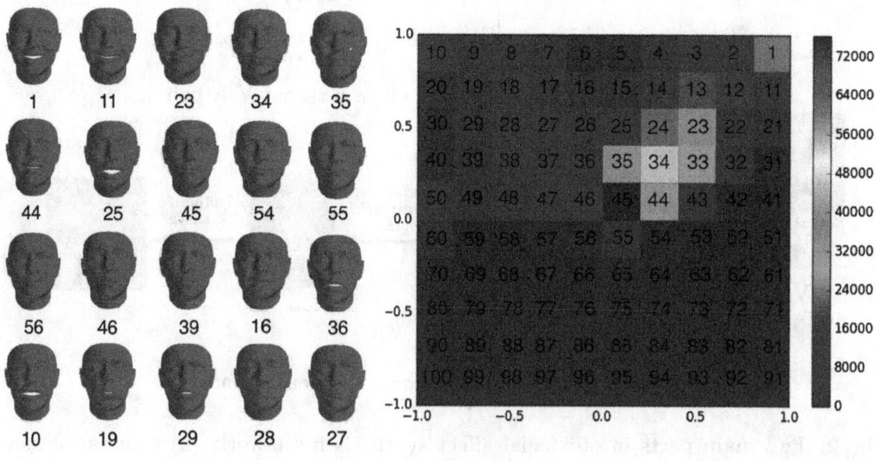

Fig. 3. The mean shapes of our blendshape models and their corresponding areas in the 2D Valence-Arousal Space, which is shown as a 2D histogram of annotations of the 4DFAB database.

the localized blendshape model [27] to describe our selection of V-A examples. For each 3D mesh, we subtracted it from the neutral mesh of the corresponding sequence and created a set of m difference vectors $\mathbf{d}_i \in \mathbb{R}^{3n}$ which were then stacked into a matrix $\mathbf{D} = [\mathbf{d}_1, ..., \mathbf{d}_m] \in \mathbb{R}^{3n \times m}$, where n is number of vertices in our mesh. Afterwards, a variant of sparse Principal Component Analysis (PCA) was applied to our data matrix $\mathbf{D}$ to identify sparse deformation components $\mathbf{C} \in \mathbb{R}^{h \times 1}$:

$$\arg\min \|\mathbf{D} - \mathbf{BC}\|_F^2 + \Omega(\mathbf{C}) \quad \text{s.t. } \mathcal{V}(\mathbf{B}), \tag{1}$$

here, the constraint $\mathcal{V}$ can be either $\max(|\mathbf{B}_k|) = 1,\ \forall k$ or $\max(\mathbf{B}_k) = 1,\ \mathbf{B} \geq 1,\ \forall k$, where $\mathbf{B}_k \in \mathbb{R}^{3n \times 1}$ denotes the kth components of sparse weight matrix $\mathbf{B} = [\mathbf{B}_1, \cdots, \mathbf{B}_h]$. The selection of these two constraints depends on our actual usage; the major difference is that the latter one allows negative weights and therefore enables deformation towards both directions, which is useful for describing shapes like muscle bulges. The regularization of sparse components $\mathbf{C}$ is performed with $\ell 1/\ell 2$ norm [1,40]. To permit more local deformations from the model, additional regularization parameters were added into $\Omega(\mathbf{C})$. To solve for the optimal $\mathbf{C}$ and $\mathbf{B}$, an iterative alternating optimization is employed, please refer to [27] for more details.

3.4 Facial Affect Synthesis for Arbitrary 2D Image

Given a facial expression synthesis based on the valence-arousal value pair, we aim at modifying the face in an arbitrary 2D image and generating a new facial image with affect. This procedure consists of three steps: (1) fit a 3D morphable model on the image; (2) generate facial affect on the reconstructed 3D face; (3) blend the new face into the original image. Specifically, we started by performing a 3DMM fitting [4] on a 2D facial image, and retrieved a reconstructed 3D face with the texture sampled from the original image. Next, we calculated the facial deformation by subtracting the synthetic face with the LSFM template, and imposed this deformation on the reconstructed mesh. This far, we have generated a new 3D face with certain affect; the last step would be rendering it back to the original 2D image, where a Poisson image blending [29] is employed to produce a natural and realistic result.

4 Experimental Study

4.1 Discovering Shared Information Between 3D Data and Valence-Arousal

In the first experiment, we wanted to prove the validity of our Valence-Arousal modeling and synthesis approach. This could be verified by showing that there is shared information between our 3D data and Valence-Arousal through a correlation analysis.

Due to the high volume and dimensionality of our 3D data, it is intractable to directly perform typical correlation analysis. Hence, we first built a powerful expression blendshape model using the apex frames of posed expression sequences from the 4DFAB; in total, 12,000 expressive 3D meshes are selected, with 2,000 for each of the six basic expressions. Then, we projected our 3D data to its subspace and retrieved the sparse representations for future analysis. We experimented with different number of components (i.e. 84, 150, 200, 300, 500) of the blendshape model to select the best configuration.

Next, we split the data into 2 sets: the training and the test set, containing 480,000 and 120,000 frames respectively, in a subject independent manner, meaning that one person could only appear in the training or test set, but not on both of them. As we have found a compact representation of our data, Canonical Correlation Analysis (CCA) [15] can be performed on the training set and their corresponding valence and arousal values. CCA is a shared-space component analysis method, which recovers the loadings to project two data matrices on a subspace where the linear correlation is maximized. This can be interpreted as discovering the shared information conveyed by all the data (or views).

After CCA, we reduced the dimensions of our data to 2. Then, on the training set, we performed Support Vector Regression (SVR) [2] with Radial Basis Function (RBF) kernel to map those 2 dimensions to the valence and arousal values. In order to examine whether our 3D data highly correlate to the Valence-Arousal labels, we predicted the V-A values of the test data using the aforementioned models (CCA and SVR), and compare the predictions with our annotated V-A labels. This comparison was performed with respect to two criteria: Concordance Correlation Coefficient and the usual Mean Squared Error. The Concordance Correlation Coefficient (CCC) can be defined as follows:

$$\rho_c = \frac{2s_{xy}}{s_x^2 + s_y^2 + (\bar{x} - \bar{y})^2}, \tag{2}$$

where s_x and s_y are the variances of the ground truth and predicted values of the regression respectively, $\bar{x}$ and $\bar{y}$ are the corresponding mean values and s_{xy} is the respective covariance value.

Table 1 shows those two criteria for the test set when we keep different numbers of principal components for our expression blendshape model. We can observe that with 200 components, highest correlation between the data and V-A labels was achieved, as well as lowest prediction error. By selecting this value, we ensured that the proposed synthesis approach is valid.

4.2 Databases Used for Affect Synthesis Evaluation

To evaluate our facial affect synthesis method in different scenarios (e.g. controlled laboratory environment, uncontrolled in-the-wild setting), we utilized neutral facial images from as many as 10 databases.

(1) Multi-PIE [14]**:** It contains 755,370 images (3072 × 2048) of 337 people. Pose, illumination, and expression are the key factors of the database. 15 view points, 19 illuminations and 7 expressions are recorded in a controlled environment.

Table 1. CCC and MSE evaluation of valence & arousal predictions on the test set when we keep different number of principal components in PCA

No. of principal components to keep	CCC		MSE	
	Valence	Arousal	Valence	Arousal
84	0.63	0.68	0.107	0.046
150	0.65	0.68	0.099	0.041
200	**0.66**	**0.69**	**0.097**	**0.040**
300	0.35	0.30	0.127	0.058
500	0.31	0.22	0.129	0.061

(2) Face place: This database [2] contains photographs of many different individuals in various types of disguises, such that, for each individual, there are multiple photographs in which hairstyle and/or eyeglasses have been changed/added. It consists of 1,284 images of Asian, 937 images of African-American, 3,362 images of Caucasian, 494 images of Hispanic and 497 images of multiracial people. All images show posed expression.

(3) 2D Face Sets: We used 3 subsets from the 2D Face Sets database[3].

Iranian women: It consists of 369 color images (1200 × 900) of 34 women. People display mostly smile and neutral expression in each of five poses.

Nottingham scans: It has 100 monochrome images (50 men, 50 women) in neutral and frontal pose. The image resolution varies from 358 × 463 to 468 × 536.

Pain expressions: It consists of 599 color images (720 × 576) of 13 women and 10 men. They usually display two of the six basic emotions (anger, disgust, fear, sad, happy, surprise) plus pain 10 expressions. Profile neutral and 45° images are available.

(4) FEI: The FEI database [38] is a Brazilian face database that contains a set of face images taken between June 2005 and March 2006. 200 individuals were recorded, and each one has 14 images, resulting in 2,800 images of size 640 × 480. All images were color and taken against a white background in an upright frontal position with profile rotation of up to 180°. The subjects are mostly students and staff at FEI, between 19 and 40 years old with distinct appearance, hairstyle and adorns. The number of male and female subjects are both 100.

(5) Aff-Wild: Aff-Wild [20,46] consists of 298 Youtube videos, with 1,200,000 frames in total. The length of each video varies from 10 s to 15 min. These videos contain spontaneous facial behaviors elicited by a variety of stimuli in arbitrary recording conditions. There are 200 subjects (130 males and 70 females) from

[2] Stimulus images courtesy of Michael J. Tarr, Center for the Neural Basis of Cognition and Department of Psychology, Carnegie Mellon University, http://www.tarrlab.org/.

[3] http://pics.stir.ac.uk.

different ethnicities. Aff-Wild serves as the benchmark of the first Affect-in-the-wild Challenge[4] [18]. For each video, there are 8 annotators to annotate the valence and arousal, in the range of [−1, +1].

(6) AFEW 5.0: This database is a dynamic facial expressions corpus (used in EmotiW Challenge 2017 [9]) consisting of 1,809 nearly real world scenes from movies and reality TV shows. There are over 330 subjects aging from 1 to 77. The database is split into three sets: training (773 videos), validation (383 videos) and test set (653 videos). It is a challenging database because both training and validation sets are mainly from the movies, while 114 out of 653 test videos are from TV. Annotations of neutral and 6 basic expressions are provided.

(7) AFEW-VA: Recently, a part of the AFEW database has been annotated in terms of Valence and Arousal, thus creating the AFEW-VA [23] database. It includes 600 video clips selected from films with real-world conditions, i.e., occlusions, illumination and body movements. The length of each video ranges from around 10 frames to over 120 frames. This database consists of per-frame annotations of V-A. In total, more than 30,000 frames were annotated for affect prediction of V-A, using discrete values in the range of [−10, +10].

(8) BU-3DFE: BU-3DFE database [45] is the first 3D facial expression database, which includes 2,500 expressive meshes from 100 subjects (56 females, 44 males) with age from 18 to 70. The subjects are from various ethnic/racial ancestries. They recorded 6 articulated expressions (happiness, disgust, fear, angry, surprise and sadness) with 4 intensities; also, there is a neutral 3D scan per subject.

(9) Kinect Fusion ITW: The KF-ITW database [4] is the first Kinect 3D database captured under relatively unconstrained conditions. This database consists of 17 different subjects performing some expressions (neutral, happy, surprise) under various illumination conditions.

(10) Bosphorus: The Bosphorus database [32] consists of 105 subjects in various poses, expressions and occlusion conditions. 18 men had beard/moustache and 15 others had short facial hair. There are 60 men and 45 women, they are mostly between 25 and 35. Majority of them are Caucasian. 27 professional actors/actresses are incorporated in the database. The number of total face scans is 4,652, each scan has been manually labeled with 24 facial landmarks.

4.3 Qualitative Evaluation of the Facial Affect Synthesis

We used all the above-mentioned databases to supply the proposed approach with 'input' neutral faces. We synthesized the emotional state of specific V-A value pairs for these images. One important task during this facial affect synthesis procedure is to preserve identity, age and gender of the original face. Instead of finding the closest matching sample (or K-nearest samples) for the given V-A pair, we categorized our 3D data based on the 2D Valence-Arousal Space (as shown in Fig. 3) and employed the mean expression of the area that contains the target V-A pair.

[4] https://ibug.doc.ic.ac.uk/resources/first-affect-wild-challenge.

Figure 4 is split into three parts. In each part, the top row illustrates some neutral images sampled from each of the aforementioned databases and the bottom one shows the respective synthesized images. Figure 5 shows the neutral

(a)

(b)

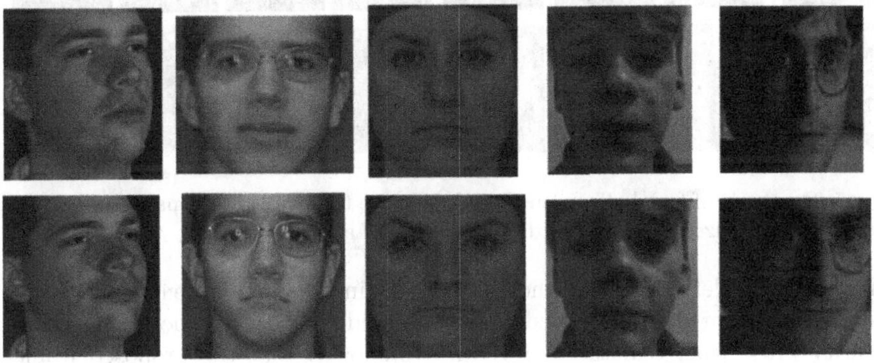

(c)

Fig. 4. (a)–(c). Synthesis of facial affect across all databases: on top rows are the neutral and on the bottom are the corresponding synthesized images.

Fig. 5. Synthesis of facial affect: on the left side are the neutral 2D images and on the right the synthesized images with different levels of affect

images on the left side, and the synthesized images of different valence and arousal values on the right. It could be observed that our synthetic images are identity preserving, realistic and vivid. We showed that the proposed framework works well for images from both in-the-wild and controlled databases. This suggests that we could effectively synthesize facial affect regardless of different image conditions (e.g., occlusions, illumination and head poses).

4.4 Quantitative Evaluation of the Facial Affect Synthesis

Leveraging Synthetic Data for Training Deep Neural Networks. We used the synthetic faces to train deep neural networks for valence and arousal prediction on two facial affect databases annotated in terms of valence and arousal, the Aff-Wild and AFEW-VA. Our first step is to select neutral frames from these two databases. Specifically, we selected frames with zero valence and arousal (human inspection was also conducted to make sure they are neutral faces), then, for each frame, we synthesized facial affect using the mean blend-shape (as shown in Fig. 3) and assigned the median valence and arousal value of that class.

Experiments and Data Augmentation on the AFEW-VA. Following our approach, we created 108,864 synthetic images from the AFEW-VA database, a number that is 3.5 times bigger than its original size. For training, we used the CNN-RNN (VGG-Face-GRU) architecture described in [18]. Similarly to [23], we used a 5-fold person-independent cross-validation strategy and at each fold we augmented the training set with the synthesized images of people appearing only in that set (preserving the person independence). Table 2 shows a comparison of the performance of our network with the best results reported in [23]. Those results are in terms of the Pearson Correlation Coefficient criterion (Pearson CC), defined as follows:

$$\rho_{xy} = \frac{s_{xy}}{s_x s_y} \tag{3}$$

where s_x and s_y are the variances of the ground truth and predicted values respectively and s_{xy} is the respective covariance value.

Table 2. Pearson Correlation Coefficient evaluation of valence & arousal predictions provided by the best architecture in [23] vs the network trained on the augmented dataset created by our approach. Note that valence and arousal values are in $[-10, 10]$.

Group	Pearson CC		MSE	
	Valence	Arousal	Valence	Arousal
Best of [23]	0.407	0.45	6.96	4.97
Our network (trained on the augmented dataset)	**0.542**	**0.589**	4.75	2.74

Experiments and Data Augmentation on the Aff-Wild. Following our approach, we created 60,135 synthetic images from the Aff-Wild database. We added those images to the training set of the first Affect-in-the-wild Challenge. It should be noticed that these images were synthesized from neutral faces found only in the training set of the challenge. The network we employed here was the same CNN-RNN (VGG-Face-GRU) architecture described in [18]. Table 3 shows a comparison of the performance of our network trained with the augmented data with the best results reported in [18] and the results of the winner of the Aff-Wild Challenge [7] (Method FATAUVA-Net).

Table 3. Concordance Correlation Coefficient evaluation of valence & arousal predictions provided by the CNN-RNN trained on the Aff-Wild dataset augmented with images synthesized by our approach vs methods [7] and [18]. Note that valence and arousal values are in $[-1, 1]$.

	CCC		MSE	
	Valence	Arousal	Valence	Arousal
FATAUVA-Net [7]	0.396	0.282	0.123	0.095
[18]	0.570	0.430	0.080	0.060
Our network trained on the augmented dataset	**0.591**	**0.442**	0.074	0.051

From both tables, it can be verified that the network trained on the augmented, with synthetic images, dataset, outperformed the networks trained without them. This implies that, by augmenting the original training set, our methodology improved the network performance. It should be noted that the boost in performance is greater when the number of augmented images is much greater than the number of images in the dataset (which is the case of AFEW-VA that contains 30,000 frames, while the augmented set included 109,000 more frames).

5 Conclusions and Future Work

A novel approach to generate facial affect in faces has been presented in this paper. It leverages a dimensional emotion model in terms of valence and arousal, and a large scale 4D face database, the 4DFAB. An efficient method has been developed for matching different blendshape models on large amounts of images extracted from the database and using these to render the appropriate facial affect on a selected face. A variety of faces and facial expressions has been examined in the experimental study, from ten databases showing expressions according to dimensional, but also categorical emotion models. The proposed approach has been successfully applied to faces from all databases, being able to render photorealistic facial expressions on them.

In our future work we will extend this approach to synthesize, not only dimensional affect in faces, but also Facial Action Units. In this way a Global Local synthesis of facial affect will be possible, through a unified modeling of global dimensional emotion and local action unit based facial expression synthesis.

Acknowledgements. The authors would also like to thank Evangelos Ververas for assisting with the affect synthesis. The work of Dimitris Kollias was funded by a Teaching Fellowship of Imperial College London. The work of S. Cheng is funded by the EPSRC project EP/J017787/1 (4D-FAB) and EP/N007743/1 (FACER2VM).

References

1. Bach, F., Jenatton, R., Mairal, J., Obozinski, G.: Optimization withsparsity-inducing penalties. Found. Trends Mach. Learn. **4**(1), 1–106 (2012). https://doi.org/10.1561/2200000015
2. Basak, D., Pal, S., Patranabis, D.C.: Support vector regression. Neural Inf. Process.-Lett. Rev. **11**(10), 203–224 (2007)
3. Blanz, V., Basso, C., Poggio, T., Vetter, T.: Reanimating faces in images and video. In: Computer Graphics Forum, vol. 22, pp. 641–650. Wiley Online Library (2003)
4. Booth, J., Antonakos, E., Ploumpis, S., Trigeorgis, G., Panagakis, Y., Zafeiriou, S.: 3D face morphable models "in-the-wild". In: IEEE Conference on Computer Vision and Pattern Recognition (CVPR), July 2017. https://arxiv.org/abs/1701.05360
5. Booth, J., Roussos, A., Ponniah, A., Dunaway, D., Zafeiriou, S.: Large scale 3D morphable models. Int. J. Comput. Vis. **126**(2–4), 233–254 (2018)
6. Cao, Q., Shen, L., Xie, W., Parkhi, O.M., Zisserman, A.: Vggface2: a dataset for recognising faces across pose and age. In: 2018 13th IEEE International Conference on Automatic Face & Gesture Recognition (FG 2018), pp. 67–74. IEEE (2018)
7. Chang, W.Y., Hsu, S.H., Chien, J.H.: Fatauva-net: an integrated deep learning framework for facial attribute recognition, action unit (au) detection, and valence-arousal estimation. In: Proceedings of the IEEE Conference on Computer Vision and Pattern Recognition Workshop (2017)
8. Cheng, S., Kotsia, I., Pantic, M., Zafeiriou, S.: 4DFAB: a large scale 4D database for facial expression analysis and biometric applications. In: 2018 IEEE Conference on Computer Vision and Pattern Recognition, CVPR 2018, Salt Lake City, Utah, US, June 2018
9. Dhall, A., Goecke, R., Ghosh, S., Joshi, J., Hoey, J., Gedeon, T.: From individual to group-level emotion recognition: Emotiw 5.0. In: Proceedings of the 19th ACM International Conference on Multimodal Interaction, pp. 524–528. ACM (2017)
10. Ding, H., Sricharan, K., Chellappa, R.: Exprgan: Facial expression editing with controllable expression intensity. arXiv preprint arXiv:1709.03842 (2017)
11. Du, S., Tao, Y., Martinez, A.: Compound facial expressions of emotion. Proc. Natl. Acad. Sci. U.S.A. **111**(15), 1454–1462 (2014). https://doi.org/10.1073/pnas.1322355111
12. Ghodrati, A., Jia, X., Pedersoli, M., Tuytelaars, T.: Towards automatic image editing: Learning to see another you. arXiv preprint arXiv:1511.08446 (2015)
13. Goodfellow, I., et al.: Generative adversarial nets. In: Advances in Neural Information Processing Systems, pp. 2672–2680 (2014)
14. Gross, R., Matthews, I., Cohn, J., Kanade, T., Baker, S.: Multi-pie. Image Vis. Comput. **28**(5), 807–813 (2010)
15. Hardoon, D.R., Szedmak, S., Shawe-Taylor, J.: Canonical correlation analysis; an overview with application to learning methods. Technical report, Royal Holloway, University of London, May 2003. http://eprints.soton.ac.uk/259225/
16. Huang, R., Zhang, S., Li, T., He, R., et al.: Beyond face rotation: Global and local perception gan for photorealistic and identity preserving frontal view synthesis. arXiv preprint arXiv:1704.04086 (2017)
17. Jonze, S., Cusack, J., Diaz, C., Keener, C., Kaufman, C.: Being John Malkovich. Universal Studios (1999)

18. Kollias, D., Nicolaou, M.A., Kotsia, I., Zhao, G., Zafeiriou, S.: Recognition of affect in the wild using deep neural networks. In: 2017 IEEE Conference on Computer Vision and Pattern Recognition Workshops (CVPRW), pp. 1972–1979. IEEE (2017)
19. Kollias, D., Tagaris, A., Stafylopatis, A.: On line emotion detection using retrainable deep neural networks. In: 2016 IEEE Symposium Series on Computational Intelligence (SSCI), pp. 1–8. IEEE (2016)
20. Kollias, D., et al.: Deep affect prediction in-the-wild: Aff-wild database and challenge, deep architectures, and beyond. arXiv preprint arXiv:1804.10938 (2018)
21. Kollias, D., Yu, M., Tagaris, A., Leontidis, G., Stafylopatis, A., Kollias, S.: Adaptation and contextualization of deep neural network models. In: 2017 IEEE Symposium Series on Computational Intelligence (SSCI), pp. 1–8. IEEE (2017)
22. Kollias, D., Zafeiriou, S.: Training deep neural networks with different datasets in-the-wild: the emotion recognition paradigm. In: 2018 International Joint Conference on Neural Networks (IJCNN), pp. 1–8. IEEE (2018)
23. Kossaifi, J., Tzimiropoulos, G., Todorovic, S., Pantic, M.: AFEW-VA database for valence and arousal estimation in-the-wild. Image Vis. Comput. **65**, 23–36 (2017)
24. Larsen, A.B.L., Sønderby, S.K., Larochelle, H., Winther, O.: Autoencoding beyond pixels using a learned similarity metric. arXiv preprint arXiv:1512.09300 (2015)
25. Makhzani, A., Shlens, J., Jaitly, N., Goodfellow, I., Frey, B.: Adversarial autoencoders. arXiv preprint arXiv:1511.05644 (2015)
26. Mohammed, U., Prince, S.J., Kautz, J.: Visio-lization: generating novel facial images. ACM Trans. Graph. (TOG) **28**(3), 57 (2009)
27. Neumann, T., Varanasi, K., Wenger, S., Wacker, M., Magnor, M., Theobalt, C.: Sparse localized deformation components. ACM Trans. Graph. (TOG) **32**(6), 179 (2013)
28. Parkhi, O.M., Vedaldi, A., Zisserman, A.: Deep face recognition. In: BMVC, vol. 1, p. 6 (2015)
29. Pérez, P., Gangnet, M., Blake, A.: Poisson image editing. In: ACM SIGGRAPH 2003 Papers, SIGGRAPH 2003, pp. 313–318. ACM, New York (2003). https://doi.org/10.1145/1201775.882269
30. Pighin, F., Hecker, J., Lischinski, D., Szeliski, R., Salesin, D.H.: Synthesizing realistic facial expressions from photographs. In: ACM SIGGRAPH 2006 Courses, p. 19. ACM (2006)
31. Russell, J.A.: Evidence of convergent validity on the dimensions of affect. J. Pers. Soc. Psychol. **36**(10), 1152 (1978)
32. Savran, A., et al.: Bosphorus database for 3D face analysis. In: Schouten, B., Juul, N.C., Drygajlo, A., Tistarelli, M. (eds.) BioID 2008. LNCS, vol. 5372, pp. 47–56. Springer, Heidelberg (2008). https://doi.org/10.1007/978-3-540-89991-4_6
33. Sun, Y., Chen, Y., Wang, X., Tang, X.: Deep learning face representation by joint identification-verification. In: Advances in Neural Information Processing Systems, pp. 1988–1996 (2014)
34. Susskind, J.M., Hinton, G.E., Movellan, J.R., Anderson, A.K.: Generating facial expressions with deep belief nets. In: Affective Computing. InTech (2008)
35. Taigman, Y., Yang, M., Ranzato, M., Wolf, L.: Deepface: closing the gap to human-level performance in face verification. In: Proceedings of the IEEE Conference on Computer Vision and Pattern Recognition, pp. 1701–1708 (2014)
36. Theobald, B.J., et al.: Mapping and manipulating facial expression. Lang. Speech **52**(2–3), 369–386 (2009)

37. Thies, J., Zollhöfer, M., Nießner, M., Valgaerts, L., Stamminger, M., Theobalt, C.: Real-time expression transfer for facial reenactment. ACM Trans. Graph. **34**(6), 183–1 (2015)
38. Thomaz, C.E., Giraldi, G.A.: A new ranking method for principal components analysis and its application to face image analysis. Image Vis. Comput. **28**(6), 902–913 (2010)
39. Whissell, C.M.: The dictionary of affect in language. In: The Measurement of Emotions, pp. 113–131. Elsevier (1989)
40. Wright, S.J., Nowak, R.D., Figueiredo, M.A.T.: Sparse reconstruction by separable approximation. IEEE Trans. Sig. Process. **57**(7), 2479–2493 (2009). https://doi.org/10.1109/TSP.2009.2016892
41. Yan, X., Yang, J., Sohn, K., Lee, H.: Attribute2Image: conditional image generation from visual attributes. In: Leibe, B., Matas, J., Sebe, N., Welling, M. (eds.) ECCV 2016. LNCS, vol. 9908, pp. 776–791. Springer, Cham (2016). https://doi.org/10.1007/978-3-319-46493-0_47
42. Yang, F., Bourdev, L., Shechtman, E., Wang, J., Metaxas, D.: Facial expression editing in video using a temporally-smooth factorization. In: 2012 IEEE Conference on Computer Vision and Pattern Recognition (CVPR), pp. 861–868. IEEE (2012)
43. Yang, F., Wang, J., Shechtman, E., Bourdev, L., Metaxas, D.: Expression flow for 3D-aware face component transfer. ACM Trans. Graph. (TOG) **30**(4), 60 (2011)
44. Yeh, R., Liu, Z., Goldman, D.B., Agarwala, A.: Semantic facial expression editing using autoencoded flow. arXiv preprint arXiv:1611.09961 (2016)
45. Yin, L., Wei, X., Sun, Y., Wang, J., Rosato, M.J.: A 3D facial expression database for facial behavior research. In: 7th International Conference on Automatic Face and Gesture Recognition, FGR 2006, pp. 211–216. IEEE (2006)
46. Zafeiriou, S., Kollias, D., Nicolaou, M.A., Papaioannou, A., Zhao, G., Kotsia, I.: Aff-wild: Valence and arousal 'in-the-wild' challenge. In: 2017 IEEE Conference on Computer Vision and Pattern Recognition Workshops (CVPRW), pp. 1980–1987. IEEE (2017)
47. Zhang, Q., Liu, Z., Quo, G., Terzopoulos, D., Shum, H.Y.: Geometry-driven photorealistic facial expression synthesis. IEEE Trans. Vis. Comput. Graph. **12**(1), 48–60 (2006)
48. Zhang, S., Wu, Z., Meng, H.M., Cai, L.: Facial expression synthesis based on emotion dimensions for affective talking avatar. In: Nishida, T., Jain, L.C., Faucher, C. (eds.) Modeling Machine Emotions for Realizing Intelligence, pp. 109–132. Springer, Heidelberg (2010)
49. Zhang, Z., Song, Y., Qi, H.: Age progression/regression by conditional adversarial autoencoder. In: The IEEE Conference on Computer Vision and Pattern Recognition (CVPR), vol. 2 (2017)

Generating Synthetic Video Sequences by Explicitly Modeling Object Motion

S. Palazzo[1], C. Spampinato[1,2(✉)], P. D'Oro[1], D. Giordano[1], and M. Shah[2]

[1] Pattern Recognition and Computer Vision (PeRCeiVe) Lab, University of Catania, Catania, Italy
cspampin@dieei.unict.it

[2] Center for Research in Computer Vision, University of Central Florida, Orlando, USA
http://crcv.ucf.edu, http://www.perceivelab.com/

Abstract. Recent GAN-based video generation approaches model videos as the combination of a time-independent scene component and a time-varying motion component, thus factorizing the generation problem into generating background and foreground separately. One of the main limitations of current approaches is that both factors are learned by mapping one source latent space to videos, which complicates the generation task as a single data point must be informative of both background and foreground content. In this paper we propose a GAN framework for video generation that, instead, employs two latent spaces in order to structure the generative process in a more natural way: (1) a latent space to generate the static visual content of a scene (background), which remains the same for the whole video, and (2) a latent space where motion is encoded as a trajectory between sampled points and whose dynamics are modeled through an RNN encoder (jointly trained with the generator and the discriminator) and then mapped by the generator to visual objects' motion. Performance evaluation showed that our approach is able to control effectively the generation process as well as to synthesize more realistic videos than state-of-the-art methods.

1 Introduction

Generative Adversarial Networks (GANs) [1] are a recent trend in computer vision and machine learning that advanced the state of the art on image and video generation to unprecedented levels of accuracy and realism. New adversarial models [2–8] are proposed at an accelerating pace, both to increase the diversity and resolution of generated images and to tackle theoretical issues on training and convergence. GANs have been applied mainly to image generation, and naively extending image generation methods to videos is not sufficient, as it jointly attempts at handling both the spatial component of the video, describing object and background appearance, and the temporal one, representing object motion and consistency across frames. Building on these considerations, recent generative efforts [9,10] have attempted to factor the latent representation of

L. Leal-Taixé and S. Roth (Eds.): ECCV 2018 Workshops, LNCS 11130, pp. 492–499, 2019.
https://doi.org/10.1007/978-3-030-11012-3_37

each video frame into two components that model a time-independent background of the scene and the time-varying foreground elements. We argue that the main limitation of these methods is that both factors are learned by mapping a single point of a source latent space (sampled as random noise) to a whole video. This, indeed, over-complicates the generation task as two videos depicting the same scene with different object trajectories or the same trajectory on different scenes are represented as different points in the latent space, although they share a common factor (in the former case the background, in the latter case object motion). To address this limitation, in this paper we propose a GAN-based generation approach that employs two latent spaces (as shown in Fig. 1) to improve the video generation process: (1) one latent space to model the static visual content of the scene (background), and (2) a foreground latent space to learn object motion dynamics. In particular, these dynamics are modeled as point trajectories in the second latent space, with each point representing the foreground content in a scene and each latent trajectory ensuring regularity and realism of the generated motion across frames. Variations in the scene latent space result in different scenes, while variations in the trajectories of the foreground latent space result in different object motion. We demonstrate the effectiveness of the proposed approach by extensively evaluating the realism of the generated videos and compared the videos generated by state of the art methods [9,10], which, conversely to our method, learn a mapping between a single latent space and video data distribution instead of learning to generate specific motion and eventually object behaviour.

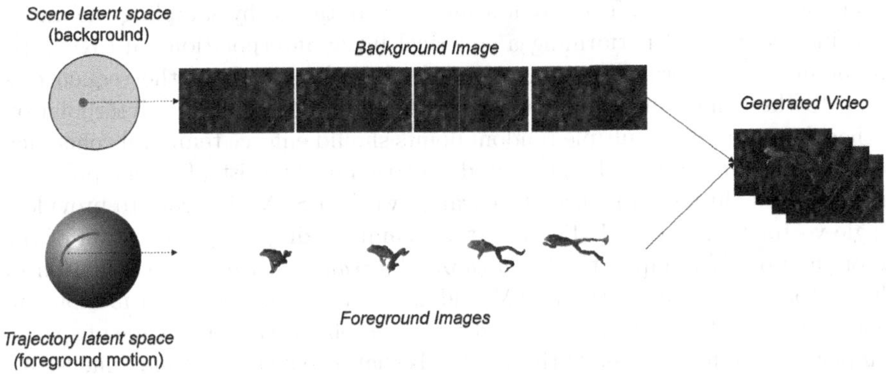

Fig. 1. Video Generation in VOS-GAN: we employ a scene latent space to generate background and a foreground latent space to generate object appearance and motion.

2 Video Generation Model

The video generation architecture presented in this work is based on a GAN framework consisting of the following two modules:

- a *generator*, implemented as a hybrid deep CNN-RNN, that receives two kinds of input: (1) a noise vector from a latent space that models scene background; (2) a sequence of vectors that model foreground motion as a trajectory in another latent space. The output of the generator is a video with its corresponding foreground mask.
- a *discriminator*, implemented as a deep CNN, that receives an input video and predicts whether it is real or not.

The architecture of the generator, inspired by the two-stream approach in [9], is shown in Fig. 2. Specifically, our generation approach factorizes the process into separate background and foreground generation, on the assumption that the world is generally stationary and the presence of informative motion can be constrained only to a set of objects of interest in a semi-static scenery. However, unlike [9], we separate the latent spaces for scene and foreground generation, and explicitly represent the latter as a temporal quantity, thus enforcing a more natural correspondence between the latent input and the frame-by-frame motion output.

Hence, the generator receives two inputs: $z_C \in \mathcal{Z}_C = \mathbb{R}^d$ and $z_M = \{z_{M,i}\}_{i=1}^t$, with each $z_{M,i} \in \mathcal{Z}_M = \mathbb{R}^d$. A point z_C in the latent space $\mathcal{Z}_C$ encodes the general scene to be applied to the output video, and is mainly responsible for driving the *background stream* of the model. This stream consists of a cascade of transposed convolutions, which gradually increase the spatial dimension of the input in order to obtain a full-scale background image $b(z_C)$ that is used for all frames in the generated video.

The set of $z_{M,i}$ points from the latent space $\mathcal{Z}_M$ defines the objects motion to be applied in the video. The latent sequence is obtained by sampling the initial and final points and performing a spherical linear interpolation (SLERP [11]) to compute all intermediate vectors, such that the length of the sequence is equal to the length (in frames) of the generated video. Using an interpolation rather than sampling multiple random points should enforce temporal coherency between appearances in the generated foreground. The list of latent points is then encoded through a recurrent neural network (LSTM) in order to provide a single vector (i.e., the LSTM's final state) summarizing a representation of the whole motion. The input to the *foreground stream* is then a concatenation of the vector coming out of the LSTM and z_C, so that the generated motion can take into account the scene to which it will be applied. After a cascade of spatio-temporal convolutions (i.e., with 3D kernels that also span the time dimension), the foreground stream provides a set of frames $f(z_C, z_M)$ with foreground content and binary masks $m(z_C, z_M)$ defining motion pixel location.

The two streams are finally combined as

$$G(z_C, z_M) = m(z_C, z_M) \odot f(z_C, z_M) + (1 - m(z_C, z_M)) \odot b(z_C) \qquad (1)$$

Foreground generation can be directly controlled acting on z_M. Indeed, varying z_M for a fixed value of z_C results in videos with the same background and different foreground appearance and motion. Thus, z_C can be seen as a condition for the foreground stream, in a similar way to conditional generative adversarial networks for restricting generation process to a specific class.

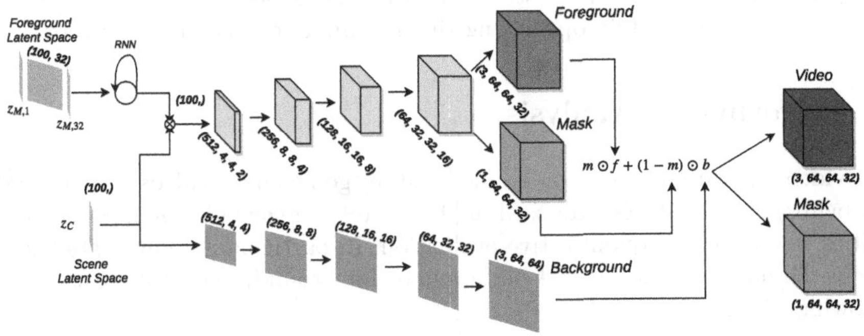

Fig. 2. Generator architecture: the *background stream* (bottom) is conditioned by a latent vector defining the general scene of the video, and produces a background image; the *foreground stream* (top) processes a sequence of latent vectors, obtained by spherically interpolating the start and end points, and the scene latent vector to generate frame-by-frame foreground appearance and motion masks. Information about dimensions of intermediate outputs is given in the figure by (*channels, height, width, duration*) tuples.

The primary goal of the discriminator network is to distinguish between generated and real videos, in order to push the generator towards more realistic outputs. The architecture of our discriminator follows a standard architecture for video discrimination [9]. The input to the model is a video clip (either real or produced by the generator), that goes first through a series of convolutional layers, encoding the video dynamics in a more compact representation, which is provided to a *discrimination stream* (bottom), which applies a 3D convolution to the intermediate representation and then makes a prediction on whether the input video is real or fake.

We jointly train the generator and the discriminator in a GAN framework, with the former trying to maximize the probability that the discriminator predict fake outputs as real, and the latter trying to minimize the same probability.

The discriminator loss is then defined as follows (for the sake of compactness, we will define $z = (z_C, z_M)$):

$$\mathcal{L}_D = -\mathbb{E}_{x \sim p_{\text{real}}} \left[\log D_{\text{adv}} (x) \right] - \mathbb{E}_{x \sim p_z} \left[\log \left(1 - D_{\text{adv}} \left(G \left(z\right)\right)\right)\right] \tag{2}$$

In the equation above, the first line encodes the adversarial loss, which pushes the discriminator to return high likelihood scores for real videos and low ones for the generated videos.

The generator loss is, more traditionally, defined as:

$$\mathcal{L}_G = -\mathbb{E}_{z \sim p_z} \left[\log D_{\text{adv}} \left(G \left(z\right)\right)\right] \tag{3}$$

In this case, the generator tries to push the discriminator to increase the likelihood of its output being real.

During training, we follow the common approach for GAN training, by sampling real videos (from an existing dataset) and generated videos (from the generator) and alternately optimizing the discriminator and the generator.

3 Performance Analysis

Our video generation model was trained on the "golf course" videos (over 600,000 videoclips) of the dataset proposed in [9]. For testing the video generation capabilities we performed quantitative evaluation. In particular, we evaluated separately the quality of generated background, foreground, and motion using the following metrics:

- **Foreground Content Distance (FCD)**. This score aims at assessing the consistency between visual appearance of foreground objects in consecutive figures and is measured by computing the average L2 distance between visual features, extracted from a fully-connected layer of a pre-trained Inception network [12], of foreground objects in two consecutive figures. The input to the Inception model is the bounding box containing the foreground region, defined as the discriminator's segmentation output.
- **Motion coherency (MC)**. While the previous score describes the quality of the generated visual appearance of moving objects, this one aims at evaluating how realistic the generated motion is, and is computed as the KL-divergence between magnitude/orientation histograms of optical flows of real and generated videos.
- **Inception score (IS)** [13] is the most adopted metric in GAN literature. In our case, we compute the Inception score by sampling a random frame from each video of a pool of generated ones.

During GAN training, we performed gradient-descent using ADAM, with an initial learning rate of 0.0002, $\beta_1 = 0.5$, $\beta_2 = 0.999$ and batch size of 16 for 25 epochs.

FCS, MC and IS scores were computed on a set of 50,000 videos generated by the compared models trained on "golf course" [9], and on the same number of random real videos as a baseline. The results in Table 1 shows that our approach significantly outperformed VGAN and TGAN on the three metrics, achieving closer values to those yielded by real videos, indicating a higher realism in scene appearance and object motion. Samples of generated videos on for VGAN, TGAN and our method are shown in Fig. 3.

Table 1. Quantitative evaluation of video generation capabilities measured by foreground content distance (FCD), motion coherency (MC) and Inception Score (IS).

	FCD	MC	IS
VGAN [9]	10.61	0.017	1.74
TGAN [10]	3.74	0.011	2.02
Our approach	**4.80**	**0.002**	**2.90**
Real videos	4.59	0.0001	4.59

Fig. 3. Frame samples. (First and forth row) VGAN-generated video figures show very little object motion, while (second and fifth row) TGAN-generated video figures show motion, but the quality of foreground appearance is low. Our approach (third and sixth row) generates video figures with a good compromise between object motion and appearance.

4 Conclusion

We propose a novel GAN-based video generation approach that employs two input latent spaces: one for modeling the background, and one to model foreground motion and appearance. Extensive experimental evaluation showed that our VOS-GAN outperforms significantly existing GAN-based methods, VGAN [9] and TGAN [10], on the video generation process, by creating videos with more realistic motion measured quantitatively.

References

1. Goodfellow, I., et al.: Generative adversarial nets. In: Ghahramani, Z., Welling, M., Cortes, C., Lawrence, N.D., Weinberger, K.Q. (eds.) Advances in Neural Information Processing Systems 27, pp. 2672–2680. Curran Associates, Inc., New York (2014)
2. Denton, E.L., Chintala, S., Szlam, A., Fergus, R.: Deep generative image models using a Laplacian pyramid of adversarial networks. In: Cortes, C., Lawrence, N.D., Lee, D.D., Sugiyama, M., Garnett, R. (eds.) Advances in Neural Information Processing Systems 28, pp. 1486–1494. Curran Associates, Inc., New York (2015)
3. Radford, A., Metz, L., Chintala, S.: Unsupervised representation learning with deep convolutional generative adversarial networks. In: ICLR (2016)
4. Zhang, H., et al.: StackGAN: text to photo-realistic image synthesis with stacked generative adversarial networks. In: The IEEE International Conference on Computer Vision (ICCV), October 2017
5. Arjovsky, M., Chintala, S., Bottou, L.: Wasserstein generative adversarial networks. In: Precup, D., Teh, Y.W. (eds.) Proceedings of the 34th International Conference on Machine Learning, International Convention Centre, Sydney, Australia, PMLR, 06–11 Aug 2017, vol. 70, pp. 214–223
6. Mao, X., Li, Q., Xie, H., Lau, R.Y., Wang, Z., Paul Smolley, S.: Least squares generative adversarial networks. In: The IEEE International Conference on Computer Vision (ICCV), October 2017
7. Roth, K., Lucchi, A., Nowozin, S., Hofmann, T.: Stabilizing training of generative adversarial networks through regularization. In: Guyon, I., et al. (eds.) Advances in Neural Information Processing Systems 30, pp. 2018–2028. Curran Associates, Inc., New York (2017)
8. Huang, X., Li, Y., Poursaeed, O., Hopcroft, J., Belongie, S.: Stacked generative adversarial networks. In: The IEEE Conference on Computer Vision and Pattern Recognition (CVPR), July 2017
9. Vondrick, C., Pirsiavash, H., Torralba, A.: Generating videos with scene dynamics. In: Lee, D.D., Sugiyama, M., Luxburg, U.V., Guyon, I., Garnett, R. (eds.) Advances in Neural Information Processing Systems 29, pp. 613–621. Curran Associates, Inc., New York (2016)
10. Saito, M., Matsumoto, E., Saito, S.: Temporal generative adversarial nets with singular value clipping. In: The IEEE International Conference on Computer Vision (ICCV), October 2017

11. Shoemake, K.: Animating rotation with quaternion curves. SIGGRAPH Comput. Graph. **19**(3), 245–254 (1985)
12. Szegedy, C., et al.: Going deeper with convolutions. In: Computer Vision and Pattern Recognition (CVPR) (2015)
13. Salimans, T., et al.: Improved techniques for training GANs. In: Lee, D.D., Sugiyama, M., Luxburg, U.V., Guyon, I., Garnett, R. (eds.) Advances in Neural Information Processing Systems 29, pp. 2234–2242. Curran Associates, Inc., New York (2016)

A Semi-supervised Deep Generative Model for Human Body Analysis

Rodrigo de Bem[1,2(✉)], Arnab Ghosh[1], Thalaiyasingam Ajanthan[1], Ondrej Miksik[1], N. Siddharth[1], and Philip Torr[1]

[1] Department of Engineering Science, University of Oxford, Oxford, UK
{rodrigo,arnabg,ajanthan,omiksik,nsid,phst}@robots.ox.ac.uk

[2] Center of Computational Sciences, Federal University of Rio Grande, Rio Grande, Brazil

Abstract. Deep generative modelling for human body analysis is an emerging problem with many interesting applications. However, the latent space learned by such models is typically not interpretable, resulting in less flexible models. In this work, we adopt a structured semi-supervised approach and present a deep generative model for human body analysis where the body pose and the visual appearance are disentangled in the latent space. Such a disentanglement allows independent manipulation of pose and appearance, and hence enables applications such as pose-transfer without being explicitly trained for such a task. In addition, our setting allows for semi-supervised pose estimation, relaxing the need for labelled data. We demonstrate the capabilities of our generative model on the Human3.6M and on the DeepFashion datasets.

Keywords: Deep generative models · Variational autoencoders · Semi-supervised learning · Human pose estimation · Analysis-by-synthesis

1 Introduction

Human-body analysis has been a long-standing goal in computer vision, with many applications in gaming, human-computer interaction, shopping and healthcare [1,29,30,37]. Typically, most approaches to this problem have focused on supervised learning of discriminative models [4–6,41], to learn a mapping from given visual input (images or videos) to a suitable abstract form (*e.g.* human pose). While these approaches do exceptionally well on their prescribed task, as evidenced by performance on pose estimation benchmarks, they fall short due to: (a) reliance on fully-labelled data, and (b) the inability to generate novel data from the abstractions.

The former is a fairly onerous requirement, particularly when dealing with real-world visual data, as it requires many hours of human-annotator time and effort to collect. Thus, being able to relax the reliance on labelled data is a highly desirable goal. The latter addresses the ability to manipulate the abstractions

L. Leal-Taixé and S. Roth (Eds.): ECCV 2018 Workshops, LNCS 11130, pp. 500–517, 2019.
https://doi.org/10.1007/978-3-030-11012-3_38

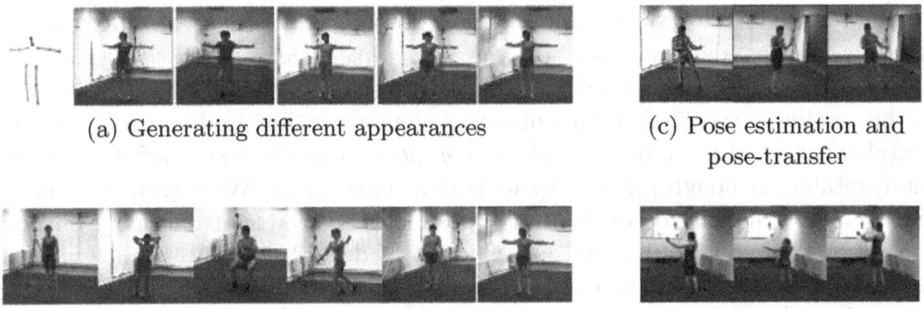

(a) Generating different appearances

(b) Generating different poses

(c) Pose estimation and pose-transfer

(d) Direct manipulation

Fig. 1. Sampled results from our deep generative model for natural images of people. (a) For a given pose (first image), we show some samples of appearance. (b) For a given appearance (first image), samples of different poses. (c) For an estimated pose (first image) and an estimated appearance (second image), we show a generated sample combining the pose of the first image with the appearance of the second. (d) For a given pose and appearance (first image), by the direct manipulation of pose, we can modify the body size, while the appearance is kept the same.

directly, with a view to *generating* novel visual data; *e.g.* moving the pose of an arm results in generation of images or videos where that arm is correspondingly displaced. Such *generative* modelling, in contrast to discriminative modelling, enables an *analysis-by-synthesis* approach to human-body analysis, where one can generate images of humans in combinations of poses and clothing unseen during training. This has many potential applications. For instance, it can be used for performance capture and reenactment of RGB videos, as already possible for faces [34], and still incipient for human bodies. It can also be used to generate images in a user specified pose to enhance datasets with minimal annotation effort. Such an approach is typically tackled using deep generative models (DGMs) [9,18,27] – an extension of standard generative models that incorporate neural networks as flexible function approximators. Such models are particularly effective in complex perceptual domains such as computer vision [19], language [25], and robotics [40], effectively delegating bottom-up feature learning to neural networks, while simultaneously incorporating top-down probabilistic semantics into the model. They solve both the deficiencies of discriminative approach discussed above by (a) employing unsupervised learning, thereby removing the need for labels, and (b) embracing a fully generative approach.

However, DGMs introduce a new problem – the learnt abstractions, or latent variables, are not *human-interpretable.* This lack of interpretability is a by-product of the unsupervised learning of representations from data. The learnt latent variables, typically represented as some smooth high-dimensional manifold, do not have consistent semantic meaning – different sub-spaces in this manifold can encode arbitrary variations in the data. This is particularly unsuitable for our purposes as we would like to view and manipulate the latent variables, *e.g.* the body pose.

In order to ameliorate the aforementioned issue, while still eschewing reliance on fully-labelled data, we rely on the *structured semi-supervised* variational autoencoder (VAE) framework [17,32]. Here, the model structure is assumed to be *partially specified*, with consistent semantics imposed on some interpretable subset of the latent variables (*e.g.* pose), and the rest is left to be non-interpretable, although referred by us here as *appearance*. Weak (semi) supervision acts as a means to constrain the pose latent variables to actually encode the pose. This gives us the full complement of desirable features, allowing (a) semi-supervised learning, relaxing the need for labelled data, (b) generative modelling through stochastic computation graphs [28], and (c) interpretable subset of latent variables defined through model structure.

In this work, we introduce a structured semi-supervised VAEGAN [20] architecture, Semi-DGPose, in which we further extend previous structured semi-supervised models [17,32] with a discriminator-based loss function [9,20]. We show some results on human pose in Fig. 1. It is formulated in a principled, unified probabilistic framework. To our knowledge, it is the first structured semi-supervised deep generative model of people in natural images, directly learned in the image space. In contrast to previous work [21,23,24,31,38], it directly enables: (i) *semi-supervised pose estimation* and (ii) *indirect pose-transfer* across domains without explicit training for such a task, both of which are tested and verified by experimental evidence.

In summary, our main contributions are: (i) a real-world application of structured semi-supervised deep generative model of natural images, separating pose from appearance in the analysis of the human body; (ii) a quantitative and qualitative evaluation of the generative capabilities of such model; and (iii) a demonstration of its utility in performing semi-supervised pose estimation and indirect pose-transfer.

2 Preliminaries

Deep generative models (DGMs) come in two broad flavours – Variational Autoencoders (VAEs) [18,27], and Generative Adversarial Networks (GANs) [9]. In both cases, the goal is to learn a generative model $p_\theta(\mathbf{x}, \mathbf{z})$ over data $\mathbf{x}$ and latent variables $\mathbf{z}$, with parameters θ. Typically the model parameters θ are represented in the form of a neural network.

VAEs learn the parameters θ that maximise the marginal likelihood (or evidence) of the model denoted as $p_\theta(\mathbf{x}) = \int p_\theta(\mathbf{x}|\mathbf{z})p_\theta(\mathbf{z})dz$. They introduce a conditional probability density $q_\phi(\mathbf{z}|\mathbf{x})$ as an approximation to the unknown and intractable model posterior $p_\theta(\mathbf{z}|\mathbf{x})$, employing the variational principle in order to optimise a surrogate objective $\mathcal{L}_{\text{VAE}}(\phi, \theta; \mathbf{x})$, called the evidence lower bound (ELBO), as

$$\log p_\theta(\mathbf{x}) \geq \mathcal{L}_{\text{VAE}}(\phi, \theta; \mathbf{x}) = \mathbb{E}_{q_\phi(\mathbf{z}|\mathbf{x})}\left[\log \frac{p_\theta(\mathbf{x}, \mathbf{z})}{q_\phi(\mathbf{z}|\mathbf{x})}\right]. \quad (1)$$

The conditional density $q_\phi(\mathbf{z}|\mathbf{x})$ is called the recognition or inference distribution, with parameters ϕ also represented in the form of a neural network.

To enable structured semi-supervised learning, one can factor the latent variables into unstructured or non-interpretable variables $\mathbf{z}$ and structured or interpretable variables $\mathbf{y}$ without loss of generality [17,32]. For learning in this framework, the objective can be expressed as the combination of supervised and unsupervised objectives. Let $\mathcal{D}_u$ and $\mathcal{D}_s$ denote the unlabelled and labelled subset of the dataset $\mathcal{D}$, and let the joint recognition network factorise as $q_\phi(\mathbf{y},\mathbf{z}|\mathbf{x}) = q_\phi(\mathbf{y}|\mathbf{x})q_\phi(\mathbf{z}|\mathbf{x},\mathbf{y})$. Then, the combined objective summed over the entire dataset corresponds to

$$\mathcal{L}_{\text{SS}}(\theta,\phi;\mathcal{D}) = \sum_{\mathbf{x}_u\in\mathcal{D}_u} \mathcal{L}_u(\theta,\phi;\mathbf{x}_u) + \gamma \sum_{(\mathbf{x}_s,\mathbf{y}_s)\in\mathcal{D}_s} \mathcal{L}_s(\theta,\phi;\mathbf{x}_s,\mathbf{y}_s), \tag{2}$$

where $\mathcal{L}_u$ and $\mathcal{L}_s$ are defined as

$$\mathcal{L}_u(\theta,\phi;\mathbf{x}_u) = \mathcal{L}_{\text{VAE}}(\theta,\phi;\mathbf{x}_u), \tag{3}$$

$$\mathcal{L}_s(\theta,\phi;\mathbf{x}_s,\mathbf{y}_s) = \mathbb{E}_{q_\phi(\mathbf{z}|\mathbf{x}_s,\mathbf{y}_s)}\left[\log \frac{p_\theta(\mathbf{x}_s,\mathbf{z}|\mathbf{y}_s)}{q_\phi(\mathbf{z}|\mathbf{x}_s,\mathbf{y}_s)}\right] + \alpha \log q_\phi(\mathbf{y}_s|\mathbf{x}_s). \tag{4}$$

Here, the hyper-parameter γ (Eq. 2) controls the relative weight between the supervised and unsupervised dataset sizes, and α (Eq. 4) controls the relative weight between generative and discriminative learning.

Note that by the factorisation of the generative model, VAEs require the specification of an explicit likelihood function $p_\theta(\mathbf{x}|\mathbf{z})$, which can often be difficult. GANs [9] on the other hand, attempt to sidestep this requirement by learning a surrogate to the likelihood function, while avoiding the learning of a recognition distribution. Here, the generative model $p_\theta(\mathbf{x},\mathbf{z})$, viewed as a mapping $G : \mathbf{z} \mapsto \mathbf{x}$, is setup in a two-player minimax game with a "discriminator" $D : \mathbf{x} \mapsto \{0,1\}$, whose goal is to correctly identify if a data point $\mathbf{x}$ came from the generative model $p_\theta(\mathbf{x},\mathbf{z})$ or the true data distribution $p(\mathbf{x})$. Such objective is defined as

$$\mathcal{L}_{\text{GAN}}(D,G) = \mathbb{E}_{p(\mathbf{x})}\left[\log D(\mathbf{x})\right] + \mathbb{E}_{p_\theta(\mathbf{z})}\left[1 - \log D(G(\mathbf{z}))\right]. \tag{5}$$

In fact, in our structured model, generation is defined as a function of pose and appearance as $G(\mathbf{y},\mathbf{z})$. Crucially, learning a customised approximation to the likelihood can result in a much higher quality of generated data, particularly for the visual domain [15].

A more recent family of DGMs, VAEGANs [20], bring together these two different approaches into a single objective that combines both the VAE and GAN objectives directly as

$$\mathcal{L} = \mathcal{L}_{\text{VAE}} + \mathcal{L}_{\text{GAN}}. \tag{6}$$

This marries better the likelihood learning with the inference-distribution learning, providing a more flexible family of models.

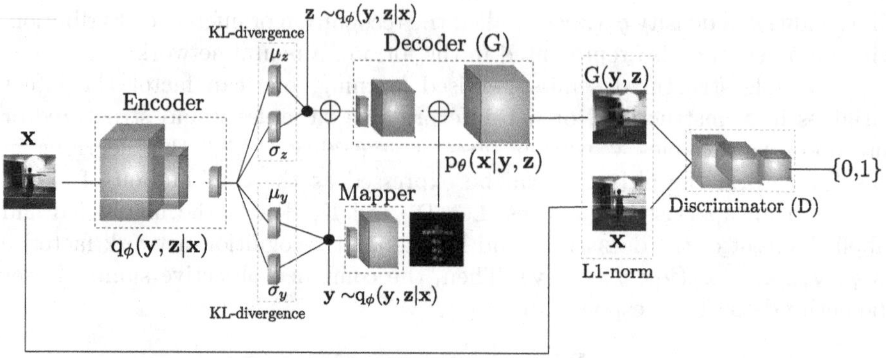

Fig. 2. Semi-DGPose architecture. The Encoder receives $\mathbf{x}$ as input. The KL-divergence losses between the Gaussian distribution $q_\phi(\mathbf{y}, \mathbf{z}|\mathbf{x})$ and the weak Gaussian priors $p(\mathbf{y})$ and $p(\mathbf{z})$ works as a regulariser for unsupervised training samples (see Eq. 3). The sampling of appearance and pose is done using the reparametrization trick [18] and propagated to the Decoder. For the supervised training (not shown above for simplicity, see Eq. 4), a regression loss between the estimated pose and the pose ground-truth label substitutes the KL-divergence over the pose distribution. In both, supervised and unsupervised training, the low-dimensional pose vector $\mathbf{y}$ is mapped to a heatmap representation by the Mapper module. The L1-norm and the Discriminator losses are computed over the reconstructed $\mathrm{G}(\mathbf{y}, \mathbf{z})$ and the original $\mathbf{x}$ images. G denotes Generator (see Eq. 5).

3 Semi-DGPose Network

Our structured semi-supervised VAEGAN model consists of two tasks: (i) learning of a recognition network (Encoder) estimating pose $\mathbf{y}$ and appearance $\mathbf{z}$ from a given RGB image $\mathbf{x}$ and (ii) learning of a generative network (Decoder) combining pose and appearance to generate corresponding RGB images. Overview of our model is shown in Fig. 2. In our model, Eq. 2 is used the aforementioned tasks, while Eq. 5 learns to discriminate between real and generated images. In contrast to the standard VAEGAN objective (Eq. 6), the structured semi-supervised VAEGAN objective is given by

$$\mathcal{L} = \mathcal{L}_{\mathrm{SS}} + \mathcal{L}_{\mathrm{GAN}}. \tag{7}$$

Pose Representation and the Mapper Module. Pose can be represented either using the 2D (x, y) positions of the joints themselves in vector form, or using Gaussian heatmaps of the joints, which is a preferred variant successfully used in many discriminative pose estimation approaches [2,6,26,35,41]. The heatmaps $\mathbf{y} \in \mathcal{R}^{P \times H \times W}$ consists of P channels, each one corresponding to a distinct body part, where $H = 64$ and $W = 64$ are the heatmaps' height and width, respectively. As the set of joints are sparse discrete points in the image, we use heatmaps for J joints, R rigid parts and $B = 1$ whole body, such that $P = J + R + B$ (see Appendix A). It covers the entire area of the body in the image, as in [2]. Our preliminary experiments showed that heatmaps led to better quality results, in contrast to the vector-based representation. On the other hand, a low-dimensional representation is more suitable and desirable as a latent variable, since human pose lies in a low-dimensional manifold embedded in the high-dimensional image space [7,8].

To cope with this mismatch, we introduce the Mapper module, which maps 2D pose-vectors to heatmaps. Ground-truth heatmaps are constructed from manually annotated ground-truth 2D joints labels, by means of a simple weak annotation strategy described in [2]. The Mapper module is then trained to map 2D joints to heatmaps, minimizing the L2-norm between predicted and ground-truth heatmaps. This module is trained separately with the same training hyper-parameters used for our full architecture, described later in Sect. 4. In the training of the full Semi-DGPose architecture, the Mapper module is integrated to it with its weights fixed, since the mapping function has been learned already. As it is illustrated in Fig. 2, the Mapper allows us to keep a low-dimensional representation in the latent space, at the same time that a dense high-dimensional "spatial" heatmap representation facilitates the generation of accurate images by the Decoder. As it is fully differentiable, the module allows the gradients to be backpropagated normally from the Decoder to the Encoder, when it is required during the training of the full architecture.

We have extensively tested several architectures of our model. All of its modules are deep CNNs and their details are in Tables 2 and 1 (Sect. A, Appendix).

Training. The terms of Eq. 2 correspond to two training routines which are alternately employed, according to the presence of ground-truth labels. In the *unsupervised case*, when no label is available, it is similar to the standard VAE (see Eq. 3). Specifically, given the image $\mathbf{x}$, the Encoder estimates the posterior distribution $q_\phi(\mathbf{y}, \mathbf{z}|\mathbf{x})$, where both appearance $\mathbf{z}$ and pose $\mathbf{y}$ are assumed to be independent given the image $\mathbf{x}$. Then, pose and appearance are sampled from the posterior, while the KL-divergences between the posterior and the prior distributions, $\mathrm{KL}[q_\phi(\mathbf{y}|\mathbf{x})|p(\mathbf{y})]$ and $\mathrm{KL}[q_\phi(\mathbf{z}|\mathbf{x})|p(\mathbf{z})]$, are used as regularisers. The samples $\mathbf{y}$ and $\mathbf{z}$ are passed through the Decoder to generate a reconstructed image. Finally, the unsupervised loss function minimized during training is composed of the L1-norm reconstruction loss, the KL-divergences and the cross-entropy Discriminator loss. In the *supervised case*, when the pose label is available, the KL-divergence between the posterior pose distribution and the pose prior, $\mathrm{KL}[q_\phi(\mathbf{y}|\mathbf{x})|p(\mathbf{y})]$, is replaced with a regression loss between the estimated pose and the given label (see Eq. 5). Now, only the appearance $\mathbf{z}$ is sampled from the posterior distribution and passed to the Decoder, along with the ground-truth pose label. Finally, the supervised loss function minimized during training is composed of the L1-norm reconstruction loss, the KL-divergence over the appearance distribution, the regression loss over the pose vector and the cross-entropy Discriminator loss. In this case, gradients are not backpropagated from the Decoder to the Encoder, through the pose posterior distribution, since pose was not estimated. In both *unsupervised* and *supervised* cases, the Mapper module, which is trained *offline*, is used to map the 2D pose-vector in the latent space to a dense heatmap representation, as illustrated in Fig. 2.

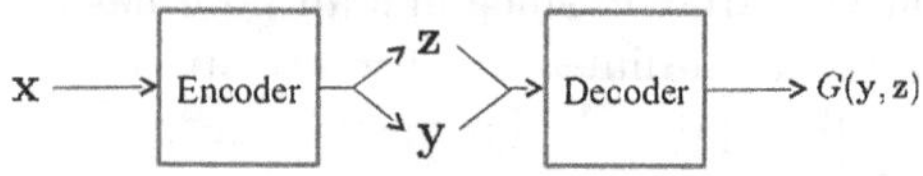

Fig. 3. Reconstruction at test time.

Reconstruction. At test time, only an image $\mathbf{x}$ is given as input, and the reconstructed image $G(\mathbf{y}, \mathbf{z})$ is obtained from the Decoder. In the reconstruction process, *direct manipulation* of the pose representation $\mathbf{y}$ allows image generations with varying body pose and size while the appearance is kept the same (see Fig. 8, Sect. 4.1) (Fig. 3).

Indirect Pose-Transfer. Our method allows us to do *indirect* pose-transfer without explicit training for such task. In this case, (i) an image $\mathbf{x}_1$ is first passed through the Encoder network, from which the target pose $\mathbf{y}_1$ is kept. (ii) In the second step, another image $\mathbf{x}_2$ is propagated through the Encoder, from which the appearance encoding $\mathbf{z}_2$ is kept. (iii) Finally, $\mathbf{z}_2$ and $\mathbf{y}_1$ are jointly propagated through the Decoder, and an image $\mathbf{x}_3$ is reconstructed, containing a person in the pose $\mathbf{y}_1$ estimated from the first image, but with the appearance $\mathbf{z}_2$ defined by the second image. This is a novel application that our approach enables; in contrast to prior art, our network neither rely on any external pose estimator nor on conditioning labels to perform pose-transfer (see Fig. 13, Sect. 4.1) (Fig. 4).

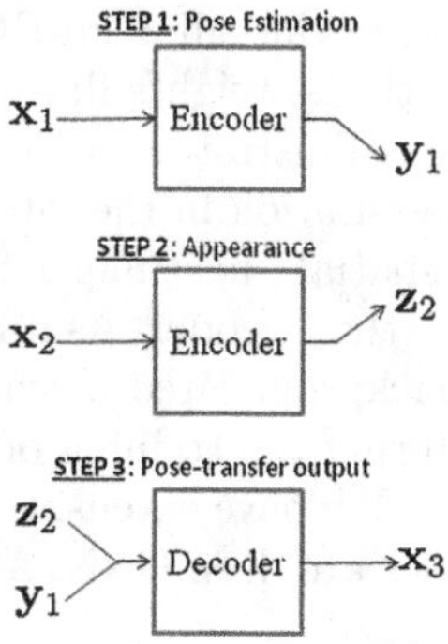

Fig. 4. Indirect pose-transfer at test time.

Sampling. When no image is given as input, we can jointly or separately sample pose $\mathbf{y}$ and appearance $\mathbf{z}$ from the posterior distribution. They may be sampled at the same time or one may be kept fixed while the other distribution is sampled. In all cases, the encodings are passed through the Decoder network to generate a corresponding RGB image (Fig. 5).

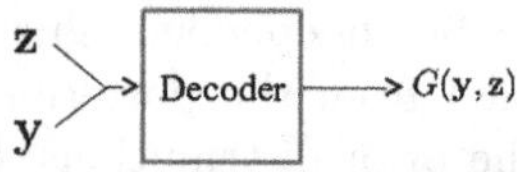

Fig. 5. Sampling at test time.

Pose Estimation. One of the main differences between our approach and prior art is the ability of our model to estimate human-body pose as well. In our model, given an input image $\mathbf{x}$, it is possible to perform pose estimation by regressing to the pose representation vector $\mathbf{y}$. In this case, the appearance encoding $\mathbf{z}$ is disregarded and the Decoder, Mapper and Discriminator networks are not used (Fig. 6).

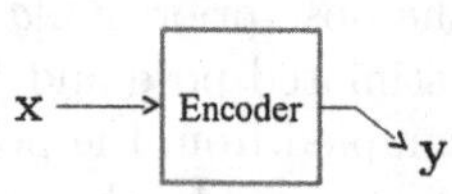

Fig. 6. Pose estimation at test time.

4 Experiments and Discussion

In this section, we present the datasets, metrics and training hyper-parameters used in our work. Finally, quantitative and qualitative results show the effectiveness and novelty of our Semi-DGPose architecture.

Human3.6M Dataset. Human3.6M [11] is a widely used benchmark for human body analysis. It contains 3.6 million images acquired by recording 5 female and 6 male actors performing a diverse set of motions and poses corresponding to 15 activities, under 4 different viewpoints. We followed the standard protocol and used sequences of 2 out of 11 actors as our test set, while the rest of the data was used for training. We use a subset of 14 (out of 32) body joints represented by their (x, y) 2D image coordinates as our ground-truth data, neglecting minor body parts (*e.g.* fingers). Due to the high frequency of the video acquisition (50 Hz), there is a considerable level of practically redundant images. Thus, out of images from all 4 cameras, we subsample frames in time, producing subsets for training and test, with 317, 989 and 1, 280 images, respectively. All the images have resolution of 1000×1000 pixels.

DeepFashion Dataset. The DeepFashion dataset (In-shop Clothes Retrieval Benchmark) [22] consists of 52,712 images of people in a variety of clothing and poses. We follow [23], using their joints' annotations obtained with an off-the-shelf pose estimator [5], and divide the dataset into training (44,950 images) and test (6,560 images) subsets. Images with wrong pose estimations were suppressed, with all original images having 256×256 pixels. Note, we aim to learn a complete generative model of people in natural images, which is significantly more complex, compared to models focusing on a particular task, such as pose-transfer. For this reason, we do not restrict our training set to pairs of images of the same person and use individual images, in contrast to [23,31].

Metrics. Since our model explicitly represents *appearance* and *body pose* as separate variables, we evaluate its performance with respect to two different aspects: (i) *image quality* of reconstructions, evaluated using the standard Peak Signal-to-Noise Ratio (PSNR) and Structural Similarity Index (SSIM) [39] metrics and (ii) *accuracy of pose estimation*, obtained by the Semi-DGPose model, measured using the Percentage of Correct Keypoints (PCK) metric [43], which computes the percentage of 2D joints correctly located by a pose estimator, given the *ground-truth* and a normalized distance threshold corresponding to the size of the person's torso.

Training Parameters. All models were trained with mini-batches consisting of 64 images. We used the Adam optimizer [16] with initial learning rate set to 10^{-4}. The weight decay regulariser was set to 5×10^{-4}. Network weights were initialized randomly for fully-connected layers and with robust initialization [10] for convolutional and transposed-convolutional layers. Except when stated differently, for all images and all models, we used a 64×64 pixel crop, centring the person of interest. We did not use any form of data augmentation or preprocessing except for image normalisation to zero mean and unit variance. All models were implemented in Caffe [14] and all experiments ran on an NVIDIA Titan X GPU.

4.1 Semi-DGPose Results

Here we evaluate our Semi-DGPose model on the Human3.6M [11] and on the DeepFashion [22] datasets. The Human3.6M is well-suited for pose estimation evaluation, since it has joints' annotations obtained in studio by mean of an accurate motion capture system. We show quantitative and qualitative results, focusing particularly on pose estimation and on *indirect* pose transfer capabilities, described later in this section. We show qualitative experiments on the DeepFashion, comparing reconstructions with original images. Our experiments and results show the effectiveness of the Semi-DGPose method.

Results on Human3.6M. To evaluate the efficacy of our model, we perform a "relative" comparison. In other words, we first train our model with full supervision (*i.e.* all data points are labelled) to evaluate performance in an ideal case and then we train the model with other setups, using labels only for 75%, 50% and 25% data points. Such an evaluation allows us to decouple the efficacy of the model itself and the semi-supervision to see how the gradual decrease in the level of supervision affects the final performance of the method on the same validation set. We first cross-validated the hyper-parameter α which weights the regression loss (see Eq. 4, in Sect. 2) and found that $\alpha = 100$ yields the best results, as shown in Fig. 7b. Following [32], we keep $\gamma = 1$ in all experiments (see Eq. 2, in Sect. 2). In Fig. 7a, we show reconstructed images along with the heatmap pose representation. When pose representation is *directly manipulated* during the reconstruction process, appearance can be kept the same while the body pose can modified, as shown in Fig. 8.

We evaluated it across different levels of supervision, with the PSNR and SSIM metrics and show results in Fig. 9a. We also evaluated the pose estimation accuracy of the Semi-DGPose model. It achieves 93.85% PCK score, normalized at 0.5, in the fully-supervised setup (100% of supervision over the training data). This pose estimation accuracy is on par with the state-of-the-art pose estimators on unconstrained images [42]. However, since the Human3.6M was captured in a controlled environment, a standard (discriminative) pose estimator can be expected to perform better. The overall PCK curves corresponding to each percentage of supervision in the training set is shown in Fig. 9b. Note that, even with 25% supervision, our model still obtains 88.35% PCK score, normalized at 0.5, showing the effectiveness of the semi-supervised approach. Finally, we show the pose estimation accuracy for different samples in Fig. 10. In Fig. 11, we show reconstructed images obtained with different levels of supervision. It

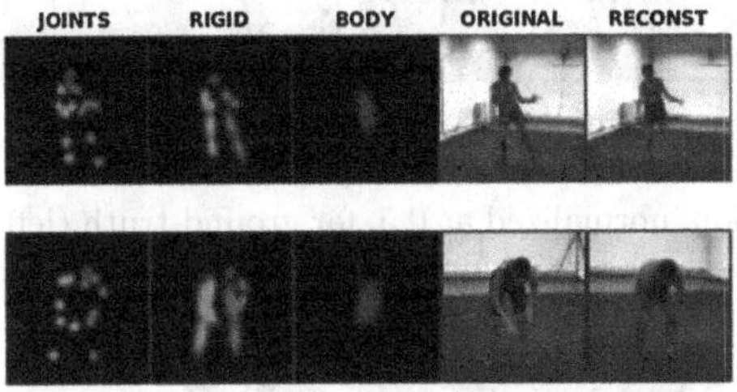

(a)

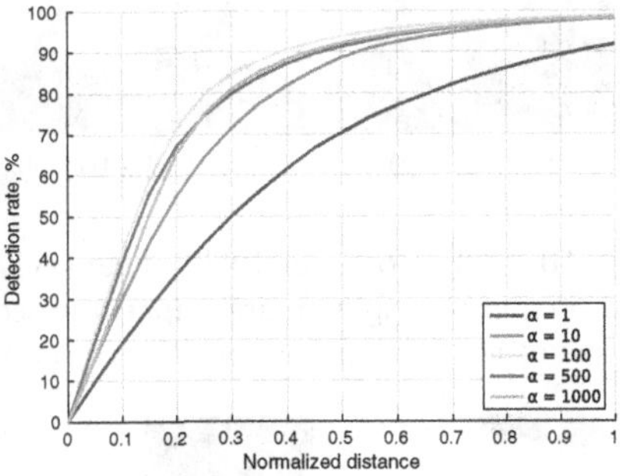

(b)

Fig. 7. (a) Qualitative reconstructions with full supervision. (b) PCK scores for the cross-validation adjustment of the regression loss weight α.

(a) (b) (c) (d) (e)

Fig. 8. Direct manipulation. Original image (**a**), followed by reconstructions in which the person's height was changed to a percentage of the original, as: (**b**) 80%, (**c**) 95%, (**d**) 105% and (**e**) 120%. The same procedure may be applied to produce different changes in the body size and aspect ratio.

Level of supervision	PSNR	SSIM
100%	22.27	0.89
75%	21.36	0.86
50%	21.49	0.87
25%	20.06	0.83

(a)

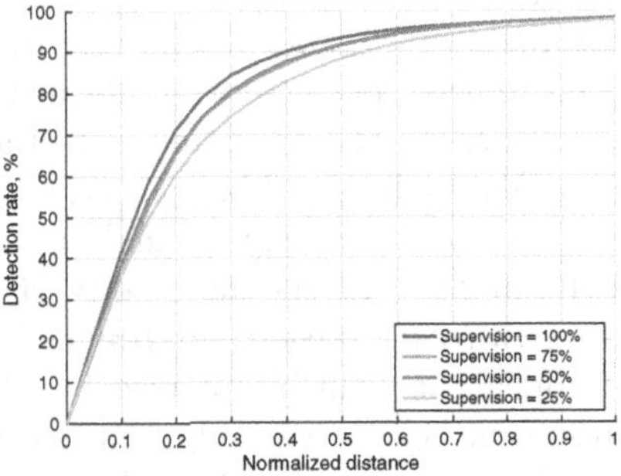

(b)

Fig. 9. Quantitative evaluations of Semi-DGPose on Human3.6M: (**a**) PSNR and SSIM measures for different levels of supervision, (**b**) PCK scores for different levels of supervision. Note that, even with 25% supervision, our Semi-DGPose obtains 88.35% PCK score, normalized at 0.5.

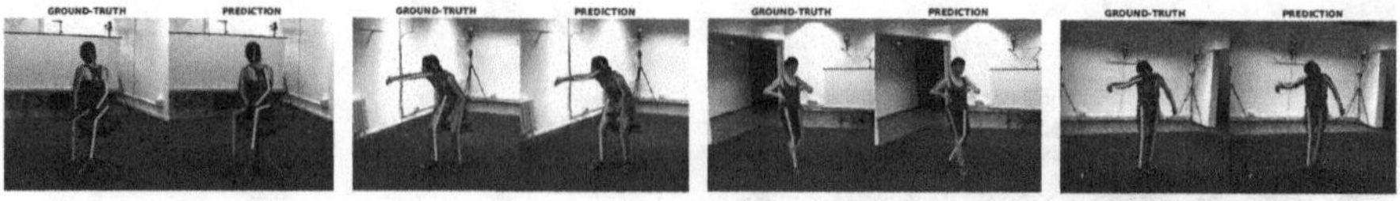

(a) PCK=92.9% (b) PCK=100.0% (c) PCK=96.4% (d) PCK=100.0%

Fig. 10. PCK scores for 100% of supervision, normalized at 0.5, for ground-truth (left) and prediction (right) pairs, superimposed on the original images. Each pair correspond to one of the 4 cameras from the Human3.6M dataset.

(a) (b) (c) (d) (e) (f)

Fig. 11. Semi-DGPose reconstructions: (**a**) original image, and (**b**) heatmap pose representation, followed by reconstructions with different levels of supervision: (**c**) 100%, (**d**) 75%, (**e**) 50%, (**f**) 25%.

(a) (b) (c) (d) (e)

Fig. 12. Pose estimation. Original image (**a**), followed by estimations, over the original image, with: (**b**) 100%, (**c**) 75%, (**d**) 50% and (**e**) 25% of supervision.

allows us to observe how image quality is affected when we gradually reduce the availability of labels. Following that, we evaluate results on pose estimation and on *indirect* pose transfer. Regarding **semi-supervised pose estimation**, we complement the previous quantitative evaluation with the results shown in Fig. 12. We highlight this distinctive capability of our Semi-DGPose generative model. Again, we aimed to analyse how the gradual decrease of supervision in the training set affects the quality of pose estimation on the test images. Concerning ***indirect pose-transfer***, as both latent variables corresponding to pose and appearance can be inferred by the model's Encoder (recognition network) at test time, latent variables extracted from different images can be combined in a subsequent step, and employed together as inputs for the Decoder (generative network). The result of that is a generated image combining appearance and body pose, extracted from two different images. The process is done in three phases, as illustrated in Fig. 13: (i) the latent pose representation $\mathbf{y}_1$ is estimated from the first input image through the Encoder; (ii) the latent *appearance* representation $\mathbf{z}_2$ is estimated from a second image, also through the Encoder, (iii) $\mathbf{y}_1$ and $\mathbf{z}_2$ are propagated through the Decoder, and a new image is generated,

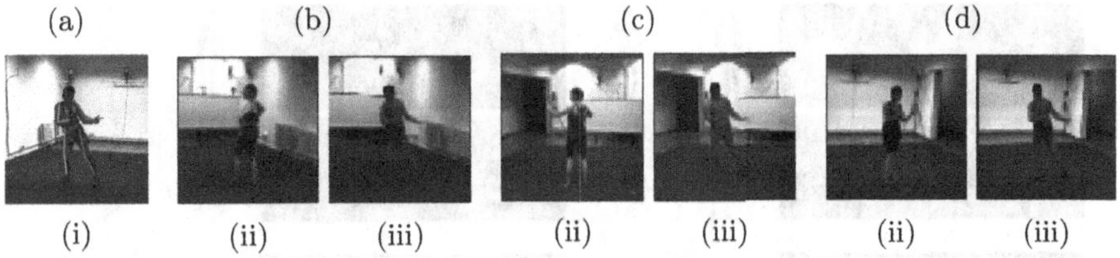

Fig. 13. ***Indirect*** **pose transfer:** **(i)** the latent target pose representation $\mathbf{y}_1$ is estimated (Encoder). The pairs **(b)**, **(c)** and **(d)**, show **(ii)** the image from which the latent *appearance* $\mathbf{z}_2$ is estimated (Encoder); **(iii)** the output image generated as a combination of $\mathbf{y}_1$ and $\mathbf{z}_2$ (Decoder). The person's outfit in the output images **(iii)** is approximated to the ones in images **(ii)**, however restricted by the low diversity of outfits observed in Human3.6M training data. Backgrounds of images **(ii)** are reproduced in the output images **(iii)** and all them differ from the one in image **(i)**.

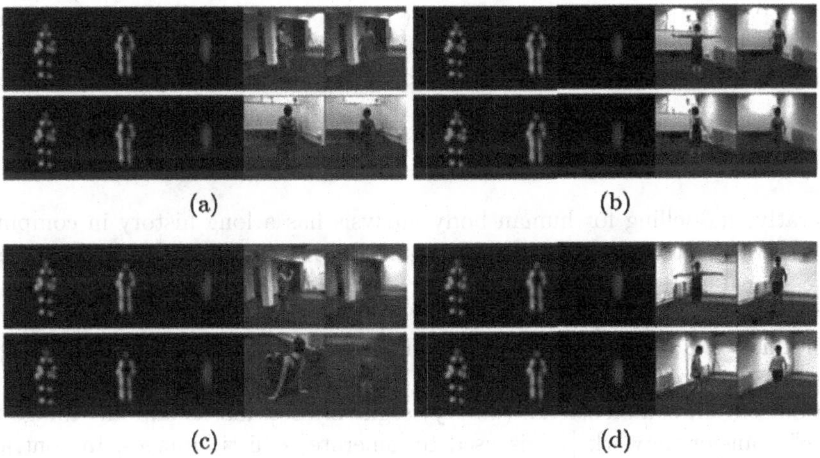

Fig. 14. Indirect pose-transfers with different levels of supervision: (a) 100%; (b) 75%; (c) 50%; (d) 25%.

combining body pose and appearance, respectively, from the first and second *encoded* images. We evaluate qualitatively the effects of semi-supervision over the indirect pose-transfer in Fig. 14.

Results on DeepFashion. To show the generality of the Semi-DGPose model we show in Fig. 15 reconstructed images on the DeepFashion dataset. The same hyper-parameters described before were used in training. Related methods in the literature [23,31] focus only on pose-transfer, training on pairs of images from the same person, which is a simpler task in comparison to ours. Such difference prevents a direct fair comparison with these methods.

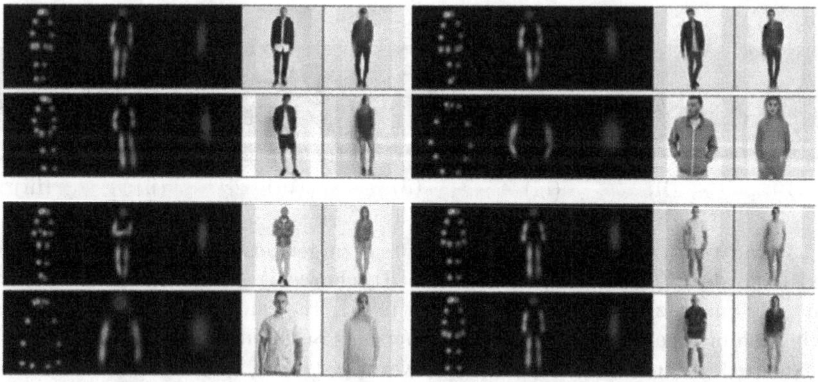

Fig. 15. Semi-DGPose DeepFashion reconstructions with 100% of supervision during training. Heatmaps are only shown as references, since the only input of the Semi-DGPose is the original image. At test time, as pose is estimated in the latent space, discrepancies between the original and reconstructed poses may be observed. Reconstructed images have 64 × 64 pixels. Best viewed if zoomed in digital version.

5 Related Work

Generative modelling for human body analysis has a long history in computer vision [13,33]. However, in the past years, deep generative models have been far less investigated compared to their discriminative counterparts [4–6,41]. Recently, Lassner *et al.* [21] presented a deep generative model based on a CVAE conditioned on human pose which allowed generating images of segmented people and their clothing. However, this model does not encode pose using raw image data but only low dimensional (binary) segmentation masks and an "image-to-image" transfer network [12] is used to generate realistic images. In contrast, we learn the generative model directly on the raw image data without the need of body parts segmentation. A closely related model is introduced in [3], but it is again a conditional model which does not allow for pose estimation neither semi-supervision. Difficulty of generating poses and detailed appearance simultaneously in an end-to-end fashion is admitted by Ma *et al.* [23]. In order to tackle this issue, they proposed a two stage image-to-image translation model. However, their model does not allow sampling, thus in its essence it is not a generative model, which is again in contrast to our approach.

In a concurrent work to ours, Siarohin *et al.* [31] improves approach of [23] by making it single-stage and trainable end-to-end. While this approach is relatively similar to ours, the key difference is that the human body joints (keypoints) are given to the algorithm (detected by another off-the-shelf discriminative method) while our method learns to encode them directly from the raw image data. Hence, our model allows sampling of different poses independent of appearance. Finally, Ma *et al.* [24] proposed a model for learning image embeddings of foreground, background and pose variables encoded as interpretable variables. However, this model has to rely on an off-the-shelf pose estimator to perform pose-transfer but our model can perform pose estimation even in a semi-supervised setting in addition to image generation. The existing approaches do not have the flexibility to manipulate pose independently of appearance and they have to be explicitly trained with pairs of images to allow pose transfer. This is in sharp contrast to our approach, where we learn pose *estimation* and pose transfer is a by-product.

Apart from this, Walker *et al.* [38] proposed a hybrid VAEGAN architecture for forecasting future poses in a video. Here, a low-dimensional pose representation is learned using a VAE and once the future poses are predicted, they are mapped to images using a GAN generator. Following [20], we use a discriminator in our training to improve the quality of the generated images, however, in contrast to [20], the latent space of our approach is interpretable which enables us to sample different poses and appearance. Considering GAN based generative models, Tulyakov *et al.* [36] presents a GAN network that learns motion and content in two separate latent spaces in an unsupervised manner. However it does not allow an explicit manipulation over the human pose.

6 Conclusions

In this paper we have presented a deep generative model for human pose analysis in natural images. To this end, we have proposed a structured semi-supervised VAEGAN approach. Our model allows independent manipulation of pose and appearance and hence enables applications such as pose-transfer without being explicitly trained for such a task. In addition to that, the semi-supervised setting relaxes the need for labelled data. We have systematically evaluated our model on the Human3.6M and DeepFashion datasets, showing applications such as indirect pose-transfer and semi-supervised pose estimation.

Acknowledgements. Rodrigo Andrade de Bem is a CAPES Foundation scholarship holder (Process no: 99999.013296/2013-02, Ministry of Education, Brazil). Ondrej Miksik is currently with Emotech Labs. This work was supported by the EPSRC, ERC grant ERC-2012-AdG 321162-HELIOS, EPSRC grant Seebibyte EP/M013774/1 and EPSRC/MURI grant EP/N019474/1.

A Semi-DGPose Architecture

The heatmaps correspond to: **(i)** 14 joints (head top, neck, right{shoulder, elbow, wrist, hip, knee, ankle}, left{shoulder, elbow, wrist, hip, knee, ankle}); **(ii)** 9 rigid parts (head, right{upper arm, lower arm, upper leg, lower leg}, left{upper arm, lower arm, upper leg, lower leg}); **(iii)** 1 whole body position. In the DeepFashion dataset, extra facial keypoints are used [23].

Table 1. Semi-DGPose architecture for 64 × 64 input images. Abbreviations: N for number of kernels/neurons, K for kernel size, S for stride and P for zero padding. CONCAT means concatenation layer, CONV means convolutional layer, BN means batch normalization layer with running average coefficient $\beta = 0.9$ and learnable affine transformation, DECONV means transpose convolutional layer, FC means fully connected layer, SUM corresponds to element-wise sum layer and RESIDUAL denotes a residual block (Table 2). The additional layers can be clearly understood.

Encoder	
Input: *images*(batch_size=64, channels=3, height=64, width=64)	
Layer	**Definition**
1	CONV-(N64, K7, S2, P1), LeakyReLU(0.01)
2	CONV-(N128, K3, S2, P1), BN, ReLU
3	CONV-(N256, K3, S2, P1), BN, ReLU
4-6	CONV-(N512, K3, S2, P1), BN, ReLU
7-9	RESIDUAL-(N512, K3, S1, P1)
10	RESIDUAL-(N512, K3, S1, P1), SIGMOID
μ_z	FC-(N100)
σ_z	FC-(N100)
μ_y	FC-(N48)
σ_y	FC-(N48)
Mapper	
Input: *pose_vector*(batch_size=64, channels=48)	
Layer	**Definition**
1	RESHAPE(batch_size=64, channels=48, height=1, width=1)
2	DECONV-(N512, K4, S1, P0), BN, LeakyReLU(0.2)
3	DECONV-(N256, K4, S2, P1), BN, LeakyReLU(0.2)
4	DECONV-(N128, K4, S2, P1), BN, LeakyReLU(0.2)
5	DECONV-(N64, K4, S2, P1), BN, LeakyReLU(0.2)
pose_heatmaps	DECONV-(N24, K4, S2, P1), SIGMOID
Decoder	
Input: *sample*(batch_size=64, channels=100); *pose_heatmaps*(batch_size=64, channels=24, height=64, width=64);	
Layer	**Definition**
1	RESHAPE(batch_size=64, channels=100, height=1, width=1)
2	DECONV-(N512, K4, S1, P0), BN, LeakyReLU(0.2)
3	DECONV-(N256, K4, S2, P1), BN, LeakyReLU(0.2)
4	DECONV-(N128, K4, S2, P1), BN, LeakyReLU(0.2)
5	DECONV-(N64, K4, S2, P1), BN, LeakyReLU(0.2)
6	DECONV-(N128, K4, S2, P1), BN, LeakyReLU(0.2)
7	CONCAT(*deconv6_output*, *pose_heatmaps*)
8	CONV-(N512, K5, S1, P2), BN, LeakyReLU(0.2)
9	CONV-(N256, K5, S1, P2), BN, LeakyReLU(0.2)
10-11	CONV-(N128, K5, S1, P2), BN, LeakyReLU(0.2)
$G(\mathbf{y}, \mathbf{z})$	CONV-(N3, K5, S1, P2), TANH

(*continued*)

Table 1. (*continued*)

Discriminator	
Input: *decoder_output*(batch_size=64, channels=3, height=64, width=64); *images*(batch_size=64, channels=3, height=64, width=64)	
Layer	**Definition**
1	CONV-(N64, K4, S2, P1), LeakyReLU(0.2)
2	CONV-(N128, K4, S2, P1), BN, LeakyReLU(0.2)
3	CONV-(N256, K4, S2, P1), BN, LeakyReLU(0.2)
4	CONV-(N512, K4, S2, P1), BN, LeakyReLU(0.2)
5	CONV-(N1, K4, S1, P0), SIGMOID

Table 2. Architecture of the residual block employed in the Semi-DGPose encoder.

RESIDUAL Layer	
Input: *previous_layer_output*	
Layer	**Definition**
1	CONV-(N512, K3, S1, P1), BN, ReLU
2	CONV-(N512, K3, S2, P1), BN
3	SUM(*conv2_output*, *previous_layer_output*)

References

1. Achilles, F., Ichim, A.-E., Coskun, H., Tombari, F., Noachtar, S., Navab, N.: Patient MoCap: human pose estimation under blanket occlusion for hospital monitoring applications. In: Ourselin, S., Joskowicz, L., Sabuncu, M.R., Unal, G., Wells, W. (eds.) MICCAI 2016. LNCS, vol. 9900, pp. 491–499. Springer, Cham (2016). https://doi.org/10.1007/978-3-319-46720-7_57
2. de Bem, R., Arnab, A., Sapienza, M., Golodetz, S., Torr, P.: Deep fully-connected part-based models for human pose estimation. In: ACML (2018)
3. de Bem, R., Ghosh, A., Ajanthan, T., Siddharth, N., Torr, P.: A conditional deep generative model of people in natural images. In: WACV (2019)
4. Bulat, A., Tzimiropoulos, G.: Human pose estimation via convolutional part heatmap regression. In: Leibe, B., Matas, J., Sebe, N., Welling, M. (eds.) ECCV 2016. LNCS, vol. 9911, pp. 717–732. Springer, Cham (2016). https://doi.org/10.1007/978-3-319-46478-7_44
5. Cao, Z., Simon, T., Wei, S.E., Sheikh, Y.: Realtime multi-person 2D pose estimation using part affinity fields. In: CVPR (2017)
6. Chu, X., Yang, W., Ouyang, W., Ma, C., Yuille, A.L., Wang, X.: Multi-context attention for human pose estimation. In: CVPR (2017)
7. Elgammal, A., Lee, C.S.: Inferring 3D body pose from silhouettes using activity manifold learning. In: CVPR (2004)
8. Goodfellow, I., Bengio, Y., Courville, A., Bengio, Y.: Deep Learning. MIT press, Cambridge (2016)
9. Goodfellow, I., et al.: Generative adversarial nets. In: NIPS (2014)

10. He, K., Zhang, X., Ren, S., Sun, J.: Delving deep into rectifiers: surpassing human-level performance on ImageNet classification. In: ICCV (2015)
11. Ionescu, C., Papava, D., Olaru, V., Sminchisescu, C.: Human3.6M: large scale datasets and predictive methods for 3D human sensing in natural environments. TPAMI **36**, 1325–1339 (2014)
12. Isola, P., Zhu, J.Y., Zhou, T., Efros, A.A.: Image-to-image translation with conditional adversarial networks. In: CVPR (2017)
13. Jaeggli, T., Koller-Meier, E., Van Gool, L.: Learning generative models for monocular body pose estimation. In: Yagi, Y., Kang, S.B., Kweon, I.S., Zha, H. (eds.) ACCV 2007. LNCS, vol. 4843, pp. 608–617. Springer, Heidelberg (2007). https://doi.org/10.1007/978-3-540-76386-4_57
14. Jia, Y., et al.: Caffe: convolutional architecture for fast feature embedding. In: ACMMM (2014)
15. Karras, T., Aila, T., Laine, S., Lehtinen, J.: Progressive growing of GANs for improved quality, stability, and variation. In: ICLR (2018)
16. Kingma, D., Ba, J.: Adam: a method for stochastic optimization. In: ICLR (2015)
17. Kingma, D.P., Mohamed, S., Rezende, D.J., Welling, M.: Semi-supervised learning with deep generative models. In: NIPS (2014)
18. Kingma, D.P., Welling, M.: Auto-encoding variational Bayes. In: ICLR (2014)
19. Kulkarni, T.D., Whitney, W.F., Kohli, P., Tenenbaum, J.: Deep convolutional inverse graphics network. In: NIPS (2015)
20. Larsen, A.B.L., Sønderby, S.K., Larochelle, H., Winther, O.: Autoencoding beyond pixels using a learned similarity metric. In: ICML (2016)
21. Lassner, C., Pons-Moll, G., Gehler, P.V.: A generative model for people in clothing. In: ICCV (2017)
22. Liu, Z., Luo, P., Qiu, S., Wang, X., Tang, X.: DeepFashion: powering robust clothes recognition and retrieval with rich annotations. In: CVPR (2016)
23. Ma, L., Jia, X., Sun, Q., Schiele, B., Tuytelaars, T., Gool, L.V.: Pose guided person image generation. In: NIPS (2017)
24. Ma, L., Sun, Q., Georgoulis, S., Van Gool, L., Schiele, B., Fritz, M.: Disentangled person image generation. In: CVPR (2018)
25. Massiceti, D., Siddharth, N., Dokania, P., Torr, P.H.: FlipDial: a generative model for two-way visual dialogue. In: CVPR (2018)
26. Newell, A., Yang, K., Deng, J.: Stacked hourglass networks for human pose estimation. In: Leibe, B., Matas, J., Sebe, N., Welling, M. (eds.) ECCV 2016. LNCS, vol. 9912, pp. 483–499. Springer, Cham (2016). https://doi.org/10.1007/978-3-319-46484-8_29
27. Rezende, D.J., Mohamed, S., Wierstra, D.: Stochastic backpropagation and approximate inference in deep generative models. In: ICML (2014)
28. Schulman, J., Heess, N., Weber, T., Abbeel, P.: Gradient estimation using stochastic computation graphs. In: NIPS (2015)
29. Seemann, E., Nickel, K., Stiefelhagen, R.: Head pose estimation using stereo vision for human-robot interaction. In: FG (2004)
30. Shotton, J., et al.: Real-time human pose recognition in parts from single depth images. In: CVPR (2011)
31. Siarohin, A., Sangineto, E., Lathuiliere, S., Sebe, N.: Deformable GANs for pose-based human image generation. In: CVPR (2018)
32. Siddharth, N., et al.: Learning disentangled representations with semi-supervised deep generative models. In: NIPS (2017)
33. Sigal, L., Balan, A., Black, M.J.: Combined discriminative and generative articulated pose and non-rigid shape estimation. In: NIPS (2008)

34. Thies, J., Zollhöfer, M., Stamminger, M., Theobalt, C., Nießner, M.: Face2Face: real-time face capture and reenactment of RGB videos. In: CVPR (2016)
35. Tompson, J., Jain, A., LeCun, Y., Bregler, C.: Joint Training of a Convolutional Network and a Graphical Model for Human Pose Estimation. In: NIPS (2014)
36. Tulyakov, S., Liu, M., Yang, X., Kautz, J.: MoCoGAN: decomposing motion and content for video generation. In: CVPR (2018)
37. von Marcard, T., Rosenhahn, B., Black, M., Pons-Moll, G.: Sparse inertial poser: automatic 3D human pose estimation from sparse IMUs. Eurographics (2017)
38. Walker, J., Marino, K., Gupta, A., Hebert, M.: The pose knows: video forecasting by generating pose futures. In: ICCV (2017)
39. Wang, Z., Bovik, A.C., Sheikh, H.R., Simoncelli, E.P.: Image quality assessment: from error visibility to structural similarity. TIP **13**, 600–612 (2004)
40. Wang, Z., Merel, J.S., Reed, S.E., de Freitas, N., Wayne, G., Heess, N.: Robust imitation of diverse behaviors. In: NIPS (2017)
41. Wei, S.E., Ramakrishna, V., Kanade, T., Sheikh, Y.: Convolutional pose machines. In: CVPR (2016)
42. Yang, W., Li, S., Ouyang, W., Li, H., Wang, X.: Learning feature pyramids for human pose estimation. In: ICCV (2017)
43. Yang, Y., Ramanan, D.: Articulated pose estimation with flexible mixtures-of-parts. In: CVPR (2011)

Role of Group Level Affect to Find the Most Influential Person in Images

Shreya Ghosh(✉) and Abhinav Dhall

Learning Affect and Semantic Image analysIs (LASII) Group,
Indian Institute of Technology Ropar, Rupnagar, India
{shreya.ghosh,abhinav}@iitrpr.ac.in
http://iitrpr.ac.in/lasii/

Abstract. Group affect analysis is an important cue for predicting various group traits. Generally, the estimation of the group affect, emotional responses, eye gaze and position of people in images are the important cues to identify an important person from a group of people. The main focus of this paper is to explore the importance of group affect in finding the representative of a group. We call that person the "Most Influential Person" (for the first impression) or "leader" of a group. In order to identify the main visual cues for "Most Influential Person", we conducted a user survey. Based on the survey statistics, we annotate the "influential persons" in 1000 images of Group AFfect database (GAF 2.0) via LabelMe toolbox and propose the **"GAF-personage database"**. In order to identify "Most Influential Person", we proposed a DNN based Multiple Instance Learning (Deep MIL) method which takes deep facial features as input. To leverage the deep facial features, we first predict the individual emotion probabilities via CapsNet and rank the detected faces on the basis of it. Then, we extract deep facial features of the top-3 faces via VGG-16 network. Our method performs better than maximum facial area and saliency-based importance methods and achieves the human-level perception of "Most Influential Person" at group-level.

Keywords: Important person · Group of people · Group level affect

1 Introduction

Nowadays, Social Networking sites have created a huge audience for everyone. A large number of images are uploaded every day on various social portals such as Facebook, Instagram, Google+, LinkedIn and others. These images mainly contain multiple subjects with a nice variety of context, lighting conditions, camera quality and other factors. Due to the above-mentioned reasons, affective computing community gets an opportunity to analyze the pattern of these data in terms of affect, behaviour, cohesiveness, event information, kinship, group norms and culture for a group of people. Moreover, when a group of people pose for a photograph, there exists some reason behind it. It may be some sort of

L. Leal-Taixé and S. Roth (Eds.): ECCV 2018 Workshops, LNCS 11130, pp. 518–533, 2019.
https://doi.org/10.1007/978-3-030-11012-3_39

social events (birthday, wedding, cultural festival, meetings after a long time and so on), professional reasons (office meetings, office party, interview etc.) or something else. Thus, it will be interesting to find out who is most "important" personality in the above-mentioned context-photographs.

Fig. 1. The left image is a group where the baby in the centre is the most "important". In the centre image, although it is a friend circle, still from the survey the boy holding the phone is the "important" one. Finally, in the rightmost image it's about socially prominent people but without this info, our model tries to predict **"Who is the most important person?"**

"Importance" is an ambiguous term in case of real-world images. It has many perspectives such as photographer's point of view, social norms and viewers' (third person) perspective. When a photographer takes some photographs, he/she aims to capture some sort of "importance" in that image. Sometimes the main aim of the photographer remains unknown to the third person or viewer. In most of the cases, the camera angle and focus play a vital role in the perception of importance. Generally, human being pays attention to the larger object in an image instead of the background i.e. size and sharpness of an object draws attention. According to social norms, the relative position of people also matters a lot. Especially in the case of social events and office party, mostly the important one will be in the centre. Although in family scenarios, these things vary a lot. In many cases, like the rightmost image of Fig. 1, there is a presence of socially prominent personality. While annotating those images, people presume them to be most important. Predicting an important person in such images is really a challenging task. Our proposed method does not have such bias as it tried to predict "important" person on the basis of visual cues and group emotion intensities without any prior information.

Despite the above-mentioned challenge, there are several other challenges, such as diverse changes in human pose, action, appearance and occlusion involved in this task. Moreover, there is a lot of variation in context, background, illumination and lighting conditions. The automated system has to take care of facial and image level information to deal with these challenges. In some recent works, [25] attempted to detect "key actors" via attention model which takes human action and appearance as input. Solomon et al. [30] trained a regression model on spatial and saliency information to infer relative importance between two people. [22] used semantic information such as interactions between persons, eye gaze information which is essentially used to infer about the importance of persons. Some psychological studies [26] reveal that group emotion also plays a vital role in the identification of most influential[1] person (in other words leader).

The main objective of our study is to answer the following questions-

- How useful are face-level and group affect features for predicting an important person in an image?
- What are the factors, which affect the perception of the important person in a group image?

Automatic identification of the most influential person at first impression (first look) has several real-world applications. It can be used for im2text applications [30] (generating sentences that describe an image), event summarization, image retrieval, web crawling, "smart-cropping" of images [30] and ranking of personal photos etc.

Our contributions in this paper are as follows:

(1) We propose an automatic "Most Influential Person" detection method via group level emotion. It performs better than our three baselines as mentioned in Sect. 3.
(2) We labelled GAF 2.0 [5] dataset with "influential person" annotation and proposed "GAF-personage" database.

The rest of the paper structure is as follows: Sect. 2 is all about the prior work in this field. Section 3 describes the dataset, data annotation and survey statistics. Section 4 is about our approach towards this problem. Section 5 contains the details of the experiments we conducted on behalf of our method. Finally, Sect. 6 states the conclusion and future scope of this project.

2 Prior Work

One of the first group related analysis was proposed by Ge et al. [12] using a bottom-up hierarchical clustering algorithm. The motivation of the paper is to spread situation awareness and evacuation planning in real-time especially in case of huge conjugation. Further, several studies are conducted in order to understand several group traits.

2.1 Finding Important Persons

Recently, Li et al. [22] propose a Hybrid Interaction Graph (HIG) to rank people present in an image. This HIG includes spatial score, action score, appearance score and attention score. Spatial score and appearance score correspond to the location and attributes of the persons respectively. Action score indicates pose of the person and attention score includes eye gaze as an attribute.

[1] Please note that we use important and influential terms interchangeably throughout the paper.

In another interesting work, Solomon Mathialagan et al. [30] propose a measure of importance in terms of person level features such as position, scale, sharpness, facial pose and occlusion. Results show that there is a small correlation between importance and visual saliency. A text corresponding to each image is also generated which describes the image.

2.2 Importance in Images

Several works [18,31,35] study the importance of objects in an image. Yamaguchi et al. [35] define "importance" via several human perceived factors which are related to compositions (i.e. size and location of objects), semantics (i.e. object type, scene type along with its description strength) and context of the given image. The results also state that in any image "person" can be classified as the most important.

There is a huge difference between the "image level importance" and "important person" [22,30] as it requires a more coarse level understanding of the image.

2.3 Image Saliency

Several studies [8,14] try to figure out the part of the image which draws the viewer's attention. Mostly, human mind judges on the basis of image saliency. Jiang et al. [20] study image level saliency in crowd images. The main objective of the paper [20] is to find salient regions in images and use these as a feature to predict the crowded context as well as the crowd levels. Here, multiple kernel learning (MKL) is used for feature integration and extraction of important information.

However, there is a significant difference between image saliency and importance. Saliency [16] tries to predict the most eye-catching regions in image whereas importance takes context and other factors into account.

2.4 Group Affect

The first group affect analysis was conducted by Dhall et al. [6] where both facial and contextual information are taken into consideration. [4] divides group affect analysis approaches into two broad categories: bottom-up and top-down approach. The bottom-up approaches first analyze the group-members individually and then evaluate the contribution of these members towards the overall group's mood. The main motivation behind the top-down approach is to determine global factors and it's impacts on the perception of group level emotion. Dhall et al. [4] propose the use of low-level features for inferring an individual's happiness intensity and then pooled it at a global level.

In another interesting study, Hernandez et al. [15] conduct an interesting experiment at MIT, where the facial expression of the people passing through the corridor was analyzed for the presence of smile. The number of smiles are averaged at a given point to decide the overall group-level mood. Barsade et al. [2]

propose that the social norms and its constraints (i.e. interpersonal cohesion and individual emotional responses) are the important cues for group emotion. In another paper, Gallagher et al. [10] argue that social context plays an important role in group-level scenarios. They modelled the group as a min-span tree. The task in the paper is to infer the gender and age of group members using the group-level contextual information. Dhall et al. [5] compute a scene level descriptor to encode the background information along with the facial and body cues. Huang et al. [17] model the group using a conditional random field and represent faces with a local binary pattern variant.

Mou et al. [23] perform an interesting study of human-affect on individual and group scenarios. They create three models as mentioned below:

(1) An individual model which is trained with an individual level dataset.
(2) Group model which is trained with a group dataset and
(3) Combined model is the hybrid fused model of above two.

Smith et al. [29] argue that the group-level emotion is different from individual emotion. In order to predict an individual's role in the overall group emotion, one should study two factors.

First, a person's involvement in a group.

Second, his/her behaviour with the group members.

2.5 Multiple Instance Learning

Multiple Instance Learning was introduced by Dietterich et al. [7] for drug activity prediction. Andrews et al. [1] propose two SVM based MIL methods for classification. The methods are named mi-SVM (for instance-level classification) and MI-SVM (bag-level classification). There are several papers [11,38] which use neural networks to explore this problem. Most of the computer vision tasks such as face detection [36], segmentation [33] and so on can fit into multiple instance learning framework.

In a recent paper, Xu et al. [34] propose a weakly supervised deep learning based MIL method in medical image processing. Further, Zhu et al. [39] propose a multiple instance learning methods with salient windows. The main aim of this method is unsupervised object detection. Wu et al. [32] use both CNN and DNN based multiple instance learning methods for image classification as well as image auto-annotation task. Zhu et al. [40] propose a deep multi-instance framework (sparse label assignment) for the breast cancer classification task. In a recent archive paper, Ilse et al. [19] propose attention based multiple instance learning framework for learning Bernoulli's distribution (at bag label).

3 Dataset Collection

Group AFfect dataset (GAF 2.0) is proposed by Dhall et al. [5] which contains group images in real-world scenarios. The images are collected via web crawling. Event and group related keywords such as party, family, protest, club, graduation ceremony and so on are used to find group images. These images are labelled into three group level emotion categories (positive, negative and neutral). We choose 1000 images from GAF 2.0 dataset[2] which uniformly belongs to three classes i.e. positive, negative and neutral respectively. We use MTCNN face detection library [37] to select those 1000 images which contains three and more than three faces. Further, we conduct a survey to observe how people decide the "importance" in a given group image.

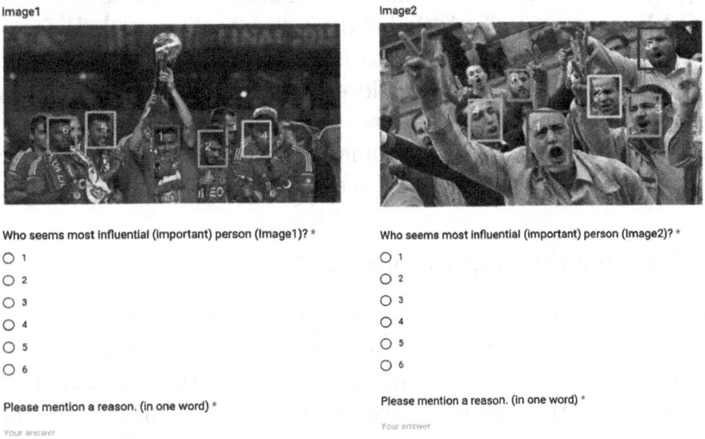

Fig. 2. These are the snapshots of the survey form.

3.1 Survey and Data Annotation

We conduct a survey of 10 images via Google form over 50 people having different occupations (for example student, corporate employee, govt. employee, professor and manager). The snapshots of the form is shown in Fig. 2. One has to choose an option on the support of "who seems to be most influential person?" Besides, one has to give reasons regarding his/her choice. The order of the faces in survey images are selected at random and the number assigned to a face in an image remains same throughout the survey.

The survey statistics and results are shown in Fig. 3. The first row in Fig. 3 describes the age distribution and gender distribution of the participants respectively. From the top left image of Fig. 3, it is observed that the age of the participants are varied from 17–57 years. There are 59.6% male participants and 40.4% females participants (in the top right image of Fig. 3). From the participants' responses regarding their respective choices, we form a word cloud (in the middle images of 2nd, 3rd and 4th rows of Fig. 3). From this statistics, we

[2] The datasets mentioned in [22,30] are not publicly available in the respective websites.

observed that people labelled on the basis of the image level, face level and position features. For example, the image present in 2nd row, the main focus is on the context feature i.e. trophy. The frequent occurrence of *'happy'*, *'smiling'*, *'angry'*, *'front'* and *'centre'* keywords throughout the responses indicate group level emotion and position information. We use group affect for choosing the same number of faces across images for further analysis because in the survey result people mention emotion attributes for choosing a particular face (for example 'happy', 'smiling' and 'angry').

Keeping all of this factors in mind, 3 annotators annotate the proposed dataset **"GAF-personage"** via LabelMe online toolbox [27]. Before starting annotation, we explained the survey statistics and the trends of the choices (for example in family scenarios mainly children are given preference, socially prominent people present in an image get preference and so on). For the baseline, we choose the central face of the image, image saliency and maximum facial area which will be discussed in the next subsection.

3.2 Baselines for the Importance Model

From the survey statistics, we observe that people mainly focus on the center of an image. To consider the central face of an image as baseline, we first determine the central pixel of the image. Then, we find the nearby face via the distance between the center of the image and the tip of the nose of the detected face. This is a very weak baseline because in the real world scenarios it is not necessary that the photographer is in front of the main subject.

We choose image saliency as another baseline because generally people judges on the basis of salient regions. The five-fold cross-validation accuracy of the saliency based prediction and ground truth is shown in Table 2.

Similarly, we choose the maximum facial area as another baseline because it is also an important factor to identify most important person [35]. The five-fold cross-validation accuracy of the maximum facial area based prediction and ground truth is shown in Table 2.

Thus, we choose three baselines for the "importance-model":

(1) Center of the image,
(2) Image Saliency and
(3) Maximum facial area.

4 Proposed Network

In this section, we describe our proposed method. Our proposed pipeline is shown in Fig. 4 which consists of two structures. The top box predicts individual-level emotion and the bottom coloured network is deep MIL based DNN which is used for final prediction.

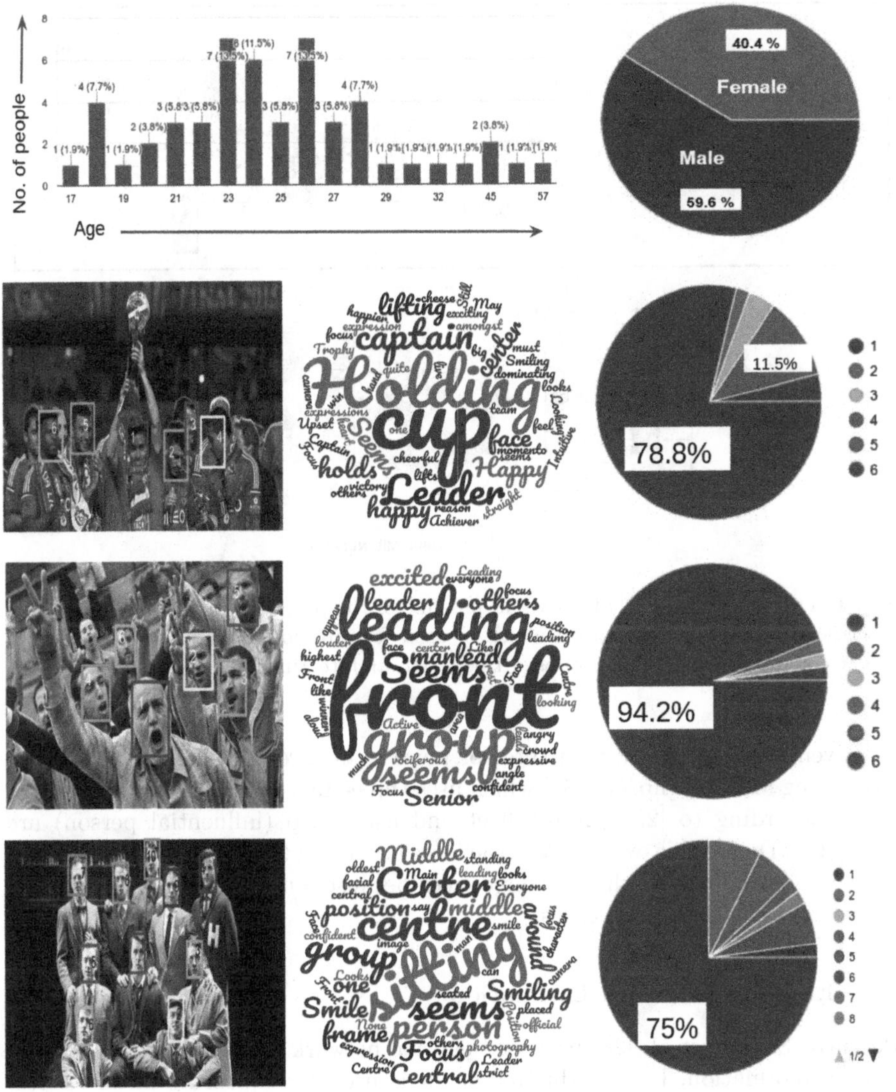

Fig. 3. This figure describes the survey results. The top left image describes the age distribution and top right image describes the gender distribution of the participants. In case of the top left figure, the x-axis indicates the age distribution and y-axis indicates percentage. For the 2nd, 3rd and 4th row, the first column is the given survey image, the second column is the reason specified in the survey to choose "influential" person and the third column is about the voting results.

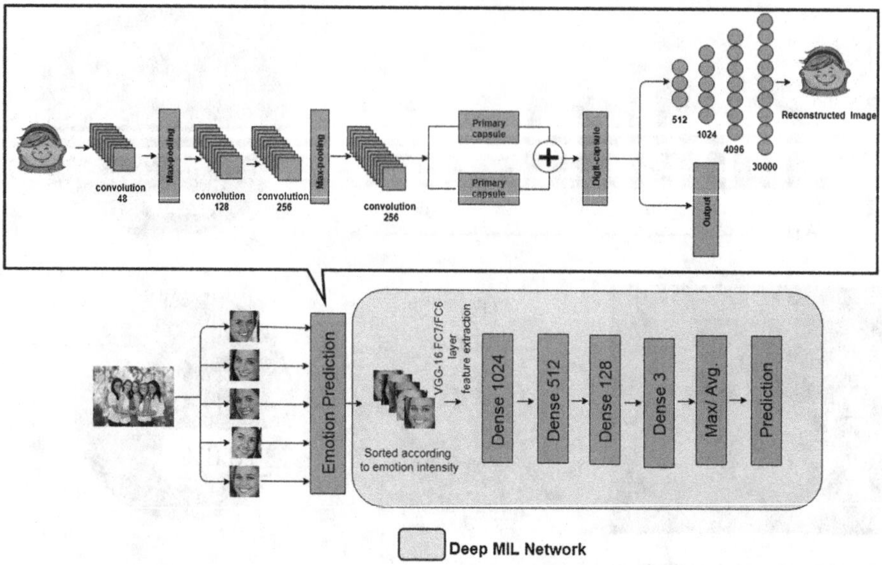

Fig. 4. This figure describes the overall pipeline of the proposed method. The top box describes the CapsNet structure which is used for emotion prediction. The bottom yellow coloured DNN is our proposed Deep MIL architecture. (Color figure online)

Given an image containing three or more than three people, we first detect faces using MTCNN library [37] which uses three-stage cascaded CNN to detect faces. According to [26], group affect and leadership (influential person) are correlated. Due to this, we first sort the faces according to the emotional intensity of each face and choose the top three faces because our labelled images contain three and more than three faces.

4.1 Emotion Intensity Estimation

Recently, Sabour et al. [28] proposed capsule network which is able to capture spatial information. Due to this reason, it is used for capturing facial expressions [13] and AU detection [9] in recent studies. There are several challenges in leveraging facial information as it can be occluded, blurred or rotated. We trained the model structure as mentioned in [13] (refer Fig. 4 upper box). From this model, we get class wise group affect probabilities of each face which gives us the information about which face contributes more to the group affect. After sorting, we take only top three faces because the minimum three faces are present in our dataset images.

4.2 Deep MIL (DNN) for Importance Estimation

In **Multiple Instance Learning** [32] terms, the image is considered as a bag $X = \{X_1, .., X_N\}$, where each X_i is the elements inside the bag (also called instance/ feature vector) where X_i's are the ith element in the bag and N is the total number of elements in the bag. In our case, the group image stands for the bag which contains N elements (faces).

In order to keep the number of elements in each bag uniform, we sort the faces according to their respective emotional intensity provided by CapsNet. Further, we extracted VGG-16 FC7 and FC6 layer features of the top 3 faces sorted by the method mentioned above. This VGG-16 network is pre-trained on the VGG-face dataset which contains identity corresponding to faces. Thus, the FC layers of the VGG network contains high-level facial features which leverage facial structure and pose related information.

From the FC7 and FC6 layers of VGG face network, we got 4096-dimensional facial information which is further passed through several FC layers as shown in Table 1. At last, we took the maximum and average of the features to predict the overall concept of the most influential person.

For our experiment, we use Swish [24] as an activation function instead of ReLU. The Swish activation function is defined as $f(x) = x.sigmoid(x)$. It has few properties (like unbounded above and bounded below) similar to ReLU and few different properties (like smooth and non-monotonic). The bounded below property of the above function helps in regularization of the network. Similarly, it does not reach near zero gradient due to its "unbounded above" property. Thus, the network can train at a faster rate. Besides, it's self-gating properties allows scaler values only instead of multiple gating inputs.

Table 1. This is the detail architecture of the proposed network. Here, b refer to the batch size.

Layers	Input	Output	Layer details
Dense	b, 3, 4096	b, 3, 1024	1024
Activation	b, 3, 1024	b, 3, 1024	ReLU/Swish
Dense	b, 3, 1024	b, 3, 512	512
Activation	b, 3, 512	b, 3, 512	ReLU/Swish
Dropout	b, 3, 512	b, 3, 512	0.5
Dense	b, 3, 512	b, 3, 128	128
Activation	b, 3, 128	b, 3, 128	ReLU/Swish
Dropout	b, 3, 128	b, 3, 128	0.3
Dense	b, 3, 128	b, 3, 3	3
Activation	b, 3, 3	b, 3, 3	ReLU/Swish
Max-pooling & flatten	b, 3, 3	b, 3	3(1-D)

5 Experiments and Results

In this section, we will describe experimental details. For implementation, we use Keras [3] deep learning library with Tensorflow backend. The data, labels and code will be made publicly available (link).

5.1 Emotion Prediction Network

We train a capsule network to predict emotions. The structure of the network is mentioned in the Fig. 4. We train the network on RAF-DB [21] dataset which contains approximately 30k facial images with 7-dimensional expression distribution (happy, sad, surprise, neutral, fear, angry and disgust). The input image passes through several convolution layers followed by max pooling layer before entering into two parallel primary capsule layers. A capsule is a set of nested neural network layers where a neural layer resides inside another. We use 'adam' optimizer with its default settings in keras library to train this network. The loss is the same as the original paper [28], that is margin loss for classification and mean square error for image reconstruction. It reaches the accuracy within 20–25 epochs without any data augmentation.

From group images, we detect faces via MTCNN [37] face detection library. We resize the detected faces to 100 × 100 dimension and predict corresponding emotion probabilities. Then, we sort the faces according to this probabilities and take the top three faces for further analysis. We observe that among 1000 images 713 images (approx. 71.3%) have their respective ground truth in this top-3 category.

5.2 Deep MIL Network (DNN)

First, we extract the VGG-16 FC7 and FC6 layer features of each top 3 faces which passes through several dense layers as mentioned in the Table 1 before prediction. We first use parallel three networks for each top 3 faces. Then, we take maximum and average of the outputs to predict final "influential person".

In order to train this Deep MIL network, we use mean square error as loss function and SGD optimizer with learning rate 0.01 and momentum 0.9 without any learning rate decay. Instead of avg-pooling, we also tried with max-pooling before prediction but the results are better in terms of accuracy in case of avg-pooling.

5.3 Result Analysis

From the Table 2, we can conclude that our method is performing better than the maximum facial area concept as well as the saliency concept. Although saliency plays an important part in case of labelling as human mind make the first perception mostly by judging saliency of an image. Similarly, the maximum facial area also plays an important role in the perception of "most influential person"

Table 2. Experimental results for finding the most "influential person" in an image.

MIL fold	Accuracy (%) (for VGG16 FC7 feature with max-pooling)	Accuracy (%) (for VGG16 FC7 feature with avg-pooling)	Accuracy (%) (for VGG16 FC6 feature with max-pooling)	Accuracy (%) (for VGG16 FC6 feature with avg-pooling)	Accuracy (%) (max facial area)	Accuracy (%) (saliency [16])
1st fold	57.49	62.50	76.00	73.50	57.20	55.20
2nd fold	65.00	60.00	73.00	73.50	57.20	60.40
3rd fold	66.50	60.00	71.50	73.50	55.82	56.30
4th fold	56.49	65.50	77.00	76.00	49.30	50.50
5th fold	62.50	75.00	74.50	76.00	53.40	56.30
Avg	**61.60**	**64.60**	**74.40**	**74.50**	**53.32**	**55.74**

Table 3. This table contains the precision of emotion wise person prediction because GAF 2.0 dataset consists of group emotion images which consists of three classes (positive, negative and neutral).

Class	Precision (most important)	Precision (2nd most important)
Negative	0.6667	0.6667
Positive	0.4530	0.3125
Neutral	0.8547	0.6837
Overall	**0.6520**	**0.5479**

because in the survey results for second image, people choose both the frontal face (having maximum area as well) to be important. We also observe that the average pooling before prediction performs better than max pooling because average pooling infers overall statistics from an image where max pooling deals with specific statistics from images.

From the Table 3, we can say that our model can detect most important person more precisely than 2nd most important person. In a more fine-grained analysis, we can observe that in case of negative group-affect scenario it is almost similar in both cases because of expression intensity and camera angle. The situation changes in the case of happy images where the precision is relatively lower. The main reason behind this is that the smile intensity changes a lot over images and the classifier get confused to choose the "influential person" (Fig. 5).

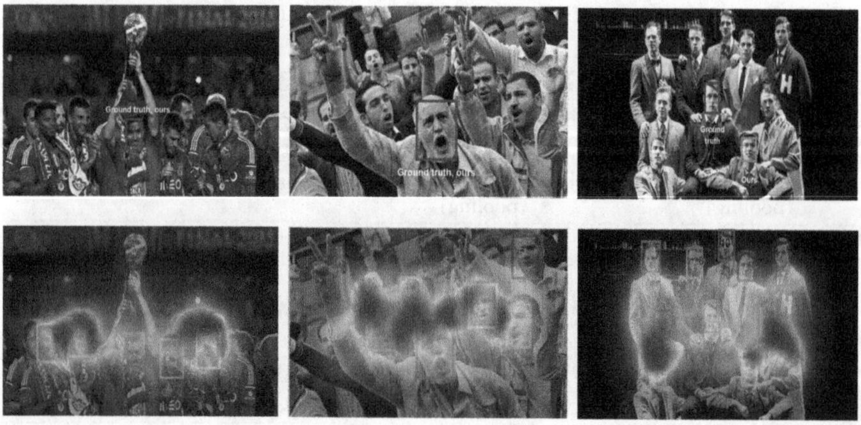

Fig. 5. This figure shows the output of our model. The left and middle image of the first row predicts the most important person correctly but for the first row rightmost image it selects the person with green boundary box as the most important person. We computed the saliency map via Matlab toolbox proposed by Hou et al. [16]. From saliency map, it is clear that there is a difference between saliency and importance.

6 Conclusion and Future Work

We study the importance of group affect to predict the most influential person. We first sort the faces according to the emotional intensity and then treat the problem as multiple instance learning problem. The results are better than the maximum facial area in the image and image saliency. Thus, we conclude that -

- Both face-level and group level features are important for predicting an important person in an image. When we sort the top three faces, we observed that 73.3% important people are included. Thus, it is clear that group level feature (here group affect) is important. Similarly, we perform our MIL experiments on the basis of deep facial features and results show that it is an important feature.
- From the survey, it is observed that the position of the person is an important motivation behind the "important" perception. Along with that facial cues, overall group affect is also a relevant indication.

In our pipeline, we have not included the position, body-pose, personal attributes, personality and eye gaze information. Besides, we can also analyze the fashion quotient of the group image especially in some social context such as a wedding, prize distribution ceremony, birthday party and so on. It will be interesting to combine all these factors to predict the probable "Leader" of a group.

Acknowledgement. We acknowledge the support of NVIDIA for providing us TITAN Xp G5X 12 GB GPU for the research purpose. We are thankful to the anonymous reviewers for their insightful comments and helpful suggestions to improve the quality of this paper. We would also like to thank the members of LASII lab for their support.

References

1. Andrews, S., Tsochantaridis, I., Hofmann, T.: Support vector machines for multiple-instance learning. In: Advances in Neural Information Processing Systems, pp. 577–584 (2003)
2. Barsade, S.G., Gibson, D.E.: Group emotion: a view from top and bottom. Composition (1998)
3. Chollet, F., et al.: Keras (2015)
4. Dhall, A., Goecke, R., Gedeon, T.: Automatic group happiness intensity analysis. IEEE Trans. Affect. Comput. **6**(1), 13–26 (2015)
5. Dhall, A., Goecke, R., Ghosh, S., Joshi, J., Hoey, J., Gedeon, T.: From individual to group-level emotion recognition: EmotiW 5.0. In: ACM ICMI (2017)
6. Dhall, A., Joshi, J., Radwan, I., Goecke, R.: Finding happiest moments in a social context. In: Lee, K.M., Matsushita, Y., Rehg, J.M., Hu, Z. (eds.) ACCV 2012. LNCS, vol. 7725, pp. 613–626. Springer, Heidelberg (2013). https://doi.org/10.1007/978-3-642-37444-9_48
7. Dietterich, T.G., Lathrop, R.H., Lozano-Pérez, T.: Solving the multiple instance problem with axis-parallel rectangles. Artif. Intell. **89**(1–2), 31–71 (1997)
8. Elazary, L., Itti, L.: Interesting objects are visually salient. J. Vis. **8**(3), 3–3 (2008)
9. Ertugrul, I.O., Jeni, L.A., Cohn, J.F.: FACSCaps: pose-independent facial action coding with capsules
10. Gallagher, A.C., Chen, T.: Understanding images of groups of people. In: IEEE CVPR (2009)
11. Garcez, A.D., Zaverucha, G.: Multi-instance learning using recurrent neural networks. In: 2012 International Joint Conference on Neural Networks (IJCNN), pp. 1–6. IEEE (2012)
12. Ge, W., Collins, R.T., Ruback, R.B.: Vision-based analysis of small groups in pedestrian crowds. IEEE Trans. Pattern Anal. Mach. Intell. **34**(5), 1003–1016 (2012)
13. Ghosh, S., Dhall, A., Sebe, N.: Automatic group affect analysis in images via visual attribute and feature networks. In: IEEE International Conference on Image Processing (ICIP). IEEE (2018)
14. Harel, J., Koch, C., Perona, P.: Graph-based visual saliency. In: Advances in Neural Information Processing Systems, pp. 545–552 (2007)
15. Hernandez, J., Hoque, M.E., Drevo, W., Picard, R.W.: Mood meter: counting smiles in the wild. In: ACM UbiComp (2012)
16. Hou, X., Harel, J., Koch, C.: Image signature: highlighting sparse salient regions. IEEE Trans. Pattern Anal. Mach. Intell. **34**(1), 194–201 (2012)
17. Huang, X., Dhall, A., Zhao, G., Goecke, R., Pietikäinen, M.: Riesz-based volume local binary pattern and a novel group expression model for group happiness intensity analysis. In: BMVC (2015)
18. Hwang, S.J., Grauman, K.: Learning the relative importance of objects from tagged images for retrieval and cross-modal search. Int. J. Comput. Vis. **100**(2), 134–153 (2012)

19. Ilse, M., Tomczak, J.M., Welling, M.: Attention-based deep multiple instance learning. arXiv preprint arXiv:1802.04712 (2018)
20. Jiang, M., Xu, J., Zhao, Q.: Saliency in crowd. In: Fleet, D., Pajdla, T., Schiele, B., Tuytelaars, T. (eds.) ECCV 2014. LNCS, vol. 8695, pp. 17–32. Springer, Cham (2014). https://doi.org/10.1007/978-3-319-10584-0_2
21. Li, S., Deng, W., Du, J.: Reliable crowdsourcing and deep locality-preserving learning for expression recognition in the wild. In: 2017 IEEE Conference on Computer Vision and Pattern Recognition (CVPR), pp. 2584–2593. IEEE (2017)
22. Li, W.H., Li, B., Zheng, W.S.: PersonRank: detecting important people in images. In: 2018 13th IEEE International Conference on Automatic Face & Gesture Recognition (FG 2018), pp. 234–241. IEEE (2018)
23. Mou, W., Gunes, H., Patras, I.: Alone versus in-a-group: a comparative analysis of facial affect recognition. In: ACM Multimedia (2016)
24. Ramachandran, P., Zoph, B., Le, Q.V.: Swish: a self-gated activation function. arXiv preprint arXiv:1710.05941 (2017)
25. Ramanathan, V., Huang, J., Abu-El-Haija, S., Gorban, A., Murphy, K., Fei-Fei, L.: Detecting events and key actors in multi-person videos. In: Proceedings of the IEEE Conference on Computer Vision and Pattern Recognition, pp. 3043–3053 (2016)
26. Redl, F.: Group emotion and leadership. Psychiatry **5**(4), 573–596 (1942)
27. Russell, B.C., Torralba, A., Murphy, K.P., Freeman, W.T.: LabelMe: a database and web-based tool for image annotation. Int. J. Comput. Vis. **77**(1–3), 157–173 (2008)
28. Sabour, S., Frosst, N., Hinton, G.E.: Dynamic routing between capsules. In: Advances in Neural Information Processing Systems, pp. 3856–3866 (2017)
29. Smith, E.R., Seger, C.R., Mackie, D.M.: Can emotions be truly group level? Evidence regarding four conceptual criteria. J. Pers. Soc. Psychol. **93**(3), 431–446 (2007)
30. Solomon Mathialagan, C., Gallagher, A.C., Batra, D.: VIP: finding important people in images. In: Proceedings of the IEEE Conference on Computer Vision and Pattern Recognition, pp. 4858–4866 (2015)
31. Spain, M., Perona, P.: Measuring and predicting object importance. Int. J. Comput. Vis. **91**(1), 59–76 (2011)
32. Wu, J., Yu, Y., Huang, C., Yu, K.: Deep multiple instance learning for image classification and auto-annotation. In: Proceedings of the IEEE Conference on Computer Vision and Pattern Recognition, pp. 3460–3469 (2015)
33. Wu, J., Zhao, Y., Zhu, J.Y., Luo, S., Tu, Z.: MILCut: a sweeping line multiple instance learning paradigm for interactive image segmentation. In: Proceedings of the IEEE Conference on Computer Vision and Pattern Recognition, pp. 256–263 (2014)
34. Xu, Y., et al.: Deep learning of feature representation with multiple instance learning for medical image analysis. In: 2014 IEEE International Conference on Acoustics, Speech and Signal Processing (ICASSP), pp. 1626–1630. IEEE (2014)
35. Yamaguchi, K., et al.: Understanding and predicting importance in images. In: 2012 IEEE Conference on Computer Vision and Pattern Recognition, pp. 3562–3569. IEEE (2012)
36. Zhang, C., Platt, J.C., Viola, P.A.: Multiple instance boosting for object detection. In: Advances in Neural Information Processing Systems, pp. 1417–1424 (2006)
37. Zhang, K., Zhang, Z., Li, Z., Qiao, Y.: Joint face detection and alignment using multitask cascaded convolutional networks. IEEE Sig. Process. Lett. **23**(10), 1499–1503 (2016)

38. Zhou, Z.H., Zhang, M.L.: Neural networks for multi-instance learning. In: Proceedings of the International Conference on Intelligent Information Technology, Beijing, China, pp. 455–459 (2002)
39. Zhu, J.Y., Wu, J., Xu, Y., Chang, E., Tu, Z.: Unsupervised object class discovery via saliency-guided multiple class learning. IEEE Trans. Pattern Anal. Mach. Intell. **37**(4), 862–875 (2015)
40. Zhu, W., Lou, Q., Vang, Y.S., Xie, X.: Deep multi-instance networks with sparse label assignment for whole mammogram classification. In: Descoteaux, M., Maier-Hein, L., Franz, A., Jannin, P., Collins, D.L., Duchesne, S. (eds.) MICCAI 2017. LNCS, vol. 10435, pp. 603–611. Springer, Cham (2017). https://doi.org/10.1007/978-3-319-66179-7_69

Residual Stacked RNNs for Action Recognition

Mohamed Ilyes Lakhal[1(✉)], Albert Clapés[2], Sergio Escalera[2], Oswald Lanz[3], and Andrea Cavallaro[1]

[1] CIS, Queen Mary University of London, London, UK
{m.i.lakhal,a.cavallaro}@qmul.ac.uk

[2] Computer Vision Centre, University of Barcelona, Barcelona, Spain
aclapes@gmail.com, sergio.escalera.guerrero@gmail.com

[3] TeV, Fondazione Bruno Kessler, Trento, Italy
lanz@fbk.eu

Abstract. Action recognition pipelines that use Recurrent Neural Networks (RNN) are currently 5–10% less accurate than Convolutional Neural Networks (CNN). While most works that use RNNs employ a 2D CNN on each frame to extract descriptors for action recognition, we extract spatiotemporal features from a 3D CNN and then learn the temporal relationship of these descriptors through a stacked residual recurrent neural network (Res-RNN). We introduce for the first time residual learning to counter the degradation problem in multi-layer RNNs, which have been successful for temporal aggregation in two-stream action recognition pipelines. Finally, we use a late fusion strategy to combine RGB and optical flow data of the two-stream Res-RNN. Experimental results show that the proposed pipeline achieves competitive results on UCF-101 and state of-the-art results for RNN-like architectures on the challenging HMDB-51 dataset.

Keywords: Action recognition · Deep residual learning · Two-stream RNN

1 Introduction

An important challenge in action recognition is to effectively model temporal dynamics and long-term dependencies. If the temporal evolution of actions is unaccounted for, similar actions (e.g. *answering phone* and *hanging-up phone*) may be confused. Also to encode discriminative spatiotemporal descriptors from the high-dimensional input video stream is key to address the recognition task.

Action recognition methods based on hand-crafted features [1,2] have recently been surpassed, in terms of recognition accuracy, by end-to-end trainable deep architectures [3]. Earlier deep learning approaches use convolutional neural networks to classify individual frames based on appearance information only, and then average their class scores to expose the video prediction [4]. To

L. Leal-Taixé and S. Roth (Eds.): ECCV 2018 Workshops, LNCS 11130, pp. 534–548, 2019.
https://doi.org/10.1007/978-3-030-11012-3_40

complement appearance information, low-level motion descriptors can be produced by feeding short clips as input to the network [5] instead of single frames, or by exploiting optical flow [6]. Integrating flow and appearance at the appropriate stage of the network can boost performance significantly [7]. Moreover, 3D ConvNets extend the convolutions in time to extract features from video segments [3,5,8]. To deal with the increased complexity of 3D ConvNets, pre-trained 2D image recognition-based CNNs can be inflated to 3D (Two-Stream Inflated 3D ConvNets (I3D) [3]). Residual networks [9] use skip connections to address the *degradation problem* (increasing the number of layers in a feed-forward network leads to a decrease in performance on both test and training data), allowing to effectively increase the depth of the network without augmenting the number of parameters.

The temporal evolution of the output of deep convolutional networks that use frames can be modeled by sequence models, e.g. Long-Short Term Memory (LSTM) [10]. To increase the depth of sequential models, LSTM layers can be stacked [11], but might suffer from the *degradation problem*. Networks with a large number of parameters or layers starve with action datasets, because of the limited training data (e.g. 10K videos in the most popular benchmarking datasets, UCF-101 and HMDB-51). It is therefore important not to increase the number of optimizable parameters.

In this paper, we extend multi-layer LSTMs with residual connections and explicitly learn *appearance* and *motion* in two separate streams. To the best of our knowledge, this is the first time Residual LSTMs are applied to video action recognition, as they were only applied to speech processing [12]. We use as input features extracted from a 3D CNN, which provides a much richer representation than a 2D CNN and reduces redundancy observed by the LSTMs on top. The predictions of the two-stream residual LSTMs are late fused using element-wise dot aggregation, as opposed to adding the final score predictions. The proposed architecture achieves competitive results on the UCF-101 dataset and outperforms state-of-the-art methods for RNN-like architecture on the HMDB-51 dataset.

The paper is organized as follows: Sect. 2 reviews related work. Section 3 introduces the proposed two-stage pipeline and data generation. Section 4 covers the experimental protocol and discusses the results. Finally, Sect. 5 concludes the paper.

2 Related Work

Spatiotemporal features can be learned by extending over time the connectivity of a 2D CNN and fusing responses from subsequent frames in short fix-length clips. This fusion leads to marginal gains over averaging predictions from a set of uniformly sampled frames [4]. 3D CNN [5] extend convolutional kernels and pooling operations over time, e.g. on 16-frame clips [13]. Increasing the temporal interval can improve recognition, except for actions with periodic patterns, by encoding longer temporal dynamics [8]. Improved results are obtained by combining long-term convolution networks with different temporal intervals, e.g. 60

and 100 frames [8]. Averaging predictions from a few random frames (or clips) may select samples that are uninformative for the action class. Max-pooling can be applied to the last convolutional layer map responses of a 2D CNN across all the frames of the video (*Conv Pooling*) [11]. Subaction patterns shared by actions classes may uniquely be assigned to a particular class, instead of to multiple classes, using frames or clips classification. To address this problem, local spatiotemporal descriptors can be aggregated over the video by softly assigning them to subaction anchors, as in ActionVLAD [14].

Temporal dynamics can be handled by sequence modeling via recurrent neural networks. Each frame can be processed in a shallow 3D CNN and the output responses modeled with an LSTM trained separately [15]. End-to-end trained architectures exists that combine a 2D CNN and a 5-layer LSTM [11]. Gated-recurrent Units (GRU) [16], a simpler variant of LSTMs with similar performance [17], consist of two gates only (*update* and *reset* gates) and the internal state (*output state*) is fully exposed. We refer the reader to [18] for an in-depth survey on recent advances in the subject.

Convolutional LSTMs [19] replace the fully connected layers in input-to-state and state-to-state transitions with convolutional layers, thus maintaining the spatial structure of input frames or convolutional maps from input to output. Spatial data redundancy can be reduced by substituting the fully connected layer with convolutions. Each pair of frames can be passed through two 2D CNNs with shared weights, whose outputs are then connected in a 3D convolutional layer and passed to a ConvLSTM [20]. ConvALSTM [21] combines the benefits of both ConvLSTM and Attention-LSTM [22,23], but relies on a shallow convolutional network for the soft-attention mechanism, unlike the Attention-LSTM. L^2STM [24] extends the LSTM formulation to learn independent hidden state transitions of memory cells for individual spatial locations.

Motion information (e.g. optical flow) and appearance (e.g. RGB data) can be modeled in two separate classification models and then the two independent softmax predictions are (late) fused. Examples of architectures include a two-stream 2D CNN [6], a long-term convolutional network [8], and ActionVLAD [14]. Moreover, spatial and temporal streams can also be fused after the last convolutional layer [7]. Cross-modal training is also possible on sequential models: L^2STM [24] modifies the gradient update equations for the input and forget gates to jointly adapt their parameters accounting for the loss of both streams during back-propagation. Motion information is easier for training from scratch with limited training data [6,8], and is useful for attentional mechanisms and action localization [21].

3 Residual Learning with RNNs

In this section we present the proposed stacked residual network (depicted in Fig. 1) and the data generation process. We also present our approach for model selection and evaluation.

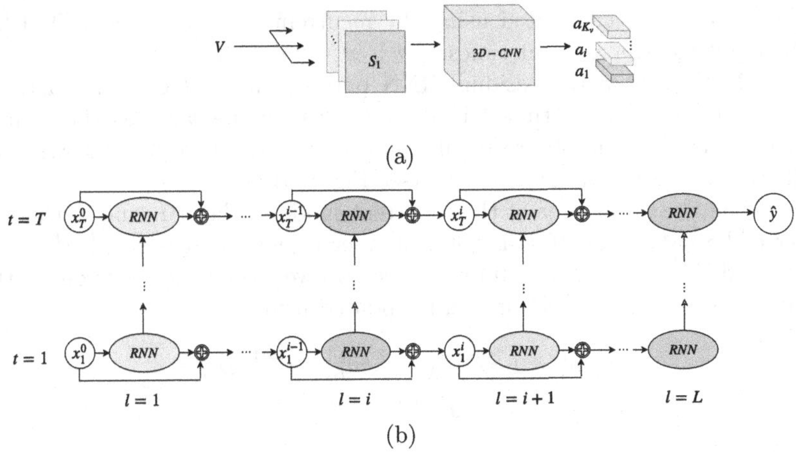

Fig. 1. The proposed residual stacked RNN architecture. The input video, V, is divided into clips from which spatiotemporal features are extracted with a 3D CNN. The residual stacked RNN learns temporal dependencies between an action class and elements of a sampled subset of features, x^0, of duration T.

3.1 The Two-Stage Pipeline

Let $V \in \mathbb{R}^{m_x \times m_y \times l_v}$ be a video of duration l_v that represents an action and whose frames have size $m_x \times m_y$ pixels. Let $K_v = \lfloor \frac{l_v}{r} \rfloor - 1$, be the number of clips in V, where r is the stride between each clip. Let each clip $S_i \in \mathbb{R}^{m_x \times m_y \times s}$ have a duration s empirically defined so that S_i captures a gesture in V. A gesture is a movement of body parts that can be used to control and to manipulate, or to communicate. A temporal concatenation of gestures composes an action [25]. Unlike frame-level predictions [11], we aim to encapsulate each S_i with a latent representation of much lower dimension, $a_i \in \mathbb{R}^{d_f}$, which is expected to encode a gesture.

Let the spatiotemporal features of S_i be extracted[1] with a 3D CNN [3,26], as $a_i = E(S_i) \in \mathbb{R}^{d_f}$, thus obtaining $a = \{a_i | i = 1 \dots K_v; a_i \in \mathbb{R}^{d_f}\}$, from which we extract a subset x^0 of size T: $x^0 = \{x_t^0 = a_{\sigma(t)} | t = 1, \dots, T; a_{\sigma(t)} \in a\}$, where $\sigma(t) = 1 + \lfloor (t-1)\frac{K_v - 1}{T-1} \rfloor$.

The final step learns the temporal dependencies between the input sequence x^0 using the residual recurrent neural network. Instead of fitting an underlying mapping $H(x)$, the same stack of layers in residual learning generates $H(x)$ to fit another mapping $F(x) = H(x) + x$. The network learns a residual mapping $F(x)$ to approximate $H(x)$ rather than $F(x)$. Given a stack of recurrent neural units of depth L, at layer l and timestep t the input is x_t^{l-1}. The previous memory and cell states for layer l from timestep $t-1$ are m_{t-1}^l and c_{t-1}^l, respectively.

[1] Note that our architecture is independent from the particular CNN structure and other models can be used as extractor, e.g. TSN [26] or I3D [3] (see Fig. 1(a)).

Then, m_t^l and c_t^l are calculated using the recurrent equations *e.g.* LSTM [27], and the input to layer $l+1$ at timestep t is $x_t^l = m_t^l + x_t^{l-1}$.

Each RNN layer in the residual RNN part has index $l \in \{1, \ldots, L\}$. The dimension of the input at time t in layer l must be the same as the memory m_t^l since the addition in the residual equation is performed element-wise. The overall structure is the same as in [28] (see Fig. 1(b)).

Let Θ^l be the parameter of the recurrent model at layer l, and L the total number of LSTM layers. If P is total number of action classes, $m_t^l, x_t^l \in \mathbb{R}^{d_f}$, $y \in \mathbb{R}^P$, and $W_y \in \mathbb{R}^{d_f \times P}$ is a fully connected layer, then the recurrent part of our hierarchical residual RNN model is updated using:

$$\begin{aligned} c_t^l, m_t^l &= LSTM_l(c_{t-1}^l, m_{t-1}^l, x_t^{l-1}; \Theta^l) \\ x_t^l &= m_t^l + x_t^{l-1} \end{aligned} \tag{1}$$

where T is the number of time steps. At the l-th layer we obtain the hidden state from $LSTM_l$ using the input x_t^{l-1}, the input at the $(l+1)$-th layer is the residual equation: $x_t^l = m_t^l + x_t^{l-1}$. We obtain the final score $\hat{y}$ through a softmax layer at the last time step T using

$$\hat{y} = \texttt{softmax}((m_T^L)^\top . W_y). \tag{2}$$

Under this formulation, our residual RNN model will learn the temporal dependencies of each clip S_i and perform a video level prediction by adding a softmax layer on top of the last LSTM unit at the last time step T (see Fig. 1(b)).

3.2 Fusion

We extend the multi-layer residual LSTM to handle two streams, namely the RGB video, V, and the optical flow, which has been shown to be useful for CNN based models [7]. Girdhar [14] explored three fusion methods to combine RGB and Flow CNN models.

Given two feature vectors $u, v \in \mathbb{R}^m$, we consider for fusion the element-wise sum and the element-wise product. For the element-wise sum, $\oplus$, the fusion is $u \oplus v = (u_1 + v_1, \ldots, u_m + v_m)$. This method is expected to help if the two responses have high scores, whereas small perturbations in either vector will be ignored. The element-wise product, $\odot$, is $u \odot v = (u_1.v_1, \ldots, u_m.v_m)$. This scheme encourages the highest scores and tends to diminish small responses.

We feed the input video, V, to a pre-trained 3D-CNN, $x^c = \text{3D-CNN}^c(V)$, and the optical flow, V^f, through a pre-trained flow model, $x^f = \text{3D-CNN}^f(V^f)$ (see Fig. 2(a)). With *mid fusion*, $x^0 = \{x_t^0 = x_t^c \circ x_t^f | t = 1, \ldots, T\}$, where $\circ \in \{\oplus, \odot\}$. We then train a Res-LSTM model using x^0 as input. With *late fusion*, we use the input x^c (x^f) to train a Res-LSTM for the appearance (optical flow) network. Once the models are trained we obtain the softmax predictions, $\hat{y}^c$ and $\hat{y}^f$, for each modality network. The final prediction is $\hat{y} = \hat{y}^c \circ \hat{y}^f$, where $\circ \in \{\oplus, \odot\}$ (see Fig. 2(b)). Results of these fusion methods are shown in Table 2.

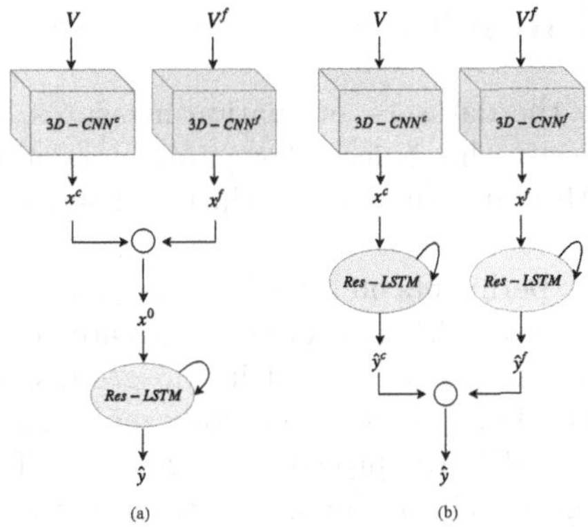

Fig. 2. Fusion schemes on two-stream Res-LSTM: (a) in *mid fusion* after obtaining the spatiotemporal features from the RGB(Flow) network we combine the features using either element-wise or dot product to produce a single vector x^0 that serves as the input to a Res-LSTM model, (b) *late fusion* on the other hand trains a separate Res-LSTM for each modality input, the predictions of each modality network are then combined for a final prediction.

3.3 Data Generation

We consider two strategies of data augmentation [24], depending on the CNN architecture used. The first strategy consists of fixing the spatial dimension and varying the temporal axis of the input stream,

$$V_S = \{V_{clip}^{(1)}, V_{clip}^{(2)}, \ldots, V_{clip}^{(v)} | V_{clip}^{(i)} \in \mathbb{R}^{m_x \times m_y \times l_t}\}, \tag{3}$$

where $l_t \leq l_v$ and we let r to be a fixed stride between each clip $V_{clip}^{(i)} \subset V$. The second strategy consists of sampling a fixed set of spatial crops with a temporal length of $T < l_v$. We select 10 crops from four corners and the center of each frame, along with their mirrors. We thus sample a new set $V_S \in \mathbb{R}^{10 \times m_x \times m_y \times T}$ for a given input video V. After a forward pass through the CNN, we obtain our spatiotemporal matrix of descriptors $\mathbf{A} \in \mathbb{R}^{10 \times T \times d_f}$, where d_f is the spatiotemporal feature dimension. Finally, the input to the recurrent network is obtained as follows:

$$x^0 = \{x_t^0 \in \mathbb{R}^{d_f} | t = 1, \ldots, T\}, \tag{4}$$

where

$$x_t^0 = \frac{1}{K_c} \sum_{k=1,\ldots,K_c} \mathbf{A}(k, t, :), \tag{5}$$

where K_c is the number of crops (in our case $K_c = 10$). We found that the mean over the features of crops is preferable to just considering each crop separately.

4 Experimental Results

We will first introduce the datasets, evaluation measures, and implementation details. Then we will discuss the choice of key parameters of the proposed method and compare with both static (non-sequential) and sequential state-of-the-art approaches.

We carried out the experiments on HMDB-51 [29] and UCF-101 [30]. HMDB-51 consists of 6,849 videos of 51 categories, each category containing at least 101 instances. Actions can be categorized into 5 groups: facial actions, facial actions involving objects, body movements, body movements involving objects, and human interactions. UCF-101 provides 13,320 videos from 101 action categories, that can be categorized into: human-object interaction, body-motion only, human-human interaction, playing musical instruments, and sports. Results will be reported in terms of accuracy (%) over the split-1 on both datasets, as in [13].

For the parameter discussion in the next section we used as feature extractor a C3D pre-trained on Sports-1M [13]. Input clips were of temporal length $|S_i| = 16$, with a stride of $r = 8$ between them. For our final architecture features were extracted using the TSN [26] model, and the sparse features were of size 25. For training the residual recurrent network we used the RMSProp optimizer [31] with a learning rate of $\epsilon = 10^{-3}$.

4.1 Discussion on Parameters

In this section we discuss the choice of the hidden layer size, the depth, the duration, and the fusion strategy for the deep residual network.

We varied the hidden layer size h, given the 4,096-dimensional spatiotemporal features extracted by the pre-trained C3D [13]. The best validation performance of the model increased before $h = 1024$ and stagnated after this value (Fig. 3(a)). We therefore used $h = 1024$ as a base parameter to our models.

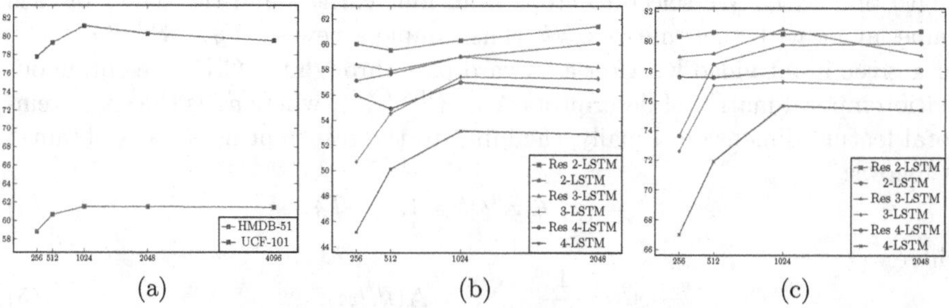

(a) (b) (c)

Fig. 3. Influence of size and depth on the performance of the LSTM. (a) Dimension of the hidden layers; (b) residual depth on HMDB-51; (c) residual depth on UCF-101.

A number of works [3,32,33] have shown that longer temporal window over the input of the 3D-CNN input leads to better performance. In Table 1, we can see that even for LSTM, longer time inputs lead to better performance. However, we may face the vanishing gradient problem using this class of model for very long sequence input. As for the temporal duration, $T = 25$ and $T = 35$[2] are the best choices for HMDB-51 and UCF-101, respectively. After these values the model starts overfitting.

To analyze the impact of the *residual connections* in the stacked recurrent neural networks context, we reduce the dimensionality of the 4,096 input features. The dimensionality of input and output need to match in order to perform the residual addition. To do so, we apply PCA over the initial feature of shape 4,096 (extracted from a pre-trained C3D model) to fit with the dimension of the residual RNN. We select a set of dimensions $\mathcal{D} = \{\mathbb{R}^{d_m} | d_m \in [256, 512, 1024, 2048]\}$, and we train our hierarchical RNN, with and without residual part[3]. Figure 3 shows that the residual connections help generalization in both datasets: even when dropping on performance, the residual RNN still performs better.

We tested stacking 2, 3, and 4 recurrent layers (Fig. 3(b)–(c)): stacking only two layers provides the best depth for the residual model as working with 3D-CNN reduces the number of feature samples per-video and thus a model with more layers is more likely to overfit the data. In contrast, for 2D-CNN feature extraction, the dataset is quite large because each frame is a feature and therefore the residual RNN model will have enough data to tune its parameters for more layers. This is why the authors in [11] were able to train 5-layers RNN.

Table 1. Impact of the value of the time step T on accuracy.

T	5	15	25	35
HMDB-51	59.5	60.2	61.5	61.4
UCF-101	77.9	79.9	79.5	80.9

Finally, late fusion outperforms mid fusion on HMDB-51 using Res-LSTM. For point-wise addition the gain is near 6% and for point-wise product it is 13%, with a clear benefit of the product aggregation "$\odot$". We use the same weights as the original TSN [26], *i.e.*, $(w_1, w_2) \in (1.5, 1)$ (see Table 2).

Table 2. Impact on accuracy of different mid and late fusion strategies on the 2-layer Res-LSTM on the HMDB-51 dataset.

Strategy	Mid fusion	Late fusion
$\oplus$ (element-wise sum)	59.3	65.2
$\odot$ (element-wise product)	56.5	68.0
$w_1.Flow + w_2.RGB$	–	63.3

[2] Note however, that the final scores we report are for $T = 25$ to allow for a fair comparison with the TSN model [26].

[3] We discarded the 4,096 feature vector because of computational requirements.

4.2 Final Model Evaluation

We evaluate our model on coarse UCF-101 categories as well as on complex action classes, following [24]. Table 3 shows that our model outperforms L^2STM in the coarse categories they reported and also in *Mixing Batter* with a gain of 4.41. However, the performance drops for the complex classes *Pizza Tossing* and *Salsa Spins*, probably because of the speed of the actions that our model was not able to capture well. Figure 4 shows the classification of some of the examples with the top confidences for each video example.

Table 3. Comparison on Split-1 of UCF-101 with complex movements.

Data types	L^2STM	Res-LSTM	Gain
Human-object interaction	86.7	88.2	↑ **1.5**
Human-human interaction	95.4	96.9	↑ **1.5**
Body-motion only	88.6	90.7	↑ **2.1**
Playing instrument	-	97.3	-
Sports	-	93.2	-
Pizza tossing	72.7	66.7	↓ 6.0
Mixing batter	86.7	91.1	↑ **4.4**
Playing dhol	100	100	≡
Salsa spins	100	97.7	↓ 2.3
Ice dancing	100	100	≡

Also, we compare our final model to other RNN-like architectures. Table 4 lists the performances and pre-training used by each solution. Our Res-LSTM outperforms the LSTM solutions in HMDB-51, while still being close to L^2STM [24] and Pre-RNN [34] performances on UCF-101.

In addition, Fig. 5 reports the confusion matrices of our model on UCF-101 and HMDB-51. The classes in both datasets are rearranged using the coarse category labels provided in each dataset.

We also combined our method with IDT, following other state-of-the-art approaches [8,14,21]. From the combination, we obtained an improvement of accuracy of, respectively, +0.5% and +8.9% in UCF-101 and HMDB-51. In order to analyze the larger improvement in HMDB-51, we illustrate the confusion matrix for the combination in Fig. 6a and the subtraction of the confusion matrices before and after the combination in Fig. 6b. Finally, Fig. 6c illustrates the per-class accuracy improvement on the HMDB-51 categories after the combination with IDT which improved (or maintained) the accuracy on 45 of the 51 categories, while only getting worse performance on 7.

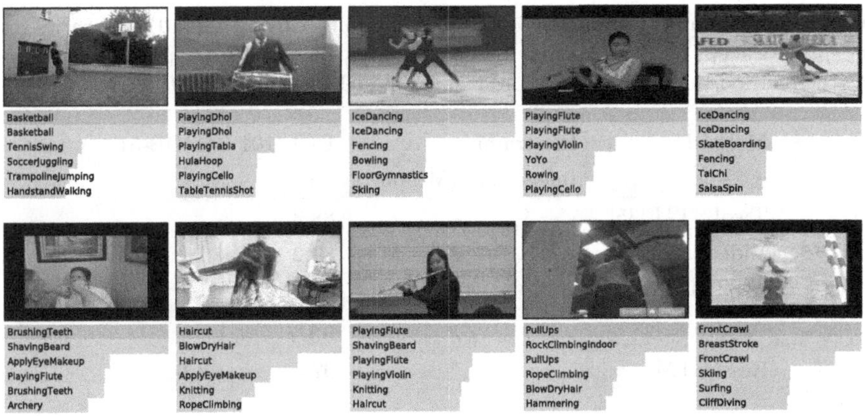

Fig. 4. Sample video classification results showing the top-5 class predictions based on confidence. First row: correctly classified videos; second row: miss-classified videos. Key – blue bar: ground-truth class; green bar: correct class prediction; red bar: incorrect class prediction. (Color figure online)

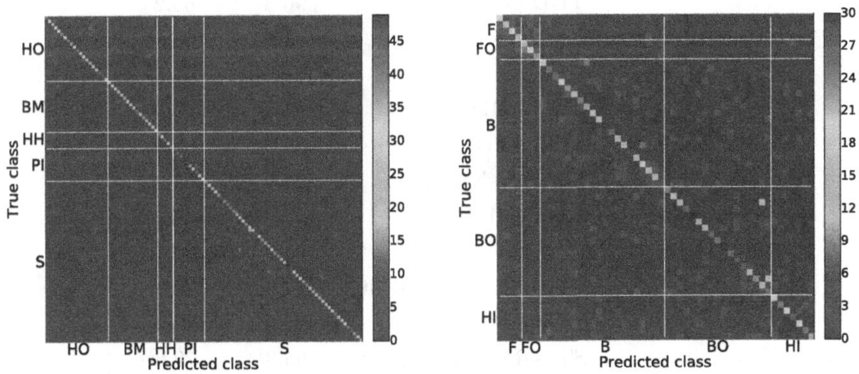

(a) (b)

Fig. 5. Confusion matrices with rearranged classes to group coarse categories. For UCF-101: human-object interaction (HO), body-motion only (BM), human-human interaction (HH), playing musical instrument (PI), and sports (S). For HMDB-51: facial actions (F), facial actions w/ object manipulation (FO), body movements (BM), body movements w/ object interaction (BO), and body movements for human interaction (HH). (a) Res-LSTM confusion matrix on UCF-101, (b) Res-LSTM confusion matrix on HMDB51

Finally, we compare to a broader set of works, either sequential or non-sequential (static) models in Table 5. Most of them only report results over the three splits in both UCF-101 and HMDB-51. Those that provide the accuracy in Split-1 are marked with '*'.

Table 4. Performance comparison of RNN-like architectures. UCF-101 accuracies are over split-1, except for [24] that only reports accuracy over the three splits. '*' indicates that the method may or not use a pre-trained model, depending on the CNN used.

Method	Pre-training		UCF-101	HMDB-51
	ImageNet	1M Sports		
TwoLSTM [35]	✓	✓	88.3	-
VideoLSTM [21]	✓	✗	89.2	56.4
L^2STM [24]	✓	✗	**93.6**	66.2
Pre-RNN [34]	✓	✗	**93.7**	-
Res-LSTM	*	*	92.5	**68.0**

Table 5. Comparison on UCF-101 and HMDB-51.

Model	Method	UCF-101	HMDB-51
Static models	FST-CNN [36]	88.1	59.1
	TDD [37]	90.3	63.2
	KV-CNN [38]	93.1	63.3
	LTC [39]	91.7	64.8
	TDD + IDT [37]	91.5	65.9
	ST-ResNet [40]	93.4	66.4
	STM-ResNet [41]	94.2	68.2
	LTC + IDT [39]	92.7	67.2
	TSN [26]	94.2	69.4
	ST-ResNet + IDT [40]	94.6	70.3
	STM-ResNet + IDT [41]	94.9	72.2
	STC-ResNext [33]	95.8‡	72.6‡
	I3D [3]	**98.0**	**80.7**
Sequential models	LRCN [42]	82.9	-
	AttLSTM [23]	77.0*	41.3
	UnsuperLSTM [43]	84.3*	44.0‡
	RLSTM-g3 [44]	86.9	55.3
	TwoLSTM [35]	88.3*	-
	VideoLSTM [21]	89.2*	56.4
	VideoLSTM + IDT [21]	91.5*	63.0
	L^2STM [24]	**93.6**	66.2
	PreRNN [34]	**93.7***	–
	Res-LSTM (ours)	92.5*	68.0*
	Res-LSTM (ours) $\odot$ IDT	93.0*	**76.9***

‡Only RGB modality is used
*Evaluation on split-1

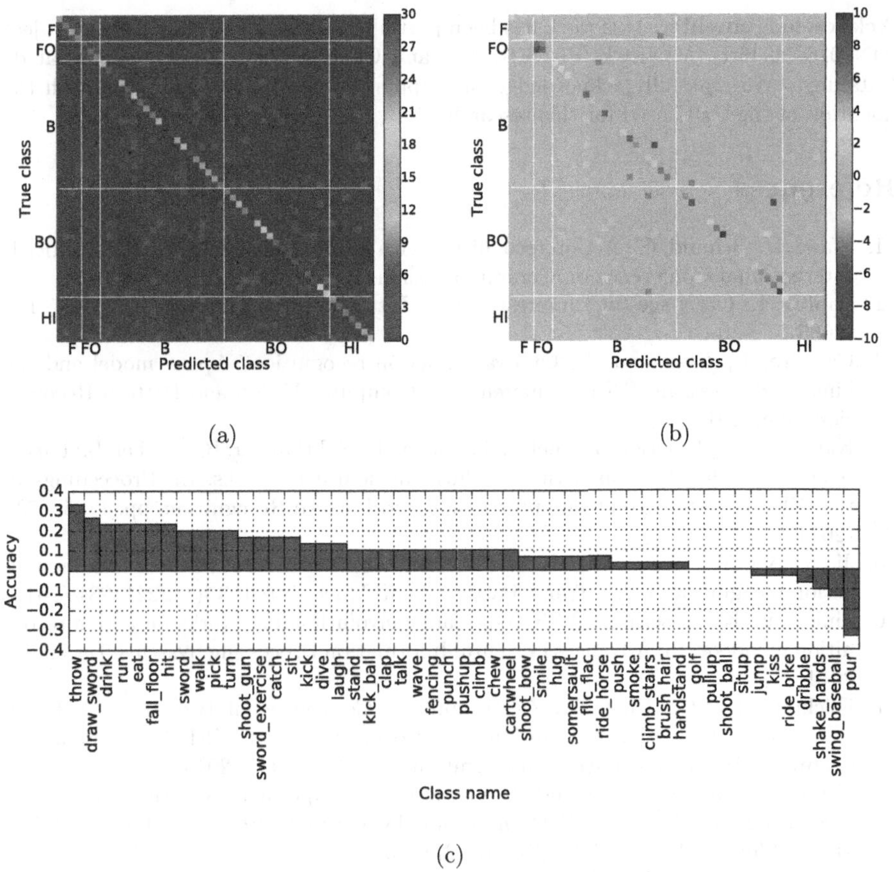

Fig. 6. Confusion matrices and per-class accuracy improvement after combining our Res-LSTM with IDT on HMDB-51. The ordering of classes in (a) and (b) is rearranged as in (a). (a) Res-LSTM ⊙ IDT confusion matrix on HMDB-51, (b) Subtraction of Res-LSTM ⊙ IDT and Res-LSTM confusion matrices on HMDB-51, (c) Per-class accuracy improvement after combining with IDT.

5 Conclusion

We have shown the benefits of the residual connection and of the fusion of appearance and motion features for an action recognition pipeline with a stacked recurrent neural network. Our solution obtained state-of-the-art against LSTM solutions on the HMDB-51 dataset.

Compared to CNN-like state-of-the-art, the RNN based models are still challenging. As future work, we will investigate the joint learning strategy by merging the spatiotemporal features from the 3D CNN directly with the RNN layer in an end-to-end learning pipeline. The end-to-end learning framework between CNN and RNN has been successfully applied to sound classification [45], we believe that this may help to reduce the gap for RNN solution in action recognition problem as well.

Acknowledgements. This work has been partially supported by the Spanish project TIN2016-74946-P (MINECO/FEDER, UE) and CERCA Programme/Generalitat de Catalunya. We gratefully acknowledge the support of NVIDIA Corporation with the donation of the GPU used for this research.

References

1. Wang, H., Schmid, C.: Action recognition with improved trajectories. In: The IEEE International Conference on Computer Vision, ICCV, pp. 3551–3558 (2013)
2. Laptev, I.: On space-time interest points. Int. J. Comput. Vis. **64**(2–3), 107–123 (2005)
3. Carreira, J., Zisserman, A.: Quo vadis, action recognition? A new model and the kinetics dataset. In: IEEE Conference on Computer Vision and Pattern Recognition, June 2017
4. Karpathy, A., Toderici, G., Shetty, S., Leung, T., Sukthankar, R., Fei-Fei, L.: Large-scale video classification with convolutional neural networks. In: Proceedings of the IEEE conference on Computer Vision and Pattern Recognition, pp. 1725–1732 (2014)
5. Ji, S., Xu, W., Yang, M., Yu, K.: 3D convolutional neural networks for human action recognition. IEEE Trans. Pattern Anal. Mach. Intell. **35**(1), 221–231 (2013)
6. Simonyan, K., Zisserman, A.: Two-stream convolutional networks for action recognition in videos. In: Advances in Neural Information Processing Systems, December 2014
7. Feichtenhofer, C., Pinz, A., Zisserman, A.: Convolutional two-stream network fusion for video action recognition. In: Proceedings of the IEEE Conference on Computer Vision and Pattern Recognition, pp. 1933–1941 (2016)
8. Varol, G., Laptev, I., Schmid, C.: Long-term temporal convolutions for action recognition. IEEE Trans. Pattern Anal. Mach. Intell. **40**(6), 1510–1517 (2018). https://doi.org/10.1109/TPAMI.2017.2712608
9. He, K., Zhang, X., Ren, S., Sun, J.: Deep residual learning for image recognition. In: IEEE Conference on Computer Vision and Pattern Recognition, June 2016
10. Hochreiter, S., Schmidhuber, J.: Long short-term memory. Neural Comput. **9**(8), 1735–1780 (1997)
11. Ng, J.Y.-H., Hausknecht, M., Vijayanarasimhan, S., Vinyals, O., Monga, R., Toderici, G.: Beyond short snippets: deep networks for video classification. In: IEEE Conference on Computer Vision and Pattern Recognition, June 2015
12. Kim, J., El-Khamy, M., Lee, J.: Residual LSTM: design of a deep recurrent architecture for distant speech recognition. arXiv preprint arXiv:1701.03360 (2017)
13. Tran, D., Bourdev, L., Fergus, R., Torresani, L., Paluri, M.: Learning spatiotemporal features with 3D convolutional networks. In: IEEE International Conference on Computer Vision, December 2015
14. Girdhar, R., Ramanan, D., Gupta, A., Sivic, J., Russell, B.: ActionVLAD: learning spatio-temporal aggregation for action classification. In: IEEE Conference on Computer Vision and Pattern Recognition, June 2017
15. Baccouche, M., Mamalet, F., Wolf, C., Garcia, C., Baskurt, A.: Sequential deep learning for human action recognition. In: Salah, A.A., Lepri, B. (eds.) HBU 2011. LNCS, vol. 7065, pp. 29–39. Springer, Heidelberg (2011). https://doi.org/10.1007/978-3-642-25446-8_4
16. Cho, K., Van Merriënboer, B., Bahdanau, D., Bengio, Y.: On the properties of neural machine translation: encoder-decoder approaches. arXiv:1409.1259 (2014)

17. Chung, J., Gulcehre, C., Cho, K., Bengio, Y.: Empirical evaluation of gated recurrent neural networks on sequence modeling. arXiv:1412.3555 (2014)
18. Asadi-Aghbolaghi, M., et al.: A survey on deep learning based approaches for action and gesture recognition in image sequences. In: IEEE International Conference on Automatic Face & Gesture Recognition, pp. 476–483 (2017)
19. Shi, X., Chen, Z., Wang, H., Yeung, D.Y., Wong, W., Woo, W.: Convolutional LSTM network: a machine learning approach for precipitation nowcasting. In: Advances in Neural Information Processing Systems, December 2015
20. Sudhakaran, S., Lanz, O.: Convolutional long short-term memory networks for recognizing first person interactions. In: IEEE International Conference on Computer Vision Workshops, October 2017
21. Li, Z., Gavrilyuk, K., Gavves, E., Jain, M., Snoek, C.G.: VideoLSTM convolves, attends and flows for action recognition. Comput. Vis. Image Underst. **166**, 41–50 (2018)
22. Xu, K., et al.: Show, attend and tell: neural image caption generation with visual attention. In: International Conference on Machine Learning, pp. 2048–2057 (2015)
23. Sharma, S., Kiros, R., Salakhutdinov, R.: Action recognition using visual attention. arXiv preprint arXiv:1511.04119 (2015)
24. Sun, L., Jia, K., Chen, K., Yeung, D.Y., Shi, B.E., Savarese, S.: Lattice long short-term memory for human action recognition. In: IEEE International Conference on Computer Vision, October 2017
25. Borges, P.V.K., Conci, N., Cavallaro, A.: Video-based human behavior understanding: a survey. IEEE Trans. Circ. Syst. Video Technol. **23**, 1993–2008 (2013)
26. Wang, L., et al.: Temporal segment networks: towards good practices for deep action recognition. In: Leibe, B., Matas, J., Sebe, N., Welling, M. (eds.) ECCV 2016. LNCS, vol. 9912, pp. 20–36. Springer, Cham (2016). https://doi.org/10.1007/978-3-319-46484-8_2
27. Hochreiter, S., Schmidhuber, J.: Long short-term memory. Neural Comput. **9**, 1735–1780 (1997)
28. Wu, Y., et al.: Google's neural machine translation system: bridging the gap between human and machine translation. CoRR (2016)
29. Kuehne, H., Jhuang, H., Garrote, E., Poggio, T., Serre, T.: HMDB: a large video database for human motion recognition. In: IEEE International Conference on Computer Vision, November 2011
30. Soomro, K., Zamir, A.R., Shah, M.: UCF101: a dataset of 101 human actions classes from videos in the wild. CoRR (2012)
31. Tijmen, T., Geoffrey, H.: Lecture 6.5-RmsProp: divide the gradient by a running average of its recent magnitude. In: COURSERA: Neural Networks for Machine Learning (2012)
32. Hara, K., Kataoka, H., Satoh, Y.: Can spatiotemporal 3D CNNs retrace the history of 2D CNNs and ImageNet? In: The IEEE Conference on Computer Vision and Pattern Recognition, CVPR, June 2018
33. Diba, A., et al.: Spatio-temporal channel correlation networks for action classification. In: Ferrari, V., Hebert, M., Sminchisescu, C., Weiss, Y. (eds.) ECCV 2018. LNCS, vol. 11208, pp. 299–315. Springer, Cham (2018). https://doi.org/10.1007/978-3-030-01225-0_18
34. Yang, X., Molchanov, P., Kautz, J.: Making convolutional networks recurrent for visual sequence learning. In: The IEEE Conference on Computer Vision and Pattern Recognition, CVPR, June 2018

35. Ng, J.Y.H., Hausknecht, M., Vijayanarasimhan, S., Vinyals, O., Monga, R., Toderici, G.: Beyond short snippets: deep networks for video classification. In: IEEE Conference on Computer Vision and Pattern Recognition, June 2015
36. Sun, L., Jia, K., Yeung, D.Y., Shi, B.E.: Human action recognition using factorized spatio-temporal convolutional networks. In: Proceedings of the 2015 IEEE International Conference on Computer Vision, ICCV, ICCV 2015, Washington, DC, USA, pp. 4597–4605. IEEE Computer Society (2015)
37. Wang, L., Qiao, Y., Tang, X.: Action recognition with trajectory-pooled deep-convolutional descriptors. In: IEEE Conference on Computer Vision and Pattern Recognition, June 2015
38. Zhu, W., Hu, J., Sun, G., Cao, X., Qiao, Y.: A key volume mining deep framework for action recognition. In: 2016 IEEE Conference on Computer Vision and Pattern Recognition, CVPR, pp. 1991–1999, June 2016
39. Varol, G., Laptev, I., Schmid, C.: Long-term temporal convolutions for action recognition. IEEE Trans. Pattern Anal. Mach. Intell. **PP**(99), 1 (2017)
40. Feichtenhofer, C., Pinz, A., Wildes, R.: Spatiotemporal residual networks for video action recognition. In: Advances in Neural Information Processing Systems, pp. 3468–3476 (2016)
41. Feichtenhofer, C., Pinz, A., Wildes, R.P.: Spatiotemporal multiplier networks for video action recognition. In: The IEEE Conference on Computer Vision and Pattern Recognition, CVPR, July 2017
42. Donahue, J., et al.: Long-term recurrent convolutional networks for visual recognition and description. IEEE Trans. Pattern Anal. Mach. Intell. **39**(4), 677–691 (2017)
43. Srivastava, N., Mansimov, E., Salakhudinov, R.: Unsupervised learning of video representations using LSTMs. In: Blei, D., Bach, F. (eds.) Proceedings of the 32nd International Conference on Machine Learning, ICML 2015, JMLR Workshop and Conference Proceedings, pp. 843–852 (2015)
44. Mahasseni, B., Todorovic, S.: Regularizing long short term memory with 3D human-skeleton sequences for action recognition. In: Proceedings of the IEEE Conference on Computer Vision and Pattern Recognition, pp. 3054–3062 (2016)
45. Choi, K., Fazekas, G., Sandler, M., Cho, K.: Convolutional recurrent neural networks for music classification. In: IEEE International Conference on Acoustics, Speech and Signal Processing, March 2017

W12 – 1st Person in Context Workshop and Challenge

W12 – 1st Person in Context Workshop and Challenge

The first Person in Context Workshop and Challenge (PIC 2018) was organised in the context of ECCV 2018 in Munich, Gemany. Analysing relations in image has known to be the first step from perception to cognition. The ultimate purpose of this workshop was therefore to push the process of visual understanding on middle level and encourage researchers within computer vision to showcase their research on relation prediction. In paritcular, this workshop narrowed the task down to only focus relations around person and aimed to make it available for industry application.

PIC 2018 had received 9 submissions, out of which 5 (56%) were accepted. The selection process was double-blind. Each paper was solicited by at least 2 reviewers.

This workshop featured six keynotes by distinguished invited speakers: B Schiele (Max-Planck-Institut fr Informatik, Gemany), MH Yang (University of California at Merced, USA), A Yuille (Johns Hopkins University, USA), J Deng (Princeton University, USA), WJ Zeng (Microsoft Research Asia, China), T Yao (JD.com, China), who delivered outstanding talks covering both the industry and academia viewpoints.

We would like to thank the workshop chairs of ECCV 18 for giving us the opportunity to run the first PIC workshop, and we also want to thank the speakers for their kind presence and excellent talks. Finally, We really appreciate MadaCode and QiHu360 for sponsoring the challenge and invited talks.

September 2018

Si Liu
Jiashi Feng
Jizhong Han
Shuicheng Yan
Yao Sun
Yue Liao
Lejian Ren
Guanghui Ren

Semantically Selective Augmentation for Deep Compact Person Re-Identification

Víctor Ponce-López(✉), Tilo Burghardt, Sion Hannunna, Dima Damen, Alessandro Masullo, and Majid Mirmehdi

Department of Computer Science, Faculty of Engineering, University of Bristol, Merchant Venturers Building, Woodland Road, Bristol BS8 1UB, UK
vponcelop@gmail.com, {v.poncelopez,tb2935,sh1670,dima.damen, a.masullo,m.mirmehdi}@bristol.ac.uk

Abstract. We present a deep person re-identification approach that combines semantically selective, deep data augmentation with clustering-based network compression to generate high performance, light and fast inference networks. In particular, we propose to augment limited training data via sampling from a deep convolutional generative adversarial network (DCGAN), whose discriminator is constrained by a semantic classifier to explicitly control the domain specificity of the generation process. Thereby, we encode information in the classifier network which can be utilized to steer adversarial synthesis, and which fuels our CondenseNet ID-network training. We provide a quantitative and qualitative analysis of the approach and its variants on a number of datasets, obtaining results that outperform the state-of-the-art on the LIMA dataset for long-term monitoring in indoor living spaces.

Keywords: Person re-identification · Selective augmentation · Face filtering · Adversarial synthesis · Deep compression

1 Introduction

Person re-identification (Re-ID) across cameras with disjoint fields of view, given unobserved intervals and varying appearance (*e.g.* change in clothing), remains a challenging subdomain of computer vision. The task is particularly demanding whenever facial biometrics [29] are not explicitly applicable, be that due to very low resolution [7] or non-frontal shots. Deep learning approaches have recently been customized, moving the domain of person Re-ID forward [1] with potential impact on a wide range of applications, for example, CCTV surveillance [5] and e-health applications for living and working environments [23]. Yet, obtaining cross-referenced ground truth over long term [17,27], realising deployment of inexpensive inference platforms, and establishing visual identities from strongly limited data – all remain fundamental challenges. In particular, the dependency of most deep learning paradigms on vast training data pools and high computational requirements for heavy inference networks appear as significant challenges to many person Re-ID settings.

L. Leal-Taixé and S. Roth (Eds.): ECCV 2018 Workshops, LNCS 11130, pp. 551–561, 2019.
https://doi.org/10.1007/978-3-030-11012-3_41

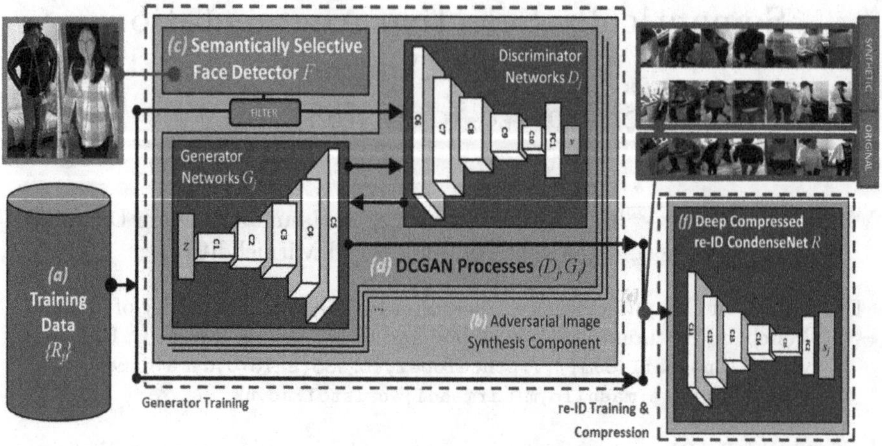

Fig. 1. Framework overview. Visual deep learning pipeline at the core of our approach: inputs (dark gray) are semantically filtered via a face detector (green) to enhance adversarial augmentation via DCGANs (blue). Original and synthetic data are combined to train a compressed CondenseNet (red) for light and fast ID-inference. (Color figure online)

In this paper, we introduce an approach for producing high performance, light and fast deep Re-ID inference networks for people - built from limited training data and not explicitly dependent on face identification. To achieve this, we propose an interplay of three recent deep learning technologies as depicted in Fig. 1: deep convolutional adversarial networks (DCGANs) [21] as class-specific sample generators (in blue); face detectors [25] used as semantic guarantors to steer synthesis (in green); and a clustering-based CondenseNet [10] as a compressor (in red). We show that the proposed face-selective adversarial synthesis allows to generate new, semantically selective and meaningful artificial images that can improve subsequent training of compressive ID networks. Whilst the training cost of our approach can be significant due to the adversarial networks' slow and complicated convergence process [6], our parameter count of final CondenseNets is approximately one order of magnitude smaller than those of other state-of-the-art systems, such as ResNet50 [33]. We provide a quantitative and qualitative analysis over different adversarial synthesis paradigms for our approach, obtaining results that outperform the highest achievements on the LIMA dataset [14] for long-term monitoring in indoor living environments.

2 Related Work

Performing person Re-ID is a popular and long-standing research area with considerable history and specific associated challenges [32]. Low-resolution face recognition [7], gait and behaviour analysis [26], as well as full-person, appearance-based recognition [32] all offer routes to performing 'in-effect' person ID or Re-ID. Here we will review particular technical aspects most relevant to the work at hand, *i.e.* looking specifically at recent augmentation and deep learning approaches for appearance-based methods.

Augmentation. Despite improvements in methods for high-quality, high-volume ground truth acquisition [17,19], input data augmentation [18] remains a key strategy to support generalisation in deep network training generally. The use of synthetic training data presents several advantages, such as the ability to reduce the effort of labeling images and to generate customizable domain-specific data. It has been noted that combining synthetic and measured input often shows improved performance over using synthetic images only [24]. Recent examples of non-augmented, innovative approaches in the person Re-ID domain include feature selection strategies [8,12], anthropometric profiling [2] using depth cameras, and multi-modal tracking [19], amongst many others. Augmentation has long been used in Re-ID scenarios too, for instance in [1], the authors consider structural aspects of the human body by exploiting mere RGB data to fully generate semi-realistic synthetic data as inputs to train neural networks, obtaining promising results for person Re-ID. Image augmentation techniques have also demonstrated effectiveness in improving the discriminative ability of learned CNN embeddings for person Re-ID, especially on large-scale datasets [1,3,33].

Adversarial Synthesis. Generative Adversarial Networks (GANs) [6] in particular have been widely and successfully applied to deliver augmentation – mainly building on their ability to construct a latent space that underpins the training data, and to sample from it to produce new training information. DCGANs [21] pair the GAN concept with compact convolutional operations to synthesise visual content more efficiently. The DCGAN's ability to organise the relationship between a latent space and an actual image space associated to the GAN input has been shown in a wide variety of applications, including face and pose analysis [16,21]. In these and other domains, latent spaces have been constructed that can convincingly model and parameterise object attributes such as scale, rotation, and position from unsupervised models, and hence dramatically reduce the amount of data needed for conditional generative modeling of complex image distributions.

Compression and Framework. Given ever-growing computational requirements for very-deep inference networks, recent research into network compression and optimisation has produced a number of approaches capable of compactly capturing network functionality. Some examples include ShuffleNet [30], MobileNet [9], and CondenseNet [10], which have proven to be effective even when operating on small devices where computational resources are limited.

In our work, we combine semantic data selection for data steering, adversarial synthesis for training space expansion, and CondenseNet compression to sparsify the built Re-ID classifier representation. Our solution operates on single images during inference, able to perform the Re-ID step in a one-shot paradigm[1].

3 Methodology and Framework Overview

Figure 1 illustrates our methodology pipeline, which follows a generative - discriminative paradigm: *(a)* training data sets $\{X_j\}$ of image patches are produced by a person detector, where each image patch set is either associated to a known person identity label $j \in \{1, .., N\}$, or an 'unknown' identity label $j = 0$. *(b)* An image augmentation component then expands on this dataset. This component consists of *(c)* a facial filter network F based on multi-view bootstrapping and OpenPose [25]; and *(d)* DCGAN [21] processes, whose discriminator networks D_j are constrained by the semantic selector F to control domain specificity. The set of DCGANs, namely network pairs (D_j, G_j), are employed to train generator networks G_j that synthesise unseen samples x associated with labels $j \in \{0, .., N\}$. These generators G_j are then used to produce large sets of samples. We focus on two types of scenarios: **(1)** a setup where we synthesize content for each identity class j individually, and **(2)** one where only a single 'unlabeled person' generator G is produced using all classes $\{X_j\}$ as input, with the aim to generate generic identity content, rather than individual-specific imagery. Sampled output from generators is *(e)* unified with the original frame sets and labels, forming the input data for *(f)* training a Re-ID CondenseNet R that learns to map sample image patches x_j to ID score vectors $s_j \in \mathbb{R}_+^{(N+1)}$ over all identity classes. This yields the sparse inference network R built implicitly compressed in order to support lightweight inference and deployment via a single network.

3.1 Adversarial Synthesis of Training Information

Adversarial Network Setup. We utilise the generic adversarial training process of DCGANs [21] and its suggested network design in order to construct a de-convolutional, generative function G_j per synthesised label class $j \in \{1, .., N\}$ that *after training* can produce new images x by sampling from a sparse latent space Z. Instead, a single 'generic person' network G is built in some experiments utilising all $\{X_j\}$. As in all adversarial setups, generative networks G or $\{G_j\}$ are paired with discriminative networks D or $\{D_j\}$, respectively. The latter map from images x to an 'is synthetic' score $v = D(x) > 0$, reflecting network support for $x \notin \{X_j\}$. Essentially, the discriminative networks then learn to differentiate generator-produced patches ($v \gg$) from original patches ($v \ll$). However, we add to this classic dual network setup [16], a third externally trained classifier F that filters and thereby controls/selects the input to D_j - in our case one that restricts input to those samples where the presence of faces can be established[2].

[1] Whilst results are competitive in this setting, discovering and matching segments during inference [14, 15, 20, 28, 34] is not used and could potentially further improve performance.

[2] We also modify the initial layer of the DCGAN to deal with a temporal gap of the specified number of frames. https://github.com/vponcelo/DCGAN-tensorflow.

Facial Filtering. We use the face keypoint detector from OpenPose [25] as the filter network F to semantically constrain the input to D_j and D. If at least one such keypoint can be established then face detection is defined as successful, where formally $F(x_j \in X_j) \in [0, 1]$ is assigned to reflect either the absence (0) or presence (1) of a face.

Training Process. All networks then engage in an adversarial training process utilising Adam [13] to optimise the networks D, $\{D_j\}$, and G, $\{G_j\}$, respectively, according to the discussion in [21], whilst enforcing the domain semantics via F. The following detailed process describes this training regime: **(1)** each D or D_j is optimised towards minimising the negative log-likelihood $-log(D(x))$ based on the relevant inputs from $\{X_j\}$ iff $F(x_j) = 1$, *i.e.* on original samples that are found to contain faces. **(2)** Network optimisation then switches to back-propagating errors into the entire networks $D(G(z))$ or $D_j(G_j(z))$, respectively, where z is sampled from a randomly initialised Gaussian to generate synthetic content. Consider that whilst the generator weights are adjusted to minimise the negative log-likelihood $-log(D(G(z)))$, encouraging v to get lower scores, the discriminator weights are adjusted to maximise it, prompting v to get higher scores. DCGAN training then proceeds by alternating between **(1)** and **(2)** until acceptable convergence.

3.2 Re-ID Network Training and Compression

Once the synthesis networks G and $\{G_j\}$ are trained, we sample their output and combine it with all original training images (withholding 15% per class for testing) to train R as a CondenseNet [10], optimised via standard stochastic gradient decent with Nestrov momentum. Structurally, R maps from 256×256-sized RGB-tensors to a score vector over all identity classes. We perform 120 epochs of training on all layers, where layer-internal grouping is applied to the dense layers in order to actively structure network pathways by means of clustering [10]. This principle has been proven effective in DenseNets [11], ShuffleNets [30], and MobileNets [9]. However, CondenseNets extend this approach by introducing a compression mechanism to remove low-impact connections by discarding unused weights. As a consequence, the approach produces an ID inference network[3] which is implicitly compressed and supports lightweight deployment.

4 Datasets

DukeMTMC-reID. First we confirm the viability of a GAN-driven CondenseNet application in a traditional Re-ID setting (*e.g.* larger cardinality of identities, outdoor scenes) via the DukeMTMC-reID [22] dataset, which is a subset of a multi-target, multi-camera pedestrian data corpus. It contains eight

[3] https://github.com/vponcelo/CondenseNet/.

Fig. 2. DCGAN synthesis examples. Samples generated by $G(z)$ with (b) or without (a) semantic controller. (c) 1st row: examples of generated images from G_0 and G_j without semantic controller; 2nd row: with semantic controller; 3rd row: original samples from X_0 and $\{X_j\}$. Columns in (c) are, from left to right, 'unknown' identity 0 and identities $j \in \{1, ..., N\}$, respectively.

85-min high-res videos with pedestrian bounding boxes. It covers 1,812 identities, where 1,404 identities appear in more than two cameras and 408 identities (distractor IDs) appear in only one[4].

Market1501. We also use a large-scale person Re-ID dataset called Market1501 [31] collected from 6 cameras covering 1,501 different identities across 19,732 images for testing and 12,936 images for training generated by a deformable part model [4].

LIMA. The **L**ong term **I**dentity aware **M**ulti-target multi-camer**A** tracking dataset [14], provides us with our main testbed for the approach. In contrast to previous datasets, image resolution is high enough in this dataset to effectively apply face detection as a semantic steer. LIMA contains a large set of 188,427 images of identity-tagged bounding boxes gathered over 13 independent sessions, where bounding boxes are estimated based on OpenNI NiTE operating on RGB-D and are grouped into time-stamped, local tracklets. The dataset covers a small set of 6 individuals filmed in various indoor environments, plus an additional 'unknown' class containing either background noise or multiple people in the same bounding box. Note that the LIMA dataset is acquired over a significant time period capturing actual people present in a home (*e.g.* residents and 'guests'). This makes the dataset interesting as a test bed for long-term analysis, where people's appearance varies significantly, including changes in clothing. In our experiments, we use a train-test ratio of 12:1 implementing a leave-one-session-out approach for cross-validation in order to probe how well performance generalises to different acquisition days.

5 Experiments and Results

We perform an extensive system analysis by applying the proposed pipeline mainly to the LIMA dataset. We define as the LIMA baseline the best so-far

[4] Evaluation protocol located at: https://github.com/layumi/DukeMTMC-reID_evaluation.

reported micro precision metric on the dataset achieved by a hybrid M2&ME approach given in [14] - that is via tracking by recognition-enhanced constrained clustering with multiple enrolment. This approach assigns identities to frames where the accuracy of picking the correct identity as the top-ranking estimate is reported. Against this, we evaluate performance metrics for our approach judging either the performance over all ground truth labels j, including the 'unknown content' class (**ALL**), that is $j \in \{0, ..., N\}$, or only for known identity ground-truth (**p-ID**), that is $j \in \{1, ..., N\}$. We use two metrics: **prec@1** as the rank-one precision, *i.e.* the accuracy of selecting the correct identity for test frames according to the highest class score produced by the final Re-ID CondenseNet R, and **mAP** as mean Average Precision over all considered classes. Table 1 provides an overview of the results.

Deep CondenseNet without Augmentation (R only). The baseline (Table 1, row 1) is first compared to results obtained when training CondenseNet (R) on original data only (Table 1, row 2). This deep compressed network outperforms the baseline **ALL prec@1** by 2.88%, in particular generalising better for cases of significant appearance change such as wearing different clothes over the session (*e.g.* without jacket and wearing a jacket afterwards. The **p-ID mAP** results (*i.e.* discarding the 'unknown' class) at 96.28% show that removing distracting content, *i.e.* manual semantic control during the test procedure, can produce scenarios of enhanced performance over filtered test subsets. We will now investigate how semantic control can be encoded via externally trained networks applied during training.

Direct Semantic Control (FR). Simply introducing a semantic controller F to face-filter the input of R is, however, counter-productive and reduces performance significantly across all metrics (Table 1, row 5). Restricting R to train on only 39% of the input this way withholds critical identity information.

Augmentation via DCGANs (G). Instead of restricting training input to the Re-ID network R, we therefore analyse how Re-ID performance is affected when semantic control is applied to generic DCGAN-synthesis via G of a cross-identity person class as suggested in [33]. Figure 2 shows examples of generated images and how the semantic controller affects the synthesis appearance. Augmentation of training data with 24k synthesised samples without semantic control (Table 1, row 3) improves performance slightly across all metrics, confirming benefits discussed in more detail in [33]. Table 2 confirms that applying such DCGAN synthesis together with CondenseNet compression to the DukeMTMC-reID dataset produce results comparable to [31]. Note that whilst the large deep ResNet50+LSRO [33] approach outperforms our compressed network significantly (Table 2, row 6), this comes at a cost of increasing the parameter cardinality by about an order of magnitude[5]. Moreover, non-controlled synthesis is generally limited. Indeed, on LIMA no further improvements can be made

[5] Require approximately 8× fewer parameters and operations to achieve comparable accuracy *w.r.t.* other dense nets (*i.e.* 600 million less operations to perform inference on a single image) [10].

Table 1. Results for LIMA - top rank precision (**prec@1**) and mean Average Precision (**mAP**) for baseline (row 1), non-semantically controlled deep CondenseNet approaches (rows 2–4), and various forms of semantic control (rows 5–7). Note improvements across all metrics when utilising: compressed deep learning (row 2), augmentation (row 3), and semantically selective filtering (rows 6–7).

	ALL prec@1	p-ID prec@1	ALL mAP	p-ID mAP
No semantic control				
1: Baseline (M2&ME) [14]	89.1	-	-	-
2: No augmentation (R)	91.98	93.49	90.90	96.28
3: Augmentation 24k$G \rightarrow R$	*92.43*	*94.27*	*91*	*96.95*
4: Augmentation 48k$G \rightarrow R$	91.74	93.48	90.61	96.54
Semantic control via F				
5: No augmentation (FR)	82.02	92.14	72.90	95.48
6: Augment. F322k$G \rightarrow R$	**92.58**	**94.57**	**91.14**	97.02
7: (24kG_0+F24kG_j) $\rightarrow R$	92.44	94.37	90.96	**97.04**

Table 2. Results for DukeMTMC-reID - top rank precision (**prec@1**) for classification and Single-Query (S-Q) performance with **No Semantic Control***. Our results outperform [31] when using augmentation (row 4), or using Market1501 as synthesis input (row 5). However, the performance of the 8× larger ResNet50+LSRO [33] cannot be achieved in our setting of compression for lightweight deployment.

Method/NSC*	prec@1	prec@5	mAP	CMC@1 S-Q	mAP S-Q
1: Baseline BoW+KISSME [31]	-	-	-	25.13	12.17
2: Baseline LOMO+XQDA [31]	-	-	-	30.75	17.04
3: No augmentation (R)	87.70	95.54	87.79	*29.04*	*15.99*
4: Augmentation 24k$G \rightarrow R$	88.08	95.73	88.26	**36.45**	**21.11**
5: Transfer 24k (Market)$G \rightarrow R$	**88.84**	**95.82**	**88.64**	*35.95*	*20.6*
6: ResNet50+LSRO [33] ($\gg$ 8x)	-	-	-	67.68	47.13

by scaling up synthesis beyond 24k, whereby performance drops slightly across all metrics and overfitting to the synthetised data can be observed (Table 1, row 4). We now introduce semantic control to the input of augmentation and observe that the scaling-up limit can be lifted. Diminishing returns take over at levels above 300k though (*i.e.* 54% of synthesis *w.r.t.* original training data). We report results when synthesising 322k of imagery via G, improving results for all metrics (Table 1, row 6). We note that these improvements are achieved by synthesising distractors rather than individual-specific augmentations.

Individual-Specific Augmentation ($G_0 + G_j$). To explore class-specific augmentation we train an entire set of DCGANs, *i.e.* produce generators G_j and G_0, respectively as specific identity and non-identity synthesis networks, and apply semantic control F to the identity classes $j \in \{1, ..., N\}$. We observe that when balancing the synthesis of training imagery across all classes equally only slightly improves on **p-ID mAP**, whilst other measures cannot be advanced (Table 1,

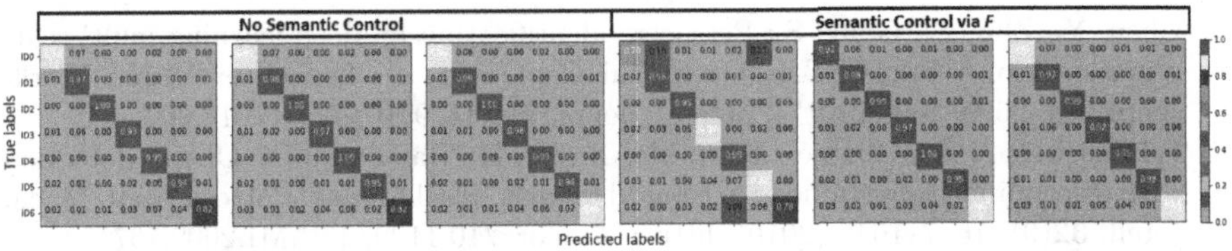

Fig. 3. Some results as confusion matrices. Columns from left to right correspond to the experimental settings grouped by the presence of semantic selection, according to Table 1 rows 2–4 and 5–7, respectively.

row 7). Figure 3 provides further result visualisations. The limited improvements of this approach compared to non-identity-specific training (despite synthesis of overall more training data) suggest that, for the LIMA setup at least, person individuality can indeed be encoded by augmentation-supported modelling of a large, generic 'person' class against a more limited, non-augmented representation of individuals. Furthermore, experiments on the most challenging LIMA sessions demonstrate that the pre-trained generator G can generalize at re-training individual-specific generators G_0 and G_j so as to reduce training cost of DCGAN indvidual-specific augmentation.

6 Conclusion

We introduced a deep person Re-ID approach that brought together semantically selective data augmentation with clustering-based network compression to produce light and fast inference networks. In particular, we showed that augmentation via sampling from a DCGAN, whose discriminator is constrained by a semantic face detector, can outperform the state-of-the-art on the LIMA dataset for long-term monitoring in indoor living environments. To explore the applicability of our framework without face detection in outdoor scenarios, we also considered well-known datasets for person Re-ID aimed at people matching, achieving competitive performance on the DukeMTMC-reID dataset.

Acknowledgements. This work was performed under the SPHERE IRC funded by the UK Engineering and Physical Sciences Research Council (EPSRC), Grant EP/K031910/1.

References

1. Barbosa, I.B., Cristani, M., Caputo, B., Rognhaugen, A., Theoharis, T.: Looking beyond appearances: synthetic training data for deep CNNs in re-identification. Comput. Vis. Image Underst. **167**, 50–62 (2018). https://doi.org/10.1016/j.cviu.2017.12.002
2. Bondi, E., Pala, P., Seidenari, L., Berretti, S., Del Bimbo, A.: Long term person re-identification from depth cameras using facial and skeleton data. In: Wannous, H., Pala, P., Daoudi, M., Flórez-Revuelta, F. (eds.) UHA3DS 2016. LNCS, vol. 10188, pp. 29–41. Springer, Cham (2018). https://doi.org/10.1007/978-3-319-91863-1_3

3. Chen, Y., Zhu, X., Gong, S.: Person re-identification by deep learning multi-scale representations. In: IEEE International Conference on Computer Vision Workshops, pp. 2590–2600 (2017). https://doi.org/10.1109/ICCVW.2017.304
4. Felzenszwalb, P.F., Girshick, R.B., McAllester, D., Ramanan, D.: Object detection with discriminatively trained part-based models. IEEE Trans. Pattern Anal. Mach. Intell. **32**(9), 1627–1645 (2010). https://doi.org/10.1109/TPAMI.2009.167
5. Filković, I., Kalafatić, Z., Hrkać, T.: Deep metric learning for person re-identification and de-identification. In: 2016 39th International Convention on Information and Communication Technology, Electronics and Microelectronics, pp. 1360–1364 (2016). https://doi.org/10.1109/MIPRO.2016.7522351
6. Goodfellow, I., et al.: Generative Adversarial Nets. In: Advances in Neural Information Processing Systems, vol. 27, pp. 2672–2680. Curran Associates, Inc. (2014)
7. Haghighat, M., Abdel-Mottaleb, M.: Low resolution face recognition in surveillance systems using discriminant correlation analysis. In: 2017 12th IEEE International Conference on Automatic Face Gesture Recognition, pp. 912–917 (2017). https://doi.org/10.1109/FG.2017.130
8. Hasan, M., Babaguchi, N.: Long-term people reidentification using anthropometric signature. In: 2016 IEEE 8th International Conference on Biometrics Theory, Applications and Systems, pp. 1–6 (2016). https://doi.org/10.1109/BTAS.2016.7791184
9. Howard, A.G., et al.: MobileNets: efficient convolutional neural networks for mobile vision applications. CoRR abs/1704.04861 (2017)
10. Huang, G., Liu, S., van der Maaten, L., Weinberger, K.Q.: CondenseNet: an efficient densenet using learned group convolutions. preprint arXiv:1711.09224 (2017)
11. Huang, G., Liu, Z., van der Maaten, L., Weinberger, K.Q.: Densely connected convolutional networks. In: Proceedings of the IEEE Conference on Computer Vision and Pattern Recognition (2017)
12. Khan, F.M., Brèmond, F.: Multi-shot person re-identification using part appearance mixture. In: 2017 IEEE Winter Conference on Applications of Computer Vision, pp. 605–614 (2017). https://doi.org/10.1109/WACV.2017.73
13. Kingma, D.P., Ba, J.: Adam: a method for stochastic optimization. CoRR abs/1412.6980 (2014)
14. Layne, R., et al.: A dataset for persistent multi-target multi-camera tracking in RGB-D. In: IEEE Conference on Computer Vision and Pattern Recognition Workshops, pp. 1462–1470 (2017). https://doi.org/10.1109/CVPRW.2017.189
15. Liu, X., Ma, X., Wang, J., Wang, H.: M3l: multi-modality mining for metric learning in person re-identification. Pattern Recognit. **76**, 650–661 (2018). https://doi.org/10.1016/j.patcog.2017.09.041
16. Ma, L., Jia, X., Sun, Q., Schiele, B., Tuytelaars, T., Van Gool, L.: Pose guided person image generation. In: Guyon, I., et al. (eds.) Advances in Neural Information Processing Systems, vol. 30, pp. 406–416. Curran Associates, Inc., New York (2017)
17. McConville, R., Byrne, D., Craddock, I., Piechocki, R., Pope, J., Santos-Rodriguez, R.: Understanding the quality of calibrations for indoor localisation. In: IEEE 4th World Forum on Internet of Things (2018). https://doi.org/10.1109/WF-IoT.2018.8355159
18. Perez, L., Wang, J.: The effectiveness of data augmentation in image classification using deep learning. CoRR abs/1712.04621 (2017)
19. Pham, T.T.T., Le, T.L., Dao, T.K.: Improvement of person tracking accuracy in camera network by fusing WiFi and visual information. Informatica **41**, 133–148 (2017)

20. Ponce-López, V., Escalante, H.J., Escalera, S., Baró, X.: Gesture and action recognition by evolved dynamic subgestures. In: Proceedings of the British Machine Vision Conference, pp. 129.1–129.13 (2015). https://dx.doi.org/10.5244/C.29.129
21. Radford, A., Metz, L., Chintala, S.: Unsupervised representation learning with deep convolutional generative adversarial networks. In: Proceedings of the International Conference on Learning Representations (2015)
22. Ristani, E., Solera, F., Zou, R., Cucchiara, R., Tomasi, C.: Performance measures and a data set for multi-target, multi-camera tracking. In: Hua, G., Jégou, H. (eds.) ECCV 2016. LNCS, vol. 9914, pp. 17–35. Springer, Cham (2016). https://doi.org/10.1007/978-3-319-48881-3_2
23. Sadri, F.: Ambient intelligence: a survey. ACM Comput. Surv. **43**(4), 36:1–36:66 (2011). https://doi.org/10.1145/1978802.1978815
24. Shrivastava, A., Pfister, T., Tuzel, O., Susskind, J., Wang, W., Webb, R.: Learning from simulated and unsupervised images through adversarial training. In: Proceedings of the Computer Vision and Pattern Recognition Conference, pp. 2107–2116 (2017)
25. Simon, T., Joo, H., Matthews, I., Sheikh, Y.: Hand keypoint detection in single images using multiview bootstrapping. In: Proceedings of the Computer Vision and Pattern Recognition Conference (2017)
26. Takemura, N., Makihara, Y., Muramatsu, D., Echigo, T., Yagi, Y.: Multi-view large population gait dataset and its performance evaluation for cross-view gait recognition. IPSJ Trans. Comput. Vis. Appl. **10**(1), 4 (2018). https://doi.org/10.1186/s41074-018-0039-6
27. Twomey, N., et al.: The SPHERE challenge: activity recognition with multimodal sensor data. preprint arXiv:1603.00797 (2016)
28. Wu, L., Wang, Y., Li, X., Gao, J.: What-and-where to match: deep spatially multiplicative integration networks for person re-identification. Pattern Recognit. **76**, 727–738 (2018). https://doi.org/10.1016/j.patcog.2017.10.004
29. Yu, S.I., Meng, D., Zuo, W., Hauptmann, A.: The solution path algorithm for identity-aware multi-object tracking. In: The IEEE Conference on Computer Vision and Pattern Recognition (2016). https://doi.org/10.1109/CVPR.2016.420
30. Zhang, X., Zhou, X., Lin, M., Sun, J.: ShuffleNet: an extremely efficient convolutional neural network for mobile devices. CoRR abs/1707.01083 (2017). https://arXiv.org/abs/1707.01083
31. Zheng, L., Shen, L., Tian, L., Wang, S., Wang, J., Tian, Q.: Scalable person re-identification: A benchmark. In: 2015 IEEE International Conference on Computer Vision, pp. 1116–1124 (2015). https://doi.org/10.1109/ICCV.2015.133
32. Zheng, L., Yang, Y., Hauptmann, A.G.: Person re-identification: past, present and future. arXiv preprint arXiv:1610.02984 (2016)
33. Zheng, Z., Zheng, L., Yang, Y.: Unlabeled samples generated by GAN improve the person re-identification baseline in vitro. In: Proceedings of the IEEE International Conference on Computer Vision, pp. 3754–3762 (2017). https://doi.org/10.1109/ICCV.2017.405
34. Zhou, S., et al.: Deep self-paced learning for person re-identification. Pattern Recognit. **76**, 739–751 (2018). https://doi.org/10.1016/j.patcog.2017.10.005

Recognizing People in Blind Spots Based on Surrounding Behavior

Kensho Hara[1(✉)], Hirokatsu Kataoka[1], Masaki Inaba[2], Kenichi Narioka[2], and Yutaka Satoh[1]

[1] National Institute of Advanced Industrial Science and Technology (AIST), Tsukuba, Ibaraki, Japan
{kensho.hara,hirokatsu.kataoka}@aist.go.jp

[2] DENSO CORPORATION, Chuo-ku, Tokyo, Japan
{MASAKI_INABA,KENICHI_NARIOKA}@denso.co.jp

Abstract. Recent advances in computer vision have achieved remarkable performance improvements. These technologies mainly focus on recognition of visible targets. However, there are many invisible targets in blind spots in real situations. Humans may be able to recognize such invisible targets based on contexts (e.g. visible human behavior and environments) around the targets, and used such recognition to predict situations in blind spots on a daily basis. As the first step towards recognizing targets in blind spots captured in videos, we propose a convolutional neural network that recognizes whether or not there is a person in a blind spot. Based on the experiments that used the volleyball dataset, which includes various interactions of players, with artificial occlusions, our proposed method achieved 90.3% accuracy in the recognition.

Keywords: Action recognition · Convolutional Neural Networks

1 Introduction

Performance of many computer vision tasks, such as object recognition in images and action recognition in videos, has been remarkably improved [3,6,12]. Most approaches try to recognize targets captured in images and videos. In other words, they mainly focus on recognition of targets visible in images and videos.

There are many invisible targets in blind spots in real situations. Such blind spots are caused by occlusions and angle of view of a camera. It is difficult to observe the blind spots without special equipments. Humans, however, may be able to recognize such invisible targets based on contexts (e.g. visible human behavior and environments) around the targets. For example, as shown in Fig. 1 (left), we can know there is at least one person on the left even though the left side is a blind spot because the man on the right looks and talks to others on the left. In addition, we can easily know such things if the scenes are given as videos, which capture dynamic information of human behavior. The recognition in blind spots is useful for various situations, such as avoiding traffic accidents to

L. Leal-Taixé and S. Roth (Eds.): ECCV 2018 Workshops, LNCS 11130, pp. 562–570, 2019.
https://doi.org/10.1007/978-3-030-11012-3_42

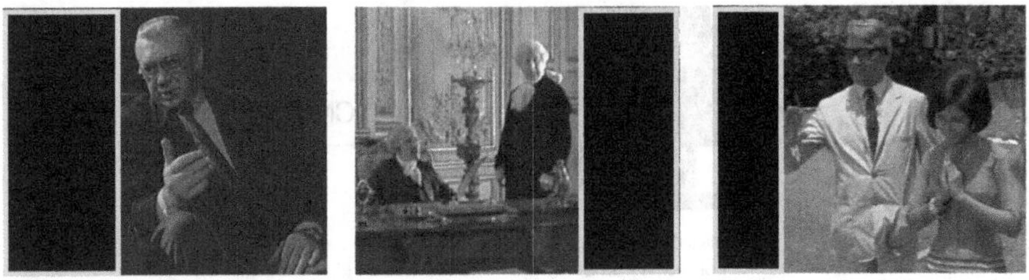

Fig. 1. This is scenes including interactions of some people (included in the AVA dataset [5]). Let us consider the black rectangles as blind spots. Based on the behavior, such as gestures and gaze directions, of people visible in the frames, we can know there is at least one person in the blind spot.

pedestrians running out from behind buildings, understanding crowded scenes with heavy occlusions, and achieving low cost surveillance by reducing the number of cameras. Because such recognition can be extended to various objects and environments besides recognizing people, it is important to develop this topic.

As the first step towards recognizing targets in blind spots, we propose a method that recognize whether or not there is a person in a blind spot captured in videos. We use a spatiotemporal 3D convolutional neural network (3D CNN) [6] to represent features of behavior of visible environments. Our proposed method uses a video with a blind spot as an input, and outputs a label, which indicate whether or not there is a person in the blind spot. Though our network cannot directly describes features in blind spots, it represents visible human behavior and environments around the blind spots, which include useful information for the recognition. We experimentally evaluated our proposed method using the volleyball dataset [9], which includes various interactions of players, with artificial blind spots.

2 Related Work

The use of large-scale datasets, such as ImageNet [4] and Kinetics [11], and deep CNNs [3,6,7,12,15] have contributed substantially to the creation of successful vision-based algorithms for images and videos. These technologies mainly focus on recognition of targets visible in images and videos whereas we focus on recognition of invisible targets in blind spots.

Some works tried to estimate information in blind spots. Bouman et al. and Baradad et al. proposed estimation methods that use observations of light [1,2]. Mak et al. tried to estimate location of sound source without visual information [13]. Zhao et al. and used radio frequency signals to estimate human pose over a wall [16]. In contrast, our recognition method is based on behavior of visible people described by a 3D CNN.

He et al. [8] experimentally showed recent action recognition method can recognize human actions based on background information without observations of

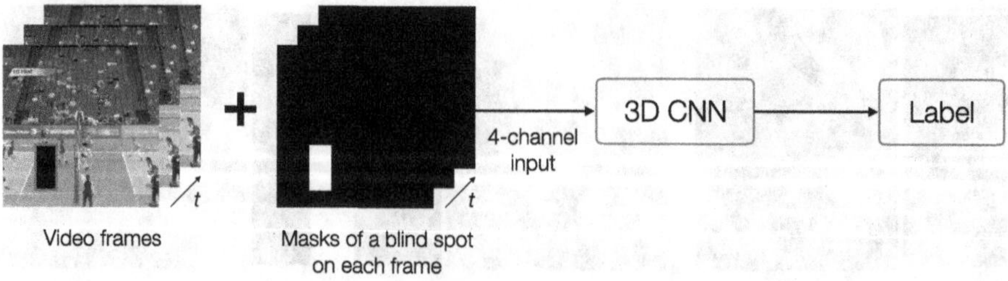

Fig. 2. Overview of our proposed method. The method uses the input video with bounding boxes of the blind spot in each frame, and outputs whether or not there is a person on the blind spot.

humans. Motivated by this work, we propose a action recognition based method to recognize a person in a blind spot.

3 Method

In this study, we propose a spatiotemporal 3D CNN based method to recognize a person in a blind spot in a video. We assume that an input video captures an activity scene with people, objects, and a blind spot. Our proposed method uses the input video with bounding boxes of the blind spot in each frame, and outputs whether or not there is a person on the blind spot. Figure 2 shows an overview of our proposed method.

In this study, we use the volleyball dataset [9] for the evaluation experiment. Because the situation of the dataset is restricted, the people captured in videos interact with each other, and it includes bounding boxes of each person in videos, it is good for the experiment in this study. A dataset for this experiment should include ground truth labels in blind spots though the volleyball dataset does not include such labels. Therefore, we add two types of artificial occlusions, similar to [8], as blind spots for positive and negative samples. We fill bounding boxes of a randomly selected person in each frame of a video to generate positive samples, which mean there is a person in the blind spot, whereas we fill randomly selected regions that do not cover any people to generate negative samples, which mean there is not a person in the blind spot. We evaluate our method by recognizing such samples in the experiment as a first step towards recognition of people in blind spots. Though the configuration of this experiment is not the same as real situations because a blind spot that track a person does not exist, we expect that this experiment shows the effectiveness of our method, which tries to represent human behavior around the targets in order to recognize a person in a blind spot.

In this section, we first explain the network architecture of 3D CNN, and then describe the detail implementation of training and testing.

3.1 Network Architecture

We use 3D ResNet [6], which is a spatiotemporal extension of original 2D ResNet [7]. ResNet, which is one of the most successful architectures in image classification, provides shortcut connections that allow a signal to bypass one layer and move to the next layer in the sequence. Since these connections pass through the networks' gradient flows from the later layers to the early layers, they can facilitate the training of very deep networks. Because 3D ResNet achieved good performance in action recognition, as shown in [6], we adopt the ResNet architecture.

We use the 18-layer ResNet with basic blocks and deeper 50-layer ResNet with bottleneck blocks as shown in Table 1. A basic block consists of two convolutional layers, and each convolutional layer is followed by batch normalization [10] and a ReLU [14]. The sizes of convolutional kernels in the blocks are $3 \times 3 \times 3$. We use identity connections and zero padding for the shortcuts of the ResNet block (type A in [7]) to avoid increasing the number of parameters. Strides of first convolutional layers of conv3, conv4, and conv5 are set to two to perform down-sampling of the inputs. A max pooling layer in conv2 also down-samples the inputs with a stride of two. Different from other convolutional layers, the size of conv1 is $7 \times 7 \times 7$. The temporal stride of conv1 is 1 whereas the spatial one is 2, similar to C3D [15].

A bottleneck block consists of three convolutional layers. The kernel sizes of the first and third convolutional layers are $1 \times 1 \times 1$, whereas those of the second are $3 \times 3 \times 3$. The shortcut pass of this block is the same as that of the basic block. We use identity connections except for those that are used for increasing dimensions (type B in [7]). Other settings are the same as the basic blocks.

The number of dimensions of a video input is four, which includes one channel, one temporal, and two spatial dimensions. The channel dimension consists of three RGB and one binary mask channels. The mask channel is used to specify where the blind spot of the input is (1 for a pixel on the spot). The number of dimensions of the output layer is two, which indicates whether or not there is a person in the blind spot.

3.2 Implementation

Training We use stochastic gradient descent with momentum to train the networks and randomly generate training samples from videos in training data in order to perform data augmentation. First, we select a temporal position in a video by uniform sampling in order to generate a training sample. A 16-frame clip is then generated around the selected temporal position. Each clip is cropped around a center position with the maximum scale (i.e. the sample width and height are the same as the short side length of the frame). We spatially resize the sample at 112×112 pixels. We then randomly decide the sample as positive or negative ones. Note that we can arbitrary set class labels for each video because we add artificial occlusions and class labels are decided based on the positions of artificial occlusions in this experiment. If the label is positive, we

Table 1. Network architectures. The dimensions of output sizes are $T \times Y \times X$,and the sizes are calculated based on a $16 \times 112 \times 112$-input. We represent $x \times x \times x, F$ as the kernel size, and the number of feature maps of the convolutional filter are $x \times x \times x$ and F, respectively. Each convolutional layer is followed by batch normalization and a ReLU. Spatio-temporal down-sampling is performed by conv3_1, conv4_1, and conv5_1 with a stride of two. A max-pooling layer (stride 2) is also located before conv2_x for down-sampling. In addition, conv1 spatially down-samples inputs with a spatial stride of two.

Layer Name	Output Size	Architecture	
		18-layer	50-layer
conv1	$16 \times 64 \times 64$	$7 \times 7 \times 7, 64$, stride 1 (T), 2 (XY)	
		$3 \times 3 \times 3$ max pool, stride 2	
conv2	$8 \times 32 \times 32$	$\begin{bmatrix} 3 \times 3 \times 3, 64 \\ 3 \times 3 \times 3, 64 \end{bmatrix} \times 2$	$\begin{bmatrix} 1 \times 1 \times 1, 64 \\ 3 \times 3 \times 3, 64 \\ 1 \times 1 \times 1, 256 \end{bmatrix} \times 3$
conv3	$4 \times 16 \times 16$	$\begin{bmatrix} 3 \times 3 \times 3, 128 \\ 3 \times 3 \times 3, 128 \end{bmatrix} \times 2$	$\begin{bmatrix} 1 \times 1 \times 1, 128 \\ 3 \times 3 \times 3, 128 \\ 1 \times 1 \times 1, 512 \end{bmatrix} \times 4$
conv4	$2 \times 8 \times 8$	$\begin{bmatrix} 3 \times 3 \times 3, 256 \\ 3 \times 3 \times 3, 256 \end{bmatrix} \times 2$	$\begin{bmatrix} 1 \times 1 \times 1, 256 \\ 3 \times 3 \times 3, 256 \\ 1 \times 1 \times 1, 1024 \end{bmatrix} \times 6$
conv5	$1 \times 4 \times 4$	$\begin{bmatrix} 3 \times 3 \times 3, 512 \\ 3 \times 3 \times 3, 512 \end{bmatrix} \times 2$	$\begin{bmatrix} 1 \times 1 \times 1, 512 \\ 3 \times 3 \times 3, 512 \\ 1 \times 1 \times 1, 2048 \end{bmatrix} \times 3$
		average pool, 2-d fc, softmax	

randomly select a person in the sample and fill the bounding boxes of the person in each frame as a blind spot. If the label is negative, we fill a region that is randomly selected in each frame. Note that relative movements of the blind spot of negative samples in each frame are based on a person that is randomly selected to reduce the information based on the movements of blind spots. We generate a binary mask channel based on the blind spots on each frame. The size of each sample is 4 channels $\times$ 16 frames $\times$ 112 pixels $\times$ 112 pixels, and each sample is horizontally flipped with 50% probability. All generated samples retain the same class labels as their original videos.

In our training, we use cross-entropy losses and back-propagate their gradients. The training parameters include a batch size of 64, weight decay of 0.01, and 0.9 for momentum. When training the networks from scratch, we start from learning rate 0.01, and divide it by 10 at 500 epochs. Training is done for 600 epochs. When performing fine-tuning, we start from a learning rate of 0.001 and divide it by 10 at 200 epochs. Training of fine-tuning is done for 300 epochs.

Testing We recognize people in blind spots in videos using the trained model. We adopt the sliding window manner to generate input clips, (i.e. videos are split into non-overlapped 16 frame clips.) Each clip is cropped around a center position and combined with a binary mask channel similar to the training step. We estimate class probabilities of each clip using the trained model, and average them to recognize people in blind spots in videos.

4 Experiments

4.1 Dataset

In the experiments, we used the volleyball dataset [9]. The volleyball dataset contains 55 videos, which captures volleyball game scenes. 4,830 frames in the videos are annotated with players' bounding boxes, individual action labels, and group activity labels. The videos are separated based on the annotations frames into 4,830 sequences. Each sequence contains 41 frames, which consist of the annotated frame and 20 frames before and after it. We used one sequence as one video input. We followed the split of training, validation, and testing sets provided in [9]. We randomly selected positive and negative sequences with 50% probability in the testing set, and selected one of the bounding boxes in each sequence of the positives as the blind spot. We also randomly generated a blind spot for the negative sequences.

4.2 Results

Table 2 shows the recognition accuracies of ResNet-18 and -50 with or without pretraining on the Kinetics dataset [11]. In addition, we show the results of 2D AlexNet [12] and 2D ResNet-18 as baselines. The 2D models used each frame as an input, output recognition scores, and recognize a video based on the averaged the scores over all frames in the video.

Table 2. Recognition accuracies of each method.

Model	2D AlexNet	2D ResNet-18	3D ResNet-18		3D ResNet-50	
Pretraining				✓		✓
Accuracy	80.7	88.3	89.4	89.2	90.3	89.2

The accuracies of 3D ResNets, which are around 90%, indicate that our method can correctly recognize a person on a blind spot in many video sequences in this experimental configuration. We can see that ResNet-50 trained from scratch achieved the highest accuracy among the methods. This result indicate that using a deeper model improves recognition accuracy. On the other hand, the pretraining on Kinetics did not improve the recognition accuracies. This result indicates that the recognition in this experiment requires different feature representations to action recognition. Compared with the baselines, our 3D ResNets achieved higher accuracies. This result indicates that spatiotemporal feature representations are effective to this task.

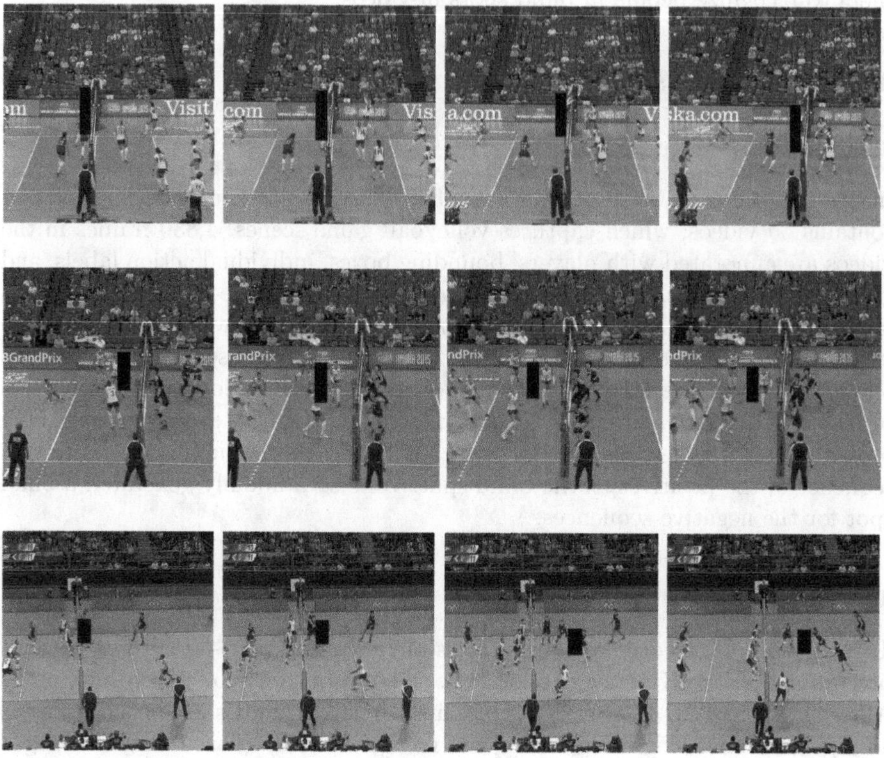

Fig. 3. Recognition examples. (top) True positive. (middle) False positive. (bottom) False negative.

Figure 3 shows recognition examples of 3D ResNet-50 trained from scratch. The example of top row, which is a true positive, is a attack scene from right. Because the player on the right attacked but the visible players on the left did not receive a ball, we can estimate there is a player on the blind spot. The result indicate that the model could understand such activities in the scene. The middle row in Fig. 3 shows the example, which is a crowded scene near the net. The model wrongly recognized the video as a positive. We can see that it is difficult to recognize there is other people in a crowded scene. The bottom row shows a false negative example. Though this example is a positive one, the blind spot did not locate on a player in many frames, which indicate a negative sample. Because the annotations of volleyball dataset include some noise, annotations of some samples in this experiment also include noises.

5 Conclusion

In this study, we proposed a method that recognize whether or not there is a person in a blind spot in videos, as the first step towards recognizing targets in blind spots. The proposed method adopts a spatiotemporal 3D CNN to learn features of videos with blind spots. We confirmed the effectiveness of the proposed method using the volleyball dataset [9] with artificial blind spots.

In our future work, we will further investigate more natural experimental settings to achieve recognition in blind spots in the wild.

References

1. Baradad, M., et al.: Inferring light fields from shadows. In: Proceedings of the IEEE Conference on Computer Vision and Pattern Recognition (CVPR), pp. 6267–6275 (2018)
2. Bouman, K.L., et al.: Turning corners into cameras: Principles and methods. In: Proceedings of the International Conference on Computer Vision (ICCV), pp. 2289–2297 (2017)
3. Carreira, J., Zisserman, A.: Quo vadis, action recognition? A new model and the Kinetics dataset. In: Proceedings of the IEEE Conference on Computer Vision and Pattern Recognition (CVPR), pp. 4724–4733 (2017)
4. Deng, J., Dong, W., Socher, R., Li, L.J., Li, K., Fei-Fei, L.: ImageNet: a large-scale hierarchical image database. In: Proceedings of the IEEE Conference on Computer Vision and Pattern Recognition (CVPR) (2009)
5. Gu, C., et al.: AVA: a video dataset of spatio-temporally localized atomic visual actions. In: Proceedings of the IEEE Conference on Computer Vision and Pattern Recognition (CVPR), pp. 6047–6056, June 2018
6. Hara, K., Kataoka, H., Satoh, Y.: Can spatiotemporal 3D CNNs retrace the history of 2D CNNs and imageNet? In: Proceedings of the IEEE Conference on Computer Vision and Pattern Recognition (CVPR), pp. 6546–6555 (2018)
7. He, K., Zhang, X., Ren, S., Sun, J.: Deep residual learning for image recognition. In: Proceedings of the IEEE Conference on Computer Vision and Pattern Recognition (CVPR), pp. 770–778 (2016)
8. He, Y., Shirakabe, S., Satoh, Y., Kataoka, H.: Human action recognition without human. In: Proceedings of the ECCV Workshop on Brave New Ideas for Motion Representations in Videos, pp. 11–17 (2016)
9. Ibrahim, M.S., Muralidharan, S., Deng, Z., Vahdat, A., Mori, G.: A hierarchical deep temporal model for group activity recognition. In: Proceedings of the IEEE Conference on Computer Vision and Pattern Recognition (CVPR), pp. 1971–1980 (2016)
10. Ioffe, S., Szegedy, C.: Batch normalization: accelerating deep network training by reducing internal covariate shift. In: Proceedings of the International Conference on Machine Learning, pp. 448–456 (2015)
11. Kay, W., et al.: The Kinetics human action video dataset. arXiv preprint arXiv:1705.06950 (2017)
12. Krizhevsky, A., Sutskever, I., Hinton, G.E.: ImageNet classification with deep convolutional neural networks. In: Proceedings of the Advances in Neural Information Processing Systems (NIPS), pp. 1097–1105 (2012)

13. Mak, L.C., Furukawa, T.: Non-line-of-sight localization of a controlled sound source. In: Proceedings of the IEEE/ASME International Conference on Advanced Intelligent Mechatronics, pp. 475–480 (2009)
14. Nair, V., Hinton, G.E.: Rectified linear units improve restricted boltzmann machines. In: Proceedings of the International Conference on Machine Learning, pp. 807–814. Omnipress (2010)
15. Tran, D., Bourdev, L., Fergus, R., Torresani, L., Paluri, M.: Learning spatiotemporal features with 3D convolutional networks. In: Proceedings of the International Conference on Computer Vision (ICCV), pp. 4489–4497 (2015)
16. Zhao, M., et al.: Through-wall human pose estimation using radio signals. In: Proceedings of the IEEE Conference on Computer Vision and Pattern Recognition (CVPR), pp. 7356–7365 (2018)

Visual Relationship Prediction via Label Clustering and Incorporation of Depth Information

Hsuan-Kung Yang, An-Chieh Cheng, Kuan-Wei Ho, Tsu-Jui Fu, and Chun-Yi Lee(✉)

Elsa Lab, Department of Computer Science, National Tsing Hua University, Hsinchu, Taiwan
{hellochick,anjiezheng,firewings89504,rayfu1996ozig, cylee}@gapp.nthu.edu.tw

Abstract. In this paper, we investigate the use of an unsupervised label clustering technique and demonstrate that it enables substantial improvements in visual relationship prediction accuracy on the Person in Context (PIC) dataset. We propose to group object labels with similar patterns of relationship distribution in the dataset into fewer categories. Label clustering not only mitigates both the large classification space and class imbalance issues, but also potentially increases data samples for each clustered category. We further propose to incorporate depth information as an additional feature into the instance segmentation model. The additional depth prediction path supplements the relationship prediction model in a way that bounding boxes or segmentation masks are unable to deliver. We have rigorously evaluated the proposed techniques and performed various ablation analysis to validate the benefits of them.

Keywords: Relationship prediction · Instance segmentation · Semantic segmentation · Unsupervised clustering · Depth information

1 Introduction

This paper describes an effective methodology to perform relationship prediction for the Person in Context (PIC) dataset [7]. In this dataset, the primary objective is to estimate human-centric relations, such as human-to-human and human-to-object relations (e.g., relative positions and activities). Different from the previous datasets (e.g., the Visual Genome dataset [5] and the Open Images dataset [6]) which only concern the relations between different bounding boxes in an image, PIC focuses on the relations between different instance segmentation. This is especially challenging for complex scenes containing various sizes of

A.-C. Cheng and K.-W. Ho—Equal contribution.

L. Leal-Taixé and S. Roth (Eds.): ECCV 2018 Workshops, LNCS 11130, pp. 571–581, 2019.
https://doi.org/10.1007/978-3-030-11012-3_43

overlapped objects, as they require a series of procedures in order to accurately predict the instance segmentation masks as well as evaluate their relations.

There have been a number of research works proposed in recent years aiming at solving the visual relationship prediction tasks [8–10]. The authors in [8] introduced a sequential architecture called MotifNet for capturing the contextual information between the bounding boxes of the objects in an image. The contextual information is then used to construct a graph for representing the relationships of the objects in the image. Relation network [9] embraces a lightweight object relation module for modeling the relations between the objects in an image via the use of their appearance and geometric features. A deep structured model is proposed in [10] for predicting visual relationships at both the feature and label levels. While the above techniques have shown significant promise in predicting relations between the bounding boxes in an image [8–10], several key issues remain unsolved and can be summarized in three aspects. First, the size of the classification space of the possible relations in a dataset is typically large. As relationship prediction is essentially a classification problem [8,9], the large classification space usually leads to insufficient samples for each class and thus difficulties in training a classification model. Second, significant class imbalance exists in most of the datasets [5–7]. The uneven distribution of data samples further exacerbates the above issue of insufficient training data, resulting in a serious drop in prediction accuracy for certain infrequent classes. Third, to the best of our knowledge, the visual relationship prediction task based on instance segmentations has yet been well explored. As instance segmentation has attracted considerable attention in the past few years [4,16], this special relationship prediction task calls for an approach toward tackling the above issues.

In order to address the first two issues mentioned above, we investigate the use of an unsupervised label clustering technique and demonstrate that it enables substantial improvements in both accuracy and training efficiency. We observe that in human-centric datasets such as PIC, a number of human-object pairs share similar patterns of relationship distribution, leaving significant opportunities for label clustering and data augmentation. For example, small objects such as 'bottle', 'cellphone', and 'plate' are extremely likely to have a 'hold' relation with human beings. Motivated by this observation, we investigate the use of k-means clustering technique to group object labels with similar patterns of relationship distribution in the dataset into fewer categories. Label clustering not only mitigates both the large classification space and class imbalance issues, but also potentially increases data samples for each clustered category. This provides the relationship prediction model more opportunities to improve its accuracy.

To further enhance the relationship prediction model based on instance semantic segmentation, we additionally explore the use of depth information in relationship prediction. We propose to incorporate depth information as an additional feature into the instance segmentation model. We observe that depth information is crucial in determining the spatial relations between objects such as 'in-front-of', 'next-to', 'behind', and so on. As a result, we integrate into our backbone instance segmentation model [13] with an auxiliary depth prediction path [12]. The additional depth prediction path supplements the relationship prediction model in a way that bounding boxes [8–10] or segmentation masks are unable to deliver. This is due to the fact that they lack the three-dimensional information required for determining the spatial relations between objects. We have rigorously evaluated the proposed techniques and performed various ablation analysis to demonstrate the benefits of them.

The contributions of this paper include the following:

- A demonstration of visual relationship prediction based on semantic information extracted by an instance semantic segmentation model.
- A method considering both the model architecture and data distribution.
- A simple approach for dealing with the large classification space and class imbalance issues by clustering labels with similar relationship distribution.
- An investigation into a novel concept of applying depth information into the relationship prediction task so as to provide additional spatial information.

The rest of this paper is organized as follows. Section 2 introduces background material. Section 3 walks through the proposed methodology, its implementation details, and the training procedure. Section 4 presents the experimental results and an ablation study of the proposed method. Section 5 concludes this paper.

2 Background

In this section, we introduce the knowledge background regarding relation prediction. We first provide an overview of instance segmentation. Then, we briefly review related works that focus on visual relation prediction. Finally, we introduce depth prediction which is applied in our method.

2.1 Instance Segmentation

Inspired by R-CNN [14] and Faster R-CNN [11], many approaches to instance segmentation are based on segment proposals. DeepMask [15] learns to produce segment candidates and then do classification. Dai *et al.* [16] presented a multi-stage cascade that predicts segment proposals based on bounding-box. In those methods, segmentation followed by recognition, which is slow and less accurate. Recently, FCIS [4] combines segment proposal and object detection for fully convolutional instance segmentation. They predict different position-based output channels which are respectively for object class, bounding-box, and segmentation in fully convolutional way. In contrast to segmentation-first strategy, Mask R-CNN [13] is an instance-first one. Based on Faster R-CNN, Mask R-CNN adds a new branch for object segmentation. They adopt two-stage process, with a Region Proposal Network (RPN) at first, followed by a sub-network which predicts object class and segmentation. In our proposed method, we apply Mask R-CNN, which is also a state-of-the-art network, as our instance segmentation network.

2.2 Visual Relation

Visual relation not only extracts objects' ground region but also describes their interactions. Yao *et al.* [3] first considers relation as hidden variables. Nowadays, there are several explicit relation extraction methods which can be divided into two categories: joint and separate. Joint methods [1,2] usually consider relation triplet as an unique class and generate class and relation information together. However, joint methods are faced with class imbalance problem and easily dominated by major class-relation triplet, which causes low accurate for minor ones. Conversely, separate models [17,18] first detect objects, and extract their relations individually.

Liang *et al.* [19] presented a separate way for extracting visual relation. They applied Faster R-CNN for object detection and then feed object visual features into following CNN blocks to extract relation for each pair of object. Furthermore, Neural-Motifs [8] adopted two-stage bidirectional LSTM to model both global context and pair-wise object relation. The first stage of the network is for object recognition and the second stage is for relation extraction. In our baseline approach, we feed in visual features from Mask R-CNN and apply the second stage of Neural-Motifs as our relation extraction model.

2.3 Depth Prediction

Depth estimation from images has a long history in computer vision. In PIC challenge, we do not have scene geometry or other information for an image, so we only consider monocular depth estimation methods. Make3D [20] over-segments input image into patches and then estimates the 3D location and orientation of local planes to explain each patch. Based on Make3D, Liu *et al.* [21] use a CNN model to learn the global context and help generate more realistic output. Karsch *et al.* [22] further produces more consistent prediction via copying parts of depth images from training set.

Different from supervised-based monocular depth prediction, MonoDepth [23] presents a unsupervised method. The author of MonoDepth train an FCN end-end to predict the pixel-level correspondence between pairs of stereo images and can perform single image depth estimation during testing. In our paper, we use the depth estimation from MonoDepth which is trained on Cityscapes [24] dataset as the auxiliary information for visual relation extraction.

3 Methodology

3.1 Architecture Overview

Figure 1 illustrates the proposed architecture. It consists of three components: an instance segmentation network (blue part), a depth prediction network (red part), and a gradient boosting classifier (purple part). The instance segmentation network is based on the implementation of Mask R-CNN [13], which includes

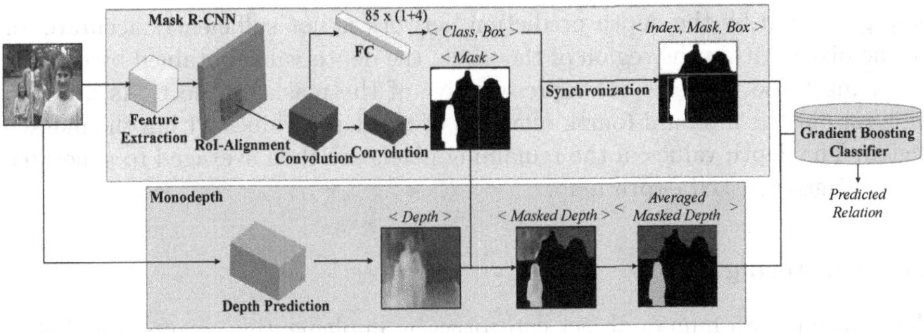

Fig. 1. The proposed framework for relationship prediction. (Color figure online)

feature extraction layers, a region of interest (RoI) alignment layer, two convolutional layers for mask prediction, and a fully-connected (FC) layer for predicting class labels and bounding boxes for the objects contained in the figure. A special synchronization procedure is used to align the indices of the bounding box and mask for each object in the figure. Please note that the class labels here stand for clustered labels, which is explained in detail in Sect. 3.4. The depth prediction network is based on the implementation of Monodepth [12], which evaluates a depth map for the input image. The depth map is then averaged within the mask region predicted by the instance segmentation network to generate an averaged masked depth map for the corresponding object instance. Finally, the bounding boxes, masks, and the averaged masked depth maps are all fed into the gradient boosting classifier to predict relations between the objects in the input image.

3.2 Instance Segmentation Network

We use Mask R-CNN [13] as our instance segmentation network. Mask R-CNN employs a two-stage structure, which includes a region proposal network (RPN) followed by a network consisting of a classification branch and a mask branch. As plotted in Fig. 1, the classification branch is used to predict classification scores and bounding boxes for the objects contained in the image. On the other hand, the mask branch predicts an instance segmentation masks for each object. As the indices of the objects from the two branches are different, a synchronization procedure is necessary so as to match the bounding boxes and masks.

3.3 Depth Prediction Network

We use Monodepth [12] to implement the depth prediction network. The network serves as an auxiliary path to the instance segmentation network and evaluates a depth map for each input image. As illustrated in Fig. 1 and discussed in Sect. 3.1, the output of the depth prediction network is an averaged masked depth map. This averaged masked depth map is generated from a portion of the pixels within the masked region contained in the raw masked depth map. As the raw depth map generated by the depth prediction network is not sufficiently accurate for all the pixels within the region of the mask, the depth value obtained by directly averaging these pixels is not representative of the masked object. As a result, we filter out the first and fourth quartiles of the depth values within the masked region. The depth values of the remaining pixels are then averaged to generated the averaged masked depth map.

3.4 Clustering

We reduce the 85 human-object categories by implementing unsupervised clustering on 85 human-object categories based on their relation's frequency distribution. The unsupervised clustering approach is based on the thought that "multiple objects might share the same frequency distribution of relations". The clustering in advance helps model to reduce the computation space when outputting relation label as classification and augment categories with less data by clustering them with other categories to accumulate data at the same time.

We choose K-means clustering as our clustering algorithm. K-means provides a simple strategy to cluster vectors quickly in a neat way. Our frequency distribution of 85 human-object categories will be normalized before sent into K-means. Moreover, we evaluate our unsupervised clustering with custom constraints. Because K-means require specific number of clusters ($n = k$) as parameter, we propose a few constraints to determine whether the clustered result is best for the training and search for the optimal interval of n. The clustering evaluation is conducted under three constraints:

1. Objects inside the same group are similar enough with each other regarding frequency distribution
2. The number of clusters is small enough to benefit model's computation
3. The total number of data inside each clusters are expected to be maximized.

The number of clusters most suitable under the three constraints lies in the range of 8 clusters to 10 clusters. The clustering curtails the original classification space (85 in original) in a significant range (8 after clustering). The optimal choice of number of clusters might vary depending on the attributes and distribution of the data.

3.5 Relation Prediction

In the PIC Challenge, every relations is human-centered. In other words, every relation candidates is predicted based on the previously generated pairs of each human in the instance and the rest of other objects. Say there is n instances in the image, and k human among the instances. In this case, the number of relation candidates will be $(n-1) * k$.

The subject in each relation prediction must be human, so we only need to check out which pseudo label groups the object is to make decision. If action relations (non-geometric relation) are more frequent or serious class imbalance happens in the group, frequency based prediction will be adopted. The frequency based prediction method is a probability model whose every prediction is totally based on the distribution of each relation's frequency. That is to say, the more frequent a relation is the more probability it is predicted as answer. We also have the other form of frequency based method where only the most frequent relation label is predicted, discarding the rest of other less frequent relations. On the other hand, if geometric relations (especially 'in-front-of', 'next-to' and 'behind') are the major composition of the group's relation distribution, we will take the previously taken features (total 10 values) into training:

1. The bounding box difference (y1, x1, y2, x2) - 4 values
2. The bounding box overlap between subject and object
3. The pseudo label group of the object
4. The depth means and medians of subject and object - 4 values.

Those features will then be sent to gradient boosting classifier to train for the final relation prediction.

4 Experimental Results

We have tried several different approaches on the PIC dataset. In this section, we will shed light on the big picture of our clustered results, and then we will break into the details of the approaches we mainly propose. Finally, we will show and compare every approaches we've experimented in an ablative analysis way.

Before we dive into the details of our relation prediction method, we will introduce the result after clustering human-object categories into several pseudo label groups.

The clustering results is shown in Fig. 2. Before the clustering, although there are 85 categories, only few category actually possesses significant relation numbers for the training, such as 'human'. After the clustering, we still can't say that the total numbers of each cluster are average enough, but the pseudo label group do augment the data similar in frequency distribution together. We hope the clustered result to meet the three constraints we proposed above as possible as they can.

We evaluate the similarity within each cluster by the standard deviation of every cosine distance between every frequency normalized vectors and the mean vectors. Finally, we pick the number of clusters as 8, which is the optimal choice we've tried so far. The clustered result is also shown in Fig. 2.

We attempted several different approaches on relation prediction part. First, we build the neural motifs [8] model on the dataset as the baseline, and the instance segmentation model in this case we choose is Mask R-CNN. However, suffering from the large classification space and the class imbalance issues, neural motifs can't reach its full potential on the dataset. At first, we build a totally

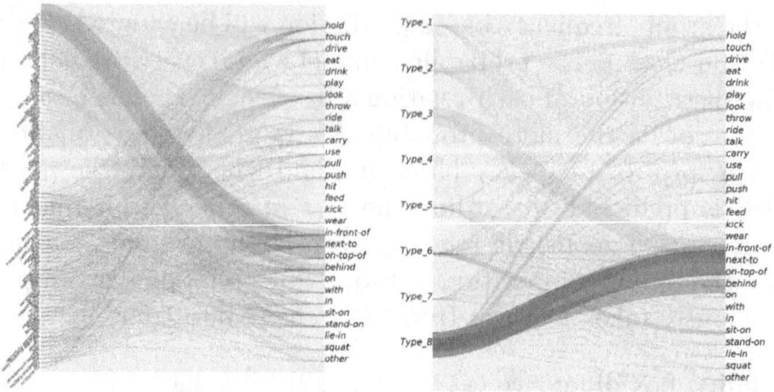

(a) Before Clustering (b) After Clustering

Fig. 2. Our proposed method clusters the 85 human-object categories into several pseudo label groups.

frequency based probability model to establish another baseline. Then we conduct experiments on the relation prediction we mentioned above, including the prediction path decision regarding using frequency based prediction or gradient boosting. We also train the gradient boosting model with or without the mean and median of each instance depth to compare the performance. The results are shown in Table 1).

The results of each approaches are shown in the table. The score metric *IoU@n* means that only predictions with *IoU* metrics above threshold will be computed its relation accuracy. We can see the improvement from freq-85 to freq-8 in the table. The improvement indicates that clustering do improve the performance. Second, from the 3rd column to the 4th column, the performance is improved because of the additional depth information.

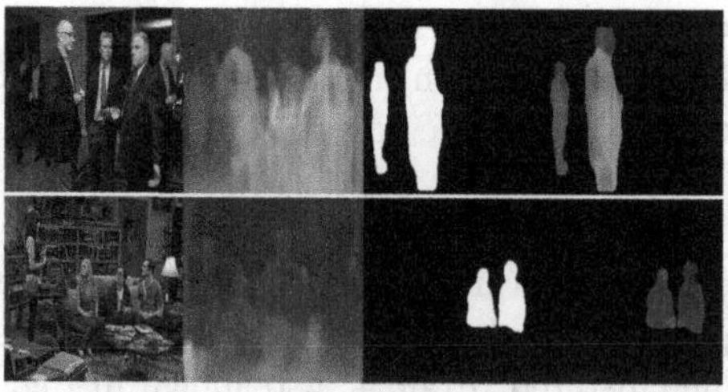

Fig. 3. The illustration of masked depth. Those images from the 1st column to 4th column are raw images, depth images extracted from the raw image, instance segmentation of the images and the combined masked depth.

Table 1. 'Baseline' in the method means Neural-Motifs; 'Freq-85' means frequency-based method on 85 categories; 'Freq-8' means 8 pseudo type; 'Gb' means gradient boosting; 'Gb-Depth' means with the depth information. The two scores under the same column are the validation score and test score. In PIC Challenge, the time of submission is limited, so not every method can be tested.

Method	IoU(0.25)	IoU(0.5)	IoU(0.75)	Average
Baseline	0.156/0.139	0.137/0.125	0.089/0.083	0.127/0.116
Freq-85	0.312/-	0.242/-	0.133/-	**0.229/-**
Freq-8	0.317/0.186	0.246/0.151	0.134/0.082	**0.232/0.140**
Gb	0.323/-	0.256/-	0.140/-	**0.240/-**
Gb-Depth	0.324/0.314	0.258/0.251	0.140/0.131	**0.241/0.232**

5 Conclusions

In this paper, we showed that unsupervised clustering can be effective in mitigating the large classification space and class imbalance issues in visual relationship prediction tasks. We proposed a technique to cluster object labels of similar relationship distribution with human beings in the same dataset into categories. In order to enhance the accuracy of instance segmentation based relationship prediction tasks, we further proposed to incorporate an auxiliary depth prediction path into our instance segmentation model. We demonstrated the effectiveness of the proposed techniques on the PIC dataset, with a detailed ablation study.

References

1. Sadeghi, M.A., Farhadi, A.: Recognition using visual phrases. In: Proceedings of IEEE Conference on Computer Vision and Pattern Recognition, CVPR, pp. 1745–1752, June 2011
2. Ramanathan, V., et al.: Learning semantic relationships for better action retrieval in images. In: Proceedings of IEEE Conference on Computer Vision and Pattern Recognition, CVPR, pp. 1100–1109, June 2015
3. Yao, B., Fei-Fei, L.: Modeling mutual context of object and human pose in human-object interaction activities. In: Proceedings of IEEE Conference on Computer Vision and Pattern Recognition, CVPR, pp. 17–24, June 2010
4. Li, Y., Qi, H., Dai, J., Ji, X., Wei, Y.: Fully convolutional instance-aware semantic segmentation. In: Proceedings of IEEE Conference on Computer Vision and Pattern Recognition, CVPR, pp. 4438–4446, July 2017
5. Krishna, R., et al.: Visual genome: connecting language and vision using crowdsourced dense image annotations. Int. J. Comput. Vis. (IJCV) **123**, 32–73 (2017)
6. Krasin, I., et al.: OpenImages: a public dataset for large-scale multi-label and multi-class image classification (2017). https://storage.googleapis.com/openimages/web/index.html
7. PIC - Person In Context. http://picdataset.com/challenge/index/

8. Zellers, R., Yatskar, M., Thomson, S., Choi, Y.: Neural motifs: scene graph parsing with global context. In: Proceedings of IEEE Conference on Computer Vision and Pattern Recognition, CVPR, pp. 5831–5840, June 2018
9. Hu, H., Gu, J., Zhang, Z., Dai, J., Wei, Y.: Relation networks for object detection. In: Proceedings of IEEE Conference on Computer Vision and Pattern Recognition, CVPR, pp. 3588–3597, June 2018
10. Zhu, Y., Jiang, S.: Deep structured learning for visual relationship detection. In: Proceedings of AAAI Conference on Artificial Intelligence, AAAI, pp. 7623–7630, February 2018
11. Ren, S., He, K., Girshick, R., Sun, J.: Faster R-CNN: towards real-time object detection with region proposal networks. IEEE Trans. Pattern Anal. Mach. Intell. (TPAMI) **39**, 1137–1149 (2017)
12. Godard, C., Aodha, O.M., Brostow, G.J.: Unsupervised monocular depth estimation with left-right consistency. In: Proceedings of IEEE Conference on Computer Vision and Pattern Recognition, CVPR, pp. 270–279, July 2017
13. He, K., Gkioxari, G., Dollár, P., Girshick, R.: Mask R-CNN. In: Proceedings of IEEE International Conference on Computer Vision, ICCV, pp. 2961–2969, October 2017
14. Girshick, R., Donahue, J., Darrell, T., Malik, J.: Rich feature hierarchies for accurate object detection and semantic segmentation. In: Proceedings of IEEE Conference on Computer Vision and Pattern Recognition, CVPR, pp. 580–587, June 2014
15. Pinheiro, P.O., Collobert, R., Dollár, P.: Learning to segment object candidates. In: Proceedings of International Conference on Neural Information Processing Systems, NIPS, pp. 1990–1998, December 2015
16. Dai, J., He, K., Sun, J.: Instance-aware semantic segmentation via multi-task network cascades. In: Proceedings of IEEE Conference on Computer Vision and Pattern Recognition, CVPR, pp. 3150–3158, June 2016
17. Sadeghi, F., Kumar Divvala, S.K., Farhadi, A.: VisKE: visual knowledge extraction and question answering by visual verification of relation phrases. In: Proceedings of the IEEE Conference on Computer Vision and Pattern Recognition, pp. 1456–1464, May 2015
18. Lu, C., Krishna, R., Bernstein, M., Fei-Fei, L.: Visual relationship detection with language priors. In: Proceedings of the IEEE Conference on Computer Vision and Pattern Recognition, pp. 852–869 (2016)
19. Liang, X., Lee, L., Xing, E.: Deep variation-structured reinforcement learning for visual relationship and attribute detection. In: 2017 IEEE Conference on Computer Vision and Pattern Recognition, CVPR, pp. 4408–4417 (2017)
20. Sun, M., Ng, A.Y., Saxena, A.: Make3D: learning 3D scene structure from a single still image. IEEE Trans. Pattern Anal. Mach. Intell. **31**, 824–840 (2008)
21. Liu, F., Shen, C., Lin, G., Reid, I.: Learning depth from single monocular images using deep convolutional neural fields. IEEE Trans. Pattern Anal. Mach. Intell. **38**, 2024–2039 (2016)
22. Karsch, K., Liu, C., Kang, S.B.: Depth extraction from video using non-parametric sampling. In: Proceedings of International Conference on Neural Information Processing Systems, NIPS, pp. 2144–2158, May 2017

23. Godard, C., Mac Aodha, O., Brostow, G.J.: Unsupervised monocular depth estimation with left-right consistency. In: Proceedings of IEEE Conference on Computer Vision and Pattern Recognition, CVPR, pp. 6602–6611, November 2017
24. Cordts, M., et al.: The cityscapes dataset for semantic urban scene understanding. In: Proceedings of the IEEE Conference on Computer Vision and Pattern Recognition, CVPR, pp. 3213–3223, December 2017

Human-Centric Visual Relation Segmentation Using Mask R-CNN and VTransE

Fan Yu, Xin Tan, Tongwei Ren(✉), and Gangshan Wu

State Key Laboratory for Novel Software Technology, Nanjing University, Nanjing, China
{yf,tx}@smail.nju.edu.cn, {rentw,gswu}@nju.edu.cn

Abstract. In this paper, we propose a novel human-centric visual relation segmentation method based on Mask R-CNN model and VTransE model. We first retain the Mask R-CNN model, and segment both human and object instances. Because Mask R-CNN may omit some human instances in instance segmentation, we further detect the omitted faces and extend them to localize the corresponding human instances. Finally, we retrain the last layer of VTransE model, and detect the visual relations between each pair of human instance and human/object instance. The experimental results show that our method obtains 0.4799, 0.4069, and 0.2681 on the criteria of R@100 with the m-IoU of 0.25, 0.50 and 0.75, respectively, which outperforms other methods in Person in Context Challenge.

Keywords: Human-centric · Visual relation segmentation
Mask R-CNN · VTransE

1 Introduction

Visual relation detection attracts much attention from both academic and industry recently because it provides more comprehensive visual content understanding beyond objects. A visual relation involves a relation triple represented by <subject, predicate, object> together with two bounding boxes to localize the subject and the object. Researchers have made efforts to analyse visual relations in both images [4,7,8] and videos [9]. It can effectively support various computer vision applications, such as image/video captioning [10], visual question answering [11] and visual search [12].

Current research aims to extract all the visual relations between each pair of subject and object. Though it may benefit to some applications, such as visual content indexing, it has obvious limitation in emphasizing the main content of images and videos. Many visual relations between an arbitrary pair of subject

Electronic supplementary material The online version of this chapter (https://doi.org/10.1007/978-3-030-11012-3_44) contains supplementary material, which is available to authorized users.

L. Leal-Taixé and S. Roth (Eds.): ECCV 2018 Workshops, LNCS 11130, pp. 582–589, 2019.
https://doi.org/10.1007/978-3-030-11012-3_44

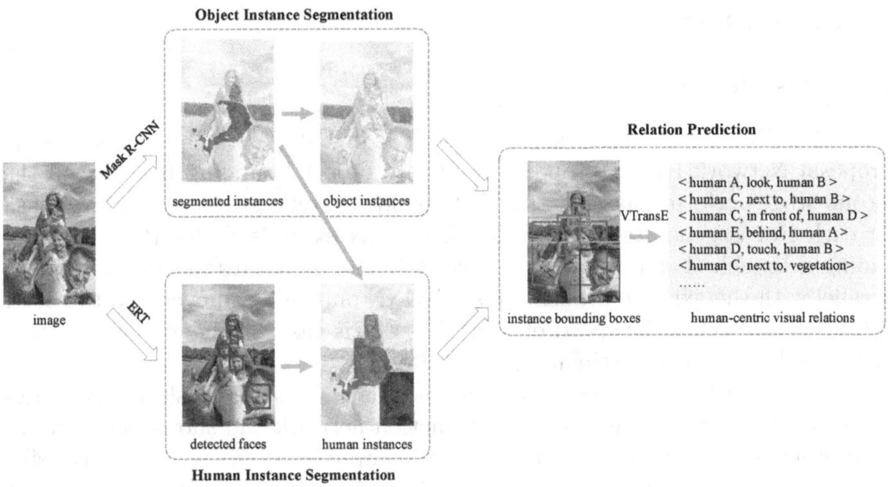

Fig. 1. An overview of the proposed method.

and object are usually meaningless to represent visual content. For example, to two distant objects, they only have spatial relation and the relation is omitted in captioning or visual question answering. Instead, a viewer concerns the human-centric visual relations, *i.e.*, the subjects in the triples of these relations are *human instances*. Moreover, human-centric relations involves more predicates as compared to the visual relations between two object, because a person may perform different actions in the interactions with objects. It means human-centric visual relation detection is more meaningful and challenging than traditional visual object detection. Based the above observation, Person in Context (PIC) Challenge aims to promote the progress of human-centric visual relation detection. Beyond human-centric visual relation detection, PIC Challenge focuses on *human-centric visual relation segmentation*, *i.e.*, the subject and the object of each visual relation should be localized with masks instead of bounding boxes.

In this paper, we propose a novel human-centric visual relation segmentation method using Mask R-CNN model and VTransE model. These two models are the state-of-the-art in instance segmentation and visual relation detection, respectively. Figure 1 shows an overview of our method. We first retain the last layer of Mask R-CNN model, fine-tune its parameters and utilize it for instance segmentation on an input image, which can generate the object instances. Then, we detect face using ensemble of regression trees method (ERT), and fuze the human instance segmented by Mask R-CNN model and the ones localized based on face detection. After this, we retrain the last layer of VTransE model and apply it on the bounding boxes of human instances and object instances to detect human-centric visual relations. Finally, we score the visual relations according to their confidences and relation prior, and return the top 100 visual relations as our result.

2 Preliminary

2.1 Mask R-CNN

Mask R-CNN is a two-stage framework [1]. The first stage, which is called Region Proposal Network(RPN), proposes candidate object bounding boxes. And the second stage performs classification and bounding-box regression, a binary mask for each RoI is generated as well. Mask R-CNN extends Faster R-CNN [2] by adding a branch that takes the positive RoIs and generates masks for them in parallel with the existing branch. Mask R-CNN only adds an overhead to Faster R-CNN and reaches the speed of 5 fps. Also, it is easily to be applied to other tasks like human poses estimation. Mask R-CNN.

Mask R-CNN has three technical essentials. Firstly, Mask R-CNN uses ResNeXt-101 and FPN as a feature extraction network and shows better result than other models. Secondly, Mask R-CNN improves the pooling net by using ROIAlign instead of ROIPooling, and solves the misalignment resulting from direct sampling by pooling net. Experiment shows that the bigger the stride, the more obvious the improvement. Thirdly, the special loss function designed by Mask R-CNN has a better result than softmax.

2.2 Face Detection by ERT

Many methods have been proposed to handle face detection and face alignment. As one of the state-of-the-arts, ERT method uses the ensemble of regression trees to estimate the faces landmark positions and proposed a framework based on gradient boosting [3]. The method uses a cascade of regression functions and each regression function efficiently estimates the shape. During the learning period, ERT save the value of shape into leaf node. After learning the tree, the initial landmark positions will be gradually improved by adding all the updated shape value. Each of the regressors is composed of many trees, and the parameters of each tree are generated after training the model using the coordinate differences of current shape and ground truth and the pixel pairs which are randomly chose.

The boosting algorithm applied in this method has a good performance in classification and regression by reducing the sum of square error of initial shape and ground truth. The method performs face alignment in one millisecond on average. Also, the missing and uncertain labels are handled. The dlib library has implemented this algorithm.

2.3 VTransE

Many research works are afforded to visual relation detection in images, and most of them focus on predicting the huge number of relations by learning from few training data. Lots of methods have been proposed to reduce the complexity from $O(N^2R)$ to $O(N+R)$ where N and R are the numbers of objects and predicates respectively.

A Visual Translational Embedding network (VTransE) [4] has been proposed for visual relation detection. This model predicts relations from an image in an end-to-end fashion and refers to a visual relation as a subject-predicate-object triple. VTransE proposes to model visual relations by mapping the features of objects and predicates in a low-dimensional space, which greatly reduces the volume of data to process. Simultaneously, VTransE incorporates knowledge transfer between objects and predicates. VTransE has been demonstrate its effectiveness on two datasets: Visual Relationship and Visual Genome and performs great.

3 Our Method

3.1 Object Instance Segmentation

We first conduct instance segmentation on an input image using Mask R-CNN model implemented with ResNet-101 network, which was pre-trained on MS COCO dataset. Considering the detected object categories in our task is different to that on MS COCO dataset, we retrain the last layer of Mask R-CNN model with the following loss function:

$$L = L_{class} + L_{box} + L_{mask}, \tag{1}$$

where the classification loss L_{class} and bounding-box loss L_{box} are defined as those in [5]; the mask loss L_{mask} is defined as that in [1].

We use a mini-batch size of 2 images on 1 GPU, starting from a learning rate of 0.001 to train the network. A weight decay of 0.0001 is used as well as a momentum of 0.9. All layers are fine-tuned using stochastic gradient descent for 500K iterations with a mini-batch size of 2, and a learning rate of 0.0001. The total training time is approximately one day on a 1080Ti GPU.

To the instance segmentation result, we retain the segmented instances belong to object but not human as our object instance segmentation result.

3.2 Human Instance Segmentation

Though the instance segmentation result generated by Mask R-CNN model includes human instance, some human instances may be omitted in instance segmentation. It leads to serious decrease on our performance because a visual relation cannot be detected if the corresponding human instance to its subject is omitted. In order to address this problem, we use ERT method to detect the faces on a given image. To each detected face, if its bounding box has not been covered by the bounding box of a segmented human instance largely, we treat it belonging to an omitted human instance. In our experiments, the coverage threshold for omitted face filtering is 0.8.

According to the location of human faces and the common sense about the proportion of human body, we estimate the location of the whole human roughly. On average, the height of persons' bounding boxes in image equals three times the height of their heads. Considering that the mask exporting from Mask R-CNN is more accurate and should have a higher priority, we add the expanding of face detection as a supplementary result. The final result of mask will be the result given by Mask R-CNN and the area covered by the bounding boxes of the estimated additional human bodies.

3.3 Relation Prediction

We use VTransE model to predict the relations between the pairs of human-human and human-object. The inputs of VTransE are the original images and bounding boxes exporting from the result of human and object segmentation.

According to the visual relations appearing in the training dataset, we retain the last layer of VTransE model with the following loss function:

$$L = \sum_{(s,p,o)\in\mathbf{R}} - \; log\ softmax(\mathbf{t}_p^T(\mathbf{W}_o\mathbf{x}_o - \mathbf{W}_s\mathbf{x}_s)), \tag{2}$$

where s, p and o represent subject, predicate and object, respectively; $\mathbf{x}_o, \mathbf{x}_s \in \mathbb{R}^M$ denote the M-dimensional features of subject and object, and $\mathbf{R}$ is the set of valid relations; $\mathbf{t}_p \in \mathbb{R}^r$ $(r \ll M)$ is relation translation vector as the one in [6]. $\mathbf{W}_o, \mathbf{W}_s \in \mathbb{R}^{r\times M}$ are two projection matrices from the feature space to the relation space. We predict the candidate relation of every pair of human-human and human-object and compute the probability score. Instead of keeping the relation of each pair with the higher score, we mix all of the predicted relations and filter out the triples with little probability and keep the triples with the same subject and object but higher score. To make the result more accurate, we remove some the result according to language prior.

4 Experiments

4.1 Dataset and Experimental Settings

We validated the proposed method on the dataset provided by PIC Challenge in ECCV 2018. The dataset has three parts: training dataset, validation dataset, and test dataset. The number of subject/object categories and relation categories on the three parts are all 85 and 31, respectively. Specifically, the training dataset contains 10,000 images, in which there are 106,959 segments and 167,916 relation instances; the validation dataset contains 1,135 images, in which there are 12,061 segments and 18,729 relation instances; the test dataset contains 2,998 images, and its details are not released.

We used Recall@100 (R@100) under different mean Intersection of Union (m-IoU) as the evaluation criteria in our experiments. Here, R@K denotes the fraction of the correct relation instances in the top K predicated relation instances in an image. Three m-IoUs were used in our experiments, namely 0.25, 0.5 and 0.75. We also evaluate the mean score of R@100 under different m-IoUs.

All the experiments were conducted on a computer with i7 3.5 GHz CPU, 32 GB memory, and one 1080Ti GPU. The average time cost in processing each image is 1.9 s.

4.2 Component Analysis

Our proposed method contains three key modules: object instance segmentation, human instance segmentation and visual relation prediction. To validate the effectiveness of each key module, we generate three baselines: (1) Mask+VTransE: using the retrained Mask R-CNN model for object instance segmentation and human instance segmentation, and using the retrained VTransE model for visual relation prediction; (2) Mask*+VTransE: using the fine-tuned Mask R-CNN model to replace the retrained one in Mask+VTransE; (3) Mask*+RelPrior+VTransE: using relation prior to filter the infrequent <predicate, object> pairs on the object instance and human instance segmentation results in Mask*+VTransE, and further using the retrained VTransE model for visual relation prediction. As compared to Mask*+relation prior+VTransE, our method extends the human instance segmentation result by fuzing the results of human instance segmentation by the fine-tuned Mask R-CNN and face detection based person localization.

Because the groundtruths in the test dataset is not available, we carried out the component analysis on the validation dataset. Table 1 shows the performance of our method and these three baselines. We can see that: (1) The fine-tuned Mask R-CNN model only improves the performance by 0.0003 in mean score. It shows that object instance segmentation cannot be easily improved by global parameter adjustment and it requires further studies for performance improvement. (2) Face detection based person localization improves the performance by 0.016 in R@100 under m-IoU 0.25 but only by 0.003 in R@100 under m-IoU 0.75. It means that face detection based person localization can find some persons omitted in human instance segmentation, but it cannot accurately localize the persons by simply extending the face locations. (3) <predicate, object> pair filtering improves the performance by 0.055 in mean score, which is the obvious improvement in our component analysis. It shows that relation prior is effective to visual relation prediction.

Table 1. Evaluation of our method with different components on the validation dataset.

Method	R@100 (m-IoU: 0.25)	R@100 (m-IoU: 0.5)	R@100 (m-IoU: 0.75)	Mean score
Mask+VTransE	0.3828	0.3330	0.2203	0.3120
Mask*+VTransE	0.3831	0.3334	0.2204	0.3123
Mask*+RelPrior+VTransE	0.4534	0.3915	0.2545	0.3673
Our	0.4693	0.3933	0.2571	0.3724

4.3 Comparison with the State-of-the-Arts

Because the implementation of other methods are not released in PIC Challenge, we use the comparison results provided by the leaderboard of PIC Challenge. We select the top 3 methods in PIC Challenge exclude our method in comparison: Cluster, Depth and Greedy (CDG), iCAN, and A context-aware top-down model (CATD).

Table 2 shows the performance of our method and these three methods. We can see that: (1) Our method outperforms other methods in all the criteria, which shows the effectiveness of our method. (2) Comparing the last rows in Tables 1 and 2, it shows that our method obtains similar performance on the validation dataset and the test dataset. It shows that our method has good generalization ability. (3) Though our method obtains the first place in PIC Challenge, its performance is far from the requirements in real applications. Human-centric visual relation segmentation is still a challenging task which requires much research attention.

Table 2. Evaluation of different methods on the test dataset.

Method	R@100 (m-IoU: 0.25)	R@100 (m-IoU: 0.5)	R@100 (m-IoU: 0.75)	Mean score
CDG	0.3140	0.2515	0.1313	0.2323
iCAN	0.2499	0.1641	0.0939	0.1693
CATD	0.1493	0.1277	0.0879	0.1216
Our	0.4799	0.4069	0.2681	0.3850

5 Conclusion

We proposed a method handling human-centric relation segmentation, which is based on Mask R-CNN and VTransE model. We use fine-tuned Mask R-CNN model to detect and segment humans and objects in images. To remedy the defect that Mask R-CNN omits some persons in the instance segmentation results, we use face detection in addition and estimate the location of human body. After exporting the result of human and object segmentation, we fine-tuned VTransE model and get the prediction of relations. The results on the test dataset are fairly good, but we can still improve the method.

Acknowledgements. This work is supported by National Science Foundation of China (61202320), the Fundamental Research Funds for the Central Universities (021714380011), and Collaborative Innovation Center of Novel Software Technology and Industrialization.

References

1. He, K., Gkioxari, G., Dollr, P., Girshick, R.: Mask R-CNN. In: IEEE International Conference on Computer Vision. IEEE (2017)

2. Ren, S., He, K., Girshick, R., Sun, J.: Faster R-CNN: towards real-time object detection with region proposal networks. In: Conference and Workshop on Neural Information Processing Systems. MIT Press (2015)
3. Zhang, H., Kyaw, Z., Chang, S.-F., Chua, T.-S.: Visual translation embedding network for visual relation detection. In: IEEE Conference on Computer Vision and Pattern Recognition. IEEE (2017)
4. Kazemi, V., Sullivan, J.: One millisecond face alignment with an ensemble of regression trees. In: IEEE Conference on Computer Vision and Pattern Recognition. IEEE (2014)
5. Girshick, R.: Fast R-CNN. In: IEEE International Conference on Computer Vision. IEEE (2015)
6. Bordes, A., Usunier, N., Garcia-Duran, A., Weston, J., Yakhnenko, O.: Translating embeddings for modeling multi-relational data. In: Conference and Workshop on Neural Information Processing Systems. MIT Press (2013)
7. Lu, C., Krishna, R., Bernstein, M., Fei-Fei, L.: Visual relationship detection with language priors. In: Leibe, B., Matas, J., Sebe, N., Welling, M. (eds.) ECCV 2016. LNCS, vol. 9905, pp. 852–869. Springer, Cham (2016). https://doi.org/10.1007/978-3-319-46448-0_51
8. Liang, X., Lee, L., Xing, E.P.: Deep variation-structured reinforcement learning for visual relationship and attribute detection. In: IEEE Conference on Computer Vision and Pattern Recognition. IEEE (2017)
9. Shang, X., Ren, T., Guo, J., Zhang, H., Chua, T.-S.: Video visual relation detection. In: ACM International Conference on Multimedia. ACM (2017)
10. Li, X., Song, X., Herranz, L., Zhu, Y., Shuqiang, J.: Image captioning with both object and scene information. In: ACM International Conference on Multimedia. ACM (2016)
11. Antol, S., et al.: VQA: visual question answering. In: IEEE International Conference on Computer Vision. IEEE (2015)
12. Guo, H., Wang, J., Xu, M., Zha, Z.-J., Lu, H.: Learning multi-view deep features for small object retrieval in surveillance scenarios. In: ACM International Conference on Multimedia. ACM (2015)

Learning Spatiotemporal 3D Convolution with Video Order Self-supervision

Tomoyuki Suzuki[1(✉)], Takahiro Itazuri[2], Kensho Hara[1], and Hirokatsu Kataoka[1]

[1] National Institute of Advanced Industrial Science and Technology (AIST), Tokyo, Japan
{suzuki-tomo,kensho.hara,hirokatsu.kataoka}@aist.go.jp
[2] Waseda University, Tokyo, Japan
s132800732@fuji.waseda.jp

Abstract. The purpose of this work is to explore self-supervised learning (SSL) strategy to capture a better feature with spatiotemporal 3D convolution. Although one of the next frontier in video recognition must be spatiotemporal 3D CNN, the convergence of the 3D convolutions is really difficult because of their enormous parameters or missing temporal(motion) feature. One of the effective solutions is to collect a 10^5-order video database such as Kinetics/Moments in Time. However, this is not an efficient with burden of manual annotations. In the paper, we train 3D CNN on wrong video-sequence detection tasks in a self-supervised manner (without any manual annotation). The shuffling and verification of consecutive video-frame-order is effective for 3D CNN to capture temporal feature and get a good start point of parameters to be fine-tuned. In the experimental section, we verify that our pretrained 3D CNN on wrong clip detection improves the level of performance on UCF101 (+3.99% better than baseline, namely training 3D convolution from scratch).

Keywords: 3D Convolutional Neural Network · Self-supervised learning · Motion feature · Human action recognition

1 Introduction

Spatiotemporal 3D Convolutional Neural Network (3DCNN) have been successful in video understanding and it is expected to further develop [4]. Recent researches [1,4] have shown that 3DCNN have beat 2DCNN [11], which are conventional state-of-the-art methods in video recognition task. Against to the difficulty of 3D conv optimization, there are mainly two factors as follows: (i) Carreira *et al.* proposed a parameter inflation [1] which is a method for knowledge transfer from 2D pretrained model into 3D initialized parameters, (ii) large-scale (over 10^5-order) and clearly annotated video datasets have been released [6,10].

However, while inflation makes *appearance* feature easier to capture for 3DCNN, the suspicion that 3DCNN does not capture the *motion* (temporal)

L. Leal-Taixé and S. Roth (Eds.): ECCV 2018 Workshops, LNCS 11130, pp. 590–598, 2019.
https://doi.org/10.1007/978-3-030-11012-3_45

feature effectively. In the recent study, Huang *et al.* pointed out that the 3DCNN with consecutive frames only selects effective frame(s) to contribute the video classification [5].

On one hand, Two-Stream 3DCNN, which is ensemble method of RGB- and flow-input achieved significantly better performance than single RGB-input in action recognition [1] (Two-stream 98.0 vs. RGB-stream 95.6 on UCF101). This result indicates that a 3DCNN with consecutive RGB frames cannot completely capture a motion feature like optical flows. We believe that acquiring motion feature like optical flows with 3DCNN from only RGB-input is the key to further progress of 3DCNN in action recognition.

Also, manual annotations are time-consuming. To effectively optimize 3DCNN, we require over 10^5-order video database such as Kinetics. The burden of human labeling has contributed to the advanced video recognition model, however, any further annotations are obstacles of training of video understanding. Namely, we must consider an effective learning method for 3D convolution without any human supervisions.

In this study, we focus on self-supervised learning (SSL) with video order to optimize 3D convolution without any manual annotations on pretrained 3DCNN. We here propose the shuffling and detecting of wrong video order to learn a 3D convolution. The video order is a high-confidence context to enoughly train 3D convolutional filters. According to the experimental results, we confirm that easily solvable SSL tasks can improve an optimization of 3DCNN. The performance rate with 3DCNN on UCF101 is improved with our self-supervision. Our self-supervision is +3.99% better than a baseline, training 3DCNN from scratch.

2 Related Works

2.1 CNN Based Action Recognition on Videos

One of the most popular approach to action recognition is Two-Stream 2DCNN [11]. This is the ensemble of spatial-stream which takes RGB frame as input and temporal-stream which takes stacked optical flow frames as input. Spatial-stream can get the benefits from ImageNet pretraining which captures strong appearance feature, while temporal-stream captures motion feature by hand-craft optical flow and temporal stacked input. Also, the variants of this model were proposed.

One of the recent trends of action recognition is the use of 3D convolution to capture spatio-temporal feature. Tran et al. trained (relatively shallow) 3DCNN on Sports 1M dataset to extract spatio-temporal feature from videos [12]. However in several years ago, unlike 2DCNN which has several large-scale image datasets, optimization of deeper architecture of 3DCNN was difficult due to the luck of the dataset including sufficient *video* instances. In recent study, several huge datasets [6,10] were released. In addition, Inflation [1], which is the method to transfer appearance knowledge from pretrained 2DCNN by expanding 2D kernels into 3D was proposed. Under favor of these factors, as deep 3D architectures as 2D became able to provide powerful performances.

On the other hand, Huang et al. provided interesting discussion that 3DCNN does not necessarily capture *temporal* information well in action recognition [5]. From the results of their experiments, it can be considered that 3DCNN focuses on key frame selection from *set* of images rather than motion information from video clip, namely relationship between frames. Moreover, Two-Stream 3DCNN, which is ensemble method of RGB input and optical flow input achieved significantly better performance than only RGB input [1]. This result indicates that from consecutive RGB frames 3DCNN can not capture complete motion which contributes to classify actions.

Based on these insights, we believe that motion information can be still disputable to explore in contrast to appearance one and contribute to further progress of 3DCNN. In this research, we provide experiments about influence of pretraining procedures which encourage 3DCNN to consider relationship between frames.

2.2 Self-supervised Representation Learning

The main goal of self-supervised learning (SSL) is to transfer a model trained on a pretext task which is defined without manual annotation to a target task. Because of no cost of annotation and fine-tuning which is compatible transfer strategy, self-supervised learning is one of the focuses of attention in computer vision. Many of pretext tasks are defined using image data. For instance, colorization, inpainting, solving puzzles and counting. Another direction is the use of video-sequence. Misra et al. trained SiameseNet to verify the order of video frames [9] and Lee et al. trained to sort frames in correct order [8]. While their approaches focus on capturing appearance feature from single frame as a result of video-sequence based pretext task, in order to capture motion feature Fernando et al. trained a model to verify video-order taking multiple subtraction images of consecutive frames as input [2]. While they used 2DCNN, currently it is said that 3DCNN is more suitable for capturing spatio-temporal feature [5]. In this research, we focus on exploring the potential of SSL using video-sequence towards motion feature on 3DCNN.

3 SSL for 3D CNN

In order to explore self-supervised learning strategy towards motion feature, we first trained a 3DCNN model on pretext task and fine-tune it on action recognition task without freezing any weights of layers. This means that in this experiments we assume capturing efficient representation provides good start point of optimization.

3.1 Pretext Tasks

According to previous works [2,8,9], we define classification task based on SiameseNet which is consist of several branch networks with shared weights and one

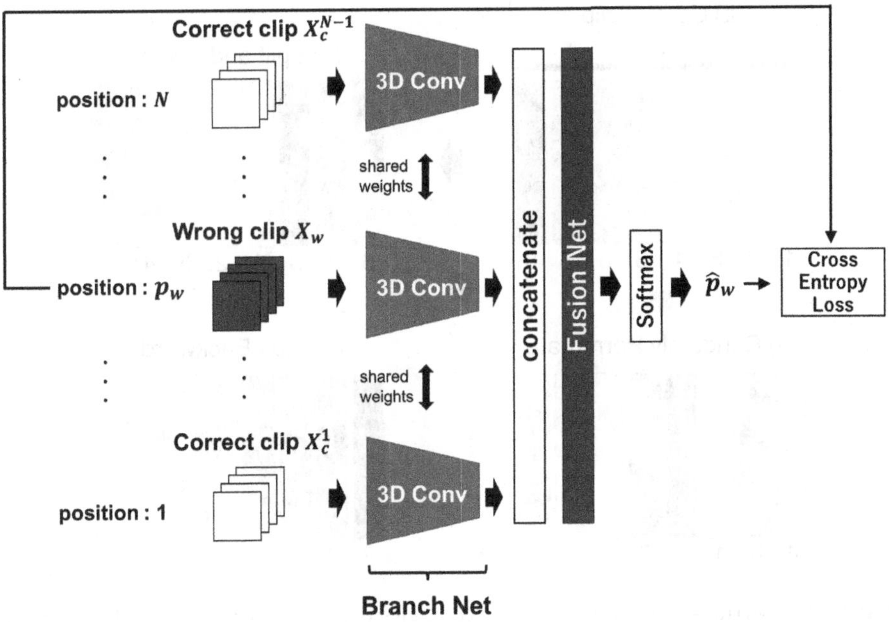

Fig. 1. Overview of pretraining strategy: Each branch network (3DCNN) takes a clip from a set of wrong one and several correct ones as input and their outputs are concatenated as input of fusion network. Here, N represents total number of input clips as well as branch network. And then, fusion network outputs estimated wrong position $\hat{p_w}$ In each question we permutate branch positions where each clip is input. Once we define the scheme of making a wrong clip, all of this task can be designed without any manual annotation.

fusion network (see Fig. 1). In this research, each branch network takes a different clip from wrong one (X_w) and several correct ones ($\{X_c^i\}_{i=1}^{N-1}$) as input and their outputs are concatenated as input of fusion network. Here, N represents total number of input clips as well as branch network. To establish problem, in each question we permutate branch positions where each clip is input, and obtain the position of a wrong clip $p_w \in \{1, ..., N\}$. And then, fusion network predicts p_w, as N-way classification problem. Note that while a wrong clip is modified in some way on temporal order (discussed below), a correct one is not modified at all.

Finally, we train a model by standard maximum likelihood estimation. Given X^j and p_w^j are j-th samples of permutation of clip set $\{X_w, X_1, ..., X_{N-1}\}$ and corresponding wrong position,

$$\theta^* = \arg\max_{\theta} \sum_j \mathcal{L}(f_\theta; X^j, p_w^j) \quad (1)$$

where $\mathcal{L}$ is likelihood function (cross entropy), and f_θ is our model parameterized by θ. Since we focus on motion feature, pretext tasks should be solved by *motion*

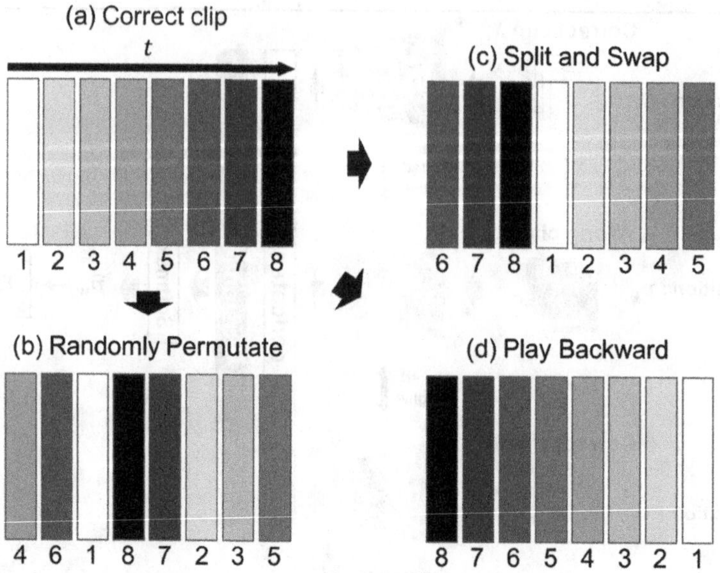

Fig. 2. The settings of wrong clip: The rectangles denote the frames in a clip ($D = 8$) and rectangles which have same color and index indicates that each of them is identical frame. We make three types of wrong clips from a correct ordered clip (a). (b) Randomly Permutate. (c) Split and Swap where p_s is set to 6. (d) Play Backward.

cue in input clips. With this in mind, we define several settings of wrong clip using unlabeled videos as below (see also Fig. 2).

Randomly Permutate (RP). This setting is similar to Fernando's [2], where they aimed at capturing video representation by 2DCNN. We first select a video clip of size W as a constrained window, then we sample different N clips including D consecutive frames from this window. We randomly choose one of the clips as a candidate of wrong clip $X'_w = \langle x_1, ..., x_i, ..., x_D \rangle$ where x_i denote the i-th frame of the clip. Then we permutate its frames randomly as a wrong clip X_w, while the rest of clips are correct clips. Note that since wrong clips differ in only temporal order, a model is required to utilize temporal information in other to detect wrong one. In this setting, our major concern is that a model captures relatively low-level temporal feature (e.g. detecting temporal blur) only, not high-level (semantic) feature which is intuitively effective for action recognition.

Split and Swap (SS). As with RP setting, we sample one candidate of wrong clip X'_w and $N - 1$ correct clips from constrained window. In this setting, we randomly choose a split position $p_s \in \{2, ..., D-1\}$, and swap two split clips to make a wrong clip.

$$\begin{aligned} X_w &= \mathrm{SS}(X'_w, p_s) \\ &= \langle x_{p_s}, ..., x_D, x_1, ..., x_{p_s-1} \rangle \end{aligned} \tag{2}$$

In contrast to RP setting, a wrong clip has only one temporal inconsistency, and it is considered that this makes pretext task somewhat more difficult than RP.

Play Backward (PB). In this setting, we play wrong clip backward, in other words apply temporal-flip.

$$\begin{aligned} X_w &= \mathrm{PB}(X'_w) \\ &= \langle x_D, x_{D-1}, ..., x_2, x_1 \rangle \end{aligned} \tag{3}$$

This is inspired by Gidaris's research [3], where they defined classification of image rotation as pretext task. The intuition behind this setting is related to the fact that in other to detect temporal-flipped videos a model is forced to capture more semantic information. In more detail, a model localizes moving subject (e.g. human, car, animal), recognizes the type and pose (e.g. where is it facing) of them, detects the direction they are moving to, and then results in successful classification. Specifically, since we use the videos for human action recognition, the subject a model detects may be often human. The most important concern of this setting is possibility of ambiguity. The distributions of videos belonging to some classes (e.g. jumping on the spot) is much the same as that of temporal-flipped videos and this means it is difficult for a model to solve the task.

3.2 Implementation

Following previous experiments of SSL [2,3,8,9] where AlexNet [7] is used as a baseline model, we construct 3D-AlexNet. The detail of architecture is shown in Table 1. Based on original architecture, 2D convolutional and pooling kernels are expanded to 3D spatio-temporal kernels, and dropout layers are replaced by batch normalization layers. This model takes 8 frames as input. During self-supervised learning, to construct SiameseNet, we use layers from `conv1` to `pool3` (denoted by `conv1-pool3`) of 3D-AlexNet followed by `fc4` as branch model, and `fc5`, `fc6` as fusion model. Training is run with $W = 20$, $D = 8$ and $N = 6$ on UCF101 train set of split1. The initial learning rate is 0.0001 and batch size is 64.

When fine-tuning on action recognition, we initialize 3D-AlexNet with pre-trained `conv1-pool3` and random initialized `fc1-fc3` followed by softmax function. We fine-tune the 3D-AlexNet on UCF101 train set of split1 and set the initial learning rate to 0.001 on `fc6-fc8` and 0.0001 on `conv1-pool6`, and batch-size to 64.

During final evaluation, we sample all non-overlapping clips from UCF101 test set of split1 as input and compute accuracy for each clip (clip-accuracy) from the maximum conditional probabilistic estimate. Also, to compute accuracy for each video (video-accuracy), we calculate arithmetic mean of the output from all clips in the video, as conditional probabilistic.

Table 1. Network architecture: In our experiments, $C = 101$ and $N = 6$.

Model	Layer name	Kernel		Stride
		Size	Channel	
3D-AlexNet	`conv1`	$(5, 11, 11)$	$3 \rightarrow 64$	$(1, 4, 4)$
	`pool1`	$(2, 3, 3)$	–	$(2, 2, 2)$
	`conv2`	$(3, 5, 5)$	$64 \rightarrow 192$	$(1, 2, 2)$
	`pool2`	$(2, 3, 3)$	–	$(2, 2, 2)$
	`conv3`	$(3, 3, 3)$	$192 \rightarrow 384$	$(1, 1, 1)$
	`conv4`	$(3, 3, 3)$	$384 \rightarrow 256$	$(1, 1, 1)$
	`conv5`	$(3, 3, 3)$	$256 \rightarrow 256$	$(1, 1, 1)$
	`pool3`	$(2, 3, 3)$	–	$(2, 2, 2)$
	`fc1`	–	$9216 \rightarrow 4096$	–
	`fc2`	–	$9216 \rightarrow 4096$	–
	`fc3`	–	$4096 \rightarrow C$	–
for SiameseNet	`fc4`	–	$9216 \rightarrow 128$	–
	`fc5`	–	$128N \rightarrow 128N$	–
	`fc6`	–	$128N \rightarrow N$	–

4 Results and Discussion

The results are reported in Table 2, where "Scratch" means training 3D-AlexNet on UCF101 without any pretraining and "Inflated" represents inflating from 2D version pretrained on ImageNet as a guide.

Table 2. Results.

Setting	Pretrain acc.(%)	Fine-tune acc.(%)	
		Clip	Video
Scratch	–	40.98	45.21
RP	99.21	**44.96**	**49.20**
SS	98.00	44.75	49.07
PB	17.65	40.01	44.97
Inflated	–	55.12	60.13

First, focusing on accuracy of pretext tasks, RP and SS setting are performed in high accuracy and seem to be solved almost perfectly. From this observation, it is expected that these settings is too easy for 3DCNN to capture efficient motion feature. On the other hand, PB is performed in near chance rate ($1/6 \approx 16.67\%$), and this implies that it is too difficult because of abovementioned ambiguity.

In spite of this expectation, as we can see in results of fine-tuning, pretraining on RP and SS improves performance of action recognition compared with Scratch, even though still can not compete against Inflated. This improvement implies that low-level and easily available temporal feature can contributes to better optimization of 3DCNN, and conversely this also means it is possible that ordinary training strategy of action recognition misses this feature. Meanwhile, we can not observe improvement by PB. The cause of this is considered to be the fact that 3DCNN can not detect wrong clips. We confirm that certain performance on pretext task is a necessary condition for improvement on target task. Throughout the whole, our strategies still can not compete against Inflated.

5 Conclusion and Future Works

In this study, we evaluate the effectiveness of self-supervised representation learning methods using temporal-sequence for 3DCNN. From results of experiments, we obtain the knowledge that low-level and easily available temporal feature from RP and SS improves optimization for 3DCNN and too difficult task to solve can not contribute to improvement.

We discuss the future research below:

Analyzing effect of motion feature: Although we show the effectiveness of SSL on 3DCNN in the form of improvement on accuracy, we should also explore how captured motion feature affects 3DCNN and action recognition on other experiments such as Huang et al.'s [5].

Removing ambiguity of PB: Despite intuition that PB setting can give semantic information to 3DCNN, this setting did not make an improvement. However, removing ambiguity of this task may lead to better result. For example, limiting dataset, action class or spatial region to ones including more intense motions.

Training on more large-scale DB: Since we set self-supervised manner, we can assume getting the benefit of more large-scale data without manual annotation. In previous work [4], training on immense number of *video* is significantly effective for 3DCNN. This is worth trying on SSL for novel knowledge of motion feature.

Fusing benefits of two features: Although we focus on motion feature, appearance feature obtained by Inflation is also strong. While we consider temporal SSL and Inflation separately now, there may be an effective method to fuse benefits of both initialization strategies.

References

1. Carreira, J., Zisserman, A.: Quo vadis, action recognition? A new model and the kinetics dataset. In: 2017 IEEE Conference on Computer Vision and Pattern Recognition (CVPR), pp. 4724–4733. IEEE (2017)
2. Fernando, B., Bilen, H., Gavves, E., Gould, S.: Self-supervised video representation learning with odd-one-out networks. In: 2017 IEEE Conference on Computer Vision and Pattern Recognition (CVPR), pp. 5729–5738. IEEE (2017)

3. Gidaris, S., Singh, P., Komodakis, N.: Unsupervised representation learning by predicting image rotations. arXiv preprint arXiv:1803.07728 (2018)
4. Hara, K., Kataoka, H., Satoh, Y.: Can spatiotemporal 3D CNNs retrace the history of 2D CNNs and ImageNet. In: Proceedings of the IEEE Conference on Computer Vision and Pattern Recognition, Salt Lake City, UT, USA, pp. 18–22 (2018)
5. Huang, D.A., et al.: What makes a video a video: analyzing temporal information in video understanding models and datasets. In: Proceedings of the IEEE Conference on Computer Vision and Pattern Recognition, pp. 7366–7375 (2018)
6. Kay, W., et al.: The kinetics human action video dataset. arXiv preprint arXiv:1705.06950 (2017)
7. Krizhevsky, A., Sutskever, I., Hinton, G.E.: ImageNet classification with deep convolutional neural networks. In: Advances in Neural Information Processing Systems, pp. 1097–1105 (2012)
8. Lee, H.Y., Huang, J.B., Singh, M., Yang, M.H.: Unsupervised representation learning by sorting sequences. In: 2017 IEEE International Conference on Computer Vision (ICCV), pp. 667–676. IEEE (2017)
9. Misra, I., Zitnick, C.L., Hebert, M.: Shuffle and learn: unsupervised learning using temporal order verification. In: Leibe, B., Matas, J., Sebe, N., Welling, M. (eds.) ECCV 2016. LNCS, vol. 9905, pp. 527–544. Springer, Cham (2016). https://doi.org/10.1007/978-3-319-46448-0_32
10. Monfort, M., et al.: Moments in time dataset: one million videos for event understanding. arXiv preprint arXiv:1801.03150 (2018)
11. Simonyan, K., Zisserman, A.: Two-stream convolutional networks for action recognition in videos. In: Advances in Neural Information Processing Systems, pp. 568–576 (2014)
12. Tran, D., Bourdev, L., Fergus, R., Torresani, L., Paluri, M.: Learning spatiotemporal features with 3D convolutional networks. In: Proceedings of the IEEE International Conference on Computer Vision, pp. 4489–4497 (2015)

W13 – 4th Workshop on Computer Vision for Art Analysis

W13 – 4th Workshop on Computer Vision for Art Analysis

Following the success of the 1st, 2nd and 3rd Workshops on Computer VISion for ART Analysis held in 2012 (together with ECCV 2012), in 2014 (together with ECCV 2014) and in 2016 (together with ECCV 2016) respectively, we present VISART IV at ECCV 2018. The use of Computer Vision for analysis of art has firmly taken hold, with highly active research in the complementary fields of Digital Art History and Digital Humanities. The benefits of advancements in Computer Vision techniques is directly effecting these fields taking advantage of invariance to style through style transfer guided methods for example in enhanced retrieval, or robust deformation of historical maps to modern topology informing historians. Bringing communities together to address the interdisciplinary nature of this research provides mutual benefits where VISART represents a forum for reflection and to inform on future advancements.

This workshop is relevant because it brings together leading researchers in the fields of computer vision, machine learning, art history, and multimedia information retrieval, with a special emphasis on art and cultural heritage applications. Following the trend from prior editions of this workshop, the scope has been further extended to include a track on the uses and reflection of Computer Vision for Art, encouraging interdisciplinary collaborations and expose the audience to an interactive perspective between technology and the arts. As with prior workshops the chairs comprise of a mixture of Art History and Computer Vision, and the invited keynote speakers are: Björn Ommer (Professor of Computer Vision, University of Heidelberg, Germany), Peter Bell (Professor of Digital Humanities, Friedrich-Alexander-University, Erlangen-Nurnberg, Germany), and John Collomosse (Professor of Computer Vision, University of Surrey, UK) providing an enlightening and broad synopsis of the intersection of Vision and Art.

September 2018

Stuart James
Leonardo Impett
Peter Hall
João Paulo Costeira
Peter Bell
Alessio Del Bue

What Was Monet Seeing While Painting? Translating Artworks to Photo-Realistic Images

Matteo Tomei, Lorenzo Baraldi(✉), Marcella Cornia, and Rita Cucchiara

University of Modena and Reggio Emilia, Modena, Italy
{matteo.tomei,lorenzo.baraldi,marcella.cornia,rita.cucchiara}@unimore.it

Abstract. State of the art Computer Vision techniques exploit the availability of large-scale datasets, most of which consist of images captured from the world as it is. This brings to an incompatibility between such methods and digital data from the artistic domain, on which current techniques under-perform. A possible solution is to reduce the domain shift at the pixel level, thus translating artistic images to realistic copies. In this paper, we present a model capable of translating paintings to photo-realistic images, trained without paired examples. The idea is to enforce a patch level similarity between real and generated images, aiming to reproduce photo-realistic details from a memory bank of real images. This is subsequently adopted in the context of an unpaired image-to-image translation framework, mapping each image from one distribution to a new one belonging to the other distribution. Qualitative and quantitative results are presented on Monet, Cezanne and Van Gogh paintings translation tasks, showing that our approach increases the realism of generated images with respect to the CycleGAN approach.

1 Introduction

In recent years, the Computer Vision community has converged towards unified approaches for image classification and understanding problems. As a matter of fact, architectures such as VGG [22] and ResNet [5] are now the standard de-facto for tackling most of the tasks in which an high-level understanding of the image is needed. Nevertheless, the application of state-of-the-art techniques to the domain of Digital Humanities and art is not trivial, as much of the development of the recent years is also due to the availability of large annotated datasets which consist of natural images or videos. This creates strong biases in the trained models, which limit the applicability of current solutions to the artistic domain [1].

A clear visualization of the domain shift between real and artistic data can be obtained by extracting high-level convolutional features from the two domains and visualizing them in a lower-dimensional projection which maintains the structure of the input space, *e.g.* by using a t-SNE transform [15]. In Fig. 2, we

L. Leal-Taixé and S. Roth (Eds.): ECCV 2018 Workshops, LNCS 11130, pp. 601–616, 2019.
https://doi.org/10.1007/978-3-030-11012-3_46

Fig. 1. A sample result from our approach. We propose a method which is capable of generating images with photo-realistic details, preserving the content of an artwork.

show the projections of visual features extracted from VGG-19 [22] and ResNet-152 [5] on real and artistic images which roughly describe the same visual domain (in this case, that of landscapes). As it can be observed, even though the content of all distributions is almost identical, features extracted from artistic images are shifted with respect to those extracted from real images, with a distance that increases when selecting less realistic styles, such as those of Cezanne and Van Gogh.

Reducing the domain shift at the pixel level, *i.e.* transforming artistic images to photo-realistic visualizations, is the objective of this paper (Fig. 1). The task has been tackled recently in literature as an instance of a more general domain translation task in unpaired settings [29]; we are not aware, however, of other works which have specifically tackled the translation between art and real. Here, our main source of intuition is that high model capacity is mandatory to memorize the details needed to perform photo-realistic generation. Therefore, instead of delegating the task of learning photo-realistic details exclusively to the min-max game of a generative adversarial model, we empower our model with an external memory of real images, and a search strategy to retrieve elements from the memory when needed to condition the generation.

Our model builds upon a Cycle-GAN [29], which consists of two Generative Adversarial Networks to align two unpaired domains. We extend and improve this approach by building external memory banks of real patches, and conditioning the learning to maximize the similarity of generated patches with respect to real patches. To this end, we devise a differentiable association strategy which, given a generated patch, retrieves the most similar real patch in the external memory. An additional loss term is then used to reduce the distance between generated and real patches. The same strategy is applied at multiple scales, to remove possible artifacts in the generation and increase the quality of the final results. To reduce the computational complexity of the approach, we also build an efficient version of our objective which is coupled with an approximated k-NN search.

Beyond presenting quantitative results obtained using state of the art metrics for image generation [6], we also perform careful perceptual experiments conducting a user study to compare the proposed approach to common unpaired translation models, under different settings. The experiments indicate that the images synthesized by our model are more realistic than those generated by a simple image-to-image translation approach.

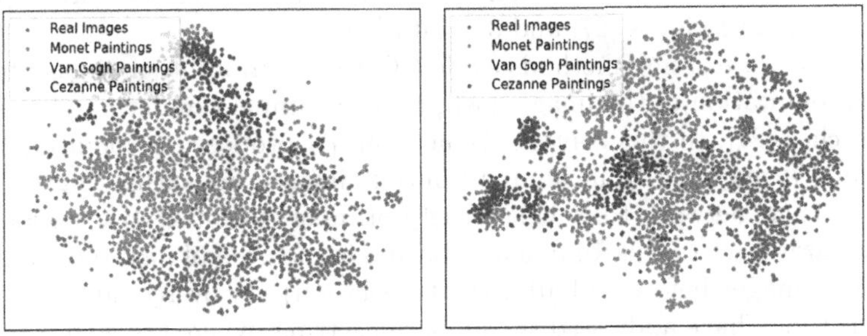

(a) VGG-19 (b) ResNet-152

Fig. 2. Domain shift visualization between real images and artistic paintings of different artists. Visualization is obtained by extracting visual features from both real and artistic images and by running the t-SNE algorithm on top of that. To encode images, we extract visual features from layer *fc7* of the VGG-19 [22] and from the final average pooling layer of the ResNet-152 [5]. To ensure a fair comparison, images are taken from roughly the same distribution of paintings: both represent landscapes. Best seen in color.

2 Related Work

The literature for image-to-image translation can be roughly categorized into style transfer [2] approaches and methods based on Generative Adversarial Networks (GANs) [4]. In the first case, the rationale is to synthesize a novel image by combining features of one image with features of another image, extracted at different semantic levels [2,3,9,25]. In the seminal work of Gatys *et al.* [2], a realistic input image was modified by minimizing a cost function aiming to preserve the content of the original image, and the style of a target artistic image, encoded via the Gram matrix of activations of a lower CNN layer.

Johnson *et al.* [9], on the same line, proposed the use of perceptual loss functions for training feed-forward encoders for the style-transfer task. Their method showed very similar qualitative results with respect to previous approaches, and significantly reduced the computational cost. The same problem of improving the overall computational efficiency of [2,3] was addressed in [25], in which a compact feed-forward network was designed to transfer the style of a given image to another one using complex and expressive loss functions. While these approaches have been successful in transferring the global texture properties of artworks to realistic images, mimicking the appearance of the brush strokes, they are not well suited for transferring from the artistic to the real domain, as texture properties are generally encoded in a translation invariant manner, and generating photo-realistic details by inverting CNN activations remains difficult.

On a different note, GANs [4] generate realistic images by aligning the distributions of real and generated images. They have been adopted for conditional image generation problems such as text to image synthesis [19], image inpainting [18] and future frame prediction [16], and have been successfully applied to other domains like videos [27] and 3D data [28].

A large set of existing methods exploit GANs to translate an image to a different representation of the image itself, as for example generating photographs from sketches [21]. In this context, Isola *et al.* [7] proposed a conditional GAN for learning a mapping from input to output images demonstrating the applicability of their network to a wide variety of image-to-image translation tasks. The main drawback of this kind of approaches is the need of paired training data (*i.e.* paired images before and after the translation). To overcome this problem, several methods have addressed the unpaired setting, where the goal is to translate images from a domain to another without leveraging on paired data to learn the corresponding translation. In particular, Liu *et al.* [14] introduced a coupled generative adversarial network that, thanks to a weight sharing strategy, is able to learn a joint distribution of multi-domain images. An extension of this work for unpaired image-to-image translation was presented in [13], exploiting a combination of variational autoencoders and GANs.

Zhu *et al.* [29] instead proposed CycleGAN, a model based on generative adversarial networks that, given two unpaired image collections, automatically translates an image from one domain to the other and vice versa. This is achieved by forcing the translation to be cycle consistent in the sense that if an image is translated from a domain to another, and translated back to the original domain, the result should be consistent with the original image. This cycle consistency criterion has been demonstrated to be effective for several tasks where paired training data does not exist, including style transfer, object transfiguration, season transfer, and photo enhancement.

3 Proposed Approach

Given an input painting, our goal is to generate a photo-realistic image representing the same content, without leveraging paired training data. In contrast to style transfer approaches [2], the objective is not to transfer a specific artistic style to an image, but rather to remove any artistic style from the painting, bringing the content back to a photo-realistic visualization. In other words, our model tries to show what reality the artist was observing or imagining while drawing.

The model is built on a cycle-consistent framework [29], which is endowed with an external memory of photo-realistic images and a patch-level retrieval strategy. At training time, real patches can be retrieved at multiple scales thanks to an assignment loss between real and generated patches. A summary of the approach is presented in Fig. 3.

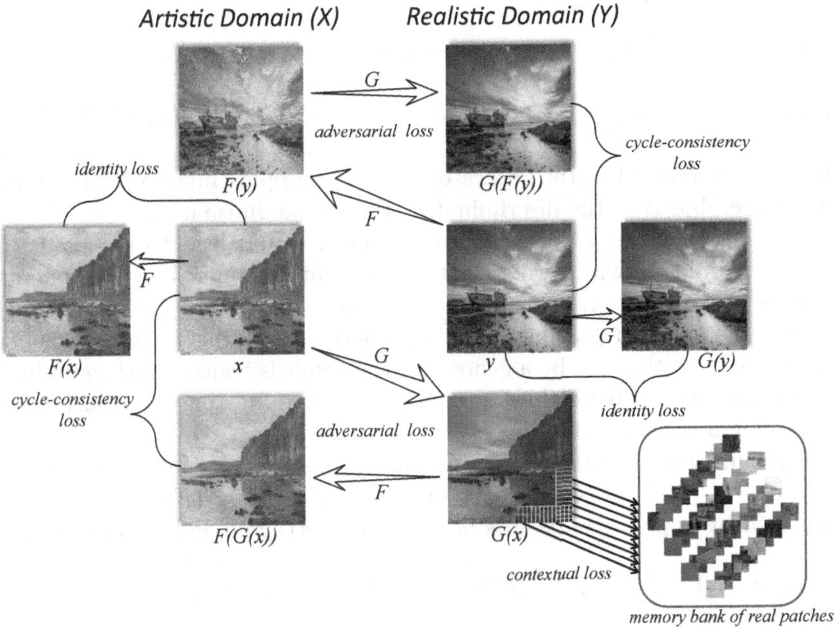

Fig. 3. Overall representation of our model. The model contains two generators (G and F) and two discriminators (not shown in the figure). The adversarial losses [4], combined with cycle-consistency losses, push the generators to produce images belonging to their corresponding target distributions, while imposing a pairing between the two domains. Every generated patch is also associated with respect to a memory bank of real patches, in a multi-scale and differentiable way. An additional cost term minimizes the distance between generated and real patches retrieved from the memory.

3.1 Unpaired Image to Image Translation

Our model needs to learn a mapping between the domain of paintings from a specific artist, which we call X, and the domain of real images, Y. Denoting the data distributions as $x \sim p_{data}(x)$ and $y \sim p_{data}(y)$, two mapping functions are built to translate data from one domain to another, $G : X \rightarrow Y$ and $F : Y \rightarrow X$. Following the Cycle-GAN approach, we realize the two mapping functions through learnable generators, which are paired with two discriminators D_X and D_Y at training time. The Cycle-Consistent Adversarial Objective features the following losses:

- Two *adversarial losses* [4] to generate images indistinguishable from those in the target domain. For both (G, D_Y) and (F, D_X), the generator is trained to reproduce the target data distribution, creating images that are difficult for the discriminator to distinguish from the real ones, while the discriminator is trained to differentiate between real and synthetic images. In this setting, the generator and the discriminator play a two-player minimax game through the following objective functions:

$$\mathcal{L}_{GAN}(G, D_Y, X, Y) = \mathbb{E}_{y\sim p_{data}(y)}[logD_Y(y)]+\mathbb{E}_{x\sim p_{data}(x)}[log(1-D_Y(G(x)))] \quad (1)$$

$$\mathcal{L}_{GAN}(F, D_X, Y, X) = \mathbb{E}_{x\sim p_{data}(x)}[logD_X(x)]+\mathbb{E}_{y\sim p_{data}(y)}[log(1-D_X(F(y)))] \quad (2)$$

During training, while the generator (*i.e.* the mapping function) tries to minimize the objective, the discriminator tries to maximize it.

- Observing that the adversarial losses, alone, would lead to an under constrained problem, which would not ensure that the input and the generated images share the same content, a *cycle consistency loss* [29] is applied to reduce the space of possible mapping functions. For this purpose, whenever an image is synthesized by a generator, the result is transformed again by the other generator, taking the image back into the starting distribution, thus obtaining a reconstructed image.
  We require the original image and the reconstructed one to be the same, *i.e.* $x \rightarrow G(x) \rightarrow F(G(x)) \approx x$ and $y \rightarrow F(y) \rightarrow G(F(y)) \approx y$. This is imposed by applying an ℓ_1-loss between reconstructed and original images:

$$\mathcal{L}_{cyc}(G, F) = \mathbb{E}_{x\sim p_{data}(x)}[\|F(G(x)) - x\|] + \mathbb{E}_{y\sim p_{data}(y)}[\|G(F(y)) - y\|] \quad (3)$$

- An *identity mapping loss* [24] helps to preserve the color distributions between input and output images. This is done by forcing the generators to behave like an identity function when their input are images from their target domain, through the following loss:

$$\mathcal{L}_{id}(G, F) = \mathbb{E}_{y\sim p_{data}(y)}[\|G(y) - y\|] + \mathbb{E}_{x\sim p_{data}(x)}[\|F(x) - x\|] \quad (4)$$

The full Cycle-Consistent Adversarial Loss [29] can therefore be written as follows:

$$\begin{aligned}\mathcal{L}_{cca}(G, F, D_X, D_Y) = \mathcal{L}_{GAN}(G, D_Y, X, Y) + \mathcal{L}_{GAN}(F, D_X, Y, X) \\ + \mathcal{L}_{cyc}(G, F) + \mathcal{L}_{id}(G, F).\end{aligned} \quad (5)$$

Alone, this objective sets an unpaired image-to-image translation setting between artistic and real images, suitable for performing translations in both directions. In the following, we discuss the incorporation of an external memory and of a retrieval strategy to condition the model on real image elements.

3.2 Retrieving Real Patches from an External Memory

Our goal is to translate images from the artistic domain to the realistic domain. To do so, we rely on the hypothesis that realistic images can be effectively generated by copying visual elements from real images, instead of optimizing the cycle-consistent generative objectives alone.

Given a set of real images, we build a memory bank M by extracting fixed-size patches from each image in a sliding window manner. When the number of real images is sufficiently large and their content is sufficiently aligned with the distribution represented by the paintings, the memory bank can effectively model a distribution of real patches which can drive the training of the generative model. To do so, each generated image $G(x)$ is split into patches as well, following the same patch size and stride as in the memory bank. Then, a retrieval strategy is designed to pair each generated patch with the most similar in the memory bank M, while an assignment loss is in charge of maximizing the similarity between generated and real patches, under the previously computed assignment. Since we focus on appearance, each patch is encoded with its RGB values, thus obtaining a dimensionality of $l \times l \times 3$ for a patch size of $l \times l$.

Reading from the External Memory. Given the set of real patches from M, $M = \{m_j\}$ and the set of patches from $G(x)$, $K = \{k_i\}$, a pairwise cosine distance function is defined after centering the distributions of real and generated patches with respect to the mean of real patches.

$$d_{ij} = \left(1 - \frac{(k_i - \mu_m) \cdot (m_j - \mu_m)}{\|k_i - \mu_m\|_2 \|m_j - \mu_m\|_2}\right), \text{ where } \mu_m = \frac{1}{N}\sum_j m_j \tag{6}$$

Each generated patch is then assigned to its most similar counterpart in the memory bank with a differential assignment strategy. In particular, we first normalize the pairwise distances and then compute pairwise affinities $A_{ij} \in [0, 1]$ as follows:

$$\tilde{d}_{ij} = \frac{d_{ij}}{\min_l d_{il} + \epsilon}, \text{ where } \epsilon = 1e-5 \tag{7}$$

$$A_{ij} = \frac{\exp(1 - \tilde{d}_{ij}/h)}{\sum_l \exp(1 - \tilde{d}_{il}/h)} = \begin{cases} \approx 1 & \text{if } \tilde{d}_{ij} \ll \tilde{d}_{il} \ \forall\, l \neq j \\ \approx 0 & \text{otherwise} \end{cases} \tag{8}$$

where $h > 0$ is a bandwidth parameter. In practice, each generated patch k_i is softly assigned to the most similar real patch, as determined by the affinity matrix A_{ij}. In other words, k_i will be assigned prominently to the real patch corresponding to $\max_j A_{ij}$, and to others near real patches which happen to have an high degree of affinity with k_i.

Reducing the Computational Overhead. Computing the assignments between real and generated patches requires to compute the entire affinity matrix A_{ij}, which leads to an intractable process when the number of real patches is large. The size of A_{ij}, in fact, grows linearly with the number of patches, which grows linearly with the number of images and quadratically when decreasing the stride.

To reduce the computational overhead, we build a suboptimal Nearest Neighbors index with real patches. Then, for each generated patch k_i, we conduct a

k-NN search to get the k nearest samples from the memory bank. We subsequently estimate the affinity matrix A_{ij} by reducing the computation only on the retrieved real patches, thus getting a sparse matrix in which the affinities for non retrieved patches are set to zero. Notice that, when the results of the k-NN search are reliable, the estimation of A_{ij} is close to the exact results, thanks to the Softmax normalization in Eq. 8.

To speed up the computation of the distances when the number of real images used to generate the memory bank is large, we adopt a suboptimal inverted index with exact post-verification (IndexIVFFlat), which has an high-performance implementation in the Faiss library [8].

Fig. 4. Comparison between (left) original Monet painting and (right) an image generated by minimizing the contextual loss on real patches, plus a content loss regularization, updating pixel values directly. As shown in the zoomed patches, many brush strokes disappear, recovering realistic textures.

Maximizing the Similarity with Real Patches. Once affinities are computed, we maximize the similarity between each generated patch and its corresponding assignments from the memory bank. To this aim, we employ the contextual loss [17] as follows.

$$\mathcal{L}_{CX}(K, M) = -\log\left(\frac{1}{N}\left(\sum_i \max_j A_{ij}\right)\right) \tag{9}$$

With the contextual loss, we aim to reduce the distance between two distributions: the distribution of the generated image features (*i.e.*, that of generated patches) and that of the memory bank features (*i.e.*, real patches).

Multi-scale. To better translate artistic details to real details we adopt a multi-scale variant of the proposed approach, thus building multiple memory banks, each with different patch sizes and strides. During training, we compute the contextual loss for each scale separately, and define the final objective as the sum of the losses obtained at each scale. In practice, we adopt three scales, as follows:

$$\mathcal{L}_{CXMS}(K, M) = \sum_{s=1}^{3} -\log\left(\frac{1}{N_s}\left(\sum_i \max_j A_{ij}^s\right)\right) \tag{10}$$

where A^s is the affinity matrix computed between patches with scale s and N_s is the number of real patches of the memory bank for scale s.

The Role of the Contextual Loss. For the ease of the reader, we showcase the benefit of this strategy in a simpler setting which does not employ a min-max generative game. Taking inspiration from style-transfer works [2], we build a cost function and minimize it by back-propagating directly on the pixel values of the source image. In particular, a content loss is placed to regularize the training and to maintain the semantic content of the original image, while the contextual loss is applied to maximize the patch-level similarity with respect to a memory bank of real images. A sample result on a Monet painting is shown in Fig. 4. As it can be observed, the contextual loss on real patches helps to obtain realistic and plausible results, removing stroke textures in large portions of the image.

3.3 Full Objective

We combine together the unpaired image-to-image translation framework and our retrieval and assignment strategy between real and generated patches, thus obtaining the following overall training loss:

$$\mathcal{L}(G, F, D_X, D_Y, K, M) = \mathcal{L}_{cca}(G, F, D_X, D_Y) + \lambda \mathcal{L}_{CXMS}(K, M) \tag{11}$$

where λ is the contextual loss weight. During our preliminary tests, we found that good values for λ, in the multi-scale version of the approach, lie around 0.1 or less. As a final side note, it is important to underline that we are interested only in generating real images from paintings and not also in the opposite task. For this reason, we do not include a second set of memory banks for the artistic features, and we do not compute the contextual loss also in the opposite direction.

4 Experimental Results

In this section, we provide qualitative and quantitative results of the proposed solution as well as implementation details and datasets used in our experiments.

4.1 Datasets and Implementation Details

To evaluate our approach, we use a set of paintings from Monet, Cezanne and Van Gogh and a set of real images. To keep the distribution of paintings and real images roughly aligned, real images are selected from landscape pictures: paintings are downloaded from Wikiart.org, and photos are taken from Flickr using the combination of tags `landscape` and `landscapephotography`. Black-and-white photos were pruned, and the images were scaled to 256×256 pixels. The number of samples for each training set are Monet: 1072, Cezanne: 583, Van Gogh: 400, Photographs: 2048.

CycleGAN Parameters. To build the Cycle-GAN part of our model, we keep the same networks and training parameters as in [29]. The generative networks architecture is adapted from Johnson *et al.* [9] and contains two stride-2 convolutions to downsample the input, followed by several residual blocks and then two convolutional layers with stride 1/2 for upsampling. The discriminative networks are PatchGANs [7,11,12] which try to classify if each square patch in an image is real or fake.

Contextual Loss Parameters. We extract patches at three different scales, to fill our memory banks, from 100 different real images. Keeping the size of the image constant, we extracted real patches of size 4×4, 8×8 and 16×16, using stride values of 4, 5 and 6 respectively. During training, at each iteration we extract patches with the same sizes and strides from the generated image and compute the contextual loss. The contextual loss weight λ in Eq. 11 was fixed to 0.1.

We train the model for 200 epochs by using the Adam optimizer [10] with a batch size of 1, keeping a learning rate of 0.0002 for the first 100 epochs and then linearly decaying it to zero over the next 100 epochs. Weights are initialized from a Gaussian distribution with 0 mean and standard deviation 0.02.

4.2 Qualitative Results

We compare our results with those from a CycleGAN [29], trained exactly with the same parameters used for our model. Given the subjective nature of the task, before presenting a quantitative discussion, we show some examples of generated images starting from Monet, Cezanne and Van Gogh paintings in Fig. 5. Additional qualitative results are reported in Fig. 6.

We observe that our results generally preserve the colors of the original paintings and contain less artifacts than images generated by CycleGAN. This quality improvement is particularly manifest in the details of sky and sea (Fig. 5, first and fourth rows), in the preservation of colors (Fig. 5, third row), and in the smoothness of objects which do not have well defined edges in the original painting, as in the smoke of Fig. 5, second row.

Fig. 5. Results of applying our method to Monet (first and second rows), Van Gogh (third row) and Cezanne (fourth row) paintings. (left) Original painting, (center) CycleGAN [29] output, (right) our method output.

4.3 Quantitative Results

To numerically evaluate the visual quality of the results, we adopt the Fréchet Inception Distance (FID) [6], which has been recently emerging as a reliable metric for evaluating generated images and has been proven to be more consistent with human judgments than the Inception score [20]. FID corresponds to a Wasserstein-2 distance [26] between two multivariate Gaussian distributions fitted on real and generated data, using activations from layers of the Inception-v3 model [23].

In Table 1, we show FID values obtained under different settings. In particular, we measure the FID distance with real images using the original paintings, fake paintings generated using style transfer, and the recovered real images generated with CycleGAN and our approach. Also, we employ three different Inception-v3 layers to assess the distance using both low-level and high-level visual features. As it can be observed, our model is able to further reduce the distance with real images, when compared to CycleGAN, thus confirming the effectiveness of the approach. The same trend is observable with both low-level and high-level Inception features, and for all the artists.

While being a well-grounded metric for image generation, the FID score cannot be as effective as human judgment. Therefore, we further evaluate our results by conducting a user study. All the tests have involved five volunteering people who were not aware of the details of the proposed approach, and thus not trained to distinguish between our results and those of CycleGAN. In each test, evaluators were presented with different real and generated images, and asked to click on the most realistic one using a web interface. Our tests were structured as follows.

Realism of the Generation – users were presented our result and the CycleGAN output for a given input painting, which was not shown in the interface. Generated images were presented in their full size (256×256) and chosen randomly from the dataset. Each user was given 100 image pairs, and asked to select which of the two images seemed more realistic.

Coherency with the Source Painting – in this test, the interface also showed the original painting to the user, who was asked to click on the generated image that best represented the painting. With this test, we aim to investigate whether our results are more faithful to the original painting colors and composition. Again, 100 image triplets were shown to each user.

Multi-scale Comparison with Real Images – to assess to what extent the generated images look realistic, we also asked the users to rank the realism of the generated images with respect to real images. In this test, the interface showed two images to the user, one generated by our method and the other randomly extracted from the real images dataset. The user was asked to select the more realistic one, and presented with 100 image pairs. The same test was repeated in three different runs, in which images were resized with a ratio of 1, 2/3, 1/2, and ensuring that different real-generated pairs were presented to the same user in different runs.

Tables 2 and 3 show the results of our tests. As it can be observed from Table 2, images generated by our method were evaluated as more realistic than those of CycleGAN 58.4% of the times, thus beating the baseline with a margin of 17%. Also, when showing the input painting to the user, images generated by our method were ranked as more coherent with the input painting, thus underlying that our method is able to preserve color and texture from the painting.

Finally, we also had some chances to win the comparison with real images. As reported in Table 3, even when comparing the results of our generation with real landscapes, sometimes the user was fooled and selected the generated image. As it can be expected, this behavior becomes more frequent when the images are downsized to a small scale. Nevertheless, it is significant to observe that, even at full scale, the user was fooled about 5% of the times.

Table 1. Fréchet Inception Distance (FID) [6] computed between real images (landscape pictures) and different sets: artist's original paintings, images obtained transferring the artist's style to the real images through Gatys *et al.* [2], images generated with CycleGAN [29] and with our method. The FID is computed using different feature layers of Inception-v3: the second max pooling (192-d), the pre-auxiliary classifier layer (768-d) and the final average pooling layer (2048-d). FIDs computed at different Inception-v3 layers are not directly comparable [6].

	Monet	Cezanne	Van Gogh
2048 dimensions			
Original paintings	74.45	176.51	166.72
Style transfer [2]	58.02	91.23	101.54
CycleGAN [29]	55.26	83.62	86.82
Our model	**54.43**	**77.01**	**81.74**
768 dimensions			
Original paintings	0.52	1.26	1.39
Style transfer [2]	0.50	1.01	1.18
CycleGAN [29]	0.41	0.49	0.48
Our model	**0.34**	**0.37**	**0.41**
192 dimensions			
Original paintings	0.94	1.67	3.96
Style transfer [2]	0.71	1.49	3.33
CycleGAN [29]	0.31	0.28	0.19
Our model	**0.16**	**0.13**	**0.11**

Table 2. Results of the user tests on realism and coherency. Values are reported as the percentage of images chosen with respect to the total.

Test	Scale	CycleGAN [29]	Our method
Realism of the generation	256 × 256	41.6%	58.4%
Coherency with the painting	256 × 256	41.2%	58.8%

Table 3. Results of the multi-scale comparison with real images. Values are reported as the percentage of images chosen with respect to the total.

Scale	Random real image	Generated image
256 × 256	95.1%	4.9%
170 × 170	88.2%	11.8%
128 × 128	88.0%	12.0%

Fig. 6. Sample results generated by our method.

5 Conclusions

We presented a novel method for artistic-to-realistic domain translation. Since paired training data is not available for this task, our approach is based on an unpaired framework. In particular, we built upon the CycleGAN architecture, and enriched it with multi-scale memory banks of real images, to drive the generation at the patch level. To make the approach computationally feasible, we also provided an approximated version of the association strategy. Results, presented both qualitatively and quantitatively, show that our method outperforms the CycleGAN baseline, leading to more realistic results. Despite the increased quality, failure cases are still frequent, and the task is still far from being solved. In particular, we noticed that the method often fails to translate portraits and images with blurry foreground objects. Future works will explore this direction, also tackling the generation of higher resolution images.

Acknowledgments. This work was supported by the CultMedia project (CTN02_00015_9852246), co-founded by the Italian MIUR. We also acknowledge the support of Facebook AI Research with the donation of the GPUs used for this research.

References

1. Baraldi, L., Cornia, M., Grana, C., Cucchiara, R.: Aligning text and document illustrations: towards visually explainable digital humanities. In: International Conference on Pattern Recognition (2018)
2. Gatys, L.A., Ecker, A.S., Bethge, M.: A neural algorithm of artistic style. arXiv preprint arXiv:1508.06576 (2015)
3. Gatys, L.A., Ecker, A.S., Bethge, M.: Image style transfer using convolutional neural networks. In: IEEE International Conference on Computer Vision and Pattern Recognition (2016)
4. Goodfellow, I., et al.: Generative adversarial nets. In: Advances in Neural Information Processing Systems (2014)
5. He, K., Zhang, X., Ren, S., Sun, J.: Deep residual learning for image recognition. In: IEEE International Conference on Computer Vision and Pattern Recognition (2016)
6. Heusel, M., Ramsauer, H., Unterthiner, T., Nessler, B., Klambauer, G., Hochreiter, S.: GANs trained by a two time-scale update rule converge to a Nash equilibrium. In: Advances in Neural Information Processing Systems (2017)
7. Isola, P., Zhu, J.Y., Zhou, T., Efros, A.A.: Image-to-image translation with conditional adversarial networks. In: IEEE International Conference on Computer Vision and Pattern Recognition (2017)
8. Johnson, J., Douze, M., Jégou, H.: Billion-scale similarity search with gpus. arXiv preprint arXiv:1702.08734 (2017)
9. Johnson, J., Alahi, A., Fei-Fei, L.: Perceptual losses for real-time style transfer and super-resolution. In: Leibe, B., Matas, J., Sebe, N., Welling, M. (eds.) ECCV 2016. LNCS, vol. 9906, pp. 694–711. Springer, Cham (2016). https://doi.org/10.1007/978-3-319-46475-6_43
10. Kingma, D.P., Ba, J.: Adam: A method for stochastic optimization. arXiv preprint arXiv:1412.6980 (2014)

11. Ledig, C., et al.: Photo-realistic single image super-resolution using a generative adversarial network. In: IEEE International Conference on Computer Vision and Pattern Recognition (2017)
12. Li, C., Wand, M.: Precomputed real-time texture synthesis with Markovian generative adversarial networks. In: Leibe, B., Matas, J., Sebe, N., Welling, M. (eds.) ECCV 2016. LNCS, vol. 9907, pp. 702–716. Springer, Cham (2016). https://doi.org/10.1007/978-3-319-46487-9_43
13. Liu, M.Y., Breuel, T., Kautz, J.: Unsupervised image-to-image translation networks. In: Advances in Neural Information Processing Systems (2017)
14. Liu, M.Y., Tuzel, O.: Coupled generative adversarial networks. In: Advances in Neural Information Processing Systems (2016)
15. van der Maaten, L., Hinton, G.: Visualizing data using t-SNE. J. Mach. Learn. Res. **9**(Nov), 2579–2605 (2008)
16. Mathieu, M., Couprie, C., LeCun, Y.: Deep multi-scale video prediction beyond mean square error. In: International Conference on Learning Representations (2016)
17. Mechrez, R., Talmi, I., Shama, F., Zelnik-Manor, L.: Learning to maintain natural image statistics. arXiv preprint arXiv:1803.04626 (2018)
18. Pathak, D., Krahenbuhl, P., Donahue, J., Darrell, T., Efros, A.A.: Context encoders: Feature learning by inpainting. In: European Conference on Computer Vision (2016)
19. Reed, S., Akata, Z., Yan, X., Logeswaran, L., Schiele, B., Lee, H.: Generative adversarial text to image synthesis. In: International Conference on Machine Learning (2016)
20. Salimans, T., Goodfellow, I., Zaremba, W., Cheung, V., Radford, A., Chen, X.: Improved techniques for training GANs. In: Advances in Neural Information Processing Systems (2016)
21. Sangkloy, P., Lu, J., Fang, C., Yu, F., Hays, J.: Scribbler: controlling deep image synthesis with sketch and color. In: IEEE International Conference on Computer Vision and Pattern Recognition (2017)
22. Simonyan, K., Zisserman, A.: Very deep convolutional networks for large-scale image recognition. arXiv preprint arXiv:1409.1556 (2014)
23. Szegedy, C., Vanhoucke, V., Ioffe, S., Shlens, J., Wojna, Z.: Rethinking the inception architecture for computer vision. In: IEEE International Conference on Computer Vision and Pattern Recognition (2016)
24. Taigman, Y., Polyak, A., Wolf, L.: Unsupervised cross-domain image generation. In: International Conference on Learning Representations (2017)
25. Ulyanov, D., Lebedev, V., Vedaldi, A., Lempitsky, V.S.: Texture networks: feed-forward synthesis of textures and stylized images. In: International Conference on Machine Learning (2016)
26. Vaserstein, L.N.: Markov processes over denumerable products of spaces, describing large systems of automata. Probl. Peredachi Informatsii **5**(3), 64–72 (1969)
27. Vondrick, C., Pirsiavash, H., Torralba, A.: Generating videos with scene dynamics. In: Advances in Neural Information Processing Systems (2016)
28. Wu, J., Zhang, C., Xue, T., Freeman, B., Tenenbaum, J.: Learning a probabilistic latent space of object shapes via 3D generative-adversarial modeling. In: Advances in Neural Information Processing Systems (2016)
29. Zhu, J.Y., Park, T., Isola, P., Efros, A.A.: Unpaired image-to-image translation using cycle-consistent adversarial networks. In: IEEE International Conference on Computer Vision (2017)

Saliency-Driven Variational Retargeting for Historical Maps

Filippo Bergamasco[1,2(✉)], Arianna Traviglia[1], and Andrea Torsello[1]

[1] DAIS - Università Ca'Foscari, Via Torino 155, 30172 Venice, Italy
{filippo.bergamasco,traviglia,andrea.torsello}@unive.it
[2] Istituto Italiano di Tecnologia (IIT), Center for Cultural Heritage Technology (CCHT), Via della Libertà 12, 30175 Venice, Italy

Abstract. We study the problem of georeferencing artistic historical maps. Since they were primarily conceived as work of art more than an accurate cartographic tool, the common warping approaches implemented in Geographic Application Systems (GIS) usually lead to an overly-stretched image in which the actual pictorial content (like written text, compass roses, buildings, etc.) is un-naturally deformed. On the other hand, domain transformation of images driven by the perceived salient visual content is a well-known topic known as "image retargeting" which has been mostly limited to a change of scale of the image (i.e. changing the width and height) rather than a more general control-points based warping.

In this work we propose a variational image retargeting approach in which the local transformations are estimated to accommodate a set of control points instead of image boundaries. The direction and severity of warping is modulated by a novel tensor-based saliency formulation considering both the visual content and the shape of the underlying features to transform. The optimization includes a flow projection step based on the isotonic regression to avoid singularities and flip overs of the resulting distortion map.

Keywords: Image retargeting · Warping · Historical maps

1 Introduction

Content-aware image warping and retargeting has drawn significant attention so that many studies have been proposed in recent years.

Broadly speaking, the main target application in existing literature has almost exclusively been the change of scale or aspect ratio of images, producing "retargeted" outputs that kept in a tight rectangular image the unmodified perceptually salient features of the source image, while eliminating or distorting the less salient portions. Common to these applications is a constrained rectangular boundary resulting in induced deformations that are mostly axis-aligned. Emblematic of this class of approaches is seam carving [3], which allows to shrink

L. Leal-Taixé and S. Roth (Eds.): ECCV 2018 Workshops, LNCS 11130, pp. 617–630, 2019.
https://doi.org/10.1007/978-3-030-11012-3_47

or expand images by removing or adding whole columns or rows of pixel found through a minimum saliency path from the top to bottom or left to right boundaries of the image.

Existing image retargeting approaches can be classified into two categories: discrete and continuous [10]. Discrete approaches alter the image size by eliminating pixels through cropping or seam carving. Recently, Rubinstein et al. [9] presented a multi-operator algorithm that combines cropping, linear scaling, and seam carving while Pritch et al. [8] remove repeated patterns in homogeneous regions.

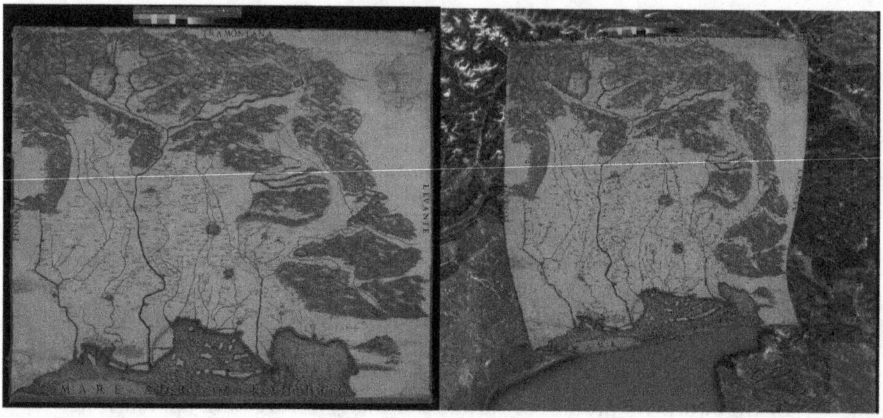

Fig. 1. Example of an historical map georeferencing process. Left: original map (1682, Sebastiano Alberti, ASV). Right: georeferenced map with respect to 15 manually-defined control points overlapped to a satellite view of the area (Google Earth basemap). Map image courtesy of State Archive of Venice.

Conversely, continuous approaches optimize mapping or warping using smoothness and salient-region preserving constraints to retain perceptual content. Wolf et al. [12] retargeted an image by merging less important pixels to reduce distortion. In this way, the distortion is propagated only along the resizing direction. Wang et al. [11] warp local regions to match optimal scaling factors, thus distributing the distortion in all directions. However, large salient objects may undergo inconsistent deformation throughout their extent. To ease this problem, Zhang et al. [13] and Guo et al. [6] force highly salient objects to undergo similarity transformations when resizing images, resulting in good preservation of local shape. However, inconsistent deformations can occur along elongated structures. Lin et al. [7] propose an approach to preserve both the visually salient objects and structure lines by constraining patches of high saliency to undergo similarity transformations. It is noteworthy to say that all the approaches are designed to give their best on photographic content rather than human-made drawings.

In this paper we address a different application for Content-aware image warping: the georeferencing of historical maps (Fig. 1). Historical maps provide vital evidence to scholars in disciplines as diverse as history, archaeology, and environmental sciences, which routinely use them to identify and map information on past landscapes that is no more available on the ground and to compare their content with current geomorphological and spatial data within GIS platforms, where historical maps can be georeferenced. A number of tools available in these platforms enable warping images to fit control points to known coordinates; generally, however, these are limited to global context-independent transformations such as polynomial or spline based image warping. These global transformations provide sufficiently accurate results with historical maps produced starting from beginning/middle of 18th century, which where originated using more or less accurate topographic criteria.

Maps created in previous centuries, instead, where generally conceived more like a pictorial depiction of the landscape rather than a rigorous topographical representation of it. In this case, global context-independent transformations tend to destroy the information-rich pictorial content, failing to warp the features over the actual landscape due to the limited degrees of freedom of the transformations available.

A retargeting process enabling the georeferencing of historical maps will differ from traditional retargeting approaches in several key elements. First, the transformation is driven by control points resulting in different boundary conditions: Dirichelet for the control points and Neumann for the actual boundary. Second, salient visual content must be preserved after the transformation. Third, the map has an orientation, so the warp should be smooth and non-decreasing in both horizontal and vertical directions. Fourth, each iconographic element should maintain the original shape and orientation. (eg. the compass rose present in many historical maps should preserve its original direction and be minimally distorted). Finally, maps are rich in linear elements, which can be stretched along their direction, but not orthogonally. Hence, context-based constraint should be directional.

In accordance to the these requirements, our approach provides three novel contributions. First, we defined a continuous image retargeting approach based on a set of control points. Second, we consider a tensor-based characterization of the saliency map to favor or penalize strong warping across salient edges. In other words, we generalize the saliency map from a scalar to a tensor field to control both the amount of stretching and its directionality among the image domain. Finally, we avoid the possible fold overs by embedding isotonic regression during the variational map optimization. This enables extreme stretches on possibly small parts of the images, avoiding folds and guaranteeing orientation and monotonicity of the map.

2 Problem Formulation

We suppose to have a *source* image I_s defined over a spatial scale-independent domain $\Omega_s \subset \mathbb{R}^2$. Our goal is to transform the image on a new scale-independent domain Ω_t (which can be affinely mapped to world coordinates) according to some point-to-point correspondences $C_p = \{(p_1, q_1), (p_2, q_2), \ldots, (p_n \in \Omega_s, q_n \in \Omega_t)\}$ that are manually defined with respect of some visual features that a human operator has identified in I_s. In Fig. 1 (Left) we have a typical example of an historical map held at the State Archive of Venice and drawn by geographer Sebastiano Alberti in 1682. To georeference the picture, an algorithm should ideally map each pixel of I_s to a new world coordinate system so that the geographical features (like the rivers, islands, city locations etc.) are mapped to their corresponding places. Since the historical map was not intended for cartographic purposes, local scale of the pictorial content is subject to a certain degree of freedom introduced by the artist. In other words, we do not expect to have a single explicit function to map the whole image into the world reference frame. In this specific example, distances between the cities and the actual shape of the shoreline is not consistent across the image.

Our objective is to find a function $f : \Omega_t \rightarrow \mathbb{R}^2$ defining the displacement of each point from target to source domain. This allows the creation of a *target* image I_t by interpolating all the points of the source image with the mapping function $M(q) = q + f(q)$ such that

$$I_t(q) = I_s\big(M(q)\big) \tag{1}$$

and $M(q_i) = p_i \;\; \forall (p_i, q_i) \in Cp$ (i.e. all the control points are mapped exactly between source and destination). In computer-vision terms, f is the optical-flow function densely mapping pixels from I_t to I_s.

2.1 Saliency Tensor Map

The fact that the important pictorial information should be preserved when transforming the source image implies a concept of *perceptually salient content* that must be identified a-priori. In the field of image retargeting, the problem is usually addressed by defining a saliency map $S(p) : \Omega_s \rightarrow [0, 1]$ to quantify the importance of each point of the source image. Such saliency map can be computed automatically from the source image [2] or obtained by directly drawing on it to customize the importance of each pixel [3]. In both the cases, the saliency map is a scalar field over the image domain used to weight the amount of stretching allowed in an area.

Since we require directional context-based constraints, we explicitly model a possible non isotropic response of the saliency map. In other words, the amount of stretching is made not only spatially but also directionally dependent. We start by considering a scalar saliency field S provided by the user to create a rank-2 tensor field T on Ω_t. Such tensor assign to each point $q \in \Omega_t$ a 2×2 matrix defined as:

$$T(q) = k_1 S\big(M(q)\big)\mathbf{I} + k_2 H(q), \quad H = W \star \left(\nabla I_t \nabla I_t^T\right) \tag{2}$$

where k_1 and k_2 are two parameters to weight the scalar and directional contribution of the saliency, $\mathbf{I}$ is the identity matrix and H is a structure tensor computed over a window W.

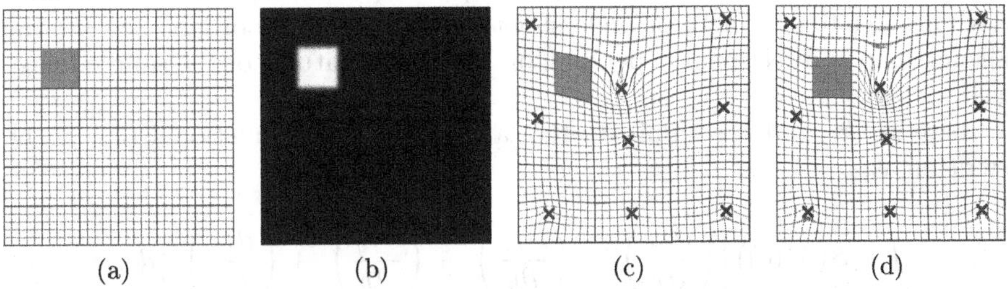

Fig. 2. Effect of the saliency map in our approach. (a) Synthetically generated source image showing a regular grid. (b) A toy-sample saliency map with high values for the pixels corresponding with the coloured square on the source image. (c) Retargeted image with constant saliency (i.e. all the pixels have the same visual importance). Retargeted image using the saliency map in (b) (Color figure online)

3 Variational Functional

We pose our retargeting problem as the minimization of the functional:

$$E(f) = \int_{\Omega_t} \text{trace}\left(\mathbf{J}_f^T T(q) \mathbf{J}_f\right) dq \tag{3}$$

where $\mathbf{J}_f = \begin{pmatrix} \partial f_x/\partial x & \partial f_x/\partial y \\ \partial f_y/\partial x & \partial f_y/\partial y \end{pmatrix}$ is the Jacobian of f. Equation (3) leads to a variational optimization problem in which we set Neumann boundary conditions for the image borders and Dirichlet boundary conditions $f(q_i) = p_i - q_i$ on the control points. The idea is to find a displacement function f between source and target domains with pre-defined values on the control points and for which the first-order partial derivatives (i.e. the local stretching caused by the mapping) is small in a quadratic sense. Additionally, the amount of stretching allowed in each direction is modulated by the saliency tensor field computed as in (2). According to the calculus of variations, $E(f)$ has a stationary value if the corresponding Euler-Lagrange equations:

$$\begin{aligned} \frac{\partial E}{\partial f_x} - \frac{\partial}{\partial x}\frac{\partial E}{\partial f_x/\partial x} - \frac{\partial}{\partial y}\frac{\partial E}{\partial f_x/\partial y} &= 0 \\ \frac{\partial E}{\partial f_y} - \frac{\partial}{\partial x}\frac{\partial E}{\partial f_y/\partial x} - \frac{\partial}{\partial y}\frac{\partial E}{\partial f_y/\partial y} &= 0 \end{aligned} \tag{4}$$

are satisfied. This lead to a set of PDEs which are solved numerically as described in the following sections.

3.1 Special Cases

In its formulation, our method generalizes other variational warp-based image retargeting techniques [5,10] but with two main differences. First, the Dirichlet boundary conditions are set on the control points and not the image boundaries which are free to overshoot or undershoot the source image borders. Second, the saliency map is directional depending on the linear features of the source image itself.

If we set $k_2 = 0$, we eliminate the latter so that the functional (3) can be rewritten as:

$$\int k_1 S(M(q)) \left[\left(\frac{\partial f_x}{\partial x}\right)^2 + \left(\frac{\partial f_x}{\partial y}\right)^2 + \left(\frac{\partial f_y}{\partial x}\right)^2 + \left(\frac{\partial f_y}{\partial y}\right)^2 \right] dq.$$

To simplify, we assume to already have a saliency map $\hat{S}(q)$, in target space, giving a reasonable approximation of $S\big(M(q)\big)$. According to the Euler-Lagrange equations, the resulting system of PDEs is:

$$\begin{aligned} -2k_1 \hat{S} \Delta f_x &= 0 \\ -2k_1 \hat{S} \Delta f_y &= 0 \end{aligned} \tag{5}$$

where Δ is the Laplace operator. Since the off-diagonal elements of $T(q)$ are equal to 0, each equation depends only on the horizontal and vertical component of f respectively and thus can be computed in parallel as set of elliptic PDEs. The only case in which $\hat{S}(q) = S\big(M(q)\big)$ is when the saliency is constant everywhere. In this case, the deformation is not saliency aware but only depends on the local deformation of the control points (Fig. 2(c)). For all the other cases, we start from an initial approximation of f and we alternate the computation of f and $\hat{S}(q)$ until convergence (See Sect. 4 for details).

4 Numerical Solution

To solve the general problem numerically, we consider a discrete approximation of Ω_s and Ω_t into a regular grid with arbitrary resolution, depending on the required level of detail. Consequently, we transform f into a $M \times N \times 2$ tensor and transform the functional (3) to:

$$\begin{aligned} E(f) = \sum_{u=0}^{N-1} \sum_{v=0}^{M-1} \operatorname{trace}\left(\mathbf{J}_f^T \hat{T}(u,v) \mathbf{J}_f\right) \\ + \sum_{(p,q)\in C_p} \alpha \big(p - M(q)\big)^2. \end{aligned} \tag{6}$$

To let the computation more stable, we substituted the Dirichlet boundary conditions on the control points with a soft $L2$ constraint on the flow values on the control points. Note that, while with this formulation the exact mapping of control points is not guaranteed, for high values of α the effect is negligible. The corresponding Euler-Lagrange equations are thus:

$$\begin{aligned} L_x = 2\delta\alpha(f_x - \hat{f}_x)^2 - 2\hat{T}_{11}\Delta f_x - 2\hat{T}_{12}\Delta f_y &= 0 \\ L_y = 2\delta\alpha(f_y - \hat{f}_y)^2 - 2\hat{T}_{21}\Delta f_x - 2\hat{T}_{22}\Delta f_y &= 0 \end{aligned} \tag{7}$$

where δ is a mixture of Kronecker Deltas centered at $q_1 \dots q_n$ and $\hat{f}$ is the known value of f at the control points. We consider an initial approximation of f obtained by interpolating the control points via multiquadric *radial basis functions* and iteratively modify f over time so that $\partial f_x/\partial t = -L_x$ and $\partial f_y/\partial t = -L_y$. We use a discrete approximation of the Laplace operator computed by convolution and forward finite differences for the time differentiation to solve the PDEs via forward Euler scheme. At each step t, we consider the function computed at previous step $f^{(t-1)}$ to obtain $\hat{T}$ according to Eq. (2).

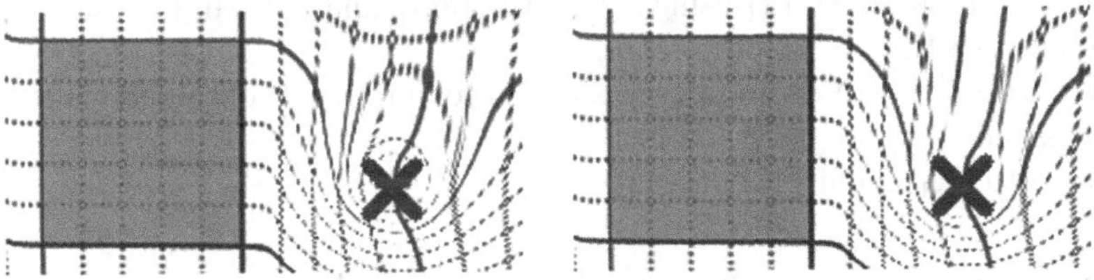

Fig. 3. Effect of the isotonic regression on the resulting distortion map. Left: with no monotonicity constraint singular solutions may cause bubbles around a control point. Right: The isotonic regression step force the resulting mapping to a non-decreasing solution thus removing such artifacts.

4.1 Avoiding the Fold Overs

Variational functional of Eq. (6) pose only constraints on the smoothness of the obtained warp but not on its monotonicity. Before starting the optimization, we compute an initial global affine transformation of the control points so that global rotations or flips of the source domain with respect to target domain are eliminated. After that, we expect that $M(u,v) \leqslant M(u+1,v)$ and $M(u,v) \leqslant M(u,v+1)$ for each point of the domain. If such constraint is violated, the resulting topology of the retargeted I_t will be no longer consistent with the original image lattice. In particular, we obtain flip overs on the warped image that manifest themselves as bubbles around the control points (See Fig. 3).

To avoid this, during the optimization we alternate the computation of f with a projection to a new space to obtain the closest approximation f^i of f (in $L2$ terms) but with the additional constraint that each row of f^i_y and each column of f^i_x are non-decreasing. This is performed by using the isotonic regression technique [4] applied in parallel to the rows and columns of f. Overall, the numerical optimization is performed by alternating the following steps:

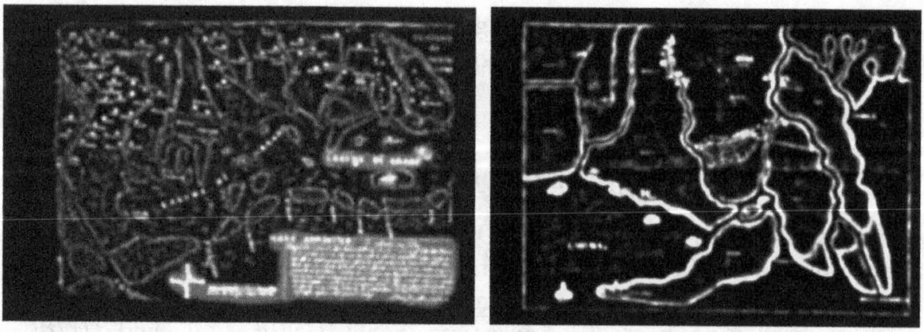

Fig. 4. The saliency map of Faventini 1734 (Left) and Unknown 1624 (Right) used for our experiments

1. Let f^0 be an initial interpolation of the control points using RBF
2. Compute $\hat{T}$ as in Eq. (2) using $f^{(t-1)}$ to approximate M and ∇I_t
3. Use forward Euler schema to compute $f^{(t)}$
4. Substitute $f^{(t)}$ with its non-decreasing approximation f^i obtained via isotonic regression
5. Return to step 2 until convergence.

5 Experimental Evaluation

We qualitatively tested our approach on three historical maps held at the State Archive of Venice (Italy). The first, (Fig. 5, left), drawn by Giovanni Battista Faventini in 1734, represents the costal line of the Marano and Grado's lagoon (NE Italy) and the mainland comprised between Tagliamento and Isonzo rivers[1]; the second (Fig. 5, right), drawn by unknown artist in 1624 circa, characterizes the town of Grado and surrounding territories up to Terzo and Fiumicello villages[2]. The third map, (Fig. 7, top-left) also sketched by unknown artist in the 17th century, depicts the lower part of the Friuli region up to the marshes surrounding Grado. These maps were chosen as good example of map content rich of iconographic elements and loosely accurate with respect to the real cartographic features.

In all the cases, the saliency map was generated in a semi-supervised way. Specifically, we first computed the Difference of Gaussian of the input images and then re-normalized the result in range $[0 \ldots 1]$. Then, we manually painted on top of the saliency map the areas in which interesting iconographic features (like the compass rose or the place names) were present. For reference, saliency maps for the images used in our experiments are shown in Figs. 4 and 7 (top-right) respectively. Note that the intended usage of the saliency is not to define areas of the historical map in which the cartographic information is more accurate but

[1] Gio. Battista Faventini in 1734, ASV, Senato Rettori, F. 232, d. 1.
[2] Unknown,1624, Dispacci Rettori di Palma, F.21, d. 1 + part.

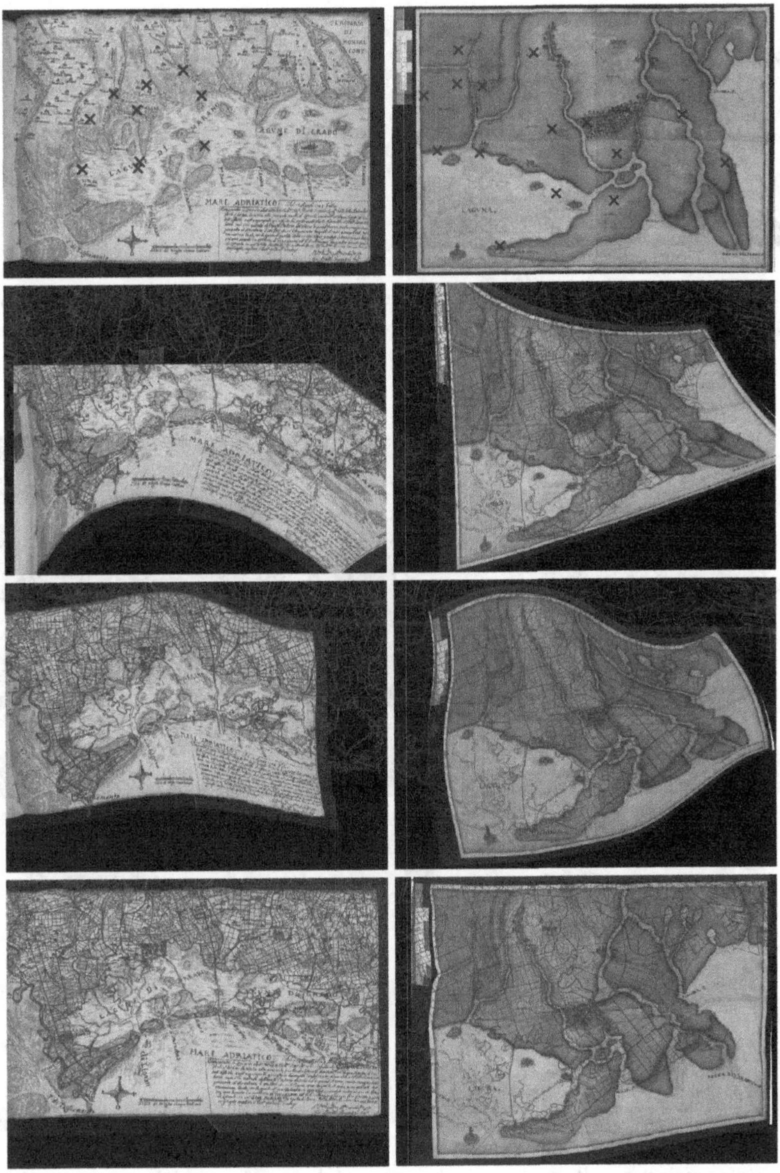

Fig. 5. Comparison between our algorithm and point-based warping methods for two different historical maps (left column: Faventini, 1734; right column: Unknown, 1624). First row: original map with the control points and saliency map superimposed. Second row: Second degree polynomial warping. Third row: Thin-plate spline warping. Fourth row: our proposed method. Note how our retargeting approach enables a better georeferentiation of the input picture while minimizing local distortions of the symbolism, geomorphology and the place names. Images courtesy of State Archive of Venice. (Color figure online)

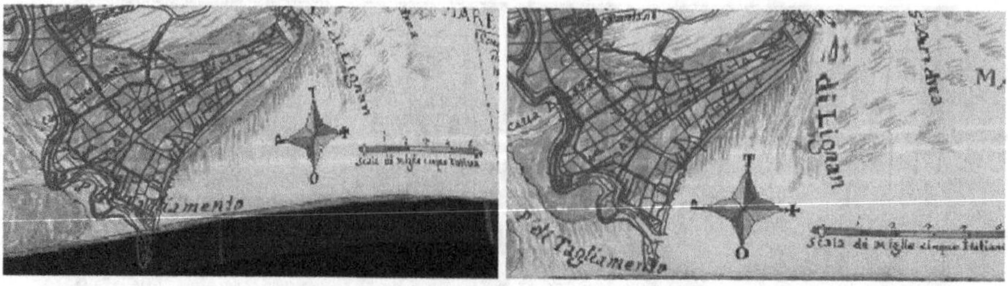

Fig. 6. Detail of the local stretching affecting the compass rose on the bottom of the Faventini 1734 map shown in Fig. 5 after processing with TPS (Left) and our method (Right).

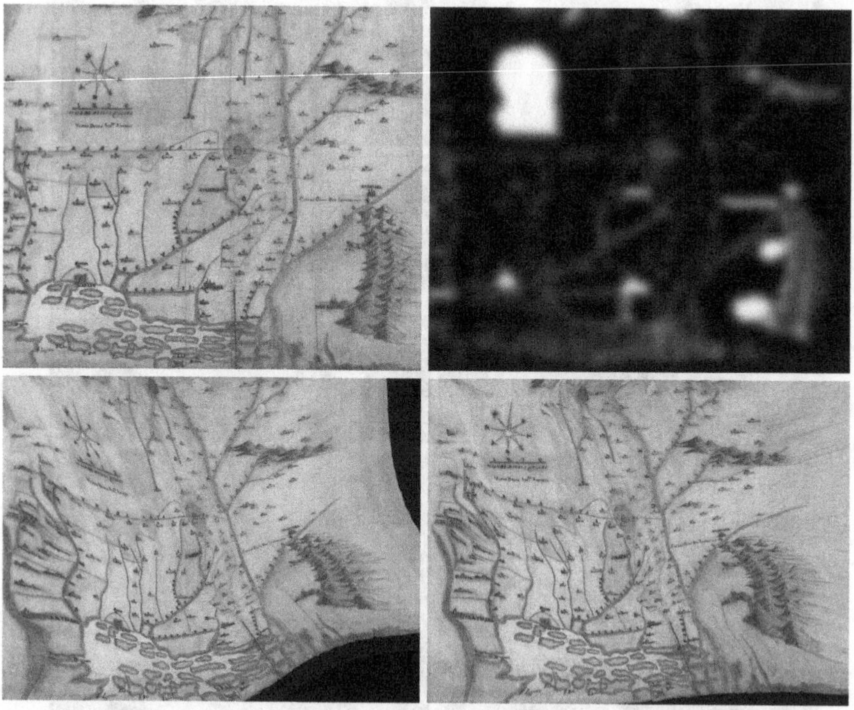

Fig. 7. Retargeting result on a complex pictorial map for which the control point placement causes a highly non-uniform distortion. Top-left: Original image. Top-right: Saliency map in which we manually gave high importance to the pictorial content of the map (see the white blob corresponding to the compass rose). Bottom-left: warping via cubic thin-plate spline. Bottom-right: retargeting computed with our proposed method. Note how our result is less "extreme" while still preserving the correct positioning of the elements. Moreover, the purely pictorial content expressed by the saliency map is retargeted with almost no distortion. Images courtesy of State Archive of Venice (Raccolta Terkuz, n. 34)

simply to mark the elements (mostly iconographic) for which the local deformation should be minimum. We ran our optimization using $k_1 = 1.0$, $k_2 = 10$, $\alpha = 100$ and a Gaussian 5×5 window W for the computation of structure tensor in all the cases.

In Fig. 5 we compare the result obtained with our technique (bottom row) against two common image warping techniques implemented in QGIS, namely: second degree polynomial and thin plate splines (TPS). We superimposed the actual national base map of the area (red lines) to highlight the overall map fitting accuracy to the geographical features. Since both polynomial and TPS are designed to work with cartographic maps and satellite images, they give the same importance to each pixel of the map. This result in often too exaggerated distortions in the attempt to satisfy each control point constraint. In both the cases, our approach gives a more natural result minimizing the local stretch for areas both far from the control points or subject to low visual saliency.

To better highlight this behavior, in Fig. 6 we show a magnification of the bottom area of the first map comprising both the shoreline and purely iconographic elements (i.e. the compass rose and the scale bar). While the shoreline correctly overlaps the actual cartography in both the cases, the shape and orientation of the two iconographic elements are better preserved with our method. In particular, the direction of the compass rose is correctly aligned with the cardinal directions and the scale bar is maintained horizontal and free to strong deformations. This is a peculiar feature of our method, that can exploit a saliency tensor field to selectively limit the distortion on specific parts of the map. In fact, we observe an actual re-positioning of all the high-saliency elements of the map more than a typical warping we obtain with interpolation approaches commonly implemented in GIS. This is further shown in Fig. 7 where we compare our method against cubic thin-plate splines on what we consider the most challenging historical map in our set.

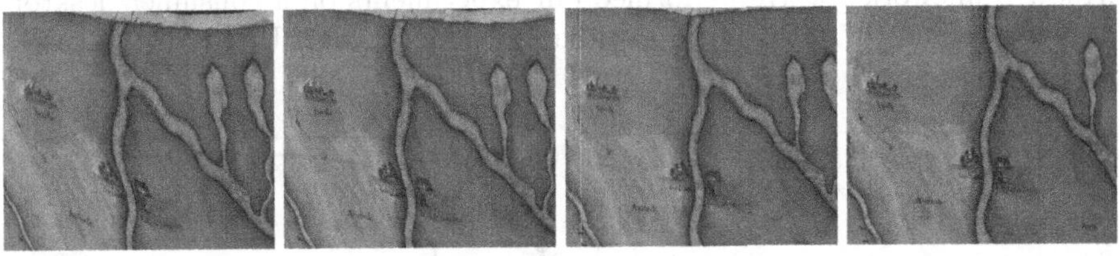

Fig. 8. Detail of the local stretching of the upper part of the 1624 (Unknown) map shown in Fig. 5 (right column) throughout the optimization. From left to right: retargeted image after 0, 5000, 20000 and 40000 iterations. The saliency tensor allows the rivers to warp more freely along their extent instead of between the banks. This way, the thickness of the linear features is preserved. Note also how the appearance of the two cities evolve toward a low distortion configuration without changing their relative position in the georeferenced image.

To visualize the evolution of the flow during the optimization, in Fig. 8 we show a magnification of the top area of the map shown in Fig. 5 (Left) at different iterations of our algorithm. The process starts with an RBF interpolation (left-most image) of the displacement computed for each control point. Since the interpolation is not aware of the saliency map, we can observe a strong deformation of the two stylized cities and their related captions. During the iterations, the stretching affecting the two cities is smoothly reduced in accordance to the high value on the saliency map. The effect is particularly visible on the most southern city (Grado), far from any control point and hence implicitly allowed to move. On the other hand, the control point just on top on the north-west city cause a strong deformation of the land eastbound it since no salient content is present. Other interesting observations can be made by analyzing the shape of the rivers among the cities. Consistent with placement of the control points, the intersection of the two main rivers moves easterly during the optimization. However, thanks to the tensor form of the saliency component, the algorithm smoothly modifies the relative angle of the two rivers (and thus their length) without changing their thickness. This is notably evident on the river oriented north-south for which the relative movement is orthogonal to its linear extent. This behavior is remarkably important as it contributes to preserve the overall visual appearance of the original map.

5.1 Implementation Details and Running Times

We designed our method so that it can be implemented in terms of convolutions and simple arithmetical operations among tensors of rank 2 and 3. In practice, we observed that is computationally more efficient to use a very simple variational solver (Forward-Euler) with a small time-step instead of a sophisticated integration scheme that do not scale well when retargeting high resolution maps.

We implemented our method using the Python version of the popular TensorFlow framework [1]. We performed our experiments on a consumer desktop PC, with an Intel i7 CPU and a Nvidia GeForce 1060 GPU. In all the cases,

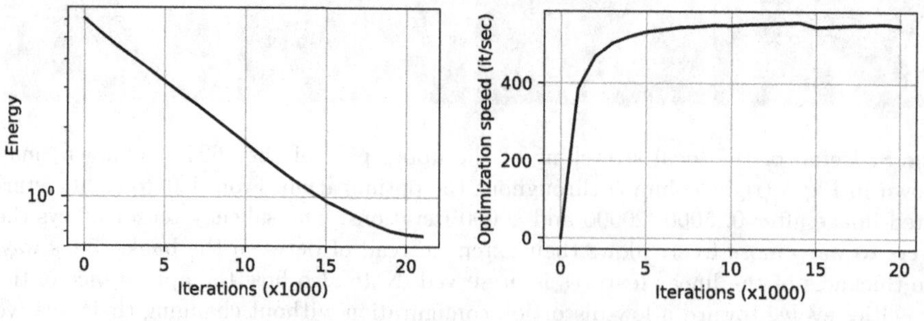

Fig. 9. Left: Evolution of the energy functional (6) throughout the iterations. Right: Optimization speed in iterations per second. Both plots refer to the map (Raccolta Terkuz, n. 34) presented in Fig. 7

flow function was scaled during the optimization to a rank-3 tensor with shape $(256, 256, 2)$ and the time delta Δ_t for the Forward-Euler scheme was set to $5E - 6$. In Fig. 9 we plotted the value of the energy functional (6) during the optimization (left plot) and the number of iterations per second (right plot) while optimizing the map presented in Fig. 7. With the parameters used for our tests, the whole optimization took 25000 to converge to a minimum at a speed of 520 iterations per second on average. This implies a total time ranging between 40 s to a minute to perform a full map retargeting.

6 Conclusion

We proposed a novel technique to perform dense continuous image retargeting driven by a set of control points. It was designed at georeferencing historical maps for which the local distortion of the pictorial content is dynamically adjusted according to a saliency tensor depending both on a saliency map defined by the user and the structure tensor computed on the image itself. This allows part of the map to be warped smoothly to accomodate the control points while preserving the local stretching of purely pictorial content (like the common compass roses) that are seamlessly re-positioned in the resulting image.

Our algorithm involves an optimization of an energy functional based on the calculus of variation that can be efficiently implemented in GPU by means of convolutions and tensor operations, commonly implemented in many frameworks designed for Convolutional Neural Networks and Deep Learning. During the optimization, we included an isotonic regression step to avoid visual artifact in the resulting displacement map. The isotonic regression guarantees that no flip-overs will be present in the retargeted output, even in presence of extreme local stretching that may happen when warping maps not created for cartographic purposes. Qualitative tests performed on original historical maps demonstrate the effectiveness of our approach especially when handling multiple pictorial elements. At the present state, our method still requires human intervention in the definition of the control points and the saliency map. For the near future, we plan to automate the saliency map creation by exploiting some of the existing approaches in the literature and implement our method as a QGIS plugin.

References

1. Abadi, M., et al.: TensorFlow: Large-scale machine learning on heterogeneous systems (2015). https://www.tensorflow.org/. Software available from tensorflow.org
2. Achanta, R., Süsstrunk, S.: Saliency detection for content-aware image resizing. In: Proceedings of the 16th IEEE International Conference on Image Processing, ICIP 2009, pp. 1001–1004. IEEE Press, Piscataway (2009)
3. Avidan, S., Shamir, A.: Seam carving for content-aware image resizing. ACM Trans. Graph. **26**(3) (2007). https://doi.org/10.1145/1276377.1276390
4. Chakravarti, N.: Isotonic median regression: a linear programming approach. Math. Oper. Res. **14**(2), 303–308 (1989). https://doi.org/10.1287/moor.14.2.303

5. Gal, R., Sorkine, O., Cohen-Or, D.: Feature-aware texturing. In: Proceedings of the 17th Eurographics Conference on Rendering Techniques, EGSR 2006, Eurographics Association, Aire-la-Ville, Switzerland, Switzerland, pp. 297–303 (2006). https://doi.org/10.2312/EGWR/EGSR06/297-303
6. Guo, Y., Liu, F., Shi, J., Zhou, Z.H., Gleicher, M.: Image retargeting using mesh parametrization. IEEE Trans. Multimedia **11**(5), 856–867 (2009). http://dblp.uni-trier.de/db/journals/tmm/tmm11.html#GuoLSZG09
7. Lin, S.S., Yeh, I.C., Lin, C.H., Lee, T.Y.: Patch-based image warping for content-aware retargeting. IEEE Trans. Multimedia **15**(2), 359–368 (2013). http://dblp.uni-trier.de/db/journals/tmm/tmm15.html#LinYLL13
8. Pritch, Y., Kav-Venaki, E., Peleg, S.: Shift-map image editing. In: ICCV, pp. 151–158. IEEE Computer Society (2009). http://dblp.uni-trier.de/db/conf/iccv/iccv2009.html#PritchKP09
9. Rubinstein, M., Shamir, A., Avidan, S.: Multi-operator media retargeting. ACM Trans. Graph. **28**(3) (2009). http://dblp.uni-trier.de/db/journals/tog/tog28.html#RubinsteinSA09
10. Shamir, A., Sorkine, O.: Visual media retargeting. In: ACM SIGGRAPH ASIA 2009 Courses, SIGGRAPH ASIA 2009, pp. 11:1–11:13. ACM, New York (2009). https://doi.org/10.1145/1665817.1665828
11. Wang, Y.S., Tai, C.L., Sorkine, O., Lee, T.Y.: Optimized scale-and-stretch for image resizing. ACM Trans. Graph. **27**(5), 118 (2008). http://dblp.uni-trier.de/db/journals/tog/tog27.html#WangTSL08
12. Wolf, L., Guttmann, M., Cohen-Or, D.: Non-homogeneous content-driven video-retargeting. In: ICCV, pp. 1–6. IEEE Computer Society (2007). http://dblp.uni-trier.de/db/conf/iccv/iccv2007.html#WolfGC07
13. Zhang, G.X., Cheng, M.M., Hu, S.M., Martin, R.R.: A shape-preserving approach to image resizing. Comput. Graph. Forum **28**(7), 1897–1906 (2009)

Deep Transfer Learning for Art Classification Problems

Matthia Sabatelli[1(✉)], Mike Kestemont[2], Walter Daelemans[3], and Pierre Geurts[1]

[1] Montefiore Institute, Department of Electrical Engineering and Computer Science, Université de Liège, Liège, Belgium
{m.sabatelli,p.geurts}@uliege.be

[2] Antwerp Center for Digital Humanities and Literary Criticism (ACDC), Universiteit Antwerpen, Antwerp, Belgium
mike.kestemont@uantwerpen.be

[3] CLiPS, Computational Linguistics Group, Universiteit Antwerpen, Antwerp, Belgium
walter.daelemans@uantwerpen.be

Abstract. In this paper we investigate whether Deep Convolutional Neural Networks (DCNNs), which have obtained state of the art results on the ImageNet challenge, are able to perform equally well on three different art classification problems. In particular, we assess whether it is beneficial to fine tune the networks instead of just using them as off the shelf feature extractors for a separately trained softmax classifier. Our experiments show how the first approach yields significantly better results and allows the DCNNs to develop new selective attention mechanisms over the images, which provide powerful insights about which pixel regions allow the networks successfully tackle the proposed classification challenges. Furthermore, we also show how DCNNs, which have been fine tuned on a large artistic collection, outperform the same architectures which are pre-trained on the ImageNet dataset only, when it comes to the classification of heritage objects from a different dataset.

Keywords: Deep Convolutional Neural Networks · Art classification
Transfer learning · Visual attention

1 Introduction and Related Work

Over the past decade Deep Convolutional Neural Networks (DCNNs) have become one of the most used and successful algorithms in Computer Vision (CV) [10,18,30]. Due to their ability to automatically learn representative features by incrementally down sampling the input via a set of non linear transformations, these kind of Artificial Neural Networks (ANNs) have rapidly established themselves as the state of the art algorithm on a large set of CV problems. Within different CV testbeds large attention has been paid to the ImageNet challenge [9], a CV benchmark that aims to test the performances of different image classifiers on a dataset that contains one million natural images distributed over thousand different classes. The availability of such a large dataset, combined with the possibility of training ANNs in parallel over several GPUs [17], has lead

L. Leal-Taixé and S. Roth (Eds.): ECCV 2018 Workshops, LNCS 11130, pp. 631–646, 2019.
https://doi.org/10.1007/978-3-030-11012-3_48

to the development of a large set of different neural architectures that have continued to outperform each other over the years [7,13,14,25,27].

A promising research field in which the classification performances of such DCNNs can be exploited is that of *Digital Heritage* [22]. Due to a growing and rapid process of digitization, museums have started to digitize large parts of their cultural heritage collections, leading to the creation of several digital open datasets [3,20]. The images constituting these datasets are mostly matched with descriptive metadata which, as presented in e.g. [20], can be used to define a set of challenging machine learning tasks. However, the number of samples in these datasets is far smaller than those in, for instance, the ImageNet challenge and this can become a serious constraint when trying to successfully train DCNNs from scratch.

The lack of available training data is a well known issue in the Deep Learning community and is one of the main reasons that has led to the development of the research field of Transfer Learning (TL). The main idea of TL consists of training a machine learning algorithm on a new task (e.g. a classification problem) while exploiting knowledge that the algorithm has already learned on a previously related task (a different classification problem). This machine learning paradigm has proved to be extremely successful in Deep Learning, where it has been shown how DCNNs that were trained on many large datasets [15,26], were able to achieve very promising results on classification problems from heterogeneous domains, ranging from medical imaging [28] or gender recognition [32] over plant classification [24] to galaxy detection [2].

In this work we explore whether the TL paradigm can be successfully applied to three different art classification problems. We use four neural architectures that have obtained strong results on the ImageNet challenge in recent years and we investigate their performances when it comes to attributing the *authorship* to different artworks, recognizing the *material* which has been used by the artists in their creations, and identifying the *artistic category* these artworks fall into. We do so by comparing two possible approaches that can be used to tackle the different classification tasks. The first one, known as off the shelf classification [23], simply retrieves the features that were learned by the DCNNs on other datasets and uses them as input for a new classifier. In this scenario the weights of the DCNN do not change during the training phase, and the final, top-layer classifier is the only component of the architecture which is actually trained. This changes in our second explored approach, known as fine tuning, where the weights of the original DCNNs are "unfrozen" and the neural architectures are trained together with the final classifier.

Recent work [16] has shown the benefits that this particular pre-training approach has. In particular, DCNNs which have been trained on the ImageNet challenge typically lead to superior results when compared to the same architectures trained from scratch. However, this is not necessarily beneficial and in some cases DCNNs that are randomly initialized are able to achieve the same performances as ImageNet pre-trained models. However, none of the results presented in [16] have been applied to datasets containing heritage objects, it is thus still an open question how such pre-trained DCNNs would perform in such a classification scenario. Below, we extensively study the performance of these DCNNs; at the same time we assess whether better TL performances can be obtained when using DCNNs that, in addition to the ImageNet dataset, have additionally been pre-trained on a large artistic collection.

Contributions and Outline: This work contributes to the field of (Deep) TL applied to art classification problems. It does so by investigating if DCNNs, which have been originally trained on problems that are very dissimilar and far from art classification, can still perform well in such a different domain. Moreover, assuming this is the case, we explore if it is possible to improve on such performances. The paper is structured as follows: in Sect. 2 we present a theoretical introduction to the field of TL, a description of the datasets that we have used and the methodological details about the experiments that we have performed. In Sect. 3 we present and discuss our results. A summary of the main contributions of this work together with some ideas for possible future research is finally presented in Sect. 4.

2 Methods

We now present the methods that underpin our research. We start by giving a brief formal definition of TL. We then introduce the three classification tasks under scrutiny, together with a brief description of the datasets. Finally, we present the neural architectures that we have used for our experiments.

2.1 Transfer Learning

A supervised learning (SL) problem can be identified by three elements: an input space $\mathcal{X}_t$, an output space $\mathcal{Y}_t$, and a probability distribution $p_t(x,y)$ defined over $\mathcal{X}_t \times \mathcal{Y}_t$ (where t stands for 'target', as this is the main problem we would like to solve). The goal of SL is then to build a function $f : \mathcal{X}_t \rightarrow \mathcal{Y}_t$ that minimizes the expectation over $p_t(x,y)$ of a given loss function ℓ assessing the predictions made by f:

$$E_{(x,y)\sim p_t(x,y)}\{\ell(y, f(x))\}, \tag{1}$$

when the only information available to build this function is a learning sample of input-output pairs $LS_t = \{(x_i, y_i)|i = 1, \ldots, N_t\}$ drawn independently from $p_t(x,y)$. In the general transfer learning setting, one assumes that an additional dataset LS_s, called the source data, is available that corresponds to a different, but related, SL problem. More formally, the source SL problem is assumed to be defined through a triplet $(\mathcal{X}_s, \mathcal{Y}_s, p_s(x,y))$, where at least either $\mathcal{X}_s \neq \mathcal{X}_t$, $\mathcal{Y}_s \neq \mathcal{Y}_t$, or $p_s \neq p_t$. The goal of TL is then to exploit the source data LS_s together with the target data LS_t to potentially find a better model f in terms of the expected loss (1) than when only LS_t is used for training this model. Transfer learning is especially useful when there is a lot of source data, whereas target data is more scarce.

Depending on the availability of labels in the target and source data and on how the source and target problems differ, one can distinguish different TL settings [21]. In what follows, we assume that labels are available in both the source and target data and that the input spaces $\mathcal{X}_t$ and $\mathcal{X}_s$, that both correspond to color images, match. Output spaces and joint distributions will however differ between the source and target problems, as they will typically correspond to different classification problems (ImageNet object recognition versus art classification tasks). Our problem is thus an instance of *inductive transfer learning* [21]. While several inductive transfer learning algorithms exist, we focus here on model transfer techniques, where information between the source and target problems is exchanged in the form of a DCNN model pre-trained on the source data. Although potentially suboptimal, this approach has the advantage of being more computationally efficient, as it does not require to train a model using both the source and the target data.

2.2 Datasets and Classification Challenges

For our experiments we use two datasets which come from two different heritage collections. The first one contains the largest number of samples and comes from the Rijksmuseum in Amsterdam[1]. On the other hand, our second 'Antwerp' dataset is much smaller. This dataset presents a random sample that is available as open data from a larger heritage repository: DAMS (Digital Asset Management System)[2]. This repository can be searched manually via the web-interface or queried via a Linked Open Data API. It aggregates the digital collections of the foremost GLAM institutions (Galleries, Libraries, Archives, Museums) in the city of Antwerp in Belgium. Thus, this dataset presents a varied and representative sample of the sort of heritage data that is nowadays being collected at the level of individual cities across the globe. While it is much smaller, its coverage of cultural production is similar to that of the Rijksmuseum dataset and presents an ideal testing ground for the transfer learning task under scrutiny here.

Both image datasets come with metadata encoded in the Dublin Core metadata standard [31]. We selected three well-understood classification challenges: (1) "material classification" which consists in identifying the material the different heritage objects are made of (e.g. paper, gold, porcelain, ...); (2) "type classification" in which the DCNNs have to classify in which artistic category the samples fall into (e.g. print, sculpture, drawing, ...), and finally (3) "artist classification", where the main goal is to appropriately match each sample of the dataset with its creator (from now on we refer to these classification tasks as challenge 1, 2 and 3 respectively). As reported in Table 1 we can see how the Rijksmuseum collection is the dataset with the largest amount of samples per challenge (N_t) and the highest amount of labels to classify (Q_t). Furthermore it is also worth noting that there was no metadata available when it comes to the first classification challenge for the Antwerp dataset (as marked by the $\times$ symbol), and how there are some common labels between the two heritage collections when it comes to challenge 2. A visualization reporting some of the images present in both datasets can be seen in Fig. 1.

We use 80% of the datasets for training while the remaining 2 x 10% is used for validation and testing respectively. Furthermore, we ensure that only classes which occur at least once in all the splits are used for our experiments. Naturally, in order to keep all comparisons fair between neural architectures and different TL approaches, all experi-

[1] https://staff.fnwi.uva.nl/t.e.j.mensink/uva12/rijks/.

[2] https://dams.antwerpen.be/.

Table 1. An overview of the two datasets that are used in our experiments. Each color of the table corresponds to a different classification challenge, starting from challenge 1 which is represented in yellow, challenge 2 in blue and finally challenge 3 in red. Furthermore we represent with N_t the amount of samples constituting the datasets and with Q_t the number of labels. Lastly, we also report if there are common labels between the two heritage collections.

Challenge	Dataset	N_t	Q_t	% of overlap
Material	Rijksmuseum	110,668	206	None
	Antwerp	$\times$	$\times$	
Type	Rijksmuseum	112,012	1,054	
	Antwerp	23,797	920	≈ 15%
Artist	Rijksmuseum	82,018	1,196	None
	Antwerp	18,656	903	

Fig. 1. A visualization of the images that are used for our experiments. It is possible to see how the samples range from images representing plates made of porcelain to violins, and from Japanese artworks to a more simple picture of a key.

ments have been performed on the exact same data splits which, together with the code used for all our experiments, are publicly released to the CV community[3].

2.3 Neural Architectures and Classification Approaches

For our experiments we use four pre-trained DCNNs that have all obtained state of the art results on the ImageNet classification challenge. The neural architectures are VGG19 [25], Inception-V3 [27], Xception [7] and ResNet50 [34]. We use the implementations of the networks that are provided in the Keras Deep Learning library [8]

3 https://github.com/paintception/Deep-Transfer-Learning-for-Art-Classification-Problems.

together with their appropriate `Tensorflow` weights [1] that come from the `Keras` official repository as well. Since all architectures have been built in order to deal with the ImageNet dataset we replace the final classification layer of each network with a new one. This final layer simply consists of a new *softmax* output, with as many neurons as there are classes, which follows a 2D global average pooling operation. We rely on this dimensionality reduction step because we do not add any fully connected layers between the last convolution block and the *softmax* output. Hence, in this way we are able to obtain a feature vector, $\mathcal{X}$, out of the rectified activation feature maps of the network that can be properly classified. Since all experiments are treated as a multi-class classification problem we use the *categorical crossentropy* function as the loss function of the DCNNs.

We investigate two possible classification approaches that are based on the previously mentioned pre-trained architectures. The first one, denoted as off the shelf classification, only trains a final *softmax* classifier on $\mathcal{X}$, which is retrieved from the different DCNNs after performing one forward pass of the image through the network[4]. This approach is intended to explore whether the features that are learned by the DCNNs on the ImageNet challenge are informative enough in order to properly train a machine learning classifier on the previously introduced art classification challenges. If this would be the case, such pre-trained models could be used as appropriate feature extractors without having to rely on expensive `GPU` computations for training. Naturally, they would only require the training of the final classifier without having to compute any backpropagation operations over the entire network.

Our second approach is generally known as fine tuning and differs from the previous one by the fact that together with the final *softmax* output the entire DCNN is trained as well. This means that unlike the off the shelf approach, the entirety of the neural architecture gets "unfrozen" and is optimized during training. The potential benefit of this approach lies in the fact that the DCNNs are independently trained on samples coming from the artistic datasets, and thus their classification predictions are not restricted by what they have previously learned on the ImageNet dataset only. Evidently, such an approach is computationally more demanding.

In order to maximize the performances of the DCNNs we take the work presented in [19] into consideration and train them with a relatively small batch size of 32 samples. We do not perform any data augmentation operations besides a standard pixel normalization to the $[0,1]$ range and a re-scaling operation which resizes the images to the input size that is required by the different DCNNs. Regarding the stochastic optimization procedures of the different classifiers, we use two different optimizers, that after preliminary experiments, turned out to be the best performing ones. For the off the shelf approach we use the RMSprop optimizer [29] which has been initialized with its default hyperparameters (learning rate = 0.001, a *momentum* value $\rho = 0.9$ and $\varepsilon = 1e-08$). On the other hand, when we fine tune the DCNNs we use the standard (and less greedy) Stochastic Gradient Descent (SGD) algorithm with the same learning rate, 0.001, and a

[4] Please note how instead of a *softmax* layer any kind of machine learning classifier can be used instead. We experimented with both Support Vector Machines (SVMs) and Random Forests but since the results did not significantly differ between classifiers we decided to not include them here.

Nesterov Momentum value set to 0.9. Training has been controlled by the *Early Stopping* method [6] which interrupted training as soon as the validation loss did not decrease for 7 epochs in a row. The model which is then used on the testing set is the one which obtained the smallest validation loss while training.

To the best of our knowledge, so far no work has been done in systematically assessing to which extent DCNNs pre-trained on the ImageNet dataset could also be used as valuable architectures when tackling art classification problems. Furthermore, it is also not known whether the fine tuning approach would yield better results when compared to the off the shelf one and if using such pre-trained ANNs would yield better performances than training the same architectures from scratch as observed by [16]. In the coming section we present new results that aim to answer these research questions.

3 Results

Our experimental results are divided in two different sections, depending on which kind of dataset has been used. We first report the results that we have obtained when using architectures that were pre-trained on the ImageNet dataset only, and aimed to tackle the three classification problems of the Rijksmuseum dataset that were presented in Sect. 2.2. We report these results in Sect. 3.1 in which we explore the benefits of using the ImageNet dataset as the TL source data, and how well such pre-trained DCNNs generalize when it comes to artistic images. We then present the results from classifying the Antwerp dataset, using DCNNs that are both pre-trained on the ImageNet dataset and on the Rijksmuseum collection in Sect. 3.3. We investigate whether these neural architectures, which have already been trained to tackle art classification problems before, perform better than the ones which have been trained on the ImageNet dataset only.

All results show comparisons between the off the shelf classification approach and the fine tuning scenario. In addition to that, in order to establish the potential benefits that TL from ImageNet has over training a DCNN from scratch, we also report the results that have been obtained when training one DCNN with weights that have been initially sampled from a "He-Uniform" distribution [12]. Since we take advantage of work [4] we use the Inception-V3 architecture. We refer to it in all figures as Scratch-V3 and visualize it with a solid orange line. Figures 2 and 3 report the performances in terms of accuracies that the DCNNs have obtained on the validation sets. While the performances that the neural architectures have obtained on the final testing set are reported in Tables 2 and 3.

3.1 From Natural to Art Images

The first results that we report have been obtained on the "material" classification challenge. We believe that this can be considered as the easiest classification task within the ones that we have introduced in Sect. 2.2 for two main reasons. First, the number of possible classes the ANNs have to deal with is more than five times smaller when compared to the other two challenges. Furthermore, we also believe that this classification task is, within the limits, the most similar one when compared to the original ImageNet challenge. Hence, the features that might be useful in order to classify the different natural images on the latter classification testbed might be not too dissimilar from the ones that are needed to properly recognize the material that the different samples of the Rijksmuseum collection are made of. If this would be the case we would expect very close performances between the off the shelf classification approach and the fine tuning one. Comparing the learning curves of the two classification strategies in Fig. 2, we actually observe that the fine tuning approach leads to significant improvements when compared to the off the shelf one, for three architectures out of the four tested ones. Note however that, in support of our hypothesis, the off the shelf approach can still reach high accuracy values on this problem and is also competitive with the DCNN trained from scratch. This suggests that features extracted from networks pretrained on ImageNet are relevant for material classification.

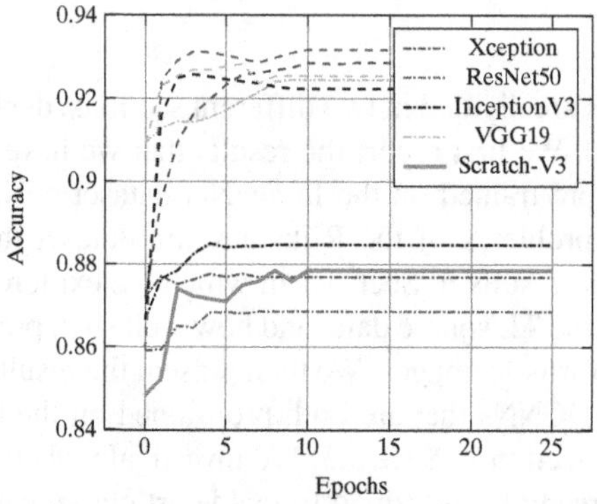

Fig. 2. Comparison between the fine tuning approach versus the off the shelf one when classifying the material of the heritage objects of the Rijksmuseum dataset. We observe how the first approach (as reported by the dashed lines) leads to significant improvements when compared to the latter one (reported by the dash-dotted lines) for three out of four neural architectures. Furthermore, we can also observe how training a DCNN from scratch leads to worse results when compared to fine-tuned architectures which have been pre-trained on ImageNet (solid orange line). (Color figure online)

The ResNet50 architecture is the DCNN which, when fine tuned, performs overall best when compared to the other three ANNs. This happens despite it being the DCNN that initially performed worse as a simple feature extractor in the off the shelf experiments. As reported in Table 2 we can see how this kind of behavior reflects itself on the separated testing set as well, where it obtained the highest testing set accuracy when fine tuned (92.95%), and the lowest one when the off the shelf approach was used (86.81%). It is worth noting how the performance between the different neural architectures do not strongly differ between each other once they are fine tuned, with all DCNNs performing around ≈92% on the final testing set. Furthermore, special attention needs to be given to the VGG19 architecture, which does not seem to benefit from the fine tuning approach as much as the other architectures do. In fact, its off the shelf performance on the testing set (92.12%) is very similar to its fine tuned one (92.23%). This suggests that this neural architecture is actually the only one which, in this task, and when pre-trained on ImageNet, can successfully be used as a simple feature extractor without having to rely on complete retraining.

When analyzing the performances of the different neural architectures on the "type" and "artist" classification challenges (respectively the left and right plots reported in Fig. 3), we observe how the fine tuning strategy leads to even more significant improvements when compared to what has been observed in the previous experiment. The results obtained on the second challenge show again how the ResNet50 architecture is the DCNN which leads to the worse results if the off the shelf approach is used (its testing set accuracy is as low as 71.23%) and similarly to what has been observed before, it then becomes the best performing ANN when fine tuned, with a final accuracy of 91.30%. Differently from what has been observed in the previous experiment, the VGG19 architecture, despite being the ANN performing best when used as off the shelf feature extractor, this time performs significantly worse than when it is fine tuned, which highlights the benefits of this latter approach. Similarly to what has been observed before, our results are again not significantly in favor of any neural architecture once they are fine tuned, with all final accuracies being around ≈91%.

If the classification challenges that we have analyzed so far have highlighted the significant benefits of the fine tuning approach over the off the shelf one, it is also important to note that the latter approach is still able to lead to satisfying results. In fact, accuracies of 92.12% have been obtained when using the VGG19 architecture on the first challenge and a classification rate of 77.33% was reached by the same architecture on the second challenge. Despite the latter accuracy being very far in terms of performance from the one obtained when fine tuning the network (90.27%), it still shows how DCNNs pre-trained on ImageNet do learn particular features that can also be used for classifying the "material" and the "type" of heritage objects. However, when analyzing the results from the "artist" challenge, we can see that this is partially not the case anymore.

For the third classification challenge, the Xception, ResNet50, and Inception-V3 architectures all perform extremely poorly if not fine tuned, with the latter two DCNNs not being able to even reach a 10% classification rate. Better results are obtained when using the VGG19 architecture, which reaches a final accuracy of 38.11%. Most importantly, all performances are again significantly improved when the networks are fine tuned. As already observed in the previous experiments, ResNet50 outperforms the others on the validation set. However, on the test set (see Table 2), the overall best performing network is Inception-V3 (with a final accuracy of 51.73%), which suggests that ResNet50 suffered from overfitting. It is important to state two major important points about this set of experiments. The first one relates to the final classification accuracies which have been obtained, and that at first sight might seem disappointing. It is true that these classification rates are significantly lower when compared to the ones obtained in the previous two experiments. However, it is important to highlight how a large set of artists present in the dataset are associated to an extremely limited amount of samples. This reflects a lack of appropriate training data which does not allow the DCNNs to learn all the features that are necessary to successfully deal with this particular classification challenge. In order to do so, we believe that more training data is required.

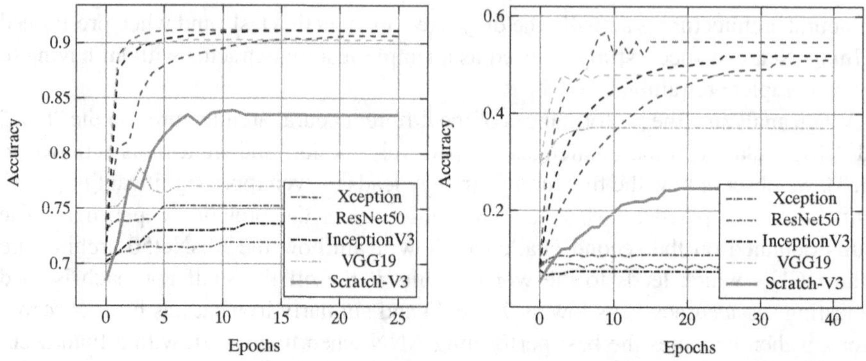

Fig. 3. A similar analysis as the one which has been reported in Fig. 2 but for the second and third classification challenges (left and right figures respectively). The results show again the significant benefits that fine tuning (reported by the dashed line plots) has when compared to the off the shelf approach (reported by the dash-dotted lines) and how this latter strategy miserably under-performs when it comes to artist classification. Furthermore we again see the benefits that using a pre-trained DCNN has over training the architecture from scratch (solid orange line). (Color figure online)

Moreover, it is worth pointing out how despite performing very poorly when used as off the shelf feature extractors, ImageNet pre-trained models do still perform better once they are fine tuned than the DCNN which is trained from scratch. This suggests that these networks do learn potentially representative features when it comes to challenge 3, but in order to properly exploit them, the DCNNs need to be fine tuned.

3.2 Discussion

In the previous section, we have investigated whether four different DCNNs pre-trained on the ImageNet dataset can be successfully used to address three art classification problems. We have observed how this is particularly the case when it comes to classifying the material and types, where in fact, the off the shelf approach can already lead to satisfactory results. However, most importantly, we have also shown how these performances are always significantly improved if the DCNNs are fine tuned and how an ImageNet initialization is beneficial over training the networks from scratch. Furthermore, we have discovered how the pre-trained DCNNs fail if used as simple feature extractors when having to attribute the authorship to the different heritage objects. In the next section, we want now to explore if the fine tuned DCCNs can lead to better performances, when tackling two of the already seen classification challenges on a different heritage collection. For this problem, we will again compare the off the shelf approach with the fine tuning one.

3.3 From One Art Collection to Another

Table 3 compares the results that have been obtained on the Antwerp dataset when using ImageNet pre-trained DCNNs (which are identified by θ) versus the same architectures

Table 2. An overview of the results obtained by the different DCNNs on the testing set when classifying the heritage objects of the Rijksmuseum. Bold results report the best performing architectures overall. The additional columns "Params" and "$\mathcal{X}$" report the amount of parameters the ANNs have to learn and the size of the feature vector which is used as input for the softmax classifier.

Challenge	DCNN	off the shelf	fine tuning	Params	$\mathcal{X}$
1	Xception	87.69%	92.13%	21K	2048
1	InceptionV3	88.24%	92.10%	22K	2048
1	ResNet50	86.81%	**92.95%**	24K	2048
1	VGG19	**92.12%**	92.23%	20K	512
2	Xception	74.80%	90.67%	23K	2048
2	InceptionV3	72.96%	91.03%	24K	2048
2	ResNet50	71.23%	**91.30%**	25K	2048
2	VGG19	**77.33%**	90.27%	20K	512
3	Xception	10.92%	51.43%	23K	2048
3	InceptionV3	.07%	**51.73%**	24K	2048
3	ResNet50	.08%	46.13%	26K	2048
3	VGG19	**38.11%**	44.98%	20K	512

fine tuned on the Rijksmuseum dataset ($\widehat{\theta}$). Similarly to the results presented in the previous section the first blue block of the table refers to the "type" classification task, while the red one reports the results obtained on the "artist" classification challenge.

While looking at the performances of the different neural architectures two interesting results can be highlighted. First, DCNNs which have been fine tuned on the Rijksmuseum dataset outperform the ones pre-trained on ImageNet in both classification challenges. This happens to be the case both when the DCNNs are used as simple feature extractors and when they are fine tuned. On the "type" classification challenge, this result is not surprising since, as discussed in Sect. 2.2, the types corresponding to the heritage objects of the two collections partially overlap. This is more suprising on the "artist" classification challenge however, since there is no overlap at all between the artists of the Rijksmuseum and the ones from the Antwerp dataset. A second interesting result, which is consistent with the results in the previous section, is the observation that it is always beneficial to fine tune the DCNNs over just using them as off the shelf feature extractors. Once the ANNs get fine tuned on the Antwerp dataset, these DCNNs, which have also been fine tuned on the Rijksmuseum dataset, outperform the architectures which have been pre-trained on ImageNet only. This happened to be the case for both classification challenges and for all considered architectures, as reported in Table 3. This demonstrates how beneficial it is for DCNNs to have been trained on a similar source task and how this can lead to significant improvements both when the networks are used as feature extractors and when they are fine tuned.

Table 3. The results obtained on the classification experiments performed on the Antwerp dataset with DCNNs which have been initially pre-trained on ImageNet (θ) and the same architectures which have been fine tuned on the Rijksmuseum dataset ($\widehat{\theta}$). Our results show how the latter pre-trained DCNNs yield better results both if used as off the shelf feature extractors and if fine tuned.

Challenge	DCNN	θ + off the shelf	$\widehat{\theta}$ + off the shelf	θ + fine tuning	$\widehat{\theta}$ + fine tuning
2	Xception	42.01%	62.92%	69.74%	72.03%
2	InceptionV3	43.90%	57.65%	70.58%	71.88%
2	ResNet50	41.59%	**64.95%**	76.50%	**78.15%**
2	VGG19	38.36%	60.10%	70.37%	71.21%
3	Xception	48.52%	**54.81%**	58.15%	58.47%
3	InceptionV3	21.29%	53.41%	56.68%	57.84%
3	ResNet50	22.39%	31.38%	62.57%	**69.01%**
3	VGG19	49.90%	53.52%	54.90%	60.01%

3.4 Selective Attention

The benefits of the fine tuning approach over the off the shelf one are clear from our previous experiments. Nevertheless, we do not have any insights yet as to what exactly allows fine tuned DCNNs to outperform the architectures which are pre-trained on ImageNet only. In order to provide an answer to that, we investigate which pixels of each input image contribute the most to the final classification predictions of the DCNNs. We do this by using the "VisualBackProp" algorithm presented by [5], which is able to identify which feature maps of the DCNNs are the most informative ones with respect to the final predictions of the network. Once these feature maps are identified, they get backpropagated to the original input image, and visualized as a saliency map according to their weights. The higher the activation of the filters, the brighter the set of pixels covered by these filters are represented.

The results that we have obtained provide interesting insights about how fine tuned DCNNs develop novel selective attention mechanisms over the images, which are very different from the ones that characterize the networks that are pre-trained on ImageNet. We report the existence of these mechanisms in Fig. 4 where we visualize the different saliency maps between a DCNN pre-trained on ImageNet and the same neural architecture which has been fine tuned on the Rijksmuseum collection (specifically renamed RijksNet[5]). On the left side of Fig. 4 we visualize which sets of pixels allow the fine tuned DCNN to successfully classify an artist of the Rijksmuseum collection that the same architecture was not able to initially recognize. It is possible to notice how the saliency maps of the latter architecture either correspond to what is more similar to a natural image, as present in the ImageNet dataset (e.g. the buildings of the first and third images), or even to non informative pixels at all, as shown by the second image. However, the fine tuned DCNN shows how these saliency maps change towards the set

[5] To show these results we have used the VGG19 architecture since it provided a better integration with the publicly available source code of the algorithm which can be found at https://github.com/raghakot/keras-vis.

of pixels that correspond to the portions of the images representing people in the bottom, suggesting that this is what allows the DCNN to appropriately recognize the artist. Similarly, on the right side of the figure we report which parts of the original image are the most useful ones when it comes to classify the type of the reported heritage object, which in this case corresponds to a glass wall of a church. We can see how the pre-trained architecture only identifies as representative pixels the right area above the arch, which turned out to be not informative enough for properly classifying this sample of the Rijksmuseum dataset. However, once the DCNN gets fine tuned we clearly see how in addition to the previously highlighted area a new saliency map occurs on the image, corresponding to the text description below the represented scene. It turns out that the presence of text is a common element below the images that represent clerical glass windows and as a consequence it is recognized by the fine tuned DCNN as a representative feature.

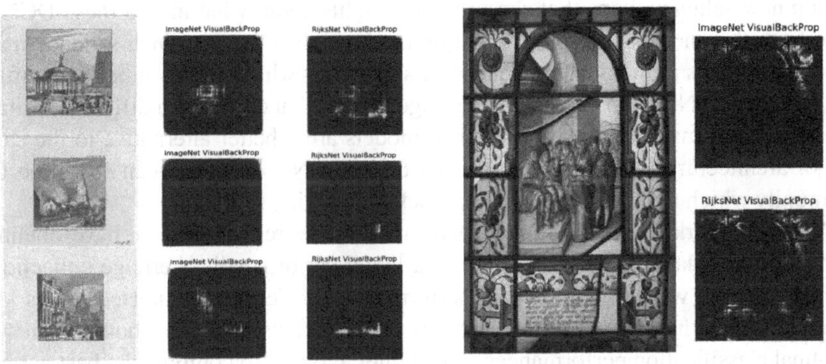

Fig. 4. A visualization that shows the differences between which sets of pixels in an image are considered informative for a DCNN which is only pre-trained on ImageNet, compared to the same architecture which has also been fine tuned on the Rijksmuseum collection. It is clear how the latter neural network develops novel selective attention mechanisms over the original image.

These observations can be related to parallel insights in authorship attribution research [11], an established task from Natural Language Processing that is highly similar in nature to artist recognition. In this field, preference is typically given to high-frequency function words (articles, prepositions, particles etc.) over content words (nouns, adjectives, verbs, etc.), because the former are generally considered to be less strongly related to the specific content or topic of a work. As such, function words or stop words lend themselves more easily to attribution across different topics and genres. In art history, strikingly similar views have been expressed by the well-known scholar Giovanni Morelli (1816–1891), who published seminal studies in the field of artist recognition [33]. In Morelli's view too, the attribution of a painting could not happen on the basis of the specific content or composition of a painting, because these items were too strongly influenced by the topic of a painting or the wishes of a patron. Instead, Morelli proposed to base attributions to so-called *Grundformen* or small, seemingly insignificant details that occur frequently in all paintings and typically show clear traces of an artist's individual style, such as ears, hands or feat, a painting's function words, so to speak. The saliency maps above reveal a similar shift in attention when the ImageNet weights are adapted on the Rijksmuseum data: instead of focusing on higher-level content features, the network shifts its attention to lower layers in the network, seemingly focusing on insignificant details, that nevertheless appear crucial to perform artist attribution.

4 Conclusion

This paper provides insights about the potential that the field of TL has for art classification. We have investigated the behavior of DCNNs which have been originally pre-trained on a very different classification task and shown how their performances can be improved when these networks are fine tuned. Moreover, we have observed how such neural architectures perform better than if they are trained from scratch and develop new saliency maps that can provide insights about what makes these DCNNs outperform the ones that are pre-trained on the ImageNet dataset. Such saliency maps reflect themselves in the development of new features, which can then be successfully used by the DCNNs when classifying heritage objects that come from different heritage collections. It turns out that the fine tuned models are a better alternative to the same kind of architectures which are pre-trained on ImageNet only, and can serve the CV community which will deal with similar machine learning problems.

As future work, we aim to investigate whether the results that we have obtained on the Antwerp dataset will also apply to a larger set of smaller heritage collections. Furthermore, we want to explore the performances of densely connected layers [14] and understand which layers of the currently analyzed networks contribute the most to their final classification performances. This might allow us to combine the best parts of each neural architecture into one single novel DCNN which will be able to tackle all three classification tasks at the same time.

Acknowledgements. The authors wish to acknowledge Jeroen De Meester (Museums and Heritage Antwerp) for sharing his expertise on the Antwerp dataset. The research for this project was financially supported by BELSPO, Federal Public Planning Service Science Policy, Belgium, in the context of the BRAIN-be project: "INSIGHT. Intelligent Neural Systems as InteGrated Heritage Tools".

References

1. Abadi, M., Barham, P., Chen, J., Chen, Z., Davis, A., Dean, J., Devin, M., Ghemawat, S., Irving, G., Isard, M., et al.: Tensorflow: a system for large-scale machine learning. In: OSDI, vol. 16, pp. 265–283 (2016)
2. Ackermann, S., Schawinksi, K., Zhang, C., Weigel, A.K., Turp, M.D.: Using transfer learning to detect galaxy mergers. Mon. Not. Roy. Astronom. Soc. **479**, 415–425 (2018)
3. Allen, N.: Collaboration through the colorado digitization project. First Monday **5**(6) (2000)
4. Bidoia, F., Sabatelli, M., Shantia, A., Wiering, M.A., Schomaker, L.: A deep convolutional neural network for location recognition and geometry based information. In: Proceedings of the 7th International Conference on Pattern Recognition Applications and Methods, ICPRAM 2018, 16–18 January 2018, Funchal, Madeira, Portugal, pp. 27–36 (2018)

5. Bojarski, M., et al.: Visualbackprop: efficient visualization of CNNs. arXiv preprint arXiv:1611.05418 (2016)
6. Caruana, R., Lawrence, S., Giles, C.L.: Overfitting in neural nets: backpropagation, conjugate gradient, and early stopping. In: Advances in Neural Information Processing Systems, pp. 402–408 (2001)
7. Chollet, F.: Xception: Deep learning with depthwise separable convolutions. arXiv preprint (2016)
8. Chollet, F., et al.: Keras (2015)
9. Deng, J., Dong, W., Socher, R., Li, L.J., Li, K., Fei-Fei, L.: Imagenet: a large-scale hierarchical image database. In: IEEE Conference on Computer Vision and Pattern Recognition, CVPR 2009, pp. 248–255. IEEE (2009)
10. Donahue, J., et al.: DeCAF: a deep convolutional activation feature for generic visual recognition. In: International Conference on Machine Learning, pp. 647–655 (2014)
11. Efstathios, S.: A survey of modern authorship attribution methods. J. Am. Soc. Inf. Sci. Technol. **3**, 538–556 (2009). https://doi.org/10.1002/asi.21001
12. He, K., Zhang, X., Ren, S., Sun, J.: Delving deep into rectifiers: surpassing human-level performance on imagenet classification. In: Proceedings of the IEEE International Conference on Computer Vision, pp. 1026–1034 (2015)
13. He, K., Zhang, X., Ren, S., Sun, J.: Deep residual learning for image recognition. In: Proceedings of the IEEE Conference on Computer Vision and Pattern Recognition, pp. 770–778 (2016)
14. Huang, G., Liu, Z., Weinberger, K.Q., van der Maaten, L.: Densely connected convolutional networks. In: Proceedings of the IEEE Conference on Computer Vision and Pattern Recognition, vol. 1 (2017)
15. Huang, G.B., Ramesh, M., Berg, T., Learned-Miller, E.: Labeled faces in the wild: a database for studying face recognition in unconstrained environments. Technical report 07–49, University of Massachusetts, Amherst (2007)
16. Kornblith, S., Shlens, J., Le, Q.V.: Do better imagenet models transfer better? arXiv preprint arXiv:1805.08974 (2018)
17. Krizhevsky, A., Sutskever, I., Hinton, G.E.: Imagenet classification with deep convolutional neural networks. In: Advances in Neural Information Processing Systems, pp. 1097–1105 (2012)
18. Ma, L., Lu, Z., Shang, L., Li, H.: Multimodal convolutional neural networks for matching image and sentence. In: Proceedings of the IEEE International Conference on Computer Vision, pp. 2623–2631 (2015)
19. Masters, D., Luschi, C.: Revisiting small batch training for deep neural networks. arXiv preprint arXiv:1804.07612 (2018)
20. Mensink, T., Van Gemert, J.: The rijksmuseum challenge: museum-centered visual recognition. In: Proceedings of International Conference on Multimedia Retrieval, p. 451. ACM (2014)
21. Pan, S.J., Yang, Q.: A survey on transfer learning. IEEE Trans. Knowl. Data Eng. **22**, 1345–1359 (2010)
22. Parry, R.: Digital heritage and the rise of theory in museum computing. In: Museum Management and Curatorship, pp. 333–348 (2005)
23. Razavian, A.S., Azizpour, H., Sullivan, J., Carlsson, S.: CNN features off-the-shelf: an astounding baseline for recognition. In: 2014 IEEE Conference on Computer Vision and Pattern Recognition Workshops (CVPRW), pp. 512–519. IEEE (2014)
24. Reyes, A.K., Caicedo, J.C., Camargo, J.E.: Fine-tuning deep convolutional networks for plant recognition. In: CLEF (Working Notes) (2015)
25. Simonyan, K., Zisserman, A.: Very deep convolutional networks for large-scale image recognition. arXiv preprint arXiv:1409.1556 (2014)

26. Stallkamp, J., Schlipsing, M., Salmen, J., Igel, C.: The German traffic sign recognition benchmark: a multi-class classification competition. In: The 2011 International Joint Conference on Neural Networks (IJCNN), pp. 1453–1460. IEEE (2011)
27. Szegedy, C., Vanhoucke, V., Ioffe, S., Shlens, J., Wojna, Z.: Rethinking the inception architecture for computer vision. In: Proceedings of the IEEE Conference on Computer Vision and Pattern Recognition, pp. 2818–2826 (2016)
28. Tajbakhsh, N., et al.: Convolutional neural networks for medical image analysis: full training or fine tuning? IEEE Trans. Med. Imaging **35**, 1299–1312 (2016)
29. Tieleman, T., Hinton, G.: Lecture 6.5-rmsprop: divide the gradient by a running average of its recent magnitude. In: COURSERA: Neural Networks for Machine Learning, pp. 26–31 (2012)
30. Tomè, D., Monti, F., Baroffio, L., Bondi, L., Tagliasacchi, M., Tubaro, S.: Deep convolutional neural networks for pedestrian detection. Sig. Process.: Image Commun. **47**, 482–489 (2016)
31. Weibel, S., Kunze, J., Lagoze, C., Wolf, M.: Dublin core metadata for resource discovery. Technical report (1998)
32. van de Wolfshaar, J., Karaaba, M.F., Wiering, M.A.: Deep convolutional neural networks and support vector machines for gender recognition. In: 2015 IEEE Symposium Series on Computational Intelligence, pp. 188–195. IEEE (2015)
33. Wollheim, R.: On Art and the Mind. Essays and Lectures. Allen Lane, London (1972)
34. Xie, S., Girshick, R., Dollár, P., Tu, Z., He, K.: Aggregated residual transformations for deep neural networks. In: 2017 IEEE Conference on Computer Vision and Pattern Recognition (CVPR), pp. 5987–5995. IEEE (2017)

Reflecting on How Artworks Are Processed and Analyzed by Computer Vision

Sabine Lang(✉) and Björn Ommer

Heidelberg Collaboratory for Image Processing, IWR, Heidelberg University, Heidelberg, Germany
{sabine.lang,bjorn.ommer}@iwr.uni-heidelberg.de

Abstract. The intersection between computer vision and art history has resulted in new ways of seeing, engaging and analyzing digital images. Innovative methods and tools have assisted with the evaluation of large datasets, performing tasks such as classification, object detection, image description and style transfer or assisting with a form and content analysis. At this point, in order to progress, past works and established practices must be revisited and evaluated on the ground of their usability for art history. This paper provides a reflection from an art historical perspective to point to erroneous assumptions and where improvements are still needed.

Keywords: Computer vision · Art history · Critical reflection · Distant viewing · Close reading · Object detection · Image description · Style transfer

1 Introduction

For some time, computer vision and art history are in close collaboration: scholars from both fields work together to find innovative ways to process large digital image sets. These new approaches are beneficial for research, because they offer new modes of how digital images can be seen or analyzed. Computational technologies enable a large scale evaluation and a close-up study, including classification, object retrieval, or a form and content analysis. For computer vision a collaboration is beneficial, since existing algorithms are tested and modified due to new requirements imposed by artistic data. In parallel, art history is compelled to question established methods and terms: how do we describe images and what do we mean by 'style'? At this point, in order to progress, we must revisit past works: how are images produced, processed and understood? Which problematic assumptions have been held? The objective of this paper is to provide a critical

Electronic supplementary material The online version of this chapter (https://doi.org/10.1007/978-3-030-11012-3_49) contains supplementary material, which is available to authorized users.

L. Leal-Taixé and S. Roth (Eds.): ECCV 2018 Workshops, LNCS 11130, pp. 647–652, 2019.
https://doi.org/10.1007/978-3-030-11012-3_49

reflection, point to problems and research gaps. The paper especially focuses on aspects of distant viewing versus close reading, object detection, image description and style transfer.

2 Image Analysis in Computer Vision and the Arts

Digital art history, which refers to the "use of analytical techniques enabled by computational technology" [6], is the result of the meeting between computer vision and art history. The presence of large art datasets eventually required efficient computational methods and tools to process and evaluate them. Works included diverse tasks, such as classification, object detection, image description or style transfer. Karayev et al. [15] classified artworks according to style; [27] used a deep convolutional model to categorize images according to genre, style and artist. Other works performed object detection in paintings: classifiers were trained on natural images [4] and paintings or on both to measure the domain shift problem [5]. Karpathy et al. [16] addressed the task of an automatic image description; [21] simultaneously annotated, classified and segmented objects in natural images. Recently, scholars focused on transferring artistic styles to natural images, utilizing deep neural networks [10] or generative adversarial networks [32] – most relied on a single input image. In art history, scholars have been concerned with similar topics for a long time: Warburg (1866–1929) used reproductions of artworks to map 'the afterlife of antiquity' [29], resembling current distant viewing efforts [13]. Art historians also discussed topics of image analysis or style: contributions have been made by Riegl (1858–1905) [25] or Wölfflin (1864–1945), who used a comparative method to study artworks and formulated his five principles of art history [31]. With his iconographical-iconological method, Erwin Panofsky (1892–1968) established a framework for image understanding and description [12]. Digital humanities scholars have (critically) reflected on the impact of technologies on these traditional practices [1,17], for example, pointed to the loose usage of terms and uninterrogative nature of many works. On the basis of current works in computer vision, the paper engages in a critical discussion.

3 Reflecting on a Computer-Based Image Analysis

Distant Viewing and Close Reading. Art historians aim to understand works of art: why did artists depict a certain subject matter or use a specific color? To find answers, they study images in detail and within a wider context. In the past, scholars in digital art history have commented on the fact that computer-based works focused on a quantitative analysis of data, thus only identifying patterns without providing an interpretation [1,17]. While more recently, a qualitative analysis has been added, scholars either facilitate a distant viewing approach or answer more pointed questions on the basis of individual artworks. Works, such as the analysis of strokes in a limited collection of drawings by Picasso, Matisse, Egon Schiele and Modigliani to identify forgeries [8] or an 'Automatic Thread-Level Canvas Analysis' to conclude whether or not two paintings were made from the same canvas [22], evaluate artworks in detail and show impressive results, but are not applicable on a large scale, because they require specific, costly data, and lack contextualization. Similar, projects utilizing distant viewing mostly remain pure visualizations [23], produce little new knowledge and rarely add a top-down approach to explain origins of patterns [7]. However for art history, an either-or-stance is insufficient [3]; in order to be relevant, an analysis must be quantitative and qualitative.

Finding Objects in Paintings. Object detection in paintings has been based on a quantitative analysis [4,5], where retrieval systems are mostly conditioned on ImageNet. The visual database contains over fourteen millions of well-aligned natural images gathered alongside pre-defined contemporary categories. While systems confidently detect objects, such as dogs, persons or other modern categories, in naturalistic images, they fail, when confronted with objects belonging to pre-modern times. Failure cases occur for medieval objects or clothing and pre-modern architecture, because systems are simply unfamiliar with these categories. Algorithms are further challenged by less standardized and complex compositions, which are manifold in art. Further complications arise, when the content of an artwork is distorted due to perspective or abstraction. In its current state, many models for object detection are not feasible for art history; to train models directly on art data would be one solution to overcome some limitations [30].

Describing Artworks. Art history and computer vision are both concerned with image description and work has been done to automatize this step [14,16]. While results on natural images may be convincing, the question remains, if the variety of subject matters, objects or styles in art can be correctly grasped by models and descriptions resemble those of art historians. A full image description of Gustave Courbet's *La Rencontre* (1854), using Panofsky's iconographical-iconological method, can be found in the supplementary material and establishes requirements of an art historical description: the method includes a pre-iconographical description, which identifies the manner in which objects are expressed, an iconographical analysis of symbols and motifs, and a placement within a wider historic and biographical context – the iconological analysis [12]. A model for an automatic image description must be able to perform a formal and semantic analysis of the artwork, preferably considering fore-, middle-, and background, understand its composition and relations between objects. Also, it must recognize symbols and cultural conventions and place the image in a wider context. What is possible so far? Works [16] have proven that models can generate descriptions of regions, thereby providing formal descriptors of, for example, color or material and identifying objects correctly. Thus, approaches mostly provide a formal description, but are unable to produce an iconographical or iconological analysis. Although the linkage to other historical digital sources might give further information about artworks, networks do not possess knowledge about symbols and pictorial or cultural conventions. A closer evaluation of works from an art historical perspective reveals further issues: most examples lack to provide an account of the image's composition or relations between objects; also computer vision mainly performs a single image description and misses a comparison or broader contextualization. However, some works have addressed these issues and studied how objects in images are related by utilizing relative attributes, thereby capturing semantic relationships [24], and identified salient regions [19]. Also, instead of images with simple compositions, more challenging datasets [18] were used, where the complexity is representative of those in artworks. While these approaches are first steps, they are still not sufficient. Automatic models might create a descriptive list of image components, however, it remains the task of art historians to create the story: to interpret artworks and position them within a wider context.

Style Refers to Formal Qualities. Style transfer is a current task in computer vision, where a natural image is being rendered in, for example, the style of Picasso or van Gogh [10,32]. For art history, these works are relevant, because they lead to a reassessment of the term style; however, works are based on some problematic assumptions. The often used expression 'in the style of...' implies that an artist is bound to a single style. However, if we look at Picasso, we find works in many different styles: in an academic, Cubist or Surrealist manner. In the context of style transfer, style mainly refers to color, shape or brush stroke; other formal features, such as composition or modeling of figures, and content are neglected. This is again highlighted, when we look at the referenced styles: most common are Impressionism, Post-Impressionism, Expressionism, Cubism or Abstract Art; less visually distinct and content-based styles, such as Gothic Art, Renaissance, Baroque or Surrealism, are absent. Results then illustrate that style transfer works best with heavy visual styles and when naturalistic images display structure on planar regions the network produces random artifacts. In computer vision artistic style is assumed to be static, but not as it is its nature dynamic and evolving. A last point refers to the fact that style transfer is mostly based on one image [10,11]. However, a single artwork might not display all aspects of a style; a portrait in an Impressionistic style accentuates different style constituents, which a landscape painting in the same style does not. Just as one has to look at the whole image to make a style judgment, because shape or light contrasts vary in different regions, it is necessary to utilize a collection of images in the same style. The work by [26] shows that using multiple instead of single images produces stylistically more convincing results.

4 Conclusion

The paper reflected on the topics of distant viewing versus close reading, object detection, an automatic image description and style transfer. It aimed to highlight problematic assumptions and where work has yet to be done. Computer vision has provided powerful tools to analyze artworks quantitatively and qualitatively, thereby creating verification and new knowledge for art history. In turn, the discipline contributes from how art history approaches, describes and interprets images. An evaluation of previous work is valuable in that it forces both disciplines to reflect on existing terms and practices. Eventually, there is great potential, when scholars from both fields work together, and there are still topics, which require our attention: the study of sculptures [9] or architecture, preservation and documentation of cultural heritage through digital reconstruction and 3D modeling [2,28], detection of forgeries [20] or provenance research being some examples.

References

1. Bishop, C.: Against digital art history. Int. J. Digi. Art Hist. (3), 123–133 (2018)
2. Boeykens, S., Maekelberg, S., De Jonge, K.: (Re-) creating the past: 10 years of digital historical reconstructions using bim. Int. J. Digit. Art Hist. (3), 63–87 (2018)
3. Bonfiglioli, R., Nanni, F.: From close to distant and back: how to read with the help of machines. In: Gadducci, F., Tavosanis, M. (eds.) HaPoC 2015. IAICT, vol. 487, pp. 87–100. Springer, Cham (2015). https://doi.org/10.1007/978-3-319-47286-7_6
4. Crowley, E.J., Zisserman, A.: In search of art. In: Agapito, L., Bronstein, M.M., Rother, C. (eds.) ECCV 2014. LNCS, vol. 8925, pp. 54–70. Springer, Cham (2015). https://doi.org/10.1007/978-3-319-16178-5_4
5. Crowley, E.J., Zisserman, A.: The art of detection. In: Hua, G., Jégou, H. (eds.) ECCV 2016. LNCS, vol. 9913, pp. 721–737. Springer, Cham (2016). https://doi.org/10.1007/978-3-319-46604-0_50
6. Drucker, J.: Is there a "digital" art history? Visual Resour. **29**(1–2), 5–13 (2013)
7. Drucker, J., Helmreich, A., Lincoln, M., Rose, F.: Digital art history: la scène américaine. une discussion entre johanna drucker, anne helmreich et matthew lincoln, introduite et modérée par francesca rose. Perspective. Actualité en histoire de l'art (2), 27–42 (2015)
8. Elgammal, A., Kang, Y., Leeuw, M.D.: Picasso, matisse, or a fake? Automated analysis of drawings at the stroke level for attribution and authentication. arXiv preprint arXiv:1711.03536 (2017)
9. Fouhey, D.F., Gupta, A., Zisserman, A.: 3D shape attributes. In: Proceedings of the IEEE Conference on Computer Vision and Pattern Recognition, pp. 1516–1524 (2016)
10. Gatys, L.A., Ecker, A.S., Bethge, M.: A neural algorithm of artistic style. arXiv preprint arXiv:1508.06576 (2015)
11. Gatys, L.A., Ecker, A.S., Bethge, M., Hertzmann, A., Shechtman, E.: Controlling perceptual factors in neural style transfer. In: IEEE Conference on Computer Vision and Pattern Recognition (CVPR), pp. 3730–3738 (2017)
12. Hatt, M., Klonk, C.: Art History: A Critical Introduction to Its Methods. Manchester University Press, Manchester (2006)
13. Hristova, S.: Images as data: cultural analytics and Aby Warburg's Mnemosyne. Int. J. Digit. Art Hist. (2), 117–135 (2016)
14. Johnson, J., Karpathy, A., Fei-Fei, L.: DenseCap: fully convolutional localization networks for dense captioning. In: Proceedings of the IEEE Conference on Computer Vision and Pattern Recognition, pp. 4565–4574 (2016)
15. Karayev, S., et al.: Recognizing image style. arXiv preprint arXiv:1311.3715 (2013)
16. Karpathy, A., Fei-Fei, L.: Deep visual-semantic alignments for generating image descriptions. In: Proceedings of the IEEE conference on Computer Vision and Pattern Recognition, pp. 3128–3137 (2015)

17. Kienle, M.: Digital art history "beyond the digitized slide library": an interview with Johanna Drucker and Miriam Posner. Artl@s Bull. **6**(3), 9 (2017)
18. Kinghorn, P., Zhang, L., Shao, L.: A region-based image caption generator with refined descriptions. Neurocomputing **272**, 416–424 (2018)
19. Krause, J., Johnson, J., Krishna, R., Fei-Fei, L.: A hierarchical approach for generating descriptive image paragraphs. In: 2017 IEEE Conference on Computer Vision and Pattern Recognition (CVPR), pp. 3337–3345. IEEE (2017)
20. Li, J., Yao, L., Hendriks, E., Wang, J.Z.: Rhythmic brushstrokes distinguish van Gogh from his contemporaries: findings via automated brushstroke extraction. IEEE Tran. Pattern Anal. Mach. Intell. **34**(6), 1159–1176 (2012)
21. Li, L.J., Socher, R., Fei-Fei, L.: Towards total scene understanding: classification, annotation and segmentation in an automatic framework. In: IEEE Conference on Computer Vision and Pattern Recognition, CVPR 2009, pp. 2036–2043. IEEE (2009)
22. van der Maaten, L., Erdmann, R.G.: Automatic thread-level canvas analysis: a machine-learning approach to analyzing the canvas of paintings. IEEE Signal Process. Mag. **32**(4), 38–45 (2015)
23. Manovich, L.: How to compare one million images? In: Berry, D.M. (ed.) Understanding Digital Humanities, pp. 249–278. Palgrave Macmillan, London (2012). https://doi.org/10.1057/9780230371934_14
24. Parikh, D., Grauman, K.: Relative attributes. In: 2011 IEEE International Conference on Computer Vision (ICCV), pp. 503–510. IEEE (2011)
25. Riegl, A., Castriota, D., Zerner, H.: Problems of Style: Foundations for a History of Ornament. Princeton University Press, Princeton (1992)
26. Sanakoyeu, A., Kotovenko, D., Lang, S., Ommer, B.: A style-aware content loss for real-time HD style transfer. In: Ferrari, V., Hebert, M., Sminchisescu, C., Weiss, Y. (eds.) ECCV 2018. LNCS, vol. 11212, pp. 715–731. Springer, Cham (2018). https://doi.org/10.1007/978-3-030-01237-3_43
27. Tan, W.R., Chan, C.S., Aguirre, H.E., Tanaka, K.: Ceci n'est pas une pipe: a deep convolutional network for fine-art paintings classification. In: 2016 IEEE International Conference on Image Processing (ICIP), pp. 3703–3707. IEEE (2016)
28. Underhill, J.: In conversation with CyArk: digital heritage in the 21st century. Int. J. Digit. Art Hist. (3), 111–123 (2018)
29. Warburg, A.: Der Bilderatlas Mnemosyne, vol. 2. Akademie Verlag, Berlin (2008)
30. Wilber, M.J., Fang, C., Jin, H., Hertzmann, A., Collomosse, J., Belongie, S.: BAM! the behance artistic media dataset for recognition beyond photography. In: Proceedings of the ICCV, vol. 1, pp. 1211–1220 (2017)
31. Wölfflin, H.: Principles of Art History. Courier Corporation, Chelmsford (2012)
32. Zhu, J.Y., Park, T., Isola, P., Efros, A.A.: Unpaired image-to-image translation using cycle-consistent adversarial networks. In: 2017 IEEE International Conference on Computer Vision (ICCV), pp. 2242–2251. IEEE, October 2017

Seeing the World Through Machinic Eyes: Reflections on Computer Vision in the Arts

Marijke Goeting[1,2](✉)

[1] Radboud University, Nijmegen, The Netherlands
m.goeting@artez.nl
[2] ArtEZ Institute of the Arts, Arnhem, The Netherlands

Abstract. Today, computer vision is broadly implemented and operates in the background of many systems. For users of these technologies, there is often no visual feedback, making it hard to understand the mechanisms that drive it. When computer vision is used to generate visual representations like Google Earth, it remains difficult to perceive the particular process and principles that went into its creation. This text examines computer vision as a medium and a system of representation by analyzing the work of design studio Onformative, designer Bernhard Hopfengärtner and artist Clement Valla. By using technical failures and employing computer vision in unforeseen ways, these artists and designers expose the differences between computer vision and human perception. Since computer vision is increasingly used to facilitate (visual) communication, artistic reflections like these help us understand the nature of computer vision and how it shapes our perception of the world.

Keywords: Art · Design · Perception · Computer vision · Google Earth · Media · Representation · Digital Image

Once we are definitively removed from the realm of direct or indirect observation of synthetic images created by the machine for the machine, instrumental virtual images will be for us the equivalent of what a foreigner's mental pictures already represent: an enigma.

–Paul Virilio

1 Introduction

In his 1994 book *The Vision Machine*, French cultural theorist Paul Virilio worried about the way automated artificial perception might come to influence our perception of the world. His idea of *vision machines* "that would be capable not only of recognising the contours of shapes, but also of completely interpreting the visual field" and that could "analyse the ambient environment and automatically interpret the meaning of events" [1] seems to have become reality. Today,

L. Leal-Taixé and S. Roth (Eds.): ECCV 2018 Workshops, LNCS 11130, pp. 653–670, 2019.
https://doi.org/10.1007/978-3-030-11012-3_50

computer vision is broadly implemented – from automatic passport control to self-driving cars and interactive video games – and used for a variety of tasks: from collecting, processing and analyzing images to even understanding them.

It is significant that Virilio uses the word "interpretation" – a term normally applied to human understanding – to describe the ability of machinic vision. And he is not alone in this. Descriptions of advanced technologies such as computer vision often involve words that are usually associated with human experience. Many writers whose imagination has been captured by recent developments in the field of artificial intelligence, for example, have described intelligent systems like Google's AlphaGo and DeepDream and Apple's Siri as "intuitive", "creative", and even "funny".[2] But applying human characteristics to computers is misleading: it blurs the distinction between the two and creates the illusion that man could be replaced, or at least rivaled, by machines.

For Virilio the threat of computer-based, artificial vision lies in its ability to create mechanized imagery from which we are often excluded. Virilio was concerned at the prospect of automatic perception needing no graphic or videographic output, therewith totally excluding us.[3] And indeed, there are many systems that use computer vision without producing any visual output (think of machine vision used in factories and self-driving cars), and it is true that visual output is not a necessity. Other systems do, however, create visual output that is meant to be seen by both humans and computers (for example QR codes), while yet other systems are designed especially to generate visual output to be seen by us (for example Google Earth). Regardless, with the advent of computer vision, we find ourselves in a new situation. For the first time in history, we are dealing with images that are not only *created* by machines, but that are also meant to be *seen* by machines. We are now in a situation in which we share the perception of our environment with our machinic other. This has given rise to the philosophical problem that Virilio called the "splitting of viewpoint."[1] How can we understand a world seen by a synthetic, sightless vision? What modes of representation are created by it? And how does this affect the way we see the world?

This paper examines computer vision as a medium; as an extension of our sense of sight, as well as of our ability to analyze and recognize what we see, in other words our visual perception as a whole. As media theorist Marshall McLuhan already explained in *Understanding Media: The Extensions of Man* (1964), any extension of our body or mind can be regarded as a medium.[4] Computer vision is such an extension: it is an externalization and automation of visual perception by technological means. Like McLuhan and Virilio, I believe it is important to examine the specific characteristics of computer vision in order to understand its effect on our senses, on our perception of the world, and how it influences a society that increasingly relies on computers to do the looking for us.

For artists and designers who are in the business of not only producing images, but also (and perhaps more importantly) of looking at and understanding images and their effect on us, computer vision has become an important medium – to use *and* to understand. For that reason, I will analyze the work of contemporary artists and designers that are already exploring the possibilities and effects of computer vision. In the past few years, designers and artists like Bernhard Hopfengärtner, studio Onformative, and Clement Valla have been experimenting with the specific characteristics of automated artificial perception and have even viewed computer vision as a particular system of representation. Although the works I have selected are not the most recent works in the field of design and media art, I have chosen them for their capacity to reflect on a diverse range of applications of computer vision (mapping, object recognition, Semacode/QR code and face recognition) while still connected by their use of Google Earth as an artistic medium, and for their ability to shed light on the differences between human and artificial perception. While the advent of convolutional neural networks entails a paradigm shift in the field of computer vision, this technique does not change the basic insights into the nature of perception and computer vision that these artworks provide.

In order to analyze and expand on the ideas that these designers and artists have explored in their work, I will use concepts from the field of media theory and philosophy as developed by Jay David Bolter and Richard Grusin, Beatrice Colomina and Mark Wigley, Anke Coumans, Vilém Flusser, Marc Hansen, Marshall McLuhan, Anna Munster, and Paul Virilio. By looking critically at computer vision as a medium and a system of representation, I hope to advance our understanding of the nature of artificial perception as well as its effect on image culture and visual communication.

2 Gaps in the Landscape: The Paradox of Perspective Imagery as Data

One artwork that investigates the nature of computer vision and its system of representation, is the project *Postcards from Google Earth* (2010-present) by French, Brooklyn-based artist Clement Valla. The work consists of screenshots of strange images found on Google Earth (Fig. 1). While navigating the virtual globe, Valla discovered landscapes that did not meet his expectations, such as bridges that appeared to droop down into valleys they were supposed to cross – like Salvador Dali's watches melting over tables and trees. To Valla, the images he collected felt alien, because they seem to be incorrect representations of the earth's surface.[5] At first, he thought they were glitches or errors, but later he realized that they were not: they were actually the logical results of the system. "These jarring moments," Valla writes, "expose how Google Earth works, focusing our attention on the software."[6]

The way Google Earth's imagery is created is a rather complex process. Google uses a variety of sources (from space shuttle shots, satellite imagery and airplane photography to GPS data) and a range of techniques (from digital imaging, image stitching, image rendering, and 3D modeling to texture mapping) supported by computer vision.[7] As Valla makes clear, the images produced by Google Earth "are hybrid images, a patchwork of two-dimensional photographic data and three-dimensional topographic data extracted from a slew of sources, data-mined, pre-processed, blended and merged in real-time." [5] With the help of computer vision, Google is able to automatically locate features within overlapping photos of the earth's surface that are the same. By connecting these features to GPS data, it becomes possible to know where photos were taken and from which angle. This allows Google to generate depth maps from different cameras and then automatically stitch these together into one big 3D reconstruction, which can subsequently be textured: photographs can now be applied to the 3D model. Together, tens of millions of images make up Google Earth, whose structure resembles a series of interconnected Russian dolls all made up out of puzzle pieces.[8] Consequently, the imagery found on Google Earth can no longer be regarded as an index of the world (a physical trace of light), but is instead a calculated rendering of data. Thus, even though it seems counter-intuitive, we should not think of Google Earth's imagery (or in effect any kind of digital image) as a photograph that is simply digital, for it is something else entirely.[6] It is the result of the way the computer is programmed to "see" and how it represents this information visually. According to Valla, Google Earth is a database *disguised* as a photographic representation.[6]

Fig. 1. Clement Valla, *Postcards from Google Earth*, 2010-present.

The illusion of reality created by Google Earth is based on its aspiration to be seamless, continuous, complete and up-to-date. In order to achieve this, the computer vision software, which Google uses to automatically generate its virtual globe, selectively chooses its data and creates a very specific representation of the earth. It does this by training on a few basic traits – it learns to recognize and select images that contain no clouds, high contrast, shallow depth and daylight – to give us a smooth and continuous 24-hour, cloudless, day-lit world.[5] The inclusiveness and presentness of this idealized representation is the result of the speed by which it comes into being. Accordingly, the imagery of Google Earth cannot be defined in relation to a particular time or place, but rather in relation to the speed of calculation.

The effect of this is that Google Earth does not privilege a particular viewpoint, but aims at a *universal perspective* – which is exactly why it needs to be collected, processed, analyzed and rendered by a computer, instead of seen from the limited viewpoint of an embodied observer. Not only is perspective arbitrary when it comes to 3D modeled imagery, it is actually considered an obstacle to the total automation of sight by vision researchers and programmers. As media theorist Marc Hansen points out in his article "Seeing with the Body: The Digital Image in Postphotography" (2001), it is only by deprivileging the particular perspectival image that a totally and fully manipulable grasp of the entire data space becomes possible. Hence, "[w]ith this deterritorialization of reference," Hansen writes, "we reach [...] the moment when a computer can 'see' in a way profoundly liberated from the optical, perspectival, and temporal conditions of human vision."[10]

As art historian Jonathan Crary has remarked in the introduction of his book *Techniques of the Observer: On Vision and Modernity in the Nineteenth Century* (1990), with the advent of techniques like computer-aided design and robotic image recognition, "[m]ost of the historically important functions of the human eye are being supplanted by practices in which visual images no longer have any reference to the position of an observer in a 'real,' optically perceived world."[11] Consequently, according to Crary, these techniques "are relocating vision to a plane severed from a human observer".[11] I, however, would argue that this does not happen entirely or definitively. Although Google Earth's imagery is indeed both "seen" and represented by technology, its *raison d'être* is that it will be perceived by a human observer. Thus, while computer vision operates independently from human perception (in terms of its opticality, perspective and speed), it is paradoxically also (still) bound to it: the human observer remains the prime focus of these images; s/he forms both its starting and end point.

This paradox is exactly what Valla's *Postcards from Google Earth* reveal. They show how the imagery of Google Earth is the result of a double recoding – from image to data, and from data to image – by using photographs as textures to decorate the surface of a 3D model. The problem, however, is that we – as humans – see *through* a photograph, and unconsciously look *at* a surface. "Most of the time this doubling of spaces in Google Earth goes unnoticed," Valla explains.[5] But when the photographs are taken from a particular angle and contain depth and shadows, suddenly the two spaces do not align. At that moment, "we are both looking *at* the distorted picture plane," the artist writes, "and *through* the same picture plane at the space depicted in the texture. In other words, we are looking at two spaces simultaneously."[5] This clash of embodied perception (with its sense of perspective and experience of space) and computer vision (with its mathematical calculation of data), reveals the friction inherent in a human-computer connected perception of the world.

In their book *Remediation: Understanding New Media* (2001), media theorists Jay David Bolter and Richard Grusin state that (new) media often strive for what they call "immediacy": to ignore, deny or erase the presence of the medium and the act of mediation, so that the viewer or user appears to stand in an immediate relationship with what is represented. According to Bolter and Grusin, digital technologies such as virtual reality and three-dimensional computer graphics are seeking to make themselves "transparent". However, often, the desire to achieve immediacy involves a large amount of (re)mediation, of combining many different media – what Bolter and Grusin call "hypermediacy" – to produce this effect.[12] This can also be seen in the example of Google Earth, which uses a combination of many different media and techniques (satellite images, airplane photography, GPS data, 3D modeling, image stitching, image rendering and texture mapping) in order to create one single, apparently seamless, "transparent" and immersive visual space. According to Bolter and Grusin, such immediacy is therefore paradoxical by nature: to achieve it, especially in new digital media, hypermediacy is required. In some cases, the experience of immediacy can even flip to an experience of hypermediacy when the viewer suddenly becomes aware of the medium and the act of mediation.

An example that Bolter and Grusin use to explain the coexistence and interdependency of immediacy and hypermediacy is the photomontage, or collage. This medium incorporates a tension between looking *at* a mediated surface and looking *through* to a "real" space beyond the surface.[13] "We become hyperconscious of the medium in photomontage," Bolter and Grusin write, "precisely because conventional photography is a medium with such loud historical claims to transparency."[14] As explained earlier, Google Earth is also a kind of photomontage or collage. However, in Google Earth the user is not aware that s/he is actually looking at a photomontage – which is, of course, the intention. The experience of transparent immediacy dominated Google's hypermediated virtual space,[15] until Valla exposed the unintentional moments of obvious mediation in an otherwise seemingly transparent, unmediated Google Earth. By selecting moments when the technology "fails," the illusion of immediacy is immediately breached. In so doing, Valla makes viewers aware of the nature of the medium, while simultaneously reminding them of their desire for – and habitual reliance on – "transparent" photorealistic imagery.

In her text "De stem van de grafisch ontwerper" (The voice of the graphic designer), film theorist Anke Coumans explains how "bad" images – meaning images that do not successfully use or fully employ the possibilities of the technical apparatus by which they are made – reveal the apparatus itself. In other words, a bad image reveals how the image was programmed, but also how it programs us. For instance, bad lighting in a photo, she writes, draws the viewers' attention to the lighting, making them aware of the distinction between a photo and reality, as well as of the reality that existed before the camera.[16] With

Valla's work, the distorted images reveal how Google Earth was programmed (literally) and how it programs us to see it as an indexical photographic representation of the world. However, in the case of Valla's *Postcards*, one could wonder if there ever was a reality before the camera. Although Google uses satellite images, Google Earth's "universal texture", as Valla calls it, is in fact a computational model.

Coumans' analysis builds on the philosophy of Vilém Flusser, who has examined the nature of "Technobilder". Technical images like photographs, film, video and computer graphics are not surfaces that represent objects or scenes, Flusser argues, but rather mosaics, visualizations of numerical code.[17] Likewise, the highly technical image of Google Earth does not represent the surface of the earth, but a programming language that constructs a computational model. As Flusser writes, "technical images [...] are produced, reproduced and distributed by apparatuses, and technicians design these apparatuses."[18] Addressees of technical images are therefore often unaware of the specific program, of the level of consciousness that went into the creation of these apparatuses, Flusser argues.[19]

Through specific design strategies, artists and designers are able to "break" the program, Coumans argues, allowing space for the viewer to enter into dialog with the otherwise predetermined visual communication.[16] Instead of images that affirm, they create "transapparatic images,"[20] which transcend the technical program and evoke contemplation. The difference between the graphic design strategies that Coumans discusses and the work of Valla is that Valla simply selected the right "wrong" images. Consequently, these images do not point to the artist, but rather to the technician. In this sense, discovering the technical "failures" or glitches[21] of the apparatus can provide rare moments in which the viewer can suddenly see through the image and glimpse its origin, i.e. its technical production and the programmer's intention.

Fig. 2. Bernhard Hopfengärtner, *Hello, World!*, 2006.

3 Perception in an Expanded Field: Between Technology and the Body

Another "transapparatic" image that transcends its technical program and reflects on the collision of human perception and computer vision, is the design project *Hello, world!* (2006) by German designer Bernhard Hopfengärtner. The work consists of a graphical pattern that the designer mowed into a wheat field near the town of Ilmenau in Thuringia, Germany (Fig. 2). The 324 bright and dark squares together form a 160×160 meter-wide Semacode, a machine-readable pattern, similar to a QR-code, which is used to connect online information to objects and locations in the real world.[22] The code translates into the phrase "Hello, world!".[23] Without the aid of computer vision, however, it is very difficult, if not impossible, to read and understand this abstract code.

By enlarging the pattern to a size beyond human scale, Hopfengärtner highlighted the fact that these visual codes are strictly speaking not meant to be seen and read by humans, but by computers. The work can really only be seen from an airplane, drone, or satellite – as a photograph. Its perception, seeing the work visually and as a whole, is therefore dependent on technological mediation. Its interpretation in turn is dependent on computer vision: algorithms are needed to extract the meaning of the pattern. As such, this work calls into question the role of the viewer, or even the viewer itself, which, arguably, need not be human at all. On the other hand, when seen from ground level, from within the field, the work had a specific tactile, olfactory, auditory, spatial and temporal nature. When walking through the extensive field, people were able to feel and smell the wheat, hear the wind whistling through it. They could get a different view of the field from different angles and under different weather conditions. Over a period of time, the wheat grew and changed color, and eventually the pattern disappeared. This particular perception of the work, this bodily experience, can really only be had by a human viewer.

Hansen argues how, in contrast to computer vision, human perception is always contaminated with affection. Hansen writes: "human perception takes place in a rich and evolving field to which bodily modalities of tactility, proprioception, memory, and duration – what I am calling affectivity – make an irreducible and constitutive contribution."[24] In other words, duration (how long something takes, but also intervals in occurrences), the position from which we view something and the movement of the body through space, the way things feel, the memories of previous encounters and the associations these memories trigger: all these aspects are meaningful to an embodied viewer. They are inextricably linked to, and therefore greatly influence not only *what* we see, but also *how* we interpret it.

Computer vision of course lacks this bodily perception and consequently it sees and interprets the world quite differently. As Virilio already observed, computers do not so much look at images (in the sense that they see and perceive images as humans do), as process data. According to Virilio, the word "image" in this context is empty, and perhaps even deceptive, since in reality the computer is rapidly decoding information and analyzing it statistically.[25] So not only does computer vision lack the position of an embodied viewer in a real, multi-sensorial perceivable world, it is also looking at a remediation of the world that consists exclusively of data.[26]

Hopfengärtner's work points to the differences between computer vision and human perception – between a mediated, disembodied, data-driven gaze and bodily experience. Whether the perception of this work can be best arrived at through computer vision or human experience remains a question, although I would argue that it lies precisely in between. This is explained in part by the fact that the "real" space where this work exists – or at least where it was meant to be seen is online, in the virtual world of Google Earth.

The project's aim was to send a message – "Hello, world!" – to the world via the digital globe of Google Earth. This message – a reference to mastering a programming language[27] – can be said to be directed both at the technology itself and the users of that technology, the designer included. In this sense, the project can be seen as a way to gain access to, control, or at least engage in a dialog with the complex and omnipresent digital realm of technology giant Google. Hopfengärtner did this not by working directly in the program of Google Earth, but by altering a part of the physical landscape, assuming that it would be automatically integrated in the satellite images Google uses to construct its virtual globe, because we do not only watch Google Earth, it also watches us.[28] Whether users of Google Earth were/are actually able to see Hopfengärtner's message is unlikely, since Google updates its aerial views regularly.[29] In this way, his message is more a statement about "self-determination and possessions in the digital world," as the designer describes it.[30]

Since the industrial revolution, writers Beatrice Colomina and Mark Wigley argue in *Are We Human? Notes on an Archeology of Design*, the debate about design has centered on the complex relationship between humans and technology. Designers and thinkers like William Morris, for example, suggested that the machine was no longer a human tool, but had become a new life-form that was turning humans into its tools.[31] According to Colomina and Wigley, "[d]esign was framed as a way to deal with the increasingly dominant logic of the industrialized and globalized world while resisting the perceived dehumanizing impact of that world. [...] The word *design* was called on in the 1830 s to explicitly negotiate between human and machine".[32] Today, a large and important part of design still focuses on precisely this balancing act. With Hopfengärtner's outcry "Hello, world!" (perhaps a question mark – "Hello, world?" – would have struck a more fitting tone), the designer lays bare some essential questions about the relationship between humans and their technology.

Today we literally live inside design, Colomina and Wigley make clear. For them, design includes everything, from the materials and objects that we use to network systems and the process of bioengineering. In this sense, Colomina and Wigley's definition of design resembles McLuhan's definition of media as any extension of our body and mind that "gradually creates a totally new human environment" which in turn "shapes and controls the scale and form of human association and action."[33] As a result of the continuous process of redesigning the human by design, Colomina and Wigley argue, there is no longer an outside to design: the whole planet is covered in countless overlapping and interacting webs, from underground transit systems and submarine communications cables to buildings, cities, transportation infrastructure and cell phone towers to satellites and space stations that circle the earth.[34]

The parallel world of Google Earth reflects this, with its interwoven layers of satellite images, 3D textures, and GEO-specific information. But what kind of planet is Google Earth exactly? In her book *An Aesthesia of Networks: Conjunctive Experience in Art and Technology* (2013), media artist and theorist Anna Munster describes the particular nature of Google's virtual globe. While at first it may appear to be the ultimate simulation of the world, she observes, one crucial aspect is missing: collective human sociality. The experience of Google Earth is solitary: you "fly" around from location to location without ever encountering others.[35] "Instead of producing a heterogeneously populated world," Munster writes, "Google Earth produces a world and its peoples as a loose database of individual users initiating and retrieving their individual queries bereft of any sociality".[36]

Even though Google Earth is made by/of us (because we both contribute content to it and produce the world that is its subject), the experience of this parallel world remains a solitary one. In Google Earth, the liveliness and messiness of social relations seems to be forever just out of reach. It does not seem to matter how detailed Google Earth becomes, it never really turns into a social place. Instead, it is a beautiful clean image of the globe, which can be consumed by nomadic, solitary individuals who live a database-mode of existence and for whom the Google Earth experience has become an end in itself.[37]

Hopfengärtner's message tries to cut through this and reach others: "Hello, world!" But in the solitary world of Google Earth, it becomes little more than a faint echo of the designer's presence. Yet at the same time its encoding as abstract visual pattern suggests that its receiver is not human, but machine – or some kind of mix. In this sense, his work is perhaps a message to the humans we have become. "What makes the human human is not inside the body or brain, or even inside the collective social body, but in our interdependency with artifacts", Colomina and Wigley state.[38] "Artifacts are interfaces," they write, "enabling different forms of human engagement with the world but equally enabling the world to engage with the human differently."[39] The increasing use of – and dependency on – computer vision technology, however, begs the question of how the world is increasingly engaging with us and how our engagement with others is being shaped by it.

4 Looking for Faces: Statistics and the Imagination

The conflation of human perception and extended technological perception is at the heart of another work, entitled *Google Faces* (2013). This digital design project consists of a computer vision program that autonomously searches for faces hidden in the surface of the earth (Fig. 3). Its makers, German designers

Julia Laub and Cedric Kiefer, who founded design studio Onformative, developed an application that automatically analyzes satellite images from Google Maps by using a face-detection algorithm.[40] As the designers explain on their website, their aim was "to explore how the cognitive experience of pareidolia can be generated by a machine".[41]

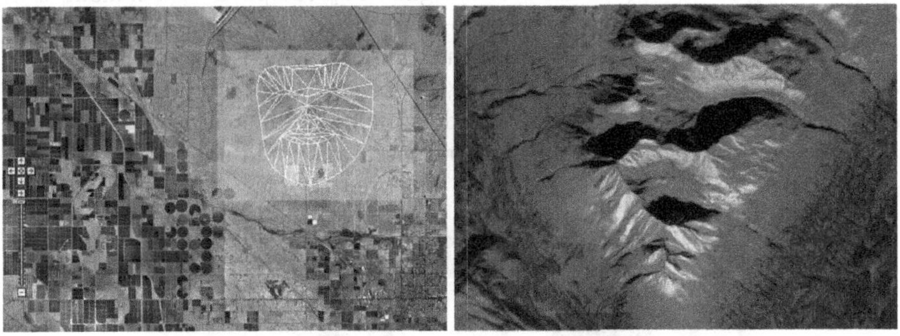

Fig. 3. Studio Onformative, *Google Faces*, 2013.

Pareidolia is a psychological phenomenon used to describe the human tendency to detect meaning in vague visual (or auditory) stimuli. Whenever we navigate our surroundings, it is of vital importance that we identify and recognize visual patterns, whether it is the face of a friend in a crowd or the speed of an approaching car. Sometimes this mechanism continues to work in situations where it should not, and we recognize a face in the shape of a mountain. Onformative's fascination is with such erroneous and seemingly useless pattern recognition. According to the designers, "we also tend to use this ability [pattern detection] to enrich our imagination. Hence we recognize meaningful shapes in clouds or detect a great bear upon astrological observations."[42] Consequently, pattern recognition can be considered an important faculty when it comes to looking at art, and is responsible for our ability to infuse certain landscapes and objects with symbolic meaning.

Pattern recognition is something computers share with us, even, as it turns out, the ability to see faces when there are none. In fact, it was the high rate of false positives (the detection of a face when there is none) that Laub and Kiefer noticed when they worked with face-tracking technology for an earlier project, which led them to further investigate this phenomenon with *Google Faces*.[43] But the similarity between computer vision and human perception is only superficial. In looking for faces in landscapes, Onformative's application *simulates* our tendency to see meaningful patterns, while in fact it is calculating the number of light and dark spots which together pass for a face-like configuration in the form of two eyes, a nose and a mouth. As Virilio already observed, "blindness is thus very much at the heart of the coming 'vision machine'. The production of *sightless vision* is itself merely the reproduction of an intense blindness that will become the latest and last form of industrialization: *the industrialization of the non-gaze*" [44] (original italics).

An adaptation of René Magritte's painting *The Treachery of Images*, posted by the Computer Vision Group of the University of California Berkeley, also – perhaps unintentionally – points to a fundamental blind spot in the way computers see the world.[45] In this image, the painting of Magritte is overlaid with a pink rectangle, referring to the field recognized by computer vision, along with its estimation of the subject – "pipe" – and its correspondence rate: 94 percent (Fig. 4). Amusingly, in this image the computer itself is not completely sure whether this is a pipe or not, providing a 94 percent accuracy. Arguably, this has little to do with the fact that it understands the difference between object and representation, since it knows only representation and not the world.

Fig. 4. Contemporary adaptation of René Magritte's painting *The Treachery of Images* (1928–1929). (Color figure online)

Thus, while Magritte's painting makes the viewer aware of the difference between object and representation – emphasized by the caption *Ceci n'est pas une pipe* (This is not a pipe) – this image makes us aware of how far a computer-interpreted version of the world is removed from the rich field of human perception and interpretation. While an image of something is not the thing itself, but a representation, what the computer "sees" is a pre-established category, based on a large number of representations applied to yet another representation. It compares a representation of a pipe with a database of representations of pipes. It therefore knows not the object nor reality, but only the pattern "pipe" – an abstracted and reduced version of reality. Paradoxically, a man-made artistic interpretation of the world, such as Magritte's painting, is therefore closer to reality than a computer's calculated account of it.

Consequently, we should be careful not to confuse human interpretation with statistical calculation or to contribute human abilities to the computer. Some of the less recognizable results of *Google Faces*, for example, have been described by writer Margaret Rhodes as "subjective," and the machine's eye as "more conceptually artistic" than ours.[46] In so doing, we are not only anthropomorphizing the landscape, we are also anthropomorphizing the computer. While we might feel we have found "faces staring back,"[46] it is in fact *we* that *project* our gaze: not only on the landscape that appears to be looking back at us, but also on the computer that is doing the looking for us.

If we consider computer vision a medium – an extension of visual perception – we realize that what Onformative is doing with *Google Faces* is examining what happens when we delegate our perception *along with our imagination* to a computer. The result is, as Kiefer and Laub describe it, an inseparable process in which objective investigations (computers) and subjective imagination (humans) collide.[41] It is important to remember, however, that in the end, it is the human observer that contributes meaning to these images, not the computer.[47] While a computer might be able to detect a face in a landscape, it is (as of yet) not able to detect this recognition itself as an instance of pareidolia or an act of the imagination.[48]

5 Conclusion

When Virilio wrote *The Vision Machine*, he worried that artificial vision would leave humans out of the perceptual loop altogether, i.e. that we would share the perception and even the interpretation of our environment with machines without any need for visual feedback. While this is still cause for concern, artists like Clement Valla, studio Onformative, and Bernhard Hopfengärtner, who explore the nature of Google Earth, show that computer vision is also used to construct images that are especially meant to be seen by us, humans. Instead of solving the problem of exclusion, however, this application of computer vision creates problems of its own – particularly when it comes to generating a visual system of representation that is used to understand the world and even more so when that system of representation simulates another. The resulting trouble is that we fail to perceive, and therefore understand, the technical program that shapes our communication.

As Valla's *Postcards from Google Earth* show, Google Earth is neither a photographic, indexical representation of the world, nor connected to the position of a real embodied observer. Google Earth does not reflect a particular perspective, but instead aims at an idealized and universal depiction of the earth's surface. Its aim, however, is strongly contrasted by its method. As Bolter and Grusin make clear, the desire for immediacy is often approached through hypermediacy. Similarly, Google Earth's smooth, continuous space is actually a patchwork of tens of millions – very selective! – images all stitched together through processes of automated visual analysis. This disguise, this illusion of reality, serves to counter or transcend our own "limited" (perhaps"undesired" is the better word) perception of the world by filtering out clouds, depth, strange angles, darkness, or any kind of obscurity or ambiguity.

But it doesn't stop here. Its speed of calculation, combined with automation, is one of the reasons why computer vision is called upon to do the looking for us. This means that the convoluted and slow process of human perception, which involves duration, tactility, movement, changing perspectives, memories and associations, is left out of the loop. As Hopfengärtner's work *Hello, world!* shows, in machine vision, our rich field of interpretation is reduced to a coded pattern that contains only a limited amount of information. In addition, Hopfengärtner's failure to get his message into Google Earth reflects how the speed of artificial perception can work against an often less efficient or predictable human communication. Perhaps this is why human sociality is lacking in a place like Google Earth. As Munster argues, the messiness of human social relations becomes an obstacle to the consumption of Google's nice, clean image of the globe.

The risk is that, despite all these deficiencies and due to complex and opaque technical processes, we start to project our own gaze onto the technology. As studio Onformative has shown with *Google Faces*, it is not difficult to anthropomorphize computer vision, to regard its outcome as subjective or to add human characteristics to it. However, as Virilio rightfully pointed out, blindness is at the heart of any vision machine – not only because it statistically calculates data, but also because this calculation is based on representation and not the world. In this sense, any artificial visual analysis is at least twice removed from reality: first, by looking only at representations, second, by comparing those representations to other representations, but also to predetermined patterns and concepts. For that reason, to describe the process of computer vision as a process of interpretation is anthropomorphic, since there really is no understanding involved, only (an intricate process of) selection. By examining what happens when we use computer vision to simulate our tendency to see meaningful patterns in random data, studio Onformative demonstrates that we are all too willing to conflate human perception and computer vision.

As McLuhan, Colomina and Wigley make clear, any technology gradually creates a totally new human environment that shapes and controls human thought and action. This is as true for computer vision, as it is for any other technology – perhaps even more so, since it externalizes and automates one of our most dominant faculties: visual perception. It is therefore important to fully understand the nature of computer vision and the way it analyzes and represents our world. By exposing unintentional moments of mediation, by highlighting the frictions that are part of a human-computer connected perception and by discovering technical failures, artists and designers allow us to peak through the cracks of otherwise often hermetically sealed technical processes. For them, technical failures and "bad" images do not need to be eradicated or quickly fixed. Instead, these instances are valuable. They not only reveal the particular nature of the apparatus itself, but also how it programs us to see the technology and the world it creates.

References

1. Virilio, P.: The Vision Machine, p. 59. Indiana University Press, Indianapolis (1994)
2. Shubber, K.: Artificial artists: when computers become creative. Wired. 7 Aug 2013. http://www.wired.co.uk/article/can-computers-be-creative. Naughton, J.: Can Google's AlphaGo really feel it in its algorithms? The Guardian. 31 Jan 2016. http://www.theguardian.com/commentisfree/2016/jan/31/google-alphago-deepmind-artificial-intelligence-intuititive. Titcomb, J.: The best of Siri: 11 funny responses from the iPhone's virtual assistant. The Telegraph. 1 Jul 2015. http://www.telegraph.co.uk/technology/apple/11709991/The-best-of-Siri-11-funny-responses-from-the-iPhones-virtual-assistant.html
3. Virilio: The Vision Machine. 60
4. McLuhan, M.: Understanding Media: The Extensions of Man. Ginko Press, Berkeley (1964). 5, 19, 34
5. Valla, C.: The Universal Texture. Rhizome, 31 July 2012. http://rhizome.org/editorial/2012/jul/31/universal-texture/
6. Postcards from Google Earth. http://www.postcards-from-google-earth.com/info/. Accessed 1 Mar 2016
7. In 2012, Google switched from using its geo-modeling community (which consists of many volunteers that manually created detailed 3D models of buildings) to automatic image rendering and computer vision techniques to create a 3D representation of entire metropolitan areas. The Never-Ending Quest for the Perfect Map. https://googleblog.blogspot.com/2012/06/never-ending-quest-for-perfect-map.html. Accessed 15 Mar 2016
8. Google Earth's Incredible 3D Imagery, Explained (Youtube). https://bit.ly/2pnyZsG. Accessed 26 Jun 2018
9. See also Goeting, M.: Digital fluidity: the performative and reconfigurable nature of the digital image in contemporary art and design. Int. J. New Media Technol. Arts **11**(4), 27–46 (2016)
10. Hansen, M.: Seeing with the body: the digital image in postphotography. Diacritics **31**(4), 54–84 (2001)
11. Crary, J.: Techniques of the Observer: On Vision and Modernity in the Nineteenth Century, p. 2. MIT Press, Cambridge (1990)
12. Bolter, J.D., Grusin, R.: Remediation: Understanding New Media. MIT Press, Cambridge (2000). 5–6, 22–23
13. Bolter, Grusin: Remediation. 38–41
14. Bolter, Grusin: Remediation. 38
15. In this regard, Google Earth departs from the tradition of cartography. Cartography's aim to map places always involves a form of reduction; relevant geographical information is collected and transformed into a schematic representation of an area. Traditionally, what gets on the map are distinctive elements, not uniformity, because including sameness hinders the functionality of a map. The aim of Google Earth, however, is to "build the most photorealistic version of our planet," as one of Google's developers makes clear, and this involves including as much (overlapping) information as possible. See Adams, C.: Imagery update: Explore your favorite places in Google Earth. Medium. https://medium.com/google-earth/imagery-update-explore-your-favorite-places-in-google-earth-5da3b28e4807. Accessed 19 Sep 2018. Consequently, Google Earth can no longer be considered a map. Instead, it functions as an all-encompassing virtual image space that builds on the photographic paradigm and owes more to the history of immersive (virtual) spaces than cartography

16. Coumans, A.: De stem van de grafisch ontwerper, drie vormen van dialogische verbeelding in het publieke domein. Esthetica. http://estheticatijdschrift.nl/wp-content/uploads/sites/175/2014/09/5-Esthetica-Destemvandegrafischontwerper-Drievormenvandialogischeverbeeldinginhetpubliekedomein-2010-12-20.pdf. Accessed 29 May 2018
17. For this reason, the distinction between "real" and "virtual" had lost its meaning to Flusser. He preferred to talk about the distinction between gestures of "abstraction" and "concretion"
18. Flusser, V.: Writings, p. 128. University Minnesota Press, Minneapolis (2002)
19. Flusser: Writings. 129–130
20. The term "transapparatische Bilder" was originally conceived by Flusser. Flusser, V.: Medienkultur. Fischer Taschenbuche Verlag, Frankfurt am Main (2005). 75, 77
21. According to Dutch glitch artist Rosa Menkman, "Glitch, an unexpected occurrence, unintended result, or break or disruption in a system, cannot be singularly codified, which is precisely its conceptual strength and dynamical contribution to media theory." Menkman, R.: The Glitch Moment(um). Institute of Network Cultures, Amsterdam (2011) 26. "It [the glitch] is the moment at which this flow [of technology] is interrupted that a counter-experience becomes possible. [...] the possibility for an alternative message unfolds. Through the distorted lens of the glitch, a viewer can perceive images of machinic inputs and outputs. The interface no longer behaves the way it is programmed to; the uncanny encounter with a glitch produces a new mode that confounds an otherwise predictable masquerade of human-computer relations." Skyers, E. I.: Vanishing Acts. Link Editions, Brescia (2015). 48–49
22. The Semacode was originally designed to encode Internet URLs, but it is also used by postal services to automate the distribution of parcels and letters, and by the railway and concert venues to sell tickets online
23. Hello, world! http://hello.w0r1d.net/description.html. Accessed 16 May 2018
24. Hansen: Seeing with the Body. 61–62
25. Virilio: The Vision Machine. 75 However, one could question whether the computational algorithms employed in computer vision are really that different from how we as humans perceive and analyze the world. After all, many of these technologies are modeled after us. Like us, they work with pattern recognition, although of course not as advanced as humans. However, although many scientists now agree that the human brain works similar to computers/algorithms, there is a risk in using this analogy. It may cause us to overlook the differences. As historian Yuval Noah Harari explains, during the Industrial Revolution scientists described the human body and mind as a steam engine because it was the dominant technology at the time. While this sounded logical in the nineteenth century, it seems naïve today and the same thing most likely applies to the human-computer analogy. It explains only a very small part of the human, and even less about what it means to be human. See Harari, Y. N.: Homo Deus: A Brief History of Tomorrow. Random House, New York (2016)
26. The digital photograph taken of the wheat field is actually a list of data that describes values of color, contrast, size, etc. It is only after using software to convert this data into an image that we can talk about an image. See also Goeting: Digital Fluidity
27. The phrase "hello, world" was first used by Canadian computer scientist Brian Kernighan in 1978 in his instruction manual The C Programming Language as a small test program to display a basic understanding of the programming language.

It was subsequently used by many others as a symbolic first step in mastering a programming language

28. Dambeck, H.: Code in Kornfeld: Gre an die Welt ber Google Earth. Spiegel Online, 9 May 2006. http://www.spiegel.de/netzwelt/web/code-im-kornfeld-gruesse-an-die-welt-ueber-google-earth-a-415135.html
29. It is unclear whether Bernhard Hopfengärtner succeeded in getting his design recorded by the satellites Google uses and consequently on Google Earth, since the satellites scan the globe with intervals of approximately one year, by which time the pattern might have faded. Moreover, the satellite images are updated with the same interval, so if it did get on to Google Earth, it was only visible for a short period of time. That is, for those people who managed to find it among the vast imagery of Google's virtual globe
30. Bauhaus-Universitt Weimar. http://www.uni-weimar.de/projekte/iwantmymkg/en/hello-world. Accessed 18 May 2018
31. Colomina, B., Wigley, M.: Are We Human? Notes on an Archeology of Design, p. 80. Lars Mller Publishers, Zrich (2016)
32. Colomina, Wigley: Are We Human? 76–77
33. McLuhan: Understanding Media. 12, 20
34. Colomina, Wigley: Are We Human? 9
35. Munster, A.: An Aesthesia of Networks Conjunctive Experience in Art and Technology, pp. 45–55. MIT Press, Cambridge (2013)
36. Munster: An Aesthesia of Networks. 53
37. Munster: An Aesthesia of Networks. 51–61
38. Colomina, Wigley: Are We Human? 23 See also Stiegler, B.: Time and Technics 1: The Fault of Epimetheus. Stanford University Press, Stanford (1998)
39. Colomina, Wigley. Are We Human? 25 The following text by Bernhard Hopfengärtner can be connected to this: "The interaction with our environment is producing our mental representation of it. Designing objects of interaction, be it physical objects, services or cultural technologies, is also a method of generating new or alternative ways of thinking. As interaction design can be used as an approach to explore this field, it also allows the incorporation social [sic] or philosophical observations and ideas into a tangible form." Royal College of Art. https://www.rca.ac.uk/students/bernhard-hopfengartner/. Accessed 22 May 2018
40. Their "algorithmic robot," as Kiefer and Laub call it, browses Google Earth day in, day out, continuously scanning the virtual globe by moving along the latitude and longitude of the earth. After it has circled the globe, it starts again, zooming in closer every time, which exponentially increases the number of images that need to be analyzed. After running the bot non-stop for several weeks, it only traveled a small part of the globe. Kiefer quoted in Solon, O.: Google Faces searches for Faces in Google Maps, and finds Forever Alone Guy. Wired. 23 May 2013. http://www.wired.co.uk/news/archive/2013-05/23/google-faces
41. Google Faces. http://onformative.com/work/google-faces. Accessed 7 Mar 2016
42. Onformative quoted in Garber, M.: These Artists are Mapping the Earth with Facial Recognition Software. The Atlantic, 21 May 2013. http://www.theatlantic.com/technology/archive/2013/05/these-artists-are-mapping-the-earth-with-facial-recognition-software/276101/
43. Kiefer quoted in Solon, O.: Google Faces searches for Faces in Google Maps
44. Virilio: The Vision Machine. 72–73
45. Berkeley Computer Vision Group. https://www2.eecs.berkeley.edu/Research/Projects/CS/vision/shape/. Accessed 2 Jun 2018

46. Rhodes, M.: Finding Hidden Faces in Google Earth's Landscapes. Fast Company, 6 October 2013. http://www.fastcodesign.com/1672781/finding-hidden-faces-in-google-earths-landscapes
47. Likewise we can delegate our wish to achieve chance or randomness in the production of artworks to computers, believing the computer to be the better instrument to achieve this goal. While computational algorithms can produce long sequences of apparently random results, they are in fact based on deterministic logic. Because these computational algorithms can never be regarded as a "true" random number source (as tossing a coin or rolling dice are), they are called pseudorandom number generators. Here again, it is our desire to perceive randomness and our inability to discern patterns and predict the outcome of a computational algorithm, that creates the impression or illusion of randomness
48. Moreover, as Stuart Hall makes clear, we humans are able to form concepts of rather obscure and abstract things, which we can't in any simple way see, have never seen and possibly can't or won't ever see. Examples are concepts like war, death, friendship or love. Hall, S.: Representation: Cultural Representations and Signifying Practices. Open University, London (1997) 17 For instance, how would computer vision be able to detect an image as a representation or expression of love or revenge?

A Digital Tool to Understand the Pictorial Procedures of 17th Century Realism

Francesca Di Cicco[1(✉)], Lisa Wiersma[2], Maarten Wijntjes[1], Joris Dik[1], Jeroen Stumpel[2], and Sylvia Pont[1]

[1] Delft University of Technology, Delft, The Netherlands
f.dicicco@tudelft.nl
[2] Utrecht University, Utrecht, The Netherlands

Abstract. To unveil the mystery of the exquisitely rendered materials in Dutch 17th century paintings, we need to understand the pictorial procedures of this period. We focused on the Dutch master Jan de Heem, known for his highly convincing still-lifes. We reconstructed his systematic multi-layered approach to paint grapes, based on pigment distribution maps, layers stratigraphy, and a 17th century textual source. We digitised the layers reconstruction to access the temporal information of the painting procedure. We combined the layers via optical mixing into a digital tool that can be used to answer "what if" art historical questions about the painting composition, by editing the order, weight and colour of the layers.

Keywords: Optical mixing · Convincing rendering · Painting reconstruction · Jan de Heem

1 Introduction

Dutch Golden Age still life painters are typically acknowledged for their meticulous rendering of reality, especially regarding material properties. How were these successfully painted? And where and how could knowledge about this procedure be applied today? With the help of a digital tool, we aim to answer our research questions. Also, we aim to serve the development of rendering reality in computer graphics [1].

Jan de Heem (1606–1684) is considered to be one of the greatest masters of the Dutch Golden Age, especially known for his fruits and flowers [2]. His technique consisted of a multi-layered systematic approach, which was shown by Wallert [3,4] to match the painting recipe given by Willem Beurs (1656–ca.1711) in the treatise *The big world painted small* [5].

Can his technique disclose the convincing visual effects he was able to achieve? Understanding the painting procedures underlying the masterful rendering of materials in 17th century Dutch paintings, is still a challenge in art history (but see [6,7]). We addressed this question by combining a scientifically

L. Leal-Taixé and S. Roth (Eds.): ECCV 2018 Workshops, LNCS 11130, pp. 671–675, 2019.
https://doi.org/10.1007/978-3-030-11012-3_51

truthful reconstruction of paintings, based on chemical data and the abovementioned art historical written source, with imaging science to develop a digital visualisation tool for the painting procedure of Jan de Heem. In the field of technical art history, painting methods are usually investigated by the use of diagnostic techniques to identify the pigments and layers beneath the visible surface. The development of non-destructive imaging methods, like X-ray and infrared-based techniques (see [8] for an exhaustive review), gave access to a wealth of knowledge about paintings stratigraphy and pigments distribution.

Fig. 1. Jan Davidsz. de Heem (a) *Festoon of Fruits and Flowers*, 16601670, oil on canvas, Rijksmuseum; (b) *Garland of Fruit and Flowers*, 16501660, oil on canvas, Mauritshuis.

We made use of such chemical data to reproduce the red grapes from two paintings by De Heem (Fig. 1). We collected data from cross-sections [3], MA-XRF scans [9] and OCT scans, and referred to Beurs' recipe for the order of the layers.

2 Digitalisation of the Layers Building-Up

The reconstruction process entailed that a skilled painter (the second author) followed the recipe using oil paint and template drawings for the De Heem grapes' outline. To reconstruct the temporal information of the multi-layered painting procedure of De Heem, we acquired high resolution digital photographs of the reconstruction process at intervals of 10 s, in a controlled environment with constant lighting.

The reconstructed sequences of layers are shown in Fig. 2. Since we aim to understand the success of the procedure, we need to access both the individual layers and their combination. In order to see the visual effect of each layer, one could paint the image several times leaving out one layer each time. But this would lead to inconsistent results given the impossibility to repaint the same image over and over with exactly the same colour mixtures and brushstrokes. The new versions of the painting may unconsciously be adapted to the fact that one step was being deliberately skipped.

Fig. 2. Sequence of layers reconstruction of red grapes in *Festoon of Fruits and Flowers*. Paintings reconstruction by Lisa Wiersma. (Color figure online)

To overcome these issues, we built an interface using optical mixing [10], which is an image combination process that recalls the systematic layering procedure used by painters [11]. The elements combined in the optical mixing tool were obtained by subtracting the first reconstructed image in Fig. 2 from the second, the second from the third, etc. The individual elements corresponding to the steps of the recipe are shown in Fig. 3.

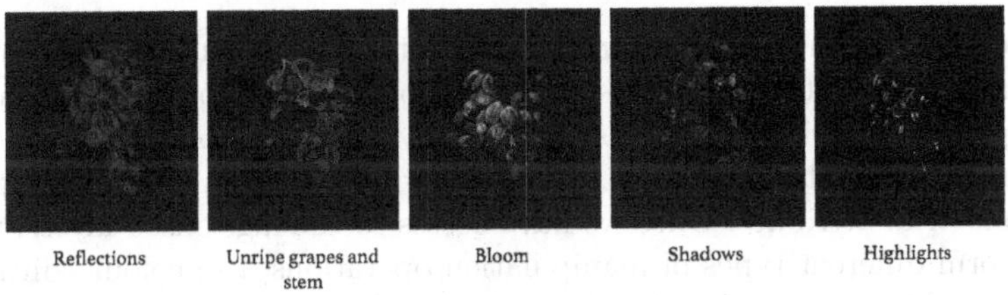

Fig. 3. Sequence of elements obtained from the layers reconstruction and combined in the optical mixing.

3 The Tool Applications

Several approaches have been used in literature to decompose images into layers via for example vectorization [12], segmentation [13], the Porter-Duff "over" operation [14,15] or the physical Kubelka-Munk model [16,17]. The retrieval of layers is usually done with the main intent of allowing image editing and manipulation.

Similarly, the aim of our layers' reconstruction was not only to see the building-up of the paintings, but also to provide a tool to explore and open up new possibilities for art historical investigation. The sliders can be used to manipulate and adjust the weights of the layers and therefore change the final appearance of the painting. For example, we can see what the painting would have looked like if the layer of vermilion would not have been applied (Fig. 4a). And what if the grapes would have been painted without the bloom layer (Fig. 4b)? Please note that the weights of all layers can be changed between 0 and 100%, allowing also subtle variations that correspond to layers thickness variations. Skipping one of the steps of De Heem's systematic procedure affects the final rendering and the realistic illusion.

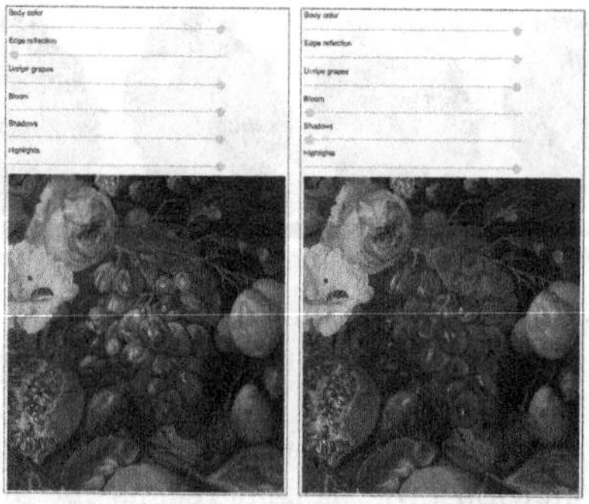

Fig. 4. Optical mixing interface for manipulation of the layers' weights. (a) Final appearance of the grapes without the second layer that corresponds to the edge reflections; (b) Final appearance of the grapes when the bloom and the shadow layers are removed. The reproduction is superposed on the real painting.

Understanding the contribution of each layer to the convincing representation of materials is an extremely interesting question not only for art historians but also for perception scientists. We assume that every layer resonates with a certain perceived material attribute and that the layer may contain the key image cues of that material attribute. Once we have access to the digitalised layers, we can also perform different types of manipulation operations, like colour editing. We can thus enable the use of counterfactual painting process scenarios to improve the knowledge and insights into the success and failure of pictorial steps. Our tool can be used by artists and art historians, conservators, scientists and a broader audience to find out how a masterpiece was made. In the context of museums, our tool can be applied for an interactive experience of the artwork. Finally, the tool can prove to be particularly useful in the field of art conservation and restoration. For example, when restoring a discoloured or damaged image, the colour editing possibilities offered by the tool can be used to check the relevance of additions or alterations.

4 Conclusions

By using the tool in visual perception experiments, we have proved that the compelling realism of Jan de Heem roots in a pictorial formula, consisting of the systematic application of necessary layers. De Heem was a meticulous and efficient painter: all the steps he made and that were described in the 17th century textual source were relevant. The computational result is an imaging technique beyond pixel values, showing actual colour layers which are editable. The assets of the digital tool, the clear-cut visualisation, practice, and testing of the Old Master's successful colour formulas, are of relevance to an interdisciplinary audience that consists of scientists, scholars, (digital) artists and interested lay persons.

Acknowledgements. This work is part of the research program NICAS "Recipes and Realities" with project number 628.007.005, which is partly financed by the Netherlands Organization for Scientific Research (NWO) and partly by Delft University of Technology. Maarten Wijntjes was financed by the VIDI project "Visual communication of material properties", number 276.54.001.

References

1. Ferwerda, J.A.: Three varieties of realism in computer graphics. In: Proceedings of SPIE 5007, Human Vision and Electronic Imaging VIII (2003)
2. Houbraken, A.: De groote schouburgh der Nederlantsche konstschilders en schilderessen. B.M. Israel, Amsterdam (1976)
3. Wallert, A.: Still Lifes: Techniques and Style, An Examination of Paintings of the Rijksmuseum. Rijksmuseum, Waanders, Amsterdam (1999)
4. Wallert, A.: De Groote Waereld in 't Kleen Geschildert (the big world painted small): a Dutch 17th century treatise on oil painting technique. In: The Artist's Process: Technology and Interpretation. Archetype, London (2012)
5. Beurs, W., Scholz, M.T.: The big world painted small. The Getty Research Institute, Los Angeles (in preparation)
6. Vandivere, A.: From the ground up. Surface and sub-surface effects in fifteenth- and sixteenth-century Netherlandish paintings. Ph.D. thesis, University of Amsterdam (2013)
7. Bol, M.: Oil and the translucent: varnishing and glazing in practice, recipes and historiography, 1100–1600. Ph.D. thesis, Utrecht University (2012)
8. Legrand, S., et al.: Examination of historical paintings by state-of-the-art hyperspectral imaging methods: from scanning infra-red spectroscopy to computed X-ray laminography. Heritage Sci. **2**(1), 1–11 (2014)
9. Keyser, N.D., Snickt, G.V.D., Loon, A.V., Legrand, S., Wallert, A.: Jan Davidsz. de Heem (1606–1684): a technical examination of fruit and flower still lifes combining MA-XRF scanning, cross-section analysis and technical historical sources. Heritage Sci. **5**(38), 1–13 (2017)
10. Pont, S., Koenderink, J., Doorn, A., Wijntjes, M., te Pas, S.: Mixing material modes. In: Proceedings of SPIE-IS&T Electronic Imaging, vol. 8291, p. 82910D (2012)
11. Zhang, F., de Ridder, H., Fleming, R.W., Pont, S.: MatMix 1.0: using optical mixing to probe visual material perception. J. Vis. **16**(6), 1–18 (2016)
12. Favreau, J.D., Lafarge, F., Bousseau, A.: Photo2Clipart: image abstraction and vectorization using layered linear gradients. ACM Trans. Graph. **36**(6), 1–11 (2017)
13. Aksoy, Y., Aydin, T.O., Smolic, A., Pollefeys, M.: Unmixing-based soft color segmentation for image manipulation. ACM Trans. Graph. **36**(2), 1–19 (2017)
14. Porter, T., Duff, T.: Compositing digital images. ACM SIGGRAPH Comput. Grap. **18**(3), 253–259 (1984)
15. Tan, J., Lien, J.M., Gingold, Y.: Decomposing images into layers via RGB-space geometry. ACM Trans. Graph. **36**(1), 1–14 (2016)
16. Kubelka, P., Munk, F.: An article on optics of paint layers. Zeitschrift fr Technische Physik **12**, 593–601 (1931)
17. Tan, J., Dvoronk, M., Skora, D., Gingold, Y.: Decomposing time-lapse paintings into layers. ACM Trans. Graph. **34**(4), 1–10 (2015)

How to Read Paintings: Semantic Art Understanding with Multi-modal Retrieval

Noa Garcia(✉) and George Vogiatzis

Aston University, Birmingham, UK
{garciadn,g.vogiatzis}@aston.ac.uk

Abstract. Automatic art analysis has been mostly focused on classifying artworks into different artistic styles. However, understanding an artistic representation involves more complex processes, such as identifying the elements in the scene or recognizing author influences. We present SemArt, a multi-modal dataset for semantic art understanding. SemArt is a collection of fine-art painting images in which each image is associated to a number of attributes and a textual artistic comment, such as those that appear in art catalogues or museum collections. To evaluate semantic art understanding, we envisage the Text2Art challenge, a multi-modal retrieval task where relevant paintings are retrieved according to an artistic text, and vice versa. We also propose several models for encoding visual and textual artistic representations into a common semantic space. Our best approach is able to find the correct image within the top 10 ranked images in the 45.5% of the test samples. Moreover, our models show remarkable levels of art understanding when compared against human evaluation.

Keywords: Semantic art understanding · Art analysis · Image-text retrieval · Multi-modal retrieval

1 Introduction

The ultimate aim of computer vision has always been to enable computers to understand images the way humans do. With the latest advances in deep learning technologies, the availability of large volumes of training data and the use of powerful graphic processing units, computer vision systems are now able to locate and classify objects in natural images with high accuracy, surpassing human performance in some specific tasks. However, we are still a long way from human-like analysis and extraction of high-level semantics from images. This work aims to push high-level image recognition by enabling machines to interpret art.

To study automatic interpretation of art, we introduce SemArt[1], a dataset for semantic art understanding. We build SemArt by gathering a collection of fine-art images, each with its respective attributes (author, type, school, etc.) as well

[1] http://noagarciad.com/SemArt/.

L. Leal-Taixé and S. Roth (Eds.): ECCV 2018 Workshops, LNCS 11130, pp. 676–691, 2019.
https://doi.org/10.1007/978-3-030-11012-3_52

as a short artistic comment or description, such as those that commonly appear in art catalogues or museum collections. Artistic comments involve not only descriptions of the visual elements that appear in the scene but also references to its technique, author or context. Some examples of the dataset are shown in Fig. 1.

Fig. 1. SemArt dataset samples. Each sample is a triplet of image, attributes and artistic comment.

We address semantic art understanding by proposing a number of models that map paintings and artistic comments into a common semantic space, thus enabling comparison in terms of semantic similarity. To evaluate and benchmark the proposed models, we design the Text2Art challenge as a multi-modal retrieval task. The aim of the challenge is to evaluate whether the models capture enough of the insights and clues provided by the artistic description to be able to match it to the correct painting.

A key difference with previously proposed methods for semantic understanding of natural images (e.g. MS-COCO dataset [15]) is that our system relies on background information on art history and artistic styles. As already noted in previous work [3–5], paintings are substantially different from natural images in several aspects. Firstly, paintings, unlike natural images, are figurative representations of people, objects, places or situations which may or may not correspond to the real world. Secondly, the study of fine-art paintings usually requires previous knowledge about history of art, different artistic styles as well as contextual information about the subjects represented. Thirdly, paintings commonly exhibit one or more layers of abstraction and symbolism which creates ambiguity in interpretation.

In this work, we harness existing prior knowledge about art and deep neural networks to model understanding of fine-art paintings. Specifically, our contributions are:

1. to introduce the first dataset for semantic art understanding in which each sample is a triplet of images, attributes and artistic comments,
2. to propose models to map fine-art paintings and their high-level artistic descriptions onto a joint semantic space,

3. to design an evaluation protocol based on multi-modal retrieval for semantic art understanding, so that future research can be benchmarked under a common, public framework.

Table 1. Datasets for art analysis. *Meta* and *Text* columns state if image metadata and textual information are provided, respectively.

Dataset	#Paintings	Meta	Text	Task
PRINTART [2]	988	✓	✗	Classification and retrieval
Painting-91 [12]	4,266	✓	✗	Classification
Rijksmuseum [19]	3,593	✓	✗	Classification
Wikipaintings [11]	85,000	✓	✗	Classification
Paintings [3]	8,629	✗	✗	Object recognition
Face paintings [4]	14,000	✗	✗	Face retrieval
VisualLink [22]	38,500	✓	✗	Instance retrieval
Art500k [18]	554,198	✓	✗	Classification
SemArt	21,383	✓	✓	Semantic retrieval

2 Related Work

With the digitalization of large collections of fine-art paintings and the emergence of publicly available online art catalogs such as WikiArt[2] or the Web Gallery of Art[3], computer vision researchers become interested in analyzing fine-art paintings automatically. Early work [2,10,12,23] proposes methods based on handcrafted visual features to identify an author and/or a specific style in a piece of art. Datasets used in these kinds of approaches, such as PRINTART [2] and Painting-91 [12], are rather small, with 988 and 4,266 painting images, respectively. Mensink and Van Gemert introduce in [19] the large-scale Rijksmuseum dataset for multi-class prediction, consisting on 112,039 images from artistic objects, although only 3,593 are from fine-art paintings. With the success of convolutional neural networks (CNN) in large-scale image classification [14], deep features from CNNs replace handcrafted image representations in many computer vision applications, including painting image classification [1,11,16,18,21,25], and larger datasets are made publicly available [11,18]. In these methods, paintings are fed into a CNN to predict its artistic style or author by studying its visual aesthetics.

Besides painting classification, other work is focused on exploring image retrieval in artistic paintings. For example, in [2], monochromatic painting images are retrieved by using artistic-related keywords, whereas in [22] a pre-trained

[2] http://www.wikiart.org.

[3] https://www.wga.hu/.

CNN is fine-tuned to find paintings with similar artistic motifs. Crowley and Zisserman [4] explore domain transfer to retrieve image of portraits from real faces, in the same way as [3] and [6] explore domain transfer to perform object recognition in paintings.

A summary of the existing datasets for fine-art understanding is shown in Table 1. In essence, previous work studies art from an aesthetics point of view to classify paintings according to author and style [2,11,12,18,19], to find relevant paintings according to a query input [2,4,22] or to identify objects in artistic representations [3]. However, understanding art involves also identifying the symbolism of the elements, the artistic influences or the historical context of the work. To study such complex processes, we propose to interpret fine-art paintings in a semantic way by introducing SemArt, a multi-modal dataset for semantic art understanding. To the best of our knowledge, SemArt is the first corpus that provides not only fine-art images and their attributes, but also artistic comments for the semantic understanding of fine-art paintings.

3 SemArt Dataset

3.1 Data Collection

To create the SemArt dataset, we collect artistic data from the Web Gallery of Art (WGA), a website with more than 44,809 images of European fine-art reproductions between the 8th and the 19th century. WGA provides links to all their images in a downloadable comma separated values file (CSV). In the CSV file, each image is associated with some attributes or metadata: author, author's birth and death, title, date, technique, current location, form, type, school and time-line. Following the links provided in the CSV file, we only collect images from artworks whose field *form* is set as painting, as opposite to images of other forms of art such as sculpture or architecture.

We create a script to collect artistic comments for each painting image, as they are not provided in the aforementioned CSV file. We omit images that are not associated to any comment and we remove irrelevant metadata fields, such as author's birth and death and current location. The final size of the cleaned collection is downsampled to 21,384 triplets, where each triplet is formed by an image, a text and a number of attributes.

3.2 Data Analysis

For each sample, the metadata is provided as a set of seven fields, which describe the basic attributes of its associated painting: *Author*, *Title*, *Date*, *Technique*, *Type*, *School* and *Timeframe*. In total, there are 3,281 different authors, the most frequent one being Vincent van Gogh with 327 paintings. There are 14,902 different titles in the dataset, with 38.8% of the paintings presenting a non-unique title. Among all the titles, Still-Life and Self-Portrait are the most common ones. *Technique* and *Date* fields are not available for all samples, but provided for completeness. *Type* field classifies paintings according to ten different genres, such as religious, landscape or portrait. There are 26 artistic schools in the collection, Italian being the most common, with 8,860 paintings and Finnish the least frequent with just 5 samples. Also, there are 22 different timeframes, which are periods of 50 years evenly distributed between 801 and 1900. The distribution of values over the fields *Type*, *School* and *Timeframe* is shown in Fig. 2. With respect to artistic comments, the vocabulary set follows the Zipf's law [17]. Most of the comments are relatively short, with almost 70% of the them containing 100 words or less. Images are provided in different aspect ratios and sizes. The dataset is randomly split into training, validation and test sets with 19,244, 1,069 and 1,069 triplets, respectively.

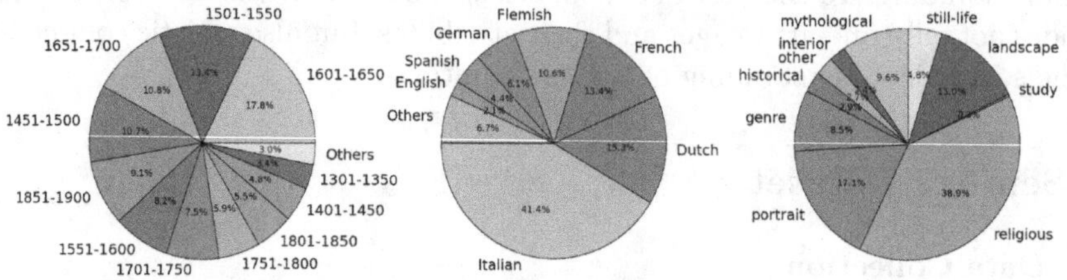

Timeframe School Type

Fig. 2. Metadata distribution. Distribution of samples within the SemArt dataset in Timeframe, School and Type attributes.

4 Text2Art Challenge

In what follows, we use bold style to refer to vectors and matrices (e.g. $\boldsymbol{x}$ and $\boldsymbol{W}$). Given a collection of artistic samples K, the k-th sample in K is given by the triplet (img_k, com_k, att_k), being img_k the artistic image, com_k the artistic comment and att_k the artistic attributes. Images, comments and attributes are input into specific encoding functions, f_{img}, f_{com}, f_{att}, to map raw data from the corpus into vector representations, $\boldsymbol{i}_k$, $\boldsymbol{c}_k$, $\boldsymbol{a}_k$, as:

$$\boldsymbol{i}_k = f_{img}(img_k; \phi_{img}) \tag{1}$$

$$\boldsymbol{c}_k = f_{com}(com_k; \phi_{com}) \tag{2}$$

$$\boldsymbol{a}_k = f_{att}(att_k; \phi_{att}) \tag{3}$$

where ϕ_{img}, ϕ_{com} and ϕ_{att} are the parameters of each encoding function.

As comment encodings, $\boldsymbol{c}_k$, and attribute encodings, $\boldsymbol{a}_k$, are both from textual data, a joint textual vector, $\boldsymbol{t}_k$ can be obtained as:

$$\boldsymbol{t}_k = \boldsymbol{c}_k \oplus \boldsymbol{a}_k \tag{4}$$

where $\oplus$ is vector concatenation.

The transformation functions, g_{vis} and g_{text}, can be defined as the functions that project the visual and the textual encodings into a common multi-modal space. The projected vectors $\boldsymbol{p}_k^{vis}$ and $\boldsymbol{p}_k^{text}$ are then obtained as:

$$\boldsymbol{p}_k^{vis} = g_{vis}(\boldsymbol{i}_k; \theta_{vis}) \tag{5}$$

$$\boldsymbol{p}_k^{text} = g_{text}(\boldsymbol{t}_k; \theta_{text}) \tag{6}$$

being θ_{vis} and θ_{text} the parameters of each transformation function.

For a given similarity function d, the similarity between any text (i.e. pair of comments and attributes) and any image in K is measured as the distance between their projections:

$$d(\boldsymbol{p}_k^{text}, \boldsymbol{p}_j^{vis}) = d(g_{text}(\boldsymbol{t}_k; \theta_{text}), g_{vis}(\boldsymbol{i}_j; \theta_{vis})) \tag{7}$$

In semantic art understanding, the aim is to learn f_{img}, f_{com}, f_{att}, g_{vis} and g_{text} such that images, comments and attributes from the same sample are mapped closer in terms of d than images, texts and attributes from different samples:

$$d(\boldsymbol{p}_k^{text}, \boldsymbol{p}_k^{vis}) < d(\boldsymbol{p}_k^{text}, \boldsymbol{p}_j^{vis}) \text{ for all } k, j \leq |K| \tag{8}$$

and

$$d(\boldsymbol{p}_k^{text}, \boldsymbol{p}_k^{vis}) < d(\boldsymbol{p}_j^{text}, \boldsymbol{p}_k^{vis}) \text{ for all } k, j \leq |K| \tag{9}$$

To evaluate semantic art understanding, we propose the Text2Art challenge as a multi-modal retrieval problem. Within Text2Art, we define two tasks: text-to-image retrieval and image-to-text retrieval. In text-to-image retrieval, the aim is to find the most relevant painting in the collection, $img^* \in K$, given a query comment and its attributes:

$$img^* = \operatorname*{argmin}_{img_j \in K} d(\boldsymbol{p}_k^{text}, \boldsymbol{p}_j^{vis}) \tag{10}$$

Similarly, in the image-to-text retrieval task, when a painting image is given, the aim is to find the comment and the attributes, $com^* \in K$ and $att^* \in K$, that are more relevant to the visual query:

$$com^*, att^* = \operatorname*{argmin}_{com_j, att_j \in K} d(\boldsymbol{p}_j^{text}, \boldsymbol{p}_k^{vis}) \tag{11}$$

5 Models for Semantic Art Understanding

We propose several models to learn meaningful textual and visual encodings and transformations for semantic art understanding. First, images, comments and attributes are encoded into visual and textual vectors. Then, a multi-modal transformation model is used to map these visual and textual vectors into a common multi-modal space where a similarity function is applied.

5.1 Visual Encoding

We represent each painting image as a visual vector, $\boldsymbol{i}_k$, using convolutional neural networks (CNNs). We use different CNN architectures, such as VGG16 [24], different versions of ResNet [8] and RMAC [26].

VGG16 [24] contains 13 3×3 convolutional layers and three fully-connected layers stacked on top of each other. We use the output of one of the fully connected layers as the visual encoding.

ResNet [8] uses shortcut connections to connect the input of a layer to the output of a deeper layer. There exist many versions depending on the number of layers, such as ResNet50 and ResNet152 with 50 and 152 layers, respectively. We use the output of the last layer as the visual encoding.

RMAC is a visual descriptor introduced by Tolias et al. in [26] for image retrieval. The activation map from the last convolutional layer from a CNN model is max-pooled over several regions to obtain a set of regional features. The regional features are post-processed, sum-up together and normalized to obtain the final visual representation.

5.2 Textual Encoding

With respect to the textual information, comments are encoded into a comment vector, $\boldsymbol{c}_k$, and attributes are encoded into an attribute vector, $\boldsymbol{a}_k$. To get the joint textual encoding, $\boldsymbol{t}_k$, both vectors are concatenated.

Comment Encoding. To encode comments into a comment vector, $\boldsymbol{c}_k$, we first build a comment vocabulary, V_C. V_C contains all the alphabetic words that appear at least ten times in the training set. The comment vector is obtained using three different techniques: a comment bag-of-words (BOWc), a comment multi-layer perceptron (MLPc) and a comment recurrent model (LSTMc).

BOWc each comment is encoded as a *term frequency - inverse document frequency* (tf-idf) vector by weighting each word in the comment by its relevance within the corpus.

MLPc comments are encoded as a tf-idf vectors and fed into a fully connected layer with tanh activation[4] and ℓ_2-normalization. The output of the normalization layer is used as the comment encoding.

LSTMc each sentence in a comment is encoded into a sentence vector using a 2,400 dimensional pre-trained skip-thought model [13]. Sentence vectors are input into a long short-term memory network (LSTM) [9]. The last state of the LSTM is ℓ_2-normalized and used as the comment encoding.

[4] $\tanh(z) = \frac{e^z - e^{-z}}{e^z + e^{-z}}$.

Attribute Encoding. We use the attribute field *Title* in the metadata to provide an extra textual information to our model. We propose three different techniques to encode titles into attribute encodings, $\boldsymbol{a}_k$: an attribute bag-of-words (BOWa) an attribute multi-layer perceptron (MLPa) and an attribute recurrent model (LSTMa).

BOWa as in comments, titles are encoded as a tf-idf-weighted vector using a title vocabulary, V_T. V_T is built with all the alphabetic words in the titles of the training set.

MLPa also as in comments, tf-idf encoded titles are fed into a fully connected layer with tanh activation and a ℓ_2-normalization. The output of the normalization layer is used as the attribute vector.

LSTMa in this case, each word in a title is fed into an embedding layer followed by a LSTM network. The output of the last state of the LSTM is ℓ_2-normalized and used as the attribute encoding.

5.3 Multi-modal Transformation

The visual and textual encodings, $\boldsymbol{i}_k$ and $\boldsymbol{t}_k$ respectively, encode visual and textual data into two different spaces. We use a multi-modal transformation model to map the visual and textual representations into a common multi-modal space. In this common space, textual and visual information can be compared in terms of the similarity function d. We propose three different models, which are illustrated in Fig. 3.

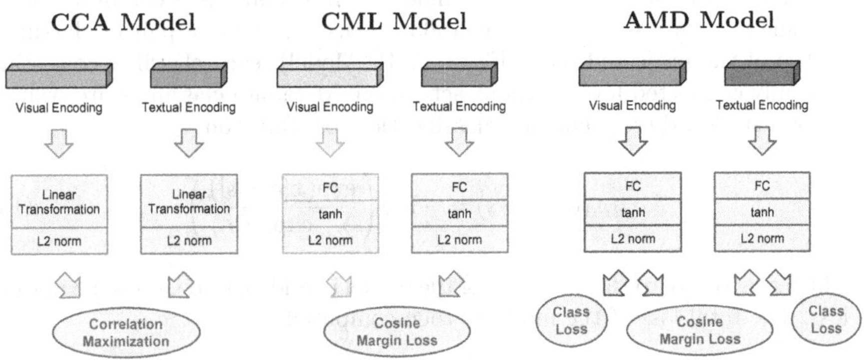

Fig. 3. Multi-modal transformation models. Models for mapping textual and visual representations into a common multi-modal space.

CCA Canonical Correlation Analysis (CCA) [7] is a linear approach for projecting data from two different sources into a common space by maximizing the normalized correlation between the projected data. The CCA projection matrices are learnt by using training pairs of samples from the corpus. At test time, the textual and visual encodings from a test sample are projected using these CCA matrices.

CML Cosine Margin Loss (CML) is a deep learning architecture trained end-to-end to learn the visual and textual encodings and their projections all at once. Each image encoding is fed into a fully connected layer followed by a tanh activation function and a ℓ_2-normalization layer to project the visual feature, $\boldsymbol{i}_j$, into a D-dimensional space, obtaining the projected visual vector $\boldsymbol{p}_j^{vis}$. Similarly, each textual vector $\boldsymbol{t}_k$, is input into another network with identical layer structure (fully connected layer with tanh activation and ℓ_2-normalization) to map the textual feature into the same D-dimensional space, obtaining the projected textual vector $\boldsymbol{p}_k^{text}$. We train the CML model with both positive ($k = j$) and negative ($k \neq j$) pairs of textual and visual data and cosine similarity with margin as the loss function:

$$L_{CML}(\boldsymbol{p}_k^{vis}, \boldsymbol{p}_j^{text}) = \begin{cases} 1 - \cos(\boldsymbol{p}_k^{vis}, \boldsymbol{p}_j^{text}), & \text{if } k = j \\ \max(0, \cos(\boldsymbol{p}_k^{vis}, \boldsymbol{p}_j^{text}) - m), & \text{if } k \neq j \end{cases} \tag{12}$$

where cos is the cosine similarity between two normalized vectors and m is the margin hyperparameter.

AMD Augmented Metadata (AMD) is a model in which the network is informed with attribute data for an extra alignment between the visual and the textual encodings. The AMD model consists on a deep learning architecture that projects both visual and textual vectors into the common multi-modal space whereas, at the same time, ensures that the projected encodings are meaningful in the art domain. As in the CML model, image and textual encodings are projected into D-dimensional vectors using fully connected layers, and the loss between the multi-modal transformations is computed using a cosine margin loss. Attribute metadata is used to train a pair of classifiers on top of the projected data (Fig. 3, AMD Model), each classifier consisting of a fully connected layer without activation. Metadata classifiers are trained using a standard cross entropy classification loss function:

$$L_{META}(\boldsymbol{x}, class) = -\log\left(\frac{\exp(\boldsymbol{x}[class])}{\sum_j \exp(\boldsymbol{x}[j])}\right) \tag{13}$$

which contribute to the total loss of the model in addition to the cosine margin loss. The total loss of the model is then computed as:

$$\begin{aligned} L_{AMD}(\boldsymbol{p}_k^{text}, \boldsymbol{p}_j^{vis}, l_{\boldsymbol{p}_k^{text}}, l_{\boldsymbol{p}_j^{vis}}) = (1 - 2\alpha)L_{CML}(\boldsymbol{p}_k^{text}, \boldsymbol{p}_j^{vis}) \\ + \alpha L_{META}(\boldsymbol{p}_k^{text}, l_{\boldsymbol{p}_k^{text}}) \\ + \alpha L_{META}(\boldsymbol{p}_j^{vis}, l_{\boldsymbol{p}_j^{vis}}) \end{aligned} \tag{14}$$

where $l_{\boldsymbol{p}_k^{text}}$ and $l_{\boldsymbol{p}_j^{vis}}$ are the class labels of the k-th text and the j-th image, respectively, and α is the weight of the classifier loss.

6 Experiments

Experimental Details. In the image encoding part, each network is initialized with its standard pre-trained weights for image classification. Images are scaled down to 256 pixels per side and randomly cropped into 224×224 patches. Visual data is augmented by randomly flipping images horizontally. In the textual encoding part, the dimensionality of LSTM hidden state for comments is 1,024, whereas in the LSTM for titles is 300. The title vocabulary size is 9,092. Skip thoughts dimensionality is set to 2,400. In the multi-modal transformation part, the CCA matrices are learnt using scikit-learn [20]. For the deep learning architectures, we use Adam optimizer and the learning rate is set to 0.0001, m to 0.1 and α to 0.01. Training is conducted in mini batches of 32 samples. Cosine similarity is used as the similarity function d in all of our models.

Text2Art Challenge Evaluation. Painting images are ranked according to their similarity to a given text, and vice versa. The ranking is computed on the whole set of test samples and results are reported as median rank (MR) and recall rate at K (R@K), with K being 1, 5 and 10. MR is the value separating the higher half of the relevant ranking position amount all samples, so the lower the better. Recall at rate K is the rate of samples for which its relevant image is in the top K positions of the ranking, so the higher the better.

6.1 Visual Domain Adaptation

We first evaluate the transferability of visual features from the natural image domain to the artistic domain. In this experiment, texts are encoded with the BOW_{C} approach with $V_C = 3{,}000$. As multi-modal transformation model, a 128-dimensional CCA is used. We extract visual encodings from networks pre-trained for classification of natural images without further fine-tunning or refinement. For the VGG16 model, we extract features from the first, second and third fully connected layer ($\text{VGG16}_{\text{FC1}}$, $\text{VGG16}_{\text{FC2}}$ and $\text{VGG16}_{\text{FC3}}$). For the ResNet models, we consider the visual features from the output of the networks (ResNet50 and ResNet152). Finally, RMAC representation is computed using a VGG16, a ResNet50 and a ResNet152 ($\text{RMAC}_{\text{VGG16}}$, $\text{RMAC}_{\text{Res50}}$ and $\text{RMAC}_{\text{Res152}}$). Results are detailed in Table 2. As semantic art understanding is a high-level task, it is expected that representations acquired from deeper layers perform better, as in the VGG16 models, where the deepest layer of the network obtains the best performance. RMAC features respond well when transferring from natural images to art, although ResNet models obtain the best performance. Considering these results, we use ResNets as visual encoders in the following experiments.

6.2 Text Encoding in Art

We then compare the performance between the different text encoding models in the Text2Art challenge. In this experiment, images are encoded with a ResNet50

Table 2. Visual Domain Adaptation. Transferability of visual features from the natural image classification domain to the Text2Art challenge.

Encoding		Text-to-image				Image-to-text			
Img	Dim	R@1	R@5	R@10	MR	R@1	R@5	R@10	MR
VGG16 FC1	4,096	0.069	0.129	0.174	115	0.061	0.129	0.180	121
VGG16 FC2	4,096	0.051	0.097	0.109	278	0.051	0.085	0.103	275
VGG16 FC3	1,000	0.101	0.211	0.285	44	0.094	0.217	0.283	51
ResNet50	1,000	0.114	0.231	0.304	42	0.114	0.242	0.318	44
ResNet152	1,000	0.108	**0.254**	**0.343**	**36**	**0.118**	**0.250**	**0.321**	**36**
RMAC VGG16	512	0.092	0.206	0.286	41	0.084	0.202	0.293	44
RMAC Res50	2,048	0.084	0.202	0.293	48	0.097	0.215	0.288	49
RMAC Res152	2,048	**0.115**	0.233	0.306	44	0.103	0.238	0.305	44

Table 3. Text Encoding in Art. Comparison between different text encodings in the Text2Art challenge.

Encoding		Text-to-image				Image-to-text			
Com	Att	R@1	R@5	R@10	MR	R@1	R@5	R@10	MR
LSTMc	LSTMa	0.053	0.162	0.256	33	0.053	0.180	0.268	33
MLPc	LSTMa	0.089	0.260	0.376	21	0.093	0.249	0.363	21
MLPc	MLPa	0.137	0.306	0.432	16	**0.140**	0.317	0.436	15
BOWc	BOWa	**0.144**	**0.332**	**0.454**	**14**	0.138	**0.327**	**0.457**	**14**

network and the CML model is used to learn the mapping of the visual and the textual encodings into a common 128-dimensional space. The different encoding methods are compared in Table 3. The best performance is obtained when using the simplest bag-of-words approach both for comments and titles (BOWc and BOWa), although the multi-layer perceptron model (MLPc and MLPa) obtain similar results. Models based on recurrent networks (LSTMc and LSTMa) are not able to capture the insights of semantic art understanding. These results are consistent with previous work [27], which shows that text recurrent models perform worse than non-recurrent methods for multi-modal tasks that do not require text generation.

6.3 Multi-modal Models for Art Understanding

Finally, we compare the three proposed multi-modal transformation models in the Text2Art challenge: CCA, CML and AMD. For the AMD approach, we use four different attributes to inform the model: Type (AMDT), TimeFrame (AMDTF), School (AMDS) and Author (AMDA). ResNet50 is used to encode visual features. Results are shown in Table 4. Random ranking results are provided as reference. Overall, the best performance is achieved with the CML

Title: Still-Life of Apples, Pears and Figs in a Wicker Basket on a Stone Ledge
Comment: The large dark vine leaves and fruit are back-lit and are sharply silhouetted against the luminous background, to quite dramatic effect. Ponce's use of this effect strongly indicates the indirect influence of Caravaggio's Basket of Fruit in the Pinacoteca Ambrosiana, Milan, almost 50 years after it was created.

0.778 0.772 0.767 0.754 0.754

Title: A Saddled Race Horse Tied to a Fence
Comment: Horace Vernet enjoyed royal patronage, one of his earliest commissions was a group of ten paintings depicting Napoleon's horses. These works reveal his indebtedness to the English tradition of horse painting. The present painting was commissioned in Paris in 1828 by Jean Georges Schickler, a member of a German based banking family, who had a passion for horse racing.

0.755 **0.732** 0.718 0.662 0.660

Title: Portrait of a Girl
Comment: This painting shows a girl in a yellow dress holding a bouquet of flowers. It is a typical portrait of the artist showing the influence of his teacher, Agnolo Bronzino.

0.870 0.848 0.847 0.827 0.825

Title: The Kreuzkirche in Dresden
Comment: A few years later, during his second stay in Saxony, Bellotto depicted the demolition of this Gothic church. There exists an almost identical version in the Gemldegalerie, Dresden.

0.841 0.834 0.803 0.800 0.799

Fig. 4. Qualitative positive results. For each text (i.e. title and comment), the top five ranked images, along with their score, are shown. The ground truth image is highlighted in green. (Color figure online) model and bag-of-words encodings. CCA achieves the worst results among all the models, which suggests that linear transformations are not able to adjust properly to the task. Surprisingly, adding extra information in the AMD models does not lead to further improvement over the CML approach. We suspect that this might be due to the unbalanced number of samples within the classes of the dataset. Qualitative results of the CML model with ResNet50 and bag-of-words encodings are shown in Figs. 4 and 5. In the positive examples (Fig. 4), not only the ground truth painting is ranked within the top five returned images, but also all the images within the top five are semantically similar to the query text. In the unsuccessful examples (Fig. 5), although the ground truth image is not ranked in the top positions of the list, the algorithm returns images that are semantically meaningful to fragments of the text, which indicates how challenging the task is.

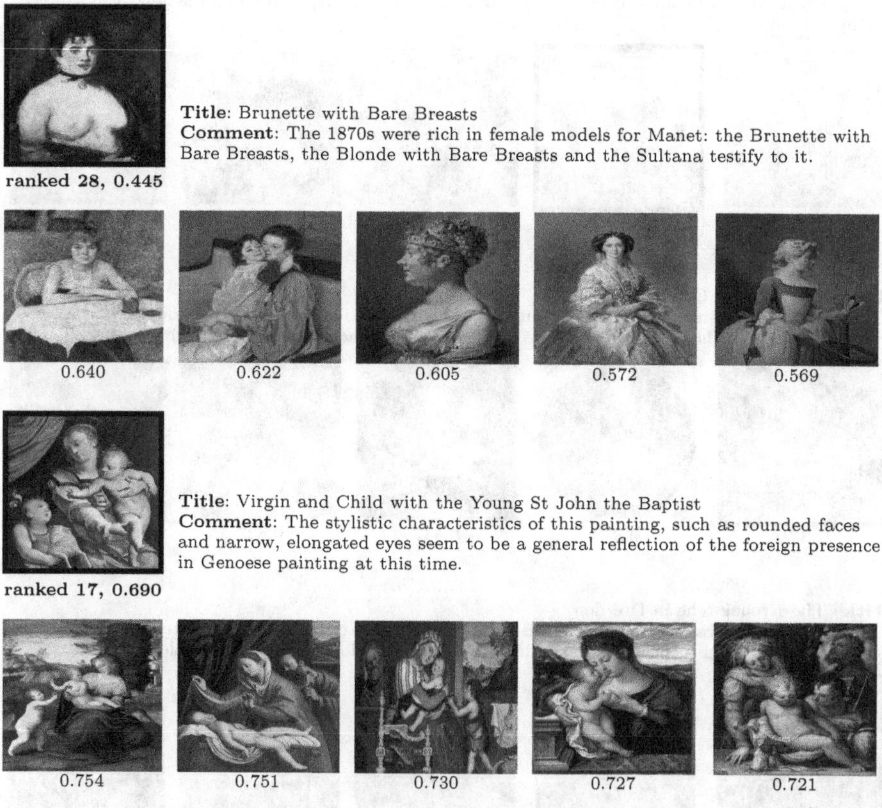

Title: Brunette with Bare Breasts
Comment: The 1870s were rich in female models for Manet: the Brunette with Bare Breasts, the Blonde with Bare Breasts and the Sultana testify to it.
ranked 28, 0.445
0.640
0.622
0.605
0.572
0.569
Title: Virgin and Child with the Young St John the Baptist
Comment: The stylistic characteristics of this painting, such as rounded faces and narrow, elongated eyes seem to be a general reflection of the foreign presence in Genoese painting at this time.
ranked 17, 0.690
0.754
0.751
0.730
0.727
0.721

Fig. 5. Qualitative negative result. For each text, the ground truth image is shown next to it, along with its ranking position and score. Below, the five top ranked images.

Table 4. Multi-modal transformation models. Comparison between different multi-modal transformation models in the Text2Art challenge.

Technique			Text-to-image				Image-to-text			
Model	Com	Att	R@1	R@5	R@10	MR	R@1	R@5	R@10	MR
Random	–	–	0.0008	0.004	0.009	539	0.0008	0.004	0.009	539
CCA	MLPc	MLPa	0.117	0.283	0.377	25	0.131	0.279	0.355	26
CML	BOWc	BOWa	**0.144**	**0.332**	**0.454**	**14**	0.138	**0.327**	**0.457**	**14**
CML	MLPc	MLPa	0.137	0.306	0.432	16	**0.140**	0.317	0.436	15
AMDT	MLPc	MLPa	0.114	0.304	0.398	17	0.125	0.280	0.398	16
AMDTF	MLPc	MLPa	0.117	0.297	0.389	20	0.123	0.298	0.413	17
AMDS	MLPc	MLPa	0.103	0.283	0.401	19	0.118	0.298	0.423	16
AMDA	MLPc	MLPa	0.131	0.303	0.418	17	0.120	0.302	0.428	16

Table 5. Human Evaluation. Evaluation in both the easy and the difficult sets.

	Technique				Text-to-image					
	Model	Img	Com	Att	Land	Relig	Myth	Genre	Port	Total
Easy	CCA	ResNet152	MLPc	MLPa	0.708	0.609	0.571	0.714	0.615	0.650
	CML	ResNet50	BOWc	BOWa	0.917	0.683	0.714	1	0.538	0.750
	Human	–	–	–	0.918	0.795	0.864	1	1	0.889
Diff.	CCA	ResNet152	MLPc	MLPa	0.600	0.525	0.400	0.300	0.400	0.470
	CML	ResNet50	BOWc	BOWa	0.500	0.875	0.600	0.200	0.500	0.620
	Human	–	–	–	0.579	0.744	0.714	0.720	0.674	0.714

6.4 Human Evaluation

We design a task in Amazon Mechanical Turk[5] for testing human performance in the Text2Art challenge. For a given artistic text, which includes comment, title, author, type, school and timeframe, human evaluators are asked to choose the most appropriate painting from a pool of ten images. The task has two different levels: *easy*, in which the pool of images is chosen randomly from all the paintings in test set, and *difficult*, in which the ten images in the pool share the same attribute type (i.e. portraits, landscapes, etc.). For each level, evaluators are asked to perform the task in 100 artistic texts. Accuracy is measured as the ratio of correct answers over the total number of answers. Results are shown in Table 5. Although human accuracy is considerable high, reaching 88.9% in the easiest set, there is a drop in performance in the difficult level, mostly because images from the same type contain more similar comments than images from different types. We evaluate a CCA and a CML model in the same data split as humans. The CML model with bag-of-words and ResNet50 is able to find the relevant image in the 75% of the samples in the easy set and in the 62% of the cases in the difficult task. There is around ten points of difference between CML model and the human evaluation, which suggests that, although there is still room for improvement, meaningful art representations are being obtained.

[5] https://www.mturk.com/.

7 Conclusions

We presented the SemArt dataset, the first collection of fine-art images with attributes and artistic comments for semantic art understanding. In SemArt, comments describe artistic information of the painting, such as content, techniques or context. We designed the Text2Art challenge to evaluate semantic art understanding as a multi-modal retrieval task, whereby given an artistic text (or image), a relevant image (or text) is found. We proposed several models to address the challenge. We showed that for visual encoding, ResNets perform the best. For textual encoding, recurrent models performed worse than multi-layer preceptron or bag-of-words. We projected the visual and textual encodings into a common multi-modal space using several methods, the one with the best results being a neural network trained with cosine margin loss. Experiments with human evaluators showed that current approaches are not able to reach human levels of art understanding yet, although meaningful representations for semantic art understanding are being learnt.

References

1. Bar, Y., Levy, N., Wolf, L.: Classification of artistic styles using binarized features derived from a deep neural network. In: Agapito, L., Bronstein, M.M., Rother, C. (eds.) ECCV 2014. LNCS, vol. 8925, pp. 71–84. Springer, Cham (2015). https://doi.org/10.1007/978-3-319-16178-5_5
2. Carneiro, G., da Silva, N.P., Del Bue, A., Costeira, J.P.: Artistic image classification: an analysis on the PRINTART database. In: Fitzgibbon, A., Lazebnik, S., Perona, P., Sato, Y., Schmid, C. (eds.) ECCV 2012. LNCS, vol. 7575, pp. 143–157. Springer, Heidelberg (2012). https://doi.org/10.1007/978-3-642-33765-9_11
3. Crowley, E., Zisserman, A.: The state of the art: object retrieval in paintings using discriminative regions. In: BMVC (2014)
4. Crowley, E.J., Parkhi, O.M., Zisserman, A.: Face painting: querying art with photos. In: BMVC, pp. 65.1–65.13 (2015)
5. Crowley, E.J., Zisserman, A.: In search of art. In: Agapito, L., Bronstein, M.M., Rother, C. (eds.) ECCV 2014. LNCS, vol. 8925, pp. 54–70. Springer, Cham (2015). https://doi.org/10.1007/978-3-319-16178-5_4
6. Crowley, E.J., Zisserman, A.: The art of detection. In: Hua, G., Jégou, H. (eds.) ECCV 2016. LNCS, vol. 9913, pp. 721–737. Springer, Cham (2016). https://doi.org/10.1007/978-3-319-46604-0_50
7. Gong, Y., Ke, Q., Isard, M., Lazebnik, S.: A multi-view embedding space for modeling internet images, tags, and their semantics. Int. J. Comput. Vis. **106**(2), 210–233 (2014)
8. He, K., Zhang, X., Ren, S., Sun, J.: Deep residual learning for image recognition. In: Proceedings of the IEEE Conference on Computer Vision and Pattern Recognition (2016)
9. Hochreiter, S., Schmidhuber, J.: Long short-term memory. Neural Comput. **9**(8), 1735–1780 (1997)
10. Johnson, C.R., et al.: Image processing for artist identification. IEEE Signal Process. Mag. **25**(4) (2008)
11. Karayev, S., et al.: Recognizing image style. In: BMVC (2014)

12. Khan, F.S., Beigpour, S., Van de Weijer, J., Felsberg, M.: Painting-91: a large scale database for computational painting categorization. Mach. Vis. Appl. **25**, 1385–1397 (2014)
13. Kiros, R., et al.: Skip-thought vectors. In: Advances in Neural Information Processing Systems (2015)
14. Krizhevsky, A., Sutskever, I., Hinton, G.E.: ImageNet classification with deep convolutional neural networks. In: NIPS (2012)
15. Lin, T.-Y., et al.: Microsoft COCO: common objects in context. In: Fleet, D., Pajdla, T., Schiele, B., Tuytelaars, T. (eds.) ECCV 2014. LNCS, vol. 8693, pp. 740–755. Springer, Cham (2014). https://doi.org/10.1007/978-3-319-10602-1_48
16. Ma, D., et al.: From part to whole: who is behind the painting? In: Proceedings of the 2017 ACM on Multimedia Conference. ACM (2017)
17. Manning, C.D., Schütze, H.: Foundations of statistical natural language processing. Inf. Retrieval **4**, 80–81 (2001)
18. Mao, H., Cheung, M., She, J.: DeepArt: learning joint representations of visual arts. In: ACM on Multimedia Conference (2017)
19. Mensink, T., Van Gemert, J.: The Rijksmuseum challenge: museum-centered visual recognition. In: ICMR (2014)
20. Pedregosa, F., et al.: Scikit-learn: machine learning in Python. J. Mach. Learn. Res. **12**, 2825–2830 (2011)
21. Saleh, B., Elgammal, A.M.: Large-scale classification of fine-art paintings: learning the right metric on the right feature. CoRR (2015)
22. Seguin, B., Striolo, C., diLenardo, I., Kaplan, F.: Visual link retrieval in a database of paintings. In: Hua, G., Jégou, H. (eds.) ECCV 2016. LNCS, vol. 9913, pp. 753–767. Springer, Cham (2016). https://doi.org/10.1007/978-3-319-46604-0_52
23. Shamir, L., Macura, T., Orlov, N., Eckley, D.M., Goldberg, I.G.: Impressionism, expressionism, surrealism: automated recognition of painters and schools of art. ACM Trans. Appl. Percept. **7**, 8 (2010)
24. Simonyan, K., Zisserman, A.: Very deep convolutional networks for large-scale image recognition. In: International Conference on Learning Representations (2015)
25. Tan, W.R., Chan, C.S., Aguirre, H.E., Tanaka, K.: Ceci n'est pas une pipe: a deep convolutional network for fine-art paintings classification. In: ICIP (2016)
26. Tolias, G., Sicre, R., Jégou, H.: Particular object retrieval with integral max-pooling of CNN activations. In: International Conference on Learning Representations (2015)
27. Wang, L., Li, Y., Huang, J., Lazebnik, S.: Learning two-branch neural networks for image-text matching tasks. IEEE Trans. Pattern Anal. Mach. Intell. (2018)

Weakly Supervised Object Detection in Artworks

Nicolas Gonthier[1(✉)], Yann Gousseau[1], Said Ladjal[1], and Olivier Bonfait[2]

[1] LTCI, Telecom ParisTech, Universite Paris-Saclay, 75013 Paris, France
{nicolas.gonthier,yann.gousseau,said.ladjal}@telecom-paristech.fr
[2] Universite de Bourgogne, UMR CNRS UB 5605, 21000 Dijon, France

Abstract. We propose a method for the weakly supervised detection of objects in paintings. At training time, only image-level annotations are needed. This, combined with the efficiency of our multiple-instance learning method, enables one to learn new classes on-the-fly from globally annotated databases, avoiding the tedious task of manually marking objects. We show on several databases that dropping the instance-level annotations only yields mild performance losses. We also introduce a new database, IconArt, on which we perform detection experiments on classes that could not be learned on photographs, such as Jesus Child or Saint Sebastian. To the best of our knowledge, these are the first experiments dealing with the automatic (and in our case weakly supervised) detection of iconographic elements in paintings. We believe that such a method is of great benefit for helping art historians to explore large digital databases.

Keywords: Weakly supervised detection · Transfer learning · Art analysis · Multiple instance learning

1 Introduction

Several recent works show that recycling analysis tools that have been developed for natural images (photographs) can yield surprisingly good results for analysing paintings or drawings. In particular, impressive classification results are obtained on painting databases by using convolutional neural networks (CNNs) designed for the classification of photographs [10,55]. These results occur in a general context were methods of transfer learning [14] (changing the task a model was trained for) and domain adaptation (changing the nature of the data a model was trained on) are increasingly applied. Classifying and analysing paintings is of course of great interest to art historians, and can help them to take full advantage of the massive artworks databases that are built worldwide.

More difficult than classification, and at the core of many recent computer vision works, the object detection task (classifying and localising an object) has been less studied in the case of paintings, although exciting results have been obtained, again using transfer techniques [11,28,52].

L. Leal-Taixé and S. Roth (Eds.): ECCV 2018 Workshops, LNCS 11130, pp. 692–709, 2019.
https://doi.org/10.1007/978-3-030-11012-3_53

Methods that detect objects in photographs have been developed thanks to massive image databases on which several classes (such as cats, people, cars) have been manually localised with bounding boxes. The PASCAL VOC [17] and MS COCO [34] datasets have been crucial in the development of detection methods and the recently introduced Google Open Image Dataset (2M images, 15M boxes for 600 classes) is expected to push further the limits of detection. Now, there is no such database (with localised objects) in the field of Art History, even though large databases are being build by many institutions or academic research teams, e.g. [16,38,39,43,44,53]. Some of these databases include image-level annotations, but none includes location annotations. Besides, manually annotating such large databases is tedious and must be performed each time a new category is searched for. Therefore, it is of great interest to develop *weakly supervised* detection methods, that can learn to detect objects using image-level annotations only. While this aspect has been thoroughly studied for natural images, only a few studies have been dedicated to the case of painting or drawings.

Moreover, these studies are mostly dedicated to the cross depiction problem: they learn to detect the same objects in photographs and in paintings, in particular man-made objects (cars, bottles ...) or animals. While these may be useful to art historians, it is obviously needed to detect more specific objects or attributes such as ruins or nudity, and characters of iconographic interest such as Mary, Jesus as a child or the crucifixion of Jesus, for instance. These last categories can hardly be directly inherited from photographic databases.

For these two reasons, the lack of location annotations and the specificity of the categories of interest, a general method allowing the weakly supervised detection on specific domains such as paintings would be of great interest to art historians and more generally to anyone needing some automatic tools to explore artistic databases. We propose some contributions in this direction:

- We introduce a new multiple-instance learning (MIL) technique that is simple and quick enough to deal with large databases,
- We demonstrate the utility of the proposed technique for object detection on weakly annotated databases, including photographs, drawings and paintings. These experiments are performed using image-level annotations only.
- We propose the first experiments dealing with the recognition and detection of iconographic elements that are specific to Art History, exhibiting both successful detections and some classes that are particularly challenging, especially in a weakly supervised context.

We believe that such a system, enabling one to detect new and unseen category with minimal supervision, is of great benefit for dealing efficiently with digital artwork databases. More precisely, iconographic detection results are useful for different and particularly active domains of humanities: Art History (to gather data relative to the iconography of recurrent characters, such as the Virgin Mary or San Sebastian, as well as to study the formal evolution of their representations), Semiology (to infer mutual configurations or relative dimensions of the iconographic elements), History of Ideas and Cultures (with category such as nudity, ruins), Material Culture Studies, etc.

In particular, being able to detect iconographic elements is of great importance for the study of spatial configurations, which are central to the reading of images and particularly timely given the increasing importance of Semiology. To fix ideas, we can give two examples of potential use. First, the order in which iconographic elements are encountered (e.g. Gabriel and Mary), when reading an image from left to right, has received much attention from art historians [20]. In the same spirit, recent studies [5] on the meaning of mirror images in early modern Italy could benefit from the detection of iconographic elements.

2 Related Work

Object Recognition and Detection in Artworks. Early works on cross-domain (or cross-depiction) image comparisons were mostly concerned with sketch retrieval, see e.g. [12]. Various local descriptors were then used for comparing and classifying images, such as part-based models [46] or mid-level discriminative patches [2,9]. In order to enhance the generalisation capacity of these approaches, it was proposed in [54] to model object through graphs of labels. More generally, it was shown in [25] that structured models are more prone to succeed in cross-domain recognition than appearance-based models.

Next, several works have tried to transfer the tremendous classification capacity of convolutional neural networks to perform cross-domain object recognition, in particular for paintings. In [10], it is shown that recycling CNNs directly for the task of recognising objects in paintings, without fine-tuning, yields surprisingly good results. Similar conclusions were also given in [55] for artistic drawings. In [32], a robust low rank parametrized CNN model is proposed to recognise common categories in an unseen domain (photo, painting, cartoon or sketch). In [53], a new annotated database is introduced, on which it is shown that fine-tuning improves recognition performances. Several works have also successfully adapted CNNs architectures to the problem of style recognition in artworks [3,31,36]. More generally, the use of CNNs opens the way to other artwork analysis tasks, such as visual links retrieval [45], scene classification [19], author classification [51] or possibly to generic artwork content representation [48].

The problem of *object detection* in paintings, that is, being able to both localise and recognise objects, has been less studied. In [11], it is shown that applying a pre-trained object detector (Faster R-CNN [42]) and then selecting the localisation with highest confidence can yield correct detections of PASCAL VOC classes. Other works attacked this difficult problem by restricting it to a single class. In [22], it is shown that deformable part model outperforms other approaches, including some CNNs, for the detection of people in cubist artworks. In [40], it is shown that the YOLO network trained on natural images can, to some extend, be used for people detection in cubism. In [52], it is proposed to perform people detection in a wide variety of artworks (through a newly introduced database) by fine-tuning a network in a supervised way. People can be detected with high accuracy even though the database has very large stylistic variations and includes paintings that strongly differs from photographs in the way they represent people.

Weakly supervised detection refers to the task of learning an object detector using limited annotations, usually image-level annotations only. Often, a set of detections (e.g. bounding boxes) is considered at image level, assuming we only know if at least one of the detection corresponds the category of interest. The corresponding statistical problem is referred to as multiple instance learning (MIL) [13]. A well-known solution to this problem through a generalisation of Support Vector Machine (SVM) has been proposed in [1]. Several approximations of the involved non-convex problem have been proposed, see e.g. [21] or the recent survey [6].

Recently, this problem has been attacked using classification and detection neural networks. In [47], it is proposed to learn a smooth version of an SVM on the features from R-CNN [23] and to focus on the initialisation phase which is crucial due to the non-convexity of the problem. In [41], it is proposed to learn to detect new specific classes by taking advantage of the knowledge of wider classes. In [4] a weakly supervised deep detection network is proposed based on Fast R-CNN [24]. Those works have been improved in [50] by adding a multi-stage classifier refinement. In [8] a multi-fold split of the training data is proposed to escape local optima. In [33], a two step strategy is proposed, first collecting good regions by a mask-out classification, then selecting the best positive region in each image by a MIL formulation and then fine-tuning a detector with those propositions as "ground truth" bounding boxes. In [15] a new pooling strategy is proposed to efficiently learn localisation of objects without doing bounding boxes regression.

Weakly supervised strategies for the cross domain problem have been much less studied. In [11], a relatively basic methodology is proposed, in which for each image the bounding box with highest (class agnostic) "objectness" score is classified. In [28], it is proposed to do mixed supervised object detection with cross-domain learning based on the SSD network [35]. Object detectors are learnt by using instance-level annotations on photographs and image-level annotations on a target domain (watercolor, cartoon, etc.). We will perform comparisons of our approach with these two methods in Sect. 4.

3 Weakly Supervised Detection by Transfer Learning

In this section, we propose our approach to the weakly supervised detection of visual category in paintings. In order to perform transfer learning, we first apply Faster R-CNN [42] (a detection network trained on photographs) which is used as a feature extractor, in the same way as in [11]. This results in a set of candidate bounding boxes. For a given visual category, the goal is then, using image-level annotations only, to decide which boxes correspond to this category. For this, we propose a new multiple-instance learning method, that will be detailed in Sect. 3.1. In contrast with classical approaches to the MIL problem such as [1] the proposed heuristic is very fast. This, combined with the fact that we do not need fine-tuning, permits a flexible on-the-fly learning of new category in a few minutes.

Figure 1 illustrates the situation we face at training time. For each image, we are given a set of bounding boxes which receive a label +1 (the visual category of interest is present at least once) or −1 (the category is not present in this image).

Fig. 1. Illustration of positive and negative sets of detections (bounding boxes) for the *angel* category.

3.1 Multiple Instance Learning

The usual way to perform MIL is through the resolution of a non-convex energy minimisation [1], although efficient convex relaxations have been proposed [29]. One disadvantage of these approaches is their heavy computational cost. In what follows, we propose a simple and fast heuristic to this problem.

For simplicity of the presentation, we assume only one visual category. Assume we have N images at hand, each of which contains K bounding boxes. Each image receives a label $y = +1$ when it is a positive example (the category is present) and $y = -1$ otherwise. We denote by n_1 the number of positive examples in the training set, and by n_{-1} the number of negative examples.

Images are indexed by i, the K regions provided by the object detector are indexed by k, the label of the i-th image is denoted by y_i and the high level semantic feature vector of size M associated to the k-th box in the i-th image is denoted $X_{i,k}$. We also assume that the detector provides a (class agnostic) "objectness" score for this box, denoted $s_{i,k}$.

We make the (strong) hypothesis that if $y_i = +1$, then there is at least one of the K regions in image i that contains an occurrence of the category. In a sense, we assume that the region proposal part is robust enough to transfer detections from photography to the target domain.

Following this assumption, our problem boils down to the classic multiple-instance classification problem [13]: if for image i we have $y_i = +1$, then at least one of the boxes contains the category, whereas if $y_i = -1$ no box does. The goal is then to decide which boxes correspond to the category. Instead of the classical SVM generalisation proposed in [1] and based on an iterative procedure, we look for an hyperplan minimising the functional defined below. We look for $w \in \mathbf{R}^M$, $b \in \mathbf{R}$ achieving

$$min_{(w,b)}\mathcal{L}(w,b) \tag{1}$$

with

$$\phi(w,b) = \sum_{i=1}^{N} \frac{-y_i}{n_{y_i}} Tanh\left\{\max_{k\in\{1..K\}} \left(w^T X_{i,k} + b\right)\right\} \tag{2}$$

and

$$\mathcal{L}(w,b) = \phi(w,b) + C * ||w||^2, \tag{3}$$

where C is a constant balancing the regularisation term. The intuition behind this formulation is that minimising $\mathcal{L}(w,b)$ amounts to seek a hyperplan separating the most positive element of each positive image from the least negative element of the negative image, sharing similar ideas as in MI-SVM [1] or Latent-SVM [18]. The $Tanh$ is here to mimic the SVM formulation in which only the worst margins count. We divide by n_{y_i} to account for unbalanced data. Indeed most example images are negative ones ($n_{-1} \gg n_1$)).

The main advantage of this formulation is that it can be realised by a simple gradient descent, therefore avoiding costly multiple SVM optimisation. If the dataset is too big to fit in the memory, we switch to a stochastic gradient descent by considering random batches in the training set.

As this problem is non-convex, we try several random initialisation and we select the couple w, b minimising the classification function $\phi(w,b)$. Although we did not explore this possibility it may be interesting to keep more than one vector to describe a class, since one iconographic element could have more that one specific feature, each stemming from a distinctive part.

In practice, we observed consistently better results when modifying slightly the above formulation by considering the (class-agnostic) "objectness" score associated to each box (as returned by Faster R-CNN). Therefore we modify function ϕ to

$$\phi^s(w,b) = \sum_{i=1}^{N} \frac{-y_i}{n_{y_i}} Tanh\left\{\max_{k\in\{1..K\}} \left((s_{i,k} + \epsilon)\left(w^T X_{i,k} + b\right)\right)\right\} \tag{4}$$

with $\epsilon \geq 0$. The motivation behind this formulation is that the score $s_{i,k}$, roughly a probability that there is an object (of any category) in box k, provides a prioritisation between boxes.

Once the best couple $(w^\star, b^\star)$ has been found, we compute the following score, reflecting the meaningfulness of category association:

$$S(x) = Tanh\{(s(x) + \epsilon)\left(w^{\star T} x + b^\star\right)\} \tag{5}$$

At test time, each box with a positive score (5) (where $s(x)$ is the objectness score associated to x) is affected to the category. The approach is then straightforwardly extended to an arbitrary number of categories, by computing a couple $(w^\star, b^\star)$ per category. Observe, however, that this leads to non-comparable scores between categories. Among all boxes affected to each class, a non-maximal suppression (NMS) algorithm is then applied in order to avoid redundant detections. The resulting multiple instance learning method is called **MI-max**.

3.2 Implementation Details

Faster R-CNN. We use the detection network Faster R-CNN [42]. We only keep its region proposal part (RPN) and the features corresponding to each proposed region. In order to yield and efficient and flexible learning of new classes, we choose to avoid retraining or even fine-tuning. Faster R-CNN is a meta-network in which a pre-trained network is enclosed. The quality of features depends on the enclosed network and we compare several possibility in the experimental part.

Images are resized to 600 by 1000 before applying Faster R-CNN. We only keep the 300 boxes having best "objectness" scores (after a NMS phase), along with their high-level features[1]. An example of extracted boxes is shown in Fig. 2. About 5 images per second can be obtained on a standard GPU. This part can be performed offline since we don't fine-tune the network.

As mentioned in [30], residual network (ResNet) appears to be the best architecture for transfer learning by feature extractions among the different ImageNet models, and we therefore choose these networks for our Faster R-CNN versions. One of them (denoted RES-101-VOC07) is a 101 layers ResNet trained for the detection task on PASCAL VOC2007. The other one (denoted RES-152-COCO) is a 152 layers ResNet trained on MS COCO [34]. We will also compare our approach to the plain application of these networks for the detection tasks when possible, that is when they were trained on classes we want to detect. We refer to these approaches as FSD (fully supervised detection) in our experiments.

For implementation, we build on the Tensorflow[2] implementation of Faster R-CNN of Chen et al. [7][3].

MI-max. When a new class is to be learned, the user provides a set of weakly annotated images. The MI-max framework described above is then run to find a linear separator specific to the class. Note that both the database and the library of classifiers can be enriched very easily. Indeed, adding an image to the database only requires running it through the Faster R-CNN network and adding a new class only requires a MIL training.

For training the MI-max, we use a batch size of 1000 examples (for smaller sets, all features are loaded into the GPU), 300 iterations of gradient descent

[1] The layer $fc7$ of size $M = 2048$ in the ResNet case, often called 2048-D.
[2] https://www.tensorflow.org/.
[3] Code can be found on GitHub https://github.com/endernewton/tf-faster-rcnn.

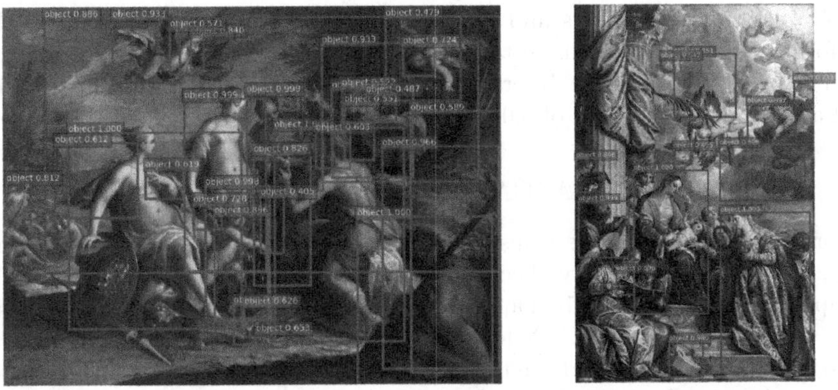

Fig. 2. Some of the regions of interest generated by the region proposal part (RPN) of Faster R-CNN.

with a learning rate of 0.01 and $\epsilon = 0.01$ (4). The whole process takes 750 s for 20 classes on PASCAL VOC07 trainval (5011 images) with 12 random start points per class, on a consumer GPU (GTX 1080Ti). Actually the random restarts are performed in parallel to take advantage of the presence of the features in the GPU memory since the transfer of data from central RAM to the GPU memory is a bottleneck for our method. The 20 classes can be learned in parallel.

For the experiments of Sect. 4.3, we also perform a grid search on the hyper-parameter C (3) by splitting the training set into training and validation sets. We learn several couples (w, b) for each possible value of C (different initialisation) and the one that minimises the loss (4) for each class is selected.

4 Experiments

In this section, we perform weakly supervised detection experiments on different databases, in order to illustrate different assets of our approach.

In all cases, and besides other comparisons, we compare our approach (MI-max) to the following baseline, which is actually the approach chosen for the detection experiments in [11] (except that we do not perform box expansion): the idea is to consider that the region with the best "objectness" score is the region corresponding to the label associated to the image (positive or negative). This baseline will be denoted as MAX. Linear-SVM classifier are learnt using those features per class in a one-vs-the-rest manner. The weight parameter that produces the highest AP (Average Precision) score is selected for each class by a cross validation method[4] and then a classifier is retrained with the best hyper-parameter on all the training data per class. This baseline requires to train several SVMs and is therefore costly.

[4] We use a 3-fold cross validation while [11] use constant training and validation set.

At test time, the labels and the bounding boxes are used to evaluate the performance of the methods in term of AP par class. The generated boxes are filtered by a NMS with an Intersection over Union (IoU) [17] threshold of 0.3 and a confidence threshold of 0.05 for all methods.

4.1 Experiments on PASCAL VOC

Before proceeding with the transfer learning and testing our method on paintings, we start with a sanity check experiment on PASCAL VOC2007 [17]. We compare our weakly supervised approach, MI-max, to the plain application of the fully supervised Faster R-CNN [42] and to the weakly supervised MAX procedure recalled above. We perform the comparison using two different architectures (for the three methods), RES-101-VOC07 and RES-512-COCO, as explained in the previous section.

Table 1. VOC 2007 test Average precision (%) Comparison of the Faster R-CNN detector (trained in a fully supervised manner: FSD) and our MI-max algorithm (trained in a weakly supervised manner) for two networks RES-101-VOC07 and RES-152-COCO.

Net	Method	aero	bicy	bird	boa	bot	bus	car	cat	cha	cow	dtab	dog	hors	mbik	pers	plnt	she	sofa	trai	tv	mean
RES-101-VOC07	FSD [26]	73.6	82.3	75.4	64.0	57.4	80.2	86.5	86.2	52.7	85.2	66.9	87.0	87.1	82.9	81.2	45.7	76.8	71.2	82.6	75.5	75.0
	MAX	20.8	47.0	26.1	20.2	8.3	41.1	44.9	60.1	31.7	54.8	46.4	42.9	62.2	58.7	20.9	21.6	37.6	16.7	42.0	19.8	36.2
	MI-max[a]	63.5	78.4	68.5	54.0	50.7	71.8	85.6	77.1	52.7	80.0	60.1	78.3	80.5	73.5	74.7	37.4	71.2	65.2	75.7	67.7	68.3 ± 0.2
RES-152-COCO	FSD [26]	91.0	90.4	88.3	61.2	77.7	92.2	82.2	93.2	67.0	89.4	65.8	88.0	92.0	89.5	88.5	56.9	85.1	81.0	89.8	85.2	82.7
	MAX [11]	58.8	64.7	52.4	8.6	20.8	55.2	66.8	76.1	19.4	66.3	6.7	59.7	56.4	43.3	15.5	18.3	80.3	7.6	71.8	32.6	44.1
	MI-max[a]	88.0	90.2	84.3	66.0	78.7	93.8	92.7	90.7	63.7	78.8	61.5	88.4	90.9	88.8	87.9	56.8	75.5	81.3	88.4	86.1	81.6 ± 0.3

[a]It is the average performance on 100 runs of our algorithm.

As shown in Table 1 our weakly supervised approach (only considering annotations at the image level[5]) yields performances that are only slightly below the ones of the fully supervised approach (using instance-level annotations). On the average, the loss is only 1.1% of mAP when using RES-512-COCO (for both methods). The baseline MAX procedure (used for transfer learning on paintings in [10]) yields notably inferior performances.

4.2 Detection Evaluation on Watercolor2k and People-Art Databases

We compare our approach with two recent methods performing object detection in artworks, one in a fully supervised way [52] for detecting people, the other using a (partly) weakly supervised method to detect several VOC classes on watercolor images [28]. For the learning stage, the first approach uses instance-level annotations on paintings, while the second one uses instance-level annotations on photographs and image-level annotations on paintings. In both cases, it

[5] However, observe that since we are relying on Faster R-CNN, our system uses a subpart trained using class agnostic bounding boxes.

is shown that using image-level annotations only (our approach, MI-max) only yields a light loss of performances.

Experiment 1: Watercolor2k. This database, introduced in [28], and available online[6], is a subset of watercolor artworks from the **BAM!** database [53] with instance-level annotations for 6 classes (bike, bird, dog, cat, car, person) that are included in the PASCAL VOC, in order to study cross-domain transfer learning. On this database, we compare our approach to the methods from [28] and from [4], to the baseline MAX discussed above, as well as to the classical MIL approach MI-SVM [1] (using a maximum of 50 iterations and no restarts).

In [28], a style transfer transformation (Cycle-GAN [56]) is applied to natural images with instance-level annotation. The images are transferred to the new modality (i.e. watercolor) in order to fine-tune a detector pre-trained on natural images. This detector is used to predict localisation of objects on watercolor images annotated at the image level. The detector is then fine-tuned on those images in a fully supervised manner. Bilen and Vedaldi [4] proposed a Weakly Supervised Deep Detection Network (WSDDN), which consists in transforming a pre-trained network by replacing its classification part by a two streams network (a region proposal stream and a classification one) combined with a weighted MIL pooling strategy.

Table 2. Watercolor2k (test set) Average precision (%). Comparison of the proposed MI-max method to alternative approaches.

Net	Method	bike	bird	car	cat	dog	person	Mean
VGG	WSDDN [4][a]	1.5	26.0	14.6	0.4	0.5	33.3	12.7
SSD	DT+PL [28][a]	76.5	54.9	46.0	37.4	38.5	72.3	54.3
RES-152-COCO	MAX [11]	74.0	34.5	26.8	17.8	21.5	21.0	32.6
	MI-SVM [1]	66.8	23.5	6.7	13.0	8.4	14.1	22.1
	MI-max [our][b]	85.2	48.2	49.2	31.0	30.0	57.0	50.1 ± 1.1

[a]The performance come from the original paper [28].
[b]Standard deviation computed on 100 runs of the algorithm.

From Table 2, one can see that our approach performs clearly better than the other ones using image-level annotations only ([4], MAX, MI-SVM). We also observe only a minor degradation of average performances (54.3% versus 48.9%) with respect to the method [28], which is retrained using style transfer and instance-level annotations on photographs.

Experiment 2: People-Art. This database, introduced in [52], is made of artistic images and bounding boxes for the single class *person*. This database is particularly challenging because of its high variability in styles and depiction techniques. The method introduced in [52] yields excellent detection performances on this database, but necessitates instance-level annotations for training.

[6] https://github.com/naoto0804/cross-domain-detection.

The authors rely on Fast R-CNN [24], of which they only keep the three first layers, before re-training the remaining of the network using manual location annotations on their database.

In Table 3, one can see that our approach MI-max yields detection results that are very close to the fully supervised results from [52], despite a much lighter training procedure. In particular, as already explained, our procedure can be trained directly on large, globally annotated database, for which manually entering instance-level annotations is tedious and time-costly.

Table 3. People-Art (test set) Average precision (%). Comparison of the proposed MI-max method to alternative approaches.

Net	Method	Person
Fast R-CNN (VGG16)	Fine tuned [52][a]	59
RES-152-COCO	MAX [11]	25.9
	MI-SVM [1]	13.3
RES-152-COCO	MI-max [our]	55.4 ± 0.7

[a]The performance come from the original paper.

4.3 Detection on IconArt Database

In this last experimental section, we investigate the ability of our approach to learn and detect new classes that are specific to the analysis of artworks, some of which cannot be learnt on photographs. Typical such examples include iconic characters in certain situations, such as Child Jesus, the crucifixion of Jesus, Saint Sebastian, etc. Although there has been a recent effort to increase open-access databases of artworks by academia and/or museums workforce [10,16, 31,36–38,44,48], they usually don't include systematic and reliable keywords. One exception is the database from the Rijkmuseum, with labels based on the IconClass classification system [27], but this database is mostly composed of prints, photographs and drawings. Moreover, these databases don't include the localisation of objects or characters.

In order to study the ability of our (and other) systems to detect iconographic elements, we gathered 5955 painting images from Wikicommons[7], ranging from the 11th to the 20th century, which are partially annotated by the Wikidata[8] contributors. We manually checked and completed image-level annotations for 7 classes. The dataset is split in training and test sets, as shown in Table 4. For a subset of the test set, and only for the purpose of performance evaluation, instance-level annotations have been added. The resulting database is called

[7] https://commons.wikimedia.org/wiki/Main_Page.

[8] https://www.wikidata.org/wiki/Wikidata:Main_Page.

IconArt[9]. Example images are shown in Fig. 3. To the best of our knowledge, the presented experiments are the first investigating the ability of modern detection tools to classify and detect such iconographic elements in paintings. Moreover, we investigate this aspect in a weakly supervised manner.

Table 4. Statistics of the IconArt database

Class	Angel	Child Jesus	Crucifixion	Mary	nudity	ruins	Saint Sebastian	None	Total
Train	600	755	86	1065	956	234	75	947	2978
Test for classification	627	750	107	1086	1007	264	82	924	2977
Test for detection	261	313	107	446	403	114	82	623	1480
Number of instances	1043	320	109	502	759	194	82		3009

Fig. 3. Example images from the IconArt database. Angel on the first line, Saint Sebastian on the second. We can see some of the challenges posed by this database: tiny objects, occlusions and large pose variability.

To fix ideas on the difficulty of dealing with iconographic elements, we start with a classification experiment. For this, we use the same classification approach as in [10], using InceptionResNetv2 [49] as a feature extractor[10]. We also perform classification-by-detection experiments, using the previously described MAX approach (as in [11]) and our approach, MI-max. In both cases, for each class, the score at the image level is the highest confidence detection score for this class on all the regions of the image. Results are displayed in Table 5. First, we observe that classification results are very variable depending on the class.

[9] The database is available online https://wsoda.telecom-paristech.fr/downloads/dataset/IconArt_v1.zip.

[10] Only the center of the image is provided to the network and extracted features are 1536-D.

Classes such as Jesus Child, Mary or crucifixion have relatively high classification scores. Others, such as Saint Sebastian, are only scarcely classified, probably due to a limited quantity of examples and a high variability of poses, scales and depiction styles. We can also observe that, as mentioned in [11], the classification by detection can provide better scores than global classification, possibly because of small objects, such as angels in our case. Observe that these classification scores can probably be increased using multi-scale learning (as in [51]), augmentation schemes and an ensemble of networks [11].

Table 5. IconArt classification test set *classification* average precision (%).

Net	Method	angel	JCchild	crucifixion	Mary	nudity	ruins	StSeb	Mean
InceptionResNetv2 [49]		44.1	77.2	57.8	81.1	77.4	74.6	26.8	62.7
RES-152-COCO	MAX [11]	49.3	74.7	30.3	67.5	57.4	43.2	7.0	47.1
	MI-max [our]	57.4	60.7	79.9	70.4	65.3	45.9	17.0	56.7 ± 1.0
	MI-max-C [our]	61.0	68.9	80.2	71.4	66.3	51.7	14.8	59.2 ± 1.2

Next, we evaluate the detection performance of our method, first with a restrictive metric: AP per class with an IoU $\geqslant 0.5$ (as in all previous detection experiments in this paper), then with a less restrictive metric with IoU $\geqslant 0.1$. Results are displayed in Table 6. Results on this very demanding experiment are a mixed-bag. Some classes, such as crucifixion, and to a less extend nudity or Jesus Child are correctly detected. Others, such as angel, ruins or Saint Sebastian, hardly get it up to 15% detection scores, even when using the relaxed criterion IoU $\geqslant 0.1$. Beyond a relatively small number of examples and very strong scale and pose variations, there are further reasons for this:

- The high in-class depiction variability (for Saint Sebastian for instance)
- The many occlusions between several instances of a same class (angel)
- The fact that some parts of an object can be more discriminative than the whole object (nudity).

Illustrations of successes and failures are displayed, respectively on Figs. 4 and 5. On the negative examples, one can see that often a larger region than

Table 6. IconArt detection test set *detection* average precision (%). All methods based on RES-152-COCO.

Method	Metric	angel	JCchild	crucifixion	Mary	nudity	ruins	StSeb	Mean
MAX [11]	AP IoU $\geqslant$ 0.5	1.4	3.9	7.4	2.8	3.9	0.3	0.9	2.9
	AP IoU $\geqslant$ 0.1	10.1	36.2	28.2	18.4	14.0	1.6	2.8	15.9
MI-max [our]	AP IoU $\geqslant$ 0.5	0.3	0.9	37.3	3.8	21.2	0.5	10.9	10.7 ± 1.7
	AP IoU $\geqslant$ 0.1	6.4	25.3	74.4	44.6	30.9	6.8	17.2	29.4 ± 1.7
MI-max-C [our]	AP IoU $\geqslant$ 0.5	3.0	17.7	32.6	4.8	23.5	1.1	9.6	13.2 ± 3.1
	AP IoU $\geqslant$ 0.1	12.3	41.2	74.4	46.3	31.2	13.6	16.1	33.6 ± 2.2

the element of interest is selected or that a whole group of instances is selected instead of a single one. Future work could focus on the use of several couples (w, b) instead of one to prevent those problems.

Fig. 4. Successful examples using our MI-max-C detection scheme. We only show boxes whose scores are over 0.75.

Fig. 5. Failure examples using our MI-max-C detection scheme. We only show boxes whose scores are over 0.75.

5 Conclusion

Results from this paper confirm that transfer learning is of great interest to analyse artworks databases. This was previously shown for classification and fully supervised detection schemes, and was here investigated in the case of weakly supervised detection. We believe that this framework is particularly suited to develop tools helping art historians, because it avoids tedious annotations and opens the way to learning on large datasets. We also show, in this context, experiments dealing with iconographic elements that are specific to Art History and cannot be learnt on natural images.

In future works, we plan to use localisation refinement methods, to further study how to avoid poor local optima in the optimisation procedure, to add contextual information for little objects, and possibly to fine-tune the network (as in [15]) to learn better features on artworks. Another exciting direction is to investigate the potential of weakly supervised learning on large databases with image-level annotations, such as the ones from the Rijkmuseum [44] or the French Museum consortium [43].

Acknowledgements. This work is supported by the "IDI 2017" project funded by the IDEX Paris-Saclay, ANR-11-IDEX-0003-02.

References

1. Andrews, S., Tsochantaridis, I., Hofmann, T.: Support vector machines for multiple-instance learning. In: Advances in Neural Information Processing Systems, pp. 577–584 (2003)
2. Aubry, M., Russell, B.C., Sivic, J.: Painting-to-3D model alignment via discriminative visual elements. ACM Trans. Graph. (ToG) **33**(2), 14 (2014)
3. Bianco, S., Mazzini, D., Schettini, R.: Deep multibranch neural network for painting categorization. In: Battiato, S., Gallo, G., Schettini, R., Stanco, F. (eds.) ICIAP 2017. LNCS, vol. 10484, pp. 414–423. Springer, Cham (2017). https://doi.org/10.1007/978-3-319-68560-1_37
4. Bilen, H., Vedaldi, A.: Weakly supervised deep detection networks. In: IEEE Conference on Computer Vision and Pattern Recognition (2016)
5. de Bosio, S.: Master and judge: the mirror as dialogical device in Italian renaissance art theory. In: Zimmermann, M. (ed.) Dialogical Imaginations: Debating Aisthesis as Social Perception. Diaphanes (2017)
6. Carbonneau, M.A., Cheplygina, V., Granger, E., Gagnon, G.: Multiple instance learning: a survey of problem characteristics and applications. Pattern Recogn. **77**, 329–353 (2016). https://doi.org/10.1016/j.patcog.2017.10.009
7. Chen, X., Gupta, A.: An implementation of faster RCNN with study for region sampling. arXiv:1702.02138 [cs], February 2017
8. Cinbis, R.G., Verbeek, J., Schmid, C.: Weakly supervised object localization with multi-fold multiple instance learning. IEEE Trans. Pattern Anal. Mach. Intell. **39**(1), 189–203 (2016). https://doi.org/10.1109/TPAMI.2016.2535231
9. Crowley, E., Zisserman, A.: The state of the art: object retrieval in paintings using discriminative regions. In: BMVC (2014)
10. Crowley, E.J., Zisserman, A.: In search of art. In: Agapito, L., Bronstein, M.M., Rother, C. (eds.) ECCV 2014. LNCS, vol. 8925, pp. 54–70. Springer, Cham (2015). https://doi.org/10.1007/978-3-319-16178-5_4
11. Crowley, E.J., Zisserman, A.: The art of detection. In: Hua, G., Jégou, H. (eds.) ECCV 2016. LNCS, vol. 9913, pp. 721–737. Springer, Cham (2016). https://doi.org/10.1007/978-3-319-46604-0_50
12. Del Bimbo, A., Pala, P.: Visual image retrieval by elastic matching of user sketches. IEEE Trans. Pattern Anal. Mach. Intell. **19**(2), 121–132 (1997)
13. Dietterich, T.G., Lathrop, R.H., Lozano-Pérez, T.: Solving the multiple instance problem with axis-parallel rectangles. Artif. Intell. **89**(1–2), 31–71 (1997)
14. Donahue, J., et al.: DeCAF: a deep convolutional activation feature for generic visual recognition. In: Xing, E.P., Jebara, T. (eds.) Proceedings of the 31st International Conference on Machine Learning. Proceedings of Machine Learning Research, PMLR, Bejing, China, vol. 32, pp. 647–655, 22–24 June 2014. http://proceedings.mlr.press/v32/donahue14.html

15. Durand, T., Mordan, T., Thome, N., Cord, M.: WILDCAT: weakly supervised learning of deep ConvNets for image classification, pointwise localization and segmentation. In: IEEE Conference on Computer Vision and Pattern Recognition (CVPR 2017). IEEE, Honolulu, July 2017
16. Europeana: collections Europeana (2018). https://www.europeana.eu/portal/en
17. Everingham, M., Van Gool, L., Williams, C.K.I., Winn, J., Zisserman, A.: The PASCAL visual object classes challenge 2007 (VOC2007) results (2007). http://www.pascal-network.org/challenges/VOC/voc2007/workshop/index.html
18. Felzenszwalb, P.F., Girshick, R.B., McAllester, D., Ramanan, D.: Object detection with discriminatively trained part-based models. IEEE Trans. Pattern Anal. Mach. Intell. **32**(9), 1627–1645 (2010)
19. Florea, C., Badea, M., Florea, L., Vertan, C.: Domain transfer for delving into deep networks capacity to de-abstract art. In: Sharma, P., Bianchi, F.M. (eds.) SCIA 2017. LNCS, vol. 10269, pp. 337–349. Springer, Cham (2017). https://doi.org/10.1007/978-3-319-59126-1_28
20. Gasparro, D.: Dal lato dell'immagine: destra e sinistra nelle descrizioni di Bellori e altri. Ed. Belvedere (2008)
21. Gehler, P.V., Chapelle, O.: Deterministic annealing for multiple-instance learning. In: Artificial Intelligence and Statistics, pp. 123–130 (2007)
22. Ginosar, S., Haas, D., Brown, T., Malik, J.: Detecting people in cubist art. In: Agapito, L., Bronstein, M.M., Rother, C. (eds.) ECCV 2014. LNCS, vol. 8925, pp. 101–116. Springer, Cham (2015). https://doi.org/10.1007/978-3-319-16178-5_7
23. Girshick, R., Donahue, J., Darrell, T., Malik, J.: Rich feature hierarchies for accurate object detection and semantic segmentation. In: 2014 IEEE Conference on Computer Vision and Pattern Recognition, pp. 580–587, June 2014. https://doi.org/10.1109/CVPR.2014.81
24. Girshick, R.: Fast R-CNN. In: International Conference on Computer Vision (ICCV) (2015)
25. Hall, P., Cai, H., Wu, Q., Corradi, T.: Cross-depiction problem: recognition and synthesis of photographs and artwork. Comput. Vis. Media **1**(2), 91–103 (2015)
26. He, K., Zhang, X., Ren, S., Sun, J.: Deep residual learning for image recognition. In: Proceedings of the IEEE Conference on Computer Vision and Pattern Recognition, pp. 770–778 (2016)
27. Iconclass: Home—Iconclass (2018). http://www.iconclass.nl/home
28. Inoue, N., Furuta, R., Yamasaki, T., Aizawa, K.: Cross-domain weakly-supervised object detection through progressive domain adaptation. In: IEEE Conference on Computer Vision and Pattern Recognition (CVPR 2018). IEEE (2018)
29. Joulin, A., Bach, F.: A convex relaxation for weakly supervised classifiers. arXiv preprint arXiv:1206.6413 (2012)
30. Kornblith, S., Shlens, J., Le, Q.V.: Do better ImageNet models transfer better? arXiv:1805.08974 [cs, stat], May 2018
31. Lecoutre, A., Negrevergne, B., Yger, F.: Recognizing art style automatically in painting with deep learning. In: ACML, pp. 1–17 (2017)
32. Li, D., Yang, Y., Song, Y.Z., Hospedales, T.M.: Deeper, broader and artier domain generalization. In: 2017 IEEE International Conference on Computer Vision (ICCV), pp. 5543–5551, October 2017. https://doi.org/10.1109/ICCV.2017.591
33. Li, D., Huang, J.B., Li, Y., Wang, S., Yang, M.H.: Weakly supervised object localization with progressive domain adaptation. In: Proceedings of the IEEE Conference on Computer Vision and Pattern Recognition, pp. 3512–3520 (2016)

34. Lin, T.-Y., et al.: Microsoft COCO: common objects in context. In: Fleet, D., Pajdla, T., Schiele, B., Tuytelaars, T. (eds.) ECCV 2014. LNCS, vol. 8693, pp. 740–755. Springer, Cham (2014). https://doi.org/10.1007/978-3-319-10602-1_48
35. Liu, W., et al.: SSD: single shot multibox detector. In: Leibe, B., Matas, J., Sebe, N., Welling, M. (eds.) ECCV 2016. LNCS, vol. 9905, pp. 21–37. Springer, Cham (2016). https://doi.org/10.1007/978-3-319-46448-0_2
36. Mao, H., Cheung, M., She, J.: DeepArt: learning joint representations of visual arts. In: Proceedings of the 2017 ACM on Multimedia Conference, pp. 1183–1191. ACM Press (2017). https://doi.org/10.1145/3123266.3123405
37. Mensink, T., Van Gemert, J.: The Rijksmuseum challenge: museum-centered visual recognition. In: Proceedings of International Conference on Multimedia Retrieval, p. 451. ACM (2014)
38. MET: image and data resources — the metropolitan museum of art (2018). https://www.metmuseum.org/about-the-met/policies-and-documents/image-resources
39. Pharos consortium: PHAROS: the international consortium of photo archives (2018). http://pharosartresearch.org/
40. Redmon, J., Divvala, S., Girshick, R., Farhadi, A.: You only look once: unified, real-time object detection. In: Proceedings of the IEEE Conference on Computer Vision and Pattern Recognition, pp. 779–788 (2016)
41. Redmon, J., Farhadi, A.: YOLO9000: better, faster, stronger. In: IEEE Conference on Computer Vision and Pattern Recognition (CVPR 2017). IEEE (2017)
42. Ren, S., He, K., Girshick, R., Sun, J.: Faster R-CNN: towards real-time object detection with region proposal networks. In: Cortes, C., Lawrence, N.D., Lee, D.D., Sugiyama, M., Garnett, R. (eds.) Advances in Neural Information Processing Systems, vol. 28, pp. 91–99. Curran Associates, Inc. (2015). http://papers.nips.cc/paper/5638-faster-r-cnn-towards-real-time-object-detection-with-region-proposal-networks.pdf
43. Réunion des Musées Nationaux-Grand Palais: Images d'Art (2018). https://art.rmngp.fr/en
44. Rijksmuseum: online collection catalogue - research (2018). https://www.rijksmuseum.nl/en/research/online-collection-catalogue
45. Seguin, B., Striolo, C., diLenardo, I., Kaplan, F.: Visual link retrieval in a database of paintings. In: Hua, G., Jégou, H. (eds.) ECCV 2016. LNCS, vol. 9913, pp. 753–767. Springer, Cham (2016). https://doi.org/10.1007/978-3-319-46604-0_52
46. Shrivastava, A., Malisiewicz, T., Gupta, A., Efros, A.A.: Data-driven visual similarity for cross-domain image matching. ACM Trans. Graph. (ToG) **30**(6), 154 (2011)
47. Song, H.O., Girshick, R., Jegelka, S., Mairal, J., Harchaoui, Z., Darrell, T.: On learning to localize objects with minimal supervision. In: Xing, E.P., Jebara, T. (eds.) Proceedings of the 31st International Conference on Machine Learning. Proceedings of Machine Learning Research, PMLR, Bejing, China, pp. 1611–1619, No. 2, 22–24 June 2014, http://proceedings.mlr.press/v32/songb14.html
48. Strezoski, G., Worring, M.: OmniArt: multi-task deep learning for artistic data analysis. arXiv:1708.00684 [cs], August 2017
49. Szegedy, C., Ioffe, S., Vanhoucke, V., Alemi, A.A.: Inception-v4, inception-resnet and the impact of residual connections on learning. In: AAAI, p. 4 (2017)
50. Tang, P., Wang, X., Bai, X., Liu, W.: Multiple instance detection network with online instance classifier refinement. In: 2017 IEEE Conference on Computer Vision and Pattern Recognition (CVPR), pp. 3059–3067 (2017)

51. van Noord, N., Postma, E.: Learning scale-variant and scale-invariant features for deep image classification. Pattern Recogn. **61**, 583–592 (2017). https://doi.org/10.1016/j.patcog.2016.06.005
52. Westlake, N., Cai, H., Hall, P.: Detecting people in artwork with CNNs. In: ECCV Workshops (2016)
53. Wilber, M.J., Fang, C., Jin, H., Hertzmann, A., Collomosse, J., Belongie, S.: BAM! The behance artistic media dataset for recognition beyond photography. In: IEEE International Conference on Computer Vision (ICCV). IEEE (2017)
54. Wu, Q., Cai, H., Hall, P.: Learning graphs to model visual objects across different depictive styles. In: Fleet, D., Pajdla, T., Schiele, B., Tuytelaars, T. (eds.) ECCV 2014. LNCS, vol. 8695, pp. 313–328. Springer, Cham (2014). https://doi.org/10.1007/978-3-319-10584-0_21
55. Yin, R., Monson, E., Honig, E., Daubechies, I., Maggioni, M.: Object recognition in art drawings: transfer of a neural network. In: 2016 IEEE International Conference on Acoustics, Speech and Signal Processing (ICASSP), pp. 2299–2303. IEEE (2016)
56. Zhu, J.Y., Park, T., Isola, P., Efros, A.A.: Unpaired image-to-image translation using cycle-consistent adversarial networks. In: 2017 IEEE International Conference on Computer Vision (ICCV) (2017)

Images of Image Machines. Visual Interpretability in Computer Vision for Art

Fabian Offert(✉)

University of California, Santa Barbara, Santa Barbara, CA 93106, USA
offert@ucsb.edu

Abstract. Despite the emergence of interpretable machine learning as a distinct area of research, the role and possible uses of interpretability in digital art history are still unclear. Focusing on feature visualization as the most common technical manifestation of visual interpretability, we argue that in computer vision for art visual interpretability is desirable, if not indispensable. We propose that feature visualization images can be a useful tool if they are used in a non-traditional way that embraces their peculiar representational status. Moreover, we suggest that exactly because of this peculiar representational status, feature visualization images themselves deserve more attention from the computer vision and digital art history communities.

Keywords: Interpretability · Feature visualization · Digital art history · Representation

1 Is Interpretability Necessary?

Contemporary computer vision algorithms – in the context of art and beyond – make extensive use of artificial neural networks to solve object recognition and classification tasks. The most common architecture employed for such tasks is the deep convolutional neural network (CNN) [7,9,10]. With the spread of CNNs across domains, however, a problem particular to deep neural networks has resurfaced: while we can train deep neural networks to do very well on specific tasks, it is often impossible to know how a model arrives at a decision, i.e. which features of an input image are relevant for its classification. As a response to this impasse, interpretable machine learning has grown into its own distinct area of research, with visual analytics of CNNs as an emerging field of study [5]. While much of the research in this area is concerned with the development of an empirical approach to interpretability [6,15], one of its open qualitative questions is: which machine learning models need to be interpretable?

While it is obvious that machine learning models deployed in high-stakes scenarios, like credit ratings and recidivism prediction (or predictive policing in general), deserve increased scrutiny and necessitate interpretability [12,21], it

L. Leal-Taixé and S. Roth (Eds.): ECCV 2018 Workshops, LNCS 11130, pp. 710–715, 2019.
https://doi.org/10.1007/978-3-030-11012-3_54

has been put into question [11] if models deployed in less critical contexts require interpretability at all, or if the internal "reasoning" of such models is irrelevant given a good enough error rate on the actual task. The main hypothesis of this paper is that in computer vision for art interpretability is desirable, if not indispensable, despite the lack of a need for normative assessment.

2 Representation and Interpretation

One of the most common technical approaches to increase the interpretability of CNNs is feature visualization. Feature visualization has been an important research area within machine learning in general and deep learning in particular at least since 2014 [24,27]. All feature visualization methods rely on the principle of activation maximization: learned features of a particular neuron or layer are visualized by optimizing a random noise input image to maximally activate this neuron or layer.

For instance, an image optimized for an output neuron of a neural network trained on the ImageNet dataset will intuitively show some object from the class associated with this neuron – if it is subjected to proper regularization [19,20,26]. More elaborate methods employ natural image priors to "bias" visualizations even more towards "legible" images [2,16–18]. In fact, unregularized feature visualization images will often fall into the range of adversarial examples [4] for a given class, i.e. they will not be visually related to natural images from this class but still activate the output neuron for this class with very high confidence. Moreover, as [19] and many others have observed, many feature visualization images are "strange mixtures of ideas" that seem to blend features from many different natural images. This suggests that individual neurons are not necessarily the right semantic units for understanding neural nets. In fact, as [25] show, looking for meaningful features does not necessarily lead to more meaningful visualizations than looking for any combination of features, i.e. producing arbitrary activation maximizations. While some recent results [1] seem to weaken the assumption of a distributed representational structure of CNNs, the assumption has nevertheless given rise to a number of highly visible critical interventions suggesting that it will be necessary to augment deep learning methods with more symbolic approaches [8,13,22].

From this indispensability of regularization we can construct a technical argument about the notion of representation as it applies to feature visualization. Johanna Drucker has described the act of interpretation as the collapse of the probability distribution of all possible interpretations [3] for an aesthetic artifact. For feature visualization images, this metaphor applies literally, as feature visualization images are literal samples from the probability distribution that is approximated by the whole model. Somewhat counter-intuitively, feature visualization images, despite being technical images, are thus arbitrary *interpretations* in the exact sense suggested by Drucker. Interpretations based on feature visualization images thus become (human) interpretations of (technical) interpretations. One possible conclusion to draw from this peculiar representational character of feature visualization images would be that visual interpretability as a concept is critically flawed. We propose to draw the opposite conclusion, suggesting that exactly this "subjective" nature of feature visualization images makes visual interpretability useful for computer vision for art.

3 A Non-traditional Approach to Visual Interpretability

Our suggestion is to use feature visualization images to "augment" the original dataset under investigation. Concretely this would mean that, in assessing a dataset with the help of machine learning, the digital art historian would not only take the model's results into account but also include a large set of feature visualization images in the analysis. In this "non-traditional" approach, the digital art historian's hermeneutic work would extend back into the very technical system that enables it, operating on both the original dataset and the feature visualization dataset. The technical system, rather than being an opaque tool, would become an integral part of the interpretative process.

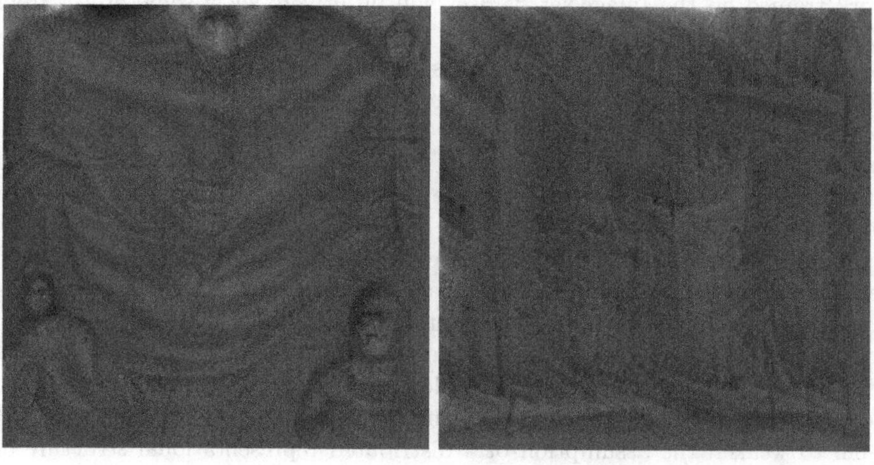

Fig. 1. Feature visualization images for the "portrait" and "landscape" classes of an InceptionV3 neural network. The network was trained on ImageNet and then fine-tuned for ten epochs on an art historical dataset. The dataset, a subset of the web gallery of art dataset, consists of three classes (portrait, landscape, and still life) with 1400 images per class. The resulting classifier reaches 95% validation accuracy. Only minimal regularization was used in the production of the feature visualization images (a 5×5 median filter was applied every four iterations). High resolution was achieved through multi-scale optimization as proposed in the original implementation of the "deep dream" algorithm [14]. The color channels of the final image were normalized independently.

The toy example in Fig. 1 shows the feasibility of this approach: the model seems to have learned that faces and, surprisingly, drapery are the defining features of a portrait. The highest scoring image from the training dataset, Moretto da Brescia's *Christ with an Angel* (1550) confirms this hypothesis, as it contains two faces and three prominent drapery objects. A defining feature of a landscape painting, according to the model, seems to be an aerial perspective blue shift. Both results point to a subtle (likely historical and/or geographical) bias in the dataset that deserves further analysis. Importantly, however, it is the strangeness, the ambiguity, the "Verfremdungseffekt" of the feature visualization image that is open to the same kind of interpretation as the original image that facilitates this conclusion.

[23] have suggested to understand interpretability as a set of strategies to counteract both the inscrutability and the anti-intuitiveness of machine learning models. Inscrutability is defined as the difficulty to investigate a model with a high number of parameters and a high structural complexity. Anti-intuitiveness, on the other hand, is defined as the fact that the internal "reasoning" of a model does not necessarily correspond to intuitive methods of inference, as hidden correlations often play an essential role. Taking up this distinction, we could say that the specific non-traditional interpretability strategy described above would not try to eliminate the anti-intuitiveness of a machine learning model but put it on its feet by embracing its anti-intuitive nature and exploiting it for the benefit of interpretation.

4 Conclusion

We have shown that the representational status of feature visualization images is not as straightforward as often assumed. Based on this clarification, we have proposed that visual interpretability, understood as a method to render the anti-intuitive properties of machine learning models usable, rather than trying to eliminate them, could benefit computer vision for art by extending the reach of the digital art historian's analysis to include the machines used to facilitate this analysis. Our toy example demonstrates the feasibility of this approach.

Both digital art history and interpretable machine learning are academic fields that only emerged in the past twenty to thirty years, and experienced significant growth only in the past five years. The intimate connection of both fields through their common interest in the analysis and interpretation of images, however, makes a closer collaboration of researchers from both fields reasonable and desirable. The non-traditional interpretability strategy outlined above is only one of many possible non-traditional approaches that could significantly impact both fields, technically, as well as conceptually.

References

1. Bau, D., Zhou, B., Khosla, A., Oliva, A., Torralba, A.: Network dissection: quantifying interpretability of deep visual representations. In: 2017 IEEE Conference on Computer Vision and Pattern Recognition (CVPR), pp. 3319–3327 (2017)
2. Dosovitskiy, A., Brox, T.: Generating images with perceptual similarity metrics based on deep networks. In: Advances in Neural Information Processing Systems, pp. 658–666 (2016). http://papers.nips.cc/paper/6157-generating-images-with-perceptual-similarity-metrics-based-on-deep-networks

3. Drucker, J.: The general theory of social relativity. The elephants (2018)
4. Goodfellow, I.J., Shlens, J., Szegedy, C.: Explaining and harnessing adversarial examples. arXiv preprint arXiv:1412.6572 (2014)
5. Hohman, F.M., Kahng, M., Pienta, R., Chau, D.H.: Visual analytics in deep learning: an interrogative survey for the next frontiers. IEEE Trans. Vis. Comput. Graph. (2018)
6. Kim, B., Doshi-Velez, F.: Towards a rigorous science of interpretable machine learning. arXiv preprint arXiv:1702.08608 (2017)
7. Krizhevsky, A., Sutskever, I., Hinton, G.E.: Imagenet classification with deep convolutional neural networks. In: Advances in Neural Information Processing Systems, pp. 1097–1105 (2012)
8. Lake, B.M., Ullman, T.D., Tenenbaum, J.B., Gershman, S.J.: Building machines that learn and think like people. Behav. Brain Sci. **40**, e253 (2017)
9. LeCun, Y., Bengio, Y., Hinton, G.: Deep learning. Nature **521**(7553), 436–444 (2015)
10. LeCun, Y., et al.: Backpropagation applied to handwritten zip code recognition. Neural Comput. **1**(4), 541–551 (1989)
11. Lipton, Z.C.: The mythos of model interpretability. In: 2016 ICML Workshop on Human Interpretability in Machine Learning (WHI 2016), New York, NY (2016)
12. Lum, K., Isaac, W.: To predict and serve? Significance **13**(5), 14–19 (2016)
13. Marcus, G.: Deep learning: a critical appraisal. arXiv preprint arXiv:1801.00631 (2018). https://arxiv.org/abs/1801.00631v1
14. Mordvintsev, A., Olah, C., Tyka, M.: Inceptionism: going deeper into neural networks (2015). https://research.googleblog.com/2015/06/inceptionism-going-deeper-into-neural.html
15. Narayanan, M., Chen, E., He, J., Kim, B., Gershman, S., Doshi-Velez, F.: How do humans understand explanations from machine learning systems? arXiv preprint arXiv:1802.00682 (2018). https://arxiv.org/abs/1802.00682v1
16. Nguyen, A., Dosovitskiy, A., Yosinski, J., Brox, T., Clune, J.: Synthesizing the preferred inputs for neurons in neural networks via deep generator networks. In: Advances in Neural Information Processing Systems, pp. 3387–3395 (2016). http://papers.nips.cc/paper/6519-synthesizing-the-preferred-inputs-for-neurons-in-neural-networks-via-deep-generator-networks
17. Nguyen, A., Yosinski, J., Bengio, Y., Dosovitskiy, A., Clune, J.: Plug and play generative networks: conditional iterative generation of images in latent space. arXiv preprint (2017). https://arxiv.org/abs/1612.00005
18. Nguyen, A., Yosinski, J., Clune, J.: Multifaceted feature visualization: uncovering the different types of features learned by each neuron in deep neural networks. arXiv preprint arXiv:1602.03616 (2016)
19. Olah, C., Mordvintsev, A., Schubert, L.: Feature visualization. Distill (2017). https://distill.pub/2017/feature-visualization
20. Olah, C., et al.: The building blocks of interpretability. Distill (2018). https://distill.pub/2018/building-blocks
21. Pasquale, F.: The Black Box Society: The Secret Algorithms That Control Money and Information. Harvard University Press, Cambridge (2015)
22. Pearl, J., Mackenzie, D.: The Book of Why: The New Science of Cause and Effect. Basic Books, New York (2018)
23. Selbst, A.D., Barocas, S.: The intuitive appeal of explainable machines. Fordham Law Rev. **87** (2018)

24. Simonyan, K., Vedaldi, A., Zisserman, A.: Deep inside convolutional networks: visualising image classification models and saliency maps. arXiv preprint arXiv:1312.6034 (2014)
25. Szegedy, C., et al.: Intriguing properties of neural networks. arXiv preprint arXiv:1312.6199 (2013)
26. Yosinski, J., Clune, J., Nguyen, A., Fuchs, T., Lipson, H.: Understanding neural networks through deep visualization. In: 2015 31st International Conference on Machine Learning Deep Learning Workshop, Lille, France (2015)
27. Zeiler, M.D., Fergus, R.: Visualizing and understanding convolutional networks. In: Fleet, D., Pajdla, T., Schiele, B., Tuytelaars, T. (eds.) ECCV 2014. LNCS, vol. 8689, pp. 818–833. Springer, Cham (2014). https://doi.org/10.1007/978-3-319-10590-1_53

Author Index

Ajanthan, Thalaiyasingam 500
Akpinar, M. Akif 100
Alberti, Michele 296
Ali, Feroz 30
Amato, Giuseppe 313
Azimi, Seyed Majid 88

Balamuralidhar, P. 129
Banerjee, Biplab 30
Baraldi, Lorenzo 601
Becarelli, Rudy 313
Belouadah, Eden 151
Bergamasco, Filippo 617
Berretti, Stefano 441
Beyan, Cigdem 364
Boccignone, Giuseppe 331
Bonfait, Olivier 692
Bouillon, Manuel 296
Bulò, Samuel Rota 180
Burghardt, Tilo 551

Caldelli, Roberto 313
Canévet, Olivier 346
Caputo, Barbara 180
Carissimi, Nicolò 364
Carrara, Fabio 313
Casser, Vincent 11
Cavallaro, Andrea 380, 534
Chahl, Javaan 117
Chaudhuri, Subhasis 30
Chen, Riwei 209
Cheng, An-Chieh 571
Cheng, Shiyang 475
Clapés, Albert 534
Cornia, Marcella 601
Costea, Dragoş 43
Cucchiara, Rita 601
Cuculo, Vittorio 331
Cun, Xiaodong 252

D'Amelio, Alessandro 331
D'Oro, P. 492
Daelemans, Walter 631
Damen, Dima 551
Davis, Larry 280
de Bem, Rodrigo 500
Del Bimbo, Alberto 441
Devanne, Maxime 190
Dhall, Abhinav 518
Di Cicco, Francesca 671
Dik, Joris 671
Duan, Lixin 172

Erdem, Aykut 100
Erdem, Erkut 100
Escalera, Sergio 534
Esser, Patrick 409

Falchi, Fabrizio 313
Fan, Xiaochuan 227
Ferrari, Claudio 441
Fu, Tsu-Jui 571

Garcia, Noa 676
Gavves, Efstratios 158
Geurts, Pierre 631
Ghanem, Bernard 11
Ghosh, Arnab 500
Ghosh, Shreya 518
Giordano, D. 492
Goedemé, Toon 3
Goeting, Marijke 653
Gonthier, Nicolas 692
Gousseau, Yann 692
Grossi, Giuliano 331
Gubbi, Jayavardhana 129
Guo, Hengkai 209

Hannunna, Sion 551
Hanson, Alex 280
Hara, Kensho 562, 590
Hardt-Stremayr, Alexander 73
Haux, Johannes 409
Ho, Kuan-Wei 571

Hofmann, Michael 158
Honda, Hiroto 217
Huang, Yi 426
Humenberger, Martin 73

Inaba, Masaki 562
Ingold, Rolf 296
Itazuri, Takahiro 590

Kataoka, Hirokatsu 562, 590
Kato, Tomohiro 217
Kestemont, Mike 631
Kollias, Dimitrios 475
Koniusz, Piotr 198
Krishnagopal, Sanjukta 280
Kumar, Saurabh 30

Ladjal, Said 692
Lai, Shang-Hong 426
Lakhal, Mohamed Ilyes 380, 534
Lang, Sabine 647
Lanz, Oswald 380, 534
Lanzarotti, Raffaella 331
Law, Yee Wei 117
Lee, Chun-Yi 571
Leordeanu, Marius 43
Lezki, Hazal 100
Lian, Qing 172
Licăreţ, Vlad 43
Lin, Guosheng 172
Liu, Bo 237
Liu, Gang 456
Liu, Ping 227
Liu, Shuangjun 395
Liwicki, Marcus 296
Logoglu, K. Berker 100
Lu, Yongchen 209
Luo, Guozhong 209
Lv, Fengmao 172

Mancini, Massimiliano 180
Marcu, Alina 43
Martínez-González, Angel 346
Masullo, Alessandro 551
Michels, Dominik L. 11
Miksik, Ondrej 500
Milbich, Timo 409
Milz, Stefan 59
Mirmehdi, Majid 551
Müller, Matthias 11
Murino, Vittorio 364

Narioka, Kenichi 562
Nguyen, Sao Mai 190
Ning, Guanghan 227

Odobez, Jean-Marc 346, 456
Offert, Fabian 710
Ommer, Björn 409, 647
Ostadabbas, Sarah 395
Ozturk, I. Ahu 100

Pala, Pietro 441
Palazzo, S. 492
Pan, Sinno Jialin 172
Pantic, Maja 475
Perera, Asanka G. 117
Pîrvu, Mihai 43
PNVR, Koutilya 280
Ponce-López, Víctor 551
Pondenkandath, Vinaychandran 296
Pont, Sylvia 671
Popescu, Adrian 151
Pun, Chi-Man 237, 252

Ramaswamy, Akshaya 129
Ren, Tongwei 582
Rezaeifar, Shideh 267
Ricci, Elisa 180
Rota, Paolo 364
Rüdiger, Tobias 59

Sabatelli, Matthia 631
Satoh, Yutaka 562
Scarramuza, Davide 3
Schörghuber, Matthias 73
Seuret, Mathias 296
Shah, M. 492
Shkodrani, Sindi 158
Siddharth, N. 500
Sluşanschi, Emil 43
Smith, Neil 11
Spampinato, C. 492
Stumpel, Jeroen 671
Su, Kai 221
Sun, Jia 221
Süss, Sebastian 59
Suzuki, Tomoyuki 590

Tai, Shao-Heng 426
Tan, Xin 582
Tang, Tang 209
Taran, Olga 267
Tomei, Matteo 601
Torr, Philip 500
Torsello, Andrea 617
Traviglia, Arianna 617
Tuytelaars, Tinne 3

Uchida, Yusuke 217

Van Beeck, Kristof 3
Varghese, Ashley 129
Villamizar, Michael 346
Vogiatzis, George 676
Voloshynovskiy, Slava 267

Wang, Changhu 221
Weiss, Stephan 73
Wen, Linfu 209
Wiersma, Lisa 671
Wijntjes, Maarten 671
Wu, Gangshan 582
Würsch, Marcel 296

Yang, Guowu 172
Yang, Hsuan-Kung 571
Yu, Dongdong 221
Yu, Fan 582
Yu, Yu 456
Yucel, M. Kerim 100

Zafeiriou, Stefanos 475
Zhang, Chi 227
Zhang, Hongguang 198

Printed in the United States
By Bookmasters